AF785162

2017 Medicare Handbook

Judith A. Stein and Alfred J. Chiplin, Jr., Editors-in-Chief

Challenging improper denials of Medicare for necessary health services remains essential to obtaining coverage. This is particularly important in light of the settlement agreement in *Jimmo v. Sebelius* and the resulting Medicare policy changes clarifying that improvement is not a prerequisite for coverage for most nursing and therapy services. The *2017 Medicare Handbook* continues to provide key coverage information and practical advocacy tips for all care settings with new and updated information. As with previous editions, the *2017 Medicare Handbook* provides ready access to relevant Medicare law and regulations, case law developments, agency policies, and other program-implementing materials. Armed with this information, beneficiary advocates can formulate effective strategies to secure necessary Medicare-covered services.

2017 EDITION HIGHLIGHTS

Implementing the Affordable Care Act (ACA) remains an ongoing focus, particularly in matters concerning quality of care, program transitions, and cost-containment. A key concern is that the integrity of the Medicare program remain intact, even as we strive to expand its benefits to address the health care needs of an increasingly diverse Medicare population, many of whom are dually eligible for Medicare and Medicaid.

We also note a surge in problems related to the interaction of the Medicare program and the Consolidated Omnibus Budget Reconciliation Act of 1985, commonly referred to as COBRA. The COBRA program extends the opportunity to stay on one's employer's health plan and pay the insurance premiums privately for a period of time, but only if the employer is of a certain size and if the employer offers health insurance to its active employees and their families. Because COBRA coverage is not considered coverage due to current employment, an individual is not entitled to a special enrollment period (SEP) for Medicare when COBRA coverage ends. In addition, the former employee is not permitted to enroll in Medicare until the next general enrollment period, which runs January through March of the year, with coverage beginning July 1.

The *2017 Medicare Handbook* also continues the authors' efforts to help advocates contest limited oversight of and access to coverage under private Medicare Advantage (MA) plans (Part C) and to understand initiatives to reduce overpayments to MA plans.

Wolters Kluwer

Other Medicare developments discussed in the *2017 Medicare Handbook* include:

- Developments in the Medicare home health and hospice benefits, particularly the ongoing implementation of the face-to-face review requirements and increasing problems accessing necessary Medicare-covered home care.
- Reducing beneficiary confusion about hospital outpatient "observation status" as opposed to inpatient admission and the impact on accessing Medicare coverage for necessary skilled nursing facility care.
- Assuring appropriate coverage and services for persons with long-term and chronic conditions.
- Ongoing implementation of important provisions of the Affordable Care Act.

12/16

For questions concerning this shipment, billing, or other customer service matters, call our Customer Service Department at 1-800-234-1660.

For toll-free ordering, please call 1-800-638-8437.

Copyright © 2017 CCH Incorporated. All Rights Reserved.

2017 MEDICARE HANDBOOK

Center for Medicare Advocacy, Inc.

Editors-in-Chief

Judith A. Stein, Esq.

and

Alfred J. Chiplin, Jr., Esq.

Contributing Authors

Mary A. Ashkar

Alfred J. Chiplin, Jr.

Toby S. Edelman

Kathleen Holt

Kata M. Kertesz

Wey-Wey Kwok

David A. Lipschutz

Judith A. Stein

Wolters Kluwer

This publication is designed to provide accurate and authoritative information in regard to the subject matter covered. It is sold with the understanding that the publisher and the author(s) are not engaged in rendering legal, accounting, or other professional services. If legal advice or other professional assistance is required, the services of a competent professional should be sought.

—From a *Declaration of Principles* jointly adopted by
a Committee of the American Bar Association and
a Committee of Publishers and Associations

Copyright © 2017 CCH Incorporated. All Rights Reserved.

No part of this publication may be reproduced or transmitted in any form or by any means, including electronic, mechanical, photocopying, recording, or utilized by any information storage or retrieval system, without written permission from the publisher. For information about permissions or to request permissions online, visit us at *http://www.wklawbusiness.com/footer-pages/permissions*, or a written request may be faxed to our permissions department at 212-771-0803.

Published by Wolters Kluwer in New York.

Wolters Kluwer Legal & Regulatory U.S. serves customers worldwide with CCH, Aspen Publishers and Kluwer Law International products.

Printed in the United States of America

1 2 3 4 5 6 7 8 9 0

ISBN 978-1-4548-7117-0

ISSN 1530-8979

SUSTAINABLE FORESTRY INITIATIVE Certified Sourcing
www.sfiprogram.org
SFI-00756

About Wolters Kluwer Legal & Regulatory U.S.

Wolters Kluwer Legal & Regulatory U.S. delivers expert content and solutions in the areas of law, corporate compliance, health compliance, reimbursement, and legal education. Its practical solutions help customers successfully navigate the demands of a changing environment to drive their daily activities, enhance decision quality and inspire confident outcomes.

Serving customers worldwide, its legal and regulatory portfolio includes products under the Aspen Publishers, CCH Incorporated, Kluwer Law International, ftwilliam.com and MediRegs names. They are regarded as exceptional and trusted resources for general legal and practice-specific knowledge, compliance and risk management, dynamic workflow solutions, and expert commentary.

WOLTERS KLUWER SUPPLEMENT NOTICE

This product is updated on a periodic basis with supplements and/or new editions to reflect important changes in the subject matter.

If you would like information about enrolling this product in the update service, or wish to receive updates billed separately with a 30-day examination review, please contact our Customer Service Department at 1-800-234-1660 or email us at: *customer.service@wolterskluwer.com*. You can also contact us at:

Wolters Kluwer
Distribution Center
7201 McKinney Circle
Frederick, MD 21704

Important Contact Information

- To order any title, go to *www.wklawbusiness.com* or call 1-800-638-8437.
- To reinstate your manual update service, call 1-800-638-8437.
- To contact Customer Service, e-mail *customer.service@wolterskluwer.com*, call 1-800-234-1660, fax 1-800-901-9075, or mail correspondence to: Order Department—Wolters Kluwer, PO Box 990, Frederick, MD 21705.
- To review your account history or pay an invoice online, visit *www.WKLawBusiness.com/payinvoices.*

Wolters Kluwer

CONTENTS

A complete table of contents for each chapter is included at the beginning of the chapter.

Chapter 4
HOME HEALTH COVERAGE

Chapter 5
HOSPICE COVERAGE

Chapter 11
PRESCRIPTION DRUG COVERAGE

PREFACE

The Medicare program continues to provide reliable, defined health care benefits for older and disabled people. Nonetheless, improper denials of Medicare coverage continue with surprising frequency, especially for services needed by people with long-term and chronic conditions. Challenges to improper denials remain essential to ensure fair access to coverage and necessary care—for individual beneficiaries, for all those who rely on Medicare for their health insurance coverage, and for the integrity of the Medicare program as a whole. The *2017 Medicare Handbook* serves as a foundation for this work.

Intended as a guide for attorneys and other advocates, the *Medicare Handbook* provides comprehensive, up-to-date information about Medicare coverage and appeals. Its goal is to provide important information and assist advocates with practical tips. The *2017 Medicare Handbook* continues this work and pays particular attention to the issues that face Medicare beneficiaries with chronic conditions.

Knowledgeable advocates, working in concert with physicians and other health care providers, can help ensure access to necessary Medicare-covered services. This is one of the reasons a standard set of benefits and coverage rules is so important, particularly as the original Medicare program has been fragmented into numerous private plan options. Armed with the *Handbook's* information, practical tools, and primary source materials, attorneys and advocates will be better able to protect the rights of Medicare beneficiaries.

The authors also hope the *2017 Medicare Handbook* will continue to illuminate the importance of preserving Medicare as a broad and universal health insurance program.

Judith A. Stein, Esq.
Executive Director
Center for Medicare Advocacy, Inc.
November 2016

ABOUT THE CENTER FOR MEDICARE ADVOCACY, INC.

The Center for Medicare Advocacy (the Center), is a national, nonprofit, nonpartisan law organization. The Center provides education, advocacy, and analysis to help older people and people with disabilities obtain Medicare and quality health care. Established in 1986, the Center focuses on the needs of Medicare beneficiaries, people with chronic conditions, and those in need of long-term care. Our work includes writing, consulting, and legal assistance regarding issues of importance to Medicare beneficiaries nationwide.

The Center's primary offices are in Connecticut and Washington, D.C., with additional attorneys in Massachusetts, New Jersey, and California. The Center is staffed by attorneys, nurses, legal assistants, and information management specialists, and includes staff members who are fluent in Spanish. In addition, a translation service is available to help people in other languages. We also have TDD equipment to assist people who are deaf. Substantive material and examples of the Center's publications, products, and services are available upon request and on our website at *www.MedicareAdvocacy.org*.

The work, expertise, and commitment of the Center have been described as follows:

> You can always count on the Center for Medicare Advocacy for the most up-to-date and accurate information out there. The Center employs some of the brightest minds around and their top priority is helping folks—whether it's sorting through the everyday complexities of Medicare or digging into funding issues, this is the place to go.
>
> – Senator (Now Secretary of State) John Kerry (2012)

The Center's policy work is driven by the concerns and stories of the real people with whom we speak daily. Annually, we respond to approximately 7,000 telephone and email inquiries and appeal thousands Medicare denials. Center staff write and speak extensively about Medicare and related topics; produce a wide array of electronic and hard copy periodicals and educational materials; advocate in administrative and legislative forums; pursue class action litigation on behalf of individuals and groups improperly denied access to Medicare and health care; provide webinars, seminars, and support nationally, including serving as the primary training source for Connecticut's State Health Insurance and Assistance Program (SHIP, known as CHOICES in Connecticut).

When necessary the Center pursues strategic litigation to ensure fair access to coverage, health care, and due process for Medicare beneficiaries. In October 2012, the Center and CMS settled the national class action law suit, *Jimmo v. Sebelius*, which promises to remove the improvement standard as a barrier to Medicare coverage. *Jimmo* clarifies that coverage is available for skilled nursing and therapy to maintain a patients' condition.

Center staff members regularly speak about Medicare and health care to a wide array of audiences. The organization also sponsors an annual conference in Washington, D.C., that connects advocates, scholars, and policy-makers to advance the interests of older and disabled people, their families, and caregivers.

ACKNOWLEDGMENTS

The authors gratefully acknowledge the staff members of the Center for Medicare Advocacy, for their many contributions to the development and maintenance of this book. In particular, we thank Matthew Hubbard for his patient and varied assistance. We also thank our Health Fellow, Dara Valanejad, and writers of significant portions of earlier versions of this *Handbook*: Brad Plebani, Patricia Nemore, Vicki Gottlich, Sally Hart, Mary T. Bethelot, Margaret Murphy, and Pam Meliso.

The Center for Medicare Advocacy also recognizes and thanks Legal Counsel for the Elderly, Inc., of AARP, which published the original version of this book, then the *Medicare Practice Manual,* written in 1990 by the Center for Medicare Advocacy. It was the genesis of our current publication. Legal Counsel for the Elderly graciously released its copyright control over the *Medicare Practice Manual* and encouraged the Center for Medicare Advocacy to update and expand the earlier material as the Medicare program evolves.

Finally, we acknowledge the coordinator of this project for the Center for Medicare Advocacy, Alfred J. Chiplin, Jr. He has led this project for over a decade, keeping us on track and reasonably on time, with his special blend of intelligence, decency, and good humor.

The Authors
November 2016

CHAPTER 1

AN INTRODUCTION TO MEDICARE COVERAGE AND APPEALS

§ 1.01 HISTORY AND OVERVIEW

Medicare is the country's flagship national health insurance program for older people and people with disabilities. Individuals entitled to Social Security retirement insurance who are 65 years of age or older and individuals entitled to Social Security disability benefits for not less than 24 months are eligible to participate in Medicare. Individuals entitled to Railroad Retirement benefits or Railroad Retirement disability benefits and individuals with end-stage renal disease (ESRD) and amyotrophic lateral sclerosis (ALS, also known as Lou Gehrig's disease), are also entitled to participate.[1] In addition, individuals who are not otherwise eligible for Medicare, but who are over age 65, may purchase coverage by paying a monthly premium.[2] Since January 1, 1983, most federal employees may count their government work toward eligibility for the Medicare hospital insurance program, Medicare Part A.[3]

Medicare is a health insurance program based on a private health insurance model. Passed in 1965 as Title 18 of the Social Security Act,[4] the program is intended to pay some of the cost of some health care services in order to ensure access to a basic level of health care for older people.[5] Medicare requires deductibles and copayments and pays only a portion of the cost of certain services for certain patients. Claims are submitted to an insurance company or other entity that acts as an agent for the federal government for the approval of coverage and payment for health care services.[6]

---

[1] 42 U.S.C. § 1395c. *See* 42 C.F.R. §§ 406.12 and 406.13, regarding qualifying due to disability or end-stage renal disease (ESRD). Persons with ALS can qualify for Medicare without the 24-month waiting period, effective July 1, 2001. *See* the Benefits Improvement and Protection Act (BIPA), Pub. L. No. 106-554 (Dec. 21, 2000), §§ 115, 116.

[2] 42 U.S.C. § 1395i-2. The individual must be a U.S. citizen or a permanent resident for five years.

[3] 42 U.S.C. § 426(a)(2)(c), (b)(2)(c); 42 C.F.R. § 406.15.

[4] 42 U.S.C. §§ 1395 *et seq., available at* https://www.ssa.gov/OP_Home/ssact/title18/1848.htm (site visited Aug. 10, 2016); *see also* "Basic Introduction to Medicare," *available at* http://www.medicareadvocacy.org/medicare-info/medicare-basics-2/ (site visited Aug. 10, 2012).

[5] Whitman v. Weinberger, 382 F. Supp. 256, 262 (E.D. Va. 1974). Coverage for certain individuals deemed permanently disabled for 24 months was added in 1972. Social Security Amendments of 1972, Pub. L. No. 92-603 (Oct. 30, 1972), § 201(a). Medicare celebrated its 50th anniversary in 2015. *See* http://www.cms.gov/Outreach-and-Education/Look-Up-Topics/50th-Anniversary/Medicare-and-Medicaid-50th-Anniversary.html (site visited June 8, 2016).

[6] For beneficiaries in traditional Medicare, doctors and suppliers are required by law to file Medicare claims for covered services and supplies a beneficiary receives. *See* https://www.medicare.gov/claims-and-appeals/file-a-claim/file-a-claim.html (site visited June 8, 2016). For information on filing a claim, see Patient's Request for Medical Payment form, *available at* http://www.medicare.gov/claims-and-appeals/file-a-claim/file-a-claim.html (site visited May 16, 2016). Note that beneficiaries in a Medicare Advantage Plan (Part C) do not have to file claims because Medicare pays these private insurance companies a set amount each month.

Unlike Medicaid, Title 19 of the Social Security Act,[7] neither Medicare eligibility nor coverage is predicated on the income or assets of the beneficiary.[8] Medicaid is a shared state-federal program, paid in part by both entities and administered by state agencies with federal oversight. Medicare, on the other hand, is entirely a federal program. Its benefits are paid from entirely federal sources. Both programs are overseen by the Centers for Medicare & Medicaid Services (CMS), formerly known as the Health Care Financing Administration (HCFA), see https://www.federalregister.gov/agencies/health-care-finance-administration (site visited Aug. 15, 2016), a component of the United States Department of Health and Human Services (HHS).

Because Medicare is a national program, Medicare procedures and qualifying criteria should not vary significantly from state to state. When they do, advocates should be certain that there are valid reasons for the discrepancies and assure that such discrepancies do not inappropriately result in a denial of coverage for necessary services.

[A] The Medicare Program in Transition

Over the past decades, Congress has added new features and limitations to the Medicare program. The Balanced Budget Act of 1997 (BBA '97)[9] created Medicare Part C, then known as the Medicare+Choice program and now known as Medicare Advantage (MA).[10] Medicare Part C added a variety of coordinated care and other financing options for Medicare-covered services, while retaining the original (or traditional) Medicare program.

Medicare Part C allows for coordinated care plans, including Health Maintenance Organizations (HMOs), Provider Service Organizations (PSOs), Special Needs Plans (SNPs), and both local and regional Preferred Provider Organizations (PPOs), as options for receiving coverage. Other options include Medical Savings Accounts (MSAs),[11] Health Savings Accounts (HSAs) under the

---

[7] 42 U.S.C. §§ 1396 *et seq. available at* https://www.gpo.gov/fdsys/pkg/USCODE-2011-title42/pdf/USCODE-2011-title42-chap7-subchapXIX-sec1396a.pdf (site visited Aug. 10, 2016).

[8] Starting in January 2007, however, individuals and couples with incomes over $85,000 for individuals and $170,000 for couples pay more for the Part B premium and, starting in January 2011, more for the Part D premium. Additionally, individuals with incomes *below* a certain threshold may receive a subsidy to help pay premiums and cost-sharing under Part D. *See* **Chapter 6** of this Handbook for Part B details and Chapter 11 for Part D details.

[9] The Balanced Budget Act of 1997 (BBA '97), Pub. L. No. 105-33 (Aug. 5, 1997).

[10] Medicare Part C, *see* BBA '97 § 4001, enacting Social Security Act §§ 1851–1859. As discussed later, Medicare+Choice was renamed "Medicare Advantage" (MA) in December 2003. *See* the Medicare Prescription Drug, Improvement, and Modernization Act of 2003 (MMA), Pub. L. No. 108-173 (Dec. 8, 2003), § 201, *see* https://www.congress.gov/bill/108th-congress/house-bill/1 (site visited Aug. 10, 2016).

[11] MSA plans were made available for the first time in January 2006.

Internal Revenue Code (I.R.C.),[12] Private Fee-for-Service (PFFS) plans,[13] and Private Religious-Fraternal Order plans.[14] While these options were allowed commencing January 1999, in most areas of the country only managed care plans, including HMOs and PPOs, and PFFS plans have developed.

BBA '97 also created, outside the MA program, an option for "private contracts between physicians and their Medicare patients for the receipt of Medicare-covered services for which no Medicare payment will be made." And physicians entering into such contracts must agree not to accept Medicare reimbursement for any Medicare-covered service for two years.[15]

In December 2000, Congress passed legislation that made significant adjustments to the Medicare Program in the form of the Medicare, Medicaid, and SCHIP Benefits Improvement & Protection Act of 2000 (BIPA),[16] which returned some of the funds to providers and HMOs that were reduced by BBA '97 and made minor enhancements for beneficiaries. More changes occurred at the end of 2003 with the enactment of the Medicare Prescription Drug, Improvement, and Modernization Act of 2003 (MMA),[17] including providing Medicare beneficiaries with assistance to pay for prescription drugs through a new Medicare Part D. The law also changed the name of private plans offered under Medicare Part C, from "Medicare+Choice" (M+C) to "Medicare Advantage (MA)."

The 2003 MMA also began a major restructuring of the traditional Medicare program, relying heavily on private insurance to deliver benefits through increased payments to Part C plans and increased beneficiary cost-sharing responsibilities. The Medicare Improvements for Patients and Providers Act of 2008 (MIPPA),[18] primarily designed to address problems with the way Medicare pays physicians, also made modest improvements for beneficiaries, including reducing the cost-sharing for mental health services and increasing the asset limits for eligibility for programs that assist with Part B premiums and cost-sharing.

---

[12] Medicare Prescription Drug, Improvement, and Modernization Act of 2003 (MMA), Pub. L. No. 108-173 (Dec. 8, 2003), § 1201, amending Internal Revenue Code (I.R.C.) of 1986 by redesignating § 223 as § 224 and by inserting new I.R.C. § 223 after § 222.

[13] *See* http://www.cms.gov/Medicare/Health-Plans/PrivateFeeforServicePlans/index.html (site visited June 8, 2016).

[14] *See* https://www.cms.gov/Regulations-and-Guidance/Guidance/Manuals/downloads/mc86c01.pdf (site visited May 16, 2016).

[15] BBA '97 § 4507, amending § 1802 of the Social Security Act, 42 U.S.C. § 1395a(b)(3)(B)(ii). *See also* **§ 6.04[E]** of this Handbook.

[16] Pub. L. No. 106-554 (Dec. 21, 2000).

[17] Pub. L. No. 108-173 (Dec. 8, 2003).

[18] Pub. L. No. 110-275 (July 15, 2008). *See also* the Center for Medicare Advocacy's "Weekly Alerts," which describe MIPPA provisions of importance to beneficiaries and their advocates, *available at* www.medicareadvocacy.org (site visited June 8, 2016).

The Patient Protection and Affordable Care Act of 2010 (PPACA)[19] and the Health Care and Education Reconciliation Act of 2010 (HCERA),[20] together known as the Affordable Care Act (ACA), contain significant changes to the Medicare program, particularly with regard to reimbursement for Medicare Advantage plans and to providers. The ACA also provides for system delivery mechanisms and demonstrations and pilot projects to improve coordination of care; other initiatives to improve quality of care; and initiatives to reduce unnecessary hospital readmissions. The law adds coverage for an annual wellness visit, eliminates cost-sharing for most preventive services, adds some consumer protections to Medicare Advantage, and phases out the Part D coverage gap known as the "Donut Hole."[21]

[B] A Historical Perspective

BBA '97, BIPA, MMA, MIPPA, and the Affordable Care Act are not the only alterations of the Medicare program. Since its enactment in 1965, Medicare has been revised several times by Congress, often to increase coverage. In 1972, for example, coverage was extended to people with disabilities.[22] Also in 1972, coverage was extended to skilled nursing facility (SNF) patients needing skilled rehabilitation rather than only to those in need of skilled nursing.[23] In 1980, Congress removed the requirement that home health patients have a prior hospitalization in order to receive Medicare home health coverage; Congress also removed the 100-visit limitation on home health coverage.[24] Despite this apparent congressional intent to increase coverage, Medicare coverage criteria are often strictly interpreted by those who administer the program, with denials for many types of care being the norm rather than the exception.

---

[19] Pub. L. No. 111-148 (Mar. 23, 2010), *available at* http://www.gpo.gov/fdsys/pkg/PLAW-111publ148/pdf/PLAW-111publ148.pdf (site visited June 8, 2016). The ACA is also known as Obamacare.

[20] Pub. L. No. 111-152 (Mar. 30, 2010), *available at* http://www.gpo.gov/fdsys/pkg/PLAW-111publ152/pdf/PLAW-111publ152.pdf (site visited May 11, 2016).

[21] *See* https://www.medicare.gov/part-d/costs/coverage-gap/part-d-coverage-gap.html (site visited Aug. 10, 2016).

[22] Social Security Amendments of 1972 § 201(a).

[23] Social Security Amendments of 1972 § 238(a), Social Security Act § 1814, 42 U.S.C. § 1395f, *available at* https://www.law.cornell.edu/uscode/text/42/1395f (site visited May 23, 2016).

[24] Omnibus Budget Reconciliation Act of 1980 (OBRA '80), Pub. L. No. 96-499 (Dec. 5, 1980), § 930(b), (g); 94 Stat. 2599, 2631 (1980). Note that BBA '97 § 4611 established a prior institutionalization requirement for payment of home health services and a 100-visit limit on post-institutional home health services for payment under Part A for persons entitled to benefits under Parts A and B. Other home health care for these individuals is paid under Part B. See discussion of the Medicare home health benefit at **§ 1.05[A][3]** of this Handbook. See also, discussion of plan costs, "How ACA Marketplace Premiums Measure Up to Expectations," available at http://kff.org/health-reform/perspective/how-aca-marketplace-premiums-measure-up-to-expectations/ (site visited Aug. 3, 2016).

A significant exception to the movement by Congress to enlarge Medicare coverage occurred in 1989, with the repeal of the Medicare Catastrophic Coverage Act of 1988 (MCCA).[25] Signed into law in July 1988, MCCA was the most significant revision and enhancement of the Medicare program since its inception. The law increased the amount of coverage available in all care settings, established some limits on beneficiary cost-sharing responsibilities, and added new benefits. The law also altered the manner in which Medicare was financed by looking only to those eligible for the program to pay for the new benefits. MCCA increased the monthly Part B premium and required a payment of a set amount for every $150 of tax liability, not to exceed a certain limit each year. This payment, which quickly became known as the Medicare surtax, was mandatory for all those eligible for Medicare, even if they did not participate in the program or did not need the new benefits. This payment mechanism proved to be the death knell of MCCA; almost all the Medicare components of MCCA were repealed in December 1989.[26]

As discussed above, Congress altered the Medicare program again in the BBA '97. This Act created a variety of private options for receiving Medicare coverage. It also made other significant changes, which have had the effect of limiting some payments and services.[27]

In 2003, the MMA greatly expanded the role of private health insurance providers in Medicare.[28] Prescription drug benefits under the ACA's Part D system are available only through private insurance companies and not through Medicare itself.[29] In an effort to increase enrollment in managed care and other private insurance plans, Congress created new private options under Part C. Congress also further increased funding to all private plans, paying them about 14 percent more per enrollee than Medicare would pay if the enrollee had remained in the traditional program. In addition, in the MMA, Congress changed the way actuaries calculate the solvency of the Medicare program, which raised concerns about the security of Medicare and the possibility of benefit reductions and increased cost-sharing in future years.

The Affordable Care Act (ACA) addresses many of the payment and solvency issues created in 2003 by the MMA. The health care reform law changes the payment structure for private Medicare Advantage plans to reduce

[25] Pub. L. No. 100-360 (July 1, 1988).

[26] Medicare Catastrophic Repeal Act of 1989, Pub. L. No. 101-234 (Dec. 13, 1989). Note that the Qualified Medicare Beneficiary program and the Medicaid spousal impoverishment provisions were not repealed.

[27] *See* BBA '97 § 4611 *et seq.*, amending Social Security Act § 1812, 42 U.S.C. §§ 1395d *et seq.* *See also* BBA '97 home health care discussion at **§ 1.05[A][3]** of this Handbook.

[28] *See* http://www.cms.gov/Medicare/Health-Plans/HealthPlansGenInfo/index.html (site visited May 11, 2016).

[29] *See* http://kff.org/medicare/fact-sheet/the-medicare-prescription-drug-benefit-fact-sheet/ (site visited May 11, 2016).

the overpayments and create greater payment equity with the traditional Medicare program. This change actually increases the number of years that the Medicare Part A trust fund is projected to remain solvent by about 12 years. Instead of changing the way that actuaries calculate Medicare solvency, however, the Affordable Care Act created a new entity, the Independent Payment Advisory Board (IPAB), to make recommendations to limit cost growth in Medicare beginning in 2014. IPAB recommendations will be adopted unless Congress takes action.[30] The IPAB does not have authority to change Medicare eligibility and benefit structures; however, there is concern that IPAB recommendations might result in changes that create barriers for beneficiaries to receive needed health care. With Medicare experiencing savings to its trust funds, the IPAB has not made cost-cutting recommendations and may yet be phased out.

§ 1.02 FINANCING

Part A of the Medicare program is financed largely through federal payroll taxes paid by employers and employees into Social Security's Federal Hospital Insurance Trust Fund. Parts B and D are financed by monthly premiums paid by Medicare beneficiaries and by general revenues from the federal government. In addition, Medicare beneficiaries share the cost of the program through copayments and deductibles that are required for many of the services covered under Parts A, B, and D.

Medicare beneficiaries also share in the costs of the Medicare Advantage program (Medicare Part C). In these plans the beneficiary's cost-sharing may be modest for some services; however, cost-sharing may exceed that of traditional Medicare for other, more expensive services.[31] The beneficiary share is permitted to increase under the law as long as overall the increases do not exceed the actuarial value of the cost-sharing that would be applicable, on average, to individuals who are in traditional Medicare.[32] Since January 2011, however, MA plans cannot impose cost-sharing for chemotherapy administration services, renal dialysis services, and skilled nursing care services that exceed the cost-sharing for those services under traditional Medicare.[33]

---

[30] The Patient Protection and Affordable Care Act (also known as the Affordable Care Act, or ACA), § 3403, *available at* http://www.gpo.gov/fdsys/pkg/PLAW-111publ148/pdf/PLAW-111publ148.pdf (site visited May 11, 2016).

[31] *See* "Medicare Advantage Fact Sheet," *available at* http://kff.org/medicare/fact-sheet/medicare-advantage-fact-sheet/ (site visited May 11, 2016).

[32] 42 U.S.C. § 1395w-24(e).

[33] ACA § 3203; Health Care and Education Reconciliation Act (HCERA) § 1102.

§ 1.03 ADMINISTRATION

The Medicare program is administered by CMS, under the direction of the Secretary of HHS. It has 10 regional offices throughout the country that oversee the program in their areas. CMS contracts with private organizations, usually insurance companies, to review claims and make payments. These entities were known as fiscal intermediaries for Part A hospital, SNF, home health, and hospice cases and as carriers for all Part B cases, but they are now all known as Medicare Administrative Contractors (MACs), most of which process claims under *both* Part A and Part B.[34] Quality Improvement Organizations (QIOs), formerly Peer Review Organizations (PROs), are responsible for "quality oversight in all traditional Medicare settings, provider-requested higher-weighed DRG [diagnosis-related group] reviews, EMTALA [Emergency Medical Treatment and Active Labor Act] reviews, provider education regarding quality of care issues, and expedited determinations."[35]

In 2012, CMS issued Transmittal 17, which revised and created new procedures for the review of quality of care concerns[36] by QIOs.[37] The new procedures

---

[34] *See* http://www.cms.gov/Medicare/Medicare-Contracting/Medicare-Administrative-Contractors/MedicareAdministrativeContractors.html (site visited May 11, 2016).

[35] CMS, "Inpatient Prospective Payment System Hospital and Long-Term Care Hospital Review and Measurement Fact Sheet," *available at* www.cms.hhs.gov/AcuteInpatientPPS/downloads/InpatientReviewFactSheet.pdf (site visited May 11, 2016). *See* Social Security Act, § 1154(a), 42 U.S.C. § 1320c-3, for a full description of the QIO function. The language of § 1154(a)(1) gives the Secretary broad authority to limit or expand QIO functions by contract.

[36] For purposes of Transmittal 17, quality of care concerns relate to a range of matters from how a beneficiary is or was treated by provider staff, whether the beneficiary is receiving or received the treatment or services requested or expected, and/or whether the services in question are or were provided in a way that meets accepted standards of care. *See* 42 U.S.C § 1320c-3. Matters of premature discharge from a Medicare-covered care setting may often start with a QIO complaint. Even so, with respect to matters of premature discharge or where there has been a denial of a continuing stay in a Medicare-participating hospital, skilled nursing facility, home health agency, or hospice, advocates should use the standard or expedited appeals process. *See* 42 U.S.C. § 1395ff, 42 C.F.R. §§ 405.900 *et seq.* (Traditional Medicare) and §§ 422.560 *et seq.* (Medicare Advantage).

[37] CMS, Transmittal 17: QIO Manual Chapter 5, "Quality of Care Review" (Apr. 6, 2012), *available at* http://www.cms.gov/Regulations-and-Guidance/Guidance/Transmittals/Downloads/R17QIO.pdf (site visited May 11, 2016). On May 9, 2014, the Centers for Medicare & Medicaid Services (CMS) announced the first phase of its restructuring of the QIO functions. In the first phase, CMS has contracted with Livanta LLC (for geographic areas 1 and 5), located in Annapolis Junction, Maryland, and KePRO (for geographic areas 2, 3, and 4), located in Seven Hills, Ohio. These contractors will be responsible for ensuring consistency in the review process with respect to beneficiary complaints. CMS describes these two contractors as its Beneficiary and Family-Centered Care (BFCC) QIO contractors. The states in the designated geographic areas are Area 1: Connecticut, Maine, Massachusetts, New Hampshire, New Jersey, New York, Pennsylvania, Puerto Rico, Rhode Island, Vermont, Virgin Islands; Area 2: District of Columbia, Delaware, Florida, Georgia, Maryland, North Carolina, South Carolina, Virginia, West Virginia; Area 3: Alabama, Arkansas, Colorado, Kentucky, Louisiana, Mississippi, Montana, North Dakota, New Mexico, Oklahoma,

apply to QIO review of the quality of services "among different cases and settings (including post-acute-care settings, ambulatory settings, and health maintenance organizations)."[38]

Qualified Independent Contractors (QICs) began reviewing Part A reconsiderations in 2005; they began reviewing Part B reconsiderations in 2006. MA determinations are made by the private insurance companies that offer the plans and then by a private entity under contract with CMS.[39] Under the traditional Medicare program, MACs review coverage decisions issued by providers and issue notices known as initial determinations from which a beneficiary can appeal. These entities make initial determinations and issue payments when Medicare coverage is available.

Initial coverage determinations for beneficiaries enrolled in MA plans are made by the plan itself. The MA plan is required to apply CMS policy and coverage rules when making coverage decisions. Reviews of unfavorable plan decisions are handled by the private contractor. CMS guides the claim review, decision, and payment process by issuing health insurance coverage manuals as well as various mailings, bulletins, "guidance," and memoranda. These CMS instructions purport to interpret the statute and regulations, but they sometimes go

---

South Dakota, Tennessee, Texas, Utah, Wyoming; Area 4: Iowa, Illinois, Indiana, Kansas, Michigan, Minnesota, Missouri, Nebraska, Ohio, Wisconsin; and Area 5: Alaska, Arizona, California, Hawaii, Idaho, Nevada, Oregon, Washington. The CMS announcement is *available at* https://www.cms.gov/Newsroom/Newsroom-Center.html (site visited May 11, 2016). Details are *available at* http://www.cms.gov/Center/Provider-Type/All-Fee-For-Service-Providers-Center.html (site visited June 8, 2016) and http://www.medicareadvocacy.org/cms-restructures-quality-improvement-organization-qio-program/ (site visited May 11, 20016).

On July 18, 2014, as part of the restructuring of the QIO program—separating the beneficiary quality of care complaint review process from provider quality improvement functions—CMS awarded additional contracts to assist providers with quality improvement matters. The new contracts represent the second phase of QIO restructuring. These QIOs will be known as Quality Innovation Network (QIN)-QIOs. *See* http://cms.gov/Newsroom/MediaReleaseDatabase/Press-releases/2014-Press-releases-items/2014-07-18.html?DLPage=1&DLSort=0&DLSortDir=descending (site visited May 11, 2016). Each QIN-QIO will work on strategic quality improvement initiatives. *See also* CMS, Quality Improvement Organization Manual, Ch. 1, *available at* http://www.cms.gov/Regulations-and-Guidance/Guidance/Manuals/Downloads/qio110c01.pdf (site visited, May 11, 2016).

[38] *See* Social Security Act, § 1154(a)(4)(A), *available at* https://www.ssa.gov/OP_Home/ssact/title11/1154.htm (site visited May 11, 2015), 42 U.S.C. § 1320c–3(a)(4)(A); Transmittal 17, § 5020. *See* http://www.medicareadvocacy.org/new-procedures-for-review-of-quality-of-care-complaints/ (site visited May 11, 2016). QIOs are entities comprising health care professionals—physicians, nurses, and other clinical professionals—who contract with the Medicare agency to review quality of care concerns, including beneficiary-generated complaints. *See also* https://www.cms.gov/Newsroom/Newsroom-Center.html (site visited Aug. 10, 2016).

[39] The MMA also included changes to the administration of Medicare. As of 2011, all claims are reviewed by MACs chosen by CMS through a competitive bidding process, replacing the current structure of intermediaries and carriers.

beyond interpretation and create criteria that are more restrictive than the Medicare Act. Practically, the manuals and other, often unpublished, directives from CMS form the basis for the coverage decisions that affect most beneficiaries.

Advocates should be alert to discrepancies between standards established by CMS and those established by the Medicare Act and regulations.[40] Where detrimental discrepancies exist, they may be the grounds for appeals or federal court challenges. Importantly, Administrative Law Judges (ALJs) and federal judges rely on the Medicare statute and regulations, not on CMS's guidelines, although regulatory changes require ALJs to give greater deference to CMS guidelines than was given in the past. Still, many cases are won on appeal to an ALJ that were denied initially and through reconsideration based on CMS rules. Furthermore, successful challenges to CMS's restrictive criteria have been brought in United States district court as violating the due process clause of the Fifth Amendment to the United States Constitution, the Medicare Act and regulations, and the Administrative Procedure Act.[41]

Advocates should also watch for discrepancies that may exist between standards enforced by CMS's regional offices and MACs. Since Medicare is a federal program, beneficiaries should not be subject to more restrictive criteria in one region of the country than in another.

§ 1.04 ENROLLMENT AND ELIGIBILITY

Generally, individuals who are 65 and are entitled to and receiving Social Security or Railroad Retirement benefits are automatically entitled to and enrolled in Medicare Part A and will be deemed to have also enrolled in Part B unless they opt out.[42] Persons who are not yet receiving Social Security or Railroad Retirement benefits must enroll in Part A during an initial enrollment period, which begins in the third month before the person reaches age 65 (or reaches age 65 and becomes a U.S. citizen, or a permanent resident who has lived continually in the United States for the five years immediately preceding application for Medicare). The initial enrollment period extends for the next seven months.[43]

---

[40] Medicare appeals regulations require Administrative Law Judges (ALJs) to give deference to CMS program guidance. 42 C.F.R. §§ 405.1062 and 405.1063.

[41] *See* Grijalva v. Shalala, 153 F.3d 1115 (9th Cir. 1998), *vacated and remanded,* 526 U.S. 1096, 119 S. Ct. 1573, 143 L. Ed. 2d 669 (1999); Healey v. Shalala, Civ. Action No. 3:98 CV 418 (DJS) (Mar. 2000); Linoz v. Heckler, Medicare & Medicaid Guide (CCH) 35,876 (9th Cir. 1986); Duggan v. Bowen, 691 F. Supp. 1487 (D.D.C. 1988); Fox v. Bowen, 656 F. Supp. 1236 (D. Conn. 1987); Hooper v. Sullivan, Medicare & Medicaid Guide (CCH) 37,985 (D. Conn. 1989); Sarrassat v. Bowen, No. C88-20161 (N.D. Cal. 1989).

[42] Social Security Act, § 206, 42 U.S.C. § 1395p(f). *See* **Appendix 1-1** of this Handbook for a summary of the traditional Medicare program (Parts A & B).

[43] 42 U.S.C. § 1395i-2(a); 42 C.F.R. § 406.21(b). On June 26, 2015, the Supreme Court ruled favorably in Obergefell v. Hodges, Dir., Ohio Dep't of Health, Nos. 14-556, 14-562, 14-571, and

An application for Social Security or Railroad Retirement will also suffice for Medicare. A separate application is not necessary. Individuals who take early retirement under Social Security will be automatically enrolled in Medicare when they attain age 65.

Individuals who are receiving Social Security benefits cannot waive their entitlement to Medicare Part A. In order to waive Part A, they must withdraw their Social Security application and return any retirement or disability benefits they have received.[44] Because Part B is voluntary, an individual may always decline Part B.

Those who are 65 years of age and are not receiving Social Security benefits may still enroll in Medicare but must file an application.[45] As the age of eligibility is gradually increasing to 67, this is an important point. Every year more

---

14-574, 576 U. S. ___ (2015), *available at* http://www.supremecourt.gov/opinions/14pdf/14-556_3204.pdf (site visited June 8, 2016). The Court found that the failure to grant same-sex couples a marriage license is a violation of equal protection under the United States Constitution. Advocates should pay close attention to implementation issues as they arise.

For background on the tortuous history of the recognition of same-sex marriages at the federal level and access to benefits, see United States v. Windsor, 570 U.S. ___ (2013), 133 S. Ct. 2675, *available at* http://www.supremecourt.gov/opinions/12pdf/12-307_6j37.pdf (site visited June 8, 2016). The *Windsor* decision holds Section 3 of the Defense of Marriage Act (DOMA) unconstitutional because DOMA limited a valid marriage to being only between a man and a woman. With respect to *Windsor*, persons in state-recognized same-sex marriages (and equivalent relationships as defined in states) should consider filing for spousal benefits as appropriate.

Same-sex spouses of Medicare beneficiaries who are in valid marriages may be eligible for benefits as a spouse and should apply for benefits as appropriate. *See* "Demise of DOMA: Implementing Federal Benefits for Same-Sex Spouses," *available at* http://www.medicareadvocacy.org/demise-of-doma-implementing-federal-benefits-for-same-sex-spouses/ (site visited June 8, 2016); *see also* Attorney General Holder's Memorandum to the President, "Implementation of *United States v. Windsor* (June 20, 2014)." The Holder Memorandum, which summarizes various agencies' practices with respect to following the law of celebration or the law of domicile in determining a valid same-sex marriage, is *available at* http://www.justice.gov/iso/opa/resources/972201462010393090 4785.pdf (site visited June 8, 2016). In addition, the Social Security Administration (SSA), on August 23, 2013, added two Program Operation Manual Systems (POMS) provisions: GN 00210.005, "Holding Claims, Appeals, and Post-Entitlement Actions Involving Same-Sex Marriages or Legal Same-Sex Relationships other than Marriage," *available at* https://secure.ssa.gov/apps10/poms.nsf/lnx/0200210005 (site visited May 11, 2016), and GN 00210.010, "Interviewing Individuals with Claims Involving Same-Sex Relationships," *available at* https://secure.ssa.gov/apps10/poms.nsf/lnx/0200210010 (site visited May 11, 2016)). *See also* LGBT Protections In Affordable Care Act Section 1557, *available at* https://www.federalregister.gov/articles/2016/05/18/2016-11458/nondiscrimination-in-health-programs-and-activities?utm_campaign=subscription+mailing+list&utm_medium=email&utm_source=federalregister.gov (site visited July 25, 2016); and *see* http://healthaffairs.org/blog/2016/06/06/lgbt-protections-in-affordable-care-act-section-1557/ (site visited July 25, 2016). *See also* https://www.gpo.gov/fdsys/pkg/FR-2016-05-18/pdf/2016-11458.pdf (site visited July 27, 2016).

[44] Social Security Program Operations Manual System (POMS), § HI 000801.002; Hall v. Sebelius, 2011 WL 891818 (D.D.C. Mar. 16, 2011).

[45] The Social Security Administration (SSA) began accepting on-line Medicare applications in March 2010. *See* www.ssa.gov.

people reaching age 65 must apply for Medicare because they are not yet eligible for Social Security. Individuals who have been entitled to Social Security or Railroad Retirement disability benefits for 24 months are entitled to Medicare but also must apply to enroll in the program. Applications may be made with Social Security after receiving disability benefits for 21 months.[46] Effective July 1, 2001, the 24-month waiting period is eliminated for disabled persons diagnosed with ALS.[47] Persons under age 65 and entitled, for more than 24 months, to monthly Social Security or Railroad Retirement benefits based on disability do not need to file an application for hospital insurance.[48]

Medicare coverage can be extended up to 93 months after disability benefits are terminated if the beneficiary is engaged in an approved nine-month trial work period (TWP) after a period of disability.[49] The previous period of disability benefits will count toward the 24-month eligibility requirement, should the beneficiary seek to reestablish Medicare eligibility.[50]

Individuals who miss their initial enrollment period must wait for a general enrollment period to enter Medicare Part B. The general enrollment period is the first three months of each calendar year (January 1 through March 31). Medicare Part B benefits do not begin until July of that year.[51]

The Part D prescription drug benefit, which became effective January 1, 2006, requires individuals who want drug coverage to affirmatively enroll in a prescription drug plan (PDP) or a Part C MA plan with prescription drug coverage (MA-PD). The initial enrollment period for Part D corresponds to the individual's initial enrollment period for Part A.[52] Individuals who do not enroll during their initial enrollment period or who want to change the plan in which they have enrolled may do so during the annual coordinated enrollment period (ACEP), October 15 through December 7 of each year.[53]

---

[46] 42 U.S.C. § 1395p(g).

[47] BIPA, § 115.

[48] 42 C.F.R. § 406.6.

[49] 42 C.F.R. § 406.12(e)(2).

[50] Note that most people with disabilities who choose to work will continue to receive at least 93 consecutive months of hospital and supplemental medical insurance under Medicare Parts A and B after completing a trial work period (TWP). *See* Center for Medicare Advocacy, "Medicare Coverage for People with Disabilities" (Aug. 21, 2008), *available at* http://www.medicareadvocacy.org/medicare-info/medicare-coverage-for-people-with-disabilities/# (site visited June 8, 2016). Additional discussion is available in Vol. VII, No. 4 of the Center's "Healthcare Rights Review" (Winter 2007). *See* the Medicare statute at 42 U.S.C. § 422(c) and implementing regulations at 20 C.F.R. § 404.1592; 42 C.F.R. § 406.12(e) (individual under age 65 who is entitled to social security or railroad retirement disability benefits); 20 C.F.R. § 220.170 (the trial work period). *See also* http://www.ssa.gov/oact/cola/twp.html (site visited May 11, 2016) and http://www.ssa.gov/redbook/eng/ssdi-only-employment-supports.htm#1 (site visited May 11, 2016).

[51] 42 C.F.R. §§ 406.21(c) and 407.12(a)(2).

[52] 42 C.F.R. § 423.38(a).

[53] 42 U.S.C. § 1395w-101(b).

Penalties apply for late enrollment under Part A, Part B, and Part D. Under Part A, a 10 percent penalty, based on the monthly Part A premium price, is imposed for every month of late enrollment up to twice the number of months for which the beneficiary has failed to enroll.[54] Under Part B, a 10 percent penalty is also imposed. The Part B penalty is for each full year (12-month gap) of late enrollment.[55] Unlike Part A, there is no end point to the penalty under Part B. Under Part D, the penalty is the greater of an amount that is actuarially sound for each uncovered month or 1 percent of the national average monthly beneficiary base premium for each uncovered month, whichever is greater. As with Part B, there is no end point to the penalty.[56]

Individuals who receive Medicare based on disability have a new initial enrollment period when they become eligible for Medicare based on age. Any late enrollment penalty they are paying because of delayed enrollment in Part B and/or Part D when they became eligible based on disability will be eliminated during the enrollment period based on age.[57]

Medicare has established a special enrollment period (SEP) for persons who do not purchase Medicare Part B at age 65 because they (or their spouse) are covered under an employer's large group health plan.[58] The SEP is generally defined to include each month in which a person is enrolled in a group health plan as described in Sections 1862(b)(1)(A)(v) and 1862(b)(1)(B)(iv) of the Social Security Act and to end with the last day of the eighth consecutive month after the person is no longer enrolled.[59]

A SEP is also available for eligible Medicare beneficiaries who are members of a qualified HMO.[60] In addition, BBA '97 created a six-month SEP for disabled workers who lose benefits under a group health plan. The SEP for these individuals starts the first day of the month in which the termination of benefits occurs.[61]

Individuals who delay enrolling in a Part D plan because they have creditable drug coverage, that is, drug coverage that is as good as Medicare, through another source also have a SEP if that drug coverage ends. There are additional SEPs that allow individuals to change drug plans at times other than the annual enrollment period, under limited circumstances.[62]

---

[54] 42 U.S.C. § 1395i-2(c)(6).
[55] 42 U.S.C. § 1395r (b); 42 C.F.R. § 408.22.
[56] 42 U.S.C. § 1395w-113(b).
[57] 42 U.S.C. § 1395w-113(b).
[58] 42 U.S.C. § 1395p(i); 42 C.F.R. § 406.24.
[59] 42 U.S.C. § 1395p(i)(3)(A), (B).
[60] 42 U.S.C. § 1395i-2(c)(7); *see* definition of "eligible individual," 42 U.S.C. § 1395i-2(a).
[61] 42 U.S.C. § 1395i-2(c)(7); *see* definition of "eligible individual," 42 U.S.C. § 1395i-2(a).
[62] Medicare Managed Care (MC) Manual, Ch. 2, § 30.4, *available at* https://www.cms.gov/Medicare/Eligibility-and-Enrollment/MedicareMangCareEligEnrol/Downloads/FINALMAEnrollmentandDisenrollmentGuidanceUpdateforCY2012-REV11162011.pdf (site visited May 11, 2016).

[A] Medicare Advantage (HMO, PPO, SNP, and PFFS) Eligibility and Enrollment

Beneficiaries have the option to receive their Medicare coverage through a participating private MA plan in areas where those plans are available. In order to do so, beneficiaries must be enrolled in both Part A *and* Part B.[63] The beneficiary must live within the service area served by the MA plan[64] and must not be enrolled in any other Medicare-participating plan.[65]

MA plans must cover the services currently available under Medicare Parts A and B. Plans must pass on to beneficiaries any cost savings achieved through efficient plan administration in the form of additional benefits, including a reduction in the Part B premium. MA plans may offer supplemental benefits for which a separate premium is charged, but the separate premium may not vary among individuals within the plan and must not exceed certain actuarial and community rating requirements.

To enroll, a beneficiary must file an application with a participating MA plan. Filing an application does not guarantee enrollment. To ensure fairness in the enrollment process, each application must be dated when it is received by the MA plan and processed in chronological order by date of receipt. Under Medicare regulations, the MA plan is required to provide prompt notification to the applicant in writing of acceptance or denial.[66]

The MA plan may deny enrollment only if acceptance of the individual (1) would require the plan to exceed its overall enrollment capacity; (2) would cause the enrollment to become substantially non-representative of the general population in the plan's geographic area; or (3) would prevent the plan from complying with the terms of its contract with CMS.[67] MA plans may choose to close enrollment. However, unless MA plans receive a "capacity waiver" from CMS, they must accept applications from certain beneficiaries, such as those who move into the geographic area.

---

[63] 42 C.F.R. § 422.50(a).

[64] Medicare Advantage (MA) plans receive a capitated payment from Medicare for each enrollee in return for providing all Medicare covered services.

[65] 42 C.F.R. §§ 422.2 and 422.50(a)(2)(iii)(3)(i). The service area, as defined by CMS, is the geographic area for which CMS grants its approval for the plan to enroll eligible individuals. A service area generally consists of a full county or counties. In 2006, regional Preferred Provider Organizations (PPOs) serving multiple states became available in some areas of the country. *See* Academy Health, "Regional PPOs in Medicare: What Are the Prospects?," *available at* http://www.hcfo.org/pdf/ppo.pdf (site visited May 11, 2016); Avalere Health LLC, "Regional and Local Preferred Provider Organizations (PPOs) Achieved Sizeable Enrollment Gains in 2008," *available at* http://avalere.com/research/docs/PPO_Growth_20080609.pdf (site visited May 11, 2016).

[66] 42 C.F.R. § 422.60.

[67] 42 C.F.R. § 422.60.

Generally, application decisions may not be based on the health of the applicant.[68] However, ESRD patients may only enroll as new enrollees in an MA SNP that serves people with chronic conditions or those dually eligible for Medicare and Medicaid. Individuals who develop ESRD while already enrolled in an MA plan may remain in the plan. If the plan requires periodic re-enrollment, they must also be permitted to re-enroll.[69] Enrollment in the MA plan continues until such time as the enrollee is disenrolled voluntarily or involuntarily.[70]

Issues of disenrollment are a critical concern, particularly when costly care and services are involved. Medicare has established specific regulatory requirements defining the circumstances for involuntary disenrollment. They include the failure to pay premiums or deductibles as required, a permanent move outside the MA plan's service area, fraudulent statements on behalf of the enrollee leading to enrollment, and disruptive behavior that impairs the plan's ability to provide services. Beneficiaries must be provided notice and appeal rights information before disenrollment.[71]

[B] Process for Exercising Choice of Medicare Advantage Plan

Beneficiaries can elect to enroll or disenroll from an MA plan only in accord with certain limitations.[72]

1. If there are one or more MA plans offered in an individual's service area at the time the individual first becomes entitled to benefits under Part A and enrolled under Part B, the individual may make an election during an initial election period. Coverage under the MA plan becomes effective as of the first date on which the individual may receive coverage, that is, the month in which the individual becomes entitled to Medicare Parts A and B.

2. "Lock-in" rules, so called because beneficiaries become "locked in" to the choices they made during the previous fall's annual enrollment period, became effective on January 1, 2006.[73] Starting in January 2011,

[68] 42 C.F.R. § 422.110.

[69] 42 C.F.R. § 422.50(a)(2). For additional exceptions to the general rule that individuals with ESRD are barred, including those converting from an employer plan offered by the MA company, see also CMS, Medicare MC Manual, Ch. 2, §§ 20.2.2 and 20.2.3, *available at* http://cms.hhs.gov/Medicare/Eligibility-and-Enrollment/MedicareMangCareEligEnrol/Downloads/FINALMAEnrollmentandDisenrollmentGuidanceUpdateforCY2012-Revised872012forCY2013.pdf (site visited May 11, 2016).

[70] 42 C.F.R. § 422.74.

[71] 42 C.F.R. § 422.74.

[72] 42 U.S.C. § 1395w-21(e).

[73] 42 U.S.C. § 1395w-21(e)(2).

the only change a beneficiary can make is to return to traditional Medicare and a PDP during the first 45 days of the year.

3. All beneficiaries may make an election during an "annual, coordinated open enrollment period." This annual election will permit beneficiaries to enroll or disenroll from the various offerings during the period from October 15 through December 7.
4. Certain "special election periods" apply only if (a) the MA plan was terminated; (b) the beneficiary ceased to be eligible for enrollment in such plan; (c) the beneficiary demonstrated that the plan violated its contract with Medicare, including marketing requirements; or (d) some other exceptional circumstance exists. Beneficiaries who reside in a nursing home or who are dually eligible for Medicare and Medicaid also have a SEP that allows them to enroll and disenroll at any time. Eligible individuals may enroll in an MA SNP for people with chronic conditions at any time; however, they may only disenroll during the annual enrollment period or the open enrollment period. A new SEP allows beneficiaries to enroll in, but not to disenroll from, an MA plan with a five-star quality rating at any time.[74]
5. Beneficiaries in the traditional Medicare program who do not make a plan election during the annual election period remain in the original program. If an individual does not make an election and is in an MA plan, that individual will remain in the MA plan. Elections become effective January 1 of the following year. However, a beneficiary who was previously covered by traditional Medicare and who elected an MA plan will, if hospitalized as of the effective date of the election, have that hospitalization covered by original Medicare until discharge. Note that this special rule applies only to hospital stays; all other ongoing Medicare-covered services should be covered by the MA plan.
6. CMS must conduct a special educational and publicity campaign every fall to inform beneficiaries about MA election procedures.[75] At the time of enrollment and every year thereafter, MA plans must disclose to enrollees in their service area the number and mix of participating doctors, emergency service options, out-of-service coverage, procedures for obtaining emergency services, optional supplemental coverage and costs, prior authorization rules, grievance and appeals procedures, quality assurance mechanisms, number of grievances and appeals and their disposition, and a summary of the method of compensating doctors.

---

[74] CMS, Medicare MC Manual, Ch. 2, § 30.4, *available at* http://www.cms.gov/Medicare/Eligibility-and-Enrollment/MedicareMangCareEligEnrol/Downloads/CY-2014-MA-Enrollment-and-Disenrollment-Guidance-r.pdf (site visited May 11, 2016).

[75] 42 C.F.R. §§ 422.50–422.80.

§ 1.05 COVERAGE

The Medicare Act allows for coverage when the services received are medically "reasonable and necessary for the diagnosis or treatment of illness or injury or to improve the functioning of a malformed body member."[76] Medicare coverage is *excluded* by statute for custodial care, except in the case of hospice services.[77] These requirements, that the care be medically reasonable and necessary for treatment or diagnosis and that the care be "skilled," are often strictly interpreted by those who administer the Medicare program; they create the most frequent obstacles to coverage.

Medicare has four parts: Part A, Part B, Part C, and Part D. Part A covers inpatient hospital care, inpatient care in a SNF, home health care services, and hospice care.[78] Part B covers medical care and services provided by physicians and other medical practitioners, durable medical equipment (DME), a variety of outpatient care services, and home health services not otherwise covered under Part A.[79] Medicare Part C, or Medicare Advantage (MA), added a variety of systems for the *financing* of Medicare-covered health services. These MA options must offer the core package of benefits available under Parts A and B, plus additional benefits.[80] In 2006, Medicare Part D added a limited prescription drug benefit offered through private insurance plans. Part D only specifies the deductible, copayment, and out-of-pocket limits for the drug benefits. The Part D plans set their own drug formularies and premiums and may vary the cost-sharing as long as the drug package they offer is the "actuarial equivalent" of the statutory standard benefit.[81]

---

[76] 42 U.S.C. § 1395y(a)(1)(A). Obtaining therapy and nursing services for ongoing chronic conditions when a patient is not improving continues to be a serious problem for Medicare beneficiaries. CMS has clarified that medical improvement has never been the basis for ongoing therapy and nursing services for a beneficiary's chronic condition. This issue is addressed in Jimmo v. Sebelius. *See* http://www.medicareadvocacy.org/medicare-info/improvement-standard/. *See also* the *Jimmo* fact sheet, *available at* http://www.medicareadvocacy.org/wp-content/uploads/2013/04/Jimmo-Fact Sheet.pdf. Clarifying language has been added to various CMS manuals. *See* CMS, MLN Matters (MM8458), "Manual Updates to Clarify Skilled Nursing Facility (SNF), Inpatient Rehabilitation Facility (IRF), Home Health (HH), and Outpatient (OPT) Coverage Pursuant to *Jimmo v. Sebelius*" (Jan. 14, 2014), *available at* http://www.cms.gov/Outreach-and-Education/Medicare-Learning-Network-MLN/MLNMattersArticles/Downloads/MM8458.pdf (site visited May 11, 2016) and the CMS Manuals website at http://cms.gov/Regulations-and-Guidance/Guidance/Manuals/Internet-Only-Manuals-IOMs-Items/CMS012673.html (site visited May 11, 2016). *See* **Appendix 1-9** of this Handbook.

[77] 42 U.S.C. § 1395y(a)(9).

[78] 42 U.S.C. §§ 1395c and 1395d.

[79] 42 U.S.C. §§ 1395j and 1395k.

[80] 42 U.S.C. §§ 1395w-21 *et seq.*

[81] *See* MMA, adding §§ 1860D-1–1860D-42 of the Social Security Act, 42 U.S.C. §§ 1395w-101–1395w-151.

[A] Part A

[1] Hospital Coverage

A beneficiary is entitled to 90 days of Medicare coverage for hospital care as an inpatient during each benefit period, or "spell of illness," after the beneficiary meets the deductible ($1,316 in 2017.)[82] If the patient remains in the hospital beyond the 60th day, he or she is responsible for a daily coinsurance amount for days 61 to 90 ($329 per day in 2017). A spell of illness begins when a beneficiary receives Medicare-covered inpatient hospital care and ends when the patient has spent 60 consecutive days outside the hospital (or SNF) or remains in a health care institution but does not receive Medicare-covered services for 60 consecutive days.[83] In addition, the beneficiary is entitled to 60 days of hospital care as a "lifetime reserve." Once exhausted, lifetime reserve days are not replenished.[84] The coinsurance for lifetime reserve days is even heftier ($658 per day in 2017).

In 1983, Congress established a prospective payment system (PPS) for Medicare reimbursement of inpatient acute care hospital services.[85] Care in

---

[82] Defining when a beneficiary is an inpatient has become increasingly difficult. Moreover, inpatient status is critical to meeting the required three-day inpatient hospitalization requirement for skilled nursing facility care. For a discussion of this issue, see "Observation Status: 'Morphed into Madness,'" *available at* http://www.medicareadvocacy.org/observation-status-morphed-into-madness/ (site visited May 11, 2016). *See also* "Observation Status and the NOTICE Act: Advocates Not over the MOON," *available at* http://www.medicareadvocacy.org/observation-status-and-the-notice-act-advocates-not-over-the-moon/ (site visited May 18, 2016). The latter piece discusses proposed rules updating Medicare reimbursement to acute care hospitals, and CMS announced how it intends to implement the Notice of Observation Treatment and Implication for Care Eligibility Act (NOTICE Act). Effective August 6, 2016, the NOTICE Act requires that hospitals provide written and oral notice, within 36 hours, to patients who are in observation or other outpatient status for more than 24 hours. The notice must explain the reason that the patient is an outpatient and describe the implications of that status both for cost-sharing in the hospital and for subsequent "eligibility for coverage" in a skilled nursing facility (SNF).

For changes due to The Consolidated Appropriations Act of 2016, see https://www.cms.gov/Medicare/Medicare-Fee-for-Service-Payment/Acute InpatientPPS/FY2016-IPPS-Final-Rule-Home-Page-Items/FY2016-IPPS-Final-Rule-Regulations.html (site visited Aug. 9, 2016). The revisions pertain to low-volume payment adjustments for hospitals based on CMS's experience with these hospitals in FY 2016.

[83] 42 U.S.C. § 1395x(b) and 42 C.F.R. §§ 409.10–409.18 (inpatient hospital services covered); 42 U.S.C. § 1395d(a) and 42 C.F.R. § 409.61 (scope of benefit); 42 C.F.R. § 409.82 (hospital deductible); 42 C.F.R. § 409.83 (hospital coinsurance); 42 C.F.R. § 409.60 (benefit period rules). *See* **Appendix 1-1** and **Appendix 1-3** of this Handbook for a summary of premiums, deductibles, and coinsurance payments. *See* http://www.medicare.gov/Pubs/pdf/11579.pdf (site visited Sept 28, 2016).

[84] For a discussion of lifetime reserve days, see CMS, Medicare Benefit Policy (BP) Manual, Ch. 5, *available at* http://www.cms.gov/Regulations-and-Guidance/Guidance/Manuals/downloads/bp102c05.pdf (site visited June 8, 2016).

[85] 42 U.S.C. § 1395ww(d).

Medicare-certified rehabilitation and psychiatric hospitals and hospital units is exempt from the diagnosis-related group (DRG) system.[86] Under PPS, Medicare payment is made at a predetermined, specific rate for each discharge.[87] All discharges are classified according to a list of DRGs. The list contains hundreds of specific DRGs. Each DRG is assigned a dollar amount based on the average cost of caring for patients with similar diagnoses in the past, regardless of whether the patient's care actually cost the hospital less, or more, to deliver.

[2] Skilled Nursing Facility Care

Medicare Part A provides payment for post-hospital care in SNFs for up to 100 days during each spell of illness.[88] If Medicare coverage requirements are met, the patient is entitled to full coverage of the first 20 days of SNF care. From day 21 through day 100, Medicare pays for all covered services except for a daily coinsurance amount ($164.50 per day in 2017). The SNF patient will not be entitled to any Medicare coverage unless he or she was hospitalized for at least three days prior to the SNF admission and was admitted to the SNF within 30 days of the hospital discharge involving an inpatient stay of three days (generally spanning three midnights).[89]

SNF coverage includes the services generally available in a SNF: nursing care provided by registered professional nurses, bed and board, physical therapy, occupational therapy, speech therapy, social services, medications, supplies, equipment, and other services necessary for the patient to attain or maintain the highest practicable level of functioning. However, "convenience" items, such as a telephone, are not covered by Medicare.

---

[86] *See* definitions at 42 C.F.R. § 412.29, Classification criteria for payment under the inpatient rehabilitation facility prospective payment system, *available at* http://www.gpo.gov/fdsys/pkg/CFR-2014-title42-vol2/xml/CFR-2014-title42-vol2-part412.xml#seqnum412.20 (site visited May 11, 2016).

[87] *See* CMS, Medicare Learning Network (MLN), "Acute Care Hospital Inpatient Prospective Payment System" (Apr. 2013), *available at* http://www.cms.gov/Outreach-and-Education/Medicare-Learning-Network-MLN/MLNProducts/downloads/AcutePaymtSysfctsht.pdf (site visited June 8, 2016).

[88] *See* "Skilled Nursing Facility (SNF) Facilities," *available at* https://www.medicare.gov/coverage/skilled-nursing-facility-care.html (site visited May 16, 2016).

[89] 42 U.S.C. § 1395x(h) and 42 C.F.R. § 409.20 (SNF services); 42 U.S.C. § 1395d(a)(2)(A) and 42 C.F.R. § 409.60 (scope of benefit); 42 U.S.C. § 1395f(a)(2)(b) (physician certification requirement); 42 C.F.R. § 409.35 (practical matter rule); 42 U.S.C. § 1395x(i) (three-day qualifying hospital stay); 42 U.S.C. § 1395x(i) (30-day rule); 42 C.F.R. §§ 409.30–409.34 (daily skilled care requirement).

There are certain requirements that must be met in order for a patient to receive Medicare coverage. These requirements include:[90]

1. A physician must certify that the patient needs SNF care;
2. The beneficiary must generally be admitted to the SNF within 30 days of a three-day inpatient hospital stay;[91]

---

[90] 42 U.S.C. § 1395x(h) and 42 C.F.R. § 409.20 (SNF services); 42 U.S.C. § 1395d(a)(2)(A) and 42 C.F.R. § 409.60 (scope of benefit); 42 U.S.C. § 1395f(a)(2)(b) (physician certification requirement); 42 C.F.R. § 409.35 (practical matter rule); 42 U.S.C. § 1395x(i) (three-day qualifying hospital stay); 42 U.S.C. § 1395x(i) (30-day rule); 42 C.F.R. §§ 409.30–409.34 (daily skilled care requirement).

[91] Defining when a beneficiary is an inpatient has become increasingly difficult. Increasingly, patients are classified as "outpatients" in observation status, even when they remain in the hospital receiving medical care for many days. Since "inpatient" status is necessary to meet the required three-day inpatient hospitalization requirement for skilled nursing facility care, these so-called outpatients are not eligible for any SNF coverage. The final rule is codified at 78 Fed. Reg. 50,495, 50,906–954 (Aug. 19, 2013). For a discussion of the final rule, see Center for Medicare Advocacy, "Observation Status: 'Morphed into Madness,'" *available at* http://www.medicareadvocacy.org/observation-status-morphed-into-madness/ (site visited May 18, 2016). *See also* https://www.cms.gov/Medicare/Medicare-Fee-for-Service-Payment/AcuteInpatientPPS/FY2016-IPPS-Final-Rule-Home-Page-Items/FY2016-IPPS-Final-Rule-Regulations.html?DLPage=1&DLEntries=10&DLSort=0&DLSortDir=ascending (site visited May 16, 2016); *see also* FY 2014 IPPS Rule Outreach (CMS 1599-F)–8-12-13, *available at* https://www.cms.gov/medicare/medicare-fee-for-service-payment/acuteinpatientpps/downloads/fy-2014-ipps-rule-outreach.pdf (site visited May 18, 2016). The final rule is codified at 78 Fed. Reg. 50,495–51,040, 50,950 (Aug. 19, 2013). For a discussion of the final rule, see http://www.medicareadvocacy.org/observation-status-new-final-rules-from-cms-do-not-help-medicare-beneficiaries/ (site visited June 8, 2016). In addition, the decision in Bagnall v. Sebelius, Civ. No. 3:11-CV-1703 (MPS) (D. Conn., Memorandum of Decision, 9/23/2013) doc. # 106, *available at* http://scholar.google.com/scholar_case?case=6608692245354306736&hl=en&as_sdt=2&as_vis=1&oi=scholarr (site visited May 16, 2016), confirms the notion that a patient must be admitted as an inpatient in order for inpatient rights to pertain; that persons who are in outpatient status do not have the rights and protections of inpatients. *See also* a discussion of *Bagnall* and the need for legislation in Center for Medicare Advocacy, "Disappointing Decision from Court in Challenge to 'Observation Status' Highlights Need to Pass Legislation," *available at* http://www.medicareadvocacy.org/disappointing-decision-from-court-in-challenge-to-observation-status-highlights-need-to-pass-legislation/ (site visited May 16, 2016). *But see* recent favorable decision, "Court Allows Medicare "Rubber Stamp" Case to Go Forward and Certifies Nationwide Class," *available at* http://www.medicareadvocacy.org/court-allows-medicare-rubber-stamp-case-to-go-forward-and-certifies-nationwide-class/ (site visited Aug. 15, 2016). In its holding, the court found that on August 8, 2016, a federal judge in Connecticut largely denied the government's motion to dismiss and granted plaintiff's motion for certification of a nationwide class. Sherman v. Burwell, No. 3:15-cv-1468 (JAM) (D. Conn. 2016). The case challenges the fact that, for the last several years, decisions at the earliest two levels of appeal in the Medicare administrative process (Redetermination and Reconsideration) have overwhelmingly resulted in upholding denials of coverage for home health care services. The judge referred to the decisions in the original named plaintiff's case (who was replaced by his wife when he died) as "unnerving." This is especially true since over 60 percent are granted if people are able to continue to the third level of appeal, the ALJ level of review).

3. The beneficiary must require daily skilled nursing or rehabilitation; and
4. The care needed by the patient must, as a practical matter, be available only in a SNF on an inpatient basis.

[3] Home Health Care

Medicare covers home health services in full, with no deductible or copayments from the beneficiary. Services must be medically necessary and reasonable, and the following criteria must be met to qualify for ("trigger") coverage:[92]

1. A physician has signed or will sign a plan of care.
2. A physician must have a face-to-face encounter with the beneficiary within 90 days prior to the start of the home health care or within 30 days of the actual start of care.
3. The patient is "confined to home," often known as "homebound." This criterion is met if leaving home requires a considerable and taxing effort, which may be shown by the patient's needing personal assistance, or the help of a wheelchair or crutches, etc. Homebound does not mean "bedbound." Absences for medical purposes and for other non-medical, but infrequent and short outings, are allowable.
4. The patient needs or will need physical or speech therapy, *or* intermittent skilled nursing (from once a day for periods of 21 days at a time if there is a predictable end to the need for daily nursing care, to once every 60 days).
5. The home health care is provided by, or under arrangement with, a Medicare-certified provider.

If the triggering conditions described above are met, the beneficiary is entitled to Medicare coverage for home health services.[93] Home health services include:[94]

---

[92] *See* 75 Fed. Reg. 70,372–486 (Nov. 17, 2010), amending 42 C.F.R. § 424.22.

[93] 42 U.S.C. § 1395x(m) and 42 C.F.R. §§ 409.40 *et seq.* (home health coverage and coverage criteria); 42 U.S.C. §§ 1395x(f)(a)(8) and 1395n(a)(2)(f) (homebound criteria). Note that BIPA amended the "homebound" definition to clarify that an individual who attends adult day centers or religious services should not be disqualified from Medicare home health coverage on grounds that he or she has violated the homebound definition.

[94] Good discharge planning is an important tool in obtaining proper home health and other post-hospital services, including SNF services and rehabilitation services. It is significantly underused as an advocacy tool. Discharge planning is available to Medicare beneficiaries and others as a condition of a hospital's participation in the Medicare program. Services should be more than a rudimentary search for the next nursing home bed or home health agency opening. *See* 42 U.S.C. § 1395x(ee) (added to the Medicare statute in OBRA '87); 42 C.F.R. §§ 482.43 *et seq.*, effective January 12, 1995. Interpretive guidelines and survey procedures for hospital discharge planning are

- Part-time or intermittent nursing care provided by or under the supervision of a registered professional nurse;
- Physical, occupational, or speech therapy;
- Medical social services under the direction of a physician; and
- To the extent permitted in regulations, part-time or intermittent services of a home health aide.[95]

In addition to the coverage criteria described above the following points are also important:[96]

1. The qualifying term "part time and intermittent," for purposes of defining the nursing services that will trigger coverage, is defined as nursing care that is provided as little as once every 60 days and as much as daily for predictable periods of 21 days at a time, with extensions in exceptional circumstances when the need for additional care is finite and predictable.
2. Part-time or intermittent services, for purposes of coverage, are defined as skilled nursing and home health aide services furnished any number of days per week so long as they are furnished fewer than eight hours

available in the Medicare State Operations Manual (SOM), CMS Pub. No. 100–07, Appendix A, § 482.43, *available at* http://www.cms.gov/Regulations-and-Guidance/Guidance/Manuals/downloads/som107ap_a_hospitals.pdf (site visited May 18, 2016). *See also* Center for Medicare Advocacy, "Discharge Planning: Tips for Evaluating a Hospital's Skilled Nursing Facility Placement Choices," *available at* http://www.medicareadvocacy.org/discharge-planning-tips-for-evaluating-a-hospitals-skilled-nursing-facility-placement-choices/ (site visited May 16, 2016).

On May 17, 2013, CMS released an update of Appendix A of the State Operations Manual (SOM) revising its interpretive guidelines for hospital discharge planning. *See* CMS's memorandum to State Survey Agency Directors about the revised discharge planning guidance, Ref: S&C: 13-32-Hospital (May 17, 2013), *available at* http://www.cms.gov/Medicare/Provider-Enrollment-and-Certification/SurveyCertificationGenInfo/Downloads/Survey-and-Cert-Letter-13-32.pdf (site visited May 18, 2016). The guidance is effective immediately and is located at http://www.cms.gov/Regulations-and-Guidance/Guidance/Manuals/downloads/som107ap_a_hospitals.pdf (site visited May 18, 2016); *see also* Alfred J. Chiplin, Jr., *Breathing Life into Discharge Planning*, 13 Elder L.J. 1, 1–83 (2005). Medicare has developed *Discharge Planning Checklist,* CMS Pub. No. 11376 (revised June 2015), *available at* https://www.medicare.gov/pubs/pdf/11376.pdf (site visited May 18, 2016). Note also that the ACA adds provisions to help with transitions from the hospital to other care settings and to prevent unnecessary re-hospitalizations.

[95] 42 CFR 405(b) importantly sets out the details of what are Medicare's coverable home health services, including "hands on personal care," which includes far more care than commonly understood.

[96] The regulations are effective January 1, 2011; however, since they clarify rather than change coverage rules, they are also applicable to services prior to that time. *See* 75 Fed. Reg. 70,461 (Nov. 17, 2010), amending 42 C.F. R. § 409.44(c), effective Jan. 1, 2011.

each day and 28 or fewer hours each week combined (or, on a case-by-case basis, up to 35 hours per week combined).

3. Individuals who attend adult day centers or religious services should *not* be disqualified from Medicare home health coverage on grounds that they violate the homebound definition.[97]

4. The Medicare capitated payment system for home health care includes incentives and disincentives provisions that have led to reductions and terminations of care for some patients, particularly those with chronic or long-term conditions.

CMS issued regulations on November 17, 2010, regarding coverage for home health services. One of the most important aspects of the home health coverage regulations is a detailed explanation clarifying when Medicare covers establishment or *performance* of therapy to maintain an individual's condition. The regulation states:

> The unique clinical condition of a patient may require the specialized skills of a qualified therapist to perform a safe and effective maintenance program required in connection with the patient's specific illness or injury. When the clinical condition of the patient is such that the complexity of the therapy services required to maintain function involve the use of complex and sophisticated therapy procedures . . . by the therapist . . . **or** the clinical condition of the patient is such that the complexity of the therapy services required to maintain function must be delivered by the therapist . . . to ensure the patient's safety and to provide an effective maintenance program, then those reasonable and necessary services shall be covered.[98]

For therapy services to be covered, the patient's clinical record must contain a plan of care established by a qualified therapist, in conjunction with the physician, which describes a course of therapy treatment and goals that are consistent with the patient's functional evaluation.[99] Documentation in the clinical record must describe the goals of the treatment plan,[100] be measurable,[101] and demonstrate that the method used to assess the patient's function, including activities of daily living (ADLs), is in accordance with acceptable practice standards.[102]

---

[97] *See* BIPA.

[98] 42 C.F.R. § 409.44(c)(2)(iii)(C).

[99] 42 C.F.R. § 409.44(c)(1)(i).

[100] 42 C.F.R. § 409.44(c)(1)(ii).

[101] 42 C.F.R. § 409.44(c)(1)(iii).

[102] 42 C.F.R. § 409.44(c)(1)(iv). *See also* CMS, Transmittal 17: QIO Manual Chapter 5—"Quality of Care Review" (Apr. 6, 2012), *available at* http://www.cms.gov/Regulations-and-Guidance/Guidance/Transmittals/Downloads/R17QIO.pdf (site visited May 18, 2016).

[4] Hospice Care

Medicare has provided coverage for hospice care since 1982. Hospice care is intended to provide palliative and supportive care for terminally ill people and their families rather than treatment for the underlying condition. Medicare covers two 90-day periods of hospice care and an unlimited number of additional periods of 60 days each.[103]

On March 10, 2014, CMS issued a memorandum entitled "Part D Payment for Drugs for Beneficiaries Enrolled in Hospice—Final 2014 Guidance."[104] The Guidance directs Part D Plan Sponsors to "place beneficiary-level prior authorization (PA) requirements on all drugs for beneficiaries who have elected hospice. . . ." As a result of advocacy, on July 18, 2014, CMS issued a memorandum to Part D Plan Sponsors and Medicare hospice providers replacing its March 10, 2014 Guidance. Pursuant to the replacement guidance, the only Part D medications requiring a "hospice prior authorization" are analgesics (medications used to treat pain), antiemetic drugs (medications used to treat nausea), laxatives, and anxiolytics (medications used to treat anxiety).[105] This means that when Medicare beneficiaries elect hospice, they should <u>not</u> have difficulty accessing medically necessary medications that are not related to their terminal condition through their Part D plans.

To receive Medicare hospice coverage, a patient must elect affirmatively to hospice services and, as a consequence, forego most other Medicare coverage for treatment of the underlying terminal condition. The hospice care must generally be provided by, or under arrangement with, one Medicare-certified hospice program during each period.

To receive Medicare coverage for hospice care, the patient must be certified as terminally ill by the patient's physician and/or the hospice staff physician,[106] and the hospice care must be part of a written plan of treatment established by

---

[103] *See* **Chapter 5** of this Handbook for a discussion of recent revisions to the Medicare conditions of participation for hospices.

[104] *See* http://www.cms.gov/Medicare/Medicare-Fee-for-Service-Payment/Hospice/Downloads/Part-D-Payment-Hospice-Final-2014-Guidance.pdf (site visited May 18, 2016).

[105] *See* Center for Medicare Advocacy, "Hospice and Access to Medications Update: CMS Replacement Guidance," *available at* http://www.medicareadvocacy.org/hospice-and-access-to-medications-update-cms-replacement-guidance/ (site visited May 18, 2016).

[106] Both the hospice physician and the patient's attending physician (if the patient has an attending physician) must certify that the patient is terminally ill for the first 90-day election period. For subsequent election periods, only a hospice physician can recertify the patient as terminally ill. 42 C.F.R. § 418.22(c). Starting January 1, 2011, prior to the 180th day recertification and for subsequent recertification, a hospice physician or nurse practitioner must have a "face-to-face encounter" with the hospice patient to determine continued eligibility for hospice coverage. ACA § 3132, HCERA § 3004, amending 42 U.S.C. § 1395f(i). *See* the Center for Medicare Advocacy, "New Hospice Regulations Are a Mixed Bag for Beneficiaries Seeking High Quality End of Life Care," *available at* http://www.medicareadvocacy.org/new-hospice-regulations-are-a-mixed-bag-for-beneficiaries-seeking-high-quality-end-of-life-care/ (site visited June 8, 2016).

the attending physician and hospice medical professionals. The hospice medical records should have clinical documentation supporting the physician's certification.

If coverage conditions are met, Medicare is available for an array of services, including:[107]

- Nursing care;
- Physician services;
- Counseling services for the patient and the family or other caretakers;
- Medical social services;
- Short-term inpatient care;
- Home health aides;
- Homemaker services;
- Medical supplies, equipment, appliances, and biologicals (including pain medication); and
- Physical, occupational, and speech therapy.

[B] Part B

Part B of Medicare provides coverage for a host of services, generally for beneficiaries who are in non-institutionalized settings. Part B is optional. It is financed by premiums paid by individuals enrolled in the program and by general revenues from the federal government. Since 1973, individuals receiving Social Security retirement benefits, individuals receiving Social Security disability benefits for 24 months, and individuals otherwise entitled to Medicare Part A are automatically enrolled in Part B unless they decline coverage. Others must enroll in Part B by filing a request with Social Security during certain designated periods.

All Medicare beneficiaries enrolled in Part B owe a monthly premium. Most participants have their premium automatically deducted from their Social Security check. Beneficiaries with low incomes and resources may be eligible for assistance in paying the Part B premium through one of the Medicare Savings Programs (MSPs).[108] The premium has been income-related for beneficiaries with higher incomes since January 2007. Individuals with incomes of $85,000 or more and couples with incomes of $170,000 or more pay higher Part B premiums than

---

[107] 42 U.S.C. § 1395x(dd) and 42 C.F.R. Pt. 418 (hospice benefit); 42 C.F.R. § 418.22 (physician certification); 42 U.S.C. § 1395d(d) (benefit periods); 42 C.F.R. § 418.24(a) (hospice election rules).

[108] *See* **§ 1.06** of this Handbook.

those below these income levels. The standard Part B premium for 2017 is $109. See **Appendix 1-3** for the premium for individuals who are not "held harmless."

Part B also has an annual deductible ($183 in 2017). Each year, before Medicare pays anything, the patient must incur medical expenses sufficient to meet the deductible, based on Medicare's approved "reasonable charge," not on the provider's actual charge.[109]

After the beneficiary meets the deductible, Part B will pay 80 percent of the reasonable charge for covered services, the reimbursement rate determined by Medicare; the beneficiary is responsible for the remaining 20 percent as coinsurance.[110] Unfortunately, the reasonable charge is often less than the provider's actual charge. If the provider agrees to "accept assignment," the provider agrees to accept Medicare's reasonable charge rate as payment in full, and the patient is responsible for only the remaining 20 percent.

If the provider does not accept assignment, the patient can be billed for a balance beyond the 20 percent coinsurance payment. There is, however, a ceiling on charges to Medicare beneficiaries even for providers who do not accept assignment. This ceiling is known as the "Limiting Charge," which is often higher than the Medicare reasonable charge but often less than the provider's actual charge, but it can be no more than 115 percent of the Medicare reasonable charge.[111]

The major benefit under Part B is payment for physicians' services. In addition, DME, outpatient therapy, diagnostic X-rays, and laboratory tests are covered. Congress has also mandated an increase in the home health services covered under Part B and added additional preventive benefits.[112] Medicare is also

---

[109] As a result of the MMA, the Part B deductible will increase yearly based on the yearly percentage increase in the monthly actuarial value of benefits paid out of the Part B trust fund. MMA, § 629, amending 42 U.S.C. §§ 1395l(b), 1395r, and 1395w.

[110] Previously, Part B paid only 50 percent (62.5 percent of the approved amount times 80 percent) of the reasonable charge for outpatient mental health treatment. As a result of MIPPA, Medicare paid 60 percent of the reasonable charge in 2012 (the beneficiary paid 50 percent). The cost-sharing slowly phases down so that, by 2014, Medicare paid 8 percent of the reasonable charge. Note, however, that diagnostic services such as psychological testing to establish a diagnosis, brief office visits to monitor or change prescriptions, and medical management furnished to someone with Alzheimer's disease or a related disorder are not subject to the additional payment limitation. 42 C.F.R. § 410.155.

[111] 42 U.S.C. § 1395w-4(g); *see* Garelick v. Sullivan, 987 F.2d 913 (2d Cir. 1993) (constitutionality of provision upheld), *cert. denied*, 510 U.S. 821, 114 S. Ct. 78, 126 L. Ed. 2d 47 (1993); *see also* A. Chiplin, *The Medicare Limiting Charge: An Issue of Implementation and Enforcement*, 26 Clearinghouse Rev. 167 (1992). *See* http://heinonline.org/HOL/LandingPage?handle=hein.journals/clear26&div=28&id=&page= (site visited May 23, 2016); and *see* further limiting charge discussion at **§ 1.05[B][2]**.

[112] 42 U.S.C. §§ 1395k and 1395x. For a list of Medicare's coverage of preventive services, see https://www.medicare.gov/coverage/preventive-and-screening-services.html (site visited June 8, 2016).

requiring a face-to-face interview with the patient as a fraud protection measure.[113]

The following is a partial list of items and services that can be covered under Part B:[114]

- Annual "Wellness Visit"
- Physicians' services;
- Home health services;
- Services and supplies, including drugs and biologicals that cannot be self-administered, furnished incidental to physicians' services;
- Diagnostic X-ray tests, diagnostic laboratory tests, and other diagnostic tests;
- X-ray therapy, radium therapy, and radioactive isotope therapy;
- Surgical dressings and splints, casts, and other devices used for fractures and dislocations;
- DME;
- Prosthetic devices;
- Braces, trusses, artificial limbs, and eyes;
- Ambulance services;
- Some outpatient and ambulatory surgical services;
- Some outpatient hospital services;
- Some physical therapy services;[115]

---

[113] *See* ACA § 6407, amending 42 U.S.C. § 1395m(a)(11)(2)(B). *See* CMS, "Face to Face Encounter Requirement for Certain Durable Medical Equipment" (Sept. 9, 2013), *available at* http://cms.gov/Research-Statistics-Data-and-Systems/Monitoring-Programs/Medicare-FFS-Compliance-Programs/Medicare-FFS-Compliance-Programs/Medical-Review/FacetoFaceEncounterRequirementforCertainDurableMedicalEquipment.html (site visited May 18, 20016).

[114] *See* Medicare.gov, "What Medicare Covers," *available at* http://www.medicare.gov/what-medicare-covers/part-b/what-medicare-part-b-covers.html (site visited June 8, 2016).

With respect to non-emergency ambulance providers, see CMS's moratorium on new non-emergency ground ambulance providers at https://www.federalregister.gov/agencies/centers-for-medicare-medicaid-serviceshttps://www.federalregister.gov/articles/2016/08/03/2016-18383/ (site visited Aug. 3, 2016).

[115] *See* CMS, "Medicare Limits on Therapy Services" (revised Jan. 2016), *available at* https://www.medicare.gov/Pubs/pdf/10988.pdf (site visited June 8, 2016). Caps on the amount Medicare will pay for outpatient therapy services went into effect on January 1, 2006. When the Medicare Access and CHIP Reauthorization Act was signed into law on April 16, 2015, the therapy caps exceptions process for PT, OT, and SLP services were extended through the remainder of CY 2015

- Some occupational therapy;[116]
- Some outpatient speech therapy;[117]
- Comprehensive outpatient rehabilitation facility (CORF) services;
- Rural health clinic services;
- Institutional and home dialysis services, supplies, and equipment;
- Ambulatory surgical center services;
- Antigens and blood-clotting factors;
- Influenza, pneumococcal, and hepatitis B vaccines;
- Some HMO services;
- Some Pap smear screenings;
- Some mammography screenings;
- Some diabetes tests;
- Some other preventive services including colorectal, prostate cancer, and glaucoma screening, smoking cessation services, and some medical nutrition therapy;
- Qualified psychologist services;

---

and for all of CY 2016 and CY 2017. *See* CMS, "Therapy Caps Exceptions Process Extended Through CY 2017," *available at* http://www.cms.gov/Medicare/Billing/TherapyServices/index.html?redirect=/TherapyServices (site visited May 18, 2016). *See also* the pamphlet "Medicare's Limits on Therapy Services," *available at* https://www.medicare.gov/Pubs/pdf/10988.pdf (site visited June 8, 2016). After the beneficiary satisfies the annual Part B deductible ($166 in 2016), Medicare pays 80 percent of the therapy costs. *See* http://www.cms.gov/Transmittals/downloads/R2073CP.pdf (site visited May 18, 2016). *See also* http://www.cms.gov/TherapyServices (site visited May 18, 2016).

[116] CMS, "Medicare Limits on Therapy Services" (revised Jan. 2016), *available at* https://www.medicare.gov/Pubs/pdf/10988.pdf (site visited May 18, 2016). Caps on the amount Medicare will pay for outpatient therapy services went into effect on January 1, 2006. When the Medicare Access and CHIP Reauthorization Act was signed into law on April 16, 2015, the therapy caps exceptions process for PT, OT, and SLP services were extended through the remainder of CY 2015 and for all of CY 2016 and CY 2017. *See* CMS, "Therapy Caps Exceptions Process Extended Through CY 2017," *available at* http://www.cms.gov/Medicare/Billing/TherapyServices/index.html?redirect=/TherapyServices (site visited May 18, 2016).

[117] CMS, "Medicare Limits on Therapy Services" (revised Jan. 2016), *available at* https://www.medicare.gov/Pubs/pdf/10988.pdf (site visited June 8, 2016). Caps on the amount Medicare will pay for outpatient therapy services went into effect on January 1, 2006. When the Medicare Access and CHIP Reauthorization Act was signed into law on April 16, 2015, the therapy caps exceptions process for PT, OT, and SLP services were extended through the remainder of CY 2015 and for all of CY 2016 and CY 2017. *See* CMS, "Therapy Caps Exceptions Process Extended Through CY 2017," *available at* http://www.cms.gov/Medicare/Billing/TherapyServices/index.html?redirect=/TherapyServices (site visited May 18, 2016).

- Therapeutic shoes for patients with severe diabetic foot disease;
- Screening for depression in adults;
- Screening and counseling to reduce alcohol misuse.

Medicare Part B is fairly comprehensive but far from complete. Certain items and services are *excluded* from coverage. They include:

- Services that are not medically reasonable or necessary;
- Custodial care;
- Personal comfort items and services;
- Care that does not meaningfully contribute to the treatment of illness, injury, or a malformed body member;
- Prescription drugs that do not require administration by a physician;
- Routine physical checkups (except for one "Welcome to Medicare" checkup when an individual first enrolls in Medicare);
- Eyeglasses or contact lenses in most cases;
- Eye examinations for the purpose of prescribing, fitting, or changing eyeglasses or contact lenses;
- Hearing aids and examinations for hearing aids;
- Orthopedic shoes and other supportive devices for the foot unless intended as an instrumental part of a leg brace;
- Cosmetic surgery;
- Most dental services; and
- Routine foot care.

[1] Preventive Services

Historically, Medicare coverage did not include much preventive care, checkups, comfort items, or respite care. However, since the late 1990s Congress has been adding preventive services to those few that already existed in the Medicare program (which included influenza, pneumococcal, and hepatitis B vaccines).[118] The Affordable Care Act removed additional barriers to accessing

---

[118] MIPPA § 101 provides that, effective January 1, 2009, CMS may use its national coverage determination (NCD) process to add coverage for additional preventive services that have been recommended by the U.S. Preventive Services Task Force that are reasonable and necessary for the prevention or early detection of an illness or a disability and that are appropriate for individuals entitled to benefits under Medicare Part A and enrolled in Medicare Part B. Also effective

preventive services, adding coverage for an annual wellness visit that includes development of a personalized prevention plan[119] and removing cost-sharing for most preventive services that receive an A or B rating by the United States Preventive Services Task Force.[120] Preventive services covered under Medicare include:[121]

- Annual wellness visit.
- Annual mammogram for women age 40 and over.
- Annual Pap smears and pelvic exams for beneficiaries considered at high risk for cervical cancer or following an abnormal Pap smear. For women not in these groups, coverage is for Pap smears and pelvic exams once every two years.
- Prostate cancer screening on an annual basis for men over age 50.
- Colorectal cancer screening tests for beneficiaries age 50 and older. Frequency and payment limits are to be determined by the Secretary.
- Outpatient diabetes self-management training services, blood testing strips, and monitors.
- Bone mass measurement tests.
- Telehealth services when a beneficiary resides in a rural county designated as a health professional shortage area and where other criteria are met.
- Coverage of screening colonoscopy once every 10 years or within four years of a screening flexible sigmoidoscopy for all persons who are *not* at high risk.
- Coverage of medical nutrition therapy services for patients with diabetes or kidney disease.

January 1, 2009, MIPPA extended eligibility for the Welcome to Medicare physical from the initial six months of Part B eligibility to the initial year, eliminated application of the Part B deductible to the initial physical, and added services to be included in the examination. The ACA also gives the Secretary discretion to modify or eliminate coverage of preventive services to the extent that the modification is consistent with recommendations of the U.S. Preventive Services Task Force ACA § 4105. *See* http://www.uspreventiveservicestaskforce.org/ (site visited May 18, 2016).

[119] ACA § 4103. *See also* Center for Medicare Advocacy, "Making Sense of Medicare's Preventive Service Benefits" (Sept. 20, 2012), *available at* http://www.medicareadvocacy.org/making-sense-of-medicares-preventive-service-benefits/ (site visited May 18, 2016).

[120] ACA § 4104. *See also* https://www.cms.gov/Regulations-and-Guidance/Guidance/Transmittals/downloads/r864otn.pdf (site visited Aug. 10, 2016).

[121] *See* Medicare.gov, "Your Medicare Coverage," *available at* http://www.medicare.gov/coverage/preventive-and-screening-services.html (site visited May 18, 2016).

- Coverage for routine glaucoma screening for persons at risk for glaucoma.
- Coverage of an initial physical examination performed within the first year of an individual's initial coverage under Part B.
- Coverage of a blood test for early detection of cardiovascular disease including tests for cholesterol levels and other lipid or triglyceride levels for individuals determined to be at risk.
- Coverage of diabetes screening tests for the purpose of early detection in individuals who are considered to be at risk for diabetes.
- Coverage of intravenous immune globulin for the treatment of primary immune deficiency diseases in the home.

[2] Limits on Physician Charges

As discussed above, when an item or a service is determined to be coverable under Medicare Part B, it is reimbursed at 80 percent of a payment rate approved by Medicare known as the "approved charge;" the patient is responsible for the remaining 20 percent. Unfortunately, the approved (or "reasonable") charge is often substantially less than the *actual* charge. The obvious result of this reimbursement system is that Medicare payment, even for items and services covered by Part B, is often inadequate. The patient is left with out-of-pocket expenses. When a physician accepts assignment, he or she agrees to accept the Medicare-approved charge as full payment for the services provided. Medicare pays 80 percent of the approved charge. Either the patient or supplemental insurance pays the remaining 20 percent copayment. No further payment is due to the physician.

Often local senior centers, area agencies on aging, and Social Security offices have lists of physicians, other providers, and medical equipment suppliers who accept Medicare assignment.[122] Also, a few states require physicians and other Part B providers who serve Medicare patients to accept assignment via their own balanced billing statutes. Massachusetts, for example, requires physicians to accept assignment for all Medicare patients; Connecticut requires the acceptance of assignment for low- and moderate-income Medicare patients. New York, Pennsylvania, Vermont, Minnesota, and Ohio also limit what physicians can charge Medicare patients.

When a physician does not accept assignment, he or she may "balance bill" the patient above the Medicare-approved charge. "Balance bill" refers to the physician's charge above the Medicare-approved rate. Federal law sets a limit known

[122] CMS provides information about the Medicare assignment program and lists of participating physicians and suppliers on its Medicare website at *www.medicare.gov*.

as the "limiting charge" on the amount a physician may balance bill. Since 1991 the limiting charge has been based on a percentage of the Medicare approved charge for physician services.

Generally, a doctor who does not accept assignment may not charge a total of more than 115 percent of the Medicare-approved amount. The patient's Medicare Summary Notice (MSN),[123] the written notice that is sent to patients after a Medicare claim is processed, will state the approved charge for the doctor's services. Usually, the patient can calculate the physician's limiting charge for the services described in the MSN by multiplying the Medicare-approved charge by 115 percent. Medicare's calculation of the limiting charge will be stated on the MSN.

For example, assume the patient goes to a doctor who does not accept assignment. The doctor's actual charge is $600, but the Medicare approved charge allows only $349.37. The doctor's total bill may not exceed $401.78 (115 percent × $349.37); this is the limiting charge. Medicare will pay $279.50 (80 percent of the $349.37 approved charge). The physician cannot charge the patient more than $122.28 ($401.78 minus Medicare payment of $279.50). If the doctor bills more than $401.78, he or she is billing above the limiting charge and is violating federal law.

In some instances, the limiting charge will be more or less than 115 percent of the approved charge. If this seems to be the case, or if other questions arise, you can obtain specific limiting charge information by calling the provider's Medicare carrier.

§ 1.06 MEDICARE SAVINGS PROGRAMS

The Qualified Medicare Beneficiary (QMB) program, the Specified Low-Income Medicare Beneficiary (SLMB) program, and the Qualified Individual (QI) program, collectively referred to as the Medicare Savings Programs (MSPs), provide varying levels of assistance to Medicare beneficiaries with low incomes.[124]

---

[123] Medicare has made revisions to the layout of its MSNs in an effort to make them more user-friendly. *See* http://www.medicare.gov/pubs/pdf/SummaryNoticeA.pdf (Part A) (site visited May 18, 20016) and http://www.medicare.gov/pubs/pdf/SummaryNoticeB.pdf (Part B) (site visited May 18, 2016); *see also* CMS's. MLN Matters, MM7676, Redesign of the Medicare Summary Notice (MSN)—Final Implementation—and Major Update to Chapter 21 of the Claims Process Manual, *available at* http://www.cms.gov/Outreach-and-Education/Medicare-Learning-Network-MLN/MLNMattersArticles/downloads/MM7676.pdf (site visited May 18, 2016).

[124] *See also* **Appendix 1-8** of this Handbook for more information on programs targeted to low-income beneficiaries.

[A] Qualified Medicare Beneficiary Program

States are required to pay the deductibles, coinsurance, and premiums for Medicare Parts A and B for certain low-income Medicare beneficiaries, under the QMB program.[125] These individuals can have incomes up to the federal poverty level (FPL), which was $1,010 per month for an individual and $1,355 per month for a couple (for 2016), indexed each year according to the Consumer Price Index.[126] States may also liberalize the income and resource criteria; advocates should check with their state for specific information about how income and resources are calculated. States that liberalized income and/or resource criteria for the QMB program generally must also do so for other MSPs.

BBA '97 made modifications to the states' payment and cost-sharing obligations under the QMB program. It also allowed states to pay no more in deductibles, coinsurance, or copayments for Medicare cost-sharing than its Medicaid program would have paid for services for its Medicaid recipients who are not eligible for QMB. These modifications were effective on August 5, 1997.[127] Since the BBA '97, many states have implemented legislation that limits these Medicare cost-sharing payments to Medicaid levels. This has created access problems for some QMB patients whose physicians do not accept Medicaid and will not accept the lower payment rate.

[B] Specified Low-Income Beneficiary Program and Qualified Individual Program

Under the SLMB program, states cover Medicare Part B premiums for persons of somewhat greater means than those who qualify just for the QMB. These are persons with incomes up to 120 percent of the FPL, or $1,208 for an individual per month in 2016, and resources at the same level as QMB[128] and $1,622 for a married couple per month.

Effective for premiums payable from January 1998 to December 2002, the BBA '97 also established a block grant to states for payment of Part B premiums for individuals with income of at least 120 percent but less than 135 percent of the FPL ($1,345/month in 2015) (the QI program).

Persons in the QI group cannot be otherwise eligible for Medicaid; the resource limit for QI is the same as for QMB. Note that the SLMB program remains an entitlement, while the BBA '97 block grant for QI is to be allotted on a first-come, first-serve basis with the number of eligible individuals who can participate in the program being limited by each state's block grant allocation for the

---

[125] 42 U.S.C. § 1395d(p).

[126] MIPPA § 112, amending 42 U.S.C. § 1396d(p)(1). *See* https://aspe.hhs.gov/basic-report/computations-2016-poverty-guidelines (site visited June 8, 2016).

[127] BBA '97 § 4714, amending 42 U.S.C. § 1396a(n).

[128] 42 U.S.C. § 1396a(a)(10)(E)(iii); 74 Fed. Reg. 4199 (Jan. 23, 2009).

fiscal year. Individuals must apply each year, and enrollment is redetermined annually.[129]

§ 1.07 THE MEDICARE APPEALS PROCESS

Because of the size and complexity of the Medicare program and because of the desire to contain costs, Medicare coverage is often denied when it should be granted. Sometimes these denials are a result of errors; sometimes they are a result of policy that places cost containment concerns over the needs of individual beneficiaries. Whatever the underlying reasons for the denial, the Medicare program includes an appeals system that is designed, at least in theory, to reverse erroneous denials and to correct mistakes.[130] If the patient's attending physician feels the care in question is medically necessary and the care is not simply excluded from Medicare coverage (e.g., hearing aids, routine dental care), the beneficiary should appeal. Unfortunately, changes to the appeals process enacted as part of BIPA and the MMA made the appeals process less friendly to beneficiaries.

BIPA unified the appeals process for claims arising under Parts A and B, other than for claims for hospital services. The Medicare statute establishes different processes for claims arising under Part C and Part D through the reconsideration level of review. For the most part, once a claim reaches the ALJ level of review and beyond, the process is the same regardless of whether the claim arises under Medicare Part A, B, C, or D.

[A] Traditional Medicare

[1] Notice of Medicare Payment

Generally, official notice from Medicare must be obtained before a beneficiary has a right to appeal. The Medicare Summary Notice (MSN) constitutes the "initial determination," or written notice that briefly explains what Medicare will

---

[129] BBA '97 § 4732, amending Social Security Act § 1902(a)(10) (42 U.S.C. § 1396(a)(10)) and enacting Social Security Act § 1933; *see also* BBA '97 § 4732(c). On December 9, 2009, CMS issued final rules to implement BIPA § 521, and MMA Title IX. *See* 74 Fed. Reg. 65,296 *et seq.* (Dec. 9, 2009), effective Jan. 8, 2010.

[130] *See* 42 U.S.C. §§ 1395ff *et seq.*; 42 C.F.R. §§ 405.904 *et seq.*, modified by final regulations at 74 Fed. Reg. 65,296 *et seq.* (Dec. 9, 2009); *see* http://edocket.access.gpo.gov/2009/pdf/E9-28707.pdf (site visited May 23, 2016) (Subpart I–Determinations, Redeterminations, Reconsiderations, and Appeals under Original Medicare (Parts A and B combined process)). The final rule clarifies that when the regulations refer to "day" that a "calendar day" is intended. This final rule also includes changes that are of a more substantive nature. *See also* https://www.cms.gov/Outreach-and-Education/Medicare-Learning-Network-MLN/MLNProducts/Downloads/MedicareAppealsProcess.pdf (site visited May 23, 2016), text update from CMS February 2015.

pay on a claim. The MSN is prepared by the Medicare contractor that reviews the claim.[131] CMS issues MSNs quarterly, rather than monthly, unless a reimbursement check is due the beneficiary.[132] Many claims are denied in whole or in part on the MSN due to insufficient information and mistakes. Determinations that find that the medical service was not medically necessary and is, therefore, not covered under Medicare should be closely examined. Errors are often made. If the claimant does not think Medicare is allowing a sufficient reimbursement amount, the claimant should also question the MSN.

It may be useful to telephone the contractor to question why Medicare benefits were denied. Sometimes the claimant will discover that inadequate information or documentation was mailed to the contractor and that the coverage denial can be resolved by providing better documentation.

It is important to note that, for all Part A claims, the first notice Medicare beneficiaries should receive informing them that care will not be covered by Medicare is from the health care provider. This is also the case for most Part B services. Before they can charge a beneficiary, providers who participate in the Medicare program must first issue a written notice to patients informing them that Medicare coverage will not be available. Providers have a financial incentive to issue denial notices because they may have to absorb the cost of the care they provide if they erroneously inform beneficiaries that the care will be covered but not if they erroneously deny coverage.

Notices from providers, however, do not form the basis for an appeal. The beneficiary must obtain a formal Medicare coverage determination or initial determination from the appropriate Medicare contractor.[133] Patients who receive denial notices from their provider must, therefore, request that a claim for payment be submitted to Medicare if they want to obtain an initial determination that can then be appealed. In addition, the initial determination does sometimes grant coverage that was denied by the provider. Note that if the beneficiary or representative requests a provider to submit a claim to Medicare, the provider is required to do so.[134]

---

[131] Claims are reviewed by contractors known as Medicare Administrative Contractors (MACs). Previously, contractors known as fiscal intermediaries reviewed Part A claims, and contractors known as carriers reviewed Part B claims.

[132] CMS, Trans. 1347 (Sept. 28, 2007) (implementation date: Oct. 29, 2007), Change Request No. 5722, *available at* https://www.cms.hhs.gov/transmittals/downloads/R1347CP.pdf (site visited May 23, 2016).

[133] Medicare Claims Processing (MCP) Manual, CMS Pub. No. 100-04, Ch. 29, §§ 10, 30.2, and 30.3, *available at* https://www.cms.gov/Regulations-and-Guidance/Guidance/Manuals/downloads/clm104c29.pdf (site visited May 23, 2016).

[134] MCP Manual, Ch. 1, § 50.1.5. (CMS implementation of this provision has been spotty.)

[2] Redeterminations

If the claimant remains dissatisfied with the initial determination, a redetermination may be requested. The redetermination is the first formal level of appeal for Medicare Part A and Part B claims.[135] The request for redetermination must be filed within 120 days of receipt of the MSN. The redetermination is performed by the entity that issued the initial determination denying benefits: the MAC for Part A SNF, home health, and hospice claims; the QIO for hospital claims,[136] and Part B claims. Generally, these appeals simply entail submitting a written request (forms are available on the Medicare.gov website at "Medicare forms")."[137] If at all possible, the claimant should attach to the redetermination request a copy of the denial notice issued by the health care provider and a supporting letter and/or documentation from the treating physician.[138]

Assistance from the attending physician is always key to a successful appeal. Claimants should include a written statement from the physician explaining the need for the service if possible and be sure to keep copies of all appeal requests and all supporting data.

Although current regulations require that redetermination decisions be issued within 60 calendar days of receipt of the redetermination request,[139] in the past it has not been unusual to wait many months for a decision from this first appeal stage. Unfortunately, it is also not unusual for meritorious claims to be

---

[135] *See* **Appendix 1-2** for a summary of the traditional Medicare appeals process and **Appendix 1-4** for a chart outlining the process.

[136] Note, too, that QIOs are tasked with reviewing quality of care concerns. *See* 42 U.S.C. § 1320c-3. Quality of care concerns relate to a range of matters from, among others, how one is or was treated by provider staff to whether one is receiving or received the treatment or services requested or expected to whether the services in question are or were provided in a way that meets accepted standards of care. *See* 42 U.S.C § 1320c-3. Matters of premature discharge from a Medicare-covered care setting may often start with a QIO complaint. Even so, with respect to matters of premature discharge or where there has been a denial of a continuing stay in a Medicare-participating hospital, SNF, home health agency, or hospice, advocates should use the standard or expedited appeals process. *See* 42 U.S.C. § 1395ff; 42 C.F.R. §§ 405.942 *et seq.* (Traditional Medicare) and 422.580–422.596 *et seq.* (Medicare Advantage). *See also* Center for Medicare Advocacy, Weekly Alert, "New Procedures for Review of Quality of Care Complaints," *available at* http://www.medicareadvocacy.org/new-procedures-for-review-of-quality-of-care-complaints/ (site visited May 23, 2016).

[137] *See* Medicare.gov, "Medicare Forms," *available at* http://www.medicare.gov/forms-help-and-resources/forms/medicare-forms.html (site visited May 23, 2016). *See also* Medicare.gov, "How do I file a complaint (also called a 'grievance')?," *available at* http://www.medicare.gov/claims-and-appeals/file-a-complaint/complaint.html (site visited May 23, 2016).

[138] *See* CMS, MLN, "Medicare Parts A & B Appeals Process" (Feb. 2015), *available at* http://www.cms.gov/Outreach-and-Education/Medicare-Learning-Network-MLN/MLNProducts/Downloads/MedicareAppealsProcess.pdf (site visited May 23, 2016).

[139] 42 C.F.R. § 405.950(a) (2009). Note that the regulations extend this time frame if the provider or supplier, as well as the beneficiary, files an appeal. However, adherence to this time frame is not enforceable by the beneficiary.

denied at the redetermination stage. However, some of these decisions do result in additional benefits, and this step is a prerequisite to move forward to the next steps in the appeal process.[140]

[3] Reconsideration

Beneficiaries dissatisfied with their redetermination decision can appeal to the next stage of the process: reconsideration. Individuals must complete the "reconsideration" step before receiving a hearing.[141] Reconsiderations are a paper review conducted by a review entity that is under contract with CMS, the QIC. A beneficiary has 180 days after receipt of an unfavorable redetermination to request a QIC reconsideration. The QIC must issue a decision within 60 days, with certain exceptions. If the QIC does not issue the decision in a timely manner, the beneficiary may request to escalate the case to an ALJ hearing. Regulations implementing the reconsideration review impose limitations on the submission of evidence on providers and suppliers, but not beneficiaries, who appeal to this level.[142] Beneficiaries may appeal an unfavorable reconsideration decision to an ALJ.

[4] Where to File an Appeal Request

Beneficiaries and their advocates must file a request for an appeal to the next level of review with the entity identified in the initial determination, redetermination, reconsideration, or ALJ decision.[143] In addition, the regulations set forth specific requirements for advocates who want to serve as appointed representatives and/or collect fees for their advocacy at the ALJ level and above.[144]

---

[140] 42 C.F.R. §§ 405.702–405.710 and 466.83 (2009) (reconsideration and appeals).

[141] 42 C.F.R. § 405.974.

[142] 42 C.F.R. §§ 405.950–405.978 (2009). Note that §§ 405.962(a) and 409.972(b)(3)(2009) now provide for a 60 calendar day filing time frame to request a reconsideration of a contractor's redetermination dismissal action, as an exception to the 180 calendar day time frame for filing a request for reconsideration of a contractor's redetermination decision. Note, too, that § 405.972(e) (2009) has been amended to clarify that a Qualified Independent Contractor's (QIC's) dismissal of a request for reconsideration of a contractor's dismissal action is binding and not subject to further review unless vacated under paragraph (d) of the section, which provides that if good and sufficient cause is established, a QIC may vacate its dismissal of a request for reconsideration within six months of the date of the notice of dismissal.

[143] 42 C.F.R. §§ 405.944 (2005); 405.964 (2009); and 405.1014 (2009). Before 2005, many beneficiaries and their advocates filed appeals through the Social Security office.

[144] 42 C.F.R. § 405.910 (2009).

[5] Summary of Expedited Appeals Process

Beneficiaries may seek expedited review of a SNF, home health, hospice, or CORF services discharge or termination.[145] The provider must give the beneficiary a general, standardized notice at least two days in advance of the proposed end of the service. If the service is fewer than two days, or if the time between services is more than two days, then notice must be given by the next to last service.[146] The notice must describe the service, the date coverage will end, the beneficiary's financial liability for continued services, and how to file an appeal.[147]

A beneficiary must request expedited review, orally or in writing, by noon of the next calendar day after receiving notice. At that time, the beneficiary is given a more specific notice that includes a detailed explanation of why services are being terminated, a description of any applicable Medicare coverage rules and information on how to obtain them, and other facts specific to the beneficiary's case. The beneficiary is not financially liable for continued services until the later of two days after receiving the notice or the termination date specified on the notice.[148]

Expedited review is available in cases involving a discharge from the provider of services, or a termination of services where "a physician certifies that failure to continue the provision of such services is likely to place the individual's health at risk."[149] Services furnished by a residential provider, such as a hospital, SNF, or hospice, are discharges for which a doctor's certificate is not required. Services furnished by a "non-residential provider," such as home health services, are treated as a termination of services for which a doctor's certificate of significant health risk must be provided.[150] A reduction in service is not considered a termination or discharge for purposes of triggering expedited review.[151]

A beneficiary who wishes to exercise the right to an expedited determination must submit a request for a determination with the QIO in the state in which the beneficiary is receiving the services at issue. The request may be made in writing or by telephone, but it must be made no later than noon of the calendar day following receipt of the provider's notice of termination. If the QIO is unavailable to accept the beneficiary's request, the beneficiary must submit the request by noon of the next day the QIO is available.[152]

---

[145] 42 U.S.C. § 1395ff(b)(1)(F), 42 C.F.R. §§ 405.1200–405.1204 (2009).

[146] 42 C.F.R. § 405.1200(b)(1).

[147] 42 C.F.R. § 405.1200(b)(2).

[148] 42 C.F.R. § 405.1202(c).

[149] 42 U.S.C. § 1395ff (b)(1)(F).

[150] 42 C.F.R. § 405.1202(a).

[151] 42 C.F.R. § 405.1200(a)(2).

[152] 42 C.F.R. § 405.1202(b). See also **§ 1.03** of this Handbook describing the QIO restructuring. The restructuring does not change the rules of the program with respect to time periods or decisional criteria. *See* CMS, "All Fee-for-Service Providers," *available at* http://www.cms.gov/Center/Provider-Type/All-Fee-For-Service-Providers-Center.html (site visited May 23, 2016); Center for Medicare Advocacy, "CMS Restructures Quality Improvement Organization (QIO) Program,"

Coverage for the services at issue will continue until the date and time designated on the termination notice, unless the QIO reverses the provider's service termination decision. If the QIO's decision is delayed because the provider did not timely supply necessary information or records, the provider may be liable for the costs of any additional coverage, as determined by the QIO.[153] If the QIO finds that the beneficiary did not receive valid notice, coverage of the provider services continues until at least two days after valid notice has been received. Continuation of coverage is not required if the QIO determines that coverage could pose a threat to the beneficiary's health or safety.[154]

If the QIO sustains the decision to terminate services or discharge the beneficiary, the beneficiary may request an expedited reconsideration, orally or in writing, by noon of the calendar day following initial notification. The reconsideration will be conducted by the QIC, which must issue a decision within 72 hours of the request. If the QIC does not comply with the time frame, the beneficiary may escalate the case to the ALJ level.[155]

Beneficiaries retain the right to utilize the standard appeals process rather than the expedited process in all situations. A QIO may review an appeal from a beneficiary, whose request is not timely filed, but the QIO does not have to adhere to the time frame for issuing a decision, and the limitation on liability does not apply.

[6] Special Rules for Hospital Claims

Hospitals must deliver a revised version of the *Important Message from Medicare* (IM) (CMS-R-193) and the *Detailed Notice of Discharge* (CMS 10066).[156] Under 42 C.F.R. § 405.1205 (for traditional Medicare) and 42 C.F.R. § 422.620 (for MA), Medicare participating hospitals must deliver the written IM notice with information about an individual's rights as a hospital patient. The information must include discharge and appeal rights and must be delivered within two calendar days of admission. A follow-up copy of the signed IM is to be given again as far as possible in advance of discharge but, in any case, no more than two calendar days prior to discharge.[157] The follow-up notice is not required

---

available at http://www.medicareadvocacy.org/cms-restructures-quality-improvement-organization-qio-program/ (site visited May. 23, 2016); and CMS Press Release, "CMS Launches Next Phase of New Quality Improvement Program" (July 18, 2014), *available at* http://cms.gov/Newsroom/MediaReleaseDatabase/Press-releases/2014-Press-releases-items/2014-07-18.html?DLPage=1&DLSort=0&DLSortDir=descending (sites visited May 23, 2016).

[153] 42 C.F.R. § 405.1202(c).

[154] 42 C.F.R. § 405.1202(c).

[155] *See* 42 C.F.R. § 405.1204.

[156] 72 Fed. Reg. 17,169 (Apr. 6, 2007).

[157] 72 Fed. Reg. 17,169 (Apr. 6, 2007).

if the admission IM was issued to the individual within two calendar days of discharge.[158]

For a hospital stay, a beneficiary must make a timely request for expedited review, orally or in writing, no later than the day of discharge. CMS, in its policy manual, interprets a "timely" request as no later than midnight of the day of discharge.[159] The beneficiary (or his or her authorized representative), upon request by the QIO, must be prepared to discuss the case with the QIO.[160] On the date that the QIO receives the beneficiary's request, the QIO must notify the hospital that the beneficiary has filed a request for intermediate review.[161] The hospital must supply any information, including medical records, that the QIO requires to conduct its review and must make it available, by phone or in writing, by the close of business of the first full working day after the day the beneficiary receives notice of the planned discharge.[162] When the beneficiary requests an expedited determination in accordance with Section 405.1206(d)(1), the QIO must make a determination and notify the beneficiary, the hospital, and the physician of its determination by close of business of the first working day after it receives all requested pertinent information.[163]

[7] Observation Notice

Until 2016, CMS required hospitals to inform patients of their outpatient status only if the hospitals' utilization review committee reversed the patient's status from inpatient to outpatient under Condition Code 44. However, effective August 6, 2016, the Notice of Observation Treatment and Implication for Care Eligibility Act (NOTICE Act) requires all hospitals to notify all patients of their outpatient status if they are in observation or other outpatient status for more than 2 hours.[164] CMS mandates use of a notice called the Medicare Outpatient Observation Notice (MOON).[165] Although final regulations implementing the NOTICE Act become effective October 1, 2016,[166] full implementation of the Act will not occur until hospitals begin using the MOON, which will not occur until 90 days

---

[158] 72 Fed. Reg. 17,169 (Apr. 6, 2007).

[159] 71 Fed. Reg. 68,721 (Nov. 27, 2007), adding a new 42 C.F.R. § 405.1205 and revising 42 C.F.R. § 405.1206. *See* revised 42 C.F.R. § 405.1206(b)(1). *See also* MCP Manual, Ch. 30, § 200.4.1.

[160] *See* revised 42 C.F.R. § 405.1206(b)(2).

[161] *See* revised 42 C.F.R. § 405.1206(e)(1).

[162] *See* revised 42 C.F.R. § 405.1206(e)(2).

[163] *See* revised 42 C.F.R. § 405.1206(d)(6).

[164] 42 U.S.C. § 1395cc(a)(1)(Y).

[165] The draft MOON notice (accessible in a zip file) is *available at* https://www.cms.gov/Regulations-and-Guidance/Legislation/PaperworkReductionActof1995/PRA-Listing-Items/CMS-10611.html (site visited Sept. 26, 2016).

[166] 81 Fed. Reg. 56761 (Aug. 22, 2016).

after the Office of Management and Budget approves the form. Realistically, the NOTICE Act will not be implemented until late 2016/early 2017.

[B] Appeal and Grievance Procedures in Medicare Part C Plans

[1] Medicare Advantage Claims

Medicare Part C establishes a different appeals process for MA cases, including those from HMOs, PPOs, SNPs, and PFFS plans.[167] In MA cases, initial determinations are known as "organization determinations." Organization and reconsideration determinations are made by the MA plan. If a reconsidered decision is denied in whole or in part, it is sent automatically to MAXIMUS Federal Services (MAXIMUS), an external review organization hired by CMS to review Medicare HMO reconsidered decisions.[168]

In addition, MA plans are required to have internal grievance procedures.[169] They must provide information to members regarding this grievance process in the plan's written membership rules, along with timetables and information about the steps necessary to utilize the grievance process.[170] The grievance procedures are to be used in all cases that do not involve an organization determination. For example, controversies about hours of service, location of facilities, or courtesy of personnel would go through the grievance process.[171]

MA plans must also inform enrollees of the appeals process in writing.[172] They are required to provide access to QIO review on issues of hospital noncoverage;[173] to provide pre-termination review of home health, SNF, and CORF services;[174] to make expedited determinations with respect to emergency or urgently needed services;[175] to provide reconsideration review;[176] and to provide

[167] *See* **Appendix 1-6** of this Handbook for a chart summarizing the Part C appeals process.

[168] 42 U.S.C. § 1395w-22(f)-(g); 42 C.F.R. §§ 422.560–422.626. Note that the MMA requires private insurance companies that offer a prescription drug plan under Part D to have grievance and appeals mechanisms that accord with the grievance and appeals mechanisms under Part C. *See also* CMS, "Medicare Managed Care Appeals," *available at* https://www.medicare.gov/claims-and-appeals/medicare-rights/medicare-rights-overview.html (site visited May 23, 2016). *See also* http://www.medicareappeals.com/ (Site visited May 23, 2016); https://www.medicare.gov/claims-and-appeals/ (site visited May, 23, 2016).

[169] 42 C.F.R. §§ 422.560 and 422.564.

[170] 42 C.F.R. § 422.111(b)(8).

[171] 42 C.F.R. § 422.564(b).

[172] 42 C.F.R. §§ 422.111(b)(8) and 422.562(a)(2). (Issues for appeal include coverage of emergency or urgently needed services, and denial or termination of other medical service, including specialist care and/or referrals.).

[173] 42 C.F.R. § 422.622.

[174] 42 C.F.R. § 422.624.

[175] 42 C.F.R. § 422.570.

[176] 42 C.F.R. §§ 422.578 and 422.580.

access to independent review outside the plan by an entity under contract with CMS for such review.[177]

If an unfavorable reconsideration determination is issued, whether through the expedited review process or within ordinary time frames, and the amount in controversy is $160.00 or more (in 2017), the enrollee has a right to a hearing before an ALJ.

The written request for a hearing must be filed within 60 days of the date of the notice of the reconsideration determination. In MA cases, the plan must be made a party to the hearing and subsequent levels of review.[178]

The following is a summary of the due process and grievance procedures required of MA plans:

1. Grievance Mechanism

   Each MA organization/plan must provide meaningful procedures for hearing and resolving grievances between the organization (including any entity or individual through which the organization/plan provides health care services) and its enrollees.[179]

2. Non-Expedited Appeals Process[180]

   An MA organization must have a procedure for making determinations regarding whether an individual enrolled with the plan is entitled to receive coverage for a health service under Medicare and the amount (if any) that the individual is required to pay with respect to the service. Decisions must be made on a timely basis.

   Determinations that deny coverage, in whole or in part, must be in writing, and must include a statement in understandable language of the reasons for the denial and a description of the reconsideration and appeals process.

   If the organization makes a decision that is completely favorable to the beneficiary, the organization must issue the determination as expeditiously as the enrollee's health condition requires, but no later than 30 calendar days from the date it receives the request for a standard reconsideration.[181]

---

[177] 42 C.F.R. § 422.592 (currently provided by MAXIMUS Federal Services), *see* http://www.externalappeal.com/Home.aspx (site visited May 23, 2016)

[178] *See* 42 C.F.R. § 422.602(b)-(c).

[179] 42 C.F.R. § 422.564.

[180] 42 C.F.R. § 422.568 (standard time frames and notice requirements for organization determinations). The MA organization must notify the enrollee of its determination as expeditiously as the enrollee's health conditions require, but no later than 14 calendar days after the date the organization receives the request for a standard organization determination. This time period can be extended for a period of 14 days upon justification by the organization.

[181] 42 C.F.R. § 422.590(a).

The organization must provide for reconsideration of an adverse determination upon request by the enrollee involved. The reconsideration decision must be made within 30 days after the date of the receipt of the request for reconsideration.[182] A reconsideration relating to a determination to deny coverage based on a lack of medical necessity must be made only by a physician with appropriate expertise in the field of medicine at issue and by other than a physician involved in the initial determination.

3. Expedited Appeals Process[183]

The MA plan must maintain procedures for expediting organization determinations and reconsiderations when, upon request of an enrollee, the organization determines that the application of the normal time frame for making determinations or reconsiderations could seriously jeopardize the life or health of the enrollee or the enrollee's ability to regain maximum function. An enrollee or a physician may request expedited consideration orally or in writing. If the physician requests an expedited determination or reconsideration, the expedited review is mandatory and commences right away.[184]

If the request is not made by or supported by a physician, it is within the discretion of the MA organization to grant the request for expedited determination or reconsideration.[185] If the MA organization denies a request for expedited determination or reconsideration, it must automatically transfer the request to the standard time frame and make the reconsideration determination within standard time frames.

If the organization expedites a request for reconsideration, it must complete its reconsideration and give the enrollee (and the physician involved, as appropriate) notice of its decision as expeditiously as the enrollee's health condition requires, but no later than 72 hours after receiving the request.[186]

4. Fast Track Review[187]

An MA organization must provide an enrollee with notice at least two days in advance of termination of home health services, SNF services, and therapy services in CORFs. The enrollee may request review by the QIO by noon of the day following receipt of the notice. The QIO

[182] The MA organization must make its reconsidered determination as expeditiously as the enrollee's health condition requires, but no later than 30 calendar days from the date it receives the request for a standard reconsideration. 42 C.F.R. § 422.590(a)(1).

[183] 42 C.F.R. §§ 422.570–422.572.

[184] 42 C.F.R. § 422.584.

[185] 42 C.F.R. § 422.584(c)(2)(i).

[186] 42 C.F.R. § 422.590(d).

[187] 42 C.F.R. §§ 422.624, 422.626.

then must request information from the plan, solicit the view of the enrollee, and issue a decision by close of business of the day after it receives the necessary information.

5. Independent Review[188]

   The Secretary contracts with an independent, outside entity, MAXIMUS, to review and resolve in a timely manner reconsiderations that affirm the denial or coverage, in whole or in part. When the independent entity makes the reconsidered determination, it is responsible for mailing a notice of its reconsidered determination to the parties and for sending a copy to CMS.[189]

6. Appeal to ALJ and Federal District Court[190]

   An enrollee in an MA plan who is dissatisfied with a MAXIMUS determination may appeal to an ALJ using the same process as is used in traditional Medicare.

7. QIO Review: An Alternative Means of Appealing Hospital Denials[191]

   An enrollee who wishes to appeal a determination by an MA plan or hospital that inpatient hospital care is no longer necessary may request immediate QIO review and may remain in the hospital without additional financial liability according to the following procedures:

   - The enrollee must submit the request for immediate review to the QIO, in writing or by telephone, by noon of the first working day after receipt of written notice that the MA plan or hospital has determined that the hospital stay is no longer necessary;
   - On the date of receipt of the request, the QIO must notify the MA plan that the enrollee has filed a request for immediate review; the organization must supply any information that the QIO requires to conduct its review, including medical records and other pertinent information; information is to be provided by telephone or in writing by the close of business of the first full working day immediately following the day the organization makes its request; the QIO must solicit the views of the enrollee with respect to the denial at issue.

Where the MA plan has authorized inpatient coverage of admission directly or by delegation, the organization continues to be financially responsible for the costs of the hospital stay when a timely appeal is filed until noon of the calendar

---

[188] 42 C.F.R. § 422.592.

[189] 42 C.F.R. §§ 422.600–422.616.

[190] 42 C.F.R. § 422.622.

[191] 42 C.F.R. § 422.622.

day following the day the QIO notifies the enrollee of its review determination. If coverage of the hospital admission was never approved by the MA plan, the MA plan is liable for the hospital costs only if it is determined on appeal that the hospital stay should have been covered under the MA plan.

[C] Appeal and Grievance Procedures in Medicare Part D Plans

[1] Coverage Determination Process

As directed by Congress, the coverage determination and appeals process for Part D PDPs[192] mirrors closely the process utilized for Medicare Part C, the MA program. The process begins when the PDP or MA-PD issues a coverage determination.[193] The plan enrollee may request a redetermination by the drug plan of an unfavorable coverage determination and then a reconsideration decision by the Independent Review Entity (IRE) of an unfavorable redetermination. Following IRE review, the enrollee may appeal to an ALJ, to the Medicare Appeals Council (MAC), and then to federal court. Expedited review is available if the Part C standards are met.

Plans must notify enrollees and the prescribing physician involved, as appropriate, of initial coverage determinations as expeditiously as the enrollee's health condition requires, but no later than 72 hours after receipt of the request. Plans must act on requests for expedited coverage determinations no later than 24 hours after receiving the request, and on expedited redeterminations within 72 hours. When a coverage determination involves a request for payment, a plan has 14 days to notify the beneficiary of its decision and to make payment, where applicable, to the beneficiary.[194] A plan may provide

[192] The coverage determinations and exceptions process for Medicare Part D, the prescription drug benefit, is authorized in the Medicare statute at 42 U.S.C. § 1395w-104(f)-(h). Implementing regulations are located at 42 C.F.R. §§ 423.560 *et seq. See* **Appendix 1-7** of this Handbook for a chart summarizing the Part D appeals process.

[193] The final regulations create a new heading for subpart M. It is now called "Grievances, Coverage Determinations, Redeterminations, and Reconsiderations." *See* 42 C.F.R. Pt. 423, subpt. M. (2009). The scope of the renamed subpart M is set out in new § 423.558 (2009) as follows: Requirements of Part D plan sponsors with respect to grievances, coverage determinations, and redeterminations are set forth in § 423.558(a)(1)(2009). The requirements of the Part D Independent Review Entity (IRE) with respect to reconsiderations are set forth in § 423.558(a)(2)(2009), and the rights of Part D enrollees with respect to grievances, coverage determinations, redeterminations, and reconsiderations are set forth in § 423.558(a)(3) (2009). The final rules also provide, in § 423.558(b) (2009), that requirements regarding reopenings, ALJ hearings, MAC review, and judicial review are set forth in subpart M.

[194] 75 Fed. Reg. 19,677 (Apr. 15, 2010), effective June 7, 2010, *available at* http://edocket.access.gpo.gov/2010/pdf/2010-7966.pdf (site visited June 8, 2016), amending 42 C.F.R. § 423.568(c). CMS in the preamble to the regulations encourages plan sponsors to issue unfavorable payment determinations sooner than 14 days, though the regulatory language does not include such a requirement. 75 Fed. Reg. at 19,677, 19,779.

oral notice of an unfavorable coverage determination as long as it also provides written notice.[195]

Coverage determinations that trigger appeal rights include a decision not to pay for or provide a Part D drug because the drug is not on the formulary, is not medically necessary, is furnished by an out-of-network pharmacy, or is not a drug for which Medicare will pay under Part D. A denial of a request for prior authorization by the plan (i.e., the plan does not approve a physician's request to pay for a formulary drug for which the plan must first grant approval) is also a coverage determination. A coverage determination also includes the failure to provide a coverage determination in a timely manner when that delay would adversely affect the health of the enrollee, a decision concerning an exception request, and a decision on the amount of cost-sharing for a drug. Affected beneficiaries may seek a coverage determination of a dispute involving the availability and amount of manufacturer discount applicable to brand name drugs provided in the coverage gap.

[2] Exceptions Process

PDPs and MA-PDs must have an exceptions process in which enrollees can ask that a formulary drug be provided at a lower tier for cost-sharing or that a non-formulary drug be covered by the plan. A beneficiary may also request an exception to a prior authorization requirement. Because exception requests are coverage determinations and governed by the rules for coverage determinations, the plan must act within the time frame for standard coverage determinations (72 hours) and expedited coverage determinations (24 hours).

The plan may grant an exception request to change the cost-sharing tier (i.e., the amount the beneficiary pays as a copayment or as coinsurance) if it determines that the non-preferred drug is medically necessary, consistent with the physician's statement in support of the exception that the preferred drug would not be as effective or would have adverse consequences. In addition, the exceptions process must address situations where a formulary's tiered structure changes during the year and an enrollee is using a drug affected by the change. However, the plan does not have to cover non-preferred drugs that have a higher cost-sharing amount at the generic drug cost-sharing level if the plan maintains a separate tier dedicated to generic drugs. Also, if the plan maintains a formulary tier in which it places very high cost and unique items, such as genomic and biotech products, it may exclude the very high cost or unique drugs from its tiered exception process.

---

[195] 76 Fed. Reg. 21,431 (Apr. 15, 2011), amending 42 U.S.C. § 423.568(f). *See also* http://www.medicareadvocacy.org/old-site/Projects/AdvocatesAlliance/IssueBriefs/10_04.12.PartDGrievancesAndAppeals.pdf (site visited May 23, 2016)

The plan may grant an exception request to cover a non-formulary drug whenever it determines that the drug is medically necessary, consistent with the physician's statement that formulary drugs would not be as effective or would have adverse consequences, and that the drug would be covered but for the fact that it is an off-formulary drug. Formulary use includes the application of cost utilization tools, such as a dose restriction, including the dosage form, that causes a particular Part D drug not to be covered for the number of doses prescribed, or a step therapy requirement that causes a particular Part D drug not to be covered until the requirements of the plan's coverage policy are met, or a therapeutic substitution requirement.

Although the regulations include some criteria for plans to consider when evaluating an exception request to change the tiered cost-sharing or to pay for a non-formulary drug, each plan has the flexibility to establish its own criteria and to develop its own exception process. In addition, the regulations leave to a plan's discretion whether, after an exception has been granted, it will continue coverage into subsequent plan years.

[3] Appeals

The first level of appeal from an unfavorable coverage determination, *including* an unfavorable exception request, is a redetermination by the drug plan. The enrollee must file a request for a redetermination with the drug plan. Drug plans have 7 days in which to notify their enrollees of a standard redetermination decision. They have 72 hours to notify the enrollee of an expedited redetermination request.

An enrollee may request a reconsideration by the IRE of an unfavorable drug plan redetermination. The reconsideration request is filed with the IRE. The Part D regulations require the IRE to issue its reconsideration decision within the time frames for issuing a redetermination.

Note that the regulations provide for an automatic reconsideration review by the IRE if the Part D plan fails to issue either a timely coverage determination or redetermination. The regulations require drug plans to forward the enrollee's request to the IRE within 24 hours if they do not act timely on the coverage determination or redetermination.[196] Advocates report, however, that drug plans that do not meet the regulatory time frames also do not comply with the requirement to send those cases to the IRE.

---

[196] 42 C.F.R. §§ 423.568(e) (2005) and 423.590(c) (2005). Reopenings, ALJ hearings, MAC review, and judicial review are available pursuant to the regulations of new subpart U. *See* 42 C.F.R. §§ 423.1968–423.2140 (2009).

[4] Notice

Plans must send written notice of a formulary change, including a change in cost-sharing tier placement, *only to those enrollees who use an affected drug*, at least 60 days in advance of the change. Notice must also be provided to CMS, state pharmacy assistance programs, pharmacies, and prescribing providers. The notice must include the name of the affected drug, whether the drug is being removed from the formulary or moved to another cost-sharing tier, the reason for the change, what alternative drugs in the same class are available to enrollees, and the right to request an exception. Alternatively, the plan may give the enrollee a 60-day supply of the drug and the 60-day notice at the time the enrollee presents a prescription for an affected drug.

The PDP or MA-PD must provide notice of appeal rights for other coverage determinations.[197] CMS does not consider the transaction at the pharmacy to be a coverage determination; thus, pharmacies have no obligation to provide individualized notice at the point of sale when coverage for a prescription is denied. However, effective January 1, 2012, plans are required to arrange with their network pharmacies to distribute general notices instructing enrollees how to contact their plan to obtain a coverage determination or to request an exception. The notices must comply with standards set by CMS, notices must be written: oral notice may only be given if the PDP mails a written notice not more than three days later.[198]

[D] Administrative Law Judge Hearings

As described above, a beneficiary who has received an unfavorable reconsideration decision for a claim under any part of Medicare may request an ALJ hearing. For all claims *except* hospital claims, in 2017 there must be at least $160 in controversy to proceed to an ALJ hearing; this amount may increase yearly.[199] Hospital claims may be appealed to an ALJ if $200 or more remains at issue. The request for hearing must be filed within 60 days of receipt of the reconsideration determination. For claims under Parts A and B, the ALJ must issue a decision within 90 days of receipt of the appeal request, with certain exceptions. The 90-day time frame applies to Part D claims other than claims in which the

---

[197] A plan sponsor may provide oral notice of a coverage determination or redetermination (either standard or expedited) provided that the plan sends written notice within three calendar days. 75 Fed. Reg. 19,677 (Apr. 15, 2010), effective June 7, 2010, *available at* http://edocket.access.gpo.gov/2010/pdf/2010-7966.pdf (site visited June 8, 2016), amending 42 C.F.R. §§ 423.568, 423.572, and 423.590.

[198] 76 Fed. Reg. 21,431 (Apr. 15, 2011), amending 42 C.F.R. § 423.562(a)(3).

[199] Section 1869(b)(1)(E) of the Social Security Act requires that the amount in controversy for ALJ hearings and for judicial review be adjusted annually. The new number can be found here: 81 Fed. Reg. 65,653 (Sept. 27, 2016).

beneficiary's prescriber indicates, or the ALJ determines, that applying the standard time frame may seriously jeopardize the beneficiary's life, health, or ability to regain maximum functioning. The ALJ must decide a request for expedited consideration within five days of receiving the request and must issue a decision as expeditiously as the beneficiary's health requires, but no later than 10 days from the date the request for the hearing is received.[200]

The ALJ hearing has traditionally been the beneficiary's best chance to win Medicare coverage previously denied. ALJs have considered the beneficiary's right to Medicare coverage in accordance with the Medicare statute and regulations (in contrast to the less formal and more restrictive guidelines and directives used by Medicare Administrative Contractors (QIOs and IREs) at their decision levels).[201] Thus, it makes sense for an advocate to expend the greatest time and energy at the hearing stage where vigorous representation will often lead to satisfying results.

The Office of Medicare Hearings and Appeals (OMHA) in HHS was created in 2005, so that all Medicare ALJ hearings are conducted by OMHA's corps of Medicare ALJs. Instead of being located throughout the country, Medicare ALJs are housed in four offices, in Arlington, Virginia; Cleveland, Ohio; Irvine, California; and Miami, Florida.

Medicare rules create a presumption that all hearings will be conducted by video teleconference (VTC) where the technology is available, although in practice many hearings are conducted by telephone. A beneficiary may request an in-person hearing, although that request is rarely granted, at the discretion of the ALJ. Even if the beneficiary appears in person, other parties to the hearing may appear by VTC or by telephone. In Part A and Part B appeals, CMS may participate in an ALJ hearing as a party, with the right to submit evidence and cross-examine witnesses; CMS cannot examine and cross-examine witnesses if the beneficiary is unrepresented.

[E] Beyond ALJ: Medicare Appeals Council and United States District Court

If the ALJ decision is unsatisfactory[202] and at least $160[203] in 2017 ($200 in hospital cases)[204] remains in controversy, the case may be further appealed to the

---

[200] 74 Fed. Reg. 65,340 *et seq.* (Dec. 9, 2009), adding 42 C.F.R. § 423.2016(b).

[201] Although ALJs are not bound by CMS policy and directives, they are required to give them deference. If an ALJ decides not to follow a policy, the ALJ must explain in the decision why the policy is not being followed.

[202] 42 C.F.R. § 478.44

[203] *See* **Appendix 1-5** of this Handbook. The update for the amount in controversy (AIC) requirement for 2017 (for ALJ and federal court review) is available at 80 Fed. Reg. 57,827–828.

[204] 42 C.F.R. § 478.46 (amount in controversy for review of unfavorable ALJ decisions in hospital cases).

Appeals Council. The Appeals Council is the final administrative appeal review for all Medicare cases under Part A, Part B, Part C, and Part D. There is one Appeals Council for all Medicare cases. Cases are almost always decided on the record; the Council may grant oral argument if it decides that the case raises important questions of policy or law or questions of fact that cannot be decided on the record. A request for Appeals Council review must be filed within 60 days of receipt of the ALJ decision. Cases are sometimes won or remanded for new hearings. The Council traditionally has taken a long time to issue decisions, although rules require decisions in Part A and Part B appeals to be issued within 90 days of receipt of the appeal, with some exceptions. As with ALJ decisions, the Council must issue a written decision within 10 days after receipt of a request for review in Part D cases involving expedited consideration.

Generally, an Appeals Council decision is a prerequisite for proceeding with an individual Medicare appeal in federal court. The required amount in controversy for federal court appeals is also $1,560 in 2017 ($2,000 for hospital cases).[205] Again, other than for hospital cases, these jurisdictional amounts will increase yearly. The complaint appealing a Medicare denial must be filed in federal court within 60 days of receipt of the Council decision and must name the Secretary of HHS, in his or her official capacity, as defendant.[206]

[F] Expedited Access to Judicial Review

A party may request expedited access to judicial review (EAJR) in place of an ALJ hearing or Appeals Council review. To do so, the party must show that there are no material facts in dispute. The party must also challenge the constitutionality of a statutory provision or the constitutionality or validity of a regulation or of a national coverage determination. After the party files a request for an ALJ hearing, the party may file a request for EAJR with the ALJ office. A determination on the request is made by a review entity consisting of up to three ALJs or members of the Appeals Council. If the review entity certifies the request, the party may file an appeal with federal district court within 60 days. If the request is denied, the case is returned to the ALJ hearing or Appeals Council if a hearing has already been held.[207]

[G] Challenges to Coverage Policies

A separate appeals process exists for beneficiaries who want to challenge the validity of a local coverage determination (LCD) or a national coverage

[205] 81 Fed. Reg. 65,653.

[206] If the defendant is not properly named, the plaintiff will be given 60 days to amend the complaint. 42 C.F.R. § 405.1136(d).

[207] 42 C.F.R. §§ 405.990 and 423.1990.

determination (NCD) which sets rules concerning Medicare payment for a particular item or service.[208] Unlike the coverage appeals process described above, a beneficiary does not have to receive a service or procedure before challenging the LCD or NCD governing the procedure as long as the beneficiary needs the service.

A beneficiary who needs, but has not yet received the service, may file an appeal with the Appeals Council within 6 months of the treating physician's written statement indicating that the service is needed. A beneficiary who has received the service must file an appeal with the DAB within 120 days of receipt of the initial determination. Someone who has received the service may appeal the claims denial at the same time as challenging the validity of the LCD or NCD used to deny the service. It is critical in both situations to include a statement from the doctor concerning the necessity of the service and other medical information to document why the LCD or NCD is no longer valid.

If the appeal involves a challenge to an LCD, it is conducted by an ALJ. The Appeals Council conducts the review if the challenge involves an NCD. If the ALJ or the Council upholds the appeal, the ALJ or the Council may order the contractor to reconsider any claim filed by the beneficiary without application of the LCD or NCD in question.

§ 1.08 CONCLUSION

Unfair denials of Medicare coverage occur with surprising frequency. Because Medicare administrators and providers often use rules and procedures that improperly restrict coverage, patients are sometimes required to pay for care that should be covered by Medicare. In addition, the Medicare law is very complicated and errors are frequently made.

The appeal system was designed to find and correct mistakes. No matter what the service at issue, assistance from the patient's *attending physician is the key* to convincing those who make coverage decisions initially, and on appeal, that the care is in fact medically necessary and/or skilled and should be covered.

[208] 42 C.F.R. §§ 426.100–426.587.

APPENDIX 1-1 2017 MEDICARE SUMMARY (TRADITIONAL PROGRAM)

Care Setting[209]	*Coverage*	*Premium*	*Deductible*	*Coinsurance*	*Appeals*
PART A		For Voluntary Enrollees Only $413/mo in 2017 if 29 or fewer quarters Soc. Sec. $227/mo in 2017 if 30 to 39 quarters Soc. Sec.			
HOSPITAL	90 days/spell of illness+60 lifetime reserve days after deductible if medically necessary and reasonable		$1,316 per spell of illness in 2017	61st-90th day: $329/day 91st-150th day: $658/day	Redetermination by QIC Hearing by ALJ (if at least $200) HHS Medicare Appeals Council Federal Court (if at least $2,000)
SKILLED NURSING FACILITY	100 days if daily skilled care and if within 30 days of 3-day hospital stay			21st-100th day: $164.50/day in 2016	Reconsideration by QIC Hearing by ALJ (if at least $160) HHS Medicare Appeals Council Federal Court (if at least $1,560 in 2017)

continues

[209] On January 1, 2006, the Medicare prescription drug program began. MA (formerly Medicare+Choice and also known as Medicare Part D) is a set of financing systems including managed care plans.

APPENDIX 1-1 continued

Care Setting	*Coverage*	*Premium*	*Deductible*	*Coinsurance*	*Appeals*
HOME HEALTH (For individuals who *also* have Part B)	100 visits if homebound and need skilled care within 14 days of 3-day hospital stay or SNF stay of any duration				Reconsideration by QIC Hearing by ALJ (if at least $160) HHS Medicare Appeals Council Federal Court (if at least $1,560 in 2017)
HOME HEALTH (For individuals who *only* have Part A)	Full coverage for undefined number of visits if homebound and need skilled care				Reconsideration by QIC Hearing by ALJ (if at least $160) HHS Medicare Appeals Council Federal Court (if at least $1,560 in 2017)
HOSPICE	Two 90-day periods+ unlimited 60-day periods if physician certifies and recertifies that patient is terminally ill and if elect palliative care only				Reconsideration by QIC Hearing by ALJ (if at least $150) HHS Medicare Appeals Council Federal Court (if at least $1,560 in 2017)

PART B		$104.90 (same as 2015)/mo in 2016* for individuals with incomes below $85,000	Part B Deductible in 2016 ($166.00, higher than in 2015)		
HOME HEALTH (If *only* have Part B *or* have used 100 Part A visits or did not meet institutionalization rules)	Full coverage for undefined number of visits if homebound and need skilled care		Deductible does *not* apply		Reconsideration by QIC Hearing by ALJ (if at least $160) HHS Medicare Appeals Council Federal Court (if at least $1,560 in 2017)
Physician Services Outpatient Services Therapy Services Durable Medical Equipment Prosthetic Devices Ambulance Services	80% of Medicare approved rate for covered services			*Assigned Claims:* 20% of Medicare approved rate *Unassigned Claims:* 20% of approved rate balance of actual charge up to an additional 15% of the approved charge	Reconsideration by QIC ALJ Hearing (if at least $160) HHS Medicare Appeals Council Federal Court (if at least $1,560 in 2017)

continues

* See **Appendix 1-3** for the premium for individuals who are not "held harmless."

APPENDIX 1-1 continued

Care Setting	*Coverage*	*Premium*	*Deductible*	*Coinsurance*	*Appeals*
Some Preventive Benefits (Including Flu Shots, Some Mammograms and Pap Smears, Bone Mass Tests, Prostate Screening, Diabetes Tests, etc.)	Some paid at 100%		Deductible waived for *some* preventive services		Reconsideration by QIC ALJ Hearing (if atleast $160), HHS Medicare Appeals Council Federal Court (if at least $1,560 in 2017)

APPENDIX 1-2 TRADITIONAL MEDICARE APPEALS PROCESS

Level[210]	*Decision Maker*	*Time Frame for Issuing Decision*	*Extension of Time Frame for Issuing Decision Availability*	*Time Frame for Requesting Next Level of Appeal*	*Escalation*
INITIAL	FI	Within 30 days of receiving "clean" claim. § 405.922		Within 120 days of receipt of initial determination to request redetermination. § 405.942(a)	No right to escalation
REDETERMINATION	FI	Within 60 calendar days of receipt of request. § 405.95(a)	If redetermination request filed untimely, time frame commences w/granting of "good cause." § 405.942(b) If multiple timely requests filed, time frame is w/in 60 days of receipt of last request.	Within 180 days of receipt of redetermination to request reconsideration. § 405.962(a)	No right to escalation

continues

[210] *See* 42 C.F.R. 405, Pt. 900, subpt. I—"Determinations, Redeterminations, Reconsiderations, and Appeals Under Original Medicare" (Part A and Part B).

APPENDIX 1-2 continued

Level	*Decision Maker*	*Time Frame for Issuing Decision*	*Extension of Time Frame for Issuing Decision Availability*	*Time Frame for Requesting Next Level of Appeal*	*Escalation*
			§ 405.950(b)(l)& (2) If additional evidence submitted by party, time frame extended for 14 calendar day for each submission. § 405.9500(3)		
RECONSIDERATION	QIC NCDs binding on QIC. § 405.968(a)(4) LCDs not binding on QIC but must give "substantial deference" to them in making decision. § 405.968	Within 60 days of receipt of request. § 405.970(a)	Same as for redeterminations § 405.970(b)	Within 60 days of receipt of reconsideration to request ALJ. § 405.1002(a)(l)	If time frame not met, have right to escalation. Must notify QIC in writing. § 405.970(d) QIC has 5 days from receipt of escalation request to issue a decision or forward to ALJ. § 405.970(d)(2)

ALJ	HHS ALJ NCDs binding on ALJ; LCDs not binding on ALJ but must give "substantial deference" to them in making decision. § 405.968 (CMS may "participate" or be "party," unless appellant is unrepresented beneficiary) § 405.1000 § 405.1010 § 405.1012	Within 90 days of timely filing of ALJ request. § 405.1016 (but requesting party may—by motion or stipulation—waive this time frame)	If ALJ request filed untimely, but "good cause" granted, time frame commences w/granting of "good cause." § 405.1016(b) If ALJ request is escalated to ALJ from QIC, time frame for issuing decision is 180 days of timely filing of request. § 405.1016(c) If CMS is a party and a party requests discovery, time frame for issuing decision is tolled. § 405.1016(d) If additional evidence submitted later than 10 days after receiving notice of hearing, period between when it should have been submitted and when	Within 60 days of receipt of ALJ decision to request MAC appeal. § 405.1102(a) [copy of request for MAC review must be sent by requestor to all parties]. § 405.1105(a)	If time frame not met, have right to escalation to MAC Must file request to escalate with ALJ in writing. § 405.1104(a)(l) ALJ has 5 days from receipt of escalation request to issue a decision or forward to ALJ. Must file escalation request w/both ALJ and MAC and copy all parties. § 405.1104(a)(2) escalation request to issue a decision or forward to ALJ. Must file escalation request w/both ALJ and MAC and copy all parties. § 405.1104(a)(2)

continues

APPENDIX 1-2 continued

Level	*Decision Maker*	*Time Frame for Issuing Decision*	*Extension of Time Frame for Issuing Decision Availability*	*Time Frame for Requesting Next Level of Appeal*	*Escalation*
			received by ALJ is not counted toward adjudication deadline. § 405.1018(b) If hearing is postponed at request of appellant, time between original hearing date and new hearing date not counted toward adjudication deadline. § 405.1020(h)		

MAC	Medicare Appeals Council (MAC) (de novo review) § 405.1108(a) (CMS may "participate" or be "party," unless appellant is unrepresented beneficiary)	Within 90 days of timely filing of MAC request (MAC may issue decision or remand to ALT). § 405.1100(c)	If appellant fails to send copy of request to escalate from ALJ or request for MAC review to all parties, deadline tolls until all parties receive notice of the request for MAC review. § 405.1106(b) Time frame tolled, if party asks to review evidence from the MAC and an opportunity to comment, beginning w/date MAC received request to review evidence through date comment received. § 405.1118 Time frame tolled, if party requests to file brief, beginning w/date request to brief received through date brief filed. § 405.1120	Within 60 days of receipt of MAC decision, can request judicial review. § 405.1102(a) (Also, can file w/in 60 days of receipt of MAC's notice that it cannot issue timely final action & cannot appeal ALJ dismissal to federal court, which, according to regs., is not available. § 405.1116)	If time frame not met, have right to escalation to federal court.§ 405.1132(a) Must file civil action w/in 60 days of receipt of MAC's notice that it cannot issue timely final action Cannot obtain Judicial review of a dismissal of a claim. § 405.1116

APPENDIX 1-3 2017 MEDICARE DEDUCTIBLE, COINSURANCE, AND PREMIUM AMOUNTS

Hospital

Deductible: $1,288.00

Coinsurance:

1st through 60th day: $0
61st through 90th day: $329.00/day
91st through 150th day: $658.00/day

Skilled Nursing Facility

Coinsurance:

1st through 20th day: $0
21st through 100th day: $164.50/day

Part A Premium (for voluntary enrollees only):

$413.00/month (if individual has 29 or fewer quarters of Social Security coverage) (an increase from 2015)

$227.00/month (if individual has 30 to 39 quarters of Social Security coverage) (an increase from 2015)

If uncertain of quarters, please call your local Social Security office.

Part B Deductible: $183.00/year

Part B Standard Premium: $109/month (same as 2015); $134 for those not held harmless*

* In July 2015, the Medicare and Social Security Trustees projected unprecedented increases in 2016 Part B premiums for some beneficiaries, as well as the 2016 deductible for all beneficiaries, as a result of unexpected increases in Part B expenditures. These projections, coupled with the Social Security Administration's (SSA's) October 2015 announcement that there would be no cost-of-living (COLA) increase in 2016, trigger the "hold harmless" provision of the Medicare statute, which prevents Medicare beneficiaries from having their monthly Social Security payment decrease as a result of an increase in Part B premiums. *See* 42 U.S.C. § 1395r(f).Check the SSA and CMS websites for updates.

APPENDIX 1-4 2017 PART B INCOME-RELATED PREMIUMS AND PART D INCOME-RELATED PREMIUM ADJUSTMENTS

Beneficiaries who file an individual tax return with income:	*Beneficiaries who file a joint tax return with income:*	*Beneficiaries who are married but file a separate tax return with income:*	*Part B income-related monthly adjustment amount:*	*Total monthly Part B premium amount:*	*Part D income-related monthly adjustment amount paid to Medicare:*
Less than or equal to $85,000	Less than or equal to $170,000	Less than or equal to $85,000	$0.00	$134	$0.00
Greater than $85,000 and less than or equal to $107,000	Greater than $170,000 and less than or equal to $214,000		$53.5	$187.50	$13.30
Greater than $107,000 and less than or equal to $160,000	Greater than $214,000 and less than or equal to $320,000		$133.9	$267.90	$34.20
Greater than $160,000 and less than or equal to $214,000	Greater than $320,000 and less than or equal to $428,000	Greater than $85,000 and less than or equal to $129,000	$214.3	$348.30	$55.20
Greater than $214,000	Greater than $428,000	Greater than $129,000	$294	$428	$76.20

continues

APPENDIX 1-4 continued

Beneficiaries who file an individual tax return with income:	*Beneficiaries who file a joint tax return with income:*	*Beneficiaries who are married but file a separate tax return with income:*	*Part B income-related monthly adjustment amount:*	*Total monthly Part B premium amount:*	*Part D income-related monthly adjustment amount paid to Medicare:*
Enrollees in Medicare Part D prescription drug plans pay premiums that vary from plan to plan. Beginning in 2011, Part D enrollees whose income exceeds the same thresholds that apply to higher income Part B enrollees must also pay a monthly adjustment amount. The regular plan premium will be paid to their Part D plan, and the income-related adjustment will be paid to Medicare. The Affordable Care Act established income-related premiums (IRPs) for Part D beginning in 2011, and it froze through 2019 the income thresholds at which IRPs begin for both Parts B and D—at $85,000 for single beneficiaries and $170,000 for married couples who file joint tax returns. Under current law, the income thresholds will revert in 2020 to the levels they would have reached had they been indexed for inflation since 2007.[211] Adjustments for Parts B and D: (a) § 1839(i)(3)(C)(i) of the Social Security Act (42 U.S.C. § 1395r(1)(3)(C)(i)) for years before 2018, and by adding at the end the following: § 402 (a) (2)(II) Subject to paragraph 5 for years beginning with 2018, and corresponding modified adjusted gross income table; and (b) conforming amendments, § (b)—Section 1839(i) of the Social Security Act (42 U.S.C. § 1395r(i)).					

[211] *See* http://www.cbo.gov/budget-options/2013/44897 (site visited June 8, 2016). *See also* Medicare Access and CHIP Reauthorization Act, Pub. L. No. 114-10 (Apr. 16, 2015), and § 402. Income Related Premium, *available at* https://www.congress.gov/114/plaws/publ10/PLAW-114publ10.pdf (site visited July 11, 2017).

APPENDIX 1-5 ORIGINAL MEDICARE (PARTS A & B) APPEALS PROCESS

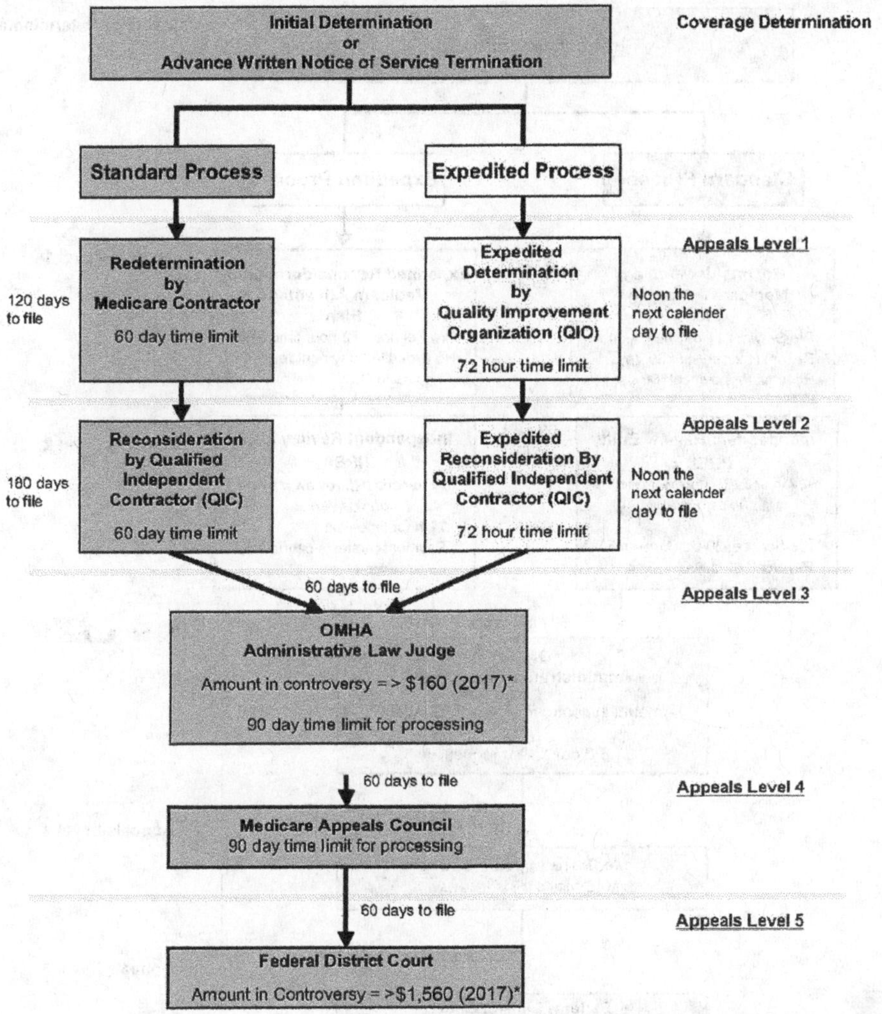

*The AIC requirements for an ALJ hearing and federal District Court are adjusted annually in accordance with the medical care component of the Consumer Price Index.

APPENDIX 1-6 MEDICARE ADVANTAGE (PART C) APPEALS PROCESS

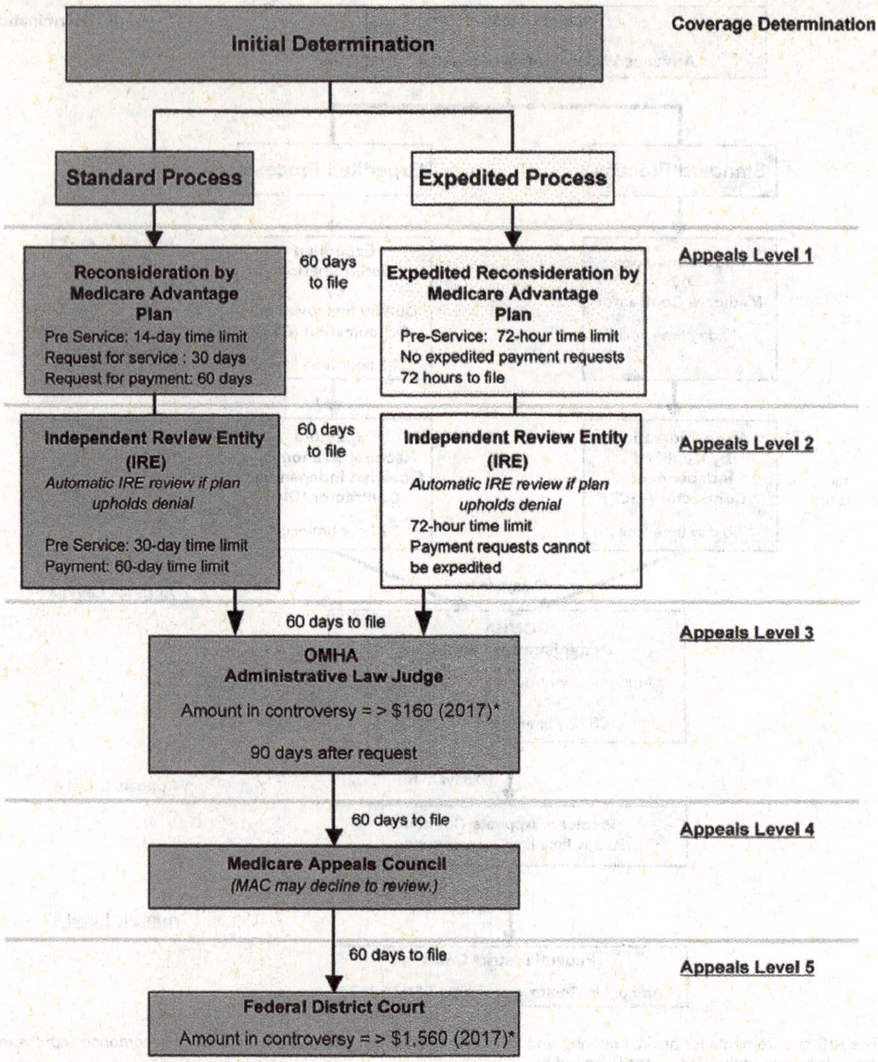

*The AIC requirements for an ALJ hearing and Federal District Court are adjusted annually in accordance with the medical care component of the Consumer Price Index.

APPENDIX 1-7 MEDICARE PRESCRIPTION DRUG PLAN (PART D) APPEALS PROCESS

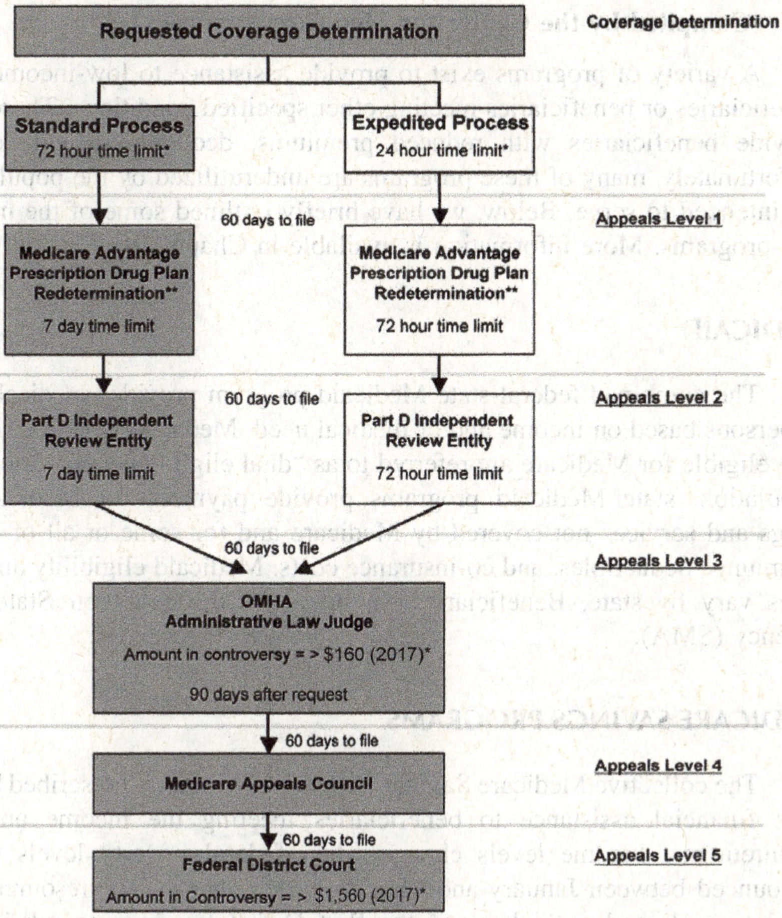

* The adjudication timeframes generally begin when the request is received by the plan sponsor. However, if the request involves an exception request, the adjudication timeframe begins when the plan sponsor receives the physician's supporting statement.

** A request for a coverage determination includes a request for a tiering exception or a formulary exception. A request for a coverage determination may be filed by the enrollee, the enrollee's appointed representative, or the enrollee's physician.

*** Starting in 2005, the AIC requirements for an ALJ hearing and Federal District Court are adjusted in accordance with the medical care component of the consumer price index.

APPENDIX 1-8 PROGRAMS TO ASSIST LOW-INCOME MEDICARE BENEFICIARIES

(Compiled by the Center for Medicare Advocacy)

A variety of programs exist to provide assistance to low-income Medicare beneficiaries or beneficiaries meeting other specified conditions. These programs provide beneficiaries with reduced premiums, deductibles, and copayments. Unfortunately, many of these programs are underutilized by the populations they are intended to serve. Below, we have briefly outlined some of the most important programs. More information is available in Chapter 10.

MEDICAID

The combined federal-state Medicaid program provides medical assistance to persons based on income and/or medical need. Medicaid beneficiaries who are also eligible for Medicare are referred to as "dual eligible beneficiaries." For this population, state Medicaid programs provide payment for Medicaid-covered drugs and services not covered by Medicare and for some or all of Medicare's premiums, deductibles, and co-insurance costs. Medicaid eligibility and coverage rules vary by state. Beneficiaries should apply through their State Medicaid Agency (SMA).

MEDICARE SAVINGS PROGRAMS

The collective Medicare Savings Programs (MSPs),[212] described below, provide financial assistance to beneficiaries meeting the income and resource requirements. Income levels change when federal poverty levels (FPLs) are announced between January and March of each year.[213] The resource (or asset) levels are aligned with those of the Part D full low-income subsidy and are indexed annually. The rules used to count income and resource levels must be at least as liberal as those for the Supplemental Security Income (SSI) program (see below), but states may use more liberal rules. Beneficiaries should apply through their SMA.[214] The chart below indicates the requirements for eligibility for each program and the assistance that each program provides.

---

[212] For ongoing information on the QI and other programs, see "Medicare Savings Programs," *available at* http://www.medicare.gov/your-medicare-costs/help-paying-costs/medicare-savings-program/medicare-savings-programs.html (site visited June 8, 2016) and "Get Health With Your Medicare Costs," https://www.medicare.gov/Pubs/pdf/10126.pdf (site visited June 8, 2016).

[213] The 2016 poverty guidelines are *available at* https://aspe.hhs.gov/poverty-guidelines (site visited Sept. 23, 2016). The 2017 poverty guidelines were not available at the time of publication.

[214] *See* "Report of the Study Panel on Medicare/Medicaid Dual Eligibles: Improving the Medicare Savings Programs" (June 2006), *available at* www.nasi.org/usr_doc/Improving_the_

LOW-INCOME SUBSIDY

The Low-Income Subsidy (LIS) was created when the Part D prescription drug benefit was added to Medicare, and the program provides assistance specifically for beneficiaries' prescription drug costs. Like the MSPs, the income levels for LIS change when new FPLs are announced between January and March of each year (the changes are effective retroactive to January 1 of that year). Like the MSPs, the resource levels for LIS change each year based on the Consumer Price Index (CPI). The rules used to count income and resources are generally the same as those of the SSI program. Beneficiaries who receive full Medicaid (dual eligible beneficiaries), SSI, or any of the MSPs are deemed eligible for the LIS and do not have to apply for it. Other beneficiaries may apply through the Social Security Administration (SSA) or through their SMA (where the state must also screen for MSP eligibility and other Medicaid benefits). The chart below indicates the requirements for eligibility for each LIS group and the assistance that each group receives as compared with the standard Part D benefit. Note that individuals in the four LIS groups do not have the "donut hole" gap in coverage.

STATE PHARMACEUTICAL ASSISTANCE PROGRAMS

Some states provide cost-sharing and supplemental drug coverage for special populations and low-income residents through their State Pharmaceutical Assistance Programs (SPAPs). Any payments made by an SPAP on behalf of a Part D enrollee will count toward the enrollee's true out-of-pocket costs, which count toward meeting the catastrophic threshold which leads to reduced or eliminated enrollee cost-sharing. Income and resource levels vary from state to state and not all states operate an SPAP.[215] Beneficiaries should contact their state to find out how to apply.

AIDS DRUG ASSISTANCE PROGRAMS

AIDS Drug Assistance Programs (ADAPs) provide crucial prescription drug coverage to patients with HIV/AIDS who have low incomes or are uninsured or underinsured. Income and resource levels vary from state to state. For more

---

Medicare_Savings_Programs.pdf (site visited June 8, 2016); *see also* MLN, "Medicaid Coverage of Medicare Beneficiaries (Dual Eligibles) At a Glance" (ICN 006977, Mar. 2013), *available at* https://www.cms.gov/Outreach-and-Education/Medicare-Learning-Network-MLN/MLNProducts/downloads/Medicare_Beneficiaries_Dual_Eligibles_At_a_Glance.pdf (site visited May 23, 2016).

[215] The most recent list of operating SPAPs can be found at http://www.medicare.gov/pharmaceutical-assistance-program/state-programs.aspx (site visited May 23, 2016).

information, see the Kaiser Family Foundation's AIDS Drug Assistance Programs (ADAPs).[216]

PHARMACY PRESCRIPTION DRUG DISCOUNT PROGRAMS

Discount drug cards offered through chain pharmacies (such as CVS and Eckerd) for a small monthly premium provide discounts on a number of services, including prescription drugs. Those with a Part D plan may use a discount card, but the two drug programs operate independently of one another. That is, drug card discounts cannot be applied to Part D prices or to Part D copayments, nor can the cost of drugs purchased using a discount card be applied toward Part D out-of-pocket costs. Discount cards may be useful for those whose drugs are excluded by Part D or for those who have reached the donut hole but will not have enough drug costs to reach catastrophic coverage. Discount cards also provide discounts on services not covered by Medicare, such as vision and dental. The utility of these cards depends on each individual's situation and will likely require detailed calculations of costs and savings. Beneficiaries and advocates should contact the pharmacy directly.

PATIENT ASSISTANCE PROGRAMS

Many pharmaceutical manufacturing companies offer Patient Assistance Programs (PAPs) to provide free or reduced-cost prescriptions to persons with low incomes and/or no insurance.[217] Some companies may be able to provide this assistance to Part D enrollees. Beneficiaries and advocates should contact the individual pharmaceutical manufacturer.

PROGRAM OF ALL-INCLUSIVE CARE FOR THE ELDERLY

The Program of All-Inclusive Care for the Elderly (PACE) provides a unique opportunity for beneficiaries with complex needs to receive their care completely from an interdisciplinary team funded by a capitated payment financed by Medicare and Medicaid. To be eligible, beneficiaries must be older than 55 years old, "meet a Nursing Facility level of care," and live in the service area of a local PACE.[218]

---

[216] AIDS Drug Assistance Programs (ADAPs), April 8, 2014, *available at* http://kff.org/hivaids/fact-sheet/aids-drug-assistance-programs/ (site visited May 23, 2016).

[217] For a directory of programs available, see http://www.medicare.gov/pharmaceutical-assistance-program/ (site visited May 23, 2016).

[218] *See* CMS, "PACE Fact Sheet," *available at* https://www.cms.gov/Medicare/Health-Plans/pace/downloads/pacefactsheet.pdf (site visited May 23, 2016). More information on the PACE program can be found at http://www.medicare.gov/your-medicare-costs/help-paying-costs/pace/pace.html (site visited May 23, 2016).

MEDICARE ADVANTAGE SPECIAL NEEDS PLANS

Certain Medicare Advantage plans are authorized by law to serve specified populations, each of which includes many low-income Medicare beneficiaries. The populations are persons dually eligible for Medicare and Medicaid, people in institutions or those in the community who need an institutional level of care, and people with severe and disabling conditions.[219] These Special Needs Plans (SNPs) are required to serve the designated population either exclusively or disproportionately.[220] Also, they must be "coordinated care" plans and they must offer the Part D prescription drug benefit.

SUPPLEMENTAL SECURITY INCOME

The SSI program makes payments to people with very low incomes and resources, and who are age 65 or older, blind, or have a disability.[221] Resources must be less than $2,000 for an individual or $3,000 for a couple. Items that are not counted as resources include the home the person lives in and the land it is on, life insurance policies with a face value of $1,500 or less, a car, burial plots, and up to $1,500 in burial funds per person. Beneficiaries may apply for SSI through the SSA.

---

[219] Special Needs Plans, *see* http://www.cms.gov/Medicare/Health-Plans/SpecialNeedsPlans/index.html (site visited May 23, 2016).

[220] *See* CMS, "Your Guide to Medicare Special Needs Plans (SNPs)" (revised Nov. 2011), *available at* http://www.medicare.gov/Pubs/pdf/11302.pdf (site visited May 23, 2016). SNP models of care summaries, *available at* http://www.cms.gov/Medicare/Health-Plans/SpecialNeedsPlans/SNP-Model-Of-Care-Summaries.html (site visited May 23, 2016).

[221] *See* Social Security, Supplemental Security Income (SSI), *available at* http://www.ssa.gov/pubs/EN-05-11000.pdf (site visited June 8, 2016); www.socialsecurity.gov (site visited June 17, 2016), or call toll-free at 1-800-772-1213; *see also* What You Need to Know When You Get Supplemental Security Income (SSI) (Publication No. 05-11011), *available at* http://www.ssa.gov/pubs/EN-05-11011.pdf (site visited May 23, 2016).

APPENDIX 1-9 CMS'S *JIMMO V. SEBELIUS* SETTLEMENT AGREEMENT PROGRAM MANUAL CLARIFICATIONS FACT SHEET

U.S. DISTRICT COURT
DISTRICT OF VERMONT
FILED
2016 AUG 17 PM 4:50
CLERK
BY LAW
DEPUTY CLERK

UNITED STATES DISTRICT COURT
FOR THE
DISTRICT OF VERMONT

GLENDA JIMMO, et al.,	)	
	)	
Plaintiffs,	)	
	)	
v.	)	Case No. 5:11-cv-17
	)	
	)	
SYLVIA MATHEWS BURWELL, Secretary of Health and Human Services,	)	
	)	
Defendant.	)	

OPINION AND ORDER GRANTING IN PART AND DENYING IN PART PLAINTIFFS' MOTION FOR RESOLUTION OF NONCOMPLIANCE WITH SETTLEMENT AGREEMENT
(Doc. 94)

This matter comes before the court on Plaintiffs' motion for resolution of noncompliance with Settlement Agreement (Plaintiffs' "motion to enforce") (Doc. 94), in which Plaintiffs assert that Defendant Sylvia Mathews Burwell, Secretary of Health and Human Services (the "Secretary"), has breached the parties' settlement agreement dated October 16, 2012 (the "Settlement Agreement"), which the court entered as a judgment on January 24, 2013 (the "Judgment"). As grounds for their motion to enforce, Plaintiffs point to the Secretary's refusal to make certain revisions to the Medicare Benefit Policy Manual (the "MBPM") and her allegedly deficient educational campaign designed to implement the Settlement Agreement.

The Secretary opposes Plaintiffs' motion, asserting that the court lacks jurisdiction to adjudicate the pending motion because Plaintiffs' notices of noncompliance are not timely. In the alternative, if jurisdiction exists, the Secretary asserts that Plaintiffs fail to establish a breach of the Settlement Agreement and their proposed remedial measures extend beyond the court's limited jurisdiction.

The court heard oral argument on May 26, 2016, at which point it took the pending motion under advisement. Plaintiffs are represented by David J. Berger, Esq., Matthew R. Reed, Esq., the Center for Medicare Advocacy, Inc., and Vermont Legal Aid, Inc. The Secretary is represented by Assistant United States Attorney M. Andrew Zee, Assistant United States Attorney Steven Y. Bressler, and Special Assistant United States Attorney Tamra Moore.

I. Factual and Procedural Background.

A. The *Jimmo* Class Action.

On January 18, 2011, six individual Medicare beneficiaries (the "Individual Plaintiffs") and seven national organizations (the "Organizational Plaintiffs") (collectively, "Plaintiffs") filed a class action suit in the District of Vermont against the Secretary, alleging, among other things, that the Secretary "impose[d] a covert rule of thumb that operate[d] as an additional and illegal condition of coverage and result[ing] in the termination, reduction, or denial of coverage for thousands of Medicare beneficiaries annually." (Doc. 13 at 2, ¶ 1.) Plaintiffs alleged this covert rule of thumb improperly imposed an "Improvement Standard," whereby coverage for certain home health care services was denied if a beneficiary's condition had not improved. *Id.* at ¶ 2. Plaintiffs further alleged that because of the Improvement Standard, Medicare contractors and adjudicators were denying Medicare coverage merely because a patient was unlikely to improve, or in retrospect failed to improve, even when the patient needed skilled care to maintain his or her condition or prevent or slow further deterioration.

The Secretary moved to dismiss Plaintiffs' claims on a number of grounds, including that they failed to allege a plausible ground for relief. The court granted the motion to dismiss in part and denied it in part. *See Jimmo v. Sebelius*, 2011 WL 5104355, at *1 (D. Vt. Oct. 25, 2011). Thereafter, without admitting liability or any wrongdoing, after several months of arms-length negotiations, the Secretary agreed to settle Plaintiffs' claims in accordance with the terms and conditions of the Settlement Agreement. The court approved the Settlement Agreement at a January 24, 2013 fairness hearing under Fed. R. Civ. P. 23(b)(2).

2

B. The Settlement Agreement.

Pursuant to the Settlement Agreement, the parties agreed to a "maintenance coverage standard" which provides that "[s]killed nursing services would be covered where such skilled nursing services are necessary to maintain the patient's current condition or prevent or slow further deterioration so long as the beneficiary requires skilled care for the services to be safely and effectively provided." (Doc. 82-1 at 13, § IX.7.a.)[1] The parties agreed to implement the maintenance coverage standard in two ways that are relevant to Plaintiffs' pending motion to enforce.

First, the Settlement Agreement required certain revisions to the MBPM in order "to clarify the coverage standards for the skilled nursing facility (SNF), home health (HH), and outpatient therapy (OPT) benefits when a patient has no restoration or improvement potential but when that patient needs skilled SNF, HH, or OPT services" and to state that Medicare coverage "does not turn on the presence or absence of an individual's potential for improvement from the nursing care, but rather on the beneficiary's need for skilled care." *Id.* at 8-9, 12, §§ IX.1, IX.7. The Secretary further agreed to "revise or eliminate any [MBPM] provisions . . . that [the Secretary] determines are in conflict" with the agreed-upon maintenance coverage standard for nursing services. *Id.* at 9, § IX.3.

The Settlement Agreement provides that the Secretary:

> will take any recommendations from Plaintiffs' Counsel under advisement and will make a good faith effort to utilize Plaintiffs' Counsel's reasonable recommendations that are limited to the coverage standards as clarified in Sections IX.6 through IX.8 and that are consistent with those coverage standards as well as all other statutory and regulatory requirements.

Id. at 10, § IX.4. Under the Settlement Agreement, the Secretary "retain[s] final authority as to the ultimate content of [MBPM] provisions." *Id.* at 9, § IX.2.

[1] To receive Medicare benefits for home health care services, a beneficiary must be: (a) confined to the home; (b) under the care of a physician; (c) in need of skilled services; and (d) under a plan of care. 42 C.F.R. § 409.42(a)-(d). "Nothing in [the] Settlement Agreement modifies, contracts, or expands the existing eligibility requirements for receiving Medicare coverage[.]" (Doc. 82-1 at 9, § IX.2.)

3

Second, the Settlement Agreement required the Secretary to engage in certain educational activities designed to implement the changes to the MBPM and to educate stakeholders regarding the maintenance coverage standard. Specifically, the Settlement Agreement requires the Secretary to "engage in a nationwide educational campaign" through the Centers for Medicare and Medicaid Services ("CMS"), and in this "Educational Campaign," "use written materials and interactive forums with providers and contractors, to communicate the SNF, home health, and OPT maintenance coverage standards and the [inpatient rehabilitation facility] coverage standards[.]" Doc. 82-1 at 14, § IX.9. The Settlement Agreement provides that "CMS shall retain final authority as to the ultimate content of the written educational materials" and the "PowerPoint slides" used in the Educational Campaign. *Id.* at 16, § IX.12.

The Settlement Agreement states that:

> The Parties recognize that Defendant's obligations are met under the Settlement Agreement once it has complied with the terms of this Settlement Agreement, and that Defendant is not guaranteeing to Plaintiffs that certain results will be achieved once the steps set forth in this Settlement Agreement have been implemented.

Id. at 23, § IX.18.

The Settlement Agreement further provides that the court will retain jurisdiction for thirty-six months after the conclusion of the Educational Campaign to "enforc[e] the provisions of the Settlement Agreement in the event that one of the Parties claims that there has been a breach of any of those provisions[.]" *Id.* at 6, § VI.3. Under the Settlement Agreement, before an aggrieved party may file a motion with the court alleging noncompliance, it must follow the dispute resolution process described in § VIII of the Settlement Agreement. The first step is to provide written notice detailing the alleged noncompliance, which must include:

> (a) a reference to all specific provisions of the Settlement Agreement that are involved; (b) a statement of the issue; (c) a statement of the remedial action sought by the Initiating Party; and (d) a brief statement of the specific facts, circumstances, and any other arguments supporting the position of the Initiating Party; and (e) if there is a good faith basis for

4

> expedited resolution, the circumstances that make expedited resolution appropriate, and the proposed date for a reasonable expedited response.

Doc. 82-1 at 7, § VIII.1. Notice of noncompliance "must be provided promptly." *Id.* Under the Settlement Agreement, "[n]otice that is not provided promptly because of a lack of diligence on the part of the Initiating Party shall not serve as a basis for the [c]ourt to exercise jurisdiction[.]" *Id.* In its Judgment, the court retained "jurisdiction over this matter for the limited purposes and time period set forth in Section VI of the [Settlement] Agreement." (Doc. 92 at 2.)

C. The Parties' Efforts to Implement the Settlement Agreement.

The Secretary made substantial revisions to chapters seven and eight of the MBPM, although many of the revisions were unrelated to the maintenance coverage standard or the Settlement Agreement and were instead made "pursuant to CMS's general authority to provide guidance on Medicare policy and implementation." (Doc. 94-5 at 2.) The Secretary issued an article regarding the revised MBPM provisions, which was disseminated to Medicare Administrative Contractors, Medicare Advantage Organizations, Qualified Independent Contractors ("QICs"), Qualified Improvement Organizations, the Chief Administrative Law Judge, the Chair of the Departmental Appeals Board, providers, suppliers, and others. The article was also posted on CMS's website.

The Secretary issued a Health Plan Management System memorandum, a Program Transmittal, and a Transmittal of Policy Systems memorandum, about the revised MBPM provisions and revised the relevant 1-800-MEDICARE customer service scripts to reflect them. The Secretary posted the Program Transmittal on CMS's website.

The Secretary conducted five open door forums and two national conference calls for the purpose of communicating the MBPM revisions and the maintenance coverage standard. The open door forums involved over 3,900 participants. During the national calls, the Secretary utilized a PowerPoint presentation that was provided to Plaintiffs' counsel in advance for comment and review. The December 19, 2013 national call was one hour in length, and approximately 3,428 participants were on the call. The Secretary

5

used CMS's regular communication channel and its website to provide notice that the calls would take place and posted an audio recording and written transcript of the call on CMS's website. The parties also discussed implementation of the Settlement Agreement during biannual meetings that occurred in January 2014, September 2014, April 2015, and September 2015.

Pursuant to the Settlement Agreement, the Secretary conducted a random sampling of 100 decisions by QICs to identify potential errors and found that fifty-six QIC decisions contained potential errors. The Secretary then determined that twenty-one of the fifty-six decisions reflected actual errors, although not all of the identified errors involved the incorrect application of the maintenance coverage standard. Another sampling identified thirty-two QIC decisions with potential errors, with four of those errors involving the incorrect application of the maintenance coverage standard.

Since publication of the MBPM revisions on December 6, 2013, Plaintiffs have repeatedly raised concerns regarding the adequacy of the revisions to reflect the maintenance coverage standard and the Secretary's allegedly deficient Educational Campaign.[2] In conjunction with their concerns, Plaintiffs have submitted to the Secretary additional proposed revisions to the MBPM, provided examples of alleged continued application of an Improvement Standard to deny Medicare coverage, and have proposed

[2] For example, on January 10, 2014, Plaintiffs raised the following concerns:

> We have a couple of suggestions and requests that we think might improve the process.
>
> First, we were struck by the fact that the Ombudsman call will not include an opportunity for questions. It's been apparent from the other calls that attendees do have a lot of questions, and so we request that that opportunity be provided in this instance as well. If that is not possible, could an e-mail address be provided so that attendees could e-mail their questions after the call?
>
> Second, in general, could CMS provide an e-mail address where anyone could send a question about the relief and the process? This would be part of the ongoing "education campaign" (small caps). Again, we believe that the questions that have been generated on the calls demonstrate that such a need exists. Those questions and answers could then be used to develop FAQ postings that would alleviate some of the confusion.

(Doc. 94-17 at 1.)

6

Frequently Asked Questions to be posted on CMS's website. The Secretary has responded to most of Plaintiffs' proposals, but has not agreed to adopt the vast majority of them, contending they are either unnecessary or are not required by the Settlement Agreement.

Plaintiffs, through counsel, also formed a *Jimmo* Implementation Council (the "Council"), a multi-disciplinary group of providers and advocates to monitor progress with the implementation of the Settlement Agreement. The Council conducted a survey of sixty interested providers, advocates, and other stakeholders, which revealed that "46% were not aware of the Education[al] Campaign provided by CMS and only 36% participated in the education efforts." (Doc. 94-50 at 4.) When asked about how the *Jimmo* settlement could be best implemented, "more education from CMS was most frequently mentioned." *Id.*

In an August 3, 2015 email, the Secretary, through counsel, stated that she had no new information to report regarding additional outreach or education. Three days later, on August 6, 2015, Plaintiffs' counsel served the Secretary with two notices of noncompliance: one addressing Plaintiffs' proposed MBPM revisions and the other identifying alleged deficiencies in the Secretary's Educational Campaign. On September 25, 2015, the Secretary responded to the notices of noncompliance. The parties then unsuccessfully attempted to resolve their differences. On November 10, 2015, the Secretary advised Plaintiffs' counsel in an email that the Secretary would engage in no additional educational activities.

On March 1, 2016, Plaintiffs filed their motion to enforce. In support of their motion, Plaintiffs submitted several coverage decisions which they contend demonstrate the persistence of confusion over the maintenance coverage standard and application of an Improvement Standard. They also submitted the declarations of certain stakeholders who opine that the Secretary did not adequately disseminate the maintenance coverage standard and conducted a confusing and inadequate Educational Campaign, and that little has changed as a result of the *Jimmo* class action settlement. As relief, Plaintiffs ask the court to require the Secretary "to revise or eliminate the specific language in the MBPM

7

that conflicts with the maintenance nursing coverage standard." (Doc. 94-1 at 25.) Plaintiffs also request that the court require the Secretary "to carry out additional educational activities to address the inaccuracies and inadequacies of the original [Educational] Campaign." *Id.*

II. Legal Analysis and Conclusions.

A. Whether the Court has Jurisdiction to Hear the Motion.

As a threshold issue, the Secretary contends that the court lacks jurisdiction to adjudicate the motion to enforce because Plaintiffs did not provide "timely" and "prompt" notice of alleged noncompliance as required by the Settlement Agreement. The Secretary points out that the allegedly deficient MBPM revisions were completed on December 6, 2013 and the Educational Campaign was completed on January 23, 2014. She asserts that Plaintiffs allowed over nineteen months to elapse before filing their notices of noncompliance. Plaintiffs counter that the record establishes they were diligent in pursuing their concerns and attempting to resolve them with the Secretary before invoking this court's jurisdiction.

Because "[f]ederal courts are courts of limited jurisdiction[,] [t]hey possess only that power authorized by Constitution and statute, which is not to be expanded by judicial decree[.]" *Kokkonen v. Guardian Life Ins. Co. of Am.*, 511 U.S. 375, 377 (1994) (internal citations omitted). For that reason, the court does not "automatically retain jurisdiction to hear a motion to enforce a settlement agreement simply by virtue of having disposed of the original case." *Hendrickson v. United States*, 791 F.3d 354, 358 (2d Cir. 2015) (internal quotation marks omitted). "[T]o retain ancillary jurisdiction over enforcement of a settlement agreement . . . a district court's order of dismissal must either (1) expressly retain jurisdiction over the settlement agreement, or (2) incorporate the terms of the settlement agreement in the order." *Id.*

The court retained jurisdiction for thirty-six months after the conclusion of the Educational Campaign to enforce the Settlement Agreement in the event that one of the parties claims that there has been a breach thereof. The Settlement Agreement requires a party seeking enforcement to do so in a timely manner. Plaintiffs satisfy this standard.

8

They raised their concerns regarding the Secretary's alleged breaches of the Settlement Agreement promptly after they occurred and repeatedly thereafter. Consistent with the Settlement Agreement, Plaintiffs attempted to resolve their concerns with the Secretary until August 3, 2015, when the Secretary advised Plaintiffs through counsel that she had no new information with respect to additional outreach or education. Three days later, Plaintiffs served two Notices of Noncompliance. On September 25, 2015, the Secretary responded in writing to Plaintiffs' Notices of Noncompliance. The parties engaged in negotiations until November 10, 2015, when the Secretary informed Plaintiffs that no further action would be taken on the Notices of Noncompliance. Plaintiffs' motion to enforce was filed less than four months thereafter.

Because Plaintiffs provided the Secretary with prompt notice of the alleged noncompliance with the Settlement Agreement, diligently pursued their concerns, and served their notices of noncompliance in a timely manner, the court retains jurisdiction to resolve the pending motion to enforce.

B. Standard of Review for Motion to Enforce.

"[A] motion to enforce a settlement agreement is fundamentally 'a claim for breach of contract, part of the consideration of which was dismissal of an earlier federal suit[.]'" *Id.* (quoting *Kokkonen*, 511 U.S. at 381). In turn, "[s]ettlement agreements are contracts and must therefore be construed according to general principles of contract law." *Red Ball Interior Demolition Corp. v. Palmadessa*, 173 F.3d 481, 484 (2d Cir. 1999). If a settlement agreement is clear and unambiguous, the court "must take care not to alter or go beyond the express terms of the agreement, or to impose obligations on the parties that are not mandated by the unambiguous terms of the agreement itself." *Id.*; *see also Cruden v. Bank of N.Y.*, 957 F.2d 961, 976 (2d Cir. 1992) ("A court may neither rewrite, under the guise of interpretation, a term of the contract when the term is clear and unambiguous, nor redraft a contract to accord with its instinct for the dispensation of equity upon the facts of a given case") (internal citation omitted).

Because the federal government is one of the contracting parties, the Settlement Agreement is "governed exclusively by federal [common] law." *Boyle v. United Techs.*

9

Corp., 487 U.S. 500, 504 (1988). Federal common law "generally adopts the relevant state law rule unless there is a significant conflict between the state rule and a federal interest." *Palmieri v. Allstate Ins. Co.*, 445 F.3d 179, 188-89 (2d Cir. 2006). In this case, there is no apparent conflict with state law.

Pursuant to Vermont law, courts "look to the plain language of a contract to discern the intent of the parties." *In re Cole*, 2008 VT 58, ¶ 13, 184 Vt. 64, 71, 954 A.2d 1307, 1311; *see also Bixler v. Bullard*, 769 A.2d 690, 695 (Vt. 2001) ("[T]he language and acts of a party to a contract are to receive such construction as the other party was fairly justified in giving to them"). In every contract governed by Vermont law, there is implied covenant of good faith and fair dealing which is "not a contractual term that the parties are free to bargain in or out [of] as they see fit." *Carmichael v. Adirondack Bottled Gas Corp. of Vt.*, 635 A.2d 1211, 1216 (Vt. 1993). The Vermont Supreme Court has described the implied covenant as follows:

> The definition of the "covenant of good faith and fair dealing" is broad. An underlying principle implied in every contract is that each party promises not to do anything to undermine to destroy the other's rights to receive the benefits of the agreement. The implied covenant of good faith and fair dealing exists to ensure that parties to a contract act with "faithfulness to an agreed common purpose and consistency with the justified expectations of the other party." . . . The implied promise by its nature protects against "a variety of types of conduct characterized as involving 'bad faith' because they violate community standards of decency, fairness or reasonableness." As the Restatement [(Second) of Contracts] points out,
>
>> [a] complete catalogue of types of bad faith is impossible, but the following types are among those which have been recognized in judicial decisions: evasion of the spirit of the bargain, lack of diligence and slacking off, willful rendering of imperfect performance, abuse of a power to specify terms, and interference with or failure to cooperate in the other party's performance.

Id. at 1216-17 (internal citations omitted).

In their pending motion, Plaintiffs seek enforcement of the Secretary's obligation to revise the MBPM and to conduct the Educational Campaign. Although Plaintiffs acknowledge that the Secretary has completed both of these obligations, they contend

10

that she has evaded the spirit of the Settlement Agreement in doing so and has thereby deprived them of the benefit of their bargain. The Secretary argues that Plaintiffs cannot establish a breach based on obligations not contained in the Settlement Agreement or merely because they are dissatisfied with the results of their agreement.

C. Whether the MBPM Revisions Violate the Settlement Agreement.

Plaintiffs concede that the Secretary made substantial changes to Chapters 7 and 8 of the MBPM, but claim that most of the changes either did not pertain to the maintenance coverage standard or did not clarify sections that arguably gave rise to the Improvement Standard. They further argue that the Secretary failed to make a good faith effort to implement Plaintiffs' recommendations to revise the MBPM as required by the Settlement Agreement. Plaintiffs assert that while the Secretary added the maintenance coverage standard to the general principles set forth in MBPM, she "did not revise or clarify any of the specific sections that govern coverage requirements for skilled nursing services to provide for maintenance nursing, [MBPM] 40.1.2.1 through [MBPM] 40.1.2.14." (Doc. 94 at 2.) The Secretary does not deny that she made no specific revisions to these sections of the MBPM to reflect the maintenance coverage standard. She contends she had no obligation to do so in the absence of a direct conflict with the maintenance coverage standard and, even in that instance, the Settlement Agreement left it to her discretion as to what, if any, revisions should be made. Two provisions of the MBPM are the subject of the pending motion to enforce.

1. MBPM § 40.1.2.1 and the "Three Week Rule."

First, Plaintiffs cite the Secretary's refusal to eliminate a reference to a "3 week rule" in MBPM § 40.1.2.1 governing skilled observation and assessment. This section provides:

> Where a patient was admitted to home health care for skilled observation because there was a reasonable potential of a complication or further acute episode, but did not develop a further acute episode or complication, the skilled observation services are still covered for 3 weeks or so long as there remains a reasonable potential for such a complication or further acute episode.

11

Id.; MBPM, Ch. 7 § 40.1.2.1. Plaintiffs argue that there is no statutory support for the "3 week rule,"[3] and that it falsely suggests that skilled observation services are limited to that time period unless the patient is at risk for future complications. They assert this language conflicts with the maintenance coverage standard which does not contain a three week limitation. They further contend that the "3 week rule" imposes an impermissible "rule of thumb" that the Settlement Agreement was intended to eliminate.

The Secretary responds that because the "3 week rule" is only one measure and because MBPM § 40.1.2.1 also provides that skilled observations will be covered "so long as there remains a reasonable potential for such a complication or further acute episode[,]" there is no direct conflict with the maintenance coverage standard. *Id.*

MBPM § 40.1.2.1 neither refers to the maintenance coverage standard nor incorporates it. As a result, it can reasonably be interpreted as endorsing standards for determining coverage for skilled observation and assessment other than the maintenance coverage standard. None of this is surprising because MBPM § 40.1.2.1 predates the parties' Settlement Agreement and the Secretary has refused to revise it. In an effort to implement the terms and conditions of the Settlement Agreement, the Secretary could have clarified how the maintenance coverage standard applies to MBPM § 40.1.2.1 and how it modifies the "3 week rule." It is a much closer question, however, whether the Secretary breached the Settlement Agreement by failing to make those revisions.

Because coverage for skilled nursing services can comply with both the maintenance coverage standard and § 40.1.2.1, there is no direct conflict between the two standards and they can be read in tandem. *See F.C.C. v. NextWave Pers. Commc'ns Inc.*, 537 U.S. 293, 304 (2003) ("[W]hen two statutes are capable of co-existence, it is the duty of the courts, absent a clearly expressed congressional intention to the contrary, to regard each as effective") (internal quotation marks omitted). Moreover, although the "3 week rule" appears to have no basis in the applicable regulations or law, it is modified by § 40.1.2.1's further provision that coverage remains available "so long as there remains a

[3] At oral argument, the only statutory or regulatory support the Secretary cited for the "3 week rule" pertained to an unrelated issue.

12

reasonable potential for . . . a complication or further acute episode." As a result, while the "3 week rule" has the potential to become an impermissible rule of thumb, this outcome is not certain. She further contends she never agreed to eliminate "rules of thumb" from the MBPM.[4]

Although the Secretary's refusal to revise § 40.1.2.1 to reflect the maintenance coverage standard is likely to cause confusion, in the absence of a direct conflict between the two provisions, the Settlement Agreement permits her to refrain from certain clarifying revisions and authorizes no recourse if she decides not to make them. The court is not empowered to revise the parties' agreement to impose a more onerous burden even if it would enhance the implementation of the maintenance coverage standard. *See Greenlaw v. United States*, 554 U.S. 237, 243-44 (2008) (describing "the principle of party presentation" whereby "as a general rule, our adversary system is designed around the premise that the parties . . . are responsible for advancing the facts and arguments entitling them to relief") (internal quotation marks and alterations omitted).

Because there is no direct conflict between the cited provision of § 40.1.2.1 and the maintenance coverage standard, the court must DENY Plaintiffs' motion to enforce insofar as it pertains to the skilled observation and assessment provision of MBPM § 40.1.2.1.

2. MBPM § 40.1.2.1 and the Maintenance Coverage Standard.

Plaintiffs also challenge a portion of MBPM § 40.1.2.1 that states:

[4] As the Secretary correctly points out, the Settlement Agreement does not prohibit rules of thumb or require her to eliminate them from the MBPM. However, the Secretary arguably has an independent duty to remove impermissible rules of thumb from the MBPM. *See* 42 C.F.R. § 409.44(a) (explaining that, under the home health benefit, Medicare coverage of skilled services is based on the "unique medical condition of the individual beneficiary"); MBPM, Ch. 7, § 20.3 (prohibiting the use of utilization screens or "'rules of thumb'" to make coverage decisions); 42 C.F.R. § 409.44(b)(3)(iii) (providing that the determination of whether a skilled service is reasonable and necessary "must be based solely upon the beneficiary's unique condition and individual needs, without regard to whether the illness or injury is acute, chronic, terminal, or expected to last a long time"); Home Health Prospective Payment System Rate Update for Calendar Year 2011, 75 Fed. Reg. 70372, 70395 (Nov. 17, 2010) ("'Rules of thumb' in the Medicare medical review process are prohibited. . . . Medical denial decisions must be based on a detailed and thorough analysis of the beneficiary's total condition and individual need for care.").

> Such signs and symptoms as abnormal/fluctuating vital signs, weight changes, edema, symptoms of drug toxicity, abnormal/fluctuating lab values, and respiratory changes on auscultation may justify skilled observation and assessment. Where these signs and symptoms are such that there is a reasonable potential that skilled observation and assessment by a licensed nurse will result in changes to the treatment of the patient, then the services would be covered. *However, observation and assessment by a nurse is not reasonable and necessary for the treatment of the illness or injury where fluctuating signs and symptoms are part of a longstanding pattern of the patient's condition which has not previously required a change in the prescribed treatment.*

(Doc. 94-8); MBPM, Ch. 7 § 40.1.2.1 (emphasis supplied).

Plaintiffs argue that the Settlement Agreement requires MBPM § 40.1.2.1 to be revised to clarify that, based on the maintenance coverage standard, it does not preclude observation and assessment "to address a long standing pattern of their condition, particularly when their treatment plan does not require changes to meet their needs or maintain their condition[.]" (Doc. 94 at 2-3.) As currently drafted, Plaintiffs contend § 40.1.2.1 erroneously suggests that the need for skilled care requires an acute episode and thus is "always episodic, temporary, [and] short-term." (Doc. 94-6 at 2.) Plaintiffs further argue that the section fails to reflect that a patient may obtain covered skilled nursing observation and assessment to maintain or prevent deterioration of his or her condition.

The Secretary responds that the challenged provision accurately indicates that when a patient's fluctuating signs and symptoms are part of a long standing pattern that remains unchanged, skilled observation and assessment services will not be reasonable and necessary, and that CMS's regulation governs when observation and assessment constitute skilled services. *See* 42 C.F.R. § 409.33(a)(2)(i).[5] She points out that "CMS

[5] 42 C.F.R. § 409.33(a)(2)(i) states:

> Observation and assessment of the patient's changing condition—(i) When observation and assessment constitute skilled services. Observation and assessment constitute skilled services when the skills of a technical or professional person are required to identify and evaluate the patient's need for modification of treatment or for additional medical procedures until his or her condition is stabilized.

14

did not agree to 'eliminate' the so-called 'Improvement Standard,' nor did it promise that the measures set forth in the [Settlement] Agreement would eliminate it." (Doc. 102 at 3.) Indeed, she denies that the Improvement Standard exists.[6]

Although not a model of clarity, § 40.1.2.1 neither expressly contains an Improvement Standard nor negates the application of the maintenance coverage standard. As a result, the Secretary did not violate the Settlement Agreement by refusing to revise this provision of the MBPM.

Finally, while Plaintiffs point to the Secretary's alleged repeated failure to clarify the application of the maintenance coverage standard in the MBPM, the Settlement Agreement required only that the Secretary take Plaintiffs' recommendations for MBPM revisions "under advisement" and make a "good faith effort to utilize" them. (Doc. 82-1 at 10, § IX.4.) The Secretary has proffered sufficient evidence that she fulfilled this duty, and Plaintiffs make no colorable claim of bad faith. The court therefore DENIES Plaintiffs' motion to enforce insofar as it pertains to revisions to the MBPM.

3. The Educational Campaign.

Plaintiffs allege that although the Secretary "checked off all the boxes set out in the Educational Campaign portion of the [Settlement] Agreement" (Doc. 103 at 4), she did not make a good faith effort to carry out the Educational Campaign with respect to both the MBPM revisions and the maintenance coverage standard. Plaintiffs also point to

[6] While it is true that the Settlement Agreement contains no concessions by the Secretary regarding the existence of the Improvement Standard, the Secretary agreed to a maintenance coverage standard which renders the use of an Improvement Standard to deny coverage impermissible. Under § IX.7 of the Settlement Agreement, the maintenance coverage standard for nursing services "does not turn on the presence or absence of an individual's *potential for improvement* from the nursing care, but rather on the beneficiary's need for skilled care." (Doc. 82-1 at 12) (emphasis supplied). Section IX.1 defines the "maintenance coverage standard as the coverage standard "when a patient has no restoration or *improvement potential* but when the patient needs skilled [services]" and provides that "[s]killed nursing services would be covered where such skilled nursing services are necessary to maintain the patient's current condition or prevent or slow further deterioration" even if the patient is unlikely to improve "so long as the beneficiary requires skilled care for the services to be safely and effectively provided." *Id.* at 9, 13 (emphasis supplied). An Improvement Standard, when used as a rule of thumb, is clearly impermissible. *See supra* note 4, at 12-13.

a number of specific alleged deficiencies in the manner in which the Secretary conducted the Educational Campaign.

For example, Plaintiffs point out that they did not have the opportunity to adequately comment on the Secretary's PowerPoint presentation because the MBPM revisions were not published until December 6, 2013. During the national call, the Secretary briefed the PowerPoint presentation, and then took questions from eighteen participants before terminating the call. Plaintiffs assert that when the Secretary terminated the call there were many participants waiting to ask questions about the Settlement Agreement and revisions to the MBPM. Plaintiffs point out that the Ombudsman call did not include any opportunity for questions, and that when they asked the Secretary to schedule another call, she refused this request. They suggested that the Secretary provide an email address for questions and post Frequently Asked Questions regarding the *Jimmo* settlement on CMS's website. Those requests were also denied.

With respect to the national calls, Plaintiffs contend that the Secretary did not effectively communicate about the calls in advance to give interested parties effective notice. The Settlement Agreement, however, only required the Secretary to "make a good faith effort to notify Plaintiffs' Lead Counsel, in advance of the National Calls[.]" (Doc. 82-1 at 19, § IX.15.) It is undisputed that the Secretary notified Plaintiffs' counsel about the calls, and provided a copy of the PowerPoint presentation utilized during the calls three weeks before the calls took place. Although not required to by the Settlement Agreement, the Secretary also noticed Medicare providers and suppliers about the national calls through her regular communications channel. These efforts were sufficient to comply with the Settlement Agreement.

Plaintiffs similarly claim that Open Door Forums ("ODFs") conducted by the Secretary pursuant to the Settlement Agreement were "problematic" because the Secretary "did not allow questions" and the publicity surrounding the ODFs "often failed to connect." (Doc. 94-1 at 11.) However, the Settlement Agreement did not require the Secretary to publicize the ODFs or ensure that the ODFs "connected" with their audience. It required only that the Secretary announce the manual revisions and reference the

16

national calls during an ODF. As the Secretary points out, she announced each ODF through targeted email, and each ODF had hundreds of participants.

Plaintiffs submit declarations from stakeholders averring that the Secretary's training regarding the maintenance coverage standard was both minimal and inadequate, that there was no follow-up, and that CMS has made little effort to address the confusion in the Medicare community regarding the import of the *Jimmo* settlement. Plaintiffs argue that there remains substantial confusion among Medicare providers, suppliers, contractors, adjudicators, and beneficiaries with respect to the maintenance coverage standard. In support of this claim, Plaintiffs cite the results of a random sampling of QIC coverage decisions which they contend demonstrate an unreasonably high error rate. They also rely on a number of individual adverse coverage decisions which they assert demonstrate that the Improvement Standard persists.[7]

Finally, Plaintiffs submit several declarations, including one from a retired administrative law judge from the Office of Medicare Hearings and Appeals who avers that after the *Jimmo* settlement, the Improvement Standard continued to be reflected in the decisions appealed to him, and that the Secretary has "paid only lip service" to the court's Judgment and has "not effectively implemented the letter or the spirit of the *Jimmo* settlement." (Doc. 94-1 at 14.)

Plaintiffs acknowledge that the Secretary did not guarantee results or the absence of mistakes, but contend that the evidence supports a conclusion that the Secretary's Educational Campaign was flawed to such an extent that it deprived them of the benefit of their bargain because "the evidence overwhelmingly indicates that the word did not get out" regarding the maintenance coverage standards. *Id.* at 11. Plaintiffs propose that the

[7] In support of this contention, Plaintiffs cite thirty-nine individual adverse decisions in which the Secretary allegedly "failed to take the patient's unique condition into consideration or to recognize that the services were needed to maintain the beneficiary's condition or to slow deterioration." *Id.* at 17. In some of the cases cited by Plaintiffs, Medicare providers stated that they had not heard of the *Jimmo* Settlement Agreement or the maintenance coverage standard.

Secretary be required to take additional steps to ensure that the Settlement Agreement has its intended effect.[8] *Id.* at 25.

In response, the Secretary sets forth in some detail the efforts she undertook to disseminate the maintenance coverage standard. She argues that what Plaintiffs actually seek is *results* and that, under the Settlement Agreement, she did not guarantee "that certain results [would] be achieved[.]" (Doc. 82-1 at 23, § IX.18.) Consequently, she asserts that adverse coverage decisions in which Medicare providers incorrectly deny coverage to beneficiaries based on the alleged "Improvement Standard" do not constitute a breach of the Settlement Agreement and, in any event, it is within her discretion to address when and how to address noncompliance. *See id.* at 22, § IX.22.e.2 ("The manner in which CMS addresses [noncompliance issues] will be within its discretion."). The Secretary notes that beneficiaries who are incorrectly denied coverage may appeal those decisions through the administrative process.

Because it is undisputed that the Secretary completed each component of the Educational Campaign, the only issue is whether the *manner* in which she conducted the campaign constitutes a breach of the Settlement Agreement. Although a close question, Plaintiffs have sustained their burden to establish that the Secretary failed to fulfill the letter and spirit of the Settlement Agreement with respect to at least one essential component of the Educational Campaign.

Plaintiffs have provided persuasive evidence that at least some of the information provided by the Secretary in the Educational Campaign was inaccurate, nonresponsive, and failed to reflect the maintenance coverage standard. The most compelling example of this is the Secretary's "Summary of the questions posed and answers provided during

[8] Plaintiffs suggest addressing the alleged inadequacies of the Educational Campaign with:

> 1) Frequently Asked Questions, drafted by [P]laintiffs' counsel and edited by CMS, posted on CMS'[s] website, and updated no less than semi-annually[;]
>
> 2) National Calls for providers and suppliers, and for contractors and adjudicators; [and]
>
> 3) A dedicated e-mail address for providers to pose questions directly to CMS.

(Doc. 94-1 at 26.)

18

the December 16, 2013 *Jimmo vs. Sebelius* National Call for contractors and adjudicators" (the "Summary") (Doc. 94-15). The Summary does not mention the maintenance coverage standard, does not provide the parties' agreed upon definition of it, and reflects virtually no effort to educate participants regarding the impact of the *Jimmo* settlement and the implementation of the maintenance coverage standard. Examples of its deficiencies are set forth below.

a. The Summary: Non-responsive answers.

When asked by contractors "how to distinguish claims where the goal is restorative from claims where the goal is maintaining or preventing decline in [the patient's] condition[,]" the Secretary did not answer this question and explain how the distinction should be drawn. Instead, she responded: "CMS believes that treatment goals should be clearly articulated in the patient's medical record. Goals should be established clearly from the beginning, in terms of maintenance or restoration. If clinical conditions change, treatment goals may change." *Id.* at 3.

When asked whether a patient can "now qualify for maintenance therapy for life assuming that therapy is necessary to prevent or slow deterioration[,]" the Secretary did not answer this question in the affirmative or negative, but instead stated that "[n]one of the existing requirements or limitations of coverage have changed." *Id.* (emphasis omitted).

When asked "[w]hen and how will the review of past claims be conducted[,]" the Secretary responded: "That aspect of the settlement agreement is relatively clear in the agreement language itself. CMS hasn't set up [a] formal timeline. The settlement agreement lays out biannual meetings at which the plaintiffs will bring additional claims." *Id.* (emphasis omitted).

When asked for guidance for determining when maintenance services would be covered for a patient that "continues to deteriorate," the Secretary advised contractors to conduct "a thorough review of the clinical record as a whole" to determine "when such a review does not support the need for skilled care." *Id.* at 2 (emphasis omitted). She did not direct them to the maintenance coverage standard which clearly provides that:

19

"Skilled nursing services would be covered where such skilled nursing services are necessary to maintain the patient's current condition or prevent or slow further deterioration so long as the beneficiary requires skilled care for the services to be safely and effectively provided." (Doc. 82-1 at 13, § IX.7.a.)

b. The Summary: Incorrect Information.

The Summary also reflects the provision of arguably incorrect information. When asked by contractors for "some examples from the settlement of where a claim was denied inappropriately[,]" and "what sort of language would be appropriate for them to use when denying claims[,]" the Secretary replied as follows:

> As stated at the beginning of my presentation, the court has not decided this case and actual claims review of cases will not begin until the second phase of the settlement agreement. As far as inappropriate examples, in some instances, contractor denials have used certain terms such as "no improvement potential," "patient plateaued"—which can serve as shorthand justifications for denying. The basis for denial should be that the beneficiary did not need skilled care. Make sure that you are not using inaccurate, shorthand terms when writing denial language—use appropriate language to describe the reason for denial (e.g., no longer need for skilled care, patient not complicated/treatment not complicated).

(Doc. 94-15 at 3.) The problem with the Secretary's response is threefold.

First, the Secretary's response may erroneously suggest that she is unaware of any claims raised in the *Jimmo* settlement of improper denials based on an Improvement Standard. *See Anderson v. Sebelius*, 2010 WL 4273238, at *8 (D. Vt. Oct. 25, 2010) (rejecting the use of an Improvement Standard and requiring the Secretary "to reexamine the need for skilled services for observation and assessment from the perspective of the condition of Plaintiff at the time the services were ordered, free from any presumption that if hindsight reveals Plaintiff's condition was stable throughout the covered period, coverage for skilled services should be denied"); *Papciak v. Sebelius*, 742 F. Supp. 2d 765, 770 (W.D. Pa. 2010) (granting plaintiff's motion for summary judgment where "the question of whether services were necessary for a maintenance program was not considered by the Secretary, and thus the Secretary failed to apply the proper legal standard"); *Rizzi v. Shalala*, 1994 WL 686630, at *5 (D. Conn. Sept. 29, 1994) (opining

20

that "the revised guidelines prohibit any arbitrary presumptions or use of illegal 'rules of thumb' to deny patients with chronic or stable illnesses home health coverage"); *Folland v. Sullivan*, 1992 WL 295230, at *7 (D. Vt. Sept. 1, 1992) (concluding the "ALJ's interpretation of [claimant's] condition [was] flawed because it impermissibly relies on the benefit of hindsight, which of course is always 20-20" and "[t]he fact that skilled care has stabilized a claimant's health does not render that level of care unnecessary. An elderly claimant need not risk a deterioration of [his or] her fragile health to validate the continuing requirement for skilled care"); *Fox v. Bowen*, 656 F. Supp. 1236, 1248 (D. Conn. 1986) ("It is clearly contrary to [Social Security] regulations for an [ALJ] to deny benefits on the basis of informal presumptions, or 'rules of thumb,' that are applied across the board without regard to the medical condition or therapeutic requirements of the individual patient").

Second, the Secretary juxtaposed "inappropriate examples" of the Improvement Standard with a statement that the inappropriate terms *can* serve as shorthand justifications for denying claims when she apparently intended to indicate that they *cannot* be used for this purpose.

And third, rather than explain that an Improvement Standard is impermissible and the maintenance coverage standard applies, the Secretary offered "denial language" that can be used to avoid "inaccurate, shorthand terms[.]" (Doc 94-15 at 3.) Her explanation that "[t]he basis for denial should be that the beneficiary did not need skilled care" is accurate, but she does not explain how this determination should be made consistent with the maintenance coverage standard. *Id.*

Section IX.9 of the Settlement Agreement requires the Secretary to use the Educational Campaign "to communicate the SNF, home health, and OPT maintenance coverage standards . . . as set forth in Sections IX.6 through IX.8" of the Settlement Agreement. (Doc. 82-1 at 14, § IX.9.) At a minimum, Plaintiffs bargained for the accurate provision of information regarding the maintenance coverage standard and their rights under the Settlement Agreement would be meaningless without it. The Secretary makes no claim to the contrary. At least insofar as the Summary is concerned, the

21

Secretary breached the Settlement Agreement by failing to convey accurate information regarding the maintenance coverage standard.

For the foregoing reasons, the court GRANTS Plaintiffs' motion to enforce with regard to the Secretary's Educational Campaign and directs the Secretary to propose corrective action for Plaintiffs' consideration within forty-five days of this Order. In the event the parties cannot agree to that corrective action, they may petition the court for a resolution of their dispute.

CONCLUSION

For the foregoing reasons, Plaintiffs' motion for resolution of noncompliance with Settlement Agreement is GRANTED IN PART and DENIED IN PART. (Doc. 94.)

SO ORDERED.

Dated at Burlington, in the District of Vermont, this 17th day of August, 2016.

Christina Reiss, Chief Judge
United States District Court

22

Secretary breached the Settlement Agreement by failing to convey accurate information regarding the maintenance coverage standard.

For the foregoing reasons, the court GRANTS Plaintiffs' motion to enforce with regard to the Secretary's Jimmo Compliant and directs the Secretary to propose corrective action for Plaintiffs' consideration within forty-five days of this Order. In the event the parties cannot agree to that corrective action, they may petition the court for a determination of their dispute.

CONCLUSION

For the foregoing reasons, Plaintiffs' motion for resolution of noncompliance with Settlement Agreement is GRANTED IN PART and DENIED IN PART. (Doc. 151).

SO ORDERED.

Dated at Burlington, in the District of Vermont, this 4th day of August, 2016.

Christina Reiss, Chief Judge
United States District Court

CHAPTER 2
HOSPITAL COVERAGE

§ 2.01 INTRODUCTION

[A] Access to Covered Services

Access to Medicare hospital coverage is essential to the financial and physical well-being of millions of aged and disabled Americans. Part A of the Medicare program is financed by the Hospital Insurance Trust Fund, which in turn is funded through a mandatory Social Security payroll tax imposed on all wage earners.[1]

Although Medicare Part A is sometimes known as "hospital insurance," coverage is available under Part A for much more than services provided by a hospital. Of course, inpatient hospital services are covered under Part A, but Medicare Part A also provides coverage for skilled nursing facility (SNF) care, home health care, and hospice care.[2] This chapter addresses eligibility for Medicare Part A as well as Medicare coverage for inpatient hospital care, including long-term care hospitals (LTCHs) and rehabilitation hospitals.

[B] Medicare Administration

Section 1874A of the Social Security Act authorizes the Secretary of the Department of Health and Human Services (HHS) to contract with entities to serve as "Medicare Administrative Contractors" to perform certain functions including determination of payment amounts and making payments; the development of local coverage determinations; beneficiary education and assistance; provider consultation, communication, education, and technical assistance; and other necessary functions, including functions concerning the Medicare Integrity Program.[3] These functions were previously performed by entities known as "fiscal intermediaries" and "carriers." Section 1874A defines the appropriate Medicare Administrative Contractor (MAC) as an entity that has a contract to perform one or more of the described functions in relation to an individual entitled to benefits under Part A or enrolled under Part B, or to a provider, supplier, or class of providers or suppliers. In addition, 42 U.S.C. §§ 1395h and 1395u specifically remove references to fiscal intermediaries and carriers, which, as noted, are now referred to as "contractors."[4]

---

[1] Social Security Act § 1817, https://www.ssa.gov/OP_Home/ssact/title18/1817.htm (site visited May 31, 2016), 42 U.S.C. § 1395i(a).

[2] 42 C.F.R. § 406.2 (Scope).

[3] 42 U.S.C. § 1395kk-1, with respect to payment functions (including the function of developing local coverage determinations, as defined in § 1869(f)(2)(B)), provider services functions, and functions relating to services furnished to individuals entitled to benefits under part A or enrolled under part B, or both.

[4] This provision was added by Sections 911 and 912 of the Medicare Prescription Drug, Improvement, and Modernization Act of 2003 (MMA), Pub. L. No. 108-173 (Dec. 8, 2003),

§ 2.02 ELIGIBILITY FOR MEDICARE HOSPITAL INSURANCE (PART A)

Medicare Part A provides basic protections against certain medical costs to persons age 65 or over who are eligible for retirement benefits under Title II of the Social Security Act (or would be eligible for such benefits if certain government employment were covered employment under Title II, or under the Railroad Retirement system); individuals under age 65 who have been entitled for not less than 24 months to benefits under Title II of the Social Security Act (or would have been so entitled if certain government employment were covered employment under Title II) or under the Railroad Retirement system on the basis of a disability;[5] and certain individuals who do not meet the requirements set out above but are medically determined to have end-stage renal disease (ESRD).[6] For people with amyotrophic lateral sclerosis (ALS) Medicare Part A begins with the first month of Social Security disability payments.[7]

Under the Medicare program, eligibility begins the first month in which an individual meets all the requirements, including application and enrollment.[8] The first month of entitlement is the first month for which the individual meets all the requirements for entitlement to Part A benefits.[9] An insured is an individual who has the number of quarters of coverage required for monthly Social Security benefits.[10] A quarter of coverage is a calendar quarter that is counted toward the

---

amending § 1874A of the Social Security Act. For a list of the Medicare Administrative Contractor (MAC) geographic jurisdictions, see http://www.cms.gov/Medicare/Medicare-Contracting/Medicare-Administrative-Contractors/A-B_MAC_Jurisdictions.html (site visited May 31, 2016).

[5] 42 C.F.R. § 406.12.

[6] Social Security Act § 1811, 42 U.S.C. § 1395c; 42 C.F.R. § 406.13 (individual who has ESRD). A three-month waiting period is provided. 42 C.F.R. § 406.13(e).

[7] Centers for Medicare & Medicaid Services (CMS), "Medicare Basics: A Guide for Families and Friends of People with Medicare," *available at* https://www.medicare.gov/Pubs/pdf/11034.pdf (site visited Sept. 7, 2016), p. 7.

[8] 42 C.F.R. § 406.3. *See also* Social Security Act § 226(c)(1)(B),42 U.S.C. § 426(c)(1)(B), which states:

> (c) For purposes of subsection (a)—
>
> (1) entitlement of an individual to hospital insurance benefits for a month shall consist of entitlement to have payment made under, and subject to the limitations in, part A of title XVIII on his behalf for inpatient hospital services, post-hospital extended care services, and home health services (as such terms are defined in part C of title XVIII) furnished him in the United States (or outside the United States in the case of inpatient hospital services furnished under the conditions described in section 1814(f)) during such month; except that (A) no such payment may be made for post-hospital extended care services furnished before January 1967, and (B) no such payment may be made for post-hospital extended care services unless the discharge from the hospital required to qualify such services for payment under part A of title XVIII occurred (i) after June 30, 1966, or on or after the first day of the month in which he attains age 65, whichever is later, or (ii) if he was entitled to hospital insurance benefits pursuant to subsection (b), at a time when he was so entitled.

[9] 42 C.F.R. § 406.3.

[10] 42 C.F.R. § 406.3.

number of covered quarters required for eligibility for monthly Social Security benefits; a quarter is counted if during that quarter (or that calendar year) the individual earned a required minimum amount of money.[11]

Persons who are age 65 or over and certain persons under age 65, who do not meet the requirements for premium-free benefits, may obtain benefits by paying a premium.[12] Monthly premium amounts are usually promulgated in October of each year, effective for the succeeding calendar year.[13]

§ 2.03 APPLICATION OR ENROLLMENT FOR MEDICARE PART A

[A] Who Must File

Most Medicare beneficiaries are eligible for Medicare Part A as a result of being age 65 or older and entitled to monthly Social Security or Railroad Retirement cash benefits.[14] Persons eligible for benefits on this basis, as well as those eligible based on disability, do not need to file an application for hospital insurance (Medicare Part A).[15]

An individual must file an application for Medicare Part A if he or she seeks entitlement on the basis of:

- Transition benefits;[16]

---

[11] 42 C.F.R. § 406.3. *See also* 20 C.F.R. Pt. 404, subpt. B (determining quarters of coverage and minimum amounts necessary).

[12] 42 C.F.R. § 406.5. For the requirements for premium hospital insurance, *see* 42 C.F.R. § 406.20. Most people do not pay a monthly Part A premium if either they or their spouse have 40 or more quarters of Medicare-covered employment. The Part A premium is $227/month in 2017 for enrollees who have 30–39 quarters of Medicare-covered employment. The Part A premium is $413/month in 2017 for those who are not otherwise eligible for premium-free hospital insurance and have fewer than 30 quarters of Medicare-covered employment.

[13] 42 C.F.R. § 406.32(a). The procedure for determining the monthly premium amount is found at 42 C.F.R. § 406.32(b)–(d); for collection of payments and payments due, see 42 C.F.R. § 406.32(e), (f); and for group payment option, see 42 C.F.R. § 406.32(g). Other premium rules are defined at § 406.33 (determination of months to be counted for premium increase: enrollment) and § 406.34 (determination of months to be counted for premium increase: reenrollment).

[14] 42 C.F.R. § 406.6. Note, however, that since the age of eligibility for Social Security benefits is floating upward depending on one's birth year, the alignment of who must file is no longer accurate. For example, for persons born between 1943 and 1954, the age of retirement for Social Security purposes is 66. See the retirement age calculator at http://www.socialsecurity.gov/retirement/1943.html (site visited May 31, 2016). Persons in this circumstance must file an application for Medicare at age 65 and may do so online. *See* http://www.ssa.gov/medicare/apply.html (site visited May 31, 2016).

[15] 42 C.F.R. § 406.6(b).

[16] 42 C.F.R. § 406.6(c)(1). *See* 42 C.F.R. § 406.11 for discussion of transition benefits.

- Deemed entitlement to disabled widow's or widower's benefits;[17]
- A diagnosis of ESRD;[18]

---

[17] 42 C.F.R. § 406.6(c)(2). *See* 42 C.F.R. § 406.12 for discussion of widow's and widower's benefits. With the June 26, 2015, favorable Supreme Court ruling in Obergefell v. Hodges, Dir., Ohio Dep't of Health, Nos. 14–556, 576 U. S. ___ (2015), same-sex spouses of Medicare beneficiaries in all states who have valid same-sex marriages may be eligible for benefits as a spouse and should apply for benefits as appropriate. *See* http://www.supremecourt.gov/opinions/14pdf/14-556_3204.pdf (site visited May 31, 2016). *Obergefell* holds that denying same-sex couples the right to marry is an improper denial of equal protection under the United States Constitution. Advocates should pay close attention to implementation issues in *Obergefell* as they arise.

For background on the tortuous history of and the recognition of same sex-marriage, see United States v. Windsor, 70 U. S. ___ (2013), *available at* http://www.supremecourt.gov/opinions/12pdf/12-307_6j37.pdf (site visited May 31, 2016). The Supreme Court in *Windsor* found unconstitutional Section 3 of the Defense of Marriage Act (DOMA). *See also* Center for Medicare Advocacy, "Demise of DOMA: Implementing Federal Benefits for Same-Sex Spouses," *available at* http://www.medicareadvocacy.org/demise-of-doma-implementing-federal-benefits-for-same-sex-spouses/ (site visited May 31, 2016).

Other useful information includes the Social Security Administration's (SSA) August 23, 2013 Program Operation Manual Systems (POMS) provisions: GN 00210.005, "Holding Claims, Appeals, and Post-Entitlement Actions Involving Same-Sex Marriages or Legal Same-Sex Relationships Other than Marriage," *available at* https://secure.ssa.gov/apps10/poms.nsf/lnx/0200210005 (site visited May 31, 2016), and GN 00210.010, "Interviewing Individuals with Claims Involving Same-Sex Relationships," *available at* https://secure.ssa.gov/apps10/poms.nsf/lnx/0200210010 (site visited May 31, 2016). Medicare has updated its information on determining who is a same-sex spouse. *See generally*, Social Security Administration (SSA), Program Operations Manual System (POMS), "Same-Sex Marriage—Determining Marital Status for Title II and Medicare Benefits" (GN 00210.002), *available at* https://secure.ssa.gov/poms.nsf/lnx/0200210002 (site visited May 31, 2016).

In addition, on June 20, 2014, Attorney General Holder published a Memorandum to the President entitled "Implementation of *United States v. Windsor*." The Holder Memorandum can be found at http://www.justice.gov/iso/opa/resources/9722014620103930904785.pdf (site visited May 31, 2016). The memorandum states that most federal agencies recognize a marriage as valid based on where the married couple currently resides (the place of domicile). Further, the memorandum states that for purposes of "processing surviving spouses' claims and appeals involving same-sex marriages, including Medicare-only claims," the SSA uses the place of domicile rule. *See also* SSA, POMS, "Same-Sex Marriage—Benefits for Surviving Spouses" (GN 00210.400), *available at* https://secure.ssa.gov/poms.nsf/lnx/0200210400 (site visited May 31, 2016).

In a separate writing, the Medicare agency is requiring skilled nursing facilities (SNFs) in the Medicare Advantage program (managed care) to allow all married Medicare beneficiaries to receive care where their spouse resides, regardless of whether they are a same- or opposite-sex couple. *See* CMS, "Memorandum to All Medicare Advantage Organizations" (Aug. 29, 2013), *available at* http://www.cms.gov/Medicare/Health-Plans/HealthPlansGenInfo/Downloads/SNF_Benefits_Post_Windsor.pdf (site visited May 31 2016), and "Important Information for Individuals in Same-Sex Marriages," *available at* thttp://www.medicare.gov/sign-up-change-plans/same-sex-marriage.html (site visited May 31, 2016). *See also* Center for Medicare Advocacy, LGBT (Lesbian, Gay, Bisexual, and Transgender) People, *available at* http://www.medicareadvocacy.org/medicare-info/lesbian-gay-bisexual-and-transgender-lgbt-seniors/ (site visited May 31, 2016).

[18] 42 C.F.R. § 406.6(c)(3). *See* 42 C.F.R. § 406.13 for discussion of end-stage renal disease (ESRD).

- Eligibility for Social Security cash benefits if the individual has attained age 65 without applying for these benefits;[19] and
- Special provisions applicable to government employment.[20]

[B] Time Periods for Filing Application

An application is deemed filed, based on the transition periods or on ESRD as described above, in the first month of eligibility if it is filed not more than three months before the first month of eligibility and is retroactive to the first month of eligibility if filed within 12 months after the first month of eligibility.[21] Similarly, an application filed more than 12 months after the first month of eligibility is retroactive to the twelfth month before the month it is filed.[22]

A valid application based on entitlement to widow's or widower's benefits is deemed filed if, before the first month in which the individual meets the conditions of eligibility, the conditions of eligibility are met before an initial determination, reconsideration, or hearing decision is made on the application.[23] An application, if validly filed within 12 months after the first month of eligibility, is deemed retroactive to that first month. If filed more than 12 months after the first month of eligibility, it is retroactive to the twelfth month before the month of filing.[24] A similar rule applies for persons eligible for Social Security benefits at or after age 65 for an application that is filed before the first month in which the individual meets all the eligibility conditions for that benefit.[25]

[C] Forms and Where to File

Forms for applying for Medicare Part A benefits may be obtained online at https://www.ssa.gov/medicare or by mail, free of charge, from the Centers for Medicare & Medicaid Services (CMS) or at any Social Security branch or district office.[26] In the alternative, an individual may use the application for monthly

[19] 42 C.F.R. § 406.6(c)(4). *See* 42 C.F.R. § 406.10(a)(3) for discussion of eligibility based on this status.

[20] 42 C.F.R. § 406.6(c)(5). *See* 42 C.F.R. § 406.15 for discussion of provisions applicable to eligibility based on government employment.

[21] 42 C.F.R. § 406.6(d)(1). *See* 42 C.F.R. § 406.21 (individual enrollment), § 406.22 (effect of month of enrollment on entitlement). *See also* 42 C.F.R. § 406.24 for a discussion of special enrollment periods (SEPs) applicable to group health plan (GHP) and large group health plan (LGHP) individuals; and *see* 42 C.F.R. § 406.26 (enrollment under state buy-in).

[22] 42 C.F.R. § 406.6(d)(1).

[23] 42 C.F.R. § 406.6(d)(2).

[24] 42 C.F.R. § 406.6(d)(2).

[25] 42 C.F.R. § 406.6(d)(3).

[26] 42 C.F.R. § 406.7. Online forms can be found at http://www.gpo.gov/fdsys/pkg/CFR-2011-title42-vol2/pdf/CFR-2011-title42-vol2-sec406-7.pdf (site visited May 31, 2016).

Social Security benefits to apply for Medicare entitlement if eligible for Medicare Part A at that time.[27]

§ 2.04 SCOPE OF BENEFITS—INPATIENT HOSPITAL COVERAGE BENEFIT PERIODS

[A] In General

An individual insured under Medicare Part A is entitled to inpatient hospital or critical access hospital (CAH) services for up to 150 days during any spell of illness (or "benefit period"), minus one day for each day of such services in excess of 90 days, which were previously used during a prior spell of illness or benefit period.[28] (These days in excess of 90 days are known as "lifetime reserve days"). This inpatient hospital coverage is available to inpatients in an acute hospital or in a rehabilitation hospital. Coverage for inpatient psychiatric hospitals is somewhat different.[29]

In any benefit period, a Medicare beneficiary is entitled to 60 fully paid days of hospital care, subject only to an initial deductible amount per benefit period; after 60 days, a beneficiary must pay a daily coinsurance amount equal to one-fourth of the initial deductible; and after 90 days, the beneficiary is entitled to 60 "lifetime reserve" days, which may be used only once during the beneficiary's lifetime.[30] The initial deductible is $1,316 in 2017 ($1,288 in 2016); the daily coinsurance amount is $329 ($322 in 2016) for days 61 to 90 of a hospital stay; and the lifetime reserve day coinsurance amount is $658 ($644 in 2016) for days

---

[27] 42 C.F.R. § 406.7.

[28] Social Security Act § 1812(a), 42 U.S.C. § 1395d(a); 42 C.F.R. § 409.61 (general limitations on amount of benefits), § 409.82 (inpatient hospital deductible), § 409.83 (inpatient hospital coinsurance). Inpatient hospital status is a critical component of accessing Medicare-covered hospital services as well as post-hospitalization services such as the skilled nursing facility benefit. Defining inpatient status has become increasingly challenging as Medicare has increased its use of "observation status" for the provision of observation services. For many patients in observation status, the care received is indistinguishable from that of persons in inpatient status, but for the status designation itself. Nonetheless, the status designation has enormous consequences in terms of the benefits and services that are available. Persons in observation status receive observation services as an outpatient (Medicare Part B). As a consequence, the right to a host of important notices and services available to inpatients is not available to persons in observation status. *See* Bagnall v. Sebelius, No. 3:11cv1703 (MPS) (D. Conn. filed Nov. 3, 2011), Memorandum of Decision dated September 23, 2013. For a discussion of *Bagnall*, see Center for Medicare Advocacy, "Disappointing Decision from Court in Challenge to 'Observation Status' Highlights Need to Pass Legislation," *available at* http://www.medicareadvocacy.org/disappointing-decision-from-court-in-challenge-to-observation-status-highlights-need-to-pass-legislation/ (site visited May 31, 2016). *See also* http://scholar.google.com/scholar_case?case=6608692245354306736&q=Bagnall+v.+Sebelius&hl=en&as_sdt=2,9&as_vis=1 (site visited May 31, 2016).

[29] *See* **§ 2.04[C]** of this Handbook.

[30] 42 C.F.R. § 409.83 (inpatient hospital coinsurance) and § 409.60 (benefit period defined).

91 to 150.[31] The deductible and coinsurance amounts and lifetime reserve day coinsurance amount are adjusted each calendar year. Each adjustment is announced in the *Federal Register*, usually in October or early November prior to the new calendar year.

[B] Benefit Period Explained

A benefit period (or "spell of illness") generally begins when a beneficiary enters a hospital and is admitted as an inpatient and has not received a hospital or SNF level of care within the prior 60 consecutive days.[32] A hospital or SNF level of care is coverable by the Medicare program.

> ■ **EXAMPLE:** Imagine that Mrs. Brown entered the hospital on January 1, 2017, and stayed for 200 days. Mrs. Brown returns home for 30 days before she is re-hospitalized. The Medicare hospital coverage available to Mrs. Brown may be described as follows: Mrs. Brown first is responsible for the $1,316 deductible before any Medicare coverage is available. She then receives 60 days of hospital coverage without coinsurance. Mrs. Brown is next responsible for $329 of coinsurance per day between days 61 and 90. On day 91 Mrs. Brown begins to use her lifetime reserve days (assuming that she has not used any of these days in prior hospital stays). The lifetime reserve days require a daily coinsurance payment of $658. After the lifetime reserve days are exhausted on the 150th day, Mrs. Brown will have exhausted her Medicare coverage for her current benefit period. When Mrs. Brown returns to the hospital after 30 days at home, she will be entitled to no additional Medicare coverage. As stated above, a beneficiary is entitled to a maximum of 150 days of hospital coverage in any one "spell of illness."[33] A spell of illness ends and a new spell of illness (with additional hospital coverage) becomes available only after the beneficiary has gone 60 consecutive days without receiving either an inpatient hospital level of care or a SNF level of care.[34] A hospital or SNF level of care is one coverable by the Medicare program. Because Mrs. Brown was at home for only 30 days, she continues in the same spell of illness and her benefits remain exhausted.

It should be noted that it is possible to have more than one benefit period in the same calendar year, requiring the payment of a new deductible and additional

---

[31] *See* http://www.medicare.gov/Pubs/pdf/11579.pdf (site visited Nov. 21, 2016).

[32] *See* CMS, Medicare General Information, Eligibility, and Entitlement, Ch. 3, §§ 10.4-10.4.4. (Benefit periods/spell of illness), *available at* https://www.cms.gov/Regulations-and-Guidance/Guidance/Manuals/downloads/ge101c03.pdf (site visited May 31, 2016).

[33] 42 U.S.C. § 1395d.

[34] Social Security Act § 1861(a), 42 U.S.C. § 1395x (a); 42 C.F.R. § 409.60(b).

coinsurance.[35] This circumstance arises when a beneficiary has two separate hospitalizations in a year, and the first hospitalization is followed by a period of 60 consecutive days without receiving an inpatient hospital or SNF level of care.

[C] Inpatient Psychiatric Services

With respect to inpatient psychiatric hospital services, a beneficiary is entitled to a total of 190 days of inpatient care during his or her lifetime.[36] Although an individual is entitled to 190 days of such care per lifetime, the individual is permitted to utilize only a maximum of 150 of these days in any given benefit period. Moreover, these 150 days are subject to the same deductible and coinsurance amounts that are applicable to care received in an acute or rehabilitation hospital setting.

> ■ **EXAMPLE:** If Mr. Jones entered a psychiatric hospital in 2017 with a full 190 lifetime days available, he would be able to use only 150 of those days and would be required to pay the $1,316 deductible. In addition, commencing with the 61st day, he would be required to pay the $329 per day coinsurance and commencing with the 91st day, he would be required to pay the $658 per day coinsurance. Because he is permitted to use only 150 of his 190 lifetime psychiatric inpatient hospital days, the remaining 40 days of available coverage can be used only in a new benefit period, that is, only after he has gone 60 consecutive days without receiving an inpatient hospital or SNF level of care.

It should be noted that if the individual was an inpatient in a psychiatric hospital on the first day of Medicare entitlement and for any of the 150 days immediately before the first day of Medicare entitlement, those days are subtracted from the 150 days that would otherwise be available in the initial benefit period for inpatient psychiatric services in a psychiatric or general hospital.[37] These subtracted days are, however, available to the individual in a subsequent benefit period. This reduction applies only if the hospital was participating in Medicare as a psychiatric hospital on the individual's first day of Medicare enrollment,[38] and only to the beneficiary's first benefit period.[39] Days spent in a general

---

[35] 42 C.F.R. § 409.80(a).

[36] 42 U.S.C. § 1395d(b)(3); 42 C.F.R. § 409.62. *See also* "Your Medicare Coverage," *available at* http://www.medicare.gov/coverage/inpatient-mental-health-care.html (site visited May 31, 2016).

[37] 42 C.F.R. § 409.63(a).

[38] 42 C.F.R. § 409.63(a)(2).

[39] 42 C.F.R. § 409.63(a)(3).

hospital before entitlements are not subtracted under this provision even if the stay was for diagnosis or treatment of mental illness.[40]

§ 2.05 MEDICARE-COVERED SERVICES

[A] In General

With respect to the provision of Medicare-covered services, "arrangements" include those arrangements that provide for Medicare payment for services delivered to Medicare beneficiaries; "covered" refers to services authorized for Medicare payment that meet Medicare coverage criteria as defined in the Medicare law and regulations;[41] "nominal charge provider" means a provider that furnishes services free of charge or at a nominal charge and is either a public provider or other provider that demonstrates to CMS's satisfaction that a significant portion of its patients are low income and requests that payment of its services be determined accordingly; "participating" refers to hospitals or other facilities that meet the conditions of participation and have in effect a Medicare provider agreement; a "qualified hospital" is one primarily engaged in providing, by or under the supervision of doctors of medicine or osteopathy, inpatient services for the diagnosis, treatment, and care or rehabilitation of persons who are sick, injured, or disabled, is not primarily engaged in providing skilled nursing care or related services, provides 24-hour nursing services, and is licensed in the United States, or in Canada or Mexico, for the purposes of furnishing non-emergency services to U.S. residents.[42]

[B] Covered Benefits

Covered benefits under Part A include the services, except for luxuries (such as a telephone or television), generally provided during a hospital or CAH stay, including use of hospital facilities, room and board in a semiprivate room, nursing and related services, medical social services, operating and recovery room costs,

---

[40] 42 C.F.R. § 409.63(b). *See also* the set of examples explaining the § 409.63 reduction rule found at 42 C.F.R. § 409.63(c); Legion v. Richardson, 354 F. Supp. 456 (S.D.N.Y.), *aff'd*, 414 U.S. 1058 (1973); and Doe v. Colautti, 592 F.2d 704 (1979).

[41] Usually, Medicare coverage results in payment by Medicare for the services or items in question. Some courts, however, have distinguished Medicare coverage from Medicare payment. This is important to a beneficiary, because once Medicare coverage is established, the beneficiary is absolved of full financial responsibility for the items or services in question, regardless of whether the provider receives Medicare payment. *See, e.g.*, New York *ex rel.* Bodnar v. Secretary of HHS, 903 F.2d 122 (2d Cir. 1990), *available at* http://openjurist.org/903/f2d/122/state-of-new-york-bodnar-v-secretary-of-health-and-human-services (site visited June 6, 2016).

[42] 42 C.F.R. § 409.3.

drugs and medical supplies furnished in the hospital, certain diagnostic or therapeutic services, laboratory tests, radiological services billed by the hospital, rehabilitation services, and blood.[43] Inpatient hospital services generally do not include SNF-type care furnished by a hospital or a CAH that has a swing-bed approval, or any nursing-facility-type care that may be furnished as a Medicaid service under the Medicaid program.[44]

§ 2.06 COVERAGE CRITERIA EXPLAINED

[A] Bed and Board

Except for applicable deductibles and coinsurance amounts, Medicare Part A covers the cost of bed and board in semiprivate (two to four beds) or ward (five or more beds) accommodations.[45] Private accommodations are covered only if the patient's treating physician concludes that the patient's condition requires isolation, if the hospital or CAH has no semiprivate or ward accommodations, or if the semiprivate and ward accommodations of the hospital or CAH are fully occupied by other patients.[46] Medicare will continue to pay for private accommodations until the patient's condition no longer requires a private room or until semiprivate or ward accommodations are available.[47] The hospital is free to charge the patient the difference between the private room rate and the semiprivate or ward accommodations rate where the patient requests a private room absent a medical need for such.[48]

[B] Nursing and Related Services

Medicare covers nursing and related services, use of hospital or CAH facilities, and medical social services as inpatient hospital or inpatient CAH services ordinarily furnished by the hospital for the care and treatment of inpatients.[49] Medicare, however, does not pay for private duty nurses or attendants.[50]

---

[43] Social Security Act § 1861(b), *available at* https://www.ssa.gov/OP_Home/ssact/title18/1861.htm (site visited June 1, 2016), 42 U.S.C. § 1395x(b); 42 C.F.R. § 409.10 (included services), § 409.11 (bed and board), § 409.12 (nursing and related services), § 409.13 (drugs and biologicals), § 409.15 (services of interns and residents-in-training), § 409.16 (other diagnostic or therapeutic services), § 409.18 (services related to kidney transplantation), and § 409.14 (services related to cardiac pacemakers and pacemaker leads).

[44] 42 C.F.R. § 409.10(b).

[45] 42 C.F.R. § 409.11(a).

[46] 42 C.F.R. § 409.11(b).

[47] 42 C.F.R. § 409.11(b)(2).

[48] 42 C.F.R. § 409.11(b)(3).

[49] 42 C.F.R. § 409.12(a).

[50] 42 C.F.R. § 409.12(b).

[C] Drugs and Biologicals

Medicare pays for drugs and biologicals as inpatient hospital or inpatient CAH services if they represent a cost to the hospital, are ordinarily furnished by the hospital or CAH for the care and treatment of inpatients, and are furnished to an inpatient for use in the hospital or CAH.[51] In addition, Medicare will pay for a limited supply of drugs for use outside the hospital or CAH if it is medically necessary to enable a beneficiary's departure from the hospital or CAH and required until the patient can obtain a continuing supply.[52]

[D] Services Furnished by an Intern or a Resident-in-Training

Inpatient hospital services include the services of medical or surgical interns or residents-in-training.[53] Services must be provided through a teaching program approved by the Council on Medical Education of the American Medical Association or the Bureau of Professional Education of the American Osteopathic Association; a program approved by the Council on Dental Education of the American Dental Association; or a program approved by the Council on Podiatry Education of the American Podiatry Association.[54]

[E] Other Diagnostic or Therapeutic Items or Services

Diagnostic or therapeutic items or services are considered inpatient hospital or inpatient CAH services if furnished by the hospital or CAH or others under arrangements made with the hospital or CAH; the billing for such services is performed through the hospital or CAH; and the services are of the kind ordinarily furnished to inpatients either by the hospital or CAH or under arrangements made by the hospital.[55]

In recent years, an increasing trend has been noted in which beneficiaries have been in hospital rooms and beds, not as "admitted" patients, but rather under "observation" status.[56] Hospitals appear to use "observation" status as a

[51] 42 C.F.R. § 409.13(a).

[52] 42 C.F.R. § 409.13(b).

[53] 42 C.F.R. § 409.15(a).

[54] 42 C.F.R. § 409.15(b), (c).

[55] 42 C.F.R. § 409.16.

[56] For information on observation status and its consequences, see Center for Medicare Advocacy, "Observation Status & *Bagnall v. Sebelius*," *available at* http://www.medicareadvocacy.org/medicare-info/observation-status/ (site visited May 31, 2016).

cost-savings mechanism to avoid Medicare hospital reimbursement complications related to CMS's Recovery Audit Contractor (RAC) program.[57]

Often, patients are not informed of their observation status. Observation status is not the same as being a hospital inpatient, although the actual services may be the same.[58] When hospital patients are classified as outpatients and are in hospitals on observation status, they may be charged for services that Medicare would have paid if they were properly admitted as hospital inpatients. Moreover, such patients will not be able to obtain Medicare coverage in SNFs if they need nursing home care after their hospital stay ends.

Medicare Part A covers nursing home care for patients who have a three-day prior inpatient hospital stay, and observation status does not count toward the three-day prior hospital stay.[59] In addition, as a result of retroactive billing practices, beneficiaries have been "admitted" to a hospital but have had that status changed to observation status before the hospital submits the bill to Medicare. The right to notice to beneficiaries in these circumstances is unclear. The Center for Medicare Advocacy continues to pursue strategies to address problems related to observation status.[60]

Beginning August 6, 2016, the Notice of Observation Treatment and Implication for Care Eligibility Act (NOTICE Act)[61] requires hospitals to provide written and oral notice, within 36 hours, to patients who are in observation or other outpatient status for more than 24 hours. The notice must explain the reason that

---

[57] *See* CMS, "Recovery Audit Program," *available at* http://www.cms.gov/Research-Statistics-Data-and-Systems/Monitoring-Programs/Medicare-FFS-Compliance-Programs/Recovery-Audit-Program/Recent_Updates.html (site visited May 31, 2016).

[58] *See* Barrows v. Burwell, No. 3:11-cv-1703 (2d Cir. Jan. 22, 2015), *available at* http://hr.cch.com/hld/BarrowsvBurwell2dCir1-22-2015.pdf (site visited May 31, 2016). *See also* Center for Medicare Advocacy, Weekly Alerts, *available at* http://www.medicareadvocacy.org and **Chapter 3** of this Handbook. The Center for Medicare Advocacy's litigation to correct this problem was unsuccessful. *See* Bagnall v. Sebelius, No. 3:11cv1703 (MPS) (D. Conn. filed Nov. 3, 2011) (Memorandum of Decision dated Sept. 23, 2013). For a discussion of *Bagnall*, see Center for Medicare Advocacy, "Disappointing Decision from Court in Challenge to 'Observation Status' Highlights Need to Pass Legislation," *available at* http://www.medicareadvocacy.org/disappointing-decision-from-court-in-challenge-to-observation-status-highlights-need-to-pass-legislation/ (site visited May 31, 2016). *See also* http://scholar.google.com/scholar_case?case=6608692245354306736&q=Bagnall+v.+Sebelius&hl=en&as_sdt=2,9&as_vis=1 (site visited May 31, 2016).

For information on the RACs, see CMS, "Recovery Audit Contractor," *available at* http://www.cms.gov/Research-Statistics-Data-and-Systems/Monitoring-Programs/Medicare-FFS-Compliance-Programs/Recovery-Audit-Program/ (site visited May 31, 2016). *See also* Tax Relief and Health Care Act of 2006 § 302, Pub. L. No. 109-432 (Dec. 20, 2006), *available at* www.cms.gov/transmittals/downloads/R139FM.pdf (site visited May 31, 2016).

[59] *See* Center for Medicare Advocacy, "Observation Status & Bagnall v. Sebelius," *available at* http://www.medicareadvocacy.org/medicare-info/observation-status/ (site visited May 31, 2016).

[60] *See* Center for Medicare Advocacy, "Observation Status & Bagnall v. Sebelius," *available at* http://www.medicareadvocacy.org/medicare-info/observation-status/ (site visited June 1, 2016).

[61] Pub. L. No. 114-42, signed by President Obama on August 6, 2015, 42 U.S.C. § 1395cc(a)(1)(Y).

the patient is an outpatient (and not an admitted inpatient) and describe the implications of that status both for cost-sharing in the hospital and for subsequent "eligibility for coverage" in a SNF. The NOTICE Act does not give patients appeal rights to challenge their observation status.[62]

In final regulations for inpatient hospital reimbursement that were put on display at the Office of Federal Register on August 2, 2016, CMS announced that the final rules, including rules to implement the NOTICE Act, would be effective October 1, 2016, and that the required written notice to patients—the Medicare Outpatient Observation Notice (MOON)—will not become effective until 90 days following approval of the MOON by the Office of Management and Budget (OMB). As of November 2016, OMB had not approved the MOON. What the CMS final rules mean is that the NOTICE Act will not be implemented until the 2017, at the earliest.

Similarly, diagnostic services of independent clinical laboratories, furnished to Medicare inpatients under arrangements with a Medicare-participating hospital, that are reimbursable under Medicare Part A are affected by observation status.[63] CMS has issued additional guidance through which it attempts to clarify when a person is an inpatient.[64] The CMS guidance is worrisome and confusing. It establishes, for example, a presumption that if a patient is in an inpatient hospital for two midnights, the patient will likely be admitted. The guidance states that claims in which a medically necessary inpatient stay spans at least two midnights after the beneficiary is formally admitted as an inpatient will be presumed appropriate for inpatient admission and inpatient hospital payment and will generally not be subject to medical review of the inpatient admission, absent evidence of systematic gaming, abuse, or delays in the provision of care in an attempt to qualify for the two-midnight presumption.[65]

Nonetheless, an order of admission remains the basis of inpatient hospital status. Furthermore, a physician's intention that his or her patient should be admitted, as expressed in the patient's medical records, is to be given weight but has no presumptive value.[66]

---

[62] https://s3.amazonaws.com/public-inspection.federalregister.gov/2016-18476.pdf at 1208.

[63] 42 C.F.R. § 482.27; *see* Medicare Benefit Policy (MBP) Manual, CMS Pub. No. 100-02, Ch. 1, § 50.3, *available at* http://cms.hhs.gov/Regulations-and-Guidance/Guidance/Manuals/Downloads/bp102c01.pdf (site visited May 31, 2016). *See also* CMS, "Are you a hospital inpatient or outpatient?" *available at* http://www.medicare.gov/Pubs/pdf/11435.pdf (site visited May 31, 2016).

[64] *See* 42 C.F.R. § 412.3(e)(1)-(2), *available at* http://www.ecfr.gov/cgi-bin/text-idx?SID=f907882f7b47ae43d815ee21bd8a9d9e&node=42:2.0.1.2.12.1.47.3&rgn=div8 (site visited June 1, 2016).

[65] 78 Fed. Reg. 50,950 (Aug. 19, 2013).

[66] *See* 78 Fed. Reg. 50,950 (Aug. 19, 2013). For further discussion of the conundrum of observation status and inpatient status, see Center for Medicare Advocacy, "Observation Status: OIG Provides an Analysis and CMS Issues Final Regulations," *available at* http://www.medicareadvocacy.org/observation-status-oig-provides-an-analysis-and-cms-issues-final-regulations/ (site visited June 1, 2016).

[F] Services Related to Kidney Transplantations

Medicare only pays for kidney transplantations performed in a Medicare-approved renal transplantation center.[67] Provided that the kidney is intended for an individual who has ESRD and is eligible for Medicare, Medicare payment is available for the evaluation or preparation of a potential or actual donor, for the donation of the kidney, or for postoperative recovery services directly related to the kidney donation.[68] The Medicare deductible and coinsurance requirements do not apply to services furnished to an individual in connection with the donation of a kidney for transplant surgery.[69]

[G] Blood Services

With respect to blood, the patient must pay a deductible for the first three units of whole blood or units of packed red cells that a beneficiary receives during a calendar year as an inpatient of a hospital, CAH, or SNF, or on an outpatient basis under Medicare Part B.[70] A unit of packed red cells is treated as the equivalent of a unit of whole blood.[71] Generally, a provider may charge the patient its customary charge for any of the first three units.[72] The deductible does not apply to other blood components such as platelet, fibrinogen, plasma, gamma globulin, and serum albumin, or to the cost of storing and administering blood.[73] The beneficiary also has the option to arrange for the blood to be replaced rather than paying for it.[74]

The blood deductible is in addition to the inpatient hospital deductible and daily coinsurance.[75] The Part A blood deductible is reduced to the extent that the Part B blood deductible has been applied; for example, the beneficiary has received one unit under Medicare Part B.

The Medicare hospital benefit does not include coverage for physicians' services while in the hospital. Those services are covered under Medicare Part B.[76] The surgeon and anesthesiologist, for example, will bill the patient separately (the cost of physicians' services deemed reasonable and necessary would be covered under Part B of the Medicare program).

---

[67] 42 C.F.R. § 409.18(a).

[68] 42 C.F.R. § 409.18(b).

[69] 42 C.F.R. § 409.89.

[70] 42 U.S.C. § 1395e (a)(2); 42 C.F.R. § 409.87(a)(3).

[71] 42 C.F.R. § 409.87(a)(2).

[72] 42 C.F.R. § 409.87(c).

[73] 42 C.F.R. § 409.87(a)(4).

[74] 42 C.F.R. § 409.87(b).

[75] 42 C.F.R. § 409.87(a)(5).

[76] 42 U.S.C. § 1395d; Social Security Act § 1812(a)(1).

§ 2.07 LIMITATIONS ON PAYMENT FOR SERVICES

[A] Physician Certification and Payment Forms

Providers of Medicare services, including hospitals, must submit payment forms indicating that the services provided were medically necessary and appropriate. The forms for submitting a request for payment are promulgated by the Secretary and must be submitted for payment no later than the calendar year following the year in which such services are furnished. Services furnished in the last quarter of a calendar year, however, are deemed to have been delivered in the following calendar year.[77]

■ **EXAMPLE:** If a patient receives services in October 2016, those services will be viewed for billing purposes (but not for deductible purposes) as having been delivered during the calendar year 2017 and, therefore, can properly be billed through the end of 2018. By contrast, services in the calendar year 2016 that were delivered on or before September 2016 could properly be billed only through the end of 2017.

The physician must certify that the inpatient hospital services provided over a period of time are required to be given on an inpatient basis for such individual's medical treatment, or that inpatient diagnostic study is medically required and such services are necessary for such purposes.[78] This certification must be furnished in such cases, and with such frequency and with supporting material, as appropriate to the case involved and as provided by the Secretary's regulations. The first such certification must be furnished no later than the 20th day of the period in which services are being provided.[79] A similar certification is required for inpatient psychiatric hospital services.[80]

Physicians must also certify that dental services performed in the hospital setting, in connection with the care, treatment, filling, removal, or replacement of teeth or structures that directly support teeth, are such that the services must be performed in the hospital setting.[81] The certification must state that because of the

[77] 42 C.F.R. § 424.44.

[78] 42 U.S.C. § 1395f (a)(2), (a)(3). *See also* 42 U.S.C. § 1395f(a)(6) (physician certification where no utilization review committee findings have been made), § 1395f(a)(8) with respect to inpatient critical access hospital services, requiring physician certification that the patient may reasonably be expected to be transferred to a hospital within 96 hours after admission to the critical access hospital.

[79] 42 U.S.C. § 1395f (a)(3).

[80] 42 U.S.C. § 1395f (a)(2)(A).

[81] 42 U.S.C. § 1395f (a)(2)(D). Access to dental services generally is problematic in Medicare as Medicare does not cover routine dental services. Advocates have found that sustaining coverage for such services is less complicated where the procedures are part of services performed on an inpatient hospital basis. Even so, the setting is not necessarily determinative of coverage. It is whether the nonroutine dental services were part of treating a recognized Medicare-covered condition that is

underlying medical condition and clinical status of the patient, or the severity of the dental procedure, hospitalization is required.[82]

[B] Payment for Services Performed Outside the United States

Payment is available for inpatient hospital services furnished to Medicare beneficiaries in a hospital located outside the United States, or under arrangements with it, if such individual is a resident of the United States and only if such hospital is closer to, or substantially more accessible from, the residence of such individual than the nearest United States hospital adequately equipped to deal with and available to treat the beneficiary's illness or injury.[83]

§ 2.08 THE MEDICAL NECESSITY STANDARD FOR INPATIENT HOSPITAL STAYS

[A] In General

The substantive standard for Medicare coverage for general hospital services (also called acute hospital care) is one of "medical necessity."[84] A physician must certify that hospital "services are required to be given on an inpatient basis for such individual's medical treatment, or that inpatient diagnostic study is medically required. . . ."[85] The regulations provide that inpatient hospital care includes cases where a beneficiary needs a SNF level of care, but under Medicare criteria, a Medicare certified SNF-level bed is not available.[86] The Medicare statute requires that the beneficiary is "entitled to have payment made" for SNF care although remaining in the hospital awaiting an available SNF bed. Therefore, in addition to requiring a SNF level of care, a beneficiary must also have been covered by Medicare for at least three days during the hospital stay in question.[87] A patient must accept the first Medicare-certified bed available[88] or lose continued Medicare inpatient hospital coverage. However, an offer of a non-certified bed

determinative. *See also* Center for Medicare Advocacy, "New Report: Expanded Dental Coverage Needed to Confront Health Crisis," *available at* http://www.medicareadvocacy.org/new-report-expanded-dental-coverage-needed-to-confront-health-crisis/ (site visited June 1, 2016).

[82] 42 U.S.C. § 1395f (a)(2)(D).

[83] 42 U.S.C. § 1395f (f).

[84] 42 U.S.C. § 1395f (a)(3).

[85] 42 U.S.C. § 1395f (a)(3).

[86] 42 C.F.R. § 412.42(c)(1); *see also* 42 C.F.R. § 424.13(b).

[87] 42 U.S.C. § 1395x(v)(1)(G)(i)(III); *see also* 42 C.F.R. § 409.30.

[88] Occasionally, the question arises as to how geographically distant the SNF bed can be and still be deemed "available" to the patient. For example, can a patient be required to accept a SNF bed that is 300 miles from the patient's home? While there is no unequivocal answer to this question in the Medicare statute or regulations, past Medicare policy stated that this requirement "is not defined to require a patient to be taken away from his family and transported over great distances." *See*

may be rejected with no risk to continued inpatient hospital coverage.[89] In addition, the statute explicitly excludes from coverage any expenses incurred for items or services "not reasonable and necessary for the diagnosis or treatment of illness or injury or to improve the functioning of a malformed body member. . ."[90]

■ **EXAMPLE:** Mrs. Smith sustains a fall and fractures her leg. Surgery is required to repair the fracture, and she is admitted to the hospital in order to receive such treatment. Close monitoring of her post-surgical condition is required because she has a history of peripheral vascular disease, venous thrombosis, and leg edema. Her treating physician has prescribed continuous intravenous anticoagulation therapy in order to prevent a stroke and is unable to accurately discern whether the swelling in her leg is attributable to swelling relative to the fracture or to the venous thrombosis. During this entire time, a span of eight days, the services Mrs. Smith is receiving in the hospital could be performed only in a hospital, where 24-hour availability of a physician exists and the requisite close physician monitoring is available. Following resolution of these medical issues, Mrs. Smith's physician orders physical therapy five times per week and includes a statement that Mrs. Smith can be transferred to a SNF. However, no Medicare-certified SNF bed is immediately available. Under these circumstances, Mrs. Smith is still eligible to receive Medicare inpatient hospital coverage, because she needs a SNF level of care, but no Medicare-certified SNF bed is available to her and she has been receiving Medicare covered inpatient hospital care for 3 days or more. The days that Mrs. Smith spends in the hospital waiting for a Medicare-certified SNF bed to become available are covered hospital days, subject to any applicable hospital coinsurance amounts, as well as the 150-day-per-benefit-period inpatient hospital limitation.

[B] Additional Requirements for Rehabilitation Hospitals

Medicare imposes additional coverage requirements for care received in rehabilitation hospitals.[91] Rehabilitation hospital care may be covered when it is

---

Medicare Intermediary Manual, CMS Pub. 13, § 3421.1C, *see* http://r.search.yahoo.com/_ylt=A0LEVigLMU9Xu6sAxYYnnIlQ;_ylu=X3oDMTBybGY3bmpvBGNvbG8DYmYxBHBvcwMyBHZ0aWQDBHNlYwNzcg--/RV=2/RE=1464836491/RO=10/RU=http%3a%2f%2fwww.cms.gov%2fRegulations-and-Guidance%2fGuidance%2fTransmittals%2fdownloads%2fR420A2.pdf/RK=0/RS=qVgariw1zXNQCU5AOrMwp1cVl6g- (site visited June 1, 2016). This provision remains in the Paper-Based Manual (but still available on the Internet) as it does not appear to have been transferred to the Internet-Only Manuals, *available at* http://www.cms.gov/Regulations-and-Guidance/Guidance/Manuals/Paper-Based-Manuals.html (site visited June 1, 2016).

[89] 42 C.F.R. § 412.42(c)(1); *see also* 42 C.F.R. § 424.13(b).

[90] Social Security Act § 1862(a)(1)(A), 42 U.S.C. § 1395(a)(1)(A).

[91] *See* 42 C.F.R. Pt. 482 and all the documentation requirements specified in 42 C.F.R. § 412.622(a)(3), (4), and (5).

provided in a freestanding rehabilitation hospital, or in a distinct rehabilitation unit of an acute care hospital. Effective January 1, 2002, inpatient rehabilitation hospitals and rehabilitation units are paid under a prospective payment system (PPS). Payments are made on the basis of prospectively determined rates and applied on a diagnosis-related group (DRG) basis.[92]

For a rehabilitation hospitalization to be covered, the following requirements must be satisfied:[93]

- The physician must certify that the patient needs inpatient hospital rehabilitation;
- The hospital must be a Medicare-certified facility;
- The patient must require a relatively intense, multidisciplinary rehabilitation program provided by a coordinated team of physical therapists, occupational therapists, speech language pathologists, rehabilitation nurses, and/or training in rehabilitation medicine, which is evidenced by at least bi-weekly team meeting notes;
- The goal of the rehabilitation program must be to upgrade the patient's ability to function as independently as possible;
- The care must be reasonable and necessary, and not actually available at a lower level of care.

It should be noted that the Medicare program pays for rehabilitation services, including physical, speech, and occupational therapies, in different settings and not solely in an inpatient hospital setting. For example, various kinds of rehabilitation can be provided at home through the Medicare home health benefit, in an outpatient therapy facility, in a SNF, in a comprehensive outpatient

---

[92] 42 C.F.R. §§ 412.600 *et seq.*

[93] 42 C.F.R. § 412.23(b), § 412.29; MBP Manual, Ch. 1 §§ 110.1 *et seq., available at* https://www.cms.gov/Regulations-and-Guidance/Guidance/Manuals/downloads/bp102c01.pdf (site visited June 1, 2016). For many years CMS interpreted "relatively intense" to mean that the patient had to require and receive at least three hours per day of physical and/or occupational therapy in order to qualify for Medicare coverage for hospital-level rehabilitation. This interpretation, found in CMS's Intermediary and Hospital Manuals, was found by the United States District Court to be an arbitrary rule of thumb that could not be used to deny coverage in Hooper v. Sullivan, Medicare & Medicaid Guide (CCH) 37,985 (D. Conn. 1989). *See also* Hooper v. Sullivan, Medicare benefits, http://www.medicareadvocacy.org/wp-content/uploads/2012/02/RRF-Issue-Brief-14-Medicare-Updates-12-2011-_3_.pdf (site visited June 1, 2016). In *Hooper*, the Secretary was ordered to revise the manual provisions to reflect the fact that Medicare determinations are to be made based on an individual assessment of each patient's needs and to prohibit denials based on the three-hour rule or any other rule of thumb. *See also* CMS Ruling 85-2, Medicare & Medicaid Guide (CCH) [1986-1 Transfer Binder] 34,817; and *see* New York *ex rel.* Holland v. Sullivan, 927 F.2d 57 (2d Cir. 1991); New York *ex rel.* Stein v. Secretary, Dep't of Health & Human Servs., 924 F.2d 431 (2d Cir. 1991); Probstein v. Sullivan, Medicare & Medicaid Guide (CCH) 41,423 (D. Conn. 1993).

rehabilitation facility (CORF), in an inpatient rehabilitation facility (IRF),[94] or in a long-term care hospital (LTCH). A patient's medical needs and condition should dictate the setting in which rehabilitation services are provided. In addition, the type and amount of care a person receives varies by setting. Federal regulations published in 2004 began a three-year phase-in of the requirement that to qualify as an IRF, 75 percent of the IRF's patients must have one or more of 13 specified conditions and otherwise require intensive rehabilitation services. However, recent legislation has mandated that the compliance rate be no greater than 60 percent, and CMS has proposed regulations identifying 60 percent as the threshold.[95] There are several proposals for site-neutral payments to IRFs and SNFs. Such proposals persist even when studies indicate that care outcomes are better in IRFs.[96]

[C] Long-Term Care Hospitals

In general, LTCHs are defined in the Medicare law as hospitals that have an average inpatient length of stay greater than 25 days. They typically provide extended medical and rehabilitative care for patients with clinically complex conditions and for those who may suffer from multiple acute or chronic conditions. Services available in such facilities can include comprehensive rehabilitation, respiratory therapy, cancer treatment, head trauma treatment and pain management.[97]

---

[94] Hospitals and rehabilitation units must meet the criteria specified in 42 C.F.R. §§ 412.23(b), 412.25, 412.29. Inpatient rehabilitation hospitals and acute care hospital rehabilitation units are collectively referred to as an inpatient rehabilitation facility (IRF) under the IRF Prospective Payment System (IRF PPS). 42 U.S.C. §§ 1395ww (d)(1)(B), 1395ww(d)(1)B)(ii). *See also* the *Medlearn Matters* discussion for Medicare providers of services found at www.carefirst.com/pages/mdmedicare/pdf/MM3334.pdf (site visited June 1, 2016). Note that inpatient rehabilitation hospitals and rehabilitation units are referred to as inpatient rehabilitation facilities (IRFs). *See* Inpatient Rehabilitation Facility PPS, *available at* https://www.cms.gov/Medicare/Medicare-Fee-for-Service-Payment/InpatientRehabFacPPS/index.html?redirect=/InpatientRehabFacPPS/ (site visited June 1, 2016).

[95] *See* Medicare, Medicaid, and SCHIP Extension Act of 2007 § 115, Pub. L. No. 110-173 (Dec. 29, 2007). The proposed regulations can be found at 73 Fed. Reg. 22,687–22,688. The 75 percent rule was originally established in 1983 but was suspended by CMS in 2002 after it found inconsistent use of the criteria by inpatient rehabilitation facilities. Government Accountability Office, *Medicare: More Specific Criteria Needed to Classify Inpatient Rehabilitation Facilities* 8-10, GAO-05-366 (Apr. 2005), *available at* www.gao.gov/new.items/d05366.pdf (site visited June 1, 2016). *See also* https://www.cms.gov/InpatientRehabFacPPS/03_Criteria.asp (site visited June 1, 2016).

[96] *See* Center for Medicare Advocacy, "Inpatient Rehabilitation Facilities and Skilled Nursing Facilities: Vive la Difference!" *available at* http://www.medicareadvocacy.org/inpatient-rehabilitation-facilities-and-skilled-nursing-facilities-vive-la-difference/ (site visited June 1, 2016).

[97] *See* the Balanced Budget Refinement Act of 1999 (BBRA), Pub. L. No. 106-113, § 123 (Nov. 29, 1999), as amended by § 307 of BIPA. This provision directed the Secretary to develop and implement a per discharge, diagnosis-related group (DRG)–based prospective payment system

To be eligible to receive payment under the PPS for LTCHs, the facility must meet the criteria to be classified as an LTCH[98] in order to be excluded from hospital inpatient PPS.[99] This condition of payment is subject to special payment provisions,[100] provisions on change in hospital status,[101] provisions related to hospitals within hospitals,[102] and satellite facilities.[103]

LTCHs may not charge beneficiaries for any covered services for which payment is made by Medicare, even if the hospital's costs of furnishing the service are greater than the PPS amount. The facility may charge the beneficiary only for the applicable deductible and coinsurance amounts.[104]

LTCHs must have an agreement with a Quality Improvement Organization (QIO) to provide ongoing review with respect to medical necessity, reasonableness, and appropriateness of hospital admissions and discharges; appropriateness of payments under outlier provisions; the validity of the hospital's diagnostic and procedural information; the completeness, adequacy, and quality of the services furnished by the hospital; and other medical or other practices with respect to beneficiaries or billing for services furnished to beneficiaries.[105]

On July 18, 2014, as part of the restructuring of the QIO program—separating the beneficiary quality of care complaint review process from provider quality improvement functions—CMS awarded additional contracts to assist providers with quality improvement matters. The new contracts represent the second phase of QIO restructuring. These QIOs will be known as Quality Innovation Network (QIN)-QIOs.[106]

(PPS) for LTCHs for cost-reporting periods beginning on or after October 1, 2002. The system replaced the reasonable cost-based payment system over a five-year transition period through October 1, 2006. Regulations implementing PPS for LTCHs are located at 42 C.F.R. §§ 412.500–412.541, http://www.gpo.gov/fdsys/granule/CFR-2011-title42-vol2/CFR-2011-title42-vol2-sec412-500 (site visited June 1, 2016). *See also* www.cms.hhs.gov/LongTermCareHospitalPPS/ (site visited June 1, 2016). Links to LTCH PPS federal regulations and notices are available at CMS, "Long-Term Care Hospital PPS," http://www.cms.gov/Medicare/Medicare-Fee-for-Service-Payment/LongTermCareHospitalPPS/index.html?redirect=/LongTermCareHospitalPPS/LTCHPPSRN/list.asp (site visited June 1, 2016). LTCHs are sometimes referred to as long-term acute care hospitals, although they are referred to by CMS as long-term care hospitals.

[98] 42 C.F.R. §§ 412.505, 412.23(e).

[99] 42 C.F.R. §§ 412.505, 412.1(a)(1).

[100] 42 C.F.R. §§ 412.505, 412.22(c).

[101] 42 C.F.R. §§ 412.505, 412.22(d).

[102] 42 C.F.R. §§ 412.505, 412.22(e).

[103] 42 C.F.R. §§ 412.505, 412.22(h).

[104] 42 C.F.R. § 412.507. Applicable deductible and coinsurance amounts are discussed at 42 C.F.R. §§ 409.82, 409.83, and 409.87.

[105] 42 C.F.R. § 412.508. Quality Improvement Organizations (QIOs), formerly known as Peer Review Organizations (PROs), are a creature of the Social Security Act, §§ 1151 *et seq.*, 42 U.S.C. §§ 1320 *et seq.*, and provide certain quality and utilization review oversight with respect to a range of Medicare-covered services.

[106] *See* CMS, Press Release, "CMS Launches Next Phase of New Quality Improvement Program," *available at* http://cms.gov/Newsroom/MediaReleaseDatabase/Press-releases/2014-Press-

On May 9, 2014, CMS announced the first phase of its restructuring of the QIO functions. In the first phase, CMS has contracted with Livanta LLC (for geographic areas 1 and 5), located in Annapolis Junction, Maryland, and KePRO (for geographic areas 2, 3, and 4), located in Seven Hills, Ohio. These contractors will be responsible for ensuring consistency in the review process with respect to beneficiary complaints. CMS describes these two contractors as its Beneficiary and Family-Centered Care (BFCC) QIO contractors.[107] The states in the designated geographic areas are:

- Area 1: Connecticut, Maine, Massachusetts, New Hampshire, New Jersey, New York, Pennsylvania, Puerto Rico, Rhode Island, Vermont, Virgin Islands
- Area 2: District of Columbia, Delaware, Florida, Georgia, Maryland, North Carolina, South Carolina, Virginia, West Virginia
- Area 3: Alabama, Arkansas, Colorado, Kentucky, Louisiana, Mississippi, Montana, North Dakota, New Mexico, Oklahoma, South Dakota, Tennessee, Texas, Utah, Wyoming
- Area 4: Iowa, Illinois, Indiana, Kansas, Michigan, Minnesota, Missouri, Nebraska, Ohio, Wisconsin
- Area 5: Alaska, Arizona, California, Hawaii, Idaho, Nevada, Oregon, Washington.[108]

§ 2.09 HOSPITAL PAYMENT

[A] Prospective Payment

A hospital must meet the conditions of Medicare participation under the Medicare PPS for hospital services furnished to Medicare beneficiaries,[109] If a hospital fails to comply with these conditions, CMS, which administers the Medicare program, may withhold Medicare payment, in full or in part, to the hospital

releases-items/2014-07-18.html?DLPage=1&DLSort=0&DLSortDir=descending (site visited June 1, 2016). Each QIN-QIO will work on strategic quality improvement initiatives. *See also* "Quality Improvement Organizations" on the CMS website at http://www.cms.gov/Medicare/Quality-Initiatives-Patient-Assessment-Instruments/QualityImprovementOrgs/index.html (site visited June 1, 2016).

[107] *See also* Beneficiary and Family-Centered Care (BFCC) QIO contractors, https://www.cms.gov/Newsroom/MediaReleaseDatabase/Press-releases/2014-Press-releases-items/2014-05-09.html (site visited June 1, 2016).

[108] *See* CMS, Press Release, "CMS Launches Improved Quality Improvement Program," May 9, 2014, *available at* http://www.cms.gov/Newsroom/MediaReleaseDatabase/Press-releases/2014-Press-releases-items/2014-05-09.html (site visited June 1, 2016).

[109] 42 C.F.R. § 412.40.

until the hospital provides appropriate assurances of its compliance. Otherwise, CMS may terminate the hospital's provider agreement.[110]

Historically, prior to 1983, the Medicare program paid hospitals on a retrospective basis in an amount equal to the reasonable cost of covered services. In other words, Medicare paid a hospital what it cost the hospital to deliver the service involved. Effective October 1, 1983, however, Congress instituted a new financing structure called the Perspective Payment System (PPS).[111]

[B] Diagnosis-Related Groups

The PPS applies to acute care and rehabilitation hospitals, as well as LTCHs, and to units in acute care hospitals that provide rehabilitation services.[112] Alcohol and drug treatment, psychiatric, and children's hospitals are not included in PPS, nor are units in acute care hospitals that provide alcohol and drug treatment, psychiatric, or pediatric services.[113]

PPS requires the payment of a prospectively determined amount for each Medicare discharge. All patient discharges are classified according to a list of Diagnosis-Related Groups (DRGs). The list includes approximately 490 DRGs. A DRG is assigned a particular value based on the average cost of caring for patients with similar diagnoses in the past.[114]

The DRG for a stroke, for example, might be $6,000. For every patient discharged from a hospital after treatment for a stroke, the hospital would receive,

---

[110] 42 C.F.R. § 412.40(b)(1), (2).

[111] 42 U.S.C. § 1395ww(d). Note that, generally, PPSs exist across a range of care settings, including hospitals, SNFs, home health, hospice, and outpatient hospital services. CMS provides updated PPS rates, rules, and data on an ongoing basis. Discussion of PPS is generally incorporated as relevant to a particular care setting.

[112] Regulations establishing a prospective payment system for rehabilitation hospitals were issued by the CMS and became effective on January 1, 2002. 42 C.F.R. §§ 412.600 *et seq.* CMS regularly updates its lists of DRGs and other codes.

[113] 42 U.S.C. § 1395ww(d)(1)(B); 42 C.F.R. §§ 412.20–412.32. *See also* 45 C.F.R. Pt. 170 *available at* http://www.gpo.gov/fdsys/pkg/FR-2015-04-30/pdf/2015-09245.pdf (site visited June 1, 2016)

[114] 42 U.S.C. § 1395ww(e). In recent years an increasing trend has been noted in which beneficiaries have been in hospital rooms and beds, not as "admitted" patients, but rather under "observation" status. Hospitals appear to use "observation" status as a cost-saving mechanism and often do not inform beneficiaries of the "observation" status. As a result, more beneficiaries are finding themselves exposed to additional expenses that are not covered by Medicare Part A for observation status. For example, beneficiaries hospitalized under observation status do not meet the three-day prior hospitalization requirement for purposes of accessing the Medicare-covered SNF benefit. In addition, beneficiaries have been "admitted" to a hospital but have had that status changed to observation status before the hospital submits the bill to Medicare. The right to notice to a beneficiary in these circumstances is unclear because the beneficiary has not been admitted as an inpatient. *See also Bagnall,* No. 3:11cv1703(MPS) (D. Conn. filed Nov. 3, 2011) (Memorandum of Decision dated Sept. 23, 2013), *available at* http://scholar.google.com/scholar_case?case=6608692245354306736&q=Bagnall+v.+Sebelius&hl=en&as_sdt=20006&as_vis=1 (site visited June 1, 2016).

for example, $6,000 in Medicare reimbursement even if the patient's care had actually cost the hospital less, or more, than $6,000 to deliver.

Only when a beneficiary has a medically necessary stay that is much longer or more expensive for the hospital than an average case covered by the appropriate DRG can the hospital receive additional Medicare coverage, called "outlier payments." The outlier payments amount to 60 percent of the average daily cost of caring for a patient with the diagnosis involved.[115] Because the hospital usually receives only the single predetermined DRG amount for a given hospital discharge, the hospital comes under severe pressure to discharge patients at the earliest possible time, thereby maximizing profit or minimizing loss.

[C] Limits on Charges to Beneficiaries

Hospitals may not charge a beneficiary for services that are paid for by Medicare, even if the hospital's cost of furnishing such services to the beneficiary is greater than the amount the hospital is paid under PPS.[116]

Under PPS, a hospital may charge a beneficiary during a covered stay, which includes at least one covered day, only for the following:

- Applicable deductible and coinsurance amounts;[117]
- Custodial care provided that is not part of medically necessary hospital services provided to the patient;[118]
- Items and services that are not medically necessary;[119]
- Non-physician services furnished to hospital inpatients by other than the hospital or a provider or supplier under arrangements made by the hospital;[120]
- Items and services provided when a patient is not entitled to Medicare Part A benefits;[121] and
- Items and services provided after Medicare Part A benefits have been exhausted.[122]

---

[115] 42 C.F.R. §§ 412.80–412.84.

[116] 42 C.F.R. § 412.42(a).

[117] *See* 42 C.F.R. §§ 409.82, 409.83, and 409.87.

[118] 42 C.F.R. § 412.42(b)(2)(i). *See also* 42 C.F.R. § 411.15(g).

[119] 42 C.F.R. § 412.42(b)(2)(ii). *See also* 42 C.F.R. § 411.15(k).

[120] 42 C.F.R. § 412.42(b)(2)(iii). *See* http://www.gpo.gov/fdsys/pkg/CFR-2011-title42-vol2/pdf/CFR-2011-title42-vol2-sec412-42.pdf (site visited June 1, 2016). *See also* Electronic Code of Federal Regulations, http://www.ecfr.gov/cgi-bin/text-idx?tpl=/ecfrbrowse/Title42/42tab_02.tpl (site visited June 1, 2016).

[121] 42 C.F.R. § 412.42(b)(2)(iv). *See also* 42 C.F.R. Pt. 408 subpt. A.

[122] 42 C.F.R. § 412.42(b)(2)(v). *See also* 42 C.F.R. § 409.61.

[D] Inpatient Hospitalization No Longer Necessary (Notice to Beneficiaries)

A hospital may charge a beneficiary for items and services provided after the hospital (acting directly or through its utilization review committee) has determined that the beneficiary does not or no longer requires inpatient hospital care;[123] or where the attending physician agrees with the hospital determination in writing (e.g., by issuing a written discharge order) that inpatient hospital services are no longer necessary.[124] Before a hospital can charge the beneficiary under these circumstances, the hospital must notify the beneficiary (or person acting on his or her behalf) in writing that:

- In the opinion of the hospital, and with the concurrence of the physician or the QIO, customary charges will be made for continued hospital care beyond the second day following the date of the notice.[125]
- The QIO will make a formal determination under the appeals procedures that apply to QIO determinations affecting Medicare Part A payment.[126]

---

[123] 42 C.F.R. § 412.42(c)(1), (2). Note that inpatient hospital care includes care where a beneficiary needs a SNF level of care and a Medicare-certified SNF bed is not available. 42 C.F.R. § 412.42(b)(2)(v). Occasionally, the question arises as to how distant the SNF bed can be, in order for it to be deemed "available" to the patient. For example, can a patient be required to accept a SNF bed that is 300 miles from the patient's home? The argument from the advocate and patient is that the location of the placement must be reasonable, that it allow family and friends to visit; that options closer by should be explored and used where appropriate. *See* Revision to State Operations Manual (SOM), Ref: S&C:13-32, "Hospital Appendix A–Interpretive Guidelines for 42 CFR 482.43, Discharge Planning," *available at* http://www.cms.gov/Medicare/Provider-Enrollment-and-Certification/SurveyCertificationGenInfo/Downloads/Survey-and-Cert-Letter-13-32.pdf (site visited June 1, 2016). According to § 482.43(c)(6): "The hospital must include in the discharge plan a list of HHAs or SNFs that are available to the patient, that are participating in the Medicare program, and that serve the geographic area (as defined by the HHA) in which the patient resides, or in the case of a SNF, in the geographic area requested by the patient. HHAs must request to be listed by the hospital as available." *See also* Alfred J. Chiplin, Jr., "Breathing Life into Discharge Planning," *The Elder L.J.* (13)1, *available at* http://publish.illinois.edu/elderlawjournal/files/2015/02/Chiplin.pdf (site visited June 1, 2016).

[124] 42 C.F.R. § 412.42(c)(2). If the hospital believes the patient no longer needs inpatient hospital care and the physician does not concur, the hospital may request immediate review by the appropriate QIO.

[125] *See* 42 C.F.R. § 405.1206(d)(6)(ii).

[126] The QIO or contractor may review any cases in which the hospital advises the beneficiary (or the person acting on the beneficiary's behalf) of the non-coverage of the services. The hospital must identify such cases to the QIO or contractor in accordance with CMS instructions. 42 C.F.R. § 412.42(g); *available at* http://www.ecfr.gov/cgi-bin/text-idx?SID=ba2c595cb77ac7cc63b26ad69e535425&mc=true&node=se42.2.412_142&rgn=div8 (site visited June 1, 2016). A variety of procedural due process issues are raised with respect to when notice is given and the level of detail describing the medical rationale for discharge that is required in the notice (42 C.F.R. § 412.42(c)(1)–(4)); *see also* 42 C.F.R. §§ 412.42–412.48, and time frames (42 C.F.R. § 478.32) for

- The charges for continued payment will be invalid and refunded if collected by the hospital, to the extent that a finding is made that the beneficiary required continued care beyond the point indicated by the hospital.[127]

[E] Medically Unnecessary Diagnostic Procedures and Services

A hospital may charge a beneficiary for diagnostic procedures and studies and therapeutic procedures and courses of treatment (such as experimental procedures and treatments) that are excluded from coverage as medically unnecessary items and services.[128] This is true even when the beneficiary receives continued inpatient hospital care, if those services are furnished after the beneficiary (or person acting on his or her behalf) has acknowledged in writing that the hospital has informed him or her that the services are not considered reasonable and necessary under Medicare.[129] The written acknowledgment must state that the services are not considered reasonable and necessary; that customary charges will be made if the services are provided; that if the services are received, a formal determination on the validity of the hospital's finding is made by the Medicare contractor or QIO, as appropriate; and that the determination is appealable by the hospital, the attending physician, or the beneficiary under the appeals procedure that applies to determinations affecting Medicare Part A payment.[130]

[F] Beneficiary Not Entitled to Medicare Part A or Exhaustion of Part A Benefits

A hospital may charge a Medicare beneficiary its usual charges for noncovered items and services furnished on outlier days for which payment is denied because the beneficiary is not entitled to Medicare Part A or has exhausted benefits.[131] If payment is considered for outlier days, the entire stay is reviewed, and days up to the number of days in excess of the outlier threshold may be denied on

beneficiaries to pursue legal remedies. Advocates should look closely to see that rules on hospital discharge notices are strictly followed.

[127] 42 C.F.R. § 412.42(c)(3)(i)–(v); Revised Advance Beneficiary Notice Forms must be used (mandatory) starting September 4, 2012; *see* http://www.cms.gov/Regulations-and-Guidance/Guidance/Transmittals/Downloads/R2480CP.pdf (site visited June 7, 2016); *see also* Center for Medicare Advocacy, "CMS Clarifies When the Advance Beneficiary Notice of Non-Coverage (ABN) Must be Issued," *available at* http://www.medicareadvocacy.org/cms-clarifies-when-the-advance-beneficiary-notice-of-non-coverage-abn-must-be-issued/ (site visited June 1, 2016).

[128] 42 C.F.R. § 412.42(d).

[129] 42 C.F.R. § 412.42(d).

[130] 42 C.F.R. § 412.42(d).

[131] 42 C.F.R. § 412.42(e). Outlier days are defined in 42 C.F.R. §§ 412.82 and 412.84.

the basis of the beneficiary's lacking entitlement to Part A or having exhausted benefits.[132] Under this rule, the latest days will be denied first.[133]

In addition, hospitals are required to notify patients who have used or will use 90 days of benefits (lifetime reserve days) in a benefit period, thus exhausting their Part A benefits, that they can elect not to use their reserve days for all or part of a stay. The notice should be given when the beneficiary has five regular coinsurance days left and is expected to be hospitalized beyond that period, or immediately, when fewer days are left. A Medicare beneficiary who is eligible for medical assistance (Medicaid) under a state plan should be advised that such assistance would not be available if the beneficiary elects not to use the lifetime reserve days. The restriction does not apply to cases where the beneficiary is deemed to have elected not to use lifetime reserve days.[134]

[G] Private Rooms and Luxury Services

A hospital may charge a Medicare beneficiary for the differential for a private room or other luxury service that is more expensive than is medically required and is furnished for the personal comfort of the beneficiary at his or her request (or the request of the person acting on his or her behalf).[135]

[H] Admission Denials

As described above, if Medicare coverage is granted, the hospital will generally receive a predetermined DRG amount. The QIO, which functions as a watchdog agency seeking to ensure that the hospital does not claim Medicare coverage for medically unnecessary care, will often deny coverage retroactively in certain types of cases. When retroactive denials occur, the hospital loses the entire DRG payment. Moreover, because the hospital had, until the issuance of the QIO denial, considered the case to be covered by Medicare, it has not complied with the required denial notice process and therefore may not charge the patient for the cost of care.[136] This danger of financial penalty is so extreme that hospitals are inhibited from admitting patients whose medical conditions resemble those of patients whose cases have been denied retroactively by the QIO.

■ **EXAMPLE:** Many hospitals have received retroactive QIO denials for hospital care delivered to patients suffering from compression fractures of

[132] 42 C.F.R. § 412.42(e).

[133] 42 C.F.R. § 412.42(e).

[134] *See* MBP Manual, Ch. 5, § 30. Lifetime reserve days are discussed at 42 C.F.R. § 409.65.

[135] 42 C.F.R. § 412.42(f).

[136] Social Security Act § 1879, 42 U.S.C. § 1395pp; 42 C.F.R. §§ 411.400–411.406, *available at* http://www.gpo.gov/fdsys/pkg/CFR-2011-title42-vol2/pdf/CFR-2011-title42-vol2-sec411-400.pdf (site visited June 1, 2016).

the spine. Although a substantial proportion of such patients do indeed require a hospital level of care, many QIOs arbitrarily deny such claims on the theory that they constitute "social" admissions for which hospital services are not really necessary. After being intimidated by the QIO, hospitals will often decline to admit spinal compression fracture patients to the hospital unless the patient agrees to accept personal financial liability for the cost of care. In effect, arbitrary denial practices by the QIO can force hospitals to deny access to care for classes of vulnerable and coverage-worthy patients.

[I] Loss of Access to Expensive Care

Even where the DRG amount is paid, the predetermined figure may be inadequate to compensate the hospital for the expense of essential, but expensive, technology, procedure, equipment, and services. Since the advent of PPS, beneficial but cost-increasing medical advances are occasionally assigned to DRGs that do not cover costs. These costs are not to be passed on to beneficiaries but absorbed in the DRG rates.[137] Note, however, Medicare does make provision for additional payment for certain extraordinary high-cost hospital stays and services.[138] Advocates need to remain vigilant about the effects of payment and access to service.

The question of the adequacy of PPS rates for purposes of diagnostic-related groups is ongoing. The focus is on the underlying cost assumptions in setting rates, on geographic variations in costs and wages, and on whether the appropriate national averages have been set for hospital wage levels. In response to these concerns, the Medicare program is continually adjusting and updating these rates.[139]

§ 2.10 UTILIZATION REVIEW AND QUALITY OF SERVICES

[A] Hospital Utilization Review Committees

Each Medicare participating hospital must have a Utilization Review Committee (URC) that reviews services furnished by the hospital and members of its medical staff.

At least two members of the URC must be physicians. URC members are generally hospital medical and administrative staff with medical oversight responsibilities. They work closely with the respective QIOs in their geographic location. Before making a determination that an admission or continued stay is not medically necessary, the URC must consult a practitioner responsible for the care of the patient and afford that practitioner the opportunity to present his or her

---

[137] *See* 42 C.F.R. §§ 412.80 *et seq.*

[138] *See* 42 C.F.R §§ 412.87–412.88.

[139] *See* www.cms.hhs.gov/AcuteInpatientPPS/ (site visited June 1, 2016).

views. If the URC decides that coverage should be denied, written notification must be given within two days of its decision to the hospital, the patient, and the attending physician.[140] As a practical matter, hospitals tend to notify beneficiaries of the decision that a Medicare admission or continued stay is not medically necessary as soon as possible, usually on the day the determination has been made. The patient's liability for the cost of inpatient hospital care does not begin until the patient has received the required legal notice in writing that Medicare coverage will be denied.[141] Once the beneficiary has been notified of the determination of the URC, the beneficiary may exercise certain appeal rights, described at **§ 2.11**.

[B] Recovery Audit Contractors

In Section 302 of the Tax Relief and Health Care Act of 2006, Congress required that its Recovery Audit Contractors (RACs) demonstration be made national and permanent by January 1, 2010.[142] The RAC demonstration focused on overpayments and underpayments by health care providers and suppliers in California, Florida, New York, Massachusetts, South Carolina, and Arizona.[143]

The impact of the RAC program on access to the Medicare hospital benefit is unfolding. As described earlier in this chapter, many beneficiaries are not being admitted as inpatients to Medicare-participating hospitals; and in some cases where they have been admitted, that status has been changed to observation before a payment request has been submitted to Medicare. Some posit that RAC concerns are deterring hospital admissions. Some believe that since the institution of the RAC program, there has been an increase in the number of Medicare beneficiaries being inappropriately classified as outpatients rather than as inpatients. Note that on July 10, 2015, CMS announced that "effective June 4, 2015, CMS has withdrawn the Requests for Quotes for the next round of Recovery Auditor contracts. CMS plans to update the Statement of Work and release new Requests for Proposals shortly. In the meantime, the current Recovery Auditors

---

140 42 C.F.R. § 482.30(d).

141 Social Security Act § 1879, 42 U.S.C. § 1395 pp; 42 C.F.R. §§ 411.400–411.406. *See also* 42 C.F.R. § 412.42.

142 *See* § 1893 of the Social Security Act (42 U.S.C. § 1395ddd). *See also* CMS report on the three-year RAC demonstration at http://www.cms.gov/Research-Statistics-Data-and-Systems/Monitoring-Programs/Medicare-FFS-Compliance-Programs/Recovery-Audit-Program/ (site visited June 6, 2016). This site provides comprehensive links to the RAC program and its expansion schedule.

143 *See* § 1893 of the Social Security Act (42 U.S.C. § 1395ddd). *See also* CMS report on the three-year RAC demonstration at http://www.cms.gov/Research-Statistics-Data-and-Systems/Monitoring-Programs/Medicare-FFS-Compliance-Programs/Recovery-Audit-Program/ (site visited June 1, 2016).

will continue active recovery auditing through at least December 31, 2015."[144] Patient advocates have argued that the zeal of hospitals to avoid RAC problems has gone too far; that patients would otherwise have been classified as inpatients but for RAC fears; that some patients kept in observation status for multiple days, sometimes weeks, are skewing readmission rates and hospital quality data.

[C] Quality Improvement Organizations

In 1982, as part of the Tax Equity and Fiscal Responsibility Act of 1982, Congress established the Peer Review Organizations (PROs), now called Quality Improvement Organizations (QIOs). This act established a peer review program to perform utilization and quality review of hospital services provided to Medicare beneficiaries.[145] Congress authorized the Secretary of the Department of Health and Human Services (HHS) to contract with private physician-controlled QIOs by region of the country to carry out such utilization and quality improvement functions.[146]

Each Medicare-participating hospital must have an agreement with a QIO for review of medical appropriateness and utilization of Medicare-covered services on an ongoing basis.[147] The QIO is to review the medical necessity, reasonableness, and appropriateness of hospital admissions and discharges; the appropriateness of inpatient care for which additional payment is sought under the outlier provisions; the validity of the hospital's diagnostic and procedural information; the completeness, adequacy, and quality of the services furnished in the hospital; and other medical or other practices related to beneficiaries or billing for services furnished to them.[148] QIOs have authority to deny Medicare payment for inappropriate or unnecessary services and to recommend that certain providers

---

[144] *See* CMS.gov, Recovery Audit Program, *available at* http://www.cms.gov/Research-Statistics-Data-and-Systems/Monitoring-Programs/Medicare-FFS-Compliance-Programs/Recovery-Audit-Program/Recent_Updates.html (site visited June 1, 2016).

[145] 42 U.S.C. §§ 1320c-1–1320c-12; *see also* QIO Manual, Ch. 5 (quality of care review), *see* https://search.yahoo.com/yhs/search?p=QIO+Manual%2C+Ch.+5&ei=UTF-8&hspart=mozilla&hsimp=yhs-002 (site visited June 6, 2016). QIOs also review the appropriateness of hospital discharge notices. *See* 42 U.S.C. § 1302c-3(e).

[146] On July 18, 2014, as part of the restructuring of the QIO program—separating the beneficiary quality of care complaint review process from provider quality improvement functions—CMS awarded additional contracts to assist providers with quality improvement matters. The new contracts represent the second phase of QIO restructuring. These QIOs are known as Quality Innovation Network (QIN)-QIOs. *See* CMS, "Press Release: CMS Launches Next Phase of New Quality Improvement Program," *available at* http://cms.gov/Newsroom/MediaReleaseDatabase/Press-releases/2014-Press-releases-items/2014-07-18.html?DLPage=1&DLSort=0&DLSortDir=descending (site visited June 1, 2016). Each QIN-QIO will work on strategic quality improvement initiatives.

[147] 42 C.F.R. § 412.44.

[148] 42 C.F.R. § 412.44.

and physicians be excluded from the Medicare program because of their utilization patterns and practices.[149]

QIOs also have responsibility to monitor hospital performance under PPS. Specifically, QIOs are charged with reviewing and determining for payment purposes "the validity of diagnostic information provided by a hospital, the completeness, adequacy and quality of care provided, and the appropriateness of care for which additional payments are sought."[150] The QIO also has quality of care review and oversight responsibility, an area of importance to Medicare beneficiaries who are concerned about the quality of care they have received in the hospital or other care settings.[151]

[D] Hospital Discharge Planning as an Advocacy Tool

Federal law requires a discharge planning process for identifying and planning for the post-hospital care needs of Medicare patients.[152] The Secretary

---

[149] 42 U.S.C. § 1320c-5(b)(1); 42 C.F.R. § 412.48. CMS continues to make changes in the functions of the QIO with respect to the scope of the QIO hospital review function. CMS has created a Hospital Payment Monitoring Program (HPMP) as part of its fiscal oversight responsibilities. These entities perform utilization review of randomly selected claims for payment purposes and measure the accuracy of Medicare fee-for-service (FFS) payments to acute inpatient prospective payment (IPPS) hospitals and LTCHs. The QIOs retain responsibility for quality oversight in all Medicare FFS settings, provider requested higher-weighted DRG reviews, reviews under the Emergency Medical Treatment and Active Labor Act (EMTALA), provider education on quality of care issues, and expedited determinations. *See* https://www.cms.gov/AcuteInpatientPPS/downloads/InpatientReviewFactSheet.pdf (site visited June 1, 2016). *See also* Social Security Act § 1154(a), https://www.ssa.gov/OP_Home/ssact/title11/1154.htm (site visited June 6, 2016), 42 U.S.C. § 1320c-3, for a full description of the QIO function. The language of § 1154(a)(1) gives the Secretary broad authority to limit or expand QIO functions by contract. Note, too, that carriers and intermediaries are gradually being re-designated as Medicare Administrative Contractors (MACs) as described in **§ 2.01[B]** of this Handbook.

[150] Social Security Act § 1866(a)(1)(F), 42 U.S.C. § 1395cc(a)(1)(f).

[151] *See* 42 U.S.C. § 1320c-3(a)(14), § 1154(a)(14) of the Social Security Act. See the conference findings of the Center for Medicare Advocacy and its citation to relevant documentation of problems with the QIO and its review and oversight of quality of care concerns, *available at* http://www.medicareadvocacy.org/medicare-info/quality-of-care/ (site visited June 1, 2016). *See also* https://www.cms.gov/Medicare/Quality-Initiatives-Patient-Assessment-Instruments/QualityImprovementOrgs/index.html (site visited June 1, 2016). *See* http://www.cms.gov/Regulations-and-Guidance/Guidance/Transmittals/Downloads/R17QIO.pdf (site visited June 1, 2016). The transmittal includes a new oral review option called "Immediate Advocacy" (*see* § 5120). Its approach is much like that of an alternative dispute resolution inquiry. Other features include, among others, a Retrospective Beneficiary Complaint Review, § 5200; Concurrent Beneficiary Complaint Review, § 5300; and Direct Advocacy Review, § 5400. Generally, these new devices are designed to give beneficiaries faster and more complete information about quality of care concerns. *See* http://www.medicareadvocacy.org/new-procedures-for-review-of-quality-of-care-complaints/ (site visited June 6, 2016).

[152] 42 U.S.C. § 1395x(ee). On November 3, 2015, CMS published in the *Federal Register*, 80 Fed. Reg. 68,126, proposed revisions to requirements for discharge planning for hospitals, CAHs,

has developed guidelines and standards for the discharge planning process in order to ensure a timely and smooth transition to the most appropriate type of follow-up care for post-hospital or rehabilitative care. The guidelines and standards address the following:[153]

- The hospital must identify, at an early stage of hospitalization, those patients who are likely to suffer adverse health consequences upon discharge in the absence of adequate discharge planning.
- Hospitals must provide a discharge planning evaluation for patients identified under subparagraph (1) and for other patients upon the request of the patient, patient's representative, or patient's physician.
- Any discharge planning evaluation must be made on a timely basis to ensure that appropriate arrangements for post-hospital care will be made before discharge and to avoid unnecessary delays in discharge.

---

and HHAs. *See* https://www.nhpf.org/library/the-basics/Basics_HospitalDischargePlanning_02-09-16.pdf (site visited June 6, 2016); http://www.gpo.gov/fdsys/pkg/FR-2015-11-03/pdf/2015-27840.pdf (site visited June 6, 2016). The proposed rule is designed to reduce avoidable hospital readmissions and improve patient care with a focus on improvements for psychiatric and behavioral health patients, including those with substance abuse disorders. The proposed rule calls for coordination, consultation, and using information from community-based service providers as recognized by the Improving Medicare Post-Acute Care Transformation Act of 2014 (Impact Act) (Pub. L. No. 113-185 (Oct. 6, 2014)); *see* http://www.medicareadvocacy.org/october-2014-the-improving-medicare-post-acute-care-transformation-act-of-2014-impact-act-other-isues/ (site visited June 6, 2016). The proposed rule fits within the framework of existing discharge planning regulations that are found at 42 C.F.R. § 482.43, applicable to all inpatients. *See also* Social Security Act § 1861(e), 42 U.S.C. § 1395x(ee).

[153] 42 C.F.R. § 482.43 (Condition of Participation: Discharge Planning). *See* CMS's discharge planning checklist, *available at* http://www.medicare.gov/Publications/Pubs/pdf/11376.pdf (site visited June 6, 2016). An expanded version of this content, dated December 2014, is available at http://www.cms.gov/outreach-and-education/medicare-learning-network-mln/mlnproducts/downloads/discharge-planning-booklet-icn908184.pdf (site visited June 7, 2016). For a discussion of discharge planning issues, see Center for Medicare Advocacy, "Medicare and Discharge Planning: Thinking Through Your Needs," *available at* http://www.medicareadvocacy.org/medicare-and-discharge-planning-thinking-through-your-needs/ (site visited June 6, 2016). In addition, CMS has offered further clarification of discharge planning responsibilities of hospitals and others in a survey and certification letter, Ref: S&C: 13-32-Hospital, *available at* http://www.cms.gov/Medicare/Provider-Enrollment-and-Certification/SurveyCertificationGenInfo/Downloads/Survey-and-Cert-Letter-13-32.pdf (site visited June 6, 2016). *See also* Center for Medicare Advocacy, "CMS Updates Guidance for Hospital Discharge Planning," *available at* http://www.medicareadvocacy.org/cms-updates-guidance-for-hospital-discharge-planning/ (site visited June 6, 2016). The Center for Medicare Advocacy has expanded its discharge planning materials on its website. *See* http://www.medicareadvocacy.org/medicare-info/discharge-planning/ (site visited June 6, 2016). *See also* Alfred J. Chiplin, Jr., "Breathing Life into Discharge Planning," The Elder L.J. (13)1, *available at* http://publish.illinois.edu/elderlawjournal/files/2015/02/Chiplin.pdf (site visited June 6, 2016).

- A discharge planning evaluation must include an evaluation of a patient's likely need for appropriate post-hospital services and the availability of those services.
- The discharge planning evaluation must be included in the patient's medical record for use in establishing an appropriate discharge plan, and the results of the evaluation must be discussed with the patient (or the patient's representative).
- Upon the request of patient's physician, the hospital must arrange for the development and initial implementation of a discharge plan for the patient.
- Any discharge planning evaluation or discharge plan must be developed by, or under the supervision of, a registered professional nurse, social worker, or other appropriately qualified personnel.

Notice about the right to hospital discharge planning is problematic. The only notice provided is a mention of discharge planning in the Medicare-required hospital notice that is given to Medicare patients on admission, a notice entitled "An Important Message from Medicare."[154] Unfortunately, neither the notice of appeal rights upon hospital discharge (when and if the hospital attempts to charge the patient privately for the cost of care involved)[155] nor the QIO determination notice[156] discusses discharge planning rights other than to say that the "hospital should arrange the services you will need after you leave the hospital."

Thus, it is important that advocates work with discharge planners and physicians to ensure that discharge planning services are requested as discussed above.[157] Advocates may wish to consider approaching the failure to provide discharge planning services as a violation of the Medicare conditions of participation and consider the sanctioning process available there, culminating in the ultimate sanction of a facility's losing its participation agreement.[158]

---

[154] Social Security Act § 1866(a)(1)(M), 42 U.S.C. § 1395cc(a)(1)(M); 42 C.F.R. § 476.78(b)(3).

[155] 42 C.F.R. § 476.94 (Notice of QIO Initial Denial Determination and Changes as a Result of a DRG).

[156] 42 C.F.R. §§ 478.40–478.42 (Beneficiary Hearing Rights).

[157] *See* Center for Medicare Advocacy, "Discharge Planning: Tips for Evaluating a Hospital's Skilled Nursing Facility Placement Choices," *available at* http://www.medicareadvocacy.org/discharge-planning-tips-for-evaluating-a-hospitals-skilled-nursing-facility-placement-choices/ (site visited June 6, 2016).

[158] 42 C.F.R. Pt. 488 (Survey, Certification, and Enforcement Procedures).

§ 2.11 APPEALING COVERAGE DENIALS

[A] Overview of an Appeal for Inpatient Hospital Services

[1] Notice and Appeal Rights Generally

Usually, the first notice a Medicare beneficiary receives that care will not be covered by Medicare is from the health care provider, in this case the hospital. As noted,[159] each hospital is required to have as a condition of participation in the Medicare program a Utilization Review Committee (URC), which is charged with making preliminary determinations regarding Medicare coverage for hospital stays.[160] The URC must make such decisions at the time of admission of a patient and, if it determines that Medicare coverage is not warranted, issue a written notice to the beneficiary or someone acting on his/her behalf ("admission denials"). Similarly, the URC must issue a written notice if it decides that Medicare coverage is no longer warranted, after the patient has been admitted and has received some coverage by Medicare ("continued stay denials").[161]

Since July 1, 2007, Medicare-participating hospitals have been required to deliver valid, written notice, the "Important Message from Medicare" (IM), of a patient's rights as a hospital patient including discharge appeal rights, within two calendar days of admission. A follow-up copy of the signed IM is given again as far as possible in advance of discharge, but no more than two calendar days prior to discharge. Follow-up notice is not required if the provision of the admission IM falls within two calendar days of discharge.[162]

Hospitals, as with all Medicare Part A providers, have a financial incentive to issue denial notices because they may have to absorb the cost of the care they provide if they erroneously inform the beneficiary that the care will be covered, but not if they erroneously deny coverage.[163]

In issuing a continued stay denial, a hospital must obtain the concurrence of the patient's treating physician before it can issue the written denial notice. If the treating physician does not concur, the hospital cannot issue the written notice,

---

[159] *See* **§ 2.10[A]** of this Handbook.

[160] 42 C.F.R. § 482.30 (Condition of Participation: Utilization Review).

[161] *See* 42 C.F.R. § 482.30 (Condition of Participation: Utilization Review). *See also* discussion in **§ 2.10[B]** of this Handbook on the impact of the RAC program, as such reviews may have an effect on admission and may frustrate the receipt of a notice of denial.

[162] *See* 42 C.F.R. § 405.1205 (Traditional Medicare) and 42 C.F.R. § 422.620 (Medicare Advantage); *see also* **Appendix 2-3** or www.cms.hhs.gov/transmittals/downloads/R1257CP.pdf (site visited June 6, 2016). *See also* www.cms.gov/Outreach-and-Education/Medicare-Learning-Network-MLN/MLNMattersArticles/downloads/MM5622.pdf (updating website addresses) (site visited June 6, 2016).

[163] 42 U.S.C. § 1395pp; *see* https://www.ssa.gov/OP_Home/ssact/title18/1879.htm (site visited May 7, 2016).

but instead must refer the case to the BFCC-QIO or QIO,[164] which will review the medical records of the patient and decide whether Medicare coverage should continue. If the QIO decides that Medicare coverage should not continue, then the QIO itself issues a notice to the beneficiary. Note that no physician concurrence is required if the URC issues a Medicare denial at the time of the patient's admission to the hospital.

Because of the requirement for physician concurrence, the Medicare patient's treating physician is a key person in the coverage determination. The regulations require that the treating physician be given an opportunity to justify the medical necessity of hospital admissions or continued stays.[165] In practice, however, this often means that the treating physician receives a telephone call informing him or her that a coverage denial is about to be issued in a given case. The treating physician may or may not attempt to convince the URC or QIO reviewer that coverage should be continued. In any event, the written record may not contain any notation beyond a terse statement that "the views of the attending physician were solicited."

As a practical matter, a beneficiary can appeal a denial of coverage of only those services actually received. Therefore, a beneficiary who is being informed that Medicare will not cover his or her stay upon admission must insist on admission anyway.[166] For a continuing hospital stay, the beneficiary must remain in the hospital in order to seek additional Medicare coverage through the appeals process.

When a patient receives a denial notice from the hospital URC at the time of admission, or a continued stay denial notice has been issued with the concurrence of the treating physician, the patient must request that the case be submitted to the Medicare QIO for its review. This patient request will trigger an initial determination that can then be appealed. (In addition, the QIO's initial determination does sometimes grant coverage that was denied by the hospital.) If the beneficiary or the beneficiary's representative requests the hospital to submit a case to the Medicare QIO, the hospital is required to do so.

For a continuing stay denial, actual written concurrence by the attending physician with the denial determination is required before the hospital may issue

---

[164] *See* **§ 2.11[B]** of this Handbook.

[165] 42 C.F.R. §§ 412.42(c) and 482.30.

[166] 42 U.S.C. § 1395ff (b) provides for a limited prior determination process regarding physician services determined by the Secretary to be subject to the process. Under the process, a participating physician who has permission from the patient or an individual who has received an advanced beneficiary notice (ABN) may ask the appropriate Medicare contractor for a determination of whether Medicare will pay for a service before actually receiving the service. *See also* QIO Manual, Ch. 7, §§ 7005 and 7015, providing for inpatient hospital preadmission review, *available at* https://www.cms.gov/Regulations-and-Guidance/Guidance/Manuals/Downloads/qio110c07.pdf (site visited June 6, 2016).

a Medicare notice of non-coverage.[167] If the attending physician does not concur, the URC may not issue a notice of non-coverage. Instead, it must refer the case to the QIO. The QIO will review the case and, if warranted, will issue a Medicare denial. This denial is the "initial determination."[168]

[2] Expedited Review Requests in Hospital Settings

For a hospital stay, a beneficiary must request expedited review of a discharge decision, orally or in writing, no later than the day of the discharge. A

[167] 42 C.F.R. § 412.42(c)(2). The patient becomes financially responsible for the services provided beyond the second day following the date of the notice. § 412.42(c)(3)(ii). *See also* discussion of § 422.620 in **Chapter 7** of this Handbook and 42 C.F.R. § 489.27 (Beneficiary Notice of Discharge Rights), *see* https://www.gpo.gov/fdsys/granule/CFR-2010-title42-vol5/CFR-2010-title42-vol5-sec489-27/content-detail.html (site visited June 6, 2016).

[168] 42 C.F.R. § 412.42(c)(2). Note modified notice requirements discussed above with respect to the use of the Revised Important Message from Medicare (IM), *see* https://www.cms.gov/Medicare/Medicare-General-Information/BNI/HospitalDischargeAppealNotices.html (site visited May 7, 2016). Moreover, CMS notes "Providers, suppliers, Medicare Advantage Organizations and Prescription Drug Plans should update their Medicare notices with the correct Quality Improvement Organization (QIO) contact information as quickly as possible and **no later than September 1, 2014**. *See* http://www.qioprogram.org (site visited June 7, 2016)/ for QIO details. Note: Providers, suppliers, Medicare Advantage Organizations, and Prescription Drug Plans should update their Medicare notices with the correct QIO contact information as quickly as possible and by September 1, 2014. *See* http://www.qioprogram.org/ (site visited June 7, 2016).

On May 9, 2014, CMS announced the first phase of its restructuring of the QIO functions. In the first phase, CMS has contracted with Livanta LLC (for geographic areas 1 and 5), located in Annapolis Junction, Maryland, and KePRO (for geographic areas 2, 3, and 4), located in Seven Hills, Ohio. These contractors will be responsible for ensuring consistency in the review process with respect to beneficiary complaints. CMS describes these two contractors as its Beneficiary and Family-Centered Care (BFCC) QIO contractors, *see* https://www.cms.gov/Newsroom/MediaReleaseDatabase/Press-releases/2014-Press-releases-items/2014-05-09.html (site visited June 6, 2016).

The states in the designated geographic areas are Area 1: Connecticut, Maine, Massachusetts, New Hampshire, New Jersey, New York, Pennsylvania, Puerto Rico, Rhode Island, Vermont, Virgin Islands; Area 2: District of Columbia, Delaware, Florida, Georgia, Maryland, North Carolina, South Carolina, Virginia, West Virginia; Area 3: Alabama, Arkansas, Colorado, Kentucky, Louisiana, Mississippi, Montana, North Dakota, New Mexico, Oklahoma, South Dakota, Tennessee, Texas, Utah, Wyoming; Area 4: Iowa, Illinois, Indiana, Kansas, Michigan, Minnesota, Missouri, Nebraska, Ohio, Wisconsin; and Area 5: Alaska, Arizona, California, Hawaii, Idaho, Nevada, Oregon, Washington.

On July 18, 2014, as part of the restructuring of the QIO program—separating the beneficiary quality of care complaint review process from provider quality improvement functions—CMS awarded additional contracts to assist providers with quality improvement matters. The new contracts represent the second phase of QIO restructuring. These QIOs will be known as Quality Innovation Network (QIN)-QIOs. *See* CMS, "Press Release: CMS Launches Next Phase of New Quality Improvement Program," *available at* https://www.cms.gov/Newsroom/MediaReleaseDatabase/Press-releases/2014-Press-releases-items/2014-07-18.html?DLPage=1&DLSort=0&DLSortDir=descending (site visited June 6, 2016). Each QIN-QIO will work on strategic quality improvement initiatives. The restructuring does not alter functions or patient's rights.

"timely request" is being interpreted by CMS as by midnight of the day of the discharge.[169] The beneficiary (or his or her authorized representative), upon request by the QIO, must be prepared to discuss the case with the QIO.[170] On the date that the QIO receives the beneficiary's request, the QIO must notify the hospital that the beneficiary has filed a request for intermediate review.[171] The hospital must supply any information, including medical records, that the QIO requires to conduct its review and must make the information available, by phone or in writing, by the close of business of the first full working day after the day the beneficiary receives notice of the planned discharge.[172] When the beneficiary requests an expedited determination in accordance with § 405.1206(d)(1), the QIO must make a determination and notify the beneficiary, the hospital, and the physician of its determination by close of business of the first working day after it receives all requested pertinent information.[173]

[3] Expedited Review Requests in Non-Hospital Settings

In addition to expedited reviews in inpatient hospital cases, beneficiaries may seek expedited review of a SNF, home health, hospice or CORF services discharge or termination.[174] The provider must give the beneficiary a general, standardized notice at least two days in advance of the proposed end of the service. If the service is fewer than two days, or if the time between services is more than two days, then notice must be given by the next-to-last service.[175] The notice describes the service, the date coverage ends, the beneficiary's financial liability for continued services, and how to file an appeal.[176]

A beneficiary must request expedited review, orally or in writing, by noon of the next calendar day after receiving notice. At that time, the beneficiary is given a more specific notice that includes a detailed explanation of why services are being terminated, a description of any applicable Medicare coverage rules and information on how to obtain them, and other facts specific to the beneficiary's case. The beneficiary is not financially liable for continued services until the later of two days after receiving the notice or the termination date specified on the notice.[177]

---

[169] *See* 71 Fed. Reg. 68,721 (Nov. 27, 2007), adding a new 42 C.F.R. § 405.1205 and revising 42 C.F.R. § 405.1206. *See also* Medicare Claims Processing (MCP) Manual, CMS Pub. 100-04, Ch. 30, § 200.4.1; 42 C.F.R. § 405.1206(b)(1).

[170] *See* revised 42 C.F.R. § 405.1206(d)(2).

[171] *See* revised 42 C.F.R. § 405.1206(e)(1).

[172] *See* revised 42 C.F.R. § 405.1206(e)(2).

[173] *See* revised 42 C.F.R. § 405.1206(e)(5).

[174] *See* 42 C.F.R. §§ 405.1200–405.1204, to implement 42 U.S.C. § 1395ff (b)(1)(F).

[175] 42 C.F.R. § 405.1200(b)(1).

[176] 42 C.F.R. § 405.1200(b)(2).

[177] 42 C.F.R. § 405.1202(b).

Expedited review is available in cases involving a discharge from the provider of services, or a termination of services where "a physician certifies that failure to continue the provision of such services is likely to place the individual's health at risk."[178] Services furnished by a residential provider, such as a hospital, a SNF, or a hospice, are discharges for which a doctor's certificate is not required. Services furnished by a "non-residential provider," such as home health services, are treated as a termination of services for which a doctor's certificate of significant health risk must be provided.[179] A reduction in service is not considered a termination or discharge for purposes of triggering expedited review.[180]

A beneficiary who wishes to exercise the right to an expedited determination must submit a request for a determination of the QIO in the state in which the beneficiary is receiving those provider services, in writing or by telephone, no later than noon of the calendar day following receipt of the provider's notice of termination. If the QIO is unable to accept the beneficiary's request, the beneficiary must submit the request by noon of the next day the QIO is available to accept a request.[181]

Coverage of provider services continues until the date and time designated on the termination notice, unless the QIO reverses the provider's service termination decision. If the QIO's decision is delayed because the provider did not timely supply necessary information or records, the provider may be liable for the costs of any additional coverage, as determined by the QIO.[182] If the QIO finds that the beneficiary did not receive valid notice, coverage of the provider services continues until at least 2 days after valid notice has been received. Continuation of coverage is not required if the QIO determines that coverage could pose a threat to the beneficiary's health or safety.[183]

If the QIO sustains the decision to terminate services or discharge the beneficiary, the beneficiary may request expedited reconsideration, orally or in writing, by noon of the calendar day following the notification of the QIO's decision. The reconsideration will be conducted by the Qualified Independent Contractor (QIC), which must issue a decision within 72 hours of the request. If the QIC does not comply with the time frame, the beneficiary may escalate the case to the Administrative Law Judge (ALJ) level.[184]

Beneficiaries retain the right to utilize the standard appeals process rather than the new expedited process in all situations. A QIO may review an appeal from a beneficiary whose request is not timely filed, but the QIO does not have

[178] 42 U.S.C. § 1395ff(b)(1).
[179] 42 C.F.R. § 405.1202(a).
[180] 42 C.F.R. § 405.1200(a)(2).
[181] 42 C.F.R. § 405.1202(b).
[182] 42 C.F.R. § 405.1202(c).
[183] 42 C.F.R. § 405.1202(c).
[184] *See* 42 C.F.R. § 405.1204.

to adhere to the time frame for issuing a decision, and the limitation on liability does not apply.

In those circumstances, however, where the attending physician does concur with the URC's determination, the URC will issue a Medicare notice of noncoverage.[185] In such cases, the beneficiary has the right to request an expedited review by the QIO. If the patient requests QIO review before noon of the first working day after the denial notice was delivered to the patient, and the patient is still in the facility, the QIO must issue a review decision within one full working day after the QIO received the review request and records.[186]

If the QIO upholds the denial of Medicare coverage by the facility's URC, the denial is effective commencing with the third day following the date of the URC's original notice, and the beneficiary is required to pay for the services he or she received commencing with that date. If the beneficiary is dissatisfied with the initial determination, he or she may request a redetermination. Patient requests for redetermination about facility services are filed with the QIO.[187] In hospital cases, the redetermination may be requested on an expedited basis.[188] This is followed by a request for a hearing before an ALJ (if at least $200 is in controversy), review by the Medicare Appeals Council (MAC), and finally judicial review (if at least $2,000 is in controversy).[189]

[B] The QIO Reconsideration and Financial Liability for the Beneficiary

A request for reconsideration must be filed within 120 days of receipt of the initial determination unless "good cause" can be shown.[190] Hospital inpatients denied Medicare during their stay may also request an "expedited reconsideration" of a Medicare denial. These expedited requests must be decided by the QIO within three working days. Under previous regulations, a hospital inpatient who

---

[185] 42 C.F.R. § 412.42(c)(2).

[186] 42 C.F.R. § 476.94.

[187] A beneficiary has 120 days from the date of the initial determination to request a determination. *See* CMS Program Memorandum (PM) AB-02-111 (July 31, 2002), *available at* https://www.cms.gov/Regulations-and-Guidance/Guidance/Transmittals/Downloads/AB02111.pdf (site visited June 6, 2016). This PM provision, of course, does not apply to expedited reconsideration requests. *See also* 42 C.F.R. § 478.20(a), which CMS PM AB-02-111 amends. *See also* appeals information in chart form in appendices accompanying this chapter.

[188] 42 C.F.R. §§ 478.12(c) and 480.20(c).

[189] 42 C.F.R. §§ 478.12, 478.18, and 478.32 (time limits for issuance of reconsideration decisions). This jurisdictional amount does not change annually.

[190] *See* 74 Fed. Reg. 65,296 (Dec. 9, 2009) (effective Jan. 8, 2010), *available at* http://edocket.access.gpo.gov/2009/pdf/E9-28707.pdf (site visited June 6, 2016). Note, too, that CMS has issued final rules for appeals of Part D claims. These rules are discussed in **Chapter 11** of this Handbook. The rules create a subpart M called "Grievances, Coverage Determinations, Redeterminations, and Reconsiderations," 42 C.F.R. Pt. 423, subpt. M (2009). *See* http://www.gpo.gov/fdsys/pkg/FR-2009-12-09/pdf/E9-28710.pdf (site visited June 6, 2016).

received a denial notice from the hospital and requested review immediately avoided being charged until the QIO issued an initial determination. The expedited appeals regulations protect from liability only those inpatients who did not know or could not reasonably have been expected to know that payment would not be made.[191]

[C] Appeals Arising Under Parts A and B of Medicare

Rules regarding the combined Medicare Parts A and B appeals are found in Subpart G of Part 405.[192] These regulations implement statutory changes to the appeals process for Medicare Part A and Part B claims and to the ALJ hearing process for all Medicare claims, including managed care claims and prescription drug claims.[193] CMS issued final rules for the combined Part A and B appeals process (non-expedited) that were effective January 8, 2010.[194] CMS has created an additional chart showing appeals processes across Parts A, B, C, and D.[195]

[D] Initial Determinations and Redeterminations

The claims process begins when the Medicare contractor issues a Medicare Summary Notice (MSN), which is an initial determination of the claim submitted by the hospital.[196] The regulations make clear that the initial determination goes only to the beneficiary, even when the contractor is aware that the beneficiary has an appointed representative.[197] Someone who wants to appeal from the initial determination must submit a written, signed request for a redetermination within 120 days of receipt of the initial determination. The regulations assume the notice is received 5 days after the actual date of the notice.[198] Requests for

---

[191] *See* 42 C.F.R. § 405.1206(f)(2).

[192] *See* 42 C.F.R. §§ 405.701 *et seq.*

[193] 70 Fed. Reg. 11,420 (Mar. 8, 2005). *See* https://www.cms.gov/Outreach-and-Education/Medicare-Learning-Network-MLN/MLNProducts/Downloads/MedicareAppealsProcess.pdf (site visited Sept. 30, 2016).

[194] *See* http://www.gpo.gov/fdsys/pkg/FR-2009-12-09/pdf/E9-28707.pdf (site visited June 6, 2016).

[195] *See* https://www.cms.gov/Outreach-and-Education/Training/CMSNationalTrainingProgram/Training-Library-Items/CMS1190652.html (site visited June 7, 2016).

[196] *See* https://www.cms.gov/Outreach-and-Education/Medicare-Learning-Network-MLN/MLN Products/downloads/BenePubFS-ICN905183.pdf (site visited June 6, 2016). To obtain various Medicare appeals forms, visit https://www.medicare.gov/forms-help-and-resources/ (site visited June 6, 2016).

[197] 42 C.F.R. §§ 405.921 and 405.910(i)(1); *see also* CMS PM AB-02-111 (July 31, 2002), *available at* http://www.cms.gov/Regulations-and-Guidance/Guidance/Manuals/downloads/bp102c15.pdf (site visited June 6, 2016).

[198] 42 C.F.R. § 405.942(a); *see also* 41 C.F.R. § 405.904, *available at* https://www.cms.gov/Regulations-and-Guidance/Guidance/Manuals/downloads/bp102c15.pdf (site visited June 6, 2016).

redeterminations in this scenario must be filed with the Medicare contractor; beneficiaries can no longer file requests with Social Security offices.[199]

The regulations also allow hospital providers to request appeal of a denial of an initial determination, raising the possibility that both the beneficiary and the hospital will initiate the appeals process.[200] In such a case, the QIO is required to consolidate the appeals.[201] The contractor has 60 days from receipt of the redetermination request to issue a decision.[202] If more than one party files a request, the time period runs from the date the last request is received.[203] For example, if a beneficiary files a redetermination request on day 1, but the hospital files on day 50, the 60-day time period for the contractor to act starts on day 50.

Unlike the initial determination, the notice of the redetermination is sent to a beneficiary's appointed representative.[204] The notice must include an explanation of the facts, policies, and law relied upon in making the redetermination decision; the right to request a reconsideration decision and the process for doing so; and a statement of specific missing documents that must be submitted.[205] The notice must state that the hospital, but not the beneficiary[206] (unless the beneficiary is represented by a provider), must submit all of its evidence by the next level of review in order for the evidence to be considered at any further stage of the appeals process. As a practical matter, the same notice is sent to beneficiaries and hospital providers, with a statement that evidentiary time limits do not apply to beneficiaries. However, in some instances the contractors and ALJs have confused this requirement. The advocate should be certain to point out to the adjudicator that a beneficiary is not required to submit all evidence until the ALJ level of appeal.

Contractors are not required to send redetermination notices to multiple beneficiaries in overpayment cases brought by hospital providers if the beneficiary allegedly has no liability for the claim.[207] The regulations create a reopening process to be used instead of the redetermination process to correct minor errors or omissions in initial determinations.[208] This process responds to a section of the Medicare law that allows providers to correct minor mistakes without going through the appeals process. A reopening can also be used at subsequent levels of review. Questions remain concerning the relationship of the new reopening

---

[199] 42 C.F.R. § 405.944(a).

[200] 42 C.F.R. § 405.940.

[201] 42 C.F.R. § 405.944(c).

[202] 42 C.F.R. § 405.950(a).

[203] 42 C.F.R. § 405.950(b)(2).

[204] 42 C.F.R. § 405.910(h)(2).

[205] 42 C.F.R. § 405.956(b), (c); § 405.966(a).

[206] 42 C.F.R. § 405.966(c).

[207] 42 C.F.R. § 405.956(a)(2).

[208] 42 C.F.R. §§ 405.980 *et seq.*

process and the process for deciding remanded cases, as well as the ability of a contractor to reopen a decision in favor of the beneficiary.[209]

[E] The QIC—Reconsideration Determinations

The 2000 law created a third level of review, the reconsideration. Reconsiderations are conducted by a relatively new group of Medicare contractors called QICs.[210] Beneficiaries and other parties to the redetermination have 180 days from the date of receipt of the redetermination decision to request a reconsideration by filing a request at the location indicated on the redetermination notice.[211] Again, reconsiderations filed by beneficiaries and the hospital will be consolidated, and the time for issuing a decision runs from receipt of the last-filed appeal.[212] Appeals of redeterminations issued by the QIO in inpatient hospital cases go to the QIC for a requested reconsideration determination.[213]

The reconsideration level of review is a paper review. The QIC, however, may solicit the views of the beneficiary.[214] As noted above, if hospital providers appeal from the QIO to the QIC, they are required to submit all of the evidence they want considered in the claim to the QIC. Evidence not submitted by the hospital to the QIC may be excluded at subsequent levels of review.[215] However, beneficiaries who appeal (except those who are represented by a provider) may present evidence at further levels of appeal.[216]

The QIC must complete its reconsideration within 60 days of the reconsideration request.[217] The time frame runs from the last request filed if more than one party seeks reconsideration; the QIC must so notify a party who filed an

---

[209] *See, e.g.*, CMS Transmittal 1069 (Sept. 29, 2006), *available at* http://www.cms.gov/Regulations-and-Guidance/Guidance/Transmittals/downloads/R1069CP.pdf (site visited June 6, 2016).

[210] 42 C.F.R. § 405.960. The jurisdiction of the QICs over reconsideration determinations commenced May 1, 2005, for all Part A determinations and those Part B determinations made by a QIO or Medicare Administrative Contractor (MAC). The jurisdiction of the QIC over Part B reconsideration determinations for all determinations currently made by a Medicare Part B MAC commenced January 1, 2006. 70 Fed. Reg. 11,424–11,426 (Mar. 8, 2005). *See* CMS, *Medicare Basics* (revised May 2011), *available at* http://www.medicare.gov/Pubs/pdf/11034.pdf (site visited June 7, 2016).

[211] 42 C.F.R. § 405.962.

[212] 42 C.F.R. § 405.964(c).

[213] 70 Fed. Reg. 11,424–11,426 (Subpart I—Determinations, Redeterminations, Reconsiderations, and Appeals Under Original Medicare (Part A and Part B)), *available at* http://www.ecfr.gov/cgi-bin/retrieveECFR?gp=&SID=373c3d21e4887af412d996502310b8a7&mc=true&n=sp42.2.405.i&r=SUBPART&ty=HTML (Mar. 8, 2005) (site visited June 6, 2016).

[214] 70 Fed. Reg. 11,447–11,478.

[215] 42 C.F.R. § 405.966(a), (c).

[216] 42 C.F.R. § 405.966(c). *See also* Center for Medicare Advocacy, "Hull v. Sebelius," discussing its recently filed lawsuit challenging inordinately low favorable appeals, *available at* http://www.medicareadvocacy.org/hull-v-sebelius/ (site visited June 6, 2016).

[217] 42 C.F.R. § 405.970(a).

earlier request.[218] The regulations do not indicate how QICs must document receipt of requests or how beneficiaries are to know when the 60-day period ends. Although the statute allows a party to the reconsideration to ask for an extension of not more than 14 days for the QIC to conclude the reconsideration, the regulations add 14 days to the reconsideration time frame each time that additional evidence is submitted.[219]

In making its reconsideration determination, the QIC is bound by national coverage determinations (NCDs) promulgated by Medicare and CMS Rulings, as well as statute and regulations.[220] It is not bound by local coverage determinations made by Medicare contractors, nor by Medicare policy issued by CMS itself, and must give "substantial deference" to these determinations and policy in making its decision.[221] If the QIC declines to apply them, the QIC's decision must state the reason why they were not followed.[222]

[F] Escalation

The Medicare Prescription Drug, Improvement, and Modernization Act of 2003 (MMA) introduced the concept of "escalation" into the Medicare appeals process. Commencing at the reconsideration level of appeal, if a decision is not rendered within a set time frame,[223] a party to the appeal may "escalate" the appeal to the next level. Many possible situations in which extensions of the time frame for the adjudicator to render its decision may occur.[224] Among these situations is the submission of additional evidence to the adjudicator by a party.

Generally, however, if a QIC does not issue a timely reconsideration decision (60 days from the date of its receipt of the request for reconsideration), the statute and regulations allow a party to request that the appeal be escalated to the next level of review, the ALJ level. The regulations give the QIC 5 days to either issue a decision or acknowledge the escalation request and send it to the ALJ level of review. The regulations indicate that an appeal escalated to the ALJ level must be completed within 180 days of receipt, rather than the statutorily mandated

---

[218] 42 C.F.R. § 405.970(b)(2).

[219] 42 C.F.R. § 405.970(b)(3).

[220] 42 C.F.R. § 405.1050(a)(4).

[221] 42 C.F.R. § 405.968(b)(1) and (2).

[222] 42 C.F.R. § 405.968(b)(3).

[223] The time frames are 60 days for the QIC to render a reconsideration determination; 90 days for an ALJ to issue a hearing decision; 180 days for the MAC to issue its decision. *See* 42 C.F.R. § 405.970 (Timeframe for making a reconsideration), *available at* http://www.ecfr.gov/cgi-bin/text-idx?SID=1542ce7fdf8a9c88f8d2b85d614172a2&mc=true&node=se42.2.405_1970&rgn=div8 (site visited June 6, 2016).

[224] 42 C.F.R. §§ 405.970(b) and 405.1002(a) (reconsideration level); 42 C.F.R. §§ 405.1016(a)–(d) and 405.1104 (ALJ level); 42 C.F.R. §§ 405.1106(b) and 405.1132 (MAC level).

90 days for ALJ decisions. Even at the ALJ level, however, additional extensions of the time frame for issuing a decision can occur.[225]

[G] Administrative Law Judge Appeals

Beneficiaries and other parties have 60 days from receipt of the reconsideration determination to file a request for an ALJ hearing.[226] Amount in controversy requirements apply at the ALJ level of appeal.[227] As noted previously, whether an individual seeking redress from a denial of inpatient hospital coverage pursues an appeal through the QIO process, or pursues an appeal in response to an MSN, the ALJ appeals level (and beyond) is the same. The request for hearing must be filed at the address indicated on the reconsideration determination.[228] In addition, a party may escalate to the ALJ hearing from the QIC, when the QIC fails to issue a timely decision.[229] However, if an appeal is escalated to the ALJ, the 90-day time frame for deciding an ALJ appeal is automatically extended to 180 days, with the possibility for additional extensions beyond the 180 days.[230]

The MMA and the regulations promulgated pursuant to it made significant changes to the ALJ appeal level.[231] An important change mandated the transfer of jurisdiction for ALJ hearings from the Social Security Administration to HHS. Currently, ALJs operate out of five field office locations: Miami, Florida; Cleveland, Ohio; Irvine, California; and Arlington, Virginia, and Kansas City, MO. These are the hearing offices in which Medicare ALJs are currently housed.[232]

Under the regulations, in-person hearings are rare and are provided only in "special or extraordinary circumstances."[233] Instead, beneficiaries will be offered a video teleconference (VTC) hearing, or if no VTC technology exists near the beneficiary, a telephone hearing.[234] The regulations do not spell out what

---

[225] 42 C.F.R. §§ 405.970(b) and 405.1002(a) (reconsideration level); 42 C.F.R. §§ 405.1016(a)–(d) and 405.1104 (ALJ level); 42 C.F.R. §§ 405.1106(b) and 405.1132 (MAC level).

[226] Extension of this 60-day time frame may be granted upon a showing of good cause. 42 C.F.R. § 405.1014(c).

[227] 42 C.F.R. § 405.1006. The amount in controversy in 2017 is $160, MCP Manual, Ch. 29, § 330.1. *See* 81 Fed. Reg. 185, P. 65653 (Sept. 28, 2012).

[228] 42 C.F.R. § 405.1014(b).

[229] 42 C.F.R. § 405.1002(b)(1)–(3).

[230] 42 C.F.R. § 405.1016(c). Among the bases for an extension are CMS is a party and a party requests discovery against another party (42 C.F.R. § 405.1016(d)); submission of additional evidence by a party later than 10 days after receiving a notice of hearing (42 C.F.R. § 405.1018(b)); a party's request for a copy of all or part of the administrative record (42 C.F.R. § 405.1042(b)(2)); and a granted request for postponement of the hearing (42 C.F.R. § 405.1020(h)).

[231] 42 C.F.R. §§ 405.1004 *et seq.*

[232] *See* the Office of Medicare Hearings and Appeals (OMHA) website: www.hhs.gov/omha/ (site visited June 6, 2016).

[233] 42 C.F.R. § 405.1020(b)(2).

[234] 42 C.F.R. § 405.1020(b).

constitutes a "special circumstance" that would justify an in-person hearing.[235] Even if such special circumstances are established, the in-person hearing will be afforded for the requestor's own testimony, but the entire hearing will not necessarily be in-person.[236] In addition, when an in-person hearing is requested and granted, the limited time frame for an ALJ to render a decision is deemed waived.[237]

Another important change is that CMS or its contractors may participate in or be made a party to the ALJ hearings, with rights to submit "position papers" and present witnesses (if they are "participants") and the right to cross-examine other party's witnesses (if they are "parties").[238] An ALJ may seek to have CMS or its contractors participate or joined as parties and CMS or one of its contractors can request that it be a participant or party.[239] Under the regulations, an ALJ must permit CMS or its contractors to participate or be joined as parties if they so request.

A notice of the hearing must be given to all parties, the Medicare contractor and the QIC, advising them of the time and date for the hearing at least 20 days prior to the date of its scheduled date.[240] All of those receiving a notice of hearing are required to acknowledge whether they plan to attend the hearing or object to the proposed time and/or place of the hearing.[241] An objection to the time and/or place must be in writing and state the reasons for the objection.[242] If a party objects to the issues as stated in the notice of hearing, that party must notify the ALJ in writing no later than five days prior to the hearing of the objections, and send a copy of the objections to all other parties to the appeal.[243] The ALJ will make a decision regarding the objections either in writing or at the hearing.[244]

Any new written evidence that a beneficiary wishes to submit must be submitted with the request for hearing or within 10 days prior to the scheduled date

---

[235] The OMHA website contains Frequently Asked Questions (FAQs) designed to be helpful when using the appeals process, *available at* http://www.hhs.gov/omha/faq/Requesting%20an%20ALJ%20Hearing/requesting_an_alj_hearing.html (site visited June 6, 2016).

[236] 42 C.F.R. § 405.1020(c).

[237] 42 C.F.R. § 405.1020(i)(4).

[238] 42 C.F.R. §§ 405.1010 (participants) and 405.1012 (parties).

[239] 42 C.F.R. §§ 405.1010, 405.1010(a), 405.1012.

[240] 42 C.F.R. §§ 405.1020(c) and 405.1022(a).

[241] 42 C.F.R. § 405.1020(c)(2). On occasion, a party may not receive the notice of hearing. The OMHA is required to attempt to contact the party who has not responded to the notice of hearing to find out why. 42 C.F.R. § 405.1022(c)(1) If the OMHA fails to make such contact, and the ALJ dismisses the appeal for failure of that party to attend the hearing, advocates have found that the OMHA's failure to attempt such contact is grounds for reversal of the dismissal.

[242] 42 C.F.R. § 405.1020(e).

[243] 42 C.F.R. § 405.1024(a), (b).

[244] 42 C.F.R. § 405.1024(c).

of the hearing.[245] Evidence may be submitted later than 10 days prior to the hearing, but the time frame for the ALJ to issue his or her decision is tolled for the period between when the evidence was required to be submitted and when it was actually received.[246] Although providers are generally required to submit all their relevant evidence at the QIC level of appeal, they may submit additional evidence if they establish "good cause" for failing to do so earlier.[247] The ALJ must review the new evidence submitted by the provider and notify all parties whether it is excluded.[248]

Although generally the issues at the hearing will include all issues brought out at any prior level of appeal that were not decided in a party's favor, the ALJ may also include as an issue any portion of any prior determination that was decided favorably.[249] The parties must be notified of all issues before the hearing.[250] New issues may be raised at any time prior to the start of the hearing, if those new issues could have a material impact on the claims that are the subject of the request for hearing.[251]

Discovery at the ALJ level of appeal is permissible only when CMS elects to be made a party to the hearing.[252] Discovery is permissible with respect to any matter that is relevant to the subject matter of the hearing, although the party from whom discovery is sought may raise objections based on the assertion that the material sought is privileged or otherwise protected.[253] Additionally, an ALJ may deny a request for discovery if the ALJ concludes that the discovery request is unreasonable, unduly burdensome or expensive, or otherwise inappropriate.[254] Discovery is limited. A party may request reasonable production of documents for inspection and copying, but depositions may not be taken unless the deponent agrees or the ALJ finds the proposed deposition is appropriate and necessary.[255] Similarly, requests for admissions and interrogatories are generally not permitted.[256]

---

[245] 42 C.F.R. § 405.1018(a). Evidence may be submitted beyond this period, but it has the effect of tolling the time frame for the ALJ to render a decision. This provision does not apply to unrepresented beneficiaries. 42 C.F.R. § 405.1018(d).

[246] 42 C.F.R. § 405.1018(b).

[247] 42 C.F.R. § 405.1018(c).

[248] 42 C.F.R. § 405.1028(a)–(d).

[249] 42 C.F.R. § 405.1032(a).

[250] 42 C.F.R. § 405.1032.

[251] 42 C.F.R. § 405.1032(b). Certain limitations apply to this. *See* 42 C.F.R. § 405.980, *see* https://www.gpo.gov/fdsys/pkg/CFR-2011-title42-vol2/pdf/CFR-2011-title42-vol2-sec405-980.pdf (site visited June 6, 2016).

[252] 42 C.F.R. § 405.1037(a).

[253] 42 C.F.R. § 405.1037(a)(2).

[254] 42 C.F.R. § 405.1037(a)(2).

[255] 42 C.F.R. § 405.1037(b)(1), (2).

[256] 42 C.F.R. § 405.1037(b)(3).

The ALJ may hold a pre-hearing or a post-hearing conference, either at his or her own initiative or at the request of a party.[257] The ALJ must inform the parties of the time, place, and purpose of the conference at least seven calendar days prior to the conference date.[258] The ALJ may consider matters in addition to those stated on the notice of hearing, if the parties consent in writing.[259] A record of the hearing will be made, and the ALJ must issue an order stating all agreements and actions resulting from the conference.[260]

An administrative record, including marked exhibits, will be made.[261] Under the interim final regulations, a party may review the record at the hearing or, if a hearing is not held, at any time prior to the issuance of an ALJ decision.[262] However, given that hearings will most often not be held in-person, the regulations offer no explanation as to how such a review can be accomplished. A party may request and receive a copy of all or part of the record; however, the party can be asked to pay the costs associated with generating the requested items.[263]

Once a hearing has been held,[264] the ALJ must issue a written decision that sets out findings of fact, conclusions of law, and the reasons for the decision.[265] The decision must be mailed to each party, the Medicare contractors, and the QIC.[266]

If an ALJ decision is not rendered within the appropriate time frame for the circumstances of the case, a party may escalate the appeal to the Medicare Appeals Council (MAC).[267] The request for escalation must be filed with the ALJ.[268] Once the request is received, the ALJ has five days to either issue a decision, remand the case to the QIC,[269] or notify the parties that a timely decision cannot be issued.[270] At that point, the QIC decision becomes the decision which

---

[257] 42 C.F.R. § 405.1040.

[258] 42 C.F.R. § 405.1040(b).

[259] 42 C.F.R. § 405.1040(c).

[260] 42 C.F.R. § 405.1040(c), (d).

[261] 42 C.F.R. § 405.1042. In practice, advocates have found that the exhibit lists are sometimes haphazardly assembled and often insufficiently detailed. If the exhibit list is ambiguous prior to hearing, the advocate should make a written request to the ALJ seeking a copy of the administrative record.

[262] 42 C.F.R. § 405.1042(a)(3), *see* http://www.ecfr.gov/cgi-bin/text-idx?SID=1197736ae810cfc056809936f54b0216&mc=true&node=se42.2.405_11042&rgn=div8 (site visited June 6, 2016).

[263] 42 C.F.R. § 405.1042(b)(1).

[264] Parties are free to waive their right to a hearing and have a decision issued solely on the administrative record. 42 C.F.R. §§ 405.1020(d) and 405.1038(b). In addition, an ALJ may, without holding a hearing, issue a decision that is fully favorable to the appellant(s) if the hearing record supports such a finding. 42 C.F.R. § 405.1038(a).

[265] 42 C.F.R. § 405.1046(a).

[266] 42 C.F.R. § 405.1046(a).

[267] 42 C.F.R. § 405.1104.

[268] 42 C.F.R. § 405.1104(a)(1).

[269] 42 C.F.R. §§ 405.1104(a)(2) and 405.1034.

[270] 42 C.F.R. § 405.1104(b)(2), (3).

the MAC will review.[271] In addition, the MAC may, on its own initiative, remove a case from the ALJ and assume responsibility for holding a hearing and adjudicating the case itself.[272]

[H] Medicare Appeals Council Review

A party dissatisfied with an ALJ decision may request review by the MAC.[273] A written request for MAC review must be filed with the MAC or the appropriate ALJ office.[274] The request must identify those parts of the ALJ decision (or other determination being appealed, if the case is before the MAC due to escalation) to which the party objects, and state the reasons for those objections.[275] Unless the appellant is an unrepresented beneficiary, the MAC will limit its review to those parts of the decision below specifically identified as objectionable in the request for review.

If a party has requested review because he or she is dissatisfied with an ALJ decision or has escalated an appeal from the ALJ to the MAC, the MAC will review *de novo* the decision below.[276] A party seeking MAC review does not have a right to a new hearing; however, the MAC, in its discretion, may conduct any additional proceedings, including holding a hearing.[277]

Generally, absent good cause,[278] no additional evidence may be introduced at the MAC level of appeal, unless the ALJ decision being reviewed decides a new issue that the parties were not afforded an opportunity to address before the ALJ.[279] However, a party to the MAC review, which is before the MAC because of escalation, may file a request for a subpoena of specified documents within 10 days of the request for escalation.[280]

The parties have the right to file briefs or other written statements with the MAC.[281] In addition, the MAC may request (but cannot require) CMS or its

---

[271] 42 C.F.R. § 405.1104(b)(3).

[272] 42 C.F.R. § 405.1050.

[273] The MAC may also exercise its "own motion" review. 42 C.F.R. § 405.1110. This review can occur upon the MAC's own initiative or when CMS (or any of its contractors) refers a case to the MAC that it thinks has been erroneously decided or the decision presents a broad policy or procedural issue that may affect the public interest. This, of course, we fear, gives CMS the ability to tightly control the decision-making process and its outcomes, even though the MMA requires the independence of ALJs.

[274] 42 C.F.R. § 405.1112(a).

[275] 42 C.F.R. § 405.1112(b).

[276] 42 C.F.R. § 405.1108.

[277] 42 C.F.R. § 405.1108(a), (d)(3).

[278] 42 C.F.R. § 405.1122(c).

[279] 42 C.F.R. § 405.1122(a).

[280] 42 C.F.R. § 405.1122(d)(1)–(4).

[281] 42 C.F.R. § 405.1120.

contractors to file a brief or position paper, if the MAC determines that it is necessary to resolve the issues in the case.[282] In some instances, the MAC may permit, or seek, oral argument on the appeal.[283]

The MAC may dispose of the case in a number of ways: it may remand the case to the ALJ;[284] it may dismiss the request for MAC review;[285] or it may issue a decision.[286] If the MAC fails to issue its decision within the required 90-day time frame from its receipt of the request for MAC review,[287] the appellant may request escalation to federal court.[288] If, upon filing of the escalation request and the lapse of the permissible time plus five additional days, the MAC is unable to issue a decision, remand, or dismissal, it must notify the appellant informing him or her that it is not able to do so.[289] A party may file an action in federal district court within 60 days after the date it receives this notification from the MAC.[290]

[I] Judicial Review

A party to a MAC decision who is dissatisfied with the decision may obtain judicial review if the amount in controversy requirement is met (the amount for 2017 is $1,560).[291] The civil action must be filed within 60 days after receipt of notice of the MAC decision.[292] Provisions exist in the regulations for applying to the MAC for extension of the filing time.[293] The civil action must be filed in the district court for the judicial district in which the beneficiary resides or, if filed by a provider, in the judicial district where it has its principal place of business.[294] The Secretary of HHS in his or her official capacity is the proper defendant.[295] The standard of review for the court is whether the decision of the Secretary of HHS is supported by substantial evidence.[296]

---

[282] 42 C.F.R. § 405.1120.

[283] 42 C.F.R. § 405.1124.

[284] 42 C.F.R. § 405.1108(d)(3).

[285] 42 C.F.R. § 405.1108(c), (d)(4)–(5).

[286] 42 C.F.R. § 405.1108(a), (d)(1).

[287] 42 C.F.R. § 405.1132. As with the other levels of appeal, the time frame for issuing a determination is subject to various extensions. *See, e.g.*, 42 C.F.R. § 405.1114 (extension when party seeks evidence from the MAC); 42 C.F.R. § 405.1120 (extension when briefs are filed); 42 C.F.R. § 405.1122(e)(2)(ii) (stay upon issuance of subpoena).

[288] 42 C.F.R. § 405.1132.

[289] 42 C.F.R. § 405.1132(a)(2).

[290] 42 C.F.R. § 405.1132(b).

[291] 42 C.F.R. § 405.1136. The amount in controversy required to proceed to federal court in 2017 is $1,560 (81 Fed. Reg. 65,653 (Sept. 27, 2016)), MCP Manual, Ch. 29, § 345.1.

[292] 42 C.F.R. § 405.1130.

[293] 42 C.F.R. § 405.1134.

[294] 42 C.F.R. § 405.1136(b).

[295] 42 C.F.R. § 405.1136(d).

[296] 42 C.F.R. § 405.1136(f).

In addition, Section 932 of the MMA modified 42 U.S.C. § 1395ff(b) to create expedited access to the judicial review process whereby beneficiaries, providers, and suppliers can have expedited access to judicial review in certain appeals of Medicare Part A or Part B claims.[297] The new expedited appeals process also applies to provider contract disputes—primarily nursing home enforcement cases.[298] Expedited review is available when it is determined both that the MAC lacks authority to decide a question of law or regulation relevant to the case and that there is no material issue of fact in dispute.[299]

A beneficiary may file a request for expedited access to judicial review at the same time as, or after, filing a request for an ALJ hearing.[300] A review entity made up of three reviewers who are ALJs or members of the HHS Departmental Appeals Board (DAB) has 60 days after receipt of the request to issue a written decision.[301] The review entity may request appropriate documents and materials from the beneficiary to support his or her contention that (1) no material issues of fact exist and (2) the MAC lacks authority to decide the relevant question of law or regulations.[302] If the review entity agrees with the beneficiary's request for expedited review, or if the review entity fails to act within 60 days of receipt of the request, the beneficiary skips ALJ and DAB review and may go directly to district court.[303] If the review entity finds against the beneficiary, she has no further recourse and may not make another request for expedited review regarding the matter in dispute.[304]

[J] Appointments of Representatives and Attorneys' Fees

The final regulations also specify the elements of a proper appointment of representative, its duration, and rules about collection of fees for representing Medicare beneficiaries in an appeal of a Medicare denial.[305]

A valid appointment of representation form must:[306]

- Be in writing and signed and dated by both the beneficiary and the representative.

---

[297] 42 C.F.R. § 405.990.

[298] 42 C.F.R. §§ 405.906(a)–(c) and 405.990(e).

[299] 42 C.F.R. § 405.990(a)(2).

[300] 42 C.F.R. § 405.990(d)(2).

[301] 42 C.F.R. § 405.990(a)(1).

[302] 42 C.F.R. § 405.990(c).

[303] 42 C.F.R. § 405.990(f)(4).

[304] 42 C.F.R. § 405.990(h)(3)(i).

[305] 42 C.F.R. §§ 405.910 and 405.912, *available at* http://www.ecfr.gov/cgi-bin/retrieveECFR?gp=&SID=0e66ad9153c83c7c9310a7f478459f1c&mc=true&n=sp42.2.405.i&r=SUBPART&ty=HTML#se42.2.405_1910 (site visited June 6, 2016).

[306] 42 C.F.R. § 405.910(c). The appointment of representation form can be found at https://www.cms.gov/Medicare/CMS-Forms/ (site visited June 6, 2016).

- Authorize the representative to act on behalf of the beneficiary and authorize the adjudicator to release identifiable health information to the representative.
- Include an explanation of the purpose and scope of the representation.
- Include the name, phone number, and address for the beneficiary and the representative.
- Include the beneficiary's Medicare health insurance claim number.
- Include the representative's professional status or relationship to the beneficiary.
- Be filed with the entity processing the party's initial determination or appeal.

If a form is defective, the representative will be given an opportunity to correct the defect. Otherwise, the representative will not have the authority to act on behalf of the beneficiary or to receive health information.[307]

The regulations limit the duration of the appointment of representation form to one year. A duly appointed representative may file multiple appeals on behalf of an individual beneficiary during the course of that year but must submit a copy of the original appointment form with each additional appeal filed. Once an appointment of representation form has been filed in a case, the appointment lasts for the duration of the appeal unless it is revoked.[308]

The regulations prohibit an appointed representative from delegating the appointment to another person without the beneficiary's consent. Thus, a family member who already serves as an appointed representative cannot delegate that appointment to an advocate for purposes of pursing an appeal unless the beneficiary signs a written notice. A signed statement is not required where both the appointed and new representatives are attorneys (but not paralegals) in the same law firm or organization. When a beneficiary lacks the capacity to sign an appointment of representation form or form acknowledging delegation of the appointment, state law determines who has authority to authorize representation on his or her behalf.[309]

Under the regulations, a beneficiary's appointed representative (but not a provider or supplier's representative) who wishes to charge a fee for services at the ALJ and MAC levels of review must obtain approval of the fee from the Secretary of HHS. The regulations also say that no award of fees or costs may be made against the Medicare trust fund, and that limitations on the amount of fees

[307] 42 C.F.R. § 405.910(d).
[308] 42 C.F.R. §§ 405.910(e) and 405.912(e).
[309] 42 C.F.R. § 405.911(l).

that apply in Social Security and SSI disability cases do not apply to Medicare appeals.[310]

The regulations do not contain any standard by which fee requests will be judged. However, the preamble indicates that guidelines for the application of Equal Access to Justice Act (EAJA) claims before HHS may be applicable to Medicare appeals.[311] The preamble further states that HHS will review the guidelines to determine whether they need to be changed in light of the new provision.[312]

The preamble justifies the policy change by saying that a change in the Medicare Act makes provisions concerning approval of fee arrangements from back awards of Social Security disability benefits applicable to Medicare appeals.[313] The preamble goes on to acknowledge, however, that, unlike Social Security cases, there is no back award of benefits from which attorneys can be paid, and that the limitation on Social Security attorneys' fees does not apply.[314]

[K] QIO Appeals for Denial of Hospital Services to Beneficiaries Enrolled in a Medicare Advantage Plan

The appeals system for beneficiaries enrolled in a Medicare Advantage (MA) plan is different, at least through the reconsideration level of appeal. The appeal rules in MA plan cases that reach the ALJ level of appeal or beyond are the same as described above. Beneficiaries who receive Medicare-covered hospital services through MA plans are entitled to QIO review of denied, reduced, or terminated care. These regulations include the right to a grievance process for non-appealable complaints, specific time frames for each step in the appeals process, and the right to appeal hospital coverage determinations to the QIO, including expedited review.[315]

At the initial stage, MA plans should have a more specific process for addressing grievances, but beneficiaries should be provided, at a minimum level, with the same number of notices as those beneficiaries who receive care under

---

[310] 42 C.F.R. § 405.910(f). *See also* http://www.ssa.gov/forms/ssa-1560.html (Petition to obtain approval of a fee for representing a claimant-SSA) (site visited June 6, 2016). The appointment of representative in Medicare appeals form refers to the SSA "Petition to Obtain Representative Fee" as the form to use to provide information in support of a petition for fees (no standard form) in Medicare appeals. It should accompany the fee petition.

[311] 70 Fed. Reg. 11,430 (Mar. 8, 2005).

[312] 70 Fed. Reg. 11,430 (Mar. 8, 2005).

[313] 70 Fed. Reg. 11,429 (Mar. 8, 2005).

[314] 70 Fed. Reg. 11,429 (Mar. 8, 2005).

[315] *See also* Weichardt v. Thompson, C.A. No. 03 5490 VRW (N.D. Cal. Settlement Agreement, Oct. 28, 2005). *See* Medicare Program; Notification Procedures for Hospital Discharges, 71 Fed. Reg. 17,052–17,062 (Apr. 5, 2006), 42 C.F.R. §§ 405.1205, 405.1206, 422.620, and 422.622, *inter alia*. *See also* 72 Fed. Reg. 17,169 (Apr. 6, 2007) and discussion at **§ 2.11[N]** of this Handbook.

traditional Medicare. The process for higher level appeals for MA plans was originally governed by a different set of provisions; however, CMS changed this to apply the same regulations to both sets of appeals at this level.[316]

Under the MA program, managed care plans are required to provide procedural protections for beneficiaries, including meaningful grievance procedures and appeal rights.[317] These protections include the right to receive notice of an adverse "organization determination" regarding services or payment;[318] the right to an internal plan appeal (called a "reconsideration");[319] a final reconsidered determination by CMS;[320] and further review by an ALJ (if $160.00 or more is in controversy in 2017),[321] by the HHS DAB,[322] and by a federal district court (if $1,560 or more is in dispute in 2017).[323]

[L] Time Frames (Medicare Advantage)

All determinations and reconsiderations must be made "as expeditiously as the enrollee's health condition requires" but not to exceed a stated number of days.[324] Notice of organization determinations (initial decisions regarding the benefits an enrollee is entitled to receive) must be provided no later than 14 days after the initial request,[325] reduced from the previous 60-day limit. Expedited organization determinations must be made within 72 hours.[326] Reconsidered determinations must be issued no later than 30 calendar days from the request for a standard reconsideration,[327] reduced from the previous 60-day time limit. If the reconsideration is expedited, the deadline is 72 hours,[328] with extensions up to 14 days upon enrollee or MA organization requests, and the delay is in the enrollee's interest.[329]

The regulations require CMS to contract with an independent outside entity to conduct a second level of review when the internal reconsideration remains, in

---

[316] CMS opted to change this part of the process to reflect exactly the process for appeals for individuals who have traditional Medicare. *See* 42 C.F.R. § 417.600(b)(1) and 70 Fed. Reg. 4588-01 (Jan. 28, 2005).

[317] 42 U.S.C. § 1395(c)(5).

[318] 42 C.F.R. §§ 422.566–422.576.

[319] 42 C.F.R. § 422.578, *available at* http://www.gpo.gov/fdsys/pkg/CFR-2010-title42-vol3/pdf/CFR-2010-title42-vol3-sec422-578.pdf (site visited June 6, 2016).

[320] 42 C.F.R. § 422.592.

[321] 42 C.F.R. § 422.600.

[322] 42 C.F.R. § 422.608.

[323] 42 C.F.R. § 422.612. *See* 81 Fed. Reg. 185, p. 65653 (Sept. 27, 2016).

[324] *See, e.g.*, 42 C.F.R. § 422.568, regarding organization determinations.

[325] 42 C.F.R. § 422.568.

[326] 42 C.F.R. § 422.572.

[327] 42 C.F.R. § 422.590(a)(1).

[328] 42 C.F.R. § 422.590(d)(1).

[329] 42 C.F.R. §§ 422.572(b) and 422.590(d)(2).

whole or in part, adverse to the enrollee.[330] Review must be conducted as expeditiously as the enrollee's health condition requires, but the regulations do not specify a maximum time frame. Contractor deadlines are to be specified in the contract.[331]

[M] Effectuation of Appeal Decisions (Medicare Advantage)

The regulations mandate that if an MA organization reverses its original determination, it must authorize or provide the service under dispute as expeditiously as the enrollee's health requires, but no later than 30 days after the beneficiary requests reconsideration.[332] If the original denial is reversed by the independent outside entity, the MA organization must comply within 60 days.[333]

[N] Non-Coverage of Inpatient Hospital Care (Medicare Advantage)

Notice requirements are slightly different for persons in a hospital that is part of a Health Maintenance Organization (HMO), Preferred Provider Organization (PPO), or Private Fee-for-Service (PFFS) plan sponsored by an MA organization. The MA organization, or the hospital that has been delegated the authority to make the discharge decision, must provide the beneficiary with written notice of non-coverage, but only if and when the beneficiary disagrees with the discharge decision. Notice and appeal rights also arise if the MA organization, or the hospital that has been delegated the authority to make the discharge decision, is not discharging the individual but no longer intends to continue coverage of the inpatient stay.[334]

The "Revised Important Message from Medicare,"[335] a broad, general information notice that is given upon admission, or within two days of admission, is the written notice that an inpatient will receive. Since July 1, 2007, Medicare-participating hospitals, including MA plans, have been required to deliver valid, written notice, in the form of the "Important Message from Medicare" (IM), of a patient's rights as a hospital patient including discharge appeal rights, within two calendar days of admission. A follow-up copy of the signed IM is given again as far as possible in advance of discharge, but no more than two calendar days prior to the proposed date of discharge. Follow-up notice is not required if the provision

---

[330] 42 C.F.R. § 422.592.

[331] 42 C.F.R. § 422.592(b).

[332] 42 C.F.R. § 422.618(a). Reversals on a request for payment must be acted upon within 60 days. 42 C.F.R. § 422.618(b).

[333] 42 C.F.R. § 422.618(c).

[334] Revised 42 C.F.R. § 422.620(a)(i), (ii).

[335] *See* CMS's corpus of Hospital Discharge Appeal Notices at http://www.cms.gov/Medicare/Medicare-General-Information/BNI/HospitalDischargeAppealNotices.html (site visited June 6, 2016).

of the admission IM falls within two calendar days of discharge.[336] If, upon being told that he or she is about to be discharged, the patient disagrees, he or she is to be given a notice of non-coverage with specific information about the basis of the hospital's discharge decision and about appeal rights. Therefore, as a practical matter, an enrollee who wishes to challenge a determination that the hospital stay is no longer necessary may need to remain in the hospital beyond the date on which Medicare non-coverage is slated to commence.

- An enrollee is entitled to coverage until at least noon of the day after the above notice is provided;[337]
- If QIO review is requested under 42 C.F.R § 422.622 (requesting immediate QIO review of non-coverage of inpatient care), coverage is extended, and:

  The enrollee must submit a request for immediate review to the QIO that has an agreement with the hospital;

  The request must be in writing or by telephone;

  The request must be submitted by noon of the first working day after the patient receives written notice that the MCO hospital has determined that the hospital stay is no longer necessary; and

  The QIO must make a determination and notify the enrollee, or the hospital and the MA plan by the close of business of the first working day after it receives all necessary information from the hospital, or the organization, or both.

  Before a notice of non-coverage is provided, the entity that makes the non- coverage/discharge determination must obtain the concurrence of the physician who is responsible for the enrollee's inpatient care.[338]

The written notice of non-coverage must be issued no later than the day before hospital coverage ends. The written notice must include the following elements[339]

1. The reason inpatient hospital care is no longer needed;
2. The effective date and time of the enrollee's liability for continued inpatient care;

[336] *See* 72 Fed. Reg. 17,169 (Apr. 6, 2007).
[337] 42 C.F.R. § 422.620(a)(2).
[338] 42 C.F.R. § 422.620(b).
[339] *See* 42 C.F.R. § 422.622(c).

3. The enrollee's appeal rights; and
4. Additional information specified by CMS.

[O] Grievances (Medicare Advantage)

MA organizations must have "meaningful procedures for timely hearing and resolution of grievances," which are complaints or disputes other than those involving organization determinations,[340] expressing dissatisfaction with any aspect of an MA organization or provider's operations, activities, or behaviors, regardless of whether remedial action is requested.

The regulation distinguishes between a grievance and appeal,[341] and requires MA organizations to inform beneficiaries whether their complaint is subject to the grievance procedure or the appeals procedure. It further distinguishes quality of care complaints,[342] and includes a process for expedited grievances,[343] requiring completion in 24 hours.

[P] Identifying Coverable Cases

Medicare claims for inpatient hospital care are suitable for Medicare coverage, and appeal if they have been denied, if they meet the following test:

The patient's condition must have been such that the care he required could only have been provided in a hospital, *or* he required a SNF level of care, and no SNF bed was actually available. (Note: A SNF level of care means that the patient required skilled services—from a physical therapist or a registered nurse, for example—on a daily basis.)[344]

§ 2.12 DENIAL AND APPEAL PROCESS

Table 2-1 depicts the complex coverage determination and appeals process in Medicare hospital cases. The text that follows the chart describes the various steps in detail.

---

[340] 42 C.F.R. § 422.564.
[341] 42 C.F.R. § 422.561.
[342] 42 C.F.R. § 422.564.
[343] 42 C.F.R. § 422.564(d)(1), (2).
[344] *See* 42 C.F.R. §§ 409.30 *et seq.*

[A] Medicare Hospital Coverage Determination and Appeals Process

See Table 2-1.

TABLE 2-1
MEDICARE PART A APPEALS
HOSPITAL CARE

Stage of Appeal:	*Reconsideration Request*	*Hearing Request*	*Request for Dept. Appeals Board Review*	*Request for Judicial Review*
Time Deadline for Filing Appeal:	60 Days After Receipt of "Notice of Medicare Claim Determination" (or within 3 Days if You Request an "Expedited Appeal")	60 Days After Receipt of "Reconsideration Determination"	60 Days After Receipt of "Hearing Decision"	60 Days After Receipt of "Appeals Board Decision"
Amount of Claim:	No Minimum	$200 Minimum*	$200 Minimum*	$2,000 Minimum
xFile Appeal Request With:	Quality Improvement Organization (QIO) or Local Social Security Office	Quality Improvement Organization (QIO) or Local Social Security Office (processed & forwarded to Social Security's Office of Hearings & Appeals)	U.S. Dept. of Health and Human Services	United States District Court
Appeal Reviewed & Decided By:	Quality Improvement Organization (QIO)	Administrative Law Judge from Social Security Departmental Office of Hearings and Appeals	U.S. Dept. of Health and Human Services Appeals Board	United States District Court

continues

TABLE 2-1 continued

Stage of Appeal:	*Reconsideration Request*	*Hearing Request*	*Request for Dept. Appeals Board Review*	*Request for Judicial Review*
Time Deadline For Decision:	3 Days If Inpatient or Pre-Admission; 30 Days for All Others	None	None	None

* If the appeal is on a question of entitlement to Part A benefits, there is no minimum amount required.

[B] The Appeals Process in Operation

The determination and appeals process depicted in **Table 2-1** is as follows:

1. The patient appears at the hospital seeking admission.

■ **EXAMPLE:** Mr. Brown and Mrs. Smith both are driven to the hospital by car. Mr. Brown, whose daughter takes him to the hospital, is having chest pains and has a history of a stroke and severe hypertension that is controlled by oral medications. By contrast, Mrs. Smith was found by a stranger wandering in the middle of a four-lane highway, dressed in a nightgown. Mrs. Smith, who lives alone, was incoherent and had a superficial wound on her leg. The stranger called the police, who took her to the hospital.

2. When confronted by a patient seeking admission, a hospital can choose one of these courses of action:
   a. The hospital may decide that the patient will be covered by Medicare and admit the patient.
   b. The hospital may decide that Medicare coverage is not available but permit the patient to enter the hospital anyway. Under such circumstances, the hospital is required to issue the patient a notice of admission denial, informing the patient that the cost of hospital care will be the patient's responsibility. Written notice of noncoverage to the patient is necessary because the patient is not liable for the cost of care and may not be charged by the hospital until he or she has been given written notice that the services involved are not covered by the Medicare program.[345]

[345] 42 C.F.R. §§ 411.404 and 412.42(c)(3); *see also* Social Security Act § 1879, 42 U.S.C. § 1395pp.

c. Finally, the hospital may deny Medicare coverage and not admit the patient. Often the patient will balk at assuming responsibility for expensive care, or the hospital may simply refuse to allow the patient to enter. Usually no written Medicare denial notice is issued, and the patient has no right to appeal. An exception exists, however, where the QIO has a pre-procedure or preadmission review process in place. Although unusual, involvement of the QIO at the preadmission stage is good news for the advocate because appeal is possible. In such cases the QIO reviews the medical necessity or appropriateness of some or all of the Medicare admissions before they occur. If the QIO determines that Medicare coverage is not available, it issues an appealable initial determination notice to the beneficiary.[346]

■ **EXAMPLE:** Upon arriving at the hospital, Mr. Brown is examined in the emergency room and admitted to the hospital. By contrast, Mrs. Smith is examined and a determination is made that she does not need hospital care, but since she cannot be safely sent home, she will be admitted to the hospital. Mrs. Smith is given a written notice of Medicare non-coverage and placed in one of the hospital's beds.

3. All patients actually admitted to the hospital must be given a special notice entitled "An Important Message from Medicare."[347] The mandatory notice is very explicit about a patient's rights while in the hospital. Most of the information in the "Important Message from Medicare" concerns the procedure to be followed when the hospital issues a continuing care denial of Medicare coverage. A continuing care denial occurs when the patient has been granted Medicare coverage on admission, but the hospital, usually acting through its URC, eventually determines that the patient no longer needs a hospital level of care.

■ **EXAMPLE:** After three days of tests, Mr. Brown is determined to require transfer to a nursing home. The hospital URC determines that he can be terminated from Medicare coverage because he no longer requires inpatient hospital care. A written continuing stay denial is issued to him.

4. Utilization review of a continuing stay often occurs because the stay is longer or more expensive than the average for that DRG. In such instances, the hospital may be motivated to avoid the financial loss

---

[346] MCP Manual, Ch. 30, §§ 240–240.6. *See also* **Appendix 2-3** in this Handbook.

[347] Social Security Act § 1866(a)(1)(M), 42 U.S.C. § 1395cc(a)(1)(M); 42 C.F.R § 412.42(c)(3); MCP Manual, Ch. 30, §§ 200–200.6. *See also* **Appendix 2-3** in this Handbook.

represented by the gap between the DRG amount paid and the cost of the patient's care as the stay continues. Before issuing a determination that an admission or a continuing stay is not medically necessary, the URC must consult the attending physician and afford an opportunity to present his or her point of view.[348] Moreover, before a hospital may bill a patient for the cost of services rendered, however, the hospital must comply with a complex coverage determination, notice, and appeals process.

Federal regulations are quite specific concerning when a hospital may charge a Medicare-eligible patient for hospital services rendered. Generally, a hospital may not charge a beneficiary for any service for which payment is made by Medicare, even if the hospital's cost of furnishing services to the patient is greater than the amount the hospital is paid under PPS.[349] The hospital is always permitted to charge the patient the applicable deductible and coinsurance amounts. The hospital is not permitted to charge the patient for care excluded from Medicare coverage as custodial care or medically unnecessary care[350] unless the following specific steps are followed:

The hospital must decide that the patient no longer requires inpatient hospital care. Inpatient hospital care includes cases where a beneficiary needs a SNF level of care, but, under Medicare criteria, a SNF level bed is not available.[351]

■ **EXAMPLE:** Mr. Brown receives three days of Medicare hospital coverage, following which a determination is made that he can be transferred to a nursing home. Transfer to a nursing home does not necessarily mean that Mr. Brown requires a SNF level of care under Medicare criteria. Therefore, an inquiry into the nature of the care that Mr. Brown requires will have to be made.

If the attending physician agrees with the hospital's determination in writing, the hospital may immediately issue a continuing care denial to the patient.[352]

■ **EXAMPLE:** Mr. Brown's treating physician, who ordered that Mr. Brown could be discharged to a nursing home, agrees that he no longer requires a hospital level of care. Therefore, the hospital URC issues a denial notice to Mr. Brown.

---

348 42 C.F.R. § 482.30(d)(2).
349 42 C.F.R. § 412.42(a).
350 42 C.F.R. §§ 411.400, 489.21(d)(1).
351 42 C.F.R. § 412.42(c)(1).
352 42 C.F.R. § 412.42(c)(2).

The continuing care denial notice given the patient must inform the patient that customary charges will be assessed against the patient only *after the second day following the date of the notice.*[353] For example, if a patient receives a denial notice on Monday, the patient may not be charged for the cost of care until Thursday.

■ **EXAMPLE:** Mr. Brown was admitted to the hospital on Thursday and was determined to be suitable for nursing home placement on Saturday. The hospital URC, therefore, with Mr. Brown's physician's concurrence, issued a denial notice on Saturday. If Mr. Brown does nothing to appeal this denial, he could stay in the hospital, without incurring any financial liability, through Monday. He could be charged for his stay commencing on Tuesday.

For a case where coverage is denied on admission and no covered days whatsoever are granted, the hospital may not charge the patient for hospital care that is not medically necessary until the patient has been notified in writing that Medicare coverage is not available.[354] The notice must also inform the patient concerning the appeal rights described below.

■ **EXAMPLE:** Mrs. Smith was given a denial notice immediately prior to her admission. The hospital would be able to charge her for her stay from the date of admission.

5. The right to appeal for a patient given a continuing care denial differs according to whether the attending physician has concurred with the URC's denial decision or whether the URC was required to obtain QIO approval of the proposed denial determination.[355]

   If the attending physician has agreed with the hospital determination of non-coverage, the QIO has not yet been required to review the case. In this situation the patient is entitled to an expedited QIO review if the patient is still an inpatient in the hospital and requests an expedited review not later than noon of the first working day after the date the patient receives the URC denial notice.[356] The hospital is required to provide the QIO with a copy of the medical records by the close of business of such working day, and the QIO must issue a determination not later than one full working day after the date the QIO has received the

[353] This limitation on charges to beneficiaries applies only where Medicare coverage was originally granted on admission, that is, where the patient's stay included at least one covered day. 42 C.F.R. § 412.42(b).

[354] 42 C.F.R. § 411.404(b).

[355] 42 C.F.R. § 412.42(c).

[356] Social Security Act § 1154(e), 42 U.S.C. § 1320c–3(c).

request for expedited review and the medical records.[357] If the patient is no longer in the hospital, or fails to request an expedited determination by noon of the first working day after the notice of no coverage is received, the QIO is required to issue a review decision within 30 days of the request.

■ **EXAMPLE:** Mr. Brown receives his continuing stay denial notice on Saturday. He must request an expedited review by the QIO by no later than noon on Monday, which he does. The QIO issues, and Mr. Brown receives, a decision that upholds the denial on Tuesday. The hospital may begin charging Mr. Brown for his stay on Tuesday. Under the Medicare regulations, an appeal to the QIO does not result in an extension of the hospital's inability to charge Mr. Brown, beyond two days after the original hospital URC notice was given to him, unless the QIO finds that, in fact, he required continued hospital care.[358] As can be seen, simply by requesting the expedited review, Mr. Brown has received an additional day of Medicare coverage in the hospital.

If the patient's attending physician does not concur with the hospital's determination of non-coverage, the hospital must obtain the QIO's concurrence before it can bill the patient.[359] The QIO must give an opportunity to the provider and to the physician to discuss the merits of the case.[360] If the QIO concurs with the hospital's determination, the hospital is so informed by the QIO, and the hospital will issue a notice to the patient.[361] The QIO's concurrence is binding upon the beneficiary unless the beneficiary is dissatisfied with this determiniation.[362] If still in the hospital, the beneficiary may request reconsideration by asking the QIO to review the case.[363] If the beneficiary is no longer in the hospital, the determination is subject to the general claims appeal process.[364]

It is unclear to what extent a hospital is required to notify the family members or legal representative of ill or incompetent patients. In one case the court found that the hospital had a duty to provide written, not oral, notice of the denial of Medicare coverage to the friend of an incompetent patient, where the hospital knew that the friend was acting on the patient's behalf.[365] In practice, hospitals usually attempt to notify

[357] Social Security Act § 1154(e), 42 U.S.C. § 1320c–3(c).

[358] 42 C.F.R. § 412.42(c)(3)(v).

[359] 42 U.S.C. § 1320c-3(e)(2); 42 C.F.R. § 412.42(c)(2).

[360] 42 C.F.R. § 412.42.

[361] 42 U.S.C. § 1320c-3(e)(2);42 C.F.R. § 412.42(c)(2).

[362] 42 C.F.R. § 405.1208.

[363] 42 C.F.R. § 405.1204.

[364] 42 C.F.R. § 405.1208(e)(2).

[365] Carpenter v. Secretary of HHS, Medicare & Medicaid Guide (CCH) 38,621 (D. Conn. 1990).

both the patient and the relative or representative who has been acting on the patient's behalf.

> ■ **EXAMPLE:** Mrs. Smith arrived at the hospital in an incoherent state, yet the hospital delivered a denial notice to her. The notice would not be deemed effective if it could be shown that Mrs. Smith's medical condition prevented her from understanding the denial notice. As an alternative, the hospital could try to locate a family member willing and able to act on Mrs. Smith's behalf, and deliver the denial notice to the family member. As a further alternative, if state law permits, the hospital could go to a court of appropriate jurisdiction to petition for appointment of a conservator or guardian for Mrs. Smith. The conservator or guardian could then be given the denial notice.

6. If the QIO reconsideration is unfavorable, the beneficiary may request a hearing before an ALJ of the HHS OMHA. The amount in controversy must be at least $200. The administrative hearing will be held by an ALJ of the OMHA. The hearing request must be filed within 60 days of receipt of the notice of the QIO reconsideration determination, unless the time is extended for good cause.[366] The request for reconsideration must be filed with the QIO.[367]

§ 2.13 HOW TO DEVELOP A WINNING APPEAL

While a denial of Medicare inpatient hospital coverage can occur for many reasons, frequently patients are denied coverage (1) in rehabilitation hospitals, (2) when, following at least three days of Medicare coverage in the hospital their condition improves, but they still require a SNF level of care after a hospital stay and no SNF bed is available, or (3) when the hospital determines that the patient requires admission for "social" reasons. The stated reason for denials of rehabilitation hospital care are often based upon the purported lack of intensity of the patient's rehabilitation program; the alleged absence of "sufficient" improvement in the patient's rehabilitation status; or a notion that the overall condition of the patient was such that the rehabilitation services could have been provided in a SNF, instead of a hospital. Denials of hospital coverage when a SNF bed is not available often occur because the hospital is simply unaware of the availability of continued Medicare coverage under such circumstances; or because the hospital improperly believes that, although a patient requires a nursing home placement, the patient's

---

[366] 42 C.F.R. § 478.42(b).

[367] Social Security Act § 1861(ee), 42 U.S.C. § 1395x(ee); 42 C.F.R. § 482.43.

condition does not rise to the level of requiring SNF care. When faced with these bases for denials of Medicare coverage, the advocate must be prepared to analyze thoroughly the facts and the applicable Medicare coverage criteria.

Denial of so-called social admissions (as in the previous example of Mrs. Smith) is often based upon the hospital's assessment that no other support system is available to the patient to assure the patient's overall safety, even though the patient—in the hospital's view—could properly receive medical treatment in some other setting. One argument that has been used successfully in such cases is that Medicare regulations require that care be provided to patients in the most economically feasible manner.[368] "Economically" is defined in the Medicare regulations as "provided at the least expensive, medically appropriate type of setting or care available."[369] Consequently, if it can be established that an inpatient hospital was the only medically appropriate type of setting or care available (and the simple fact that the patient was admitted to the hospital, rather than discharged home or sent to some other, less intensive care setting, is evidence of this fact), then the services received by the patient as a hospital inpatient are medically reasonable and necessary, in the absence of availability of any alternative care.

Of course, in any Medicare inpatient hospital appeal, as is usually the case in other areas of advocacy, effective analysis and factual development will greatly improve your chances of prevailing. Address these areas:

1. Recognize an unfair coverage denial by comparing the facts of the case with the legal criteria of coverage. In acute hospital cases medical necessity is the amorphous standard. This is a two-part standard: (a) Is it medically necessary for the patient to be treated in a hospital[370] and (b) if the patient no longer requires treatment in the hospital and could be treated outside the hospital, does the patient need at least a SNF level of care, and is there no SNF bed available in a participating facility?[371]
2. Build an alliance with the attending physician. The statute and regulations repeatedly require the involvement of the attending physician in the decision-making process. Physicians will typically feel divided loyalties. They do not want to see their hospital lose money, but they also want to protect their patients from unfair charges for care. It is the advocate's job to educate the physician concerning the legitimate rules of Medicare coverage and to encourage the physician to support the patient's claim by expressing an opinion, preferably in writing, that it is medically necessary for the patient to be treated in the hospital, or that the patient requires a SNF level of care and that no SNF bed in a

[368] 42 C.F.R. § 1004.10.

[369] 42 C.F.R. § 1004.1(b).

[370] 42 U.S.C. § 1395f (a)(3).

[371] 42 C.F.R. §§ 412.42(c)(1) and 424.13(b).

participating facility is available. Often an explicit and detailed letter from the attending physician becomes the deciding factor in a successful Medicare appeal.

3. Evaluate the medical record for a hospital level of care. The degree and intensity of skill delivered to a patient is the central factor in determining what level of care the patient requires. If the patient requires a degree of skill and intensity of services available only in a hospital, then it is medically necessary for the patient to be treated in a hospital. One benchmark, although not the exclusive one, is whether the beneficiary required the 24-hour availability of a physician. Such physician availability usually exists only in a hospital. If the patient requires daily skilled care in an institutional setting, then that patient requires a SNF level of care. The details found in the written medical record will often provide the evidence necessary to substantiate the patient's claim.
4. Determine where one is in the process. You will notice that the coverage determination and appeals process is quite complex; your client's rights depend upon where in the process his or her claim happens to be. The advocate must gather all available notices and documentation to determine the present status of the appeal. Generally, it is in the beneficiary's interest for an advocate to take action at the earliest possible time. For example, patients and their families often hear word of an impending continued care denial before a written notice is actually received. By encouraging the attending physician to support the claim at an early stage, an advocate can often delay or even prevent the issuance of the denial notice.

Hospital care is generally the most expensive care that a patient can receive. Because of the expense involved, denials of Medicare inpatient hospital coverage, or the threat of such a denial, can often lead patients to forgo necessary medical care. The result frequently can be a deteriorated and untreated state of health. The availability of advocacy on the patient's behalf, therefore, may mean the difference between the patient's receiving needed care or accepting and living with unnecessarily poor health. Hence, an advocate's role where Medicare hospital coverage is concerned is, first, to make sure the patient receives the care he or she requires, and second, to ensure that the patient is not charged for services that should be covered by Medicare.

As observed, economic considerations often override a purely medical perspective when it comes to access to Medicare-covered hospital care. However, a well-prepared advocate who is familiar with the Medicare inpatient hospital coverage criteria and the patient's medical condition and treatment can fight against this tide and ensure that the patient receives appropriate health care. By allying oneself with the patient in this way, the advocate may also influence and inform

Medicare coverage determinations made in general by providers and, so, prevent future improper denials of Medicare coverage.

§ 2.14 LINKING PAYMENT TO QUALITY OUTCOMES UNDER THE MEDICARE PROGRAM

President Obama signed into law the Patient Protection and Affordability Care Act of 2010[372] (PPACA, or the Affordable Care Act, or ACA) on March 23, 2010, and the Health Care and Education Reconciliation Act of 2010[373] (HCERA) on March 30, 2010. Changes in the ACA address measuring the quality of care that is received by Medicare beneficiaries and linking payment to those measures. In the legislation, Congress has placed emphasis on efforts to measure quality and to provide payment for only those services and procedures that meet certain quality of care standards.[374] For an update of CMS activities, review the materials on Medicare Quality Initiatives in the area of Hospital Value Based Purchasing (HVBP).[375] The Secretary is to coordinate the value-based payment modifier with the Physician Feedback Program.[376]

The Secretary must specify an initial performance period for application of the payment modifier for 2015. The Secretary must apply the payment modifier, beginning on January 1, 2015, to specific physicians and groups of physicians the Secretary determines appropriate and, beginning not later than January 1, 2017, to all physicians and groups of physicians.[377]

The Secretary is to create incentives for applicable hospitals to reduce hospital-acquired conditions with respect to discharges occurring during fiscal year 2015 and subsequent fiscal years. The amount of payment for such discharges during the fiscal year must be equal to 99 percent of the amount of payment that would otherwise apply. An applicable hospital is one that is in the top quartile of hospitals (that receive inpatient hospital service payments on the basis of prospective rates as set by the Medicare Geographical Classification Review Board) relative to the national average of hospital-acquired conditions during the

---

[372] Pub. L. No. 111-148 (Mar. 23, 2010).

[373] Pub. L. No. 111-152 (Mar. 30, 2010).

[374] *See* Center for Medicare Advocacy, "Changes to Medicare Advantage Plans And Prescription Drug Plans Under Health Care Reform," Apr. 8, 2010, for a discussion of quality bonus payments for Medicare Advantage plans, *available at* http://www.medicareadvocacy.org/InfoByTopic/Reform/10_04.08.MAandPDChanges.htm (site visited June 6, 2016).

[375] *See* CMS.gov, "Hospital Value-Based Purchasing," *available at* https://www.cms.gov/Medicare/Quality-Initiatives-Patient-Assessment-Instruments/hospital-value-based-purchasing/index.html?redirect=/Hospital-Value-Based-Purchasing/ (site visited June 6, 2016).

[376] *See* CMS, https://www.cms.gov/medicare/medicare-fee-for-service-payment/physicianfeedbackprogram/valuebasedpaymentmodifier.html (site visited June 6, 2016).

[377] *See* CMS.gov, "Value-Based Payment Modifier," *available at* http://www.cms.gov/Medicare/Medicare-Fee-for-Service-Payment/PhysicianFeedbackProgram/ValueBasedPaymentModifier.html (site visited June 6, 2016).

applicable period, as determined by the Secretary. The term "hospital-acquired condition" means a condition identified or determined by the Secretary that an individual acquires during a stay in an applicable hospital. The term "applicable period" means, with respect to a fiscal year, a period specified by the Secretary.[378]

Prior to fiscal year 2015 and in each subsequent fiscal year, the Secretary must provide confidential reports to applicable hospitals with respect to hospital-acquired conditions of the applicable hospital and make information available to the public regarding hospital-acquired conditions of each applicable hospital.[379] Information for the public shall also be posted on the Hospital Compare Internet website.[380]

The Secretary must conduct a study on expanding the health care–acquired conditions policy to payments made to other facilities under the Medicare program. The report, together with recommendations, was to be submitted to Congress not later than January 1, 2012.[381]

[A] National Legislative Strategy to Improve Health Care Quality

- **ACA § 3011. National Strategy.** The Secretary, through a transparent collaborative process, is to establish a national strategy to improve the delivery of health care services, patient health outcomes, and population health. The national strategy must include a comprehensive strategic plan to achieve the priorities described above.[382]

- **ACA § 3012. Interagency Working Group on Health Care Quality.** The President must convene a working group to be known as the Interagency Working Group on Health Care Quality (referred to in this section as the "Working Group"). Not later than December 31, 2010, and annually thereafter, the Working Group must submit to the relevant Committees of Congress and make public on an Internet website a report describing the progress and recommendations of the Working Group. The

---

[378] *See* CMS, Medicare Learning Network, "Hospital-Acquired Conditions and Present on Admission Indicator Reporting Provision," *available* https://www.cms.gov/Outreach-and-Education/Medicare-Learning-Network-MLN/MLNProducts/Downloads/wPOA-Fact-Sheet.pdf (site visited June 6, 2016)).

[379] *See* Center for Medicare Advocacy, "Health Reform: Linking Payments to Quality Outcome," *available at* http://www.medicareadvocacy.org/health-reform-linking-medicare-payment-to-quality-outcome/ (site visited June 6, 2016).

[380] *See* https://www.medicare.gov/hospitalcompare/search.html (site visited June 6, 2016).

[381] *See* CMS, Medicare Learning Network, "Hospital-Acquired Conditions Present on Admission Indicator Reporting Provision," see Hospital-Acquired Conditions Present on Admission Indicator Reporting Provision (site visited June 6, 2016).

[382] *See* CMS, "Quality Measurement Impact Reports," *available at* http://www.cms.gov/Medicare/Quality-Initiatives-Patient-Assessment-Instruments/QualityMeasures/QualityMeasurementImpactReports.html (site visited June 6, 2016).

goals of the Working Group are to achieve collaboration, cooperation, and consultation between federal departments and agencies with respect to developing and disseminating strategies, goals, models, and timetables that are consistent with the national priorities identified above.[383]

[383] *See* http://www.ahrq.gov/workingforquality/reports/annual-reports/nqs2014annlrpt.htm (site visited June 6, 2016).

APPENDIX 2-1 TITLE 42—PUBLIC HEALTH (CODE OF FEDERAL REGULATIONS):

PART 405—FEDERAL HEALTH INSURANCE FOR THE AGED AND DISABLED*

Subpart J—Expedited Determinations and Reconsiderations of Provider Service Terminations, and Procedures for Inpatient Hospital Discharges

Sec. 405.1200 Notifying beneficiaries of provider service terminations.

(a) Applicability and scope. (1) For purposes of §§ 405.1200 through 405.1204, the term, provider, is defined as a home health agency (HHA), skilled nursing facility (SNF), comprehensive outpatient rehabilitation facility (CORF), or hospice.

(2) For purposes of §§ 405.1200 through 405.1204, a termination of Medicare-covered service is a discharge of a beneficiary from a residential provider of services, or a complete cessation of coverage at the end of a course of treatment prescribed in a discrete increment, regardless of whether the beneficiary agrees that the services should end. A termination does not include a reduction in services. A termination also does not include the termination of one type of service by the provider if the beneficiary continues to receive other Medicare-covered services from the provider.

(b) Advance written notice of service terminations. Before any termination of services, the provider of the service must deliver valid written notice to the beneficiary of the provider's decision to terminate services. The provider must use a standardized notice, as specified by CMS, in accordance with the following procedures:

(1) *Timing of notice.* A provider must notify the beneficiary of the decision to terminate covered services no later than 2 days before the proposed end of the services. If the beneficiary's services are expected to be fewer than 2 days in duration, the provider must notify the beneficiary at the time of admission to the provider. If, in a non-residential setting, the span of time between services exceeds 2 days, the notice must be given no later than the next to last time services are furnished.

(2) *Content of the notice.* The standardized termination notice must include the following information:

(i) The date that coverage of services ends;

(ii) The date that the beneficiary's financial liability for continued services begins;

---

* *See* http://www.gpo.gov/fdsys/pkg/CFR-2007-title42-vol2/pdf/CFR-2007-title42-vol2-part405-subpartJ.pdf (site visited Sept. 15, 2016).

(iii) A description of the beneficiary's right to an expedited determination under § 405.1202, including information about how to request an expedited determination and about a beneficiary's right to submit evidence showing that services must continue;

(iv) A beneficiary's right to receive the detailed information specified under § 405.1202(f); and

(v) Any other information required by CMS.

(3) *When delivery of the notice is valid.* Delivery of the termination notice is valid if—

(i) The beneficiary (or the beneficiary's authorized representative) has signed and dated the notice to indicate that he or she has received the notice and can comprehend its contents; and

(ii) The notice is delivered in accordance with paragraph (b)(1) of this section and contains all the elements described in paragraph (b)(2) of this section.

(4) *If a beneficiary refuses to sign the notice.* The provider may annotate its notice to indicate the refusal, and the date of refusal is considered the date of receipt of the notice.

(5) *Financial liability for failure to deliver valid notice.* A provider is financially liable for continued services until 2 days after the beneficiary receives valid notice as specified under paragraph (b)(3) of this section, or until the service termination date specified on the notice, whichever is later. A beneficiary may waive continuation of services if he or she agrees being discharged sooner than the planned service termination date.

Sec. 405.1202 Expedited determination procedures.

(a) Beneficiary's right to an expedited determination by the QIO. A beneficiary has a right to an expedited determination by a QIO under the following circumstances:

(1) services furnished by a non-residential provider, the beneficiary disagrees with the provider of those services that services should be terminated, and a physician certifies that failure to continue the provision of the service(s) may place the beneficiary's health at significant risk.

(2) For services furnished by a residential provider or a hospice, the beneficiary disagrees with the provider's decision to discharge the beneficiary.

(b) Requesting an expedited determination. (1) A beneficiary who wishes to exercise the right to an expedited determination must submit a request for a determination to the QIO in the State in which the beneficiary is receiving those provider services, in writing or by telephone, by no later than noon of the calendar day following receipt of the provider's notice of termination. If the QIO is unable to accept the beneficiary's request, the beneficiary must submit the request by noon of the next day the QIO is available to accept a request.

(2) The beneficiary, or his or her representative, must be available to answer questions or to supply information that the QIO may request to conduct its review.

(3) The beneficiary may, but is not required to, submit evidence to be considered by a QIO in making its decision.

(4) If a beneficiary makes an untimely request for an expedited determination by a QIO, the QIO will accept the request and make a determination as soon as possible, but the 72-hour time frame under paragraph (e)(6) and the financial liability protection under paragraph (g) of this section do not apply.

(c) Coverage of provider services. Coverage of provider services continues until the date and time designated on the termination notice, unless the QIO reverses the provider's service termination decision. If the QIO's decision is delayed because the provider did not timely supply necessary information or records, the provider may be liable for the costs of any additional coverage, as determined by the QIO in accordance with paragraph (e)(7) of this section. If the QIO finds that the beneficiary did not receive valid notice, coverage of provider services continues until at least 2 days after valid notice has been received. Continuation of coverage is not required if the QIO determines that coverage could pose a threat to the beneficiary's health or safety.

(d) Burden of proof. When a beneficiary requests an expedited determination by a QIO, the burden of proof rests with the provider to demonstrate that termination of coverage is the correct decision, either on the basis of medical necessity, or based on other Medicare coverage policies.

(1) In order for the QIO to determine whether the provider has met the burden of proof, the provider should supply any and all information that a QIO requires to sustain the provider's termination decision, consistent with paragraph (f) of this section.

(2) The beneficiary may submit evidence to be considered by a QIO in making its decision.

(e) Procedures the QIO must follow. (1) On the day the QIO receives the request for an expedited determination under paragraph (b) of this section, it must immediately notify the provider of those services that a request for an expedited determination has been made.

(2) The QIO determines whether the provider delivered valid notice of the termination decision consistent with § 405.1200(b) and paragraph (f) of this section.

(3) The QIO examines the medical and other records that pertain to the services in dispute. If applicable, the QIO determines whether a physician has certified that failure to continue the provision of services may place the beneficiary's health at significant risk.

(4) The QIO must solicit the views of the beneficiary who requested the expedited determination.

(5) The QIO must provide an opportunity for the provider/practitioner to explain why the termination or discharge is appropriate.

(6) No later than 72 hours after receipt of the request for an expedited determination, the QIO must notify the beneficiary, beneficiary's physician, and the provider of services of its determination whether termination of Medicare coverage is the correct decision, either on the basis of medical necessity or based on other Medicare coverage policies.

(7) If the QIO does not receive the information needed to sustain a provider's decision to terminate services, it may make its determination based on the evidence at hand, or it may defer a decision until it receives the necessary information. If this delay results in extended Medicare coverage of an individual's provider services, the provider may be held financially liable for these services, as determined by the QIO.

(8) The QIO's initial notification may be by telephone, followed by a written notice including the following information:

(i) The rationale for the determination;

(ii) An explanation of the Medicare payment consequences of the determination and the date a beneficiary becomes fully liable for the services; and

(iii) Information about the beneficiary's right to a reconsideration of the QIO's determination, including how to request a reconsideration and the time period for doing so.

(f) Responsibilities of providers. (1) When a QIO notifies a provider that a beneficiary has requested an expedited determination, the provider must send a detailed notice to the beneficiary by close of business of the day of the QIO's notification. The detailed termination notice must include the following information:

(i) A specific and detailed explanation why services are either no longer reasonable and necessary or are no longer covered;

(ii) A description of any applicable Medicare coverage rule, instruction, or other Medicare policy, including citations to the applicable Medicare policy rules or information about how the beneficiary may obtain a copy of the Medicare policy;

(iii) Facts specific to the beneficiary and relevant to the coverage determination that are sufficient to advise the beneficiary of the applicability of the coverage rule or policy to the beneficiary's case; and

(iv) Any other information required by CMS.

(2) Upon notification by the QIO of the request for an expedited determination, the provider must supply all information that the QIO needs to make its expedited determination, including a copy of the notices required under § 405.1200(b) and under paragraph (f)(1) of this section. The provider must furnish this information as soon as possible, but no later than by close of business of the day the QIO notifies the provider of the request for an expedited determination. At the discretion of the QIO, the provider may make the information available by phone or in writing (with a written record of any information not transmitted initially in writing).

(3) At a beneficiary's request, the provider must furnish the beneficiary with a copy of, or access to, any documentation that it sends to the QIO including records of any information provided by telephone. The provider may charge the beneficiary a reasonable amount to cover the costs of duplicating the documentation and/or delivering it to the beneficiary. The provider must accommodate such a request by no later than close of business of the first day after the material is requested.

(g) Coverage during QIO review. When a beneficiary requests an expedited determination in accordance with the procedures required by this section, the provider may not bill the beneficiary for any disputed services until the expedited determination process (and reconsideration process, if applicable) has been completed.

Sec. 405.1204 Expedited reconsiderations.

(a) Beneficiary's right to an expedited reconsideration. A beneficiary who is dissatisfied with a QIO's expedited determination may request an expedited reconsideration by the appropriate QIC.

(b) Requesting an expedited reconsideration. (1) A beneficiary who wishes to obtain an expedited reconsideration must submit a request for the reconsideration to the appropriate QIC, in writing or by telephone, by no later than noon of the calendar day following initial notification (whether by telephone or in writing) receipt of the QIO's determination. If the QIC is unable to accept the beneficiary's request, the beneficiary must submit the request by noon of the next day the QIC is available to accept a request.

(2) The beneficiary, or his or her representative, must be available to answer questions or supply information that the QIC may request to conduct its reconsideration.

(3) The beneficiary may, but is not required to, submit evidence to be considered by a QIC in making its decision.

(4) A beneficiary who does not file a timely request for an expedited QIC reconsideration subsequently may request a reconsideration under the standard claims appeal process, but the coverage protections described in paragraph (f) of this section would not extend through this reconsideration, nor would the timeframes or the escalation process described in paragraphs (c)(3) and (c)(5) of this section, respectively.

(c) Procedures the QIC must follow. (1) On the day the QIC receives the request for an expedited determination under paragraph (b) of this section, the QIC must immediately notify the QIO that made the expedited determination and the provider of services of the request for an expedited reconsideration.

(2) The QIC must offer the beneficiary and the provider an opportunity to provide further information.

(3) Unless the beneficiary requests an extension in accordance with paragraph (c)(6) of this section, no later than 72 hours after receipt of the request for an expedited reconsideration, and any medical or other records needed for such reconsideration, the QIC must notify the QIO, the beneficiary, the beneficiary's physician, and the provider of services, of its decision on the reconsideration request.

(4) The QIC's initial notification may be done by telephone, followed by a written notice including:

(i) The rationale for the reconsideration decision;

(ii) An explanation of the Medicare payment consequences of the determination and the beneficiary's date of liability; and

(iii) Information about the beneficiary's right to appeal the QIC's reconsideration decision to an ALJ, including how to request an appeal and the time period for doing so.

(5) Unless the beneficiary requests an extension in accordance with paragraph (c)(6) of this section, if the QIC does not issue a decision within 72 hours of receipt of the request, the QIC must notify the beneficiary of his or her right to have the case escalated to the ALJ hearing level if the amount remaining in controversy after the QIO determination is $100 or more.

(6) A beneficiary requesting an expedited reconsideration under this section may request (either in writing or orally) that the QIC grant such additional time as the beneficiary specifies (not to exceed 14 days) for the reconsideration. If an extension is granted, the deadlines in paragraph (c)(3) of this section do not apply.

(d) Responsibilities of the QIO. (1) When a QIC notifies a QIO that a beneficiary has requested an expedited reconsideration, the QIO must supply all information that the QIC needs to make its expedited reconsideration as soon as possible, but no later than by close of business of the day that the QIC notifies the QIO of the request for an expedited reconsideration.

(2) At a beneficiary's request, the QIO must furnish the beneficiary with a copy of, or access to, any documentation that it sends to the QIC. The QIO may charge the beneficiary a reasonable amount to cover the costs of duplicating the documentation and/or delivering it to the beneficiary. The QIO must accommodate the request by no later than close of business of the first day after the material is requested.

(e) Responsibilities of the provider. A provider may, but is not required to, submit evidence to be considered by a QIC in making its decision. If a provider fails to comply with a QIC's request for additional information beyond that furnished to the QIO for purposes of the expedited determination, the QIC makes its reconsideration decision based on the information available.

(f) Coverage during QIC reconsideration process. When a beneficiary requests an expedited reconsideration in accordance with the deadline specified in (b)(1) of this section, the provider may not bill the beneficiary for any disputed services until the QIC makes its determination.

Sec. 405.1205 Notifying beneficiaries of hospital discharge appeal rights.

(a) Applicability and scope. (1) For purposes of § 405.1204, § 405.1205, § 405.1206, and § 405.1208, the term "hospital" is defined as any facility providing care at the inpatient hospital level, whether that care is short term or long term, acute or non-acute, paid through a prospective payment system or other reimbursement basis, limited to specialty care or providing a broader spectrum of services. This definition includes critical access hospitals.

(2) For purposes of § 405.1204, § 405.1205, § 405.1206, and § 405.1208, a discharge is a formal release of a beneficiary from an inpatient hospital.

(b) Advance written notice of hospital discharge rights. For all Medicare beneficiaries, hospitals must deliver valid, written notice of a beneficiary's rights as a hospital inpatient, including discharge appeal rights. The hospital must use a standardized notice, as specified by CMS, in accordance with the following procedures:

(1) *Timing of notice.* The hospital must provide the notice at or near admission, but no later than 2 calendar days following the beneficiary's admission to the hospital.

(2) *Content of the notice.* The notice must include the following information:

(i) The beneficiary's rights as a hospital inpatient including the right to benefits for inpatient services and for post-hospital services in accordance with 1866(a)(1)(M) of the Act.

(ii) The beneficiary's right to request an expedited determination of the discharge decision including a description of the process under § 405.1206, and the availability of other appeals processes if the beneficiary fails to meet the deadline for an expedited determination.

(iii) The circumstances under which a beneficiary will or will not be liable for charges for continued stay in the hospital in accordance with 1866(a)(1)(M) of the Act.

(iv) A beneficiary's right to receive additional detailed information in accordance with § 405.1206(e).

(v) Any other information required by CMS.

(3) *When delivery of the notice is valid.* Delivery of the written notice of rights described in this section is valid if—

(i) The beneficiary (or the beneficiary's representative) has signed and dated the notice to indicate that he or she has received the notice and can comprehend its contents, except as provided in paragraph (b)(4) of this section; and

(ii) The notice is delivered in accordance with paragraph (b)(1) of this section and contains all the elements described in paragraph (b)(2) of this section.

(4) *If a beneficiary refuses to sign the notice.* The hospital may annotate its notice to indicate the refusal, and the date of refusal is considered the date of receipt of the notice.

(c) Follow up notification. (1) The hospital must present a copy of the signed notice described in paragraph (b)(2) of this section to the beneficiary (or beneficiary's representative) prior to discharge. The notice should be given as far in advance of discharge as possible, but not more than 2 calendar days before discharge.

(2) Follow up notification is not required if the notice required under § 405.1205(b) is delivered within 2 calendar days of discharge.

[71 FR 68720, Nov. 27, 2006]

Sec. 405.1206 Expedited determination procedures for inpatient hospital care.

(a) Beneficiary's right to an expedited determination by the QIO. A beneficiary has a right to request an expedited determination by the QIO when a hospital (acting directly or through its utilization review committee), with physician concurrence, determines that inpatient care is no longer necessary.

(b) Requesting an expedited determination. (1) A beneficiary who wishes to exercise the right to an expedited determination must submit a request to the QIO that has an agreement with the hospital as specified in § 476.78 of this chapter. The request must be made no later than the day of discharge and may be in writing or by telephone.

(2) The beneficiary, or his or her representative, upon request by the QIO, must be available to discuss the case.

(3) The beneficiary may, but is not required to, submit written evidence to be considered by a QIO in making its decision.

(4) A beneficiary who makes a timely request for an expedited QIO review in accordance with paragraph (b)(1) of this section is subject to the financial liability protections under paragraphs (f)(1) and (f)(2) of this section, as applicable.

(5) A beneficiary who fails to make a timely request for an expedited determination by a QIO, as described in paragraph (b)(1) of this section, and remains in the hospital without coverage, still may request an expedited QIO determination at any time during the hospitalization. The QIO will issue a decision in accordance with paragraph (d)(6)(ii) of this section, however, the financial liability protection under paragraphs (f)(1) and (f)(2) of this section does not apply.

(6) A beneficiary who fails to make a timely request for an expedited determination in accordance with paragraph (b)(1) of this section, and who is no longer an inpatient in the hospital, may request QIO review within 30 calendar days after the date of discharge, or at any time for good cause. The QIO will issue a decision in accordance with paragraph (d)(6)(iii) of this section; however, the financial liability protection under paragraphs (f)(1) and (f)(2) of this section does not apply.

(c) Burden of proof. When a beneficiary (or his or her representative, if applicable) requests an expedited determination by a QIO, the burden of proof rests with the hospital to demonstrate that discharge is the correct decision, either on the basis of medical necessity, or based on other Medicare coverage policies. Consistent with paragraph (e)(2) of this section, the hospital should supply any and all information that a QIO requires to sustain the hospital's discharge determination.

(d) Procedures the QIO must follow. (1) When the QIO receives the request for an expedited determination under paragraph (b)(1) of this section, it must immediately notify the hospital that a request for an expedited determination has been made.

(2) The QIO determines whether the hospital delivered valid notice consistent with § 405.1205(b)(3).

(3) The QIO examines the medical and other records that pertain to the services in dispute.

(4) The QIO must solicit the views of the beneficiary (or the beneficiary's representative) who requested the expedited determination.

(5) The QIO must provide an opportunity for the hospital to explain why the discharge is appropriate.

(6)(i) When the beneficiary requests an expedited determination in accordance with paragraph (b)(1) of this section, the QIO must make a determination and notify the beneficiary, the hospital, and physician of its determination within one calendar day after it receives all requested pertinent information.

(ii) When the beneficiary makes an untimely request for an expedited determination, and remains in the hospital, consistent with paragraph (b)(5) of this section, the QIO will make a determination and notify the beneficiary, the hospital, and the physician of its determination within 2 calendar days following receipt of the request and pertinent information.

(iii) When the beneficiary makes an untimely request for an expedited determination, and is no longer an inpatient in the hospital, consistent with paragraph (b)(6) of this section, the QIO will make a determination and notify the beneficiary, the hospital, and physician of its determination within 30 calendar days after receipt of the request and pertinent information.

(7) If the QIO does not receive the information needed to sustain a hospital's decision to discharge, it may make its determination based on the evidence at hand, or it may defer a decision until it receives the necessary information. If this delay results in extended Medicare coverage of an individual's hospital services, the hospital may be held financially liable for these services, as determined by the QIO.

(8) When the QIO issues an expedited determination, the QIO must notify the beneficiary, the physician, and hospital of its decision by telephone, followed by a written notice that must include the following information:

(i) The basis for the determination.

(ii) A detailed rationale for the determination.

(iii) An explanation of the Medicare payment consequences of the determination and the date a beneficiary becomes fully liable for the services.

(iv) Information about the beneficiary's right to a reconsideration of the QIO's determination as set forth in § 405.1204, including how to request a reconsideration and the time period for doing so.

(e) Responsibilities of hospitals. (1) When a QIO notifies a hospital that a beneficiary has requested an expedited determination, the hospital must deliver a detailed notice to the beneficiary as soon as possible but no later than noon of the day after the QIO's notification. The detailed notice must include the following information:

(i) A detailed explanation why services are either no longer reasonable and necessary or are otherwise no longer covered.

(ii) A description of any applicable Medicare coverage rule, instruction, or other Medicare policy, including information about how the beneficiary may obtain a copy of the Medicare policy.

(iii) Facts specific to the beneficiary and relevant to the coverage determination that are sufficient to advise the beneficiary of the applicability of the coverage rule or policy to the beneficiary's case.

(iv) Any other information required by CMS.

(2) Upon notification by the QIO of the request for an expedited determination, the hospital must supply all information that the QIO needs to make its expedited determination, including a copy of the notices required as specified in § 405.1205 (b) and (c) and paragraph (e)(1) of this section. The hospital must furnish this information as soon as possible, but no later than by noon of the day after the QIO notifies the hospital of the request for an expedited determination. At the discretion of the QIO, the hospital must make the information available by phone or in writing (with a written record of any information not transmitted initially in writing).

(3) At a beneficiary's (or representative's) request, the hospital must furnish the beneficiary with a copy of, or access to, any documentation that it sends to the QIO, including written records of any information provided by telephone. The hospital may charge the beneficiary a reasonable amount to cover the costs of duplicating the documentation and/or delivering it to the beneficiary. The hospital must accommodate such a request by no later than close of business of the first day after the material is requested.

(f) Coverage during QIO expedited review—(1) *General rule and liability while QIO review is pending.* If the beneficiary remains in the hospital past midnight of the discharge date ordered by the physician, and the hospital, the physician who concurred with the discharge determination, or the QIO subsequently finds that the beneficiary requires inpatient hospital care, the beneficiary is not financially responsible for continued care (other than applicable coinsurance and deductible) until the hospital once again determines that the beneficiary no longer requires inpatient care, secures concurrence from the physician responsible for the beneficiary's care or the QIO, and notifies the beneficiary with a notice consistent with 405.1205(c).

(2) *Timely filing and limitation on liability.* If a beneficiary files a request for an expedited determination by the QIO in accordance with paragraph (b)(1) of this section, the beneficiary is not financially responsible for inpatient hospital services (other than applicable coinsurance and deductible) furnished before noon of the calendar day after the date the beneficiary (or his or her representative) receives notification (either orally or in writing) of the expedited determination by the QIO.

(3) *Untimely request and liability.* When a beneficiary does not file a request for an expedited determination by the QIO in accordance with paragraph (b) of this section, but remains in the hospital past the discharge date, that beneficiary may be held responsible for charges incurred after the date of discharge or as otherwise stated by the QIO.

(4) *Hospital requests an expedited review.* When the hospital requests a review in accordance with § 405.1208, and the QIO concurs with the hospital's discharge determination, a hospital may not charge the beneficiary until the date specified by the QIO.

(g) Effect of an expedited QIO determination. The QIO determination is binding upon the beneficiary, physician, and hospital, except in the following circumstances:

(1) *Right to request a reconsideration.* If the beneficiary is still an inpatient in the hospital and is dissatisfied with the determination, he or she may request a reconsideration according to the procedures described in § 405.1204.

(2) *Right to pursue the general claims appeal process.* If the beneficiary is no longer an inpatient in the hospital and is dissatisfied with this determination, the determination is subject to the general claims appeal process.

[71 FR 68721, Nov. 27, 2006]

Sec. 405.1208 Hospital requests expedited QIO review.

(a) General rule. (1) If the hospital (acting directly or through its utilization review committee) believes that the beneficiary does not require further inpatient hospital care but is unable to obtain the agreement of the physician, it may request an expedited determination by the QIO.

(2) When the hospital requests review, and the QIO concurs with the hospital's discharge determination, a hospital may not charge a beneficiary until the date specified by the QIO in accordance with 405.1206(f)(4).

(b) Procedures hospital must follow. (1) The hospital must (acting directly or through its utilization review committee) notify the beneficiary (or his or her representative) that it has requested that review.

(2) The hospital must supply any pertinent information the QIO requires to conduct its review and must make it available by phone or in writing, by close of business of the first full working day immediately following the day the hospital submits the request for review.

(c) Procedures the QIO must follow. (1) The QIO must notify the hospital that it has received the request for review and must notify the hospital if it has not received all pertinent records.

(2) The QIO must examine the pertinent records pertaining to the services.

(3) The QIO must solicit the views of the beneficiary in question.

(4) The QIO must make a determination and notify the beneficiary, the hospital, and physician within 2 working days of the hospital's request and receipt of any pertinent information submitted by the hospital.

(d) Notice of an expedited determination. (1) When a QIO issues an expedited determination as stated in paragraph (c)(4) of this section, it must notify the beneficiary, physician, and hospital of its decision, by telephone and subsequently in writing.

(2) A written notice of the expedited initial determination must contain the following:

(i) The basis for the determination;

(ii) A detailed rationale for the determination;

(iii) A statement explaining the Medicare payment consequences of the expedited determination and date of liability, if any; and

(iv) A statement informing the beneficiary of his or her appeal rights and the timeframe for requesting an appeal.

(e) Effect of an expedited determination. The expedited determination under this section is binding upon the beneficiary, physician, and hospital, except in the following circumstances:

(1) *When a beneficiary remains in the hospital.* If the beneficiary is still an inpatient in the hospital and is dissatisfied with this determination, he or she may request a reconsideration according to the procedures described in § 405.1204. The procedures described in § 405.1204 will apply to reconsiderations requested under this section. If the beneficiary does not make a request in accordance with § 405.1204(b)(1), the time frames described in § 405.1204(c)(3), the escalation procedures described in § 405.1204(c)(5), and the coverage rule described in § 405.1204(f) will not apply.

(2) *When a beneficiary is no longer an inpatient in the hospital.* If the beneficiary is no longer an inpatient in the hospital and is dissatisfied with this determination, this determination is subject to the general claims appeal process.

[69 FR 69624, Nov. 26, 2004, as amended at 71 FR 68722, Nov. 27, 2006]

APPENDIX 2-2 TITLE 42—PUBLIC HEALTH (CODE OF FEDERAL REGULATIONS): PART 412—PROSPECTIVE PAYMENT SYSTEMS FOR INPATIENT HOSPITAL SERVICES*

Subpart A—General Provisions

Sec. 412.10 Changes in the DRG classification system.

(a) General rule. CMS issues changes in the DRG classification system in a Federal Register notice at least annually. Except as specified in paragraphs (c) and (d) of this section, the DRG changes are effective prospectively with discharges occurring on or after the same date the payment rates are effective.

(b) Basis for changes in the DRG classification system. All changes in the DRG classification system are made using the principles established for the DRG system. This means that cases are classified so each DRG is—

(1) Clinically coherent; and

(2) Embraces an acceptable range of resource consumption.

(c) Interim coverage changes—(1) *Criteria.* CMS makes interim changes to the DRG classification system during the Federal fiscal year to incorporate items and services newly covered under Medicare.

(2) *Implementation and effective date.* CMS issues interim coverage changes through its administrative issuance system and makes the change effective as soon as is administratively feasible.

(3) *Publication for comment.* CMS publishes any change made under paragraph (c)(1) of this section in the next annual notice of changes to the DRG classification system published in accordance with paragraph (a) of this section.

(d) Interim changes to correct omissions and inequities—(1) *Criteria.* CMS makes interim changes to the DRG classification system to correct a serious omission or inequity in the system only if failure to make the changes would have—

(i) A potentially substantial adverse impact on the health and safety of beneficiaries; or

(ii) A significant and unwarranted fiscal impact on hospitals or the Medicare program.

(2) *Publication and effective date.* CMS publishes these changes in the Federal Register in a final notice with comment period with a prospective effective date. The change is also published for public information in the next annual notice of changes to the DRG classification system published in accordance with paragraph (a) of this section.

---

* *See* http://www.ecfr.gov/cgi-bin/retrieveECFR?gp=&SID=e07cf54a2d15ed24befdd2ed32aee68f&mc=true&n=pt42.2.412&r=PART&ty=HTML#_top (site visited June 6, 2016).

(e) Review by ProPAC. Changes published annually in accordance with paragraph (a) of this section are subject to review and comment by ProPAC upon publication. Interim changes to the DRG classification system that are made in accordance with paragraphs (c) and (d) of this section are subject to review by ProPAC before implementation.

[50 FR 35688, Sept. 3, 1985, as amended at 51 FR 31496, Sept. 3, 1986; 57 FR 39820, Sept. 1, 1992]
***

Subpart B—Hospital Services Subject to and Excluded from the Prospective Payment Systems for Inpatient Operating Costs and Inpatient Capital-Related Costs

Sec. 412.20 Hospital services subject to the prospective payment systems.

(a) Except for services described in paragraphs (b), (c), (d), and (e) of this section, all covered hospital inpatient services furnished to beneficiaries during the subject cost reporting periods are paid under the prospective payment system as specified in § 412.1(a)(1).

(b) Effective for cost reporting periods beginning on or after January 1, 2005, covered inpatient hospital services furnished to Medicare beneficiaries by an inpatient psychiatric facility that meets the conditions of § 412.404 are paid under the prospective payment system described in subpart N of this part.

(c)(1) Effective for cost reporting periods beginning on or after January 1, 2002, covered inpatient hospital services furnished to Medicare beneficiaries by a rehabilitation hospital or rehabilitation unit that meet the conditions of § 412.604 are paid under the prospective payment system described in subpart P of this part.

(2) CMS will not pay for services under subpart P of this part if the services are paid for by a health maintenance organization (HMO) or competitive medical plan (CMP) that elects not to have CMS make payments to an inpatient rehabilitation facility for services, which are inpatient hospital services, furnished to the HMO's or CMP's Medicare enrollees, as provided under part 417 of this chapter.

(d) Effective for cost reporting periods beginning on or after October 1, 2002, covered inpatient hospital services furnished to Medicare beneficiaries by a long-term care hospital that meets the conditions for payment of §§ 412.505 through 412.511 are paid under the prospective payment system described in subpart O of this part.

(e) Inpatient hospital services will not be paid under the prospective payment systems specified in § 412.1(a)(1) under any of the following circumstances:

(1) The services are furnished by a hospital (or hospital unit) explicitly excluded from the prospective payment systems under §§ 412.23, 412.25, 412.27, and 412.29.

(2) The services are emergency services furnished by a nonparticipating hospital in accordance with § 424.103 of this chapter.

(3) The services are paid for by an HMO or competitive medical plan (CMP) that elects not to have CMS make payments directly to a hospital for inpatient hospital services furnished to the HMO's or CMP's Medicare enrollees, as provided in § 417.240(d) and § 417.586 of this chapter.

[50 FR 12741, Mar. 29, 1985, as amended at 53 FR 6648, Mar. 2, 1988; 57 FR 39820, Sept. 1, 1992; 59 FR 45400, Sept. 1, 1994; 66 FR 41386, Aug. 7, 2001; 67 FR 56048, Aug. 30, 2002; 68 FR 45698, Aug. 1, 2003; 69 FR 66976, Nov. 15, 2004]

***

Sec. 412.22 Excluded hospitals and hospital units: General rules.

(a) Criteria. Subject to the criteria set forth in paragraph (e) of this section, a hospital is excluded from the prospective payment systems specified in § 412.1(a)(1) of this part if it meets the criteria for one or more of the excluded classifications described in § 412.23. For purposes of this subpart, the term "hospital" includes a critical access hospital (CAH).

(b) Cost reimbursement. Except for those hospitals specified in paragraph (c) of this section, and § 412.20(b), (c), and (d), all excluded hospitals (and excluded hospital units, as described in § 412.23 through § 412.29) are reimbursed under the cost reimbursement rules set forth in part 413 of this chapter, and are subject to the ceiling on the rate of hospital cost increases as specified in § 413.40 of this chapter.

(c) Special payment provisions. The following classifications of hospitals are paid under special provisions and therefore are not generally subject to the cost reimbursement or prospective payment rules of this chapter.

(1) Veterans Administration hospitals.

(2) Hospitals reimbursed under State cost control systems approved under part 403 of this chapter.

(3) Hospitals reimbursed in accordance with demonstration projects authorized under section 402(a) of Public Law 90—248 (42 U.S.C. 1395b—1) or section 222(a) of Public Law 92—603 (42 U.S.C. 1395b—1 (note)).

(4) Nonparticipating hospitals furnishing emergency services to Medicare beneficiaries.

(d) Changes in hospitals' status. For purposes of exclusion from the prospective payment systems under this subpart, the status of each currently participating hospital (excluded or not excluded) is determined at the beginning of each cost reporting period and is effective for the entire cost reporting period. Any changes in the status of the hospital are made only at the start of a cost reporting period.

(e) Hospitals-within-hospitals. Except as provided in paragraphs (e)(1) (vi) and (f) of this section, a hospital that occupies space in a building also used by another hospital, or in one or more separate buildings located on the same campus as buildings used by another hospital, must meet the following criteria in order to be excluded from the prospective payment systems specified in § 412.1(a)(1):

(1) Except as specified in paragraph (f) of this section, for cost reporting periods beginning on or after October 1, 1997—

(i) *Separate governing body.* The hospital has a governing body that is separate from the governing body of the hospital occupying space in the same building or on the same campus. The hospital's governing body is not under the control of the hospital occupying space in the same building or on the same campus, or of any third entity that controls both hospitals.

(ii) *Separate chief medical officer.* The hospital has a single chief medical officer who reports directly to the governing body and who is responsible for all medical staff activities of the hospital. The chief medical officer of the hospital is not employed by or under contract with either the hospital occupying space in the same building or on the same campus or any third entity that controls both hospitals.

(iii) *Separate medical staff.* The hospital has a medical staff that is separate from the medical staff of the hospital occupying space in the same building or on the same campus. The hospital's medical staff is directly accountable to the governing body for the quality of medical care provided in the hospital, and adopts and enforces by-laws governing medical staff activities, including criteria and procedures for recommending to the governing body the privileges to be granted to individual practitioners.

(iv) *Chief executive officer.* The hospital has a single chief executive officer through whom all administration authority flows, and who exercises control and surveillance over all administrative activities of the hospital. The chief executive officer is not employed by, or under contract with, either the hospital occupying space in the same building or on the same campus or any third entity that controls both hospitals.

(v) *Performance of basic hospital functions.* The hospital meets one of the following criteria:

(A) The hospital performs the basic functions specified in §§ 482.21 through 482.27, 482.30, 482.42, 482.43, and 482.45 of this chapter through the use of employees or under contracts or other agreements with entities other than the hospital occupying space in the same building or on the same campus, or a third entity that controls both hospitals. Food and dietetic services and housekeeping, maintenance, and other services necessary to maintain a clean and safe physical environment could be obtained under contracts or other agreements with the hospital occupying space in the same building or on the same campus, or with a third entity that controls both hospitals.

(B) For the same period of at least 6 months used to determine compliance with the criterion regarding the age of patients in § 412.23(d)(2) or the length-of-stay criterion in § 412.23(e)(2), or for hospitals other than children's or long-term care hospitals, for a period of at least 6 months immediately preceding the first cost reporting period for which exclusion is sought, the cost of the services that the hospital obtains under contracts or other agreements with the hospital occupying space in the same building or on the same campus, or with a third entity that controls both hospitals, is no more than 15 percent of the hospital's total inpatient operating costs, as defined in § 412.2(c). For purposes of this paragraph (e)(1)(v)(B), however, the costs of preadmission services are those specified under § 413.40(c)(2) rather than those specified under § 412.2(c)(5).

(C) For the same period of at least 6 months used to determine compliance with the criterion regarding the age of inpatients in § 412.23(d)(2) or the length-of-stay criterion in § 412.23(e)(2), or for hospitals other than children's or long-term care hospitals, for the period of at least 6 months immediately preceding the first cost reporting period for which exclusion is sought, the hospital has an inpatient population of whom at least 75 percent were referred to the hospital from a source other than another hospital occupying space in the same building or on the same campus.

(vi) Effective October 1, 2008, if a State hospital that is occupying space in the same building or on the same campus as another State hospital cannot meet the criterion under paragraph (e)(1)(i) of this section solely because its governing body is under the control of the State hospital with which it shares a building or a campus, or is under the control of a third entity that also controls the State hospital with which it shares a building or a campus, the State hospital can nevertheless qualify for an exclusion if it meets the other applicable criteria in this section and—

(A) Both State hospitals occupy space in the same building or on the same campus and have been continuously owned and operated by the State since October 1, 1995;

(B) Is required by State law to be subject to the governing authority of the State hospital with which it shares space or the governing authority of a third entity that controls both hospitals; and

(C) Was excluded from the inpatient prospective payment system before October 1, 1995, and continues to be excluded from the inpatient prospective payment system through September 30, 2008.

(2) Effective for long-term care hospitals-within-hospitals for cost reporting periods beginning on or after October 1, 2004, the hospital must meet the governance and control requirements at paragraphs (e)(1)(i) through (e)(1)(iv) of this section.

(3) *Notification of co-located status.* A long-term care hospital that occupies space in a building used by another hospital, or in one or more entire buildings located on the same campus as buildings used by another hospital and that meets the criteria of paragraphs (e)(1) or (e)(2) of this section must notify its fiscal intermediary and CMS in writing of its co-location and identify by name, address, and Medicare provider number those hospital(s) with which it is co-located.

(f) Application for certain hospitals. Except as provided in paragraph (f)(3) of this section, if a hospital was excluded from the prospective payment systems under the provisions of this section on or before September 30, 1995, and at that time occupied space in a building also used by another hospital, or in one or more buildings located on the same campus as buildings used by another hospital, the criteria in paragraph (e) of this section do not apply to the hospital as long as the hospital—

(1) Continues to operate under the same terms and conditions, including the number of beds and square footage considered to be part of the hospital for purposes of Medicare participation and payment in effect on September 30, 1995; or

(2) In the case of a hospital that changes the terms and conditions under which it operates after September 30, 1995, but before October 1, 2003, continues to operate under the same terms and conditions, including the number of beds and square footage considered to be part of the hospital for purposes of Medicare participation and payment in effect on September 30, 2003.

(3) For cost reporting periods beginning on or after October 1, 2006, in applying the provisions of paragraph (f)(1) or (f)(2) of this section, any hospital that was excluded from the prospective payment systems under the provisions of this section on or before September 30, 1995, and at that time occupied space in a building also used by another hospital, or in one or more buildings located on the same campus as buildings used by another hospital may increase or decrease the square footage or decrease the number of beds considered to be part of the hospital at any time without affecting the provisions of paragraph (f)(1) or (f)(2) of this section.

(i) If a hospital to which the provisions of paragraph (f)(1) of this section applies decreases its number of beds below the number of beds considered to be part of the hospital on September 30, 1995, it may subsequently increase the number of beds at any time as long as the resulting total number of beds considered to be part of the hospital does not exceed the number of beds at the hospital on September 30, 1995.

(ii) If a hospital to which the provisions of paragraph (f)(2) of this section applies decreases its number of beds below the number of beds considered to be part of the hospital on September 30, 2003, it may subsequently increase the number of beds at any time as long as the resulting total number of beds considered to be part of the hospital does not exceed the number of beds at the hospital on September 30, 2003.

(g) Definition of control. For purposes of this section, control exists if an individual or an organization has the power, directly or indirectly, significantly to influence or direct the actions or policies of an organization or institution.

(h) Satellite facilities. (1) For purposes of paragraphs (h)(2) through (h)(5) of this section, a satellite facility is a part of a hospital that provides inpatient services in a building also used by another hospital, or in one or more entire buildings located on the same campus as buildings used by another hospital.

(2) Except as provided in paragraphs (h)(3), (h)(4), (h)(5), (h)(7) and (h)(8) of this section, effective for cost reporting periods or after October 1, 1999, a hospital that has a satellite facility must meet the following criteria in order to be excluded from the acute care hospital inpatient prospective payment systems for any period:

(i) In the case of a hospital (other than a children's hospital) that was excluded from the prospective payment systems for the most recent cost reporting period beginning before October 1, 1997, the hospital's number of State-licensed and Medicare-certified beds, including those at the satellite facilities, does not exceed the hospital's number of State-licensed and Medicare-certified beds on the last day of the hospital's last cost reporting period beginning before October 1, 1997.

(ii) The satellite facility independently complies with—

(A) For psychiatric hospitals, the requirements under § 412.23(a);

(B) For rehabilitation hospitals, the requirements under § 412.23(b)(2);

(C) For the children's hospitals, the requirements under § 412.23(d)(2); or

(D) For long-term care hospitals, the requirements under §§ 412.23(e)(1) through (e)(3)(i).

(iii) The satellite facility meets all of the following requirements:

(A) Effective for cost reporting periods beginning on or after October 1, 2002, it is not under the control of the governing body or chief executive officer of the hospital in which it is located, and it furnishes inpatient care through the use of medical personnel who are not under the control of the medical staff or chief medical officer of the hospital in which it is located.

(*1*) Except as provided in paragraph (h)(2)(iii)9A)(*2*) of this section, effective for cost reporting periods beginning on or after October 1, 2009, the governing body of the hospital of which the satellite facility is a part is not under the control of any third entity that controls both the hospital of which the satellite facility is a part and the hospital with which the satellite facility is co-located.

(*2*) If a hospital and its satellite facility were excluded from the inpatient prospective payment system under the provisions of this section for the most recent cost reporting period beginning prior to October 1, 2009, the hospital does not have to meet the requirements of paragraph (h)(2)(iii)(A)(*1*) of this section, with respect to that satellite facility, in order to retain its IPPS-excluded status.

(*3*) A hospital described in paragraph (h)(2)(iii)(A)(*2*) of this section that establishes an additional satellite facility in a cost reporting period beginning on or after October 1, 2009, must meet the criteria in this section, including the provisions of paragraph (h)(2)(iii)(A)(*1*) of this section with respect to the additional satellite facility, in order to be excluded from the inpatient prospective payment system.

(B) It maintains admission and discharge records that are separately identified from those of the hospital in which it is located and are readily available.

(C) It has beds that are physically separate from (that is, not commingled with) the beds of the hospital in which it is located.

(D) It is serviced by the same fiscal intermediary as the hospital of which it is a part.

(E) It is treated as a separate cost center of the hospital of which it is a part.

(F) For cost reporting and apportionment purposes, it uses an accounting system that properly allocates costs and maintains adequate statistical data to support the basis of allocation.

(G) It reports its costs on the cost report of the hospital of which it is a part, covering the same fiscal period and using the same method of apportionment as the hospital of which it is a part.

(3) Except as provided in paragraphs (h)(4) and (h)(5) of this section, the provisions of paragraph (h)(2) of this section do not apply to—

(i) Any hospital structured as a satellite facility on September 30, 1999, and excluded from the prospective payment systems on that date, to the extent the hospital continues operating under the same terms and conditions, including the number of beds and square footage considered, for the purposes of Medicare participation and payment, to be part of the hospital, in effect on September 30, 1999; or

(ii) Any hospital excluded from the prospective payment systems under § 412.23(e)(2)(ii).

(4) For cost reporting periods beginning before October 1, 2006, in applying the provisions of paragraph (h)(3) of this section, any hospital structured as a satellite facility on September 30, 1999, may increase or decrease the square footage of the satellite facility or may decrease the number of beds in the satellite facility if these changes are made necessary by relocation of a facility—

(i) To permit construction or renovation necessary for compliance with changes in Federal, State, or local law; or

(ii) Because of catastrophic events such as fires, floods, earthquakes, or tornadoes.

(5) For cost reporting periods beginning on or after October 1, 2006, in applying the provisions of paragraph (h)(3) of this section—

(i) Any hospital structured as a satellite facility on September 30, 1999, may increase or decrease the square footage or decrease the number of beds considered to be part of the satellite facility at any time without affecting the provisions of paragraph (h)(3) of this section; and

(ii) If the satellite facility decreases its number of beds below the number of beds considered to be part of the satellite facility on September 30, 1999, it may subsequently increase the number of beds at any time as long as the resulting total number of beds considered to be part of the satellite facility does not exceed the number of beds at the satellite facility on September 30, 1999.

(6) *Notification of co-located status.* A satellite of a long-term care hospital that occupies space in a building used by another hospital or in one or more entire buildings located on the same campus as buildings used by another hospital and that meets the criteria of paragraphs (h)(1) through (h)(5) of this section must notify its fiscal intermediary and CMS in writing of its co-location and identify by name, address, and Medicare provider number, those hospital(s) with which it is co-located.

(7) The provisions of paragraph (h)(2)(i) of this section do not apply to any long-term care hospital that is subject to the long-term care hospital prospective payment system under Subpart O of this subpart, effective for cost reporting periods occurring on or after October 1, 2002, and that elects to be paid based on 100 percent of the Federal prospective payment rate as specified in § 412.533(c), beginning with the first cost reporting period following that election, or when the LTCH is fully transitioned to 100 percent of the Federal prospective rate, or to a new long-term care hospital, as defined in § 412.23(e)(4).

(8) The provisions of paragraph (h)(2)(i) of this section do not apply to any inpatient rehabilitation facility that is subject to the inpatient rehabilitation facility prospective payment system under subpart P of this part, effective for cost reporting periods beginning on or after October 1, 2003.

[50 FR 12741, Mar. 29, 1985]
Editorial Note: For Federal Register Citations affecting § 412.22, see the List of CFR Sections Affected, which appears in the Finding Aids section of the printed volume and at *www.fdsys.gov* (site visited Aug. 14, 2014).

Sec. 412.23 Excluded hospitals: Classifications.

Hospitals that meet the requirements for the classifications set forth in this section are not reimbursed under the prospective payment systems specified in § 412.1(a)(1):

(a) Psychiatric hospitals. A psychiatric hospital must—

(1) Meet the following requirements to be excluded from the prospective payment system as specified in § 412.1(a)(1) and to be paid under the prospective payment system as specified in § 412.1(a)(2) and in subpart N of this part;

(2) Be primarily engaged in providing, by or under the supervision of a psychiatrist, psychiatric services for the diagnosis and treatment of mentally ill persons; and

(3) Meet the conditions of participation for hospitals and special conditions of participation for psychiatric hospitals set forth in part 482 of this chapter.

(b) Rehabilitation hospitals. A rehabilitation hospital must meet the requirements specified in § 412.29 of this subpart to be excluded from the prospective payment systems specified in § 412.1(a)(1) of this subpart and to be paid under the prospective payment system specified in § 412.1(a)(3) of this subpart and in Subpart P of this part:

(c) [Reserved]

(d) Children's hospitals. A children's hospital must—

(1) Have a provider agreement under part 489 of this chapter to participate as a hospital; and

(2) Be engaged in furnishing services to inpatients who are predominantly individuals under the age of 18.

(e) Long-term care hospitals. A long-term care hospital must meet the requirements of paragraph (e)(1) and (e)(2) of this section and, when applicable, the additional requirement of § 412.22(e), to be excluded from the prospective payment system specified in § 412.1(a)(1) and to be paid under the prospective payment system specified in § 412.1(a)(4) and in Subpart O of this part.

(1) ***Provider agreements.*** The hospital must have a provider agreement under Part 489 of this chapter to participate as a hospital; and

(2) ***Average length of stay.*** (i) The hospital must have an average Medicare inpatient length of stay of greater than 25 days (which includes all covered and non-covered days of stay of Medicare patients) as calculated under paragraph (e)(3) of this section; or

(ii) For cost reporting periods beginning on or after August 5, 1997, a hospital that was first excluded from the prospective payment system under this section in 1986 meets the length of stay criterion if it has an average inpatient length of stay for all patients, including both Medicare and non-Medicare inpatients, of greater than 20 days and demonstrates that at least 80 percent of its annual Medicare inpatient discharges in the 12-month cost reporting period ending in fiscal year 1997 have a principal diagnosis that reflects a finding of neoplastic disease as defined in paragraph (f)(1)(iv) of this section.

(3) ***Calculation of average length of stay.*** (i) Subject to the provisions of paragraphs (e)(3)(ii) through (v) of this section, the average Medicare inpatient length of stay specified under paragraph (e)(2)(i) of this section is calculated by dividing the total number of covered and noncovered days of stay of Medicare inpatients (less leave or pass days) by the number of total Medicare discharges for the hospital's most recent complete cost reporting period. Subject to the provisions of paragraphs (e)(3)(ii) through (v) of this section, the average inpatient length of stay specified under paragraph (e)(2)(ii) of this section is calculated by dividing the total number of days for all patients, including both Medicare and non-Medicare inpatients (less leave or pass days) by the number of total discharges for the hospital's most recent complete cost reporting period.

(ii) Effective for cost reporting periods beginning on or after July 1, 2004, in calculating the hospital's average length of stay, if the days of a stay of an inpatient involves days of care furnished during two or more separate consecutive cost reporting periods, that is, an admission during one cost reporting period and a discharge during a future consecutive cost reporting period, the total number of days of the stay are considered to have occurred in the cost reporting period during which the inpatient was discharged. However, if after application of this provision, a hospital fails to meet the average length of stay specified under paragraphs (e)(2)(i) and (ii) of this section, Medicare will determine the hospital's average inpatient length of stay for cost reporting periods beginning on or after July 1, 2004, but before July 1, 2005, by dividing the applicable total days for Medicare inpatients under paragraph (e)(2)(i) of this section or the total days for all inpatients under paragraph (e)(2)(ii) of this section, during the cost reporting period when they occur, by the number of discharges occurring during the same cost reporting period.

(iii) If a change in a hospital's average length of stay specified under paragraph (e)(2)(i) or paragraph (e)(2)(ii) of this section is indicated, the calculation is made by the same method for the period of at least 5 months of the immediately preceding 6-month period.

(iv) If a hospital seeks exclusion from the inpatient prospective payment system as a long-term care hospital and a change of ownership (as described in § 489.18 of this chapter) occurs within the period of at least 5 months of the 6-month period preceding its petition for long-term care hospital status, the hospital may be excluded from the inpatient prospective payment system as a long-term care hospital for the next cost reporting period if, for the period of at least 5 months of the 6 months immediately preceding the start of the cost reporting period for which the hospital is seeking exclusion from the inpatient prospective payment system as a long-term care hospital (including time before the change of ownership), the hospital has met the required average length of stay, has continuously operated as a hospital, and has continuously participated as a hospital in Medicare.

(v) For periods beginning on or after October 1, 2011, a hospital that is excluded from the inpatient prospective payment system as a long-term care hospital that plans to undergo a change of ownership (as described in § 489.18 of this chapter) must notify its fiscal intermediary or MAC within 30 days of the effective date of such change of ownership, as specified § 424.516(e) of this subchapter. The hospital will continue to be excluded from the inpatient prospective payment system as a long-term care hospital for the cost reporting period following the change of ownership only if, for the period of at least 5 months of the 6 months immediately preceding the change of ownership, the hospital meets the required average length of stay (calculated in accordance with paragraph (e)(3)(i) of this section).

(4) ***Rules applicable to new long-term care hospitals***—(i) ***Definition.*** For purposes of payment under the long-term care hospital prospective payment system under subpart O of this part, a new long-term care hospital is a provider of inpatient hospital services that meets the qualifying criteria in paragraphs (e)(1) and (e)(2) of this section and, under present or previous ownership (or both), its first cost reporting period as a LTCH begins on or after October 1, 2002.

(ii) ***Satellite facilities and remote locations of hospitals seeking to become new long-term care hospitals.*** Except as specified in paragraph (e)(4)(iii) of this section, a satellite facility (as defined in § 412.22(h)) or a remote location of a hospital (as defined in § 413.65(a)(2) of this chapter) that voluntarily reorganizes as a separate Medicare participating hospital, with or without a concurrent change in ownership, and that seeks to qualify as a new long-term care hospital for Medicare payment purposes must demonstrate through documentation that it meets the average length of stay requirement as specified under paragraphs (e)(2)(i) or (e)(2)(ii) of this section based on discharges that occur on or after the effective date of its participation under Medicare as a separate hospital.

(iii) ***Provider-based facility or organization identified as a satellite facility and remote location of a hospital prior to July 1, 2003.*** Satellite facilities and remote locations of hospitals that became subject to the provider-based status rules under § 413.65 as of July 1, 2003, that become separately participating hospitals, and that seek to qualify as long-term care hospitals for Medicare payment purposes may submit to the fiscal intermediary discharge data gathered during 5 months of the immediate 6 months preceding the facility's separation from the main hospital for calculation of the average length of stay specified under paragraph (e)(2)(i) or paragraph (e)(2)(ii) of this section.

(5) ***Freestanding long-term care hospital.*** For purposes of this paragraph, a freestanding long-term care hospital means a hospital that meets the requirements of paragraph (e)(1) and (2) of this section and all of the following:

(i) Does not occupy space in a building also used by another hospital.

(ii) Does not occupy space in one or more separate or entire buildings located on the same campus as buildings used by another hospital.

(iii) Is not part of a hospital that provides inpatient services in a building also used by another hospital.

(6) ***Moratorium on the establishment of new long-term care hospitals and long-term care hospital satellite facilities***—(i) ***General rule.*** Except as specified in paragraph (e)(6)(ii) of this paragraph, for the period beginning December 29, 2007 and ending December 28, 2012, a moratorium applies to the establishment and classification of a long-term care hospital or long-term care hospital satellite facility as described in § 412.23(e).

(ii) ***Exception.*** The moratorium specified in paragraph (e)(6)(i) of this section is not applicable to the establishment and classification of a long-term care hospital that meets the requirements in paragraph (e) of this section or a long-term care hospital satellite facility that meets the requirements in § 412.22(h), if the long-term care hospital met one of the following criteria on or before December 29, 2007:

(A) Began its qualifying period for payment in accordance with paragraph (e) of this section.

(B)(*1*) Has a binding written agreement with an outside, unrelated party for the actual construction, renovation, lease or demolition for a long-term care hospital; and

(*2*) Has expended, before December 29, 2007, at least 10 percent (or, if less, $2.5 million) of the estimated cost of the project specified in paragraph (ii)(B)(1) of this paragraph.

(C) Had obtained an approved certificate of need from the State, when required by State law.

(7) ***Moratorium on increasing the number of beds in existing long-term care hospitals and existing long-term care hospital satellite facilities.*** (i) For purposes of this paragraph, an existing long-term care hospital or long-term care hospital satellite facility means a long-term care hospital that meets the requirements of paragraph (e) of this section or long-term care hospital satellite facility that meets the requirements of § 412.22(h) of this part and received payment under the provisions of subpart O of this part on or before December 29, 2007.

(ii) Effective for the period beginning December 29, 2007 and ending December 28, 2012—

(A) Except as specified in paragraph (e)(7)(ii)(B) and (C) of this section, the number of Medicare-certified beds in an existing long-term care hospital or an existing long-term care hospital satellite facility as defined in paragraph (e)(7)(i) of this section must not be increased beyond the number of Medicare-certified beds on December 29, 2007.

(B) Except as specified in paragraph (e)(7)(ii)(C) of this section, the moratorium specified in paragraph (e)(7)(ii)(A) of this section is not applicable to—

(*1*) An existing long-term care hospital or existing long-term care hospital satellite facility as defined in paragraph (e)(7)(i) of this section that meets both of the following requirements:

(*i*) Is located in a State where there is only one other long-term care hospital that meets the criteria specified in § 412.23(e) of this subpart.

(*ii*) Requests an increase in the number of Medicare-certified beds after the closure or decrease in the number of Medicare-certified beds of another long-term care hospital in the State; or

(*2*) An existing long-term care hospital or existing long-term care hospital satellite facility as defined in paragraph (e)(7)(i) of this section that obtained a certificate of need for an increase in beds and that meets both of the following requirements:

(*i*) Is in a State for which such certificate of need is required, and

(*ii*) Such certificate was issued on or after April 1, 2005, and before December 29, 2007.

(C) The exceptions specified in paragraph (e)(7)(ii)(B) of this section do not affect the limitation on increasing beds under § 412.22(f) and § 412.22(h)(3) of subpart.

(8) ***Application of LTCH moratorium on the increase in beds at section 114(d)(1)(B) of Public Law 110-173 to LTCHs and LTCH satellite facilities established or classified as such under section 114(d)(2) of Public Law 110-173.*** Effective for the period beginning October 1, 2011, and ending December 28, 2012, for long-term care hospitals and long-term care hospital satellite facilities established under paragraph (e)(6)(ii) of this section for the period beginning December 29, 2007, and ending September 30, 2011, the moratorium under paragraph (e)(7) of this section applies and the number of Medicare-certified beds must not be increased beyond the number of beds that were certified by Medicare at the long-term care hospital or the long-term care hospital satellite facility as of October 1, 2011.

(f) Cancer hospitals—(1) *General rule.* Except as provided in paragraph (f)(2) of this section, if a hospital meets the following criteria, it is classified as a cancer hospital and is excluded from the prospective payment systems beginning with its first cost reporting period beginning on or after October 1, 1989. A hospital classified after December 19, 1989, is excluded beginning with its first cost reporting period beginning after the date of its classification.

(i) It was recognized as a comprehensive cancer center or clinical cancer research center by the National Cancer Institute of the National Institutes of Health as of April 20, 1983.

(ii) It is classified on or before December 31, 1990, or, if on December 19, 1989, the hospital was located in a State operating a demonstration project under section 1814(b) of the Act, the classification is made on or before December 31, 1991.

(iii) It demonstrates that the entire facility is organized primarily for treatment of and research on cancer (that is, the facility is not a subunit of an acute general hospital or university-based medical center).

(iv) It shows that at least 50 percent of its total discharges have a principal diagnosis that reflects a finding of neoplastic disease. (The principal diagnosis for this purpose is defined as the condition established after study to be chiefly responsible for occasioning the admission of the patient to the hospital. For the purposes of meeting this definition, only discharges with ICD-9-CM principal diagnosis codes of 140 through 239, V58.0, V58.1, V66.1, V66.2, or 990 will be considered to reflect neoplastic disease.)

(2) *Alternative.* A hospital that applied for and was denied, on or before December 31, 1990, classification as a cancer hospital under the criteria set forth in paragraph (f)(1) of this section is classified as a cancer hospital and is excluded from the prospective payment systems beginning with its first cost reporting period beginning on or after January 1, 1991, if it meets the criterion set forth in paragraph (f)(1)(i) of this section and the hospital is—

(i) Licensed for fewer than 50 acute care beds as of August 5, 1997;

(ii) Is located in a State that as of December 19, 1989, was not operating a demonstration project under section 1814(b) of the Act; and

(iii) Demonstrates that, for the 4-year period ending on December 31, 1996, at least 50 percent of its total discharges have a principal diagnosis that reflects a finding of neoplastic disease as defined in paragraph (f)(1)(iv) of this section.

(g) Hospitals outside the 50 States, the District of Columbia, or Puerto Rico. A hospital is excluded from the prospective payment systems if it is not located in one of the fifty States, the District of Columbia, or Puerto Rico.

(h) Hospitals reimbursed under special arrangements. A hospital must be excluded from prospective payment for inpatient hospital services if it is reimbursed under special arrangement as provided in § 412.22(c).

(i) Changes in classification of hospitals. For purposes of exclusions from the prospective payment system, the classification of a hospital is effective for the hospital's entire cost reporting period. Any changes in the classification of a hospital are made only at the start of a cost reporting period.

[50 FR 12741, Mar. 29, 1985]
Editorial Note: For Federal Register Citations affecting § 412.23, see the List of CFR Sections Affected, which appears in the Finding Aids section of the printed volume and at *www.fdsys.gov* (site visited June 7, 2016).
* * *

Subpart C—Conditions for Payment under the Prospective Payment Systems for Inpatient Operating Costs and Inpatient Capital-Related Costs

Sec. 412.42 Limitations on charges to beneficiaries.

(a) Prohibited charges. A hospital may not charge a beneficiary for any services for which payment is made by Medicare, even if the hospital's costs of furnishing services to that beneficiary are greater than the amount the hospital is paid under the prospective payment systems.

(b) Permitted charges—Stay covered. A hospital receiving payment under the prospective payment systems for a covered hospital stay (that is, a stay that includes at least one covered day) may charge the Medicare beneficiary or other person only for the following:

(1) The applicable deductible and coinsurance amounts under §§ 409.82, 409.83, and 409.87 of this chapter.

(2) Noncovered items and services, furnished at any time during a covered stay, unless they are excluded from coverage only on the basis of the following:

(i) The exclusion of custodial care under § 405.310(g) of this chapter (see paragraph (c) of this section for when charges may be made for custodial care).

(ii) The exclusion of medically unnecessary items and services under § 405.310(k) of this chapter (see paragraphs (c) and (d) of this section for when charges may be made for medically unnecessary items and services).

(iii) The exclusion under § 405.310(m) of this chapter of non-physician services furnished to hospital inpatients by other than the hospital or a provider or supplier under arrangements made by the hospital.

(iv) The exclusion of items and services furnished when the patient is not entitled to Medicare Part A benefits under subpart A of part 406 of this chapter (see paragraph (e) of this section for when charges may be made for items and services furnished when the patient is not entitled to benefits).

(v) The exclusion of items and services furnished after Medicare Part A benefits are exhausted under § 409.61 of this chapter (see paragraph (e) of this section for when charges may be made for items and services furnished after benefits are exhausted).

(c) Custodial care and medically unnecessary inpatient hospital care. A hospital may charge a beneficiary for services excluded from coverage on the basis of § 411.15(g) of this chapter (custodial care) or § 411.15(k) of this chapter (medically unnecessary services) and furnished by the hospital after all of the following conditions have been met:

(1) The hospital (acting directly or through its utilization review committee) determines that the beneficiary no longer requires inpatient hospital care. (The phrase "inpatient hospital care" includes cases where a beneficiary needs a SNF level of care, but, under Medicare criteria, a SNF-level bed is not available. This also means that a hospital may find that a patient awaiting SNF placement no longer requires inpatient hospital care because either a SNF-level bed has become available or the patient no longer requires SNF-level care.)

(2) The attending physician agrees with the hospital's determination in writing (for example, by issuing a written discharge order). If the hospital believes that the beneficiary does not require inpatient hospital care but is unable to obtain the agreement of the physician, it may request an immediate review of the case by the QIO as described in § 405.1208 of this chapter. Concurrence by the QIO in the hospital's determination will serve in lieu of the physician's agreement.

(3) The hospital (acting directly or through its utilization review committee) notifies the beneficiary (or his or her representative) of his or her discharge rights in writing consistent with § 405.1205 and notifies the beneficiary, in accordance with § 405.1206 of this chapter (if applicable) that in the hospital's opinion, and with the attending physician's concurrence or that of the QIO, the beneficiary no longer requires inpatient hospital care.

(4) If the beneficiary remains in the hospital after the appropriate notification, and the hospital, the physician who concurred in the hospital determination on which the notice was based, or QIO subsequently finds that the beneficiary requires an acute level of inpatient hospital care, the hospital may not charge the beneficiary for continued care until the hospital once again determines that the

beneficiary no longer requires inpatient care, secures concurrence, and notifies the beneficiary, as required in paragraphs (c)(1), (c)(2), and (c)(3) of this section.

(d) Medically unnecessary diagnostic and therapeutic services. A hospital may charge a beneficiary for diagnostic procedures and studies, and therapeutic procedures and courses of treatment (for example, experimental procedures) that are excluded from coverage under § 411.15(k) of this chapter (medically unnecessary items and services), even though the beneficiary requires continued inpatient hospital care, if those services are furnished after the beneficiary (or the person acting on his or her behalf) has acknowledged in writing that the hospital (acting directly or through its utilization review committee and with the concurrence of the intermediary) has informed him or her as follows:

(1) In the hospital's opinion, which has been agreed to by the intermediary, the services to be furnished are not considered reasonable and necessary under Medicare.

(2) Customary charges will be made if he or she receives the services.

(3) If the beneficiary receives the services, a formal determination on the validity of the hospital's finding is made by the intermediary and, to the extent that the decision requires the exercise of medical judgment, the QIO.

(4) The determination is appealable by the hospital, the attending physician, or the beneficiary under the appeals procedure that applies to determinations affecting Medicare Part A payment.

(5) The charges for the services will be invalid and, to the extent collected, will be refunded by the hospital if the services are found to be covered by Medicare.

(e) Services furnished on days when the individual is not entitled to Medicare Part A benefits or has exhausted the available benefits. The hospital may charge the beneficiary its customary charges for non-covered items and services furnished on outlier days (as described in Subpart F of this part) for which payment is denied because the beneficiary is not entitled to Medicare Part A or his or her Medicare Part A benefits are exhausted. (1) If payment is considered for outlier days, the entire stay is reviewed and days up to the number of days in excess of the outlier threshold may be denied on the basis of non-entitlement to Part A or exhaustion of benefits. (2) In applying this rule, the latest days will be denied first.

(f) Differential for private room or other luxury services. The hospital may charge the beneficiary the customary charge differential for a private room or other luxury service that is more expensive than is medically required and is furnished for the personal comfort of the beneficiary at his or her request (or the request of the person acting on his or her behalf).

(g) Review. (1) The QIO or intermediary may review any cases in which the hospital advises the beneficiary (or the person acting on his or her behalf) of the non-coverage of the services in accordance with paragraph (c)(3) or (d) of this section.

(2) The hospital must identify such cases to the QIO or intermediary in accordance with CMS instructions.

[50 FR 12741, Mar. 29, 1985, as amended at 50 FR 35688, Sept. 3, 1985; 54 FR 41747, Oct. 11, 1989; 57 FR 39821, Sept. 1, 1992; 71 FR 48137, Aug. 18, 2006; 71 FR 68722, Nov. 27, 2006]
***

Subpart D—Basic Methodology for Determining Prospective Payment Federal Rates for Inpatient Operating Costs

Sec. 412.60 DRG classification and weighting factors.

(a) Diagnosis-related groups. CMS establishes a classification of inpatient hospital discharges by Diagnosis-Related Groups (DRGs).

(b) DRG weighting factors. CMS assigns, for each DRG, an appropriate weighting factor that reflects the estimated relative cost of hospital resources used with respect to discharges classified within that group compared to discharges classified within other groups.

(c) Assignment of discharges to DRGs. CMS establishes a methodology for classifying specific hospital discharges within DRGs which ensures that each hospital discharge is appropriately assigned to a single DRG based on essential data abstracted from the inpatient bill for that discharge.

(1) The classification of a particular discharge is based, as appropriate, on the patient's age, sex, principal diagnosis (that is, the diagnosis established after study to be chiefly responsible for causing the patient's admission to the hospital), secondary diagnoses, procedures performed, and discharge status.

(2) Each discharge is assigned to only one DRG (related, except as provided in paragraph (c)(3) of this section, to the patient's principal diagnosis) regardless of the number of conditions treated or services furnished during the patient's stay.

(3) When the discharge data submitted by a hospital show a surgical procedure unrelated to a patient's principal diagnosis, the bill is returned to the hospital for validation and re-verification. CMS's DRG classification system provides a DRG, and an appropriate weighting factor, for the group of cases for which the unrelated diagnosis and procedure are confirmed.

(d) Review of DRG assignment. (1) A hospital has 60 days after the date of the notice of the initial assignment of a discharge to a DRG to request a review of that assignment. The hospital may submit additional information as a part of its request.

(2) The intermediary reviews the hospital's request and any additional information and decides whether a change in the DRG assignment is appropriate. If the intermediary decides that a higher-weighted DRG should be assigned, the case

will be reviewed by the appropriate QIO as specified in Sec. 466.71(c)(2) of this chapter.

(3) Following the 60-day period described in paragraph (d)(1) of this section, the hospital may not submit additional information with respect to the DRG assignment or otherwise revise its claim.

(e) Revision of DRG classification and weighting factors. Beginning with discharges in fiscal year 1988, CMS adjusts the classifications and weighting factors established under paragraphs (a) and (b) of this section at least annually to reflect changes in treatment patterns, technology, and other factors that may change the relative use of hospital resources.

[50 FR 12741, Mar. 29, 1985, as amended at 52 FR 33057, Sept. 1, 1987; 57 FR 39821, Sept. 1, 1992; 59 FR 45397, Sept. 1, 1994]

APPENDIX 2-3 MEDICARE CLAIMS PROCESSING MANUAL

Chapter 30—Financial Liability Protections[377]

200—Expedited Review Process for Hospital Inpatients in Original Medicare
- 200.1—Scope of the Instructions
- 200.2—Special Considerations
- 200.3—Notifying Beneficiaries of their Right to an Expedited Review
  - 200.3.1—Delivery of the Important Message from Medicare
  - 200.3.2—The Follow-Up Copy of the Signed Important Message from Medicare
- 200.4—Rules and Responsibilities when a Beneficiary Requests an Expedited Review
  - 200.4.1—The Role of the Beneficiary and Liability
  - 200.4.2—The Responsibilities of the Hospital
  - 200.4.3—The Role of the QIOs
  - 200.4.4—Effect of a QIO Expedited Determination
- 200.5—General Notice Requirements
  - 200.5.1—Number of Copies
  - 200.5.2—Reproduction
  - 200.5.3—Length and Page Size
  - 200.5.4—Contrast of Paper and Print
  - 200.5.5—Modification
  - 200.5.6—Font
  - 200.5.7—Customization
  - 200.5.8—Retention of the Notices
- 200.6—Completing the Notices
  - 200.6.1—Translated Notices
  - 200.6.2 Exhibit 1—An Important Message from Medicare (CMS-R-193) and Form Instructions
  - 200.6.3 Exhibit 2—The Detailed Notice of Discharge (CMS 10066) and Form Instructions

220—Hospital Requested Expedited Review
- 220.1—Responsibilities of the Hospital
- 220.2—Responsibilities of the QIO

[377] *See* https://www.cms.gov/Regulations-and-Guidance/Guidance/Manuals/Downloads/clm104c30.pdf (site visited June 7, 2016).

200—Expedited Review Process for Hospital Inpatients in Original Medicare (Rev. 1257, Issued: 05-25-07; Effective: 07-01-07; Implementation: 07-02-07)

Medicare beneficiaries who are hospital inpatients have a statutory right to appeal to a QIO for an expedited review when a hospital, with physician concurrence, determines that inpatient care is no longer necessary. The instructions that follow stem directly from regulations at 42 CFR 405.1205 and 405.1206 and are effective July 1, 2007. These regulations are also referenced at 42 CFR 489.27 and 412.42 (c)(3). The authority for these instructions stems from Sections 1866(a)(1)(M), 1869(c)(3)(C)(iii)(III), and 1154(e) of the Social Security Act. Instructions for managed care will be located in Chapter 13 of the Medicare Managed Care Manual.

Hospitals must notify Medicare beneficiaries who are hospital inpatients about their hospital discharge appeal rights. Hospitals will use a revised version of the Important Message from Medicare (IM) a statutorily required notice, to explain the beneficiary's rights as a hospital patient, including discharge appeal rights. Hospitals must issue the IM within 2 calendar days of admission, must obtain the signature of the beneficiary or his or her representative and provide a copy at that time. Hospitals will also deliver a copy of the signed notice as far in advance of discharge as possible, but not more than 2 calendar days before discharge.

For those beneficiaries who request a QIO review, hospitals must deliver a Detailed Notice of Discharge as soon as possible, but no later than noon of the day after the QIO's notification. Both the IM and the Detailed Notice must be the standardized notices provided by CMS.

200.1—Scope of the Instructions (Rev. 1257, Issued: 05-25-07; Effective: 07-01-07; Implementation: 07-02-07)

These instructions implement 42 CFR 405.1205 and 405.1206 which require hospitals to inform Medicare beneficiaries who are hospital inpatients of their right to a QIO review. These instructions delineate the expectations of beneficiaries (or their representative, if applicable), responsibilities of hospitals, and the role of the QIOs when the beneficiary requests an expedited review by a QIO of the discharge decision. For purposes of this instruction, the term "beneficiary" means either beneficiary or representative, when a representative is acting for a beneficiary.

Hospitals Affected by These Instructions. The term hospital is defined in the regulation as any facility providing care at the inpatient hospital level, whether that care is short term or long term, acute or non acute, paid through a prospective payment system or other reimbursement basis, limited to specialty care or providing a broader spectrum of services. This definition includes critical access hospitals. This means all hospitals paid under the Inpatient Acute Prospective Payment System (IPPS), sole community hospitals/regional referrals centers or any other type of hospital receiving special consideration under IPPS (for example, Medicare dependent hospitals, Indian Health Service hospitals); hospitals not under IPPS, including, but not limited to: hospitals paid under State or United States territory waiver programs, hospitals paid under certain demonstration projects cited in regulation (§ 489.34), rehabilitation hospitals, long-term care hospitals, psychiatric hospitals, critical access hospitals, children's hospitals, and cancer hospitals. Swing beds in hospitals are excluded, because they are considered a lower level of care. Religious nonmedical health care institutions are also excluded.

Hospital Inpatients Who Are Medicare Beneficiaries. These instructions apply to beneficiaries in original Medicare who are hospital inpatients. Hospital outpatients who are receiving Part B services, such as those in observation stays or in the emergency department, do not receive these notices, unless they subsequently require inpatient care. Medicare beneficiaries in hospital swing beds or custodial care beds do not receive these notices when they are receiving services at a lower level of care.

Definition of Discharge. The term "discharge" is defined as a formal release of a beneficiary from an inpatient hospital. This includes when the beneficiary is physically discharged from the hospital as well as when the beneficiary is discharged "on paper"—meaning that the beneficiary remains in the hospital, but at a lower level of care (for example, the beneficiary is moved to a swing bed or to custodial care).

200.2—Special Considerations
(Rev. 1257, Issued: 05-25-07; Effective: 07-01-07; Implementation: 07-02-07)

Other Insurers. Section 1866(a)(1)(M), delivery of the Important Message from Medicare, applies to each individual who is entitled to benefits under Medicare Part A. Therefore, these requirements apply if a beneficiary is eligible for both Original Medicare and Medicaid (a dual eligible), is eligible for Original Medicare and another insurance program or payer, or has Medicare as a secondary payer. No matter where in the sequence of payers Medicare falls, these requirements still apply.

Inpatient to Inpatient Transfers. Beneficiaries who are being transferred from one inpatient hospital setting to another inpatient hospital setting, do not need to be provided with the follow-up copy of the notice prior to leaving the original hospital, since this is considered to be the same level of care. Beneficiaries always have the right to refuse care and may contact the QIO if they have a quality of care issue. The receiving hospital must deliver the Important Message from Medicare again according to the procedures in these instructions.

Preadmission/Admissions for Services that are Not Reasonable and Necessary. When a Medicare beneficiary is planning to be hospitalized for services that Medicare usually pays for, but are not considered to be reasonable and necessary in this particular situation, hospitals must deliver a Preadmission/Admission Hospital Issued Notice of Noncoverage (HINN). (See Section 240 of this Chapter.) The Important Message from Medicare would be delivered only if the stay became a covered stay.

Admissions for Services that Medicare Never Covers. When a Medicare beneficiary is admitted for hospital services that are never covered by Medicare, hospitals may deliver the Preadmission/Admission HINN. The IM would be delivered only if the stay became a covered stay.

Change of Status from Inpatient to Outpatient. When a hospital utilization review committee determines that an inpatient admission does not meet the hospital's inpatient criteria, the hospital may change the beneficiary's status from inpatient to outpatient. See CR 3444 (Use of Condition Code 44) and MedLearn Matters article, SE0622, published on March 22, 2006, for notification requirements in this situation.

End of Part A days. For purposes of this instruction, the term discharge does not include exhaustion of Part A days, therefore, when a beneficiary exhausts Part A days, these requirements do not apply.

Hospital Requests QIO Review when the Physician does not Concur. There are separate existing requirements under 405.1208 for notifying a beneficiary when the hospital requests a QIO review. Hospitals should deliver the Notice of a Hospital Requested Review (HRR). (See Section 220 of this chapter.)

200.3—Notifying Beneficiaries of their Right to an Expedited Review
(Rev. 1257, Issued: 05-25-07; Effective: 07-01-07; Implementation: 07-02-07)

Hospitals must notify Medicare beneficiaries who are hospital inpatients about their hospital discharge appeal rights. Hospitals will use a revised version of the Important Message from Medicare (IM) a statutorily-required notice, to explain the beneficiary's rights as a hospital patient, including discharge appeal rights. Hospitals must issue the IM within 2 calendar days of admission, must obtain the signature of the beneficiary or his or her representative and provide a copy at that time. Hospitals will also deliver a copy of the signed notice as far in advance of discharge as possible, but not more than 2 calendar days before discharge.

200.3.1—Delivery of the Important Message from Medicare (Rev. 1257, Issued: 05-25-07; Effective: 07-01-07; Implementation: 07-02-07)

Hospitals must follow the procedures listed below in delivering the Important Message from Medicare (IM). Valid Notice consists of:

Use of Standardized Notice. Hospitals must use the standardized form (CMS-R-193), see Section 200.6.2. The notices are also available on *www.cms.hhs.gov/bni* at the Link for Hospital Discharge Appeal Notices. Hospitals may not deviate from the content of the form except where indicated (see Section 200.6 on Completing the Notice). The OMB control number must be displayed on the notice.

Delivery Timeframe. Hospitals must deliver the original copy of the IM at or near admission, but no later than 2 calendar days following the date of the beneficiary's admission to the hospital.

Hospitals may deliver the initial copy of the notice if the beneficiary is seen during a preadmission visit, but not more than 7 calendar days in advance of admission. If a beneficiary receives and signs the initial copy of the IM as part of the preadmission process, the follow-up copy of the notice must be delivered if delivery of the initial copy occurred more than 2 calendar days prior.

In-Person Delivery. The IM must be delivered to the beneficiary in person. However, if the beneficiary is not able to comprehend the notice, it must be delivered to and signed by the beneficiary's representative.

Notice Delivery to Representatives. CMS requires that notification of a beneficiary who is not competent be made to a representative of the beneficiary. A representative is an individual who, under State or other applicable law, may make health care decisions on a beneficiary's behalf (e.g., the beneficiary's legal guardian, or someone appointed in accordance with a properly executed "durable medical power of attorney").

Otherwise, a person (typically, a family member or close friend) whom the beneficiary has indicated may act for him or her, but who has not been named in any legally binding document may be a representative for purpose of receiving the notices described in this section. Such representatives should have the beneficiary's best interests at heart and must act in a manner that is protective of the beneficiary and the beneficiary's rights. Therefore, a representative should have no relevant conflict of interest with the beneficiary. A notifier (including the notifier's employees) that has a conflicting interest (such as shifting financial liability to the beneficiary) is not qualified to be a representative. (Note: If the beneficiary wishes to appoint a representative to file an appeal on his/her behalf, a valid Form 1696 or a conforming written instrument must be signed by both the beneficiary and the prospective representative and filed with the appeal request. See Medicare Claims Processing Manual, Publication 100-4, Ch. 29, Section 270 for specific instructions related to the use of Form 1696 and the appointment of representatives).

Notification to the representative may be problematic because that person may not be available in person to acknowledge receipt of the required notification. Hospitals are required to develop procedures to use when the beneficiary is incapable of receiving or incompetent to receive the notice, and the hospital cannot obtain the signature of the beneficiary's representative through direct personal contact.

Regardless of the competency of a beneficiary, if the hospital is unable to personally deliver a notice to a representative, then the hospital should telephone the representative to advise him or her of the beneficiary's rights as a hospital patient, including the right to appeal a discharge decision.

The information provided should include the following at a minimum:

- The name and telephone number of a contact at the hospital;
- The beneficiary's planned discharge date, and the date when the beneficiary's liability begins;
- The beneficiary's rights as a hospital patient, including the right to appeal a discharge decision;
- How to get a copy of a detailed notice describing why the hospital and physician believe the beneficiary is ready to be discharged;
- A description of the steps for filing an appeal;
- When (by what time/date) the appeal must be filed to take advantage of the liability protections;
- The entity required to receive the appeal, including any applicable name, address, telephone number, fax number or other method of communication the entity requires in order to receive the appeal in a timely fashion;
- Direction to the 1-800-MEDICARE number for additional assistance to the representative in further explaining and filing the appeal; and

The date the hospital conveys this information to the representative, whether in writing or by telephone, is the date of receipt of the notice. Confirm the telephone contact by written notice mailed on that same date. Place a dated copy of the notice in the beneficiary's medical file, and document the telephone contact with the beneficiary's representative (as listed above) on either the notice itself, or in a separate entry in the beneficiary's file or attachment to the notice. The documentation should indicate that the staff person told the representative the planned discharge date, the date the beneficiary's financial liability begins, the beneficiary's appeal rights, and how and when to initiate an appeal. The documentation should also include the name of the staff person initiating the contact, the name of the representative contacted by phone, the date and time of the telephone contact, and the telephone number called.

When direct phone contact cannot be made, send the notice to the representative by certified mail, return receipt requested, or other delivery method that requires signed verification of delivery. The date that someone at the representative's address signs (or refuses to sign) the receipt is the date received. Place a copy of the notice in the beneficiary's medical file, and document the attempted telephone contact to the members' representative. The documentation should include: the name of the staff person initiating the contact, the name of the representative you attempted to contact, the date and time of the attempted call, and the telephone number called.

If both the hospital and the representative agree, hospitals may send the notice by fax or email, however, hospitals must meet the HIPAA privacy and security requirements.

Ensuring Beneficiary Comprehension. Hospitals must make every effort to ensure the beneficiary comprehends the contents of the notice before obtaining the beneficiary's signature. This includes explaining the notice to the beneficiary if necessary and providing an opportunity for the beneficiary to ask questions. The hospital should answer all the beneficiary's questions orally to the best of its ability. The beneficiary should be able to understand that he or she may appeal a discharge decision without financial risk, but may have to pay for any services received after the discharge date if he or she stays in the hospital and does not appeal. Notices should not be delivered during an emergency, but should be delivered once the beneficiary is stable.

These instructions do not preclude the use of assistive devices, witnesses, or interpreters for notice delivery. Thus, if a beneficiary is able to comprehend the notice, but either is physically unable to sign it or needs the assistance of an interpreter to translate it or an assistive device to read or sign it, valid delivery may be achieved by documenting use of such assistance.

Beneficiary Signature and Date. The IM must be signed and dated by the beneficiary to indicate that he or she has received the notice and can comprehend its contents, unless an appropriate reason for the lack of signature is recorded on the IM, such as a properly annotated signature refusal (see below).

Refusal to Sign and Annotation. If a beneficiary refuses to sign the notice, hospitals may annotate the notice to indicate the refusal, and the date of refusal is considered the date of receipt of the notice. The annotation may be placed in the unused patient signature line, in the "Additional Information" section on page 2 of the notice or another sheet of paper may be attached to the notice, if necessary.

Any insertions on the notice must be easy for the beneficiary to read in order for the notice to be considered valid. See also Section 200.5.6—Insertions in Blanks.

Notice Delivery and Retention. Hospitals must give the original copy of the signed or annotated notice to the patient. Hospitals must retain a copy of the signed notice and may determine the method of storage that works within their existing processes, for example, storing a copy in the medical record or electronically.

200.3.2—The Follow-Up Copy of the Signed Important Message from Medicare
(Rev. 1257, Issued: 05-25-07; Effective: 07-01-07; Implementation: 07-02-07)

A "follow-up" copy of the signed IM must be delivered to the beneficiary using the following guidelines:

Delivery Timeframe. The follow-up copy must be delivered as far in advance of discharge as possible, but no more than 2 calendar days before the planned date of discharge. Thus, when discharge seems likely within 1-2 calendar days, hospitals should make arrangements to deliver the follow-up copy of the notice, so that the beneficiary has a meaningful opportunity to act on it. However, when discharge cannot be predicted in advance, the follow-up copy may be delivered as late as the day of discharge, if necessary. If the follow-up copy of the notice must be delivered on the day of discharge, hospitals must give beneficiaries who need it at least 4 hours to consider their right to request a QIO review. Beneficiaries may choose to leave prior to that time, however, hospitals must not pressure a beneficiary to leave during that time period. If the hospital delivers the follow-up copy, and the beneficiary status subsequently changes, so that the discharge is beyond the 2-day timeframe, hospitals must deliver another copy of the signed notice again within 2 calendar days of the new planned discharge date. Hospitals may not develop procedures for delivery of the follow up copy routinely on the day of discharge.

Alternative to Delivery of the Signed Copy. A hospital may choose to deliver a new copy of the IM (not a copy of the signed IM) during the required timeframes; however, the hospital must obtain the beneficiary's or representative's signature and date on the notice again at that time.

Exception to Delivery of the Follow-Up Copy. If delivery of the original IM is within 2 calendar days of the date of discharge, no follow-up notice is required. For example, if a beneficiary is admitted on Monday, the IM is delivered on Wednesday and the beneficiary is discharged on Friday, no follow-up notice is required.

If a beneficiary receives and signs the initial copy of the IM as part of the preadmission process, the follow-up copy of the notice must be delivered if delivery of the initial copy occurred more than 2 calendar days prior.

Documentation. Hospitals must document timely delivery of the follow-up copy of the IM in the patient records, when applicable. Hospitals are responsible for demonstrating compliance with this requirement. If hospitals have processes in place to document delivery of other information related to discharge that includes a beneficiary signature and date, hospitals may include the follow-up copy of the notice in those documents. If there are no other existing processes in place, hospitals may use the "Additional Information" section of the IM to document delivery of the follow-up copy, for example, by adding a line for the beneficiary's or representative's initials and date.

200.4—Rules and Responsibilities when a Beneficiary Requests an Expedited Review
(Rev. 1257, Issued: 05-25-07; Effective: 07-01-07; Implementation: 07-02-07)

A beneficiary has a right to request an expedited review by the QIO when a hospital (acting directly or through its utilization review committee), with physician concurrence, determines that inpatient care is no longer necessary.

200.4.1—The Role of the Beneficiary and Liability
(Rev. 1257, Issued: 05-25-07; Effective: 07-01-07; Implementation: 07-02-07)

Submitting a Request: A beneficiary who chooses to exercise the right to an expedited review must submit a request to the QIO that has an agreement with the hospital where the beneficiary is an inpatient. In order to be considered timely, the request must be made no later than midnight of the day of discharge, may be in writing or by telephone, and must be before the beneficiary leaves the hospital. The beneficiary, upon request of the QIO, should be available to discuss the case. The beneficiary may, but is not required to, submit written evidence to be considered by the QIO.

Timely Requests: When the beneficiary makes a timely request for a QIO review—that is, requests a review no later than midnight of the day of discharge—the beneficiary is not financially responsible for inpatient hospital services (except applicable coinsurance and deductibles) furnished before noon of the calendar day after the date the beneficiary receives notification of the expedited determination from the QIO. Liability for further inpatient hospital services depends on the QIO decision:

- **Unfavorable determination:** If the QIO notifies the beneficiary that the QIO did not agree with the beneficiary, liability for continued services begins at noon of the day **after** the QIO notifies the beneficiary that the QIO agreed with the hospital's discharge determination, or as otherwise determined by the QIO.

- **Favorable determination:** If the QIO notifies the beneficiary that the QIO agreed with the beneficiary, the beneficiary is not financially responsible for continued care (other than applicable coinsurance and deductibles) until the hospital once again determines that the beneficiary no longer requires inpatient care, secures the concurrence of the physician responsible for the beneficiary's care or the QIO, and notifies the beneficiary with a follow-up copy of the IM.

Untimely Requests: When the beneficiary fails to make a timely request for an expedited review, and remains in the hospital, he or she still may request an expedited review at any time, but the beneficiary may be held responsible for charges incurred after the day of discharge, or as otherwise stated by the QIO. If the QIO finds that the patient should have remained an inpatient, the hospital will refund the beneficiary any funds that were collected. When the beneficiary fails to make a timely request for an expedited review and is no longer an inpatient at the hospital, he or she may still request a QIO review within 30 calendar days of the date of discharge, or at any time for good cause.

200.4.2—The Responsibilities of the Hospital (Rev. 1257, Issued: 05-25-07; Effective: 07-01-07; Implementation: 07-02-07)

Provide the Detailed Notice of Discharge: When a QIO notifies the hospital that a beneficiary has requested an expedited review, the hospital must deliver a Detailed Notice of Discharge (the Detailed Notice) to the beneficiary as soon as possible but not later than noon of the day after the QIO's notification. If a beneficiary requests more detailed information prior to requesting a review, hospitals may deliver the detailed notice in advance of the beneficiary requesting a review.

Use of Standardized Notice. Hospitals must use the standardized form (CMS-10066), see Section 200.6.2. This notice is also available on *www.cms.hhs.gov/bni* at the Link for Hospital Discharge Appeal Notices. Hospitals may not deviate from the content of the form except where indicated (see Section 200.6.2 on Completing the Notice). The OMB control number must be displayed on the notice.

The Detailed Notice must be the standardized notice provided by CMS and contain the following:

- A detailed explanation why services are either no longer reasonable and necessary or are otherwise no longer covered.
- A description of any applicable Medicare coverage rule, instruction, or other Medicare policy, including information about how the beneficiary

may obtain a copy of the Medicare policy. (See instructions for the Detailed Notice of Discharge at Section 200.6.3, Exhibit 2)

- Facts specific to the beneficiary and relevant to the coverage determination that are sufficient to advise the beneficiary of the applicability of the coverage rule or policy to the beneficiary's case.
- Any other information required by CMS.

Hospitals must follow requirements in Section 200.5.6 on Insertions in Blanks and Section 200.6. on Completing the Notices.

Provide Information to the QIO. Upon notification by the QIO of the beneficiary's request for an expedited review, the hospital must supply any and all information that the QIO needs to make the expedited determination, including copies of both the IM and the Detailed Notices. The hospital must furnish this information as soon as possible, but no later than noon of the day after the QIO notifies the hospital of the request. At the discretion of the QIO, the hospital may make the information available by telephone or in writing. A written record of any information not transmitted in writing should be sent as soon as possible. If the hospital fails to provide the needed information, the QIO may make a decision based on evidence at hand or defer the decision until it receives the necessary information. If this delay results in extended coverage of an individual's hospital services, the hospital may be held financially liable for those services, as determined by the QIO.

Burden of Proof. The burden of proof lies with the hospital to demonstrate that discharge is the correct decision, either on the basis of medical necessity or based on other Medicare coverage policies.

Provide the Beneficiary with Documentation if Requested. At the request of the beneficiary, the hospital must furnish the beneficiary with a copy of, or access to, any documentation that it sends to the QIO, including written records of any information provided by telephone. The hospital may charge the beneficiary a reasonable amount to cover the costs of duplicating the documentation and/or delivering it to the beneficiary. The hospital must accommodate the request by no later than the first day after the material is requested.

200.4.3—The Role of the QIOs

QIO Availability. The QIO should have methods in place to accept requests for reviews outside of normal business hours, such as an answering machine message. QIOs will issue decisions within one calendar day after it receives all pertinent information.

Notify the hospital of the beneficiary's request for an expedited review. When the QIO receives the request from the beneficiary, the QIO must notify the hospital of the request immediately, or immediately in the morning if the request is received after the QIO's business hours.

Receive and Examine records. The QIO will examine medical and other records that pertain to the services in dispute.

Determine if the hospital delivered valid notice. The QIO will determine whether the hospital delivered valid notice, meaning that the notice is the standardized notice published by CMS, meets the notice delivery timeframes, and has been signed and dated by the beneficiary. If the QIO determines that the hospital did not deliver valid notice, the QIO will instruct the hospital to reissue the notice if necessary, proceed with the review, and educate the hospital retrospectively. If the beneficiary or representative makes an untimely request for a review, and the QIO determines that the beneficiary did not receive valid notice, the QIO will determine the date the beneficiary becomes fully liable for the services.

Solicit the views of the beneficiary. The QIO must solicit views of the beneficiary who requested the expedited review.

Solicit the views of the hospital. The QIO must provide an opportunity for the hospital to explain why the hospital and physician believe discharge is appropriate. The QIO may develop guidelines as to the form and extent of this opportunity.

If needed information is not received. If the QIO does not receive the information from the hospital needed to sustain the discharge decision, it may make its determination based on the evidence at hand or it may defer a decision until it receives the necessary information. If this delay results in extended Medicare coverage of an individual's hospital services, the hospital may be held financially responsible for these services as determined by the QIO.

QIO Determination. QIOs make their determinations based on criteria in § 1154(a) of the Act, which specifies that QIOs will determine whether:

- the services are reasonable and medically necessary,
- the services meet professionally recognized standards of care, and
- the services could be safely be delivered in another setting.

Notification following a timely request. When the beneficiary makes a timely request for an expedited review, the QIO must make its determination and notify the beneficiary, the hospital, and the physician of its determination within one calendar day after it receives all requested pertinent information. When the QIO issues an expedited determination, the QIO must notify the beneficiary, the hospital and the physician of its decision by telephone, followed by a written notice that must include the following information:

- The basis for the determination.
- A detailed rationale for the determination.
- An explanation of the Medicare payment consequences of the determination and the date a beneficiary becomes fully liable for services.
- Information about the beneficiary's right to an reconsideration of the QIO's determination, including how to request the reconsideration and the timeframe for doing so.

Notification following an untimely request. When the beneficiary makes an untimely request for an expedited review, and remains in the hospital, the QIO will make its determination and notify the beneficiary, the hospital, and the physician of its determination within 2 calendar days after it receives all requested pertinent information. When the beneficiary makes an untimely request for an expedited review, and is no longer an inpatient in the hospital, the QIO will make its determination and notify the beneficiary, the hospital, and the physician of its determination within 30 calendar days after it receives all requested pertinent information.

200.4.4—Effect of a QIO Expedited Determination
(Rev. 1257, Issued: 05-25-07; Effective: 07-01-07; Implementation: 07-02-07)

The QIO determination is binding on the beneficiary, the physician, and hospital except in the following circumstances:

Right to pursue a reconsideration. If the beneficiary is still an inpatient in the hospital and is dissatisfied with the determination, he or she may request a reconsideration according to the procedures described in 405.1204.

Right to pursue the general claims appeal process. If the beneficiary is no longer an inpatient in the hospital and is dissatisfied with this determination, the determination is subject to the general claims appeal process (See Chapter 29 of this manual.).

200.5—General Notice Requirements
(Rev. 1257, Issued: 05-25-07; Effective: 07-01-07; Implementation: 07-02-07)

Since the Important Message from Medicare and the Detailed Notice of Discharge are OMB approved, standardized notices, hospitals must comply with the following General Notice Requirements:

200.5.1—Number of Copies
(Rev. 1257, Issued: 05-25-07; Effective: 07-01-07; Implementation: 07-02-07)

The Important Message from Medicare: In most cases, a minimum of three copies of the Important Message from Medicare, including the original, will be needed. The beneficiary keeps the original signed notice and will receive a follow-up copy of the signed notice, except when delivery of the original notice falls within two days of discharge. The hospital must retain a copy of the signed IM and may do so electronically.

The Detailed Notice: A minimum of two copies of the Detailed Notice, including the original, will be needed. The beneficiary keeps the original notice. The hospital must retain a copy of the signed document and may do so electronically.

Providing Copies to the QIO: In addition to the above, if a beneficiary requests a review, hospitals are required to provide copies of both notice described in this section to the QIO.

200.5.2—Reproduction
(Rev. 1257, Issued: 05-25-07; Effective: 07-01-07; Implementation: 07-02-07)

Hospitals may reproduce the notices by using self-carbonizing paper, photocopying the IM, or using another appropriate method. All reproductions must conform to applicable instructions.

200.5.3—Length and Page Size
(Rev.1587, Issued: 09-05-08, Effective: 03-03-08, Implementation: 03-01-09)

The Important Message from Medicare: The IM must NOT exceed two sides of a page in length. The IM is designed as a letter-sized form. If necessary, it may be expanded to a legal-sized page to accommodate information hospitals insert in the notice.

The Detailed Notice: The Detailed Notice must NOT exceed one side of a page in length. The Detailed Notice is designed as a letter-sized form. If necessary, it may be expanded to a legal-sized page to accommodate information hospitals may insert in the notice. Hospitals may attach applicable Medicare policies to the notice.

200.5.4—Contrast of Paper and Print
(Rev. 1257, Issued: 05-25-07; Effective: 07-01-07; Implementation: 07-02-07)

A visually high-contrast combination of dark ink on a pale background must be used. Do not use reversed print (e.g., white on black), or block-shade (highlight) notice text.

200.5.5—Modification
(Rev. 1257, Issued: 05-25-07; Effective: 07-01-07; Implementation: 07-02-07)

The notices described in this section may not be modified, except as specifically allowed by these instructions. In no case may either notice be condensed.

200.5.6—Font
(Rev. 1257, Issued: 05-25-07; Effective: 07-01-07; Implementation: 07-02-07)

The IM and the Detailed Notice must meet the following font requirements in order to facilitate beneficiary understanding:

- **Font Type:** To the greatest extent practicable, the fonts as they appear in the notices on the CMS website should be used. Any changes in the font type should be based solely on software and/or hardware limitations of the notices. Examples of easily readable alternative fonts include: Arial, Arial Narrow, Times New Roman, and Courier.
- **Font Effect/Style:** Any changes to the font, such as italics, embossing, bold, etc., should not be used since they can make the notices more difficult to read.
- **Font Size:** The font size generally should be 12 point. Titles should be 18 point, but handwritten insertions in blanks of the IM can be as small as 10 point if needed.
- **Insertions in Blanks:** Information inserted by hospitals in the blank spaces on the IM and the Detailed Notice may be typed or legibly handwritten using the guidelines above.

200.5.7—Customization
(Rev. 1257, Issued: 05-25-07; Effective: 07-01-07; Implementation: 07-02-07)

Hospitals are permitted to do some customization of IM or the Detailed Notice such as pre-printing agency-related information to promote efficiency and to ensure clarity for beneficiaries. Guidelines for customization are:

- Maintaining underlines in the blank spaces is not required.
- Information in blanks that is constant can be pre-printed, such as the hospital's name, QIO name and telephone number. Note the TTY phone number also needs to be entered.

200.5.8—Retention of the Notices
(Rev. 1257, Issued: 05-25-07; Effective: 07-01-07; Implementation: 07-02-07)

Hospitals are required to retain copies of the signed notices and may do so either in hardcopy or electronically.

200.6—Completing the Notices
(Rev. 1257, Issued: 05-25-07; Effective: 07-01-07; Implementation: 07-02-07)

When completing the Important Message from Medicare and the Detailed Notice of Discharge, hospitals must utilize the following instructions:

200.6.1—Translated Notices
(Rev. 1257, Issued: 05-25-07; Effective: 07-01-07; Implementation: 07-02-07)

Both the "Important Message from Medicare" and the "Detailed Notice of Discharge" are available at http://www.cms.hhs.gov/BNI/ [site visited July 28, 2016]. The notices will be available in English and Spanish, and in PDF and Word formats, under a dedicated link on the left hand margin: "Hospital Discharge Appeal Notices." Hospitals should choose the appropriate version of the Important Message from Medicare and the Detailed Notice of Discharge based on the language the beneficiary best understands. When Spanish-language notices are used, the hospital should make insertions on the notice in Spanish. If this is impossible, additional steps need to be taken to ensure that the beneficiary comprehends the content of the notice.

200.6.2—Exhibit 1—An Important Message from Medicare (CMS-R-193) and Form Instructions
(Rev. 1257, Issued: 05-25-07; Effective: 07-01-07; Implementation: 07-02-07)

Patient Name: DEPARTMENT OF HEALTH & HUMAN SERVICES
Patient ID Number: Centers for Medicare & Medicaid Services
Physician: OMB Approval No. 0938-0692

AN IMPORTANT MESSAGE FROM MEDICARE ABOUT YOUR RIGHTS

AS A HOSPITAL INPATIENT, YOU HAVE THE RIGHT TO:

- Receive Medicare covered services. This includes medically necessary hospital services and services you may need after you are discharged, if ordered by your doctor. You have a right to know about these services, who will pay for them, and where you can get them.
- Be involved in any decisions about your hospital stay, and know who will pay for it.
- Report any concerns you have about the quality of care you receive to the Quality Improvement Organization (QIO) listed here {Insert Name and Telephone Number of the QIO}. [For the QIO Directory, see http://www.qualitynet.org/dcs/ContentServer?cid=1228774346765&pagename=QnetPublic%2FPage%2FQnetTier4&c=Page (site visited June July 28, 2016).]

YOUR MEDICARE DISCHARGE RIGHTS

Planning For Your Discharge: During your hospital stay, the hospital staff will be working with you to prepare for your safe discharge and arrange for services you may need after you leave the hospital. When you no longer need inpatient hospital care, your doctor or the hospital staff will inform you of your planned discharge date.

If you think you are being discharged too soon:

- You can talk to the hospital staff, your doctor and your managed care plan (if you belong to one) about your concerns.
- You also have the right to an appeal, that is, a review of your case by a Quality Improvement Organization (QIO). The QIO is an outside reviewer hired by Medicare to look at your case to decide whether you are ready to leave the hospital.

- **If you want to appeal, you must contact the QIO no later than your planned discharge date and before you leave the hospital.**
  - If you do this, you will not have to pay for the services you receive during the appeal (except for charges like copays and deductibles).
- If you do not appeal, but decide to stay in the hospital past your planned discharge date, you may have to pay for any services you receive after that date.
- **Step by step instructions for calling the QIO and filing an appeal are on page 2.**

To speak with someone at the hospital about this notice, call

____

Please sign and date here to show you received this notice and understand your rights.

______________________________ ______________

Signature of Patient or Representative Date

CMS-R-193 (approved 05/2007)

STEPS TO APPEAL YOUR DISCHARGE

- **STEP 1**: You must contact the QIO no later than your planned discharge date and before you leave the hospital. If you do this, you will not have to pay for the services you receive during the appeal (except for charges like copays and deductibles).
    - Here is the contact information for the QIO:
    - **{insert name of QIO in bold}**
    - **{insert telephone number of QIO}**
    - You can file a request for an appeal any day of the week. **Once you speak to someone or leave a message, your appeal has begun.**
    - Ask the hospital if you need help contacting the QIO.
    - The name of this hospital is __________ {insert the name of the hospital and the provider ID number} __________.
- **STEP 2**: You will receive a detailed notice from the hospital or your Medicare Advantage or other Medicare managed care plan (if you belong to one) that explains the reasons they think you are ready to be discharged.
- **STEP 3**: The QIO will ask for your opinion. You or your representative need to be available to speak with the QIO, if requested. You or your representative may give the QIO a written statement, but you are not required to do so.
- **STEP 4**: The QIO will review your medical records and other important information about your case.
- **STEP 5**: The QIO will notify you of its decision within **1 day after** it receives all necessary information.
    - If the QIO finds that you are not ready to be discharged, Medicare will continue to cover your hospital services.
    - If the QIO finds you are ready to be discharged, Medicare will continue to cover your services until noon of the day **after** the QIO notifies you of its decision.

IF YOU MISS THE DEADLINE TO APPEAL, YOU HAVE OTHER APPEAL RIGHTS:

- You can still ask the QIO or your plan (if you belong to one) for a review of your case:
    - If you have Original Medicare: Call the QIO listed above.

- If you belong to a Medicare Advantage Plan or other Medicare managed care plan: Call your plan.
- If you stay in the hospital, the hospital may charge you for any services you receive after your planned discharge date.

For more information, call 1-800-MEDICARE (1-800-633-4227), or TTY: 1-877-486-2048.

Additional Information:

According to the Paperwork Reduction Act of 1995, no persons are required to respond to a collection of information unless it displays a valid OMB control number. The valid OMB control number for this information collection is 0938-0692. The time required to complete this information collection is estimated to average 15 minutes per response, including the time to review instructions, search existing data resources, gather the data needed, and complete and review the information collection. If you have comments concerning the accuracy of the time estimate(s) or suggestions for improving this form, please write to: CMS, 7500 Security Boulevard, Attn: PRA Reports Clearance Officer, Mail Stop C4-26-05, Baltimore, Maryland 21244-1850.

Notice Instructions

The Important Message from Medicare (OMB #0938-0692) (CMS-R-193)

Completing the Notice

PAGE 1 of the Important Message from Medicare

A. Header

Hospitals must display "DEPARTMENT OF HEALTH & HUMAN SERVICES, Centers for Medicare & Medicaid Services" and the OMB number.

The following blanks must be completed by the hospital. Information inserted by hospitals in the blank spaces on the IM may be typed or legibly handwritten in 12-point font or the equivalent. Hospitals may also use a patient label that includes the following information:

Patient Name: Fill in the patient's full name.

Patient ID number: Fill in an ID number that identifies this patient. This number should not be, nor should it contain, the social security number.

Physician: Fill in the name of the patient's physician.

B. Body of the Notice

Bullet # 3 Report any concerns you have about the quality of care you receive to the Quality Improvement Organization (QIO) listed here __________. Hospitals may preprint or otherwise insert the name and telephone number (including TTY) of the QIO.

To speak with someone at the hospital about this notice call: Fill in a telephone number at the hospital for the patient or representative to call with questions about the notice. Preferably, a contact name should also be included.

Patient or Representative Signature: Have the patient or representative sign the notice to indicate that he or she has received it and understands its contents.

Date: Have the patient or representative place the date he or she signed the notice.

PAGE 2 of the Important Message from Medicare

First sub-bullet—Insert name and telephone number of QIO in BOLD: Insert name and telephone number (including TTY), in bold, of the Quality Improvement Organization that performs reviews for the hospital.

Second sub-bullet—The name of this hospital is: Insert/preprint the name of the hospital, including the Medicare provider ID number (not the telephone number).

Additional Information: Hospitals may use this section for additional documentation, including, for example, obtaining beneficiary initials to document delivery of the follow-up copy of the IM, or documentation of refusals.

200.6.3—Exhibit 2—The Detailed Notice of Discharge (CMS 10066) and Form Instructions
(Rev. 1257, Issued: 05-25-07; Effective: 07-01-07; Implementation: 07-02-07)

Patient Name: OMB Approval No. 0938-1019
Patient ID Number: Date Issued:
Physician:

{Insert Hospital or Plan Logo here}
DETAILED NOTICE OF DISCHARGE

You have asked for a review by the Quality Improvement Organization (QIO), an independent reviewer hired by Medicare to review your case. This notice gives you a detailed explanation about why your hospital and your managed care plan (if you belong to one), in agreement with your doctor, believe that your inpatient hospital services should end on ___________. This is based on Medicare coverage policies listed below and your medical condition.

This is not an official Medicare decision. The decision on your appeal will come from your Quality Improvement Organization (QIO).

- Medicare Coverage Policies:
  ___________ Medicare does not cover inpatient hospital services that are not medically necessary or could be safely furnished in another setting. (Refer to 42 Code of Federal Regulations, 411.15 (g) and (k)).
  ___________ Medicare Managed Care policies, if applicable: (insert specific managed care policies)
  ___________ Other ___________ {insert other applicable policies} ___________
- Specific information about your current medical condition:
- If you would like a copy of the documents sent to the QIO, or copies of the specific policies or criteria used to make this decision, please call {insert hospital and/or plan telephone number}.

According to the Paperwork Reduction Act of 1995, no persons are required to respond to a collection of information unless it displays a valid OMB control number. The valid OMB control number for this information collection is 0938-1019. The time required to complete this information collection is estimated to average 60 minutes per response, including the time to review instructions, search existing data resources, gather the data needed, and complete and review the information collection. If you have comments concerning the accuracy of the time estimate(s) or suggestions for improving this form, please write to: CMS, 7500 Security Boulevard, Attn: PRA Reports Clearance Officer, Mail Stop C4-26-05, Baltimore, Maryland 21244-1850.

CMS 10066 (approved 5/2007)

Instructions for Completing the Detailed Notice of Discharge (CMS 10066)

This is a standardized notice. Hospitals may not deviate from the content of the form except where indicated. Please note that the OMB control number must be displayed on the notice. Insertions must be typed or legibly hand-written in 12-point font or the equivalent.

Hospitals or plans may modify the following sections to incorporate use of a sticker or label that includes this information:

Patient Name: Fill in the patient's full name.

Patient ID number: Fill in the patient's ID number. This should not be, nor should it contain, the patient's social security or HICN number.

Physician: Fill in the name of the patient's physician.

Date Issued: Fill in the date the notice is delivered to the patient by the hospital/plan.

Insert logo here: Hospitals/plans may elect to place their logo in this space. However, the name, address, and telephone number of the hospital/plan must be immediately under the logo, if not incorporated into the logo. If no logo is used, the name and address and telephone number (including TTY) of the hospital/plan must appear above the title of the form.

BLANK 1: **This notice gives you a detailed explanation of why your hospital and your managed care plan (if you belong to one), in agreement with your doctor, believe that your inpatient hospital services should end on ___________ .** In the space provided, fill in planned date of discharge.

Bullet # 1: **Medicare Coverage Policies:** Place a check next to the applicable Medicare and/or managed care policies. If necessary, hospitals may also use the selection "Other" to list other applicable policies, guidelines or instructions. Hospitals or plans may also preprint frequently used coverage policies or add more space below this line, if necessary. Policies should be written in full sentences and in plain language. In addition, the hospital or plan may attach additional pages or specific policies or discharge criteria to the notice. Any attachments must be included with the copy sent to the QIO as well.

Bullet # 2: **Specific information about your current medical condition"** Fill in detailed and specific information about the patient's current medical condition and the reasons why services are no longer reasonable or necessary for this patient or are no longer covered according to Medicare or Medicare managed care coverage guidelines. Use full sentences and plain language.

Bullet # 3: **If you would like a copy of the documents sent to the QIO, or copies of the specific policies or criteria used to make this decision, please call ___________ .** The hospital/plan should also supply a telephone number for patients to call to get a copy of the relevant documents sent to the QIO. If the hospital/plan has not attached the Medicare policies and/or the Medicare managed care plan policies used to decide the discharge date, the hospital should supply a telephone number for patients to call to obtain copies of this information.

Hospitals or plans may add space below this section to insert a signature line and date, if they so choose.

220—Hospital Requested Expedited Review
(Rev. 1257, Issued: 05-25-07; Effective: 07-01-07; Implementation: 07-02-07)

When a hospital determines that a beneficiary no longer needs inpatient care, but is unable to obtain the agreement of the physician, the hospital may request a QIO review. Hospitals must notify the beneficiary that the review has been requested. These instructions stem directly from Section 1154(e) of the Act and 42 CFR Part 405.1208.

220.1—Responsibilities of the Hospital
(Rev. 1257, Issued: 05-25-07; Effective: 07-01-07; Implementation: 07-02-07)

The hospital must comply with the following procedures when requesting a QIO review:

Notify the Beneficiary. Hospitals must notify the beneficiary that the hospital has requested a review using a model language notice called the Hospital Requested Review (HRR) described in this section. See Section 220.4 for General Notice Requirements.

Supply information to the QIO. Hospitals must supply any pertinent information the QIO needs to conduct its review and must make it available by phone or in writing, by close of business on the first full day immediately following the day the hospital submits the request for review.

220.2—Responsibilities of the QIO
(Rev. 1257, Issued: 05-25-07; Effective: 07-01-07; Implementation: 07-02-07)

The QIO's responsibilities are as follows:

Receive request and examine records. The QIO must notify the hospital that it has received the request for review and must notify the hospital if it has not received pertinent records, examine the pertinent records pertaining to the services, and solicit the views of the beneficiary.

Issue a determination. QIOs make their determinations based on criteria in § 1154(a) of the Act, which specifies that QIOs will determine whether:

- the services are reasonable and medically necessary,
- the services meet professionally recognized standards of care, and
- the services could be safely be delivered in another setting.

The QIO will make a determination and notify the beneficiary, the hospital, and the physician of its decision within 2 days of the hospital's request and receipt of any pertinent information submitted by the hospital.

Notification. When the QIO issues the determination, it must notify the beneficiary, the hospital, and the physician of its decision by telephone and subsequently in writing. The written notice of the expedited initial determination must contain the following:

- The basis for the determination;
- A detailed rationale for the determination;
- A statement explaining the Medicare payment consequences of the expedited determination and the date of liability if any; and
- A statement informing the beneficiary of his or her appeal rights and the timeframe for requesting an appeal.

220.3—Effect of the Hospital Requested Expedited Determination (Rev. 1257, Issued: 05-25-07; Effective: 07-01-07; Implementation: 07-02-07)

The expedited determination is binding on the beneficiary, physician, and hospital, except in the following circumstances:

When the beneficiary remains in the hospital. When the beneficiary is still an inpatient in the hospital and is dissatisfied with this determination, he or she may request a reconsideration according to the procedures described in Section 300 of this Chapter.

When the beneficiary is no longer an inpatient in the hospital. If the beneficiary is no longer an inpatient in the hospital and is dissatisfied with this determination, this determination is subject to the general claims appeal process (See Chapter 29 of this manual).

220.4—General Notice Requirements (Rev. 1257, Issued: 05-25-07; Effective: 07-01-07; Implementation: 07-02-07)

Providers should use the HRR to notify a beneficiary that it has requested a QIO review. This notice can be found at *www.cms.hhs.gov/bni.* Since the HRR uses model language, providers have some flexibility in the preparation of this notice. However, it is highly recommended that hospitals use the model language provided in this instruction, or by their QIO, in order to avoid questions of invalid notice. Providers should utilize the General Notice Requirements in Section 200.5 and the Translation requirements in Section 200.6.1 when preparing the notice.

220.5—Exhibit 3—Model Language for Notice of Hospital Requested Review (Rev. 1257, Issued: 05-25-07; Effective: 07-01-07; Implementation: 07-02-07)

Hospital Identifier

Model Notice of Hospital Requested Review (HRR)

Name of Patient: ___________ Name of Physician: ___________
Patient ID Number: ___________ Date Issued: ___________

We believe that Medicare will not continue to cover your hospital care because these services are no longer considered medically necessary in your case. Because your doctor disagreed with our finding, the hospital is asking the quality improvement organization (QIO) to review your case. The QIO is an outside reviewer hired by Medicare to look at your case to decide if you are ready to leave the hospital. The name of the QIO is ___________ **(insert the name of the QIO)** ___________.

- The QIO will contact you to solicit your views about your case and the care you need.
- You do not need to take any action until you hear from the QIO.

For more information about this notice, call 1-800-MEDICARE (1-800-633-4227), or TTY: 1-877-486-2048.

Please sign your name, the date and time. Your signature does not mean that you agree with this notice, just that you received the notice and understand it.

______________________ ___________ ___________

Signature of Patient or Representative Date Time

240—Preadmission/Admission Hospital Issued Notice of Noncoverage (HINN)
(Rev. 1257, Issued: 05-25-07; Effective: 07-01-07; Implementation: 07-02-07)

Regulations found at 42 CFR Part 476.71 require QIOs to review the medical necessity of hospital discharges **and admissions**, in addition to other requirements specified in that section of the regulation. Therefore, a beneficiary has a right to request an expedited review by the QIO when a hospital (acting directly or through its utilization review committee) has determined at the time of preadmission or admission, that the beneficiary is facing a non-covered hospital stay because the services are not considered to be reasonable and necessary in this case, the services could be safely provided in another setting, or the care is considered custodial in nature.

The utilization review committee or the hospital may issue a preadmission/admission HINN. QIOs may also issue such notices after having been contacted by a hospital regarding care believed to be medically unnecessary, inappropriate, or custodial. The hospital need not obtain the attending physician's concurrence, or the QIO's, prior to issuing the preadmission/admission HINN. This also applies to direct admissions to swing beds (i.e., the beneficiary is admitted to the swing bed when the hospital determines that the beneficiary does not need hospital-level care, but instead needs only skilled nursing (SNF) or custodial nursing (NF) level services).

240.1—Delivery of the Preadmission/Admission HINN
(Rev. 1257, Issued: 05-25-07; Effective: 07-01-07; Implementation: 07-02-07)

When delivering the Preadmission/Admission HINN, hospitals must follow the notice delivery requirements in Section 200.3.1 regarding:

- In-Person Delivery,
- Notice Delivery to Representatives,
- Ensuring Beneficiary Comprehension.
- Beneficiary Signature and Date.
- Refusal to Sign.
- Notice Delivery and Retention.

240.2—Notice Delivery Timeframes and Liability
(Rev. 1257, Issued: 05-25-07; Effective: 07-01-07; Implementation: 07-02-07)

Preadmission: In preadmission situations, the beneficiary is liable, if admitted, for customary charges for all services furnished during the stay, except for those services for which he or she is eligible to receive payment under Part B.

Admission: If the admission notice is issued at 3 p.m. or earlier on the day of admission, the beneficiary is liable for customary charges for all services furnished after receipt of the notice, except for those services for which the beneficiary is eligible to receive payment under Part B.

If the admission notice is issued after 3 p.m. on the day of admission, the beneficiary is liable for customary charges for all services furnished on the day following the day of receipt of the notice, except for those services for which the beneficiary is eligible to receive payment under Part B.

240.3—Timeframes for Submitting a Request for a QIO Review
(Rev. 1257, Issued: 05-25-07; Effective: 07-01-07; Implementation: 07-02-07)

Preadmission: In preadmission situations, a beneficiary who chooses to exercise the right to a QIO review should request immediately, but no later than 3 calendar days after receipt of the notice, or if admitted, at any point during the stay, an immediate review of the facts related to the admission.

Admission: In admission situations, a beneficiary who chooses to exercise the right to a QIO review should request immediately, or at any point in the stay, an immediate review of the facts related to the admission.

240.4—Results of the QIO Review
(Rev. 1257, Issued: 05-25-07; Effective: 07-01-07; Implementation: 07-02-07)

If the QIO disagrees with the hospital's determination and says the stay is reasonable and necessary, the beneficiary will be refunded any amount collected except applicable coinsurance and deductibles, and convenience items or services not covered by Medicare.

If the QIO agrees with the hospital determination and says the stay is not reasonable and necessary, the beneficiary will be responsible for all services on the date specified by the QIO.

240.5—Effect of the QIO Review
(Rev. 1257, Issued: 05-25-07; Effective: 07-01-07; Implementation: 07-02-07)

The QIO will send the beneficiary a formal determination of the medical necessity and appropriateness of the hospitalization determination is binding on the beneficiary, the physician, and hospital except in the following circumstances:

Right to pursue a reconsideration. If the beneficiary is still an inpatient in the hospital and is dissatisfied with the determination, he or she may request a reconsideration according to the procedures described in § 405.1204 (See Section 300 of this chapter.)

Right to pursue the general claims appeal process. If the beneficiary is no longer an inpatient in the hospital, the determination is subject to the general claims appeal process (See Chapter 29 of this manual.)

240.6—Exhibit 4—Model Language for Preadmission/Admission Hospital Issued Notice of Noncoverage
(Rev. 1257, Issued: 05-25-07; Effective: 07-01-07; Implementation: 07-02-07)

Hospital Identifier
Preadmission or Admission Hospital-Issued Notice of Noncoverage (HINN)
Model Language

Name of Patient: ___________ Name of the Physician:___________
Patient ID Number: ___________ Date Issued: ___________

We believe that Medicare is not likely to pay for your admission for ___________ (specify service or condition) ___________ because:

___________ it is not considered to be medically necessary
___________ it could be furnished safely in another setting
___________ other ______________________________.

However, this notice is not an official Medicare decision.

If you disagree with our finding:

- You should talk to your doctor about this notice and any further health care you may need.
- You also have the right to an appeal, that is, an immediate review of your case by a Quality Improvement Organization (QIO). The QIO is an outside reviewer hired by Medicare to make a formal decision about whether your admission is covered by Medicare. **See page 2 for instructions on how to request a review and contact the QIO.**
- If you decide to go ahead with the hospitalization, you will have to pay for it. ______________________________[378]

CONTINUED ON PAGE 2

---

[378] *For preadmission notices, insert:* "customary charges for all services furnished during the stay, except for those services for which you are eligible under Part B."

For admission notices issued not later than 3:00 P.M. on the date of admission, insert: "customary charges for all services furnished after receipt of this hospital notice, except for those services for which you are eligible under Part B." *(If these requirements are not met, insert the liability phrase below.)*

For admission notices issued after 3:00 P.M. on the day of admission, insert: "customary charges for all services furnished on the day following the day of receipt of this notice, except for those services for which you are eligible to receive payment under Part B."

If you want an immediate review of your case:

__________ (insert one of the following as appropriate) __________

Preadmission:

- Call the QIO immediately at the number listed below, but no later than 3 calendar days after you receive this notice. If you are admitted, you may call the QIO at any point in the stay.

Admission:

- Call the QIO immediately at the number listed below or you may call the QIO at any point during your stay.
- You may also call the QIO for quality of care issues.

QIO Contact Information: _______ (insert name of QIO in bold) _______

_______ (insert telephone number of QIO) _______

If you do not want an immediate review:

- You may still request a review within 30 calendar days from the date of receipt of this notice by calling the QIO at the number below.

Results of the QIO Review:

- The QIO will send you a formal decision about whether your hospitalization is appropriate according to Medicare's rules, and will tell you about your reconsideration and appeal rights.
    - IF THE QIO FINDS YOUR HOSPITAL CARE IS COVERED, you will be refunded any money you may have paid the hospital except for any applicable copays, deductibles, and convenience items or services normally not covered by Medicare.
    - IF THE QIO FINDS THAT YOUR HOSPITAL CARE IS NOT COVERED, you are responsible for payment for all services beginning on (specify date). (see footnote 1 on page 1).

For more information, call 1-800-MEDICARE (1-800-633-4227), or TTY: 1-877-486-2048.

Please sign your name, the date and time. Your signature does not mean that you agree with this notice, just that you received the notice and understand it.

________________	________	________
Signature of Patient or Representative	Date	Time

260—Expedited Determination Process for Provider Services Terminations (Rev. 2711, Issued: 05-24-13; Effective: 08-26-13; Implementation: 08-26-13)

260.1—Statutory Authority
(Rev. 2711, Issued: 05-24-13; Effective: 08-26-13; Implementation: 08-26-13)

Section 1869(b)(1)(F) of the Social Security Act (the Act), as amended by section 521 of the Medicare, Medicaid, and SCHIP Benefits Improvement and Protection Act of 2000 (BIPA) (Pub. L. 106-554) granted beneficiaries in Original Medicare the right to an expedited determination process to dispute the end of their Medicare covered care in certain provider settings.

This process was implemented through a final rule with comment period, CMS-4004-FC (69 FR 69252, November 26, 2004), effective July 1, 2005. The resulting regulations are located at 42 CFR Part 405, §§ 405.1200-405.1204. There is a parallel process for beneficiaries enrolled in Medicare health plans (See §§ 90.2-90.8 in Chapter 13 of the Medicare Managed Care Manual (CMS Pub. 100-16).)

260.2—Scope
(Rev. 2711, Issued: 05-24-13; Effective: 08-26-13; Implementation: 08-26-13)

The expedited determination process is available to beneficiaries in Original Medicare whose covered services are being terminated in the following settings. All beneficiaries receiving services in these settings must receive a Notice of Medicare Non-Coverage (NOMNC) before their services end: For purposes of this instruction, the term "Beneficiary" means either beneficiary or representative, when a representative is acting for a beneficiary.

- Home Health Agencies (HHAs)
- Comprehensive Outpatient Rehabilitation Services (CORFs)
- Hospice
- Skilled Nursing Facilities (SNFs—Includes services covered under a Part A stay, as well as Part B services provided under consolidated billing (i.e., physical therapy, occupational therapy, and speech therapy). A NOMNC must be delivered by the SNF at the end of a Part A stay or when all of Part B therapies are ending. For example, a beneficiary exhausts the SNF Part A 100-day benefit, but remains in the facility under a private pay stay and receives physical and occupational therapy covered under Medicare Part B. A NOMNC must be delivered by the SNF when both Part B therapies are ending.

Skilling Nursing Facilities includes beneficiaries receiving Part A and B services in Swing Beds.

260.2.1—Exceptions
(Rev. 2711, Issued: 05-24-13; Effective: 08-26-13; Implementation: 08-26-13)

The following service terminations, reductions, or changes in care are not eligible for an expedited review. Providers should not deliver a NOMNC in these instances.

When services are being reduced (e.g., an HHA providing physical therapy and occupational therapy discontinues the occupational therapy).

When beneficiaries are moving to a higher level of care (e.g., home health care ends because a beneficiary is admitted to a SNF).

When beneficiaries exhaust their benefits (e.g., a beneficiary reaches 100 days of coverage in a SNF, thus exhausting their Medicare Part A SNF benefit).

When beneficiaries end care on their own initiative (e.g., a beneficiary decides to revoke the hospice benefit and return to standard Medicare coverage).

When a beneficiary transfers to another provider at the same level of care (e.g., a beneficiary transfers from one SNF to another while remaining in a Medicare-covered SNF stay).

When a provider discontinues care for business reasons (e.g., an HHA refuses to continue care at a home with a dangerous animal or because the beneficiary was receiving physical therapy and the provider's physical therapist leaves the HHA for another job).

260.3—Notice of Medicare Non-Coverage
(Rev. 2711, Issued: 05-24-13; Effective: 08-26-13; Implementation: 08-26-13)

The notice is subject to the Paperwork Reduction Act Process and approval by the Office for Management and Budget. OMB-approved notices may only be modified as per their accompanying instructions. Unapproved modifications may invalidate the NOMNC. The notice and accompanying instructions may be found online at *http://www.cms.gov/Medicare/Medicare-General-Information/BNI* [site visited Sept. 18, 2016]

260.3.1—Alterations to the NOMNC

(Rev. 2711, Issued: 05-24-13; Effective: 08-26-13; Implementation: 08-26-13)

The NOMNC must remain two pages. The notice can be two sides of one page or one side of two separate pages, but must not be condensed to one page.

Providers may include their business logo and contact information on the top of the NOMNC. Text may not be shifted from page 1 to page 2 to accommodate large logos, address headers, etc.

Providers may include information in the optional "Additional information" section relevant to the beneficiary's situation.

Note: Including information normally included in the Detailed Explanation of Non-Coverage (DENC) in the "Additional information" section does not satisfy a provider's responsibility to deliver the DENC, if otherwise required.

260.3.2—Completing the NOMNC
(Rev. 2711, Issued: 05-24-13; Effective: 08-26-13; Implementation: 08-26-13)

Providers must use the OMB-approved NOMNC (CMS-10123). Providers must type or write the following information in the corresponding blanks of the NOMNC:

- Patient name
- Medicare patient number
- Type of coverage (SNF, Home Health, CORF, or Hospice)
- Effective date (last day of coverage)

Note: The effective date is always the last day beneficiaries will receive coverage for their services. Beneficiaries have no liability for services received on this date, but may face charges for services received the day following the effective date of the NOMNC for home health, hospice, and CORF services. Because SNFs cannot bill the beneficiary for services furnished on the day of (but before the actual moment of) discharge, beneficiaries may leave a SNF the day after the effective date and not face liability for such services.

260.3.3—Provider Delivery of the NOMNC
(Rev. 2711, Issued: 05-24-13; Effective: 08-26-13; Implementation: 08-26-13)

Providers must deliver the NOMNC to all beneficiaries eligible for the expedited determination process per § 260.2. A NOMNC must be delivered even if the beneficiary agrees with the termination of services.

Medicare providers are responsible for the delivery of the NOMNC. Providers may formally delegate the delivery of the notices to a designated agent such as a courier service; however, all of the requirements of valid notice delivery apply to designated agents.

The provider must ensure that the beneficiary or representative signs and dates the NOMNC to demonstrate that the beneficiary or representative received the notice and understands that the termination decision can be disputed Use of assistive devices may be used to obtain a signature. Electronic issuance of NOMNCs is not prohibited. If a provider elects to issue a NOMNC that is viewed on an electronic screen before signing, the beneficiary must be given the option of requesting paper issuance over electronic if that is what is preferred. Regardless of whether a paper or electronic version is issued and regardless of whether the signature is digitally capture or manually penned, the beneficiary must be given a paper copy of the NOMNC, with the required beneficiary-specific information inserted, at the time of notice delivery.

260.3.4—Required Delivery Timeframes
(Rev. 2711, Issued: 05-24-13; Effective: 08-26-13; Implementation: 08-26-13)

The NOMNC should be delivered to the beneficiary at least two calendar days before Medicare covered services end or the second to last day of service if care is not being provided daily. For example, if the last day of covered SNF care is a Friday, the NOMNC should be delivered no later than the preceding Wednesday.

Note: The two day advance requirement is NOT a 48 hour requirement. For example, if a patient's last covered home health service is at 10AM on Wednesday and the notice is delivered at 4PM on the prior Monday, it is considered timely.

If home health services are being provided less frequently than daily, the notice must be delivered no later than the next to last visit before Medicare covered services end. For example, if home health care is provided on Tuesdays and Thursdays, and Tuesday is the last day of Medicare services, the notice must be delivered no later than the preceding Thursday.

The NOMNC may be delivered earlier than two days preceding the end of covered services. However, delivery of the notice should be closely tied to the impending end of coverage so a beneficiary will more likely understand and retain the information regarding the right to an expedited determination.

The notice may not be routinely given at the time services begin. An exception is when the services are expected to last fewer than two days. In these instances, the notice may be given by the provider when services begin.

There is an accepted circumstance when the NOMNC may be delivered sooner than two days or the next to last visit before coverage ends. This exception is limited to cases where a beneficiary receiving home health services is found to be no longer be homebound, and thus ineligible for covered home health care. In this circumstance, the NOMNC should be immediately delivered to the beneficiary upon discovery of the loss of homebound status. We expect that in the vast majority of cases, in all settings, the decision of a physician to end care will be based on medical necessity, and thus, foreseeable by the provider within the required time frames for notice delivery.

260.3.5—Refusal to Sign the NOMNC
(Rev. 2711, Issued: 05-24-13; Effective: 08-26-13; Implementation: 08-26-13)

If the beneficiary refuses to sign the NOMNC, the provider should annotate the notice to that effect, and indicate the date of refusal on the notice. The date of refusal is considered to be the date of notice receipt. Beneficiaries who refuse to sign the NOMNC remain entitled to an expedited determination.

260.3.6—Financial Liability for Failure to Deliver a Valid NOMNC (Rev. 2711, Issued: 05-24-13; Effective: 08-26-13; Implementation: 08-26-13)

If a Qualified Independent Contractor (QIO) determines that a provider did not deliver a valid NOMNC to a beneficiary, the provider is financially liable for continued services until two days after the beneficiary receives valid notice, or until the effective date of the valid notice, whichever is later.

260.3.7—Amending the Date of the NOMNC (Rev. 2711, Issued: 05-24-13; Effective: 08-26-13; Implementation: 08-26-13)

If the initial NOMNC was delivered to a beneficiary and the effective date was changed, the provider may amend the notice to reflect the new date. The newer effective date may not be earlier than the effective date of the original notice except in those cases involving the abrupt end of services, as discussed in § 260.3.4.

The beneficiary must be verbally notified as soon as possible after the provider is aware of the change. The amended NOMNC must be delivered or mailed to the beneficiary and a copy retained in the beneficiary's file.

If an expedited determination is already in progress, the provider must immediately notify the QIO of the change and provide an amended notice to the QIO.

260.3.8—NOMNC Delivery to Representatives (Rev. 2711, Issued: 05-24-13; Effective: 08-26-13; Implementation: 08-26-13)

The NOMNC may be delivered to a beneficiary's appointed or authorized representative. Appointed representatives are individuals designated by beneficiaries to act on their behalf during the appeal process. A beneficiary may designate an appointed representative via the "Appointment of Representative" form, the CMS-1696. *http://www.cms.hhs.gov/cmsforms/downloads/cms1696.pdf* [site visited June 7, 2016. See Chapter 29 of the Medicare Claims Processing Manual, section 270.1, for more information on appointed representatives.

CMS usually requires that notification to a beneficiary who has been deemed legally incompetent be made to an authorized representative of the beneficiary. Generally, an authorized representative is an individual who, under State or other applicable law, may make health care decisions on a beneficiary's behalf (e.g., the beneficiary's legal guardian, or someone appointed in accordance with a properly executed durable medical power of attorney). However, if a beneficiary is temporarily incapacitated, a person (typically, a family member or close friend) whom the provider has determined could reasonably represent the beneficiary, but who has not been named in any legally binding document, may be a representative for the purpose of receiving the notices described in this section.

Such a representative should have the beneficiary's best interests at heart and must act in a manner that is protective of the beneficiary and the beneficiary's rights. Therefore, a representative should have no relevant conflict of interest with the beneficiary.

In these instances of delivering a notice to an unnamed representative, the provider should annotate the NOMNC with the name of the staff person initiating the contact, the name of the person contacted, and the date, time, and method (in person or telephone) of the contact. A copy of the NOMNC with this information should be retained in the beneficiary's record.

Note – Exceptions to in-person notice delivery. If the NOMNC must be delivered to a representative not living with the beneficiary, the provider is not required to make off-site in-person notice delivery to the representative. The provider must complete the NOMNC as required and telephone the representative at least two days prior to the end of covered services. The provider should inform the representative of the beneficiary's right to appeal a coverage termination decision.

The information provided should include the following:

- The beneficiary's last day of covered services, and the date when the beneficiary's liability is expected to begin.
- The beneficiary's right to appeal a coverage termination decision.
- A description of how to request an appeal by a QIO.
- The deadline to request a review as well as what to do if the deadline is missed.
- The telephone number of the QIO to request the appeal.

The date the provider communicates this information to the representative, whether by telephone or in writing, is considered the receipt date of the NOMNC.

The NOMNC must be annotated with the following information on the day that the provider makes telephone contact:

- Reflect that all of the information indicated above was communicated to the representative;
- Note the name of the staff person initiating the contact, the name of the representative contacted by phone, the date and time of the telephone contact, and the telephone number called.

A copy of the annotated NOMNC should be mailed to the representative the day telephone contact is made and a dated copy should be placed in the beneficiary's medical file.

If the provider chooses to communicate the information in writing, a hard copy of the NOMNC must be sent to the representative by certified mail, return receipt requested, or any other delivery method that can provide signed verification of delivery (e.g., FedEx, UPS). The burden is on the provider to demonstrate that timely contact was attempted with the representative and that the notice was delivered.

The date that someone at the representative's address signs (or refused to sign) the receipt is considered the date received. Place a copy of the annotated NOMNC in the beneficiary's medical file.

If both the provider and the representative agree, providers may send the notice by fax or e-mail; however, provider's fax and e-mail systems must meet the Health Insurance Portability and Accountability Act of 1996 (HIPAA) privacy and security requirements.

260.3.9—Notice Retention for the NOMNC
(Rev. 2711, Issued: 05-24-13; Effective: 08-26-13; Implementation: 08-26-13)

The provider must retain the original signed NOMNC in the beneficiary's file. The beneficiary should receive a paper copy of the NOMNC that includes all of the required information such as the effective date and covered service at issue. Electronic notice retention is permitted if the NOMNC was delivered electronically.

260.3.10—Hours of NOMNC Delivery
(Rev. 2711, Issued: 05-24-13; Effective: 08-26-13; Implementation: 08-26-13)

Notice delivery should occur within the normal operating hours of the provider. Providers are not expected to extend their hours or days of business solely to meet the requirements of the expedited determination process. However, it is expected that all notices be provided as timely as possible within these constraints.

260.4—Expedited Determination Process
(Rev. 2711, Issued: 05-24-13; Effective: 08-26-13; Implementation: 08-26-13)

260.4.1—Beneficiary Responsibilities
(Rev. 2711, Issued: 05-24-13; Effective: 08-26-13; Implementation: 08-26-13)

260.4.1.1—Timeframe for Requesting an Expedited Determination
(Rev. 2711, Issued: 05-24-13; Effective: 08-26-13; Implementation: 08-26-13)

A beneficiary who receives a NOMNC and disagrees with the termination of services may request an expedited determination by the appropriate QIO for the state where the services were provided. The beneficiary must contact the QIO by noon of the day before the effective date on the NOMNC. The beneficiary may contact the QIO by telephone or in writing. If the QIO is unable to accept the request, the beneficiary must submit the request by noon of the next day the QIO is available.

260.4.1.2—Provide Information to QIO
(Rev. 2711, Issued: 05-24-13; Effective: 08-26-13; Implementation: 08-26-13)

The beneficiary must be available to answer questions or supply information requested by the QIO. The beneficiary may, but is not required to, supply additional information to the QIO that he or she believes is pertinent to the case.

260.4.1.3—Obtain Physician Certification of Risk (Home Health and CORF services only)
(Rev. 2711, Issued: 05-24-13; Effective: 08-26-13; Implementation: 08-26-13)

A beneficiary must obtain a physician certification stating that failure to continue home health or CORF services is likely to place the beneficiary's health at significant risk. Without such a certification statement a QIO may not make a determination for service terminations in these settings.

The physician certification is a written statement from any licensed physician contacted by a beneficiary. This is a special certification required only in this expedited determination process for expedited determinations in home health and CORF settings.

A beneficiary may request an expedited determination from a QIO before obtaining this certification of risk. Once the QIO is aware of a review request, it will instruct the beneficiary on how to obtain the necessary certification from a physician.

260.4.2—Beneficiary Liability During QIO Review
(Rev. 2711, Issued: 05-24-13; Effective: 08-26-13; Implementation: 08-26-13)

A provider may not bill a beneficiary who has timely filed an expedited determination for disputed services until the review process, including a reconsideration by a Qualified Independent Contractor (QIC), if applicable, is complete.

260.4.3—Untimely Requests for Review
(Rev. 2711, Issued: 05-24-13; Effective: 08-26-13; Implementation: 08-26-13)

If the beneficiary makes an untimely request to the QIO, the QIO will accept the request for review, but is not required to complete the review within its usual 72-hour deadline. The QIO will make a determination as soon as possible upon receipt of the request. Beneficiaries have up to 60 days from the effective date of the NOMNC to make an untimely request to a QIO. When the beneficiary is still receiving services, the QIO must make a determination and notify the parties within 7 days of receipt of the request. When the beneficiary is no longer receiving services, the QIO will make a determination within 30 days of the request.

The coverage protections discussed in § 260.4.2 do not apply to a beneficiary who makes an untimely request to the QIO.

260.4.4—Provider Responsibilities
(Rev. 2711, Issued: 05-24-13; Effective: 08-26-13; Implementation: 08-26-13)

When a provider is notified by a QIO of a beneficiary request for an expedited determination, the provider must—

- Deliver the beneficiary a DENC (see § 260.4.5) by close of business the day they are notified;
- Supply the QIO with copies of the NOMNC and DENCs by close of business of the day of the QIO notification;
- Supply all information, including medical records, requested by the QIO. The QIO may allow this required information to be supplied via phone, writing, or electronically. If supplied via phone, the provider must keep a written record of the information it provides within the patient record; and
- Furnish the beneficiary, at their request, with access to or copies of any documentation it provides to the QIO. The provider may charge the beneficiary a reasonable amount to cover the costs of duplicating and delivering the documentation. This documentation must be provided to the beneficiary by close of business of the first day after the material is requested.

260.4.5—The Detailed Explanation of Non-Coverage
(Rev. 2711, Issued: 05-24-13; Effective: 08-26-13; Implementation: 08-26-13)

The DENC is subject to the Paperwork Reduction Act Process and approval by the office of Management and Budget. OMB-approved notices may only be modified as per their accompanying instructions. Unapproved modifications may invalidate the DENC. The notice and accompanying instructions may be found online at *http://www.cms.gov/Medicare/Medicare-General-Information/BNI*. Medicare providers are responsible for the delivery of the DENC to beneficiaries who request an expedited determination by the QIO.

The DENC must contain the following information:

- The facts specific to the beneficiary's discharge and provider's determination that coverage should end.
- A specific and detailed explanation of why services are either no longer reasonable and necessary or no longer covered.
- A description of, and citations to, the Medicare coverage rule, instruction, or other policies applicable to the review.

The provider should make insertions on the notice in Spanish, if necessary. If this is impossible, additional steps should be taken to ensure that the beneficiary comprehends the content of the notice. Providers may resource CMS multilingual services provided through the 1-800-MEDICARE help line if needed.

The delivery must occur in person by close of business of the day the QIO notifies the provider that the beneficiary has requested an expedited determination. A provider may also choose to deliver the DENC with the NOMNC.

The DENC does not require a signature but should be annotated in the event of a beneficiary's refusal to accept the notice upon delivery.

Note: An HHA is not required to make a separate trip to the beneficiary's residence solely to deliver a DENC. Upon notification from the QIO of a beneficiary's request for an expedited determination, an HHA may telephone the beneficiary to provide the information contained on the DENC, annotate the DENC with the date and time of telephone contact and file with the beneficiary's records. A hard copy of the DENC should be sent to the beneficiary via tracked mail or other personal courier method by close of business of the day the QIO notifies the provider that the beneficiary has requested an expedited determination. The burden is on the provider to demonstrate that timely contact was attempted with the beneficiary and that the notice was delivered.

DENC delivery to representatives, DENC hours of delivery, and DENC retention requirements are the same as the NOMNC requirements outlined in § 260.3.

Expedited Determination Scenario in a Skilled Nursing Facility – Example

On June 2nd, the SNF delivers a NOMNC to Bob Mills notifying him that his Medicare covered stay will end on June 4th. Bob decides to request an expedited determination.

June 2nd	June 3rd	June 4th	June 4th	June 6th
NOMNC Delivered Bob receives a NOMNC indicating that his coverage is ending June 4th.	**Bob must** request an expedited determination by noon today.	**NOMNC Effective Date** This is the last day of coverage, as stated on the NOMNC.	**If Bob made his request on June 2nd:** The QIO makes its decision and notifies Bob and SNF by COB.	**If Bob made his request on June 3rd:** The QIO makes its decision and notifies Bob and the SNF by COB.
	The QIO must notify the SNF of Bob's request for an expedited determination. **The SNF must deliver the DENC to Bob by COB today.** **The SNF must provide relevant medical records to the QIO by COB today.**	**The beneficiary has no liability for this day as this is the last day of coverage in the SNF.**	**If QIO decision is unfavorable:** Beginning today Bob is liable for his stay if he does not leave the SNF.	

260.5—QIO Responsibilities
(Rev. 2711, Issued: 05-24-13; Effective: 08-26-13; Implementation: 08-26-13)

260.5.1—Receive Beneficiary Requests for Expedited Review
(Rev. 2711, Issued: 05-24-13; Effective: 08-26-13; Implementation: 08-26-13)

QIOs must be available to receive beneficiary requests for review 24 hours a day, 7 days a week.

260.5.2—Notify Providers and Allow Explanation of Why Covered Services Should End
(Rev. 2711, Issued: 05-24-13; Effective: 08-26-13; Implementation: 08-26-13)

When the QIO receives a request from a beneficiary, the QIO must immediately notify the provider of services that a request for an expedited determination was made. If the request is received after normal working hours, the QIO should notify the provider as soon as possible on the morning after the request was made.

260.5.3—Validate Delivery of NOMNC
(Rev. 2711, Issued: 05-24-13; Effective: 08-26-13; Implementation: 08-26-13)

The QIO must validate that the NOMNC included the required elements outlined below:

- Date that coverage of services ends.
- Date that beneficiary's financial liability begins.
- Description of right to an expedited determination (and how to request an expedited determination) and the right to submit relevant information to the QIO.
- Right to detailed information on why the provider believes Medicare will no longer cover services.
- Contact information for QIO in the state where services were delivered.

The QIO should determine that NOMNC delivery was valid of all of the following criteria are met:

- All elements stated above are included.
- The beneficiary signed and dated the notice. If the NOMNC was annotated because the beneficiary refused to sign the notice upon delivery, the QIO may still conduct an expedited determination in these instances.
- Notice was delivered at least two days before services terminate. For a non-residential provider, the notice may be delivered at the next to last visit before services terminate.

Invalidating a NOMNC should be a rare occurrence. The only reasons to invalidate are the lack of one of the criteria stated above or a pattern of minor errors as established by the provider.

If a QIO invalidates a NOMNC, a new NOMNC must be issued to the beneficiary with an effective date at least two days after the beneficiary receives valid notice. If the beneficiary again disagrees with the termination of care, a new request to the QIO must be made.

260.5.4—Solicit the Views of the Beneficiary
(Rev. 2711, Issued: 05-24-13; Effective: 08-26-13; Implementation: 08-26-13)

The QIO must solicit the views of the beneficiary who requested the expedited determination.

260.5.5—Solicit the Views of the Provider
(Rev. 2711, Issued: 05-24-13; Effective: 08-26-13; Implementation: 08-26-13)

The QIO must afford the provider an opportunity to explain why the discharge is appropriate.

260.5.6—Make Determination and Notify Required Parties
(Rev. 2711, Issued: 05-24-13; Effective: 08-26-13; Implementation: 08-26-13)

No later than 72 hours after receipt of the request for an expedited determination, the QIO must make its determination on whether the discharge is appropriate based on medical necessity or other Medicare coverage policies.

Note: If the QIO does not receive supporting information from the provider, it may make its determination based on the evidence at hand, or defer a decision until it receives the necessary information. If this delay results in continued services for the beneficiary, the provider may be held financially liable for these services as determined by the QIO.

The QIO must notify the beneficiary, the beneficiary's physician, and the provider of services of its determination. This notification must include the rationale for the determination and an explanation of Medicare payment consequences and beneficiary liability. QIOs must also inform the beneficiary of the right to an expedited reconsideration by the Qualified Independent Contractor (QIC) and how to request a timely expedited reconsideration. The QIO will make its initial notification via telephone and will follow up with a written determination letter.

260.6—Effect of a QIO Expedited Determination
(Rev. 2711, Issued: 05-24-13; Effective: 08-26-13; Implementation: 08-26-13)

The QIO determination is binding unless the beneficiary pursues an expedited reconsideration per section 270 of this chapter.

260.6.1—Right to Pursue an Expedited Reconsideration
(Rev. 2711, Issued: 05-24-13; Effective: 08-26-13; Implementation: 08-26-13)

If dissatisfied with the expedited determination, the beneficiary may request an expedited reconsideration according to the procedures described in section 270 of this chapter.

260.6.2—Effect of QIO Determination on Continuation of Care
(Rev. 2711, Issued: 05-24-13; Effective: 08-26-13; Implementation: 08-26-13)

If the QIO decision extends coverage to a period where a physician's ordered do not exist, either because of the duration of the expedited determination process, or because the physician has already concurred with the termination of care, providers cannot deliver care. In the event of a QIO decision favorable to a beneficiary without physician orders, the ordering physician should be made aware the QIO has ruled coverage should continue, and be given the opportunity to reinstate orders. The beneficiary may also seek other personal physicians to write orders for care as well as find another service provider. The expedited determination process does not override regulatory or State requirements that physician orders are required for a provider to deliver care.

If a QIO decision is favorable to the beneficiary and the beneficiary resumes covered services, a new NOMNC should be delivered if that care is later terminated, per the requirements of this section. If the beneficiary again disagrees with the termination of care, a new request to the QIO must be made.

The QIO decision will affect the necessity of subsequent Advance Beneficiary Notice of Noncoverage (ABN) deliveries.

Example: If covered home health care continues following a favorable QIO decision for the beneficiary, the HHA would resume issuance of Home Health Advanced Beneficiary Notices (HHABNs) as warranted for the remainder of this home health episode. If the QIO decides that Medicare covered care should end and the patient wishes to continue receiving care from the HHA, even though Medicare will not pay, an HHABN with Option Box 1 must be issued to the beneficiary since this would be an initiation of non-covered care.

Example: If covered Skilled Nursing Facility (SNF) care continues following a favorable QIO decision for the beneficiary but later ends due to the end of Medicare coverage, and the patient wishes to continue receiving uncovered care at the SNF, a SNFABN must be issued to the beneficiary.

260.6.3—Right to Pursue the Standard Claims Appeal Process
(Rev. 2711, Issued: 05-24-13; Effective: 08-26-13; Implementation: 08-26-13)

If a beneficiary receives services of the type at issue in the expedited determination after the coverage end date, and coverage is denied, the beneficiary may appeal the denial within the standard claims appeal process (see Chapter 29 of this manual).

261—Expedited Determination Notice Association with Advance Beneficiary Notices
(Rev. 2711, Issued: 05-24-13; Effective: 08-26-13; Implementation: 08-26-13)

Delivery of the NOMNC does not replace the required delivery of other mandatory notices, including ABNs. Notice delivery must be determined by the individual NOMNC requirements per this section and ABN delivery requirements per § 1879 of the Act and per guidance in this chapter. Both the NOMNC and an ABN may be required in certain instances.

Only one notice may be required when Medicare covered care is ending.

Example: A beneficiary is receiving CORF services and all covered CORF care is ending. A NOMNC must be delivered at least two days, or two visits, prior to the end of coverage. If the beneficiary does not continue the CORF services, an ABN should not be issued.

Some situations may require two notices at the end of Medicare covered care.

Example: A beneficiary's Part A stay is ending because skilled level care is no longer medically necessary and the beneficiary wishes to remain in the SNF receiving custodial care. The beneficiary must receive the NOMNC two days prior to the end of coverage. A SNFABN must also be delivered before custodial care begins.

It is also possible that no notice is required when Medicare coverage is ending.

Example: A beneficiary exhausts the 100 day benefit in a SNF. In this instance, the NOMNC should not be delivered. The SNFABN is not required in this situation. However, it can be issued voluntarily, as a courtesy to the beneficiary.

300—Expedited Reconsiderations
(Rev. 1257, Issued: 05-25-07; Effective: 07-01-07; Implementation: 07-02-07)

A beneficiary who is dissatisfied with a QIO determination can request a reconsideration by an independent review entity (IRE). Such reconsiderations are codified in regulations effective July 1, 2005 (42 CFR 405.1204) but are familiar to inpatient hospital providers as the process previously available under § 1155 of the Act. This reconsideration process is the same for hospital and non-hospital providers.

300.1—The Role of the Beneficiary and Liability
(Rev. 1257, Issued: 05-25-07; Effective: 07-01-07; Implementation: 07-02-07)

Submitting a Request: A beneficiary who chooses to exercise the right to an expedited reconsideration must submit a request to the appropriate IRE in writing or by telephone no later than noon of the calendar day following the initial notification (whether by telephone or in writing) of the QIO's determination. The beneficiary, upon request of the QIO, should be available to discuss the case or supply information that the IRE may request. The beneficiary may, but is not required to, submit written evidence to be considered by the IRE.

Untimely Requests: When the beneficiary fails to make a timely request for an expedited reconsideration subsequently may request a reconsideration under the standard claims appeal process (See Chapter 29 of this Manual), but the coverage protection described in Section 300.5 would not extend through this reconsideration, nor would the notification timeframes or the escalation process described in Section 300.2 apply.

300.2—The Responsibilities of the IRE
(Rev. 1257, Issued: 05-25-07; Effective: 07-01-07; Implementation: 07-02-07)

Receipt of the Request. On the day the IRE receives the request for an expedited reconsideration, the IRE must immediately notify the QIO that made the expedited determination and the provider of services of the request for the expedited reconsideration.

Examine Records and Other Information. The IRE must offer the beneficiary and the provider an opportunity to provide further information.

Notification. Unless the beneficiary requests an extension (see below), the IRE must notify the QIO, the beneficiary, and the provider of services of its decision no later than 72 hours after receipt of the request for an expedited reconsideration, and any such records needed for the reconsideration. The initial notification may be done by telephone followed by a written notice that includes:

- The rationale for the reconsideration decision,
- An explanation of the Medicare payment consequences of the determination and the beneficiary's date of liability,
- Information about the beneficiary's right to appeal the IRE's reconsideration decision to an ALJ, including how to request an appeal and the time period for doing so.

Escalation. Unless the beneficiary requests an extension, if the IRE does not issue a decision within 72 hours of receipt of the request, the IRE must notify the beneficiary of his or her right to have the case escalated to the ALJ hearing level if the amount remaining in controversy is $100 or more.

Extensions. A beneficiary who requests an expedited reconsideration may request (either in writing or orally) that an IRE grant such additional time as the beneficiary specifies (not to exceed 14 days) for the reconsideration. If an extension is granted, the deadlines described above under notification, do not apply.

300.3—The Responsibilities of the QIO
(Rev. 1257, Issued: 05-25-07; Effective: 07-01-07; Implementation: 07-02-07)

When an IRE notifies the QIO that a beneficiary has requested an expedited reconsideration, the QIO must supply all information that the IRE needs to make its expedited reconsideration as soon as possible, but no later than by close of business of the day that the IRE notifies the QIO of the request for the reconsideration.

At the beneficiary's request, the QIO must furnish the beneficiary with a copy of, or access to, any documentation that it sends to the IRE. The QIO may charge the beneficiary a reasonable amount to cover the costs of duplicating the documentation and/or delivering it to the beneficiary. The QIO must accommodate the request by no later than close of business of the first day after the material is requested.

300.4—The Responsibilities of the Provider
(Rev. 1257, Issued: 05-25-07; Effective: 07-01-07; Implementation: 07-02-07)

The provider may, but is not required to, submit evidence to be considered by an IRE in making its decision. If a provider fails to comply with an IRE's request for additional information beyond that furnished by the QIO for purposes of the expedited determination, the IRE makes its reconsideration decision based on the information available.

300.5—Coverage During an Expedited Reconsideration
(Rev. 1257, Issued: 05-25-07; Effective: 07-01-07; Implementation: 07-02-07)

When a beneficiary makes a timely request for an expedited determination, the provider may not bill the beneficiary for any disputed services until the IRE makes its determination. Beneficiary liability for continued services is based on the QIO's decision.

Transmittals Issued for this Chapter Rev #	*Issue Date*	*Subject*	*Impl Date*	*CR#*
R3187CP	02/06/2015	Language Only Update to Pub 100-04, Chapter 30 for ASC X12 and Claim References	03/06/2015	8992
R2911CP	03/14/2014	Manual Updates to Clarify Skilled Nursing Facility Advanced Beneficiary Notice (SNFABN Requirements pursuant to Jimmo vs. Sebelius	03/25/2014	8644

continues

Transmittals Issued for this Chapter Rev #	*Issue Date*	*Subject*	*Impl Date*	*CR#*
R2872CP	02/21/2014	Correction CR – Advance Beneficiary Notice of Noncoverage (ABN), Form CMS-R-131	05/15/2013	8597
R2782CP	09/06/2013	Advance Beneficiary Notice of Noncoverage (ABN), Form CMS-R-131	12/09/2013	8404
R2781CP	09/06/2013	Home Health Change of Care Notice (HHCCN), Form CMS-10280, Manual Instructions. This CR rescinds and fully preplaces CR 7323.	12/09/2013	8403
R2711CP	05/24/2013	Expedited Determinations for Provider Service Terminations	08/26/2013	7903
R2480CP	06/01/2012	Advanced Beneficiary Notice of Noncoverage (ABN, Form CMS-R-131, Updated Manual Instructions	09/04/2012	7821
R2362CP	12/01/2011	Home Health Advance Beneficiary Notice, (HHABN), Form CMS-R-296	02/03/2012	7323

continues

Transmittals Issued for this Chapter Rev #	*Issue Date*	*Subject*	*Impl Date*	*CR#*
R1983CP	06/11/2010	Clarification on Use of the SNF ABN and Denial Letters	03/01/2010	6987
R1587CP	09/05/2008	Revised Form CMS-R-131 Advance Beneficiary Notice of Noncoverage	03/01/2009	6136
R1257CP	05/25/2007	Important Message From Medicare (IM) and Expedited Determination Procedures for Hospital Discharges	7/02/2007	5622
R1186CP	02/23/2007	Changes to Chapter 30—Updates to Amount in Controversy Requirement and Correction of Appeals Terminology	05/23/2007	5348
R1035CP	08/18/2006	Updating Publication 100-04, Chapter 30 Regarding the CD ROM Initiative for the Annual "Dear Doctor" Mailing	09/18/2006	5214
R1025CP	08/11/2006	Revised Home Health Advance Beneficiary Notice	09/01/2006	5009

continues

Transmittals Issued for this Chapter Rev #	*Issue Date*	*Subject*	*Impl Date*	*CR#*
R994CP	06/30/2006	Special Issues Associated with the Advance Beneficiary Notice (ABN) for Hospice Providers and Comprehensive Outpatient Rehabilitation Facilities (CORFs)	09/29/2006	5117
R594CP	06/24/2005	Preliminary Instructions: Expedited Determinations/ Reviews for Original Medicare	07/01/2005	3903
R577CP	06/03/2005	Preliminary Instructions: Expedited Determinations/ Reviews for Original Medicare	07/01/2005	3903
R001CP	11/01/2003	Initial Publication of Manual	NA	NA

CHAPTER 3

SKILLED NURSING FACILITY COVERAGE

§ 3.01 INTRODUCTION

The Medicare skilled nursing facility (SNF) benefit provides limited but valuable health care benefits for Medicare beneficiaries. It is, however, one of the most misunderstood areas of Medicare. Many people mistakenly believe that Medicare does not cover nursing home care at all. Others believe that Medicare covers long-term care. Still others realize there is limited coverage, but they do not understand that the level of care received (e.g., skilled versus only custodial care) affects coverage.

Medicare coverage under Part A is available for up to 100 days per benefit period if the patient has had a qualifying three-day hospital stay and requires daily skilled care. If a SNF stay is covered by traditional Medicare, the first 20 days are paid in full and the patient must meet a copayment obligation for days 21 through 100. Medicare Advantage plans may have different copayment rules, but they must be actuarially equivalent to copayments under traditional Medicare.

SNF patients who are not in a Part A stay (because, for example, they have used the 100-day benefit or they do not need daily skilled rehabilitation services) may be eligible for Part B coverage of their less-than-daily skilled rehabilitation services. SNF patients cannot use Parts A and B for their SNF care at the same time.

§ 3.02 COVERAGE

Medicare covers necessary post-hospital extended care services for up to 100 days in a benefit period.[1] Extended care services are defined in the statute as nursing care and rehabilitation provided to a Medicare beneficiary who is an inpatient in a SNF.[2] Such services must be provided daily, and the condition treated in the SNF must be either a condition for which the patient received hospital services or a condition that arose at the SNF while the individual was being treated for a condition for which the hospital services were received.[3] Traditional Medicare covers the first 20 days in full; however, there is a copayment for the next 80 days. The daily copayment is equal to one-eighth of the hospital deductible amount.[4] Accordingly, for a 100-day stay in 2017, the patient would be responsible for $13,160.00 (80 coinsurance days × $164.50/day). For information about Medicare Advantage, see **Chapter 7**.

This is a significant amount of money, which is either paid out-of-pocket by the patient or covered by a Medigap insurance policy. The copayment obligation can present problems for Medicare patients. Although a patient's Medigap policy

[1] 42 U.S.C. § 1395d(a)(2)(A).

[2] 42 U.S.C. § 1395x(h).

[3] 42 U.S.C. § 1395f(a)(2)(B); 42 C.F.R. § 409.31(b).

[4] 42 C.F.R. § 409.85(a)(2).

may cover the SNF copayment, the patient must pay premiums for private supplemental insurance coverage. Moreover, if Medicare does not cover the stay, neither does a Medigap policy. Long-term care insurance policies are offered in many states, but these policies are generally medically underwritten and may have expensive premiums and limited coverage.

Regulations promulgated by the Secretary of the Department of Health and Human Services (HHS)[5] define covered skilled *nursing* services, which include overall management and evaluation of a care plan, observation and assessment of a patient's changing condition, and patient education services.[6]

Medicare coverage is also available for *rehabilitation* services for the ongoing assessment of rehabilitation needs and potential, therapeutic exercises or activities, gait evaluation and training, range of motion exercises, *and* maintenance therapy.[7]

Services may be considered skilled, and therefore coverable by Medicare, if they are necessary to *maintain* current status or to prevent further decline or deterioration[8] and if they are provided by, or under the supervision of, a registered nurse or therapist.[9] The regulations explicitly state that in determining whether skilled rehabilitation services are required, the restoration potential of the individual is not dispositive.[10] These are particularly important sections of the regulations since those who administer the Medicare program have regularly denied coverage on the grounds that the care or therapy required is "maintenance only" and that the patient's underlying condition will not improve. The court-approved Settlement in *Jimmo v. Sebelius*[11] ends the myth that Medicare coverage depends solely on the patient's potential for improvement. *Jimmo* confirms that Medicare pays for maintenance care and that coverage depends on a patient's need for skilled nursing care or skilled rehabilitation services or both. Implementation of *Jimmo* remains an on-going concern.

---

[5] 42 C.F.R. §§ 409.20 *et seq.* and 409.30 *et seq. See also* the Medicare Benefit Policy (MBP) Manual, CMS Pub. 100-02, Ch. 8, §§ 10, *et seq.*, *available at* http://www.cms.gov/manuals/Downloads/bp102c08.pdf (site visited May 16, 2016).

[6] 42 C.F.R. §§ 409.21 and 409.33(a)(1)–(3). The regulations implementing a prospective payment system, a system based on resource utilization groups (RUGs), deleted these examples. (*See* preamble to May 12, 1998, regulations, 63 Fed. Reg. 26,284–26,285, noting an intent that the RUGs act as proxies for observation, assessment, management, and patient education.) In July 1999, these examples were reinstated into the regulations. 64 Fed. Reg. 41,670 (July 30, 1999); 42 C.F.R. § 409.33(a)(1)–(3).

[7] 42 C.F.R. § 409.33(c).

[8] 42 C.F.R. §§ 409.32(c) and 409.33(c)(5).

[9] 42 C.F.R. §§ 409.32 and 409.33(a), (b).

[10] 42 C.F.R. §§ 409.32(c).

[11] Civil Action No. 5:11-CV-17-CR (D. Vt. Jan. 24, 2013), *available at* http://www.medicareadvocacy.org/wp-content/uploads/2012/12/Jimmo-Settlement-Agreement-00011764.pdf (site visited May 16, 2016).

§ 3.03 QUALIFYING CRITERIA

[A] Basic Eligibility and Coverage

With respect to the Medicare SNF benefit:[12]

- Only admissions after a three-day inpatient hospital stay are covered;
- Ordinarily, post-hospital transfer to a SNF must be made within 30 days after leaving the hospital;
- The patient must require and receive skilled services on a daily basis—skilled nursing seven days per week or rehabilitation five days per week or a combination of the two for seven days per week—in order to qualify for coverage;
- Skilled care must be related to the condition for which the patient was hospitalized;
- A maximum of 100 days per benefit period (also called spell of illness) may be covered;
- As a practical matter, the care must be required to be provided on an inpatient basis.

[B] Three-Day Test

The Medicare statute limits coverage of SNF stays to:

> extended care services furnished [to] an individual after transfer from a hospital in which he was an inpatient for not less than three consecutive days before his discharge from the hospital in connection with such transfer. For purposes of the preceding sentence, items and services shall be deemed to have been furnished to an individual after transfer from a hospital, and he shall be deemed to have been an inpatient in the hospital immediately before transfer there from, if he is admitted to the skilled nursing facility within 30 days after discharge from such hospital. . . .[13]

To qualify for coverage, a Medicare patient first must be an inpatient of a hospital for three consecutive days.[14] The Centers for Medicare & Medicaid Services (CMS) defines "days" as midnights, not 24-hour periods. A patient admitted to the hospital at 11:55 p.m. will have that day counted as the first day of admission The day of discharge does not count as one of the three qualifying

---

[12] See citations in the discussion below.

[13] 42 U.S.C. § 1395x(i).

[14] 42 U.S.C. § 1395x(i); MBP Manual, Ch. 8, § 20.1, *available at* http://www.cms.gov/manuals/Downloads/bp102c08.pdf (site visited May 16, 2016).

days—hence, the requirement is often referred to as the "three-midnights" rule. If a patient was in the hospital as an inpatient for a time period that crossed three midnights, the patient has satisfied the three-day test.

Language added to the Medicare Benefit Policy (MBP) Manual in 2013 confirms that the three-day test is satisfied when the patient has at least three consecutive days of medically necessary inpatient hospital services, even if the patient's care becomes "less intensive during the latter part of the stay."[15] Similarly, hospital days can be included in the three-day count for a patient whose care needs drop to a SNF level, when no SNF bed is available and the physician certifies that continued stay in the hospital is medically necessary.[16]

A stay in a psychiatric hospital qualifies for the three-day test, although CMS cautions that a patient with "only a psychiatric condition . . . is likely to receive only non-covered care" in a SNF.[17]

Frequently, a patient is first treated in a hospital emergency department. Hospitals may keep patients in the emergency department for lengthy periods of time, even after a decision has been made to admit. Sometimes delays occur because hospital personnel have not had time to do the paperwork for admission. If an admission is logged in by hospital staff after midnight, the admission date is set as the calendar day when the paperwork is actually completed.

An early case held that if the care in the emergency department constitutes one part of a course of treatment that continues after the formalities of admission are completed, time spent by the patient in the emergency department should count toward the required three-day hospital stay.[18] This decision was explicitly overruled by a later case.[19]

Another frequent pattern is that patients move from the emergency department to a bed in the acute care hospital, where they receive "observation services," an outpatient benefit under Medicare Part B. Patients may be formally admitted to inpatient status after receiving observation services. CMS does not count time spent in either the emergency department or observation status in determining whether a patient meets the qualifying three-day hospital stay requirement.[20] A nationwide class action challenging CMS's policy of refusing to count *all* time in the hospital toward meeting the qualifying hospital stay

---

[15] MBP Manual, Ch. 8, § 20.1, *available at* http://www.cms.gov/manuals/Downloads/bp102c08.pdf (site visited May 16, 2016).

[16] MBP Manual, Ch. 8, § 20.1, *available at* http://www.cms.gov/manuals/Downloads/bp102c08.pdf (site visited May 16, 2016).

[17] MBP Manual, Ch. 8, § 20.1. NOTE, *available at* http://www.cms.gov/manuals/Downloads/bp102c08.pdf (site visited May 16, 2016).

[18] Jenkel v. Shalala, 845 F. Supp. 69 (D. Conn. 1994).

[19] Landers v. Leavitt, 545 F.3d 98 (2d Cir. 2008).

[20] MBP Manual, Ch. 8, § 20.1, *available at* http://www.cms.gov/manuals/Downloads/bp102c08.pdf (site visited May 16, 2016).

requirement when a patient was, at some point, admitted to inpatient status was not successful.[21]

Increasingly, Medicare beneficiaries are never formally admitted to inpatient status in acute care hospitals. They remain, instead, under observation for their entire hospital stay. Although the Medicare Manuals provide that observation status should "usually" not continue beyond 24 hours or, at most, 48 hours,[22] many beneficiaries are kept on observation status or are otherwise called outpatients for considerably longer periods. Remaining on observation or outpatient status has significant financial consequences for beneficiaries.[23] They must pay for services that would be covered by a Part A hospital stay, copayments for Part B services, and prescription drugs received in the hospital. In addition, they are denied Medicare coverage for their subsequent SNF stay, with limited ability to get the matter before the Medicare agency for an initial determination of whether the beneficiary was "admitted" to the hospital for purposes of SNF coverage. A federal district court dismissed litigation, *Bagnall v. Sebelius*,[24] that challenged observation status as violating the Medicare statute, the Administrative Procedures Act, and the Due Process Clause of the Fifth Amendment.[25] In 2015, a court of appeals reversed and remanded on the due process issues appealed by plaintiffs: notice and opportunity for hearing.[26] The case is now known as *Barrows v. Burwell* and is currently back in district court.

Physicians may order observation services for their patients instead of admitting them as inpatients. Often, however, the decision is made by the hospital in an effort to avoid Medicare audits and denials. Since 2004, CMS has authorized hospitals' utilization review committees to retroactively reverse a physician's inpatient admission of his or her patient, although since 2011, the practitioner responsible for the patient's care must agree to the change in the patient's status.[27]

---

[21] *Landers*, 545 F.3d 98 (2d Cir. 2008).

[22] MBP Manual, Ch. 6, § 20.6, *available at* https://www.cms.gov/Regulations-and-Guidance/Guidance/Manuals/Downloads/bp102c06.pdf (site visited May 16, 2016).

[23] Although the primary consequences of observation services have been financial, the quality of hospital care provided to beneficiaries during observation or outpatient status may become an increasing problem as hospitals establish separate observation units.

[24] 2013 WL 5346659, No. 3:11cv1703(MPS) (D. Conn., Sept. 23, 2013).

[25] For additional information about observation status, including the aspects of the *Bagnall* decision that are being appealed, see http://www.medicareadvocacy.org/medicare-info/observation-status/.

[26] Barrows v. Burwell, 777 F.3d 106 (2d Cir. 2015).

[27] Under Condition Code 44, an inpatient admission may be changed retroactively to outpatient when (1) the change in status is made while the patient is still in the hospital; (2) the hospital has not submitted a claim to Medicare for inpatient admission; (3) "the practitioner responsible for the care of the patient" and the utilization review committee "concur with the decision;" and (4) the "the concurrence of the practitioner and UR committee is documented in the patient's medical record." Medicare Claims Processing (MCP) Manual, CMS Pub. 100-04, Ch. 1, § 50.3, originally issued as Inpatient Admission Changed to Outpatient, Transmittal 299 (Sept. 10, 2004), revised by Transmittal 2296 (Sept. 2, 2011) and Transmittal 2386 (Jan. 13, 2012). In 2004, Condition Code 44

Regulations published in August 2013[28] defining inpatient hospital status according to time-based factors (i.e., a physician who expects that a patient will remain hospitalized for two midnights should admit the patient as an inpatient, under a *presumption* of inpatient care) are intended, in part, to reduce lengthy observation stays and may indirectly affect the three-day test. Preamble language suggests that time spent in the emergency department or in outpatient status (including observation status) is relevant for the two-midnight *benchmark* for inpatient care. That is, CMS auditors should not review inpatient admission decisions if the patient was in the hospital at least two midnights, even if both midnights were not inpatient. Enforcement of the two-midnight rule was stayed for many years by CMS[29] and by Congress,[30] but the rule is now fully in effect.[31] Effective January 1, 2016, a minor modification to the two-midnight rule allows physicians to order an inpatient stay for a patient whose expected length of stay is less than two midnights.[32]

Until 2016, CMS required hospitals to inform patients of their outpatient status only if the hospitals' utilization review committee reversed the patient's status from inpatient to outpatient under Condition Code 44. However, effective August 6, 2016, the Notice of Observation Treatment and Implication for Care Eligibility Act (NOTICE Act) requires all hospitals to notify all patients of their outpatient status if they are in observation or other outpatient status for more than 2 hours.[33] CMS mandates use of a notice called the Medicare Outpatient Observation Notice (MOON).[34] Although final regulations implementing the NOTICE Act become

---

allowed a patient's status to be changed from inpatient to outpatient if "a physician," not necessarily the practitioner responsible for the patient's care, agreed to the change.

[28] 74 Fed. Reg. 50,495, 50,938–954 (especially 50,944–949) (Aug. 19, 2013).

[29] Centers for Medicare & Medicaid Services (CMS), Frequently Asked Questions, "2 Midnight Inpatient Admission Guidance & Patient Status Reviews for Admissions on or After October 1, 2013," *available at* http://www.cms.gov/Research-Statistics-Data-and-Systems/Monitoring-Programs/Medical-Review/Downloads/QAsforWebsitePosting_110413-v2-CLEAN.pdf; CMS, "Selecting Hospital Claims for Patient Status Reviews: Admissions on or After October 1, 2013" (last updated: Nov. 4, 2013), *available at* http://www.cms.gov/Research-Statistics-Data-and-Systems/Monitoring-Programs/Medical-Review/Downloads/SelectingHospitalClaimsforAdmissionsonorafterOctober1st2013forReviewForWebPostingCLEAN.pdf; CMS, "Inpatient Hospital Reviews" (Dec. 31, 2015 update), *available at* https://www.cms.gov/Research-Statistics-Data-and-Systems/Monitoring-Programs/Medicare-FFS-Compliance-Programs/Medical-Review/InpatientHospitalReviews.html (sites visited May 16, 2016).

[30] 42 U.S.C. § 1395ddd note, extending moratorium through March 31, 2015 (added by § 111 of the Protecting Access to Medicare Act of 2014, Pub. L. No. 113-93); 42 U.S.C. § 1395ddd note (as amended), extending moratorium through September 30, 2015 (added by § 521 of the Medicare Access and CHIP Reauthorization Act of 2015, Pub. L. No. 114-10.

[31] 80 Fed. Reg. 70,297, 70538-70549 (Nov. 13, 2015).

[32] 42 C.F.R. § 412.3(d)(3), 80 Fed. Reg. 70,297, 70,538-70,549 (Nov. 13, 2015).

[33] 42 U.S.C. § 1395cc(a)(1)(Y).

[34] The draft MOON notice (accessible in a zip file) is *available at* https://www.cms.gov/Regulations-and-Guidance/Legislation/PaperworkReductionActof1995/PRA-Listing-Items/CMS-10611.html (site visited Sept. 26, 2016).

effective October 1, 2016,[35] full implementation of the Act will not occur until hospitals begin using the MOON, which will not occur until 90 days after the Office of Management and Budget approves the form. Realistically, the NOTICE Act will not be implemented until 2017.

Medicare Advantage (MA) plans may provide SNF coverage without a prior three-day hospital stay,[36] but they are not required to do so.[37] Most do, but some MA plans charge copayments earlier in a patient's stay.

[C] Thirty-Day Test

Part A coverage requires that a patient be admitted to the SNF within 30 days of discharge from the hospital, not counting the day of discharge.[38] The regulations and Medicare Benefit Policy (MBP) Manual recognize limited exceptions to the 30-day rule. If it is not "medically appropriate" to begin the post-hospital SNF care within the 30-day period and if it is "medically predictable" at the time of discharge from the hospital that the patient will need covered care in a "predeterminable time period," treatment may begin at a later date when it is medically appropriate to begin an active course of treatment or therapy.[39] For example, a patient recovering from a hip fracture will require skilled therapy services. However, the patient may be non-weight-bearing during the 30-day period after discharge from the hospital. In this case, it may not be appropriate to begin therapy until the fracture has had time to heal and the patient achieves a weight-bearing status. The MBP Manual recognizes four to six weeks after hospital discharge as an appropriate and predictable time to begin therapy for a hip fracture. Accordingly, admission to the SNF four to six weeks after discharge from the hospital could be considered timely.[40]

Even if the patient with a hip fracture goes to a SNF, leaves after two days, and returns five weeks later for predictable rehabilitative care, both SNF stays are covered by Medicare.[41] Similarly, a patient who is immediately admitted to a SNF following discharge from a hospital and receives *non-covered care* will get Medicare coverage at a later time if it was "medically predictable that covered SNF care would be required at a predeterminable time interval."[42] The example in the

---

[35] 81 Fed. Reg. 56,761 (Aug. 22, 2016).

[36] 42 C.F.R. § 422.101(c).

[37] Rapport v. Leavitt, 564 F. Supp. 2d 186 (W.D.N.Y. 2008).

[38] 42 U.S.C. § 1395x(i).

[39] 42 C.F.R. § 409.30(b)(2); MBP Manual, Ch. 8, § 20.2.2.

[40] MBP Manual, Ch. 8, § 20.2.2.1, *available at* http://www.cms.gov/manuals/Downloads/bp102c08.pdf (site visited May 17, 2016).

[41] MBP Manual, Ch. 8, § 20.2.2.3, Example 1, *available at* http://www.cms.gov/manuals/Downloads/bp102c08.pdf (site visited May 17, 2016).

[42] MBP Manual, Ch. 8, § 20.2.2.3, Example 3, *available at* http://www.cms.gov/manuals/Downloads/bp102c08.pdf (site visited May 17, 2016).

MBP Manual is a patient whose leg is amputated and who, after the stump is healed, requires daily skilled rehabilitative services to learn how to use a prosthesis.[43] The MBP Manual further recognizes that if "complications" prevent initiation of deferred care—for example, the amputee's stump becomes infected—the SNF stay may be covered "even though care is not started within the usual anticipated time frame."[44]

However, if a patient's medical needs are *not* predictable at the time of discharge from the hospital, admission to a SNF after 30 days will *not* fall within the exception to the 30-day rule.[45] The MBP Manual's example is a patient who receives covered care for three weeks but, six weeks later, experiences an unexpected change in condition and again requires skilled care. The patient's second need for skilled care is not covered by Medicare.[46]

The 30-day transfer requirement is also considered met if a patient receiving covered SNF care "leaves a SNF and is readmitted to the same or any other participating SNF for further covered care within 30 days of the last covered skilled day."[47] The brief interruption of covered care does not require rehospitalization before Medicare will cover the SNF care. Similarly, a patient whose SNF stay is covered on admission but who subsequently does not require skilled care may resume Medicare coverage as long as the break in covered care does not exceed 30 days.[48] Language added to the MBP Manual in 2015 confirms that coverage under Part A may be resumed "if the beneficiary remains in the SNF to receive custodial care following a covered stay, and subsequently develops a renewed need for covered care there within 30 consecutive days."[49]

[D] Skilled Level-of-Care Requirement

Once a patient has established a qualifying hospital stay, Medicare payment for post-hospital extended care services will be available only when:

---

[43] MBP Manual, Ch. 8, § 20.2.2.3, Example 3, *available at* http://www.cms.gov/manuals/Downloads/bp102c08.pdf (site visited May 17, 2016).

[44] MBP Manual, Ch. 8, § 20.2.2.4, *available at* http://www.cms.gov/manuals/Downloads/bp102c08.pdf (site visited May 17, 2016).

[45] MBP Manual, Ch. 8, § 20.2.2.2, *available at* http://www.cms.gov/manuals/Downloads/bp102c08.pdf (site visited May 17, 2016).

[46] MBP Manual, Ch. 8, § 20.2.2.3, Example 2, *available at* http://www.cms.gov/manuals/Downloads/bp102c08.pdf (site visited May 17, 2016).

[47] MBP Manual, Ch. 8, § 20.2.3, *available at* http://www.cms.gov/manuals/Downloads/bp102c08.pdf (site visited May 18, 2016).

[48] MBP Manual, Ch. 8, § 20.2, *available at* http://www.cms.gov/manuals/Downloads/bp102c08.pdf (site visited May 18, 2016).

[49] MBP Manual, Ch. 8, § 20.2.3, *available at* http://www.cms.gov/manuals/Downloads/bp102c08.pdf (site visited May 18, 2016).

> such services are or were required to be given because the individual needs or needed on a daily basis skilled nursing care (provided directly by or requiring the supervision of skilled nursing personnel) or other skilled rehabilitation services, which as a practical matter can only be provided in a skilled nursing facility on an inpatient basis, for any of the conditions with respect to which he was receiving inpatient hospital services . . . prior to transfer to the skilled nursing facility. . . .[50]

The statute requires that (1) the patient needs skilled nursing services or skilled rehabilitation services, which must be performed by or under the supervision of professional or technical personnel and ordered by a physician; (2) the patient needs the services on a daily basis; (3) services can be provided, as a practical matter, only on an inpatient basis in a SNF; and (4) services are reasonable and necessary. Analysis begins with whether the patient needs skilled care.[51]

A patient admitted directly to a SNF after an inpatient hospital stay of three or more days is presumed to meet the level of care for SNF coverage for the first five days if he or she is assigned to one of the upper 52 Resource Utilization Groups (RUG-IV) identified under Medicare's prospective payment system (PPS) for SNFs.[52] A patient assigned to one of the lower 14 RUG-IV categories may receive Medicare-covered care; for such a patient, an individual level of care determination must be made "using existing administrative criteria and procedures."[53] The presumption of coverage for the SNF stay does *not* apply if the patient is discharged from the hospital to another setting and then, within 30 days from the hospital discharge, goes to the SNF.[54] The presumption of coverage applies to a patient who is rehospitalized and returns directly to the SNF for care, although a new Medicare five-day assessment is required.[55]

A patient must receive *skilled*, as opposed to *custodial*, care. Medicare will not reimburse any expenses when the level of care is only custodial.[56] However, custodial services are often provided in addition to skilled care. The key is that the patient must require and receive skilled care, not just custodial care, on a daily basis. If skilled services are provided frequently, but not on a daily basis, Medicare coverage for the stay under Part A will not be available.

---

[50] 42 U.S.C. § 1395f(a)(2)(B).

[51] MBP Manual, Ch. 8, § 30, *available at* http://www.cms.gov/manuals/Downloads/bp102c08.pdf (site visited May 18, 2016).

[52] MBP Manual, Ch. 8, § 30.1, *available at* http://www.cms.gov/manuals/Downloads/bp102c08.pdf (site visited May 18, 2016); 79 Fed. Reg. 45,627, 45,640–41 (Aug. 5, 2014).

[53] MBP Manual, Ch. 8, § 30.1, *available at* http://www.cms.gov/manuals/Downloads/bp102c08.pdf (site visited May 18, 2016).

[54] MBP Manual, Ch. 8, § 30.1, *see* 2, *available at* http://www.cms.gov/manuals/Downloads/bp102c08.pdf (site visited May 18, 2016).

[55] MBP Manual, Ch. 8, § 30.1, *see* 3, *available at* http://www.cms.gov/manuals/Downloads/bp102c08.pdf (site visited May 18, 2016).

[56] 42 U.S.C. § 1395y(a)(9).

[1] Skilled Nursing or Rehabilitation Services

The regulations state that the patient must require skilled nursing or rehabilitation services that are ordered by the attending physician.[57] The skilled services must be provided on a daily basis by, or furnished under the supervision of, skilled personnel.[58] Skilled services may be provided directly by the therapist or under the "general supervision" of the skilled personnel. "'General supervision' requires initial direction and periodic inspection of the actual activity," but "the supervisor need not always be physically present or on the premises when the assistant is performing the services."[59] In addition, the skilled services must be related to a condition for which the patient received inpatient hospital care or that arose at the SNF while the patient was being treated for such a condition.[60]

The inherent complexity of a service must be evaluated in the context of the patient's need for safe and effective service delivery.[61] Special medical complications may substantiate the need for skilled services that are not ordinarily required.[62] For example, while a qualified physical therapist is not usually required to give whirlpool baths, professional therapy services may be needed for a beneficiary whose condition "is complicated by circulatory deficiency, areas of desensitization, or open wounds."[63] Similarly, skilled management of unskilled services may justify the need for Medicare-covered care.[64] When rehabilitation services are the primary services supporting Medicare coverage, "the key issue is whether the skills of a therapist are needed," not whether the patient has "potential for recovery."[65]

Language added to the MBP Manual in 2014 stresses the importance of thorough and timely documentation of treatment goals and the need for skilled services.[66]

---

[57] 42 C.F.R. § 409.31(a)(1).

[58] 42 C.F.R. § 409.31(a)(3) and (b); MBP Manual, Ch. 8, § 30.2.1 *available at* http://www.cms.gov/manuals/Downloads/bp102c08.pdf (site visited May 18, 2016).

[59] MBP Manual, Ch. 8, § 30.2.1, NOTE, *available at* http://www.cms.gov/manuals/Downloads/bp102c08.pdf (site visited May 18, 2016).

[60] 42 U.S.C. §§ 1395f(a)(2)(B) and 1395x(i); 42 C.F.R. §§ 409.31(b)(2)(i)–(ii) and 424.20.

[61] 42 C.F.R. § 409.32(a).

[62] 42 C.F.R. § 409.32(b).

[63] MBP Manual, Ch. 8, § 30.2.2 (second example), *available at* http://www.cms.gov/manuals/Downloads/bp102c08.pdf (site visited May 18, 2016).

[64] MBP Manual, Ch. 8, § 30.2.2 (third example, describing resident with multiple physical and mental impairments), *available at* http://www.cms.gov/manuals/Downloads/bp102c08.pdf (site visited May 18, 2016).

[65] MBP Manual, Ch. 8, § 30.2.2 (first example), *available at* http://www.cms.gov/manuals/Downloads/bp102c08.pdf (site visited May 18, 2016).

[66] MBP Manual, Ch. 8, § 30.2.2.1, *available at* http://www.cms.gov/manuals/Downloads/bp102c08.pdf.

The regulations contain examples of skilled nursing and rehabilitation services.[67] Some of the examples constitute skilled nursing care only if the services of a skilled or professional person are required. Other examples automatically constitute covered skilled nursing services. Skilled rehabilitation services are separately described.

Skilled *nursing* services may include the following activities when the skills of a technical or professional person are needed:[68]

- **Overall management and evaluation of care plan.**[69] Managing and evaluating a care plan constitutes skilled nursing services when skilled nursing personnel are required "to meet the patient's [] needs, promote recovery, and ensure medical safety."[70] Medicare coverage is available for management and evaluation of a care plan "only when, in light of the patient's condition, the aggregate of those services requires the involvement of technical or professional personnel."[71] Nonskilled services may require skilled management "when the condition of the beneficiary is such that there is an expectation that a change in condition is likely without that intervention."[72] The regulation's sole example and the MBP Manual's first example find skilled personnel are necessary, based on the patient's condition, age, and immobility, which together create "a high potential for serious complications."[73] The second MBP Manual example also supports a finding of skilled oversight based on the patient's immobility, confusion, and chest congestion, which create "high probability of relapse."[74] If the patient's record "clearly establishes that there was a likely potential for serious complications without skilled management," the Medicare contractor will assume that skilled care was provided even

[67] 42 C.F.R. § 409.33. *See also* MBP Manual, Ch. 8, § 30.2.3 (Skilled Nursing and Skilled Rehabilitation Services), *available at* http://www.cms.gov/manuals/Downloads/bp102c08.pdf (site visited May 18, 2016).

[68] 42 C.F.R. § 409.33(a). *See also* MBP Manual, Ch. 8, § 30.2.3, *available at* http://www.cms.gov/manuals/Downloads/bp102c08.pdf (site visited May 18, 2016).

[69] 42 C.F.R. § 409.33(a)(1); MBP Manual, Ch. 8, § 30.2.3.1, *available at* http://www.cms.gov/manuals/Downloads/bp102c08.pdf (site visited May 18, 2016).

[70] 42 C.F.R. § 409.33(a)(1)(i); MBP Manual, Ch. 8, § 30.2.3.1, *available at* http://www.cms.gov/manuals/Downloads/bp102c08.pdf (site visited May 18, 2016).

[71] 42 C.F.R. § 409.33(a)(1).

[72] MBP Manual, Ch. 8, § 30.2.3.1, *available at* http://www.cms.gov/manuals/Downloads/bp102c08.pdf (site visited May 18, 2016).

[73] 42 C.F.R. § 409.33(a)(1)(ii); MBP Manual, Ch. 8, § 30.2.3.1 (example 1), *available at* http://www.cms.gov/manuals/Downloads/bp102c08.pdf (site visited May 18, 2016).

[74] MBP Manual, Ch. 8, § 30.2.3.1 (example 2), *available at* http://www.cms.gov/manuals/Downloads/bp102c08.pdf (site visited May 18, 2016).

when the patient's clinical record does not "specifically identify 'skilled planning and management activities' as such."[75]

- **Observation and assessment of the patient's changing condition** if treatment may need to be modified, new medical procedures may need to be initiated, or the patient's condition needs to be stabilized.[76] The regulations provide the example of a patient with congestive heart failure who requires close nursing observation "to detect signs of decompensation, abnormal fluid balance, or adverse effects from medications."[77] A patient with acute psychological symptoms in addition to physical problems, such as depression, anxiety, or agitation, may require skilled nursing care to ensure their safety or the safety of others.[78] The examples in the regulations and MBP Manual illustrate the fact-specific nature of the inquiry.[79] Skilled observation is appropriate if there is a "reasonable probability" of a potential complication or further acute episode, even if the complication or acute episode never develops.[80]
- **Patient education services** to train and teach patients "self-maintenance" and "how to manage their treatment regimen."[81] The regulations provide two examples: a patient with a recent leg amputation who needs skilled personnel to provide gait training and to teach care of the prosthesis and a newly-diagnosed diabetic patient who needs skilled personnel to teach self-administration of insulin and foot-care precautions.[82] Additional examples in the MBP Manual include teaching patients to self-administer medications, insulin injections, or medical gases; to care for a prosthesis, colostomy, or ileostomy; to perform self-catheterization; to self-administer gastrostomy feedings; to use and care for braces, splints, and orthotics and associated skin care; and to care for specialized dressings or skin treatments.[83]

---

[75] MBP Manual, Ch. 8, § 30.2.3.1, *available at* http://www.cms.gov/manuals/Downloads/bp102c08.pdf (site visited May 18, 20016).

[76] 42 C.F.R. § 409.33(a)(2); MBP Manual, Ch. 8, § 30.2.3.2, *available at* http://www.cms.gov/manuals/Downloads/bp102c08.pdf (site visited May 18, 2016).

[77] 42 C.F.R. § 409.33(a)(2)(ii).

[78] 42 C.F.R. § 409.33(a)(2)(ii); MBP Manual, Ch. 8, § 30.2.3.2, *available at* http://www.cms.gov/manuals/Downloads/bp102c08.pdf (site visited May 18, 2016).

[79] 42 C.F.R. § 409.33(1)(2)(ii); MBP Manual, Ch. 8, § 30.2.3.2, *available at* http://www.cms.gov/manuals/Downloads/bp102c08.pdf (site visited May 18, 2016).

[80] MBP Manual, Ch. 8, § 30.2.3.2, *available at* http://www.cms.gov/manuals/Downloads/bp102c08.pdf (site visited May 18, 2016).

[81] 42 C.F.R. § 409.33(a)(3); MBP Manual, Ch. 8, § 30.2.3.3, *available at* http://www.cms.gov/manuals/Downloads/bp102c08.pdf (site visited July 20, 2015).

[82] 42 C.F.R. § 409.33(a)(3)(ii).

[83] MBP Manual, Ch. 8, § 30.2.3.3.

The MBP Manual describes as "questionable situations" those involving patients whose primary need is oral medication or who are "capable of independent ambulation, dressing, feeding, and hygiene."[84]

The regulations provide that the restoration potential of a patient is not the controlling factor in determining whether skilled care is necessary.[85] The maintenance standard of coverage is confirmed by *Jimmo v. Sebelius.*[86] Skilled care may be necessary to preserve the patient's current status or to slow or prevent further decline or deterioration of the patient's medical condition.[87] Similarly, physical therapy to maintain the patient's present level of functioning may be a covered service when the skills and knowledge of a therapist are needed.[88]

Language added to the MBP Manual in 2014 as a result of *Jimmo* stresses that maintenance nursing services are covered by Medicare.

> Skilled nursing services would be covered where such skilled nursing services are necessary to maintain the patient's current condition or prevent or slow further deterioration so long as the beneficiary requires skilled care for the services to be safely and effectively provided, and all other requirements for coverage under the SNF benefit are met.[89]

The MBP Manual firmly ends the myth of improvement as the sole basis for Medicare coverage: "Coverage does not turn on the presence or absence of an

---

[84] MBP Manual, Ch. 8, § 30.2.4, *available at* http://www.cms.gov/manuals/Downloads/bp102c08.pdf (site visited May 18, 2016).

[85] 42 C.F.R. § 409.32(c) ("The restoration potential of a patient is not the deciding factor in determining whether skilled services are needed."); MBP Manual, Ch. 8, § 30.2.2 (first example) ("When rehabilitation services are the primary services, . . . [t]he deciding factor is not the patient's potential for recovery, but whether the services needed require the skills of a therapist or whether they can be provided by nonskilled personnel."); MBP Manual, Ch. 8, § 30.4 ("Coverage for such skilled therapy services does not turn on the presence or absence of a beneficiary's potential for improvement from therapy services, but rather on the beneficiary's need for skilled care. Therapy services are considered skilled when they are so inherently complex that they can be safely and effectively performed only by, or under the supervision of, a qualified therapist."); Papciak v. Sebelius, 742 F. Supp. 2d 765 (W.D. Pa. 2010) (The Secretary failed to apply the correct legal standard when she considered only the patient's restoration potential, not whether the patient needed SNF care to maintain her level of functioning following hip replacement surgery.).

[86] Civil Action No. 5:11-CV-17-CR (D. Vt. Jan. 24, 2013). *See* http://www.medicareadvocacy.org/wp-content/uploads/2012/12/Jimmo-Settlement-Agreement-00011764.pdf (site visited May 18, 2016). *See also* CMS, *Jimmo v. Sebelius* Settlement Agreement: Program Manual Clarifications Fact Sheet, https://www.cms.gov/medicare/medicare-fee-for-service-payment/snfpps/downloads/jimmo_fact_sheet2_022014_final.pdf. *See* **Appendix 1-9.**

[87] 42 C.F.R. § 409.32(c).

[88] 42 C.F.R. § 409.33(c)(5) (describing when maintenance therapy qualifies as skilled rehabilitation services).

[89] MBP Manual, Ch. 8, § 30.3, *available at* http://www.cms.gov/manuals/Downloads/bp102c08.pdf (site visited May 18, 2016).

individual's potential for improvement from nursing care, but rather on the beneficiary's need for skilled care."[90]

If a patient is receiving one or more of the following skilled nursing services on a daily basis, the requirement for receiving daily skilled care is met per se:[91]

- "Intravenous/intramuscular injections and intravenous feeding."
- "Enteral feeding that comprises at least 26 percent of daily calorie requirements and provides at least 501 milliliters of fluid per day."
- "Naso-pharyngeal and tracheostomy aspiration."
- "Insertion, sterile irrigation, and replacement of suprapubic catheters."
- "Application of dressings involving prescription medications and aseptic techniques."
- "Treatment of extensive decubitus ulcers" (the MBP Manual says stage 3 or worse) or "other widespread skin disorders."
- "Heat treatments which have been specifically ordered by a physician as part of active treatment and which require observation by skilled nursing personnel to evaluate the patient's progress adequately."
- "Rehabilitation nursing procedures, including the related teaching and adaptive aspects of nursing, that are part of active treatment and require the presence of skilled nursing personnel; e.g., the institution and supervision of bowel and bladder training programs."
- "Initial phases of a regimen involving administration of medical gases."
- "Care of a colostomy during the early post-operative period in the presence of associated complications," which is added by the MBP Manual (justification and documentation in the medical record are required).[92]

Language added to the MBP Manual as a result of *Jimmo* also confirms that maintenance therapy services are covered by Medicare: "Coverage for such skilled therapy services does not turn on the presence or absence of a beneficiary's potential for improvement from therapy services, but rather on the beneficiary's need for skilled care."[93] Skilled therapy services are covered if they are necessary "to improve the patient's current condition, to maintain the patient's

---

[90] MBP Manual, Ch. 8, § 30.3, *available at* http://www.cms.gov/manuals/Downloads/bp102c08.pdf (site visited May 18, 2016).

[91] 42 C.F.R. § 409.33(b). MBP Manual, Ch. 8, § 30.3, *available at* http://www.cms.gov/manuals/Downloads/bp102c08.pdf (site visited May 18, 2016).

[92] MBP Manual, Ch. 8, § 30.3, *available at* http://www.cms.gov/manuals/Downloads/bp102c08.pdf (site visited May 18, 2016).

[93] MBP Manual, Ch. 8, § 30.4, *available at* http://www.cms.gov/manuals/Downloads/bp102c08.pdf (site visited May 18, 2016).

current condition, or to prevent or slow further deterioration of the patient's condition."[94]

Skilled physical therapy services must be related to "an active written treatment plan" and must require "the judgment, knowledge, and skills of a qualified physical therapist."[95] The services must be needed either to improve or to establish or perform "a safe and effective maintenance program."[96] The services must also be considered specific and effective treatment for the patient's condition under accepted standards of medical practice, as well as reasonable and necessary for the treatment of the patient's condition.[97] The MBP Manual cautions that many SNF patients require services that may be provided by supportive personnel, without the supervision of a physical therapist, and that these services are not covered by Medicare as skilled physical therapy.[98]

The regulations identify services that qualify as skilled rehabilitation services,[99] with elaboration provided in the MBP Manual:[100]

- "Ongoing assessment of a patient's rehabilitation needs and potential."
- "Therapeutic exercises" that require skilled personnel "due either to the type of exercise employed or to the condition of the patient."
- "Gait evaluation and training furnished to a patient whose ability to walk has been impaired by neurological, muscular, or skeletal abnormality." The MBP Manual elaborates that while gait evaluation and training by a therapist is skilled physical therapy, activities of an aide ("repetitious exercises to improve gait, or to maintain strength and endurance, and assistive walking") are not.
- "Range of motion exercises." The MBP Manual elaborates that range of motion *tests* are skilled physical therapy; range of motion *exercises* generally are not, unless specific circumstances make them skilled for a particular patient. Passive range of motion is not skilled physical therapy.

---

[94] MBP Manual, Ch. 8, § 30.4, *available at* http://www.cms.gov/manuals/Downloads/bp102c08.pdf (site visited May 18, 2016).

[95] MBP Manual, Ch. 8, § 30.4.1.1, *available at* http://www.cms.gov/manuals/Downloads/bp102c08.pdf (site visited May 18, 2016).

[96] MBP Manual, Ch. 8, § 30.4.1.1, *available at* http://www.cms.gov/manuals/Downloads/bp102c08.pdf (site visited May 18, 2016).

[97] MBP Manual, Ch. 8, § 30.4.1.1, *available at* http://www.cms.gov/manuals/Downloads/bp102c08.pdf (site visited May 18, 2016).

[98] MBP Manual, Ch. 8, § 30.4.1.1, *available at* http://www.cms.gov/manuals/Downloads/bp102c08.pdf (site visited May 18, 2016).

[99] 42 C.F.R. § 409.33(c)(1)–(7).

[100] MBP Manual, Ch. 8, § 30.4.1.2.A-G, *available at* http://www.cms.gov/manuals/Downloads/bp102c08.pdf (site visited May 18, 2016).

- "Maintenance therapy" when the services "are so inherently complex that they can be safely and effectively performed only by, or under the supervision of, a qualified therapist." The MBP Manual says, "a maintenance program to maintain the patient's current condition or to prevent or slow further deterioration is covered so long as the beneficiary requires skilled care for the safe and effective performance of the program." It further provides, "If the specialized knowledge and judgment of a qualified therapist are required," the design of the maintenance program, instruction of the patient or appropriate caregiver, and "necessary periodic reevaluations" of the patient and the program are all considered skilled therapy services. As an example of covered maintenance therapy, the MBP Manual describes determining the exercises required to maintain the present level of function for a patient with Parkinson's disease, including conducting an initial evaluation, designing a maintenance program, and instructing the patient or supportive personnel to carry out the maintenance program.

- Ultrasound, shortwave, and microwave diathermy treatments.

- "Hot packs, hydrocollator, infra-red treatments, paraffin baths, and whirlpool baths." The MBP Manual explains that although these treatments do not ordinarily require skilled therapists, skilled therapy services may be necessary "where the patient's condition is complicated by circulatory deficiency, areas of desensitization, open wounds, fractures, or other complications."

- Speech pathologist or audiologist services.[101] The MBP Manual defines speech-language pathology and occupational therapy by reference to Inpatient Hospital Services, Chapter 1 of the MBP Manual.[102]

Except in certain circumstances,[103] personal care services do not qualify as skilled services:[104]

- "Administration of routine oral medication, eye drops and ointments." The MBP Manual confirms that these are not skilled services, even if the

---

[101] 42 C.F.R. § 409.33(c); MBP Manual, Ch. 8, § 30.4.2, *available at* http://www.cms.gov/manuals/Downloads/bp102c08.pdf (site visited May 18, 2016).

[102] MBP Manual, Ch. 8, §§ 30.4.2 and 30.4.3, respectively, *available at* http://www.cms.gov/manuals/Downloads/bp102c08.pdf (site visited May 18, 2016).

[103] 42 C.F.R. § 409.32(b) (exceptions allowing services usually viewed as nonskilled to be considered skilled); MBP Manual, Ch. 8, § 30.5 (nonskilled supportive or personal services), *available at* http://www.cms.gov/manuals/Downloads/bp102c08.pdf (site visited May 18, 2016).

[104] 42 C.F.R. § 409.33(d)(1)–(13); MBP Manual, Ch. 8, § 30.5, *available at* http://www.cms.gov/manuals/Downloads/bp102c08.pdf (site visited May 18, 2016).

patient is unable to self-administer these medications or state law requires a nurse to dispense them.

- "General maintenance care of colostomy and ileostomy."
- "Routine services to maintain satisfactory functioning of indwelling bladder catheters."
- "Changes of dressing for uninfected post-operative or chronic conditions."
- "Prophylactic and palliative skin care, including bathing and application of creams, or treatment of minor skin problems."
- Routine incontinence care.
- General maintenance of a plaster cast. The MBP Manual notes that a patient with a preexisting skin or circulatory condition, or who needs adjustment of traction, may require skilled services.
- Routine care of braces and similar devices.
- "Use of heat as a palliative and comfort measure" (e.g., whirlpool or hydrocollator).
- "Routine administration of medical gases after a regimen of therapy has been established."
- "Assistance in dressing, eating, and going to the toilet."
- "Periodic turning and positioning in bed."
- "General supervision of exercises," including carrying out of repetitious exercises in a maintenance program.[105]

[2] Daily Skilled Services

To meet the definition of *daily*, skilled nursing care, or a combination of skilled nursing services and rehabilitation services, must be provided seven days per week.[106] Skilled rehabilitation services provided five days per week satisfy the daily requirement.[107] The MBP Manual advises that there must be "a valid medical reason" for scheduling therapies on different days and that "arbitrarily

[105] MBP Manual, Ch. 8, § 30.5, *available at* http://www.cms.gov/manuals/Downloads/bp102c08.pdf (site visited May 18, 2016).

[106] 42 C.F.R. §§ 409.30 (basic requirements), 409.31 (skilled level of care requirement), and 409.34 (definition of "daily").

[107] 42 C.F.R. § 409.34(a)(2); MBP Manual, Ch. 8, § 30.6, *available at* http://www.cms.gov/manuals/Downloads/bp102c08.pdf (site visited May 18, 2016).

staggering the timing of various therapy modalities through the week" to achieve five days of therapy would not qualify a beneficiary for Medicare coverage.[108]

The MBP Manual cautions against applying the "daily" requirement too "strictly," recognizing that the requirement may be met even when therapy is suspended in an "isolated break" for a day or two (e.g., due to a resident's extreme fatigue).[109]

A temporary absence to attend "a special religious service, holiday meal, family occasion, going on a car ride, or for a trial visit home" is not by itself evidence that a beneficiary does not need skilled care.[110] The MBP Manual cautions facilities against taking a "conservative approach" and notifying patients "that leaving the facility will result in denial of coverage."[111] "Frequent or prolonged" absences, however, may suggest that the beneficiary's care needs can be met outside a SNF.[112]

The Medicare Claims Processing (MCP) Manual does not permit SNFs to bill the Medicare program or the beneficiary for care during a beneficiary's brief leave of absence "where the patient is absent, but not discharged, for reasons other than admission to a hospital, other SNF, or distinct part of the same SNF."[113] There is an exception, however. A provision of the MCP Manual authorizes SNFs to bill beneficiaries for bed-hold during a temporary "SNF absence" if the SNF informs patients in advance of both their option to make bed-hold payments and the amount of the charge and if the patients "affirmatively elect" to make bed-hold payments prior to being charged.[114]

[3] "Practical Matter" Test

Even if daily skilled services are medically necessary, Medicare coverage may still be denied unless the services, "as a 'practical matter,' can only be provided in a SNF on an inpatient basis."[115] Whether the "practical matter" test is

[108] MBP Manual, Ch. 8, § 30.6, *available at* http://www.cms.gov/manuals/Downloads/bp102c08.pdf (site visited May 18, 2016).

[109] MBP Manual, Ch. 8, § 30.6, *available at* http://www.cms.gov/manuals/Downloads/bp102c08.pdf (site visited May 18, 2016).

[110] MBP Manual, Ch. 8, § 30.7.3, *available at* http://www.cms.gov/manuals/Downloads/bp102c08.pdf (site visited May 18, 2016).

[111] MBP Manual, Ch. 8, § 30.7.3, *available at* http://www.cms.gov/manuals/Downloads/bp102c08.pdf (site visited May 18, 2016).

[112] MBP Manual, Ch. 8, § 30.7.3, *available at* http://www.cms.gov/manuals/Downloads/bp102c08.pdf (site visited May 18, 2016).

[113] MCP Manual, CMS Pub. 100-04, Ch. 6, § 40.3.5.2, *available at* http://www.cms.gov/Regulations-and-Guidance/Guidance/Manuals/Downloads/clm104c06.pdf (site visited May 18, 2016).

[114] MCP Manual, Ch. 1, § 30.1.1.1, *available at* https://www.cms.gov/Regulations-and-Guidance/Guidance/Manuals/Downloads/clm104c01.pdf (site visited May 18, 2016).

[115] 42 C.F.R. § 409.31(b)(3). *See also* 42 C.F.R. § 409.35; MBP Manual, Ch. 8, § 30.7, *available at* http://www.cms.gov/manuals/Downloads/bp102c08.pdf (site visited May 18, 2016).

met depends on consideration of "the availability and feasibility of using more economical alternative facilities or services'" specifically, whether more economical services are *actually available* to *this* beneficiary.[116]

If the daily skilled services are not available on an outpatient basis where the patient lives, the "practical matter" test is satisfied and inpatient care in a SNF is covered. However, in evaluating the availability of alternative care, the issue is the feasibility of the alternative care, not whether Medicare will pay for it. As a result, if a physical therapist could provide daily physical therapy to a patient, it is not relevant to the "practical matter" determination that the patient has exceeded the outpatient therapy cap or does not participate in Medicare Part B.[117]

If transportation to the outpatient services would pose "an excessive physical hardship" to the patient or would be "less economical" or "less efficient or effective" than inpatient services in the SNF, the practical matter test is satisfied.[118] "Less economical" is determined from the perspective of the health care delivery system. If getting services in a hospital outpatient department would require an ambulance ride and providing care in a SNF would be more economical, the "economy and efficiency" test is met. Similarly, "inordinate travel costs" to a patient's isolated residence also satisfy the "economy and efficiency" test.[119]

The patient's medical condition is critical to the "practical matter" determination. If an alternative care setting would "adversely affect a patient's medical condition," care in a SNF is appropriate.[120] The MBP Manual provides the example of "a 75-year old woman who has suffered a cerebrovascular accident and cannot climb stairs safely." If the patient lives alone in a second-floor apartment, which is accessible only by climbing a flight of stairs, she is eligible for SNF care, even when the physical and occupational therapy she needs is available one mile from her apartment. The MBP Manual concludes, "because of her inability to negotiate the stairs, the daily skilled services she requires cannot, as a practical matter, be provided to the patient outside the SNF."[121]

Goodrich v. Bowen[122] involved Medicare coverage of daily insulin injections for 17 SNF patients. The court appropriately noted that the administration

---

[116] 42 C.F.R. § 409.35(a).

[117] MBP Manual, Ch. 8, § 30.7.1, *available at* http://www.cms.gov/manuals/Downloads/bp102c08.pdf (site visited May 18, 2016).

[118] MBP Manual, Ch. 8, § 30.7, *available at* http://www.cms.gov/manuals/Downloads/bp102c08.pdf (site visited May 18, 2016).

[119] MBP Manual, Ch. 8, § 30.7.2 (examples 1 and 2, respectively), *available at* http://www.cms.gov/manuals/Downloads/bp102c08.pdf (site visited May 18, 2016).

[120] MBP Manual, Ch. 8, § 30.7.3, *available at* http://www.cms.gov/manuals/Downloads/bp102c08.pdf (site visited May 18, 2016).

[121] MBP Manual, Ch. 8, § 30.7.3 (example), *available at* http://www.cms.gov/manuals/Downloads/bp102c08.pdf (site visited May 18, 2016).

[122] 1988 WL 235577 (D. Conn. May 31, 1988); *see also* Hoye v. Sebelius, 2011 WL 1467636 (D. Mass. Mar. 31, 2011).

of subcutaneous injections, at that time, was presumed to be a skilled nursing service pursuant to the Medicare regulations.[123] *Goodrich* addressed the criteria for establishing "practical matter," discussing the availability and feasibility of using alternative services:

> [T]he "practical matter" criteria [sic] requires an individual assessment of each claimant's overall condition and actual investigation into the availability and feasibility of alternatives to inpatient SNF care. It is not sufficient for the Secretary to look at only one aspect of a claimant's care such as the need for daily insulin injections. The Secretary must assess the need for skilled service along with the other services the claimant requires, both skilled and custodial, and then arrive at a determination of the "practical matter" requirement.[124]

As with the skilled care determination, the patient's total condition is important in assessing the practical matter standard. Here, however, the patient's custodial needs may be as important as the need for skilled care.

Finally, home care is not an alternative to SNF care if the patient does not have sufficient assistance at home from "capable and willing family" or others, such as a home health agency.[125] In assessing the practicalities of providing the needed care at home, rather than in a SNF, relevant questions include whether outpatient or home health care services are actually available, whether the patient has access to such services even if they are available, and whether the patient is able to be maintained at home in order to receive the skilled outpatient or home health care services.

[E] The Benefit Period or "Spell of Illness"

Medicare covers a maximum of 100 days of SNF care during a benefit period, also known as the "spell of illness."[126] A benefit period begins the first day a Medicare beneficiary enters a hospital or SNF and ends when he or she has been receiving less than a skilled level of care, or is not receiving care in a hospital or SNF, for 60 consecutive days. It is theoretically possible for a beneficiary to have more than one benefit period during a calendar year. However, the patient

---

[123] 42 C.F.R. § 409.33(b)(1). *But see* 63 Fed. Reg. 26,284 (May 12, 1998) regarding insulin injections and the skilled care concept.

[124] *See also Hoye*, 2011 WL 1467636 (remand; burden should be on Secretary "to demonstrate the availability and feasibility of outpatient services, and to engage in the practical matter inquiry"); Mazzella v. Heckler, 1985 WL 77596 (D. Conn. Aug. 18, 1985).

[125] MBP Manual, Ch. 8, §§ 30.7, 30.7.1, *available at* http://www.cms.gov/manuals/Downloads/bp102c08.pdf (site May 18, 2016).

[126] 42 U.S.C. §§ 1395d(a)(2)(A) and 1395x(a); 42 C.F.R. § 409.60; *see* Matthews v. Leavitt, 452 F.3d 145 (2d Cir. 2006); Mayburg v. Secretary of HHS, 740 F.2d 100 (1st Cir. 1984); Levi v. Heckler, 736 F.2d 848 (2d Cir. 1984).

must remain outside a hospital or SNF for 60 consecutive days, or, if remaining in a nursing facility, must receive less than a SNF level of care for 60 consecutive days, in order to end a benefit period and be eligible to begin a new one.[127]

■ **EXAMPLE:** Mrs. Jones is admitted to the hospital and, after a four-day inpatient stay, is transferred to the SNF on March 25. Medicare coverage is granted for 100 days, through July 3. Mrs. Jones remains in the SNF through August 28 but does not receive either daily skilled nursing or rehabilitation services. She is then readmitted to the hospital. Following discharge from the hospital, she is readmitted to the SNF.

Mrs. Jones will not be entitled to Medicare coverage for her second SNF admission because she did not have a "break" in her benefit period and has already received 100 days of coverage during this benefit period. (She did not receive daily skilled care in a hospital or SNF for only 58 days, from July 3 to August 28, rather than for the required 60 days.) Mrs. Jones would have to receive a custodial level of care in the SNF for 60 consecutive days and then require inpatient hospital care for at least three days in order to qualify for Medicare SNF coverage under a new benefit period.

[F] Care in a SNF Must Be Related to Condition for Which the Patient Was Hospitalized

To meet Medicare's level of care requirements, a patient must receive services for either a condition for which the patient received inpatient hospital services or a condition that arose while the patient was receiving care in a SNF for a condition for which the patient received inpatient hospital services.[128] In other words, there must be some connection between the patient's condition during the qualifying hospital stay and subsequent SNF admission. A problem that occasionally arises is establishing that the SNF patient is receiving skilled care that is related to the patient's prior hospitalization. The problem most often encountered is a fact-finder's requiring that a SNF patient receive exactly the same services for exactly the same condition as provided in the hospital. Such an interpretation of the law is inappropriate and should be challenged.

---

[127] 42 C.F.R. § 409.60(b); Medicare General Information, Eligibility, and Entitlement Manual, CMS Pub. 100-01, Ch. 3, §§ 10.4.3.2 and 10.4.4, *available at* http://www.cms.gov/Regulations-and-Guidance/Guidance/Manuals/Downloads/ge101c03.pdf (site visited May 18, 2016).

[128] 42 U.S.C. § 1395f(a)(2)(B); 42 C.F.R. § 409.31(b)(2)(i)–(ii); MBP Manual, Ch. 8, § 20.1, *available at* http://www.cms.gov/manuals/Downloads/bp102c08.pdf (site visited May 18, 2016) (New language added in 2013 provides: "In this context, the applicable hospital condition need not have been the principal diagnosis that actually precipitated the beneficiary's admission to the hospital, but could be any one of the conditions present during the qualifying hospital stay.").

In *Sowell v. Richardson*,[129] the court found that hospitalization was due to the patient's general physical condition. In *Hayner v. Weinberger*,[130] the patient's underlying condition was related to the condition subsequently treated at the SNF. Both courts found the patients eligible for Medicare coverage. In *Shepack v. Bowen*,[131] the court noted, "it is critical to ascertain the interrelationship between a claimant's various illnesses in order to determine if the condition for which a claimant received skilled nursing services in a SNF was a condition for which he or she received inpatient hospital services."[132] The court remanded the case to the Administrative Law Judge (ALJ) to obtain further medical documentation. Upon rehearing, the ALJ found the services received at the SNF were for a condition previously treated at the hospital.

A district court liberally construed 42 C.F.R. § 409.31(b)(2) in *Stefanko v. Secretary of HHS*.[133] The patient was treated in the hospital for a primary condition of a fractured knee and secondary conditions of congestive heart failure, diabetes, and kidney failure. The court found that treatment in the SNF of the surgical wound and insulin injections constituted skilled care for conditions that were treated in the hospital.

As a practical matter, it is useful to collect documentation to establish that the SNF stay was for a condition treated or diagnosed, or both, in the hospital. It is important to document all the conditions treated during the hospitalization. Treatment may consist of monitoring a cardiac or pulmonary condition. A person with diabetes experiencing unstable blood sugar levels while in the hospital may require careful monitoring. The patient may be generally weak or may present complexities due to multiple conditions that require skilled management.

§ 3.04 IDENTIFYING COVERABLE CASES

Medicare SNF claims are suitable for Medicare coverage, and appealable if they have been denied, if they meet the following criteria:

1. The patient was hospitalized as an inpatient for at least three consecutive days not including the day of discharge and, in most cases, was admitted to the SNF within 30 days of hospital discharge.

2. A physician certified that the patient needs SNF care.

3. The beneficiary required "skilled nursing or skilled rehabilitation services, or both, on a daily basis." Skilled nursing and skilled rehabilitation services are those that require the skills of technical or professional

---

[129] 319 F. Supp. 689, 692 (D.S.C. 1970).

[130] 382 F. Supp. 762, 765 (E.D.N.Y. 1974).

[131] No. N-85-157 (JAC) (D. Conn. Mar. 16, 1987).

[132] *Shepack*, No. N-85-157 (JAC), slip. op. at 11.

[133] 1990 U.S. Dist. LEXIS 21041 (D. Conn. Mar. 27, 1990).

personnel such as registered nurses, licensed practical nurses, physical therapists, and occupational therapists. In order to be deemed skilled, the service must be so inherently complex that it can be safely and effectively performed only by, or under the supervision of, professional or technical personnel.

4. The SNF is a Medicare-certified facility.

Other Important Points

1. The restoration potential of a patient is not the deciding factor in determining whether skilled services are needed.
2. The management of a plan involving only a variety of "custodial" personal care services is skilled when, in light of the patient's total condition, the aggregate of those services requires the involvement of skilled personnel.
3. The requirement that a patient receive "daily" skilled services will be met if skilled *rehabilitation* services are provided *five days* per week.
4. Examples of skilled services:
    a. Overall management and evaluation of care plan;
    b. Observation and assessment of the patient's changing condition;
    c. Levin tube and gastrostomy feedings;
    d. Ongoing assessment of rehabilitation needs and potential;
    e. Therapeutic exercises or activities;
    f. Gait evaluation and training.
5. The doctor is the patient's most important ally. If it appears that Medicare coverage will be denied, ask the doctor to help demonstrate that the standards described above are met.
6. If the SNF issues a notice saying Medicare coverage is not available and the patient seems to satisfy the criteria above, ask the facility to submit a claim for a formal Medicare coverage determination. The SNF must submit a claim at the patient's or representative's request; the patient is not required to pay until he or she receives a formal determination from Medicare.
7. Do not be satisfied with a Medicare determination unreasonably limiting coverage; appeal for the benefits the patient deserves. It will take some time, but you may win your case.

§ 3.05 SNF PROSPECTIVE PAYMENT SYSTEM AND RESOURCE UTILIZATION GROUPS

[A] Prospective Payment System Mandated as of July 1, 1998

The Balanced Budget Act of 1997 mandated a prospective payment system (PPS) for the Medicare SNF benefit.[134] The per diem rates cover all routine service, ancillary, and capital-related costs for Part A-covered stays.

The PPS uses case-mix adjustments to relate payments to resident needs. The system accounts for the relative resource use of different types of patients, based on acuity, as determined by a patient classification system now called Resource Utilization Groups-IV (RUG-IV). Each Medicare-coverable patient is placed into one of ten major classifications and then into one of 66 groups. Originally and until January 1, 2006, the SNF PPS used seven major classifications and 44 groups. Effective January 1, 2006, PPS was expanded into 53 groups.[135] In fiscal year 2011, RUG-IV expanded to 66 case-mix groups.[136] The classifications are mutually exclusive; every patient is placed into only one classification at a time.[137]

The process of placing patients into the RUG-IV classifications requires accurate and comprehensive information-gathering about a patient's characteristics and needs. A patient's RUG-IV classification has implications for both reimbursement and Medicare coverage.

---

[134] The Balanced Budget Act of 1997 (BBA '97), Pub. L. No. 105-33 (Aug. 5, 1997), § 4432(a), amending § 1888 of the Social Security Act, by adding subsection (e), 42 U.S.C. § 1395yy, effective on or after July 1, 1998 (depending on SNFs' cost-reporting periods).

[135] 70 Fed. Reg. 45,025, 45,045–46 (Aug. 4, 2005).

[136] CMS announced in August 2009 that RUG-IV would be implemented in fiscal year 2011. 74 Fed. 40,288 (Aug. 11, 2009). Section 10325 of the Patient Protection and Affordable Care Act (PPACA) (known as the Affordable Care Act, or ACA), Pub. L. No. 111-148, delayed the implementation date for most of RUG-IV by one year. Section 10325 was repealed by § 202 of the Medicare and Medicaid Extenders Act of 2010, Pub. L. No. 111-309, allowing full implementation of the RUG-IV system as of FY 2011. 76 Fed. Reg. 26,364, 26,367–68 (May 6, 2011).

[137] 63 Fed. Reg. 26,251 (May 12, 1998); 64 Fed. Reg. 41,643 (July 30, 1999); 65 Fed. Reg. 46,769 (July 31, 2000); 66 Fed. Reg. 39,561 (July 31, 2001); 67 Fed. Reg. 49,797 (July 31, 2002); 68 Fed. Reg. 46,035 (Aug. 4, 2003), 68 Fed. Reg. 55,882 (Sept. 29, 2003) (correction notice), 69 Fed. Reg. 45,775 (July 30, 2004); 70 Fed. Reg. 45,026 (Aug. 4, 2005); 71 Fed. Reg. 43,158 (July 31, 2006); 71 Fed. Reg. 57,519 (Sept. 29, 2006) (correction notice); 72 Fed. Reg. 43,411 (Aug. 3, 2007); 73 Fed. Reg. 46,415 (Aug. 8, 2008); 74 Fed. Reg. 40,288 (Aug. 11, 2009); 75 Fed. Reg. 42,885 (July 22, 2010 (notice); 76 Fed. Reg. 48,486 (Aug. 8, 2011); 77 Fed. Reg. 46,213 (Aug. 2, 2012); 78 Fed. Reg. 47,936 (Aug. 6, 2013); 79 Fed. Reg. 45,627 (Aug. 5, 2014); 80 Fed. Reg. 46,389, 46,405 (Aug. 4, 2015); 81 Fed. Reg. 51,969, 51,976 (Aug. 5, 2016).

[B] Impact on Nursing Home Reimbursement

The RUG classifications are hierarchical, with higher categories providing greater reimbursement. The prospective payment system was phased in over a three-year transition period. Depending upon when a facility's cost-reporting period ends, the phase-in began either October 1, 1998, or January 1, 1999.

[C] The Ten Major RUG-IV Categories

The ten major RUG-IV categories, in hierarchical order based upon intensity of resource utilization, are:

1. Rehabilitation Plus Extensive Services
2. Ultra High Rehabilitation
3. Very High Rehabilitation
4. High Rehabilitation
5. Medium Rehabilitation
6. Low Rehabilitation
7. Extensive Services
8. Special Care High
9. Special Care Low
10. Clinically Complex

A patient classified into one of the upper 52 RUG-IV classifications following a qualifying hospital stay is presumed to meet a Medicare level of care during the first five-day assessment period.[138] A patient classified into one of the remaining 14 categories qualifies for Medicare coverage based upon the statutory and regulatory criteria for the SNF level of care.[139]

[D] Impact on Medicare Coverage: A Presumption of Medicare Coverage for "Upper 52"

A Medicare beneficiary who is classified into one of the top 52 RUG-IV categories may nevertheless experience barriers to SNF admission. These barriers

[138] MBP Manual, Ch. 8, § 30.1, *available at* http://www.cms.gov/manuals/Downloads/bp102c08.pdf (site visited May 25, 2016); 81 Fed. Reg. 51,969, 51,984 (Aug. 5, 2016).

[139] These Medicare-covered groups may be redesignated on an annual basis, 63 Fed. Reg. 26,251, 26,283 (May 12, 1998) (citing 42 C.F.R. §§ 409.31–35 and Medicare manuals). *See also* 81 Fed. Reg. 51,969, 51,984 (Aug. 5, 2016).

are often caused by the high cost to SNFs of caring for certain groups of individuals seeking admission.

When the RUGs system was first implemented, patients who met the SNF coverage criteria experienced difficulty gaining admission to a SNF if they required complex nursing care and expensive medications or if they had high transportation costs, often related to dialysis. Hospital discharge planners reported that they were having more difficulty placing some Medicare patients and that facilities were changing their admissions practices in response to the new reimbursement system.[140] Since virtually all costs of providing services needed by patients are covered by the SNF's Medicare prospective per diem rate under consolidated billing, many SNFs were reluctant to admit individuals needing the services described above, when Medicare was the apparent payment source, because of the costs involved.

In the Medicare, Medicaid, and SCHIP Balanced Budget Refinement Act of 1999 (BBRA),[141] Congress amended the Medicare statute in an effort to address these access problems. Effective April 1, 2000, the cost of an ambulance ride to a hospital for the purpose of obtaining kidney dialysis or radiation therapy for cancer treatment was "unbundled" from the SNF's Medicare payment. As a result, the per diem RUG reimbursement for SNF patients needing ambulance transportation for these purposes was no longer required to pay for the ambulance in addition to the services provided in the SNF. Instead, ambulance costs are billed separately.

The BBRA also excluded certain "high-cost, low probability" services from consolidated billing: certain chemotherapy items, chemotherapy administration services, radioisotope services, and customized prosthetic devices.[142] Despite these exclusions from consolidated billing, beneficiaries needing chemotherapy are often denied admission by SNFs that do not know that some of these drugs are excluded from the daily SNF rate. CMS has declined to exclude additional "high cost, low probability services" from consolidated billing unless they fall within one of the four categories specified in the BBRA.[143]

In September 2001, the HHS Office of Inspector General (OIG) reported that Medicare beneficiaries were difficult to place in SNFs if they needed IV antibiotics or expensive drugs or if they were medically complex, needed a ventilator,

---

[140] Office of Inspector General (OIG), *Early Effects of the Prospective Payment System on Access to Skilled Nursing Facilities*, OEI-02-99-00400 (Aug. 1999).

[141] Medicare, Medicaid, and SCHIP Balanced Budget Refinement Act of 1999 (BBRA), Pub. L. No. 106-113 (Nov. 29, 1999).

[142] BBRA § 103, 42 U.S.C. § 1395yy(e)(2)(A)(iii)(II), (III), (IV), (V); 79 Fed. Reg. 45,627, 45,641-644 (Aug. 5, 2014); 80 Fed. Reg. 46,389, 46,406-407 (Aug. 4, 2015).

[143] *See. e.g.,* 81 Fed. Reg. 51,9969, 51,984-51,986 (Aug. 5, 2016).

had an infectious disease or needed isolation, had renal failure or needed dialysis, had behavior problems, or needed total parental feedings.[144]

Later statutory and regulatory revisions to the SNF PPS excluded additional services from the PPS rates. At present, services excluded from the SNF rate,[145] and separately billed to Medicare,[146] include:

- Certain cardiac catheterizations;
- Certain computerized axial topography (CT) scans;
- Certain magnetic resonance imaging (MRIs);
- Certain ambulatory surgeries involving the use of a hospital operating room;
- Certain radiation therapies;
- Certain angiographies, and lymphatic and venous procedures;
- Emergency services;
- Ambulance services when related to an excluded service within this list; and
- Ambulance transportation related to dialysis services.

The Medicare Prescription Drug, Improvement, and Modernization Act of 2003 (MMA) provided for a temporary 128 percent increase in the PPS per diem for any SNF patient with Acquired Immune Deficiency Syndrome (AIDS).[147] CMS has continued this add-on each year.[148]

Payment issues may be important when benefits are sought for SNF patients, especially for those who are not classified into one of the 52 RUG-IV categories that carry a presumption of Medicare coverage.

§ 3.06 PROBLEM AREAS OF CONCERN FOR THE ADVOCATE

Frequent problems that stand in the way of Medicare SNF coverage are addressed below.

---

[144] OIG, *Medicare Beneficiary Access to Skilled Nursing Facilities*, OEI-02-0330, p. 7 (Sept. 2000). In July 2001, the OIG found similar difficulties and also identified residents as difficult to place if they had decubitus ulcers and needed wound care. OIG, *Medicare Beneficiary Access to Skilled Nursing Facilities*, OEI-02-01-00160, p. 7 (July 2001).

[145] MCP Manual, Ch. 6, § 20.1.2, *available at* http://www.cms.gov/Regulations-and-Guidance/Guidance/Manuals/Downloads/clm104c06.pdf (site visited May 25, 2016).

[146] MBP Manual, Ch. 8, § 10.2, *available at* http://www.cms.gov/manuals/Downloads/bp102c08.pdf (site visited May 25, 2016).

[147] The Medicare Prescription Drug, Improvement, and Modernization Act (MMA), Pub. L. No. 108-173 (Dec. 8, 2003), § 511, 42 U.S.C. § 1395yy(e)(12). The increase remains in effect.

[148] 81 Fed. Reg. 51,969, 51,976 (Aug. 5, 2016).

[A] Skilled Versus Custodial Care

The critical question in every Medicare SNF coverage determination is whether the patient was receiving a skilled level of care on a daily basis. The type of skilled care may be either nursing or rehabilitation services, or a combination of the two. Rehabilitation services include physical therapy, occupational therapy, and speech therapy. Rehabilitation services need only be provided five days per week to qualify as "daily," while nursing services, or a combination of nursing and therapy, must be provided seven days per week to meet the "daily" test.[149]

For example, a patient who receives physical therapy three days per week and occupational therapy two other days would be eligible for coverage. This patient has received skilled rehabilitation services five days per week. Similarly, a patient who receives physical therapy three days per week and skilled nursing care the other four days would be eligible for coverage. The key is that the patient is receiving skilled care each day of the week.

Most Medicare SNF patients require custodial care in addition to daily skilled care. Frequently these patients are nonambulatory or semiambulatory. For example, a stroke patient will require physical therapy to learn how to walk again and to rebuild muscle strength. In meeting the practical-matter requirement for inpatient coverage, it is often necessary to establish that the needed custodial care can only be provided, as a practical matter, on an inpatient basis.[150]

An assessment of whether care is skilled focuses on the inherent complexity of the service. This line of analysis has been adopted by courts in making level of care determinations.[151] Courts have also noted that a commonsense, nontechnical consideration of the patient's condition as a whole must be made in determining the level of care.[152]

There is no definition of custodial care in the law. The regulations merely state that custodial care is care that does not meet the definition of SNF care.[153] As a general rule, custodial care is interpreted to be care that a layperson without any special skills or training can safely and effectively perform.[154]

A systematic assessment of which services have actually been provided to the patient and careful review of the medical record can help determine whether

---

[149] 42 C.F.R. § 409.34. *See also* MBP Manual, Ch. 8, § 30.6, *available at* http://www.cms.gov/manuals/Downloads/bp102c08.pdf (site visited May 25, 2016).

[150] The "practical matter" criterion for coverage requires that the beneficiary need care on an inpatient basis. 42 C.F.R. § 409.35; MBP Manual, Ch. 8, § 30.7, *available at* http://www.cms.gov/manuals/Downloads/bp102c08.pdf (site visited May 25, 2016).

[151] Hurley v. Bowen, 857 F.2d 907, 911 (2d Cir. 1988); Hirsch v. Bowen, 655 F. Supp. 342, 344 (S.D.N.Y. 1987).

[152] Friedman v. Secretary of HHS, 819 F.2d 42, 45 (2d Cir. 1987); *Papciak*, 742 F. Supp. 2d 765, 769; Pfalzgraf v. Shalala, 997 F. Supp. 360, 365 (W.D.N.Y. 1998); Landa v. Shalala, 900 F. Supp. 628, 635 (E.D.N.Y. 1995); Walsh v. Secretary of HHS, 636 F. Supp. 358, 360 (E.D.N.Y. 1986).

[153] 42 C.F.R. § 411.15(g).

[154] *Hirsch*, 655 F. Supp. 342.

the patient received a Medicare-covered level of care. A checklist may be a useful tool in evaluating level of care:

- Is this a rehabilitation or nursing patient (or both)?
- Which rehabilitation services have been provided (i.e., physical, occupational, or speech therapy)?
- Check the list of *per se* skilled therapy services.
- Is skilled development, management, and evaluation of the patient care plan required?
- Is skilled observation and assessment of the patient's changing or unstable condition required?
- Which specific nursing services have been provided (e.g., injections, decubitus ulcer care, dressing changes)?
- Are there any special medical complications that require the services of skilled personnel (e.g., multiple medications with potential adverse reactions, psychiatric components)?[155]
- Have the services been provided by or under the supervision of certified skilled personnel?
- Is there sufficient medical evidence to support a claim for Medicare coverage?

[B] Total Condition of the Patient

Courts have consistently taken the position that a patient's total condition must be taken into consideration, not merely each individual service provided.[156] In assessing the Medicare patient's total condition, the records should be examined to determine the need for management and evaluation of the patient's care plan or observation or monitoring, or both, of the patient's medical condition. As part of the "total condition" analysis, a recent federal court decision recognized

[155] 42 C.F.R. § 409.33(a)(2); MBP Manual, Ch. 8, § 30.2.2, *available at* http://www.cms.gov/manuals/Downloads/bp102c08.pdf (site visited May 25, 2016).

[156] *Papciak*, 742 F. Supp. 2d 765; *Pfalzgraf*, 997 F. Supp. 360, 365; Yuknat v. Bowen, 1989 WL 265508 (D. Conn. Mar. 31, 1989); Stearns v. Sullivan, 1989 WL 141736 (D. Mass. Nov. 6, 1989); Perales v. Sullivan, 1989 WL 111087 (S.D.N.Y. Sept. 19, 1989); Scotto v. Bowen, 1989 WL 32805 (E.D.N.Y. Mar. 30 1989); Olson v. Bowen, 1988 WL 235560 (W.D. Wis. May 31, 1988); Babula v. Secretary of HHS, 655 F. Supp. 1117 (W.D.N.Y. 1987); *Hirsch*, 655 F. Supp. 342; Israel v. Bowen, 669 F. Supp. 61 (W.D.N.Y. 1987); Gartmann v. Secretary of HHS, 633 F. Supp. 671, 679 (E.D.N.Y. 1986); Howard v. Heckler, 618 F. Supp. 1333 (E.D.N.Y. 1985); Roth v. Secretary of HHS, 606 F. Supp. 636 (W.D.N.Y. 1985); Kuebler v. Secretary of HHS, 579 F. Supp. 1436 (E.D.N.Y. 1984).

the need to consider whether situational depression and anxiety were temporarily limiting a patient's ability to progress in her functional capacity.[157]

[C] Management and Evaluation of the Patient Care Plan

SNF patients are entitled to Medicare coverage if they need and receive skilled observation, assessment, management of care plan, or patient education services, even if they do not require or receive specific nursing services, such as injections or catheter irrigation, and even if they do not fall within the top 52 RUG-IV categories.[158] Documentation to support coverage on these bases must be kept by the facility and should be found in the medical record, including the doctor's order, nurses' notes, and any medical assessment data that the SNF is required to keep for transmittal to the Medicare contractors for payment.[159]

Overall management and evaluation of a patient's care plan may involve skilled services, even when the individual services are not skilled. The need for skilled care may be inferred from the services provided, even when the skilled planning and management activities are not specifically identified in the patient's clinical record.[160] One or more of the following nursing services may qualify a patient for Medicare coverage of his or her SNF stay:

- Involvement of skilled nursing personnel to develop, manage, and evaluate a care plan formulated through physician orders;
- Involvement of skilled nursing personnel to meet the patient's needs, promote recovery, and ensure medical safety when considering the patient's physical and mental condition;
- Management by skilled nursing personnel of personal care services when the patient's condition and aggregate of services require technical or professional intervention;
- Involvement of skilled nursing personnel to understand the relationship between services and evaluate the ultimate effect of one service on another;
- Involvement of skilled nursing personnel required, even though each individual service is not considered skilled by itself;

[157] *Papciak*, 742 F. Supp. 2d 765.

[158] 42 C.F.R. § 409.33(a)(1) and (3); MBP Manual, Ch. 8, § 30.1, *available at* http://www.cms.gov/manuals/Downloads/bp102c08.pdf (site May 25, 2016).

[159] *See generally* 42 C.F.R. §§ 413.343 and 483.20.

[160] 42 C.F.R. § 409.33(a)(1)(ii); MBP Manual, Ch. 8, § 30.2.3.1, *available at* http://www.cms.gov/manuals/Downloads/bp102c08.pdf (site visited May 25, 2016).

- Skilled planning and management services not specifically articulated as such in the clinical record, if the patient's overall condition is documented as justifying the need for technical or professional services.[161]

Cases that rest solely on management and evaluation of the skilled service are among the most difficult to win because the standard is ambiguous and the qualifying factors are not easy to define. Certain factors are important in this type of case: age, number of medical conditions, mental impairment, patient safety, and actual professional staff involvement. An individual with medical problems involving vital organs and systems is more likely to require skilled management and evaluation. Very often a case rests on the fact that skilled nursing personnel are involved in the development, management, and evaluation of the patient's care plan.

The MBP Manual provides as an example "an aged patient with a history of diabetes mellitus and angina pectoris who is recovering from an open reduction of the neck of the femur."[162] He requires "skin care, appropriate oral medications, a diabetic diet, a therapeutic exercise program to preserve muscle tone and body condition, and observation to notice signs of deterioration . . . or complications. . . ."[163] Although the individual services could be provided by nonskilled personnel, the patient's condition, age, and immobility "create a high potential for serious complications" and justify skilled care until the patient's treatment regimen is stabilized.[164]

Every aspect of the patient's condition, including the variety and intensity of services being performed by nursing personnel, should be carefully evaluated. The review should include the following steps:

- Checking the written care plan[165] and how plan elements are reflected in the ongoing medical assessment data.
- Checking whether the patient manifested behavioral symptoms of psychological or mental impairments and whether the patient had such a condition in addition to physical problems.

---

161 42 C.F.R. § 409.33(a)(1)(ii); MBP Manual, Ch. 8, § 30.2.3.1, *available at* http://www.cms.gov/manuals/Downloads/bp102c08.pdf (site visited May 25, 2016).

162 42 C.F.R. § 409.33(a)(1)(ii); MBP Manual, Ch. 8, § 30.2.3.1 (example 1), *available at* http://www.cms.gov/manuals/Downloads/bp102c08.pdf (site visited July 5, 2016).

163 MBP Manual, Ch. 8, § 30.2.3.1 (example 1), *available at* http://www.cms.gov/manuals/Downloads/bp102c08.pdf (site visited May 25, 2016).

164 MBP Manual, Ch. 8, § 30.2.3.1 (example 1), *available at* http://www.cms.gov/manuals/Downloads/bp102c08.pdf (site visited May 25, 2016).

165 42 C.F.R. § 483.20(k). Often the plan of care alone will not have sufficient information to be helpful. Physician's orders, medical treatment records, and nursing or therapy notes, or both, may contain additional and more specific proof that daily skilled care was needed and provided.

- Checking whether nursing intervention was necessary to ensure patient safety and promote recovery.
- Carefully assessing the aggregate of services in light of the patient's total condition. A patient may need assessment, observation, and other interventions related to a refusal of medication and nutrition, and at the same time, may require occupational therapy twice weekly as well as a variety of personal care services.
- Checking the interrelationship of services. One example is the frequent need for a nurse to assess the interaction of various medications taken simultaneously for different conditions.

Several *per se* nonskilled services may require skilled management even if each service is nonskilled. Multiple medical diagnoses and a great deal of professional nursing services may support the need for skilled management. A need for skilled management services may also be established, even without explicit clinical references to skilled planning and management services, "if the record as a whole clearly establishes that there was a likely potential for serious complications without skilled management."[166]

Management and evaluation services are closely related to observation and assessment services.[167] Often a patient will require a combination of management and observation services. Medicare coverage is more likely to be granted when a patient requires skilled observation in addition to management of the care plan.

[D] Observation and Assessment of the Patient's Changing or Unstable Condition

Many SNF patients require skilled nursing monitoring of their overall medical condition.[168] An individual's condition may change, necessitating a change in the plan of care or additional medical interventions. Medicare covers such nursing care if the care is required and performed on a daily basis.

The Medicare statute and regulations do not require that frail or chronically ill persons deteriorate or suffer a medical setback in order to invoke Medicare coverage for skilled nursing observation and assessment. The risk of potential instability is sufficient to cover services that are needed to maintain a fragile person at the maximum medical and functional status.

---

[166] MBP Manual, Ch. 8, § 30.2.3.1, *available at* http://www.cms.gov/manuals/Downloads/bp102c08.pdf (site visited May 25, 2016).

[167] MBP Manual, Ch. 8, § 30.2.3.2, *available at* http://www.cms.gov/manuals/Downloads/bp102c08.pdf (site visited May 25, 2016).

[168] 42 C.F.R. § 409.33(a)(2); MBP Manual, Ch. 8, § 30.2.3.2, *available at* http://www.cms.gov/manuals/Downloads/bp102c08.pdf (site visited May 25, 2016).

The regulation and MBP Manual give examples when observation and assessment constitute skilled services.[169] Stabilizing a patient's treatment regimen and observing a patient in an unstabilized post-operative period are examples.

An analysis of the record to determine the need for observation and assessment should demonstrate the following:

- Medical necessity was documented by physician orders and nursing or therapy notes;
- Skilled personnel were utilized to identify and evaluate the patient's needs;
- Modification of treatment was needed for additional medical procedures;
- Care was necessary until the patient's condition stabilized or to ensure the patient remained stable;
- There was a reasonable probability of a potential complication or a new acute episode that required monitoring by skilled personnel (even if such complication or episode did not occur);
- Where applicable, acute psychological symptoms were present in addition to physical problems.

A SNF patient with acute psychological symptoms may not have the ability to cooperate with SNF personnel in the same way as patients without such symptoms. For example, a patient may have an order for pain medication, as needed. Due to psychological factors, the patient may not be able to express the need clearly. The patient's nonverbal expressions or behaviors may require skilled interpretation and interventions. Similarly, for a patient with an "as needed" order for medication for agitation or anxiety, the skill of a nurse may be needed to determine, after careful observation and assessment, when to administer such medications. These cases require careful and comprehensive development of the facts to support Medicare coverage.[170]

---

[169] 42 C.F.R. § 409.33(a)(2); MBP Manual, Ch. 8, § 30.2.3.2, *available at* http://www.cms.gov/manuals/Downloads/bp102c08.pdf (site visited May 25, 2016).

[170] *Compare* Gregorace v. Bowen, 1988 WL 95306 (E.D.N.Y. Sept. 1, 1988) [1989-1 Transfer Binder] Medicare & Medicaid Guide (CCH) ¶ 37,444 (Medicare coverage was appropriate, based on observation and assessment, where three of the patient's medications could be administered only under certain circumstances and medications needed to be modified within 24 hours of the patient's admission because of the patient's changing condition) *and* Frohnhoefer v. Leavitt, No. 06-CV-1236 (SJF) (E.D.N.Y. Mar. 19, 2007) (Medicare coverage denied; monitoring and nursing notes, required by state law, did not mean skilled observation and assessment services were provided).

[E] Patient Education

Patient education services may be skilled services if technical or professional personnel are needed to teach a patient self-maintenance and how to manage his or her treatment regimen.[171] Illustrative examples include:

- Teaching self-administration of injectable medications;
- Teaching self-administration of a complex range of medications;
- "Teaching a newly diagnosed diabetic to administer insulin injections, to prepare and follow a diabetic diet, and to observe foot-care precautions;"
- "Teaching self-administration of medical gases;"
- "Gait training and teaching of prosthesis care for a patient who has had a recent leg amputation;"
- Teaching colostomy or ileostomy care;
- "Teaching patients how to perform self-catheterization and self-administration of gastrostomy feedings;"
- "Teaching patients how to care for and maintain central venous lines, such as Hickman catheters;"
- "Teaching patients the use and care of braces, splints and orthotics, and any associated skin care;" and
- "Teaching patients the proper care of any specialized dressings or skin treatments."[172]

[F] Opinion of the Attending Physician

A critical question is how much weight should be given to various types of evidence. The concept or rule of law that the opinion of an attending or treating physician should be given special consideration was first developed in the context of Social Security disability cases.[173]

---

[171] 42 C.F.R. § 409.33(a)(3); MBP Manual, Ch. 8, § 30.2.3.3, *available at* http://www.cms.gov/manuals/Downloads/bp102c08.pdf (site visited May 25, 2016).

[172] MBP Manual, Ch. 8, § 30.2.3.3, *available at* http://www.cms.gov/manuals/Downloads/bp102c08.pdf (site visited May 25, 2016).

[173] Schisler v. Heckler, 787 F.2d 76, 81–85 (2d Cir. 1986). *See also Schisler II*, 851 F.2d 43 (2d Cir. 1988). In response to the first two *Schisler* decisions, the Secretary of HHS promulgated regulations establishing an administrative treating physician rule. These regulations were upheld in the *Schisler III* decision, 3 F.3d 563 (2d Cir. 1993). *See also* Executive Dir. of Office of Vt. Health Access *ex rel.* Carey v. Sebelius, 698 F. Supp. 2d 436, 441 (D. Vt. 2010).

Although most courts have held that the opinion of a Medicare attending physician is not binding, the preponderance of judicial authority is that the opinion of an attending physician must be given great weight when there is no directly conflicting evidence.[174]

The U.S. Court of Appeals for the Second Circuit has twice addressed the treating physician rule in the context of Medicare.[175] In response, the Health Care Financing Administration (HCFA, now CMS) issued a formal administrative ruling concerning the weight to be given a treating physician's opinion in determining hospital and SNF coverage.[176]

The ruling sets out four specific points:

1. No *presumptive* weight may be given to the opinion of a treating physician in determining the medical necessity of inpatient hospital or SNF services.
2. The treating physician's opinion must be evaluated in the context of all the evidence contained in the administrative record.
3. Treating physician certification is required for Medicare *payment;* however, *coverage* decisions are not based solely on physician certification.
4. Coverage decisions are based upon objective medical information available from claims forms and, when necessary, the medical record, which includes the physician certification.

Although CMS's rule is consistent with the great weight that must be afforded to the opinion of the treating physician, the attending physician's opinion may be contradicted at the hearing by a medical adviser who has been retained as a consultant by the ALJ. Cross-examination of the medical adviser is likely to establish that the medical adviser has not treated or even examined the patient. The medical adviser's opinion is totally derived from a review of the documentary medical evidence.

Courts have recognized that the opinion of a nontreating physician, which is based only on review of medical records, should not be accorded as much evidentiary weight as the opinion of an attending physician.[177] In *Gartmann v.*

---

[174] *See, e.g., Hirsch*, 655 F. Supp. 342; *Israel*, 669 F. Supp. 61; *Gartmann*, 633 F. Supp. 671; *Walsh*, 636 F. Supp. 358, *aff'd by* New York *ex rel.* Bodnar, 903 F.2d 122 (2d Cir. 1990) (determination not binding on factfinder). *See also* Bodnar v. Secretary of HHS, [1989 Transfer Binder] Medicare & Medicaid Guide (CCH) ¶ 38,274 (N.D.N.Y. Aug. 1, 1989); Mazzella v. Heckler, No. H-83-953 (PCD) (D. Conn. Aug. 18, 1985) [1986-1 Transfer Binder] Medicare & Medicaid Guide (CCH) ¶ 34,863.

[175] New York *ex rel.* Holland v. Sullivan, 927 F.2d 57 (2d Cir. 1991); New York *ex rel.* Stein v. Sullivan, 924 F.2d 431 (2d Cir. 1991).

[176] HCFA Ruling, No. HCFA R93-1, [1993 Transfer Binder] Medicare & Medicaid Guide (CCH) 41,444 (May 18, 1993).

[177] Stenger v. Bowen, 692 F. Supp. 1474, 1476 (E.D.N.Y. 1988).

Secretary of HHS,[178] the court found that the opinion of the medical adviser could not be considered substantial evidence to support a denial of coverage because it was not supported by the findings or opinions of the treating physician. If the only medical testimony is presented by the non-treating medical advisor, however, it may be persuasive to the ALJ.[179] Presenting evidence from the attending physician is important, and especially so when a medical advisor testifies.

[G] Restoration Potential of the Rehabilitation Patient

Most Medicare patients qualifying for SNF coverage are rehabilitation patients. Most of these patients receive physical therapy. The regulations recognize rehabilitation services as skilled services, including cases in which *maintenance* therapy is required to be provided by skilled personnel.[180] Over the years, Medicare contractors often, but erroneously, required that a patient show significant rehabilitation potential and steady improvement in order to receive Medicare coverage. This was not the appropriate legal standard. The nationwide class action *Jimmo v. Sebelius* has now unequivocally confirmed that maintenance nursing and maintenance therapy are covered by Medicare.[181]

An earlier case, *Fox v. Bowen*,[182] successfully challenged Medicare's policy and practice of denying coverage of SNF physical therapy services, based upon arbitrary rules of thumb and without consideration of the patient's individual condition. The court found that Medicare intermediaries were improperly denying Medicare coverage for physical therapy for maintenance therapy, non-weight-bearing therapy to patients with fractures, and passive range-of-motion exercises. Patients who were able to ambulate 50 feet with supervision, patients with amputations who were not yet fitted with prostheses, and patients who required daily skilled physical therapy for a period longer than two weeks were also improperly denied coverage.[183]

The *Fox* ruling struck down these arbitrary rules of thumb and mandated that each patient's individual medical condition be carefully assessed to determine whether skilled physical therapy services are required. Implicit in this ruling is that coverage cannot be denied merely because an individual's restoration potential is not sufficient or because insufficient progress has been achieved. Such

[178] 633 F. Supp. 671, 680 (E.D.N.Y. 1986).

[179] *Frohnhoefer*, No. 06-CV-1236 (SJF) (E.D.N.Y. Mar. 19, 2007) (outside medical expert's testimony was uncontradicted when treating physician did not testify and beneficiary did not present evidence contrary to outside expert; Medicare coverage denied).

[180] 42 C.F.R. § 409.33(c)(5).

[181] *Jimmo*, Civil Action No. 5:11-CV-17-CR. *See* http://www.medicareadvocacy.org/wp-content/uploads/2012/12/Jimmo-Settlement-Agreement-00011764.pdf (site visited July 20, 2015).

[182] 656 F. Supp. 1236 (D. Conn. 1987). This case was certified as a statewide class action in Connecticut; however, the ruling has affected Medicare coverage standards nationwide.

[183] *Fox*, 656 F. Supp. 1236, 1252 (D. Conn. 1987).

blanket restrictions are arbitrary and contrary to the provisions of the Medicare regulations pertaining to restoration potential, which explicitly state:

> The restoration potential of a patient is not the deciding factor in determining whether skilled services are needed. Even if full recovery or medical improvement is not possible, a patient may need skilled services to prevent further deterioration or preserve current capabilities.[184]

The MBP Manual similarly provides: "When rehabilitation services are the primary services, . . . [t]he deciding factor is not the patient's potential for recovery. . . ."[185] Despite these explicit principles, Medicare coverage over the years was often denied for beneficiaries who reached a "plateau."[186] The *Jimmo* case should, once and for all, end denials of coverage on this erroneous basis.

[H] Noncertified Bed

In order for Medicare to pay for a SNF stay, the patient must be in a bed that is certified for Medicare participation. Medicare will not cover skilled care if the patient is in a noncertified bed unless it can be shown that the placement was erroneous and the patient was not aware that he or she was in a noncertified bed or did not consent to the placement.[187]

The patient may inadvertently be placed in a non-Medicare-certified bed but receive a SNF level of care. The law provides that when the sole reason for denial of Medicare coverage is an unintentional, inadvertent, or erroneous action concerning transfer to a noncertified bed, payment may be made.[188] This application of waiver of liability applies only when a patient has not consented to the transfer to a noncertified bed and the only reason for denial is the fact that the patient was in a noncertified bed.[189] The patient must still establish eligibility for, and receipt of, daily skilled care.

The bed certification issue declined in significance as a concern when the Medicare program began paying SNFs on the basis of patients' assessments, rather than on the certification status of patients' beds. Today, most SNFs and beds are certified for Medicare.

---

[184] 42 C.F.R. § 409.32(c).

[185] MBP Manual, Ch. 8, § 30.2.2 (example), *available at* http://www.cms.gov/manuals/Downloads/bp102c08.pdf (site visited May 25, 2016).

[186] Bohlin v. Leavitt, 2006 WL 2360058 (D. Mass. Aug. 16, 2006).

[187] 42 U.S.C. § 1395pp(e); MCP Manual, Ch. 30, § 20; Hendry Convalescent Ctr. v. Harris, [1982 Transfer Binder] Medicare & Medicaid Guide (CCH) 31,934(A) (E.D. Mich. 1982); Wright v. Califano, [1979-1 Transfer Binder] Medicare & Medicaid Guide (CCH) 29,643.

[188] 42 U.S.C. § 1395pp(e); *Wright*, [1979-1 Transfer Binder] Medicare & Medicaid Guide (CCH) 29,643.

[189] MCP Manual, Ch. 30, §§ 30.1 and 40.

§ 3.07 PRE-APPEALS ADVOCACY

[A] Overview

Coverage decisions for SNF care are made at various levels, first by the provider, then by the administrative appeal system,[190] and, finally, by the federal courts. A decision by a SNF is separate from a decision made by Medicare. Only a formal Medicare decision triggers the appeals process. If a patient requests that the SNF submit a claim to Medicare despite the facility's belief that Medicare will not cover the stay under Part A, the facility must submit a claim.[191] A Medicare contractor then issues a Medicare initial determination. Following the initial determination, an appeal can be taken to "redetermination" and "reconsideration," then on to an ALJ hearing, the Medicare Appeals Council (MAC), and, finally, federal district court.

[B] The Importance of No-Payment or Demand Bill

SNFs submit consolidated bills to the Medicare contractor for payment in accordance with CMS requirements.[192] They must submit claims to the Medicare contractor, *even when* they believe that the patient's stay will not be covered, in order for Medicare to make a determination about coverage. This procedure, referred to as "no-payment" or "demand" billing, was not changed by the consolidated billing process. SNFs are required to submit demand bills at the request of a patient.[193] Furthermore, SNFs cannot bill the patient until the Medicare contractor issues a formal claim determination.[194] If the SNF does not submit a bill to the Medicare contractor, however, the patient's right to appeal is lost, because the Medicare contractor will never have made an initial Medicare determination from which an appeal may be taken.

Although Medicare contractors perform the first official assessment of a patient's level of care, the experience of beneficiaries is that contractors often rubber-stamp the SNF's denial.

Beneficiaries have the right to demand that Medicare be billed for services already provided to them, even when they request expedited review.[195] Submission of a demand bill is necessary because the two appeals processes have different functions. The expedited review, which seeks to keep services in place,

---

[190] *See* **§ 3.08** of this Handbook.

[191] Sarrassat v. Sullivan, 1989 WL 208444 (N.D. Cal. May 17, 1989).

[192] BBA '97, § 4432(b); HCFA, Program Memorandum A-98-18 (Apr. 1998).

[193] MCP Manual, Ch. 6, § 10, *available at* http://www.cms.gov/Regulations-and-Guidance/Guidance/Manuals/Downloads/clm104c06.pdf (site visited May 25, 2016), and Ch. 30, § 70; *Sarrassat*, 1989 WL 208444 (N.D. Cal. May 17 1989).

[194] MCP Manual, Ch. 30, § 70.6.1.3.

[195] *See* **§ 3.08[C].**

determines eligibility or entitlement to continued coverage; the demand bill determines whether the ongoing services the beneficiary already received are coverable by Medicare. Consequently, if a beneficiary prevails on expedited review at a later stage, such as an ALJ hearing, Medicare would still not have determined whether the ongoing services provided to the beneficiary met the Medicare coverage criteria unless a demand bill had been submitted for an official determination. A Medicare beneficiary may request that a demand bill be submitted to Medicare for an official determination by checking the appropriate box on the SNFABN, the notice that SNFs must provide to beneficiaries in advance of furnishing what the SNF believes to be noncovered care. However, a demand bill may be requested at any point in a beneficiary's stay.[196]

[C] Waiver of Liability

A related issue involves the "waiver of liability" provision in the Medicare statute.[197] Pursuant to this provision, a patient's responsibility for the cost of care not covered by Medicare (known as "financial liability") may be waived under certain circumstances. In general, liability will be waived when it is found that the patient did not know, or have reason to know, that Medicare would not cover the services.[198]

In order for liability to be waived, there must be a determination that Medicare will not cover the services, based upon a finding that the care was not medically reasonable and necessary or that it was custodial.[199] If both the patient and provider did not know or could not be reasonably expected to know that services would not be covered, liability will rest with the Medicare program.[200]

In some instances, the patient is relieved of liability but the provider is not. Such a situation occurs, for example, when a provider has reason to know that Medicare will not cover the services because the provider has received denial notices for patients with similar medical conditions. In this situation, Medicare will indemnify the patient and reimburse him or her for any amounts he or she paid to the provider during the period for which liability was waived. Medicare will then treat the payment to the provider as an overpayment and recoup the difference from later billings.[201]

---

196 MCP Manual, 100-04, Ch. 30, § 70.6.2.

197 42 U.S.C. § 1395pp.

198 42 U.S.C. § 1395pp; *see also* MCP Manual, Ch. 30, § 70.

199 42 U.S.C. § 1395y(a)(1)(A) and (9).

200 42 U.S.C. § 1395pp(a)(2); 42 C.F.R. § 411.400.

201 42 U.S.C. § 1395pp(b); 42 C.F.R. § 411.402.

[D] Notice Issues

[1] Function of the Notice

Notice plays a key role in determining waiver of liability issues, that is, whether a patient knew or could be expected to know that Medicare would not cover the service. Medicare patients are not medical experts and cannot be expected to know whether a service is medically necessary or the difference between skilled and custodial care. Accordingly, the patient must be notified in advance that Medicare will not cover the SNF services. Notice also informs a patient of his or her right to request a demand bill so that the Medicare contractor will issue an initial determination from which the beneficiary can file an appeal, if necessary. CMS uses one notice to inform the beneficiary of both the potential liability if a claim is submitted to Medicare and Medicare determines noncoverage and the right to request a demand bill to initiate an appeal.

A SNF must give a beneficiary a notice if it intends to deny, reduce, or terminate Medicare Part A–covered services.[202]

[2] Form of Notice

Although the statute is not specific about what notice is appropriate, the regulations require that notice of noncoverage be given to the patient in writing.[203] Generally, oral notice is not legally sufficient.[204] Someone who is admitted as a Medicare patient will receive a written denial notice when the SNF believes Medicare will not pay for the care. If the reason for the noncoverage is statutory—either "medical necessity" (the services are "not reasonable and necessary") or level of care (the care is custodial, rather than skilled)—the SNF must use either the SNF Advance Beneficiary Notice (SNFABN)[205] or the appropriate letter of the five denial letters.[206]

[202] MCP Manual, Ch. 30, § 70.2.3.1.

[203] 42 C.F.R. § 411.404; MCP Manual, Ch. 30, §§ 40.3, 70.1.

[204] *See Sarrassat*, 1989 WL 208444 (N.D. Cal. May 17, 1989), establishing that a beneficiary must receive a notice of noncoverage, including notice of the opportunity to request an appeal of the SNF's noncoverage determination and establishing that where the beneficiary requests an appeal, services continue through the issuance of the formal Medicare finding of noncoverage. *But see* HCFA Ruling 95-1 (Dec. 22, 1995); MCP Manual, Ch. 30, §§ 30.1 (establishing when beneficiary is on notice of noncoverage) and 40.2 (presumption that beneficiary did not know services were not covered unless there is evidence of written notice to beneficiary). Often SNF staff will note on the written notice, included in the patient's record, that oral notice was provided over the telephone. These cases require close scrutiny.

[205] CMS Form No. CMS-10055, *available at* http://www.cms.hhs.gov/BNI/Downloads/SNF-DENIAL-LETTERS.pdf (site visited May 25, 2016). *See also* http://www.cms.gov/Medicare/Medicare-General-Information/BNI/FFSSNFABNandSNFDenialLetters.html (site visited May 25, 2016).

[206] The five denial notices are available at http://www.cms.gov/Medicare/Medicare-General-Information/BNI/Downloads/SNF-DENIAL-LETTERS.pdf (site visited May 25, 2016). *See also*

The notice must include an explanation in lay language[207] that the patient and his or her authorized representative "can comprehend"[208] and must be given to the patient or the patient's authorized representative.[209] If the patient "is not capable of receiving the notice," the patient has not received "proper notice" and the facility may be financially responsible.[210]

A SNF using the model SNFABN form must give specific reasons in the "Because" section explaining why it believes that Medicare payment will be denied.[211] The SNF's refusal to respond to inquiries from the patient or authorized representative about the notice and its meaning may result in the notice's invalidation.[212]

The MCP Manual states that the SNFABN must meet its standards for cultural competency, clearly identify the particular item or service, and include the reasons the SNF believes Medicare will not pay for the SNF stay.[213] The notice should not include abbreviations, diagnosis codes, or technical language. A SNFABN that a beneficiary cannot understand is defective and will not protect the SNF from financial liability.[214]

CMS has issued another notice—the Notice of Exclusion from Medicare Benefits (SNF-NEMB)—that facilities may use with "technical" denials, such as failure to meet the three-day qualifying inpatient hospital stay or absence of days left in the benefit period.[215]

Another CMS form—the Notice of Medicare Provider Non-Coverage—is used for expedited appeals, discussed below.[216]

In guidance to state survey agencies, CMS clarifies that beneficiaries have two separate types of appeals—standard claim appeals (the SNFABN or Denial Letters) and expedited appeals (Notice of Medicare Provider Non-Coverage)—each with its own notice.[217]

---

http://www.cms.gov/Medicare/Medicare-General-Information/BNI/FFSSNFABNandSNFDenialLetters.html (site visited May 25, 2016).

[207] MCP Manual, Ch. 30, § 70.3.1.

[208] MCP Manual, Ch. 30, § 70.3.4. *See also* § 70.3.5.

[209] MCP Manual, Ch. 30, § 70.3.1.

[210] MCP Manual, Ch. 30, § 70.3.4.

[211] MCP Manual, Ch. 30, § 70.4.3.3.

[212] MCP Manual, Ch. 30, § 70.4.3.4.

[213] MCP Manual, Ch. 30, § 70.3.2.

[214] MCP Manual, Ch. 30, § 70.3.5.

[215] Notice of Exclusions from Medicare Benefits, Skilled Nursing Facility (SNF-NEMB), CMS Form No. CMS-20014, *available at* http://www.cms.hhs.gov/BNI/Downloads/CMS20014.pdf (site visited May 25, 2016); MCP Manual, Ch. 30, §§ 70.2.2.2 and 90.

[216] Notice of Medicare Provider Non-Coverage, OMB No. 0938-0953. *See* **§ 3.08[C]** of this Handbook for discussion of expedited appeals.

[217] CMS, "Survey and Certification Issues Related to Liability Notices and Beneficiary Appeal Rights in Nursing Homes," S&C-09-20 (Jan. 9, 2009), *available at* http://www.cms.hhs.gov/SurveyCertificationGenInfo/downloads/SCLetter09-20.pdf (site visited May 25, 2016).

[3] SNF Billing Notices

CMS has established a standard process requiring SNFs to submit bills to Medicare contractors for beneficiaries who "started a spell of illness under a SNF Part A benefit for every month of the related stay even though no benefits may be payable."[218] The bills are required when a patient has exhausted his or her 100-day SNF benefit (*benefits exhaust*) and when a patient no longer needs a Medicare-covered level of care but continues to reside in a Medicare-certified part of the SNF (*no payment*). When a SNF patient dropped to nonskilled care in a previous month, the SNF is allowed to submit a final discharge bill spanning multiple months through the month of discharge. CMS intends to use *benefits exhaust* and *no payment* bills to track patients' benefit periods and for purposes of national health care planning.

In considering waiver of the patient's liability, review:

- Whether Medicare coverage was denied upon admission or at a later date.
- Whether the denial was because the services were not skilled or because they were not reasonable and necessary.
- Whether written notice was given by the SNF.
- Who received the notice.
- Whether the patient was capable of understanding the notice (e.g., are there language barriers).
- Whether the notice was mailed to a family member.
- When the notice was received.

When Medicare coverage is denied at admission, the Medicare denial notice is one of many documents presented to the patient's representative on the day of admission. Consequently, people often do not remember receiving this notice. The advocate should request a copy from the provider even if a family member does not remember receiving a notice. A copy might be found in the patient's file that is signed by the patient or family member. Review the notice to determine whether it complies with the forms approved by CMS.

[218] MCP Manual 100-04, Ch. 6, § 40.8, originally issued as "Benefits Exhaust and No-Payment Billing Instructions for Medicare Fiscal Intermediaries (FIs) and Skilled Nursing Facilities (SNFs)," MCP Manual, Transmittal No. 930 (Apr. 28, 2006), *available at* http://www.cms.gov/Regulations-and-Guidance/Guidance/Manuals/Downloads/clm104c06.pdf (site visited May 25, 2016).

§ 3.08 APPEALS

[A] Medicare Advantage

If the beneficiary has enrolled in a Medicare Advantage plan, Medicare Advantage appeal rights apply.[219]

[B] Appeals Process for Traditional Medicare

[1] Initial Determinations

The claims process begins when the Medicare contractor issues an initial determination of a claim submitted by the SNF or with respect to a demand bill requested by the beneficiary.[220] The initial determination, which is issued as the Medicare Summary Notice (MSN), goes only to the beneficiary, even when the contractor is aware that the beneficiary has an appointed representative.[221] An appeal from the initial determination requires submission of a written, signed request for a redetermination within 120 days of the initial determination;[222] the regulations assume the notice is received five days after the date of the notice. Requests for redeterminations must be filed with the office indicated on the MSN.[223]

The regulations also allow SNFs to request appeal of a denial of an initial determination,[224] raising the possibility that both the beneficiary and the SNF will initiate the appeals process. In such a case, the contractor must consolidate the appeals. The contractor has 60 days from receipt of the redetermination request to issue a decision.[225] If more than one party files a request, the time period runs from the date the last request is received.[226] For example, if a beneficiary files a redetermination request on day 1, but the SNF files on day 50, the 60-day time period for the contractor to act starts on day 50.

[2] Redeterminations

Unlike the MSN, the notice of the redetermination is sent to a patient's appointed representative. The notice explains the facts, policies, and law relied on

[219] *See* **§ 7.04[G]**; Giesse v. Secretary of the Dep't of HHS, 476 F. Supp. 2d 734 (N.D. Ohio 2006).

[220] 42 C.F.R. §§ 405.920 and 405.921.

[221] 42 C.F.R. § 405.921(a).

[222] 42 C.F.R. § 405.942(a).

[223] 42 C.F.R. § 405.944(a).

[224] 42 C.F.R. § 405.906(a)(3).

[225] 42 C.F.R. § 405.950(a).

[226] 42 C.F.R. § 405.950(b)(2).

in making the redetermination decision; the right to request a reconsideration and the process for doing so; and a statement of specific missing documents that must be submitted. The notice states that SNFs, but not patients (unless they are represented by a SNF), must submit all their evidence at the next level of review in order for the evidence to be considered at any further stage of the appeals process.[227] Contractors are not required to send redetermination notices to multiple patients in overpayment cases brought by SNFs if the patient allegedly has no liability for the claim. It is unclear how the contractor determines in such cases whether the patient has already paid for the service in question.

A reopening process may be used instead of the redetermination process to correct minor errors or omissions in initial determinations.[228] Reopenings can also be used at subsequent levels of review. Questions remain concerning the relationship of the reopening process and the process for deciding remanded cases, as well as the ability of a contractor to reopen a decision in favor of the beneficiary.

[3] Reconsiderations

A third level of review, reconsideration,[229] is conducted by Medicare contractors called Qualified Independent Contractors (QICs). Patients and other parties to the redetermination have 180 days to request a reconsideration by filing a request at the location indicated on the redetermination notice.[230] Again, reconsiderations filed by patients and the SNF are consolidated, and the time for issuing a decision runs from receipt of the last-filed appeal.

Appeals of redeterminations by the Medicare contractors concerning SNF care go through the QIC reconsideration. The reconsideration level of review is a paper review;[231] CMS states in the preamble to the final regulations that QICs will not conduct hearings. However, the QIC is supposed to solicit the view of the patient. Patients may submit additional evidence at subsequent levels of review.[232] SNFs are required to submit all the evidence they want considered in the claim to the QIC.

The QIC is required to complete its reconsideration within 60 days of the reconsideration request.[233] Again, the time runs from the last request filed if more than one party seeks reconsideration; the QIC must so notify a party who filed an earlier request. The regulations do not indicate how QICs will document receipt or how patients will know when the 60-day period ends. Although the statute allows a party to the reconsideration to ask for an extension of not more than 14

---

[227] 42 C.F.R. § 405.956.

[228] 42 C.F.R. § 405.980.

[229] 42 C.F.R. §§ 405.960–978.

[230] 42 C.F.R. § 405.962(a).

[231] 42 C.F.R. § 405.968(a)(1).

[232] 42 C.F.R. § 405.966(c).

[233] 42 C.F.R. § 405.970(a).

days for the QIC to conclude the reconsideration, the regulations add 14 days to the reconsideration time frame each time additional evidence is submitted.[234]

If a QIC does not issue a timely decision, a party may request that the appeal be escalated to the next level of review, the ALJ level. The regulations give the QIC five days to either issue a decision or acknowledge the escalation request and send the appeal to the ALJ level of review.[235] The regulations indicate that an appeal escalated to the ALJ level will be completed within 180 days of receipt, rather than the statutorily mandated 90 days for ALJ decisions.

[4] ALJ Hearing and Beyond

If the reconsideration decision by the QIC is unsatisfactory and at least $160 (in 2017) remains in controversy, the beneficiary has 60 days in which to request an ALJ hearing.[236] The hearing request should be made in writing and should be filed with the entity identified in the reconsideration notice.[237] If the hearing decision is unsatisfactory, a beneficiary may request a review from the Medicare Appeals Council (MAC).[238] The request must be made within 60 days of receipt of the hearing decision.[239] If $1,560 (in 2017) remains in controversy after the hearing, the case may proceed to a federal district court.[240]

In *Chamberlain v. Leavitt*,[241] the federal district court applied "a heightened standard of review" when a beneficiary was not represented by counsel at the administrative hearing. Heightened review required the ALJ "to ensure that the claimant secures all of the relevant medical testimony; the duty to call the claimant's physicians to testify; and the duty to instruct the claimant of his right to subpoena and cross-examine physicians." Among the key issues not considered by the ALJ were "the identity of the patient's attending physicians, therapists or nurses; the patient's daily activities, care and medications; the monitoring of the patient's nutrition and eating; and the number of times plaintiff received intramuscular injections." The court remanded the case to the ALJ for further development of the administrative hearing record.

---

[234] 42 C.F.R. § 405.970(b)(3).

[235] 42 C.F.R. § 405.970(e)(2).

[236] 42 C.F.R. § 405.1014(b)(1). Section 940 of the MMA required that, starting in 2005, the amount in controversy for ALJ hearings and for judicial review be adjusted annually by the percentage increase in the medical care component of the consumer price index for urban consumers and be rounded to the nearest multiple of $10.

[237] 42 C.F.R. § 405.1014.

[238] 42 C.F.R. §§ 405.1100–1130.

[239] 42 C.F.R. § 405.1102(a).

[240] 42 C.F.R. § 405.1136(a)(1).

[241] No. 06-CV-0646 (N.D.N.Y. Feb. 10, 2009), Medicare & Medicaid Guide (CCH) 302,759.

ALJs lack authority to address breach of contract, negligence, or other claims for damages in the administrative appeal.[242]

[C] Expedited Appeals Process in Traditional Medicare

Patients in traditional Medicare may seek expedited review of a SNF's discharge from care under Part A in order to continue covered care without interruption.[243] The SNF must give the patient a general, standardized notice at least two days in advance of the proposed end of the service. If the service is fewer than two days, notice must be given by the next-to-last day of service. The notice describes the service, the date coverage ends, the patient's financial liability for continued services, and how to file an appeal.

A patient must request expedited review, orally or in writing, by noon of the next calendar day after receiving notice. At that time, the patient is given a Detailed Explanation of Non-coverage (DENC),[244] a more specific notice that includes a detailed explanation of why services are being terminated, a description of any applicable Medicare coverage rules and information on how to obtain them, and other facts specific to the patient's case. The patient is not financially liable for continued services until the later of two days after receiving the notice or the termination date specified in the notice.

A reduction in service where Medicare coverage continues is not considered a termination or discharge for purposes of triggering expedited review. If the reduction in service results in a loss of Medicare coverage (e.g., the patient no longer receives seven days per week of skilled nursing care or five days per week of rehabilitation services), expedited review may be available.[245] In addition, if the SNF proposes to transfer the patient to a non-Medicare certified part of the SNF, the patient is entitled to notice and opportunity for a hearing under the Nursing Home Reform Law's transfer and discharge rules.[246]

Expedited review will be conducted by the Beneficiary and Family Centered Care Quality Improvement Organization (BFCC-QIO), which has 72 hours in which to make a decision.[247] When the BFCC-QIO receives the request for review, it must contact the provider, which then must supply the BFCC-QIO with information supporting its determination by the close of the same business day.[248] The BFCC-QIO must solicit the views of the patient and review the notice to

[242] Matthews v. Leavitt, 452 F.3d 145 (2d Cir. 2006).

[243] 42 C.F.R. §§ 405.1200–.1204.

[244] *Available at* https://www.cms.gov/Medicare/Medicare-General-Information/BNI/FFSEDNotices.html.

[245] 42 C.F.R. § 405.1202(a)(2).

[246] 42 U.S.C. § 1395i-3(c)(2); 42 C.F.R. § 483.12.

[247] 42 C.F.R. § 405.1202(e)(6).

[248] 42 C.F.R. §§ 405.1202(e)(1), 405.1202(f), BFCC-QIOs and SNFs, respectively.

determine whether it meets CMS requirements.[249] The patient may not incur liability if the BFCC-QIO decision is delayed because the provider did not get the necessary information to the reviewer in a timely manner.[250]

If the BFCC-QIO sustains the decision to terminate/discharge services, the patient may request expedited reconsideration, orally or in writing, by noon of the calendar day following initial notification.[251] The reconsideration will be conducted by the QIC, which must issue a decision within 72 hours of the request.[252] If the QIC does not comply with the time frame, the beneficiary may escalate the case to the ALJ level.[253]

A BFCC-QIO may review an appeal from a patient whose request is not timely filed, but the BFCC-QIO does not have to adhere to the time frame for issuing a decision, and the limitation on liability does not apply.[254]

Patients retain the right to utilize the standard appeals process as well as the new expedited process in all situations. Moreover, even if a beneficiary requests an expedited review, the beneficiary should also request that a demand bill be submitted, unless the beneficiary prevails at expedited review and Medicare-covered services are continued without interruption. Indeed the importance of invoking both the expedited appeals process as well as the demand bill process is illustrated by the fact that some Medicare contractors and ALJs have limited their decisions solely to a review of whether the beneficiary was entitled to continued coverage of the services in question and have refused to look at any care that was given after the decision was made to end coverage for services that may have continued. Using the demand bill process ensures that an appealable decision will be made for all of the services a patient continues to receive.

[D] Which Cases to Appeal

The success of an appeal will be determined by the strength of the nursing and medical evidence, particularly the statements of treating physicians. Favorable decisions are more likely at higher levels of the appeals process.

When assessing a case for appeal, review whether there are technical problems with the case (e.g., whether the patient had a qualifying hospital stay and was transferred to the SNF in a timely fashion). Next, determine whether the case involves rehabilitation or skilled nursing care, or a combination of both. Cases with daily rehabilitation services, especially physical therapy, are generally good cases for appeal. The services must be provided by, or under the supervision of, a professional physical therapist.

---

[249] 42 C.F.R. § 405.1202(e)(4), (2), respectively.

[250] 42 C.F.R. § 405.1202(e)(7).

[251] 42 C.F.R. § 405.1204.

[252] 42 C.F.R. § 405.1204(c)(3).

[253] 42 C.F.R. § 405.1202(c)(5).

[254] 42 C.F.R. § 405.1202(b)(2).

When assessing a skilled nursing claim, determine whether the patient received daily *per se* nursing services as listed in the regulation. If not, take a closer look at the patient's total condition. A "total condition" case should be documented by sufficient daily nursing notes. If the nursing notes are sparse or skip days, it will be more difficult to establish daily monitoring or management.

It is common for a patient to receive physical therapy three times per week. A claim for Part A coverage may be worth appealing if skilled nursing services can be documented during the other four days. Unless skilled rehabilitation therapy was provided five days per week, the skilled nursing care must be provided seven *days* per week, not seven *times* each week (five days per week in rehabilitation therapy cases).

APPENDIX 3-1 REVIEWING SKILLED NURSING FACILITY MEDICAL RECORDS

Introduction

Medicare skilled nursing facility (SNF) case files contain several types of medical records. Common medical records include hospital discharge summaries, SNF admission notes, physical examinations, physician orders, physician progress notes, daily nursing notes, medication charts, wound care charts, therapy evaluations, and therapy flow sheets (which could include physical, occupational, and speech therapy).

Hospital Discharge Summary

The hospital discharge summary contains a great deal of valuable information, including the patient's diagnoses and treatment received in the hospital. The discharge summary also lists all diagnostic procedures and a brief medical history. The patient's age and a brief statement of the events that preceded hospitalization are usually included. Look for any reference to future treatments to be performed at the SNF and for a listing of all discharge medications.

SNF Admission Notes

SNF admission notes or physical examination forms are generally completed by nursing staff. Sometimes a full physical examination is done by the patient's treating physician. These records provide assessments related to the patient's functional status upon admission, including vital sign data. Any functional or perceptual deficits are noted. Many forms include a body chart with specific references to skin problems or decubitus ulcers.

Physician's Orders

The initial admission orders may be handwritten. It is important to make every effort to decipher these orders because of the important information they contain. If necessary, a call to the doctor's office or review by another physician or a nurse may help in reading the writing or interpreting the abbreviations, or both. The initial orders include the patient's primary and secondary diagnoses. Medications are listed with instructions for administration. For example, an order written "Inderal, PO, q.i.d." means the patient is taking Inderal, an antihypertensive medication, orally, four times daily. Some physicians will use the brand name (e.g., Inderal), while others may use the generic name (propranolol). An order for a drug "prn" means the patient is given the drug on an as-needed basis. The *Physicians' Desk Reference* and *Mosby's Nursing Drug Reference* are useful reference materials for prescription drugs.

Physician's orders include the physician certification for the required level of care. Most physician order sheets indicate whether the patient is certified for a SNF level of care. Orders are usually renewed every calendar month or 30 days and are signed by the treating physician.

The physician's orders also include all other treatments and services provided to the patient. The orders indicate skilled services, such as physical therapy treatments, as well as orders for services that may not necessarily be considered skilled services, such as the administration of over-the-counter (OTC) artificial tear drops. References such as the *Lippincott Manual of Nursing Practice* can help the advocate determine whether the level of care performed is skilled nursing care. The orders may also include quality of life information, such as whether a patient is allowed any alcoholic beverages or a leave of absence from the facility.

The file contains physician progress notes and notations from other specialists that see the patient (e.g., a consultation with an ear, nose, and throat physician or a dietitian). Often the treating physician goes to the facility only once per month to see the patient. An increase in frequency of visits may indicate that the patient needs more skilled care or that the patient's medical condition is deteriorating. The notes are helpful to define the medical issues and to indicate the frequency with which the patient's medical condition required physician intervention.

Nurses' Notes and Other Treatment Records

Other areas of the medical file may identify information about the patient's specific treatments. These areas include flow sheets and drug and treatment records. The daily nursing notes are also important. These clinical records reveal the day-to-day treatments as well as the patient's status. Some facilities keep better records than others and some nurses document patient care more thoroughly than others. First determine whether there are daily entries. Each entry is signed by the nurse on duty for the particular shift. Sometimes there may several days with no entry at all. A pattern of missing daily entries may indicate that the SNF felt the level of care was no longer skilled, which may or may not actually be the case. Unfortunately, it is difficult to document observation and assessment or management of a care plan without detailed daily nursing notes. Examining other documentation, such as wound care or medication sheets, may help substantiate daily skilled care.

A patient in a SNF may suffer from pressure sores, or decubitus ulcers. These indicate the general debility, loss of mobility, and compromised nutritional status of the patient. Specific treatments for pressure sores should be documented in the physician orders and nursing notes. A wound care chart or treatment record has a diagram of the body showing the location of the ulcers or wounds. Entries in these records indicate the location, size, and depth of the wound. They also reveal whether there is any drainage from the wound and the "stage" of the wound. Skin ulcers are classified as stages I to IV, with stages indicating progressive degeneration of the wound. Stage I is inflammation or reddening of the skin. Stage IV is skin breakdown with deep tissue involvement and the presence of necrotic or dead tissue. Treatment progress is noted in these records.

Medication Charts

Medication charts document the daily administration of prescribed medications. These records reveal the drug, dose, mode, and frequency of administration. The original date of prescription, renewal date, and administration dates are noted. The administration of other treatments may also be noted. For example, daily decubitus ulcer care may be documented in the medication chart as opposed to a separate wound care chart, or a patient's bowel movements may be monitored through entries in the medication chart. There is usually a separate chart to document medication that is administered on an as-needed basis or medication that is withheld for any reason. Nurses' initials usually appear each time a medication is administered.

Therapy Records

Patients receiving therapy have therapy evaluations and progress flow sheets. These are the most important records in cases that rely on daily physical therapy as the qualifying skilled service. The evaluation portion assesses the patient's functional problems and need for rehabilitative physical therapy. The care plan addresses the patient's specific treatments and their frequency and identifies both short-term and long-term rehabilitation goals and their frequency. Therapy records may be signed by both the registered physical therapist and the treating physician. Daily progress notes or flow sheets document the treatments actually received by the patient. These records include the dates of services, mobility status, specific rehabilitation modalities, and patient endurance. Some records also have brief narrative notes concerning each treatment. These are signed or initialed by the treating physical therapist.

Nonskilled Services

Documentation of nonskilled services, such as care provided by certified nurse aides (CNAs), may be present in the record. The records may contain valuable information regarding the total condition of the patient, for example, input and output (I&O), pattern of bowel elimination, urinary incontinence, and mobility patterns. Their value should not be overlooked in supplementing the licensed nurses' notes.

Conclusion

A careful review and understanding of the beneficiary's medical records is key to a successful Medicare appeal. Once significant portions of the medical record are identified, be certain they are available to the ALJ or other decision-makers and that they become part of the formal Medicare appeal record.

APPENDIX 3-2 WORKSHEETS

1. Reviewing Skilled Nursing Facility Records

Documents Contained in a Skilled Nursing Facility Record:

- Hospital Discharge Summary (W-10)
- Skilled Nursing Facility Admission Notes
- Physician Orders
- Nurses' Notes & Other Treatment Records
- Medication Charts
- Therapy Records
- Nonskilled Services

2. Establishing Medical Necessity

- Review patient's demographics, e.g., age, gender
- Compare assistive devices, functional limitations, and activities permitted with patient's age, disability, and diagnoses
- Note complexity of diagnoses and conditions that interact with each other
- Group medications by classification, noting multiple drugs for the same diagnosis
- Look for new medications or changes in doses of existing medications
- New physician orders may indicate a change in patient's condition
- Note changes in vital signs
- Look for increases in frequency of visits by skilled staff, which may indicate deterioration of the patient or need for skilled observation
- Examine visit documentation for evidence of observation and assessment, management of a care plan, and patient education
- Review therapy narratives, ventilator settings, wound care charts, gastric tube feedings, and medical social worker records for changes in patient condition
- Review wound care charts and diagrams, which show healing and treatment changes
- Compare therapeutic diets and fluid restrictions with patient's diagnoses, nutritional status, height, and weight
- Review nonskilled records for evidence of changes in patient's condition

3. Skilled Nursing Facility Review

Center Case No:

Date Reviewed:

Advocate:

Patient:

HIC#:

Provider:

Period at Issue:

Services at Issue/Delivered:

☐ SN ☐ PT ☐ OT ☐ ST ☐ Other

Age:

Diagnoses:

1.

2.

3.

4.

Surgical Procedures:

1.

2.

Functional Limitations:

Activities Permitted:

Mental Status:

Therapeutic Diet:

Case No.:

Reasonableness and Necessity:

- ☐ Obs. & Assess:
- ☐ Mgmt. of Care Plan:
- ☐ PT Teaching:

Skilled Nursing Services:

- ☐ IV or IM injections or IV feedings
- ☐ Enteral feedings (at least 26% of caloric requirements and at least 501 ml of fluid)
- ☐ Nasopharyngeal or tracheostomy aspiration
- ☐ Sterile insertion, irrigation, and replacement of catheters
- ☐ Dressings involving medications and aseptic technique
- ☐ Treatment of decubitus ulcers or widespread skin disorders
- ☐ Heat treatments ordered by MD
- ☐ Administration of medical gases
- ☐ Rehabilitation nursing

Therapy Services:

- ☐ Therapeutic exercises
- ☐ Gait evaluation & training
- ☐ ROM/Exercise
- ☐ Maintenance therapy
- ☐ Ultrasound, shortwave, and microwave therapy
- ☐ Hot pack, hydrocollator, infrared treatment, paraffin baths, and whirlpool
- ☐ Speech pathologist

Number of Days Used:
Dates of Discontinuation of Therapy Services:

- ☐ PT ____________ ____________
- ☐ OT ____________ ____________
- ☐ ST ____________ ____________

Case No.:

SNF Level of Care Required ☐ Yes ☐ No

Notice Issues:

Notice Adequate ☐ Yes ☐ No

- ☐ Unsigned Notice
- ☐ Telephone Notification Only
- ☐ No Evidence Notice Mailed/Received

Perceived issue for which claim may have been denied:

- ☐ No three-day qualifying hospital stay
- ☐ Not Reasonable and Necessary
- ☐ Non-Medicare-Certified Bed

Is documentation adequate to succeed on coverage appeal to ALJ?

- ☐ Yes
- ☐ No

If no, specify:

APPENDIX 3-3 IMPORTANT SELECTIONS FROM THE MEDICARE BENEFIT POLICY MANUAL

Chapter 8—Coverage of Extended Care (SNF) Services Under Hospital Insurance

Skilled Nursing and Rehabilitation Definitions

30. Skilled Nursing Facility Level of Care—General

(Rev. 179, Issued: 01-14-14, Effective: 01-07-14, Implementation: 01-07-14) A3-3132, SNF-214

Care in a SNF is covered if all of the following four factors are met:

- The patient requires skilled nursing services or skilled rehabilitation services, i.e., services that must be performed by or under the supervision of professional or technical personnel (see §§ 30.2–30.4); are ordered by a physician and the services are rendered for a condition for which the patient received inpatient hospital services or for a condition that arose while receiving care in a SNF for a condition for which he received inpatient hospital services;
- The patient requires these skilled services on a daily basis (see § 30.6); and
- As a practical matter, considering economy and efficiency, the daily skilled services can be provided only on an inpatient basis in a SNF. (See § 30.7.)
- The services delivered are reasonable and necessary for the treatment of a patient's illness or injury, i.e., are consistent with the nature and severity of the individual's illness or injury, the individual's particular medical needs, and accepted standards of medical practice. The services must also be reasonable in terms of duration and quantity.

If any one of these four factors is not met, a stay in a SNF, even though it might include the delivery of some skilled services, is not covered. For example, payment for a SNF level of care could not be made if a patient needs an intermittent rather than daily skilled service.

In reviewing claims for SNF services to determine whether the level of care requirements are met, the intermediary of Medicare Administrative Contractor (MAC) first considers whether a patient needs skilled care. If a need for a skilled service does not exist, then the "daily" and "practical matter" requirements are not addressed. See section 30.2.2.1 for a discussion of the role of appropriate documentation in facilitating accurate coverage determinations for claims involving skilled care. Additional material on documentation appears in the various clinical scenarios that are presented throughout these level of care guidelines.

Coverage of nursing care and/or therapy to perform a maintenance program does not turn on the presence or absence of an individual's potential for improvement from the nursing care and/or therapy, but rather on the beneficiary's need for skilled care.

Eligibility for SNF Medicare A coverage has not changed with the inception of PPS. However, the skilled criteria and the medical review process have changed slightly. For Medicare to render payment for skilled services provided to a beneficiary during a SNF Part A stay, the facility must complete and MDS.

■ **EXAMPLE:** Even though the irrigation of a suprapubic catheter may be a skilled nursing service, daily irrigation may not be "reasonable and necessary" for the treatment of a patient's illness or injury.

30.1 Administrative Level of Care Presumption

(Rev. 57, Issued: 11-08-06, Effective: 07-27-06, Implementation: 12-14-06)

Under the SNF PPS, beneficiaries who are admitted (or readmitted) directly to a SNF after a qualifying hospital stay are considered to meet the level of care requirements of 42 CFR 409.31 up to and including the assessment reference date (ARD) for the 5-day assessment prescribed in 42 CFR 413.343(b), when correctly assigned to one of the Resource Utilization Groups (RUGs) that is designated (in the annual publication of Federal prospective payment rates described in 42 CFR 413.345) as representing the required level of care. If the beneficiary is not admitted (or readmitted) directly to a SNF after a qualifying hospital Stay, the administrative level of care presumption does not apply.

For purposes of this presumption, the assessment reference date is defined in accordance with 42 CFR 483.315(d), and must occur no later than the eighth day of posthospital SNF care. Consequently, of the ARD for the 5-day assessment* prescribed in 42 CFR 413.343(b) is set on day 9, or later, the administrative level of care presumption does not apply. The coverage that arises from this presumption remains in effect for as long thereafter as it continues to be supported by the facts of the beneficiary's condition and care needs. However, this administrative presumption does not apply to any of the subsequent assessments.

To be correctly assigned, the data coded on the Resident Assessment Instrument (RAI) must be accurate and meet the definitions described in the Long Term Care Facility RAI User's Manual. The beneficiary must receive services in the SNF that are reasonable and necessary. Services provided to the beneficiary during the hospital stay are reviewed to ensure proper coding of the most recent

---

* Includes Medicare Readmission/Return Assessment.

version of the RAI. The two examples illustrated below demonstrate a correct assignment and an incorrect assignment.

Incorrect Assignment:	IV med provided in hospital coded on MDS, but IV was for a surgical procedure only—as a consequence, the MDS is on accurate and the presumption does not apply (see Chapter 3, Section P of the RAI).
Correct Assignment:	Beneficiary is receiving oxygen therapy as well as rehab service. The respiratory therapy services are found reasonable and necessary; however, the rehab services are found not reasonable and necessary, resulting in a revised RUG. Beneficiary was and is now correctly assigned—presumption applies.

A beneficiary who groups into other than one of the RUGs designated as representing the required level of care on the 5-day assessment prescribed in 42 CFR 413.343(b) is not automatically classified as meeting or not meeting the SNF level of care definition. Instead, the beneficiary must receive an individual level of care determination using existing administrative criteria and procedures.

The following scenarios further clarify that a beneficiary's correct classification to one of the RUGs that is designated (in the annual publication of Federal prospective payment rates described in 42 CFR 413.345) as representing the required level of care triggers the coverage presumption under the initial 5-day, Medicare-required assessment only when that assessment occurs directly following the beneficiary's hospital discharge.

1. Routine SNF Admission Directly From Qualifying Hospital Stay. If the beneficiary is admitted to the SNF immediately following a 3-day qualifying hospital stay, there is a presumption that he or she meets the Medicare level of care criteria when correctly assigned to one of the RUGs that is designated (in the annual publication of Federal prospective payment rates described in 42 CFR 413.345) as representing the required level of care. The presumption lasts through the assessment reference date of the 5-day assessment, which must occur no later than the eighth day of the stay.
2. Admission to SNF does not immediately follow discharge from the qualifying hospital stay, but occurs within 30 days (as required under the "30 day transfer rule). If the beneficiary is discharged from the hospital to a setting other than the SNF, the presumption of coverage does not apply, even if the beneficiary's SNF admission occurs within 30 days of discharge from the qualifying hospital stay. Accordingly, coverage would be determined based on a review of the medical evidence in the file.

3. SNF Resident is Re-Hospitalized and Then Returns Directly to the SNF. If a beneficiary who has been in a covered Part A stay required readmission to a hospital, and subsequently returns directly to the SNF for continuing care, there is a presumption that he or she meets the level of care criteria upon readmission to the SNF when correctly assigned to one of the RUGs that is designated (in the annual publication of Federal prospective payment rates described in 42 CFR 413.345) as representing the required level of care. A new Medicare 5-day assessment is required and the presumption of coverage lasts through the assessment reference date of that assessment, which must occur no later than the eighth day of the stay.
4. Routine SNF Admission Directly From Qualifying Hospital Stay, but Initial Portion of SNF Stay Covered by Another Insurer (Medicare as Secondary Payer). When a beneficiary goes directly from a qualifying hospital stay to the SNF, but the initial portion of the SNF stay is covered by another insurer that is primary to Medicare, Medicare coverage would not start until coverage by the primary insurer ends. Accordingly, the Medicare required schedule of the assessment is not required to begin until the first day of Medicare coverage. If a beneficiary met the level of care criteria for Medicare coverage during the first 8 days of the stay following a qualifying hospital stay, and the other insurer covered this part of the stay, there is no presumption. If Medicare becomes primary before the eighth day of the stay following a qualifying hospital stay, the presumption would apply through the assessment reference date on the 5-day assessment or, if earlier, the eighth day of the stay.
5. Readmission to SNF Within 30 Days After Discharge From Initial SNF Stay—No Intervening Hospitalization. As noted in scenario 1, if a beneficiary is initially admitted to the SNF directly from the hospital for a covered Part A stay, the presumption for that stay is applicable when the
6. Initial, Non-Medicare SNF Stay Followed by Qualifying Hospitalization and Readmission to SNF for Medicare Stay. Dually eligible (Medicare/Medicaid) Beneficiaries whose initial stay in the SNF is either Medicaid-covered or private pay, are eligible for the Medicare presumption of coverage when readmitted to the SNF following a qualifying hospitalization, when correctly assigned to one of the RUGs that is designated (in the annual publication of Federal prospective payment rates described in 42 CFR 413.234) are representing the required level of care. (Of course, in order to qualify for Medicare coverage upon readmission, the beneficiary must be placed in the portion of the institution that is actually certified by Medicare as a SNF.)

   No presumption of coverage applies when Medicare is the secondary payer for days 1 through 8 of the covered stay where Medicare becomes primary after day 8 due to a reversal or denial by the secondary insurer.

7. Transfer From One SNF to Another. There is no presumption of coverage in cases involving the transfer of a beneficiary from one SNF to another or from SNF-level care in a swing bed to a SNF. The presumption only applies to the SNF stay that immediately follows the qualifying hospital stay when the beneficiary is correctly assigned to one of the RUGs that is designated (in the annual publication of Federal prospective payment rates described in 2 CFR 413.345) as representing the required level of care. Therefore, in cases involving transfer of a beneficiary from a swing-bed hospital to a SNF, the presumption only applies if the beneficiary was receiving acute care (rather than SNF-level care) immediately prior to discharge from the swing-bed hospital.

30.2 Skilled Nursing and Skilled Rehabilitation Services

(Rev. 1, 10-01-03)

30.2.1 Skilled Services Defined

(Rev. 179, Issued: 01-14-14, Effective: 01-07-14, Implementation: 01-07-14)

Skilled nursing and/or skilled rehabilitation services are those services, furnished pursuant to physician orders, that:

- Require the skills of qualified technical or professional health personnel such as registered nurses, licensed practical (vocational) nurses, physical therapists, occupational therapists, and speech pathologists or audiologists; and
- Must be provided directly by or under the general supervision of these skilled nursing or skilled rehabilitation personnel to assure the safety of the patient and to achieve the medically desired result.

■ **NOTE:** "General supervision" requires initial direction and periodic inspection of the actual activity. However, the supervisor need not always be physically present or on the premises when the assistant is performing services.

Skilled care may be necessary to improve a patient's current condition, to maintain the patient's current condition, or to prevent or slow further deterioration of the patient's condition.

30.2.2 Principles for Determining Whether a Service is Skilled

(Rev. 179, Issued: 01-14-14, Effective, 01-07-14, Implementation: 01-07-14) A3-3132.1B, SNF-214.1.B

- If the inherent complexity of a service prescribed for a patient is such that it can be performed safely and/or effectively only by or under the general supervision of skilled nursing or skilled rehabilitation personnel, the service is a skilled service; e.g., the administration of intravenous feedings and intramuscular injections; the insertion of suprapubic catheters; and ultrasound, shortwave, and microwave therapy treatments.
- The intermediary or MAC considers the nature of the service and the skills required for safe and effective delivery of that service in deciding whether a service is a skilled service. While a patient's particular medical condition is a valid factor in deciding if skilled services are needed, a patient's diagnosis or prognosis should never be the sole factor in deciding that a service is not skilled.

  ■ **EXAMPLE:** When rehabilitation services are the primary services, the key issue is whether the skills of a therapist are needed. The deciding factor is not the patient's potential for recovery, but whether the services needed require the skills of a therapist or whether they can be provided by nonskilled personnel. (See § 30.5.)

- A service that is ordinarily considered nonskilled could be considered a skilled service in cases in which, because of special medical complications, skilled nursing or skilled rehabilitation personnel are required to perform or supervise it or to observe the patient. In these cases, the complications and special services involved must be documented by physicians' orders and nursing or therapy notes.

  ■ **EXAMPLE:** Whirlpool baths do not ordinarily require the skills of a qualified physical therapist. However, the skills, knowledge, and judgment of a qualified physical therapist might be required where the patient's condition is complicated by circulatory deficiency, areas of desensitization, or open wounds. The documentation needs to support the severity of the circulatory condition that requires skilled care (see section 30.2.2.1).

- In determining whether services rendered in a SNF constitute covered care, it is necessary to determine whether individual services are skilled, and whether, in light of the patient's total condition, skilled management of the services provided is needed even though many or all of the specific services were unskilled.

■ **EXAMPLE:** An 81-year-old woman who is aphasic and confused, suffers from hemiplegia, congestive heart failure, and atrial fibrillation, has suffered a cerebrovascular accident, is incontinent, has a Stage 1 decubitus ulcer, and is unable to communicate and make her needs known. Even though no specific service provided is skilled, the patient's condition requires daily skilled nursing involvement to manage a plan for the total care needed, to observe the patient's progress, and to evaluate the need for changes in the treatment plan. As discussed in section 30.2.2.1 below, the medical condition of the patient must be described and documented to support the goals for the patient and the need for skilled nursing services.

- The importance of a particular service to an individual patient, or the frequency with which it must be performed, does not, by itself, make it a skilled service.

■ **EXAMPLE:** A primary need of a nonambulatory patient may be frequent changes of position in order to avoid development of decubitus ulcers. However, since such changing of position does not ordinarily require skilled nursing or skilled rehabilitation personnel, it would not constitute a skilled service, even though such services are obviously necessary.

- The possibility of adverse effects from the improper performance of an otherwise unskilled service does not make it a skilled service unless there is documentation to support the need for skilled nursing or skilled rehabilitation personnel. Although the act of turning a patient normally is not a skilled service, for some patients the skills of a nurse may be necessary to assure proper body alignment in order to avoid contractures and deformities. In all such cases, the reasons why skilled nursing or skilled rehabilitation personnel are essential must be documented in the patient's record.

30.2.2.1 Documentation to Support Skilled Care Determinations

(Rev. 179, Issued: 01-14-14, Effective: 01-07-14, Implementation: 01-07-14) A3-3132.1.C, SNF-214.1.C

Claims for skilled care coverage need to include sufficient documentation to enable a reviewer to determine whether—

- Skilled involvement is required in order for the services in question to be furnished safely and effectively; and
- The services themselves are, in fact, reasonable and necessary for the treatment of a patient's illness or injury, i.e., are consistent with the

> nature and severity of the individual's illness or injury, the individual's particular medical needs, and accepted standards of medical practice. The documentation must also show that the services are appropriate in terms of duration and quantity, and that the services promote the documented therapeutic goals.

Such determinations would be made from the perspective of the patient's condition when the services were ordered and what was, at that time, reasonably expected to be appropriate treatment for the illness or injury. Thus, when a service appears reasonable and necessary from that perspective, it would not then be appropriate to deny the service retrospectively merely because the goals of treatment have not yet been achieved. However, if it becomes apparent at some point that the goal set for the patient is no longer a reasonable one, then the treatment goal itself should be promptly and appropriately modified to reflect this, and the patient should then be reassessed to determine whether the treatment goal as revised continues to require the provision of skilled services. By the same token, the **treatment goal itself** cannot be modified retrospectively, e.g., when it becomes apparent that the initial treatment goal of restoration is no longer a reasonable one, the provider cannot retroactively alter the initial goal of treatment from restoration to maintenance. Instead, it would make such a change on a prospective basis only.

Although the presence of appropriate documentation is not, in and of itself, an element of the definition of a "skilled" service, such documentation serves as the means by which a provider would be able to establish and a contractor would be able to confirm that skilled care is, in fact, needed and received in a given case.

It is expected that the documentation in the patient's medical record will reflect the need for the skilled services provided. The patient's medical record is also expected to provide important communication among all members of the care team regarding the development, course, and outcomes of the skilled observations, assessments, treatment, and training performed. Taken as a whole, then, the documentation in the patient's medical record should illustrate the degree to which the patient is accomplishing the goals as outlined in the care plan. In this way, the documentation will serve to demonstrate why a skilled service is needed.

Thorough and timely documentation with respect to treatment goals can help clearly demonstrate a beneficiary's need for skilled care in situations where such need might not otherwise be readily apparent, as when the treatment's purpose changes (for example, from restoration to maintenance), as well as in establishing the efficacy of care that serves to prevent or slow decline—where, by definition, there would be no "improvement" to evaluate. For example, when skilled services are necessary to maintain the patient's current condition, the documentation would need to substantiate that the services of skilled personnel are, in fact, required to achieve this goal. Similarly, establishing that a maintenance program's services are reasonable and necessary would involve regularly documenting the degree to which the program's treatment goals are being accomplished. In situations where the maintenance program is performed to maintain the patient's current condition, such documentation would serve to demonstrate the program's effectiveness in achieving this goal. When the maintenance program is intended to slow further deterioration of the patient's condition, the efficacy of the services could be established by documenting that the natural progression of the patient's medical or functional decline has been interrupted. Assessments of all goals must be performed in a frequent and regular manner so that the resulting documentation provides a sufficient basis for determining the appropriateness of coverage.

Therefore the patient's medical record must document as appropriate:

- The history and physical exam pertinent to the patient's care, (including the response or changes in behavior to previously administered skilled services);
- The skilled services provided;
- The patient's response to the skilled services provided during the current visit;
- The plan for future care based on the rationale of prior results.
- A detailed rationale that explains the need for the skilled service in light of the patient's overall medical condition and experiences;
- The complexity of the service to be performed;
- Any other pertinent characteristics of the beneficiary.

The documentation in the patient's medical record must be accurate, and avoid vague or subjective descriptions of the patient's care that would not be sufficient to indicate the need for skilled care. For example, the following terminology does not sufficiently describe the reaction of the patient to his/her skilled care:

- Patient tolerated treatment well
- Continue with POC
- Patient remains stable

Such phraseology does not provide a clear picture of the results of the treatment, nor the "next steps" that are planned. Objective measurements of physical outcomes of treatment should be provided and/or a clear description of the changed behaviors due to education programs should be recorded so that all concerned can follow the results of the provided services.

30.2.3 Specific Examples of Some Skilled Nursing or Skilled Rehabilitation Services

(Rev. 179, Issued: 01-14-14, Effective: 01-07-14, Implementation: 01-07-14) A3-3132.1.C, SNF-214.1.C

30.2.3.1 Management and Evaluation of a Patient Care Plan

(Rev. 179, Issued: 01-14-14, Effective: 01-07-14, Implementation: 01-07-14) A3-3132.1.C.1, SNF-214.1.C.1

The development, management, and evaluation of a patient care plan, based on the physician's orders and supporting documentation, constitute skilled nursing services when, in terms of the patient's physical or mental condition, these services require the involvement of skilled nursing personnel to meet the patient's medical needs, promote recovery, and ensure medical safety. However, the planning and management of a treatment plan that does not involve the furnishing of skilled services may not require skilled nursing personnel; e.g., a care plan for a patient with organic brain syndrome who requires only oral medication and a protective environment. The sum total of nonskilled services would only add up to the need for skilled management and evaluation when the condition of the beneficiary is such that there is an expectation that a change in condition is likely without that intervention.

The patient's clinical record may not always specifically identify "skilled planning and management activities" as such. Therefore, in this limited context, if the documentation of the patient's overall condition substantiates a finding that the patient's medical needs and safety can be addressed only if the total care, skilled or not, is planned and managed by skilled nursing personnel, it is appropriate to infer that skilled management is being provided, but only if the record as a whole clearly establishes that there was a likely potential for serious complications without skilled management, as illustrated in the following Examples.

■ **EXAMPLE 1:** An aged patient with a history of diabetes mellitus and angina pectoris is recovering from an open reduction of the neck of the femur. He requires, among other services, careful skin care, appropriate oral medications, a diabetic diet, a therapeutic exercise program to preserve muscle tone and body condition, and observation to notice signs of deterioration in his condition or complications resulting from his restricted (but increasing) mobility. Although any of the required services could be performed by a properly instructed person, that person would not have the capability to understand the relationship among the services and their effect on each other. Since the nature of the patient's condition, his age, and his immobility create a high potential for serious complications, such an understanding is essential to assure the patient's recovery and safety. The management of this plan of care requires skilled nursing personnel until such time as skilled care is no longer required in coordinating the patient's treatment regimen, even though the individual services involved are supportive in nature and do not require skilled nursing personnel. The documentation in the medical record as a whole is essential for this determination and must illustrate the complexity of the unskilled services that are a necessary part of the medical treatment and which require the involvement of skilled nursing personnel to promote the stabilization of the patient's medical condition and safety.

■ **EXAMPLE 2:** An aged patient is recovering from pneumonia, is lethargic, is disoriented, has residual chest congestion, is confined to bed as a result of his debilitated condition, and requires restraints at times. To decrease the chest congestion, the physician has prescribed frequent changes in position, coughing, and deep breathing. While the residual chest congestion alone would not represent a high risk factor, the patient's immobility and confusion represent complicating factors which, when coupled with the chest congestion, could create high probability of a relapse. In this situation, skilled overseeing of the nonskilled services would be reasonable and necessary, pending the elimination of the chest congestion, to assure the patient's medical safety. The documentation in the medical record as a whole is essential for this determination and must illustrate the complexity of the unskilled services that are a necessary part of the medical treatment and which require the involvement of skilled nursing personnel to promote the patient's recovery and medical safety in view of the patient's overall condition.

30.2.3.2 Observation and Assessment of Patient's Condition

(Rev. 179, Issued: 01-14-14, Effective: 01-07-14, Implementation: 01-07-14) A3-3132.1.C.2, SNF-214.1.C.2

Observation and assessment are skilled services when the likelihood of change in a patient's condition requires skilled nursing or skilled rehabilitation personnel to identify and evaluate the patient's need for possible modification of treatment or initiation of additional medical procedures, until the patient's treatment regimen is essentially stabilized.

■ **EXAMPLE 1:** A patient with arteriosclerotic heart disease with congestive heart failure requires close observation by skilled nursing personnel for signs of decompensation, abnormal fluid balance, or adverse effects resulting from prescribed medication. Skilled observation is needed to determine whether the digitalis dosage should be reviewed or whether other therapeutic measures should be considered, until the patient's treatment regimen is essentially stabilized. The medical documentation must describe the skilled services that require the involvement of nursing personnel to promote the stabilization of the patient's medical condition and safety.

■ **EXAMPLE 2:** A patient has undergone peripheral vascular disease treatment including revascularization procedures (bypass) with open or necrotic areas of skin on the involved extremity. Skilled observation and monitoring of the vascular supply of the legs is required. The medical documentation must describe the skilled services that require the involvement of nursing personnel to promote the patient's recovery and medical safety in view of the patient's overall condition.

■ **EXAMPLE 3:** A patient has undergone hip surgery and has been transferred to a SNF. Skilled observation and monitoring of the patient for possible adverse reaction to the operative procedure, development of phlebitis, or skin breakdown is both reasonable and necessary. The medical documentation must describe the skilled services that require the involvement of nursing personnel to promote the patient's recovery and medical safety in view of the patient's overall condition.

■ **EXAMPLE 4:** A patient has been hospitalized following a heart attack, and following treatment but before mobilization, is transferred to the SNF. Because it is unknown whether exertion will exacerbate the heart disease, skilled observation is reasonable and necessary as mobilization is initiated, until the patient's treatment regimen is essentially stabilized. The medical documentation must describe the skilled services that require the involvement of nursing personnel to promote the stabilization of the patient's medical condition and safety.

■ **EXAMPLE 5:** A frail 85-year-old man was hospitalized for pneumonia. The infection was resolved, but the patient, who had previously maintained adequate nutrition, will not eat or eats poorly. The patient is transferred to a SNF for monitoring of fluid and nutrient intake, assessment of the need for tube feeding and forced feeding if required. Observation and monitoring by skilled nursing personnel of the patient's oral intake is required to prevent dehydration. The medical documentation must describe the skilled services that require the involvement of nursing personnel to promote the patient's recovery and medical safety in view of the patient's overall condition.

■ **EXAMPLE 6:** A patient with congestive heart failure may require continuous close observation to detect signs of decompensation, abnormal fluid balance, or adverse effects resulting from prescribed medication(s) that serve as indicators for adjusting therapeutic measures. The medical documentation must describe the skilled services that require the involvement of nursing personnel to promote the patient's recovery and medical safety in view of the patient's overall condition, to maintain the patient's current condition, or to prevent or slow further deterioration in the patient's condition.

If a patient was admitted for skilled observation but did not develop a further acute episode or complication, the skilled observation services still are covered so long as there was a reasonable probability for such a complication or further acute episode. "Reasonable probability" means that a potential complication or further acute episode was a likely possibility.

Information from the patient's medical record must document that there is a reasonable potential for a future complication or acute episode sufficient to justify the need for continued skilled observation and assessment.

Such signs and symptoms as abnormal/fluctuating vital signs, weight changes, edema, symptoms of drug toxicity, abnormal/fluctuating lab values, and respiratory changes on auscultation may justify skilled observation and assessment. Where these signs and symptoms are such that there is a reasonable potential that skilled observation and assessment by a licensed nurse will result in changes to the treatment of the patient, then the services are reasonable and necessary. However, observation and assessment by a nurse is not reasonable and necessary to the treatment of the illness or injury where these characteristics are part of a longstanding pattern of the patient's waxing and waning condition which by themselves do not require skilled services and there is no attempt to change the treatment to resolve them.

Skilled observation and assessment may also be required for patients whose primary condition and needs are psychiatric in nature or for patients who, in addition to their physical problems, have a secondary psychiatric diagnosis. These patients may exhibit acute psychological symptoms such as depression, anxiety or agitation, which require skilled observation and assessment such as observing for indications of suicidal or hostile behavior. However, these conditions often require considerably more specialized, sophisticated nursing techniques and physician attention than is available in most participating SNFs. (SNFs that are primarily engaged in treating psychiatric disorders are precluded by law from participating in Medicare.) Therefore, these cases must be carefully documented.

30.2.3.3 Teaching and Training Activities

(Rev. 179, Issued: 01-14-14, Effective: 01-07-14, Implementation: 01-07-14) A3-3132.1.C.3, SNF-214.1.C.3

Teaching and training activities, which require skilled nursing or skilled rehabilitation personnel to teach a patient how to manage their treatment regimen, would constitute skilled services. Some examples are:

- Teaching self-administration of injectable medications or a complex range of medications;
- Teaching a newly diagnosed diabetic to administer insulin injections, to prepare and follow a diabetic diet, and to observe foot-care precautions;

- Teaching self-administration of medical gases to a patient;
- Gait training and teaching of prosthesis care for a patient who has had a recent leg amputation;
- Teaching patients how to care for a recent colostomy or ileostomy;
- Teaching patients how to perform self-catheterization and self-administration of gastrostomy feedings;
- Teaching patients how to care for and maintain central venous lines, such as Hickman catheters;
- Teaching patients the use and care of braces, splints and orthotics, and any associated skin care; and
- Teaching patients the proper care of any specialized dressings or skin treatments.

The documentation must thoroughly describe all efforts that have been made to educate the patient/caregiver, and their responses to the training. The medical record should also describe the reason for the failure of any educational attempts, if applicable.

■ **EXAMPLE:** A newly diagnosed diabetic patient is seen in order to learn to self-administer insulin injections, to prepare and follow a diabetic diet, and to observe foot-care precautions. Even though the patient voices understanding of the nutritional principles of his diabetic diet, he expresses dissatisfaction with his food choices and refuses to comply with the education he is receiving. This refusal continues, notwithstanding efforts to counsel the patient on the potentially adverse consequences of the refusal and to suggest alternative dietary choices that could help to avoid or alleviate those consequences. The patient's response to the recommended treatment plan as well as to all educational attempts is documented in the medical record.

30.2.4 Questionable Situations

(Rev. 1, 10-01-03)
A3-3132.1.D, SNF-214.1.D

There must be specific evidence that daily skilled nursing or skilled rehabilitation services are required and received if:

- The primary service needed is oral medication; or
- The patient is capable of independent ambulation, dressing, feeding, and hygiene.

30.3 Direct Skilled Nursing Services to Patients

(Rev. 179, Issued: 01-14-14, Effective: 01-07-14, Implementation: 01-07-14) A3-3132.2, SNF-214.2

Nursing services are considered skilled when they are so inherently complex that they can be safely and effectively performed only by, or under the supervision of, a registered nurse or, when provided by regulation, a licensed practical (vocational) nurse. (See 42 CFR § 409.32.) If all other requirements for coverage under the SNF benefit are met, skilled nursing services are covered when an individualized assessment of the patient's clinical condition demonstrates that the specialized judgment, knowledge, and skills of a registered nurse or, when provided by regulation, a licensed practical (vocational) nurse are necessary. Skilled nursing services would be covered where such skilled nursing services are necessary to maintain the patient's current condition or prevent or slow further deterioration so long as the beneficiary requires skilled care for the services to be safely and effectively provided, and all other requirements for coverage under the SNF benefit are met. Coverage does not turn on the presence or absence of an individual's potential for improvement from nursing care, but rather on the beneficiary's need for skilled care.

A condition that would not ordinarily require skilled nursing services may nevertheless require them under certain circumstances. In such instances, skilled nursing care is necessary only when (a) the particular patient's special medical complications require the skills of a registered nurse or, when provided by regulation, a licensed practical nurse to perform a type of service that would otherwise be considered nonskilled; or (b) the needed services are of such complexity that the skills of a registered nurse or, when provided by regulation, a licensed practical nurse are required to furnish the services.

A service is not considered a skilled nursing service merely because it is performed by or under the direct supervision of a nurse. If a service can be safely and effectively performed (or self-administered) by an unskilled person, the service cannot be regarded as a skilled nursing service although a nurse actually provides the service. Similarly, the unavailability of a competent person to provide a nonskilled service, regardless of the importance of the service to the patient, does not make it a skilled service when a nurse provides the service.

Some examples of direct skilled nursing services are:

- Intravenous or intramuscular injections and intravenous feedings;
- Enteral feeding that comprises at least 26 percent of daily caloric requirements and provides at least 501 milliliters of fluid per day;
- Naso-pharyngeal and tracheotomy aspiration;
- Insertion, sterile irrigation, and replacement of suprapubic catheters;

- Application of dressings involving prescription medications and aseptic techniques (see § 30.5 for exception);
- Treatment of decubitus ulcers, of a severity rated at Stage 3 or worse, or a widespread skin disorder (see § 30.5 for exception);
- Heat treatments which have been specifically ordered by a physician as part of active treatment and which require observation by skilled nursing personnel to evaluate the patient's progress adequately (see § 30.5 for exception);
- Rehabilitation nursing procedures, including the related teaching and adaptive aspects of nursing, that are part of active treatment and require the presence of skilled nursing personnel; e.g., the institution and supervision of bowel and bladder training programs;
- Initial phases of a regimen involving administration of medical gases such as bronchodilator therapy; and
- Care of a colostomy during the early postoperative period in the presence of associated complications. The need for skilled nursing care during this period must be justified and documented in the patient's medical record.

30.4 Direct Skilled Rehabilitation Services to Patients

(Rev. 179, Issued: 01-14-14, Effective: 01-07-14, Implementation: 01-07-14) A3-3132.1.C, SNF-214.1.C

The following sections contain examples and guidelines concerning direct skilled therapy services to patients, including skilled physical therapy, occupational therapy, and speech/language pathology therapy.

Coverage for such skilled therapy services does not turn on the presence or absence of a beneficiary's potential for improvement from therapy services, but rather on the beneficiary's need for skilled care. Therapy services are considered skilled when they are so inherently complex that they can be safely and effectively performed only by, or under the supervision of, a qualified therapist. (See 42 CFR § 409.32.) These skilled services may be necessary to improve the patient's current condition, to maintain the patient's current condition, or to prevent or slow further deterioration of the patient's condition.

If all other requirements for coverage under the SNF benefit are met, such skilled therapy services are covered when an individualized assessment of the patient's clinical condition demonstrates that the specialized judgment, knowledge, and skills of a qualified therapist are necessary for the performance of the rehabilitation services.

30.4.1 Skilled Physical Therapy

(Rev. 1, 10-01-03)
A3-3132.3.A, SNF-214.3.A

30.4.1.1 General

(Rev. 179, Issued: 01-04-14, Effective: 01-07-14, Implementation: 01-07-14)

Skilled physical therapy services must meet all of the following conditions:

- The services must be directly and specifically related to an active written treatment plan that is based upon an initial evaluation performed by a qualified physical therapist after admission to the SNF and prior to the start of physical therapy services in the SNF that is approved by the physician after any needed consultation with the qualified physical therapist. In those cases where a beneficiary is discharged during the SNF stay and later readmitted, an initial evaluation must be performed upon readmission to the SNF, prior to the start of physical therapy services in the SNF;
- The services must be of a level of complexity and sophistication, or the condition of the patient must be of a nature that requires the judgment, knowledge, and skills of a qualified physical therapist;
- The services must be provided with the expectation, based on the assessment made by the physician of the patient's restoration potential, that the condition of the patient will improve materially in a reasonable and generally predictable period of time; or, the services must be necessary for the **establishment** of a safe and effective maintenance program; or, the services must require the skills of a qualified therapist for the **performance** of a safe and effective maintenance program. **NOTE:** See Section E. Maintenance Therapy for more guidance regarding when skilled therapy services are necessary for the performance of a safe and effective maintenance program.
- The services must be considered under accepted standards of medical practice to be specific and effective treatment for the patient's condition; and
- The services must be reasonable and necessary for the treatment of the patient's condition; this includes the requirement that the amount, frequency, and duration of the services must be reasonable.

■ **EXAMPLE 1:** An 80-year-old, previously ambulatory, post-surgical patient has been bedbound for one week and, as a result, has developed muscle atrophy, orthostatic hypotension, joint stiffness, and lower extremity edema. To the extent that the patient requires a brief period of daily skilled physical therapy services to restore lost functions, those services are reasonable and necessary and must be documented in the medical record (see § 30.2.2.1).

■ **EXAMPLE 2:** A patient with congestive heart failure also has diabetes and previously had both legs amputated above the knees. Consequently, the patient does not have a reasonable potential to achieve ambulation, but still requires daily skilled physical therapy to learn bed mobility and transferring skills, as well as functional activities at the wheelchair level. If the patient has a reasonable potential for achieving those functions in a reasonable period of time in view of the patient's total condition, the physical therapy services are reasonable and necessary and must be documented in the medical record (see § 30.2.2.1).

Physical therapy services are not reasonable and necessary and would not be covered if the expected results are insignificant in relation to the extent and duration of physical therapy services that would be required to achieve those results.

Some SNF inpatients do not require skilled physical therapy services but do require services, which are routine in nature. When services can be safely and effectively performed by supportive personnel, such as aides or nursing personnel, without the supervision of a physical therapist, they do not constitute skilled physical therapy. Additionally, services involving activities for the general good and welfare of the patient (e.g., general exercises to promote overall fitness and flexibility and activities to provide diversion or general motivation) do not constitute skilled physical therapy.

30.4.1.2 Application of Guidelines

(Rev. 179, Issued: 01-14-14, Effective: 01-07-14, Implementation: 01-07-14) A3-3132.3.A.2, SNF-214.3.A.2

Some of the more common skilled physical therapy modalities and procedures are:

A. Assessment

The skills of a physical therapist are required for the ongoing assessment of a patient's rehabilitation needs and potential. Skilled rehabilitation services concurrent with the management of a patient's care plan include tests and measurements of range of motion, strength, balance, coordination, endurance, and functional ability.

B. Therapeutic Exercises

Therapeutic exercises, which must be performed by or under the supervision of the qualified physical therapist, due either to the type of exercise employed or to the condition of the patient.

C. Gait Training

Gait evaluation and training furnished to a patient whose ability to walk has been impaired by neurological, muscular, or skeletal abnormality often require the skills of a qualified physical therapist.

Repetitious exercises to improve gait, or to maintain strength and endurance, and assistive walking can be appropriately provided by supportive personnel, e.g., aides or nursing personnel, and would not necessarily require the skills of a physical therapist. Thus, such services are not inherently skilled. However, see § 30.2.2 for the specific circumstances in which an ordinarily nonskilled service can nevertheless be considered skilled. Documentation of the patient's condition in the medical record must describe the circumstances which delineate the need for skilled rather than unskilled services during gait training.

D. Range of Motion

Only the qualified physical therapist may perform range of motion tests and, therefore, such **tests** are skilled physical therapy. Range of motion **exercises** constitute skilled physical therapy only if they are part of active treatment for a specific disease state which has resulted in a loss or restriction of mobility (as evidenced by physical therapy notes showing the degree of motion lost, the degree to be restored and the impact on mobility and/or function).

Range of motion exercises which are not related to the restoration of a specific loss of function may be provided safely by supportive personnel, such as aides or nursing personnel, and as such would not necessarily require the skills of a physical therapist. Passive exercises to maintain range of motion in paralyzed extremities that can be carried out by aides or nursing personnel would not be considered skilled care. However, see § 30.2.2. for the specific circumstances in which an ordinarily nonskilled service can nevertheless be considered skilled. Documentation of the patient's condition in the medical record must describe the circumstances which delineate the need for skilled rather than unskilled services during range of motion training.

E. Maintenance Therapy

Therapy services in connection with a maintenance program are considered skilled when they are so inherently complex that they can be safely and effectively performed only by, or under the supervision of, a qualified therapist. (See 42 CFR § 409.32.) If all other requirements for coverage under the SNF benefit are met, skilled therapy services are covered when an individualized assessment of the patient's clinical condition demonstrates that the specialized judgment, knowledge, and skills of a qualified therapist are necessary for the performance of a safe and effective maintenance program. Such a maintenance program to maintain the patient's current condition or to prevent or slow further deterioration is covered so long as the beneficiary requires skilled care for the safe and effective performance of the program. When, however, the individualized assessment does not demonstrate such a necessity for skilled care, including when the performance of a maintenance program does not require the skills of a therapist because it could safely and effectively be accomplished by the patient or with the assistance of non-therapists, including unskilled caregivers, such maintenance services do not constitute a covered level of care.

A service is not considered a skilled therapy service merely because it is furnished by a therapist or by a therapist/therapy assistant under the direct supervision of a therapist. If a service can be self-administered or safely and effectively furnished by an unskilled person, without the direct supervision of a therapist, the service cannot be regarded as a skilled therapy service even when a therapist actually furnishes the service. Similarly, the unavailability of a competent person to provide a non-skilled service, regardless of the importance of the service to the patient, does not make it a skilled service when a therapist furnishes the service.

However, even though it would not otherwise require the skills of a therapist, the performance of a maintenance program may nevertheless require such skills under certain circumstances. Specifically, skilled therapy services are necessary for the performance of a safe and effective maintenance program only when (a) the particular patient's special medical complications require the skills of a qualified therapist to perform a therapy service that would otherwise be considered nonskilled; or (b) the needed therapy procedures are of such complexity that the skills of a qualified therapist are required to perform the procedure.

If the specialized knowledge and judgment of a qualified therapist are required, the establishment or design of a maintenance program by a qualified therapist, the instruction of the beneficiary or appropriate caregiver by a qualified therapist regarding a maintenance program, and the necessary periodic reevaluations by a qualified therapist of the beneficiary and maintenance program are considered skilled therapy services, to the extent provided by regulation.

■ **EXAMPLE:** A patient with Parkinson's disease may require the services of a physical therapist to determine the type of exercises that are required to maintain his present level of function. The initial evaluation of the patient's needs, the designing of a maintenance program which is appropriate to the capacity and tolerance of the patient and the treatment objectives of the physician, the instruction of the patient or supportive personnel (e.g., aides or nursing personnel) in the carrying out of the program, would constitute skilled physical therapy and must be documented in the medical record (see § 30.2.2.1).

While a patient is receiving a skilled physical therapy program, the physical therapist should regularly reevaluate the patient's condition and adjust any exercise program the patient is expected to carry out independently or with the aid of supportive personnel to maintain the function being restored. Consequently, by the time it is determined that no further skilled therapy services are needed, i.e., by the end of the last skilled session, the physical therapist will have already designed any maintenance program required and instructed the patient or supportive personnel in the carrying out of the program.

F. Ultrasound, Shortwave, and Microwave Diathermy Treatments

These modalities must always be performed by or under the supervision of a qualified physical therapist.

G. Hot Packs, Infra-Red Treatments, Paraffin Baths, and Whirlpool Baths

Heat treatments and baths of this type ordinarily do not require the skills of a qualified physical therapist. However, the skills, knowledge, and judgment of a qualified physical therapist might be required in the giving of such treatments or baths in a particular case, e.g., where the patient's condition is complicated by circulatory deficiency, areas of desensitization, open wounds, fractures, or other complications. There must be clear documentation in the medical record of the special medical complications that describe the need for the skilled therapy provided by the therapist.

30.4.2 Speech Pathology

(Rev. 179, Issued: 01-14-14, Effective: 01-07-14, Implementation: 01-07-14)

See Pub. 100-02, Medicare Benefit Policy Manual, Chapter 1, "Inpatient Hospital Services."

See § 30.4.1.2.E Maintenance Therapy for the specific circumstances in which speech-language pathology therapy is appropriate in connection with a maintenance program.

30.4.3 Occupational Therapy—

(Rev. 179, Issued: 01-14-14, Effective: 01-07-14, Implementation: 01-07-14) A3-3132.3.C, SNF-214.3.C

See Pub. 100-02, Medicare Benefit Policy Manual, Chapter 1, "Inpatient Hospital Services."

See § 30.4.1.2.E Maintenance Therapy for the specific circumstances in which occupational therapy is appropriate in connection with a maintenance program.

30.5 Nonskilled Supportive or Personal Care Services—

(Rev. 1, 10-01-03) A3-332.4, SNF-214.4

The following services are not skilled services unless rendered under circumstances detailed in § 30.2:

- Administration of routine oral medications, eye drops, and ointments (the fact that patients cannot be relied upon to take such medications themselves or that State law requires all medications to be dispensed by a nurse to institutional patients would not change this service to a skilled service);
- General maintenance care of colostomy and ileostomy;
- Routine services to maintain satisfactory functioning of indwelling bladder catheters (this would include emptying and cleaning containers and clamping the tubing);
- Changes of dressings for uninfected post-operative or chronic conditions;
- Prophylactic and palliative skin care, including bathing and application of creams, or treatment of minor skin problems;
- Routine care of the incontinent patient, including use of diapers and protective sheets;
- General maintenance care in connection with a plaster cast (skilled supervision or observation may be required where the patient has a preexisting skin or circulatory condition or requires adjustment of traction);
- Routine care in connection with braces and similar devices;
- Use of heat as a palliative and comfort measure, such as whirlpool or steam pack;

- Routine administration of medical gases after a regimen of therapy has been established (i.e., administration of medical gases after the patient has been taught how to institute therapy);
- Assistance in dressing, eating, and going to the toilet;
- Periodic turning and positioning in bed; and
- General supervision of exercises, which have been taught to the patient and the performance of repetitious exercises that do not require skilled rehabilitation personnel for their performance. (This includes the actual carrying out of maintenance programs where the performances of repetitive exercises that may be required to maintain function do not necessitate a need for the involvement and services of skilled rehabilitation personnel. It also includes the carrying out of repetitive exercises to improve gait, maintain strength or endurance; passive exercises to maintain range of motion in paralyzed extremities which are not related to a specific loss of function; and assistive walking.) (See Medicare Benefit Policy Manual, Chapter 1, "Inpatient Hospital Services.")

30.6 Daily Skilled Services Defined

(Rev. 179, Issued: 01-14-14, Effective: 01-07-14, Implementation: 01-07-14)

Skilled nursing services or skilled rehabilitation services (or a combination of these services) must be needed and provided on a "daily basis," i.e., on essentially a 7-days-a-week basis. A patient whose inpatient stay is based solely on the need for skilled rehabilitation services would meet the "daily basis" requirement when they need and receive those services on at least 5 days a week. (If therapy services are provided less than 5 days a week, though, the "daily" requirement would not be met.)

This requirement should not be applied so strictly that it would not be met merely because there is an isolated break of a day or two during which no skilled rehabilitation services are furnished and discharge from the facility would not be practical.

■ **EXAMPLE:** A patient who normally requires skilled rehabilitation services on a daily basis may exhibit extreme fatigue, which results in suspending therapy sessions for a day or two. Coverage may continue for these days since discharge in such a case would not be practical.

In instances when a patient requires a skilled restorative nursing program to positively affect his functional well-being, the expectation is that the program be rendered at least 6 days a week. (Note that when a patient's skilled status is based on a restorative program, medical evidence must be documented to justify the services. In most instances, it is expected that a skilled restorative program will be, at most, only a few weeks in duration.)

The daily basis requirement can be met by furnishing a single type of skilled service every day, or by furnishing various types of skilled services on different days of the week that collectively add up to "daily" skilled services. However, arbitrarily staggering the timing of various therapy modalities through the week, merely in order to have some type of therapy session occur each day, would not satisfy the SNF coverage requirement for skilled care to be needed on a "daily basis." To meet this requirement, the patient must actually **need** skilled rehabilitation services to be furnished on each of the days that the facility makes such services available.

It is not sufficient for the scheduling of therapy sessions to be arranged so that some therapy is **furnished** each day, unless the patient's medical needs indicate that daily therapy is required. For example, if physical therapy is furnished on 3 days each week and occupational therapy is furnished on 2 other days each week, the "daily basis" requirement would be satisfied only if there is a valid medical reason why both cannot be furnished on the same day. The basic issue here is not whether the services are needed, but **when** they are needed. Unless there is a legitimate medical need for scheduling a therapy session each day, the "daily basis" requirement for SNF coverage would not be met.

30.7 Services Provided on an Inpatient Basis as a "Practical Matter"

(Rev. 179, Issued: 01-14-14, Effective: 01-07-14, Implementation: 01-07-14) A-3132.6, SNF-214.6

In determining whether the daily skilled care needed by an individual can, as a "practical matter," only be provided in a SNF on an inpatient basis, the intermediary or MAC considers the individual's physical condition and the availability and feasibility of using more economical alternative facilities or services.

As a "practical matter," daily skilled services can be provided only in a SNF if they are not available on an outpatient basis in the area in which the individual resides or transportation to the closest facility would be:

- An excessive physical hardship;
- Less economical; or
- Less efficient or effective than an inpatient institutional setting.

The availability of capable and willing family or the feasibility of obtaining other assistance for the patient at home should be considered. Even though needed daily skilled services might be available on an outpatient or home care basis, as a practical matter, the care can be furnished only in the SNF if home care would be ineffective because the patient would have insufficient assistance at home to reside there safely.

■ **EXAMPLE:** A patient undergoing skilled physical therapy can walk only with supervision but has a reasonable potential to learn to walk independently with further training. Further daily skilled therapy is available on an outpatient or home care basis, but the patient would be at risk for further injury from falling, because insufficient supervision and assistance could not be arranged for the patient in his home. In these circumstances, the physical therapy services as a practical matter can be provided effectively only in the inpatient setting.

30.7.1 The Availability of Alternative Facilities or Services

(Rev. 1, 10-01-03)
A-3132.6.A, SNF-214.6.A

Alternative facilities or services may be available to a patient when health care providers such as home health agencies are utilized. These alternatives are not always available in all communities and even where they exist they may not be available when needed.

■ **EXAMPLE:** Where the residents of a rural community generally utilize the outpatient facilities of a hospital located some distance from the area, the hospital outpatient department constitutes an alternative source of care that is available to the community. Roads in winter, however, may be impassable for some periods of time and in special situations institutionalization might be needed.

In determining the availability of more economical care alternatives, the coverage or non-coverage of that alternative care is not a factor to be considered. Home health care for a patient who is not homebound, for example, may be an appropriate alternative in some cases. The fact that Medicare cannot cover such care is irrelevant.

The issue is feasibility and not whether coverage is provided in one setting and not provided in another. For instance, an individual in need of daily skilled physical therapy might be able to receive the services needed on a more economical basis from an independently practicing physical therapist. However, the fact that Medicare payment could not be made for the services because the $500 expense limitation applicable to the services of an independent physical therapist had been exceeded or because the patient was not enrolled in Part B, would not be a basis for determining that, as a practical matter, the needed care could only be provided in a SNF.

In determining the availability of alternate facilities or services, whether the patient or another resource can pay for the alternate services is not a factor to be considered.

30.7.2 Whether Available Alternatives Are More Economical in the Individual Case

(Rev. 1, 10-01-03)
A3-3132.6.B, SNF-214.6.B

If the intermediary determines that an alternative setting is available to provide the needed care, it considers whether the use of the alternative setting would actually be more economical in the individual case.

■ **EXAMPLE 1:** If a patient's condition requires daily transportation to the alternative source of care (e.g., a hospital outpatient department) by ambulance, it might be more economical from a health care delivery viewpoint to provide the needed care in the SNF setting.

■ **EXAMPLE 2:** If needed care could be provided in the home, but the patient's residence is so isolated that daily visits would entail inordinate travel costs, care in a SNF might be a more economical alternative.

30.7.3 Whether the Patient's Physical Condition Would Permit Utilization of an Available, More Economical Care Alternative

(Rev. 1, 10-01-03)
A3-3132.6.C, SNF-214.6.C

In determining the practicality of using more economical care alternatives, the intermediary considers the patient's medical condition. If the use of those alternatives would adversely affect the patient's medical condition, the intermediary concludes that as a practical matter the daily skilled services can only be provided by a SNF on an inpatient basis.

If the use of a care alternative involves transportation of the individual on a daily basis, the intermediary considers whether daily transportation would cause excessive physical hardship. Determinations on whether a patient's condition would be adversely affected if an available, more economical care alternative were utilized should not be based solely on the fact that the patient is nonambulatory. There are individuals confined to wheelchairs who, though nonambulatory, could be transported daily by automobile from their homes to alternative care sources without any adverse impact. Conversely, there are instances where an individual's condition would be adversely affected by daily transportation to a care facility, even though the individual is able to ambulate to some extent.

■ **EXAMPLE:** A 75-year-old woman has suffered a cerebrovascular accident and cannot climb stairs safely. The patient lives alone in a second-floor apartment accessible only by climbing a flight of stairs. She requires physical therapy and occupational therapy on alternate days, and they are available in a CORF one mile away from her apartment. However, because of her inability to negotiate the stairs, the daily skilled services she requires cannot, as a practical matter, be provided to the patient outside the SNF.

The "practical matter" criterion should never be interpreted so strictly that it results in the automatic denial of coverage for patients who have been meeting all of the SNF level of care requirements, but who have occasion to be away from the SNF for a brief period of time. While most beneficiaries requiring a SNF level of care find that they are unable to leave the facility, the fact that a patient is granted an outside pass or short leave of absence for the purpose of attending a special religious service, holiday meal, family occasion, going on a car ride, or for a trial visit home, is not, by itself evidence that the individual no longer needs to be in a SNF for the receipt of required skilled care. Where frequent or prolonged periods away from the SNF become possible, the intermediary may question whether the patient's care can, as a practical matter, only be furnished on an inpatient basis in a SNF. Decisions in these cases should be based on information reflecting the care needed and received by the patient while in the SNF and on the arrangements needed for the provision, if any, of this care during any absences. (*See* the Medicare Benefit Policy Manual, Chapter 3, "Duration of Covered Inpatient Services," § 20.1.2, for counting inpatient days during a leave of absence.)

A conservative approach to retain the presumption for limitation of liability may lead a facility to notify patients that leaving the facility will result in denial of coverage. Such a notice is not appropriate. If a SNF determines that covered care is no longer needed, the situation does not change whether the patient actually leaves the facility or not.

APPENDIX 3-4 TITLE 42—PUBLIC HEALTH (CODE OF FEDERAL REGULATIONS):

PART 409—HOSPITAL INSURANCE BENEFITS

Subpart C—Posthospital SNF Care

Sec. 409.20 Coverage of services.

(a) Included services. Subject to the conditions and limitations set forth in this subpart and subpart D of this part, "posthospital SNF care" means the following services furnished to an inpatient of a participating SNF, or of a participating hospital or critical access hospital (CAH) that has a swing-bed approval:

(1) Nursing care provided by or under the supervision of a registered professional nurse.

(2) Bed and board in connection with the furnishing of that nursing care.

(3) Physical therapy, occupational therapy, and speech- language pathology services.

(4) Medical social services.

(5) Drugs, biologicals, supplies, appliances, and equipment.

(6) Services furnished by a hospital with which the SNF has a transfer agreement in effect under § 483.75(n) of this chapter.

(7) Other services that are generally provided by (or under arrangements made by) SNFs.

(b) Excluded services—(1) *Services that are not considered inpatient hospital services.* No service is included as posthospital SNF care if it would not be included as an inpatient hospital service under §§ 409.11 through 409.18.

(2) *Services not generally provided by (or under arrangements made by) SNFs.* Except as specifically listed in §§ 409.21 through 409.27, only those services generally provided by (or under arrangements made by) SNFs are considered as posthospital SNF care. For example, a type of medical or surgical procedure that is ordinarily performed only on an inpatient basis in a hospital is not included as "posthospital SNF care," because such procedures are not generally provided by (or under arrangements made by) SNFs.

(c) Terminology. In § 409.21 through § 409.36—.

(1) The terms *SNF* and *swing-bed hospital* are used when the context applies to the particular facility.

(2) The term *facility* is used to mean both SNFs and swing-bed hospitals.

(3) The term *swing-bed hospital* includes a CAH with swing-bed approval under subpart F of part 485 of this chapter.

(4) The term *post-hospital SNF care* includes SNF care that does not follow a hospital stay when the beneficiary is enrolled in a plan, as defined in § 422.4 of this chapter, offered by a Medicare+Choice (M+C) organization, that includes the benefits described in § 422.101(c) of this chapter.

[48 FR 12541, Mar. 25, 1983, as amended at 50 FR 33033, Aug. 16, 1985; 58 FR 30667, May 26, 1993; 63 FR 26306, May 12, 1998; 64 FR 3648, Jan. 25, 1999; 64 FR 41681, July 30, 1999; 68 FR 46070, Aug. 4, 2003; 68 FR 50854, Aug. 22, 2003; 69 FR 35529, June 25, 2004; 75 FR 73613, Nov. 29, 2010]

Sec. 409.21 Nursing care.

(a) Basic rule. Medicare pays for nursing care as posthospital SNF care when provided by or under the supervision of a registered professional nurse.

(b) Exception. Medicare does not pay for the services of a private duty nurse or attendant. An individual is not considered to be a private duty nurse or attendant if he or she is a SNF employee at the time the services are furnished.

[63 FR 26306, May 12, 1998]
***

Sec. 409.22 Bed and board.

(a) Semiprivate and ward accommodations. Except for applicable deductible and coinsurance amounts Medicare Part A pays in full for semiprivate (2 to 4 beds), or ward (5 or more beds) accommodations.

(b) Private accommodations—(1) *Conditions for payment in full.* Except for applicable coinsurance amounts, Medicare pays in full for a private room if—

(i) The patient's condition requires him to be isolated;

(ii) The SNF has no semiprivate or ward accommodations; or

(iii) The SNF semiprivate and ward accommodations are fully occupied by other patients, were so occupied at the time the patient was admitted to the SNF for treatment of a condition that required immediate inpatient SNF care, and have been so occupied during the interval.

(2) *Period of payment.* In the situations specified in paragraph (b)(1) (i) and (iii) of this section, Medicare pays for a private room until the patient's condition no longer requires isolation or until semiprivate or ward accommodations are available.

(3) *Conditions for patient's liability.* The facility may charge the patient the difference between its customary charge for the private room furnished and its most prevalent charge for a semiprivate room if:

(i) None of the conditions of paragraph (b)(1) of this section is met, and

(ii) The private room was requested by the patient or a member of the family who, at the time of request was informed what the charge would be.
***

Sec. 409.23 Physical, occupational, and speech therapy.

Medicare pays for physical, occupational, or speech-language pathology services as posthospital SNF care if they are furnished—

(a) By (or under arrangements made by) the facility and billed by (or through) the facility;

(b) By qualified physical therapists, physical therapist assistants, occupational therapists, occupational therapy assistants or speech-language pathologists as defined in part 484 of this chapter[.]

(2) In accordance with a plan that meets the requirements of § 409.17(b) through (d) of this part.

[75 FR 73613, Nov. 29, 2010]

Sec. 409.24 Medical social services.

Medicare pays for medical social services as posthospital SNF care, including—

(a) Assessment of the social and emotional factors related to the beneficiary's illness, need for care, response to treatment, and adjustment to care in the facility;

(b) Case work services to assist in resolving social or emotional problems that may have an adverse effect on the beneficiary's ability to respond to treatment; and

(c) Assessment of the relationship of the beneficiary's medical and nursing requirements to his or her home situation, financial resources, and the community resources available upon discharge from facility care.

[63 FR 26306, May 12, 1998]

***

Sec. 409.25 Drugs, biologicals, supplies, appliances, and equipment.

(a) Drugs and biologicals. Except as specified in paragraph (b) of this section, Medicare pays for drugs and biologicals as posthospital SNF care only if—

(1) They represent a cost to the facility;

(2) They are ordinarily furnished by the facility for the care and treatment of inpatients; and

(3) They are furnished to an inpatient for use in the facility.

(b) Exception. Medicare pays for a limited supply of drugs for use outside the facility if it is medically necessary to facilitate the beneficiary's departure from the facility and required until he or she can obtain a continuing supply.

(c) Supplies, appliances, and equipment. Except as specified in paragraph (d) of this section, Medicare pays for supplies, appliances, and equipment as posthospital SNF care only if they are—

(1) Ordinarily furnished by the facility to inpatients; and

(2) Furnished to inpatients for use in the facility.

(d) Exception. Medicare pays for items to be used after the individual leaves the facility if—

(1) The item is one that the beneficiary must continue to use after leaving, such as a leg brace; or

(2) The item is necessary to permit or facilitate the beneficiary's departure from the facility and is required until he or she can obtain a continuing supply, for example, sterile dressings.

[63 FR 26307, May 12, 1998]
***

Sec. 409.26 Transfer agreement hospital services.

(a) Services furnished by an intern or a resident-in-training. Medicare pays for medical services that are furnished by an intern or a resident-in-training (under a hospital teaching program approved in accordance with the provisions of Sec. 409.15) as posthospital SNF care, if the intern or resident is in—

(1) A participating hospital with which the SNF has in effect an agreement under Sec. 483.75(n) of this chapter for the transfer of patients and exchange of medical records; or

(2) A hospital that has a swing-bed approval, and is furnishing services to a SNF-level inpatient of that hospital.

(b) Other diagnostic or therapeutic services. Medicare pays for other diagnostic or therapeutic services as posthospital SNF care if they are provided—

(1) By a participating hospital with which the SNF has in effect a transfer agreement as described in paragraph (a)(1) of this section; or

(2) By a hospital or a CAH that has a swing-bed approval, to its own SNF-level inpatient.

[63 FR 26307, May 12, 1998]
***

Sec. 409.27 Other services generally provided by (or under arrangements made by) SNFs.

In addition to those services specified in Secs. 409.21 through 409.26, Medicare pays as posthospital SNF care for such other diagnostic and therapeutic services as are generally provided by (or under arrangements made by) SNFs, including—

(a) Medical and other health services as described in subpart B of part 410 of this chapter, subject to any applicable limitations or exclusions contained in that subpart or in Sec. 409.20(b);

(b) Respiratory therapy services prescribed by a physician for the assessment, diagnostic evaluation, treatment, management, and monitoring of patients with deficiencies and abnormalities of cardiopulmonary function; and

(c) Transportation by ambulance that meets the general medical necessity requirements set forth in Sec. 410.40(d)(1) of this chapter.

[63 FR 26307, May 12, 1998, as amended at 64 FR 41681, July 30, 1999]
***

Subpart D—Requirements for Coverage of Posthospital SNF Care

Sec. 409.31 Level of care requirement.

(a) Definition. As used in this section, *skilled nursing and skilled rehabilitation services* means services that:

(1) Are ordered by a physician;

(2) Require the skills of technical or professional personnel such as registered nurses, licensed practical (vocational) nurses, physical therapists, occupational therapists, and speech pathologists or audiologists; and

(3) Are furnished directly by, or under the supervision of, such personnel.

(b) Specific conditions for meeting level of care requirements. (1) The beneficiary must require skilled nursing or skilled rehabilitation services, or both, on a daily basis.

(2) Those services must be furnished for a condition—

(i) For which the beneficiary received inpatient hospital or inpatient CAH services; or

(ii) Which arose while the beneficiary was receiving care in a SNF or swing-bed hospital for a condition for which he or she received inpatient hospital or inpatient CAH services; or

(iii) For which, for an M+C enrollee described in § 409.20(c)(4), a physician has determined that a direct admission to a SNF without an inpatient hospital or inpatient CAH stay would be medically appropriate.

(3) The daily skilled services must be ones that, as a practical matter, can only be provided in a SNF, on an inpatient basis.

[48 FR 12541, Mar. 25, 1983, as amended at 58 FR 30666, May 26, 1993; 68 FR 50854, Aug. 22, 2003; 70 FR 45055, Aug. 4, 2005]
***

Sec. 409.32 Criteria for skilled services and the need for skilled services.

(a) To be considered a skilled service, the service must be so inherently complex that it can be safely and effectively performed only by, or under the supervision of, professional or technical personnel.

(b) A condition that does not ordinarily require skilled services may require them because of special medical complications. Under those circumstances, a service that is usually nonskilled (such as those listed in Sec. 409.33(d)) may be considered skilled because it must be performed or supervised by skilled nursing or rehabilitation personnel. For example, a plaster cast on a leg does not usually require skilled care. However, if the patient has a preexisting acute skin condition or needs traction, skilled personnel may be needed to adjust traction or watch for complications. In situations of this type, the complications, and the skilled services they require, must be documented by physicians' orders and nursing or therapy notes.

(c) The restoration potential of a patient is not the deciding factor in determining whether skilled services are needed. Even if full recovery or medical improvement is not possible, a patient may need skilled services to prevent further deterioration or preserve current capabilities. For example, a terminal cancer patient may need some of the skilled services described in Sec. 409.33.

[48 FR 12541, Mar. 25, 1983, as amended at 59 FR 65493, Dec. 20, 1994]
***

Sec. 409.33 Examples of skilled nursing and rehabilitation services.

(a) Services that could qualify as either skilled nursing or skilled rehabilitation services— (1) *Overall management and evaluation of care plan.* (i) When overall management and evaluation of care plan *constitute skilled services.* The development, management, and evaluation of a patient care plan based on the physician's orders constitute skilled services when, because of the patient's physical or mental condition, those activities require the involvement of technical or professional personnel in order to meet the patient's needs, promote recovery, and ensure medical safety. Those activities include the management of a plan involving a variety of personal care services only when, in light of the patient's condition, the aggregate of those services requires the involvement of technical or professional personnel.

(ii) *Example.* An aged patient with a history of diabetes mellitus and angina pectoris who is recovering from an open reduction of a fracture of the neck of the femur requires, among other services, careful skin care, appropriate oral medications, a diabetic diet, an exercise program to preserve muscle tone and body condition, and observation to detect signs of deterioration in his or her condition or complications resulting from restricted, but increasing, mobility. Although any of the required services could be performed by a properly instructed person, such a person would not have the ability to understand the relationship between the services and evaluate the ultimate effect of one service on the other. Since the nature of the patient's condition, age, and immobility create a high potential for serious complications, such an understanding is essential to ensure the patient's recovery and safety. Under these circumstances, the management of the plan of care would require the skills of a nurse even though the individual services are not skilled. Skilled planning and management activities are not always specifically identified in the patient's clinical record. Therefore, if the patient's overall condition supports a finding that recovery and safety can be ensured only if the total care is planned, managed, and evaluated by technical or professional personnel, it is appropriate to infer that skilled services are being provided.

(2) *Observation and assessment of the patient's changing condition*—(i) *When observation and assessment constitute skilled services.* Observation and assessment constitute skilled services when the skills of a technical or professional person are required to identify and evaluate the patient's need for modification of treatment or for additional medical procedures until his or her condition is stabilized.

(ii) *Examples.* A patient with congestive heart failure may require continuous close observation to detect signs of decompensation, abnormal fluid balance, or adverse effects resulting from prescribed medication(s) that serve as indicators for adjusting therapeutic measures. Similarly, surgical patients transferred from a hospital to a SNF while in the complicated, unstabilized postoperative period, for example, after hip prosthesis or cataract surgery, may need continued close skilled monitoring for postoperative complications and adverse reaction. Patients who, in addition to their physical problems, exhibit acute psychological symptoms such as depression, anxiety, or agitation, may also require skilled observation and assessment by technical or professional personnel to ensure their safety or the safety of others, that is, to observe for indications of suicidal or hostile behavior. The need for services of this type must be documented by physicians' orders or nursing or therapy notes.

(3) *Patient education services*—(i) *When patient education services constitute skilled services.* Patient education services are skilled services if the use of technical or professional personnel is necessary to teach a patient self-maintenance.

(ii) *Examples.* A patient who has had a recent leg amputation needs skilled rehabilitation services provided by technical or professional personnel to provide gait training and to teach prosthesis care. Similarly, a patient newly diagnosed with diabetes requires instruction from technical or professional personnel to learn the self-administration of insulin or foot-care precautions.

(b) Services that qualify as skilled nursing services. (1) Intravenous or intramuscular injections and intravenous feeding.

(2) Enteral feeding that comprises at least 26% of daily calorie requirements and provides at least 501 milliliters of fluid per day.

(3) Nasopharyngeal and tracheostomy aspiration;

(4) Insertion and sterile irrigation and replacement of suprapubic catheters;

(5) Application of dressings involving prescription medications and aseptic techniques;

(6) Treatment of extensive decubitus ulcers or other widespread skin disorder;

(7) Heat treatments which have been specifically ordered by a physician as part of active treatment and which require observation by nurses to adequately evaluate the patient's progress;

(8) Initial phases of a regimen involving administration of medical gases;

(9) Rehabilitation nursing procedures, including the related teaching and adaptive aspects of nursing, that are part of active treatment, e.g., the institution and supervision of bowel and bladder training programs.

(c) Services that would qualify as skilled rehabilitation services. (1) Ongoing assessment of rehabilitation needs and potential: Services concurrent with the management of a patient care plan, including tests and measurements of range of motion, strength, balance, coordination, endurance, functional ability, activities of daily living, perceptual deficits, speech and language or hearing disorders;

(2) Therapeutic exercises or activities: Therapeutic exercises or activities which, because of the type of exercises employed or the condition of the patient, must be performed by or under the supervision of a qualified physical therapist or occupational therapist to ensure the safety of the patient and the effectiveness of the treatment;

(3) Gait evaluation and training: Gait evaluation and training furnished to restore function in a patient whose ability to walk has been impaired by neurological, muscular, or skeletal abnormality;

(4) Range of motion exercises: Range of motion exercises which are part of the active treatment of a specific disease state which has resulted in a loss of, or restriction of, mobility (as evidenced by a therapist's notes showing the degree of motion lost and the degree to be restored);

(5) Maintenance therapy; Maintenance therapy, when the specialized knowledge and judgment of a qualified therapist is required to design and establish a maintenance program based on an initial evaluation and periodic reassessment of the patient's needs, and consistent with the patient's capacity and tolerance. For example, a patient with Parkinson's disease who has not been under a rehabilitation regimen may require the services of a qualified therapist to determine what type of exercises will contribute the most to the maintenance of his present level of functioning.

(6) Ultrasound, short-wave, and microwave therapy treatment by a qualified physical therapist;

(7) Hot pack hydrocollator, infrared treatments, paraffin baths, and whirlpool in particular cases where the patient's condition is complicated by circulatory deficiency, areas of desensitization, open wounds, fractures, or other complications, and the skills, knowledge, and judgment of a qualified physical therapist are required; and

(8) Services of a speech pathologist or audiologist when necessary for the restoration of function in speech or hearing.

(d) Personal care services. Personal care services which do not require the skills of qualified technical or professional personnel are not skilled services except under the circumstances specified in Sec. 409.32(b). Personal care services include, but are not limited to, the following:

(1) Administration of routine oral medications, eye drops, and ointments;

(2) General maintenance care of colostomy and ileostomy;

(3) Routine services to maintain satisfactory functioning of indwelling bladder catheters;

(4) Changes of dressings for noninfected postoperative or chronic conditions;

(5) Prophylactic and palliative skin care, including bathing and application of creams, or treatment of minor skin problems;

(6) Routine care of the incontinent patient, including use of diapers and protective sheets;

(7) General maintenance care in connection with a plaster cast;

(8) Routine care in connection with braces and similar devices;

(9) Use of heat as a palliative and comfort measure, such as whirlpool and hydrocollator;

(10) Routine administration of medical gases after a regimen of therapy has been established;

(11) Assistance in dressing, eating, and going to the toilet;

(12) Periodic turning and positioning in bed; and

(13) General supervision of exercises which have been taught to the patient; including the actual carrying out of maintenance programs, i.e., the performance of the repetitive exercises required to maintain function do [sic] not require the skills of a therapist and would not constitute skilled rehabilitation services (see paragraph (c) of this section). Similarly, repetitious exercises to improve gait, maintain strength, or endurance; passive exercises to maintain range of motion in paralyzed extremities, which are not related to a specific loss of function; and assistive walking do not constitute skilled rehabilitation services.

[48 FR 12541, Mar. 25, 1983, as amended at 63 FR 26307, May 12, 1998; 64 FR 41681, July 30, 1999]

***

APPENDIX 3-5 SNF NOTICES OF NON-COVERAGE

Notice of Exclusions from Medicare Benefits
Skilled Nursing Facility (NEMB-SNF)*

Date of Notice: ____________

NOTE: You need to make a choice about receiving these health care items or services.

It is not Medicare's opinion, but our opinion, that Medicare will not pay for the item(s) or service(s) described below. Medicare does not pay for all of your health care costs. Medicare only pays for covered items and services when Medicare rules are met. The fact that Medicare will not pay for a particular item or service does not mean that you should not receive it. There may be a good reason to receive it. Right now, in your case, **Medicare will not pay for –**

Items or Services:

We believe that Medicare will not pay for the following reason. (See the reason checked off below.)

☐ No qualifying 3-day inpatient hospital stay.
☐ No days left in this benefit period.
☐ Care not ordered or certified by a physician.
☐ Daily skilled care not needed.
☐ SNF transfer requirement not met.
☐ Facility/Bed not certified by Medicare.
☐ Care not given by, nor supervised by, skilled nursing or rehabilitation staff.
☐ Items or services not furnished under arrangements by the skilled nursing facility.
☐ **Other:** ____________

The purpose of this notice is to help you make an informed choice about whether or not you want to receive these items or services, knowing that you will have to pay for them yourself or through other insurance that you may have. Before you make a decision about your options, you should **read this entire notice carefully.**

- Ask us to explain, if you don't understand why Medicare won't pay.
- Ask us how much these items or services will cost you (**Estimated Cost $**________.)

Your other insurance is: ____________

Please choose one option. Check on box. Sign and date this notice.

☐ **Option 1 YES** I want to receive these items or services and get an official Medicare decision about coverage. Please submit a claim, with any evidence supporting my need for these items or services, to Medicare for its official decision. I understand you will notify me when my claim is submitted and that you will not bill me for these items or services until Medicare makes its decision. If Medicare denies payment, I agree to be personally and fully responsible for payment. That is, I will pay personally, either out of pocket or through any other insurance that I have.

I understand that I can appeal if Medicare decides not to pay. Medicare will send me notice of its official decision not to pay that explains its decision in my case. That notice will explain how I can appeal Medicare's decision not to pay. If I do not hear from Medicare about its official coverage decision within 90 days, I can telephone Medicare at
( ) ____________. TTY/TDD: ( ) ____________.

☐ **Option 2. YES** I want to receive these items or services. Do NOT submit a claim to Medicare. I agree to be fully and personally responsible for payment of any amount for which my other insurance will not pay. I realize I cannot appeal to Medicare.

☐ **Option 3. NO** I will not receive these items or services. I understand that you will not be able to submit a claim to Medicare and that I will not be able to appeal your opinion that Medicare won't pay.

Patient's name	Identification Number
Signature of the patient or the authorized representative	Date

Form CMS 20014 OMB Exempt

---

* The MedLearn series is available at http://www.cms.gov/Outreach-and-Education/Medicare-Learning-Network-MLN/MLNProducts/downloads/abn_booklet_icn006266.pdf (site visited Sept. 26, 2016). *See also* the material published at http://www.cms.gov/Medicare/Medicare-General-Information/BNI/FFSSNFABNandSNFDenialLetters.html (site visited Sept. 26, 2016).

Skilled Nursing Facility's Name and Address
Telephone number and TTY/TDD number

Skilled Nursing Facility Advance Beneficiary Notice (SNFABN)

Date of Notice: ____________

NOTE: You need to make a choice about receiving these health care items or services.

It is not Medicare's opinion, but our opinion, that Medicare will not pay for the items or services described below. Medicare does not pay for all of your health care costs. Medicare only pays for covered items and services when Medicare rules are met. The fact that Medicare may not pay for a particular item or service does not mean that you should not receive it. There may be a good reason to receive it. Right now, in your case, **Medicare probably will not pay for –**

Items or Services:

Because:

The purpose of this form is to help you make an informed choice about whether or not you want to receive these items or services, knowing that you might have to pay for them yourself. Before you make a decision about your options, you should **read this entire notice carefully**.

- Ask us to explain, if you don't understand why Medicare probably won't pay.
- Ask us how much these items or services will cost you (**Estimated Cost: $** ____________), in case you have to pay for them yourself or through other insurance you may have.
  Your other insurance is: ____________
- If in 90 days you have not gotten a decision on your claim, contact the Medicare contractor at: Address: ____________
  or at: Telephone: ____________ TTY/TDD: ____________
- If you receive these items or services, we will submit your claim for them to Medicare.

PLEASE CHOOSE **ONE** OPTION. CHECK **ONE** BOX. **DATE & SIGN** THIS NOTICE.

☐ **Option 1. YES. I want to receive these items or services.** I understand that Medicare will not decide whether to pay unless I receive these items or services. I understand you will notify me when my claim is submitted and that you will not bill me for these items or services until Medicare makes its decision. If Medicare denies payment, I agree to be personally and fully responsible for payment. That is, I will pay personally, either out of pocket or through any other insurance that I have. I understand that I can appeal Medicare's decision.

☐ **Option 2. NO. I will not receive these items or services.** I understand that you will not be able to submit a claim to Medicare and that I will not be able to appeal your opinion that Medicare won't pay. I understand that, in the case of any physician-ordered items or services, should notify my doctor who ordered them that I did not receive them.

Patient's Name: ____________ **Patient Identification #:** ____________

____________ ____________

Date **Signature of the patient or of the authorized representative**

Form CMS-10055

INTERMEDIARY DETERMINATION OF NONCOVERAGE

NAME OF SNF
ADDRESS
DATE

TO: NAME
ADDRESS

RE: NAME OF BENEFICIARY
HICN
DATE OF ADMISSION

On (Date), the Medicare intermediary advised us that the services you receive will no longer qualify as covered under Medicare beginning (Date).

The Medicare intermediary will send you a formal determination as to the noncoverage of your stay after (Date). If you wish to appeal, the formal notice will contain information about how this can be done. The intermediary will inform you of the reason for denial and your appeal rights.

We regret that this may be your first notice of the noncoverage of services under Medicare. Our efforts to contact you earlier, in person or by telephone, were unsuccessful.

Please verify receipt of this notice by signing below.

Sincerely yours,

____

Signature of Administrative Officer

VERIFICATION OF RECEIPT OF NOTICE

A. This acknowledges that I received this attached notice of noncoverage of services under Medicare on (date of receipt).

____

(Signature of Beneficiary or Person
acting on Beneficiary's behalf

B. This is to confirm that you were advised of the noncoverage of the services under Medicare by telephone on (date of telephone contact).

____

(Name of Beneficiary or
Representative contacted)

____

(Signature of Administrative Officer)

KEEP A COPY OF THIS FOR YOUR RECORDS

UR COMMITTEE DETERMINATION OF ADMISSION

NAME OF SNF
ADDRESS
DATE

TO: NAME
ADDRESS

RE: NAME OF BENEFICIARY
HICN
DATE OF ADMISSION

On (Date), our Utilization Review Committee reviewed your medical information available at the time of, or prior to your admission, and advised us that the services (you or beneficiary's name) needed do not meet the requirements for coverage under Medicare. The reason is:

(Insert specific reason the services were determined to be noncovered.)

This decision has not been made by Medicare. It represents the Utilization Review Committee's judgment that the services you needed did not meet Medicare payment requirements. Normally, under this situation, a bill is not submitted to Medicare. A bill will only be submitted to Medicare if you request us to submit one. Furthermore, if you want to appeal this decision you must request that a bill be submitted. If you request a bill be submitted, the Medicare intermediary will notify you of its determination. If you disagree with that determination you may file an appeal.

You must also request that a bill be submitted to Medicare if you have questions concerning your liability for payment for the services you received.

Under a provision of the Medicare law, you do not have to pay for noncovered services determined to be custodial care or not reasonable or necessary unless you had reason to know the services were noncovered. You are considered to know that these services were noncovered effective with the date of this notice.

We regret that this may be your first notice of the noncoverage of services under Medicare. Our efforts to contact you earlier in person or by telephone were unsuccessful.

Please check one of the boxes below to indicate whether or not you want your bill submitted to Medicare and sign the notice to verify receipt.

Sincerely yours,

____

Signature of Administrative Officer

REQUEST FOR MEDICARE INTERMEDIARY REVIEW

/ / A. I want my bill submitted to the intermediary for a Medicare decision. You will be informed when the bill is submitted.

If you do not receive a formal Notice of Medicare Determination within 90 days of this request you should contact: (Name and address of intermediary).

/ / B. I do not want my bill submitted to the intermediary for a Medicare decision.

I understand that I do not have Medicare appeal rights if a bill is not submitted.

NOTE: You are not required to pay for services until a Medicare decision has been made.

VERIFICATION OF RECEIPT OF NOTICE

C. This acknowledges that I received the notice of noncoverage of services under Medicare on (date of receipt).

____
(Signature of Beneficiary or Person acting on Beneficiary's behalf)

D. This is to confirm that you were advised of the noncoverage of the services under Medicare by telephone on (date of telephone contact).

____
(Name of Beneficiary or Representative contacted)

____
(Signature of Administrative Officer)

KEEP A COPY OF THIS FOR YOUR RECORDS

UR COMMITTEE DETERMINATION ON CONTINUED STAY

NAME OF SNF
ADDRESS
DATE

TO: NAME
ADDRESS

RE: NAME OF BENEFICIARY
HICN
DATE OF ADMISSION

On (Date) our Utilization Review Committee reviewed your medical information and found that the services furnished (you or beneficiary's name) no longer qualified for payment by Medicare beginning (Date).

The reason for this is: (Insert specific reason services were determined to be noncovered).

This decision has not been made by Medicare. It represents the Utilization Review Committee's judgment that the services you needed no longer met Medicare payment requirements. A bill will be sent to Medicare for the covered services you received before (Date). Normally, the bill submitted to Medicare does not include services provided after this date. If you want to appeal this decision you must request that the bill submitted to Medicare include the services our URC determined to be noncovered. Medicare will notify you of its determination. If you disagree with that determination you may file an appeal.

Under a provision of the Medicare law, you do not have to pay for noncovered services determined to be custodial or not reasonable or necessary unless you had reason to know the services were noncovered. You are considered to know that these services were noncovered effective with the date of this notice.

We regret that this may be your first notice of the noncoverage of services under Medicare. Our efforts to contact you earlier in person or by telephone were unsuccessful.

Please check one of the boxes below to indicate whether or not you want the bill for services after (date) submitted to Medicare and sign the notice to verify receipt.

Sincerely yours,

____

Signature of Administrative Officer

REQUEST FOR MEDICARE INTERMEDIARY REVIEW

/ / A. I want my bill for services I continue to receive to be submitted to the intermediary for a Medicare decision. You will be notified when the bill is submitted.

If you do not receive a formal Notice of Medicare Determination within 90 days of this request you should contact: (Name and address of intermediary).

/ / B. I do not want my bill for services submitted to the intermediary for a Medicare decision.

I understand that I do not have Medicare appeal rights if a bill is not submitted.

NOTE: You are not required to pay for services until a Medicare decision has been made.

VERIFICATION OF RECEIPT OF NOTICE

C. This acknowledges that I received this notice of noncoverage of services under Medicare on (date of receipt).

____
(Signature of Beneficiary or Person acting on Beneficiary's behalf)

D. This is to confirm that you were advised of the noncoverage of the services under Medicare by telephone on (date of telephone contact).

____
(Name of Beneficiary or Representative contacted)

____
(Signature of Administrative Officer)

KEEP A COPY OF THIS FOR YOUR RECORDS

SNF DETERMINATION ON ADMISSION

NAME OF SNF
ADDRESS
DATE

TO: NAME
ADDRESS

RE: NAME OF BENEFICIARY
HICN
DATE OF ADMISSION

On (Date), we reviewed your medical information available at the time of, or prior to your admission, and we believe that the services (you or beneficiary's name) needed did not meet the requirements for coverage under Medicare. The reason is:

(Insert specific reason services are determined to be noncovered.)

This decision has not been made by Medicare. It represents our judgment that the services you needed did not meet Medicare payment requirements. Normally, under this situation, a bill is not submitted to Medicare. A bill will only be submitted to Medicare if you request that a bill be submitted. Furthermore, if you want to appeal this decision, you must request that a bill be submitted. If you request that a bill be submitted, the Medicare intermediary will notify you of its determination. If you disagree with that determination, you may file an appeal.

Under a provision of the Medicare law, you do not have to pay for noncovered services determined to be custodial care or not reasonable or necessary unless you had reason to know the services were noncovered. You are considered to know that these services were noncovered effective with the date of this notice.

If you have questions concerning your liability for payment for services you received prior to the date of this notice, you must request that a bill be submitted to Medicare.

We regret that this may be your first notice of the noncoverage of services under Medicare. Our efforts to contact you earlier in person or by telephone were unsuccessful.

Please check one of the boxes below to indicate whether or not you want your bill submitted to Medicare and sign the notice to verify receipt.

Sincerely yours,

____

Signature of Administrative Officer

REQUEST FOR MEDICARE INTERMEDIARY REVIEW

/ / A. I want my bill submitted to the intermediary for a Medicare decision. You will be informed when the bill is submitted.

If you do not receive a formal Notice of Medicare Determination within 90 days of this request you should contact: (Name and address of intermediary).

/ / B. I do not want my bill submitted to the intermediary for a Medicare decision.

I understand that I do not have Medicare appeal rights if no bill is submitted.

NOTE: You are not required to pay for services until a Medicare decision has been made.

VERIFICATION OF RECEIPT OF NOTICE

C. This acknowledges that I received this notice of noncoverage of services under Medicare on (date of receipt).

____

(Signature of Beneficiary or Person acting on Beneficiary's behalf)

D. This is to confirm that you were advised of the noncoverage of the services under Medicare by telephone on (date of telephone contact).

____

(Name of Beneficiary or Representative contacted)

____

(Signature of Administrative Officer)

KEEP A COPY OF THIS FOR YOUR RECORDS

SNF DETERMINATION ON CONTINUED STAY

NAME OF SNF
ADDRESS
DATE

TO: NAME
ADDRESS

RE: NAME OF BENEFICIARY
HICN
DATE OF ADMISSION

On (Date), we reviewed your medical information and found that the services furnished (you or beneficiary's name) no longer qualified as covered under Medicare beginning (Date).

The reason is: (Insert specific reason services are considered noncovered.)

This decision has not been made by Medicare. It represents our judgment that the services you needed no longer met Medicare payment requirements. A bill will be sent to Medicare for the services you received before (Date). Normally, the bill submitted to Medicare does not include services provided after this date. If you want to appeal this decision, you must request that the bill submitted to Medicare include the services we determined to be noncovered. Medicare will notify you of its determination. If you disagree with that determination you may file an appeal.

Under a provision of the Medicare law, you do not have to pay for noncovered services determined to be custodial care or not reasonable or necessary unless you had reason to know the services were noncovered. You are considered to know that these services were noncovered effective with the date of this notice.

We regret that this may be your first notice of the noncoverage of services under Medicare. Our efforts to contact you earlier in person or by telephone were unsuccessful.

Please check one of the boxes below to indicate whether or not you want your bill submitted to Medicare and sign the notice to verify receipt.

Sincerely yours,

____
Signature of Administrative Officer

REQUEST FOR MEDICARE INTERMEDIARY REVIEW

/ / A. I want my bill for services I continue to receive to be submitted to the intermediary for a Medicare decision. You will be informed when the bill is submitted.

If you do not receive a formal Notice of Medicare Determination within 90 days of this request you should contact: (Name and address of intermediary).

/ / B. I do not want my bill for services I continue to need to be submitted to the intermediary for a Medicare decision.

I understand that I do not have Medicare appeal rights if a bill is not submitted.

NOTE: You are not required to pay for services until a Medicare decision has been made.

VERIFICATION OF RECEIPT OF NOTICE

C. This acknowledges that I received this notice of noncoverage of services under Medicare on (date of receipt).

____

(Signature of Beneficiary or Person acting on Beneficiary's behalf)

D. This is to confirm that you were advised of the noncoverage of the services under Medicare by telephone on (date of telephone contact).

____

(Name of Beneficiary or Representative contacted)

____

(Signature of Administrative Officer)

KEEP A COPY OF THIS FOR YOUR RECORDS

{Insert provider contact information here}
Notice of Medicare Non-Coverage

Patient name: **Patient number:**

The Effective Date Coverage of Your Current **{insert type}**
Services Will End: **{insert effective date}**

- Your Medicare provider and/or health plan have determined that Medicare probably will not pay for your current {insert type} services after the effective date indicated above.
- You may have to pay for any services you receive after the above date.

Your Right to Appeal This Decision

- You have the right to an immediate, independent medical review (appeal) of the decision to end Medicare coverage of these services. Your services will continue during the appeal.
- If you choose to appeal, the independent reviewer will ask for your opinion. The reviewer also will look at your medical records and/or other relevant information. You do not have to prepare anything in writing, but you have the right to do so if you wish.
- If you choose to appeal, you and the independent reviewer will each receive a copy of the detailed explanation about why your coverage for services should not continue. You will receive this detailed notice only after you request an appeal.
- If you choose to appeal, and the independent reviewer agrees services should no longer be covered after the effective date indicated above;
  - Neither Medicare nor your plan will pay for these services after that date.
- If you stop services no later than the effective date indicated above, you will avoid financial liability.

How to Ask For an Immediate Appeal

- You must make your request to your Quality Improvement Organization (also known as a QIO). A QIO is the independent reviewer authorized by Medicare to review the decision to end these services.
- Your request for an immediate appeal should be made as soon as possible, but no later than noon of the day before the effective date indicated above.
- The QIO will notify you of its decision as soon as possible, generally no later than two days after the effective date of this notice if you are in Original Medicare. If you are in a Medicare health plan, the QIO generally will notify you of its decision by the effective date of this notice.
- Call your QIO at: {insert QIO name and toll-free number of QIO} to appeal, or if you have questions.

See page 2 of this notice for more information.

Form CMS 10123-NOMNC (Approved 12/31/2011) OMB approval 0938-0953

If You Miss The Deadline to Request An Immediate Appeal, You May Have Other Appeal Rights:

- If you have Original Medicare: Call the QIO listed on page 1.
- If you belong to a Medicare health plan: Call your plan at the number given below.

Plan contact information ______________________________

____

Additional Information (Optional):

Please sign below to indicate you received and understood this notice.

I have been notified that coverage of my services will end on the effective date indicated on this notice and that I may appeal this decision by contacting my QIO.

______________________________ ______________

Signature of Patient or Representative Date

Form CMS 10123-NOMNC (Approved 12/31/2011) OMB approval 0938-0953

CHAPTER 4

HOME HEALTH COVERAGE

§ 4.01 INTRODUCTION

The Medicare home health benefit is a crucial source of health care financing for Medicare beneficiaries who reside in their homes. When properly implemented, the Medicare home health benefit can provide coverage for necessary services, even if the patient has a chronic condition and even if the services are expected to extend over a long period of time. Increasingly, these services are the central component of long-term care, and are not one service, but a constellation of skilled and nonskilled services that allows a Medicare beneficiary to remain at home.

When Medicare coverage is unfairly denied, beneficiaries may be unable to afford the home health care they need. Unable to live safely in the community, they may be forced to enter a nursing home. Vigorous advocacy can protect these patients' rights to coverage and care.[1] Starting in 1998, with the implementation of the Balanced Budget Act of 1997 (BBA '97),[2] Medicare beneficiaries began experiencing increased uncertainty about the nature and extent of covered services under the Medicare home health benefit, due in large part to significant changes in the Medicare reimbursement system for home care providers that were introduced.

Even though the Medicare home health care benefit was thrown into turmoil with the passage of the BBA '97, leading to inappropriate terminations, denials, and reductions of necessary home health services,[3] other aspects of the home health benefit, such as services covered and approaches to advocacy, remain unchanged. Thoughtful, informed advocacy continues to help beneficiaries obtain the Medicare coverage to which they are entitled.

§ 4.02 COST & COVERAGE

[A] Cost

Under the law, an individual can receive the home health care benefit for as long as they continue to qualify for home health care. There is no limit on the number of visits for which Medicare will pay. With the exception of durable medical equipment (DME) and osteoporosis drugs, there is no coinsurance, copayment, or deductible for home health services and supplies.[4] The coinsurance for DME osteoporosis drugs furnished as a home health service is 20 percent of

[1] *See* the Center for Medicare Advocacy's online self-help packets and other materials for successful home health care advocacy at http://www.medicareadvocacy.org/medicare-info/home-health-care/ (site visited July 26, 2016).

[2] *See* The Balanced Budget Act of 1997 (BBA '97), Pub. L. No. 105-33 (Aug. 5, 1997), Title IV, Subtitle G, §§ 4601–4616 (Medicare Home Health Benefit), which significantly limited home health care access. *See* **§ 4.05** of this Handbook.

[3] *See* BBA '97, Title IV, Subtitle G, §§ 4601–4616. *See* **§ 4.05** of this Handbook.

[4] MBPM, Ch. 7, § 60.4,

the cost for the service. It is important to note that the Part B outpatient therapy cap that limits the amount Medicare will pay for medically necessary outpatient therapy services does not apply to therapy covered under the Part A home health benefit.

With a few exceptions, Medicare Advantage (MA) plans must provide enrollees in that plan with all Part A and Part B traditional Medicare services.[5] The MA plan can impose different cost-sharing for care provided.[6] While there is no copayment required for home health services provided under the traditional Medicare benefit, MA plans may impose cost-sharing and other restrictions such as the requirement that prior approval be obtained before the receipt of home health services.[7] It is important to review the Medicare Advantage's Evidence of Coverage to determine what the plan covers and how much an individual will be required to pay.

[B] Coverage Criteria

Medicare provides for coverage of home health services under Parts A and B when the services are medically "reasonable and necessary," and when:[8]

1. The individual is confined to his or her home (or "homebound");
2. The individual needs skilled nursing care on an intermittent basis, or physical or speech therapy or, in the case of an individual who has been furnished home health services based on such a need but no longer requires skilled nursing care or therapy, the individual continues to need occupational therapy;
3. A plan for furnishing the services has been established and is periodically reviewed by a physician; and
4. Such services are furnished by, or under arrangement with, a Medicare-certified home health agency (HHA).[9]

---

[5] 42 C.F.R. § 422.100(a).

[6] 42 C.F.R. § 422.100(f)(6).

[7] For an example regarding what MA plans can charge for home health services see Table 16, p. 171 of the 2017 Final Call Letter, https://www.cms.gov/Medicare/Health-Plans/MedicareAdvtgSpecRateStats/Downloads/Announcement2017.pdf, which states that MA plans that use voluntary maximum out-of-pocket amounts can charge 20 percent coinsurance or $35 for home health services. See **§ 7.01[A]** of this Handbook for a discussion regarding maximum out-of-pocket limits for those enrolled in an MA plan.

[8] 42 U.S.C. § 1395f(a)(2)(C); 42 C.F.R. §§ 409.42 *et seq.*

[9] 42 U.S.C. § 1395x(m).

[C] How Medicare Pays

The Medicare home health benefit is available under Parts A and B. The substantive coverage criteria are identical under both parts. However, pursuant to BBA '97, Part A coverage is sometimes limited to 100 visits and sometimes hinges on a prior hospital or skilled nursing facility (SNF) stay.[10] The BBA '97 added a prior-institutionalization requirement, established a "home health spell of illness" benefit period, and created a 100-visit coverage limitation per spell of illness for most beneficiaries seeking coverage under Part A.[11] These provisions were effective for services on or after January 1, 1998. How Medicare finances home health services depends on whether a beneficiary is enrolled in Part A and Part B or is enrolled in only Part A or only Part B.

[1] Beneficiaries Enrolled in Part A and Part B

For beneficiaries who are enrolled in Part A and Part B, Part A finances post-institutional home health services furnished during a home health spell of illness[12] for up to 100 visits during a spell of illness if the following criteria are met:

- Beneficiary is enrolled in Part A and Part B and meets home health coverage criteria;
- Beneficiary had a 3-day consecutive stay in a hospital; and
- Home health services were initiated and the first covered home health visit was rendered within 14 days of discharge from the 3-day consecutive stay in the hospital or within 14 days of discharge from a skilled nursing facility in which the individual was provided post-hospital extended care services.[13] If the first home health visit is not initiated within 14 days of discharge, then home health services are financed under Part B.

---

[10] 42 U.S.C. § 1395x. *See* **§ 4.05** of this Handbook.

[11] 42 U.S.C. § 1395d.

[12] The home health spell of illness concept is similar to that which exists for hospital and SNF care. The *home health spell of illness* is defined as a period of consecutive days beginning with the first day (not included in a previous home health spell of illness) on which the individual is furnished post-institutional home health services; and which occurs in a month for which the individual is entitled to benefits under Part A, and ending with the close of the first period of 60 consecutive days thereafter on each of which the individual is neither an inpatient of a hospital or rural primary care hospital, nor an inpatient of a skilled nursing facility, nor provided home health services.

[13] 42 U.S.C. § 1395x(tt)(1).

After an individual exhausts 100 visits of Part A post-institutional home health services, Part B will finance the balance of the home health spell of illness. A beneficiary who is enrolled in Part A and Part B and is eligible for the Medicare home health benefit but does not meet the 3-day consecutive stay requirement or the 14-day initiation of care requirements, will have their home health services financed under Part B. To the extent that all coverage requirements are met, payment may be made on behalf of eligible beneficiaries under Part B for an unlimited number of covered home health visits.[14]

[2] Beneficiaries Enrolled in Part A Only or Part B Only

If a beneficiary is enrolled only in Part A and meets the Medicare home health coverage criteria then all of the home health services will be paid for under Part A and the 100 day visit limit will not apply. If a beneficiary is enrolled only in Part B and meets the Medicare home health coverage criteria then all of the home health services will be paid for under Part B. There is no 100-visit limit under Part B.[15]

[D] Coverable Home Health Services Described

If the triggering conditions described above in **§ 4.02[B]** of this Handbook are satisfied, the beneficiary qualifies for Medicare coverage of home health services. Home health services include:[16]

1. Part-time or intermittent nursing care provided by or under the supervision of a registered professional nurse;
2. Physical, occupational, or speech therapy;
3. Medical social services under the direction of a physician;

---

[14] MBPM, Ch. 7, § 70.1.

[15] 42 U.S.C. § 1395d.

[16] 42 U.S.C. § 1395x(m)(1)–(4). On November 3, 2015, CMS published in the *Federal Register*, 80 Fed. Reg. 68,126, proposed revisions to requirements for discharge planning for hospitals, CAHs, and HHAs. *See* http://www.gpo.gov/fdsys/pkg/FR-2015-11-03/pdf/2015-27840.pdf (site visited June 7, 2016). The proposed rule is designed to reduce avoidable hospital readmissions and improve patient care with a focus on improvements for psychiatric and behavioral health patients, including those with substance abuse disorders. The proposed rule calls for coordination, consultation, and using information from community-based service providers as recognized by the Improving Medicare Post-Acute Care Transformation Act of 2014 (Impact Act) (Pub. L. No. 113-185 (Oct. 6, 2014)). The proposed rule fits within the framework of existing discharge planning regulations that are found at 42 C.F.R. § 482.43, applicable to all inpatients. *See also* Social Security Act § 1861(e), 42 U.S.C. § 1395x(ee).

4. Part-time or intermittent services of a home health aide; and

5. Medical supplies.

Note that skilled nursing and physical and speech therapy services are "qualifying skilled services" for the purpose of establishing initial eligibility for the Medicare home health benefit. A patient must initially require one of these skilled services in order to receive other covered home health services.[17] Home health aide, medical social worker, and occupational therapy services are "dependent services," along with durable medical equipment and medical supplies.[18]

In practice, the requirements that a patient be confined to the home (the "homebound" rule) and need a qualifying skilled service are of fundamental importance. Generally, if these preconditions are met, the beneficiary will qualify for the home health benefit and, thus, any dependent services and items they may need.

Medicare covers home health aide services if the patient is also in need of skilled nursing care or physical therapy or speech-language pathology or has a continuing need for occupational therapy. If the patient qualifies for Medicare coverage of home health care on another basis, such as the need for skilled nursing or skilled physical or speech therapy, then the patient will also get coverage for occupational therapy.

There are some important notable gaps in what the home health benefit will cover. A frequently asked question is whether home infusion therapy is a covered service under the home health benefit. Unfortunately, the home health benefit under traditional Medicare does not currently cover home infusion therapy. Obtaining coverage for both the medication and the professional services necessary for the infusion requires billing both Medicare Parts D and B. However, Medicare Part B only pays for the administration of certain types of drugs that cannot be self-administered, and only when provided in an outpatient setting, such as a hospital, infusion center, or doctor's office. Medicare Part D will cover the medications covered under a beneficiary's prescription drug plan, but not the skilled services and necessary supplies required to actually administer the medication. Therefore, because of the outpatient requirement under Part B, most beneficiaries in need of home infusion therapy are forced to travel to an outpatient setting to receive Part B coverage for the skilled services and equipment.[19] Importantly, most private insurance and Medicare Advantage plans do cover both the medication and professional services in the home for some time.

[17] 42 C.F.R. § 409.44.

[18] 42 C.F.R. § 409.45.

[19] CMS takes the position that it does not have authority to cover home infusions under Part D. The National Home Infusion Association (NHIA) has spearheaded efforts to change the law and is actively supporting The Medicare Home Infusion Site of Care Act of 2015 (S.275/HR 605). This legislation would allow home infusions to be covered under traditional Medicare.

§ 4.03 REQUIREMENTS FOR COVERAGE

[A] The Homebound Rule

The requirement that a patient is homebound (confined to home) is described in detail in the Medicare statute as follows:

> an individual shall be considered to be "confined to his home" if the individual has a condition, due to an illness or injury, that restricts the ability of the individual to leave his or her home except with the assistance of another individual or the aid of a supportive device (such as crutches, a cane, a wheelchair, or a walker), or if the individual has a condition such that leaving his or her home is medically contraindicated. While an individual does not have to be bedridden to be considered "confined to his home," the condition of the individual should be such that there exists a normal inability to leave home, that leaving home requires a considerable and taxing effort by the individual. Any absence of an individual from the home attributable to the need to receive healthcare treatment, including regular absences for the purpose of participating in therapeutic, psychosocial, or medical treatment in an adult day-care program that is licensed or certified by a State, or accredited, to furnish adult day-care services in the State shall not disqualify an individual from being considered to be "confined to his home." Any other absence of an individual from the home shall not so disqualify an individual if the absence is of infrequent or of relatively short duration. For purposes of the preceding sentence, any absence for the purpose of attending a religious service shall be deemed to be an absence of infrequent or short duration.[20]

As a careful reading will disclose, the statutory definition of homebound status is ambiguous. While the statute states, for example, that a patient is considered homebound if unable to leave home "except with the assistance of another individual or the aid of a supportive device," it also states that the "condition of the individual should be such that there exists a normal inability to leave home." The question often arises whether a patient in a wheelchair is homebound if he or she leaves home in a wheelchair on a regular basis.[21] Advocates often find themselves quoting one section of the statute to support such a patient's homebound

---

[20] *See* 42 U.S.C. §§ 1395f(a)(2)(C) (Part A), 1395n(a)(2)(A)(i) (Part B), and 1395n(a)(F) (further discussion of homebound criteria), as amended by the Medicare, Medicaid, and SCHIP Benefits Improvement and Protection Act of 2000 (BIPA), Pub. L. No. 106-554 (Dec. 21, 2000).

[21] *See* Center for Medicare Advocacy, "Home Health" page at http://www.medicareadvocacy.org/medicare-info/home-health-care/ *and* "Improvement Standard and *Jimmo* News," *available at* http://www.medicareadvocacy.org/medicare-info/improvement-standard/ (sites visited June 7, 2016); CMS Manual System, Trans. 179 (Jan. 14, 2014), *available at* http://www.cms.gov/Regulations-and-Guidance/Guidance/Transmittals/Downloads/R179BP.pdf (sites visited June 7, 2016). *See also* Morris v. N. Haw. Community Hosp., 37 F. Supp. 2d 1181 (D. Haw. 1999) (denying home health to a quadriplegic who could not leave his home without considerable assistance and effort

status, while Medicare decision makers attempt to justify denials with different language.

Effective November 19, 2013, CMS changed its standards for determining whether an individual meets the definition of "homebound." The new, more restrictive, policy states:[22]

> For purposes of the statute, an individual shall be considered "confined to the home" (homebound) if the following two criteria are met:
>
> 1. Criteria-One:
>
> The patient must either:
>
> - Because of illness or injury, need the aid of supportive devices such as crutches, canes, wheelchairs, and walkers; the use of special transportation; or the assistance of another person in order to leave their place of residence
>
> OR
>
> - Have a condition such that leaving his or her home is medically contraindicated.
>
> If the patient meets one of the criteria in Criteria-One, then the patient must ALSO meet two additional requirements defined in Criteria-Two below.
>
> 2. Criteria-Two:
>
> - There must exist a normal inability to leave home;
>
> AND
>
> - Leaving home must require a considerable and taxing effort.

In spite of the agency's restrictive interpretation of the law, the intent of the Medicare statute is to provide home health care to beneficiaries who lack an ordinary ability to leave home. Beneficiaries who need the assistance of another person, an assistive device, or special transportation to leave home, or for whom leaving home is medically contraindicated, are examples of people who lack an

---

would cause irreparable harm and violate the public interest in providing benefits to those who qualify for them); Dennis v. Shalala, 1994 WL 708166 (D. Vt. 1994) (infrequent trips to an adult day care program and to local supermarket held within the definition of homebound); Burgess v. Shalala, 1993 WL 327764 (D. Vt. 1993) (must consider both physical and mental effort of leaving home in determining homebound status); Labossiere v. Secretary of HHS, 1991 WL 531922 (D. Vt. 1991) (must show considerable and taxing effort in leaving the home, also must have strong evidentiary support of the nature of the assistance needed, including assistive devices); Pope v. Secretary of HHS, 1991 WL 236173 (D. Vt. 1991) (merely using a walker or wheelchair is not enough to trigger homebound status).

[22] SNFABN, CMS Pub. 100-02, Ch. 7, § 30.1.1, *available at* http://www.cms.gov/Regulations-and-Guidance/Guidance/Manuals/downloads/bp102c07.pdf (site visited July 28, 2016).

ordinary ability to leave home and thus need health services to come to them. However, they are not the *only* beneficiaries who are homebound for purposes of Medicare coverage of home health care. For example, an individual with chronic obstructive pulmonary disease may not require an assistive device, the assistance of another person, or specialized transportation in order to leave home. Nonetheless, he or she may still have an ordinary inability to leave home for multiple reasons including shortness of breath, dizziness upon exertion, or inability to climb stairs.

The Medicare Benefit Policy Manual provides examples of homebound patients that may be useful to advocates attempting to establish homebound status, including:[23]

- A beneficiary paralyzed from a stroke who is confined to a wheelchair or who requires the aid of crutches in order to walk;
- A beneficiary who is blind or senile and requires the assistance of another person in leaving his or her place of residence;
- A beneficiary who has lost the use of his or her upper extremities and, therefore, is unable to open doors, use handrails on stairways, etc., and therefore requires the assistance of another individual in leaving his or her place of residence;
- A patient with a psychiatric problem if the patient's illness is manifested in part by a refusal to leave his or her home environment or is of such a nature that it would not be considered safe for the patient to leave the home unattended, even if the patient has no physical limitations; and
- A patient in the late stages of ALS or a neurodegenerative disability.

In determining whether someone is homebound the Medicare Benefit Policy Manual (MBPM) states that it is necessary to look at the individual's overall condition over a period of time rather than looking at isolated period.[24] It is also important to note that for purposes of determining someone's homebound status an individual may have more than one "home," and an individual who resides in more than one place of residence will not be disqualified from meeting the homebound criteria. The MBPM states "[f]or example, a person may reside in a principal home and also a second vacation home, mobile home, or the home of a caretaker relative. The fact that the patient resides in more than one home and, as a result, must transit from one to the other, is not in itself, an indication that the patient is not homebound."[25]

---

[23] MBPM, Ch. 7, § 30.1.1, *available at* http://www.cms.gov/Regulations-and-Guidance/Guidance/Manuals/downloads/bp102c07.pdf (site visited July 28, 2016).

[24] MBPM, Ch. 7, § 30.1.1.

[25] MBPM, Ch. 7, § 30.1.1.

[B] Skilled Nursing Care on an Intermittent Basis, or Physical or Speech Therapy or Occupational Therapy

[1] Generally

The second principal criterion to be met to qualify for the Medicare home health benefit is that the patient needs skilled nursing care on an intermittent basis, or physical or speech therapy, or have continuing need for occupational therapy services.[26]

For nursing visits to be qualifying services, they must be skilled and furnished on an intermittent basis. "Intermittent" means skilled nursing care that is either provided or needed on fewer than seven days each week or less than eight hours each day for periods of 21 days or less (with extensions in exceptional circumstances when the need for additional care is finite and predictable).[27]

There is no intermittency requirement for therapy services. Thus, if a patient meets the requirement for skilled physical or speech therapy, the criterion is met. It is important to note that occupational therapy services cannot establish *initial* eligibility for Medicare home health coverage. Occupational therapy services may be covered when initial eligibility is established on another basis, such as the need for skilled nursing or skilled physical or speech therapy. After that, however, a continued need for occupational therapy can qualify a Medicare patient for extended home health eligibility when occupational therapy is the *only* continuing skilled service needed by a patient.[28]

[2] Defining Skilled Care

The Medicare home health regulations[29] define coverable skilled nursing services as services that must, under state law, be performed by a registered nurse or a licensed practical (vocational) nurse, be provided on a part-time or intermittent basis, be reasonable and necessary for the treatment of the illness or injury, and meet the criteria for SNFs. CMS has adopted, for purposes of defining skilled

---

[26] 42 U.S.C. § 1395f(a)(2)(C); Medicare General Information, Eligibility and Entitlement (MGIEE) Manual, CMS Pub. 100-01, Ch. 4, § 30.3; MBPM, Ch. 7, § 30.4, *available at* http://www.cms.gov/Regulations-and-Guidance/Guidance/Manuals/downloads/bp102c07.pdf (site visited July 28, 2016). Paper-Based Manuals and Internet-Only Manuals (IOMs) may be viewed at http://www.cms.hhs.gov/manuals/ (site visited June 7, 2016).

[27] 42 U.S.C. §§ 1814(a)(2)(C) and 1835(a)(2)(A).

[28] 42 C.F.R. § 409.42(c)(4) ("Subsequent to an initial covered occupational therapy service, continuing occupational therapy services which meet the requirements of § 409.44(c) are considered to be qualifying services"). *See also* MBPM, Ch. 7, § 40.24, *available at* http://www.cms.gov/Regulations-and-Guidance/Guidance/Manuals/downloads/bp102c07.pdf (site visited July 28, 2016).

[29] 42 C.F.R. § 409.44(b)(1). *See also* MBPM, Ch. 7, § 40.1 (skilled nursing care), *available at* http://www.cms.gov/Regulations-and-Guidance/Guidance/Manuals/downloads/bp102c07.pdf (site visited July 28, 2016).

nursing in the home health care context, the skilled nursing examples and definitions contained in 42 C.F.R. § 409.33, applicable to Medicare certified skilled nursing facilities.[30] These regulations contain critical examples of skilled nursing services and are relied upon extensively by home health care providers and beneficiaries. The regulations provide that the service must be so inherently complex that it can be safely and effectively performed only by, or under the supervision of, professional or technical personnel.[31]

The skilled services listed in the SNF regulations include overall management and evaluation of the patient's care plan, observation and assessment of the patient's changing condition, and patient education services, as well as specific skilled treatments including, but not limited to, intravenous or intramuscular injections, tube feedings, insertion and sterile irrigation and replacement of a suprapubic catheter, wound care involving prescription medications and aseptic techniques, and suctioning a tracheotomy.[32]

The home health regulations define coverable skilled physical and occupational therapy and speech-language pathology services as services relating directly and specifically to a treatment regimen (established by the physician, after any needed consultation with the qualified therapist) that is designed to treat the beneficiary's illness or injury. The services must be reasonable and necessary and must be considered, under accepted standards of professional clinical practice, to be a specific, safe, and effective treatment for the beneficiary's condition.[33]

[3] CMS Medicare Benefit Policy Manual, Home Health Services, Chapter 7

[a] Skilled Home Care

The MBPM defines skilled home health care in a way that parallels the SNF regulations, and includes several clinical examples to illustrate when care would or would not be covered. Some principles and guidelines from the manual follow:

1. A service that, by its nature, requires the skill of a licensed nurse to be provided safely and effectively continues to be a skilled service even if it is taught to the patient, the patient's family, or other caregivers. For instance, wound care may continue to be covered skilled nursing care, notwithstanding that the patient's family provides it part of the time.[34]

[30] 42 C.F.R. § 409.44(b).

[31] 42 C.F.R. § 409.32(a) (SNF regulations). *See also* 42 C.F.R. § 409.44(b)(1)(i).

[32] 42 C.F.R. § 409.33(a) & (b).

[33] 42 C.F.R. § 409.44(c).

[34] MBPM, Ch. 7, § 40.1.1(Example 5), *available at* http://www.cms.gov/Regulations-and-Guidance/Guidance/Manuals/downloads/bp102c07.pdf (site visited July 28, 2016).

2. A beneficiary's diagnosis should never be the sole factor in deciding that a service the beneficiary needs is either skilled or non-skilled.[35]
3. Skilled care may, depending on the unique condition of the patient, continue to be necessary for patients whose condition is stable. For example, periodic visits to change a catheter as needed, treat the symptoms of catheter malfunction, and teach proper catheter care would be covered as long as they are reasonable and necessary, even if the patient is stable and the care is expected to be needed for a long and indefinite period.[36]
4. Observation and assessment of the patient's condition by a nurse are reasonable and necessary skilled services where there is a reasonable potential for change in a patient's condition that requires skilled nursing personnel to identify and evaluate the patient's need for possible modification of treatment or initiation of additional medical procedures until the patient's clinical condition and/or treatment regimen has stabilized.[37]
5. Skilled management and evaluation of the patient's care plan are also reasonable and necessary nursing services where underlying conditions or complications require that only a registered nurse can ensure that essential non-skilled care is achieving its purpose. To be covered, the complexity of the necessary unskilled services that are a necessary part of the medical treatment must require the involvement of skilled nursing personnel to promote the patient's recovery and medical safety in view of the patient's overall condition.[38]

---

[35] MBPM, Ch. 7, § 40.1.1, *available at* http://www.cms.gov/Regulations-and-Guidance/Guidance/Manuals/downloads/bp102c07.pdf (site visited July 28, 2016).

[36] MBPM, Ch. 7, § 40.1.1(Example 8), *available at* http://www.cms.gov/Regulations-and-Guidance/Guidance/Manuals/downloads/bp102c07.pdf (site visited July 28, 2016).

[37] MBPM, Ch. 7, § 40.1.2.1, *available at* http://www.cms.gov/Regulations-and-Guidance/Guidance/Manuals/downloads/bp102c07.pdf (site visited July 28, 2016).

[38] MBPM, Ch. 7, § 40.1.2.2, *available at* http://www.cms.gov/Regulations-and-Guidance/Guidance/Manuals/downloads/bp102c07.pdf (site visited July 28, 2016). In 2009, CMS tightened the criteria for determining whether the evaluation and management of non-skilled services by a skilled nurse are considered to be a coverable skilled service. *See* 74 Fed. Reg. 58,133 (Nov. 10, 2009). The language of the final rule is included in 42 C.F.R. § 409.42(c)(1)(i), effective January 1, 2010. The final rule allows that "[i]n some cases, the condition of the patient may cause a service that would originally be considered unskilled to be considered a skilled nursing service." However, "[w]here nursing visits are not needed to observe and assess the effects of the non-skilled services being provided to treat the illness or injury," and "[w]here a service can be safely and effectively performed (or self-administered by the beneficiary) by non-licensed staff without the direct supervision of a nurse, the service cannot be regarded as a skilled service[.]"

6. Teaching or training activities constitute coverable skilled nursing services when reasonable and necessary to teach the family or caregivers how to manage the treatment regimen of the patient's illness, injury, or functional loss. The test of whether a nursing service is skilled relates to the skill required to teach and not to the nature of what is being taught. Therefore, where skilled nursing services are necessary to teach an unskilled service, the teaching may be covered. Where it becomes apparent after a reasonable period of time that the patient, family, or caregiver will not or is not able to be trained, then further teaching and training would cease to be reasonable and necessary.[39]

[b] Intermittent Skilled Nursing Care

Although a need for skilled nursing care may be identified, the question remains whether the patient needs *intermittent* skilled nursing care as required and defined by the statute. Intermittency does not apply to therapy services. For many years, Medicare claims were routinely denied on the basis that the patient needed *more* than intermittent skilled nursing care. The meaning of the term "intermittent" was nowhere adequately described.

On August 1, 1988, the United States District Court for the District of Columbia issued a decision clarifying this point, establishing that "intermittent" means "less than daily."[40] A patient will need intermittent skilled care if he or she needs skilled care visits on six or fewer days per week. If the patient requires daily skilled care on a seven-day-per-week basis, however, the patient will be found to have violated the intermittent rule and will be considered ineligible for continued home health coverage unless the certifying physician attests on the plan of care that the patient will require daily skilled care for only a relatively short time (three weeks, for example) or that the need for daily skilled care will end at a certain predictable time in the future.[41]

---

[39] MBPM, Ch. 7, § 40.1.2.3, *available at* http://www.cms.gov/Regulations-and-Guidance/Guidance/Manuals/downloads/bp102c07.pdf (site visited July 28, 2016). In 2009, CMS elaborated on the extent to which patient education services were coverable. *See* 74 Fed. Reg. 58,133 (Nov. 10, 2009). The language of the final rule is included in 42 C.F.R. § 409.42(c)(1)(ii), effective January 1, 2010. The final rule provides that "[s]killed education services are no longer needed if it becomes apparent, after a reasonable period of time, that the patient, family, or caregiver could not or would not be trained."

[40] Duggan v. Bowen, 691 F. Supp. 1487, 1511 (D.D.C. 1988). *See also* Rizzi v. Shalala, 1994 WL 686630 (D. Conn. 1994) (mooting the plaintiff's claim that the Secretary arbitrarily presumes that patients with a "chronic" or "stable" condition are ineligible for home health coverage. The court recognized that after *Duggan*, the HHA Manual was revised to clarify the standards that determine whether the skilled care requirement has been met).

[41] MBPM, Ch. 7, § 50.7, *available at* http://www.cms.gov/Regulations-and-Guidance/Guidance/Manuals/downloads/bp102c07.pdf (site visited July 28, 2016).

Congress, in BBA '97, amended the Medicare statute for purposes of Section 1861(m) of the Social Security Act to define "part-time or intermittent services" as:

> Skilled nursing and home health aide services furnished any number of days per week as long as they are furnished (combined) less than 8 hours each day and 28 or fewer hours each week (or subject to review on a case-by-case basis as to the need for care, less than 8 hours each day and 35 or fewer hours per week).[42]

In this amendment, Congress went on to define "intermittent" for purposes of Sections 1814(a)(2)(C)[43] and 1835(a)(2)(A)[44] of the Social Security Act as:

> skilled nursing care that is either provided or needed on fewer than 7 days each week, or less than 8 hours of each day for periods of 21 days or less (with extensions in exceptional circumstances when the need for additional care is finite and predictable).[45]

Together, these BBA '97 amendments codified CMS manual standards and other internal guidelines, which have been used by providers and Medicare Administrative Contractors (MACs)[46] for years to define the amount and frequency of home health nursing and aide services that are covered by Medicare.

[4] Skilled Therapy

There is no intermittency requirement for physical or speech therapy or for continuing occupational therapy. A patient's need for physical or speech therapy or for continuing occupational therapy services will, assuming the patient is homebound, trigger home health coverage even where the patient does not require skilled nursing services. In order to qualify, therapy must be skilled. The MBPM provides that the service of a physical, speech, or occupational therapist is a skilled therapy service if the inherent complexity of the service is such that it can be performed safely and/or effectively only by or under the supervision of a skilled therapist.[47]

---

[42] 42 U.S.C. § 1395x(m).

[43] *See* 42 U.S.C. § 1395f(a)(2)(C) (conditions and limitations for payment).

[44] *See* 42 U.S.C. § 1395n(a)(2)(A)(i) (payment of claims of providers of service).

[45] 42 U.S.C. § 1395x(m). CMS policy carves out a specific exception to the intermittent requirement for insulin-dependent diabetics who cannot self-administer insulin injections and for whom there is no willing caregiver to inject the insulin. In this circumstance, there is no need to demonstrate a predictable and finite end to daily nursing visits to administer insulin. *See* MBPM, Ch. 7, §§ 40.1.2.4(A.2) and 40.1.3, *available at* http://www.cms.gov/Regulations-and-Guidance/Guidance/Manuals/downloads/bp102c07.pdf (site visited July 28, 2016).

[46] "Medicare Administrative Contractors" (MACs) are private health care insurers that have been awarded a geographic jurisdiction by CMS to process claims for Medicare Fee-For-Service beneficiaries.

[47] MBPM, Ch. 7, § 40.2.1, *available at* http://www.cms.gov/Regulations-and-Guidance/Guidance/Manuals/downloads/bp102c07.pdf (site visited July 28, 2016).

To be covered, assuming all other eligibility and coverage criteria have been met, the skilled services must also be reasonable and necessary to the treatment of the patient's illness or injury or to the restoration or maintenance of function affected by the patient's illness or injury, within the context of the patient's unique medical condition. To be considered reasonable and necessary, the therapy must be consistent with the nature and severity of the illness or injury and the beneficiary's particular needs. The amount, frequency, and duration of the services must be reasonable, and the services must be considered, under accepted standards of medical practice, to be specific and effective treatment for the patient's condition.[48]

The issue of "improvement" and access to skilled therapy and nursing services is a significant problem and is the subject of litigation in *Jimmo v Sebelius*.[49] CMS has taken the position that there has never been an "improvement standard" but, in forging a settlement with plaintiffs, agreed to review and change language in its several manuals to clarify that improvement is not the standard for determining whether on-going skilled therapy and nursing services are necessary. The updated manuals and other CMS guidance became available in January 2014.[50]

In spite of *Jimmo*, MACs continue to deny coverage based on the lack of expectation of a significant improvement in the patient's condition within a reasonable and predictable period of time. Beneficiaries and advocates should bear in mind that "restoration potential" is not required by law, that a patient's diagnosis or prognosis should never be the sole factor in deciding whether or not a service is skilled, and that a maintenance program *can* be covered if skilled services are necessary to prevent further deterioration or preserve current capabilities. This *includes* visits by the therapist to design, establish, teach, perform, or supervise a maintenance program.[51]

---

[48] MBPM, Ch. 7, § 40.2.1, *available at* http://www.cms.gov/Regulations-and-Guidance/Guidance/Manuals/downloads/bp102c07.pdf (site visited July 28, 2016).

[49] *See* Jimmo v. Sebelius, 2011 WL 5104355 (D. Vt. 2011), *available at* http://www.clearinghouse.net/chDocs/public/PB-VT-0002-0002.pdf *See also* "*Jimmo v. Sebelius* Settlement Agreement Fact Sheet," *available at* http://www.cms.gov/Medicare/Medicare-Fee-for-Service-Payment/SNFPPS/Downloads/Jimmo-FactSheet.pdf (sites visited July 28, 2016).

[50] MBPM, Ch. 7, § 40.2.1. *See also* Center for Medicare Advocacy, "Improvement Standard and *Jimmo* News," *available at* http://www.medicareadvocacy.org/medicare-info/improvement-standard/ (site visited July 28, 2016). Plaintiffs remain concerned that CMS's implementation and education campaigns are inadequate.

[51] 42 C.F.R. § 409.44(c)(2)(iii); MBPManual, Ch. 7, §§ 40.2.1 and 40.2.2.E. Note that the parties in Jimmo v. Sebelius, 5:11-CV-17 (D. Vt. Jan. 18, 2011), entered into a settlement agreement affirming that improvement is an inappropriate standard in determining whether care for chronic conditions should be continued. Problems have arisen with implementation of *Jimmo*, particularly as many HHA providers do not know about the settlement, find the documentation requirements difficult, or continue to receive improper denials from Medicare contractors. *See* **Appendix 1-9** of this Handbook.

Pursuant to the MBPM, the following types of skilled therapy[52] are covered by the Medicare home health benefit:

1. Assessment by a physical therapist to determine a beneficiary's rehabilitation needs and potential, or to develop and implement a physical therapy program;
2. Therapeutic exercises that must be taught by or under the supervision of a qualified physical therapist to ensure the safety of the beneficiary and the effectiveness of the treatment;
3. Gait training furnished a beneficiary whose ability to walk has been impaired by neurological, muscular, or skeletal abnormality;
4. Range of motion tests, and range of motion exercises, if they are part of an active treatment for a specific disease, illness, or injury that has resulted in a loss or restriction of mobility;
5. Maintenance therapy required to maintain the patient's current function or to prevent or slow further deterioration;
6. Ultrasound, shortwave, and microwave diathermy treatments;
7. Hot packs, infra-red treatments, paraffin, and whirlpool baths may, depending on the special medical circumstances or complications of the particular patient, require the skills, knowledge, and judgment of a qualified physical therapist; and
8. Wound care that falls within the auspices of the physical therapist's State Practice Act.

[C] Part-Time or Intermittent Services

Once a patient has satisfied the definition of being homebound and established a need for skilled nursing care on an intermittent basis, or physical or speech therapy or occupational therapy, then home health coverage under Medicare is available for the therapy *and* for part-time or intermittent services of a home health aide or nurse. As discussed above, intermittent services are services delivered less than daily, that is, fewer than seven days per week. Part-time services are services delivered fewer than eight hours per day.[53]

Reading the part-time and intermittent standards together, a patient *should* be able to obtain coverage for home health aide or nursing service seven days a week but fewer than eight hours each day (part-time services), or six or fewer

[52] MBPM, Ch. 7, § 40.2.2, *available at* http://www.cms.gov/Regulations-and-Guidance/Guidance/Manuals/downloads/bp102c07.pdf (site visited July 28, 2016).

[53] *Duggan*, 691 F. Supp. 1487, 1511. SSA § 1861(m)(1),(4), and (7)(B); MBPM, Ch. 7, §§ 40.1.3 and 50.7-50.7.2.

times a week for as many as 24 hours per day (intermittent services). In practice, however, do not assume the availability of this heavy degree of coverage on an ongoing basis. Current law and Medicare guidelines provide that coverage may be available for up to 28 hours of aide and nurse services combined each week without the necessity of special documentation. Coverage is available for aide and nurse services totaling as many as 35 hours per week if additional medical justification is shown.[54]

§ 4.04 CHRONIC, STABLE, AND MAINTENANCE-LEVEL PATIENTS

Advocates should be aware that although Medicare home health coverage *should* be available for extended periods of care, the Medicare reimbursement system works to discourage the actual delivery of long periods of care. Fearing inadequate reimbursement, HHAs may resist serving patients who require long-term care or numerous or extended visits. Excuses used may include that the patient is "chronic" or staff shortages exist. MACs routinely deny home health coverage to patients deemed chronic, stable, or in need of care to "maintain" or "prevent deterioration"[55] of their conditions, or who otherwise are not getting better or worse at a rapid pace.

It is, therefore, particularly important to note that the federal regulation states that "[t]he determination of whether a beneficiary needs skilled nursing care should be based solely upon the beneficiary's unique condition and individual needs, without regard to whether the illness or injury is acute, chronic, terminal or expected to last a long time."[56] The MBPM also makes it clear that:

> A patient's overall medical condition, without regard to whether the illness or injury is acute, chronic, terminal, or expected to extend over a long period of time, should be considered in deciding whether skilled services are needed. A patient's diagnosis should never be the sole factor in deciding that a service the patient needs is either skilled or not skilled. Skilled care may, depending on the unique condition of the patient, continue to be necessary for patients whose condition is stable.[57]

As enunciated by these provisions, individuals with chronic conditions can be entitled to Medicare coverage, even if the care they need will continue for long

---

[54] MBPM, Ch. 7, § 50.7, *available at* http://www.cms.gov/Regulations-and-Guidance/Guidance/Manuals/downloads/bp102c07.pdf (site visited July 28, 2016).

[55] 42 C.F.R. § 409.32.

[56] 42 C.F.R. § 409.44(b)(3)(iii).

[57] MBPM, Ch. 7, § 40.1.1, *available at* http://www.cms.gov/Regulations-and-Guidance/Guidance/Manuals/downloads/bp102c07.pdf (site visited July 28, 2016). In the preamble to the final home health prospective payment regulations, CMS stated, "In order to address the needs of longer stay patients we are not limiting the number of 60-day episode re-certifications permitted in a given fiscal year assuming a patient remains eligible for the Medicare home health benefit." 65 Fed. Reg. 41,128, 41,140 (July 3, 2000). *See* **§ 4.05[D]** of this Handbook.

periods of time. Restoration should not be the decisive factor in determining entitlement to coverage.[58]

Furthermore, the United States District Court for the District of Connecticut ruled in *Fox v. Thompson (sub nom. Fox v. Bowen)*,[59] a federal class action concerning Medicare coverage for skilled nursing facility care, that the Secretary of Health and Human Services (HHS) shall not deny Medicare coverage on the basis of "arbitrary rules of thumb." Instead, as the court ruled in *Fox*, each claimant should receive an individualized assessment of his or her need for care based on the facts and circumstances of the claimant's particular case. A particular patient with multiple sclerosis, for example, may well be homebound, require intermittent skilled nursing and/or therapy, and qualify for Medicare coverage, even though the underlying medical condition will remain.[60]

Unfortunately, HHAs are often convinced that Medicare coverage is unavailable for patients who will not recover and for those in need of maintenance physical therapy. In order to avoid the financial penalties associated with a claim submission that will be denied by the MAC, many agencies deny coverage in these cases themselves and decline to submit a claim unless the patient insists. Since agencies usually rely upon the CMS manual, it is particularly important to note supportive sections of the manual and to instruct the provider that the federal regulations are clear that coverage is available even if the patient is unlikely to improve and even when the care is needed to maintain his or her condition.

In November 2010, CMS revised its regulations to clarify Medicare coverage principles for home health services, including physical therapy, occupational therapy, and speech-language pathology services.[61] Most importantly for people with long-term conditions, the revisions "clarified" that skilled care does include services that are intended to maintain a person's condition and that no "rules of thumb" should be used to deny care, including rules that require restoration potential.[62] The regulations state:

> "Rules of thumb" in the Medicare medical review process are prohibited. . . . Any "rules of thumb" that would declare a claim not covered solely on the

[58] 42 C.F.R. § 409.32, incorporated into the home health regulations at 42 C.F.R. § 409.44(b).

[59] 656 F. Supp. 1236 (D. Conn. 1986).

[60] Smith v. Shalala, 855 F. Supp. 658 (D. Vt. 1994); Bergeron v. Shalala, 855 F. Supp. 665 (D. Vt. 1994). *See also* Prendergast v. Leavitt, No. 08-cv-1148 (D. Conn. Aug. 1, 2008), which held that it is inappropriate for a Managed Care plan to terminate services for a chronically ill patient who is not likely to improve but needs services to maintain or to slow the deterioration of her chronic condition. A similar case was filed in Vermont, Anderson v. Leavitt, No. 09-cv-16 (D. Vt., filed Jan.16, 2009). The Center for Medicare Advocacy continues to pursue the revision of CMS and contractor policies that require improvement. *See* Gill Deford, Margaret Murphy, & Judith Stein, *How the "Improvement Standard" Improperly Denies Coverage to Medicare Patients with Chronic Conditions*, Clearinghouse Review, Vol. 43, No. 9-10, Jan-Feb. 2010.

[61] 75 Fed. Reg. 70,461 (Nov. 17, 2010), amending 42 C.F. R. § 409.44(c) (effective Jan. 1, 2011).

[62] 75 Fed. Reg. 70,395 (Nov. 17, 2010), 42 C.F.R. § 409.44(c)(2)(iii)(C).

> basis of elements, such as lack of restoration potential, . . . or degree of stability, is [sic] unacceptable without individual review of all pertinent facts.[63]

To determine whether a service is skilled, and therefore coverable, the regulations direct decision-makers to review accepted standards of clinical practice and to consider whether a professional is needed for the service to be safe and effective for the particular beneficiary.[64]

One of the most important aspects of the revised home health coverage regulations includes a more detailed explanation of when Medicare covers establishment or performance of therapy in the context of a maintenance program. The regulation states:

> The unique clinical condition of a patient may require the specialized skills of a qualified therapist to perform a safe and effective maintenance program required in connection with the patient's specific illness or injury. Where the clinical condition of the patient is such that the complexity of the therapy services required to maintain function involve the use of complex and sophisticated therapy procedures . . . by the therapist . . . **or** the clinical condition of the patient is such that the complexity of the therapy services required to maintain function must be delivered by the therapist . . . to ensure the patient's safety and to provide an effective maintenance program, then those reasonable and necessary services shall be covered.[65]

In 2011, the Center for Medicare Advocacy, with Vermont Legal Aid and others, filed *Jimmo,* a class action lawsuit, against the Secretary of HHS to assure the broadest possible application of the rule that improvement is not required to receive care for one's chronic condition. Following plaintiffs' successful efforts in defeating defendant's motion to dismiss, the parties entered into a settlement agreement in which the defendant agreed to revise its various manuals to clarify that Medicare coverage determinations turn on the need for skilled care—not on the ability of an individual to improve. The settlement agreement applies to skilled maintenance services provided under the Medicare home health, outpatient therapy, and skilled nursing facility benefits. The settlement applies to both Medicare Part A and B and also applies equally to Medicare Advantage as to the traditional Medicare program. The settlement agreement is not limited to particular conditions or diseases. It applies to patients who require skilled services to maintain their condition or slow deterioration regardless of their underlying illness, disability, or injury.

The manual revisions were published on December 6, 2013. As CMS states in the Transmittal announcing the manual revisions:

---

[63] 75 Fed. Reg. 70,395 (Nov. 17, 2010).

[64] 42 C.F.R. § 409.44(c)(2)(i).

[65] 42 C.F.R. § 409.44(c)(2)(iii)(C) (emphasis added).

> **No "Improvement Standard" is to be applied in determining Medicare coverage for maintenance claims that require skilled care.** Medicare has long recognized that even in situations where no improvement is possible, skilled care may nevertheless be needed for maintenance purposes (i.e., to prevent or slow a decline in condition). The Medicare statute and regulations have never supported the imposition of an "Improvement Standard" rule-of-thumb in determining whether skilled care is required to prevent or slow deterioration in a patient's condition. Thus, such coverage depends not on the beneficiary's restoration potential, but on whether skilled care is required, along with the underlying reasonableness and necessity of the services themselves. The manual revisions now being issued will serve to reflect and articulate this basic principle more clearly.[66] (emphasis in original)

In spite of the agency's clarifications in manual provisions and other guidance, claims for maintenance services continue to be denied by the MACs. Consequently, HHAs remain hesitant to provide services to patients who require maintenance care and to bill those services to Medicare. This continued loss of skilled care based on an improvement requirement is occurring despite CMS's assertion that it has completed the education campaign required by the settlement. That campaign, however, has clearly failed to educate key components of the provider community and Medicare decision-making system. As such, vigorous advocacy on behalf of beneficiaries is still required in this area to ensure access to crucial home care.[67]

On March 1, 2016, the Center for Medicare Advocacy, along with Vermont Legal Aid, filed a Motion for Resolution of Non-Compliance with the *Jimmo v. Sebelius* settlement agreement. The filing comes after three years of urging CMS to fulfill its obligation to end the continued application of the "Improvement Standard" by Medicare providers, contractors, and adjudicators to deny Medicare coverage for skilled maintenance nursing and therapy. On August 17, 2016, the judge

---

[66] CMS Transmittal 179 (Jan. 14, 2014), *available at* http://www.cms.gov/Regulations-and-Guidance/Guidance/Transmittals/Downloads/R179BP.pdf (site visited July 28, 2016). Pursuant to the settlement, CMS also issued "*Jimmo v. Sebelius* Settlement Agreement Fact Sheet," *available at* http://www.cms.gov/Medicare/Medicare-Fee-for-Service-Payment/SNFPPS/Downloads/Jimmo-FactSheet.pdf; an MLN Matters article, "Manual Updates to Clarify Skilled Nursing Facility (SNF), Inpatient Rehabilitation Facility (IRF), Home Health (HH), and Outpatient (OPT) Coverage Pursuant to *Jimmo v. Sebelius*," *available at* http://www.cms.gov/Outreach-and-Education/Medicare-Learning-Network-MLN/MLNMattersArticles/Downloads/MM8458.pdf; and "*Jimmo v. Sebelius* Settlement Agreement Program Manual Clarifications Fact Sheet," *available at* http://www.cms.gov/Medicare/Medicare-Fee-for-Service-Payment/SNFPPS/Downloads/jimmo_fact_sheet2_022014_final.pdf (sites visited July 287, 2016).

[67] *See* Center for Medicare Advocacy, "Self Help Packet for Home Health Care Appeals Including "Improvement Standard" Denials," *available at* http://www.medicareadvocacy.org/self-help-packet-for-expedited-home-health-care-appeals-including-improvement-standard-denials/ (site visited June 7, 2016); and Center for Medicare Advocacy, "*Jimmo v. Sebelius*, the Improvement Standard Case FAQs," *available at* http://www.medicareadvocacy.org/jimmo-v-sebelius-the-improvement-standard-case-faqs/ (site visited June 7, 2016).

granted, in part, the plaintiff's motion for enforcement of the settlement.[68] The judge concluded in part that some of the information provided by the Secretary in the Educational Campaign was "inaccurate, nonresponsive, and failed to reflect the maintenance standard" and ordered CMS to develop corrective action.

§ 4.05 PROSPECTIVE PAYMENT SYSTEM FOR HOME HEALTH SERVICES

BBA '97 added a requirement to the Medicare statute that all costs for Medicare home health services be reimbursed under a prospective payment system (PPS).[69] Final regulations to implement home health PPS were published in the *Federal Register* on July 3, 2000,[70] and CMS began paying HHAs under PPS on October 1, 2000.

[A] What Is PPS?

PPS is a payment system. It does not change eligibility and coverage criteria for Medicare home health benefits. Under PPS, Medicare pays a fixed rate to HHAs for the services they provide a beneficiary during a 60-day episode of care.[71] PPS covers all home health services and non-routine medical supplies including outpatient physical therapy. PPS does not cover the cost of durable medical equipment (DME) or certain osteoporosis drugs, which are reimbursed separately.[72]

[B] Determining the Amount of Payment

HHAs must use the Outcome and Assessment Information Set (OASIS) to perform a comprehensive assessment of each new patient before care is

---

[68] *See* http://www.medicareadvocacy.org/wp-content/uploads/2016/08/Jimmo-2.pdf (site visited Aug. 18, 2016).

[69] *See* 42 U.S.C. § 1395ff.

[70] 65 Fed. Reg. 41,128.

[71] 42 C.F.R. §§ 409.43(f), 424.22(b), 484.205(a). For ongoing updates on home health PPS, see http://www.cms.gov/Medicare/Medicare-Fee-for-Service-Payment/HomeHealthPPS/index.html?redirect=/homehealthpps/ (site visited July 28, 2016).

[72] 42 C.F.R. §§ 409.100(a), 410.150(b)(19), 413.1(h). Most durable medical equipment (DME) is now subject to cost limitations associated with Medicare's competitive bidding program for durable medical equipment, prosthetics, orthotics, and supplies (DMEPOS). *See* CMS, "DMEPOS Competitive Bidding—Home," *available at* http://www.cms.gov/Medicare/Medicare-Fee-for-Service-Payment/DMEPOSCompetitiveBid/index.html?redirect=/dmeposcompetitivebid/ (site visited July 28, 2016). CMS continues to roll out the congressionally mandated DMEPOS competitive bidding program.

provided.[73] The OASIS identifies the patient's medical, nursing, rehabilitation, social, and discharge planning needs. Information from the new assessment helps determine the appropriate payment amount under PPS for each patient. First, CMS determines a national prospective 60-day episode payment rate. The rate is then adjusted by two factors: (1) a wage index appropriate for the area in which the beneficiary receives the services, and (2) a case-mix adjuster consisting of selected data elements from OASIS plus an additional data element measuring therapy services.[74] The PPS rate varies, depending upon the patient's clinical condition, functional status, and service needs.

A patient is reassessed at the end of each 60-day episode of care to ensure proper payment. The reassessment also helps determine the proper payment amount for the next episode of care if more services are needed.

If a patient's care needs change substantially during the 60-day episode of care, or if the patient's care plan is completed earlier than expected,[75] CMS may change the amount of payment. CMS may also make an additional payment if the actual costs of providing services are much greater than anticipated.[76] If the patient requires four or fewer home health visits, CMS makes a low-utilization payment adjustment (LUPA), and the agency is paid on a per visit amount that changes depending on the service provided.[77]

[C] The Claims Process

The claim submission process differs under PPS from the old fee-for-service process. PPS provides for split percentage payments.[78] At the beginning of an episode of care, the HHA submits to the MAC a request for anticipated payment (RAP) for the initial percentage payment. The initial payment is 60 percent of the total PPS amount for new patients and 50 percent for ongoing patients.[79]

---

[73] 64 Fed. Reg. 32,984 (June 18, 1999). OASIS is a group of data elements for CMS to assess each home health care patient and to measure patient outcomes. *See also* 42 C.F.R. § 484.20 (requiring HHAs to electronically report data from the OASIS as a Condition of Participation). Updates on OASIS are available at www.cms.gov/Medicare/Quality-Initiatives-Patient-Assessment-Instruments/HomeHealthQualityInits/index.html?redirect=/homehealthqualityinits/ (site visited July 28, 2016).

[74] 42 C.F.R. §§ 484.210, 484.215, 484.220, and 484.250. The PPS rate is generally more for a beneficiary who needs at least eight hours, or ten visits, of therapy services.

[75] If a beneficiary changes agencies in the middle of a 60-day episode, or if a beneficiary is discharged after reaching his or her goals and then returns to the same agency during the 60-day period, the agency will receive a partial episode payment (PEP) adjustment. The agency will be paid the prorated PPS amount based on the number of days services were provided during the 60-day episode. 42 C.F.R. §§ 484.205(d) (partial episode adjustment) and 484.235 (methodology for calculating partial episode adjustment).

[76] An agency may receive an outlier payment in addition to the PPS amount if the imputed cost of the 60-day episode exceeds a threshold amount. 42 C.F.R. § 484.205(e).

[77] 42 C.F.R. §§ 484.205(c) and 484.230.

[78] 42 C.F.R. § 484.205(b)(1), (2).

[79] 42 C.F.R. § 484.205(b).

The initial request for payment does not constitute a Medicare claim.[80] At the end of the episode the agency submits a request for the residual final payment and is paid the remaining amount.

Under PPS, the RAP may be submitted without a care plan signed by a doctor. The request for payment may be based on a signed doctor's referral prescribing detailed orders or on verbal doctor's orders that are recorded in the plan of care that include a description of the patient's condition and services to be provided, that are attested to by the nurse or therapist responsible for the care, and that are included in a plan of care that is submitted to the doctor.[81] The care plan must be signed and dated by the doctor before the claim for each episode is submitted for the final percentage PPS payment.[82]

[1] Physician Certification

As a condition for payment, a physician must certify a patient's eligibility for the Medicare home health benefit.[83] CMS does not mandate a particular format for the certification, which is commonly included as a section on the plan of care. Specifically, a physician must certify (attest) that the patient is confined to the home and needs or needed intermittent skilled nursing care or physical or speech therapy, or continuing occupational therapy. The physician must also certify (attest) that the patient is under the care of a doctor of medicine, osteopathy, or podiatric medicine and that the services are being furnished under a plan of care that has been established and will be periodically reviewed by that doctor. The physician must recertify the patient for each subsequent 60-day episode of care in the same manner and, additionally, include an estimate of how much longer the skilled services will be required.[84]

Note that in 2009, CMS added a requirement for home health patients who require skilled management and evaluation of their care plan. If a patient's underlying condition or complication requires a registered nurse to ensure that essential non-skilled care is achieving its purpose and necessitates a registered nurse be involved in the development, management, and evaluation of a patient's care plan, the physician must include a brief narrative describing the clinical justification of this need, which is required for both certification and recertification.[85]

---

[80] Although the initial request for payment is not a claim for Medicare purposes, it is a claim for enforcement purposes. 42 C.F.R. § 409.43(c)(2).

[81] 42 C.F.R. § 409.43(c)(1).

[82] 42 C.F.R. § 409.43(c)(3).

[83] 42 C.F.R. § 424.22(a); MBPM, Ch. 7, § 30.5.1, *available at* http://www.cms.gov/Regulations-and-Guidance/Guidance/Manuals/downloads/bp102c07.pdf (site visited July 28, 2016). The certification must be complete prior to when an HHA bills Medicare for reimbursement; however, physicians should complete the certification when the plan of care is established, or as soon as possible thereafter.

[84] 42 C.F.R. § 424.22(b)(2); MBPM, Ch. 7, § 30.5.2, *available at* http://www.cms.gov/Regulations-and-Guidance/Guidance/Manuals/downloads/bp102c07.pdf (site visited July 28, 2016).

[85] 42 C.F.R. §§ 424.22(a), 424.22(b) (Recertification).

[a] Face-to-Face Encounter Requirement

The Affordable Care Act (ACA) added a new element to the certification requirement, mandating that the certifying physician document the occurrence of a face-to-face encounter with the patient seeking home health care.[86] The intent is to reduce fraud, waste, and abuse by assuring that a physician or other health care provider actually meet with patients to ascertain their specific care needs before ordering home health care. Implementation of the requirement began April 1, 2011.

The regulations establish that a face-to-face encounter must occur no more than 90 days prior to or within 30 days after the home health care start of care date.[87] The encounter must be performed by the certifying physician or the physician who cared for the patient in an acute or post-acute care facility. The following non-physician practitioners (NPPs) may also perform the encounter: a nurse practitioner or clinical nurse specialist working in collaboration with the certifying or facility physician and a certified nurse midwife or physician assistant working under the supervision of the certifying or facility physician.[88] Face-to-face patient encounters may occur via telehealth.[89] If the orders for home care are based on a new condition that was not evident during the encounter, then another face-to-face examination would be required within 30 days after the start of care.[90]

A face-to-face patient encounter is required only for initial certifications (i.e., any time that a Start of Care OASIS is completed to initiate home care).[91] Recertification for subsequent 60-day episodes do not require a new face-to-face encounter. However, without a complete initial certification, there cannot be payment for subsequent episodes.

---

[86] Patient Protection and Affordable Care Act (PPACA or ACA), Pub. L. No. 111-148 (Mar. 23, 2010) § 6407; 2 U.S.C. § 1395f(a)(2)(C).

[87] 42 C.F.R. § 424.22(a)(1)(v); MBPM, Ch. 7, § 30.5.1.1(2), *available at* http://www.cms.gov/Regulations-and-Guidance/Guidance/Manuals/downloads/bp102c07.pdf (site visited July 28, 2016).

[88] 42 C.F.R. § 424.22(a)(1)(v); MBPM, Ch. 7, § 30.5.1.1(1), *available at* http://www.cms.gov/Regulations-and-Guidance/Guidance/Manuals/downloads/bp102c07.pdf (site visited July 28, 2016). The home health services may not be certified or recertified by a physician who has a financial relationship with the HHA providing the services. An NPP who has a financial relationship with the HHA may not perform the face-to-face encounter. *See* 42 C.F.R. § 424.22(d).

[89] 42 C.F.R. § 424.22(a)(1)(v)(B); MBPM, Ch. 7, § 30.5.1.1(4), *available at* http://www.cms.gov/Regulations-and-Guidance/Guidance/Manuals/downloads/bp102c07.pdf (site visited July 28, 2016).

[90] MBPM, Ch. 7, § 30.5.1.1(2), *available at* http://www.cms.gov/Regulations-and-Guidance/Guidance/Manuals/downloads/bp102c07.pdf (site visited July 28, 2016).

[91] MBPM, Ch. 7, § 30.5.1, *available at* http://www.cms.gov/Regulations-and-Guidance/Guidance/Manuals/downloads/bp102c07.pdf (site visited July 28, 2016). CMS has clarified that if a home health patient is admitted to an inpatient facility and returns home from the inpatient stay after day 61 (after the first day of what would have been the next episode of care), then care would have to be initiated under a new start of care OASIS and initial certification, with a new face-to-face encounter.

From 2011 through 2014, CMS required a separate and distinct section of, or an addendum to, the certification documenting the face-to-face encounter which was clearly titled, dated, and signed by the certifying physician. CMS further required that the physician include a brief narrative statement describing how the clinical findings from the encounter supported the patient's homebound status and need for skilled services. This created a major impediment for Medicare patients' access to services and for participating HHAs' being paid. During this period, MACs denied a large percentage of home health claims on technical grounds without ever reviewing the medical record, finding that the face-to-face encounter documentation was insufficient to substantiate eligibility. Physicians were perplexed as to what was expected of them in these brief narrative statements, which never seemed to satisfy the contractors.

Effective January 1, 2015, CMS eliminated the narrative statement from the face-to-face encounter documentation requirement.[92] The current guidelines still require a physician to certify that a patient encounter was performed by a physician or allowed NPP during the prescribed time frame (and to document the date of the encounter) and was related to the primary reason for the home health services.

Although certifying physicians no longer need to compose a narrative statement describing the patient's homebound status and need for skilled care, CMS has imposed a new "supporting documentation" requirement.[93] At the request of CMS and/or its review entities, an HHA must produce the actual clinical note from the face-to-face encounter, as well as any other supporting documentation from the certifying physician's and/or the acute/post-acute care facility's medical records needed to support the patient's eligibility for Medicare home health coverage.[94] CMS policy allows physicians and facilities to incorporate (by signature) clinical records from the HHA that substantiate a patient's homebound status and need for skilled care, so long as the clinical records are corroborated by their own records.[95] As a practical matter, it could make sense for an HHA to gather this documentation when working with the physician/facility on the patient's certification and plan of care. It remains to be seen whether this new requirement will be less challenging to comply with and how much of an administrative burden it will impose.

---

[92] 76 Fed. Reg. 66,031, 66,043 (Nov. 6, 2014). *See also* MLN Matters® SE1436, "Certifying Patients for the Medicare Home Health Benefit," *available at* https://www.cms.gov/Outreach-and-Education/Medicare-Learning-Network-MLN/MLNMattersArticles/Downloads/SE1436.pdf (site visited July 28, 2016).

[93] MBPM, Ch. 7, § 30.5.1.2, *available at* http://www.cms.gov/Regulations-and-Guidance/Guidance/Manuals/downloads/bp102c07.pdf (site visited July 28, 2016).

[94] MBPM, Ch. 7, § 30.5.1.2, *available at* http://www.cms.gov/Regulations-and-Guidance/Guidance/Manuals/downloads/bp102c07.pdf (site visited July 28, 2016).

[95] MBPM, Ch. 7, § 30.5.1.2, *available at* http://www.cms.gov/Regulations-and-Guidance/Guidance/Manuals/downloads/bp102c07.pdf (site visited July 28, 2016).

[2] Pre-Claim Review Demonstration

Beginning in 2016, CMS implemented a three-year pre-claim review demonstration for home health services. The pre-claim review demonstration is described as a "process through which a request for provisional affirmation of coverage is submitted for review before a final claim is submitted for payment."[96] The process is meant to assure that all relevant coverage and clinical documentation requirements are met before the final claim is submitted for payment which will "decrease improper payments because of insufficient documentation, as well as reduce the need for HHAs to appeal claims."[97] The intent of the new pre-claim review is to help protect the Medicare Trust Funds and taxpayer funds from fraud and improper payments. The pre-claim review does not change eligibility standards or Medicare's documentation requirements. A home health agency will be required to submit information they currently submit for payment but will be required to do so earlier in the process. Home health agencies will be given the opportunity to fix home health documentation and resubmit a pre-claim as many times as possible before a final claim for payment is submitted.

The pre-claim review began in Illinois on August 3, 2016 and was scheduled to begin in Florida, Texas, Michigan and Massachusetts over the following months. CMS delayed implementing the demonstration to the other four pilot states as they determined that additional education efforts were needed before moving forward.[98]

[D] Issues Under PPS

Under PPS, HHAs are paid based on the medical and service needs (home health resource utilization groups, or HHRUGs) of a particular beneficiary. Nevertheless, some beneficiaries who otherwise meet the eligibility criteria for Medicare home health benefits report problems in getting services or in getting the level of services prescribed by their doctors. Beneficiaries reporting problems include people with chronic conditions and those who use a large amount of non-routine medical supplies. Problems in getting services or supplies may arise where the agency does not believe the PPS rate adequately covers its costs. Thus, although PPS is ostensibly only a payment system, it may deter some HHAs from serving certain beneficiaries. Advocates should continue to watch PPS closely to

---

[96] https://www.cms.gov/Research-Statistics-Data-and-Systems/Monitoring-Programs/Medicare-FFS-Compliance-Programs/Pre-Claim-Review-Initiatives/Downloads/FAQ.pdf (site visited July 28, 2016).

[97] *See* https://www.cms.gov/Research-Statistics-Data-and-Systems/Monitoring-Programs/Medicare-FFS-Compliance-Programs/Pre-Claim-Review-Initiatives/Downloads/Pre_Claim_Review_Fact_Sheet.pdf (site visited July 28, 2016).

[98] https://www.cms.gov/Research-Statistics-Data-and-Systems/Monitoring-Programs/Medicare-FFS-Compliance-Programs/Pre-Claim-Review-Initiatives/Overview.html (site visited November 9, 2016).

ensure it does not generate the same adverse consequences prompted by the interim payment system (IPS) in effect from 1998 through September 2000, when caps on reimbursement caused HHAs to reduce care, terminate services, or deny admission to patients because of their diagnosis or care needs.[99]

Recent policy changes have been made to the Home Health Prospective Payment System (HH PPS) that advocates should be aware of. CMS issued a final rule (CMS-1648-F) that updates the Medicare HH PPS rates and wage index for calendar year 2017.[100] In the final rule, CMS updates the payment rates and the case-mix weights for 2017. Areas of significant change and concern to advocates are as follows:

- Payment for high-cost outlier episodes of care will be based on visit length rather than the current cost-per-visit calculation, thus making it more difficult for individuals who need brief encounters at home to obtain care. It is expected that more than a third of beneficiaries eligible for outlier payments in 2016 will not be eligible for outlier payments as of 2017.
- Payment for Negative Pressure Wound Therapy (NPWT) using a disposable device may be obtained outside of the HH PPS bundled payment. This may drive the result of more providers using disposable NPWT devices and likely encourage home health agencies to provide more services to users of NPWT.
- Home Health Value Based Purchasing (HHVBP) continues to move forward since its implementation in January 2016. Increases in payments to providers based on HHVBP will continue to grow over the next several years. HHVBP creates incentives for increased home health payments based on narrowly defined achievements of "quality care" which are based on improvements in ambulation, bed transferring, bathing, pain interfering with activity, and shortness of breath. There are currently no HHVBP achievements that characterize functional maintenance, but comments to the final rules, addressing the Quality Reporting Program, state, "We Wish to clarify that "improvement" on a measure means an improved agency performance score and that better patient outcomes can encompass both functional stabilization and improvement." (CMS-1648-F page 188).

---

[99] *See, e.g.*, Winkler v. Interim Healthcare, Inc., 36 F. Supp. 2d 1026 (D. Tenn. 1999). This problem has taken on renewed urgency in several recent Connecticut cases, particularly where services for a chronic care patient are needed on an ongoing basis. In these situations, but for the home health care services, the patient's chronic condition would deteriorate. Note that CMS has been using its PPS rate announcement as a vehicle to introduce proposed changes to home health regulations and policies on payment, eligibility, and coverage. The rates for 2016 are *available at* https://www.gpo.gov/fdsys/pkg/FR-2015-11-05/pdf/2015-27931.pdf (site visited June 7, 2016).

[100] https://www.cms.gov/center/provider-Type/home-Health-Agency-HHA-Center.html and https://www.gpo.gov/fdsys/pkg/FR-2016-11-03/pdf/2016-26290.pdf (sites visited November 15, 2016).

- Home Health Quality Reporting Program adopted new Discharge to Community measures that will create further impediments to access home health coverage for those most at risk for unplanned hospitalization or death. If either an unplanned hospitalization or death occurs within 31 days of a beneficiary being discharged from home health care to independence in the community, this will be measured and count against a home health agency.

§ 4.06 CLAIMS SUBMISSION, DETERMINATION, AND APPEAL

[A] Generally

The home health claims submission process is complex and its reimbursement system seriously impedes the granting of appropriate coverage. The sections that follow describe the procedure in detail.

[B] Medicare Home Health Claims Submission and Appeals Process[101]

[1] Medicare Advantage

In the event that the home health beneficiary has enrolled in a Medicare Advantage plan, then the beneficiary will be afforded the Medicare Advantage appeal rights.[102]

[2] Appeals Arising Under Parts A and B of Medicare

Rules regarding Medicare appeals were published in the *Federal Register* on March 8, 2005, and codified at Subpart G of Part 405.[103] The rules establish a combined Part A and Part B appeals process. CMS's regulations implement the changes to the appeals process for Medicare Part A and Part B claims and implement changes to the administrative law judge (ALJ) hearing process for all Medicare claims, including managed care claims and prescription drug claims.[104]

---

[101] *See* Center for Medicare Advocacy, "Self Help Packet for Home Health Care Appeals Including "Improvement Standard" Denials," *available at* http://www.medicareadvocacy.org/self-help-packet-for-expedited-home-health-care-appeals-including-improvement-standard-denials/ (site visited July 28, 2016).

[102] *See* Medicare Managed Care Manual, Ch. 13, *available at* https://www.cms.gov/Regulations-and-Guidance/Guidance/Manuals/Downloads/mc86c13.pdf (site visited July 28, 2016). *See* **§ 7.04** of this Handbook for a discussion of the Medicare Advantage appeal system.

[103] *See* 42 C.F.R. §§ 405.701 *et seq.*

[104] 70 Fed. Reg. 11,420 (Mar. 8, 2005). *See* final regulations (non-expedited appeals) at http://www.gpo.gov/fdsys/pkg/CFR-2011-title42-vol2/pdf/CFR-2011-title42-vol2-part405-subpartI.pdf (site visited July 28, 2016), authorized by 42 U.S.C. §§ 1395ff, codified at 42 C.F.R. §§ 405.900 *et seq.* (Subpart I—Determinations, Redeterminations, Reconsiderations, and Appeals under Original Medicare process).

Currently, there is great concern over the staggeringly low success rate for appeals at the first two levels (redetermination and reconsideration) of appeal and the enormous backlog of appeals at the ALJ level.[105]

On October 9, 2015, the Center for Medicare Advocacy filed a class action lawsuit in federal court alleging that the 98 percent denial rate at the initial appeal levels deprives beneficiaries of a meaningful review, in violation of the Medicare Act and Due Process Clause.[106] The plaintiff seeks declaratory and injunctive relief for a nationwide class of Medicare beneficiaries who have received or will receive adverse redetermination and reconsideration decisions on their claims for coverage of home health care services. The court denied the government's motion to dismiss the due process claim, granted the motion to dismiss the statutory claim, and certified a nationwide class action on August 8, 2016.[107] On August 1, 2016, the Center settled a separate nationwide class action lawsuit in federal court that challenged the long wait times for ALJ decisions faced by beneficiaries.[108] The settlement incorporates a policy of prioritizing beneficiary appeals to ensure timely processing, as well as certain reforms to make the ALJ appeals system easier for beneficiaries to use.[109]

Since FY 2010, when Medicare Recovery Audit Contractors (RACs) began actively trying to identify and correct improper payments under the National Recovery Audit program, there has been a dramatic increase in the volume of appeals, leading to huge backlogs and long delays to obtain decisions for beneficiaries and providers alike. While there was much discussion in Congress in 2015 about how to "fix" the Medicare appeals system, many of the proposals do not reach the heart of the problem and, if implemented, could further restrict beneficiary access to meaningful reviews.[110] On July 5, 2016, CMS proposed rules to revise the procedures that HHS would follow at the various levels of appeal.[111]

---

[105] *See* Center for Medicare Advocacy, "Senate Finance Committee Holds Hearing on Medicare Appeals Backlog—Proposed Solutions Are of Great Concern," *available at* http://www.medicareadvocacy.org/senate-finance-committee-holds-hearing-on-medicare-appeals-backlog-proposed-solutions-are-of-great-concern/ (site visited July 28, 2016).

[106] *Sherman v. Burwell*, No. 3:15-CV-1468 (D. Conn., Complaint filed Oct. 9, 2015).

[107] *Sherman*, No. 3:15-CV-1468 (ruling denying motion to dismiss and granting motion for class certification issued Aug. 8, 2016).

[108] Exley v. Burwell, No. 3:14-CV-1230 (D. Conn. May 24, 2016). The settlement is *available at* http://www.medicareadvocacy.org/wp-content/uploads/2016/08/Approved-Settlement-Agreement-00201898xC6348.pdf (site visited Aug. 15, 2016).

[109] *Exley*, No. 3:14-CV-1230.

[110] *See* Center for Medicare Advocacy, "Center Attorneys Meet with Senate Finance Committee Staff Members about Changes to Medicare Appeals Process," *available at* http://www.medicareadvocacy.org/center-attorneys-meet-with-senate-finance-committee-staff-members-about-changes-to-medicare-appeals-process/ (site visited July 28, 2016).

[111] *See* Medicare Program: Changes to the Medicare Claims and Entitlement, Medicare Advantage Organization Determination, and Medicare Prescription Drug Coverage Determination Appeals Procedures, *available at* https://www.federalregister.gov/articles/2016/07/05/2016-15192/medicare-program-changes-to-the-medicare-claims-and-entitlement-medicare-advantage-organization (site visited July 28, 2016).

[3] Initial Determinations and Redeterminations

The claims process begins when the MAC issues an initial determination of a claim submitted by the home health provider or, occasionally, by the beneficiary. The regulations make clear that the initial determination, which is issued as the Medicare Summary Notice (MSN), goes only to the beneficiary, even when the contractor is aware that the beneficiary has an appointed representative.[112] Someone who wants to appeal from the initial determination must submit a written, signed request for a redetermination within 120 days of the initial determination; the regulations assume the notice is received five days after the date of the notice.[113] An extension to file a request after the deadline may be granted if good cause is shown.[114] Redetermination requests must be filed with the office indicated on the MSN; beneficiaries can no longer file requests with Social Security offices.[115]

The regulations also allow home health providers to request appeal of a denial of an initial determination. In such a case, the contractor, an entity that contracts with the federal government to review and/or adjudicate claims, determinations, and/or decisions, must consolidate the appeals. The contractor has 60 days from receipt of the redetermination request to issue a decision. If more than one party files a request, the time period runs from the date the last request is received. If, for example, a beneficiary files a redetermination request on day 1, but the home health provider files on day 50, the 60-day time period for the contractor to act starts on day 50.[116]

Unlike the MSN (now given quarterly when there is no payment due), the notice of the redetermination is sent to the appellant, and copies are mailed to each party to the initial determination and to the party's authorized representative and/or appointed representative, if applicable.[117] The notice explains the facts, policies, and law relied upon in making the redetermination decision; the right to request a reconsideration and the process for doing so; and a statement of specific missing documents that must be submitted.[118] The notice states that home health providers, but not beneficiaries (unless they are represented by a provider), must submit all their evidence at the next level of review in order for the evidence to

[112] 42 C.F.R. § 405.921(a).

[113] 42 C.F.R. § 405.942(a).

[114] 42 C.F.R. § 405.942(b).

[115] 42 C.F.R. § 405.944(a).

[116] 42 C.F.R. §§ 405.906, 405.940, 405.944(c), and 405.950. *See* "definitions" at 42 C.F.R. § 405.902.

[117] Medicare Claims Processing (MCP) Manual, Ch. 29, § 310.5, *available at* https://www.cms.gov/Regulations-and-Guidance/Guidance/Manuals/downloads/clm104c29.pdf (site visited July 28, 2016).

[118] Examples of CMS's revised MSNs are *available at* http://www.cms.gov/apps/files/msn_changes.pdf; http://www.medicare.gov/pubs/pdf/SummaryNoticeA.pdf (Part A); http://www.medicare.gov/pubs/pdf/SummaryNoticeB.pdf (Part B); and http://www.medicare.gov/pubs/pdf/SummaryNoticeDME.pdf (DME) (sites visited July 28, 2016).

be considered at any further stage of the appeals process.[119] In addition, contractors are not required to send redetermination notices to multiple beneficiaries in overpayment cases brought by home health providers if the beneficiary allegedly has no liability for the claim.

The regulations create a new reopening process to be used instead of the redetermination process to correct minor errors or omissions in initial determinations.[120] This process responds to a new section of the Medicare law that allows home health providers to correct minor mistakes without going through the appeals process.[121] Reopenings can also be used at subsequent levels of review.

[4] Reconsideration

A third level of review, the reconsideration, is conducted by a separate group of Medicare contractors called Qualified Independent Contractors (QICs). Beneficiaries and other parties to the redetermination have 180 days to request a reconsideration determination by filing a request at the location indicated on the redetermination notice.[122] An extension to file a request after the deadline may be granted if good cause is shown.[123]

The reconsideration level of review is a paper review. However, the QIC is to solicit the beneficiary's position. As noted above, home health providers are required to submit all the evidence they want considered in the claim to the QIC. Evidence not submitted may be excluded at subsequent levels of review. Beneficiaries may submit additional evidence at subsequent levels of review

The QIC is to issue a determination within 60 days of the reconsideration request.[124] Again, the time frame runs from receipt of the last request filed; the QIC must so notify a party who filed an earlier request. The regulations do not indicate how QICs are to document receipt or how beneficiaries are to know when the 60-day period ends. Although the statute allows a party to the reconsideration to ask for an extension of not more than 14 days for the QIC to conclude the reconsideration, the regulations add 14 days to the reconsideration time frame each time that additional evidence is submitted.[125]

If a QIC does not issue a timely decision, the regulations allow a party to request that the appeal be escalated to the next level of review, the ALJ level.[126] The regulations give the QIC five days to either issue a decision or acknowledge

---

[119] 42 C.F.R. § 405.956.

[120] 42 C.F.R. §§ 405.927 and 405.980.

[121] Medicare Prescription Drug Improvement and Modernization Act of 2003 § 937, 42 U.S.C. § 1395ff(b)(1)(G).

[122] 42 C.F.R. § 405.962(a).

[123] 42 C.F.R. § 405.962(b).

[124] 42 C.F.R. § 405.970(a).

[125] 42 C.F.R. § 405.970(b)(3).

[126] 42 C.F.R. § 405.970(c)(2).

the escalation request and send it to the ALJ level of review.[127] Under the regulations, an appeal escalated to the ALJ level will be completed within 180 days of receipt, rather than the statutorily mandated 90 days for ALJ decisions.

In practice, however, Medicare contractors at the two lower levels tend to issue timely decisions. It is not until Medicare beneficiaries reaches the ALJ level of review that they begin to experience significant delays in receiving decisions.[128]

[5] ALJ Hearings and Beyond

If the reconsideration decision by the QIC is unfavorable and at least $160 (in 2017) remains in controversy, the beneficiary has 60 days in which to request an ALJ hearing.[129] The hearing request should be made in writing and should be filed with the entity identified in the reconsideration notice.[130] An extension to file a request after the deadline may be granted if good cause is shown.[131] At this level of appeal a Medicare beneficiary who is dissatisfied with the previous decisions has the right to a hearing in front of an ALJ. The Office of Medicare Hearings and Appeals (OMHA) is responsible for conducting ALJ hearings. An ALJ hearing can be held by video-teleconference (VTC)[132] so that the ALJ and any parties involved can see and hear one another.

If the ALJ hearing decision is unfavorable, a beneficiary may request a review from the Medicare Appeals Council (Council).[133] The request must be made within 60 days of receipt of the hearing decision.[134] If at least $1,560 (in 2017) remain in controversy after the Council issues its review determination, the case may proceed to a federal district court.[135]

[C] Summary of Expedited Appeals Process

Expedited review is available in cases involving a discharge from the provider of services or a termination of services where "a physician certifies that failure to continue the provision of such services is likely to place the individual's health at

---

[127] 42 C.F.R. § 405.970(e)(2).

[128] The current backlog of ALJ appeals has led to untimely delays in scheduling hearings and issuing decisions. Under CMS's stated policy to prioritize appeals filed by beneficiaries, it has designated a mail stop to identify when a Request for Hearing is submitted by a Beneficiary seeking an appeal or an appointed representative filing on behalf of a Beneficiary. These individuals should add: "ATTN: Beneficiary Mail Stop" above the address line in order to ensure priority processing of their ALJ appeal request.

[129] 42 C.F.R. § 405.1014(b)(1).

[130] 42 C.F.R. § 405.1014.

[131] 42 C.F.R. § 405.1014(c).

[132] 42 C.F.R. § 405.1020(b).

[133] 42 C.F.R. §§ 405.1100–1130.

[134] 42 C.F.R. § 405.1102(a).

[135] 42 C.F.R. § 1136(a)(1).

risk."[136] Home health services are treated as a termination of services for which a doctor's certificate of significant health risk must be provided.[137] A reduction in service is not considered a termination or discharge for purposes of triggering expedited review.

Beneficiaries may seek expedited review of a home health service appeal.[138] The provider must give the beneficiary a general, standardized notice at least two days in advance of the proposed end of the service. If the service is fewer than two days, or if the time between services is more than two days, then notice must be given by the next-to-last service. The notice describes the service, the date coverage ends, the beneficiary's financial liability for continued services, and how to file an appeal.

A beneficiary must request expedited review, orally or in writing, by noon of the next calendar day after receiving notice. At that time, the beneficiary is given a more specific notice that includes a detailed explanation of why services are being terminated, a description of any applicable Medicare coverage rules and information on how to obtain them, and other facts specific to the beneficiary's case. The beneficiary is not financially liable for continued services until the later of two days after receiving the notice or the termination date specified on the notice.

Expedited review is conducted by the Beneficiary and Family Centered Care Quality Improvement Organization (BFCC-QIO), which has 72 hours in which to make a decision. When the BFCC-QIO receives the request for review, it must contact the provider, which then must supply the BFCC-QIO with information supporting its determination by the close of the same business day. The BFCC-QIO must solicit the views of the beneficiary and review the notice to determine whether it meets CMS requirements. The beneficiary does not incur liability if the BFCC-QIO decision is delayed because the provider did not get the necessary information to the reviewer in a timely manner.

If the BFCC-QIO sustains the decision to terminate or discharge services, the beneficiary may request expedited reconsideration, orally or in writing, by noon of the calendar day following initial notification. The reconsideration will be conducted by the QIC, which must issue a decision within 72 hours of the

---

[136] 42 U.S.C. § 1395ff(b)(1)(F).

[137] 42 C.F.R. § 405.1202(a).

[138] 42 C.F.R. §§ 405.1200-405.1204, implementing 42 U.S.C. § 1395ff(b)(1)(F). Notice of expedited review is not given in benefit situations (1) when the termination of covered services is the result of a beneficiary's, not a provider's, decision to end coverage; (2) when termination is for reasons other than medical necessity under Medicare coverage policy; and (3) when the beneficiary requires treatment at a higher level of care, such as transfer to an acute-care hospital. 42 C.F.R. §§ 405.1200–405.1204. *See* CMS's instructions for "Notice of Medicare Provider Non-Coverage," Form Number CMS-10123, *available at* http://www.cms.gov/Medicare/Medicare-General-Information/BNI/Downloads/UPDATED_InstructionsforNOMNC.pdf, and instructions for "Detailed Explanation of Non-Coverage," Form Number CMS-10124, *available at* http://www.cms.gov/Medicare/Medicare-General-Information/BNI/Downloads/UPDATED_InstructionsforDENC.pdf (sites visited July 28, 2016).

request. If the QIC does not comply with the time frame, the beneficiary may escalate the case to the ALJ level.

Beneficiaries retain the right to utilize the standard (non-expedited) appeals process in all situations. A BFCC-QIO may review an appeal from a beneficiary when the request is not timely filed, but the BFCC-QIO does not have to adhere to the time frame for issuing an expedited decision, and the limitation on liability does not apply.

[D] Claims Development and Submission

When a beneficiary desires Medicare home health coverage, he or she must contact an HHA certified by Medicare, present a physician's order for care, and request Medicare-covered services. Typically, the agency will evaluate the patient, determine whether coverage will be available for the needed care (including developing the plan of care that must be approved and certified by the patient's physician) and determine the home health resource utilization group (HHRUG) to which the patient will be assigned under PPS. If the HHA believes coverage will be granted by the MAC, it will submit a request for anticipated payment (RAP) for the first part of its payment under PPS. The HHA will deliver the services and then submit a claim for coverage to the MAC at the end of the 60-day episode to receive the final PPS payment.[139] The claims are usually submitted at two-month intervals.

[E] Notice and Appeal Rights in Home Health Care

The Medicare statute requires HHAs, as a condition of participation, to protect and promote the following for each individual under its care:[140]

> (A) The right to be fully informed in advance about the care and treatment to be provided by the agency, to be fully informed in advance of any changes in the care or treatment to be provided by the agency that may affect the individual's well-being, and (except with respect to an individual adjudged incompetent) to participate in planning care and treatment or changes in care or treatment;
>
> (E) The right to be fully informed orally and in writing (in advance of coming under the care of the agency) of—
>
>> (iv) any change in the charges or items described in clause (i), (ii), or (iii) [services not covered by Medicare]; and
>
> (F) The right to be fully informed in writing (in advance of coming under the care of the agency) of the individual's rights and obligations under this subchapter.

---

[139] 42 C.F.R. §§ 409.43, 424.33.

[140] 42 U.S.C. § 1395bbb(a)(1).

Medicare regulations also require HHAs to give their patients written and oral notice concerning when Medicare will pay for services initially as well as when there is a change in expectations of Medicare payment for services.[141] In addition, the Medicare Claims Processing Manual (MCPM) requires HHAs to give their patients an Advance Beneficiary Notice of Non-coverage (ABN) prior to delivering an item or a service that they don't believe Medicare will cover.[142] The key notion behind the ABN is that it enables the beneficiary to make an informed decision on whether or not to receive the service or item in question and accept potential financial liability.

Note that while the MCPM does not require HHAs to inform patients that they can demand that a claim be submitted to Medicare, it does require HHAs to submit claims if the patients learn on their own about the demand bill process.[143] HHAs are also required to issue a Home Health Change of Care Notice (HHCCN) to notify beneficiaries of care changes involving reductions or terminations of items and/or services.[144] Expedited review is available when all Medicare-covered services are ending.[145]

Unfortunately, these notice provisions are not monitored and enforced by CMS as extensively as needed, and consequently HHAs often fail to provide patients with notice of denials, reductions, or terminations of care. As a result, beneficiaries often lack information about appeal rights, including where to file, what to file, or how best to supplement one's record in support of a claim for coverage.[146] HHAs are required to use a model notice whenever a triggering event

---

[141] 42 C.F.R. § 484.10(e)(1), (2).

[142] CMS, Fee for Service Advance Beneficiary Notice, Form CMS-R-131, *available at* http://www.cms.gov/Medicare/Medicare-General-Information/BNI/ABN.html (site visited July 28, 2016). *See also* MCPM, Ch. 30, § 50 *et seq.*, *available at* https://www.cms.gov/Regulations-and-Guidance/Guidance/Manuals/downloads/clm104c30.pdf (site visited July 28, 2016).

[143] MCPM, Ch. 10, § 50, *available at* http://www.cms.gov/Regulations-and-Guidance/Guidance/Manuals/downloads/clm104c10.pdf (site visited July 28, 2016). *See also* Lutwin (Healey) v. Thompson, 361 F.3d 146 (2d Cir. 2004) (requiring notice to beneficiaries whenever home health care is denied, reduced, or terminated). For the latest developments, it is best to periodically consult CMS's notice initiative page: http://www.cms.gov/Medicare/Medicare-General-Information/BNI/ (site visited July 28, 2016). *See also* 69 Fed. Reg. 69,264 (Nov. 26, 2004), adding 42 C.F.R. §§ 405.1200–405.1204, to implement 42 U.S.C. § 1395ff(b)(1)(F).

[144] CMS, Home Health Change of Care Notice (HHCCN), Form CMS-10280, *available at* http://www.cms.gov/Medicare/Medicare-General-Information/BNI/HHCCN.html (site visited July 28, 2016). *See also* MCPM, Ch. 30, § 60, *et seq.*, *available at* https://www.cms.gov/Regulations-and-Guidance/Guidance/Manuals/downloads/clm104c30.pdf (site visited July 28, 2016).

[145] HHAs must continue to issue an expedited determination notice called the Notice of Medicare Provider Non-Coverage (NOMNC), Form CMS-10123, if applicable, when all covered services are being terminated. For more information, see http://www.cms.gov/Medicare/Medicare-General-Information/BNI/FFSEDNotices.html (site visited July 28, 2016).

[146] Program Memorandum (PM) A-01-30 (Feb. 28, 2001), reissued as PM A-02-017 (Feb. 26, 2002); PM A-01-05 (Jan. 16, 2001), reissued as PM A-02-018 (Feb. 26, 2002); Healey v. Thompson, 186 F. Supp. 2d 105 (D. Conn. 2001).

defined by CMS occurs. Note that *Lutwin (Healey) v. Thompson* requires notice in all situations where services are denied, reduced, or terminated. Issues involving CMS's monitoring and enforcement of the notice requirement are being resolved in large part through CMS Transmittal No. 1025 (Medicare Claims Processing).[147]

Although theoretically there is a procedure for appealing Medicare home health terminations and reductions, several characteristics of its design render it useless for most beneficiaries. First, appeal is permitted only with respect to services actually received; second, most HHAs will not provide services after a reduction or termination; third, agencies that agree to provide services only do so if the beneficiary pays for the services pending appeal, which most beneficiaries cannot afford; and fourth, the appeal process is slow and cumbersome and decisions often come far too long after a crisis point.[148]

[F] Liability Protections

The liability of the patient for the cost of care is waived until he or she is informed in writing, by issuance of the ABN, that coverage is not available.[149] Situations exist where PPS payment has been made for the full episode. Should additional coverage be granted, for example, additional home health aide hours, but care does not increase to outlier criteria, the HHA would not receive additional payment. But it cannot charge the beneficiary for the additional cost of care.

Whenever the HHA submits a claim to the MAC, it risks a financial penalty. If the MAC determines that the services involved should not be covered, it issues an initial determination denying the claim. The HHA may not begin to charge the patient for the cost of services until the patient is informed in writing that Medicare coverage will be denied.[150] Thus, the agency is forced to absorb the cost of the care already furnished.

If the HHA believes that coverage will be denied by the contractor, or when the agency is unsure whether coverage will be granted, it will generally seek to avoid submitting a claim in order to escape any possible financial penalty. The

---

[147] *Lutwin (Healey)*, 361 F.3d 146. Note, too, that if an HHA decides to stop providing service for a reason not related to Medicare coverage (e.g., for its own financial and business reasons), such a cessation of service is not subject to appeal. *See* **Appendix 4-7** of this Handbook, including the discussion of "option box 2" in § 60-4. The issuance of an ABN in this circumstance is voluntary.

[148] For information on developing and pursuing an appeal of a home health care denial, see Center for Medicare Advocacy, "Self Help Packet for Home Health Care Appeals Including "Improvement Standard" Denials," *available at* http://www.medicareadvocacy.org/self-help-packet-for-expedited-home-health-care-appeals-including-improvement-standard-denials/ (site visited July 28, 2016).

[149] See MCPM, Ch. 30, §§ 30.1 (beneficiary liability) and 30.2 (provider liability), *available at* http://www.cms.gov/Regulations-and-Guidance/Guidance/Manuals/downloads/clm104c30.pdf (site visited July 28, 2016).

[150] 42 C.F.R. §§ 411.400–411.406.

agency may be found liable if it failed to issue a notice or issued a defective notice. Although the beneficiary has a right to insist that a claim be submitted even where the HHA believes coverage will be denied (called a "demand bill"), often the agency will seek to discourage the patient from requiring such a no-payment claim submission because, under some circumstances, the agency may be penalized if the contractor determines that a claim should have been deemed covered initially by the agency.[151]

In many cases, this system results in a complete loss of care as well as the loss of the right to appeal. When the agency is afraid to claim coverage from the contractor, the agency usually will not deliver home health services unless the patient agrees to pay for them. If the patient is unable to afford the expensive home health care involved, the care will not be delivered even though Medicare coverage should have been granted, and could have been won on appeal had the care been delivered and a claim submitted. (Remember, the contractor will not make an initial determination on a claim until after the services involved have been rendered.)

Inappropriate restrictions on Medicare coverage can result in the complete loss of home health care or can mean that the patient will receive less care than he or she actually needs. Ultimately, the Medicare program may pay less home health coverage, but at the cost of increased disability, patient indigence, and unnecessary institutionalization.

§ 4.07 THE ROLE OF ADVOCACY

Advocacy in the home health arena, as in other Medicare areas, is often the key to the individual's ability to "access" services. Good advocacy allows people to be heard. It focuses on the important questions of whether the circumstances of a particular individual have been given full consideration with respect to coverage and services.

Effective advocates can include Medicare beneficiaries themselves as well as lawyers, paralegals, family members, friends, and treating physicians acting on the beneficiary's behalf. Effectiveness is grounded in good information about the Medicare program and in a keen appreciation of, and insistence upon, the right to be heard when services are denied, reduced, or terminated.

Advocates should develop a working knowledge of the Medicare benefit, as well as a good and supportive relationship with health care providers. This will ensure a broad knowledge base for advocates about the law and the relevant medical facts that must be demonstrated in order to prove eligibility for coverage and services. At the same time, this activity on behalf of a beneficiary will often educate medical providers about the basic legal requirements for Medicare coverage. This synergy is essential to effective advocacy.

---

[151] *See* **Appendix 4-1** of this Handbook; *see also* **Appendix 4-7** for CMS's treatment of "notice triggering" events. CMS has issued a revised ABN and HHCCN, *available at* http://www.cms.gov/Medicare/Medicare-General-Information/BNI/HHCCN.html (site visited July 28, 2016).

§ 4.08 HOW TO DEVELOP A WINNING APPEAL

[A] Sequential Approach to Case Development

Advocacy can make a crucial difference to your client's chance of success on appeal. The following approach is suggested:

1. Ascertain whether the HHA involved is certified to participate in the Medicare program.
2. Determine whether your client is homebound and whether he or she requires intermittent skilled nursing services or physical or speech therapy or continuing occupational therapy.
3. Ascertain whether the care billed to the Medicare program qualifies as part-time or intermittent nursing, or aide services.
4. Ensure that the home health care your client needs is delivered. The MAC will not issue an initial determination except where a claim for payment is submitted by a certified HHA for the cost of home health services already rendered. Unfortunately, unfair Medicare coverage denials often have an un-appealable prospective effect. The agency decides that services will henceforth not be covered by the MAC and declines to deliver the care unless payment is forthcoming. If the patient cannot pay for the care, the care will not be delivered, and a claim will not be submitted. The patient will not be able to challenge the unfair coverage denial. Accordingly, it is the advocate's first duty to make sure that care is rendered.

   Three ways to make sure that care is rendered in order to obtain an appealable initial determination are:

   a. If your client has funds sufficient to cover the cost involved, or if other public or private funds are available, urge him or her to consider paying for the care and then to file an appeal for Medicare coverage. This approach is often fruitful where there is a strong medical basis for coverage.

   b. If your client is unable to afford the care involved, attempt to convince the HHA to "carry" the case. That is, try to persuade the agency to deliver the care without receiving payment in advance while the claim and appeals process proceed. Your client may be required to assume liability for the cost of services in writing should Medicare coverage be denied.

   c. Finally, you may be able to persuade the HHA to take a chance on the claim. Especially if you can demonstrate a successful record in appeals of similar cases, the HHA may be willing to deliver the care without assurance of payment in expectation that your appeal will prove successful.

5. Provide the HHA with copies of relevant, supporting language from the federal regulations and CMS manual. If your client requires maintenance nursing or rehabilitation services, provide a copy of the *Jimmo* settlement agreement and Fact Sheet.[152]
6. Request *in writing* that the HHA submit a claim to Medicare for all the services ordered by the patient's physician that are potentially coverable by Medicare.
7. Solicit the written opinion of the attending physician. For care already initiated by the agency, the attending physician will have been required to sign a certification and plan-of-treatment form. You should obtain a copy of this document for review and for submission with your appeal if it is helpful.

A more detailed letter from the physician emphasizing the patient's homebound status, the need for skilled care, and the medical necessity of both the skilled care and the home health aide is often helpful. A persuasive attending physician's letter often encourages the contractor to grant the claim at the initial determination level, thereby avoiding the need for further appeal. If an appeal to the reconsideration or ALJ hearing levels is necessary, a strong and detailed attending physician's letter will often be the key to coverage in most cases.

[B] The Patient's Plan of Care as an Advocacy Tool

[1] Plan-of-Care Requirements

A plan of care is a prerequisite for Medicare coverage for home health services. The plan of care must include physician's orders as well as drug treatments and frequency and should explain the interrelationship of other medical/social services that the particular patient might receive, including physical therapy or speech therapy.[153] It must be signed and dated by a physician.[154]

[2] Physician Attestation Required

The plan of care must be signed by the physician before the bill for services is submitted, and any changes in the plan must be signed and dated by the

[152] *See Jimmo* settlement agreement at http://www.medicareadvocacy.org/wp-content/uploads/2014/10/Jimmo-II-Settlement-FINAL.pdf. *See also* "*Jimmo v. Sebelius* Settlement Agreement Fact Sheet," *available at* http://www.cms.gov/Medicare/Medicare-Fee-for-Service-Payment/SNFPPS/Downloads/Jimmo-FactSheet.pdf (site visited July 28, 2016).

[153] 42 C.F.R. §§ 409.43 *et seq.*

[154] *See* 42 C.F.R. § 424.22(d) (the certifying physician may not have a significant ownership interest in the HHA as defined in § 424.22(d), a 5 percent or more ownership interest, or financial or contractual relationship).

physician.[155] Orders for "as needed" services or "PRN" services must be accompanied by a description of the medical signs and symptoms that would occasion such visits and a specific number of visits that can be made under that order before an additional physician's order would have to be obtained,[156] including oral orders.[157]

[3] Plan of Care as Advocacy Tool

In some instances, HHAs, without consulting with attending physicians and obtaining their consent, are notifying patients at the end of a plan-of-care period that home health services will no longer be provided. Advocates should therefore pay particular attention to both the plan-of-care document *and* the process of its development to ensure that the physician is responsible for the plan and supports its contents. This approach may be helpful in avoiding a termination of services initiated by the HHA. Such terminations are particularly prevalent when the patient needs costly care or care that will be required for a long period of time.

[4] Continuing Need for Care

Advocates must demonstrate that the beneficiary continues to meet Medicare home health criteria, including the need for skilled care services. The plan of care should include as much detail as possible, supporting the need for the specific services to be continued.

[5] Termination of the Plan of Care

Federal regulations provide that a plan of care is considered terminated if the beneficiary does not receive at least one covered skilled nursing, physical therapy, speech-language pathology service, or occupational therapy visit in a 60-day period, unless the physician documents that the interval without such care is appropriate.[158] Medicare regulation and manual provisions anticipate at least a minimal process for recertification, to the extent that the physician is given an opportunity to review the plan of care, every 60 days, and sign a new care plan if services are needed.[159]

[6] Cycle for Plan Review

The plan of care should be reviewed by the physician in consultation with the professional staff of the HHA at least every 60 days under PPS. Each such

[155] 42 C.F.R. § 409.43(c). Under PPS, a signed plan of care is submitted at the end of the 60-day episode of care and not with the initial request for anticipated payment.
[156] 42 C.F.R. § 409.43(b).
[157] 42 C.F.R. § 409.43(d).
[158] 42 C.F.R. § 409.43(f).
[159] 42 C.F.R. § 424.22(b) (recertification).

review is to be signed and dated by the physician.[160] As discussed above, termination of a plan of care is often a tricky issue, especially as HHAs seek to divest themselves of their heavy care patients. Again, be sure that the patient's attending physician is in charge of the plan of care, supports its contents, and approves of any discharge from home care.

[C] Identifying Coverable Home Health Cases

The lists provided in the following sections can be used as a quick reference aid to help identify coverable home health claims.

[1] Coverage Criteria

Home health claims are suitable for Medicare coverage, and appeal if they have been denied, if they meet the following criteria:

1. A physician has signed or will sign a plan of care.
2. The patient is or will be homebound. This criterion can be met if: the person has a normal inability to leave the home and leaving home requires a considerable and taxing effort; and the person either requires assistance to leave the home which may be shown by the patient needing personal assistance or the help of a wheelchair or crutches, etc., or it is medically contraindicated for the person to leave home. Occasional but infrequent non-medical absences from home are allowable.
3. The patient needs or will need skilled nursing care on an intermittent basis (from as much as every day for recurring periods of 21 days—if there is a predictable end to the need for daily care—to as little as once every 60 days) or physical or speech therapy or ongoing occupational therapy services.
4. The care must be provided by, or under arrangements with, a Medicare-certified provider.

[2] Coverable Home Health Services

If the triggering conditions described above are met, the beneficiary is entitled to Medicare coverage for home health services. There is no coinsurance or deductible under traditional Medicare. Home health services include:

---

[160] 42 C.F.R. § 409.43(e). For ongoing updates to notices in the home health arena, see the CMS website http://www.cms.gov/Medicare/Medicare-General-Information/BNI/HHCCN.html (site visited July 28, 2016).

1. Part-time or intermittent nursing care provided by or under the supervision of a registered professional nurse;
2. Physical, occupational, or speech therapy;
3. Medical social services under the direction of a physician; and
4. To the extent permitted in regulations, part-time or intermittent services of a home health aide.

[3] Additional Hints for Coverage

1. Medicare coverage should not be denied simply because the patient's condition is "chronic" or "stable." "Restorative potential" is not necessary.
2. Resist arbitrary caps on coverage imposed by the MAC. For example, do not accept provider or MAC assertions that aide services in excess of one visit per day are not covered or that daily nursing visits can never be covered.
3. There is no legal limit to the duration of the Medicare home health benefit. Medicare coverage is available for necessary home care even if it is to extend over a long period of time.
4. The doctor is the patient's most important ally. If it appears that Medicare coverage will be denied, ask the doctor to help demonstrate that the standards above are met. Home care services should not be ended or reduced unless this has been ordered by the doctor.
5. In order to be able to appeal a Medicare denial, the HHA must have filed a Medicare claim for the patient's care. Request in writing that the HHA file a Medicare claim even if the agency claims that Medicare will deny coverage.

APPENDIX 4-1 CMS PROGRAM MEMORANDA, TRANSMITTALS A-01-21 (FEB. 6, 2001) AND 192 (AUG. 1, 2014)*

Program Memorandum Intermediaries

Department of Health and Human Services (DHHS)
HEALTH CARE FINANCING ADMINISTRATION (HCFA)

Transmittal A-01-21 **Date: FEBRUARY 6, 2001**

CHANGE REQUEST 1503

SUBJECT: Clarification of the Homebound Definition Under the Medicare Home Health Benefit

Background

Section 507 of the Beneficiary Improvement and Protection Act (BIPA) amends the Social Security Act (the Act) (§§1814(a) and 1835(a); (42 U.S.C. 1395f(a) and 1395n(a)), which establish the homebound requirement under the Medicare home health benefit. The statutory language of the homebound definition is amended as follows:

(A) In the last sentence, by striking, 'and that absences of the individual from home are infrequent or of relatively short duration, or are attributable to the need to receive medical treatment" and

(B) By adding at the end the following new sentences: "Any absence of an individual from the home attributable to the need to receive health care treatment, including regular absences for the purpose of participating in therapeutic, psychosocial, or medical treatment in an adult day-care program that is licensed or certified by a State, or accredited, to furnish adult day-care services in the State shall not disqualify an individual from being considered to be confined to his home. Any other absence of an individual from the home shall not so disqualify an individual if the absence is of infrequent or of relatively short duration. For purposes of the preceding sentence, any absence for the purpose of attending a religious service shall be deemed to be an absence of infrequent or short duration."

The amendments made to the Act (§1814(a); and 1835(a); (42 U.S.C. 1395n(a)), apply to home health services furnished on or after December 21, 2000 (the enactment date of BIPA).

Discussion

This Program Memorandum (PM) provides clarification of the homebound statutory eligibility requirement applicable to the Medicare home health benefit now that it has been amended by BIPA. Sections 1814 and 1835 of the Act and §1395 of the U.S.C. establish the homebound/confined to the home definition under the Medicare home health benefit. Section 507 of BIPA clarifies the statutory definition of homebound/confined to the home for purposes of eligibility under the Medicare home health benefit. To qualify for the Medicare home health benefit, §§1814(a)(2)(C) and 1835(a)(2)(A) of the Act require a Medicare beneficiary to be confined to the home, under the care of a physician, receiving services under a plan of care established and periodically reviewed by a physician, be in need of skilled nursing care on an intermittent basis (other than solely venipuncture), or physical therapy or speech-language pathology or have a continuing need for occupational therapy.

Sections 1814 and 1835 of the Act sets forth the conditions and limitations on payment for home health services. Physician certification that the beneficiary is confined to his home is an eligibility requirement for all home health services.

HCFA Pub. 60A

* *Available at* http://www.cms.gov/Transmittals/downloads/A0121.pdf (site visited July 28, 2016). Updated language can be found in § 60.4.1, Definition of Homebound Patient under the Medicare Home Health (HH) Benefit (Rev. 192, Issued: 08-01-14, Effective: 09-02-14, Implementation: 09-02-14), *available at* https://www.cms.gov/Regulations-and-Guidance/Guidance/Transmittals/downloads/R192BP.pdf (site visited July 28, 2016).

The new provision expands the list of circumstances in which absences from the home would be consistent with a determination that the patient is "confined to the home" or "homebound" for Medicare purposes, it does not change the existing homebound guidelines beyond the two specific provisions below. The new provisions include:

- Any absence of an individual from the home attributable to the need to receive health care treatment, including regular absences for the purpose of participating in therapeutic, psychosocial, or medical treatment in an adult day-care program that is licensed or certified by a State, or accredited, to furnish adult day care services in the State shall not negate the beneficiary's homebound status for purposes of eligibility.

- Any absence for religious service is deemed to be an absence of infrequent or short duration and thus does not negate the homebound status of the beneficiary.

This new statutory provision does not imply that Medicare coverage has been expanded to include adult day care services.

Implementation

The new statutory provisions replace the eligibility requirements which have been used in the course of medical review. Accordingly, replace the previous definition of "confined to the home" in your medical review guidelines with the new provisions contained in this PM. This material will subsequently be incorporated into HCFA manuals and program regulations.

Home health agencies (HHAs) enrolling patients eligible for these new provisions are responsible for demonstrating the adult day care center is licensed or certified/accredited as part of determining whether the patient is homebound for purposes of Medicare eligibility. Examples of information that could demonstrate licensure or certification/accreditation include: the license/certificate of accreditation number of the adult day care center and the effective date of the license/certificate of accreditation and the name of the authority responsible for the license/certificate or accreditation of the adult day care center.

Inform HHAs of this statutory clarification of current Medicare policy. The contents of this PM should be published in the next regularly scheduled edition of your bulletin or newsletter and should also be posted on your web-site for HHAs.

These instructions should be implemented within your current operating budget.

The *effective date* for this PM is December 21, 2000.

The *implementation date* is February 6, 2001.

The discard date for this PM is February 6, 2002.

If you have any questions, contact: Kathy Walch (410) 786-7970.

CMS Manual System	Department of Health & Human Services (DHHS)
Pub 100-02 Medicare Benefit Policy	Centers for Medicare & Medicaid Services (CMS)
Transmittal 192	**Date: August 1, 2014**
	Change Request 8818

SUBJECT: Clarification of the Confined to the Home Definition in Chapter 15, Covered Medical and Other Health Services, of the Medicare Benefit Policy Manual

I. SUMMARY OF CHANGES: This instruction clarifies the definition of the patient as being "confined to the home" to more accurately reflect the definition as articulated at Section 1835(a) of the Social Security Act. In addition, vague terms, such as "generally speaking", have been removed to ensure clear and specific requirements of the definition. These changes present the requirements first and more closely align the policy manual with the Act. This will prevent confusion, promote a clearer enforcement of the statute, and provide more definitive guidance to HHAs in order to foster compliance.

EFFECTIVE DATE: September 2, 2014
**Unless otherwise specified, the effective date is the date of service.*
IMPLEMENTATION DATE: September 2, 2014

Disclaimer for manual changes only: The revision date and transmittal number apply only to red italicized material. Any other material was previously published and remains unchanged. However, if this revision contains a table of contents, you will receive the new/revised information only, and not the entire table of contents.

II. CHANGES IN MANUAL INSTRUCTIONS: (N/A if manual is not updated)
R=REVISED, N=NEW, D=DELETED-*Only One Per Row.*

R/N/D	CHAPTER / SECTION / SUBSECTION / TITLE
R	15/60.4.1/Definition of Homebound Patient Under the Medicare Home Health (HH) Benefit

III. FUNDING:
For Medicare Administrative Contractors (MACs):
The Medicare Administrative Contractor is hereby advised that this constitutes technical direction as defined in your contract. CMS does not construe this as a change to the MAC statement of Work. The contractor is not obliged to incur costs in excess of the amounts allotted in your contract unless and until specifically authorized by the Contracting Officer. If the contractor considers anything provided, as described above, to be outside the current scope of work, the contractor shall withhold performance on the part(s) in question and immediately notify the Contracting Officer, in writing or by e-mail, and request formal directions regarding continued performance requirements.

IV. ATTACHMENTS:
Business Requirements
Manual Instruction

Attachment - Business Requirements

Pub. 100-02	Transmittal: 192	Date: August 1, 2014	Change Request: 8818

SUBJECT: Clarification of the Confined to the Home Definition in Chapter 15, Covered Medical and Other Health Services, of the Medicare Benefit Policy Manual

EFFECTIVE DATE: September 2, 2014
**Unless otherwise specified, the effective date is the date of service.*
IMPLEMENTATION DATE: September 2, 2014

I. GENERAL INFORMATION

A. Background: In the calendar year 2012 Home Health Prospective Payment System (HH PPS) proposed rule published on July 12, 2011, CMS proposed its intent to provide clarification to the Benefit Policy Manual language regarding the definition of "confined to the home". In the calendar year 2012 HH PPS final rule published on November 4, 2011 (76 FR 68599-68600), this proposal was finalized. This clarification was recommended by the Office of Inspector General (OIG).

B. Policy: This instruction clarifies the definition of the patient as being "confined to the home" to more accurately reflect the definition as articulated at Sections 1814(a) and 1835(a) of the Social Security Act. In addition, vague terms, such as "generally speaking", have been removed to ensure clear and specific requirements of the definition. These changes present the requirements first and more closely align the policy manual with the Act. This will prevent confusion, promote a clearer enforcement of the statute, and provide more definitive guidance to HHAs in order to foster compliance.

II. BUSINESS REQUIREMENTS TABLE

"Shall" denotes a mandatory requirement, and "should" denotes an optional requirement.

Number	Requirement	Responsibility								
		A/B MAC			DME	Shared-System Maintainers				Other
		A	B	HHH	DME MAC	FISS	MCS	VMS	CWF	
8818.1	Medicare contractors shall be aware of the clarification in the definition of "confined to the home" as stated in the revised Pub 100-02, Medicare Benefit Policy Manual, Chapter 15, section 60.4.1.		X							

III. PROVIDER EDUCATION TABLE

Number	Requirement	Responsibility				
		A/B MAC			DME MAC	CEDI
		A	B	HHH		
8818.2	MLN Article: A provider education article related to this instruction will be available at http://www.cms.gov/Outreach-and-Education/Medicare-Learning-Network-MLN/MLNMattersArticles/ shortly after the CR is released. You will receive notification of the article release via the established "MLN Matters" listserv. Contractors shall post this article, or a direct link to this article, on their Web sites and include information about it in a listserv message within one week of the availability of the provider education article. In addition, the provider education article shall be included in the contractor's next regularly scheduled bulletin. Contractors are free to supplement MLN Matters articles with localized information that would benefit their provider community in billing and administering the Medicare program correctly.		X			

IV. SUPPORTING INFORMATION

Section A: Recommendations and supporting information associated with listed requirements: N/A

"Should" denotes a recommendation.

X-Ref Requirement Number	Recommendations or other supporting information:
N/A	N/A

Section B: All other recommendations and supporting information: N/A

V. CONTACTS

Pre-Implementation Contact(s): Hillary Loeffler, 410-786-0456 or hillary.loeffler@cms.hhs.gov

Post-Implementation Contact(s): Contact your Contracting Officer's Representative (COR) or Contractor Manager, as applicable.

VI. FUNDING

Section A: For Medicare Administrative Contractors (MACs):
The Medicare Administrative Contractor is hereby advised that this constitutes technical direction as defined in your contract. CMS does not construe this as a change to the MAC Statement of Work. The contractor is not obligated to incur costs in excess of the amounts allotted in your contract unless and until specifically authorized by the Contracting Officer. If the contractor considers anything provided, as described above, to be outside the current scope of work, the contractor shall withhold performance on the part(s) in question

and immediately notify the Contracting Officer, in writing or by e-mail, and request formal directions regarding continued performance requirements.

ATTACHMENTS: 0

60.4.1 - Definition of Homebound Patient Under the Medicare Home Health (HH) Benefit

(Rev. 192, Issued: 08-01-14, Effective: 09-02-14, Implementation: 09-02-14)

This definition applies to homebound for purposes of the Medicare home health benefit.

For a patient to be eligible to receive covered home health services, the law requires that a physician certify in all cases that the patient is confined to his/her home. For purposes of the statute, an individual shall be considered "confined to the home" (homebound) if the following two criteria are met:

1. *Criteria-One:*

The patient must either:

- *Because of* illness or injury, need the aid of supportive devices such as crutches, canes, wheelchairs, and walkers; the use of special transportation; or the assistance of another person *in order to leave their place of residence*

OR

- *Have a* condition such that leaving his or her home is medically contraindicated.

If the patient meets one of the Criteria-One conditions, then the patient must ALSO meet two additional requirements defined in Criteria-Two below.

2. *Criteria-Two:*

- *There must exist a* normal inability to leave home*;*

AND

- *Leaving home must* require a considerable and taxing effort.

If the patient does in fact leave the home, the patient may nevertheless be considered homebound if the absences from the home are infrequent or for periods of relatively short duration, or are attributable to the need to receive health care treatment. Absences attributable to the need to receive health care treatment include, but are not limited to:

- *Attendance at adult day centers to receive medical care;*
- *Ongoing receipt of outpatient kidney dialysis; or*
- *The receipt of outpatient chemotherapy or radiation therapy.*

Any absence of an individual from the home attributable to the need to receive health care treatment, including regular absences for the purpose of participating in therapeutic, psychosocial, or medical treatment in an adult day-care program that is licensed or certified by a State, or accredited to furnish adult day-care services in a state, shall not disqualify an individual from being considered to be confined to his home. Any other absence of an individual from the home shall not so disqualify an individual if the absence is of an infrequent or of relatively short duration. *For purposes of the preceding sentence, any absence for the purpose of attending a religious service shall be deemed to be an absence of infrequent or short duration. It is expected that in most instances, absences from the home that occur will be for the purpose of receiving health care treatment.* However, occasional absences from the home for nonmedical purposes, e.g., an occasional trip to the barber, a walk around the block or a drive, attendance at a family reunion, funeral, graduation, or other infrequent or unique event would not necessitate a finding that the *patient* is not homebound if the absences are undertaken on an infrequent basis or are of relatively short duration and do not indicate that the patient has the capacity to obtain the health care provided outside rather than in the home.

Some examples of homebound patients that illustrate the factors used to determine whether a homebound condition exists would be:

- A *patient* paralyzed from a stroke who is confined to a wheelchair or requires the aid of crutches in order to walk;

- A *patient* who is blind or senile and requires the assistance of another person in leaving his or her *place of* residence;

- A *patient* who has lost the use of the upper extremities and, therefore, is unable to open doors, use handrails on stairways, etc., requires the assistance of another individual *to leave* his or her place of residence;

- A *patient* in the late stages of ALS or neurodegenerative disabilities. In determining whether the patient has the general inability to leave the home and leaves the home only infrequently or for periods of short duration, it is necessary to look at the patient's condition over a period of time rather than for short periods within the home health stay. For example, a patient may leave the home (under the conditions described above, e.g., with severe and taxing effort, with the assistance of others) more frequently during a short period when, for example, the presence of visiting relatives provides a unique opportunity for such absences, than is normally the case. So long as the patient's overall condition and experience is such that he or she meets these qualifications, he or she should be considered confined to the home.

- A *patient* who has just returned from a hospital stay involving surgery who may be suffering from resultant weakness and pain and, therefore, his or her actions may be restricted by the physician to certain specified and limited activities such as getting out of bed only for a specified period of time, or walking stairs only once a day, etc.;

- A *patient* with arteriosclerotic heart disease of such severity that the beneficiary must avoid all stress and physical activity; *and*

- A *patient* with a psychiatric illness *that* is manifested in part by a refusal to leave home *or is of such a nature that it would not be* considered safe for the *patient* to leave home unattended, even if he *or* she had no physical limitations.

The aged person who does not often travel from home because of feebleness and insecurity brought on by advanced age *would* not *be* considered confined to *the* home for purposes of this reimbursement unless they *meet one of the above conditions* above.

APPENDIX 4-2 HOME HEALTH CARE HEARING CHECKLIST

(Compiled by the Center for Medicare Advocacy)*

This checklist will help you make sure that the evidence you have gathered is sufficient to demonstrate that the patient involved is entitled to Medicare home health coverage. Each of the essential points you must prove is listed. Underneath each point you will find a description of the documents or other evidence which will help you meet the legal requirement involved.

		YES	NO
1.	The claimant is enrolled in the Medicare program. Look for the claimant's Medicare number, which can be found on the Medicare enrollment card.	[ ]	[ ]
2.	The patient is confined to his or her home. Look for documentation or testimony that the patient has a normal inability to leave his or her home without difficulty. The requirement is met if the beneficiary must be assisted by another person, or requires the help of an assistive device such as a cane or wheelchair in order to leave the home.	[ ]	[ ]
3.	The patient is under the care of a physician. Look for: (a) physician's order for home health services; and (b) physician's statement or Attending Physician Report.	[ ]	[ ]
4.	The beneficiary needs skilled nursing care on an intermittent basis or physical or speech therapy. Look for: (a) documentation or testimony that it is medically necessary that the patient receive skilled care at least once every 60 days; (b) physician's testimony or written statement that intermittent skilled care is medically necessary is the best evidence of this requirement (Attending Physician's Report, etc.); and (c) nurse or therapist notes.	[ ]	[ ]
5.	The beneficiary needs home health aide care, occupational therapy, or other home medical services (if you are seeking Medicare coverage for these services.)	[ ]	[ ]

* For additional information on home health care, see Center for Medicare Advocacy, "Home Health," *available at* http://www.medicareadvocacy.org/medicare-info/home-health-care/ (site visited July 28, 2016).

Look for:

(a) physician's testimony or written statement that home health aide or other care is medically necessary is the best evidence of this requirement (Attending Physician's Report, etc.); and

(b) home health aide notes, therapist, medical social service provider notes.

APPENDIX 4-3 ATTENDING PHYSICIAN REPORT— HOME HEALTH CARE

(Compiled by the Center for Medicare Advocacy)

Patient: HIC#

Provider: Period At Issue:

Physician:

PLEASE RESPOND TO THE FOLLOWING QUESTIONS BY CHECKING THE APPROPRIATE RESPONSES AND ELABORATING WHERE INDICATED. BE SURE YOUR RESPONSES REFER TO THE TIME PERIOD ENTERED ABOVE.

1. Were you an attending physician to this patient during the period at issue described above? ______Yes ______ No

2. Please indicate whether the patient required any of the following services during the period at issue: ______Yes ______ No

   (a) Skilled Nursing

   If yes, please specify type(s): ____

   ____

   ____

   (b) Skilled Physical Therapy ______Yes ______ No

   If yes, please specify type(s): ____

   ____

   ____

   (c) Skilled Speech Therapy ______Yes ______ No

   If yes, please specify type(s): ____

   ____

   ____

(d) Occupational Therapy ______Yes ______ No

(e) Home Health Aides ______Yes ______ No

(f) Medical Social Services ______Yes ______ No

(g) Durable Medical Equipment ______Yes ______ No

(h) Medical Supplies ______Yes ______ No

(i) Other (please specify): ____

3. During the time period at issue, was the patient confined to his/her home? (The individual had a condition that restricted the ability of the individual to leave his or her home except with the assistance of another individual or the aid of a supportive device, or the individual had a condition such that leaving his or her home was contraindicated.) ______Yes ______ No

Comment: ____

____

____

4. Was the skilled nursing which the patient required, needed on an "intermittent" basis (from once a day for a predictable period of time to once every 60 days) ______Yes ______ No

Comment: ____

____

____

5. Did the patient require the services of a "part-time" (less than 8 hours per day) or "intermittent" home health aide in addition to the skilled nursing and/or rehabilitative services? ______Yes ______ No

Comment: ____

____

____

6. Please respond to the following:

(a) Did the patient have special medical complications that required the professional or technical administration of services which are generally considered nonskilled? ______Yes ______ No

If yes, please elaborate: ____

____

____

(b) Did the patient's overall management and care plan require technical or professional personnel to assure recovery and/or safety? ______Yes ______ No

(c) Was the patient's condition such that technical or professional personnel were needed to properly *observe* and possibly *modify* treatment? ______Yes ______ No

(d) Was the use of technical or professional personnel necessary to teach the patient self-maintenance? ______Yes ______ No

FURTHER REMARKS: ____

____

____

____

____

____

____

______________________ ______________________
Date Signature of Physician

THANK YOU FOR YOUR TIME AND CONSIDERATION IN COMPLETING THIS REPORT.

APPENDIX 4-4 IMPORTANT SELECTIONS FROM THE MEDICARE BENEFIT POLICY MANUAL

CHAPTER 7 § 20—Conditions for Coverage*

CMS PUB. 100-02

(Compiled by the Center for Medicare Advocacy)

A finding that care is not reasonable and necessary must be based on information provided on the forms and in the medical record with respect to the unique medical condition of the individual beneficiary. *That is, a coverage denial may not be based solely on the reviewer's general inferences about patients with similar diagnoses or on data related to utilization generally, but must be based upon objective clinical evidence regarding the patient's individual need for care.*

20. Conditions To Be Met for Coverage of Home Health Services
(Rev. 1, 10-01-03)
A3-3116, HHA-203

Medicare covers HHA services when the following criteria are met:

1. The person to whom the services are provided is an eligible Medicare beneficiary;
2. The HHA that is providing the services to the beneficiary has in effect a valid agreement to participate in the Medicare program;
3. The beneficiary qualifies for coverage of home health services as described in §30;
4. The services for which payment is claimed are covered as described in §§40 and 50;
5. Medicare is the appropriate payer; and
6. The services for which payment is claimed are not otherwise excluded from payment.

20.1. Reasonable and Necessary Services
(Rev. 1, 10-01-03)
A3-3116.1. HHA-203.1

20.1.1. Background
(Rev. 1, 10-01-03)
A3-3116.1A, HHA-203.1A

* *See* MBPM, Ch. 7, *available at* http://www.cms.gov/Regulations-and-Guidance/Guidance/Manuals/Downloads/bp102c07.pdf (site visited July 28, 2016).

In enacting the Medicare program, Congress recognized that the physician would play an important role in determining utilization of services. The law requires that payment can be made only if a physician certifies the need for services and establishes a plan of care. The Secretary is responsible for ensuring that Medicare covers the claimed services, including determining whether they are "reasonable and necessary."

20.1.2. Determination of Coverage
(Rev. 208, Issued: 04-22-15, Effective: 01-01-15, Implementation: 05-11-15)

The *Medicare contractor's* decision on whether care is reasonable and necessary is based on information reflected in the home health plan of care, the OASIS as required by 42 CFR 484.55 or a medical record of the individual patient. Medicare does not deny coverage solely on the basis of the reviewer's general inferences about patients with similar diagnoses or on data related to utilization generally, but bases it upon objective clinical evidence regarding the patient's individual need for care. Coverage of skilled nursing care or therapy to perform a maintenance program does not turn on the presence or absence of a patient's potential for improvement from the nursing care or therapy, but rather on the patient's need for skilled care. Skilled care may be necessary to improve a patient's current condition, to maintain the patient's current condition, to prevent or slow further deterioration of the patient's condition.

20.2. Impact of Other Available Caregivers and Other Available Coverage on Medicare Coverage of Home Health Services
(Rev. 208, Issued: 04-22-15, Effective: 01-01-15, Implementation: 05-11-15)

Where the Medicare criteria for coverage of home health services are met, patients are entitled by law to coverage of reasonable and necessary home health services. Therefore, a patient is entitled to have the costs of reasonable and necessary services reimbursed by Medicare without regard to whether there is someone available to furnish the services. However, where a family member or other person is or will be providing services that adequately meet the patient's needs, it would not be reasonable and necessary for HHA personnel to furnish such services. Ordinarily it can be presumed that there is no able and willing person in the home to provide the services being rendered by the HHA unless the patient or family indicates otherwise and objects to the provision of the services by the HHA, or unless the HHA has first hand knowledge to the contrary.

Similarly, a patient is entitled to reasonable and necessary *Medicare* home health services even if the patient would qualify for institutional care (e.g., hospital care or skilled nursing facility care) *and Medicare payment should be made for reasonable and necessary home health services where the patient is also receiving supplemental services that do not meet Medicare's definition of skilled nursing care or home health aide services.*

■ **EXAMPLE 1:** A patient who lives with an adult daughter and otherwise qualifies for Medicare coverage of home health services, requires the assistance of a home health aide for bathing and assistance with an exercise program to improve endurance. The daughter is unwilling to bathe her elderly father and assist him with the exercise program. Home health aide services would be reasonable and necessary.

■ **EXAMPLE 2:** A patient who is being discharged from a hospital with a diagnosis of osteomyelitis and requires continuation of the I.V. antibiotic therapy that was begun in the hospital was found to meet the criteria for Medicare coverage of skilled nursing facility services. If the patient also meets the qualifying criteria for coverage of home health services, payment may be made for the reasonable and necessary home health services the patient needs, notwithstanding the availability of coverage in a skilled nursing facility.

■ **EXAMPLE 3:** A patient who needs skilled nursing care on an intermittent basis also hires a licensed practical (vocational) nurse to provide nighttime assistance while family members sleep. The care provided by the nurse, as respite to the family members, does not require the skills of a licensed nurse (as defined in §40.1) and therefore has no impact on the beneficiary's eligibility for Medicare payment of home health services even though another third party insurer may pay for that nursing care.

20.3. Use of Utilization Screens and "Rules of Thumb"
(Rev. 1, 10-01-03)
A3-3116.3, HHA-203.3

Medicare recognizes that determinations of whether home health services are reasonable and necessary must be based on an assessment of each beneficiary's individual care needs. Therefore, denial of services based on numerical utilization screens, diagnostic screens, diagnosis or specific treatment norms is not appropriate.

APPENDIX 4-5 IMPORTANT SELECTIONS FROM THE MEDICARE BENEFIT POLICY MANUAL

CHAPTER 7 § 40—Home Health Services*

CMS PUB. 100-02

(Compiled by the Center for Medicare Advocacy)

40. Covered Services under a Qualifying Home Health Plan of Care (Rev. 1, 10-01-03)
A3-3118, HHA-205

Section 1861(m) of the Act governs the Medicare home health services that may be provided to eligible beneficiaries by or under arrangements made by a participating home health agency (HHA). Section 1861(m) describes home health services as

- Part-time or intermittent skilled nursing care (other than solely venipuncture for the purposes of obtaining a blood sample);
- Part-time or intermittent home health aide services;
- Physical therapy;
- Speech-language pathology;
- Occupational therapy;
- Medical social services;
- Medical supplies (including catheters, catheter supplies, ostomy bags, supplies related to ostomy care, and a covered osteoporosis drug (as defined in § 1861(kk) of the Act), but excluding other drugs and biologicals);
- Durable medical equipment while under the plan of care established by physician;
- Medical services provided by an intern or resident-in-training under an approved teaching program of the hospital in the case of an HHA which is affiliated or under common control with a hospital; and
- Services at hospitals, skilled nursing facilities, or rehabilitation centers when they involve equipment too cumbersome to bring to the home.

The term "part-time or intermittent" for purposes of coverage under § 1861(m) of the Act means skilled nursing and home health aide services furnished any number of days per week as long as they are furnished (combined)

---

* See MBPM, Ch. 7, *available at* http://www.cms.gov/Regulations-and-Guidance/Guidance/Manuals/Downloads/bp102c07.pdf (site visited July 28, 2016).

less than 8 hours each day and 28 or fewer hours each week (or, subject to review on a case-by-case basis as to the need for care, less than 8 hours each day and 35 or fewer hours per week). See § 50.7

For any home health services to be covered by Medicare, the patient must meet the qualifying criteria as specified in § 30, including having a need for skilled nursing care on an intermittent basis, physical therapy, speech-language pathology services, or a continuing need for occupational therapy as defined in this section.

40.1. Skilled Nursing Care
(Rev. 179, Issued: 01-14-14, Effective: 01-07-14, Implementation: 01-07-14)
A3-3118.1, HHA-205.1

To be covered as skilled nursing services, the services must require the skills of a registered nurse, or a licensed practical (vocational) nurse under the supervision of a registered nurse, must be reasonable and necessary to the treatment of the patient's illness or injury as discussed in § 40.1.1, below, and must be intermittent as discussed in § 40.1.3. Coverage of skilled nursing care does not turn on the presence or absence of a patient's potential for improvement from the nursing care, but rather on the patient's need for skilled care.

40.1.1. General Principles Governing Reasonable and Necessary Skilled Nursing Care
(Rev. 179, Issued: 01-14-14, Effective: 01-07-14, Implementation: 01-07-14)
A3-3118.1, HHA-205.1

If all other eligibility and coverage requirements under the home health benefit are met, skilled nursing services are covered when an individualized assessment of the patient's clinical condition demonstrates that the specialized judgment, knowledge, and skills of a registered nurse or, when provided by regulation, a licensed practical (vocational) nurse ("skilled care") are necessary. Skilled nursing services are covered where such skilled nursing services are necessary to maintain the patient's current condition or prevent or slow further deterioration so long as the beneficiary requires skilled care for the services to be safely and effectively provided. When, however, the individualized assessment does not demonstrate such a necessity for skilled care, including when the services needed do not require skilled nursing care because they could safely and effectively be performed by the patient or unskilled caregivers, such services will not be covered under the home health benefit.

Skilled nursing care is necessary only when (a) the particular patient's special medical complications require the skills of a registered nurse or, when provided by regulation, a licensed practical nurse to perform a type of service that would otherwise be considered non-skilled; or (b) the needed services are of such complexity that the skills of a registered nurse or, when provided by regulation, a licensed practical nurse are required to furnish the services. To be considered a skilled service, the service must be so inherently complex that it can be safely and effectively performed only by, or under the supervision of, professional or technical personnel as provided by regulation, including42 C.F.R. 409.32.

Some services may be classified as a skilled nursing service on the basis of complexity alone (e.g., intravenous and intramuscular injections or insertion of catheters) and if reasonable and necessary to the treatment of the patient's illness or injury, would be covered on that basis. If a service can be safely and effectively performed (or self-administered) by an unskilled person, without the direct supervision of a nurse, the service cannot be regarded as a skilled nursing service although a nurse actually provides the service. However, in some cases, the condition of the patient may cause a service that would ordinarily be considered unskilled to be considered a skilled nursing service. This would occur when the patient's condition is such that the service can be safely and effectively provided only by a nurse. A service is not considered a skilled nursing service merely because it is performed by or under the supervision of a nurse. The unavailability of a competent person to provide a non-skilled service, regardless of the importance of the service to the patient, does not make it a skilled service when a nurse provides the service.

A service that, by its nature, requires the skills of a nurse to be provided safely and effectively continues to be a skilled service even if it is taught to the patient, the patient's family, or other caregivers.

The skilled nursing service must be reasonable and necessary to the diagnosis and treatment of the patient's illness or injury within the context of the patient's unique medical condition. To be considered reasonable and necessary for the diagnosis or treatment of the patient's illness or injury, the services must be consistent with the nature and severity of the illness or injury, the patient's particular medical needs, and accepted standards of medical and nursing practice. The determination of whether the services are reasonable and necessary should be made in consideration that a physician has determined that the services ordered are reasonable and necessary. The services must, therefore, be viewed from the perspective of the condition of the patient when the services were ordered and what was, at that time, reasonably expected to be appropriate treatment for the illness or injury throughout the certification period.

A patient's overall medical condition, without regard to whether the illness or injury is acute, chronic, terminal, or expected to extend over a long period of time, should be considered in deciding whether skilled services are needed. A patient's diagnosis should never be the sole factor in deciding that a service the patient needs is either skilled or not skilled. Skilled care may, depending on the unique condition of the patient, continue to be necessary for patients whose condition is stable.

As is outlined in home health regulations, as part of the home health agency (HHA) Conditions of Participation (CoPs), the clinical record of the patient must contain progress and clinical notes. Additionally, in Pub. 100-04, Medicare

Claims Processing Manual, Chapter 10; "Home Health Agency Billing", instructions specify that for each claim, HHAs are required to report all services provided to the beneficiary during each episode, which includes reporting each visit in line-item detail. As such, it is expected that the home health records for every visit will reflect the need for the skilled medical care provided. These clinical notes are also expected to provide important communication among all members of the home care team regarding the development, course and outcomes of the skilled observations, assessments, treatment and training performed. Taken as a whole then, the clinical notes are expected to tell the story of the patient's achievement towards his/her goals as outlined in the Plan of Care. In this way, the notes will serve to demonstrate why a skilled service is needed.

Therefore the home health clinical notes must document as appropriate:

- the history and physical exam pertinent to the day's visit, (including the response or changes in behavior to previously administered skilled services) and the skilled services applied on the current visit, and
- the patient/caregiver's response to the skilled services provided, and
- the plan for the next visit based on the rationale of prior results,
- a detailed rationale that explains the need for the skilled service in light of the patient's overall medical condition and experiences,
- the complexity of the service to be performed, and any other pertinent characteristics of the beneficiary or home

Clinical notes should be written so that they adequately describe the reaction of a patient to his/her skilled care. Clinical notes should also provide a clear picture of the treatment, as well as "next steps" to be taken. Vague or subjective descriptions of the patient's care should not be used. For example terminology such as the following would not adequately describe the need for skilled care:

- Patient tolerated treatment well
- Caregiver instructed in medication management
- Continue with POC

Objective measurements of physical outcomes of treatment should be provided and/or a clear description of the changed behaviors due to education programs should be recorded in order that all concerned can follow the results of the applied services.

■ **EXAMPLE 1:** The presence of a plaster cast on an extremity generally does not indicate a need for skilled nursing care. However, the patient with a preexisting peripheral vascular or circulatory condition might need skilled nursing care to observe for complications, monitor medication administration for pain control, and teach proper skin care to preserve skin integrity and prevent breakdown. The documentation must support the severity of the circulatory condition that requires skilled care. The clinical notes for each home health visit should document the patient's skin and circulatory examination as well as the patient and/or care giver application of the educational principles taught since the last visit. The plan for the next visit should describe the skilled services continuing to be required.

■ **EXAMPLE 2:** The condition of a patient, who has irritable bowel syndrome or is recovering from rectal surgery, may be such that he or she can be given an enema safely and effectively only by a nurse. If the enema were necessary to treat the illness or injury, then the visit would be covered as a skilled nursing visit. The documentation must support the skilled need for the enema, and the plan for future visits based on this information.

■ **EXAMPLE 3:** Giving a bath does not ordinarily require the skills of a nurse and, therefore, would not be covered as a skilled nursing service unless the patient's condition is such that the bath could be given safely and effectively only by a nurse (as discussed in § 30.1 above).

■ **EXAMPLE 4:** A patient with a well-established colostomy absent complications may require assistance changing the colostomy bag because they cannot do it themselves and there is no one else to change the bag. Notwithstanding the need for the routine colostomy care, changing the colostomy bag does not become a skilled nursing service when the nurse provides it.

■ **EXAMPLE 5:** A patient was discharged from the hospital with an open draining wound that requires irrigation, packing, and dressing twice each day. The HHA has taught the family to perform the dressing changes. The HHA continues to see the patient for the wound care that is needed during the time that the family is not available and willing to provide the dressing changes. The wound care continues to be skilled nursing care, notwithstanding that the family provides it part of the time, and may be covered as long as the patient requires it.

■ **EXAMPLE 6:** A physician has ordered skilled nursing visits for a patient with a hairline fracture of the hip. The home health record must document the reason skilled services are required and why the nursing visits are reasonable and necessary for treatment of the patient's hip injury.

■ **EXAMPLE 7:** A physician has ordered skilled nursing visits for teaching of self-administration and self-management of the medication regimen for a patient, newly diagnosed, with diabetes mellitus in the home health plan of care. Each visit's documentation must describe the patient's progress in this activity.

■ **EXAMPLE 8:** Following a cerebrovascular accident (CVA), a patient has an in-dwelling Foley catheter because of urinary incontinence, and is expected to require the catheter for a long and indefinite period. The medical condition of the patient must be described and documented to support the need for nursing skilled services in the home health plan of care. Periodic visits to change the catheter as needed, treat the symptoms of catheter malfunction, and teach proper catheter care would be covered as long as they are reasonable and necessary, although the patient is stable, even if there is an expectation that the care will be needed for a long and indefinite period. However, at every home health visit, the patient's current medical condition must be described and there must be documentation to support the need for continued skilled nursing services.

■ **EXAMPLE 9:** A patient with advanced multiple sclerosis undergoing an exacerbation of the illness needs skilled teaching of medications, measures to overcome urinary retention, and the establishment of a program designed to minimize the adverse impact of the exacerbation. The clinical notes for each home health visit must describe why skilled nursing services were required. The skilled nursing care received by the patient would be covered despite the chronic nature of the illness.

■ **EXAMPLE 10:** A patient with malignant melanoma is terminally ill, and requires skilled observation, assessment, teaching, and treatment. The patient has not elected coverage under Medicare's hospice benefit. The documentation should describe the goal of the skilled nursing intervention, and at each visit the services provided should support that goal. The skilled nursing care that the patient requires would be covered, notwithstanding that the condition is terminal, because the documentation and description must support that the needed services required the skills of a nurse.

* * *

40.1.2. Application of the Principles to Skilled Nursing Services (Rev. 1, 10-01-03)
A3-3118.1.B, HHA-205.1.B

The following discussion of skilled nursing services applies the foregoing principles to specific skilled nursing services about which questions are most frequently raised.

40.1.2.1 Observation and Assessment of the Patient's Condition When Only the Specialized Skills of a Medical Professional Can Determine Patient's Status

(Rev. 179, Issued: 01-14-14, Effective: 01-07-14, Implementation: 01-07-14)

Observation and assessment of the patient's condition by a nurse are reasonable and necessary skilled services where there is a reasonable potential for change in a patient's condition that requires skilled nursing personnel to identify and evaluate the patient's need for possible modification of treatment or initiation of additional medical procedures until the patient's clinical condition and/or treatment regimen has stabilized. Where a patient was admitted to home health care for skilled observation because there was a reasonable potential of a complication or further acute episode, but did not develop a further acute episode or complication, the skilled observation services are still covered for 3 weeks or so long as there remains a reasonable potential for such a complication or further acute episode.

Information from the patient's home health record must document the rationale that demonstrates that there is a reasonable potential for a future complication or acute episode and, therefore, may justify the need for continued skilled observation and assessment beyond the 3-week period. Such signs and symptoms as abnormal/fluctuating vital signs, weight changes, edema, symptoms of drug toxicity, abnormal/fluctuating laboratory values, and respiratory changes on auscultation may justify skilled observation and assessment. Where these signs and symptoms are such that there is a reasonable potential that skilled observation and assessment by a nurse will result in changes to the treatment of the patient, then the services would be covered. However, observation and assessment by a nurse is not reasonable and necessary for the treatment of the illness or injury where fluctuating signs and symptoms are part of a longstanding pattern of the patient's condition which has not previously required a change in the prescribed treatment.

■ **EXAMPLE 1:** A patient with atherosclerotic heart disease with congestive heart failure requires close observation by skilled nursing personnel for signs of decompensation or adverse effects resulting from prescribed medication. Skilled observation is needed to determine whether the drug regimen should be modified or whether other therapeutic measures should be considered until the patient's treatment regimen is essentially stabilized. The clinical notes for each home health visit should reflect the deliberations and their outcome.

■ **EXAMPLE 2:** A patient has undergone peripheral vascular disease treatment including a revascularization procedure (bypass). The incision area is showing signs of potential infection (e.g., heat, redness, swelling, drainage) and the patient has elevated body temperature. For each home health visit the clinical notes must demonstrate that the skilled observation and monitoring is required.

■ **EXAMPLE 3:** A patient was hospitalized following a heart attack. Following treatment he was discharged home. Because it is not known whether increasing exertion will exacerbate the heart disease, skilled observation is reasonable and necessary as mobilization is initiated in the patient's home. The patient's necessity for skilled observation must be documented at each home health visit until the patient's clinical condition and/or treatment regimen has stabilized.

■ **EXAMPLE 4:** A frail 85-year-old man was hospitalized for pneumonia. The infection was resolved, but the patient, who had previously maintained adequate nutrition, will not eat or eats poorly. The patient is discharged to the HHA for monitoring of fluid and nutrient intake, and assessment of the need for tube feeding. Observation and monitoring by licensed nurses of the patient's oral intake, output and hydration status is required to determine what further treatment or other intervention is needed. The patient's necessity for skilled observation and treatment must be documented at each home health visit, until the patient's clinical condition and/or treatment regimen has stabilized.

■ **EXAMPLE 5:** A patient with glaucoma and a cardiac condition has a cataract extraction. Because of the interaction between the eye drops for the glaucoma and cataracts and the beta blocker for the cardiac condition, the patient is at risk for serious cardiac arrhythmias. Skilled observation and monitoring of the drug actions is reasonable and necessary until the patient's condition is stabilized. The patient's necessity for skilled observation and treatment must be documented at each home health visit, until the patient's clinical condition and/or treatment regimen has stabilized.

■ **EXAMPLE 6:** A patient with hypertension suffered dizziness and weakness. The physician found that the blood pressure was too low and discontinued the hypertension medication. Skilled observation and monitoring of the patient's blood pressure and medication regimen is required until the blood pressure remains stable and in a safe range. The patient's necessity for skilled observation and treatment must be documented at each home health visit, until the patient's clinical condition and/or treatment regimen has stabilized.

■ **EXAMPLE 7:** A patient has chronic non-healing skin ulcers, Diabetes Mellitus Type I, and spinal muscular atrophy. In the past, the patient's wounds have deteriorated, requiring the patient to be hospitalized. Previously, a skilled nurse has trained the patient's wife to perform would care. The treating physician orders a new episode of skilled care, at a frequency of one visit every 2 weeks to perform observation and assessment of the patient's skin ulcers to make certain that they are not worsening. This order is reasonable and necessary because, although the unskilled family caregiver has learned to care for the wounds, the skilled nurse can use observation and assessment to determine if the condition is worsening.

40.1.2.2. Management and Evaluation of a Patient Care Plan
(Rev. 179, Issued: 01-14-14, Effective: 01-07-14, Implementation: 01-07-14)
A3-3118.1.B.2, HHA-205.1.B.2

Skilled nursing visits for management and evaluation of the patient's care plan are also reasonable and necessary where underlying conditions or complications require that only a registered nurse can ensure that essential unskilled care is achieving its purpose. For skilled nursing care to be reasonable and necessary for management and evaluation of the patient's plan of care, the complexity of the necessary unskilled services that are a necessary part of the medical treatment must require the involvement of licensed nurses to promote the patient's recovery and medical safety in view of the patient's overall condition.

* * *

40.2. Skilled Therapy Services
(Rev. 179, Issued: 01-14-14, Effective: 01-07-14, Implementation: 01-07-14)
A3-3118.2, HHA-205.2

To be covered as skilled therapy, the services must require the skills of a qualified therapist and must be reasonable and necessary for the treatment of the patient's illness or injury as discussed below. Coverage does not turn on the presence or absence of an individual's potential for improvement, but rather on the beneficiary's need for skilled care.

40.2.1. General Principles Governing Reasonable and Necessary Physical Therapy, Speech-Language Pathology Services, and Occupational Therapy
(Rev. 208, Issued: 04-22-15, Effective: 01-01-15, Implementation: 05-11-15)

The service of a physical therapist, speech-language pathologist, or occupational therapist is a skilled therapy service if the inherent complexity of the service is such that it can be performed safely and/or effectively only by or under the general supervision of a skilled therapist. To be covered, assuming all other eligibility and coverage criteria have been met, the skilled services must also be reasonable and necessary to the treatment of the patient's illness or injury or to the restoration or maintenance of function affected by the patient's illness or injury. It is necessary to determine whether individual therapy services are skilled and whether, in view of the patient's overall condition, skilled management of the services provided is needed.

The development, implementation, management, and evaluation of a patient care plan based on the physician's orders constitute skilled therapy services when, because of the patient's clinical condition, those activities require the specialized skills, knowledge, and judgment of a qualified therapist to ensure the effectiveness of the treatment goals and ensure medical safety. Where the specialized skills, knowledge, and judgment of a therapist are needed to manage and periodically reevaluate the appropriateness of a maintenance program, such services would be covered, even if the skills of a therapist were not needed to carry out the activities performed as part of the maintenance program.

While a patient's particular medical condition is a valid factor in deciding if skilled therapy services are needed, a patient's diagnosis or prognosis should never be the sole factor in deciding that a service is or is not skilled. The key issue is whether the skills of a therapist are needed to treat the illness or injury, or whether the services can be carried out by unskilled personnel.

A service that is ordinarily considered unskilled could be considered a skilled therapy service in cases where there is clear documentation that, because of special medical complications, skilled rehabilitation personnel are required to perform the service. However, the importance of a particular service to a patient or the frequency with which it must be performed does not, by itself, make an unskilled service into a skilled service.

Assuming all other eligibility and coverage criteria have been met, the skilled therapy services must be reasonable and necessary to the treatment of the patient's illness or injury within the context of the patient's unique medical condition. To be considered reasonable and necessary for the treatment of the illness or injury:

a. The services must be consistent with the nature and severity of the illness or injury, the patient's particular medical needs, including the requirement that the amount, frequency, and duration of the services must be reasonable; and

b. The services must be considered, under accepted standards of medical practice, to be specific, safe, and effective treatment for the patient's condition, meeting the standards noted below. The home health record must specify the purpose of the skilled service provided.

   To ensure therapy services are effective, at defined points during a course of treatment, for each therapy discipline for which services are provided, a qualified therapist (instead of an assistant) must perform the ordered therapy service. During this visit, the therapist must assess the patient using a method which allows for objective measurement of function and successive comparison of measurements. The therapist must document the measurement results in the clinical record. Specifically:

   i. **Initial Therapy Assessment**

   - For each therapy discipline for which services are provided, a qualified therapist (instead of an assistant) must assess the patient's function using a method which objectively measures activities of daily living such as, but not limited to, eating, swallowing, bathing, dressing, toileting, walking, climbing stairs, using assistive devices, and mental and cognitive factors. The measurement results must be documented in the clinical record.
   - Where more than one discipline of therapy is being provided, a qualified therapist from each of the disciplines must functionally

assess the patient. The therapist must document the measurement results which correspond to the therapist's discipline and care plan goals in the clinical record.

ii. **Reassessment at least every 30 days (performed in conjunction with an ordered therapy service)**

- At least once every 30 days, for each therapy discipline for which services are provided, a qualified therapist (instead of an assistant) must provide the ordered therapy service, functionally reassess the patient, and compare the resultant measurement to prior assessment measurements. The therapist must document in the clinical record the measurement results along with the therapist's determination of the effectiveness of therapy, or lack thereof.
- *For multi-discipline therapy cases, a qualified therapist from each of the disciplines must functionally reassess the patient. The therapist must document the measurement results which correspond to the therapist's discipline and care plan goals in the clinical record.*
- The 30-day clock begins with the first therapy service (of that discipline) and the clock resets with each therapist's visit/assessment/measurement/documentation (of that discipline).

c. Services involving activities for the general welfare of any patient, e.g., general exercises to promote overall fitness or flexibility and activities to provide diversion or general motivation do not constitute skilled therapy. Unskilled individuals without the supervision of a therapist can perform those services.

d. Assuming all other eligibility and coverage requirements have been met, in order for therapy services to be covered, one of the following three conditions must be met:

iii. **The skills of a qualified therapist are needed to restore patient function:**

- To meet this coverage condition, therapy services must be provided with the expectation, based on the assessment made by the physician of the patient's restorative potential that the condition of the patient will improve materially in a reasonable and generally predictable period of time. Improvement is evidenced by objective successive measurements.
- Therapy is not considered reasonable and necessary under this condition if the patient's expected restorative potential would be

insignificant in relation to the extent and duration of therapy services required to reach such potential.

- Therapy is not required to effect improvement or restoration of function where a patient suffers a transient or easily reversible loss of function (such as temporary weakness following surgery) which could reasonably be expected to improve spontaneously as the patient gradually resumes normal activities. Therapy in such cases is not considered reasonable and necessary to treat the patient's illness or injury, under this condition. However, if the criteria for maintenance therapy described in (3) below is met, therapy could be covered under that condition.

iv. The patient's clinical condition requires the specialized skills, knowledge, and judgment of a qualified therapist to establish or design a maintenance program, related to the patient's illness or injury, in order to ensure the safety of the patient and the effectiveness of the program, to the extent provided by regulation,

- For patients receiving rehabilitative/restorative therapy services, if the specialized skills, knowledge, and judgment of a qualified therapist are required to develop a maintenance program, the expectation is that the development of that maintenance program would occur during the last visit(s) for rehabilitative/restorative treatment. The goals of a maintenance program would be to maintain the patient's current functional status or to prevent or slow further deterioration.
- Necessary periodic reevaluations by a qualified therapist of the beneficiary and maintenance program are covered if the specialized skills, knowledge, and judgment of a qualified therapist are required.
- Where a maintenance program is not established until after the rehabilitative/restorative therapy program has been completed, or where there was no rehabilitative/restorative therapy program, and the specialized skills, knowledge, and judgment of a qualified therapist are required to develop a maintenance program, such services would be considered reasonable and necessary for the treatment of the patient's condition in order to ensure the effectiveness of the treatment goals and ensure medical safety. When the development of a maintenance program could not be accomplished during the last visits(s) of rehabilitative/restorative treatment, the therapist must document why the maintenance program could not be developed during those last rehabilitative/restorative treatment visit(s).

- When designing or establishing a maintenance program, the qualified therapist must teach the patient or the patient's family or caregiver's necessary techniques, exercises or precautions as necessary to treat the illness or injury. The instruction of the beneficiary or appropriate caregiver by a qualified therapist regarding a maintenance program is covered if the specialized skills, knowledge, and judgment of a qualified therapist are required. However, visits made by skilled therapists to a patient's home solely to train other HHA staff (e.g., home health aides) are not billable as visits since the HHA is responsible for ensuring that its staff is properly trained to perform any service it furnishes. The cost of a skilled therapist's visit for the purpose of training HHA staff is an administrative cost to the agency.

v. The skills of a qualified therapist (not an assistant) are needed to perform maintenance therapy:

- Coverage of therapy services to perform a maintenance program is not determined solely on the presence or absence of a beneficiary's potential for improvement from the therapy, but rather on the beneficiary's need for skilled care. Assuming all other eligibility and coverage requirements are met, skilled therapy services are covered when an individualized assessment of the patient's clinical condition demonstrates that the specialized judgment, knowledge, and skills of a qualified therapist ("skilled care") are necessary for the performance of a safe and effective maintenance program. Such a maintenance program to maintain the patient's current condition or to prevent or slow further deterioration is covered so long as the beneficiary requires skilled care for the safe and effective performance of the program. When, however, the individualized assessment does not demonstrate such a necessity for skilled care, including when the performance of a maintenance program does not require the skills of a therapist because it could safely and effectively be accomplished by the patient or with the assistance of non-therapists, including unskilled caregivers, such maintenance services will not be covered.

- Further, under the standard set forth in the previous paragraph, skilled care is necessary for the performance of a safe and effective maintenance program only when (a) the particular patient's special medical complications require the skills of a qualified therapist to perform a therapy service that would otherwise be considered non-skilled; or (b) the needed therapy procedures are of such complexity that the skills of a qualified therapist are required to perform the procedure.

e. The amount, frequency, and duration of the services must be reasonable.

* * *

40.2.2. Application of the Principles to Physical Therapy Services
(Rev. 179, Issued: 01-14-14, Effective: 01-07-14, Implementation: 01-07-14)

The following discussion of skilled physical therapy services applies the principles in § 40.2.1 to specific physical therapy services about which questions are most frequently raised.

A. Assessment

Assuming all other eligibility and coverage requirements have been met, the skills of a physical therapist to assess a patient's rehabilitation needs and potential or to develop and/or implement a physical therapy program are covered when they are reasonable and necessary because of the patient's condition. Skilled rehabilitation services concurrent with the management of a patient's care plan include objective tests and measurements such as, but not limited to, range of motion, strength, balance, coordination, endurance or functional ability.

As described in section 40.2.1(b), at defined points during a course of therapy, the qualified physical therapist (instead of an assistant) must perform the ordered therapy service visit, assess the patient's function using a method which allows for objective measurement of function and comparison of successive measurements, and document the results of the assessments, corresponding measurements, and effectiveness of the therapy in the patient's clinical record. Refer to § 40.2.1(b) for specific timing and documentation requirements associated with these requirements.

B. Therapeutic Exercises

Therapeutic exercises which require the skills of a qualified physical therapist to ensure the safety of the beneficiary and the effectiveness of the treatment constitute skilled physical therapy, when the criteria in § 40.2.1(d) above are met.

C. Gait Training

Gait evaluation and training furnished to a patient whose ability to walk has been impaired by neurological, muscular or skeletal abnormality require the skills of a qualified physical therapist and constitute skilled physical therapy and are considered reasonable and necessary if training can be expected to materially improve or maintain the patient's ability to walk or prevent or slow further deterioration of the patient's ability to walk. Gait evaluation and training that is furnished to a patient whose ability to walk has been impaired by a condition other than a neurological, muscular or skeletal abnormality would nevertheless be covered where physical therapy is reasonable and necessary to restore or maintain function or to prevent or slow further deterioration. Refer to § 40.2.1(d)(1) for the reasonable and necessary coverage criteria associated with restoring patient function.

■ **EXAMPLE 1:** A physician has ordered gait evaluation and training for a patient whose gait has been materially impaired by scar tissue resulting from burns. Physical therapy services to evaluate the patient's gait, establish a gait training program, and provide the skilled services necessary to implement the program would be covered. The patient's response to therapy must be documented. At appropriate intervals (see above), the qualified therapist must assess the patient with objective measurements of function.

■ **EXAMPLE 2:** A patient who has had a total hip replacement is ambulatory but demonstrates weakness and is unable to climb stairs safely. Physical therapy would be reasonable and necessary to teach the patient to safely climb and descend stairs. Once the patient has reached the goal of climbing and descending stairs safely, additional therapy services are no longer required, and this would not be covered.

■ **EXAMPLE 3:** A patient who has received gait training has reached his maximum restoration potential and the physical therapist is teaching the patient and family how to perform safely the activities that are a part of a maintenance program. The visits by the physical therapist to demonstrate and teach the activities (which by themselves do not require the skills of a therapist) would be covered since they are needed to establish the program (refer to § 40.2.1(d)(2)). The patient's and caregiver's understanding and implementation of the maintenance program must be documented. After the establishment of the maintenance program, any further visits would need to document why the skilled services of a physical therapist are still required.

D. Range of Motion

Only a qualified physical therapist may perform range of motion tests and, therefore, such tests are skilled physical therapy.

Range of motion exercises constitute skilled physical therapy only if they are part of an active treatment for a specific disease state, illness, or injury that has resulted in a loss or restriction of mobility (as evidenced by physical therapy notes showing the degree of motion lost and the degree to be restored). Unskilled individuals may provide range of motion exercises unrelated to the restoration of a specific loss of function often safely and effectively. Passive exercises to maintain range of motion in paralyzed extremities that can be carried out by unskilled persons do not constitute skilled physical therapy.

However, if the criteria in § 40.2.1(d)(3) are met, where there is clear documentation that, because of special medical complications (e.g., susceptible to pathological bone fractures), the skills of a therapist are needed to provide services that ordinarily do not need the skills of a therapist, then the services would be covered.

APPENDIX 4-6 TITLE 42—PUBLIC HEALTH (CODE OF FEDERAL REGULATIONS):

PART 409—HOSPITAL INSURANCE BENEFITS

Subpart E—Home Health Services Under Hospital Insurance*

Sec. 409.44 Skilled services requirements.

(a) General. The intermediary's decision on whether care is reasonable and necessary is based on information provided on the forms and in the medical record concerning the unique medical condition of the individual beneficiary. A coverage denial is not made solely on the basis of the reviewer's general inferences about patients with similar diagnoses or on data related to utilization generally but is based upon objective clinical evidence regarding the beneficiary's individual need for care.

(b) Skilled nursing care. (1) Skilled nursing care consists of those services that must, under State law, be performed by a registered nurse, or practical (vocational) nurse, as defined in § 484.4 of this chapter, meet the criteria for skilled nursing services specified in § 409.32, and meet the qualifications for coverage of skilled services specified in § 409.42(c). See § 409.33(a) and (b) for a description of skilled nursing services and examples of them.

(i) In determining whether a service requires the skill of a licensed nurse, consideration must be given to the inherent complexity of the service, the condition of the beneficiary, and accepted standards of medical and nursing practice.

(ii) If the nature of a service is such that it can safely and effectively be performed by the average nonmedical person without direct supervision of a licensed nurse, the service cannot be regarded as a skilled nursing service.

(iii) The fact that a skilled nursing service can be or is taught to the beneficiary or to the beneficiary's family or friends does not negate the skilled aspect of the service when performed by the nurse.

(iv) If the service could be performed by the average nonmedical person, the absence of a competent person to perform it does not cause it to be a skilled nursing service.

(2) The skilled nursing care must be provided on a part-time or intermittent basis.

(3) The skilled nursing services must be reasonable and necessary for the treatment of the illness or injury.

(i) To be considered reasonable and necessary, the services must be consistent with the nature and severity of the beneficiary's illness or injury, his or her particular medical needs, and accepted standards of medical and nursing practice.

---

* *Available at* http://www.ecfr.gov/cgi-bin/text-idx?rgn=div5&node=42:2.0.1.2.9#42:2.0.1.2.9.5 (site visited July 28, 2016).

(ii) The skilled nursing care provided to the beneficiary must be reasonable within the context of the beneficiary's condition.

(iii) The determination of whether skilled nursing care is reasonable and necessary must be based solely upon the beneficiary's unique condition and individual needs, without regard to whether the illness or injury is acute, chronic, terminal, or expected to last a long time.

(c) Physical therapy, speech-language pathology services, and occupational therapy. To be covered, physical therapy, speech-language pathology services, and occupational therapy must satisfy the criteria in paragraphs (c)(1) and (2) of this section.

(1) Speech-language pathology services and physical or occupational therapy services must relate directly and specifically to a treatment regimen (established by the physician, after any needed consultation with the qualified therapist) that is designed to treat the beneficiary's illness or injury. Services related to activities for the general physical welfare of beneficiaries (for example, exercises to promote overall fitness) do not constitute physical therapy, occupational therapy, or speech-language pathology services for Medicare purposes. To be covered by Medicare, all of the requirements apply as follows:

(i) The patient's plan of care must describe a course of therapy treatment and therapy goals which are consistent with the evaluation of the patient's function, and both must be included in the clinical record. The therapy goals must be established by a qualified therapist in conjunction with the physician.

(ii) The patient's clinical record must include documentation describing how the course of therapy treatment for the patient's illness or injury is in accordance with accepted professional standards of clinical practice.

(iii) Therapy treatment goals described in the plan of care must be measurable, and must pertain directly to the patient's illness or injury, and the patient's resultant impairments.

(iv) The patient's clinical record must demonstrate that the method used to assess a patient's function included objective measurements of function in accordance with accepted professional standards of clinical practice enabling comparison of successive measurements to determine the effectiveness of therapy goals. Such objective measurements would be made by the qualified therapist using measurements which assess activities of daily living that may include but are not limited to eating, swallowing, bathing, dressing, toileting, walking, climbing stairs, or using assistive devices, and mental and cognitive factors.

(2) Physical and occupational therapy and speech-language pathology services must be reasonable and necessary. To be considered reasonable and necessary, the following conditions must be met:

(i) The services must be considered under accepted standards of professional clinical practice, to be a specific, safe, and effective treatment for the beneficiary's condition. Each of the following requirements must also be met:

(A) The patient's function must be initially assessed and periodically reassessed by a qualified therapist, of the corresponding discipline for the type of therapy being provided, using a method which would include objective measurement as described in § 409.44(c)(1)(iv). If more than one discipline of therapy is being provided, a qualified therapist from each of the disciplines must perform the assessment and periodic reassessments. The measurement results and corresponding effectiveness of the therapy, or lack thereof, must be documented in the clinical record.

(B) At least every 30 days a qualified therapist (instead of an assistant) must provide the needed therapy service and functionally reassess the patient in accordance with § 409.44(c)(2)(i)(A). Where more than one discipline of therapy is being provided, a qualified therapist from each of the disciplines must provide the needed therapy service and functionally reassess the patient in accordance with § 409.44(c)(2)(i)(A) at least every 30 days.

(C) If a patient is expected to require 13 therapy visits, a qualified therapist (instead of an assistant) must provide all of the therapy services on the 13th therapy visit and functionally reassess the patient in accordance with § 409.44(c)(2)(i)(A). Exceptions to this requirement are as follows:

(1) The qualified therapist's visit can occur after the 10th therapy visit but no later than the 13th therapy visit when the patient resides in a rural area or when documented circumstances outside the control of the therapist prevent the qualified therapist's visit at the 13th therapy visit.

(2) Where more than one discipline of therapy is being provided, the qualified therapist from each discipline must provide all of the therapy services and functionally reassess the patient in accordance with paragraph (c)(2)(i)(A) of this section during the visit associated with that discipline which is scheduled to occur after the 10th therapy visit but no later than the 13th therapy visit per the plan of care. In instances where the frequency of a particular discipline, as ordered by a physician, does not make it feasible for the reassessment to occur during the specified time frames without providing an extra unnecessary visit or delaying a visit, then it is acceptable for the qualified therapist from that discipline to provide all of the therapy and functionally reassess the patient during the visit associated with that discipline that is scheduled to occur closest to the 14th Medicare-covered therapy visit, but no later than the 13th Medicare-covered therapy visit.

(D) If a patient is expected to require 19 therapy visits, a qualified therapist (instead of an assistant) must provide all of the therapy services on the 19th therapy visit and functionally reassess the patient in accordance with § 409.44(c)(2)(A). Exceptions to this requirement are as follows:

(1) This required qualified therapist service can instead occur after the 16th therapy visit but no later than the 19th therapy visit when the patient resides in a rural area or documented circumstances outside the control of the therapist preclude the qualified therapist service at the 19th therapy visit.

(2) Where more than one discipline of therapy is being provided, the qualified therapist from each discipline must provide all of the therapy services and functionally reassess the patient in accordance with paragraph (c)(2)(i)(A) of this section during the visit associated with that discipline which is scheduled to occur

after the 16th therapy visit but no later than the 19th therapy visit per the plan of care. In instances where the frequency of a particular discipline, as ordered by a physician, does not make it feasible for the reassessment to occur during the specified time frames without providing an extra, unnecessary visit or delaying a visit, then it is acceptable for the qualified therapist from that discipline to provide all of the therapy and functionally reassess the patient during the visit associated with that discipline that is scheduled to occur closest to the 20th Medicare-covered therapy visit, but no later than the 19th Medicare-covered therapy visit.

(E) As specified in paragraphs (c)(2)(i)(A)(B), (C), and (D) of this section, therapy visits for the therapy discipline(s) not in compliance with these policies will not be covered until the following conditions are met:

(1) The qualified therapist has completed the reassessment and objective measurement of the effectiveness of the therapy as it relates to the therapy goals. As long as paragraphs (c)(2)(i)(E)(*2*) and (c)(2)(i)(E)(*3*) of this section are met, therapy coverage resumes with the completed reassessment therapy visit.

(*2*) The qualified therapist has determined if goals have been achieved or require updating.

(3) The qualified therapist has documented measurement results and corresponding therapy effectiveness in the clinical record in accordance with § 409.44(c)(2)(i)(H) of this section.

(F) If the criteria for maintenance therapy, described at § 409.44(c)(2)(iii)(B) and (C) of this section are not met, the following criteria must also be met for subsequent therapy visits to be covered:

(1) If the objective measurements of the reassessment do not reveal progress toward goals, the qualified therapist together with the physician must determine whether the therapy is still effective or should be discontinued.

(*2*) If therapy is to be continued in accordance with § 409.44(c)(2)(iv)(B)(*1*) of this section, the clinical record must document with a clinically supportable statement why there is an expectation that the goals are attainable in a reasonable and generally predictable period of time.

(G) Clinical notes written by therapy assistants may supplement the clinical record, and if included, must include the date written, the signature, professional designation, and objective measurements or description of changes in status (if any) relative to each goal being addressed by treatment. Assistants may not make clinical judgments about why progress was or was not made, but must report the progress or the effectiveness of the therapy (or lack thereof) objectively.

(H) Documentation by a qualified therapist must include the following:

(1) The therapist's assessment of the effectiveness of the therapy as it relates to the therapy goals;

(2) Plans for continuing or discontinuing treatment with reference to evaluation results and or treatment plan revisions;

(3) Changes to therapy goals or an updated plan of care that is sent to the physician for signature or discharge;

(4) Documentation of objective evidence or a clinically supportable statement of expectation that the patient can continue to progress toward the treatment goals and is responding to therapy in a reasonable and generally predictable period of time; or in the case of maintenance therapy, the patient is responding to therapy and can meet the goals in a predictable period of time.

(ii) The services must be of such a level of complexity and sophistication or the condition of the beneficiary must be such that the services required can safely and effectively be performed only by a qualified physical therapist or by a qualified physical therapy assistant under the supervision of a qualified physical therapist, by a qualified speech-language pathologist, or by a qualified occupational therapist or a qualified occupational therapy assistant under the supervision of a qualified occupational therapist (as defined in § 484.4 of this chapter). Services that do not require the performance or supervision of a physical therapist or an occupational therapist are not considered reasonable or necessary physical therapy or occupational therapy services, even if they are performed by or supervised by a physical therapist or occupational therapist. Services that do not require the skills of a speech-language pathologist are not considered to be reasonable and necessary speech-language pathology services even if they are performed by or supervised by a speech-language pathologist.

(iii) For therapy services to be covered in the home health setting, one of the following three criteria must be met:

(A) There must be an expectation that the beneficiary's condition will improve materially in a reasonable (and generally predictable) period of time based on the physician's assessment of the beneficiary's restoration potential and unique medical condition.

(1) Material improvement requires that the clinical record demonstrate that the patient is making improvement towards goals when measured against his or her condition at the start of treatment.

(2) If an individual's expected restorative potential would be insignificant in relation to the extent and duration of therapy services required to achieve such potential, therapy would not be considered reasonable and necessary, and thus would not be covered.

(3) When a patient suffers a transient and easily reversible loss or reduction of function which could reasonably be expected to improve spontaneously as the patient gradually resumes normal activities, because the services do not require the performance or supervision of a qualified therapist, those services are not to be considered reasonable and necessary covered therapy services.

(B) The unique clinical condition of a patient may require the specialized skills, knowledge, and judgment of a qualified therapist to design or establish a safe and effective maintenance program required in connection with the patient's specific illness or injury.

(1) If the services are for the establishment of a maintenance program, they must include the design of the program, the instruction of the beneficiary, family, or home health aides, and the necessary periodic reevaluations of the beneficiary

and the program to the degree that the specialized knowledge and judgment of a physical therapist, speech-language pathologist, or occupational therapist is required.

(2) The maintenance program must be established by a qualified therapist (and not an assistant).

(C) The unique clinical condition of a patient may require the specialized skills of a qualified therapist to perform a safe and effective maintenance program required in connection with the patient's specific illness or injury. Where the clinical condition of the patient is such that the complexity of the therapy services required to maintain function involve the use of complex and sophisticated therapy procedures to be delivered by the therapist himself/herself (and not an assistant) or the clinical condition of the patient is such that the complexity of the therapy services required to maintain function must be delivered by the therapist himself/herself (and not an assistant) in order to ensure the patient's safety and to provide an effective maintenance program, then those reasonable and necessary services shall be covered.

(iv) The amount, frequency, and duration of the services must be reasonable and necessary, as determined by a qualified therapist and/or physician, using accepted standards of clinical practice.

(A) Where factors exist that would influence the amount, frequency or duration of therapy services, such as factors that may result in providing more services than are typical for the patient's condition, those factors must be documented in the plan of care and/or functional assessment.

(B) Clinical records must include documentation using objective measures that the patient continues to progress towards goals. If progress cannot be measured, and continued progress towards goals cannot be expected, therapy services cease to be covered except when—

(1) Therapy progress regresses or plateaus, and the reasons for lack of progress are documented to include justification that continued therapy treatment will lead to resumption of progress toward goals; or

(2) Maintenance therapy as described in § 409.44(c)(2)(iii)(B) or (C) is needed.

[59 FR 65494, Dec. 20, 1994, as amended at 74 FR 58133, Nov. 10, 2009; 75 FR 70461, Nov. 17, 2010; 76 FR 68606, Nov. 4, 2011; 77 FR 67162, Nov. 8, 2012]

***

Sec. 409.45 Dependent services requirements.

(a) General. Services discussed in paragraphs (b) through (g) of this section may be covered only if the beneficiary needs skilled nursing care on an intermittent basis, as described in Sec. 409.44(b); physical therapy or speech-language pathology services as described in Sec. 409.44(c); or has a continuing need for occupational therapy services as described in Sec. 409.44(c) if the beneficiary's eligibility for home health services has been established by virtue of a prior need for intermittent skilled nursing care, speech-language pathology services, or physical therapy in the current or prior certification period; and otherwise meets the qualifying criteria (confined to the home, under the care of a physician, in need of skilled services, and under a plan of care) specified in Sec. 409.42. Home health coverage is not available for services furnished to a beneficiary who is no longer in need of one of the qualifying skilled services specified in this paragraph. Therefore, dependent services furnished after the final qualifying skilled service are not covered, except when the dependent service was not followed by a qualifying skilled service as a result of the unexpected inpatient admission or death of the beneficiary, or due to some other unanticipated event.

(b) Home health aide services. To be covered, home health aide services must meet each of the following requirements:

(1) The reason for the visits by the home health aide must be to provide hands-on personal care to the beneficiary or services that are needed to maintain the beneficiary's health or to facilitate treatment of the beneficiary's illness or injury. The physician's order must indicate the frequency of the home health aide services required by the beneficiary. These services may include but are not limited to:

(i) Personal care services such as bathing, dressing, grooming, caring for hair, nail and oral hygiene that are needed to facilitate treatment or to prevent deterioration of the beneficiary's health, changing the bed linens of an incontinent beneficiary, shaving, deodorant application, skin care with lotions and/or powder, foot care, ear care, feeding, assistance with elimination (including enemas unless the skills of a licensed nurse are required due to the beneficiary's condition, routine catheter care, and routine colostomy care), assistance with ambulation, changing position in bed, and assistance with transfers.

(ii) Simple dressing changes that do not require the skills of a licensed nurse.

(iii) Assistance with medications that are ordinarily self-administered and that do not require the skills of a licensed nurse to be provided safely and effectively.

(iv) Assistance with activities that are directly supportive of skilled therapy services but do not require the skills of a therapist to be safely and effectively performed, such as routine maintenance exercises and repetitive practice of functional communication skills to support speech-language pathology services.

(v) Routine care of prosthetic and orthotic devices.

(2) The services to be provided by the home health aide must be—

(i) Ordered by a physician in the plan of care; and

(ii) Provided by the home health aide on a part-time or intermittent basis.

(3) The services provided by the home health aide must be reasonable and necessary. To be considered reasonable and necessary, the services must—

(i) Meet the requirement for home health aide services in paragraph (b)(1) of this section;

(ii) Be of a type the beneficiary cannot perform for himself or herself; and

(iii) Be of a type that there is no able or willing caregiver to provide, or, if there is a potential caregiver, the beneficiary is unwilling to use the services of that individual.

(4) The home health aide also may perform services incidental to a visit that was for the provision of care as described in paragraphs (b)(3)(i) through (iii) of this section. For example, these incidental services may include changing bed linens, personal laundry, or preparing a light meal.

(c) Medical social services. Medical social services may be covered if the following requirements are met:

(1) The services are ordered by a physician and included in the plan of care.

(2) (i) The services are necessary to resolve social or emotional problems that are expected to be an impediment to the effective treatment of the beneficiary's medical condition or to his or her rate of recovery.

(ii) If these services are furnished to a beneficiary's family member or caregiver, they are furnished on a short-term basis and it can be demonstrated that the service is necessary to resolve a clear and direct impediment to the effective treatment of the beneficiary's medical condition or to his or her rate of recovery.

(3) The frequency and nature of the medical social services are reasonable and necessary to the treatment of the beneficiary's condition.

(4) The medical social services are furnished by a qualified social worker or qualified social work assistant under the supervision of a social worker as defined in § 484.4 of this chapter.

(5) The services needed to resolve the problems that are impeding the beneficiary's recovery require the skills of a social worker or a social work assistant under the supervision of a social worker to be performed safely and effectively.

(d) Occupational therapy. Occupational therapy services that are not qualifying services under § 409.44(c) are nevertheless covered as dependent services if the requirements of § 409.44(c)(2)(i) through (iv), as to reasonableness and necessity, are met.

(e) Durable medical equipment. Durable medical equipment in accordance with Sec. 410.38 of this chapter, which describes the scope and conditions of payment for durable medical equipment under Part B, may be covered under the home health benefit as either a Part A or Part B service. Durable medical equipment furnished by an HHA as a home health service is always covered by Part A if the beneficiary is entitled to Part A.

(f) Medical supplies. Medical supplies (including catheters, catheter supplies, ostomy bags, and supplies relating to ostomy care but excluding drugs and biologicals) may be covered as a home health benefit. For medical supplies to be covered as a Medicare home health benefit, the medical supplies must be needed to treat the beneficiary's illness or injury that occasioned the home health care.

(g) Intern and resident services. The medical services of interns and residents in training under an approved hospital teaching program are covered if the services are ordered by the physician who is responsible for the plan of care and the HHA is affiliated with or under the common control of the hospital furnishing the medical services.

Approved means—

(1) Approved by the Accreditation Council for Graduate Medical Education;

(2) In the case of an osteopathic hospital, approved by the Committee on Hospitals of the Bureau of Professional Education of the American Osteopathic Association;

(3) In the case of an intern or resident-in-training in the field of dentistry, approved by the Council on Dental Education of the American Dental Association; or

(4) In the case of an intern or resident-in-training in the field of podiatry, approved by the Council on Podiatric Medical Education of the American Podiatric Medical Association.

[59 FR 65495, Dec. 20, 1994; 60 FR 39122, 39123, Aug. 1, 1995]

APPENDIX 4-7 HOME HEALTH ADVANCE BENEFICIARY NOTICE (HHABN)*

Form Instructions—Advance Beneficiary Notice of Noncoverage (ABN) OMB Approval Number: 0938-0566

Overview

The ABN is a notice given to beneficiaries in Original Medicare to convey that Medicare is not likely to provide coverage in a specific case. "Notifiers" include physicians, providers (including institutional providers like outpatient hospitals), practitioners and suppliers paid under Part B (including independent laboratories), as well as hospice providers and religious non-medical health care institutions (RNHCIs) paid exclusively under Part A. Home health agencies (HHAs) have used the HHABN Option Box 1 in the past to inform beneficiaries of liability. With the publication of these instructions, HHAs may now issue the ABN instead of the HHABN Option Box 1. In the near future, the HHABN will be discontinued and replaced with the ABN and a new change of care notice called the Home Health Change of Care Notice (HHCCN). The date for all HHAs to discontinue HHABN use will be published on the CMS website http://www.cms.gov/Medicare/Medicare-General-Information/BNI/HHABN.html and announced via Open Door Forums and Home Health Agency listservs.

All of the aforementioned physicians, suppliers, practitioners, and providers must complete the ABN as described below, and deliver the notice to affected beneficiaries or their representative before providing the items or services that are the subject of the notice. (Note that although Medicare inpatient hospitals use other approved notices for this purpose, skilled nursing facilities (SNFs) must use the revised ABN for Part B items and services.) Since March 1, 2009, the ABN-G and ABN-L are no longer valid; and notifiers must use the revised Advance Beneficiary Notice of Noncoverage (CMS-R-131).

The ABN must be verbally reviewed with the beneficiary or his/her representative and any questions raised during that review must be answered before it is signed. The ABN must be delivered far enough in advance that the beneficiary or representative has time to consider the options and make an informed choice. Employees or subcontractors of the notifier may deliver the ABN. ABNs are never required in emergency or urgent care situations. Once all blanks are completed and the form is signed, a copy is given to the beneficiary or representative. In all cases, the notifier must retain the original notice on file.

* For further information, see CMS "Beneficiary Notices Initiative (BNI)" page at https://www.cms.gov/Medicare/Medicare-General-Information/BNI/index.html?redirect=/BNI (site visited July 28, 2016).

ABN Changes

The ABN is a formal information collection subject to approval by the Executive Office of Management and Budget (OMB) under the Paperwork Reduction Act of 1995 (PRA). As part of this process, the notice is subject to public comment and re-approval every 3 years. The revised ABN included in this package incorporates: suggestions for changes made by notifiers over the past 3 years of use, refinements made to similar liability notices in the same period based on consumer testing and other means, as well as related Medicare policy changes and clarifications occurring in the same interval. We have made additional changes based on suggestions received during the recent public comment period.

This version of the ABN continues to combine the general ABN (ABN-G) and the laboratory ABN (ABN-L) into a single notice, with an identical OMB form number. As combined, however, the new notice will capture the overall improvements incorporated into the revised ABN while still permitting preprinting of the lab-specific key information and denial reasons used in the former ABN-L.

Also, note that while previously the ABN was only required for denial reasons recognized under section 1879 of the Act, the revised version of the ABN may also be used to provide voluntary notification of financial liability.

Instructions for completion of the form are set forth below. Once the new ABN approval process is completed, CMS will issue detailed instructions on the use of the ABN in Pub. 100-04 Medicare Claims Processing Manual, chapter 30, section 50. Related policy on billing and coding of claims, as well as coverage determinations, is found elsewhere in the CMS manual system or website (www.cms.hhs.gov).

Completing the Notice

OMB-approved ABNs are placed on the CMS website at: *http://www.cms.gov/Medicare/Medicare-General-Information/BNI/ABN.html.* Notices placed on this site can be downloaded and should be used as is, as the ABN is a standardized OMB-approved notice. However, some allowance for customization of format is allowed as mentioned for those choosing to integrate the ABN into other automated business processes.

ABNs must be reproduced on a single page. The page may be either letter or legal-size, with additional space allowed for each blank needing completion when a legal-size page is used.

Sections and Blanks:

There are 10 blanks for completion in this notice, labeled from (A) through (J), with accompanying instructions for each blank below. We recommend that the labels for the blanks be removed before use. Blanks (A)-(F) and blank (H) may be completed prior to delivering the notice, as appropriate. Entries in the blanks may be typed or hand-written, but should be large enough (i.e., approximately 12-point font) to allow ease in reading. (Note that 10 point font can be used in blanks when detailed information must be given and is otherwise difficult to fit in the allowed space.) The notifier must also insert the blank (D) header information into the blanks labeled (D) within the Option Box, Blank (G). The check boxes in the Option Box, Blank (G), must be completed by the beneficiary or his/her representative. Blank (I) should be a cursive signature, with printed annotation if needed in order to be understood.

A. Header

Blanks A-C, the header of the notice, must be completed by the notifier prior to delivering the ABN.

Blank (A) Notifier(s): Notifiers must place their name, address, and telephone number (including TTY number when needed) at the top of the notice. This information may be incorporated into a notifier's logo at the top of the notice by typing, hand-writing, pre-printing, using a label or other means.

If the billing and notifying entities are not the same, the name of more than one entity may be given in the Header as long as it is specified in the Additional Information (H) section who should be contacted for questions.

Blank (B) Patient Name: Notifiers must enter the first and last name of the beneficiary receiving the notice, and a middle initial should also be used if there is one on the beneficiary's Medicare (HICN) card. The ABN will not be invalidated by a misspelling or missing initial, as long as the beneficiary or representative recognizes the name listed on the notice as that of the beneficiary.

Blank (C) Identification Number: Use of this field is optional.Notifiers may enter an identification number for the beneficiary that helps to link the notice with a related claim. The absence of an identification number does not invalidate the ABN. An internal filing number created by the notifier, such as a medical record number, may be used. Medicare numbers (HICNs) or Social Security numbers **must not** appear on the notice.

B. Body

Blank (D): The following descriptors may be used in the header of Blank (D):

- Item
- Service
- Laboratory test
- Test
- Procedure
- Care
- Equipment

- The notifier must list the specific items or services believed to be noncovered under the header of Blank (D).
- In the case of partial denials, notifiers must list in Blank (D) the excess component(s) of the item or service for which denial is expected.
- For repetitive or continuous noncovered care, notifiers must specify the frequency and/or duration of the item or service. See § 50.14.3 for additional information.
- General descriptions of specifically grouped supplies are permitted. For example, "wound care supplies" would be a sufficient description of a group of items used to provide this care. An itemized list of each supply is generally not required.
- When a reduction in service occurs, notifiers must provide enough additional information so that the beneficiary understands the nature of the reduction. For example, entering "wound care supplies decreased from weekly to monthly" would be appropriate to describe a decrease in frequency for this category of supplies; just writing "wound care supplies decreased" is insufficient.

Blank (E) Reason Medicare May Not Pay: In this blank, notifiers must explain, in beneficiary friendly language, why they believe the items or services described in Blank (D) may not be covered by Medicare. Three commonly used reasons for noncoverage are:

- "Medicare does not pay for this test for your condition."
- "Medicare does not pay for this test as often as this (denied as too frequent)."
- "Medicare does not pay for experimental or research use tests."

To be a valid ABN, there must be at least one reason applicable to each item or service listed in Blank (D). The same reason for noncoverage may be applied to multiple items in Blank (D).

Blank (F) Estimated Cost: Notifiers must complete Blank (F) to ensure the beneficiary has all available information to make an informed decision about whether or not to obtain potentially noncovered services.

Notifiers must make a good faith effort to insert a reasonable estimate for all of the items or services listed in Blank (D). In general, we would expect that the estimate should be within $100 or 25% of the actual costs, whichever is greater; however, an estimate that exceeds the actual cost substantially would generally still be acceptable, since the beneficiary would not be harmed if the actual costs were less than predicted. Thus, examples of acceptable estimates would include, but not be limited to, the following:

For a service that costs $250:

- Any dollar estimate equal to or greater than $150
- "Between $150-300"
- "No more than $500"

For a service that costs $500:

- Any dollar estimate equal to or greater than $375
- "Between $400-600"
- "No more than $700"

Multiple items or services that are routinely grouped can be bundled into a single cost estimate. For example, a single cost estimate can be given for a group of laboratory tests, such as a basic metabolic panel (BMP). Average daily cost estimates are also permissible for long term or complex projections. As noted above, providers may also pre-print a menu of items or services in Blank (D) and include a cost estimate alongside each item or service. If a situation involves the possibility of additional tests or procedures (such as in reflex testing), and the costs associated with such tests cannot be reasonably estimated by the notifier at the time of ABN delivery, the notifier may enter the initial cost estimate and indicate the possibility of further testing. Finally, if for some reason the notifier is unable to provide a good faith estimate of projected costs at the time of ABN delivery, the notifier may indicate in the cost estimate area that no cost estimate is available. We would not expect either of these last two scenarios to be routine or frequent practices, but the beneficiary would have the option of signing the ABN and accepting liability in these situations.

CMS will work with its contractors to ensure consistency when evaluating cost estimates and determining validity of the ABN in general. In addition, contractors will provide ongoing education to notifiers as needed to ensure proper notice delivery. Notifiers should contact the appropriate CMS regional office if they believe that a contractor inappropriately invalidated an ABN.

C. Options

Blank (G) Options: Blank (G) contains the following three options:

☐ **OPTION 1.** I want the (D) listed above. You may ask to be paid now, but I also want Medicare billed for an official decision on payment, which is sent to me on a Medicare Summary Notice (MSN). I understand that if Medicare doesn't pay, I am responsible for payment, but **I can appeal to Medicare** by following the directions on the MSN. If Medicare does pay, you will refund any payments I made to you, less co-pays or deductibles.

This option allows the beneficiary to receive the items and/or services at issue and requires the notifier to submit a claim to Medicare. This will result in a payment decision that can be appealed. *See Ch. 30, § 50.15.1 of the online Medicare Claims Processing Manual for instructions on the notifier's obligation to bill Medicare.*

Note: Beneficiaries who need to obtain an official Medicare decision in order to file a claim with a secondary insurance should choose Option 1.

☐ **OPTION 2.** I want the (D) listed above, but do not bill Medicare. You may ask to be paid now as I am responsible for payment. **I cannot appeal if Medicare is not billed.**

This option allows the beneficiary to receive the noncovered items and/or services and pay for them out of pocket. No claim will be filed and Medicare will not be billed. Thus, there are no appeal rights associated with this option.

☐ **OPTION 3.** I don't want the (D) listed above. I understand with this choice I am not responsible for payment, and I cannot appeal to see if Medicare would pay.

This option means the beneficiary does not want the care in question. By checking this box, the beneficiary understands that no additional care will be provided and thus, there are no appeal rights associated with this option.

The beneficiary or his or her representative must choose only one of the three options listed in Blank (G). Under no circumstances can the notifier decide for the beneficiary which of the 3 checkboxes to select. Pre-selection of an option by the notifier invalidates the notice. However, at the beneficiary's request, notifiers may enter the beneficiary's selection if he or she is physically unable to do so. In such cases, notifiers must annotate the notice accordingly.

If there are multiple items or services listed in Blank (D) and the beneficiary wants to receive some, but not all of the items or services, the notifier can accommodate this request by using more than one ABN. The notifier can furnish an additional ABN listing the items/services the beneficiary wishes to receive with the corresponding option.

If the beneficiary cannot or will not make a choice, the notice should be annotated, for example: "beneficiary refused to choose an option".

D. Additional Information

Blank (H) Additional Information: Notifiers may use this space to provide additional clarification that they believe will be of use to beneficiaries. For example, notifiers may use this space to include:

- A statement advising the beneficiary to notify his or her provider about certain tests that were ordered, but not received;
- Information on other insurance coverage for beneficiaries, such as a Medigap policy, if applicable;

- An additional dated witness signature; or
- Other necessary annotations.

Annotations will be assumed to have been made on the same date as that appearing in Blank J, accompanying the signature. If annotations are made on different dates, those dates should be part of the annotations.

E. Signature Box

Once the beneficiary reviews and understands the information contained in the ABN, the Signature Box is to be completed by the beneficiary (or representative). This box cannot be completed in advance of the rest of the notice.

Blank (I) Signature: The beneficiary (or representative) must sign the notice to indicate that he or she has received the notice and understands its contents. If a representative signs on behalf of a beneficiary, he or she should write out "representative" in parentheses after his or her signature. The representative's name should be clearly legible or noted in print.

Blank (J) Date: The beneficiary (or representative) must write the date he or she signed the ABN. If the beneficiary has physical difficulty with writing and requests assistance in completing this blank, the date may be inserted by the notifier.

Disclosure Statement: The disclosure statement in the footer of the notice is required to be included on the document.

CHAPTER 5

HOSPICE COVERAGE

§ 5.01 INTRODUCTION

Medicare covers hospice care[1] for beneficiaries diagnosed as terminally ill. Terminally ill means the individual has a medical prognosis that his or her life expectancy is six months or less if the illness runs its normal course.[2] Hospice care is a comprehensive set of services identified and coordinated by an interdisciplinary group to provide for the physical, psychosocial, spiritual, and emotional needs of a terminally ill patient and the patient's family members.[3]

The hospice benefit is different from all other Medicare benefits in that it does not provide for the curative treatment of illness or injury;[4] rather, it is designed for the palliation and management of terminal illness.[5] Palliative care is defined as patient and family centered care that optimizes quality of life by anticipating, preventing, and treating suffering. Throughout the continuum of illness, it involves addressing physical, intellectual, emotional, social, and spiritual needs and facilitates patient autonomy, access to information, and choice.[6]

Medicare-covered hospice care must be provided by a Medicare-certified hospice provider. The hospice provider must comply with Medicare's conditions of participation.[7] Hospice care should "allow the patient to remain at home as long as possible by providing support to the patient and family, and by keeping the patient as comfortable as possible while maintaining his or her dignity and quality of life."[8]

One can receive covered hospice care under Medicare only after specifically opting into the hospice benefit, thereby opting out of eligibility for Medicare coverage for other medical care and services related to the terminal illness. Electing hospice care, however, does *not* mean that all curative treatment is waived. Beneficiaries who elect the Medicare hospice benefit may still receive Medicare coverage for medically reasonable and necessary treatment for diagnoses unrelated to their terminal illness.

§ 5.02 ELIGIBILITY

The Medicare hospice benefit is provided under Part A of the Medicare program. Therefore, in order to be eligible for this benefit, one must be enrolled in Medicare Part A. In addition, prior to receiving Medicare-covered hospice care, the beneficiary must be certified by the hospice physician and the individual's

[1] 42 U.S.C. § 1395x(dd).
[2] 42 C.F.R. § 418.3.
[3] 42 C.F.R. § 418.3.
[4] 42 U.S.C. § 1395y(a)(1)(A).
[5] 42 U.S.C. § 1395y(a)(1)(C).
[6] 42 C.F.R. § 418.3.
[7] 42 C.F.R. §§ 418.52–418.116.
[8] 73 Fed. Reg. 32,088 (June 5, 2008).

attending physician (if different than the hospice physician) as terminally ill.[9] The certification is based on the physician's clinical judgment regarding the normal course of the individual's illness.[10] The certification must specify that the individual's prognosis is for a life expectancy of six months or less if the terminal illness runs its normal course.[11] Nurse practitioners can act as attending physicians but they cannot certify or recertify terminal diagnosis and prognosis. In the event that a nurse practitioner is the beneficiary's attending physician, the hospice medical director or physician designee must certify or recertify the beneficiary's limited life expectancy.[12]

The certifying physician must include a brief narrative explanation of the clinical findings that support a life expectancy of six months or less as part of the certification and recertification forms or as an addendum to the certification and recertification forms.[13] Clinical information and other documentation that support the medical prognosis must be filed in the medical record with the written certification.[14] The clinical information will be part of the hospice provider's eligibility assessment for the patient.[15] The certification is filed with the hospice provider.[16]

---

[9] 42 C.F.R. § 418.22(c):

> *Sources of certification.* (1) For the initial 90-day period, the hospice must obtain written certification statements . . . from (i) [t]he medical director of the hospice or the physician member of the hospice interdisciplinary group; and (ii) [t]he individual's attending physician if the individual has an attending physician. . . . (2) For subsequent periods, the only requirement is certification by one of the physicians listed in paragraph(c)(1)(i) of this section.

[10] If a Medicare beneficiary is terminally ill and has not yet elected the hospice benefit, Medicare will pay for a consultation visit with the hospice medical director or physicians who are employees of a hospice program. During this visit, the physician may evaluate the individual's need for pain and symptom management, counsel the individual with respect to end-of-life issues and care options, and advise the individual regarding advanced care planning. Hospices receive payment for this service that is equal to the amount established for an office or other outpatient visit for evaluation and management associated with presenting problems of moderate severity under the established Medicare physician fee schedule other than the portion of the amount attributable to the practice expense component. The physician, if not a volunteer, will be paid by the hospice. Medicare Benefit Policy (MBP) Manual, Ch. 9, §§ 80–80.2.

[11] 42 C.F.R. § 418.22(b)(1). *See also* MBP Manual, Ch. 9, *available at* http://www.cms.gov/Regulations-and-Guidance/Guidance/Manuals/Downloads/bp102c09.pdf (site visited May 25, 2016).

[12] MBPM, Ch. 9, § 40.1.3.2.

[13] 42 C.F.R. § 418.22(b)(3).

[14] 42 C.F.R. § 418.22(b)(2).

[15] 42 C.F.R. § 418.22(b)(2).

[16] 42 C.F.R. § 418.22.

§ 5.03 ELECTION OF THE HOSPICE BENEFIT

An election to receive hospice care is made by filing an election statement with a hospice provider of choice.[17] An election statement may be filed by either the beneficiary or his or her legal representative.[18] Once a beneficiary elects the hospice benefit, he or she waives all rights to Medicare payment for services that are *related to the treatment of the terminal condition* or a related condition, except for services provided by the designated hospice or by another provider under arrangements made by the designated hospice, or by the individual's attending physician.[19]

The election statement itself must:

- Identify the designated hospice provider and the attending physician;[20]
- Contain an acknowledgement that:
  - — the attending physician is his or her chosen physician;
  - — he or she has a full understanding of the palliative rather than the curative nature of hospice care as it relates to the individual's terminal illness;
  - — he or she is waiving Medicare coverage for: hospice care provided by another hospice provider and for any services related to the treatment of the terminal condition for which hospice care was elected or a related condition except for care and services provided by or under arrangement with the designated hospice or provided by the beneficiary's attending physician;[21]

---

[17] 42 C.F.R. § 418.24.

[18] 42 C.F.R. § 418.24.

[19] This is only the case if the attending physician is not an employee of the designated hospice or receiving compensation from the hospice for the provided services. 42 C.F.R. § 418.24(d)(2)(iii). Furthermore, the Medicare Hospice Manual limits such services to the personal professional services of the attending physician. In other words, the costs for services such as labs or X-rays must be provided under arrangements with the hospice and will not be reimbursed by Medicare if independently ordered by the attending physician. Medicare Claims Processing (MCP) Manual, CMS Pub. 100-04, Ch. 11, § 40.1.3.

[20] This information should include, but is not limited to, the attending physician's full name, office address, NPI number, or any other detailed information to clearly identify the attending physician. MBP Manual, Ch. 9, § 20.2.1, *available at* http://www.cms.gov/Regulations-and-Guidance/Guidance/Manuals/Downloads/bp102c09.pdf (site visited May 25, 2016).

[21] Prompt filing of the hospice Notice of Election (NOE) with the Medicare contractor is required to properly enforce this waiver and prevent inappropriate payments to non-hospice providers. The effective date of hospice election is the same as the hospice admission date. A timely-filed NOE is one that is submitted to and accepted by the Medicare contractor within 5 calendar days after the hospice election. MBP Manual, Ch. 9, § 20.2.1.1.

- State the effective date of the election[22] and
- Be signed by the beneficiary or his or her representative.[23]

An individual may elect to receive hospice care during one or more of the following election periods: an initial 90-day period, a subsequent 90-day period, or an unlimited number of subsequent 60-day periods.[24] At the start of the first period, a hospice physician and the beneficiary's attending physician must certify in writing that the beneficiary is terminally ill.[25] For subsequent periods, only a hospice physician must certify the beneficiary as terminally ill.[26]

A hospice election will continue through the initial election period and through the subsequent election periods without a break in care, as long as the individual remains in the care of the hospice program, does not revoke the election, and is not discharged from the hospice.[27] Prior to each new election period, a hospice physician[28] must review the patient's clinical information[29] and, if hospice care remains appropriate, recertify in writing that the beneficiary continues to be terminally ill.[30] Hospice election periods are also called benefit periods.

Prior to the third benefit period, and for all subsequent benefit periods, a hospice physician or nurse practitioner must have a face to face encounter with the hospice patient to determine continued eligibility for Medicare coverage of hospice care.[31] Additionally, if a hospice provider is deemed to have a high percentage of patients who remain on hospice care longer than 180 days (the specific percentage is to be specified by the Secretary), the Secretary will review the medical merits of all care exceeding 180 days.[32]

---

[22] 42 C.F.R. § 418.24(b)(4).

[23] 42 C.F.R. § 418.24(b)(5).

[24] 42 C.F.R. § 418.21.

[25] 42 C.F.R. § 418.22(c)(1). *See also* MBP Manual, Ch. 9, § 20.1, *available at* http://www.cms.gov/Regulations-and-Guidance/Guidance/Manuals/Downloads/bp102c09.pdf (site visited May 25, 2016).

[26] 42 C.F.R. § 418.22(c)(2).

> *Sources of certification.* (1) For the initial 90-day period, the hospice must obtain written certification statements . . . from (i) The medical director of the hospice or the physician member of the hospice interdisciplinary group; and (ii) The individual's attending physician if the individual has an attending physician. (2) For subsequent periods, the only requirement is certification by one of the physicians listed in paragraph(c)(1)(i) of this section.

[27] 42 C.F.R. § 418.24(c).

[28] 42 C.F.R. § 418.22(c)(2).

[29] 42 C.F.R. § 418.102(c).

[30] 42 C.F.R. § 418.22(c)(2). *See also* **§ 5.02** of this Handbook.

[31] 42 C.F.R. § 418.22(a)(4). *See also* MBP Manual, Ch. 9, §§ 20.1.5 and 40.1.3.2 ("Hospice nurse practitioners [employed by the hospice] may conduct face-to-face encounters . . . as part of the certification process, but are still prohibited by statute from certifying the terminal illness.").

[32] ACA § 3132.

Because exceptional circumstances will sometimes make it impossible for providers to have face to face encounters prior to hospice admissions, the Centers for Medicare & Medicaid Services (CMS) has appropriately created the following policy:

> In cases where a hospice newly admits a patient who is in the third or later benefit period, exceptional circumstances may prevent a face to face encounter prior to the start of the benefit period. For example, if the patient is an emergency weekend admission, it may be impossible for a hospice physician or [nurse practitioner] to see the patient until the following Monday. Or, if CMS data systems are unavailable, the hospice may be unaware that the patient is in the third benefit period. In such documented cases, a face to face encounter which occurs within 2 days after admission will be considered to be timely. Additionally, for such documented exceptional cases, if the patient dies within 2 days of admission without a face to face encounter, a face to face encounter can be deemed as complete.[33]

§ 5.04 WHO MAY MAKE AN ELECTION FOR HOSPICE CARE

Medicare beneficiaries may elect hospice care for palliative treatment of a terminal illness.[34] Problems may arise when a person lacks the mental capacity to make an election. Under this circumstance, a representative may make the election. A representative is an individual who has the authority under state law (whether by statute or pursuant to an appointment by the courts of the state) to authorize or terminate medical care or to elect or revoke the election of hospice care on behalf of a terminally ill patient who is mentally or physically incapacitated. This may include a legal guardian.[35]

§ 5.05 HOSPICE ADMISSION

The hospice provider admits a patient only on the recommendation of the hospice medical director in consultation with, or input from, the patient's attending physician.[36] In reaching a decision to certify that the patient is terminally ill, the hospice medical director must consider at least the following information: diagnosis of the terminal condition of the patient; other health conditions, whether related or unrelated to the terminal condition; and current clinically relevant information supporting all diagnoses.[37]

---

[33] MBPM, Ch. 9, § 20.1.5.d (Face-to-face encounter), *available at* http://www.cms.gov/Regulations-and-Guidance/Guidance/Manuals/Downloads/bp102c09.pdf (site visited May 25, 2016).

[34] 42 C.F.R. § 418.24(b)(2).

[35] 42 C.F.R. § 418.3.

[36] 42 C.F.R. § 418.25(a).

[37] 42 C.F.R. § 418.25(b).

The hospice admission date is the first day of the benefit period, except in the case of transfers. The admission date may not precede the physician's certification date by more than two calendar days. If a new hospice admission occurs following a hospice discharge or revocation that resulted in the termination of the hospice benefit, the admission date cannot be the same as the revocation or discharge date.[38]

§ 5.06 MEDICARE ADVANTAGE

Medicare Advantage organizations must inform enrollees who are eligible for hospice care about the available Medicare hospice providers in their community.[39] Once the beneficiary elects the hospice benefit, the hospice provider will bill Medicare Part A (Medicare fee-for-service) for the beneficiary's hospice care. In other words, traditional Medicare, rather than the Medicare Advantage plan, will pay the provider for the hospice care. Also of note, if during a hospice benefit period, the beneficiary receives care from providers for care unrelated to the terminal illness, those providers will also bill traditional Medicare (Part A or B) for the care in question. While the beneficiary is on hospice, he or she is responsible for Part A and Part B cost-sharing. If the beneficiary revokes the hospice election or is discharged from hospice care, the Medicare Advantage organization will become responsible for the beneficiary's health care costs on the first day of the month after the revocation or discharge.[40]

§ 5.07 PATIENT RIGHTS

During the initial assessment visit in advance of furnishing care, the hospice provider must give the patient or representative oral and written notice of the patient's rights and responsibilities in a language and manner that the patient understands.[41] Additionally, the hospice provider must inform and distribute information concerning its policies on advance directives, including a description of applicable state law.[42] Hospice providers cannot deny care because a beneficiary has not formulated an advance directive.[43] The hospice provider must obtain

---

[38] MBPM, Ch. 9, § 20.1.2, Completing the Uniform (Institutional Provider) Bill (Form CMS-1450) for Hospice Election, Rev. 3326 (Aug. 14, 2015).

[39] 42 C.F.R. § 422.320.

[40] 42 C.F.R. §§ 417.585 and 417.531. *See also* MCP Manual, Ch. 11, § 30.4 and MBP Manual, Ch. 9, § 20.4. As the beneficiary will not have a Medigap or equivalent policy, there may be significant out-of-pocket expense for non-hospice care.

[41] 42 C.F.R. § 418.52(a)(1).

[42] 42 C.F.R. § 418.52(a)(2).

[43] 42 C.F.R. § 418.52(a)(2). *See also* 73 Fed. Reg. 32,088, 32,097 (June 5, 2008) ("Under this final rule, hospices are required to comply with 42 C.F.R. part 489 Subpart I, 'Advance directives.'

the patient's or representative's signature confirming that he or she received a copy of the notice of rights and responsibilities.[44]

[A] Hospice Patient Rights

Each hospice patient has the following rights:[45]

- To exercise his or her rights as a patient of the hospice;
- To have his or her property and person treated with respect;
- To voice grievances regarding treatment or care that is (or fails to be) furnished and the lack of respect for property by anyone who is furnishing services on behalf of the hospice;
- To be free from discrimination or reprisal for exercising his or her rights;[46]
- To receive effective pain management and symptom control from the hospice for conditions related to the terminal illness;
- To be involved in developing his or her hospice plan of care;
- To refuse care or treatment;
- To choose his or her attending physician;[47]
- To have a confidential clinical record (and access to that record);
- To be free from mistreatment, neglect, or verbal, mental, sexual, and physical abuse, including injuries of unknown source, and misappropriation of patient property;

Patients may choose to develop advance directives in accordance with applicable State requirements. Likewise, they may choose to not formulate advance directives.").

[44] 42 C.F.R. § 418.52(b)(1).

[45] If a patient has been adjudicated incompetent under state law by a court of proper jurisdiction, the rights of the patient are exercised by the person appointed pursuant to state law to act on the patient's behalf. If a state court has not adjudged a patient incompetent, any legal representative designated by the patient in accordance with state law may exercise the patient's rights to the extent allowed by state law. 42 C.F.R. § 418.52(b)(2) and (3).

[46] 42 C.F.R. § 418.52(b)(1).

[47] Medicare Prescription Drug, Improvement, and Modernization Act of 2003, Pub. L. No. 108-173 (Dec. 8, 2003), 117 Stat. 2066, *available at* http://www.gpo.gov/fdsys/pkg/PLAW-108publ173/pdf/PLAW-108publ173.pdf (site visited May 25, 2016). Section 408 authorized Medicare payments for the services of a nurse practitioner chosen by the beneficiary instead of a physician as having the most significant role in the determination and delivery of the beneficiary's medical care. The nurse is not authorized to certify the beneficiary as terminally ill but is able to review hospice plans of care. *See* MBP Manual, Ch. 9, § 40.1.3.2, *available at* http://www.cms.gov/Regulations-and-Guidance/Guidance/Manuals/Downloads/bp102c09.pdf (site visited May 25, 2016).

- To receive information about the services covered under the hospice benefit; and
- To receive information about the scope of services that the hospice will provide and specific limitations on those services.[48]

[B] Hospice Requirements

Each hospice must:[49]

- Ensure that all alleged violations involving mistreatment, neglect, or verbal, mental, sexual, and physical abuse, including injuries of unknown source, and misappropriation of patient property, are reported immediately by hospice employees and contracted staff to the hospice administrator;
- Immediately investigate all alleged violations involving anyone furnishing services on behalf of the hospice and immediately take action to prevent further potential violations while the alleged violation is being verified. Investigations and/or documentation of all alleged violations must be conducted in accordance with established procedures;
- Take appropriate corrective action in accordance with state law if the alleged violation is verified by the hospice administrator or an outside body having jurisdiction, such as the state survey agency or local law enforcement agency; and
- Ensure that the verified violations are reported to state and local bodies having jurisdiction (including to the state survey and certification agency) within five working days of becoming aware of the violation.

§ 5.08 HOSPICE REVOCATION

An individual or legal representative may revoke the election of hospice care at any time during an election period.[50] To revoke the election, the individual or legal representative must file a statement with the hospice provider that includes the following information:[51]

- The signature of the beneficiary or legal representative; and
- The date of revocation (which cannot be earlier than the date upon which the revocation is made).

---

[48] 42 C.F.R. § 418.52(c).

[49] 42 C.F.R. § 418.52(b)(4).

[50] 42 C.F.R. § 418.28(a).

[51] 42 C.F.R. § 418.28(b)(2).

Upon revocation, the beneficiary is no longer covered under Medicare for hospice care,[52] resumes Medicare coverage for benefits previously waived,[53] and may, at any time, elect to receive hospice coverage for any other hospice election periods that he or she is eligible to receive.[54]

§ 5.09 HOSPICE DISCHARGE

A hospice provider may discharge a patient if the patient moves out of the provider's service area or transfers to another provider,[55] the hospice provider determines that the patient is no longer terminally ill, or for cause if the hospice provider determines that the behavior of the patient or another person in the patient's home is disruptive, abusive, or uncooperative to the extent that delivery of care to the patient or the ability of the hospice provider to operate effectively is seriously impaired.[56]

There are no appeal rights available to beneficiaries who are discharged from hospice for cause. However, pursuant to the regulations, prior to such a discharge, the hospice provider must:[57]

- Advise the patient that a discharge for cause is being considered;
- Make a serious effort to resolve the problem(s) presented by the patient's behavior or situation;
- Ascertain that the patient's proposed discharge is not due to the patient's use of necessary hospice services; and
- Document the problem(s) and efforts made to resolve the problem(s) and enter this documentation into its medical record.
- Notify the Medicare contractor and State Survey Agency of the circumstances surrounding the impending discharge. The hospice provider may need to make referrals to other relevant state or community agencies (i.e., adult protective services) as appropriate.

Prior to discharging a patient for reasons other than revocation or transfer, the hospice must obtain a written physician's discharge order from the hospice

[52] 42 C.F.R. § 418.28(c)(1).

[53] 42 C.F.R. § 418.28(c)(2).

[54] 42 C.F.R. § 418.28(c)(3).

[55] A change of ownership of a hospice is not considered a change in the patient's designation of a hospice and requires no action on the patient's part. MBP Manual, Ch. 9, § 20.2.1.

[56] 42 C.F.R. § 418.26(a).

[57] 42 C.F.R. § 418.26(a). *See also* MBP Manual, Ch. 9, § 20.2.1 and § 20.2.3, *available at* http://www.cms.gov/Regulations-and-Guidance/Guidance/Manuals/Downloads/bp102c09.pdf (site visited May 25, 2016).

medical director.[58] If a patient has an attending physician involved in his or her care, this physician should be consulted before discharge and his or her review and decision included in the discharge note.[59]

An individual, upon discharge from the hospice during a particular election period for reasons other than immediate transfer to another hospice, is no longer covered under Medicare for hospice care, resumes previously waived Medicare coverage[60] and may at any time elect to receive hospice care if he or she is again eligible to receive the benefit.[61]

Hospice providers must have in place a discharge planning process that takes into account the prospect that a patient's condition might stabilize or otherwise change such that the patient cannot continue to be certified as terminally ill.[62] The discharge planning process must include planning for any necessary family counseling, patient education, or other services before the patient is discharged.[63]

If the hospice provider is discharging the patient because the medical director no longer believes the patient is terminally ill, the provider must issue a standardized termination notice.[64] This notice must indicate that Medicare coverage for hospice care is ending, the date coverage ends, the beneficiary's financial liability for continued service, and how to appeal the discharge.[65] This standardized termination notice is the first step in the expedited appeals process, which guarantees Medicare beneficiaries review of their cases within 72 hours of request.[66]

§ 5.10 CHANGING HOSPICE PROVIDERS

A beneficiary may change, once each election period, the designation of the particular hospice provider. The change of the designated hospice provider is not a revocation of the election of hospice benefits. In order to change the designated provider, the beneficiary or representative must file, with both the provider from which the beneficiary has been receiving care, and the new provider from which the beneficiary will be receiving care, a signed statement indicating the name of each provider and the effective date of the change.[67]

---

[58] 42 C.F.R. § 418.26(b).

[59] 42 C.F.R. § 418.26(b).

[60] *See* **§ 5.01** of this Handbook.

[61] 42 C.F.R. § 418.26(c).

[62] 42 C.F.R. § 418.26(d)(1).

[63] 42 C.F.R. § 418.26(d)(2).

[64] 42 C.F.R. § 405.1200.

[65] 42 C.F.R. § 405.1200.

[66] 70 Fed. Reg. 11,419 (Mar. 8, 2005), 42 C.F.R. § 405.1202. *See also* **§ 1.07[A][5]** and **§ 5.15[D]** of this Handbook.

[67] 42 C.F.R. § 418.30.

Note that such a change may be made only once during each election period. If an additional change were desired, the beneficiary would have to revoke the hospice coverage and then reelect hospice coverage using a new election period.

§ 5.11 HOSPICE SERVICES

[A] Interdisciplinary Group

Any hospice services that are to be provided to a Medicare beneficiary must be included in a written plan of care established by the hospice interdisciplinary group.[68] The hospice provider must designate a registered nurse who is a member of the interdisciplinary group to coordinate care and to ensure continuous assessment of each patient's and family's needs and implementation of the interdisciplinary plan of care. The interdisciplinary group must include, but is not limited to, individuals who are qualified and competent to practice in the following professional roles:[69]

- Doctor of medicine or osteopathy (who is an employee or under contract with the hospice);
- Registered nurse;
- Social worker; and
- Pastoral or other counselor.

[B] Hospice Plan of Care

The plan of care must be created in collaboration with the beneficiary's attending physician (if any), the patient or representative, and the primary caregiver in accordance with the patient's needs.[70] The plan of care must account for all services necessary for the palliation and management of the terminal illness and related conditions, including the following:[71]

- Interventions to manage pain and symptoms;
- A detailed statement of the scope and frequency of services necessary to meet the specific patient and family needs;

---

[68] 42 C.F.R. §§ 418.56, 418.58, and 418.68. "The hospice must designate an interdisciplinary group . . . which, in consultation with the patient's attending physician, must prepare a written plan of care. The plan of care must specify the hospice care and services necessary to meet the patient and family-specific needs identified in the comprehensive assessment as such needs relate to the terminal illness and related conditions."

[69] 42 C.F.R. § 418.56(a)(1).

[70] 42 C.F.R. § 418.56(b).

[71] 42 C.F.R. § 418.56(c).

- Measurable outcomes anticipated from implementing and coordinating the plan of care;
- Drugs and treatment necessary to meet the needs of the patient;
- Medical supplies and appliances necessary to meet the needs of the patient; and
- The interdisciplinary group's documentation of the patient's or representative's level of understanding, involvement, and agreement with the plan of care, in accordance with the hospice's own policies.

The plan of care must be reviewed and/or revised as the patient's condition requires, but no less frequently than every 15 calendar days.[72]

[C] Physician Services

The hospice medical director, physician employees, and contracted physician(s) of the hospice provider, in conjunction with the patient's attending physician, are responsible for the palliation and management of the terminal illness and conditions related to the terminal illness.[73]

[D] Nursing Care

The hospice provider must render nursing care and services by or under the supervision of a registered nurse. Nursing services must ensure that the nursing needs of the patient are met as identified in the patient's initial assessment,[74] comprehensive assessment,[75] and updated assessments.[76] Nursing care may be provided on a continuous basis for as much as 24 hours a day *during periods of crisis* as necessary to maintain an individual at home. A period of crisis is one in which the patient requires continuous care to achieve palliation or management of acute medical symptoms.[77]

---

[72] 42 C.F.R. § 418.56(d).

[73] 42 C.F.R. § 418.64(a). *See also* MBP Manual, Ch. 9, § 40.1.3.

[74] Initial assessment is an evaluation of the patient's physical, psychosocial, and emotional status related to the terminal illness and related conditions to determine the patient's immediate care and support needs. 42 C.F.R. § 418.3. The hospice registered nurse must complete an initial assessment within 48 hours after the election of hospice care. 42 C.F.R. § 418.54(a).

[75] Comprehensive assessment is a thorough evaluation of the patient's physical, psychosocial, emotional, and spiritual status related to the terminal illness and related conditions. This includes a thorough evaluation of the caregiver's and family's willingness and capability to take care of the patient. 42 C.F.R. § 418.3. The comprehensive assessment must be completed no later than five days after the election of hospice care. 42 C.F.R. § 418.54(b).

[76] 42 C.F.R. § 418.64(b)(1). *See also* MBP Manual, Ch. 9, § 40.1.1.

[77] 42 C.F.R. § 418.204(a). *See also* MBP Manual, Ch. 9, § 40.2.1.

[E] Medical Social Services

Medical social services must be provided by a qualified social worker, under the direction of a physician. Social work services must be based on the patient's psychosocial assessment and the patient's family's needs and acceptance of these services.[78]

[F] Counseling Services

Counseling services must be available to the patient and family to assist the patient and family in minimizing stress and problems that arise from the terminal illness, related conditions, and the dying process.[79] Counseling services must include, but are not limited to, bereavement counseling, dietary counseling, and spiritual counseling.[80]

[1] Bereavement Counseling

Bereavement counseling is emotional, psychosocial, and spiritual support and services provided before and after the death of a patient to assist with issues related to grief, loss, and adjustment.[81] Though not reimbursed by Medicare, bereavement counseling is a required hospice service.[82] Each Medicare-certified hospice provider must have an organized program for the provision of bereavement services under the supervision of a qualified professional with experience or education in grief or loss counseling.[83] Bereavement services should be made available to family and other affected individuals[84] for up to one year after the death of the patient.[85]

[2] Dietary Counseling

Dietary counseling should be provided when identified in the plan of care as a needed service. When provided, it must be performed by a qualified individual, which might be a dietitian or a nurse. The qualified individual must address and assure that the dietary needs of the patient are met.[86]

---

[78] 42 C.F.R. § 418.64(c).

[79] 42 C.F.R. § 418.64(d).

[80] 42 C.F.R. § 418.64(d). *See also* MBP Manual, Ch. 9, § 40.1.4.

[81] 42 C.F.R. § 418.3.

[82] 42 C.F.R. § 418.204(c).

[83] 42 C.F.R. § 418.64(d)(1)(i).

[84] Bereavement counseling extends to residents of a residential care center when appropriate and identified in the bereavement plan of care. 42 C.F.R. § 418.64(d)(1)(ii).

[85] 42 C.F.R. § 418.64(d)(1)(ii). *See also* MBP Manual, Ch. 9, § 40.2.3.

[86] 42 C.F.R. § 418.64(d)(2).

[3] Spiritual Counseling

Regarding spiritual counseling the hospice must:[87]

- Provide an assessment of the patient's and family's spiritual needs;
- Provide spiritual counseling to meet these needs in accordance with the patient's and family's acceptance of this service, and in a manner consistent with patient and family beliefs and desires;
- Make all reasonable efforts to facilitate visits by local clergy, pastoral counselors, or other individuals who can support the patient's spiritual needs; and
- Advise the patient and family of this service.

[G] Physical Therapy, Occupational Therapy, and Speech-Language Pathology

Physical therapy, occupational therapy, and speech-language pathology services must be available to hospice patients and, when provided, offered in a manner consistent with accepted standards of practice.[88]

[H] Hospice Aide and Homemaker Services

[1] Hospice Aides

Hospice aide training and supervision requirements are extensive and are described in the conditions of participation.[89] Hospice aides are assigned to a specific patient by a registered nurse who is a member of the interdisciplinary group.[90] The hospice aide provides services that are:[91]

- Ordered by the interdisciplinary group;
- Included in the plan of care;
- Permitted to be performed under state law by such hospice aide; and
- Consistent with the hospice aide training.

---

[87] 42 C.F.R. § 418.64(d)(3).

[88] 42 C.F.R. § 418.72. *See also* MBP Manual, Ch. 9, § 40.1.8.

[89] 42 C.F.R. § 418.76.

[90] 42 C.F.R. § 418.76(g).

[91] 42 C.F.R. § 418.76(g)(2).

The duties of the hospice aide include, but are not limited to:[92]

- Provision of hands-on personal care;
- Performance of simple procedures as an extension of therapy or nursing services;
- Assistance in ambulation or exercises; and
- Assistance in administering medications that are ordinarily self-administered.

Hospice aides must report changes in the patient's medical, nursing, rehabilitative, and social needs to a registered nurse, as the changes relate to the plan of care and quality assessment and improvement activities. Hospice aides must also complete the appropriate records in compliance with the hospice's policies and procedures.[93]

[2] Hospice Homemakers

Homemaker services must be provided by individuals who have successfully completed a hospice orientation addressing the needs and concerns of patients and families coping with a terminal illness.[94] Homemaker services must be coordinated and supervised by a member of the interdisciplinary group.[95] Instructions for homemaker duties must be prepared by a member of the interdisciplinary group.[96] Homemakers must report all concerns about the patient or family to the member of the interdisciplinary group who is coordinating homemaker services.[97]

[3] Hospice Interface with Medicaid Waiver Program

Section 1915(c) of the Social Security Act permits the Secretary of Health and Human Services (HHS) to waive Medicaid requirements in order to allow states to use Medicaid money to pay for the delivery of long-term services within community settings. The provisions waived are Section 1902(a)(1) (requirement that provisions be statewide), Section 1902(a)(10)(B) (requirement that services be comparable), and Section 1902(a)(10)(C)(i)(III) (regarding income and resource applicable in the community). Thus, Section 1915(c) waivers permit

---

[92] 42 C.F.R. § 418.76(g)(3).
[93] 42 C.F.R. § 418.76(g)(4). *See also* MBP Manual, Ch. 9, § 40.1.7.
[94] 42 C.F.R. § 418.76(j)(1).
[95] 42 C.F.R. § 418.76(k)(1).
[96] 42 C.F.R. § 418.76(k)(2).
[97] 42 C.F.R. § 418.76(k)(3). *See also* MBP Manual, Ch. 9, § 40.1.7.

states to target waivers to particular areas of the state, for instance, where the need is greatest. States are also able to make waiver services available only to certain people, such as those at risk of institutionalization, or to people with particular diseases. And finally, states are permitted to provide Medicaid to individuals in the community who otherwise would have been eligible had they been institutionalized.

Medicare beneficiaries who receive personal care services under a Medicaid Waiver Program may continue to receive those benefits after they have elected the hospice benefit.[98] Services under the Medicaid personal care benefit may be used to the extent that the hospice provider would routinely use the services of a hospice patient's family in implementing a patient's plan of care.[99] The hospice must coordinate its hospice aide and homemaker services with the Medicaid personal care benefit to ensure the patient receives the hospice aide and homemaker services he or she needs.[100]

[I] Volunteer Services

For each Medicare certified hospice program, volunteers must provide day-to-day administrative and/or direct patient care services in an amount that, at a minimum, equals 5 percent of all paid hospice employees and contract staff.[101]

[J] Medical Supplies and Durable Medical Equipment

Medical supplies and appliances and durable medical equipment (DME) related to the palliation and management of the terminal illness and related conditions must be provided by the hospice while the patient is under hospice care.[102] Medical supplies and appliances include things such as colostomy bags and supplies directly related to colostomy care.[103] DME includes items such as hospital beds and wheelchairs.[104]

[K] Drugs and Biologicals

Drugs and biologicals related to the palliation and management of the terminal condition and related conditions, as identified in the hospice plan of care,

---

[98] 42 C.F.R. § 418.76(i).
[99] 42 C.F.R. § 418.76(i)(2).
[100] 42 C.F.R. § 418.76(i)(3).
[101] 42 C.F.R. § 418.78.
[102] 42 C.F.R. § 418.106.
[103] 42 C.F.R. § 410.36.
[104] 42 C.F.R. § 410.38.

must be provided by the hospice while the patient is under hospice care.[105] A hospice provider may use chemotherapy, radiation therapy, and other modalities for palliative purposes if it determines that these services are needed.[106]

For each medication provided while the beneficiary is not an inpatient (general inpatient or respite care), the hospice program may charge the beneficiary a coinsurance payment.[107] This coinsurance cannot exceed $5.00.[108]

The hospice provider must ensure that the interdisciplinary group confers with an individual with education and training in drug management as defined in hospice policies and procedures and state law, who is an employee of or under contract with the hospice, to ensure that drugs and biologicals meet each patient's needs.[109]

The Medicare Prescription Drug,[110] Improvement, and Modernization Act of 2003[111] added prescription drug coverage as a Medicare benefit. If a hospice patient signed up for a Part D plan,[112] then whether the hospice, Medicare Part B, the beneficiary's Part D plan, or the beneficiary is responsible for paying for the hospice patient's medications will depend on the medication's purpose.

Palliative medications related to the hospice patient's terminal illness should be paid for by the beneficiary's hospice provider.[113] Curative medications related to the patient's terminal illness will not be paid for by the hospice provider, Medicare Part B, or the beneficiary's Medicare Part D plan.[114] Medications prescribed for the treatment of illness not related to the patient's terminal illness should be billed to Part B, when they are Part B medications (incident to a physician's visit);[115] when they are not Part B medications, they should be billed to the patient's Part D plan.[116] If the patient receives Medicare covered inpatient care for a condition not related to his or her terminal illness, then the medications that he or she receives in the inpatient facility that are not related to the terminal illness will be covered under the Medicare Part A benefit for hospital[117] or SNF

[105] 42 C.F.R. § 418.106.

[106] MBP Manual, Ch. 9, § 40.2.4.

[107] 42 C.F.R. § 418.400.

[108] 42 C.F.R. § 418.400(a).

[109] 42 C.F.R. § 418.106.

[110] *See* **Chapter 11** of this Handbook.

[111] Pub. L. No. 108-173 (Dec. 8, 2003), 117 Stat. 2066.

[112] *See* **§ 11.01** of this Handbook.

[113] *See* **§ 5.11[B]** of this Handbook.

[114] *See* **§ 5.01** of this Handbook.

[115] *See* **§ 6.03[A]** of this Handbook.

[116] *See* **§ 11.04** of this Handbook.

[117] *See* **§ 2.06[C]** of this Handbook.

care.[118] The medications that are related to the terminal illness should continue to be paid for by the hospice provider.

In June 2012, the Health and Human Services Office of Inspector General (OIG) issued a report suggesting that Part D plans were frequently paying for hospice medications.[119] In 2014, CMS issued a memorandum directing Part D plans to seek prior authorization after a beneficiary elects hospice care, for analgesics, antiemetics, laxatives, and anxiolytics (used to treat anxiety), because these medications are usually related to an individual's terminal condition.[120]

[L] Short-Term General Inpatient Care

Short-term general inpatient care must be made available by the hospice provider for pain control and symptom management.[121] The care must be provided in a Medicare certified inpatient hospice facility, or hospital or skilled nursing facility.[122] While an individual is receiving general inpatient care for pain control or symptom management, each shift at the facility must include a registered nurse who provides direct patient care.[123] Hospices that provide inpatient care directly in their own facilities must provide rooms that have a home-like atmosphere and are designed to preserve the dignity, comfort, and privacy of hospice patients.[124]

On August 31, 2007, CMS issued the following policy "clarification":

> To receive payment for general inpatient care under the Medicare hospice benefit, beneficiaries *must* require an intensity of care directed towards pain control and symptom management that cannot be managed in any other settings. It is the level of care provided to meet the individual's needs and not the location of where the individual resides, or caregiver breakdown, that determines payment rates for Medicare services (*Emphasis in original*).[125]

---

[118] *See* **Chapter 3** of this Handbook. *See also* CMS, SNF Consolidated Billing, "Overview on Skilled Nursing Facility (SNF) Consolidated Billing (CB)," *available at* https://www.cms.gov/Medicare/Billing/SNFConsolidatedBilling/index.html?redirect=/SNFConsolidatedBilling/ (site visited May 25, 2016).

[119] *See* OIG, HHS, "Medicare Could Be Paying Twice for Prescription Drugs for Beneficiaries in Hospice" (June 28, 2012), *available at* https://oig.hhs.gov/oas/reports/region6/61000059.asp (site visited May 25, 2016).

[120] *See* Memorandum from CMS to All Part D Plan Sponsors and Medicare Hospice Providers (July 18, 2014), *available at* http://www.cms.gov/Medicare/Medicare-Fee-for-Service-Payment/Hospice/Downloads/2014-PartD-Hospice-Guidance-Revised-Memo.pdf (site visited May 25, 2016).

[121] 42 C.F.R. § 418.108.

[122] 42 C.F.R. § 418.108.

[123] 42 C.F.R. §§ 418.108 and 418.110(b).

[124] 42 C.F.R. § 418.110(e) and (f).

[125] 72 Fed. Reg. 50,214, 50,220 (Aug. 31, 2007).

When an individual's hospice care is billed to Medicare at a general inpatient level of care, the per diem rate pays for both the beneficiary's hospice care and the beneficiary's room and board.[126]. On the other hand, if a hospice patient receives general inpatient care for three or more days and then revokes the hospice benefit, then the three day stay in the inpatient facility (although not necessarily the same as a hospital level of care in terms of kind of care provided) qualifies the beneficiary for covered SNF services.[127] In other words, the three day general inpatient hospice stay is considered, for purposes of obtaining Medicare coverage of SNF care, to be the equivalent of a three day qualifying hospital stay.

When a beneficiary has been receiving Medicare covered general inpatient care and the hospice provider determines that continued general inpatient care is no longer medically reasonable and necessary, the provider must issue an Advance Beneficiary Notice (ABN) if the beneficiary or his or her authorized representative believe the beneficiary should continue to receive that level of care.[128] If the beneficiary or the beneficiary's authorized representative indicate on the ABN that the beneficiary would like the care billed to Medicare (demand bill), the hospice provider must bill Medicare for an appealable determination.[129]

[M] Inpatient Care for Respite Purposes

Inpatient care for respite purposes is provided to the hospice patient when necessary to relieve the beneficiary's caregiver(s).[130] Respite care may be provided only on an occasional basis and is limited to no more than five consecutive days at a time.[131] The respite care must be provided in a Medicare certified hospice, a Medicare certified hospital, a Medicare certified SNF, or a Medicare or Medicaid certified nursing facility (NF).[132] Rooms must be designed to ensure the dignity, comfort, and privacy of patients.[133] The facility providing respite care must provide 24-hour nursing services that meet the nursing needs of all patients and are furnished in accordance with each patient's plan of care. Each patient must receive all nursing services as prescribed and must be kept comfortable, clean, well-groomed, and protected from accident, injury, and infection.[134]

---

[126] 42 C.F.R. § 418.302.

[127] MBPM, Ch. 9, § 40.1.5. *See also* **§ 3.03[E]** of this Handbook regarding calculating benefit periods for skilled nursing facility (SNF) care.

[128] MCP Manual, Ch. 11, § 100.2.

[129] MCP Manual, Ch. 11, § 100.2.

[130] 42 C.F.R. § 418.204(b)(1). *See also* MBP Manual, Ch. 9, § 40.2.2.

[131] 42 C.F.R. § 418.204(b)(2).

[132] 42 C.F.R. §§ 418.108(b) and 418.110(e) and (f).

[133] 42 C.F.R. §§ 418.108(b)(2) and 418.110(f).

[134] 42 C.F.R. § 418.108(b)(2).

While the beneficiary is at a respite level of care, the hospice benefit pays for both the beneficiary's medical care and the beneficiary's room and board. There is a coinsurance amount that the hospice provider may require the patient to pay if respite services are received. The daily coinsurance amount for respite care can be no more than 5 percent of the payment made by CMS for a respite day. The actual amount will vary depending on the provider. However, in no event may the total amount of the coinsurance exceed the inpatient hospital deductible in effect in the year in which the hospice benefit was elected. In 2016, this amount is $1,288. The coinsurance is payable for each coinsurance period. A coinsurance period begins on the first day an election is effective and ends with the close of the first period of 14 consecutive days on each of which an election is not in effect for the beneficiary.[135] So, for example, if the patient elected 210 consecutive days of hospice coverage, the patient would be required to pay the respite coinsurance up to the maximum only once.

§ 5.12 HOSPICE INPATIENT FACILITY RULES

The conditions of participation are extensive for hospice providers that provide inpatient care directly in their own facilities.[136] The provider must provide a home like atmosphere and ensure that patient areas are designed to preserve the dignity, comfort, and privacy of patients.[137] There must be physical space for private patient and family visiting, accommodations for family members to remain with the patient throughout the night, and physical space for family privacy after a patient's death.[138] There must be opportunity for patients to receive visitors at any hour, including infants and small children.[139]

The patient rooms must be designed and equipped for nursing care, as well as the dignity, comfort, and privacy of patients.[140] The hospice provider must accommodate a patient and family request for a single room whenever possible.[141] Each patient's room must be at or above grade level; contain a suitable bed and other appropriate furniture for each patient; have closet space that provides security and privacy for clothing and personal belongings; accommodate no more than two patients and their family members; provide at least 80 square feet for each residing patient in a double room and at least 100 square feet for each

---

[135] 42 C.F.R. § 418.400(b).
[136] 42 C.F.R. § 418.110.
[137] 42 C.F.R. § 418.110(e).
[138] 42 C.F.R. § 418.110(e)(1).
[139] 42 C.F.R. § 418.110(e)(2).
[140] 42 C.F.R. § 418.110(f)(1).
[141] 42 C.F.R. § 418.110(f)(2).

patient residing in a single room; and be equipped with an easily activated, functioning device accessible to the patient that is used for calling for assistance.[142]

§ 5.13 HOSPICE CARE FOR RESIDENTS OF FACILITIES

Medicare beneficiaries who reside in SNF/NF or intermediate care facilities for persons with mental retardation (ICF/MR) can receive Medicare covered hospice care if the hospice provider and facility have a contract.[143] Under these circumstances, the hospice provider must assume professional management of the resident's hospice services in accordance with the hospice plan of care and the hospice conditions of participation.[144] The conditions of participation mandate that the contracts include very specific information.[145] They must include, but are not limited to:

- The manner in which the facility and the hospice are to communicate with each other and document such communications to ensure that the needs of the patient are addressed and met 24 hours a day;
- A provision stating that the hospice assumes responsibility for determining the appropriate course of hospice care, including the determination to change the level of services if needed;
- An agreement that it is the hospice's responsibility to provide services at the same level and to the same extent as those services would be provided if the resident were in his or her own home;
- A provision that the hospice may use the facility staff where permitted by state law and as specified by the facility to assist in the administration of prescribed therapies included in the plan of care only to the extent that the hospice would routinely use the services of a hospice patient's family in implementing the plan of care.[146]

It is important to understand that when a Medicare beneficiary has elected hospice care, is at a routine level of care, and is residing in a nursing home, the Medicare hospice benefit will pay for the beneficiary's hospice care but **not** for the beneficiary's room and board.

Alternatively, it is possible for an individual to receive both Medicare covered SNF care and Medicare covered hospice care.[147] For this to occur, the

[142] 42 C.F.R. § 418.110(f)(3). Waivers for some of these requirements are available for hospices operating prior to December 2, 2008. 42 C.F.R. § 418.110(f)(4).

[143] 42 C.F.R. § 418.112. *See also* MBPM, Ch. 9, § 20.3.

[144] 42 C.F.R. § 418.112(b).

[145] 42 C.F.R. § 418.112(c).

[146] 42 C.F.R. § 418.112(c).

[147] 42 C.F.R. § 418.112(c).

Medicare SNF care must be for a condition unrelated to the terminal condition. For instance, if a Medicare beneficiary who has elected hospice falls and breaks a hip, has a three day qualifying hospital stay,[148] and then is transferred to a SNF, so long as the broken hip is not related to the beneficiary's underlying terminal illness, then the beneficiary may continue to receive Medicare covered hospice care for the terminal illness while also receiving Medicare covered SNF care for the broken hip. This is significant because Medicare covered SNF inpatient care includes payment for room and board.

§ 5.14 DEDUCTIBLES AND COINSURANCE FOR NONHOSPICE CARE

The hospice patient is liable for coinsurance amounts only for drugs and biologicals and respite care (*see* § **5.11[K]** and § **5.11[M]**). No other services *provided by the hospice* for the palliation and management of the patient's terminal illness may be billed to the patient.

If, while on hospice, the patient receives medical care for conditions not related to his or her terminal condition, then he or she will be liable for the standard Medicare deductibles and coinsurance payments related to that care. Also, if he or she receives care from his or her attending physician, the beneficiary will be financially responsible for any Part B cost-sharing associated with the care.[149]

§ 5.15 HOSPICE DENIALS AND APPEALS

Hospice patients are afforded the same appeal rights as those granted to other recipients of medical care under Part A of Medicare.[150]

[A] Coding Problems

Sometimes Medicare beneficiaries who elected the hospice benefit inappropriately receive coverage denials for care they received that was not related to the terminal illness. For instance, a hospice patient may have outpatient physical therapy for chronic back pain not related to the terminal illness. She might receive a denial for the physical therapy because the billing department at the therapist's office failed to code the bill correctly. Generally this problem can be solved by asking the billing department to re-bill Medicare using the code (GW Modifier) indicating that the individual is a hospice patient but that the provided care was not related to the terminal illness. In the event that the provider's billing office is not cooperative or if Medicare continues to deny the claim despite the fact that

---

[148] 42 U.S.C. § 1395x(i). *See also* § **3.03** of this Handbook.
[149] 42 C.F.R. § 418.402.
[150] *See* § **1.07** of this Handbook.

the provider has billed correctly, these claims should be appealed. As was discussed above, upon electing hospice, one does not waive all rights to Medicare coverage, only some of those rights related to the terminal illness.[151]

[B] Billing Errors

Another source of inappropriate denials also occurs through billing error. Hospice providers frequently have contractual relationships with other entities for the provision of care related to the terminal illness.[152] For instance, a provider may have a contractual relationship with a DME provider for the provision of items such as wheelchairs and hospital beds. These contracts specify that the providers of services and goods are to bill the hospice provider for the rendered services and goods. In other words, they are not to bill Medicare and they are not to bill the beneficiary. However, sometimes, through billing error, the contracted provider will bill Medicare rather than the hospice provider. This will result in a Medicare denial. Should this occur, contact the hospice provider. If the provider is unwilling or unable to remedy the problem, then the denial should be appealed.

Beneficiaries must remember that upon electing hospice, they waive their rights to Medicare coverage for treatment of the terminal illness that is not provided by their attending physician, the hospice, or under arrangement with the hospice.[153] Should beneficiaries seek out care for their terminal illness from other providers, their care will not be covered by Medicare.

[C] Terminal Status

Because Medicare coverage of hospice care hinges almost exclusively on whether the beneficiary has a life expectancy of six months or less,[154] denials of hospice coverage are most likely made based on a finding that the beneficiary's life expectancy was not six months or less. In pursuing a hospice appeal, the advocate should attempt to obtain an explicit and detailed letter from the patient's attending physician, listing specific clinical findings supporting the beneficiary's limited life expectancy. Moreover, the advocate should ask the physician to provide clinical documentation (medical records) that supports his or her clinical findings. This letter and documentation often can be the pivotal factors in achieving a successful result. In addition, the advocate should closely examine the medical record for notations indicating that the beneficiary was terminally ill with a limited life expectancy. Doctors' orders, nurses' notes, and the written care

[151] *See* **§ 5.01** of this Handbook.
[152] MBP Manual, Ch. 9, § 40.4.
[153] *See* **§ 5.01** of this Handbook.
[154] *See* **§ 5.02** of this Handbook.

plan[155] established for the patient will often be useful sources of evidence to support a claim for Medicare coverage. Any notes of the hospice's interdisciplinary group regarding the patient's care will also prove helpful.[156]

Advocates should be especially wary of hospice discharges when the beneficiary's health status has not changed and the only apparent reason for the discharge is that the beneficiary has lived "too long."[157] These discharges may be motivated by the "hospice cap." Since its inception, the Medicare regulations have included a cap limiting the average annual payment per patient a hospice can receive.[158] When the cap was first implemented, due to the structure of the election periods, few beneficiaries received more than six months of Medicare-covered hospice care. However, in 1998, the regulations were changed to increase access to hospice care. Beneficiaries became eligible for an unlimited number of 60-day certification periods so long as they have a life expectancy of 6 months or less if the terminal illness runs its course.

Since the change in the benefit structure, many hospices have exceeded the hospice cap. Consequently, they were asked to pay significant sums of money back to Medicare. As a result, to avoid this sanction in the future, hospices may inappropriately discharge patients who live beyond six months. Should this occur, the beneficiary's right to appeal should be exercised immediately.

Another potential problem might arise due to the face to face requirement that went into effect January 2011. According to the Medicare Benefit Policy Manual, if hospice providers fail to obtain the required face to face documentation, the affected Medicare beneficiaries will not be eligible for Medicare payment for their hospice care.[159] However, this should not permit hospices to shift

---

[155] 42 C.F.R. §§ 418.56, 418.58, and 418.68. The hospice must designate an interdisciplinary group . . . which, in consultation with the patient's attending physician, must prepare a written plan of care. The plan of care must specify the hospice care and services necessary to meet the patient and family-specific needs identified in the comprehensive assessment as such needs relate to the terminal illness and related conditions."

[156] 42 C.F.R. § 418.68: "The hospice must designate an interdisciplinary group or groups composed of individuals who provide or supervise the care and services offered by the hospice."

[157] MBPM, Ch. 9, § 20.2.3 reads as follows

> Once a hospice chooses to admit a Medicare beneficiary, it may not automatically or routinely discharge the beneficiary at its discretion, even if the care promises to be costly or inconvenient, or the State allows for discharge under State requirements. The election of the hospice benefit is the beneficiary's choice rather than the hospice's choice, and the hospice cannot revoke the beneficiary's election. Neither should the hospice request or demand that the patient revoke his/her election.

[158] 42 C.F.R. § 418.309.

[159] MBPM, Ch.9, § 20.1 reads as follows

> For recertifications on or after January 1, 2011, a hospice physician or hospice nurse practitioner must have a face-to-face encounter with each hospice patient prior to the beginning of the patient's third benefit period, and prior to each subsequent benefit period. Failure to meet the face-to-face encounter requirements . . . results in a failure by the hospice to meet the patient's recertification of terminal illness eligibility requirement. The patient would cease to be eligible for the benefit.

financial liability for this care to the beneficiaries. Pursuant to the regulations, the provider should be financially responsible for any uncovered care.[160] If hospice beneficiaries are held financially responsible for this care, they should certainly appeal.

[D] Expedited Appeals

In the event that the hospice provider intends to discharge a beneficiary because the medical director no longer believes he or she is terminally ill, it must first give the beneficiary a standardized termination notice.[161] The standardized termination notices are designed to inform beneficiaries that they are being discharged from hospice care and that they have a right to an expedited appeal.[162] A beneficiary who wishes to exercise the right to an expedited appeal must call the Beneficiary and Family Center Care Quality Improvement Organization (BFCC-QIO) (number supplied on the notice) by no later than noon of the calendar day following receipt of the provider's notice of termination.[163] No later than 72 hours after receipt of the request for an expedited review, the BFCC-QIO must notify the beneficiary, beneficiary's physician, and the hospice program of its determination.[164]

[E] Waiver of Liability

Section 1879 of the Social Security Act provides protections from liability for charges for claims denied by Medicare for services provided to beneficiaries who were not aware that the services would not be covered by Medicare. On August 5, 1997, the limitation of liability was extended to Medicare hospice coverage via Section 1879(g) of the Act.[165]

---

[160] 42 C.F.R. § 489.21 states that if a beneficiary "would be entitled to have payment made if the provider [h]ad in its files the required certification and recertification by a physician related to the services furnished to the beneficiary," the provider "agrees not to charge [the] beneficiary." *See also* MCP Manual, Ch. 30, § 50.15.3.1: "The ABN must not be issued when the face to face requirement is not met within the required time frame. Failure to meet the face to face requirement should not be misrepresented as a determination that the beneficiary is no longer terminally ill."

[161] 42 C.F.R. § 411.404.

[162] 42 C.F.R. § 411.404. *See also* **§ 1.07** of this Handbook for a full discussion of expedited appeals.

[163] 42 C.F.R. § 405.1202(b).

[164] 42 C.F.R. § 405.1202(e)(6).

[165] 42 U.S.C. § 1395pp(g); *see also* MBP Manual, Ch. 9, § 50.

[F] Standard Appeals

Not only do Medicare beneficiaries have a right to an expedited appeal, they also have a right to a standard appeal. To exercise the right to a standard appeal, the beneficiary must ask the hospice provider to bill Medicare for rendered hospice care (demand bill). Once the hospice receives the request, it should submit the claim to the Medicare contractor for an initial determination.[166] The Medicare contractor, upon receiving the claim, will review the medical evidence and issue an initial determination indicating whether the hospice care is covered by Medicare.[167] After this determination, a notice of initial determination will be sent to the beneficiary's last known address.[168] The notice must be written in a manner calculated to be understood by the beneficiary.[169] It must contain:[170]

- The reasons for the determination, including whether a local medical review policy, a local coverage determination, or a national coverage determination was applied;
- Procedures for obtaining additional information concerning the contractor's determination, such as a specific provision of a policy, manual, law, or regulation used in making the determination;
- Information on the right to a redetermination if the beneficiary is dissatisfied with the outcome of the initial determination and instructions on how to request a redetermination; and
- Any other requirements specified by CMS.

If the beneficiary receives a full denial, a partial denial, or a denial, but his or her liability is waived, the patient may wish to appeal.[171]

§ 5.16 ADVANCE CARE PLANNING

In November 2015, CMS issued final rules detailing how the agency will pay for services provided to beneficiaries in Medicare by physicians and other health care professionals in 2016, including information on payment for advance care planning (ACP).[172] The ACP billing codes went into effect for services to the

---

[166] MCP Manual, Ch. 11, § 30.3.

[167] 42 C.F.R. § 405.921.

[168] 42 C.F.R. § 405.921(a)(1).

[169] 42 C.F.R. § 405.921(a)(1).

[170] 42 C.F.R. § 405.921(a)(2).

[171] *See* **§ 1.07[A]** of this Handbook for a description of the appeal process.

[172] Final Rule, 80 Fed. Reg. 70,885, *available at* https://www.federalregister.gov/articles/2015/11/16/2015-28005/medicare-program-revisions-to-payment-policies-under-the-physician-fee-schedule-

Physician Fee Schedule (PFS) under CPT codes 99497 and 99498 beginning January 1, 2016.[173] These included explanation and discussion of advance directives and standard forms. Completion of an advance directive is not a requirement for billing the service.[174]

Through these codes, providers can now bill for discussions about long-term treatment options and planning, including advance care directives that outline considerations like patient preference in the event that the patient has a health event that adversely affects decision-making capacity.[175]

There are no place of service limitations on the ACP codes; ACP services may be appropriately furnished in a variety of settings depending on the needs and condition of the beneficiary.[176] The codes are separately payable to the billing physician or practitioner in both facility and non-facility settings, and are not limited to particular physician specialties.[177]

The conversations are voluntary, and can be an optional element of the Annual Wellness Visit (AWV); ACP services furnished on the same day and by the same provider as an AWV are considered a preventive service. Therefore, the deductible and coinsurance are not applied to the codes used to report ACP services when performed as part of an AWV.[178]

---

and-other-revisions?utm_campaign=pi+subscription+mailing+list&utm_medium=email&utm_source=federalregister.gov (site visited Aug. 8, 2016).

[173] Frequently Asked Questions about Billing the Physician Fee Schedule for Advance Care Planning Services, *available at* https://www.cms.gov/Medicare/Medicare-Fee-for-Service-Payment/PhysicianFeeSched/Downloads/FAQ-Advance-Care-Planning.pdf (site visited Aug. 8, 2016).

[174] Frequently Asked Questions about Billing the Physician Fee Schedule for Advance Care Planning Services, *available at* https://www.cms.gov/Medicare/Medicare-Fee-for-Service-Payment/PhysicianFeeSched/Downloads/FAQ-Advance-Care-Planning.pdf (site visited Aug. 8, 2016).

[175] *See* https://www.federalregister.gov/articles/2015/11/16/2015-28005/medicare-program-revisions-to-payment-policies-under-the-physician-fee-schedule-and-other-revisions?utm_campaign=pi+subscription+mailing+list&utm_medium=email&utm_source=federalregister.gov (site visited Aug. 8, 2016).

[176] Frequently Asked Questions about Billing the Physician Fee Schedule for Advance Care Planning Services, *available at* https://www.cms.gov/Medicare/Medicare-Fee-for-Service-Payment/PhysicianFeeSched/Downloads/FAQ-Advance-Care-Planning.pdf (site visited Aug. 8, 2016).

[177] *See* https://www.cms.gov/Medicare/Medicare-Fee-for-Service-Payment/PhysicianFeeSched/Downloads/FAQ-Advance-Care-Planning.pdf (site visited Aug. 8, 2016).

[178] CMS MLN Matter, "Advance Care Planning (ACP) as an Optional Element of an Annual Wellness Visit (AWV)," *available at* https://www.cms.gov/Outreach-and-Education/Medicare-Learning-Network-MLN/MLNMattersArticles/downloads/MM9271.pdf (site visited Aug. 8, 2016).

CHAPTER 6

MEDICARE PART B: SUPPLEMENTARY MEDICAL INSURANCE BENEFITS FOR THE AGED AND DISABLED

§ 6.01 INTRODUCTION

[A] Services

Part B of the Medicare program, Supplementary Medical Insurance (SMI) Benefits for the Aged and Disabled,[1] provides coverage for a host of services for beneficiaries, including:

- Physician services;
- Services and supplies incident to a physician's professional services, including drugs and biologicals that cannot be self-administered, including chemotherapy;
- Outpatient hospital services;
- Physical and occupational therapy services;
- Speech language pathology services;
- X-ray, laboratory, and other diagnostic tests;
- Some preventive services
- Surgical dressings and devices for reduction of fractures;
- Durable medical equipment (DME); and
- Prosthetic devices, orthotics, and supplies.

Definitions of Medicare-covered services, along with critical Medicare terms, are found at 42 U.S.C. § 1395x.[2]

---

[1] 42 U.S.C. §§ 1395k, x.

[2] 42 U.S.C. § 1395k (scope of benefits), *available at* http://www.gpo.gov/fdsys/pkg/USCODE-2010-title42/pdf/USCODE-2010-title42-chap7-subchapXVIII-partB.pdf (site visited June 7, 2016), and § 1395x (definitions), *available at* http://www.gpo.gov/fdsys/pkg/USCODE-2010-title42/pdf/USCODE-2010-title42-chap7-subchapXVIII-partE-sec1395x.pdf (site visited June 7, 2016). Definitions include § 1395x(a) (spell of illness), § 1395x(b) (inpatient hospital services), § 1395x(c) (inpatient psychiatric hospital services), § 1395x(e) (definition of hospital), § 1395x(f) (psychiatric hospital), § 1395x(g) (outpatient occupational therapy services), § 1395x(h) (extended care services), § 1395x(i) (post hospital extended care services), § 1395x(j) (skilled nursing facility), § 1395x(m) (home health services), § 1395x(o) (home health agency), § 1395x(p) (outpatient physical therapy services), § 1395x(q) (physician services), § 1395x(r) (physician), and § 1395x(s) (medical and other services, including durable medical equipment (DME), prosthetic devices, and ambulance services). *See* Centers for Medicare & Medicaid Services (CMS), "2015 Medicare & You," *available at* http://www.medicare.gov/Pubs/pdf/10050.pdf (site visited June 7, 2016); *see also* https://www.medicare.gov/what-medicare-covers/index.html (site visited June 14, 2016).

[B] Administration

Part B is financed by premiums paid by individuals enrolled in the program and by general revenues from the federal government. Since 1993, individuals receiving Social Security retirement benefits, individuals receiving Social Security disability benefits for 24 months, and individuals otherwise entitled to Medicare Part A are automatically enrolled in Part B unless they decline coverage.[3] Persons with amyotrophic lateral sclerosis (ALS) are entitled to Part A the first month that they are entitled to Social Security disability cash benefits.[4] There are also special eligibility rules for persons with end-stage renal disease (ESRD).[5]

Section 911 of the Medicare Prescription Drug, Improvement, and Modernization Act of 2003 (MMA), as part of the government's regulatory reform initiative, created a new Section 1874A of the Social Security Act that modifies and consolidates the administration of the Medicare program.[6] In particular, the Secretary of Health and Human Services (HHS) now has the authority to contract with an eligible entity known as a Medicare Administrative Contractor (MAC). These entities perform certain functions previously performed by insurance companies and other entities known as carriers (Part B) and intermediaries (Part A). Functions include determining payment amounts, local medical coverage decisions, beneficiary education, technical assistance, and other functions.[7]

The MMA also created the office of the Medicare Beneficiary Ombudsman, located in HHS. The Ombudsman is to assist beneficiaries with appeals and related matters in fee-for-service and Medicare Advantage (MA)—formerly called Medicare+Choice—settings.[8]

---

[3] 42 U.S.C. § 1395o; *see also* 42 C.F.R. § 407.10(a)(1).

[4] *See* CMS, "Original Medicare (Part A and B) Eligibility and Enrollment," *available at* http://www.cms.gov/Medicare/Eligibility-and-Enrollment/OrigMedicarePartABEligEnrol/ (site visited June 7, 2016).

[5] *See* CMS, "Original Medicare (Part A and B) Eligibility and Enrollment," *available at* http://www.cms.gov/Medicare/Eligibility-and-Enrollment/OrigMedicarePartABEligEnrol/ (site visited June 7, 2016).

[6] *See* 42 U.S.C. § 1395kk-1 (contracts with Medicare Administrative Contractors, or MACs).

[7] Sections 911 and 912 of the Medicare Prescription Drug, Improvement, and Modernization Act of 2003 (MMA), Pub. L. No. 108-173 (Dec. 8, 2003), and conforming modifications to 42 U.S.C. § 1395h and u removing references to fiscal intermediaries and carriers. CMS has consolidated the functions of intermediaries and carriers into the new MACs. *See* CMS, "Medicare Administrative Contractors" (July 2013), *available at* http://www.cms.gov/Medicare/Medicare-Contracting/Medicare-Administrative-Contractors/MedicareAdministrativeContractors.html (site visited June 7, 2016).

[8] Provision is effective one year from date of enactment of MMA. *See* § 923, amending § 1808 of the Social Security Act. *See* "Ombudsman Center," *available at* http://www.cms.hhs.gov/center/ombudsman.asp (site visited June 7, 2016). There is also an ombudsman for the competitive acquisition of durable medical equipment. *See* http://www.medicare.gov/claims-and-appeals/file-a-complaint/durable-medical-equipment/complaints-about-dme.html (site visited June 7, 2016).

§ 6.02 ENROLLMENT AND PAYMENT REQUIREMENTS

[A] Eligibility

Medicare Part B, the SMI program, is a voluntary program for eligible enrollees who enroll and pay a monthly premium.[9] An eligible enrollee is a person who is either entitled to Part A[10] or age 65 or older who is a citizen or who

---

[9] *See* 42 U.S.C. § 1395j–w. The Part B monthly premium in 2017 is $109 for an individual whose modified adjusted gross income (MAGI) is less than $85,000. *See* 80 Fed. Reg. 70,811-820 (Nov. 16, 2015). See **Appendix 1-3** for the premium for individuals not "held harmless." Premiums for a subsequent year are usually announced in the *Federal Register* prior to November of the preceding year. In subsequent years, it will be increased by the same percentage as the Part B premium (monthly actuarial value of benefits payable under Part B), rounded up to the nearest dollar. *See* MMA § 629, amending § 1833(b) of the Social Security Act, 42 U.S.C. § 1395l(b). *See* § **6.02[C][2]** of this Handbook for discussion of the Part B Income-Related Premium. *See* 77 Fed. Reg. 69,850 (Nov. 21, 2012). The program was set to expire in 2002 but has been continually extended.

[10] 42 U.S.C. § 1395o; 42 C.F.R. § 407.10(a)(1). *See* the June 26, 2015, favorable Supreme Court ruling in Obergefell v. Hodges, Dir., Ohio Dep't of Health, Nos. 14-556, 14-562, 14-571 and 14-574, 576 U.S. ____ (2015), *available at* http://www.supremecourt.gov/opinions/14pdf/14-556_3204.pdf (site visited June 7, 2016). In *Obergefell,* the Court found that the failure to grant same-sex couples a marriage license is a violation of equal protection under the United States Constitution. Advocates should pay close attention to implementation issues as they arise.

For background on the tortuous history of the recognition of same-sex marriages at the federal level and access to benefits, see United States v. Windsor, *available at* http://www.supremecourt.gov/opinions/12pdf/12-307_6j37.pdf (site visited June 7, 2016). *Windsor* holds Section 3 of the Defense of Marriage Act (DOMA) unconstitutional because DOMA limits a valid marriage as only between a man and a woman. With respect to *Windsor,* persons in state-recognized same-sex marriages should consider filing for spousal benefits as appropriate.

Same-sex spouses of Medicare beneficiaries who are in valid marriages may be eligible for benefits as a spouse and should apply for benefits as appropriate. *See* Center for Medicare Advocacy, "Demise of DOMA: Implementing Federal Benefits for Same-Sex Spouses," *available at* http://www.medicareadvocacy.org/demise-of-doma-implementing-federal-benefits-for-same-sex-spouses/ (site visited June 7, 2016); *see also* Attorney General Holder's Memorandum to the President, "Implementation of *United States v. Windsor*" (June 20, 2014), *available at* http://www.justice.gov/iso/opa/resources/9722014620103930904785.pdf (site visited June 7, 2016). The Holder Memorandum summarizes various agencies' practices with respect to following the law of celebration or the law of domicile in determining a valid same-sex marriage.

On August 23, 2013, the Social Security Administration (SSA) added two Program Operation Manual Systems (POMS) provisions: GN 00210.005, "Holding Claims, Appeals, and Post-Entitlement Actions Involving Same-Sex Marriages or Legal Same-Sex Relationships Other than Marriage," *available at* https://secure.ssa.gov/apps10/poms.nsf/lnx/0200210005 (site visited June 7, 2016), and GN 00210.010, "Interviewing Individuals with Claims Involving Same-Sex Relationships," *available at* https://secure.ssa.gov/apps10/poms.nsf/lnx/0200210010 (site visited June 7, 2016). *See also* Section 1557 of the Affordable Care Act (ACA) which prohibits discrimination on the basis of race, color, national origin, sex, age, or disability in certain health programs and

has been a lawful permanent resident for five years preceding the month of application.[11] Persons not entitled to Part A benefits may request enrollment in Part B.[12] Persons convicted of crimes against national security (subversive activity) may not enroll.[13]

An individual must enroll for SMI or must be enrolled by a state under a buy-in agreement.[14] The SMI program pays only for covered expenses incurred during an individual's period of entitlement.[15]

Persons younger than 65 may enroll in Medicare if they have been found disabled under Title II of the Social Security Act and are entitled to social security or railroad retirement disability benefits.[16] However, such persons must satisfy a 24-month waiting period (benefits begin in the 25th month after they have been entitled to Social Security cash disability benefits). An individual is entitled or deemed entitled to social security disability benefits as an insured individual, child, widow, or widower who is "under a disability" or is a disabled qualified beneficiary certified under Section 7(d) of the Railroad Retirement Act.[17]

Disabled persons[18]

> Disabled persons who are not insured for monthly social security disability benefits, but would be insured for such benefits if their QCs [quarters of coverage] from government employment were social security QCs, are deemed to be entitled to disability benefits and automatically entitled to Part A after being disabled for 29 months.
>
> Part A entitlement on the basis of disability is available, not only to the worker, but also to the widow, widower, or child of a deceased, disabled, or retired worker if any of them become disabled within the meaning of the

activities. A summary of the final rule is *available at* http://www.hhs.gov/sites/default/files/2016-06-07-section-1557-final-rule-summary-508.pdf. *See also* https://www.federalregister.gov/articles/2016/05/18/2016-11458/nondiscrimination-in-health-programs-and-activities?utm_campaign=subscription+mailing+list&utm_medium=email&utm_source=federalregister.gov (site visited June 25, 2016) and *see*, http://healthaffairs.org/blog/2016/06/06/lgbt-protections-in-affordable-care-act-section-1557/ (site visited June 25, 2016).

[11] 42 U.S.C. § 1395i-2; 42 C.F.R. § 407.10(a)(2)(i)–(iii).

[12] 42 C.F.R. § 407.22(a)(1).

[13] 42 C.F.R. § 407.10(b).

[14] 42 C.F.R. §§ 407.4(a)(2) and 407.40.

[15] 42 C.F.R. § 407.4(b). *See also* Medicare General Information, Eligibility, and Entitlement, Chapter 1, *available at* http://www.cms.gov/Regulations-and-Guidance/Guidance/Manuals/Downloads/ge101c01.pdf (site visited June 7, 2016) *and* Chapter 2, *available at* https://www.cms.gov/Regulations-and-Guidance/Guidance/Manuals/downloads/ge101c02.pdf (sites visited June 7, 2016).

[16] 42 C.F.R. § 406.12.

[17] 42 C.F.R. § 406.12.

[18] *See* CMS, "Original Medicare (Part A and B) Eligibility and Enrollment," *available at* http://www.cms.gov/Medicare/Eligibility-and-Enrollment/OrigMedicarePartABEligEnrol/ (site visited June 7, 2016). *See also* CMS, *Medicare Coverage of Kidney Dialysis and Kidney Transplant Services* (revised Aug. 2015), *available at* https://www.medicare.gov/Publications/Pubs/pdf/10128.pdf (site visited June 7, 2016).

Social Security or Railroad Retirement Acts. Beginning July 1, 2001, individuals whose disability is Amyotrophic Lateral Sclerosis (ALS) are entitled to Part A the first month they are entitled to Social Security disability cash benefits.

End-stage renal disease (ESRD)[19]

Individuals are eligible for Part A if they receive regular dialysis treatments or a kidney transplant, have filed an application, and meet one of the following conditions:

- have worked the required amount of time under Social Security, the Railroad Retirement Board, or as a government employee; or
- are getting or are eligible for Social Security or Railroad Retirement benefits; or
- are the spouse or dependent child of a person who has worked the required amount of time under Social Security, the Railroad Retirement Board, or as a government employee; or
- are getting Social Security or Railroad Retirement benefits.

Part A ESRD coverage begins:[20]

- the 3rd month after the month in which a regular course of dialysis begins; or
- the first month in which a regular course of dialysis begins of dialysis if the individual engages in self-dialysis if the individual engage in self-dialysis training; or
- the month of kidney transplant;
- two (2) months prior to the month of transplant if the individual was hospitalized during those earlier months in preparation for the transplant.

[B] Enrollment

[1] Enrollment Periods

Persons enrolled in Part A are presumed to want Part B. An individual can, however, opt out of Part B before coverage begins or within a specified period

[19] *See* CMS, "Original Medicare (Part A and B) Eligibility and Enrollment," *available at* http://www.cms.gov/Medicare/Eligibility-and-Enrollment/OrigMedicarePartABEligEnrol/ (site visited June 7, 2016).

[20] *See* CMS, "Original Medicare (Part A and B) Eligibility and Enrollment," *available at* http://www.cms.gov/Medicare/Eligibility-and-Enrollment/OrigMedicarePartABEligEnrol/ (site visited June 7, 2016). *See also* CMS, *Medicare Coverage of Kidney Dialysis and Kidney Transplant Services* (revised Aug. 2015), *available at* https://www.medicare.gov/Pubs/pdf/10128.pdf (site visited June 9, 2016).

(not less than two months) beginning after notice that Part B coverage has started.[21]

Enrollment in Part B, and Medicare generally, is automatic for most persons who qualify for Medicare Part A. For others, it is usually handled through the local office of the Social Security Administration (SSA). An application for benefits can be submitted by mail, in person, or online at socialsecurity.org. If one wishes to decline Part B, a signed statement to that effect should be sent to the local SSA office.[22]

Most beneficiaries enroll during their initial enrollment period, which includes the seven-month period beginning on the first day of the third month before the month when all eligibility requirements are met and extends for seven months from that date.[23] Generally, early application is recommended so as to avoid gaps in coverage.[24] For example, if an individual enrolls in the first three months of the initial enrollment period, entitlement begins with the first month of eligibility.[25] If the individual enrolls during the fourth month of the initial enrollment period, entitlement begins with the following month.[26] If the individual enrolls in the fifth month of the initial enrollment period, entitlement begins the second month after the month of enrollment.[27] If the individual waits until the last two months of the initial enrollment period to enroll, entitlement begins the third month after the month of enrollment.[28]

Beneficiaries age 65 or older who continue to be covered by an employer group health plan that covers any number of employees (except plans that cover only self-employed individuals and no employees) through their own active employment or the active employment of their spouse[29] may delay their enrollment in Medicare Part B without incurring a penalty.[30] Such beneficiaries will be entitled to a "special enrollment period" (SEP) when the earlier of two things

---

[21] 42 C.F.R. § 407.17(b).

[22] 42 C.F.R. § 407.17(b).

[23] 42 U.S.C. § 1395p(d); 42 C.F.R. § 407.14(a)(1). Under the Medicare Advantage (MA) program, enrollees must make an election whether to participate in an MA managed care option. *See* 42 C.F.R. §§ 422.62 *et seq.*

[24] *See* 42 U.S.C. § 1395q; 42 C.F.R. § 407.25.

[25] 42 C.F.R. § 407.25(a)(1).

[26] 42 C.F.R. § 407.25(a)(2).

[27] 42 C.F.R. § 407.25(a)(3).

[28] 42 C.F.R. § 407.25(a)(4).

[29] 42 U.S.C. § 1395p(i). Individuals entitled to Medicare on the basis of disability (except end-stage renal disease) may also qualify for a special enrollment period (SEP) if they are covered by a large group health plan (100 employees) through their own employment or the employment of a family member. 42 C.F.R. § 407.20(d)(2). *See also* "Special Circumstances (Special Enrollment Periods)," *available at* http://www.medicare.gov/sign-up-change-plans/when-can-i-join-a-health-or-drug-plan/special-circumstances/join-plan-special-circumstances.html (site visited June 7, 2016).

[30] Beneficiaries age 65 or older who are covered through active employment by an Employer Group Health Plan (EGHP) that covers fewer than 20 employees may need to enroll in Part B in spite of Medicare's SEP provisions, however, because the EGHP is a secondary payer. Under these

occurs: the employment through which they have the insurance ends or the insurance terminates. The special enrollment period runs for a period of eight months.[31] Advocates should explore the consequences of delaying enrollment in Part B at age 65 and obtaining access to Medigap insurance and its pre-existing condition exclusions and limitations.[32]

Persons enrolling late, because they missed their initial enrollment period and were not eligible for a special enrollment period, must wait for a general enrollment period to apply.[33] There is a general enrollment period each year from January 1st through March 31st.[34] There may be penalties attached to enrollment during a general enrollment period, however, as explained in detail below.

[2] Penalty for Late Enrollment

As a general matter, persons eligible for Part B should consider filing an application for benefits at the earliest possible time.[35] There is a ten percent penalty added to the premium for each full year of late enrollment.[36] The penalty has no durational limit.[37] There is no increase in premium if the late enrollment gap is less than 12 months.[38] Late enrollment is allowed only during the first three months of each calendar year (coverage becomes effective July 1 of that calendar year).[39]

---

circumstances, beneficiaries are advised to check with the EGHP's administrator to determine whether enrollment in Medicare Part B is required.

[31] 42 U.S.C. § 1395p(i); 42 C.F.R. § 406.24(b)(2). *See generally* 42 C.F.R. § 406.24 for a discussion of SEPs; *see also* HealthCare.gov, "Getting Health Coverage Outside Open Enrollment," *available at* https://www.healthcare.gov/coverage-outside-open-enrollment/special-enrollment-period/ (site visited June 7, 2016).

[32] *See* **Chapter 8** (Medigap Services) and **Chapter 9** (Medicare's Relationship with Private Insurance) of this Handbook.

[33] 42 C.F.R. §§ 406.24 and 407.25.

[34] 42 U.S.C. § 1395p(e).

[35] Advocates should advise their low-income clients of Medicaid provisions that require states to pay the premiums for Medicare beneficiaries with incomes at or below the federal poverty level and resources at or below twice the Supplemental Security Income (SSI) limit. *See* 42 U.S.C. §§ 1396a and 1396d(p) of the Medicaid statute, https://www.gpo.gov/fdsys/pkg/USCODE-2010-title42/pdf/USCODE-2010-title42-chap7-subchapXIX.pdf (site visited June 8, 2016). Medicaid buy-in for low-income Medicare beneficiaries and other Medicare Savings Programs (MSPs) are discussed in **Chapter 10** of this Handbook. In addition, **Chapter 11** discusses access to the low-income subsidy (LIS) for assistance in paying for prescription drugs under the Medicare Part D program.

[36] 42 U.S.C. § 1395(r); 42 C.F.R. § 408.22. The standard monthly premium is determined under 42 C.F.R. § 408.20.

[37] *See* §§ 408.24 and 408.25. For disabled beneficiaries under age 65, the penalty will end when they turn 65.

[38] 42 C.F.R. § 408.22. The 10 percent penalty is implemented for full 12-month periods of late enrollment.

[39] 42 C.F.R. §§ 407.15(a) and 407.25.

There is no late enrollment penalty if the delay is the result of error, fault, or delay by a federal government official or agent of the government.[40] The enrollee must establish that he or she with good cause relied on erroneous information provided by such an official, for example, an SSA or Medicare official.[41]

[C] Premiums

[1] Standard Monthly Premium

Persons enrolled in Medicare Part B are required to pay a monthly premium, the amount of which is established annually by HHS.[42] Payments are either deducted from government benefits or by direct payment or remittance as provided in the law.[43]

Premiums are deducted from Social Security, Railroad Retirement, or federal civil service retirement benefits.[44] Part B premiums submitted by direct payment are generally billed quarterly but can be billed monthly where the beneficiary is unwilling or unable to pay quarterly.[45]

If the beneficiary receives only a civil service annuity and has a spouse who is eligible for Medicare SMI, the beneficiary may authorize the deduction of the spouse's premium from the beneficiary's check.[46]

---

[40] 42 C.F.R. § 407.32. For disabled beneficiaries, the SSA's Program Operations Manual System (POMS) provides for equitable relief when the delay in enrollment was caused by incorrect information provided by their employer or group health plan. *See* SSA POMS, HI 00805.320, *available at* http://policy.ssa.gov/poms.nsf/links/0600805320 (site visited June 7, 2016).

[41] 42 C.F.R. § 407.32. For disabled beneficiaries, the POMS provides for equitable relief when the delay in enrollment was caused by incorrect information provided by their employer or group health plan. *See* SSA POMS, HI 00805.320, *available at* http://policy.ssa.gov/poms.nsf/links/0600805320 (site visited June 7, 2016).

[42] 42 U.S.C. § 1395r; *see also* 42 C.F.R. §§ 408.4(a) and 407.17(b) (automatic enrollment). (*See* discussion of special provisions for payment of Medicare premiums, copayments, and deductibles for persons with low incomes and resources found in **Chapter 10** of this Handbook). *See also* Medicare Access and CHIP Reauthorization Act, Pub. L. No.114-10 (Apr. 16, 2015), and § 402, Income Related Premium, *available at* https://www.congress.gov/114/plaws/publ10/PLAW-114publ10.pdf (site visited July 11, 2017).

[43] 42 U.S.C. § 1395r; 42 C.F.R. § 408.20 (monthly premiums); 42 C.F.R. § 408.40 (deduction from monthly benefits).

[44] 42 C.F.R. §§ 408.42, 408.43, and 408.44.

[45] 42 C.F.R. § 408.60(b).

[46] 42 C.F.R. § 408.44. The authorization is through the Office of Personnel Management (OPM).

If benefits are suspended for excess earnings and are to be resumed before the close of the taxable year, the individual is not billed for Part B premiums but can continue to pay such premiums to keep his or her coverage.[47] If payment of premiums is not to be resumed before the end of the taxable year, the individual is billed directly for premiums.[48]

The grace period for failing to pay the initial premium or subsequent monthly premium ends with the last day of the third month after the billing month; termination of coverage for nonpayment is effective with the first month following the end of the grace period.[49] Overdue payments remain an obligation and can be deducted from future Social Security or Railroad Retirement or offset against any Part B payments otherwise due, or can be collected directly from the enrollee or the enrollee's estate.[50]

In general, Medicare beneficiaries pay approximately 25 percent of Medicare Part B program costs, with some beneficiaries paying slightly more if they have incurred an increased enrollment premium for late enrollment or re-enrollment.[51] Approximately 75 percent of the Medicare Part B premium is subsidized by the federal government through contributions to the SMI trust fund.[52]

[2] "Hold Harmless" Part B Premiums

Medicare has a "hold harmless" provision that is used to protect beneficiaries from a decrease in the monthly amount of their Social Security checks from the previous year that would otherwise apply in order to cover an increase in the standard Medicare Part B premium amount.[53]

---

[47] 42 C.F.R. § 408.46(a).

[48] 42 C.F.R. § 408.46(b).

[49] 42 C.F.R. § 408.8.

[50] 42 C.F.R. § 408.4(b).

[51] 42 C.F.R. § 408.20(c)(1). Note, too, that MA plans can provide a reduction in the Medicare Part B premium as an additional benefit. *See* 42 C.F.R. § 408.21.

[52] 42 U.S.C. § 1395r. Note that since January 2003, an MA plan may elect to receive a reduction in its payments if 80 percent of the reduction is applied to reduce the standard Medicare Part B premiums of its Medicare enrollees, and the Medicare Part B premium is reduced monthly and is offered to all Medicare enrollees in a specific plan benefit package. 42 C.F.R. § 408.21(a). In addition, the reduction cannot be greater than the standard premium amount determined for the year; however, it can be less. 42 C.F.R. § 408.21(b).

[53] *See* Social Security Act § 1839(f),42 U.S.C. § 1395r(f). *See* SSA Cost-of-Living Adjustment, *available at* http://www.ssa.gov/cola/ (site visited June 7, 2016). *See also* Center for Medicare Advocacy, information about Part B, *available at* https://www.cms.gov/Medicare/Medicare.html (site visited June 8, 2016). Check website periodically for updates.

[3] Part B Income-Related Premium (Above the Standard Premium Amount)

While representing savings to the SMI trust fund, the Part B income-related premium implements a public policy shift, requiring Medicare beneficiaries to pay more in premiums depending on income. Under this provision, the responsibility for determining the income-related portion of the Part B premium resides with SSA, using individual federal income tax data from the Internal Revenue Service (IRS). In resolving administrative disputes about the amount of an income-related Part B premium, SSA must use its administrative review process for the determination of rights regarding non-medical issues.

January 2007 marked the beginning of the application of the Medicare Part B income-related premium whereby Medicare beneficiaries with higher incomes are required to pay a greater portion of the Part B premium costs.[54] This higher premium is added to the Medicare Part B standard monthly premium, plus any applicable premium increase for late enrollment or re-enrollment.[55]

The higher premium amount applies to beneficiaries with federal modified adjusted gross taxable income (as defined by the IRS) over the threshold income amount of $85,000 per individual or $170,000 for a couple.[56] The new approach was phased in from calendar year 2007 through calendar year 2009.[57] At or above this threshold amount, the beneficiary will pay an income-related monthly adjustment amount.[58] For 2011 through 2019, the monthly adjustment amounts are unchanged.[59]

The purpose of the income-related monthly adjustment amount is to reduce the federal subsidy of the Medicare Part B program for beneficiaries with modified adjusted gross income above an established threshold.[60] The Centers for

---

[54] The income-related premium is a requirement of the MMA, § 811. Final regulations implementing the Part B income-related premium can be found at 71 Fed. Reg. 62,923 (Oct. 27, 2006) and are codified at 20 C.F.R. § 418.1001 *et seq.*

[55] 20 C.F.R. § 418.1001 *et seq.* The income-related premium provision amends § 1839 of the Social Security Act, 42 U.S.C. § 1395r. The Deficit Reduction Act of 2005 (DRA), Pub. L. No. 109-171 (Feb. 8, 2006), § 5111, further amended § 1839(i) of the Social Security Act to provide that the payment of the full amount of the income-related monthly adjustment amount was phased in starting in 2007 and was completed in 2009, with a 33 percent phase-in in 2007, 67 percent in 2008, and 100 percent in 2009. Before the DRA, there was a five-year phase-in period. 42 U.S.C. § 1395r(i)(3)(B).

[56] *See* 20 C.F.R. § 418.1105(b). *See also* SSA, "Social Security: Medicare Premiums: Rules for Higher-Income Beneficiaries 2015," *available at* http://www.ssa.gov/pubs/EN-05-10536.pdf (site visited June 7, 2016). Check the SSA.gov website periodically for updates.

[57] 20 C.F.R. §§ 418.1001(b) and 418.1130.

[58] 20 C.F.R. §§ 418.1001(b) and 418.1130.

[59] *See* 20 C.F.R. § 418.1120, *available at* http://www.socialsecurity.gov/OP_Home/cfr20/418/418-1120.htm (site visited June 7, 2016).

[60] *See* 20 C.F.R. § 418.1005.

Medicare & Medicaid Services (CMS) must publish the threshold amounts annually in September in the *Federal Register*. Published threshold amounts will be effective January 1 of the next calendar year for the full calendar year.[61]

[a] Higher Income Medicare Beneficiary Payment Amount Elements

A beneficiary with income above the threshold amount must pay:[62]

1. The Medicare Part B standard monthly premium; plus
2. Any applicable increase in the standard monthly premium for late enrollment or re-enrollment; plus
3. An income-related monthly adjustment amount.

The federal premium subsidy is the portion of the full cost of providing Medicare Part B coverage that is paid by the federal government through transfers into the SMI trust fund, and the income-related monthly adjustment amount is an additional amount of premium that beneficiaries will pay for Medicare Part B coverage if they have income above the threshold. A person's income-related monthly adjustment amount is based on his or her modified adjusted gross income (MAGI).[63]

Medicare beneficiaries required to pay an income-related monthly adjustment amount are not eligible for the limitation on a Medicare Part B standard monthly premium increase beyond the amount of their Social Security (or tier 1 railroad retirement) cost-of-living adjustments.[64]

Those who enroll in Medicare after January 1, 2007, and who are determined to be responsible for an income-related Part B premium will be notified shortly after enrolling in Medicare Part B.[65] Persons who became Medicare

[61] The SSA is the agency responsible for the administration of the Part B Income-related premium process in conjunction with the Internal Revenue Service of the U.S. Department of the Treasury and CMS of the Department of Health and Human Services (HHS). *See* 20 C.F.R. § 418.1005. The modified adjusted gross income (MAGI) ranges will be adjusted annually as described in 20 C.F.R. § 418.1115(e). CMS publishes in the *Federal Register* the dollar amounts for the income-related monthly adjustment amount. For 2011 through 2019, the monthly adjustment amounts are unchanged. *See* http://www.socialsecurity.gov/OP_Home/cfr20/418/418-1120.htm (site visited June 7, 2016).

[62] 20 C.F.R. § 418.1005.

[63] *See* 20 C.F.R. § 418.1001. MAGI is defined in **§ 6.02[C][3][c]** of this Handbook.

[64] 20 C.F.R. §§ 418.1001, 418.1010 (definitions), and 418.1125 (effect on an individual's total Medicare Part B premium).

[65] 20 C.F.R. §§ 418.1001, 418.1010, and 418.1125.

beneficiaries during 2007 or thereafter are notified by the SSA prior to the start of each year if required to pay an income-related Part B premium.[66]

CMS publishes the Medicare Part B standard monthly premium each year.[67] CMS also establishes rules for entitlement to a non-standard premium as well as premium penalties for late enrollment or re-enrollment.[68]

PART B
INCOME-RELATED PREMIUM IN 2017

*Beneficiaries who file an individual tax return with income:**	*Beneficiaries who file a joint tax return with income:*	*Beneficiaries who are married, but file a separate tax return with income:*	*Income-related monthly adjustment amount*	*Total monthly Part B premium amount*
Less than or equal to $85,000	Less than or equal to $170,000	Less than or equal to $85,000	$0.00	$134.00
Greater than $85,000 and less than or equal to $107,000	Greater than $170,000 and less than or equal to $214,000	—	$53.50	$187.50
Greater than $107,000 and less than or equal to $160,000	Greater than $214,000 and less than or equal to $320,000	—	$133.90	$267.90
Greater than $160,000 and less than or equal to $214,000	Greater than $320,000 and less than or equal to $428,000	Greater than $85,000 and less than or equal to $129,000	$214.30	$348.30
Greater than $214,000	Greater than $428,000	Greater than $129,000	$294.60	$428.60

* MAGI ranges are adjusted annually and published in the *Federal Register* in September of each year. *See* 20 C.F.R. § 418.1115(e). For 2017, *see* https://www.federalregister.gov/documents/2016/11/15/2016-27425/medicare-program-medicare-part-b-monthly-actuarial-rates-premium-rate-and-annual-deductible. For 2011 through 2019, the monthly adjustment amounts are unchanged. *See* 20 C.F.R. § 418.1120, *available at* http://www.socialsecurity.gov/OP_Home/cfr20/418/418-1120.htm (site visited June 7, 2016).

[66] 20 C.F.R. §§ 418.1001, 418.1010, and 418.1125.
[67] 42 C.F.R. § 408.20.
[68] 42 C.F.R. § 408.20(e)(6).x

The SSA modified and clarified its definition of major life-changing events that allow a beneficiary to request a review of a determination that states the beneficiary must pay an income-related premium. A beneficiary may request that the SSA use more recent tax information to make the calculation if:

1. A beneficiary receives a settlement payment from a former employer in lieu of periodic pension payments and/or health insurance coverage as a result of the former employer's closure, bankruptcy, or reorganization;
2. A beneficiary experiences a loss of investment property as a result of fraud or theft due to a criminal act by a third party;
3. A beneficiary experiences a reduction in or loss of income from an employer's pension plan due to termination or reorganization of the pension plan or a scheduled cessation of pension, regardless of whether the pension is insured.[69]

A non-standard premium may be established in individual cases only if the individual is entitled to old age or disability benefits for the months of November and December, and actually receives the corresponding benefit checks in December and January.[70] For calendar years after 1988, beginning with calendar year 1989, a premium increase greater than the cost-of-living increase is still a prerequisite for a non-standard premium.[71] A non-standard premium, however, is not precluded solely because the cash benefit is further reduced as a result of government pension offset or workers' compensation payment.[72] The non-standard premium is the greater of the following: the premium paid for December; the standard premium promulgated for January, reduced as necessary to compensate for (1) the fact that the cost-of-living increase was less than the increase in the standard premium; or (2) the further reduction in benefit because of government pension offset of workers' compensation payments.[73]

[b] Determining the Amount to Be Paid

SSA uses information that it gets from the IRS to determine whether beneficiaries who are enrolled in Medicare Part B are required to pay an income-related monthly adjustment amount. SSA changes income-related monthly adjustment amount determinations using information provided by a beneficiary under circumstances. SSA also notifies beneficiaries when the Social Security benefit

[69] 75 Fed. Reg. 41,084 (July 15, 2010), amending 20 C.F.R. §§ 418.1205, 418.1210, 418.1230, 418.1255, and 418.1265.

[70] 42 C.F.R. § 408.20(e)(1) (basic rule).

[71] 42 C.F.R. § 408.20(e)(3(i).

[72] 42 C.F.R. § 408.20(e)(3)(ii).

[73] 42 C.F.R. § 408.20(e)(4).

amounts they receive will change based on its income-related monthly adjustment amount determination.[74]

SSA determines a beneficiary's income-related monthly adjustment amount using the beneficiary's tax filing status and MAGI.[75] A beneficiary's income-related premium amount is determined using a set of tables reflecting MAGI ranges. For each range, an unsubsidized Medicare Part B premium percentage is assigned. The remainder is subsidized from the SMI trust fund. The first year in which affected Part B enrollees had to pay the full amount of the income-related premiums was 2009. In 2008, if a beneficiary had to pay a Part B income-related monthly adjustment amount, he or she was responsible for 67 percent of any applicable income-related monthly adjustment amount.[76] In 2007, the beneficiary was responsible for 33 percent of the applicable amount.[77] For 2011 through 2019, the monthly adjustment amounts are unchanged.[78]

[c] Subpart B Income-Related Monthly Adjustment Amount

The Medicare Part B income-related monthly adjustment amount is codified in the Code of Federal Regulations at 20 C.F.R. Part 418. It contains the rules that SSA uses to determine when one will be required to pay an income-related monthly adjustment amount, in addition to one's Medicare Part B standard monthly premium, plus any applicable premium increase for late enrollment or reenrollment.[79]

Section 811 of the MMA amended the Social Security Act to provide that the limitation on increases in the Medicare Part B standard monthly premium for some beneficiaries will not apply to beneficiaries who are responsible for an income-related premium.[80] The standard Part B Medicare premium is set to cover

---

[74] 20 C.F.R. § 418.1005(c). *See* 20 C.F.R. § 418.1120 *available at* http://www.socialsecurity.gov/OP_Home/cfr20/418/418-1120.htm (site visited June 7, 2016). MAGI ranges are adjusted annually and generally published in the *Federal Register* in September for the following year. *See* 20 C.F.R. § 418.1115(e). The income thresholds applicable to the increased Part B premiums will stay the same as in 2010 through December 31, 2019. *See* ACA § 3402, amending § 1839(i) of the Social Security Act.

[75] 20 C.F.R. § 418.1120.

[76] 72 Fed. Reg. 57,039 (Oct. 5, 2007).

[77] 72 Fed. Reg. 57,039. Check the tables at 72 Fed. Reg. 57,041–47 (Oct. 5, 2007) for the listings of income-related premium ranges, income-related monthly adjustment amounts, and total monthly premium amounts. For 2011 through 2019, the monthly adjustment amounts are unchanged. *See* 20 C.F.R. § 418.1120 *available at* http://www.socialsecurity.gov/OP_Home/cfr20/418/418-1120.htm (site visited June 7, 2016).

[78] *See* 20 C.F.R. § 418.1120 *available at* http://www.socialsecurity.gov/OP_Home/cfr20/418/418-1120.htm (site visited June 7, 2016).

[79] *See* Table at 20 C.F.R. § 418.1120(b)(1).

[80] *See* Table at 20 C.F.R. § 418.1120(b)(1).

approximately 25 percent of the Medicare Part B program costs. The other 75 percent is subsidized in large part by the federal government by contributions to the SMI trust fund.[81]

In determining whether one is required to pay an income-related premium, SSA requests information about a beneficiary's MAGI from IRS for the tax year two years prior to the effective year of the income-related monthly adjustment amount determination.[82] If IRS does not provide information about a beneficiary's MAGI for two years prior to the effective year, then SSA will use a beneficiary's MAGI for the tax year three years prior to the effective year of the income-related monthly adjustment amount determination.[83] If the beneficiary must pay an income-related monthly adjustment amount, the beneficiary will not be eligible for the limitation on Medicare Part B standard monthly premium increase beyond the amount of his or her Social Security (or tier 1 railroad retirement) cost-of-living adjustments.[84]

MAGI is defined at 26 U.S.C. Section 62 and in related regulations and includes certain other forms of income that may be excluded from adjusted gross income for purposes of determining the amount of federal income tax that one must pay.[85] The definition includes the beneficiary's adjusted gross income as defined by the IRS, plus the following forms of tax-exempt income:[86]

1. Tax-exempt interest income;
2. Income from United States savings bonds used to pay higher education tuition and fees;
3. Foreign earned income;
4. Income derived from sources within Guam, American Samoa, or the Northern Mariana islands; and
5. Income from sources within Puerto Rico.

SSA will use three years of tax information only until information for two years prior becomes available.[87]

---

[81] 20 C.F.R. §§ 418.1115 and 418.1120.

[82] 20 C.F.R. § 418.1135(a).

[83] 20 C.F.R. § 418.1135(b).

[84] 71 Fed. Reg. 10,926 (Mar. 3, 2006); 42 C.F.R. Pt. 418, *available at* http://www.ecfr.gov/cgi-bin/retrieveECFR?gp=1&SID=2176b8f0721322be2e8bfd80a8a2881f&ty=HTML&h=L&r=PART&n=20y2.0.1.1.10#20:2.0.1.1.10.2 (site visited June 7, 2016).

[85] 71 Fed. Reg. 10,926 (Mar. 3, 2006). *See* 42 C.F.R. Pt. 418, *available at* http://www.ecfr.gov/cgi-bin/retrieveECFR?gp=1&SID=2176b8f0721322be2e8bfd80a8a2881f&ty=HTML&h=L&r=PART&n=20y2.0.1.1.10#20:2.0.1.1.10.2 (site visited June 7, 2016).

[86] *See* 20 C.F.R. § 418.1010(b)(6).

[87] *See* 20 C.F.R. §§ 418.1135–418.1150.

If three years of IRS information is used, the beneficiary may request that SSA use information provided by the beneficiary for the tax year two years before that year. SSA will use this information if it will result in a lower income-related monthly adjustment amount. In order to make an initial determination based on beneficiary-supplied information, the beneficiary must provide a retained copy of his or her signed federal income tax return for that year, a copy that the beneficiary has requested for that year from IRS, or an IRS transcript of the beneficiary's return. If the beneficiary supplies a copy of his or her retained IRS return, SSA will verify this information with IRS.[88]

In some cases, IRS will not have data to provide SSA regarding an individual's MAGI because the amount of the individual's income is below the level for which an income tax return must be filed. SSA will not be making income-related monthly adjustment amount determinations in such situations because this individual's income would also be below the MAGI threshold. If, however, SSA receives information which indicates that an individual who has not filed a tax return has income which exceeds the established threshold for an income-related monthly adjustment amount, SSA will make such a determination.[89] The statute requires that the Secretary of HHS, in conjunction with the Secretary of the Treasury, issue regulations that provide for the treatment of the premium adjustment with respect to such individuals.[90]

[d] The Sliding Scale Formula and How It Applies

Section 1839(i) of the Social Security Act, 42 U.S.C. Section 1395r, prescribes a sliding scale formula that SSA will use to establish annually four income-related monthly adjustment amounts beginning in 2007.[91] The calculation of the income-related monthly adjustment amount reduces a beneficiary's Medicare Part B premium subsidy using specified percentages, and the amount of this premium subsidy reduction is the income-related monthly adjustment amount.[92]

To determine each income-related monthly adjustment amount, CMS will use the unsubsidized Medicare Part B premium (approximately four times the Medicare Part B standard monthly premium) and multiply it by a specified percentage.[93] The percentage used in the calculation increases as the amount of MAGI increases.[94] The premium subsidy is the amount of the Part B premium

[88] *See* 20 C.F.R. § 418.1240.
[89] *See* 20 C.F.R. § 418.1135(f).
[90] 42 U.S.C. 1395r(i)(4)(B)(iii).
[91] *See* 20 C.F.R. § 418.1115.
[92] 20 C.F.R. § 418.1120.
[93] 20 C.F.R. § 418.1120.
[94] 20 C.F.R. § 418.1120.

paid by the SMI trust fund.[95] Currently, beneficiaries not subject to the Part B income-related premium pay 25 percent of monthly premium costs.[96]

The income thresholds applicable to the **increased** Part B premiums will stay the same for the period January 1, 2011, through December 31, 2019.[97]

1. Greater than $85,000 and less than or equal to $107,000;
2. Greater than $107,000 and less than or equal to $160,000;
3. Greater than $160,000 and less than or equal to $214,000; and
4. Greater than $214,000.

In 2017, the MAGI ranges for individuals who are married and file a joint tax return for the tax year used by SSA to make its income-related monthly adjustment amount determinations are as follows:[98]

1. Greater than $170,000 and less than or equal to $214,000;
2. Greater than $214,000 and less than or equal to $320,000;
3. Greater than $320,000 and less than or equal to $428,000; and
4. Greater than $428,000.

In 2017, the MAGI ranges for married individuals who file a separate return and have lived with their spouse at any time during the tax year used by SSA to make the income-related monthly adjustment amount determinations are as follows:[99]

1. Greater than $85,000 and less than or equal to $129,000; and
2. Greater than $129,000.

Section 1839(i)(3)(C)(iii) (42 U.S.C. § 1395r) provides for the MAGI ranges for individuals who file their federal income tax return with a filing status of married filing separately and who also have lived with their spouse at any time during the year to be reduced by the threshold amount established for that calendar year which may result in a higher income-related monthly adjustment amount for

[95] 20 C.F.R. § 418.1120.
[96] 20 C.F.R. § 418.1120.
[97] *See* ACA § 3402, amending § 1839(i) of the Social Security Act.
[98] 20 C.F.R. § 418.1120.
[99] 20 C.F.R. § 418.1120(b)(3).

these individuals.[100] Section 1839(i)(1), however, provides a threshold amount that is $85,000, but this may change after 2019.[101]

SSA will use this information to determine which amount applies to a beneficiary based on the beneficiary's tax filing status in the tax year SSA is using to determine the beneficiary's income-related monthly adjustment amount.[102]

[e] Applicable Modified Adjusted Gross Income Ranges

The range amounts for individuals who are married filing jointly are double the range amounts for single income tax filers, with IRS recognizing three additional filing statuses: head of household, qualifying widow(er), and married filing separately.[103]

If a beneficiary files an amended tax return for the tax year SSA used to make a determination of his or her income-related monthly adjustment amount, the beneficiary may request that SSA use his or her amended tax return for that year; the beneficiary must provide to SSA proof that he or she filed an amended tax return with IRS, including the beneficiary's retained copy of the amended tax return, and a letter from IRS verifying receipt of the return, or an IRS transcript of his or her amended tax return. If the beneficiary believes that IRS provided incorrect modified adjusted gross income information and SSA used that information to determine the beneficiary's income-related monthly adjustment amount, the beneficiary may request that SSA make a new income-related monthly adjustment amount determination.[104]

[f] Applicable Modified Adjusted Gross Income Adjustment Amount

Section 1839(i)(3)(B) requires the amount of the full income-related monthly adjustment to be phased in over a three-year period beginning in 2007. The percentage changed each year so that the income-related monthly adjustment amount was phased in starting in 2009.[105]

---

[100] 20 C.F.R. § 418.1120(b)(3).

[101] 20 C.F.R. § 418.1120(b)(3). The income thresholds applicable to the **increased** Part B premiums will stay the same as in 2010 through December 31, 2019. *See* ACA § 3402, amending § 1839(i) of the Social Security Act, *see* https://search.yahoo.com/yhs/search?p=ACA+%C2%A7%E2%80%893402%2C+amending+%C2%A7%E2%80%891839%28i%29+of+the+Social+Security+Act&ei=UTF-8&hspart=mozilla&hsimp=yhs-002 (site visited June 13, 2016).

[102] 20 C.F.R. § 418.1120(c).

[103] *See* 20 C.F.R. § 418.1120.

[104] 20 C.F.R. § 418.1150.

[105] 20 C.F.R. § 418.1120.

[g] When the Social Security Administration Will Use a More Recent Tax Year (Major Life Changing Events)

The Secretary of HHS is to establish procedures in conjunction with the Secretary of the Treasury for determining a person's MAGI for a tax year more recent than the information ordinarily provided by IRS when:[106]

- The beneficiary experiences a major life-changing event;[107]
- The major life-changing event in question results in a significant reduction in the beneficiary's MAGI;
- The beneficiary requests that SSA use a more recent tax year's MAGI; and
- The beneficiary provides evidence of the event and evidence of the reduction in MAGI.

Such events include marriage, divorce, death of a spouse; partial or full work stoppage; and loss of income from income-producing property (when the loss is not at the beneficiary's direction, for example, loss of income from real property due to a natural disaster declared by the President of the United States or by a state governor or arson, or destruction of livestock or crops).[108]

Life-changing events also include a reduction or loss of certain forms of pension income due to termination or reorganization of the pension plan, or a scheduled cessation of one's pension benefits.[109] For reductions made in income-related monthly adjustment amount determination based on one's request due to a qualifying major life-changing event, the determination will generally be effective on January 1 of the calendar year for which SSA makes the determination; and if the beneficiary enrolled in Medicare Part B after January 1 of the year for which SSA makes an income-related monthly adjustment amount determination based on the beneficiary's request due to a major life-changing event, the determination will be effective the month of the beneficiary's Medicare Part B enrollment.[110]

A life-changing event does not include events that affect expenses but not income; in addition, a life-changing event does not include events that result in the loss of dividend income.[111]

---

[106] 20 C.F.R. §§ 418.1201 and 418.1225.

[107] Form SSA-44 (11-2011) for applying for a change based on a life-changing event is *available at* http://www.ssa.gov/online/ssa-44.pdf (site visited June 7, 2016).

[108] 20 C.F.R. §§ 418.1205 and 418.1225.

[109] 20 C.F.R. § 418.1205(f).

[110] 20 C.F.R. § 418.1230. A useful SSA form for requesting a reduction in one's income-related monthly adjustment amount based on a recognized life-changing event can be found at http://www.ssa.gov/online/ssa-44.pdf (site visited June 7, 2016).

[111] 20 C.F.R. § 418.1210.

When a beneficiary asks SSA to use a more recent tax year because of a life-changing event, SSA will ask the beneficiary to provide evidence of the major life-changing event and evidence as to how the event significantly reduced the beneficiary's MAGI.[112] Unless SSA has information in its records that raises a doubt about the evidence presented, additional evidence documenting the life-changing event will not be necessary.[113]

The effective date of an income-related monthly adjustment amount initial determination based on a more recent tax year for requests made during or after 2007 and the beneficiary's MAGI for the more recent tax year can be significantly reduced as a result of a major life-changing event. SSA's initial determination is generally effective on January 1 of the year in which the beneficiary makes his or her request.[114] If the beneficiary's first month of enrollment or re-enrollment in Medicare Part B is after January of the year for which he or she makes a request for use of a more recent tax year, SSA's initial determination is effective on the first day of the beneficiary's entitlement to Medicare Part B enrollment or re-enrollment.[115]

If a beneficiary knows of changes in the information provided to SSA that will result in the use of a more recent tax year, the beneficiary is to inform SSA, allowing SSA to ascertain whether the beneficiary's income-related monthly adjustment amount should be eliminated or adjusted.[116] SSA will accept new MAGI information at any time after the beneficiary's request until the end of the calendar year following the more recent tax year(s) SSA used.[117]

[h] Appealing an Income-Related Monthly Adjustment (IRMA)

[i] General Provisions. When SSA decides that a beneficiary must pay an income-related monthly adjustment (IRMA), that decision and the amount of any adjustment, based on information SSA receives from IRS or the beneficiary, will be communicated to the beneficiary through a notice of an initial determination from SSA, explaining that if the beneficiary disagrees, he or she may request that SSA reconsider the determination.[118] This notice will also explain the beneficiary's right to reconsideration or a new determination.[119] The notice will explain that the beneficiary may request a new initial determination, rather than reconsideration, if he or she believes the information SSA used in its initial

[112] 20 C.F.R. §§ 418.1255 and 418.1265.
[113] 20 C.F.R. § 418.1250.
[114] 20 C.F.R. § 418.1230.
[115] 20 C.F.R. § 418.1230.
[116] 20 C.F.R. § 418.1240.
[117] 20 C.F.R. §§ 418.1240 and 418.1245.
[118] 20 C.F.R. § 418.1315.
[119] 20 C.F.R. § 418.1315.

determination was correct, but the beneficiary wants SSA to use different information about his or her modified adjusted gross income.[120]

In making initial determinations and reconsiderations, SSA will use the rules for the administrative review process that it uses for determinations of beneficiary rights regarding non-medical issues under Title II of the Act.[121] SSA will use its rules for determinations and decisions about a beneficiary's rights regarding non-medical issues under Title II of the Social Security Act, as described in 42 C.F.R. Part 404, Subpart J.[122] If dissatisfied with SSA's reconsideration, the beneficiary may request further review, including a hearing before an administrative law judge (ALJ) from the Office of Medicare Hearings and Appeals (OMHA) at HHS, review by the Medicare Appeals Council (MAC), and judicial review, consistent with 42 C.F.R. Part 405, subpart I.[123] As part of the request, the beneficiary will be required to provide consent to HHS for the agency to release relevant tax return information to OMHA or the MAC for the purposes of adjudicating any appeal of the amount of an income-related adjustment to the Part B premium subsidy and for any judicial review of that appeal.[124] An initial determination is the determination SSA will make about a beneficiary's income-related monthly adjustment amount that is subject to administrative review.[125] For the purposes of administering the income-related monthly adjustment amount, initial determinations include but are not limited to determinations about (1) the amount of the beneficiary's income-related monthly adjustment amount based on information provided by IRS and (2) any change in the beneficiary's income-related monthly adjustment amount based on a request for a new determination.[126]

[ii] New Initial Determination. SSA regulations provide for requesting a "new initial determination" that a beneficiary may use when he or she does not dispute the accuracy of the IRS modified adjusted gross income information SSA used, or the determination SSA made based on that information, but the beneficiary wants SSA to use different information.[127] The beneficiary may provide evidence of his or her modified adjusted gross income for a more recent tax year than the information provided by IRS when the beneficiary has experienced a major life-changing event that significantly reduces his or her income or when IRS has provided modified adjusted gross income information from three years prior to

---

[120] 20 C.F.R. §§ 418.1315, 418.1325, 418.1330, and 418.1335.

[121] 20 C.F.R. § 418.1340.

[122] 20 C.F.R. § 418.1340.

[123] 20 C.F.R. § 418.1350.

[124] 20 C.F.R. § 418.1350.

[125] 20 C.F.R. §§ 418.1301–418.1310.

[126] 20 C.F.R. § 418.1310.

[127] 20 C.F.R. § 418.1310.

the premium effective year and the beneficiary supplies a retained copy of his or her federal income tax return for the tax year two years prior.[128]

[D] Copayments and Deductibles

Under Part B, a beneficiary is responsible for an annual deductible and copayment (or coinsurance amount) for covered items and services,[129] which is based on the Medicare-approved amount (not the actual charge) for incurred expenses.[130] The annual deductible is offset against first incurred expenses in a given calendar year.[131]

Generally, Medicare requires beneficiaries to pay a 20 percent copayment amount based on the Medicare-approved amount for most Part B services.[132] Medicare then reimburses the Part B provider or supplier 80 percent of the Medicare-approved amount.[133]

Under the Outpatient Prospective Payment System (OPPS), a beneficiary's coinsurance with respect to outpatient hospital services is calculated for each

---

[128] 20 C.F.R. § 418.1310.

[129] 42 U.S.C. § 1395l.

[130] 42 U.S.C. § 1395l(b); 42 C.F.R. § 410.160. *See* 42 U.S.C. § 1395u(b)(3). The Medicare-approved charge is sometimes referred to as the Medicare reasonable charge amount. The reasonable charge amount is a complicated calculation. It is generally the (1) lowest of the physician's actual charge; (2) the physician's customary charge to other Medicare beneficiaries for similar services as determined by the contractor according to its profile of that physician's charges; and (3) the local or geographic prevailing charge recognized by the contractor for similar services provided by physicians to Medicare patients. *See also* 42 C.F.R. § 405.501.

[131] *See* 42 C.F.R. § 408.40 *et seq.*

[132] 42 U.S.C. § 1395l(a); 42 C.F.R. § 410.152(b). (Exceptions include clinical diagnostic laboratory tests provided by laboratories and physicians who participate in the Medicare assignment program; home health care; used durable medical equipment that is purchased at a price that is at least 25 percent less than the reasonable charge for comparable new equipment; outpatient and ambulatory surgical services; pneumococcal vaccine; donation of a kidney for transplant surgery.) *See also* list of covered services found below. Note, too, that with respect to outpatient hospital services reimbursed under Part B, the beneficiary copayment amount was being based on actual charges rather than the Medicare-approved amount. *See* Stephenson v. Shalala, 87 F.3d 350 (9th Cir. 1996). Also, the Balanced Budget Act of 1997 (BBA '97), Pub. L. No. 105-33 (Aug. 5, 1997), required the establishment of a Prospective Payment System for Hospital Outpatient Department Services, including fee schedules and coinsurance amounts, effective for services on or after January 1, 1999. (§ 4523(a), amending § 1833(t) of the Social Security Act, 42 U.S.C. § 1395l(t).) This payment system has resulted in beneficiaries sometimes paying substantially more than 20 percent for some outpatient services. The Middle Class Tax Relief and Job Creation Act of 2012 (Pub. L. No. 112-96 (Feb. 22, 2012), 126 Stat. 156, § 3002), *available at* http://www.gpo.gov/fdsys/pkg/PLAW-112pub l96/pdf/PLAW-112publ96.pdf (site visited June 7, 2016) made changes to the time periods that rural hospitals are able to bill for services.

[133] 42 U.S.C. § 1395l(a); 42 C.F.R. § 410.152(b). Persons using non-participating physicians may be charged 15 percent above the Medicare approved amount where the actual charge is greater than Medicare's approved amount.

ambulatory payment classification (APC), based on 20 percent of the national median APC calculation.[134] This is a different calculation from the usual 20 percent copayment amount calculation under Medicare Part B. Under OPPS, the 20 percent copayment amount could be quite large. Section 204 of the Balanced Budget Refinement Act of 1999 (BBRA) provides that no *single* APC coinsurance amount can be greater than the hospital inpatient deductible in a given year.[135] However, hospitals may charge more than one APC per beneficiary outpatient department encounter, depending on the services provided.[136]

§ 6.03 COVERED MEDICAL AND OTHER HEALTH CARE SERVICES

[A] Covered Services

[1] Medically Reasonable and Necessary Medical and Other Health Services

Medicare Part B provides coverage for expenses incurred by beneficiaries for medically reasonable and necessary medical and other health services.[137] Advocates should consult the Medicare National Coverage Determinations (NCD) Manual for updates and modifications to Medicare coverage policy.[138] Medicare provides coverage for categories of services as follows:[139]

- Physician services, including surgery, consultation, and office and institutional calls (visits), and services and supplies, including drugs and biologicals that cannot be self-administered, furnished incident to a physician's professional service;[140]

---

[134] *See* BBA '97, § 4523, amending 42 U.S.C. § 1395l.

[135] *See* BBRA 1999, Pub. L. No. 106-113, amending 42 U.S.C. § 1395l(t)(8)(C).

[136] *See* Medicare Claims Processing (MCP) Manual, Chapter 4—Part B Hospital (Including Inpatient Hospital Part B and OPPS), § 10.2 (APC Payment Groups), *available at* http://www.cms.gov/Regulations-and-Guidance/Guidance/Manuals/downloads/clm104c04.pdf (site visited June 7, 2016).

[137] 42 U.S.C. § 1395y(a)(1)(A). The reasonable and necessary determination, while informed by physician and other health care provider opinion, is ultimately a determination of the Secretary. *See, e.g.*, MedPac, "Appendix B: An Introduction to How Medicare Makes Coverage Decisions," *available at* http://www.medpac.gov/documents/reports/Mar03_AppB.pdf?sfvrsn=0 (site visited June 7, 2016); *see also* Erringer v. Thompson, 371 F.3d 625 (9th Cir. 2004), *available at* http://openjurist.org/371/f3d/625/erringer-v-thompson (site visited June 7, 2016).

[138] Medicare National Coverage Determinations (NCD) Manual, CMS Pub. 100-03, *available at* http://www.cms.gov/medicare-coverage-database/overview-and-quick-search.aspx (site visited June 7, 2016). *See also* CMS's Medicare Coverage Database Archive site, https://localcoverage.cms.gov/mcd_archive/overview.asp (site visited June 7, 2016).

[139] 42 U.S.C. §§ 1395k(a) and 1395x.

[140] *See also* 42 C.F.R. §§ 410.20(b) and 410.22–410.25.

- Outpatient rehabilitation services;[141]
- Outpatient hospital services furnished incident to physician services;[142]
- Outpatient physical therapy; outpatient speech language pathology services; and diagnostic X-ray tests, laboratory tests,[143] and other diagnostic tests;[144]
- X-ray, radium, and radioactive isotope therapy;[145]
- Surgical dressings, and splints, casts, and other devices used for reduction of fractures and dislocations;[146]

---

[141] *See also* 42 C.F.R. §§ 410.61 and 410.100.

[142] 42 U.S.C. § 1395k(a)(2)(B)(i), 42 C.F.R. § 410.27, and Medicare Benefit Policy (MBP) Manual, CMS Pub. 100-02, Ch. 6, § 10, *available at* http://www.cms.hhs.gov/manuals/Downloads/bp102c06.pdf (site visited June 7, 2016).

[143] Note, too, that the Medicare Improvements for Patients and Providers Act of 2008 (MIPPA), Pub. L. No. 110-275, (July 15, 2008), § 145 (clinical laboratory tests) repealed the Medicare Competitive Bidding Demonstration Project for Clinical Laboratory Services, effective on enactment of MIPPA.

[144] *See also* 42 C.F.R. §§ 410.61 and 410.100; MIPPA § 143 (Speech-language pathology services), which states that the term "out-patient speech-language pathology services" has the meaning given the term "outpatient physical therapy services" in § 1661(ll) of the Social Security Act, 42 U.S.C. § 1395x(ll) and that "speech-language pathology" shall be substituted for "physical therapy" each place it occurs, and that the term "speech-language pathologist" shall be substituted for "physical therapist" each place it appears. Medicare has been making decisions with respect to speech generating devices (SGDs) that are causing controversy, including limiting access to certain devices that also have smartphone technologies. *See, e.g.*, Center for Medicare Advocacy, "Medicare's Reluctance to Embrace Technology: Effects on the Coverage of Speech Generating Devices," *available at* http://www.medicareadvocacy.org/medicares-reluctance-to-embrace-technology-effects-on-the-coverage-of-speech-generating-devices/ (site visited June 7, 2016); Center for Medicare Advocacy, "CMS Rescinds Restrictive Policy and Will Reconsider Technological Advances," *available at* http://www.medicareadvocacy.org/welcome-reprieve-for-people-who-need-speech-generating-devices-sgds-to-communicate/ (site visited June 7, 2016). A final SGD NCD was published by CMS on July 29, 2015. It authorizes Medicare coverage for SGDs for other types of communication e-mail, text and phone messages- in addition to speech. Further, Congress passed, and the President signed, the Steve Gleason Act, which moves the coverage of SGDs from the rental category to the purchase category for three years, allowing SGD users to take their personalized devices into any care setting. The Steve Gleason Act also allows better access to accessories necessary to operate SGDs. *See* Center for Medicare Advocacy, "Better Medicare Coverage of Speech Generating Devices, *available at* http://www.medicareadvocacy.org/better-medicare-coverage-of-speech-generating-devices/ (site visited June 7, 2016). *See also* extended coverage of LGBT issues: http://www.hhs.gov/civil-rights/for-individuals/section-1557/index.html (site visited July 25, 2016); summary of the final rule: http://www.hhs.gov/sites/default/files/2016-06-07-section-1557-final-rule-summary-508.pdf (site visited July 25, 2016).

[145] 42 C.F.R. § 410.35 and Medicare Benefit Policy (MBP) Manual, CMS Pub. 100-02, Ch. 6, § 10, *available at* http://www.cms.gov/Regulations-and-Guidance/Guidance/Manuals/downloads/bp102c06.pdf (site visited June 7, 2016).

[146] 42 C.F.R. § 410.36(a)(1) and Medicare Benefit Policy (MBP) Manual, CMS Pub. 100-02, Ch. 6, § 10, *available at* http://www.cms.gov/Regulations-and-Guidance/Guidance/Manuals/downloads/bp102c06.pdf (site visited June 7, 2016).

- Rental or purchase of DME for use in the patient's home;[147]
- Ambulance service;[148]
- Prosthetic devices that replace all or part of an internal body organ;[149]
- Preventive benefits (discussed below);[150]
- Leg, arm, back, and neck braces and artificial legs, arms, and eyes;[151]
- Certain medical supplies used in connection with home dialysis delivery systems;[152]
- Rural health clinic (RHC) services;[153]

---

[147] Rules for customized items of DME are located at 42 C.F.R. § 414.224. Note that ACA § 6407 requires a face-to-face encounter with the patient and physician for certification of the need for DME or for home health care services. This requirement is applicable to all certifications on or after January 1, 2010. Certifications via telehealth (subject to certain limitations) are permitted. 42 C.F.R. § 414.224.

[148] *See* 42 C.F.R. § 410.40. As an additional fraud and abuse protection, the ACA states that only Medicare-enrolled physicians or other "eligible professionals" can prescribe DME and home health care. Section 6407(d) *See* 42 C.F.R. § 424.506 *et seq.* (May 5, 2010), effective July 6, 2010. CMS is using its Provider Enrollment, Chain, and Ownership System (PECOS), described in the above interim final regulations, as the vehicle through which it is an eligible professional, defined in the ACA, as one who has enrolled under Medicare's Quality Care Reporting System for providers. *See* § 6405(a), and its reference to § 1866(j) of the Social Security Act, 42 U.S.C. § 1395cc(j) (Enrollment Process for Providers of Services and Suppliers). An "enrolled physician" is defined as one who has registered with Medicare in accordance with rules established by the Secretary. *See* § 6505(a) and its reference to § 1848(k)(3)(B) of the Social Security Act, 42 U.S.C. § 1395w-4 (Payment Based on Fee Schedule). 42 U.S.C. § 1395w-4(k)(3)(B) (Covered Professional Services and Eligible Professionals Defined) describes an "eligible professional" as a physician, a practitioner (including a certified nurse anesthetist, a certified midwife, a clinical social worker, a clinical psychologist (*see* 42 U.S.C. § 1395u)), and a physical or occupational therapist or a qualified speech-language pathologist. Requests for payments need to include the national provider identifier for the physician who periodically reviews the plan for services. *See* Middle Class Tax Relief and Job Creation Act of 2012, Pub. L. No. 112-96 (Feb. 22, 2012), 126 Stat. 156.

[149] 42 C.F.R. § 410.36(a)(2) and MBP Manual, CMS Pub. 100-02, Ch. 6, § 10, *available at* http://www.cms.gov/Regulations-and-Guidance/Guidance/Manuals/downloads/bp102c06.pdf (site visited June 7, 2016).

[150] 42 C.F.R. § 410.16 and MBP Manual, CMS Pub. 100-02, Ch. 15, § 280, *available at* http://www.cms.gov/Regulations-and-Guidance/Guidance/Manuals/downloads/bp102c15.pdf (site visited June 7, 2016). It should be noted that ACA, § 4001 *et seq.* (Pub. L. No. 111-148), puts a major emphasis on preventive services and education about the value of preventive services through the creation of interagency task forces and community-based initiatives. One should look for the steady addition over time of new preventive services to Medicare's array of benefits.

[151] 42 C.F.R. § 410.36(a)(3) and MBP Manual, CMS Pub. 100-02, Ch. 6, § 10, *available at* http://www.cms.gov/Regulations-and-Guidance/Guidance/Manuals/downloads/bp102c06.pdf (site visited June 7, 2016).

[152] Special rules governing payment for suppliers of home dialysis supplies and equipment are found at 42 C.F.R. § 414.330.

[153] *See also* 42 C.F.R. §§ 405.2401–405.2417.

- Ambulatory surgical center (ASC) services;[154]
- Antigens and blood-clotting factors;[155]
- Influenza, pneumococcal, and hepatitis B vaccines;[156]
- Some health maintenance organization (HMO) services;[157]
- Some Pap smear screenings;[158]
- Some mammography screenings;[159]
- Qualified psychologist services; and[160]
- Therapeutic shoes for patients with severe diabetic foot disease.[161]

Medicare Part B also covers home health visits not covered under Part A and outpatient hospital services not reimbursed by a contractor (an entity under contract with CMS for the administration of Part A services).

It should also be noted that some medical services may be considered for coverage under more than one of the categories of services mentioned above, for example, EKG services. In those instances, if the requirements for one category of service are met, payment is available.[162]

---

[154] 42 U.S.C. § 1395k(a)(2)(F)(i), 42 C.F.R. §§ 410.3 and 410.165, and MBP Manual, CMS Pub. 100-02, Ch. 15, § 280, *available at* http://www.cms.gov/Regulations-and-Guidance/Guidance/Manuals/downloads/bp102c15.pdf (site visited June 7, 2016).

[155] 42 C.F.R. § 410.63 and MBP Manual, CMS Pub. 100-02, Ch. 15, § 50, *available at* http://www.cms.gov/Regulations-and-Guidance/Guidance/Manuals/downloads/bp102c15.pdf (site visited June 7, 2016).

[156] 42 C.F.R. § 410.57 and MBP Manual, CMS Pub. 100-02, Ch. 15, § 50, *available at* http://www.cms.gov/Regulations-and-Guidance/Guidance/Manuals/downloads/bp102c15.pdf (site visited June 7, 2016).

[157] 42 C.F.R. § 410.58.

[158] 42 C.F.R. § 410.56 and MBP Manual, CMS Pub. 100-02, Ch. 15, § 250, *available at* http://www.cms.gov/Regulations-and-Guidance/Guidance/Manuals/downloads/bp102c15.pdf (site visited June 7, 2016).

[159] 42 U.S.C. § 1395m(c)(2). Medicare will pay for one mammogram for female beneficiaries between the ages of 35 to 39 and Medicare will pay for annual mammograms for female beneficiaries age 40 and over. The Part B annual deductible is waived for these services.

[160] 42 U.S.C. § 1395k(2)(B)(iii), 42 C.F.R. § 410.71, and MBP Manual, CMS Pub. 100-02, Ch. 15, § 250, *available at* http://www.cms.gov/Regulations-and-Guidance/Guidance/Manuals/downloads/bp102c15.pdf (site visited June 7, 2016).

[161] 42 U.S.C. § 1395l(o) and MBP Manual, CMS Pub. 100-02, Ch. 15, § 290, *available at* http://www.cms.gov/Regulations-and-Guidance/Guidance/Manuals/downloads/bp102c15.pdf (site visited June 7, 2016).

[162] MBP Manual, CMS Pub. 100-02, Ch. 15, § 10, *available at* http://www.cms.gov/Regulations-and-Guidance/Guidance/Manuals/downloads/bp102c15.pdf (site visited June 7, 2016).

The Balanced Budget Act of 1997 (BBA '97)[163] added a set of "preventive services" to the Medicare program. They include:

- An annual mammogram for women age 40 and over (deductible does not apply).[164]
- Annual Pap smears and pelvic exams for beneficiaries considered at high risk or following an abnormal Pap smear; for women not in these groups, coverage is for Pap smears and pelvic exams once every two years (deductible does not apply).[165]
- Prostate cancer screening annually for men over age 50.[166]
- Colorectal cancer screening tests for beneficiaries age 50 and older except there is no minimum age for having a screening colonoscopy. Fecal occult blood tests are covered annually; flexible sigmoidoscopy is generally covered every 48 months (or every 120 months when used instead of a colonoscopy for those not at high risk); screening colonoscopy is covered every 120 months or every 24 months for those at high risk; and barium enemas are covered every 48 months (or every 24 months for those at high risk) when used instead of sigmoidoscopy or colonoscopy. The Part B related deductible for colorectal screenings was eliminated by the Deficit Reduction Act of 2005 (DRA), effective January 1, 2007.[167]
- Outpatient diabetes self-management training services, blood testing strips, and monitors.[168]
- Medical nutrition therapy services for beneficiaries who have diabetes or renal disease who have not received diabetes outpatient self-management training services within a time period determined by the Secretary, are not receiving maintenance dialysis for which Medicare payment is being made, and who meet such other criteria determined by the Secretary.

[163] *See* §§ 4101(a)–(b), 4103(a), 4104(a), 4105(a), 4106(a), and 4107 of BIPA, amending §§ 1834, 1861 of the Social Security Act.

[164] 42 U.S.C. §§ 1395l(b) and 1395m(c)(2)(A).

[165] 42 U.S.C. §§ 1395l(b) and 1395x(nn).

[166] 42 U.S.C. §§ 1395l(h)(1)(A) and 1395x(oo).

[167] DRA § 5113, amending 42 U.S.C. §§ 1395l and 1395m. In May 2009, Medicare decided that it would not cover virtual colonoscopies. *See* CMS, "Decision Memo for Screening Computed Tomography Colonography (CTC) for Colorectal Cancer" (CAG-00396N), *available at* http://www.hhs.gov/sites/default/files/2016-06-07-section-1557-final-rule-summary-508.pdf (site visited June 7, 2016).

[168] 42 U.S.C. § 1395x.

- Bone mass measurements once every two years for qualified high-risk individuals.[169]
- Glaucoma screening for individuals determined to be at high risk for glaucoma, individuals with a family history of glaucoma, and individuals with diabetes.[170]
- Telehealth services when a beneficiary resides in a rural county designated as a health professional shortage area and where other criteria are met.[171]
- Other services not otherwise described that identify medical conditions or risk factors as the Secretary determines.[172]

Advocates should be aware that in making coverage decisions, Medicare uses screens and norms of treatment. These norms and screens generally go to the issue of frequency of use of certain services and procedures. They are not to be used to deny services outright but can be used as a tool for identifying certain usage patterns and trends. When norms and screens are used, beneficiaries are to be provided an opportunity to rebut any unfavorable coverage assumptions made on the basis of such screens and norms.[173]

The MMA added more preventive services. These new services include:

- *Preventive Physical Exams.* When initially enacted, the law stated that this exam was for an initial physical exam performed no later than six months after the individual's initial date of coverage under Part B.[174]

---

[169] 42 U.S.C. § 1395x. High-risk persons include an estrogen-deficient woman at clinical risk for osteoporosis; an individual with vertebral abnormalities; an individual receiving long-term glucocorticoid steroid therapy; an individual with primary hyperparathyroidism; or an individual being monitored to assess the response to or efficacy of an approved osteoporosis drug therapy.

[170] 42 U.S.C. § 1395x(s)(2)(u).

[171] 42 U.S.C. § 1395m(m); 42 C.F.R. § 410.78. *See also* Center for Medicare Advocacy, "Medicare and Telemedicine (or Telehealth)," *available at* http://www.medicareadvocacy.org/medicare-and-telemedicine-or-telehealth/ (site visited June 7, 2016).

[172] *See* MIPPA, Pt. I (Prevention, Mental health, and Marketing), § 101 (improvements to coverage of preventive services). The Secretary has authority to add preventive services that he or she determines are reasonable and necessary for the prevention or early detection of an illness or a disability, recommended with a grade of A or B by the U.S. Preventive Services Task Force, and appropriate for individuals entitled to benefits under Part A or enrolled under Part B. In the case of additional preventive services, the Medicare agency will pay 80 percent of the lesser of the actual charge for the service or the amount determined under a fee schedule established by the Secretary.

[173] *See* Vorster v. Bowen, 709 F. Supp. 934 (C.D. Cal. 1989) (Part B—frequency of service screens); Fox v. Bowen, 656 F. Supp. 1236 (D. Conn. 1987) (Part A—access to physical therapy services in a skilled nursing facility).

[174] MMA § 611, adding § 1861(ww) and amending §§ 1861(s)(2), 1833(a)(1), and 1848(j)(3) of the Social Security Act. Effective Jan. 1, 2005, 42 U.S.C. §§ 1395x(s)(2), 1395l(a)(1), and 1395w-4(j).

The Medicare Improvements for Patients and Providers Act of 2008 (MIPPA), however, changed the time period for this exam to 12 months after the initial date of coverage under Part B, effective January 1, 2009.[175] The term "initial preventive physical examination" means physicians' services consisting of a physical examination (including measurement of height, weight, and blood pressure, and an electrocardiograph) with the goal of health promotion and disease detection and includes education, counseling, and referral with respect to screening and other preventive services described in MIPPA Section 611(b)(2) but does not include clinical laboratory tests.[176]

- *Cardiovascular Screening Blood Tests*. This is a blood test for the early detection of cardiovascular disease. The tests can only be performed once every two years. The provision was effective on January 1, 2005.[177]
- *Diabetes Laboratory Diagnostic Tests*. The tests include fasting plasma glucose tests as well as other tests and modifications. It applies to individuals at risk of diabetes or who have any combination of the following: hypertension; dyslipidemia; obesity (body mass index greater than or equal to 30kg/m2); previous identification of an elevated impaired glucose tolerance; a risk factor consisting of at least two of the following characteristics: overweight, defined as body mass index greater than 25, but less than 30, kg/m2; a family history of diabetes; a history of gestational diabetes mellitus or delivery of a baby weighing greater than 9 pounds; 65 years of age or older.[178]
- *Abdominal Aortic Aneurysm Screening*. In addition, note that the DRA adds coverage for this screening test as part of the "Welcome to Medicare" physical exam discussed above for certain Medicare beneficiaries as of January 1, 2007, and eliminates the Medicare Part B Premium for this screening test.[179]
- *Screening for Depression in Adults*. Coverage is available in primary care settings (defined in the Social Security Act at Sections 1833(u)(6), 1833(x)(2)(A)(i)(I), and 1833(x)(2)(A)(i)(II)) that have staff-assisted depression care supports in place to assure accurate diagnosis, effective treatment, and follow-up.[180]

---

175 *See* MIPPA § 101(b)(3), Pub. L. No. 110-275 (July 15, 2008).

176 *See* MMA § 611(b)(1).

177 *See* MMA § 612, amending §§ 1861(s)(2) and 1862(a)(1) and adding § 1861(xx)(1) to the Social Security Act, 42 U.S.C. §§ 1395x(s)(2), 1395l(a)(1), and 1395w-4(j).

178 *See* MMA § 613.

179 DRA § 5112, amending 42 U.S.C. § 1395x.

180 Medicare NCD Manual, § 210.9, *available at* http://www.cms.gov/Regulations-and-Guidance/Guidance/Manuals/downloads/ncd103c1_part4.pdf (site visited June 7, 2016).

- *Screening and Behavioral Counseling Interventions in Primary Care to Reduce Alcohol Misuse.* CMS will cover up to four brief, face-to-face, behavioral counseling interventions per year for Medicare beneficiaries, including pregnant women. Covered are those beneficiaries who misuse alcohol, but whose levels or patterns of alcohol consumption do not meet criteria for alcohol dependence (defined as at least three of the following: tolerance; withdrawal symptoms; impaired control; preoccupation with acquisition and/or use; persistent desire or unsuccessful efforts to quit; sustains social, occupational, or recreational disability; use continues despite adverse consequences); who are competent and alert at the time that counseling is provided; and whose counseling is furnished by qualified primary care physicians or other primary care practitioners in a primary care setting.[181]

[2] Annual Wellness Visit Added by the Patient Protection and Affordable Care Act

Medicare beneficiaries are entitled to an annual wellness visit that includes a personalized prevention plan.[182] The personalized prevention plan is based on a health risk assessment made prior to, or as part of, a visit with a health care professional (physician, health educator, registered dietician, or nutrition professional or a team of professionals).[183]

The assessment establishes or updates medical and family history; lists current providers and suppliers that are regularly involved in providing medical care to the individual (including a list of prescribed medications); lists height, weight, body mass index (or waist circumference, if appropriate), blood pressure, and other routine measurements; and indicates any cognitive impairment.[184] In addition, the health professional is to establish a screening schedule for the next five to ten years, as appropriate, based on recommendations of the United States Preventive Services Task Force and the Advisory Committee on Immunization Practices, and the individual's health status, screening history, and age-appropriate preventive services.[185]

---

[181] CMS, "Decision Memo for Screening for Depression in Adults" (CAG-00425N) (Oct. 14, 2011), *available at* http://www.cms.gov/medicare-coverage-database/details/nca-decision-memo.aspx?NCAId=251 (site visited June 7, 2016).

[182] ACA § 4103, *see* http://www.cdc.gov/policy/hst/hra/4103.html (site visited June 13, 2016) amending 42 U.S.C. § 1395x(s)(2), *see* https://www.gpo.gov/fdsys/pkg/USCODE-2010-title42/pdf/USCODE-2010-title42-chap7-subchapXVIII-partE-sec1395x.pdf (site visited June 13, 2016). The annual wellness visit became available on January 1, 2011.

[183] 42 U.S.C. § 1395x(s)(2)(hhh), *see* http://www.hhs.gov/sites/default/files/2016-06-07-section-1557-final-rule-summary-508.pdf (site visited June 13, 2016); ACA § 4103.

[184] ACA § 4103(a)(2)(A)–(D).

[185] ACA § 4103(a)(2)(E).

The annual wellness visit builds on the current "Welcome to Medicare" check-up or "initial physical examination" that is available to beneficiaries within 12 months of their becoming covered under Medicare Part B. The initial preventive physical examination consists of a physical examination, including measurement of height, weight, and blood pressure, and an electrocardiograph, with the goal of health promotion and disease detection. As discussed above, the initial preventive physical examination also includes education, counseling, and referral with respect to screening and other preventive services, although it does not include clinical laboratory tests.[186] A beneficiary is entitled to only a "Welcome to Medicare" check-up, not an annual wellness visit exam, during the 12-month period after coverage begins under Part B as described above.[187]

[3] Elimination of Cost-Sharing for Preventive Services

The Patient Protection and Affordable Care Act (PPACA, also known as the Affordable Care Act, or ACA) also eliminated cost-sharing for most of the preventive services covered under Medicare, effective January 1, 2011.[188] The services for which there will be no cost-sharing (deductible and/or copayment) are:

1. Mammograms every 12 months for eligible beneficiaries age 40 and older;
2. Colorectal cancer screening, including flexible sigmoidoscopy or colonoscopy;
3. Cervical cancer screening, including a Pap smear test and pelvic exam;
4. Cholesterol and other cardiovascular screenings;
5. Diabetes screening;

---

[186] *See* 42 U.S.C. § 1395x(ww).

[187] *See* CMS, Quick Reference Information: The ABCs of Providing the Initial Preventive Physical Examination (Jan. 2012), *available at* http://www.cms.gov/Outreach-and-Education/Medicare-Learning-Network-MLN/MLNProducts/downloads/MPS_QRI_IPPE001a.pdf (site visited June 7, 2016). *See also* CMS, Your Guide to Medicare's Preventive Benefits (revised Feb. 2013), *available at* http://www.medicare.gov/Pubs/pdf/10110.pdf (site visited June 7, 2016).

[188] *See* CMS's Prevention—General Information page, http://www.cms.gov/Medicare/Prevention/PrevntionGenInfo/ (site visited June 7, 2016). Because there is no cost-sharing for these services, providers are not required to issue an Advance Beneficiary Notice (ABN) to beneficiaries. If, however, the frequency of the services covered by Medicare is surpassed and the patient still wants to continue treatment, the provider must issue an ABN before providing the additional services in order to transfer liability to the beneficiary for the services received. *See* Center for Medicare Advocacy, "CMS Clarifies When the Advance Beneficiary Notice of Non-Coverage (ABN) Must be Issued" (Aug. 16, 2012), *available at* http://www.medicareadvocacy.org/cms-clarifies-when-the-advance-beneficiary-notice-of-non-coverage-abn-must-be-issued/ (site visited June 7, 2016). *See also* MCP Manual, CMS Pub. 100-04, *available at* http://www.cms.gov/Regulations-and-Guidance/Guidance/Transmittals/Downloads/R2480CP.pdf (site visited June 7, 2016).

6. Medical nutrition therapy to help people manage diabetes or kidney disease;
7. Prostate cancer screening (for most codes);
8. Annual flu shot, pneumonia vaccine, and the hepatitis B vaccine;
9. Bone mass measurement;
10. Abdominal aortic aneurysm screening to check for a bulging blood vessel;
11. HIV screening for people who are at increased risk or who ask for the test;
12. Smoking cessation counseling.[189]

Cost-sharing is also eliminated for the Wellness Visit and Personal Prevention Plan.

CMS indicates that the following preventive services covered by Medicare are not recommended by USPSTF with a grade of A or B for any populations or indications and will therefore *continue to be subject to cost-sharing:*[190]

1. Digital rectal examination furnished as a prostate cancer screening service;
2. Glaucoma screening;
3. Diabetes self-management training services;
4. Barium enema furnished as a colorectal cancer screening.

Note that, for all services, current coverage policies continue to apply. For example, Medicare covers bone mass measurements only once every two years for qualified high-risk individuals.[191] Testing within that time frame for people who meet the eligibility criteria will not be subject to a deductible or copayment. Bone mass measurement will not be covered for someone who is not a high-risk individual, however, regardless of the change in cost-sharing requirements.

---

[189] On August 25, 2010, CMS announced that it was extending coverage for smoking cessation counseling. *See* "HHS Announces Medicare Expands Coverage of Tobacco Cessation Counseling" (Aug. 25, 2010), *available at* http://cms.hhs.gov/Newsroom/MediaReleaseDatabase/Press-Releases/2010-Press-Releases-Items/2010-08-25.html (site visited June 7, 2016).

[190] 75 Fed. Reg. 73,169 *et seq.* (Nov. 29, 2010), amending 42 C.F.R. §§ 410.152 and 410.160, *see* http://www.ecfr.gov/cgi-bin/text-idx?SID=e13f94c394a8bf2b77a7cd15ecc417d0&mc=true&node=se42.2.410_1152&rgn=div8 (site visited June 7, 2016).

[191] 42 U.S.C. § 1395x.

[4] Implications for Medicare Advantage Plans

With the exception of hospice care, Medicare Advantage (MA) plans are required to provide all items and services that are covered under Medicare Part A and Part B.[192] Since January 1, 2011, MA plans are required to offer an Annual Wellness Visit to their enrollees.[193]

Medicare Advantage plans have more leeway with regard to elimination of cost-sharing for preventive services. Medicare Advantage plans have always been allowed to impose different cost-sharing than Part A and Part B, as long as the cost-sharing is actuarially equivalent to cost-sharing under traditional Medicare.[194] By placing limits on Medicare Advantage cost-sharing for certain costly services, ACA expands that authority by allowing plans to impose cost-sharing for services for which Part A and Part B do not have cost-sharing.[195]

While many Medicare Advantage plans have traditionally eliminated cost-sharing for preventive benefits under their authority to offer an actuarially equivalent benefit package, some have not. CMS issued regulations, effective January 2012, that prohibit plans from charging deductibles, copayments, or coinsurance for *in-network* Medicare-covered preventive services, as specified by CMS on an annual basis.[196]

[5] Medicare Caps for Physical Therapy/Speech Pathology Services and Occupational Therapy

[a] Background

The BBA '97 placed limitations on the amount of financial coverage available to Medicare beneficiaries receiving outpatient rehabilitation therapy services (except those provided under arrangements with a hospital[197]), including physical therapy, speech-language pathology services, and occupational therapy. Two categories were defined, one covering physical therapy services and speech-language pathology services combined, and the other covering occupational therapy services. These so-called therapy caps are indexed each year by the Medicare Economic Index (MEI), per the BBA '97. The caps were intended to become effective in 1999.

---

[192] 42 U.S.C. § 1395w-22(a); 42 C.F.R. § 422.101.

[193] For information on no cost-sharing services and an analysis of their use, see HHS, "The Affordable Care Act: Strengthening Medicare in 2011," *available at* http://www.cms.gov/apps/files/Medicarereport2011.pdf (site visited June 7, 2016).

[194] 42 U.S.C. § 1395w-24.

[195] PPACA § 3202, amending 42 U.S.C. § 1395w-24.

[196] 75 Fed. Reg. 71,189 (Nov. 22, 2010), amending 42 C.F.R. § 422.100(k).

[197] *See* MCP Manual, CMS Pub. 100-04, Ch. 5, § 10.2, *available at* https://www.cms.gov/manuals/downloads/clm104c05.pdf (site visited June 7, 2016).

In 1999, Congress passed a Balanced Budget Refinement Act[198] that placed a moratorium on the "therapy caps." For calendar year 2009, CMS established a combined therapy cap per beneficiary for outpatient physical therapy and speech language pathology services and a separate cap for outpatient occupational therapy services.[199] This approach has continued. For 2017 and future updates and other therapy cap developments and information, check the CMS website at https://www.cms.gov/Medicare/Billing/TherapyServices/index.html?redirect=/TherapyServices. The therapy caps exceptions process for PT, OT, and SLP services was extended through CY 2017.[200] A beneficiary must first cover the deductible and pay 20 percent coinsurance. Medicare will then cover the remaining 80 percent up to the annual cap. Either a provider or the beneficiary can submit a request for an exception. All services that require exceptions to caps are processed using the automatic exceptions process.[201]

[b] Automatic Exceptions

Automatic exceptions can cover diagnoses and procedures that are either directly related to the condition, any associated complexities that may negatively impact recovery from that condition, and/or particular evaluation services.

A list of condition codes that fall into the "automatically" excepted category can be found at *http://www.cms.hhs.gov/transmittals/downloads/R855CP.pdf.*[202] Diagnoses and procedures that qualify as automatic exceptions do not require specific documentation for submission to the Medicare contractor. Documentation must be maintained in case of a claim review though. Any documentation demonstrating the "medical necessity" of the automatically excepted diagnosis is all that needs to be submitted.

Though not specifically stated by CMS, complexities appear to be of two varieties: (1) physical ailments that lead to complexities in treating the targeted

---

[198] Medicare, Medicaid, and SCHIP Balanced Budget Refinement Act of 1999, Pub. L. No. 106-113 (Nov. 29, 1999).

[199] *See* 72 Fed. Reg. 66,356 (Nov. 27, 2007). For updated information on therapy cap changes, please check the CMS website at https://www.cms.gov/Medicare/Billing/TherapyServices/index.html?redirect=/TherapyServices (site visited June 7, 2016).

[200] *See* CMS, Therapy Services, *available at* https://www.cms.gov/Medicare/Billing/TherapyServices/index.html?redirect=/TherapyServices (site visited June 7, 2016). *See also* the Medicare Access and CHIP Reauthorization Act of 2015 (MACRA) § 202. It also extended the therapy caps exceptions process through December 31, 2017, and modified the requirement for manual review of services over the $3,700 therapy thresholds. MACRA extended the application of the therapy caps, and related provisions, to outpatient hospitals until January 1, 2018.

[201] *See* https://www.cms.gov/Medicare/Billing/TherapyServices/index.html?redirect=/TherapyServices (site visited June 7, 2016).

[202] *See also* CMS's Therapy Services page, https://www.cms.gov/Medicare/Billing/TherapyServices/index.html?redirect=/TherapyServices (site visited June 7, 2016; *and* CMS, "Medicare Limits on Therapy Services," *available at* http://www.medicare.gov/Pubs/pdf/10988.pdf (site visited June 7, 2016).

condition of the body and (2) complications of management flow leading to a potential delay in treatment.

Depending on the nature of the complexity, an exception should be approved for any complexity affecting the beneficiary's ability to recover from the condition. Complexities due to physical ailments must also be connected to a condition, especially if they are to qualify as an automatic exception. Some complexities, though, will qualify as an automatic exception even if they are connected to a condition that is not specifically listed in the 2017 ICD-10-CM codes list of automatically excepted diagnoses.[203] This can happen for an unrelated condition that causes a complexity affecting the rate of recovery for the originally diagnosed condition that is the purpose of the therapy. For example, if the beneficiary is experiencing a musculoskeletal problem that is not associated with the condition receiving therapy (example given by CMS: a wrist injury that prevents the use of a cane), but it does affect the ability of the patient to recover, then this complexity can qualify as an automatic exception for any additional treatment required because of the complexity.

"Complexities" due to management flow issues can be excepted for a variety of CMS provided reasons, such as if a beneficiary requires treatment within 30 treatment days of being discharged from a hospital or skilled nursing facility (SNF), or a beneficiary needs to return to a pre-morbid living situation, or a beneficiary is unable to reach an outpatient hospital therapy service due to lack of access (thus resulting in approval for treatment at a non-hospital based facility). Additionally, if a beneficiary requires physical therapy and speech language pathology simultaneously, this particular type of complexity will be the basis for an exception once this double treatment reaches the cap.[204]

For evaluation services to be excepted from the therapy cap, they must be contained in the following list of Outpatient Rehabilitation Healthcare Common Procedure Coding System (HCPCS) Codes and will only be excepted from the cap once the cap is reached (a retroactive exception): 92506 (evaluation of speech), 92597 (oral speech device evaluation), 92607 (evaluation for prescription for speech-generating Augmentative and Alternative Communication [AAC] device), 92608 (each additional 30 minutes required for evaluation), 92610-92611-92612-92614-92616 (swallow evaluations), 96105 (assessment of aphasia), 97001 (physical therapy evaluation), 97002 (physical therapy re-evaluation), 97003 (occupational therapy evaluation), 97004 (occupational therapy re-evaluation).[205]

---

[203] *See* https://www.cms.gov/Medicare/Coding/ICD10/2017-ICD-10-CM-and-GEMs.html (site visited Aug. 12, 2016). Follow ICD-10 developments at Medicare's ICD-10 page, https://www.cms.gov/Medicare/Coding/ICD10/index.html (site visited June 7, 2016).

[204] *See* https://www.cms.gov/Medicare/Billing/TherapyServices/index.html?redirect=/TherapyServices (site visited Aug. 9, 2016).

[205] *See* https://www.cms.gov/Medicare/Billing/TherapyServices/index.html?redirect=/TherapyServices (Site Aug. 9, 2016).

[c] Limitations

Only 15 additional days of treatment may be requested at any one time. However, a plan justifying any additional treatment days, including any days beyond the initial 15, must be submitted with the exceptions request.

[d] Contractor's Decision Process

In requesting an exception from the Medicare contractor, if the contractor does not make a decision within ten days, the services are automatically considered "medically necessary" and the requested therapy treatment is automatically approved. The CMS information on this ten-day window for contractors to make a decision though infers that the contractor does not need to notify the beneficiary of a decision within those ten days, so the beneficiary or his/her provider may need to inquire after the window has closed to ascertain the determination.

[e] Where the Outpatient Therapy Cap Applies

The therapy cap, and its exceptions process, applies to services furnished in outpatient therapy settings, which includes all Part B outpatient therapy settings and providers: therapists' private practices; offices of physicians and certain non-physician practitioners; Part B SNFs; home health agencies (Type of Bill (TOB) 34X); rehabilitation agencies, also known as outpatient rehabilitation facilities (ORFs); comprehensive outpatient rehabilitation facilities (CORFs); and hospital outpatient departments (HOPDs).[206]

[f] Appeals

CMS's notes in its therapy cap exceptions process discussion that because the caps are statutorily based, they are difficult to appeal. An appeal, nonetheless, is not precluded. Advocates should approach these appeals as they would any other Part B appeal.[207]

---

[206] Section 603 of the American Taxpayer Relief Act of 2012 (ATRA) (payment for outpatient therapy), Pub. L. No. 112-240, H.R. 8, 126 Stat. 2313 (Jan. 2, 2013), *available at* http://gpo.gov/fdsys/pkg/PLAW-112publ240/pdf/PLAW-112publ240.pdf (site visited June 7, 2016); *see* the CMS therapy cap page, *available at* http://www.cms.gov/Research-Statistics-Data-and-Systems/Monitoring-Programs/Medical-Review/TherapyCap.html (site visited June 7, 2016); *see also* the Q&As of the American Physical Therapy Association (APTA), *available at* http://www.apta.org/Medicare/TherapyCap/FAQ/ (site visited June 7, 2016); *and* CMS, "Medicare Limits on Therapy Services," *available at* http://www.medicare.gov/Pubs/pdf/10988.pdf (site visited June 7, 2016).

[207] For more discussion, see Office of Medicare Hearings and Appeals (OMHA), "Understanding the Appeals Process," *available at* http://www.hhs.gov/omha/process/index.html (site visited June 13, 2016).

[B] Excluded Services

Medicare Part B, as described above, is fairly comprehensive but not complete. Certain categories of services and procedures are excluded from its purview.[208]

Services are also denied on the basis of Local Coverage Determinations (LCDs). These policies are often hidden and not explicitly discussed in denial motions. Currently, CMS has a website for searching for National Coverage Determinations (NCDs) and LCDs.[209] Advocates should ask contractors and hearing officers whether an LCD is the basis of a denial of coverage and ask that the LCD be made available.

Among the categories of services and procedures that are excluded are the following:

- Services that are not medically reasonable or necessary;
- Custodial care;
- Personal comfort items and services;
- Care that does not meaningfully contribute to the treatment of illness, injury, or a malformed body member;
- Prescription drugs that do not require administration by a physician;
- Routine physical checkups;
- Eyeglasses or contact lenses in most cases;
- Eye examinations for purpose of prescribing, fitting, or changing eyeglasses or contact lenses;
- Hearing aids and examinations for hearing aids;
- Immunizations except for pneumococcal and hepatitis B vaccine;
- Orthopedic shoes and other supportive devices for the foot unless intended as an instrumental part of a leg brace;
- Cosmetic surgery;
- Most dental services; and
- Routine foot care.

---

[208] *See generally* 42 U.S.C. § 1395y(a).

[209] *See* the Medicare Coverage Database (MCD), *available at* http://www.cms.gov/medicare-coverage-database/overview-and-quick-search.aspx (site visited June 7, 2016). *See also* https://www.cms.gov/DeterminationProcess/Downloads/FR11072003.pdf (site visited June 7, 2016). The definitions of an NCD and an LCD are included in regulations at 42 C.F.R. § 400.202. An LCD must conform to § 1862(a)(1)(A) of the Social Security Act (reasonable and necessary criteria); it is an intermediary-wide or carrier-wide decision; and it has not gone through the full review process of an NCD and is not a decision of CMS.

[C] Waiver of Liability Payment for Certain Excluded Items and Services

As described above, Medicare pays for covered services that are deemed reasonable and necessary, and not otherwise excluded. There are circumstances, however, in which Medicare will pay for excluded services. The general rule is that neither the beneficiary nor the provider knew or should have known that the service at issue was excluded.[210] Further, if Medicare determines that the beneficiary was unaware of the exclusion, but the provider knew or should have known, Medicare will indemnify the beneficiary or release the beneficiary from liability for payment.[211]

Under these circumstances, the provider is not entitled to payment for the excluded service either from the beneficiary or from Medicare.[212] Providers with persistent problems in this regard, or with poor track records, lose the presumption of lack of knowledge of whether an item or a service is covered, and their requests for payment for excluded items and services will be denied.[213]

[D] Special Coverage Areas

[1] Ambulance Service

Ambulance service is covered under Part B of the Medicare Program if certain conditions are met.[214] Generally, the ambulance supplier must meet the

[210] 42 U.S.C. § 1395pp; 42 C.F.R. § 411.400. Provider knowledge of Medicare rules is presumed through written notices of non-coverage from Medicare contractors to providers, utilization review committees, and other communications; beneficiary knowledge is imputed through having received denials of coverage under comparable circumstances. *See* 42 C.F.R. §§ 411.404 and 411.406.

[211] 42 U.S.C. § 1395pp; 42 C.F.R. §§ 411.400 *et seq. See* New CMS Manual Issuance: Transmittal 2480 (June 1, 2012), Change Request 6136, Pub. 100-04 Medicare Claims Processing (Revised Form CMS-R-131 Advance Beneficiary Notice of Non-coverage), *available at* http://www.cms.gov/Regulations-and-Guidance/Guidance/Transmittals/Downloads/R2480CP.pdf (site visited June 7, 2016), which also includes CMS's further update to the ABN and its usages. *See also* Center for Medicare Advocacy, "CMS Clarifies When the Advance Beneficiary Notice of Non-Coverage (ABN) Must be Issued" (Aug. 16, 2012) (discussing changes that became effective on September 4, 2012), *available at* http://www.medicareadvocacy.org/cms-clarifies-when-the-advance-beneficiary-notice-of-non-coverage-abn-must-be-issued/ (site visited June 7, 2016).

[212] 42 U.S.C. § 1395pp; 42 C.F.R. §§ 411.400 *et seq.*

[213] 42 C.F.R. § 411.406.

[214] 42 C.F.R. § 410.40. CMS provides for separate reasonable charge rates for ambulance reimbursement. Rates are dependent on the level of service provided. 42 C.F.R. § 410.40 provides for seven different levels of service. *See* MCP Manual, Ch. 15, §§ 20.2–20.6, *available at* http://www.cms.gov/Regulations-and-Guidance/Guidance/Manuals/Downloads/clm104c15.pdf (site visited June 7, 2016); *see also* http://www.cms.gov/Medicare/Medicare-Fee-for-Service-Payment/AmbulanceFeeSchedule/afspuf.html (site visited June 7, 2016); for detailed information on calculating ambulance reimbursement amounts. *See also* MMA, § 415, amending 42 U.S.C. § 1395m(l), with respect to rural air ambulance.

ambulance vehicle, staff, billing, and reporting standards established by CMS in regulations,[215] and no payment is made directly or indirectly for ambulance services under Part A,[216] including a national fee schedule.[217]

Ambulance regulations clarify rules defining medical necessity for ambulance transport, amending 42 C.F.R. § 410.40 to state that for non-emergency transport, bed confinement is not the sole criterion in determining medical necessity of ambulance transport.[218] In addition, on April 1, 2002, CMS established a fee schedule for the payment of ambulance services, including requiring ambulance service providers to accept assignment, thus limiting patient liability.[219] Medical necessity, origin, and destination requirements must be met.

Payment for ambulance services under Part B is available for ambulance trips within the United States for basic life support (BLS) services and advanced life support (ALS) services, and for paramedic ALS intercept services.[220] All payments for ambulance services are made on an assignment-only basis, and

---

[215] 42 C.F.R. §§ 410.40 and 410.41. Note that MIPPA § 146(b) makes improvements to air ambulance fees. Section 146(a) extends current increases for Medicare payments for ground ambulances through 2010. *See* CMS, "Ambulance Fee Schedule Public Use Files," *available at* http://www.cms.gov/Medicare/Medicare-Fee-for-Service-Payment/AmbulanceFeeSchedule/afspuf.html (site visited June 7, 2016).

[216] 42 C.F.R. § 410.40(a)(2).

[217] *See* 42 C.F.R. § 414.615. For on-going updates from CMS, check the ambulance services center page of CMS's website at http://www.cms.gov/Center/Provider-Type/Ambulances-Services-Center.html?redirect=/center/ambulance.asp (site visited June 7, 2016)

[218] Amending 42 C.F.R. § 410.40(d). *See also* CMS's Ambulance Fee Schedule—public use file, *available at* http://www.cms.gov/Medicare/Medicare-Fee-for-Service-Payment/AmbulanceFeeSchedule/afspuf.html (site visited June 7, 2016). For further background, *see* 42 C.F.R. Pt. 414 subpt. H, ambulance services. *See* 42 C.F.R. § 414.610 (basis of payment, which requires ambulance service providers to accept Medicare assignment, including air ambulance providers). 42 C.F.R. § 414.620 requires the publication of an ambulance fee schedule. 42 C.F.R. § 414.625 provides that there is no administrative or judicial review of the amounts established under the ambulance fee schedule.

[219] 42 C.F.R. § 414.610(a)–(g). Section 414.610(b) addresses mandatory assignment for claims filed on or after April 1, 2002. *See* § 414.610(c)(5), rural adjustment factor (RAF), adding interim final rules on payment increases for rural and urban ambulance services. This notice implements MMA, § 414.

[220] 42 C.F.R. § 410.40(a)(2)(b)(1)–(3). Paramedic ALS intercept services must be furnished in a rural area as defined in 42 C.F.R. § 412.62(f) and must be furnished under contract with one or more volunteer ambulance services that are certified to furnish ambulance service; that furnish services only at the BLS level; and that are prohibited by state law from billing for any service. They can also be furnished by a paramedic ALS intercept supplier certified to furnish ALS services as provided in 42 C.F.R. § 410.41(b)(2) and that bills all the recipients who receive ALS intercept services for the entity, regardless of whether those recipients are Medicare beneficiaries. For purposes of payment for paramedic intercept ambulance services, a rural area is an area designated as a rural area by any law or regulation of the state or if it is located in a rural census tract of a metropolitan statistical area (MSA) (as determined under the most recent Goldsmith Modification). CMS defines a rural area to mean "an area located outside an urban area, or a rural census tract within an MSA as determined under the most recent version of the Goldsmith modification as determined by the Office of Rural Health Policy of the Health Resources and Services Administration." Definitions

providers can collect from beneficiaries only the unmet Part B deductible and Part B coinsurance amounts.[221]

With respect to medical necessity, ambulance service is available under Medicare only if the services are furnished to a beneficiary with a medical condition such that other modes of transportation are contraindicated.[222] If the ambulance trip is necessary for non-emergency services, the beneficiary must be unable to get up from bed without assistance; the beneficiary must be unable to ambulate; and the beneficiary must be unable to sit in a chair or wheelchair.[223] If the ambulance ride is not medically necessary and the provider has reason to know that Medicare will not cover the cost, the provider may shift liability for the cost to the beneficiary only by providing the beneficiary with an ABN. Issuance of an ABN is mandatory in such a situation if three conditions are met: (1) the service being provided is a Medicare covered ambulance ride; (2) the provider believes that the service may be denied in part or in full because it is not medically necessary; and (3) the ambulance service is being provided in a *non-emergency* situation.[224]

Medicare covers scheduled non-emergency ambulance services if the ambulance supplier, in advance of the service, obtains a written order from the treating physician certifying that the medical necessity requirements of the coverage regulations are met. The order must be dated no earlier than 60 days before the ambulance service is provided.[225]

For ambulance service for a resident of a facility who is under the care of a physician, the physician must certify that the trip meets the above-described medical necessity requirements within 48 hours after the trip.[226] If the trip is for

---

applicable to ambulance services, both land and water (referred to as "ground") are found at 42 C.F.R. § 414.605. Specialty care transport (SCT) means the hospital-to-hospital transportation of a critically injured or ill beneficiary by a ground ambulance vehicle, including medically necessary supplies and services, at a level of service beyond the scope of the EMT-Paramedic. SCT is necessary when a beneficiary's condition requires ongoing care that must be furnished by one or more health professionals in an appropriate specialty area, for example, nursing, emergency medicine, respiratory care, cardiovascular care, or a paramedic with additional training. An urban area means an MSA, as defined by the Executive Office of Management and Budget.

[221] 67 Fed. Reg. 9099, 9134, amending 42 C.F.R. § 414.610(a)–(g) by adding new § 414.610(b).

[222] 42 U.S.C. § 1395x(s)(7); 42 C.F.R. § 410.40(d).

[223] 42 C.F.R. § 410.40(d)(1)(i)–(iii).

[224] *See* New CMS Manual Issuance: Transmittal 2480 (June 1, 2012), Change Request 6136, Pub. 100-04 Medicare Claims Processing (Revised Form CMS-R-131 Advance Beneficiary Notice of Non-coverage), *available at* http://www.cms.gov/Regulations-and-Guidance/Guidance/Transmittals/Downloads/R2480CP.pdf (site visited June 7, 2016).

[225] 42 C.F.R. § 410.40(d)(2).

[226] 42 C.F.R. § 410.40(d)(3)(i). CMS is interpreting its rules such that physician certification can be signed by a physician's assistant, a nurse practitioner, or a clinical nurse specialist, acting under the supervision of the physician, as recognized under state law. Further, for purposes of certification with respect to unscheduled, non-emergency ambulance transports, a registered nurse who is employed by the attending physician or who is an employee of the hospital or facility where the

a beneficiary residing at home or in a facility and is not under the direct care of a physician, no certification is required.[227]

Origin and destination requirements for ambulance service coverage are as follows:[228]

- From any point of origin to the nearest hospital, critical access hospital (CAH), or SNF that is capable of furnishing the required level and type of care for the beneficiary's illness or injury, including the necessary physician specialists needed to treat the beneficiary's condition;
- From a hospital, CAH, or SNF to the beneficiary's home;
- From a SNF to the nearest supplier of medically necessary services not available at the SNF where the beneficiary is a resident, including the return trip;

---

patient is being treated may sign a physician certification statement on oral orders from the physician or other qualified practitioner. Also, consult the websites of the durable medical equipment regional carriers (DMERCs). Coverage criteria for DME items are generally available online. It is best to work through the resources of the DMERC handling such items for the region in which the beneficiary resides or where the equipment was obtained.

On October 23, 2015, CMS announced an expansion of the "3-year Medicare Prior Authorization Model for Repetitive Scheduled Non-Emergent Ambulance Transport" in accordance with § 515(a) of the Medicare Access and CHIP Reauthorization Act of 2015. ([CMS-6063-N2] http://www.gpo.gov/fdsys/pkg/FR-2015-10-23/pdf/2015-27030.pdf (site visited June 7, 2016)) The model is being expanded to the states of Maryland, Delaware, North Carolina, West Virginia, and Virginia and the District of Columbia. The expansion began on January 1, 2016.

Medicare may cover ambulance services, including air ambulance (fixed-wing and rotary-wing) services, if the ambulance service is furnished to a beneficiary whose medical condition is such that other means of transportation are contraindicated. The beneficiary's condition must require both the ambulance transportation itself and the level of service provided in order for the billed service to be considered medically necessary. Non-emergent transportation by ambulance is appropriate if either the (1) beneficiary is bed-confined and it is documented that the beneficiary's condition is such that other methods of transportation are contraindicated; or (2) beneficiary's medical condition, regardless of bed confinement, is such that transportation by ambulance is medically required. Thus, bed confinement is not the sole criterion in determining the medical necessity of non-emergent ambulance transportation; rather, it is one factor that is considered in medical necessity determinations.

A repetitive ambulance service is defined as medically necessary ambulance transportation that is furnished in 3 or more round trips during a 10-day period, or at least 1 round trip per week for at least 3 weeks (42 C.F.R. § 410.40(d)(l)). Repetitive ambulance services are often needed by beneficiaries receiving dialysis or cancer treatment. Medicare may cover repetitive, scheduled, non-emergent transportation by ambulance if (1) the medical necessity requirements are met; and (2) the ambulance provider/supplier, before furnishing the service to the beneficiary, obtains a written order from the beneficiary's attending physician certifying that the medical necessity requirements are met. *See* 42 C.F.R. § 410.40(d)(l), (2). *See also* 42 42 C.F.R. §§ 410.40, 410.41, and in the Medicare Benefit Policy Manual (Pub. 100-02), Chapter 10, *see* https://www.cms.gov/Regulations-and-Guidance/Guidance/Manuals/Downloads/bp102c10.pdf (site visited June 8, 2016).

[227] 42 C.F.R. § 410.40(d)(3)(ii).

[228] 42 C.F.R. § 410.40(e)(1)–(4).

- For a beneficiary who is receiving renal dialysis for treatment of ESRD, from the beneficiary's home to the nearest facility that furnishes renal dialysis, including the return trip.

[2] Durable Medical Equipment

[a] General

Coverage is available under Part B for the rental, purchase, or lease of DME for use in the home.[229] Generally, items of DME include such things as iron lungs, wheelchairs, hospital beds, walkers, canes, oxygen systems, and dialysis systems. A physician's order is generally necessary to obtain DME.[230] Under the DME rules, the Medicare program pays 80 percent of the payment basis and schedules established by the Secretary's exclusive authority to set payment amounts under the program.[231] Note that Section 6407 of ACA requires a face-to-face encounter with the patient and physician (or other recognized certifier) for certification of the need for DME or for home health care services. This requirement is applicable to all certifications on or after January 1, 2010. Certifications via telehealth (subject to certain limitations) are permitted.[232] In addition, ACA gives the Secretary the authority to apply this face-to-face requirement to other services for which payment under the Medicare program is available based upon a finding that such a decision would reduce the risk of waste, fraud, or abuse.[233] Further, the ACA gives the Secretary the authority to apply the face-to-face requirement to similar services paid for under the Medicaid program if the Secretary deems such an approach would reduce waste, fraud, and abuse.[234]

---

[229] 42 U.S.C. § 1395m(a); 42 C.F.R. § 410.38. Advocates should consult the Medicare NCD Manual to identify the sections covering the issues in question for the most up-to-date DME coverage listings. *See* http://www.cms.gov/Regulations-and-Guidance/Guidance/Manuals/Internet-Only-Manuals-IOMs-Items/CMS014961.html (site visited June 7, 2016). This listing is generally given great weight in the administrative review process and in federal court review. It is particularly helpful in understanding the specific coverage criteria, including the necessary medical factors for coverage.

[230] 42 U.S.C. § 1395m(a)(11)(B).

[231] 42 U.S.C. § 1395m(a)(1)(A), (B), (C).

[232] Amending 42 U.S.C. § 1395m(a)(11)(2)(B). The implementation of this provision has been postponed to an unspecified time in CY 2014. *See* CMS, "Face to Face Encounter Requirement for Certain Durable Medical Equipment," (updated Mar. 27, 2015), *available at* https://www.cms.gov/Research-Statistics-Data-and-Systems/Monitoring-Programs/Medicare-FFS-Compliance-Programs/Medical-Review/FacetoFaceEncounterRequirementforCertainDurableMedicalEquipment.html (site visited June 8, 2016).

[233] ACA § 6407(c).

[234] ACA § 6407(d). On November 16, 2012, CMS published a final rule to implement ACA, 6407. *See* CMS, Justification of Estimates for Appropriations Committees, Fiscal Year 2014, *available at* http://www.cms.gov/About-CMS/Agency-Information/PerformanceBudget/Downloads/FY2015-CJ-Final.pdf (site visited June 7, 2016).

The issue of whether to rent, purchase, or lease DME is often a problem. The best approach is to work closely with the contractor and physician to determine the appropriate DME for the individual and the coverage rationale for its use. It is also important to understand that Medicare, under guidelines established by the Secretary, makes the determination of whether DME should be rented, purchased, or leased, and how much Medicare will pay for such equipment.[235]

Where customized items of DME are involved, it is important to show how the item is uniquely designed to meet the needs of the particular beneficiary, consistent with Medicare's requirements of medical necessity, and not merely an item of convenience.[236]

Additions or modifications of DME that are not considered to be medically necessary will not be covered by Medicare. In order for the supplier to shield itself from liability for the cost of the improvements or modifications when it knows the modifications will not be covered by Medicare, the supplier must issue an ABN.[237] Since issuing an ABN is mandatory in this case, liability for the cost of the equipment modifications or improvements cannot be shifted to the beneficiary if the beneficiary is not provided with notice of his or her liability.

[b] Competitive Acquisition of Certain Durable Medical Equipment, Prosthetics, Orthotics, and Supplies

The implementation of CMS's competitive acquisition program, currently underway, was to begin on July 1, 2008, but, as required by MIPPA, was temporarily delayed, including the imposition of certain MIPPA-required reforms.[238] Rules describing the program and its roll out in 2009 provided important information about the structure and function of the program and are described

---

[235] 42 U.S.C. § 1395m(a)(1)(C), 1395m(a)(1)(A)–(C); 42 C.F.R. § 421.210. Also, note that CMS has a system of DMERCs. *See* 42 U.S.C. § 1395m(a)(12). These contractors have established protocols and coverage criteria that they employ in making DME coverage decisions. In many instances, the protocols reflect Medicare national coverage determinations and thus a uniform coverage policy. In other instances, from region to region, DMERCs may employ differing approaches to coverage of the same item or category of DME. *See* Durable Medical Equipment Center, http://www.cms.hhs.gov/center/dme.asp (site visited June 7, 2016); http://www.cms.gov/Center/Provider-Type/Durable-Medical-Equipment-DME-Center.html?redirect=/center/dme.asp (site visited June 7, 2016); including a link to a discussion of speech generating devices (SGDs), http://www.cms.gov/medicare-coverage-database/details/medicare-coverage-document-details.aspx?MCDId=26&ExpandComments=n&mcdtypename=National+Benefit+Category+Analyses&MCDIndexType=3&bc=AgAEAAAAACAAAA%3d%3d& (site visited June 7, 2016).

[236] *See* 42 C.F.R. § 414.224.

[237] *See* New CMS Manual Issuance: Transmittal 2480 (June 1, 2012), Change Request 6136, Pub. 100-04 Medicare Claims Processing (Revised Form CMS-R-131 Advance Beneficiary Notice of Non-coverage), *available at* http://www.cms.gov/Regulations-and-Guidance/Guidance/Transmittals/Downloads/R2480CP.pdf (site visited June 7, 2016).

[238] *See* MIPPA § 154 (Delay in and reform of Medicare DMEPOS competitive acquisition program).

throughout this section, including relevant citation.[239] Expansion of "Round 2" bidding of the DME competitive bidding program is to proceed and to expand to additional metropolitan statistical areas (MSAs).[240] Regulations implementing aspects of the program are in place.[241]

As required by Section 302 of the MMA, Medicare published final regulations establishing the requirements for a new competitive bidding program for certain durable medical equipment, prosthetics, orthotics, and supplies (DMEPOS). As required by the MMA, the competitive bidding program is being phased in with high-cost and high-volume items or those with the largest savings potential based on the following factors: total Medical expenditures (allowable charges) for the item; growth in Medicare expenditures; number of suppliers of the item; savings potential; and findings and reports and studies by the Office of Inspector General (OIG) or the Government Accountability Office (GAO).[242]

---

[239] *See* MIPPA § 154(A)(1)(D). *See also* CMS's web page materials at http://www.cms.gov/Medicare/Medicare-Fee-for-Service-Payment/DMEPOSCompetitiveBid/index.html?redirect=/DMEPOSCompetitiveBid/%20(Rules%20for%20DME%20competitive%20bidding%20project? (site visited June 7, 2016).

[240] *See* ACA § 6410, amending 42 U.S.C. § 1395w-3(a)(1). See discussion of MSAs and other aspects of the program throughout this section. Under ACA, the Secretary is to expand the program to the next 21 largest MSAs. The current list of MSAs is described in **§ 6.03[D][2][b][i]** of this Handbook. The DMEPOS program remains controversial, and there are efforts to repeal the program and replace it with a market pricing program at the manufacturer level for DMEPOS under Medicare Part B. *See* H.R. 1717, *available at* http://www.gpo.gov/fdsys/pkg/BILLS-113hr1717ih/pdf/BILLS-113hr1717ih.pdf (site visited June 7, 2016); *see also* Center for Medicare Advocacy, "Medicare's National Mail Order Program for Diabetic Testing Supplies," *available at* http://www.medicareadvocacy.org/medicares-national-mail-order-program-for-diabetic-testing-supplies/ (site visited June 7, 2016).

[241] *See* 74 Fed. Reg. 61,737– 62,206 (Nov. 25, 2009) (*see* material starting at 61,887). *See also* 75 Fed. Reg. 52,629 (Aug. 27, 2010), setting out final regulations that DMEPOS suppliers must meet. A useful overview of the Competitive Bidding program for DMEPOS and its implementation problems, potential for savings, and related issues is available from the U.S. Government Accountability Office (GAO), GAO-10-1057T, http://www.gao.gov/new.items/d101057t.pdf (site visited June 7, 2016)).

[242] *See* § 1847B of the Social Security Act, 42 U.S.C. 1395w–3b; *see also* § 1847(a)(1) of the Social Security Act, 42 U.S.C. § 1395w-3(a)(1); 72 Fed. Reg. 17,992 *et seq.* (Apr. 10, 2007). Rules were effective June 11, 2007. Ongoing standards for DMEPOS providers with respect to payment rules for items furnished by DMEPOS suppliers and issuance of DMEPOS supplier billing privileges are set out at 42 C.F.R. § 424.57. Advocates should continue to watch for emerging developments. *See also* CMS's MedLearn article, *available at* http://www.cms.hhs.gov/MLNMattersArticles/downloads/SE0820.pdf (site visited June 7, 2016) and CMS, "Durable Medical Equipment, Prosthetics, Orthotics and Supplies (DMEPOS) Competitive Bidding Program," *available at* http://www.cms.gov/Outreach-and-Education/Medicare-Learning-Network-MLN/MLNProducts/downloads/dme_ref_agt_factsheet_icn900927.pdf (site visited June 7, 2016). For more information about the accreditation and bonding requirement, *see* http://www.cms.hhs.gov/MedicareProviderSupEnroll (site June 7, 2015). On-going updates are available on CMS's competitive bidding page: http://www.cms.gov/DMEPOSCompetitiveBid/ (site visited June 7, 2016).

The basic structure of the program described below remains intact. Note, however, that all contracts issued under the first phase of the DMEPOS program were terminated by MIPPA.[243] As the program has rolled out, it has been resisted by provider and supplier associations and their members. In some instances, the authors have observed that suppliers are winning bids and then refusing to provide the required services and equipment, saying that they cannot honor their commitments because the bid prices are too low. In general, suppliers and providers are to honor their bid obligations.[244] Even as beneficiaries are bearing the brunt of provider resistance, the Office of the Inspector General (OIG) for HHS and the General Accountability Office (GAO) have issued reports stating that beneficiary access to necessary items of DMEPOS has not been compromised.[245] These reports belie beneficiary experience, particularly since January 2014.[246] Moreover, providers are continuing to push for legislation that would replace the current competitive bidding system with an auction system.[247] Beneficiary advocates are concerned that such an approach leaves too much control of the costs of and access to DMEPOS in the hands of the supplier industry.[248]

---

[243] MIPPA § 154(A)(1)(D)(ii).

[244] *See* Center for Medicare Advocacy, "Delivery and Set-Up Guidelines for Durable Medical Equipment, Prosthetics, Orthotics, and Supplies (DMEPOS)," *available at* http://www.medicareadvocacy.org/delivery-and-set-up-guidelines-for-durable-medical-equipment-prosthetics-orthotics-and-supplies-dmepos/ (site visited June 7, 2016). 42 C.F.R. § 424.57(c)(12)(delivery), *available at* http://www.ecfr.gov/cgi-bin/text-idx?SID=50cc231bebd54e92b9479bb2d43b852b&mc=true&node=se42.3.424_157&rgn=div8 (site visited June 7, 2016). Contract terms for suppliers are provided in 42 C.F.R. §§ 414.422(e) (furnishing items) and 414.422(g) (breach of contract), *available at* http://www.gpo.gov/fdsys/pkg/CFR-2011-title42-vol3/pdf/CFR-2011-title42-vol3-sec414-422.pdf (site visited June 7, 2016). Other important regulatory guidance is available in CMS's Outreach and Education/MedLearn Series.

[245] *See* Center for Medicare Advocacy's analysis of the problem, "Memorandum: GAO and OIG Reports Note No Problems in Beneficiary Access to DMEPOS. Beneficiary Advocates Disagree," *available at* http://www.medicareadvocacy.org/memorandum-gao-and-oig-reports-note-no-problems-in-beneficiary-access-to-dmepos-beneficiary-advocates-disagree/ (site visited June 7, 2016). *See also* Center for Medicare Advocacy, "The DMEPOS Competitive Bidding Process: Is It Working?" *available at* http://www.medicareadvocacy.org/the-dmepos-competitive-bidding-process-is-it-working/ (site visited June 7, 2016).

[246] *See* "Memorandum: GAO and OIG Reports Note No Problems in Beneficiary Access to DMEPOS. Beneficiary Advocates Disagree," *available at* http://www.medicareadvocacy.org/memorandum-gao-and-oig-reports-note-no-problems-in-beneficiary-access-to-dmepos-beneficiary-advocates-disagree/ (site visited June 7, 2016).

[247] *See* proposed H.R. 4920 and American Association for Homecare, "Support Medicare DMEPOS Competitive Bidding Improvement Act—H.R. 4920," *available at* https://www.aahomecare.org/pages/take-action-support-binding-bid-legislation (site visited June 7, 2016);https://www.congress.gov/bill/113th-congress/house-bill/4920 (site visited June 7, 2016).

[248] For an analysis of the earlier version of the auction approach (H.R. 1717), see Center for Medicare Advocacy, "Let DMEPOS Competitive Bidding Proceed While Addressing Identified Problems and Concerns," *available at* http://www.medicareadvocacy.org/let-dmepos-competitive-bidding-proceed-while-addressing-identified-problems-and-concerns/ (site visited June 7, 2016). The same concerns are applicable to the industry's newest proposal, H.R. 4920.

In December 2015, CMS issued a final rule establishing a prior authorization for certain durable medical equipment, prosthetics, orthotics, and supplies (CMS-6050-F).[249] A major focus of the proposal is reigning in costs of certain expensive items and services.

[i] Competitive Bidding Areas. For a list of the existing competitive bidding areas across the country, see the following link: https://www.medicare.gov/what-medicare-covers/part-b/competitive-bidding-program-areas.html#collapse-4770 (site visited Aug. 10, 2016).

[ii] Terms to Remember. The competitive acquisition program for DMEPOS has introduced new terms, including:[250]

- *contract supplier*—an entity that is awarded a contract by CMS to furnish items under a competitive bidding program;
- *non-contract supplier*—a supplier that is not awarded a contract by CMS to furnish items included in a competitive bidding program;
- *referral agents*—applies to the range of physicians, practitioners, or providers who prescribe DMEPOS (in essence, "order" or "refer") for their patients;
- *grandfathered supplier*—a non-contract supplier that chooses to continue to furnish grandfathered items to a beneficiary in a CBA;
- *grandfathered item*—means all rented items within a product category for which payment was made prior to the implementation of a competitive bidding program to a grandfathered supplier that chooses to continue to furnish the items in accordance with 42 C.F.R. § 414.408(j) of this subpart and that fall within the following payment categories for competitive bidding:
    1. An inexpensive or routinely purchased item described in 42 C.F.R. § 414.220 of this part.
    2. An item requiring frequent and substantial servicing, as described in 42 C.F.R. § 414.222 of this part.
    3. Oxygen and oxygen equipment described in 42 C.F.R. § 414.226 of this part.
    4. Other DME described in 42 C.F.R. § 414.229 of this part.
- *Single payment amount*—allowed payment for an item furnished under a competitive bidding program.

[249] CMS. "CMS-6050-F" (Dec. 30, 2015), *available at* https://www.gpo.gov/fdsys/pkg/FR-2015-12-30/pdf/2015-32506.pdf (site visited Aug.10, 2016).

[250] 42 C.F.R. § 414.402.

• *competitive bidding ombudsman*—The Secretary has provided for a competitive acquisition ombudsman within the CMS in order to respond to complaints and inquiries made by suppliers and individuals relating to the application of the competitive acquisition program under this section. The ombudsman may be within the office of the Medicare Beneficiary Ombudsman appointed under section 1808(c). The ombudsman shall submit to Congress an annual report on the activities under this subsection, which report shall be coordinated with the report provided under section 1808(c)(2)(C).[251]

[iii] Competitive Bidding Implementation Contractor. CMS has established a DMEPOS Competitive Bidding Implementation Contractor (CBIC) website and has contracted with Palmetto GBA to conduct certain functions in relation to the administration of the DMEPOS competitive bidding program.[252] The functions of the CBIC are to prepare the request for bids (RFB), perform bid evaluations, and ensure that suppliers meet all applicable financial and quality standards. The contractor is also to conduct an education program for beneficiaries, suppliers, and referral agents.

In general, competitively bid items that are related and are used to treat a similar medical condition will be grouped into product categories, for example, hospital beds and accessories. Suppliers do not have to bid on all product categories, but for those product categories for which they bid, the supplier must bid on every item in the product category. In addition, contract suppliers will be required to furnish all items within a product category.

[iv] Product Categories. For a list of the current product categories, see the following link: https://www.medicare.gov/what-medicare-covers/part-b/competitive-bidding-program-areas.html#collapse-4770 (site visited Aug. 10, 2016).

[v] Grandfathering Certain Contractors.[253] The competitive bidding rules provide for "grandfathering" the provision of certain rental items for which

---

[251] MIPPA § 154(f).

[252] *See* http://www.dmecompetitivebid.com (site visited June 7, 2016) (this site has information for beneficiaries who must use suppliers that participate in the competitive bidding process); the competitive bidding rules are located at 72 Fed. Reg. 17,991 (Apr. 10, 2007), amending 42 C.F.R. Pts. 411 and 414; *see also* http://www.cms.hhs.gov/quarterlyproviderupdates/downloads/cms1270f.pdf (site visited June 7, 2015). In addition, CMS is amending Chapter 36 of its online MCP Manual to reflect its implementation policies with respect to its DMEPOS competitive bidding program. For updates, check http://www.cms.gov/Regulations-and-Guidance/Guidance/Manuals/downloads/clm104c36.pdf (site visited June 7, 2016). *See also* http://www.cms.gov/Medicare/Medicare-Fee-for-Service-Payment/DMEPOSCompetitiveBid/index.html?redirect=/DMEPOSCompetitiveBid/%20(Rules%20for%20DME%20competitive%20bidding%20project? (site visited June 7, 2016).

[253] CMS has published several Tip Sheets for providers affected by the DMEPOS competitive bidding program. "Grandfathered" DMEPOS suppliers are non-contract suppliers that elect to continue

payment is made on a rental basis prior to the implementation of a competitive bidding program and for which payment is made after implementation of a competitive bidding program to a grandfathered supplier that continues to furnish the items as provided under the payment regulations. These items include certain inexpensive or routinely purchased items (brand name items); an item requiring frequent and substantial servicing; oxygen and oxygen equipment and other DME described in the regulations.[254] It also allows for the grandfathering of certain special physician/practitioners—nurses, physician assistants, clinical nurse specialists, physical therapists, and occupational therapists in private practice to receive payment for certain competitively bid items furnished to their own patients as part of the professional service even though they have not submitted a bid and have not been selected as a contract supplier.[255]

With respect to choice of providers, beneficiaries who are renting an item of DME or oxygen and oxygen equipment that meets the definition of a grandfathered item may elect to obtain the item from a grandfathered supplier.[256] The rules also contain special provisions for small suppliers, including the forming of networks of small suppliers.[257]

[vi] Repair and Replacement of Beneficiary-Owned Items.[258]

Repair Only

A beneficiary who owns a competitively bid item that needs to be repaired may have the repairs performed by either a contract supplier or by a non-contract supplier. Medicare will pay for reasonable and necessary labor that is not otherwise covered under a manufacturer's or supplier's warranty.

---

to provide certain rented DME or oxygen and oxygen equipment at the time the DMEPOS competitive bidding program begins in a given competitive bidding area (CBA). The grandfathering exception may also apply to beneficiaries who transition from an MA plan. "Referral agents" are to assist beneficiaries to determine whether they are seeking and using suppliers who are in the CBAs in which they reside, and with referrals to appropriate providers. In addition, CMS has issued a "Tip Sheet" to explain how certain physicians and other treating practitioners can provide certain types of competitively bid items in a CBA to their patients without submitting a bid and being selected as a contract-provider. *See* CMS, "Overview of New Medicare Competitive Bidding Program for Durable Medical Equipment, Prosthetics, Orthotics, and Supplies (DMEPOS)," SE0805 Revised, Medicare Learning Network, *available at* http://www.cms.gov/Outreach-and-Education/Medicare-Learning-Network-MLN/MLNMattersArticles/downloads/SE0805.pdf (site visited June 7, 2016) and CMS, "Durable Medical Equipment, Prosthetics, Orthotics, and Supplies (DMEPOS) Competitive Bidding Program: Grandfathering, Repair and Replacement, Mail Order Diabetic Supplies and Advance Beneficiary Notices (ABNs)," https://www.cms.gov/Medicare/Medicare-Contracting/ContractorLearningResources/Downloads/JA0806.pdf (site visited June 8, 2016).

[254] *See* 42 C.F.R. § 414.402 (definitions).

[255] 42 C.F.R. § 414.402 (definitions). *See also* 42 C.F.R. §§ 414.226–414.229.

[256] *See* 42 C.F.R. § 414.408(e)(2). *See also* 42 C.F.R. § 414.408(j)(4).

[257] *See* 42 C.F.R. § 414.418.

[258] *See* 42 C.F.R. § 414.408(k).

Repair and Replacement

If a part needs to be replaced to make the beneficiary-owned equipment serviceable, and the replacement part is also a competitively bid item for the CBA in which the beneficiary maintains a permanent residence, the part may be obtained from either a contract supplier or a non-contract supplier. In these situations, Medicare pays the single payment amount provided under the competitive bidding program for the replacement part.

Replacement Only

Beneficiaries who are permanent residents within a CBA are required to obtain replacement of all items subject to competitive bidding from a contract supplier—including replacement of base equipment and replacement of parts or accessories for base equipment that are being replaced for reasons other than servicing of the base equipment.

Beneficiaries who are not permanent residents of a CBA but require a replacement of a competitively bid item while visiting in a different CBA must obtain the replacement item from a contract supplier. The supplier will be paid the fee schedule amount for the state in which the beneficiary is a permanent resident.

[vii] Mail Order Diabetic Supplies Under the Program. Medicare beneficiaries who are permanent residents in a CBA may purchase their diabetic testing supplies from a mail order contract supplier for the area in which the beneficiary is a permanent resident or from a non-contract supplier in cases where the supplies are not furnished on a mail order basis.[259] These supplies will be reimbursed at the single payment amount for the CBA where the beneficiary maintains a permanent residence. For diabetic supplies that are not furnished through mail order, suppliers will be paid the fee schedule amount.

[viii] Competitive Bidding and Advance Beneficiary Notice Information. In general, if a non-contract supplier in a CBA furnishes a competitively bid item to any Medicare beneficiary regardless of whether that beneficiary maintains a permanent residence in the CBA or another area, and no applicable exceptions apply, Medicare will not make payment. In these circumstances, the

---

[259] *See* § 636 of the American Taxpayer Relief Act of 2012, Pub. L. No. 112-240, H.R. 8, 126 Stat. 2313 (Jan. 2, 2013), amending Social Security Act, § 1834(a)(1), 42 U.S.C. 1395m(a)(1), *available at* http://www.gpo.gov/fdsys/pkg/BILLS-112hr8eas/pdf/BILLS-112hr8eas.pdf (site visited June 7, 2016). The DMEPOS program for mail-order diabetic supplies went into effect July 1, 2013. *See* http://www.medicareadvocacy.org/medicares-national-mail-order-program-for-diabetic-testing-supplies/ (site visited June 7, 2016); *see also* http://www.cms.gov/Outreach-and-Education/Medicare-Learning-Network-MLN/MLNProducts/downloads/DME_Mail_Order_Factsheet_ICN900924.pdf (site visited June 7, 2016).

beneficiary is not liable for payment unless the non-contract supplier in a CBA obtains an ABN signed by the beneficiary.[260]

A signed ABN indicates that the beneficiary was informed in writing prior to receiving the item that there would be no Medicare coverage due to the supplier's contract status and that the beneficiary understands that he or she will be liable for all costs that the non-contract supplier may charge for the item.[261]

[ix] No Administrative or Judicial Review of Process. There is no administrative or judicial review under the DMEPOS competitive bidding process for the following: establishment of payment amounts; awarding of contracts; designation of CBAs; phase-in of the competitive bidding program; selection of items for competitive bidding; and the bidding structure and number of contract suppliers selected for a competitive bidding program.[262] In addition, a denied claim is not appealable if the denial is based on a determination by CMS that a competitively bid item was furnished in a CBA in a manner not authorized under the competitive bidding program.[263]

[c] Medicare Coverage of Power Mobility Devices

On May 5, 2005, CMS issued an NCD defining access to Medicare-covered mobility assistive equipment (MAE) such as power wheelchairs and scooters (three-wheel devices). These devices are under the broad umbrella of power mobility devices (PMDs).[264] In making its coverage determination with respect

---

[260] CMS has available a series of Fact Sheets that may help beneficiaries understand the importance of an ABN in the context of Medicare's competitive bidding program. *See* http://www.cms.gov (site visited June 7, 2016).

[261] The beneficiary must also understand that he or she can get the supplies from a Medicare-approved contractor. Although the non-contract supplier does not have to refer the beneficiary to the Medicare-approved contractor, it must at least direct the beneficiary to the 1-800-MEDICARE number. *See* CMS Transmittal 2480 Advanced Beneficiary Notice of Non-Coverage § 50.12, *available at* http://www.cms.gov/Regulations-and-Guidance/Guidance/Transmittals/Downloads/R2480CP.pdf (site visited June 7, 2016).

[262] 42 C.F.R. § 414.424.

[263] 42 C.F.R. § 414.424. Note, too, that MIPPA § 154(a)(1)(D) provides that nothing in the subsection terminating contracts awarded under the initial competition round shall be construed to provide an independent cause of action or right to administrative or judicial review with regard to the termination of the initially awarded contracts under round one.

[264] *See* CMS, Decision Memo for Mobility Assistive Equipment (CAG-00274N), *available at* http://www.cms.gov/medicare-coverage-database/details/nca-decision-memo.aspx?NCAId=143&fromdb=true (site visited June 7, 2016). Other important citations on access to power mobility devices (PMDs) under Medicare include Medicare Learning Network's "Power Mobility Devices (PMDs): Complying with Documentation & Coverage Requirements," *available at* http://www.cms.gov/Outreach-and-Education/Medicare-Learning-Network-MLN/MLNProducts/downloads/pmd_DocCvg_FactSheet_ICN905063.pdf (site visited June 7, 2016); CMS's Medicare Coverage Database, *available at* http://www.cms.hhs.gov/mcd/search.asp (site visited June 7, 2016); and the MCP

to the appropriateness of such equipment for a particular beneficiary, CMS has moved away from a chair- or bed-confined standard and is now basing coverage determinations on an evaluation of a beneficiary's ability to engage in certain mobility-related activities of daily living (MRADLs) such as toileting, feeding, and bathing in customary locations in the home. Where such criteria are met, and properly documented, CMS will consider the item of DME at issue reasonable and necessary as defined in the Medicare law.[265]

In April 2007, CMS issued, through its Medicare Learning Network, a detailed treatment of access to PMDs, including power wheelchairs and power operated vehicles (POVs).[266] It provides the following useful definitions:[267]

> **Power Mobility Devices:** PMDs are defined as covered items of Durable Medical Equipment (DME) that are in a class of wheelchairs that includes power wheelchairs (four-wheeled motorized vehicles whose steering is operated by an electronic device or joystick to control direction and turning) or POVs (three- or four-wheeled motorized scooters that are operated by a tiller) that a beneficiary uses in the home.
>
> **Power (Motorized) Wheelchairs:** Most beneficiaries who require power wheelchairs are non-ambulatory and have severe weakness of the upper extremities due to a neurologic or muscular condition. Under the MAE national coverage policy, power wheelchairs may be medically necessary for beneficiaries who cannot effectively perform Mobility-Related Activities of Daily Living (MRADLs) in the home using a cane, walker, manually operated wheelchair, or a POV/scooter. In addition, the beneficiary must demonstrate the ability to safely and effectively operate the power wheelchair in the home environment.
>
> **Power Operated Vehicles (POVs or scooters):** These vehicles have been appropriately used in the home environment to improve the ability of chronically disabled persons to cope with normal domestic, vocational, and

---

Manual, *available at* http://www.cms.gov/medicare-coverage-database/details/ncd-details.aspx?NCDId=219&ncdver=2 (site visited June 7, 2016). Advocates should check this website frequently for updates.

[265] *See* § 1862(a)(1)(A) of the Social Security Act, 42 U.S.C. § 1395y(a)(1)(A). *See also* CMS rules for an advance determination of Medicare coverage (ADMC) for customized DME, *available at* http://www.cms.gov/Regulations-and-Guidance/Guidance/Transmittals/downloads/R5PIM.pdf (site visited June 7, 2016). It is important to note that ADMCs are not initial determinations as defined at 42 C.F.R. § 405.801(a).

[266] *See* CMS Fact Sheet, "Medicare Coverage of Power Mobility Devices (PMDs): Power Wheelchairs and Power Operated Vehicles (POVs)," Medicare Learning Network, *available at* http://www.cms.hhs.gov/MLNProducts/downloads/PMDFactSheet07_Quark19.pdf (site visited June 7, 2016).

[267] *See* CMS Fact Sheet, "Medicare Coverage of Power Mobility Devices (PMDs): Power Wheelchairs and Power Operated Vehicles (POVs)," Medicare Learning Network, *available at* http://www.cms.hhs.gov/MLNProducts/downloads/PMDFactSheet07_Quark19.pdf (site visited June 7, 2016).

> social activities. Under the MAE national coverage policy, POVs may be medically necessary for beneficiaries who cannot effectively perform MRA-DLs in the home using a cane, walker, or manually operated wheelchair. In addition, the beneficiary must demonstrate sufficient strength and postural stability to safely and effectively operate the POV in the home environment.

In its NCD issuance, CMS set forth new function-based criteria for PMD, setting out an algorithmic process called the "Clinical Criteria for MAE Coverage." It replaces the older "bed or chair-confined" standard.[268] It is felt that this new approach gives greater consideration to the beneficiary's abilities to engage mobility activities within the home. Moreover, the issuance does not preclude use of the PMD outside the home. The chief concern is to establish that the beneficiary has a mobility limitation such that a PMD is medically necessary and that the beneficiary has the physical and mental ability to use the equipment in the home and is willing to do so. When these factors are appropriately documented by physicians and treating practitioners, the beneficiary is free to use the MOE both in the home, and out in the community (but not primarily for the pursuit of leisure or recreational activities).

In making an assessment whether an item of PMD is appropriate the physician or treating practitioner must conduct a face-to-face evaluation of the beneficiary before writing a prescription. The decision memorandum provides the additional clarification that Medicare no longer restricts the type of physician able to prescribe a PMD. Also, a physician assistant, nurse practitioner, or clinical nurse specialist may prescribe a PMD. In addition the prescription for the PMD must be writing and signed and dated by the physician or treating practitioner who performed the face-to-face examination, and must be received by the PMD supplier within 30 days of the face-to-face examination.[269]

Other supporting information that the physician or treating practitioner must provide the supplier of the PMD includes:[270]

- The medical necessity for the use of the PMD in the home,
- Relevant information from the beneficiary's medical record, and

---

[268] *See* CMS Fact Sheet, "Medicare Coverage of Power Mobility Devices (PMDs): Power Wheelchairs and Power Operated Vehicles (POVs)," Medicare Learning Network, *available at* http://www.cms.hhs.gov/MLNProducts/downloads/PMDFactSheet07_Quark19.pdf (site visited June 7, 2016).

[269] *See* CMS Fact Sheet, "Medicare Coverage of Power Mobility Devices (PMDs): Power Wheelchairs and Power Operated Vehicles (POVs)," Medicare Learning Network, *available at* http://www.cms.hhs.gov/MLNProducts/downloads/PMDFactSheet07_Quark19.pdf (site visited June 7, 2016).

[270] *See* CMS Fact Sheet, "Medicare Coverage of Power Mobility Devices (PMDs): Power Wheelchairs and Power Operated Vehicles (POVs)" Medicare Learning Network, *available at* http://www.cms.hhs.gov/MLNProducts/downloads/PMDFactSheet07_Quark19.pdf (site visited June 7, 2016).

- Information establishing that the beneficiary or caregiver is capable of operating the PMD.

With respect to prior documentation, CMS clarifies that the information in the record at the face-to-face evaluation will be sufficient to support medical necessity. It notes, however, that prior documentation may be necessary when the information from the face-to-face examination refers to previous notes in the medical record.[271]

[d] Medicare Payment for and Maintenance of Oxygen Equipment

Medicare provides for coverage of home oxygen therapy under the Part B DME benefit if certain medical pre-conditions are met.[272] This coverage includes the rental of oxygen delivery systems.[273]

In regulations issued November 25, 2009, and effective January 1, 2010,[274] CMS clarified that the oxygen suppler that furnishes oxygen equipment during the 36-month rental period (described below) must continue to furnish the oxygen equipment after the 36-month rental period. The supplier is required to continue to furnish the equipment during any period of medical need for the remainder of the reasonable useful life of the equipment as provided in Section 144(b) of MIPPA (discussed below).[275]

Providers are paid a monthly payment amount for furnishing medically necessary stationary oxygen equipment of a particular class—including stationary oxygen concentrators, stationary liquid oxygen systems, and gaseous oxygen systems.[276] Medicare also pays a monthly add-on payment to suppliers furnishing medically necessary portable oxygen equipment, including traditional portable liquid oxygen systems and portable gaseous oxygen systems and oxygen generating portable equipment, as well as oxygen transfilling equipment. Both the liquid and gaseous oxygen systems (stationary and portable) require ongoing delivery of oxygen contents.[277]

CMS further clarified that under no circumstance will a new period of continuous use begin following the 36-month rental period and before the end of the

---

[271] *See* CMS Fact Sheet, "Medicare Coverage of Power Mobility Devices (PMDs): Power Wheelchairs and Power Operated Vehicles (POVs)," Medicare Learning Network, *available at* http://www.cms.hhs.gov/MLNProducts/downloads/PMDFactSheet07_Quark19.pdf (site visited June 7, 2016).

[272] *See* § 1834 of the Social Security Act, 42 U.S.C. § 1395m(a)(5)(A)–(F); *see also* 42 C.F.R. § 414.226 (oxygen and oxygen equipment).

[273] *See* § 1834 of the Social Security Act, 42 U.S.C. § 1395m(a)(5)(A)–(F); *see also* 42 C.F.R. § 414.226 (oxygen and oxygen equipment).

[274] *See* 74 Fed. Reg. 61,888 (Nov. 25, 2009), discussing 42 C.F.R. § 414.226.

[275] 74 Fed. Reg. 61,888 (Nov. 25, 2009).

[276] 42 C.F.R. § 414.226(c)(1)(ii) and (iii).

[277] *See* 42 C.F.R. § 414.226.

equipment's reasonable useful lifetime; and that the supplier is responsible for furnishing the equipment after the 36-month rental period and before the end of the equipment's reasonable useful lifetime.[278] Further, regardless of any break in the medical need that occurs following the 36-month rental period, the regulations provide that once the break ends and medical need for the oxygen equipment resumes, the supplier is obligated to continue furnishing the item for no additional rental payments until the end of the equipment's reasonable useful life.[279]

Effective January 1, 2006, Medicare pays for stationary and portable oxygen equipment for a 36-month capped rental period. Under the Deficit Reduction Act (DRA) of 2005, ownership of the oxygen equipment was transferred to the beneficiary at the end of the 36-month period.[280] Section 144(b) of MIPPA repealed the transfer of ownership provision applicable to oxygen equipment created by the DRA.[281] Under MIPPA, the supplier continues to own the equipment after the 36-month capped rental period.[282]

Suppliers participating in the Medicare program are paid over a 36-month period for furnishing a beneficiary's oxygen and oxygen equipment needs for up to five years. The supplier is required to continue to maintain the oxygen equipment and is to furnish the equipment and any necessary supplies and accessories during this five-year period. For beneficiaries who use oxygen tanks or cylinders that need delivery of gaseous or liquid oxygen contents, Medicare will continue to pay each month for the delivery after the 36-month capped rental period.[283]

At the end of the five-year period, the obligation of the supplier to furnish the oxygen and oxygen equipment ends. The beneficiary may elect to obtain replacement equipment from any Medicare-certified contract supplier serving the area in which the beneficiary resides. A new 36-month payment period and five-year supplier obligation period starts at the end of the initial five-year period.

---

[278] *See* 42 C.F.R. § 414.230(h).

[279] 42 C.F.R. § 414.230.

[280] The Deficit Reduction Act (DRA) of 2005, §§ 5101(a)–(b), Pub. L. No. 109-171. *See also* CMS, MedLearn, "Oxygen Therapy Supplies: Complying with Documentation & Coverage Requirements" (Dec. 2011), *available at* https://www.scanhealthplan.com/media/1483/medicare-coverage-of-oxygen-therapy.pdf (site visited June 9, 2016), *and* Government Accountability Office, Report to Congressional Requesters, "Medicare Home Oxygen: Refining Payment Methodology Has Potential to Lower Program and Beneficiary Spending" (Jan. 2011), *available at* http://www.gao.gov/assets/320/315094.pdf (site visited June 7, 2016).

[281] MIPPA § 144(b).

[282] *See* CMS Transmittal Number 497(May 22, 2009), implementation date July 6, 2009, *available at* http://www.cms.hhs.gov/transmittals/downloads/R497OTN.pdf (site visited June 7, 2016).

[283] *See* CMS Transmittal Number 497 (May 22, 2009), implementation date July 6, 2009, *available at* http://www.cms.hhs.gov/transmittals/downloads/R497OTN.pdf (site visited June 7, 2016).

[i] CMS's Consumer Alert on Oxygen Equipment and Supplies. CMS, through its Office of Public Affairs, announced that beneficiaries should continue to receive the oxygen and oxygen supplies that they need; that Medicare is required to make 36 monthly payments to oxygen equipment suppliers; that suppliers must continue to provide beneficiaries with properly functioning oxygen equipment and associated supplies after the 36th month (three-year) payment period; that the supplier is required to perform any repairs or to provide replacements at no cost to beneficiaries until the beneficiary has used the equipment for five years; and that after five years, the supplier may replace the equipment, but a new 36-month rental period will begin at that time; that if a supplier refuses to comply with these rules, the beneficiary should notify CMS *immediately* by calling 1-800-Medicare (1-800-633-4227) or, for users of TTY, 1-877-486-2048.[284]

[ii] Payment Rules for Oxygen and Supplies. Medicare's monthly rental rate covers the beneficiary's oxygen equipment and necessary supplies and accessories such as tubing or a mouth piece, oxygen contents, maintenance, servicing, and repairs. Medicare pays 80 percent of the rental amount, and the Medicare beneficiary is responsible for any unpaid Part B deductible and the remaining 20 percent of the rental amount.[285] Medigap policies A–G and K–N pay the 20 percent cost-sharing.[286] Note that these payment rules apply to traditional Medicare. Medicare Advantage plans have their own rules concerning payment and cost-sharing for oxygen and supplies. Some plans require beneficiaries to pay more than 20 percent cost-sharing; some plans continue to impose a 20 percent cost-sharing even after the 36-month capped rental period under traditional Medicare.

[iii] No Separate Payment for Maintenance and Repairs. Under MIPPA, ownership of the oxygen equipment is retained by the supplier after the rental payments stop. The MIPPA law requires the suppliers to provide all necessary maintenance of the equipment without charge. A beneficiary may not be charged for repairing or replacing the equipment or parts necessary to make the equipment function properly. If the equipment has to be replaced because it no

---

[284] *See* CMS, Press Release, "Medicare Consumer Alert for Beneficiaries Who Use Oxygen Equipment and Supplies" (Dec. 17, 2008), *available at* http://www.cms.gov/Newsroom/MediaReleaseDatabase/Press-Releases/2008-Press-Releases-Items/2008-12-17.html (site visited June 7, 2016). *See also* Center for Medicare Advocacy, "Medicare Coverage of Home Oxygen Therapy," *available at* http://www.medicareadvocacy.org/medicare-info/medicare-part-b/#OXYGEN%20THERAPY (site visited June 7, 2016).

[285] *See* CMS, "Medicare Coverage of Durable Medical Equipment and Other Devices," *available at* http://www.medicare.gov/Pubs/pdf/11045.pdf (site visited June 7, 2016).

[286] *See* Choosing a Medigap Policy: A Guide to Health Insurance for People with Medicare," *available at* https://www.medicare.gov/Pubs/pdf/02110-Medicare-Medigap.guide.pdf (site visited June 14, 2016).

longer functions properly, the supplier must replace the equipment with the same or similar make and model of equipment at no charge.[287]

[iv] Service for Oxygen Equipment for Persons Outside Their Home Geographic Area. Persons who travel outside their home geographic areas for extensive periods of time (several weeks or more at a time) or who relocate should ask their current supplier for assistance in finding a supplier in the area where they visit extensively or in the area in which they have relocated. This can get tricky as the initial supplier has been paid for furnishing the necessary equipment and for servicing it for five years. Beneficiaries may find that some suppliers are unwilling or slow to meet their maintenance and service responsibility when the beneficiary is no longer in the area in which the supplier does business. The supplier may choose to make arrangements with a supplier in the beneficiary's new area to provide necessary maintenance and service but otherwise remains responsible for the maintenance and service functions for which it has been paid. Beneficiaries who encounter problems with their suppliers in making such arrangements should call 1-800-MEDICARE (1-800-633-4227). TTY users should call 1-877-486-2048.[288]

[v] Competitive Bidding. It is important to mention that competitive bidding (discussed in **§ 6.03[D][2][b]**) is part of the concern of many suppliers of durable medical equipment, including oxygen equipment. CMS is continuing the cost-containment steps and provisions that have been enacted over the years. Containment of costs for oxygen and oxygen equipment is part of that overall containment effort. Specifically, oxygen and oxygen equipment are included in the ten categories of items and services that are part of the constellation of services and supplies on which suppliers must bid in order to become Medicare-certified contract suppliers of durable medical equipment.[289]

---

[287] *See* CMS, Press Release, "Medicare Consumer Alert for Beneficiaries Who Use Oxygen Equipment and Supplies" (Dec. 17, 2008), *available at* http://www.cms.gov/Newsroom/MediaReleaseDatabase/Press-Releases/2008-Press-Releases-Items/2008-12-17.html (site visited June 7, 2016).

[288] *See* CMS, Press Release, "Medicare Consumer Alert for Beneficiaries Who Use Oxygen Equipment and Supplies" (Dec. 17, 2008), *available at* http://www.cms.gov/Newsroom/MediaReleaseDatabase/Press-Releases/2008-Press-Releases-Items/2008-12-17.html (site visited June 7, 2016). Note that suppliers are working with members of the United States Congress to change this rule. Many suppliers feel that this requirement is burdensome. *See* http://www.gainesvilletimes.com/news/archive/14287/ (site visited June 7, 2016).

[289] CMS. "Oxygen Equipment & Accessories," *available at* https://www.medicare.gov/coverage/oxygen-equipment-and-accessories.html (site visited Aug. 10, 2016).

[3] National Coverage Determinations

The Medicare statute gives the Secretary the obligation and authority to make determinations about what specific items and services are covered under the Medicare program.[290] CMS uses its NCD process to discharge this responsibility.[291]

Advocates should visit Medicare's Coverage Determinations web page.[292] Medicare's database of national and local coverage decisions should be consulted for updates.[293] When seeking to petition for a new coverage decision or to set aside an old one, it is important to have extensive medical support for the coverage of the item, service, or procedure at issue. In addition to one's treating physician, local and national medical societies can be helpful in such endeavors. Also, it is important to keep in mind that the removal of a negative NCD may only pave the way to assert that a more favorable NCD should be established. In any event, the removal of a negative NCD opens the way for local Medicare Administrative Contractors (MACs) to issue local coverage decisions LCDs on the matter at issue, pending the development of an NCD on the particular matter.

An NCD does not include a determination of what code, if any, is assigned to a service nor is it a determination with respect to the amount of payment to be made for the service.[294] NCDs are binding on all Medicare contractors, Quality Improvement Organizations (QIOs), HMOs, competitive medical plans, health care prepayment plans, and the MAC when published in the *Federal Register*.[295] An ALJ may not disregard, set aside, or otherwise review an NCD.[296] An ALJ may review the facts of a particular case to determine whether an NCD applies to a specific claim for benefits and, if so, whether the NCD was applied correctly to the claim.[297] A provider of services or a supplier may not introduce evidence in any appeal under Section 1395ff of the Social Security Act that was not presented at the reconsideration unless there is good cause that precluded the introduction

---

[290] 42 U.S.C. §§ 1395y(a)(1)(A), 1395ff(b)(3), 1395hh. *See also* 42 C.F.R. § 405.205. *See also* Medicare NCD Manual.

[291] *See* current Medicare authority to make NCDs without the requirement of notice-and-comment rule-making procedures, §§ 1871(a)(2), 1869(c)(3)(B) of the Social Security Act, 42 U.S.C. §§ 1395hh(a)(2) and 1395ff(b)(3)(B); procedures for maintaining code lists in the Negotiated NCDs for Clinical Diagnostic Services *and* CMS's Medicare Coverage Database, *available at* http://www.cms.gov/medicare-coverage-database/ (site visited June 7, 2016).

[292] *See* CMS, "Medicare Coverage Determination Process," *available at* http://www.cms.gov/Medicare/Coverage/DeterminationProcess/ (site visited June 7, 2016).

[293] *See* CMS's Medicare Coverage Database website at http://www.cms.gov/medicare-coverage-database/overview-and-quick-search.aspx (site visited June 7, 2016).

[294] 42 C.F.R. § 400.202 (definitions specific to Medicare); *see also* the Medicare Managed Care Manual, Ch. 4, § 90 (national and local coverage determinations), *available at* http://www.cms.gov/Regulations-and-Guidance/Guidance/Manuals/downloads/mc86c04.pdf (site visited June 7, 2016).

[295] 42 C.F.R. § 405.1060(a).

[296] 42 C.F.R. § 405.1060(b)(1).

[297] 42 C.F.R. § 1060(b)(2).

of such evidence at or before that reconsideration.[298] The federal courts may set aside an NCD only after it has received and considered the Secretary's rationale for the coverage determination.[299] Advocates encounter problems with the NCD process when they seek coverage for new procedures. Problem areas usually revolve around getting access to the national coverage process itself; the lack of the ability to participate in the process in a meaningful way such that information in support of coverage is fairly and fully heard and utilized in making NCDs; and the extremely slow nature of the process itself. The current process, and relevant definitions, effective December 8, 2003, are set out in the final regulations.[300]

An LCD is a decision by a contractor under Medicare Part A or Part B whether to cover a particular service on a contractor-wide basis in accordance with Medicare's reasonable and necessary criteria; it may provide that a service is not reasonable and necessary for certain diagnoses and/or for certain diagnosis codes; but it does not include a determination of which procedure code, if any, is assigned to a service or a determination with respect to the amount of payment to be made for the service.[301]

With respect to LCD and NCD reviews and individual claim appeals, an aggrieved party (a Medicare beneficiary or the estate of a Medicare beneficiary)[302] must notify the ALJ or the Departmental Appeals Board (DAB), as appropriate, regarding the submission and disposition of any pending claim or appeal relating to the subject of the aggrieved party's LCD and NCD complaint; this reporting obligation continues through the entire LCD and NCD review process.[303] Only an aggrieved party may initiate a review of an LCD and NCD and must do so through filing an acceptable complaint.[304] Only currently

---

[298] 42 U.S.C. § 1395ff(b)(3); 42 C.F.R. § 405.1050; Section 522 of the Medicare, Medicaid, and SCHIP Benefits Improvement and Protection Act of 2000 provides for Departmental Appeals Board (DAB) review of NCDs. *See also* 42 U.S.C. § 1395ff(f)(1)(a)(v). A DAB decision would constitute final HHS action and would be subject to limited judicial review. 42 C.F.R. §§ 405.732 and 405.860.

[299] 42 U.S.C. § 1395ff(b)(3). *See also* 42 C.F.R. § 426.100–426.587 (review of LCDs and NCDs, including the process and timelines for review).

[300] *See* 68 Fed. Reg. 63,692 (Nov. 7, 2003) (preamble), 42 C.F.R. § 405.902 (definitions), and 42 C.F.R. § 405.1050 (applicability of national coverage determinations). For further background discussion, see 64 Fed. Reg. 22,619–25 (Apr. 27, 1999). Information about the application of NCDs or LCDs in the denial of coverage should be included in Medicare Summary Notices (MSNs). See the redesigned MSN at http://www.cms.gov/apps/files/msn_changes.pdf (site visited June 7, 2016).

[301] 42 C.F.R. § 400.202 (definitions specific to Medicare).

[302] 42 C.F.R. § 426.110. *See* CMS's Local Coverage Database, *available at* http://www.cms.gov/medicare-coverage-database/indexes/national-and-local-indexes.aspx (site visited June 7, 2016).

[303] 42 C.F.R. § 426.310.

[304] 42 C.F.R. § 426.320; *see also* Hays v. Leavitt, 583 F. Supp. 2d 62 (D.D.C., Oct. 16, 2008), in which the federal district court confirmed that only the beneficiary can challenge an LCD and that the term "reasonable and necessary" refers to coverage and not to cost. The opinion is presently available at https://ecf.dcd.uscourts.gov/cgi-bin/show_public_doc?2008cv1032-22 (site visited June 7, 2016).

effective (no drafts or other predecisional material) LCDs or NCDs (or deemed NCDs) may be challenged.[305] During the review of an NCD or LCD, the aggrieved party bears the burden of proof and the burden of persuasion for the issue(s) raised in a complaint; the burden of proof is judged by a preponderance of the evidence.[306]

§ 6.04 MEDICARE PART B AND PAYMENT

[A] Medicare Assignment Program

The Medicare assignment program was established in 1984 and initially focused on physicians.[307] The program now includes both physicians and suppliers.[308] Under this program, physicians and suppliers agree to accept the Medicare reasonable charge amount (the Medicare-approved amount) as payment in full (no balance billing) with the beneficiary being responsible for a 20 percent copayment.[309]

In order to participate, physicians and suppliers must make an annual election whether to participate and sign a participation agreement. Physicians and suppliers who do not elect to participate may participate on a case-by-case basis.[310] Physicians and suppliers who participate are designated as participating physicians and suppliers, are listed in directories of Medicare participating physicians and suppliers, and receive certain insignia they can use in their offices to identify themselves as participants in the Medicare assignment program.

---

[305] 42 C.F.R. § 426.325.

[306] 42 C.F.R. § 426.330. For further discussion of the NCD process, see https://www.cms.gov/Medicare/Coverage/DeterminationProcess/ (site visited June 7, 2016; *see also* http://www.cms.gov/Medicare/Coverage/DeterminationProcess/Downloads/FR09262003.pdf (site visited June 7, 2016) and http://www.cms.gov/Medicare/Coverage/DeterminationProcess/Downloads/guidance.pdf (site visited June 7, 2016). *See also* Medicare Payment Advisory Commission (MedPac), "Appendix B: An Introduction to How Medicare Makes Coverage Decisions," *available at* http://www.medpac.gov/documents/reports/Mar03_AppB.pdf?sfvrsn=0 (site visited June 7, 2016). The *Federal Register* material on challenging an NCD/LCD can be found at http://www.cms.gov/Medicare/Coverage/DeterminationProcess/downloads/FR11072003.pdf (site visited June 7, 2016).

[307] 42 U.S.C. § 1395u(b)(4). *See also* MCP Manual, Ch. 1, §§ 30.3 *et seq.* The physician assignment form is available at https://www.cms.gov/cmsforms/downloads/cms460.pdf (site visited June 7, 2016).

[308] *See* 42 C.F.R. §§ 424.55 (payment to supplier), 414.48 (limits on actual charges of nonparticipating suppliers), and 400.202 (definition specific to Medicare, including payment on an assignment-related basis).

[309] 42 U.S.C. § 1395u(b)(3)(B)(ii); 42 C.F.R. § 410.152. *See also* 42 U.S.C. § 1395n; 42 C.F.R. § 424.55(b).

[310] 42 U.S.C. § 1395u(h)(2)–(6).

Participating physicians and suppliers also receive a five percent higher Medicare fee schedule amount.[311]

[B] Fee Schedules and Limiting Charge Amounts

Beginning in November 1989, Congress enacted additional physician payment reforms that limited what physicians who do not participate in the Medicare assignment program can charge their Medicare patients, effective January 1, 1991.[312] The limiting charge amount for non-participating physicians for their Medicare patients is no more than 115 percent above the Medicare fee schedule amount, which is the recognized payment amount or limiting charge.[313] For example, if Medicare sets the recognized payment amount for a service at $100, even though the non-participating physician might bill non-Medicare patients at $175, the physician can bill his or her Medicare patient for the service no more than $115.

Physicians who treat patients eligible for Medicaid, including qualified Medicare beneficiaries (QMBs), must bill on an assignment-only basis.[314] Moreover, if the services of a non-participating physician to Medicare beneficiaries are determined not to be medically necessary, the physician must return the billed amount to the beneficiary.[315] With respect to elective surgery costing $500 or more, nonparticipating physicians must provide the beneficiary with written information that sets out the difference in the Medicare reimbursement and the physician's full charge.[316] In addition, physicians must submit all claims, both assigned and unassigned, for their Medicare beneficiaries; they cannot charge extra for this service, and claims have to be submitted within one year of the date of providing services(s) for which reimbursement is sought.[317] All payments for

[311] 42 U.S.C. §§ 1395w-4(g), 1395u(b)(4)(A)(iv). *See also* Whitney v. Heckler, 780 F.2d 963, 970-72 (11th Cir. 1986) (upholding the five percent cost differential).

[312] *See* Omnibus Budget Reconciliation Act of 1989 (OBRA '89), Pub. L. No. 101-239, 6102 (adding § 1848(g) to the Social Security Act, 42 U.S.C. § 1395w-4(g) (limitation on beneficiary liability)); 42 C.F.R. § 414.48.

[313] 42 U.S.C. § 1395w-4(g)(2)(B), (C). It should be noted that states can establish more stringent balance billing limits, given that Congress has not totally preempted the field. *See* Pennsylvania Med. Soc'y v. Marconis, 942 F.2d 842 (3d Cir 1991); Massachusetts Med. Soc'y v. Dukakis, 815 F.2d 790 (1st Cir. 1987); Medical Soc'y of N.Y. State v. Cuomo, 777 F. Supp. 1157 (S.D.N.Y. 1991); Downhour v. Somani, 85 F.3d 261 (6th Cir.), *cert. denied*, 519 U.S. 965 (1996). In addition, New York Medicare beneficiaries have been found to have a private right of action against hospitals to seek repayment against a hospital for physician overcharges under Medicare and state law that limits charge laws. *See* Medicare Beneficiaries Def. Fund v. Memorial Sloan-Kettering Cancer Ctr., 603 N.Y.S.2d 1016 (Sup. Ct. 1993).

[314] 42 U.S.C. § 1395w-4(g)(3) (applies to services furnished on or after April 1, 1990).

[315] 42 C.F.R. § 411.408.

[316] 42 U.S.C. § 1395w-4(g).

[317] 42 U.S.C. § 1395w-4(g)(4).

ambulance services are made on an assignment-only basis. Providers can collect from beneficiaries only the unmet Part B deductible and Part B coinsurance amounts.[318]

[C] Limited Prior Determination Process

Section 938 amends the MMA[319] to create a limited prior determination process regarding physician services determined by the Secretary to be subject to the process.[320] Under the process, a participating physician who has permission from the patient or an individual who has received an ABN may ask the appropriate Medicare contractor for a determination of whether Medicare will pay for a service before actually receiving the service.[321]

The Secretary may require that the request be accompanied by a description of the physician's service, supporting medical necessity documentation, the ABN if the requester is the individual, and other appropriate documents. The contractor must then provide a written notice, within 45 days of receipt of the request, as to whether the service is covered, is not covered, or the contractor lacks sufficient information to make a coverage determination. The contractor must inform the beneficiary of the decision if the request was made by the physician.

A determination that a service is covered is binding on the contractor in the absence of fraud or misrepresentation of the facts. If the determination is not favorable, the individual has no appeal rights. However, the individual may still receive the service and have a claim submitted to the contractor. If the claim for services received is denied, the individual may then pursue an appeal through the regular appeals process. Similarly, an individual who decides not to go through the prior determination process, but who chooses instead to receive the service and seek reimbursement, retains current appeals rights.

[D] Advance Determination of Medicare Coverage

The current Advance Determination of Medicare Coverage (ADMC) is an optional process[322] that takes the place of the old "prior approval" process, but it is only for certain wheelchairs (manual or power-driven), related options, and

[318] 67 Fed. Reg. 9099, 9134, amending 42 C.F.R. § 414.610(a)–(g) by adding new § 414.610(b).

[319] 42 U.S.C. § 1395ff(b).

[320] 42 U.S.C. § 1395ff(b).

[321] 42 U.S.C. § 1395ff(b).

[322] *See* § 1834a (15) of the Social Security Act, 42 U.S.C. § 1395m(a)(15) (Advance Determinations of Coverage for Certain Items). *See also* Medicare Program Integrity Manual, Ch. 5, Items and Services Having Special DME Review Considerations, *available at* http://www.cms.gov/Regulations-and-Guidance/Guidance/Manuals/downloads/pim83c05.pdf (June 7, 2016).

accessories.[323] It is used to obtain a coverage decision from a DME MAC prior to delivery and payment for DME that is subject to the ADMC process. Requests for an ADMC are submitted to the relevant DME MAC, which will have on its web page, or will otherwise make available, a statement of the information that is required for review of an ADMC request. A negative ADMC determination is not subject to an appeal because it does not meet the definition of an initial determination, as no request for payment is being made. ADMC requests may be resubmitted only once during the six-month period following a negative determination. Likewise, if the wheelchair base is approved, but one or more accessories are denied, an ADMC request may not be resubmitted for those accessories.

[E] Private Physician Contracts

BBA '97 established an option allowing Medicare beneficiaries to enter into private contracts with their physicians (either a provider group, a network of providers, or an individual provider) to pay privately for services otherwise covered by the Medicare program.[324] Medicare limitations on actual charges and the physician requirement to submit claims do not apply.[325] For purposes of this provision, a Medicare beneficiary is an individual who is entitled to benefits under Part A or enrolled under Part B.[326]

Contracts under this provision are outside the Medicare program and physicians must agree not to bill Medicare for Medicare-covered service for a period of two years and submit a written affidavit to the Secretary of HHS to that effect.[327] A copy of the affidavit of the physician showing that the physician has advised the beneficiary of his or her rights under this provision must be filed with the Secretary of HHS within ten days after the first such contract has been signed.[328]

Moreover, the provider of service must warn the beneficiary that Medicare balance billing limits do not apply and that Medicare Supplemental Insurance

---

[323] *See* CMS Manual System, Pub. 100-08, Medicare Program Integrity Manual, Ch. 5, § 5.16, http://www.cms.gov/Regulations-and-Guidance/Guidance/Manuals/Downloads/pim83c05.pdf (site visited June 15, 2015). Relevant Wheelchair HCPCS codes are E1161, E1231–E1234, K0005, K0009, K0835–K0843, K0848–K0855 (only if an alternative drive control interface will be provided at the time of initial issue), K0856–K0864, K0868–K0871 (only if an alternative drive control interface will be provided at the time of initial issue), and K0877–K0891. When the base code is eligible, all options and accessories ordered by the physician for the chair are eligible for an ADMC. Check with the DME MAC covering your jurisdiction, *available at* https://www.cms.gov/Medicare/Medicare-Contracting/Medicare-Administrative-Contractors/Downloads/DME-MAC-Jurisdiction-Map-Jan-2016.pdf (site visited June 9, 2016).

[324] 42 U.S.C. § 1395a(b)(1)–(4); 42 C.F.R. §§ 405.400–405.450.

[325] 42 U.S.C. § 1395a(b)(4).

[326] 42 U.S.C. § 1395a(b)(4).

[327] 42 U.S.C. § 1395a(b)(3).

[328] 42 U.S.C. § 1395a(b)(3); 42 C.F.R. § 405.420 (requirements of the opt-out affidavit).

(Medigap) may not provide coverage under these circumstances.[329] In addition, the provision stipulates that a Medicare beneficiary who has entered such a contract is free to use his or her Medicare card with other physicians who have not signed such a contract.[330] The law also provides that such contracts cannot be entered when the beneficiary is facing the need for emergency or urgently needed care.[331]

Contracts must clearly indicate that the beneficiary:[332]

- Agrees not to submit a claim (or request that a physician or practitioner submit a claim) to Medicare for covered services;
- Agrees to be responsible, whether through insurance or otherwise, for payment for services provided and that no reimbursement will be provided from Medicare;
- Acknowledges that no fee schedule or balance billing limits will apply to physician or provider charges;
- Acknowledges that Medigap plans do not, and that other supplemental insurance plans may not, elect to make payments for such services because payment is not made under Medicare; and
- Acknowledges that the Medicare beneficiary has the right to use other physicians who have not entered into such contracts.

[F] Accountable Care Organizations

On November 1, 2011, the final rule establishing a Medicare Shared Savings Program (MSSP) was released.[333] An MSSP promotes accountability for a defined patient population, coordinates items and services under traditional Medicare Parts A and B, and encourages investment in infrastructure and redesigned care processes for high quality and efficient service delivery.[334] Under the MSSP, groups of providers of services and suppliers that meet criteria established by the Secretary may work together to manage and coordinate care for Medicare fee-for-service beneficiaries through an accountable care organization (ACO). An ACO that meets quality performance standards established by the Secretary is eligible to receive payments for shared savings.

---

329 42 U.S.C. § 1395a(b)(2).

330 42 U.S.C. § 1395a(b)(2).

331 42 U.S.C. § 1395a(b)(2); 42 C.F.R. § 405.420(j).

332 42 U.S.C. § 1395a(b)(2)(B); 42 C.F.R. § 405.420.

333 42 Fed. Reg. 67, 802.

334 See ACA § 3022, creating the Medicare Shared Savings Program (MSSP), effective March 23, 2010. Section 3022 amends the Social Security Act to add a new § 1899, 42 U.S.C. 1395jjj. Regulations implementing the accountable care organization (ACO) program can be found at 42 C.F.R. Pt. 425 (Nov. 2, 2011).

The provisions for the MSSP outlined below bring many of the features that are associated with Medicare Advantage (MA) coordinated care plans into the traditional Medicare program. Because the MSSP operates only in the traditional Medicare program, beneficiaries enrolled in an MA plan under Medicare Part C, a competitive medical plan, or in a Program of All-Inclusive Care for the Elderly (PACE) cannot receive services through an ACO under the MSSP.

On June 9, 2015, CMS published in the *Federal Register* a final rule concerning the workings of its ACO program.[335] With the exception of the amendments to Sections 425.312, 425.704, and 425.708, the provisions of the final rule are effective on August 3, 2015. The amendments to Sections 425.312 and 425.708 became effective November 1, 2015. The amendments to Section 425.704 became effective January 1, 2016. The rule concerns the workings of CMS's ACOs, established by Section 3022 of the Affordable Care Act.[336] ACOs, part of the Medicare Shared Savings Program, are part of Medicare's fee-for-service offerings and are designed to improve health care delivery and patient experience and to reduce costs. As discussed below, it is a voluntary program. Applications from ACOs are accepted on an annual basis for contracts of three years' duration.[337]

[1] Eligible Providers and Suppliers

As determined by the Secretary, the following groups of suppliers and providers of services, who have established a mechanism for shared governance, are eligible to participate as ACOs under the program:

- ACO professionals (physicians and other professionals recognized under the Medicare program) in group practice arrangements; networks of individual practices of ACO professionals;
- Partnerships or joint venture arrangements between hospitals and ACO professionals;
- Hospitals employing ACO professionals; and
- Such other groups of suppliers or providers of services as the Secretary determines appropriate.

---

[335] *See* http://www.gpo.gov/fdsys/pkg/FR-2015-06-09/pdf/2015-14005.pdf (site visited June 7, 2016). *See also* 42 C.F.R. Pt. 425.

[336] *See* http://www.cms.gov/Medicare/Medicare-Fee-for-Service-Payment/sharedsavingsprogram/index.html (site visited June 7, 2016).

[337] See CMS' description of the program located at http://cms.gov/Newsroom/MediaReleaseDatabase/Press-releases/2015-Press-releases-items/2015-06-04.html (site visited June 7, 2016).

[2] Ineligible Providers and Suppliers

Under the MSSP, a supplier or provider of services who participates in any of the following is *not* eligible to participate in an ACO:

- A model tested or expanded under the demonstration projects authority of the Secretary that involves shared savings under this title;
- Any other program or demonstration project that involves such shared savings; and
- The independence at home medical practice pilot program.

[3] Accountable Care Organization Contractual Requirements

An ACO must: be willing to become accountable for the quality, cost, and overall care of the Medicare fee-for-service beneficiaries assigned to it; enter into an agreement with the Secretary to participate in the program for not less than a three-year period (the agreement period); have a formal legal structure that would allow the organization to receive and distribute payments for shared savings to participating suppliers and providers of services; include primary care ACO professionals that are sufficient for the number of Medicare fee-for-service beneficiaries assigned to the ACO (at a minimum, the ACO shall have at least 5,000 beneficiaries assigned to it); provide the Secretary with information regarding professionals participating in the ACO as the Secretary determines necessary to support the assignment of Medicare fee-for-service beneficiaries to an ACO, the implementation of quality and other reporting requirements, and the determination of payments for shared savings; have in place a leadership and management structure that includes clinical and administrative systems; have a defined process to promote evidence-based medicine and patient engagement, report on quality and cost measures, and coordinate care, such as through the use of telehealth, remote patient monitoring, and other such enabling technologies; and demonstrate to the Secretary that it meets patient-centeredness criteria specified by the Secretary, such as the use of patient and caregiver assessments or the use of individualized care plans.[338]

[4] Quality Measures Reporting

The Secretary is to determine appropriate measures to assess the quality of care furnished by the ACO, including such measures as clinical processes and outcomes; patient and (where practicable) caregiver experiences; and utilization,

[338] *See also* http://oig.hhs.gov/compliance/accountable-care-organizations/index.asp (site visited June 14, 2016).

such as rates of hospital admissions for conditions for which good outpatient care could potentially prevent the need for hospitalization, or for which early intervention could prevent complications or more severe disease ("ambulatory care sensitive conditions"). The Secretary may, as she determines appropriate, incorporate reporting requirements and incentive payments related to the physician quality reporting initiative, including electronic prescribing, electronic health records, and other similar initiatives, and may use alternative criteria that would otherwise apply under for determining whether to make such payments. Incentive payments shall not be taken into consideration when calculating payments otherwise made under the ACO provision.[339]

[5] Assignment of Traditional Medicare Beneficiaries to Accountable Care Organizations

The Secretary shall determine an appropriate method to assign traditional Medicare beneficiaries to an ACO, based on their utilization of primary care services provided by an ACO professional. Under the program, payments shall continue to be made to suppliers and providers of services participating in an ACO in the same manner as they would otherwise be made except that a participating ACO is eligible to receive payment for shared savings if the ACO meets quality performance standards established by the Secretary and meets the contracting requirements above.[340]

[6] Savings Requirement and Benchmark

An ACO shall be eligible to receive payment for shared savings only if the estimated average per capita Medicare expenditures for traditional Medicare beneficiaries for Part A and Part B services under the ACO (adjusted for beneficiary characteristics), is below the applicable benchmark by at least the percentage specified by the Secretary for a given year.[341] The Secretary shall determine the appropriate percentage to account for normal variation in expenditures, based on the number of Medicare fee-for-service beneficiaries assigned to an ACO. The Secretary will estimate a benchmark for each agreement period for each ACO. The benchmark will be based on the most recent data available for three years of

[339] *See also* https://www.cms.gov/Medicare/Quality-Initiatives-Patient-Assessment-Instruments/QualityMeasures/index.html (site visited June 14, 2016).

[340] For a review of ongoing developments with respect to ACOs, see Medicare.gov, "Accountable Care Organizations (ACOs), *available at* http://www.medicare.gov/manage-your-health/coordinating-your-care/accountable-care-organizations.html (site visited June 7, 2016).

[341] *See* Center for Medicare Advocacy, "Accountable Care Organizations Should Increase Coordinated Care in Traditional Medicare," *available at* http://www.medicareadvocacy.org/accountable-care-organizations-should-increase-care-coordination-in-traditional-medicare/ (site visited June 7, 2016).

per-beneficiary expenditures for Medicare Parts A and B services for fee-for-service beneficiaries assigned to the ACO. The benchmark will be adjusted for beneficiary characteristics and other factors the Secretary determines appropriate and will be updated by the projected absolute amount of growth in national per capita expenditures for Medicare Parts A and B services under the original fee-for-service program, as estimated by the Secretary. The benchmark will be reset at the start of each agreement period.[342]

[7] Payments for Shared Savings

The Secretary will establish limits on the total amount of shared savings that may be paid to an ACO. If the Secretary determines that an ACO has taken steps to avoid more costly patients to reduce the likelihood of increasing expenses to the ACO, the Secretary may impose an appropriate sanction on the ACO, including termination from the program. Payment of shared savings to ACOs, based on meeting quality performance measures established by the Secretary, will be a percentage (as determined by the Secretary) of the difference between the estimated average per capita Medicare expenditures in a year (adjusted for beneficiary characteristics) under the ACO and the benchmark established for the ACO. The remainder of the difference will be retained by the MSSP.[343]

[8] Termination, Administration, and Waiver Authority

The Secretary may terminate an agreement with an ACO if it does not meet the Secretary's quality performance standards. Rules concerning the coordination of federal information policy and security (printing and documents) will not apply to the ACO program. In addition, the Secretary may waive civil money penalties requirements for false claims and the criminal penalties for fraud under the Medicare program as necessary to carry out the MSSP.[344]

[9] Limitations on Review

There will be no administrative or judicial review of the specific criteria for establishing an ACO; the assessment of the quality of care furnished by an ACO and the establishment of performance standards; the assignment of Medicare fee-for-service beneficiaries to an ACO; the determination of whether an ACO is

[342] *See also* https://www.cms.gov/Medicare/Medicare-Fee-for-Service-Payment/sharedsavingsprogram/Downloads/MSSP-QM-Benchmarks.pdf (site visited June 14, 2014).

[343] *See also* https://www.cms.gov/Medicare/Medicare-Fee-for-Service-Payment/sharedsavingsprogram/index.html (site visited June 14, 2014).

[344] *See also* http://www.medicareadvocacy.org/old-site/InfoByTopic/QualityOfCare/10_07.01.ACOs.htm (site visited June 14, 2016).

eligible for shared savings and the amount of such shared savings, including the determination of the estimated average per capita Medicare expenditures under the ACO for Medicare fee-for-service beneficiaries and the average benchmark for the ACO; the percent of shared savings specified by the Secretary and any limit on the total amount of shared savings established by the Secretary; and the termination of an ACO.

§ 6.05 FILING MEDICARE PART B CLAIMS

Claims for Part B services, including physician services and other services reimbursable on a charge basis or fee schedule basis, must be filed no later than the end of the calendar year following the year in which the services were furnished. The time limit on filing claims for services is the period ending one calendar year after the date of the service (the Secretary may create exceptions).[345]

For services furnished on or after September 1, 1990, physicians and suppliers are required to complete and submit both assigned and non-assigned Part B claims for their Medicare patients within 12 months of the date of the services received.[346] Physicians and suppliers who submit claims beyond this time period will have their claims reduced by 10 percent of the amount that would otherwise be paid; physicians who submit non-assigned claims late are subject to monetary penalties.[347]

With respect to the submission of claims, a claim is any writing submitted by or on behalf of the claimant, indicating a request or claim for payment from Medicare in connection with the receipt of medical services. No particular claim form is required, although a variety of Medicare billing forms are prepared and recognized by CMS. Claims should identify the beneficiary and the services received, although the identification of services does not have to be complete. Claims are considered filed when mailed or delivered to CMS or any contractor (entity under contract with CMS to administer Part A and Part B claims).[348]

---

[345] 42 C.F.R. § 424.44(1); MCP Manual, Ch. 1, § 70. ACA § 6404(a)(2)(A) (Part B) (in the case of services furnished before January 1, 2010, a bill or request for payment under § 1814(a)(1) (conditions and limitations for payment for services), § 1842(b)(3)(B) (provisions related to the administration of Part B), or § 1835(a) (procedures for the payment of claims for providers of services) shall be filed not later than December 31, 2010). *See* ACA § 6404(b)(2). For a list of exceptions, see 42 C.F.R. § 424.44(2).

[346] 42 U.S.C. § 1395w-4(g)(4). *See* https://www.gpo.gov/fdsys/pkg/USCODE-2011-title42/html/USCODE-2011-title42-chap7-subchapXVIII.htm (site visited Aug. 10, 2016). MCP Manual, Ch. 1, §§ 70 *et seq.* Claims submitted for Part B services received from a non-participating hospital or for services received out of the United States must be submitted in accordance with the rules described above. *See* 42 C.F.R. §§ 424.100 *et seq. See* MCP Manual, Ch. 1, § 10.2.1. *See also* 42 U.S.C. § 1395u(b)(6) (who can receive payment).

[347] 42 U.S.C. § 1395w-4(g)(4)(B).

[348] MCP Manual, Ch. 1, § 70.7.1.

Contractor jurisdiction for the submission and processing of claims is generally the geographic area in which the physician's or supplier's office is located. If the physician or supplier maintains offices in more than one contractor service area, each office is serviced for that area. If the physician does not maintain an office but uses his or her home address, that address determines the contractor jurisdiction. If the office where the service is rendered is in another contractor's jurisdiction, the claim must be transferred to that contractor.[349]

§ 6.06 INFORMATION ABOUT COVERAGE

[A] Annual Notice to Beneficiaries

The BBA '97 required the Secretary to provide Medicare beneficiaries with an Annual Notice to Beneficiaries, instructing beneficiaries to check carefully their explanations of benefits or itemized statements for accuracy, along with a toll-free telephone number for reporting errors and questionable charges, including fraud and abuse reporting.[350] The annual notice to beneficiaries also must tell them that they have a right to request of their physician, provider, supplier, or other entity providing services, an itemized statement of Medicare-covered items and services provided.

The requested itemization is to be provided no later than 30 days from the date of the request.[351] Failure to provide the requested itemization can result in civil money penalties of $100 for each such failure.[352] The beneficiary has 90 days from the date of receipt of the itemization to submit a written request to the Secretary for review of the itemization.[353]

[B] Medicare Summary Notices[354]

Generally, official notice from Medicare must be obtained before a beneficiary has a right to file an appeal. The Medicare Summary Notice (MSN) constitutes the "initial determination" or written notice that briefly explains what Medicare will pay on a claim. The MSN is prepared by the Medicare contractor that reviews the claim. Many claims are denied in whole or in part on the MSN

---

[349] MCP Manual, Ch. 1, § 10.1.1

[350] 42 U.S.C. § 1395b-2. The annual notice requirement became effective on the date of the enactment of BBA '97, Aug. 5, 1997.

[351] 42 U.S.C. § 1395b-7(2)(A).

[352] 42 U.S.C. § 1395b-7(2)(B). The effective date of the itemization requirement was January 1999.

[353] 42 U.S.C. § 1395b-7(3).

[354] *See* MCP Manual, Ch. 21. *See also* HHS, Office of Medicare Hearings and Appeals (OMHA), "Understanding the Appeals Process," *available at* http://www.hhs.gov/omha/process/index.html (site visited June 7. 2016).

due to insufficient information and mistakes. Determinations finding that the medical service was not medically necessary and is, therefore, not covered under Medicare should be closely examined. Errors are often made. If the claimant does not think Medicare is allowing a sufficient reimbursement amount, the claimant should also question the MSN.[355]

It is important to note that for most Part B claims, the first notice beneficiaries should receive informing them that care will not be covered by Medicare is from the health care provider. Before they can charge a beneficiary, providers who participate in the Medicare program must first issue a written notice to the patient informing him or her that Medicare coverage will not be available. Providers have a financial incentive to issue denial notices because they may have to absorb the cost of the care they provide if they erroneously inform the beneficiary that the care will be covered but not if they erroneously deny coverage.

Notices from providers, however, do not form the basis for an appeal. The beneficiary must obtain a formal Medicare coverage determination or "initial determination" from the appropriate Medicare contractor.[356]

§ 6.07 APPEALS

[A] Appeals Arising Under Parts A and B of Medicare

Rules regarding Medicare appeals are codified at Subpart G of Part 405.[357] For Part B claims, the rules were phased in over the course of 2005 and fully in place by January 1, 2006. The rules establish a combined Part A and Part B appeals process.[358] CMS's regulations, referred to above, implement the changes

---

[355] For a discussion of CMS's updates to its MSN, see Center for Medicare Advocacy, "New Medicare Summary Notice, *available at* http://www.medicareadvocacy.org/new-medicare-summary-notice/ (site visited June 7, 2016). Note that CMS has reduced the frequency of Medicare Summary Notice (MSN) deliveries. They are sent quarterly when beneficiaries are not due a payment from Medicare. *See* Transmittal 1347, September 28, 2007 (implementation date, Oct. 29, 2007), Change Request Number 5722, *available at* http://www.cms.hhs.gov/transmittals/downloads/R1347CP.pdf (site visited June 7, 2016). Beneficiaries may receive bills from providers that need to be paid before they have received an MSN. Under this circumstance, the beneficiary will not be able to verify in advance of payment whether the amount billed agrees with CMS's calculation, thus possibly increasing the number of disputes about payments. This has proved problematic, and there is an effort to return to a monthly MSN. *See* the redesigned MSN, along with the previous version, at http://www.cms.gov/apps/files/msn_changes.pdf (site visited June 7, 2016), including downloadable files at http://www.cms.gov/Medicare/Medicare-General-Information/MSN/index.html (site visited June 7, 2016).

[356] *See* http://www.cms.gov/Medicare/Appeals-and-Grievances/OrgMedFFSAppeals/RedeterminationbyaMedicareContractor.html (site visited June 7, 2016).

[357] *See* 42 C.F.R. §§ 405.900 *et seq.*

[358] The chart in **Appendix 6-9** outlines the basic structure of the Parts A & B appeals process. *See also* https://www.cms.gov/MLNProducts/downloads/MedicareAppealsprocess.pdf (site visited June 7, 2016).

to the appeals process for Medicare Part A and Part B claims and implement changes to the ALJ hearing process for all Medicare claims, including managed care claims and prescription drug claims.[359] For Part B claims that are currently decided by a Medicare carrier (or contractor), these appeal procedures are effective for redeterminations issued on or after January 1, 2006.[360]

CMS issued final regulations for the Medicare Claims Appeals Process (Parts A & B combined). The rules were effective as of January 8, 2010. Regulations governing the combined appeals process for Medicare Parts A and B, authorized by 42 U.S.C. § 1395ff, are codified at 42 C.F.R. § 405.900 et seq. (Subpart I—Determinations, Redeterminations, Reconsiderations, and Appeals under Original Medicare process).[361]

Highlights of the changes and clarifications for Parts A and B appeals are as follows:

- *Definition of a Contractor.* CMS has clarified the term contractor for purposes of Subpart I as an entity that has a contract with the federal government to review and/or adjudicate claims, determinations and/or decisions. This includes, but is not limited to, Medicare Administrative Contractors (MACs), Qualified Independent Contractors (QICs), and Quality Improvement Organizations (QIOs).
- *State Medicaid Agency as Party.* A Medicaid state agency cannot be a party to an initial determination. Rather, it can only be a party to a redetermination, reconsideration, hearing, or Medicare Appeals Council (MAC) review. Only after Medicare has issued its initial determination on a claim for items or services provided to a dually eligible beneficiary can a determination be made about a state agency's potential liability for all or part of the associated charges.
- *Appointment of Representative.* If an appeal request is filed by an individual attempting to represent a party, but the submission contains a defective Appointment of Representative (AOR) form, the adjudicator will give the party notice of the defect and time to correct it. A representative must submit, with each appeal request, a copy of the valid, effective AOR or other conforming written instrument in order to request a redetermination or other appeal on behalf of the party. A valid, executed

[359] *See* 42 C.F.R. §§ 405.900 *et seq.* (Subpart I—Determinations, Redeterminations, Reconsiderations, and Appeals under Original Medicare (Part A and Part B)), *available at* http://www.ecfr.gov/cgi-bin/text-idx?rgn=div6&node=42:2.0.1.2.5.8 (site visited June 7, 2016).

[360] *See* 42 C.F.R. §§ 405.900 *et seq.*

[361] Final regulations are at 74 Fed. Reg. 65,296 *et seq.* (Dec. 9, 2009). *See* http://edocket.access.gpo.gov/2009/pdf/E9-28707.pdf (site visited June 7, 2016). *See also* CMS, *Medicare Parts A and B Appeals Process* (Feb. 2015), *available at* https://www.cms.gov/Outreach-and-Education/Medicare-Learning-Network-MLN/MLNProducts/downloads/MedicareAppealsProcess.pdf (site visited June 7, 2016).

AOR will be honored for the duration of the initial appeal request for which it is filed, and for any subsequent appeal requests with which it is submitted, provided the initial appeal request is filed within one year of the effective date of the AOR. With respect to Medicare Secondary Payer recovery claims, the AOR is deemed valid for longer than one year because liability, no-fault, and worker's compensation claims often take more than one year to resolve.

- *Proof of Authority to Represent Where Beneficiary Has Died.* In order to prevent unauthorized disclosures, CMS contractors must obtain documentation of the status of any person attempting to appeal on behalf of a deceased beneficiary, that is, authority to administer the estate by probate or intestate provisions of the relevant state probate law.
- *Approval of Fees before Charging Beneficiary.* In these final regulations, CMS reiterates its position, as in Social Security cases, that persons, including attorneys, wishing to charge a fee for representation services before the Secretary, must obtain approval of fees before charging a beneficiary. The requirement applies to proceedings at the Administrative Law Judge (ALJ) level and beyond. CMS also clarifies that the requirement does not apply to non-beneficiary appellants.
- *Medicare Summary Notice (MSN).* This notice, and a remittance advice (RA), are only sent to parties of an initial determination. They are not sent to appointed representatives. The MSN covers the entire range of health care services and items billed to Medicare within a 90 calendar day period. An RA contains comprehensive claims information for all claims processed for a provider or supplier during a specific period.
- *Assignment of Appeal Rights.* CMS has clarified that appointing a representative and assigning appeal rights are two different and unrelated actions. Beneficiaries have the option of either (1) assigning (transferring), by a signed agreement, their appeal rights to the provider or supplier that provided the item or service at issue, if such person or entity is not a party to the initial determination, or (2) appointing a representative (by a signed writing) to act on their behalf during the appeal.
- *Clean Claims.* Claims for services that cannot be timely adjudicated at the initial determination level because they lack sufficient documentation and/or require special handling do not come within the definition of clean claims.
- *Notice of Non-coverage.* A provider's notice of non-coverage does not constitute an initial determination because it is not a determination made by the Medicare program.
- *Effect of Claim Suspended for Medical Review by Contractor Staff.* A claim suspended for medical staff review is not considered a claim that

is invalid or incomplete and would not preclude review. Rather, a claim that is suspended for development is one that appears technically sufficient on its face, but requires additional information in order to make a coverage and payment decision.

- *Calendar Days*. Throughout Subpart I, unless otherwise specified, CMS is now using the term "calendar day" to define what it means when it uses the word "day."
- *Final or Binding Decisions*. CMS is reserving the term "final" decision of the Secretary to describe those actions or decisions for which judicial review may be immediately sought. The term "binding" describes situations in which the parties are obligated to abide by the adjudicator's action or decision, unless further recourse to challenge the action or decision is available and a party exercises that right. In its comments, CMS notes that a binding decision is not a final decision of the Secretary for the purposes of exhausting administrative remedies prior to judicial review.
- *ALJ Subpoena Power*. An ALJ may not issue a subpoena to CMS or its contractors, on his or her own initiative or at the request of a party, to compel an appearance, testimony, or the production of evidence. Parties to an ALJ hearing who wish to subpoena documents or witnesses must file a written request for the issuance of a subpoena within the time period required (within ten calendar days of the receipt of the notice of the hearing).
- *Limits of ALJ and Medicare Administrative Contractors*. All laws and regulations pertaining to the Medicare and Medicaid programs, including but not limited to Titles XI, XVIII, and XIX of the Social Security Act and applicable implementing regulations, are binding on ALJs and MACs.
- *Escalation to MAC from the ALJ*. With respect to escalation, language says "if the ALJ does not issue a decision, dismissal order, or remand order within the later of 5 calendar days of receiving the request for escalation or 5 calendar days from the end of the applicable adjudication period as prescribed in the regulations at 42 C.F.R. § 405.1016,"[362] the appellant may request MAC review. In addition, the appellant must send a copy of the request for review to the other parties to the ALJ decision or dismissal who received a copy of the hearing decision or a copy of the notice of dismissal.

---

[362] 42 C.F.R. § 405.1104(b).

With respect to QIO review, the Medicare agency has now separated out the review entities that will respond to beneficiary complaints from those that are to handle quality improvement matters for providers. On May 9, 2014, CMS announced the first phase of its restructuring of the QIO functions. In the first phase, CMS has contracted with Livanta LLC (for geographic areas 1 and 5), located in Annapolis Junction, Maryland, and KePRO (for geographic areas 2, 3, and 4), located in Seven Hills, Ohio. These contractors will be responsible for ensuring consistency in the review process with respect to beneficiary complaints. CMS describes these two contractors as its Beneficiary and Family-Centered Care (BFCC) QIO contractors.[363]

The states in the designated geographic areas are Area 1: Connecticut, Maine, Massachusetts, New Hampshire, New Jersey, New York, Pennsylvania, Puerto Rico, Rhode Island, Vermont, and Virgin Islands; Area 2: District of Columbia, Delaware, Florida, Georgia, Maryland, North Carolina, South Carolina, Virginia, and West Virginia; Area 3: Alabama, Arkansas, Colorado, Kentucky, Louisiana, Mississippi, Montana, North Dakota, New Mexico, Oklahoma, South Dakota, Tennessee, Texas, Utah, and Wyoming; Area 4: Iowa, Illinois, Indiana, Kansas, Michigan, Minnesota, Missouri, Nebraska, Ohio, Wisconsin; and Area 5: Alaska, Arizona, California, Hawaii, Idaho, Nevada, Oregon, and Washington.[364]

On July 18, 2014, as part of the restructuring of the QIO program—separating the beneficiary quality of care complaint review process from provider quality improvement functions—CMS awarded additional contracts to assist providers with quality improvement matters. The new contracts represent the second phase of QIO restructuring. These QIOs are known as the Quality Innovation Network (QIN)-QIOs.[365]

[B] Initial Determinations, Redeterminations, and Appeals

The claims process begins when the Medicare contractor issues an initial determination of a claim submitted by a provider.[366] The notice of the initial

[363] *See* CMS, Press Release, "CMS Launches Improved Quality Improvement Program" (July 18, 2014), *available at* https://www.cms.gov/Newsroom/MediaReleaseDatabase/Press-releases/2014-Press-releases-items/2014-07-18.html (site visited June 9, 2016).

[364] *See* CMS, Press Release, "CMS Launches Improved Quality Improvement Program" (May 9, 2014), *available at* https://www.cms.gov/Newsroom/MediaReleaseDatabase/Press-releases/2014-Press-releases-items/2014-07-18.html (site visited June 9, 2016). *See also* http://qioprogram.org/sites/default/files/BFCC-QIO%20Provider%20and%20Practitioner%20FAQs%2011.17.15_508.pdf (site visited July 25, 2016).

[365] *See* CMS, Press Release, "CMS Launches Next Phase of New Quality Improvement Program" (July 18, 2014), *available at* http://cms.gov/Newsroom/MediaReleaseDatabase/Press-releases/2014-Press-releases-items/2014-07-18.html?DLPage=1&DLSort=0&DLSortDir=descending (site visited June 8, 2016). Each QIN-QIO will work on strategic quality improvement initiatives.

[366] 42 C.F.R. § 405.904.

determination is sent to the beneficiary.[367] This happens even when the contractor is aware that the beneficiary has an appointed representative. An initial determination is made by the appropriate contractor with respect to coverage or reimbursement under the Medicare Act, including any amounts payable.[368] An initial determination is binding unless it is revised or reconsidered or revised as a result of a reopening.[369] The contractor must make an initial decision on clean claims (generally electronically submitted and about which there are no obvious computer/clerical errors) within 30 days of receipt; otherwise, interest must be paid as specified in the regulation.[370]

Notice of the initial determination must contain the reasons for the determination, including whether a local medical review policy, a local coverage determination, or a national coverage determination was applied.[371] The notice should also contain additional information about the determination, such as specific policies, manuals, laws, or regulations used in making the determination.[372] In addition, the notice should provide information about the right to a redetermination if the beneficiary is dissatisfied with the outcome of the initial determination[373] and instructions on how to request a redetermination.

Parties to the initial determination include the beneficiary, supplier, and provider.[374] Parties to the redetermination, reconsideration, hearing, and Medicare Appeals Council (MAC) are the parties to the initial determination as provided in Section 409.906(a), except where the beneficiary has assigned his or her appeal rights to a provider or supplier under Section 409.912.[375] Parties to the redetermination, reconsideration, hearing, and MAC also can include a state agency; a provider or supplier that has accepted an assignment of appeal rights; or a nonparticipating physician or supplier not billing on an assignment basis who may be liable to refund monies collected for services furnished to the beneficiary that were deemed not reasonable and necessary.[376]

Someone who wants to appeal from the initial determination must submit a written, signed request for a redetermination within 120 days of the initial determination; the regulations assume the notice is received five days after the date of the notice. Requests for redeterminations must be filed with the contractor.[377] A request is considered as filed on the date it is received by the contractor.[378]

---

[367] 42 C.F.R. § 405.921(a)(2)(i).

[368] 42 C.F.R. § 405.920.

[369] 42 C.F.R. § 405.928. *See also* 20 C.F.R. §§ 404.907 and 404.988.

[370] 42 C.F.R. § 405.922.

[371] 42 C.F.R. § 405.921(a)(2)(ii).

[372] 42 C.F.R. § 405.921(b).

[373] 42 C.F.R. § 405.921(a)(2)(iii).

[374] 42 C.F.R. § 405.906(a).

[375] 42 C.F.R. § 409.906(b)(1).

[376] 42 C.F.R. § 409.906(b)(2).

[377] 42 C.F.R. § 405.942.

[378] 42 C.F.R. § 405.942(a)(2).

The regulations allow providers and suppliers to request appeal of a denial of an initial determination,[379] raising the possibility that both the beneficiary and the provider or supplier will initiate the appeals process. In such a case the Medicare contractor must consolidate the appeals. The contractor has 60 days from receipt of the redetermination request to issue a decision.[380] If more than one party files a request, the time period runs from the date the last request is received.[381] For example, if a beneficiary files a redetermination request on day 1, but the provider files on day 50, the 60 calendar day time period for the contractor to act starts on day 50.

The regulations create a new reopening process to be used instead of the redetermination process to correct minor errors or omissions in initial determinations, including at subsequent levels of review.[382]

It has been the experience of the Center for Medicare Advocacy (the Center) that virtually all appeals are denied at the first two levels of the administrative review process, with Medicare contractors performing only cursory reviews of the medical record and low-quality analysis. Consequently, the Center filed litigation[383] to address the problem. A critical issue is whether the Secretary of HHS's denial rate of about 98 percent at the lowest two levels of appeal in Medicare's system of administrative review (redetermination and reconsideration) violates the Medicare statute and the Due Process Clause. The plaintiff seeks declaratory and injunctive relief for a nationwide class of Medicare beneficiaries who have received or will receive adverse redetermination and reconsideration decisions on their claims for coverage of home health care services. The court denied the government's motion to dismiss the due process claim, granted the motion to dismiss the statutory claim, and certified a nationwide class action on August 8, 2016.[384]

[C] The Qualified Independent Contractors—Reconsideration Determinations

The 2000 law created a third level of review, the reconsideration. Reconsiderations are conducted by a group of Medicare contractors called Qualified Independent Contractors (QICs).[385] The use of the QICs became effective for Part B

[379] *See* 42 C.F.R. § 405.906(c).

[380] 42 C.F.R. § 405.950.

[381] 42 C.F.R. § 405.950(b)(2).

[382] 42 C.F.R. § 405.980(a)(3). *See also* 42 C.F.R. § 405.980(a)(l)(i)-(iv).

[383] Sherman v. Burwell, No. 3:15-CV-01468 (D. Conn., Complaint filed Oct. 9, 2015).

[384] *Sherman*, No. 3:15-CV-01468 (ruling denying motion to dismiss and granting motion for class certification issued Aug. 8, 2016).

[385] 42 C.F.R. § 405.960. The QIC's jurisdiction over reconsideration determinations commenced on May 1, 2005, for all Part A determinations and those Part B determinations made by a QIO or fiscal intermediary (or contractor). The QIC's jurisdiction over Part B reconsideration

claims currently handled by Medicare contractors with respect to redeterminations issued on or after January 1, 2006. Beneficiaries and other parties to the redetermination have 180 days to request reconsideration by filing a request at the location indicated on the redetermination notice.[386] Reconsiderations filed by both a beneficiary and a provider or supplier will be consolidated, and the time for the QIC to issue a decision runs from receipt of the last-filed appeal.[387]

The reconsideration level of review is a paper review; CMS states clearly in the preamble to the final regulations that QICs will not be conducting hearings. However, the QIC may solicit the view of the beneficiary.[388] As noted above, if providers or suppliers appeal from the QIO to the QIC, they are required to submit all of the evidence they want considered in the claim to the QIC. Evidence not submitted by providers or suppliers to the QIC may be excluded at subsequent levels of review.[389] However, beneficiaries who appeal (except those who are represented by a provider) may present evidence at further levels of appeal.[390]

The QIC must complete its reconsideration within 60 days of the reconsideration request.[391] Again, the time frame runs from the last request filed if more than one party seeks reconsideration; the QIC must so notify a party who filed an earlier request.[392] Although the statute allows a party to the reconsideration to ask for an extension of not more than 14 days for the QIC to conclude the reconsideration, the regulations add 14 days to the reconsideration time frame each time that additional evidence is submitted.[393]

In making its reconsideration determination, the QIC is bound by the NCDs promulgated by Medicare and CMS Rulings, as well as statute and regulations.[394] It is not bound by LCDs made by Medicare contractors nor by Medicare policy issued by CMS itself; however, the QIC must give "substantial deference" to these determinations and policy in making its decision.[395] If the QIC declines to apply them, the QIC's decision must state the reason why they were not followed.[396]

---

determinations for all determination currently made by a Medicare Part B carrier (or contractor) commenced January 1, 2006. *See* 70 Fed. Reg. 11,424–26 (Mar. 8, 2005).

[386] 42 C.F.R. § 405.962.

[387] 42 C.F.R. § 405.964(c).

[388] 70 Fed. Reg. 11,447–78 (Mar. 8, 2005).

[389] 42 C.F.R. § 405.966(a).

[390] 42 C.F.R. § 405.966(c).

[391] 42 C.F.R. § 405.970(a).

[392] 42 C.F.R. § 405.970(b)(2).

[393] 42 C.F.R. § 405.970(b)(3).

[394] 42 C.F.R. § 405.968(b).

[395] 42 C.F.R. § 405.968(b)(1), (2).

[396] 42 C.F.R. § 405.968(b)(3).

[D] Escalation

The MMA introduced the concept of "escalation" into the Medicare appeals process. Commencing at the reconsideration level of appeal, if a decision is not rendered within a set time frame,[397] a party to the appeal may "escalate" the appeal to the next level. For Part B claims currently processed by a Medicare contractor, the escalation process will not be in effect with respect to reconsiderations after January 1, 2006. If a QIC does not issue a timely reconsideration decision (60 days from the date of its receipt of the request for reconsideration), the statute and regulations allow a party to request that the appeal be escalated to the next level of review, the ALJ level. The regulations give the QIC five days to either issue a decision or acknowledge the escalation request and send it to the ALJ level of review. The regulations indicate that an appeal escalated to the ALJ level must be completed within 180 days of receipt, rather than the statutorily mandated 90 days for ALJ decisions. Even at the ALJ level, however, additional extensions of the time frame for issuing a decision can occur.[398]

[E] Administrative Law Judge Hearings

Beneficiaries and other parties have 60 days from receipt of the reconsideration determination to file a request for an ALJ hearing and if the amount in controversy is $160 or more in 2017.[399] The request for hearing must be filed at the address indicated on the reconsideration determination.[400] In addition, a party may escalate to the ALJ hearing from the QIC, when the QIC fails to issue a timely decision.[401] However, if an appeal is escalated to the ALJ, the 90 calendar day time frame for deciding an ALJ appeal is automatically extended to 180 days, with the possibility for additional extensions beyond the 180 days.[402]

---

[397] The time frames are 60 days for the QIC to render a reconsideration determination (42 C.F.R. § 405.970); 90 days for an ALJ to issue a hearing decision (42 C.F.R. § 405.1016); 180 days for the Medicare Appeals Council (MAC) to issue its decision (42 C.F.R. § 405.1100). *See* http://www.hhs.gov/dab/index.html (site visited July 8, 2016); Medicare Operations Division, *see* http://www.hhs.gov/dab/divisions/medicareoperations/index.html (site visited July 8, 2016); search MAC decisions, *available at* http://www.hhs.gov/dab/divisions/medicareoperations/macdecisions/mac_decisions.html (site visited July 8, 2016).

[398] 42 C.F.R. §§ 405.970(b) and 405.1002(a) (reconsideration level); 42 C.F.R. §§ 405.1016(a)–(d) and 405.1104 (ALJ level); 42 C.F.R. §§ 405.1106(b) and 405.1132 (MAC level).

[399] Extension of this 60-day time frame may be granted upon a showing of good cause. 42 C.F.R. § 405.1014(c). *See also* 42 C.F.R. § 405.1108(a), (d)(3) and 80 Fed. Reg. 57,827–828 (Sept. 25, 2015).

[400] 42 C.F.R. § 405.1014(b)(2).

[401] 42 C.F.R. § 405.1002.

[402] 42 C.F.R. § 405.1016(c). Among the bases for an extension are if CMS is a party and a party requests discovery against another party (42 C.F.R. § 405.1016(d)); submission of additional

The ALJ appeal level (transferred from the SSA) is under the administration of the HHS, a change which was mandated by the MMA.[403] ALJs operate out of four locations: Miami, Florida; Cleveland, Ohio; Irvine, California; and Falls Church, Virginia. These are the only hearing offices in which Medicare ALJs are housed, effective on or after July 1, 2005.[404]

In-person hearings are all but a thing of the past, except in "special or extraordinary circumstances."[405] Instead, beneficiaries are offered a video teleconference (VTC) hearing or, if no VTC technology exists in a location near the beneficiary, a telephone hearing.[406]

What constitutes a "special circumstance" that would justify an in-person hearing is illusive.[407] Even if such special circumstances are established, the in-person hearing will be for the requestor's own testimony, but not to the entire hearing.[408] In addition, when an in-person hearing is requested and granted, the limited time frame for an ALJ to render his or her decision may be waived by the party requesting the hearing.[409]

CMS or its contractors may participate in or be made a party to the ALJ hearings, with rights to submit "position papers" and present witnesses (if they are "participants") and the right to cross-examine the other party's witnesses (if they are "parties").[410] An ALJ may seek to have CMS or its contractors participate or joined as parties, and CMS itself can request that it be a participant or party.[411] Under the regulations, an ALJ must permit CMS or its contractors to participate or be joined as parties, if they so request.

A notice of the hearing must be given to all parties, the Medicare contractor, and the QIC, advising them of the time and date for the hearing at least 20 days prior to the date of its scheduled date.[412] All of those receiving a notice of hearing are required to acknowledge whether they plan to attend the hearing or object to

---

evidence by a party later than 10 days after receiving a notice of hearing (42 C.F.R. § 405.1018(b)); a party's request for a copy of all or part of the administrative record [42 C.F.R. § 405.1042(b)(2)]; and a granted request for postponement of the hearing (42 C.F.R. § 405.1020(h)).

[403] 42 C.F.R. §§ 405.1004 *et seq.*

[404] *See* 70 Fed. Reg. 11,425 (Mar. 8, 2005).

[405] 42 C.F.R. § 405.1020(b)(2).

[406] 42 C.F.R. § 405.1020(b).

[407] The preamble to the interim final regulations discusses some circumstances which might warrant an in-person hearing. Among these is when the case "presents complex challenging or novel presentation issues" or based upon "the appellant's proximity to and ability to go to the local hearing office." 70 Fed. Reg. 11,457 (Mar. 8, 2005).

[408] The provisions in 42 C.F.R. § 405.1020 apply to Part B hearings requested on or after July 1, 2005 and can be found at http://www.ecfr.gov/cgi-bin/text-idx?SID=7e296b47069a0a5b6333bf5527c3c6d7&mc=true&node=se42.2.405_11020&rgn=div8 (site visited June 8, 2016).

[409] 42 C.F.R. § 405.1020(i)(4).

[410] 42 C.F.R. §§ 405.1010 (participants) and 405.1012 (parties).

[411] 42 C.F.R. §§ 405.1010 (participants), 405.1010(a), and 405.1012 (parties).

[412] 42 C.F.R. §§ 405.1020(c) and 405.1022(a).

the proposed time and/or place of the hearing.[413] An objection to the time and/or place must be in writing and state the reasons for the objection.[414] If a party objects to the issues as stated in the notice of hearing, that party must notify the ALJ in writing no later than five days prior to the hearing of the objections, and send a copy of the objections to all other parties to the appeal.[415] The ALJ will make a decision with respect to the objections either in writing or at the hearing.[416]

Any new written evidence which a beneficiary wishes to submit must be submitted with the request for hearing or within ten days prior to the scheduled date of the hearing.[417] Evidence may be submitted later than ten days prior to the hearing, but the time frame for the ALJ's issuance of his or her decision is tolled for the period between when the evidence was required to be submitted and when it was actually received.[418] Although providers are generally required to submit all relevant evidence at the QIC level of appeal, they may submit additional evidence if they establish "good cause" for failing to do so earlier.[419] The ALJ must review the new evidence submitted by the provider and notify all parties whether it is excluded.[420]

Generally, the issues at an ALJ hearing include all issues brought out at any prior level of appeal and not decided in a party's favor; even so, the ALJ may also include as an issue any portion of any prior determination that was decided favorably.[421] The parties must be notified of all issues before the hearing.[422] New issues may be raised at any time prior to the start of the hearing, if those new issues could have a material impact on the claims that are the subject of the request for hearing.[423]

Discovery at the ALJ level of appeal is permissible only when CMS elects to be made a party to the hearing.[424] Discovery is permissible with respect to any matter that is relevant to the subject matter of the hearing, although the party from whom discovery is sought may raise objections based on the assertion that the material sought is privileged or otherwise protected.[425] Additionally, an ALJ may deny a request for discovery if he or she concludes that the discovery

[413] 42 C.F.R. § 405.1020(c)(2).
[414] 42 C.F.R. § 405.1020(e).
[415] 42 C.F.R. § 405.1024(a), (b).
[416] 42 C.F.R. § 405.1024(c).
[417] 42 C.F.R. § 405.1018(a). This provision does not apply to unrepresented beneficiaries or oral testimony given. 42 C.F.R. § 405.1018(d).
[418] 42 C.F.R. § 405.1018(b).
[419] 42 C.F.R. § 405.1018(c).
[420] 42 C.F.R. § 405.1028(a)–(d).
[421] 42 C.F.R. § 405.1032(a).
[422] 42 C.F.R. § 405.1032.
[423] 42 C.F.R. § 405.1032(b). Certain limitations apply. *See* 42 C.F.R. § 405.980.
[424] 42 C.F.R. § 405.1037(a).
[425] 42 C.F.R. § 405.1037(a)(2).

request is unreasonable, unduly burdensome or expensive, or otherwise inappropriate.[426] Discovery is limited. A party may request reasonable production of documents for inspection and copying, but depositions may not be taken unless the deponent agrees or the ALJ finds the proposed deposition is appropriate and necessary.[427] Similarly, requests for admissions and interrogatories are generally not permitted.[428]

The ALJ may hold a pre-hearing or a post-hearing conference, either at his or her own initiative or at the request of a party.[429] The ALJ must inform the parties of the time, place, and purpose of the conference at least seven calendar days prior to the conference date.[430] The ALJ may consider matters in addition to those stated on the notice of hearing, if the parties consent in writing.[431] A record of the hearing will be made, and the ALJ must issue an order stating all agreements and actions resulting from the conference.[432]

An administrative record, including marked exhibits, will be made.[433] Under the interim final regulations, a party may review the record at the hearing or, if a hearing is not held, at any time prior to the issuance of an ALJ decision.[434] However, given that hearings will most often not be held in person, the regulations offer no explanation as to how such a review can be accomplished. A party may request and receive a copy of all or part of the record; however, the party can be asked to pay the costs of providing the requested items.[435]

Once a hearing has been held,[436] the ALJ must issue a written decision that sets out findings of fact, conclusions of law, and the reasons for the decision.[437] The decision must be mailed to each party, the Medicare contractors, and the QIC.[438]

If an ALJ decision is not rendered within the appropriate time frame for the circumstances of the case, a party may escalate the appeal to the MAC.[439] The request for escalation must be filed with the ALJ.[440] Once the request is received,

---

[426] 42 C.F.R. § 405.1037(a)(2).

[427] 42 C.F.R. § 405.1037(b)(1), (2).

[428] 42 C.F.R. § 405.1037(b)(3).

[429] 42 C.F.R. § 405.1040.

[430] 42 C.F.R. § 405.1040(b).

[431] 42 C.F.R. § 405.1040(c).

[432] 42 C.F.R. §§ 405.1040(c) and 405.100(d).

[433] 42 C.F.R. § 405.1042.

[434] 42 C.F.R. § 405.1042(a)(3).

[435] 42 C.F.R. § 405.1042(b)(1).

[436] Parties are free to waive the right to a hearing, and have a decision issued solely on the administrative record. 42 C.F.R. §§ 405.1020(d) and 405.1038(b). In addition, an ALJ may, without holding a hearing, issue a decision that is fully favorable to the appellant(s) if the hearing record supports such a finding. 42 C.F.R. § 405.1038(a).

[437] 42 C.F.R. § 405.1046(a).

[438] 42 C.F.R. § 405.1046(a).

[439] 42 C.F.R. § 405.1104.

[440] 42 C.F.R. § 405.1104(a)(1).

the ALJ has five days to either issue a decision, remand the case to the QIC,[441] or notify the parties that a timely decision cannot be issued.[442] At that point, the QIC decision becomes the decision which the MAC will review.[443] In addition, the MAC may, on its own initiative, remove a case from the ALJ and assume responsibility for holding a hearing and adjudicating the case itself.[444]

[F] Medicare Appeals Council Review

A party who is dissatisfied with an ALJ decision may request review by the MAC.[445] A written request for MAC review must be filed with the MAC or the appropriate ALJ office.[446] The request must identify those parts of the ALJ decision (or other determination being appealed, if the case is before the MAC due to escalation) to which the party objects, and state the reasons for those objections.[447] Unless the appellant is an unrepresented beneficiary, the MAC will limit its review to those parts of the decision below specifically identified as objectionable in the request for review.

If a party has requested review because he or she is dissatisfied with an ALJ decision, or has escalated an appeal from the ALJ to the MAC, the MAC will review *de novo* the decision below.[448] A party seeking MAC review does not have a right to a new hearing; however, the MAC, in its discretion, may conduct any additional proceedings, including holding a hearing.[449]

Generally, absent good cause,[450] no additional evidence may be introduced at the MAC level of appeal, unless the ALJ decision being reviewed decides a new issue about which the parties were not afforded an opportunity to address before the ALJ.[451] However, a party to the MAC review which is before the MAC because of escalation may file a request for a subpoena of specified documents within 10 days of the request for escalation.[452]

---

[441] 42 C.F.R. §§ 405.1104(a)(2) and 405.1034.

[442] 42 C.F.R. § 405.1104(b)(2), (3).

[443] 42 C.F.R. § 405.1104(b)(3).

[444] 42 C.F.R. § 405.1050.

[445] The MAC may also exercise its "own motion" review. 42 C.F.R. § 405.1110. This review can occur upon the initiative of the MAC or when CMS (or any of its contractors) refers a case to the MAC that it thinks has been erroneously decided or the decision presents a broad policy or procedural issue that may affect the public interest.

[446] 42 C.F.R. § 405.1112(a).

[447] 42 C.F.R. § 405.1112(b).

[448] 42 C.F.R. § 405.1108.

[449] 42 C.F.R. § 405.1108(a), (d)(3).

[450] 42 C.F.R. § 405.1122(c).

[451] 42 C.F.R. § 405.1122(a).

[452] 42 C.F.R. § 405.1122(d)(1)–(4).

The parties have the right to file briefs or other written statements with the MAC.[453] In addition, the MAC may request (but cannot require) CMS or its contractors to file a brief or position paper, if the MAC determines that it is necessary to resolve the issues in the case.[454] In some instances, the MAC may permit, or seek, oral argument on the appeal.[455]

The MAC may dispose of the case in a number of ways: it may remand the case to the ALJ;[456] it may dismiss the request for MAC review;[457] or it may issue a decision.[458] If the MAC fails to issue its decision within the required 90 calendar day time frame from its receipt of the request for MAC review,[459] the appellant may request escalation to federal court.[460] If, upon filing of the escalation request and the lapse of the permissible time plus five additional days, the MAC is unable to issue a decision, remand, or dismissal, it must notify the appellant informing him or her that it is not able to do so.[461] A party may file an action in federal district court within 60 days after the date it receives this notification from the MAC.[462]

[G] Judicial Review

A party to a MAC decision who is dissatisfied with that decision may obtain judicial review if the amount in controversy meets established requirements.[463]

The civil action must be filed within 60 days after receipt of notice of the MAC decision.[464] Provisions exist in the regulations for applying to the MAC for extension of the filing time.[465] The civil action must be filed in the district court for the judicial district in which the beneficiary resides or, if filed by a provider,

---

[453] 42 C.F.R. § 405.1120.

[454] 42 C.F.R. § 405.1120.

[455] 42 C.F.R. § 405.1124.

[456] 42 C.F.R. § 405.1108(d)(3).

[457] 42 C.F.R. § 405.1108(c), (d)(4)–(5).

[458] 42 C.F.R. § 405.1108(a), (d)(1).

[459] 42 C.F.R. § 405.1132. As with the other levels of appeal, the time frame for issuing a determination is subject to various extensions. *See, e.g.,* 42 C.F.R. § 405.1114 (extension when party seeks evidence from the MAC), § 405.1120 (extension when briefs are filed), and § 405.1122(e)(2)(ii) (stay upon issuance of subpoena).

[460] 42 C.F.R. § 405.1132.

[461] 42 C.F.R. § 405.1132(a)(2).

[462] 42 C.F.R. § 405.1132(b).

[463] 42 C.F.R. § 405.1136. The calculation for the amount in controversy requirement is increased by the percentage increase in the medical care component of the consumer price index for all urban consumers (U.S. city average) as measured from July 2003 to the July preceding the current year involved. 42 C.F.R. § 405.1006. For calendar year (CY) 2016, the amount in controversy requirement for ALJ review is $160 or more; for judicial review, $1,560 or more.

[464] 42 C.F.R. § 405.1130.

[465] 42 C.F.R. § 405.1134.

in the judicial district where it has its principal place of business.[466] The Secretary of HHS in his or her official capacity is the proper defendant.[467] The standard of review for the court is whether the Secretary's decision is supported by substantial evidence.[468]

In addition, Section 932 of the MMA modified 42 U.S.C. § 1395ff(b) to create expedited access to the judicial review process whereby beneficiaries, providers, and suppliers can have expedited access to judicial review in certain appeals of Medicare Part A or Part B claims.[469] The expedited appeals process also applies to provider contract disputes—primarily nursing home enforcement cases.[470] Expedited review is available when it is determined both that the MAC lacks authority to decide a question of law or regulation relevant to the case and that there is no material issue of fact in dispute.[471]

A beneficiary may file a request for expedited access to judicial review at the same time as, or after, filing a request for an ALJ hearing.[472] A review entity made up of three reviewers who are ALJs or members of the DAB has 60 days after receipt of the request to issue a written decision.[473] The review entity may request appropriate documents and materials from the beneficiary to support his or her contention that (1) no material issues of fact exist and (2) the MAC lacks authority to decide the relevant question of law or regulations.[474] If the review entity agrees with the beneficiary's request for expedited review, or if the review entity fails to act within 60 days of receipt of the request, the beneficiary skips ALJ and DAB review and may go directly to district court.[475] If the review entity finds against the beneficiary, he or she has no further recourse and may not make another request for expedited review regarding the matter in dispute.[476]

§ 6.08 APPOINTMENTS OF REPRESENTATIVES AND ATTORNEYS' FEES

The regulations also specify the elements of a proper appointment of representative, its duration, and rules about collection of fees for representing Medicare beneficiaries in an appeal of a Medicare denial.[477] These rules are applicable

466 42 C.F.R. § 405.1136(b).
467 42 C.F.R. § 405.1136(d).
468 42 C.F.R. § 405.1136(f).
469 42 C.F.R. § 405.990.
470 42 C.F.R. §§ 405.906(a)–(c) and 405.990(e).
471 42 C.F.R. § 405.990(a)(2).
472 42 C.F.R. § 405.990(d)(2).
473 42 C.F.R. § 405.990(a)(1).
474 42 C.F.R. § 405.990(c).
475 42 C.F.R. § 405.990(f)(4).
476 42 C.F.R. § 405.990(h)(3)(i).
477 42 C.F.R. §§ 405.910 and 405.912.

to all Medicare appeals, including Part B appeals currently being handled by a Medicare contractor, effective May 1, 2005.[478]

A valid appointment of representation (AOR) form must:[479]

- Be in writing and signed and dated by both the beneficiary and the representative.
- Authorize the representative to act on behalf of the beneficiary and authorize the adjudicator to release identifiable health information to the representative.
- Include an explanation of the purpose and scope of the representation.
- Include the name, phone number, and address for the beneficiary and the representative.
- Include the beneficiary's Medicare health insurance claim number.
- Include the representative's professional status or relationship to the beneficiary.
- Be filed with the entity processing the party's initial determination or appeal.

If a form is defective, the representative will be given an opportunity to correct the defect. Otherwise, the representative will not have the authority to act on behalf of the beneficiary or to receive health information.[480] In addition, a representative must submit, with each appeal request, a copy of the valid, effective AOR or other conforming written instrument in order to request a redetermination or other appeal on behalf of the party. A valid, executed AOR will be honored for the duration of the initial appeal request for which it is filed, and for any subsequent appeal requests with which it is submitted, provided the initial appeal request is filed within one year of the effective date of the AOR. With respect to Medicare Secondary Payer recovery claims, the AOR is deemed valid for longer than one year because liability, no-fault, and worker's compensation claims often take more than one year to resolve.[481]

The regulations limit the duration of the appointment of representation form to one year. A duly appointed representative may file multiple appeals on behalf of an individual beneficiary during the course of that year, but must submit a copy of the original appointment form with each additional appeal filed. Once an appointment of representation form has been filed in a case, the appointment lasts

[478] 70 Fed. Reg. 11,425 (Mar. 8, 2005).

[479] 42 C.F.R. § 405.910(c).

[480] 42 C.F.R. § 405.910(d)(2); *see also* material at **§ 6.07[A]**; final regulations are at 74 Fed. Reg. 65,296 *et seq. See* http://edocket.access.gpo.gov/2009/pdf/E9-28707.pdf (site visited June 8, 2016).

[481] 74 Fed. Reg. 65,296 *et seq.*

for the duration of the appeal, even upon the death of the assignor, unless it is revoked.[482]

The regulations prohibit an appointed representative from delegating the appointment to another person without the beneficiary's consent. Thus, a family member who already serves as an appointed representative cannot delegate that appointment to an advocate for purposes of pursing an appeal unless the beneficiary signs a written notice. A signed statement is not required where both the appointed and new representatives are attorneys (but not paralegals) in the same law firm or organization. When a beneficiary lacks the capacity to sign an appointment of representation form or form acknowledging delegation of the appointment, state law determines who has authority to authorize representation on his or her behalf.[483]

Under the regulations, a beneficiary's appointed representative (but not a provider or supplier's representative) who wishes to charge a fee for services at the ALJ and MAC levels of review must obtain approval of the fee from the Secretary. The regulations also say that no award of fees or costs may be made against the Medicare trust fund, and that limitations on the amount of fees that apply in Social Security and Supplemental Security Income disability cases do not apply to Medicare appeals.[484]

The regulations do not contain a standard by which fee requests will be judged. However, attorneys are requested to submit the application for a fee form used in Social Security cases for review. The "Appointment of Representative in Medicare Appeals" form refers to the SSA "Petition to Obtain Representative Fee" as the form to use to provide information in support of a petition for fees (no standard form) in Medicare appeals. It should accompany the fee petition.[485]

In appeals brought to federal district court, attorneys' fees are generally available for cases under the Social Security Act, either through the Social Security Act Title II provisions[486] or under the EAJA.[487]

Under EAJA, fees are available to prevailing parties against the government in civil cases where the government's position is deemed not "substantially justified" or where there are special circumstances that would make an award unjust.[488] Proving entitlement to benefits is generally regarded as meeting the prevailing party

---

[482] 42 C.F.R. §§ 405.910(e) and 405.912(e).

[483] 42 C.F.R. § 405.910(l).

[484] 42 C.F.R. § 405.910(f).

[485] Attorneys should review the material at these links: http://www.ssa.gov/representation/fee_petitions.htm (petition to obtain approval of a fee for representing a claimant—SSA) (site visited July 8, 2016) and http://cms.gov/Medicare/CMS-Forms/CMS-Forms/downloads/cms1696.pdf (appointment of representative in Medicare appeals) (site visited July 8, 2016).

[486] *See* 42 U.S.C. § 406(b).

[487] *See* 28 U.S.C. § 2412.

[488] 28 U.S.C. § 2412(d)(1)(A).

status.[489] Having established prevailing party status, the burden shifts to the government to prove that its position was substantially justified.[490] The government must meet a strong burden of showing that its position was substantially justified.[491] Fees are awarded in accordance with the statute's fee provisions.[492]

[489] *See* McGill v. Secretary of HHS, 712 F.2d 28, 32 (2d Cir. 1983), *cert. denied*, 465 U.S. 1068 (1984).

[490] 28 U.S.C. § 2412(d)(1)(A).

[491] Pierce v. Underwood, 487 U.S. 552 (1988).

[492] *See* 28 U.S.C. § 2412(d)(2).

APPENDIX 6-1 TITLE 42—PUBLIC HEALTH (CODE OF FEDERAL REGULATIONS):

PART 405—FEDERAL HEALTH INSURANCE FOR THE AGED AND DISABLED

(Subpart I—Determinations, Redeterminations, Reconsiderations, and Appeals Under Original Medicare (Part A and Part B))*

[70 FR 11472, Mar. 8, 2005, unless otherwise noted.]

§ 405.900 Basis and scope.

(a) Statutory basis. This subpart is based on the provisions of sections 1869 (a) through (e) and (g) of the Act.

(1) Section 1869(a) through (e) and (g) of the Act.

(2) Section 1862(b)(2)(B)(viii) of the Act.

(b) Scope. This subpart establishes the requirements for appeals of initial determinations for benefits under Part A or Part B of Medicare, including the following:

(1) The initial determination of whether an individual is entitled to benefits under Part A or Part B. (Regulations governing reconsiderations of these initial determinations are at 20 CFR, part 404, subpart J).

(2) The initial determination of the amount of benefits available to an individual under Part A or Part B.

(3) Any other initial determination relating to a claim for benefits under Part A or Part B, including an initial determination made by a quality improvement organization under section 1154(a)(2) of the Act or by an entity under contract with the Secretary (other than a contract under section 1852 of the Act) to administer provisions of titles XVIII or XI of the Act.

[70 FR 11472, Mar. 8, 2005, as amended at 80 FR 10617, Feb. 27, 2015]

§ 405.902 Definitions.

For the purposes of this subpart, the term—

ALJ means an Administrative Law Judge of the Department of Health and Human Services.

Appellant means the beneficiary, assignee or other person or entity that has filed and pursued an appeal concerning a particular initial determination.

* *See* http://www.ecfr.gov/cgi-bin/text-idx?rgn=div5&node=42:2.0.1.2.5 (site visited June 8, 2016).

Designation as an appellant does not in itself convey standing to appeal the determination in question.

Applicable plan means liability insurance (including self-insurance), no-fault insurance, or a workers' compensation law or plan.

Appointed representative means an individual appointed by a party to represent the party in a Medicare claim or claim appeal.

Assignee means:

(1) A supplier that furnishes items or services to a beneficiary and has accepted a valid assignment of a claim or

(2) A provider or supplier that furnishes items or services to a beneficiary, who is not already a party, and has accepted a valid assignment of the right to appeal a claim executed by the beneficiary.

Assignment of a claim means the transfer by a beneficiary of his or her claim for payment to the supplier in return for the latter's promise not to charge more for his or her services than what the carrier finds to be the Medicare-approved amount, as provided in §§ 424.55 and 424.56 of this chapter.

Assignment of appeal rights means the transfer by a beneficiary of his or her right to appeal under this subpart to a provider or supplier who is not already a party, as provided in section 1869(b)(1)(C) of the Act.

Assignor means a beneficiary whose provider of services or supplier has taken assignment of a claim or an appeal of a claim.

Authorized representative means an individual authorized under State or other applicable law to act on behalf of a beneficiary or other party involved in the appeal. The authorized representative will have all of the rights and responsibilities of a beneficiary or party, as applicable, throughout the appeals process.

Beneficiary means an individual who is enrolled to receive benefits under Medicare Part A or Part B.

Carrier means an organization that has entered into a contract with the Secretary in accordance to section 1842 of the Act and is authorized to make determinations for Part B of title XVIII of the Act.

Clean claim means a claim that has no defect or impropriety (including any lack of required substantiating documentation) or particular circumstance requiring special treatment that prevents timely payment from being made on the claim under title XVIII within the time periods specified in sections 1816(c) and 1842(c) of the Act.

Contractor means an entity that contracts with the Federal government to review and/or adjudicate claims, determinations and/or decisions.

Family member means for purposes of the QIC reconsideration panel under § 405.968 the following persons as they relate to the physician or healthcare provider.

(1) The spouse (other than a spouse who is legally separated from the physician or health care professional under a decree of divorce or separate maintenance);

(2) Children (including stepchildren and legally adopted children);

(3) Grandchildren;

(4) Parents; and

(5) Grandparents.

Fiscal Intermediary means an organization that has entered into a contract with CMS in accordance with section 1816 of the Act and is authorized to make determinations and payments for Part A of title XVIII of the Act, and Part B provider services as specified in § 421.5(c) of this chapter.

MAC stands for the Medicare Appeals Council within the Departmental Appeals Board of the U.S. Department of Health and Human Services.

Party means an individual or entity listed in § 405.906 that has standing to appeal an initial determination and/or a subsequent administrative appeal determination.

Provider means a hospital, critical access hospital, skilled nursing facility, comprehensive outpatient rehabilitation facility, home health agency, or hospice that has in effect an agreement to participate in Medicare, or clinic, rehabilitation agency, or public health agency that has in effect a similar agreement, but only to furnish outpatient physical therapy or speech pathology services, or a community mental health center that has in effect a similar agreement but only to furnish partial hospitalization services.

Qualified Independent Contractor (QIC) means an entity which contracts with the Secretary in accordance with section 1869 of the Act to perform reconsiderations under § 405.960 through § 405.978.

Quality Improvement Organization (QIO) means an entity that contracts with the Secretary in accordance with sections 1152 and 1153 of the Act and 42 CFR subchapter F, to perform the functions described in section 1154 of the Act and 42 CFR subchapter F, including expedited determinations as described in § 405.1200 through § 405.1208.

Reliable evidence means evidence that is relevant, credible, and material.

Remand means to vacate a lower level appeal decision, or a portion of the decision, and return the case, or a portion of the case, to that level for a new decision.

Similar fault means to obtain, retain, convert, seek, or receive Medicare funds to which a person knows or should reasonably be expected to know that he or she or another for whose benefit Medicare funds are obtained, retained, converted, sought, or received is not legally entitled. This includes, but is not limited to, a failure to demonstrate that he or she filed a proper claim as defined in part 411 of this chapter.

Supplier means, unless the context otherwise requires, a physician or other practitioner, a facility, or other entity (other than a provider of services) that furnishes items or services under Medicare.

Vacate means to set aside a previous action.

[70 FR 11472, Mar. 8, 2005, as amended at 74 FR 65333, Dec. 9, 2009; 80 FR 10617, Feb. 27, 2015]

§ 405.904 Medicare initial determinations, redeterminations and appeals: General description.

(a) General overview—(1) *Entitlement appeals.* The SSA makes an initial determination on an application for Medicare benefits and/or entitlement of an individual to receive Medicare benefits. A beneficiary who is dissatisfied with the initial determination may request, and SSA will perform, a reconsideration in accordance with 20 CFR part 404, subpart J if the requirements for obtaining a reconsideration are met. Following the reconsideration, the beneficiary may request a hearing before an Administrative Law Judge (ALJ) under this subpart (42 CFR part 405, subpart I). If the beneficiary obtains a hearing before an ALJ and is dissatisfied with the decision of the ALJ, he or she may request the Medicare Appeals Council (MAC) to review the case. Following the action of the MAC, the beneficiary may be entitled to file suit in Federal district court.

(2) *Claim appeals.* The Medicare contractor makes an initial determination when a claim for Medicare benefits under Part A or Part B is submitted. A beneficiary who is dissatisfied with the initial determination may request that the contractor perform a redetermination of the claim if the requirements for obtaining a redetermination are met. Following the contractor's redetermination, the beneficiary may request, and the Qualified Independent Contractor (QIC) will perform, a reconsideration of the claim if the requirements for obtaining a reconsideration are met. Following the reconsideration, the beneficiary may request, and the ALJ will conduct a hearing if the amount remaining in controversy and other requirements for an ALJ hearing are met. If the beneficiary is dissatisfied with the decision of the ALJ, he or she may request the MAC to review the case. If the MAC reviews the case and issues a decision, and the beneficiary is dissatisfied with the decision, the beneficiary may file suit in Federal district court if the amount remaining in controversy and the other requirements for judicial review are met.

(b) Non-beneficiary appellants. In general, the procedures described in paragraph (a) of this section are also available to parties other than beneficiaries either directly or through a representative acting on a party's behalf, consistent with the requirements of this subpart I. A provider generally has the right to judicial review only as provided under section 1879(d) of the Act; that is, when a determination involves a finding that services are not covered because—

(1) They were custodial care (see § 411.15(g) of this chapter); they were not reasonable and necessary (see § 411.15(k) of this chapter); they did not qualify as covered home health services because the beneficiary was not confined to the home or did not need skilled nursing care on an intermittent basis (see § 409.42(a) and (c)(1) of this chapter); or they were hospice services provided to a non-terminally ill individual (see § 418.22 of this chapter); and

(2) Either the provider or the beneficiary, or both, knew or could reasonably be expected to know that those services were not covered under Medicare.

§ 405.906 Parties to the initial determinations, redeterminations, reconsiderations, hearings and reviews.

(a) *Parties to the initial determination.* The parties to the initial determination are the following individuals and entities:

(1) A beneficiary who files a claim for payment under Medicare Part A or Part B or has had a claim for payment filed on his or her behalf, or in the case of a deceased beneficiary, when there is no estate, any person obligated to make or entitled to receive payment in accordance with part 424, subpart E of this chapter. Payment by a third party payer does not entitle that entity to party status.

(2) A supplier who has accepted assignment for items or services furnished to a beneficiary that are at issue in the claim.

(3) A provider of services who files a claim for items or services furnished to a beneficiary.

(4) An applicable plan for an initial determination under § 405.924(b)(16) where Medicare is pursuing recovery directly from the applicable plan. The applicable plan is the sole party to an initial determination under § 405.924(b)(16) (that is, where Medicare is pursuing recovery directly from the applicable plan).

(b) *Parties to the redetermination, reconsideration, hearing and MAC.* The parties to the redetermination, reconsideration, hearing, and MAC review are—

(1) The parties to the initial determination in accordance with paragraph (a) of this section, except under paragraph (a)(1) of this section where a beneficiary has assigned appeal rights under § 405.912;

(2) A State agency in accordance with § 405.908;

(3) A provider or supplier that has accepted an assignment of appeal rights from the beneficiary according to § 405.912;

(4) A non-participating physician not billing on an assigned basis who, in accordance with section 1842(l) of the Act, may be liable to refund monies collected for services furnished to the beneficiary because those services were denied on the basis of section 1862(a)(1) of the Act; and

(5) A non-participating supplier not billing on an assigned basis who, in accordance with sections 1834(a)(18) and 1834(j)(4) of the Act, may be liable to refund monies collected for items furnished to the beneficiary.

(c) *Appeals by providers and suppliers when there is no other party available.* If a provider or supplier is not already a party to the proceeding in accordance with paragraphs (a) and (b) of this section, a provider of services or supplier may appeal an initial determination relating to services it rendered to a beneficiary who subsequently dies if there is no other party available to appeal the determination. This paragraph (c) does not apply to an initial determination with respect to an applicable plan under § 405.924(b)(16).

[70 FR 11472, Mar. 8, 2005, as amended at 80 FR 10617, Feb. 27, 2015]

§ 405.908 Medicaid State agencies.

When a beneficiary is enrolled to receive benefits under both Medicare and Medicaid, the Medicaid State agency may file a request for an appeal with respect to a claim for items or services furnished to a dually eligible beneficiary only for services for which the Medicaid State agency has made payment, or for which it may be liable. A Medicaid State agency is considered a party only when it files a timely redetermination request with respect to a claim for items or services furnished to a beneficiary in accordance with 42 CFR parts 940 through 958. If a State agency files a request for redetermination, it may retain party status at the QIC, ALJ, MAC, and judicial review levels.

§ 405.910 Appointed representatives.

(a) *Scope of representation.* An appointed representative may act on behalf of an individual or entity in exercising his or her right to an initial determination or appeal. Appointed representatives do not have party status and may take action only on behalf of the individual or entity that they represent.

(b) *Persons not qualified.* A party may not name as an appointed representative, an individual who is disqualified, suspended, or otherwise prohibited by law from acting as a representative in any proceedings before DHHS, or in entitlement appeals, before SSA.

(c) *Completing a valid appointment.* For purposes of this subpart, an appointment of representation must:

(1) Be in writing and signed and dated by both the party and individual agreeing to be the representative;

(2) Provide a statement appointing the representative to act on behalf of the party, and in the case of a beneficiary, authorizing the adjudicator to release identifiable health information to the appointed representative.

(3) Include a written explanation of the purpose and scope of the representation;

(4) Contain both the party's and appointed representative's name, phone number, and address;

(5) Identify the beneficiary's Medicare health insurance claim number when the beneficiary is the party appointing a representative;

(6) Include the appointed representative's professional status or relationship to the party;

(7) Be filed with the entity processing the party's initial determination or appeal.

(d) *Curing a defective appointment of representative.* (1) If any one of the seven elements named in paragraph (c) of this section is missing from the appointment, the adjudicator should contact the party and provide a description of the missing documentation or information.

(2) Unless the defect is cured, the prospective appointed representative lacks the authority to act on behalf of the party, and is not entitled to obtain or receive any information related to the appeal, including the appeal decision.

(e) *Duration of appointment.* (1) Unless revoked, an appointment is considered valid for 1 year from the date that the Appointment of Representative (AOR) form or other conforming written instrument contains the signatures of both the party and the appointed representative.

(2) To initiate an appeal within the 1-year time frame, the representative must file a copy of the AOR form, or other conforming written instrument, with the appeal request. Unless revoked, the representation is valid for the duration of an individual's appeal of an initial determination.

(3) For an initial determination of a Medicare Secondary Payer recovery claim, an appointment signed in connection with the party's efforts to make a claim for third party payment is valid from the date that appointment is signed for the duration of any subsequent appeal, unless the appointment is specifically revoked.

(4) For an initial determination of a Medicare Secondary Payer recovery claim, an appointment signed by an applicable plan which has party status in accordance with § 405.906(a)(1)(iv) is valid from the date that appointment is signed for the duration of any subsequent appeal, unless the appointment is specifically revoked.

(f) *Appointed representative fees*—(1) *General rule.* An appointed representative for a beneficiary who wishes to charge a fee for services rendered in connection with an appeal before the Secretary must obtain approval of the fee from the Secretary. Services rendered below the ALJ level are not considered proceedings before the Secretary.

(2) *No fees or costs against trust funds.* No award of attorney or any other representative's fees or any costs in connection with an appeal may be made against the Medicare trust funds.

(3) *Special rules for providers and suppliers.* A provider or supplier that furnished the items or services to a beneficiary that are the subject of the appeal may represent that beneficiary in an appeal under this subpart, but the provider or supplier may not charge the beneficiary any fee associated with the representation. If a provider or supplier furnishes services or items to a beneficiary, the provider or supplier may not represent the beneficiary on the issues described in section 1879(a)(2) of the Act, unless the provider or supplier waives the right to payment from the beneficiary for the services or items involved in the appeal.

(4) *Special rules for purposes of third party payment.* The Secretary does not review fee arrangements made by a beneficiary for purposes of making a claim for third party payment (as defined in 42 CFR 411.21) even though the representation may ultimately include representation for a Medicare Secondary Payer recovery claim.

(5) *Reasonableness of representative fees.* In determining the reasonableness of a representative's fee, the Secretary will not apply the test specified in sections 206(a)(2) and (a)(3) of the Act.

(g) *Responsibilities of an appointed representative.* (1) An appointed representative has an affirmative duty to—

(i) Inform the party of the scope and responsibilities of the representation;

(ii) Inform the party of the status of the appeal and the results of actions taken on behalf of the party, including, but not limited to, notification of appeal determinations, decisions, and further appeal rights;

(iii) Disclose to a beneficiary any financial risk and liability of a non-assigned claim that the beneficiary may have;

(iv) Not act contrary to the interest of the party; and

(v) Comply with all laws and CMS regulations, CMS Rulings, and instructions.

(2) An appeal request filed by a provider or supplier described in paragraph (f)(3) of this section must also include a statement signed by the provider or supplier stating that no financial liability is imposed on the beneficiary in connection with that representation. If applicable, the appeal request must also include a signed statement that the provider or supplier waives the right to payment from the beneficiary for services or items regarding issues described in section 1879(a)(2) of the Act.

(h) *Authority of an appointed representative.* An appointed representative may, on behalf of the party—

(1) Obtain appeals information about the claim to the same extent as the party;

(2) Submit evidence;

(3) Make statements about facts and law; and

(4) Make any request, or give, or receive, any notice about the appeal proceedings.

(i) *Notice or request to an appointed representative*—(1) *Initial determinations.* When a contractor takes an action or issues an initial determination, it sends the action or notice to the party.

(2) *Appeals.* When a contractor, QIC, ALJ, or the MAC takes an action or issues a redetermination, reconsideration, or appeal decision, in connection with an initial determination, it sends notice of the action to the appointed representative.

(3) The contractor, QIC, ALJ or MAC sends any requests for information or evidence regarding a claim that is appealed to the appointed representative. The contractor sends any requests for information or evidence regarding an initial determination to the party.

(4) For initial determinations and appeals involving Medicare Secondary Payer recovery claims where the beneficiary is a party, the adjudicator sends

notices and requests to both the beneficiary and the beneficiary's representative, if the beneficiary has a representative.

(j) *Effect of notice or request to an appointed representative.* A notice or request sent to the appointed representative has the same force and effect as if was sent to the party.

(k) *Information available to the appointed representative.* An appointed representative may obtain any and all appeals information applicable to the claim at issue that is available to the party.

(l) *Delegation of appointment by appointed representative.* An appointed representative may not designate another individual to act as the appointed representative of the party unless—

(1) The appointed representative provides written notice to the party of the appointed representative's intent to delegate to another individual. The notice must include:

(i) The name of the designee; and

(ii) The designee's acceptance to be obligated and comply with the requirements of representation under this subpart.

(2) The party accepts the designation as evidenced by a written statement signed by the party. This signed statement is not required when the appointed representative and designee are attorneys in the same law firm or organization.

(m) *Revoking the appointment of representative.* (1) A party may revoke an appointment of representative without cause at any time.

(2) *Revocation.* Revocation is not effective until the adjudicator receives a signed, written statement from the party.

(3) *Death of the party.* (i) The death of a party terminates the authority of the appointed representative, except as specified in paragraph (m)(3)(ii) of this section.

(ii) A party's death does not terminate an appeal that is in progress if another individual or entity may be entitled to receive or obligated to make payment for the items or services that are the subject of the appeal. The appointment of representative remains in effect for the duration of the appeal except for MSP recovery claims.

[70 FR 11472, Mar. 8, 2005, as amended at 80 FR 10617, Feb. 27, 2015]

§ 405.912 Assignment of appeal rights.

(a) Who may be an assignee. Only a provider, or supplier that—

(1) Is not a party to the initial determination as defined in Sec. 405.906; and

(2) Furnished an item or service to the beneficiary may seek assignment of appeal rights from the beneficiary for that item or service.

(b) Who may not be an assignee. An individual or entity who is not a provider or supplier may not be an assignee. A provider or supplier that furnishes an item or service to a beneficiary may not seek assignment for that item or service when considered a party to the initial determination as defined in § 405.906.

(c) Requirements for a valid assignment of appeal right. The assignment of appeal rights must—

(1) Be executed using a CMS standard form;

(2) Be in writing and signed by both the beneficiary assigning his or her appeal rights and by the assignee;

(3) Indicate the item or service for which the assignment of appeal rights is authorized;

(4) Contain a waiver of the assignee's right to collect payment from the assignor for the specific item or service that are the subject of the appeal except as set forth in paragraph (d)(2) of this section; and

(5) Be submitted at the same time the request for redetermination or other appeal is filed.

(d) Waiver of right to collect payment. (1) Except as specified in paragraph (d)(2) of this section, the assignee must waive the right to collect payment for the item or service for which the assignment of appeal rights is made. If the assignment is revoked under paragraph (g)(2) or (g)(3) of this section, the waiver of the right to collect payment nevertheless remains valid. A waiver of the right to collect payment remains in effect regardless of the outcome of the appeal decision.

(2) The assignee is not prohibited from recovering payment associated with coinsurance or deductibles or when an advance beneficiary notice is properly executed.

(e) Duration of a valid assignment of appeal rights. Unless revoked, the assignment of appeal rights is valid for all administrative and judicial review associated with the item or service as indicated on the standard CMS form, even in the event of the death of the assignor.

(f) Rights of the assignee. When a valid assignment of appeal rights is executed, the assignor transfers all appeal rights involving the particular item or service to the assignee. These include, but are not limited to—

(1) Obtaining information about the claim to the same extent as the assignor;

(2) Submitting evidence;

(3) Making statements about facts or law; and

(4) Making any request, or giving, or receiving any notice about appeal proceedings.

(g) Revocation of assignment. When an assignment of appeal rights is revoked, the rights to appeal revert to the assignor. An assignment of appeal rights may be revoked in any of the following ways:

(1) *In writing by the assignor.* The revocation of assignment must be delivered to the adjudicator and the assignee, and is effective on the date of receipt by the adjudicator.

(2) By abandonment if the assignee does not file an appeal of an unfavorable decision.

(3) By act or omission by the assignee that is determined by an adjudicator to be contrary to the financial interests of the assignor.

(h) Responsibilities of the assignee. Once the assignee files an appeal, the assignee becomes a party to the appeal. The assignee must meet all requirements for appeals that apply to any other party.

[70 FR 11472, Mar. 8, 2005, as amended at 70 FR 37702, June 30, 2005]

Initial Determinations

§ 405.920 Initial determinations.

After a claim is filed with the appropriate contractor in the manner and form described in subpart C of part 424 of this chapter, the contractor must—

(a) Determine if the items and services furnished are covered or otherwise reimbursable under title XVIII of the Act;

(b) Determine any amounts payable and make payment accordingly; and

(c) Notify the parties to the initial determination of the determination in accordance with § 405.921.

§ 405.921 Notice of initial determination.

(a) *Notice of initial determination sent to the beneficiary.* (1) The notice must be written in a manner calculated to be understood by the beneficiary, and sent to the last known address of the beneficiary.

(2) *Content of the notice.* The notice of initial determination must contain all of the following:

(i) The reasons for the determination, including whether a local medical review policy, a local coverage determination, or national coverage determination was applied.

(ii) The procedures for obtaining additional information concerning the contractor's determination, such as a specific provision of the policy, manual, law or regulation used in making the determination.

(iii) Information on the right to a redetermination if the beneficiary is dissatisfied with the outcome of the initial determination and instructions on how to request a redetermination.

(iv) Any other requirements specified by CMS.

(b) *Notice of initial determination sent to providers and suppliers.* (1) An electronic or paper remittance advice (RA) notice is the notice of initial determination sent to providers and suppliers that accept assignment.

(i) The electronic RA must comply with the format and content requirements of the standard adopted for national use by covered entities under the

Health Insurance Portability and Accountability Act (HIPAA) and related CMS manual instructions.

(ii) When a paper RA is mailed, it must comply with CMS manual instructions that parallel the HIPAA data content and coding requirements.

(2) The notice of initial determination must contain all of the following:

(i) The basis for any full or partial denial determination of services or items on the claim.

(ii) Information on the right to a redetermination if the provider or supplier is dissatisfied with the outcome of the initial determination.

(iii) All applicable claim adjustment reason and remark codes to explain the determination.

(iv) The source of the RA and who may be contacted if the provider or supplier requires further information.

(v) All content requirements of the standard adopted for national use by covered entities under HIPAA.

(vi) Any other requirements specified by CMS.

(c) *Notice of initial determination sent to an applicable plan*—(1) *Content of the notice.* The notice of initial determination under § 405.924(b)(16) must contain all of the following:

(i) The reasons for the determination.

(ii) The procedures for obtaining additional information concerning the contractor's determination, such as a specific provision of the policy, manual, law or regulation used in making the determination.

(iii) Information on the right to a redetermination if the liability insurance (including self-insurance), no-fault insurance, or workers' compensation law or plan is dissatisfied with the outcome of the initial determination and instructions on how to request a redetermination.

(iv) Any other requirements specified by CMS.

(2) [Reserved]

[70 FR 11472, Mar. 8, 2005, as amended at 80 FR 10617, Feb. 27, 2015]

§ 405.922 Time frame for processing initial determinations.

The contractor issues initial determinations on clean claims within 30 days of receipt if they are submitted by or on behalf of the beneficiary who received the items and/or services; otherwise, interest must be paid at the rate specified at 31 U.S.C. 3902(a) for the period beginning on the day after the required payment date and ending on the date payment is made.

[70 FR 11472m Mar 8, 2005, as amended at 74 FR 65333, Dec. 9, 2009]

§ 405.924 Actions that are initial determinations.

(a) *Applications and entitlement of individuals.* SSA makes initial determinations and processes reconsiderations with respect to an individual on the following:

(1) A determination with respect to entitlement to hospital insurance or supplementary medical insurance under Medicare.

(2) A disallowance of an individual's application for entitlement to hospital or supplementary medical insurance, if the individual fails to submit evidence requested by SSA to support the application. (SSA specifies in the initial determination the conditions of entitlement that the applicant failed to establish by not submitting the requested evidence).

(3) A denial of a request for withdrawal of an application for hospital or supplementary medical insurance, or a denial of a request for cancellation of a request for withdrawal.

(4) A determination as to whether an individual, previously determined as entitled to hospital or supplementary medical insurance, is no longer entitled to those benefits, including a determination based on nonpayment of premiums.

(b) *Claims made by or on behalf of beneficiaries.* The Medicare contractor makes initial determinations regarding claims for benefits under Medicare Part A and Part B. A finding that a request for payment or other submission does not meet the requirements for a Medicare claim as defined in § 424.32 of this chapter, is not considered an initial determination. An initial determination for purposes of this subpart includes, but is not limited to, determinations with respect to any of the following:

(1) If the items and/or services furnished are covered under title XVIII.

(2) In the case of determinations on the basis of section 1879(b) or (c) of the Act, if the beneficiary, or supplier who accepts assignment under § 424.55 of this chapter knew, or could reasonably have expected to know at the time the items or services were furnished, that the items or services were not covered.

(3) In the case of determinations on the basis of section 1842(l)(1) of the Act, if the beneficiary or physician knew, or could reasonably have expected to know at the time the services were furnished, that the services were not covered.

(4) Whether the deductible is met.

(5) The computation of the coinsurance amount.

(6) The number of days used for inpatient hospital, psychiatric hospital, or post-hospital extended care.

(7) Periods of hospice care used.

(8) Requirements for certification and plan of treatment for physician services, durable medical equipment, therapies, inpatient hospitalization, skilled nursing care, home health, hospice, and partial hospitalization services.

(9) The beginning and ending of a spell of illness, including a determination made under the presumptions established under § 409.60(c)(2) of this chapter, and as specified in § 409.60(c)(4) of this chapter.

(10) The medical necessity of services, or the reasonableness or appropriateness of placement of an individual at an acute level of patient care made by the Quality Improvement Organization (QIO) on behalf of the contractor in accordance with § 476.86(c)(1) of this chapter.

(11) Any other issues having a present or potential effect on the amount of benefits to be paid under Part A or Part B of Medicare, including a determination as to whether there was an underpayment of benefits paid under Part A or Part B, and if so, the amount thereof.

(12) If a waiver of adjustment or recovery under sections 1870(b) and (c) of the Act is appropriate—

(i) When an overpayment of hospital insurance benefits or supplementary medical insurance benefits (including a payment under section 1814(e) of the Act) was made for an individual; or

(ii) For a Medicare Secondary Payer recovery claim against a beneficiary or against a provider or supplier.

(13) If a particular claim is not payable by Medicare based upon the application of the Medicare Secondary Payer provisions of section 1862(b) of the Act.

(14) Under the Medicare Secondary Payer provisions of sections 1862(b) of the Act that Medicare has a recovery claim against a provider, supplier, or beneficiary for services or items that were already paid by the Medicare program, except when the Medicare Secondary Payer recovery claim against the provider or supplier is based upon failure to file a proper claim as defined in part 411 of this chapter because this action is a reopening.

(15) A claim not payable to a beneficiary for the services of a physician who has opted-out.

(16) Under the Medicare Secondary Payer provisions of section 1862(b) of the Act that Medicare has a recovery claim if Medicare is pursuing recovery directly from an applicable plan. That is, there is an initial determination with respect to the amount and existence of the recovery claim.

(c) *Determinations by QIOs.* An initial determination for purposes of this subpart also includes a determination made by a QIO that:

(1) A provider can terminate services provided to an individual when a physician certified that failure to continue the provision of those services is likely to place the individual's health at significant risk; or

(2) A provider can discharge an individual from the provider of services.

[70 FR 11472, Mar. 8, 2005, as amended at 74 FR 65333, Dec. 9, 2009; 79 FR 68001, Nov. 13, 2014; 80 FR 10618, Feb. 27, 2015]

§ 405.926 Actions that are not initial determinations.

Actions that are not initial determinations and are not appealable under this subpart include, but are not limited to the following:

(a) Any determination for which CMS has sole responsibility, for example one of the following:

(1) If an entity meets the conditions for participation in the program.

(2) If an independent laboratory meets the conditions for coverage of services.

(3) Determination under the Medicare Secondary Payer provisions of section 1862(b) of the Act of the debtor for a particular recovery claim.

(b) The coinsurance amounts prescribed by regulation for outpatient services under the prospective payment system.

(c) Any issue regarding the computation of the payment amount of program reimbursement of general applicability for which CMS or a carrier has sole responsibility under Part B such as the establishment of a fee schedule set forth in part 414 of this chapter, or an inherent reasonableness adjustment pursuant to § 405.502(g), and any issue regarding the cost report settlement process under Part A.

(d) Whether an individual's appeal meets the qualifications for expedited access to judicial review provided in § 405.990.

(e) Any determination regarding whether a Medicare overpayment claim must be compromised, or collection action terminated or suspended under the Federal Claims Collection Act of 1966, as amended.

(f) Determinations regarding the transfer or discharge of residents of skilled nursing facilities in accordance with § 483.12 of this chapter.

(g) Determinations regarding the readmission screening and annual resident review processes required by subparts C and E of part 483 of this chapter.

(h) Determinations for a waiver of Medicare Secondary Payer recovery under section 1862(b) of the Act.

(i) Determinations for a waiver of interest.

(j) Determinations for a finding regarding the general applicability of the Medicare Secondary Payer provisions (as opposed to the application of these provisions to a particular claim or claims for Medicare payment for benefits).

(k) Except as specified in § 405.924(b)(16), determinations under the Medicare Secondary Payer provisions of section 1862(b) of the Act that Medicare has a recovery against an entity that was or is required or responsible (directly, as an insurer or self-insurer; as a third party administrator; as an employer that sponsors, contributes to or facilitates a group health plan or a large group health plan; or otherwise) to make payment for services or items that were already reimbursed by the Medicare program.

(l) A contractor's, QIC's, ALJ's, or MAC's determination or decision to reopen or not to reopen an initial determination, redetermination, reconsideration, hearing decision, or review decision.

(m) Determinations that CMS or its contractors may participate in or act as parties in an ALJ hearing or MAC review.

(n) Determinations that a provider or supplier failed to submit a claim timely or failed to submit a timely claim despite being requested to do so by the beneficiary or the beneficiary's subrogee.

(o) Determinations with respect to whether an entity qualifies for an exception to the electronic claims submission requirement under part 424 of this chapter.

(p) Determinations by the Secretary of sustained or high levels of payment errors in accordance with section 1893(f)(3)(A) of the Act.

(q) A contractor's prior determination related to coverage of physicians' services.

(r) Requests for anticipated payment under the home health prospective payment system under § 409.43(c)(ii)(2) of this chapter.

(s) Claim submissions on forms or formats that are incomplete, invalid, or do not meet the requirements for a Medicare claim and returned or rejected to the provider or supplier.

[70 FR 11472, Mar. 8, 2005, as amended at 70 FR 37702, June 30, 2005; 80 FR 10618, Feb. 27, 2015]

§ 405.927 Initial determinations subject to the reopenings process.

Minor errors or omissions in an initial determination must be corrected only through the contractor's reopenings process under § 405.980(a)(3).

§ 405.928 Effect of the initial determination.

(a) An initial determination described in § 405.924(a) is binding unless it is revised or reconsidered in accordance with 20 CFR 404.907, or revised as a result of a reopening in accordance with 20 CFR 404.988.

(b) An initial determination described in § 405.924(b) is binding upon all parties to the initial determination unless—

(1) A redetermination is completed in accordance with § 405.940 through § 405.958; or

(2) The initial determination is revised as a result of a reopening in accordance with § 405.980.

(c) An initial determination listed in § 405.924(b) where a party submits a timely, valid request for redetermination under § 405.942 through § 405.944 must be processed as a redetermination under § 405.948 through § 405.958 unless the initial determination involves a clerical error or other minor error or omission.

Redeterminations

§ 405.940 Right to a redetermination.

A person or entity that may be a party to a redetermination in accordance with § 405.906(b) and that is dissatisfied with an initial determination may request a redetermination by a contractor in accordance with § 405.940 through § 405.958, regardless of the amount in controversy.

§ 405.942 Time frame for filing a request for a redetermination.

(a) Time frame for filing a request. Except as provided in paragraph (b) of this section, any request for redetermination must be filed within 120 calendar days from the date a party receives the notice of the initial determination.

(1) For purposes of this section, the date of receipt of the initial determination will be presumed to be 5 days after the date of the notice of initial determination, unless there is evidence to the contrary.

(2) The request is considered as filed on the date it is received by the contractor.

(b) Extending the time frame for filing a request. *General rule.* If the 120 calendar day period in which to file a request for a redetermination has expired and a party shows good cause, the contractor may extend the time frame for filing a request for redetermination.

(1) *How to request an extension.* A party may file a request for an extension of time for filing a request for a redetermination with the contractor. The party should include any evidence supporting the request for extension. The request for redetermination extension must—

(i) Be in writing;

(ii) State why the request for redetermination was not filed within the required time frame; and

(iii) Meet the requirements of § 405.944.

(2) *How the contractor determines if good cause exists.* In determining if a party has good cause for missing a deadline to request a redetermination, the contractor considers—

(i) The circumstances that kept the party from making the request on time;

(ii) If the contractor's action(s) misled the party; and

(iii) If the party had or has any physical, mental, educational, or linguistic limitations, including any lack of facility with the English language, that prevented the party from filing a timely request or from understanding or knowing about the need to file a timely request.

(3) *Examples of good cause.* Examples of circumstances when good cause may be found to exist include, but are not limited to, the following situations:

(i) The party was prevented by serious illness from contacting the contractor in person, in writing, or through a friend, relative, or other person; or

(ii) The party had a death or serious illness in his or her immediate family; or

(iii) Important records of the party were destroyed or damaged by fire or other accidental cause; or

(iv) The contractor gave the party incorrect or incomplete information about when and how to request a redetermination; or

(v) The party did not receive notice of the determination or decision; or

(vi) The party sent the request to a Government agency in good faith within the time limit, and the request did not reach the appropriate contractor until after the time period to file a request expired.

[70 FR 11472, Mar. 8, 2005, as amended at 74 FR 65333, Dec. 9, 2009]

§ 405.944 Place and method of filing a request for a redetermination.

(a) Filing location. The request for redetermination must be filed with the contractor indicated on the notice of initial determination.

(b) Content of redetermination request. The request for redetermination must be in writing and should be made on a standard CMS form. A written request that is not made on a standard CMS form is accepted if it contains the same required elements as follows:

(1) The beneficiary's name;

(2) The Medicare health insurance claim number;

(3) Specific service(s) and/or item(s) for which the redetermination is being requested and the specific date(s) of the service;

(4) The name and signature of the party or the representative of the party.

(c) Requests for redetermination by more than one party. If more than one party timely files a request for redetermination on the same claim before a redetermination is made on the first timely filed request, the contractor must consolidate the separate requests into one proceeding and issue one redetermination.

§ 405.946 Evidence to be submitted with the redetermination request.

(a) Evidence submitted with the request. When filing the request for redetermination, a party must explain why it disagrees with the contractor's determination and should include any evidence that the party believes should be considered by the contractor in making its redetermination.

(b) Evidence submitted after the request. When a party submits additional evidence after filing the request for redetermination, the contractor's 60 calendar day decision-making time frame is automatically extended for up to 14 calendar days for each submission.

[70 FR 11472, Mar. 8, 2005, as amended at 70 FR 37702, June 30, 2005; 74 FR 65333, Dec. 9, 2009]

§ 405.948 Conduct of a redetermination.

A redetermination consists of an independent review of an initial determination. In conducting a redetermination, the contractor reviews the evidence and findings upon which the initial determination was based, and any additional evidence the parties submit or the contractor obtains on its own. An individual who was not involved in making the initial determination must make a redetermination. The contractor may raise and develop new issues that are relevant to the claims in the particular case.

§ 405.950 Time frame for making a redetermination.

(a) General rule. The contractor mails, or otherwise transmits, written notice of the redetermination or dismissal to the parties to the redetermination at their last known addresses within 60 calendar days of the date the contractor receives a timely filed request for redetermination.

(b) Exceptions. (1) If a contractor grants an appellant's request for an extension of the 120 calendar day filing deadline made in accordance with § 405.942(b), the 60 calendar day decision-making time frame begins on the date the contractor receives the late-filed request for redetermination, or when the request for an extension is granted, whichever is later.

(2) If a contractor receives from multiple parties timely requests for redetermination of a claim determination, consistent with § 405.944(c), the contractor must issue a redetermination or dismissal within 60 calendar days of the latest filed request.

(3) If a party submits additional evidence after the request for redetermination is filed, the contractor's 60 calendar day decision-making time frame is extended for up to 14 calendar days for each submission, consistent with § 405.946(b).

[70 FR 11472, Mar. 8, 2005, as amended at 70 FR 37702, June 30, 2005; 74 FR 65333, Dec. 9, 2009]

§ 405.952 Withdrawal or dismissal of a request for a redetermination.

(a) Withdrawing a request. A party that files a request for redetermination may withdraw its request by filing a written and signed request for withdrawal. The request for withdrawal must contain a clear statement that the appellant is withdrawing the request for a redetermination and does not intend to proceed further with the appeal. The request must be received in the contractor's mailroom before a redetermination is issued. The appeal will proceed with respect to any other parties that have filed a timely request for redetermination.

(b) Dismissing a request. A contractor dismisses a redetermination request, either entirely or as to any stated issue, under any of the following circumstances:

(1) When the person or entity requesting a redetermination is not a proper party under § 405.906(b) or does not otherwise have a right to a redetermination under section 1869(a) of the Act;

(2) When the contractor determines the party failed to make out a valid request for redetermination that substantially complies with § 405.944;

(3) When the party fails to file the redetermination request within the proper filing time frame in accordance with § 405.942;

(4) When a beneficiary or the beneficiary's representative files a request for redetermination, but the beneficiary dies while the request is pending, and all of the following criteria apply:

(i) The beneficiary's surviving spouse or estate has no remaining financial interest in the case. In deciding this issue, the contractor considers if the surviving spouse or estate remains liable for the services for which payment was denied or a Medicare contractor held the beneficiary liable for subsequent similar services under the limitation of liability provisions based on the denial of payment for services at issue;

(ii) No other individual or entity with a financial interest in the case wishes to pursue the appeal; and

(iii) No other party filed a valid and timely redetermination request under §§ 405.942 and 405.944;

(5) When a party filing the redetermination request submits a timely written request for withdrawal with the contractor; or

(6) When the contractor has not issued an initial determination on the claim or the matter for which a redetermination is sought.

(c) Notice of dismissal. A contractor mails or otherwise transmits a written notice of the dismissal of the redetermination request to the parties at their last known addresses. The notice states that there is a right to request that the contractor vacate the dismissal action.

(d) Vacating a dismissal. If good and sufficient cause is established, a contractor may vacate its dismissal of a request for redetermination within 6 months from the date of the notice of dismissal.

(e) Effect of dismissal. The dismissal of a request for redetermination is final and binding, unless it is modified or reversed by a QIC under § 405.974(b) or vacated under paragraph (d) of this section.

[70 FR 11472, Mar. 8, 2005, as amended at 74 FR 65333, Dec. 9, 2009]

§ 405.954 Redetermination.

Upon the basis of the evidence of record, the contractor adjudicates the claim(s), and renders a redetermination affirming or reversing, in whole or in part, the initial determination in question.

§ 405.956 Notice of a redetermination.

(a) Notification to parties—(1) *General rule.* Written notice of a redetermination affirming, in whole or in part, the initial determination must be mailed or otherwise transmitted to all parties at their last known addresses in accordance with the time frames established in § 405.950. Written notice of a redetermination fully reversing the initial determination must be mailed or otherwise transmitted to the appellant in accordance with the time frames established in § 405.950. If the redetermination results in issuance of supplemental payment to a provider or supplier, the Medicare contractor must also issue an electronic or paper RA notice to the provider or supplier.

(2) *Overpayment cases involving multiple beneficiaries who have no liability.* In an overpayment case involving multiple beneficiaries who have no liability, the contractor may issue a written notice only to the appellant.

(b) Content of the notice for affirmations, in whole or in part. For decisions that are affirmations, in whole or in part, of the initial determination, the redetermination must be written in a manner calculated to be understood by a beneficiary, and contain—

(1) A clear statement indicating the extent to which the redetermination is favorable or unfavorable;

(2) A summary of the facts, including, as appropriate, a summary of the clinical or scientific evidence used in making the redetermination;

(3) An explanation of how pertinent laws, regulations, coverage rules, and CMS policies apply to the facts of the case;

(4) A summary of the rationale for the redetermination in clear, understandable language;

(5) Notification to the parties of their right to a reconsideration and a description of the procedures that a party must follow in order to request a reconsideration, including the time frame within which a reconsideration must be requested;

(6) A statement of any specific missing documentation that must be submitted with a request for a reconsideration, if applicable;

(7) A statement that all evidence the appellant wishes to introduce during the claim appeals process should be submitted with the request for a reconsideration;

(8) Notification that evidence not submitted to the QIC as indicated in paragraph (b)(6) of this section, is not considered at an ALJ hearing or further appeal, unless the appellant demonstrates good cause as to why that evidence was not provided previously; and

(9) The procedures for obtaining additional information concerning the redetermination, such as specific provisions of the policy, manual, or regulation used in making the redetermination.

(10) Any other requirements specified by CMS.

(c) Content of the notice for a full reversal. For decisions that are full reversals of the initial determination, the redetermination must be in writing and contain—

(1) A clear statement indicating that the redetermination is wholly favorable;

(2) Any other requirements specified by CMS.

(d) Exception for beneficiary appeal requests. (1) The notice must inform beneficiary appellants that the requirements of paragraph (b)(8) of this section are not applicable for purposes of beneficiary appeals.

(2) This exception does not apply for appeal requests from beneficiaries who are represented by providers or suppliers.

§ 405.958 Effect of a redetermination.

In accordance with section 1869(a)(3)(D) of the Act, once a redetermination is issued, it becomes part of the initial determination. The redetermination is binding upon all parties unless—

(a) A reconsideration is completed in accordance with § 405.960 through § 405.978; or

(b) The redetermination is revised as a result of a reopening in accordance with § 405.980.

[70 FR 11472, Mar. 8, 2005, as amended at 74 FR 65333, Dec. 9, 2009]

Reconsideration

§ 405.960 Right to a reconsideration.

A person or entity that is a party to a redetermination made by a contractor as described under § 405.940 through § 405.958, and is dissatisfied with that determination, may request a reconsideration by a QIC in accordance with § 405.962 through § 405.966, regardless of the amount in controversy.

§ 405.962 Timeframe for filing a request for a reconsideration.

(a) Timeframe for filing a request. Except as provided in paragraph (b) of this section and in § 504.974(b)(1), regarding a request for QIC reconsideration of a contractor's dismissal of a redetermination request, any request for a reconsideration must be filed within 180 calendar days from the date the party receives the notice of the redetermination.

(1) For purposes of this section, the date of receipt of the redetermination will be presumed to be 5 calendar days after the date of the notice of redetermination, unless there is evidence to the contrary.

(2) For purposes of meeting the 180 calendar day filing deadline, the request is considered as filed on the date it is received by the QIC.

(b) Extending the time for filing a request—(1) *General rule.* A QIC may extend the 180 calendar day timeframe for filing a request for reconsideration for good cause.

(2) *How to request an extension.* A party to the redetermination must file its request for an extension of the time for filing the reconsideration request with its request for reconsideration. A party should include evidence to support the request for extension. The request for reconsideration and request for extension must—

(i) Be in writing;

(ii) State why the request for reconsideration was not filed within the required timeframe; and

(iii) Meet the requirements of § 405.964.

(3) *How the QIC determines whether good cause exists.* In determining whether a party has good cause for missing a deadline to request reconsideration, the QIC applies the good cause provisions contained in § 405.942(b)(2) and (b)(3).

[70 FR 11472, Mar. 8, 2005, as amended at 74 FR 65334, Dec. 9, 2009]

§ 405.964 Place and method of filing a request for a reconsideration.

(a) Filing location. The request for reconsideration must be filed with the QIC indicated on the notice of redetermination.

(b) Content of reconsideration request. The request for reconsideration must be in writing and should be made on a standard CMS form. A written request that is not made on a standard CMS form is accepted if it contains the same required elements, as follows:

(1) The beneficiary's name;

(2) Medicare health insurance claim number;

(3) Specific service(s) and item(s) for which the reconsideration is requested and the specific date(s) of service;

(4) The name and signature of the party or the representative of the party; and

(5) The name of the contractor that made the redetermination.

(c) Requests for reconsideration by more than one party. If more than one party timely files a request for reconsideration on the same claim before a reconsideration is made on the first timely filed request, the QIC must consolidate the separate requests into one proceeding and issue one reconsideration.

§ 405.966 Evidence to be submitted with the reconsideration request.

(a) Evidence submitted with the request. When filing a request for reconsideration, a party should present evidence and allegations of fact or law related to the issue in dispute and explain why it disagrees with the initial determination, including the redetermination.

(1) This evidence must include any missing documentation identified in the notice of redetermination, consistent with § 405.956(b)(6).

(2) Absent good cause, failure to submit all evidence, including documentation requested in the notice of redetermination prior to the issuance of the notice of reconsideration precludes subsequent consideration of that evidence.

(b) Evidence submitted after the request. Each time a party submits additional evidence after filing the request for reconsideration, the QIC's 60 calendar day decisionmaking timeframe is automatically extended by up to 14 calendar days for each submission. This extension does not apply to timely submissions of documentation specifically requested by a QIC, unless the documentation was originally requested in the notice of redetermination.

(c) Exception for beneficiaries and State Medicaid Agencies that file reconsideration requests. (1) Beneficiaries and State Medicaid Agencies that file requests for reconsideration are not required to comply with the requirements of paragraph (a) of this section. However, the automatic 14 calendar day extension described in paragraph (b) of this section applies to each evidence submission made after the request for reconsideration is filed.

(2) Beneficiaries who are represented by providers or suppliers must comply with the requirements of paragraph (a) of this section.

[70 FR 11472, Mar. 8, 2005, as amended at 74 FR 65334, Dec. 9, 2009]

§ 405.968 Conduct of a reconsideration.

(a) General rules. (1) A reconsideration consists of an independent, on-the-record review of an initial determination, including the redetermination and all issues related to payment of the claim. In conducting a reconsideration, the QIC reviews the evidence and findings upon which the initial determination, including the redetermination, was based, and any additional evidence the parties submit or that the QIC obtains on its own. If the initial determination involves a finding on whether an item or service is reasonable and necessary for the diagnosis or treatment of illness or injury (under section 1862(a)(1)(A) of the Act), a QIC's reconsideration must involve consideration by a panel of physicians or other appropriate health care professionals, and be based on clinical experience, the patient's medical records, and medical, technical, and scientific evidence of record to the extent applicable.

(b) Authority of the QIC. (1) National coverage determinations (NCDs), CMS Rulings, and applicable laws and regulations are binding on the QIC.

(2) QICs are not bound by LCDs, LMRPs, or CMS program guidance, such as program memoranda and manual instructions, but give substantial deference to these policies if they are applicable to a particular case. A QIC may decline to follow a policy, if the QIC determines, either at a party's request or at its own discretion, that the policy does not apply to the facts of the particular case.

(3) If a QIC declines to follow a policy in a particular case, the QIC's reconsideration explains the reasons why the policy was not followed.

(4) A QIC's decision to decline to follow a policy under this section applies only to the specific claim being reconsidered and does not have precedential effect.

(5) A QIC may raise and develop new issues that are relevant to the claims in a particular case provided that the contractor rendered a redetermination with respect to the claims.

(c) Qualifications of the QIC's panel members. (1) Members of a QIC's panel who conduct reconsiderations must have sufficient medical, legal, and other expertise, including knowledge of the Medicare program.

(2) When a redetermination is made with respect to whether an item or service is reasonable and necessary (section 1862(a)(1)(A) of the Act), the QIC designates a panel of physicians or other appropriate health care professionals to consider the facts and circumstances of the redetermination.

(3) Where a claim pertains to the furnishing of treatment by a physician, or the provision of items or services by a physician, a reviewing professional must be a physician.

(d) Disqualification of a QIC panel member. No physician or health care professional employed by or otherwise working for a QIC may review determinations regarding—

(1) Health care services furnished to a patient if that physician or health care professional was directly responsible for furnishing those services; or

(2) Health care services provided in or by an institution, organization, or agency, if that physician or health care professional or any member of the physician's family or health care professional's family has, directly or indirectly, a

significant financial interest in that institution, organization, or agency (see the term family member as defined in § 405.902).

§ 405.970 Timeframe for making a reconsideration.

(a) General rule. Within 60 calendar days of the date the QIC receives a timely filed request for reconsideration or any additional time provided by paragraph (b) of this section, the QIC mails, or otherwise transmits to the parties at their last known addresses, written notice of—

(1) The reconsideration;

(2) Its inability to complete its review within 60 days in accordance with paragraphs (c) through (e) of this section; or

(3) Dismissal.

(b) Exceptions. (1) If a QIC grants an appellant's request for an extension of the 180 calendar day filing deadline made in accordance with Sec. 405.962(b), the QIC's 60 calendar day decision-making timeframe begins on the date the QIC receives the late filed request for reconsideration, or when the request for an extension that meets the requirements of § 405.962(b) is granted, whichever is later.

(2) If a QIC receives timely requests for reconsideration from multiple parties, consistent with § 405.964(c), the QIC must issue a reconsideration, notice that it cannot complete its review, or dismissal within 60 days for each submission of the latest filed request.

(3) Each time a party submits additional evidence after the request for reconsideration is filed, the QIC's 60 calendar day decisionmaking timeframe is extended by up to 14 days for each submission, consistent with § 405.966(b).

(c) Responsibilities of the QIC. Within 60 calendar days of receiving a request for a reconsideration, or any additional time provided for under paragraph (b) of this section, a QIC must take one of the following actions:

(1) Notify all parties of its reconsideration, consistent with § 405.976.

(2) Notify the parties that it cannot complete the reconsideration by the deadline specified in paragraph (b) of this section and offer the appellant the opportunity to escalate the appeal to an ALJ. The QIC continues to process the reconsideration unless it receives a written request from the appellant to escalate the case to an ALJ after the adjudication period has expired.

(d) Responsibilities of the appellant. If an appellant wishes to exercise the option of escalating the case to an ALJ, the appellant must notify the QIC in writing.

(e) Actions following appellant's notice. (1) If the appellant fails to notify the QIC, or notifies the QIC that the appellant does not choose to escalate the case, the QIC completes its reconsideration and notifies the appellant of its action consistent with § 405.972 or § 405.976.

(2) If the appellant notifies the QIC that the appellant wishes to escalate the case, the QIC must take one of the following actions within 5 calendar days of

receipt of the notice or 5 calendar days from the end of the applicable adjudication period under paragraph (a) or (b) of this section:

(i) Complete its reconsideration and notify all parties of its decision consistent with § 405.972 or § 405.976.

(ii) Acknowledge the escalation notice in writing and forward the case file to the ALJ hearing office.

[70 FR 11472, Mar. 8, 2005, as amended at 70 FR 37702, June 30, 2005; 74 FR 65334, Dec. 9, 2009]

§ 405.972 Withdrawal or dismissal of a request for a reconsideration.

(a) Withdrawing a request. An appellant that files a request for reconsideration may withdraw its request by filing a written and signed request for withdrawal. The request for withdrawal must—

(1) Contain a clear statement that the appellant is withdrawing the request for reconsideration and does not intend to proceed further with the appeal.

(2) Be received in the QIC's mailroom before the reconsideration is issued.

(b) Dismissing a request. A QIC dismisses a reconsideration request, either entirely or as to any stated issue, under any of the following circumstances:

(1) When the person or entity requesting reconsideration is not a proper party under § 405.906(b) or does not otherwise have a right to a reconsideration under section 1869(b) of the Act;

(2) When the QIC determines that the party failed to make out a valid request for reconsideration that substantially complies with § 405.964(a) and (b);

(3) When the party fails to file the reconsideration request in accordance with the timeframes established in § 405.962, or fails to file the request for reconsideration of a contractor's dismissal of a redetermination request in accordance with the timeframes established in § 405.974(b)(1);

(4) When a beneficiary or the beneficiary's representative files a request for reconsideration, but the beneficiary dies while the request is pending, and all of the following criteria apply:

(i) The beneficiary's surviving spouse or estate has no remaining financial interest in the case. In deciding this issue, the QIC considers if the surviving spouse or estate remains liable for the services for which payment was denied or a Medicare contractor held the beneficiary liable for subsequent similar services under the limitation of liability provisions based on the denial of payment for services at issue;

(ii) No other individual or entity with a financial interest in the case wishes to pursue the appeal; and

(iii) No other party to the redetermination filed a valid and timely request for reconsideration under §§ 405.962 and 405.964.

(5) When a party filing for the reconsideration submits a written request of withdrawal to the QIC and satisfies the criteria set forth in paragraph (a) of this section before the reconsideration has been issued; or

(6) When the contractor has not issued a redetermination on the initial determination for which a reconsideration is sought.

(c) Notice of dismissal. A QIC mails or otherwise transmits written notice of the dismissal of the reconsideration request to the parties at their last known addresses. The notice states that there is a right to request that the contractor vacate the dismissal action. The appeal will proceed with respect to any other parties that have filed a timely request for reconsideration.

(d) Vacating a dismissal. If good and sufficient cause is established, a QIC may vacate its dismissal of a request for reconsideration within 6 months of the date of the notice of dismissal.

(e) Effect of dismissal. The dismissal of a request for reconsideration is binding, unless it is modified or reversed by an ALJ under § 405.1004 or vacated under paragraph (d) of this section. The dismissal of a request for reconsideration of a contractor's dismissal of a redetermination request is binding and not subject to further review unless vacated under paragraph (d) of this section.

[70 FR 11472, Mar. 8, 2005, as amended at 74 FR 65334, Dec. 9, 2009]

§ 405.974 Reconsideration.

(a) Reconsideration of a contractor determination. Except as provided in § 405.972, upon the basis of the evidence of record, the QIC must issue a reconsideration affirming or reversing, in whole or in part, the initial determination, including the redetermination, in question.

(b) Reconsideration of contractor's dismissal of a redetermination request. (1) A party to a contractor's dismissal of a request for redetermination has a right to have the dismissal reviewed by a QIC, if the party files a written request for review of the dismissal with the QIC within 60 calendar days after receipt of the contractor's notice of dismissal.

(i) For purposes of this section, the date of receipt of the contractor's notice of dismissal is presumed to be 5 calendar days after the date of the notice of dismissal, unless there is evidence to the contrary.

(ii) For purposes of meeting the 60 calendar day filing deadline, the request is considered as filed on the date it is received by the QIC indicated on the notice of dismissal.

(2) If the QIC determines that the contractor's dismissal was in error, it vacates the dismissal and remands the case to the contractor for a redetermination.

(3) A QIC's reconsideration of a contractor's dismissal of a redetermination request is binding and not subject to further review.

[70 FR 11472, Mar. 8, 2005, as amended at 70 FR 37703, June 30, 2005; 74 FR 65334, Dec. 9, 2009]

§ 405.976 Notice of a reconsideration.

(a) Notification to parties—(1) *General rules.* (i) Written notice of the reconsideration must be mailed or otherwise transmitted to all parties at their last known addresses, in accordance with the timeframes established in § 405.970(a) or (b).

(ii) The notice must be written in a manner reasonably calculated to be understood by a beneficiary.

(iii) The QIC must promptly notify the entity responsible for payment of claims under Part A or Part B of its reconsideration. If the reconsideration results in issuance of supplemental payment to a provider or supplier, the Medicare contractor must also issue an electronic or paper RA notice to the provider or supplier.

(2) *Overpayment cases involving multiple beneficiaries who have no liability.* In an overpayment case involving multiple beneficiaries who have no liability, the QIC may issue a written notice only to the appellant.

(b) Content of the notice. The reconsideration must be in writing and contain—

(1) A clear statement indicating whether the reconsideration is favorable or unfavorable;

(2) A summary of the facts, including as appropriate, a summary of the clinical or scientific evidence used in making the reconsideration;

(3) An explanation of how pertinent laws, regulations, coverage rules, and CMS policies, apply to the facts of the case, including, where applicable, the rationale for declining to follow an LCD, LMRP, or CMS program guidance;

(4) In the case of a determination on whether an item or service is reasonable or necessary under section 1862(a)(1)(A) of the Act, an explanation of the medical and scientific rationale for the decision;

(5) A summary of the rationale for the reconsideration.

(i) If the notice of redetermination indicated that specific documentation should be submitted with the reconsideration request, and the documentation was not submitted with the request for reconsideration, the summary must indicate how the missing documentation affected the reconsideration; and

(ii) The summary must also specify that, consistent with §§ 405.956(b)(8) and 405.966(b), all evidence, including evidence requested in the notice of redetermination, that is not submitted prior to the issuance of the reconsideration will not be considered at an ALJ level, or made part of the administrative record, unless the appellant demonstrates good cause as to why the evidence was not provided prior to the issuance of the QIC's reconsideration. This requirement does not apply to beneficiaries, unless the beneficiary is represented by a provider or supplier or to State Medicaid Agencies;

(6) Information concerning to the parties' right to an ALJ hearing, including the applicable amount in controversy requirement and aggregation provisions;

(7) A statement of whether the amount in controversy needed for an ALJ hearing is met when the reconsideration is partially or fully unfavorable;

(8) A description of the procedures that a party must follow in order to obtain an ALJ hearing of an expedited reconsideration, including the time frame under which a request for an ALJ hearing must be filed;

(9) If appropriate, advice as to the requirements for use of the expedited access to judicial review process set forth in § 405.990;

(10) The procedures for obtaining additional information concerning the reconsideration, such as specific provisions of the policy, manual, or regulation used in making the reconsideration; and

(11) Any other requirements specified by CMS.

§ 405.978 Effect of a reconsideration.

A reconsideration is binding on all parties, unless—

(a) An ALJ decision is issued in accordance to a request for an ALJ hearing made in accordance with § 405.1014;

(b) A review entity issues a decision in accordance to a request for expedited access to judicial review under § 405.990; or

(c) The reconsideration is revised as a result of a reopening in accordance with § 405.980.

[70 FR 11472, Mar. 8, 2005, as amended at 74 FR 65334, Dec. 9, 2009]

Reopenings

§ 405.980 Reopenings of initial determinations, redeterminations, and reconsiderations, hearings and reviews.

(a) General rules. (1) A reopening is a remedial action taken to change a binding determination or decision that resulted in either an overpayment or underpayment, even though the binding determination or decision may have been correct at the time it was made based on the evidence of record. That action may be taken by—

(i) A contractor to revise the initial determination or redetermination;

(ii) A QIC to revise the reconsideration;

(iii) An ALJ to revise the hearing decision; or

(iv) The MAC to revise the hearing or review decision.

(2) If a contractor issues a denial of a claim because it did not receive requested documentation during medical review and the party subsequently requests a redetermination, the contractor must process the request as a reopening.

(3) Notwithstanding paragraph (a)(4) of this section, a contractor must process clerical errors (which includes minor errors and omissions) as reopenings, instead of as redeterminations as specified in § 405.940. If the contractor receives a request for reopening and disagrees that the issue is a clerical error, the contractor must dismiss the reopening request and advise the party of any appeal rights, provided the timeframe to request an appeal on the original denial has not expired. For purposes of this section, clerical error includes human or mechanical errors on the part of the party or the contractor such as—

(i) Mathematical or computational mistakes;

(ii) Inaccurate data entry; or

(iii) Denials of claims as duplicates.

(4) When a party has filed a valid request for an appeal of an initial determination, redetermination, reconsideration, hearing, or MAC review, no adjudicator has jurisdiction to reopen an issue on a claim that is under appeal until all appeal rights for that issue are exhausted. Once the appeal rights for the issue have been exhausted, the contractor, QIC, ALJ, or MAC may reopen as set forth in this section.

(5) The contractor's, QIC's, ALJ's, or MAC's decision on whether to reopen is binding and not subject to appeal.

(6) A determination under the Medicare secondary payer provisions of section 1862(b) of the Act that Medicare has an MSP recovery claim for services or items that were already reimbursed by the Medicare program is not a reopening, except where the recovery claim is based upon a provider's or supplier's failure to demonstrate that it filed a proper claim as defined in part 411 of this chapter.

(b) Time frames and requirements for reopening initial determinations and redeterminations initiated by a contractor. A contractor may reopen and revise its initial determination or redetermination on its own motion—

(1) Within 1 year from the date of the initial determination or redetermination for any reason.

(2) Within 4 years from the date of the initial determination or redetermination for good cause as defined in § 405.986.

(3) At any time if there exists reliable evidence as defined in § 405.902 that the initial determination was procured by fraud or similar fault as defined in § 405.902.

(4) At anytime if the initial determination is unfavorable, in whole or in part, to the party thereto, but only for the purpose of correcting a clerical error on which that determination was based.

(5) At any time to effectuate a decision issued under the coverage appeals process.

(c) Time frame and requirements for reopening initial determinations and redeterminations requested by a party. (1) A party may request that a contractor reopen its initial determination or redetermination within 1 year from the date of the initial determination or redetermination for any reason.

(2) A party may request that a contractor reopen its initial determination or redetermination within 4 years from the date of the initial determination or redetermination for good cause in accordance with § 405.986.

(3) A party may request that a contractor reopen its initial determination at any time if the initial determination is unfavorable, in whole or in part, to the party thereto, but only for the purpose of correcting a clerical error on which that determination was based. Third party payer error does not constitute clerical error. *See* § 405.986(c).

(d) Time frame and requirements for reopening reconsiderations, hearing decisions and reviews initiated by a QIC, ALJ, or the MAC. (1) A QIC may reopen its reconsideration on its own motion within 180 calendar days from the date of the reconsideration for good cause in accordance with § 405.986. If the QIC's reconsideration was procured by fraud or similar fault, then the QIC may reopen at any time.

(2) An ALJ or the MAC may reopen a hearing decision on its own motion within 180 calendar days from the date of the decision for good cause in accordance with § 405.986. If the hearing decision was procured by fraud or similar fault, then the ALJ or the MAC may reopen at any time.

(3) The MAC may reopen its review decision on its own motion within 180 days from the date of the review decision for good cause in accordance with § 405.986. If the MAC's decision was procured by fraud or similar fault, then the MAC may reopen at any time.

(e) Time frames and requirements for reopening reconsiderations, hearing decisions, and reviews requested by a party. (1) A party to a reconsideration may request that a QIC reopen its reconsideration within 180 calendar days from the date of the reconsideration for good cause in accordance with § 405.986.

(2) A party to a hearing may request that an ALJ or the MAC reopen a hearing decision within 180 days from the date of the hearing decision for good cause in accordance with § 405.986.

(3) A party to a review may request that the MAC reopen its decision within 180 calendar days from the date of the review decision for good cause in accordance with § 405.986.

[70 FR 11472, Mar. 8, 2005, as amended at 70 FR 37703, June 30, 2005; 74 FR 65334, Dec. 9, 2009]

§ 405.982 Notice of a revised determination or decision.

(a) When adjudicators initiate reopenings. When any determination or decision is reopened and revised as provided in § 405.980, the contractor, QIC, ALJ, or the MAC must mail its revised determination or decision to the parties to that determination or decision at their last known address. In the case of a full or partial reversal resulting in issuance of a payment to a provider or supplier, a revised electronic or paper remittance advice notice must be issued by the Medicare contractor. An adverse revised determination or decision must state the rationale and basis for the reopening and revision and any right to appeal.

(b) Reopenings initiated at the request of a party. The contractor, QIC, ALJ, or the MAC must mail its revised determination or decision to the parties to that determination or decision at their last known address. In the case of a full or partial reversal resulting in issuance of a payment to a provider or supplier, a revised electronic or paper remittance advice notice must be issued by the Medicare contractor. An adverse revised determination or decision must state the rationale and basis for the reopening and revision and any right to appeal.

§ 405.984 Effect of a revised determination or decision.

(a) Initial determinations. The revision of an initial determination is binding upon all parties unless a party files a written request for a redetermination that is accepted and processed in accordance with § 405.940 through § 405.958.

(b) Redeterminations. The revision of a redetermination is binding upon all parties unless a party files a written request for a QIC reconsideration that is accepted and processed in accordance with § 405.960 through § 405.978.

(c) Reconsiderations. The revision of a reconsideration is binding upon all parties unless a party files a written request for an ALJ hearing that is accepted and processed in accordance with § 405.1000 through § 405.1064.

(d) ALJ Hearing decisions. The revision of a hearing decision is binding upon all parties unless a party files a written request for a MAC review that is accepted and processed in accordance with § 405.1100 through § 405.1130.

(e) MAC review. The revision of a MAC review is binding upon all parties unless a party files a civil action in which a Federal district court accepts jurisdiction and issues a decision.

(f) Appeal of only the portion of the determination or decision revised by the reopening. Only the portion of the initial determination, redetermination, reconsideration, or hearing decision revised by the reopening may be subsequently appealed.

(g) Effect of a revised determination or decision. A revised determination or decision is binding unless it is appealed or otherwise reopened.

§ 405.986 Good cause for reopening.

(a) Establishing good cause. Good cause may be established when—

(1) There is new and material evidence that—

(i) Was not available or known at the time of the determination or decision; and

(ii) May result in a different conclusion; or

(2) The evidence that was considered in making the determination or decision clearly shows on its face that an obvious error was made at the time of the determination or decision.

(b) Change in substantive law or interpretative policy. A change of legal interpretation or policy by CMS in a regulation, CMS ruling, or CMS general instruction, or a change in legal interpretation or policy by SSA in a regulation, SSA ruling, or SSA general instruction in entitlement appeals, whether made in response to judicial precedent or otherwise, is not a basis for reopening a determination or hearing decision under this section. This provision does not preclude contractors from conducting re-openings to effectuate coverage decisions issued under the authority granted by section 1869(f) of the Act.

(c) Third party payer error. A request to reopen a claim based upon a third party payer's error in making a primary payment determination when Medicare processed the claim in accordance with the information in its system of records or on the claim form does not constitute good cause for reopening.

[70 FR 11472, Mar. 8, 2005, as amended at 70 FR 37703, June 30, 2005]

Expedited Access to Judicial Review

§ 405.990 Expedited access to judicial review.

(a) Process for expedited access to judicial review. (1) For purposes of this section, a "review entity" means an entity of up to three reviewers who are ALJs or members of the Departmental Appeals Board (DAB), as determined by the Secretary.

(2) In order to obtain expedited access to judicial review (EAJR), a review entity must certify that the Medicare Appeals Council (MAC) does not have the authority to decide the question of law or regulation relevant to the matters in dispute and that there is no material issue of fact in dispute.

(3) A party may make a request for EAJR only once with respect to a question of law or regulation for a specific matter in dispute in an appeal.

(b) Conditions for making the expedited appeals request. (1) A party may request EAJR in place of an ALJ hearing or MAC review if the following conditions are met:

(i) A QIC has made a reconsideration determination and the party has filed a request for—

(A) An ALJ hearing in accordance with § 405.1002 and a final decision of the ALJ has not been issued;

(B) MAC review in accordance with § 405.1102 and a final decision of the MAC has not been issued; or

(ii) The appeal has been escalated from the QIC to the ALJ level after the period described in § 405.970(a) and § 405.970(b) has expired, and the QIC does not issue a final action within the time frame described in § 405.970(e).

(2) The requestor is a party, as defined in paragraph (e) of this section.

(3) The amount remaining in controversy meets the requirements of § 405.1006(b) or (c).

(4) If there is more than one party to the reconsideration, hearing, or MAC review, each party concurs, in writing, with the request for the EAJR.

(5) There are no material issues of fact in dispute.

(c) Content of the request for EAJR. The request for EAJR must—

(1) Allege that there are no material issues of fact in dispute and identify the facts that the requestor considers material and that are not disputed; and

(2) Assert that the only factor precluding a decision favorable to the requestor is—

(i) A statutory provision that is unconstitutional, or a provision of a regulation or national coverage determination and specify the statutory provision that the requestor considers unconstitutional or the provision of a regulation or a national coverage determination that the requestor considers invalid, or

(ii) A CMS Ruling that the requester considers invalid;

(3) Include a copy of any QIC reconsideration and of any ALJ hearing decision that the requester has received;

(4) If any QIC reconsideration or ALJ hearing decision was based on facts that the requestor is disputing, state why the requestor considers those facts to be immaterial; and

(5) If any QIC reconsideration or ALJ hearing decision was based on a provision of a law, regulation, national coverage determination or CMS Ruling in addition to the one the requestor considers unconstitutional or invalid, a statement as to why further administrative review of how that provision applies to the facts is not necessary.

(d) Place and time for an EAJR request—(1) *Method and place for filing request.* The requestor may include an EAJR request in his or her request for an ALJ hearing or MAC review, or, if an appeal is already pending with an ALJ or the MAC, file a written EAJR request with the ALJ hearing office or MAC where the appeal is being considered. The ALJ hearing office or MAC forwards the request to the review entity within 5 calendar days of receipt.

(2) *Time of filing request.* The party may file a request for the EAJR—

(i) If the party has requested a hearing, at any time before receipt of the notice of the ALJ's decision; or

(ii) If the party has requested MAC review, at any time before receipt of notice of the MAC's decision.

(e) Parties to the EAJR. The parties to the EAJR are the persons or entities who were parties to the QIC's reconsideration determination and, if applicable, to the ALJ hearing.

(f) Determination on EAJR request. (1) The review entity described in paragraph (a) of this section will determine whether the request for EAJR meets all of the requirements of paragraphs (b), (c), and (d) of this section.

(2) Within 60 calendar days after the date the review entity receives a request and accompanying documents and materials meeting the conditions in paragraphs (b), (c), and (d) of this section, the review entity will issue either a certification in accordance to paragraph (g) of this section or a denial of the request.

(3) A determination by the review entity either certifying that the requirements for EAJR are met pursuant to paragraph (g) of this section or denying the request is final and not subject to review by the Secretary.

(4) If the review entity fails to make a determination within the time frame specified in paragraph (f)(2) of this section, then the requestor may bring a civil action in Federal district court within 60 calendar days of the end of the time frame.

(g) Certification by the review entity. If a party meets the requirements for the EAJR, the review entity certifies in writing that—

(1) The material facts involved in the claim are not in dispute;

(2) Except as indicated in paragraph (g)(3) of this section, the Secretary's interpretation of the law is not in dispute;

(3) The sole issue(s) in dispute is the constitutionality of a statutory provision, or the validity of a provision of a regulation, CMS Ruling, or national coverage determination;

(4) But for the provision challenged, the requestor would receive a favorable decision on the ultimate issue (such as whether a claim should be paid); and

(5) The certification by the review entity is the Secretary's final action for purposes of seeking expedited judicial review.

(h) Effect of certification by the review entity. If an EAJR request results in a certification described in paragraph (g) of this section—

(1) The party that requested the EAJR is considered to have waived any right to completion of the remaining steps of the administrative appeals process regarding the matter certified.

(2) The requestor has 60 calendar days, beginning on the date of the review entity's certification within which to bring a civil action in Federal district court.

(3) The requestor must satisfy the requirements for venue under section 1869(b)(2)(C)(iii) of the Act, as well as the requirements for filing a civil action in a Federal district court under § 405.1136(a) and § 405.1136(c) through § 405.1136(f).

(i) Rejection of EAJR. (1) If a request for EAJR request does not meet all the conditions set out in paragraphs (b), (c) and (d) of this section, or if the review entity does not certify a request for EAJR, the review entity advises in writing all parties that the request has been denied, and returns the request to the ALJ hearing office or the MAC, which will treat it as a request for hearing or for MAC review, as appropriate.

(2) Whenever a review entity forwards a rejected EAJR request to an ALJ hearing office or the MAC, the appeal is considered timely filed and the 90 calendar day decision making time frame begins on the day the request is received by the hearing office or the MAC.

(j) Interest on any amounts in controversy. (1) If a provider or supplier is granted judicial review in accordance with this section, the amount in controversy, if any, is subject to annual interest beginning on the first day of the first month beginning after the 60 calendar day period as determined in accordance with paragraphs (f)(4) or (h)(2) of this section, as applicable.

(2) The interest is awarded by the reviewing court and payable to a prevailing party.

(3) The rate of interest is equal to the rate of interest applicable to obligations issued for purchase by the Federal Supplementary Medical Insurance Trust Fund for the month in which the civil action authorized under this subpart is commenced.

(4) No interest awarded in accordance with this paragraph shall be income or cost for purposes of determining reimbursement due to providers or suppliers under Medicare.

[70 FR 11472, Mar. 8, 2005, as amended at 70 FR 37703, June 30, 2005; 74 FR 65334, Dec. 9, 2009]

ALJ Hearings

§ 405.1000 Hearing before an ALJ: General rule.

(a) If a party is dissatisfied with a QIC's reconsideration or if the adjudication period specified in § 405.970 for the QIC to complete its reconsideration has elapsed, the party may request a hearing.

(b) A hearing may be conducted in-person, by video teleconference (VTC), or by telephone. At the hearing, the parties may submit evidence (subject to the restrictions in § 405.1018 and § 405.1028), examine the evidence used in making the determination under review, and present and/or question witnesses.

(c) In some circumstances, a representative of CMS or its contractor, including the QIC, QIO, fiscal intermediary or carrier, may participate in or join the hearing as a party. (*See,* § 405.1010 and § 405.1012).

(d) The ALJ conducts a *de novo* review and issues a decision based on the hearing record.

(e) If all parties to the hearing waive their right to appear at the hearing in person or by telephone or video teleconference, the ALJ may make a decision based on the evidence that is in the file and any new evidence that is submitted for consideration.

(f) The ALJ may require the parties to participate in a hearing if it is necessary to decide the case. If the ALJ determines that it is necessary to obtain testimony from a non-party, he or she may hold a hearing to obtain that testimony, even if all of the parties have waived the right to appear. In that event, however, the ALJ will give the parties the opportunity to appear when the testimony is given, but may hold the hearing even if none of the parties decide to appear.

(g) An ALJ may also issue a decision on the record on his or her own initiative if the evidence in the hearing record supports a fully favorable finding.

[70 FR 11472, Mar. 8, 2005, as amended at 74 FR 65334, Dec. 9, 2009]

§ 405.1002 Right to an ALJ hearing.

(a) A party to a QIC reconsideration may request a hearing before an ALJ if—

(1) The party files a written request for an ALJ hearing within 60 calendar days after receipt of the notice of the QIC's reconsideration.

(2) The party meets the amount in controversy requirements of § 405.1006.

(3) For purposes of this section, the date of receipt of the reconsideration is presumed to be 5 calendar days after the date of the reconsideration, unless there is evidence to the contrary.

(4) For purposes of meeting the 60 calendar day filing deadline, the request is considered as filed on the date it is received by the entity specified in the QIC's reconsideration.

(b) A party who files a timely appeal before a QIC and whose appeal continues to be pending before a QIC at the end of the period described in § 405.970 has a right to a hearing before an ALJ if—

(1) The party files a written request with the QIC to escalate the appeal to the ALJ level after the period described in § 405.970(a) and (b) has expired and the party files the request in accordance with § 405.970(d);

(2) The QIC does not issue a final action within 5 days of receiving the request for escalation in accordance with § 405.970(e)(2); and

(3) The party has an amount remaining in controversy specified in § 405.1006.

[70 FR 11472, Mar. 8, 2005, as amended at 70 FR 37703, June 30, 2005; 74 FR 65335, Dec. 9, 2009]

§ 405.1004 Right to ALJ review of QIC notice of dismissal.

(a) A party to a QIC's dismissal of a request for reconsideration has a right to have the dismissal reviewed by an ALJ if—

(1) The party files a written request for an ALJ review within 60 calendar days after receipt of the notice of the QIC's dismissal.

(2) The party meets the amount in controversy requirements of § 405.1006.

(3) For purposes of this section, the date of receipt of the QIC's dismissal is presumed to be 5 calendar days after the date of the dismissal notice, unless there is evidence to the contrary.

(4) For purposes of meeting the 60 calendar day filing deadline, the request is considered as filed on the date it is received by the entity specified in the QIC's dismissal.

(b) If the ALJ determines that the QIC's dismissal was in error, he or she vacates the dismissal and remands the case to the QIC for a reconsideration.

(c) An ALJ's decision regarding a QIC's dismissal of a reconsideration request is binding and not subject to further review. The dismissal of a request for ALJ review of a QIC's dismissal of a reconsideration request is binding and not subject to further review, unless vacated by the MAC under § 405.1108(b).

[70 FR 11472, Mar. 8, 2005, as amended at 70 FR 37703, June 30, 2005; 74 FR 65335, Dec. 9, 2009]

§ 405.1006 Amount in controversy required to request an ALJ hearing and judicial review.

(a) Definitions. For the purposes of aggregating claims to meet the amount in controversy requirement for an ALJ hearing or judicial review:

(1) "Common issues of law and fact" means the claims sought to be aggregated are denied, or payment is reduced, for similar reasons and arise from a similar fact pattern material to the reason the claims are denied or payment is reduced.

(2) "Delivery of similar or related services" means like or coordinated services or items provided to one or more beneficiaries.

(b) ALJ review. To be entitled to a hearing before an ALJ, the party must meet the amount in controversy requirements of this section.

(1) For ALJ hearing requests, the required amount remaining in controversy must be $100 increased by the percentage increase in the medical care component of the consumer price index for all urban consumers (U.S. city average) as measured from July 2003 to the July preceding the current year involved.

(2) If the figure in paragraph (b)(1) of this section is not a multiple of $10, then it is rounded to the nearest multiple of $10. The Secretary will publish

changes to the amount in controversy requirement in the Federal Register when necessary.

(c) Judicial review. To be entitled to judicial review, a party must meet the amount in controversy requirements of this subpart at the time it requests judicial review.

(1) For review requests, the required amount remaining in controversy must be $1,000 or more, adjusted as specified in paragraphs (b)(1) and (b)(2) of this section.

(2) [Reserved]

(d) Calculating the amount remaining in controversy. (1) The amount remaining in controversy is computed as the actual amount charged the individual for the items and services in question, reduced by—

(i) Any Medicare payments already made or awarded for the items or services; and

(ii) Any deductible and coinsurance amounts applicable in the particular case.

(2) Notwithstanding paragraph (d)(1) of this section, when payment is made for items or services under section 1879 of the Act or § 411.400 of this chapter, or the liability of the beneficiary for those services is limited under § 411.402 of this chapter, the amount in controversy is computed as the amount that the beneficiary would have been charged for the items or services in question if those expenses were not paid under § 411.400 of this chapter or if that liability was not limited under § 411.402 of this chapter, reduced by any deductible and coinsurance amounts applicable in the particular case.

(e) Aggregating claims to meet the amount in controversy—(1) *Appealing QIC reconsiderations to the ALJ level.* Either an individual appellant or multiple appellants may aggregate two or more claims to meet the amount in controversy for an ALJ hearing if—

(i) The claims were previously reconsidered by a QIC;

(ii) The request for ALJ hearing lists all of the claims to be aggregated and is filed within 60 calendar days after receipt of all of the reconsiderations being appealed; and

(iii) The ALJ determines that the claims that a single appellant seeks to aggregate involve the delivery of similar or related services, or the claims that multiple appellants seek to aggregate involve common issues of law and fact. Part A and Part B claims may be combined to meet the amount in controversy requirements.

(2) *Aggregating claims that are escalated from the QIC level to the ALJ level.* Either an individual appellant or multiple appellants may aggregate two or more claims to meet the amount in controversy for an ALJ hearing if—

(i) The claims were pending before the QIC in conjunction with the same request for reconsideration;

(ii) The appellant(s) requests aggregation of the claims to the ALJ level in the same request for escalation; and

(iii) The ALJ determines that the claims that a single appellant seeks to aggregate involve the delivery of similar or related services, or the claims that multiple appellants seek to aggregate involve common issues of law and fact. Part A and Part B claims may be combined to meet the amount in controversy requirements.

(f) Content of request for aggregation. When an appellant(s) seeks to aggregate claims in a request for an ALJ hearing, the appellant(s) must—

(1) Specify all of the claims the appellant(s) seeks to aggregate; and

(2) State why the appellant(s) believes that the claims involve common issues of law and fact or delivery of similar or related services.

[70 FR 11472, Mar. 8, 2005, as amended at 74 FR 65335, Dec. 9, 2009]

§ 405.1008 Parties to an ALJ hearing.

(a) Who may request a hearing. Any party to the QIC's reconsideration may request a hearing before an ALJ. However, only the appellant (that is, the party that filed and maintained the request for reconsideration by a QIC) may request that the appeal be escalated to the ALJ level if the QIC does not complete its action within the time frame described in § 405.970.

(b) Who are parties to the ALJ hearing. The party who filed the request for hearing and all other parties to the reconsideration are parties to the ALJ hearing. In addition, a representative of CMS or its contractor may be a party under the circumstances described in § 405.1012.

§ 405.1010 When CMS or its contractors may participate in an ALJ hearing.

(a) An ALJ may request, but may not require, CMS and/or one or more of its contractors, to participate in any proceedings before the ALJ, including the oral hearing, if any. CMS and/or one or more of its contractors, including a QIC, may also elect to participate in the hearing process.

(b) If CMS or one or more of its contractors elects to participate, it advises the ALJ, the appellant, and all other parties identified in the notice of hearing of its intent to participate no later than 10 calendar days after receiving the notice of hearing.

(c) Participation may include filing position papers or providing testimony to clarify factual or policy issues in a case, but it does not include calling witnesses or cross-examining the witnesses of a party to the hearing.

(d) When CMS or its contractor participates in an ALJ hearing, the agency or its contractor may not be called as a witness during the hearing.

(e) CMS or its contractor must submit any position papers within the time frame designated by the ALJ.

(f) The ALJ cannot draw any adverse inferences if CMS or a contractor decides not to participate in any proceedings before an ALJ, including the hearing.

[70 FR 11472, Mar. 8, 2005, as amended at 74 FR 65335, Dec. 9, 2009]

§ 405.1012 When CMS or its contractors may be a party to a hearing.

(a) CMS and/or one or more of its contractors, including a QIC, may be a party to an ALJ hearing unless the request for hearing is filed by an unrepresented beneficiary.

(b) CMS and/or the contractor(s) advises the ALJ, appellant, and all other parties identified in the notice of hearing that it intends to participate as a party no later than 10 calendar days after receiving the notice of hearing.

(c) When CMS or one or more of its contractors participate in a hearing as a party, it may file position papers, provide testimony to clarify factual or policy issues, call witnesses or cross-examine the witnesses of other parties. CMS or its contractor(s) will submit any position papers within the time frame specified by the ALJ. CMS or its contractor(s), when acting as parties, may also submit additional evidence to the ALJ within the time frame designated by the ALJ.

(d) The ALJ may not require CMS or a contractor to enter a case as a party or draw any adverse inferences if CMS or a contractor decides not to enter as a party.

[70 FR 11472, Mar. 8, 2005, as amended at 74 FR 65335, Dec. 9, 2009]

§ 405.1014 Request for an ALJ hearing.

(a) Content of the request. The request for an ALJ hearing must be made in writing. The request must include all of the following—

(1) The name, address, and Medicare health insurance claim number of the beneficiary whose claim is being appealed.

(2) The name and address of the appellant, when the appellant is not the beneficiary.

(3) The name and address of the designated representatives if any.

(4) The document control number assigned to the appeal by the QIC, if any.

(5) The dates of service.

(6) The reasons the appellant disagrees with the QIC's reconsideration or other determination being appealed.

(7) A statement of any additional evidence to be submitted and the date it will be submitted.

(b) When and where to file. The request for an ALJ hearing after a QIC reconsideration must be filed—

(1) Within 60 calendar days from the date the party receives notice of the QIC's reconsideration;

(2) With the entity specified in the QIC's reconsideration. The appellant must also send a copy of the request for hearing to the other parties. Failure to do so will toll the ALJ's 90 calendar day adjudication deadline until all parties to the QIC reconsideration receive notice of the requested ALJ hearing. If the request for hearing is timely filed with an entity other than the entity specified in the QIC's reconsideration, the deadline specified in § 405.1016 for deciding the appeal begins on the date the entity specified in the QIC's reconsideration receives the request for hearing. If the request for hearing is filed with an entity, other than the entity specified in the QIC's reconsideration, the ALJ hearing office must notify the appellant of the date of receipt of the request and the commencement of the 90 calendar day adjudication time frame.

(c) Extension of time to request a hearing. (1) If the request for hearing is not filed within 60 calendar days of receipt of the QIC's reconsideration, an appellant may request an extension for good cause (See §§ 405.942(b)(2) and 405.942(b)(3)).

(2) Any request for an extension of time must be in writing, give the reasons why the request for a hearing was not filed within the stated time period, and must be filed with the entity specified in the notice of reconsideration.

(3) If the ALJ finds there is good cause for missing the deadline, the time period for filing the hearing request will be extended. To determine whether good cause for late filing exists, the ALJ uses the standards set forth in §§ 405.942(b)(2) and 405.942(b)(3).

(4) If a request for hearing is not timely filed, the adjudication period in § 405.1016 begins the date the ALJ grants the request to extend the filing deadline.

[70 FR 11472, Mar. 8, 2005, as amended at 70 FR 37703, June 30, 2005; 74 FR 65335, Dec. 9, 2009]

§ 405.1016 Time frames for deciding an appeal before an ALJ.

(a) When a request for an ALJ hearing is filed after a QIC has issued a reconsideration, the ALJ must issue a decision, dismissal order, or remand to the QIC, as appropriate, no later than the end of the 90 calendar day period beginning on the date the request for hearing is received by the entity specified in the QIC's notice of reconsideration, unless the 90 calendar day period has been extended as provided in this subpart.

(b) The adjudication period specified in paragraph (a) of this section begins on the date that a timely filed request for hearing is received by the entity specified in the QIC's reconsideration, or, if it is not timely filed, the date that the ALJ grants any extension to the filing deadline.

(c) When an appeal is escalated to the ALJ level because the QIC has not issued a reconsideration determination within the period specified in § 405.970, the ALJ must issue a decision, dismissal order, or remand to the QIC, as appropriate, no later than the end of the 180 calendar day period beginning on the date that the request for escalation is received by the ALJ hearing office, unless the 180 calendar day period is extended as provided in this subpart.

(d) When CMS or its contractor is a party to an ALJ hearing and a party requests discovery under § 405.1037 against another party to the hearing, the adjudication periods discussed in paragraphs (a) and (c) of this section are tolled.

[70 FR 11472, Mar. 8, 2005, as amended at 70 FR 37703, June 30, 2005; 74 FR 65335, Dec. 9, 2009]

§ 405.1018 Submitting evidence before the ALJ hearing.

(a) Except as provided in this section, parties must submit all written evidence they wish to have considered at the hearing with the request for hearing (or within 10 calendar days of receiving the notice of hearing).

(b) If a party submits written evidence later than 10 calendar days after receiving the notice of hearing, the period between the time the evidence was required to have been submitted and the time it is received is not counted toward the adjudication deadline specified in § 405.1016.

(c) Any evidence submitted by a provider, supplier, or beneficiary represented by a provider or supplier that is not submitted prior to the issuance of the QIC's reconsideration determination must be accompanied by a statement explaining why the evidence was not previously submitted to the QIC, or a prior decision-maker (see § 405.1028).

(d) The requirements of this section do not apply to oral testimony given at a hearing, or to evidence submitted by an unrepresented beneficiary.

[70 FR 11472, Mar. 8, 2005, as amended at 70 FR 37704, June 30, 2005; 74 FR 65335, Dec. 9, 2009]

§ 405.1020 Time and place for a hearing before an ALJ.

(a) General. The ALJ sets the time and place for the hearing, and may change the time and place, if necessary.

(b) Determining how appearances are made. The ALJ will direct that the appearance of an individual be conducted by video teleconferencing (VTC) if the ALJ finds that VTC technology is available to conduct the appearance. The ALJ may also offer to conduct a hearing by telephone if the request for hearing or administrative record suggests that a telephone hearing may be more convenient for one or more of the parties. The ALJ, with the concurrence of the Managing Field Office ALJ, may determine that an in-person hearing should be conducted if—

(1) VTC technology is not available; or

(2) Special or extraordinary circumstances exist.

(c) Notice of hearing. (1) The ALJ sends a notice of hearing to all parties that filed an appeal or participated in the reconsideration, any party who was found liable for the services at issue subsequent to the initial determination, the contractor that issued the initial determination, and the QIC that issued the reconsideration, advising them of the proposed time and place of the hearing.

(2) The notice of hearing will require all parties to the ALJ hearing (and any potential participant from CMS or its contractor who wishes to attend the hearing) to reply to the notice by:

(i) Acknowledging whether they plan to attend the hearing at the time and place proposed in the notice of hearing; or

(ii) Objecting to the proposed time and/or place of the hearing.

(d) A party's right to waive a hearing. A party may also waive the right to a hearing and request that the ALJ issue a decision based on the written evidence in the record. As provided in § 405.1000, the ALJ may require the parties to attend a hearing if it is necessary to decide the case. If the ALJ determines that it is necessary to obtain testimony from a non-party, he or she may still hold a hearing to obtain that testimony, even if all of the parties have waived the right to appear. In those cases, the ALJ will give the parties the opportunity to appear when the testimony is given but may hold the hearing even if none of the parties decide to appear.

(e) A party's objection to time and place of hearing. (1) If a party objects to the time and place of the hearing, the party must notify the ALJ at the earliest possible opportunity before the time set for the hearing.

(2) The party must state the reason for the objection and state the time and place he or she wants the hearing to be held.

(3) The request must be in writing.

(4) The ALJ may change the time or place of the hearing if the party has good cause. (Section 405.1052(a)(2) provides the procedures the ALJ follows when a party does not respond to a notice of hearing and fails to appear at the time and place of the hearing.)

(f) Good cause for changing the time or place. The ALJ can find good cause for changing the time or place of the scheduled hearing and reschedule the hearing if the information available to the ALJ supports the party's contention that—

(1) The party or his or her representative is unable to attend or to travel to the scheduled hearing because of a serious physical or mental condition, incapacitating injury, or death in the family; or

(2) Severe weather conditions make it impossible to travel to the hearing; or

(3) Good cause exists as set forth in paragraph (g) of this section.

(g) Good cause in other circumstances. (1) In determining whether good cause exists in circumstances other than those set forth in paragraph (f) of this section, the ALJ considers the party's reason for requesting the change, the facts supporting the request, and the impact of the proposed change on the efficient administration of the hearing process.

(2) Factors evaluated to determine the impact of the change include, but are not limited to, the effect on processing other scheduled hearings, potential delays in rescheduling the hearing, and whether any prior changes were granted the party.

(3) Examples of other circumstances a party might give for requesting a change in the time or place of the hearing include, but are not limited to, the following:

(i) The party has attempted to obtain a representative but needs additional time.

(ii) The party's representative was appointed within 10 calendar days of the scheduled hearing and needs additional time to prepare for the hearing.

(iii) The party's representative has a prior commitment to be in court or at another administrative hearing on the date scheduled for the hearing.

(iv) A witness who will testify to facts material to a party's case is unavailable to attend the scheduled hearing and the evidence cannot be otherwise obtained.

(v) Transportation is not readily available for a party to travel to the hearing.

(vi) The party is unrepresented, and is unable to respond to the notice of hearing because of any physical, mental, educational, or linguistic limitations (including any lack of facility with the English language) that he or she has.

(h) Effect of rescheduling hearing. If a hearing is postponed at the request of the appellant for any of the above reasons, the time between the originally scheduled hearing date and the new hearing date is not counted toward the adjudication deadline specified in § 405.1016.

(i) *A party's request for an in-person hearing.* (1) If a party objects to a VTC hearing or to the ALJ's offer to conduct a hearing by telephone, the party must notify the ALJ at the earliest possible opportunity before the time set for the hearing and request an in-person hearing.

(2) The party must state the reason for the objection and state the time or place he or she wants the hearing to be held.

(3) The request must be in writing.

(4) When a party's request for an in-person hearing is granted, the party is deemed to have waived the 90 calendar day time frame specified in § 405.1016 (including any applicable extensions provided in this subpart) unless the party requesting the hearing agrees to waive such adjudication timeframe in writing.

(5) The ALJ may grant the request, with the concurrence of the Managing Field Office ALJ, upon a finding of good cause and will reschedule the hearing for a time and place when the party may appear in person before the ALJ.

[70 FR 11472, Mar. 8, 2005, as amended at 70 FR 37704, June 30, 2005; 74 FR 65335, Dec. 9, 2009]

§ 405.1022 Notice of a hearing before an ALJ.

(a) Issuing the notice. After the ALJ sets the time and place of the hearing, notice of the hearing will be mailed to the parties and other potential participants, as provided in § 405.1020(c) at their last known addresses, or given by personal service, unless the parties have indicated in writing that they do not wish to receive this notice. The notice is mailed or served at least 20 calendar days before the hearing.

(b) Notice information. (1) The notice of hearing contains a statement of the specific issues to be decided and will inform the parties that they may designate a person to represent them during the proceedings.

(2) The notice must include an explanation of the procedures for requesting a change in the time or place of the hearing, a reminder that, if the appellant fails to appear at the scheduled hearing without good cause, the ALJ may dismiss the hearing request, and other information about the scheduling and conduct of the hearing.

(3) The appellant will also be told if his or her appearance or that of any other party or witness is scheduled by VTC, telephone, or in person. If the ALJ has scheduled the appellant or other party to appear at the hearing by VTC, the notice of hearing will advise that the scheduled place for the hearing is a VTC site and explain what it means to appear at the hearing by VTC.

(4) The notice advises the appellant or other parties that if they object to appearing by VTC or telephone, and wish instead to have their hearing at a time and place where they may appear in person before the ALJ, they must follow the procedures set forth at § 405.1020(i) for notifying the ALJ of their objections and for requesting an in-person hearing.

(c) Acknowledging the notice of hearing. (1) If the appellant, any other party to the reconsideration, or their representative does not acknowledge receipt of the notice of hearing, the ALJ hearing office attempts to contact the party for an explanation.

(2) If the party states that he or she did not receive the notice of hearing, an amended notice is sent to him or her by certified mail or e-mail, if available. (See § 405.1052 for the procedures the ALJ follows in deciding if the time or place of a scheduled hearing will be changed if a party does not respond to the notice of hearing).

[70 FR 11472, Mar. 8, 2005, as amended at 74 FR 65335, Dec. 9, 2009]

§ 405.1024 Objections to the issues.

(a) If a party objects to the issues described in the notice of hearing, he or she must notify the ALJ in writing at the earliest possible opportunity before the time set for the hearing, and no later than 5 calendar days before the hearing.

(b) The party must state the reasons for his or her objections and send a copy of the objections to all other parties to the appeal.

(c) The ALJ makes a decision on the objections either in writing or at the hearing.

[70 FR 11472, Mar. 8, 2005, as amended at 74 FR 65335, Dec. 9, 2009]

§ 405.1026 Disqualification of the ALJ.

(a) An ALJ cannot conduct a hearing if he or she is prejudiced or partial to any party or has any interest in the matter pending for decision.

(b) If a party objects to the ALJ who will conduct the hearing, the party must notify the ALJ within 10 calendar days of the date of the notice of hearing. The ALJ considers the party's objections and decides whether to proceed with the hearing or withdraw.

(c) If the ALJ withdraws, another ALJ will be appointed to conduct the hearing. If the ALJ does not withdraw, the party may, after the ALJ has issued an action in the case, present his or her objections to the MAC in accordance with § 405.1100 *et seq.* The MAC will then consider whether the hearing decision should be revised or a new hearing held before another ALJ. If the case is escalated to the MAC after a hearing is held but before the ALJ issues a decision, the MAC considers the reasons the party objected to the ALJ during its review of the case and, if the MAC deems it necessary, may remand the case to another ALJ for a hearing and decision.

§ 405.1028 Prehearing case review of evidence submitted to the ALJ.

(a) Examination of any new evidence. After a hearing is requested but before it is held, the ALJ will examine any new evidence submitted with the request for hearing (or within 10 calendar days of receiving the notice of hearing) as specified in § 405.1018, by a provider, supplier, or beneficiary represented by a provider or supplier to determine whether the provider, supplier, or beneficiary represented by a provider or supplier had good cause for submitting the evidence for the first time at the ALJ level.

(b) Determining if good cause exists. An ALJ finds good cause, for example, when the new evidence is material to an issue addressed in the QIC's reconsideration and that issue was not identified as a material issue prior to the QIC's reconsideration.

(c) If good cause does not exist. If the ALJ determines that there was not good cause for submitting the evidence for the first time at the ALJ level, the ALJ must exclude the evidence from the proceeding and may not consider it in reaching a decision.

(d) Notification to all parties. As soon as possible, but no later than the start of the hearing, the ALJ must notify all parties that the evidence is excluded from the hearing.

[70 FR 11472, Mar. 8, 2005, as amended at 74 FR 65335, Dec. 9, 2009]

***

APPENDIX 6-2 TITLE 42—PUBLIC HEALTH (CODE OF FEDERAL REGULATIONS):

PART 406—HOSPITAL INSURANCE ELIGIBILITY AND ENTITLEMENT

(Subpart C—Premium Hospital Insurance)*

[Note: These regulations have been compiled and annotated by the editors.]

Sec. 406.24 Special enrollment period related to coverage under group health plans.[1]

(a) Terminology. As used in this subpart, the following terms have the indicated meanings.

(1) Current employment status has the meaning given this term in Sec. 411.104 of this chapter.

(2) Family member has the meaning given this term in Sec. 411.201 of this chapter.

(3) Group health plan (GHP) and large group health plan (LGHP) have the meanings given those terms in Sec. 411.101 of this chapter, except that the "former employee" language of those definitions does not apply with respect to SEPs because—

(i) Section 1837(i)(1)(A) of the Act explicitly requires that GHP coverage of an individual age 65 or older be by reason of the individual's (or the individual's spouse's) current employment status; and

(ii) The sentence following section 1837(i)(1)(B) of the Act refers to "large group health plan." Under section 1862(b)(1)(B)(i), as amended by OBRA '93, LGHP coverage of a disabled individual must be "by virtue of the individual's or a family member's current employment status with an employer."

(4) Special enrollment period (SEP) is a period provided by statute to enable certain individuals to enroll in Medicare without having to wait for the general enrollment period.

(b) Duration of SEP.[2] (1) The SEP includes any month during any part of which—

(i) An individual over age 65 is enrolled in a GHP by reason of the current employment status of the individual or the individual's spouse; or

(ii) An individual under age 65 and disabled—

---

* *See* www.ecfr.gov/cgi-bin/text-idx?tpl=/ecfrbrowse/title42/42cfr406-main02.tpl (site visited Nov. 21, 2015).

[1] Before August 1986, SEPs were available only for enrollment in supplementary medical insurance, not for enrollment in premium hospital insurance.

[2] Before March 1995, SEPs began on the first day of the first month the individual was no longer covered under a GHP or LGHP by reason of current employment status.

(A) Is enrolled in a GHP by reason of the current employment status of the individual or the individual's spouse; or

(B) Is enrolled in an LGHP by reason of the current employment status of the individual or a member of the individual's family.

(2) The SEP ends on the last day of the eighth consecutive month during which the individual is at no time enrolled in a GHP or an LGHP by reason of current employment status.

(c) Conditions for use of a SEP.[3] In order to use a SEP, the individual must meet the following conditions:

(1) When first eligible to enroll for premium hospital insurance under Sec. 406.20(b) or (c), the individual was—

(i) Age 65 or over and covered under a GHP by reason of the current employment status of the individual or the individual's spouse;

(ii) Under age 65 and covered under an LGHP by reason of the current employment status of the individual or a member of the individual's family; or

(iii) Under age 65 and covered under a GHP by reason of the current employment status of the individual or the individual's spouse.

(2) For all the months thereafter, the individual has maintained coverage either under hospital insurance or a GHP or LGHP.

(d) Special rule: Additional SEPs. (1) Generally, if an individual fails to enroll during any available SEP, he or she is not entitled to any additional SEPs.

(2) However, if an individual fails to enroll during a SEP, because coverage under the same or a different GHP or LGHP was restored before the end of that particular SEP, that failure to enroll does not preclude additional SEPs.

(e) Effective date of coverage. (1) If the individual enrolls in a month during any part of which he or she is covered under a GHP or LGHP on the basis of current employment status, or in the first full month when no longer so covered, coverage begins on the first day of the month of enrollment or, at the individual's option, on the first day of any of the three following months.

(2) If the individual enrolls in any month of the SEP other than the months specified in paragraph (e)(1) of this section, coverage begins on the first day of the month following the month of enrollment.

[61 FR 40346, Aug. 2, 1996]

[3] Before August 10, 1993, an individual under age 65 could qualify for a SEP only if he or she had LGHP coverage as an "active individual," which the statute defined as "an employee, employer, self-employed individual (such as the employer), individual associated with the employer in a business relationship, or as a member of the family of any of those persons."

APPENDIX 6-3 TITLE 42—PUBLIC HEALTH (CODE OF FEDERAL REGULATIONS):

PART 407—SUPPLEMENTARY MEDICAL INSURANCE (SMI) ENROLLMENT AND ENTITLEMENT

(Subpart B—Individual Enrollment and Entitlement for SMI)*

[70 FR 11472, Mar. 8, 2005, unless otherwise noted.]

§ 407.10 Eligibility to enroll.

(a) Basic rule. Except as specified in paragraph (b) of this section, an individual is eligible to enroll for SMI if he or she—

(1) Is entitled to hospital insurance under any of the rules set forth in §§ 406.10 through 406.15 of this chapter; or

(2) Meets the following requirements:

(i) Has attained age 65. (An individual is considered to have attained age 65 on the day before the 65th anniversary of his or her birth.)

(ii) Is a resident of the United States.

(iii) Is a citizen of the United States, or an alien lawfully admitted for permanent residence who has resided continuously in the United States during the 5 years preceding the month in which he or she applies for enrollment.

(b) Exception. An individual is not eligible to enroll for SMI if he or she has been convicted of—

(1) Spying, sabotage, treason, or subversive activities under chapter 37, 105, or 115 of title 18 of the United States Code; or

(2) Conspiracy to establish dictatorship under section 4 of the Internal Security Act of 1950.

***

§ 407.12 General enrollment provisions.

(a) Opportunity to enroll. (1) An individual who is eligible to enroll for SMI may do so during an initial enrollment period or a general enrollment period as specified in §§ 407.14 and 407.15. An individual who meets the conditions specified in § 407.20 may enroll during a special enrollment period, as provided in that section.

(2) An individual who fails to enroll during his or her initial enrollment period or whose enrollment has been terminated may enroll or reenroll during a

* *See* www.ecfr.gov/cgi-bin/text-idx?tpl=/ecfrbrowse/title42/42cfr407_main_02.tpl (site visited Oct. 18, 2015).

general enrollment period, or, if he or she meets the specified conditions, during a special enrollment period.

(b) Enrollment periods ending on a nonworkday. (1) If an enrollment period ends on a Federal nonworkday, that period is automatically extended to the next succeeding workday.

(2) A Federal nonworkday is any Saturday, Sunday, or Federal legal holiday or a day that is declared by statute or executive order to be a day on which Federal employees are not required to work.

§ 407.14 Initial enrollment period.

(a) Duration. (1) The initial enrollment period is the 7-month period that begins 3 months before the month an individual first meets the eligibility requirements of § 407.10 and ends 3 months after that first month of eligibility.

(2) In determining the initial enrollment period of an individual who is age 65 or over and eligible for enrollment solely because of entitlement to hospital insurance, the individual is considered as first meeting the eligibility requirements for SMI on the first day he or she becomes entitled to hospital insurance or would have been entitled if he or she filed an application for that program.

(b) Deemed initial enrollment period. (1) SSA or CMS will establish a deemed initial enrollment period for an individual who fails to enroll during the initial enrollment period because of a belief, based on erroneous documentary evidence, that he or she had not yet attained age 65. The period will be established as though the individual had attained age 65 on the date indicated by the incorrect information.

(2) A deemed initial enrollment period established under paragraph (b)(1) of this section is used to determine the individual's premium and right to enroll in a general enrollment period if that is advantageous to the individual.

§ 407.15 General enrollment period.

(a) Except as specified in paragraph (b) of this section, the general enrollment period is January through March of each calendar year.

(b) An unlimited general enrollment period existed between April 1 and September 30, 1981. Any eligible individual whose initial enrollment period had ended, or whose previous period of entitlement had terminated, could have enrolled or reenrolled during any month of that 6-month period.

§ 407.17 Automatic enrollment.

(a) Who is automatically enrolled. An individual is automatically enrolled for SMI if he or she:

(1) Resides in the United States, except in Puerto Rico;

(2) Becomes entitled to hospital insurance under any of the provisions set forth in §§ 406.10 through 406.15 of this chapter; and

(3) Does not decline SMI enrollment.

(b) Opportunity to decline automatic enrollment. (1) SSA will notify an individual that he or she is automatically enrolled under paragraph (a) of this section and grant the individual a specified period (at least 2 months after the month the notice is mailed) to decline enrollment.

(2) The individual may decline enrollment by submitting to SSA or CMS a signed statement that he or she does not wish SMI.

(3) The statement must be submitted before entitlement begins, or if later, within the time limits set in the notice of enrollment.

***

Sec.407.20 Special enrollment period related to coverage under group health plans.

(a) Terminology—(1) *Group health plan (GHP) and large group health plan (LGHP).* These terms have the meanings given them in § 411.101 of this chapter except that the "former employee" language of those definitions does not apply with respect to SEPs for the reasons specified in § 406.24(a)(3) of this chapter.

(2) Special enrollment period (SEP). This term has the meaning set forth in § 406.24(a)(4) of this chapter. In order to use a SEP, an individual must meet the conditions of paragraph (b) and of paragraph (c) or (d) of this section, as appropriate.

(b) General rule. All individuals must meet the following conditions:

(1) They are eligible to enroll for SMI on the basis of age or disability, but not on the basis of end-stage renal disease.

(2) When first eligible for SMI coverage (4th month of their initial enrollment period), they were covered under a GHP or LGHP on the basis of current employment status or, if not so covered, they enrolled in SMI during their initial enrollment period; and

(3) For all months thereafter, they maintained coverage under either SMI or a GHP or LGHP. (Generally, if an individual fails to enroll in SMI during any available SEP, he or she is not entitled to any additional SEPs. However, if an individual fails to enroll during a SEP because coverage under the same or a different GHP or LGHP was restored before the end of that particular SEP, that failure to enroll does not preclude additional SEPs.)

(c) Special rule: Individual age 65 or over. For an individual who is or was covered under a GHP, coverage must be by reason of the current employment status of the individual or the individual's spouse.

(d) Special rules: Disabled individual.[1] Individuals entitled on the basis of disability (but not on the basis of end-stage renal disease) must meet conditions that vary depending on whether they were covered under a GHP or an LGHP.

(1) For a disabled individual who is or was covered under a GHP, coverage must be on the basis of the current employment status of the individual or the individual's spouse.

(2) For a disabled individual who is or was covered under an LGHP, coverage must be as follows:

(i) Before August 10, 1993, as an "active individual," that is, as an employee, employer, self-employed individual (such as the employer), individual associated with the employer in a business relationship, or as a member of the family of any of those persons.

(ii) On or after August 10, 1993, by reason of current employment status of the individual or a member of the individual's family.

(e) Effective date of coverage. The rule set forth in § 406.24(d) for Medicare Part A applies equally to Medicare Part B.

[61 FR 40346, Aug. 2, 1996]
***

§ 407.25 Beginning of entitlement: Individual enrollment.

The following apply whether an individual is self-enrolled or automatically enrolled in SMI:

(a) Enrollment during initial enrollment period. (1) If an individual enrolls during the first three months of the initial enrollment period, entitlement begins with the first month of eligibility.

(2) If an individual enrolls during the fourth month of the initial enrollment period, entitlement begins with the following month.

(3) If an individual enrolls during the fifth month of the initial enrollment period, entitlement begins with the second month after the month of enrollment.

(4) If an individual enrolls in either of the last two months of the initial enrollment period, entitlement begins with the third month after the month of enrollment.

(5) Example. An individual first meets the eligibility requirements for enrollment in April. The initial enrollment period is January through July. The month in which the individual enrolls determines the month that begins the period of entitlement, as follows:

---

[1] Under the current statute, the SEP provision applicable to disabled individuals covered under an LGHP expires in September 1998. Unless Congress changes that date, the last SEP available under those provisions will begin with June 1998.

Enrolls in initial enrollment period	*Entitlement begins on—*
January	April 1 (month eligibility requirements first met)
February	April 1
March	April 1
April	May 1 (month following month of enrollment)
May	July 1 (second month after month of enrollment)
June	September 1 (third month after month of enrollment)
July	October 1 (third month after month of enrollment)

(b) Enrollment or reenrollment during general enrollment period. (1) If an individual enrolls or reenrolls during a general enrollment period before April 1, 1981, or after September 30, 1981, entitlement begins on July 1 of that calendar year.

(2) If an individual enrolled or reenrolled during the general enrollment period between April 1, 1981, and September 20, 1981, entitlement began with the third month after the month in which the enrollment request was filed.

(c) Enrollment or reenrollment during a SEP. The rules set forth in § 406.24(d) of this chapter apply.

[53 FR 47204, Nov. 22, 1988, as amended at 61 FR 40347, Aug. 2, 1996]
***

§ 407.32 Prejudice to enrollment rights because of Federal Government misrepresentation, inaction, or error.

If an individual's enrollment or non-enrollment in SMI is unintentional, inadvertent, or erroneous because of the error, misrepresentation, or inaction of a Federal employee or any person authorized by the Federal Government to act in its behalf, the Social Security Administration or CMS may take whatever action it determines is necessary to provide appropriate relief. The action may include:

(a) Designation of a special initial or general enrollment period;

(b) Designation of an entitlement period based on that enrollment period;

(c) Adjustment of premiums;

(d) Any combination of actions under paragraphs (a) through (c) of this section; or

(e) Any other remedial action that may be necessary to correct or eliminate the effects of the error, misrepresentation, or inaction.

APPENDIX 6-4 TITLE 42—PUBLIC HEALTH (CODE OF FEDERAL REGULATIONS):

PART 408—PREMIUMS FOR SUPPLEMENTARY MEDICAL INSURANCE

(Subpart B—Amount of Monthly Premiums)*

§ 408.22 Increased premiums for late enrollment and for reenrollment.

For an individual who enrolls after expiration of his or her initial enrollment period or reenrolls after termination of a coverage period, the standard monthly premium determined under § 408.20 is increased by ten percent for each full twelve months in the periods specified in §§ 408.24 and 408.25.

---

* *See* www.ecfr.gov/cgi-bin/text-idx?tpl=/ecfrbrowse/title42/42cfr408-main02.tpl (site visited June 8, 2016).

APPENDIX 6-5 TITLE 42—PUBLIC HEALTH (CODE OF FEDERAL REGULATIONS):

PART 410—SUPPLEMENTARY MEDICAL INSURANCE (SMI) BENEFITS

(Subpart B—Medical and Other Health Services)*

§ 410.10 Medical and other health services: Included services.

Subject to the conditions and limitations specified in this subpart, "medical and other health services" includes the following services:

(a) Physicians' services.

(b) Services and supplies furnished incident to a physician's professional services, of kinds that are commonly furnished in physicians' offices and are commonly either furnished without charge or included in the physicians' bills.

(c) Services and supplies, including partial hospitalization services, that are incident to physician services and are furnished to outpatients by or under arrangements made by a hospital or a CAH.

(d) Diagnostic services furnished to outpatients by or under arrangements made by a hospital or a CAH if the services are services that the hospital or CAH ordinarily furnishes to its outpatients for diagnostic study.

(e) Diagnostic laboratory and X-ray tests (including diagnostic mammography that meets the conditions for coverage specified in § 410.34(b) of this subpart) and other diagnostic tests.

(f) X-ray therapy and other radiation therapy services.

(g) Medical supplies, appliances, and devices.

(h) Durable medical equipment.

(i) Ambulance services.

(j) Rural health clinic services.

(k) Home dialysis supplies and equipment; on or after July 1, 1991, epoetin (EPO) for home dialysis patients, and, on or after January 1, 1994, for dialysis patients, competent to use the drug; self-care home dialysis support services; and institutional dialysis services and supplies.

(l) Pneumococcal vaccinations.

(m) Outpatient physical therapy and speech pathology services.

(n) Cardiac pacemakers and pacemaker leads.

(o) Additional services furnished to enrollees of HMOs or CMPs, as described in Sec. 410.58.

(p) Hepatitis B vaccine.

(q) Blood clotting factors for hemophilia patients competent to use these factors without medical or other supervision.

---

* *See* www.ecfr.gov/cgi-bin/text-idx?tpl=/ecfrbrowse/title42/42cfr410_main_02.tpl (site visited June 8, 2016).

(r) Screening mammography services.

(s) Federally qualified health center services.

(t) Services of a certified registered nurse anesthetist or an anesthesiologist's assistant.

(u) Prescription drugs used in immunosuppressive therapy.

(v) Clinical psychologist services and services and supplies furnished as an incident to the services of a clinical psychologist, as provided in § 410.71.

(w) Clinical social worker services, as provided in § 410.73.

(x) Services of physicians and other practitioners furnished in or at the direction of an IHS or Indian tribal hospital or clinic.

(y) Intravenous immune globulin administered in the home for the treatment of primary immune deficiency diseases.

[51 FR 41339, Nov. 14, 1986, as amended at 52 FR 27765, July 23, 1987; 55 FR 22790, June 4, 1990; 55 FR 53522, Dec. 31, 1990; 56 FR 8841, Mar. 1, 1991; 56 FR 43709, Sept. 4, 1991; 57 FR 24981, June 12, 1992; 57 FR 33896, July 31, 1992; 58 FR 30668, May 26, 1993; 59 FR 26959, May 25, 1994; 59 FR 49833, Sept. 30, 1994; 60 FR 8955, Feb. 16, 1995; 63 FR 20128, Apr. 23, 1998; 66 FR 55328, Nov. 1, 2001; 69 FR 66420, Nov. 15, 2004]

***

§ 410.12 Medical and other health services: Basic conditions and limitations.

(a) Basic conditions. The medical and other health services specified in § 410.10 are covered by Medicare Part B only if they are not excluded under subpart A of part 411 of this chapter, and if they meet the following conditions:

(1) When the services must be furnished. The services must be furnished while the individual is in a period of entitlement. (The rules on entitlement are set forth in part 406 of this chapter.)

(2) By whom the services must be furnished. The services must be furnished by a facility or other entity as specified in § 410.14 through § 410.69.

(3) Physician certification and recertification requirements. If the services are subject to physician certification requirements, they must be certified as being medically necessary, and as meeting other applicable requirements, in accordance with subpart B of part 424 of this chapter.

(b) Limitations on payment. Payment for medical and other health services is subject to limitations on the amounts of payment as specified in § 410.152 and § 410.155 and to the annual and blood deductibles as set forth in § 410.160 and § 410.161.

[51 FR 41339, Nov. 14, 1986, as amended at 53 FR 6648, Mar. 2, 1988; 57 FR 33896, July 31, 1992]

***

§ 410.14 Special requirements for services furnished outside the United States.

Medicare Part B pays for physicians' services and ambulance services furnished outside the United States if the services meet the applicable conditions of § 410.12 and are furnished in connection with covered inpatient hospital services that meet the specific requirements and conditions set forth in subpart H of part 424 of this chapter.

[51 FR 41339, Nov. 14, 1986, as amended at 53 FR 6648, Mar. 2, 1988]
***

§ 410.20 Physicians' services.

(a) Included services. Medicare Part B pays for physicians' services, including diagnosis, therapy, surgery, consultations, and home, office, and institutional calls.

(b) By whom services must be furnished. Medicare Part B pays for the services specified in paragraph (a) of this section if they are furnished by one of the following professionals who is legally authorized to practice by the State in which he or she performs the functions or actions, and who is acting within the scope of his or her license.

(1) A doctor of medicine or osteopathy, including an osteopathic practitioner recognized in section 1101(a)(7) of the Act.

(2) A doctor of dental surgery or dental medicine.

(3) A doctor of podiatric medicine.

(4) A doctor of optometry.

(5) A chiropractor who meets the qualifications specified in § 410.22.

(c) Limitations on services. The Services specified in paragraph (a) of this section may be covered under Medicare Part B if they are furnished within the limitations specified in §§ 410.22 through 410.25.

(d) Prior determination of medical necessity for physicians' services—(1) *Definitions.* (i) A "Prior Determination of Medical Necessity" means an individual decision by a Medicare contractor, before a physician's service is furnished, as to whether or not the physician's service is covered consistent with the requirements of section 1862(a)(1)(A) of the Act relating to medical necessity.

(ii) An "eligible requester" includes the following:

(A) A participating physician (or a physician that accepts assignment), but only with respect to physicians' services to be furnished to an individual who is entitled to receive benefits under this part and who has consented to the physician making the request under this section for those physicians' services.

(B) An individual entitled to benefits under this part, but only with respect to physicians' services for which the individual receives, from a physician, an advance beneficiary notice under section 1879(a) of the Act.

(2) *General rule.* Each Medicare contractor will, through the procedures established in CMS manual instructions, allow requests for prior determinations of medical necessity from eligible requesters under its respective jurisdiction for those services identified by CMS (updated annually in conjunction with the update to the MPFS and posted on that specific Medicare contractor's Web site by the Healthcare Common Procedure Coding System procedure code and code description). Only those services listed on that Medicare contractor's Web site on the date the request for a prior determination is made are subject to prior determination. Each contractor's list will consist of the following:

(i) The national list, provided by CMS, of the most expensive physicians' services (as defined in section 1848(j)(3) of the Act) included in the MPFS which are performed at least 50 times annually.

(ii) The national list, provided by CMS, of plastic and dental surgeries that may be covered by Medicare and that have an amount of at least $1,000 on the MPFS (not including the adjustment for location by the GPCI).

(3) *Services with local coverage determinations (LCDs) or national coverage determinations (NCDs).* In instances where an LCD or an NCD exists that has sufficiently specific reasonable and necessary criteria addressing the particular clinical indication for the procedure for which the prior determination is requested, the contractor will send a copy of the LCD or NCD to the requestor along with an explanation that the LCD or NCD serves as the prior determination and that no further determination will be made.

(4) *Identification of eligible services.* CMS will identify the number of services that are eligible for a prior determination through manual instructions consistent with the criteria established in the regulation.

(5) *Statutory procedures.* Under sections 1869(h)(3) through (h)(6) of the Act, the following procedures apply:

(i) *Request for prior determination*—(A) *In general.* An eligible requester may submit to the contractor a request for a determination, before the furnishing of a physician's service, as to whether the physician's service is covered under this title consistent with the applicable requirements of section 1862(a)(1)(A) of the Act (relating to medical necessity).

(B) *Accompanying documentation.* CMS may require that the request be accompanied by a description of the physician's service, supporting documentation relating to the medical necessity of the physician's service, and other appropriate documentation. In the case of a request submitted by an eligible requester who is described in section 1869(h)(1)(B)(ii) of the Act, the Secretary may require that the request also be accompanied by a copy of the advance beneficiary notice involved.

(ii) *Response to request*—(A) *General rule.* The contractor will provide the eligible requester with written notice of a determination as to whether—

(*1*) The physician's service is covered (the physician's service is covered consistent with the requirements of section 1862(a)(1)(A) of the Act relating to medical necessity); or

(*2*) The physician's service is not covered (the physician's service is not covered consistent with the requirements of section 1862(a)(1)(A) of the Act relating to medical necessity); or

(*3*) The contractor lacks sufficient information to make a coverage determination with respect to the physician's service.

(B) *Contents of notice for certain determinations*—(*1*) *Coverage.* If the contractor makes the determination described in paragraph (d)(5)(ii)(A)(1) of this section, the contractor will indicate in the prior determination notice that the physician service is covered consistent with the requirements of section 1862(a)(1)(A) of the Act relating to medical necessity.

(*2*) *Non-coverage.* If the contractor makes the determination described in paragraph (d)(5)(ii)(A)(*2*) of this section, the contractor will include in the notice a brief explanation of the basis for the determination, including on what national or local coverage or noncoverage determination (if any) the determination is based, and a description of any applicable rights under section 1869(a) of the Act.

(*3*) *Insufficient information.* If the contractor makes the determination described in paragraph (d)(5)(ii)(A)(*3*) of this section, the contractor will include in the notice a description of the additional information required to make the coverage determination.

(C) *Deadline to respond.* The notice described in paragraphs (d)(5)(ii)(A)(1) through (d)(5)(ii)(A)(3) of this section will be provided by the contractor within 45 days of the date the request for a prior determination is received by the contractor.

(D) *Informing beneficiary in case of physician request.* In the case of a request by a participating physician or a physician accepting assignment, the process will provide that the individual to whom the physician's service is to be furnished will be informed of any determination described in paragraph (d)(5)(ii)(A)(2) of this section (relating to a determination of non-coverage). The beneficiary will also be notified that, notwithstanding the determination of non-coverage, the beneficiary has the right to obtain the physician's service in question and have a claim submitted for the physician's service.

(iii) *Binding nature of positive determination.* If the contractor makes the determination described in paragraph (d)(5)(ii)(A)(*1*) of this section, that determination will be binding on the contractor in the absence of fraud or evidence of misrepresentation of facts presented to the contractor.

(iv) *Limitation on further review*—(A) *General rule.* Contractor determinations described in paragraph (d)(5)(ii)(A)(*2*) of this section or paragraph (d)(5)(ii)(A)(*3*) of this section (relating to pre-service claims) are not subject to administrative appeal or judicial review.

(B) Decision not to seek prior determination or negative determination does not impact the right to obtain services, seek reimbursement, or appeal rights.

Nothing in this paragraph will be construed as affecting the right of an individual who—

(*1*) Decides not to seek a prior determination under this paragraph with respect to physicians' services; or

(*2*) Seeks such a determination and has received a determination described in paragraph (d)(5)(ii)(A)(*2*) of this section, from receiving (and submitting a claim for) those physicians' services and from obtaining administrative or judicial review respecting that claim under the other applicable provisions of this part 405 subpart I of this chapter. Failure to seek a prior determination under this paragraph with respect to physicians' services will not be taken into account in that administrative or judicial review.

(C) *No prior determination after receipt of services.* Once an individual is provided physicians' services, there will be no prior determination under this paragraph with respect to those physicians' services.

[51 FR 41339, Nov. 14, 1986, as amended at 73 FR 9678, Feb. 22, 2008]

§ 410.21 Limitations on services of a chiropractor.

(a) Qualifications for chiropractors. (1) A chiropractor licensed or authorized to practice before July 1, 1974, and an individual who began studies in a chiropractic college before that date, must have— .

(i) Had preliminary education equal to the requirements for graduation from an accredited high school or other secondary school;

(ii) Graduated from a college of chiropractic approved by the State's chiropractic examiners after completing a course of study covering a period of not less than 3 school years of 6 months each year in actual continuous attendance and covering adequate courses of study in the subjects of anatomy, physiology, symptomatology and diagnosis, hygiene and sanitation, chemistry, histology, pathology, and principles and practice of chiropractic, including clinical instruction in vertebral palpation, nerve tracing and adjusting; and

(iii) Passed an examination prescribed by the State's chiropractic examiners covering the subjects specified in paragraph (a)(1)(ii) of this section.

(2) A chiropractor first licensed or authorized to practice after June 30, 1974, and an individual who begins studies in a chiropractic college after that date, must have—

(i) Had preliminary education equal to the requirements for graduation from an accredited high school or other secondary school;

(ii) Satisfactorily completed 2 years of pre-chiropractic study at the college level;

(iii) Satisfactorily completed a 4-year course of 8 months each year offered by a college or school of chiropractic approved by the State's chiropractic examiners and including at least 4,000 hours in courses in anatomy, physiology, symptomatology and diagnosis, hygiene and sanitation, chemistry, histology, pathology, principles and practice of chiropractic, and clinical instruction in vertebral palpation, nerve tracing and adjusting, plus courses in the use and effect of X-ray and chiropractic analysis;

(iv) Passed an examination prescribed by the State's chiropractic examiners covering the subjects specified in paragraph (a)(2)(iii) of this section; and

(v) Attained 21 years of age.

(b) Limitations on services. (1) Medicare Part B pays only for a chiropractor's manual manipulation of the spine to correct a subluxation if the subluxation has resulted in a neuromusculoskeletal condition for which manual manipulation is appropriate treatment.

(2) Medicare Part B does not pay for X-rays or other diagnostic or therapeutic services furnished or ordered by a chiropractor.

[51 FR 41339, Nov. 14, 1986, as amended at 64 FR 59439, Nov. 2, 1999. Redesignated at 66 FR 55328, Nov. 1, 2001]

§ 410.22 Limitations on services of an optometrist.

Medicare Part B pays for the services of a doctor of optometry, which he or she is legally authorized to perform in the State in which he or she performs them, if the services are among those described in section 1861(s) of the Act and § 410.10 of this part.

[64 FR 59439, Nov. 2, 1999. Redesignated at 66 FR 55328, Nov. 1, 2001]

§ 410.23 Screening for glaucoma: Conditions for and limitations on coverage.

(a) Definitions: As used in this section, the following definitions apply:

(1) *Direct supervision in the office setting* means the optometrist or the ophthalmologist must be present in the office suite and be immediately available to furnish assistance and direction throughout the performance of the procedure. It does not mean the physician must be present in the room when the procedure is performed.

(2) *Eligible beneficiary* means individuals in the following high risk categories:

(i) Individual with diabetes mellitus.

(ii) Individual with a family history of glaucoma.

(iii) African-Americans age 50 and over.

(iv) Hispanic-Americans age 65 and over.

(3) *Screening for glaucoma* means the following procedures furnished to an individual for the early detection of glaucoma:

(i) A dilated eye examination with an intraocular pressure measurement.

(ii) A direct ophthalmoscopy examination, or a slit-lamp biomicroscopic examination.

(b) Condition for coverage of screening for glaucoma. Medicare Part B pays for glaucoma screening examinations provided to eligible beneficiaries as described in paragraph (a)(2) of this section if they are furnished by or under the direct supervision in the office setting of an optometrist or ophthalmologist who is legally authorized to perform these services under State law (or the State regulatory mechanism provided by State law) of the State in which the services are furnished, as would otherwise be covered if furnished by a physician or incident to a physician's professional service.

(c) Limitations on coverage of glaucoma screening examinations. (1) Payment may not be made for a glaucoma screening examination that is performed for an individual who is not an eligible beneficiary as described in paragraph (a)(2) of this section.

(2) Payment may be made for a glaucoma screening examination that is performed on an individual who is an eligible beneficiary as described in paragraph (a)(2) of this section, after at least 11 months have passed following the month in which the last glaucoma screening examination was performed.

[66 FR 55328, Nov. 1, 2001, as amended at 70 FR 70330, Nov. 21, 2005]

§ 410.24 Limitations on services of a doctor of dental surgery or dental medicine.

Medicare Part B pays for services furnished by a doctor of dental surgery or dental medicine within the scope of his or her license, if the services would be covered as physicians' services when performed by a doctor of medicine or osteopathy.[1]

[51 FR 41339, Nov. 14, 1986, as amended at 56 FR 8852, Mar. 1, 1991]

---

[1] For services furnished before July 1, 1981, Medicare Part B paid only for the following services of a doctor of dental surgery or dental medicine: Surgery on the jaw or any adjoining structure, and Reduction of a fracture of the jaw or other facial bone.

§ 410.25 Limitations on services of a podiatrist.

Medicare Part B pays for the services of a doctor of podiatric medicine, acting within the scope of his or her license, if the services would be covered as physicians' services when performed by a doctor of medicine or osteopathy.

§ 410.26 Services and supplies incident to a physician's professional services: Conditions.

(a) Definitions. For purposes of this section, the following definitions apply:

(1) *Auxiliary personnel* means any individual who is acting under the supervision of a physician (or other practitioner), regardless of whether the individual is an employee, leased employee, or independent contractor of the physician (or other practitioner) or of the same entity that employs or contracts with the physician (or other practitioner).

(2) *Direct supervision* means the level of supervision by the physician (or other practitioner) of auxiliary personnel as defined in § 410.32(b)(3)(ii).

(3) *Independent contractor* means an individual (or an entity that has hired such an individual) who performs part-time or full-time work for which the individual (or the entity that has hired such an individual) receives an IRS–1099 form.

(4) *Leased employment* means an employment relationship that is recognized by applicable State law and that is established by two employers by a contract such that one employer hires the services of an employee of the other employer.

(5) *Non-institutional setting* means all settings other than a hospital or skilled nursing facility.

(6) *Practitioner* means a non-physician practitioner who is authorized by the Act to receive payment for services incident to his or her own services.

(7) *Services and supplies* means any services or supplies (including drugs or biologicals that are not usually self-administered) that are included in section 1861(s)(2)(A) of the Act and are not specifically listed in the Act as a separate benefit included in the Medicare program.

(b) Medicare Part B pays for services and supplies incident to the service of a physician (or other practitioner).

(1) Services and supplies must be furnished in a non-institutional setting to non-institutional patients.

(2) Services and supplies must be an integral, though incidental, part of the service of a physician (or other practitioner) in the course of diagnosis or treatment of an injury or illness.

(3) Services and supplies must be commonly furnished without charge or included in the bill of a physician (or other practitioner).

(4) Services and supplies must be of a type that are commonly furnished in the office or clinic of a physician (or other practitioner).

(5) Services and supplies must be furnished under the direct supervision of the physician (or other practitioner). The physician (or other practitioner) directly supervising the auxiliary personnel need not be the same physician (or other practitioner) upon whose professional service the incident to service is based.

(6) Services and supplies must be furnished by the physician, practitioner with an incident to benefit, or auxiliary personnel.

(7) A physician (or other practitioner) may be an employee or an independent contractor.

(8) Claims for drugs payable administered by a physician as defined in section 1861(r) of the Social Security Act to refill an implanted item of DME may only be paid under Part B to the physician as a drug incident to a physician's service under section 1861(s)(2)(A). These drugs are not payable to a pharmacy/supplier as DME under section 1861(s)(6) of the Act.

(c) Limitations. (1) Drugs and biologicals are also subject to the limitations specified in Sec. 410.29.

(2) Physical therapy, occupational therapy and speech-language pathology services provided incident to a physician's professional services are subject to the provisions established in Secs. 410.59(a)(3)(iii), 410.60(a)(3)(iii), and 410.62(a)(3)(ii).

[51 FR 41339, Nov. 14, 1986, as amended at 66 FR 55328, Nov. 1, 2001; 67 FR 20684, Apr. 26, 2002; 69 FR 66421, Nov. 15, 2004

§ 410.27 Outpatient hospital services and supplies incident to physician services: Conditions.

(a) Medicare Part B pays for hospital services and supplies furnished incident to a physician service to outpatients, including drugs and biologicals that cannot be self-administered, if—

(1) They are furnished—

(i) By or under arrangements made by a participating hospital, except in the case of an SNF resident as provided in § 411.15(p) of this chapter;

(ii) As an integral though incidental part of a physician's services; and

(iii) In the hospital or at a department of a provider, as defined in § 413.65(a)(2) of this subchapter, that has provider-based status in relation to a hospital under § 413.65 of this subchapter; and

(2) In the case of partial hospitalization services, also meet the conditions of paragraph (d) of this section.

(b) Drugs and biologicals are also subject to the limitations specified in § 410.168.

(c) Rules on emergency services furnished to outpatients by nonparticipating hospitals are specified in § 410.168.

(d) Medicare Part B pays for partial hospitalization services if they are—

(1) Prescribed by a physician who certifies and recertifies the need for the services in accordance with subpart B of part 424 of this chapter; and

(2) Furnished under a plan of treatment as required under subpart B of part 424 of this chapter.

(e) Services furnished by an entity other than the hospital are subject to the limitations specified in § 410.42(a).

(f) Services furnished at a department of a provider, as defined in § 413.65(a)(2) of this subchapter, that has provider-based status in relation to a hospital under § 413.65 of this subchapter, must be under the direct supervision of a physician. "Direct supervision" means the physician must be present and on the premises of the location and immediately available to furnish assistance and direction throughout the performance of the procedure. It does not mean that the physician must be present in the room when the procedure is performed.

[76 FR 74580, Nov. 30, 2011]

§ 410.28 Hospital or CAH diagnostic services furnished to outpatients: Conditions.

(a) Medicare Part B pays for hospital or CAH diagnostic services furnished to outpatients, including drugs and biologicals required in the performance of the services (even if those drugs or biologicals are self-administered), if those services meet the following conditions:

(1) They are furnished by or under arrangements made by a participating hospital or participating CAH, except in the case of an SNF resident as provided in § 411.15(p) of this chapter.

(2) They are ordinarily furnished by, or under arrangements made by, the hospital or CAH to its outpatients for the purpose of diagnostic study.

(3) They would be covered as inpatient hospital services if furnished to an inpatient.

(b) Drugs and biologicals are also subject to the limitations specified in § 410.29(b) and (c).

(c) Diagnostic services furnished by an entity other than the hospital or CAH are subject to the limitations specified in § 410.42(a).

(d) Rules on emergency services furnished to outpatients by nonparticipating hospitals are set forth in subpart G of part 424 of this chapter.

(e) Medicare Part B makes payment under section 1833(t) of the Act for diagnostic services furnished at a facility (other than an RHC or an FQHC) that CMS designates as having provider-based status only when the diagnostic services are furnished under the appropriate level of physician supervision specified by CMS in accordance with the definitions in § 410.32(b)(3)(i), (b)(3)(ii), and (b)(3)(iii). Under general supervision at a facility accorded provider-based status, the training of the nonphysician personnel who actually perform the diagnostic procedure and the maintenance of the necessary equipment and supplies are the continuing responsibility of the facility. In addition—

(1) For services furnished directly or under arrangement in the hospital or in an on-campus or off-campus outpatient department of the hospital, as defined in § 413.65 of this subchapter, "direct supervision" means that the physician must be immediately available to furnish assistance and direction throughout the performance of the procedure. It does not mean that the physician must be present in the room where the procedure is performed.

(2) For services furnished under arrangement in nonhospital locations, "direct supervision" means the definition specified in § 410.32(b)(3)(ii).

(f) The rules for clinical diagnostic laboratory tests set forth in Sec. 410.32(a) and (d)(2) through (d)(4) of this subpart are applicable to those tests when furnished in hospitals and CAHs.

[51 FR 41339, Nov. 14, 1986, as amended at 58 FR 30668, May 26, 1993; 63 FR 26307, May 12, 1998; 65 FR 18536, Apr. 7, 2000; 66 FR 58809, Nov. 23, 2001; 74 FR 60680, Nov. 20, 2009; 75 FR 72259, Nov. 24, 2010]

§ 410.29 Limitations on drugs and biologicals.

Medicare Part B does not pay for the following:

(a) Except as provided in § 410.28(a) for outpatient diagnostic services and § 410.63(b) for blood clotting factors, and except for EPO, any drug or biological that can be self-administered.

(b) Any drug product that meets all of the following conditions:

(1) The drug product was approved by the Food and Drug Administration (FDA) before October 10, 1962.

(2) The drug product is available only through prescription.

(3) The drug product is the subject of a notice of opportunity for hearing issued under section 505(e) of the Federal Food, Drug, and Cosmetic Act and published in the Federal Register on a proposed order of FDA to withdraw its approval for the drug product because it has determined that the product is less than effective for all its labeled indications.

(4) The drug product is presently not subject to a determination by FDA, made under its efficacy review program, that there is a compelling justification of the drug product's medical need. (21 CFR 310.6 contains an explanation of the efficacy review program.)

(c) Any drug product that is identical, related, or similar, as defined in 21 CFR 310.6, to a drug product that meets the conditions of paragraph (b) of this section.

[51 FR 41339, Nov. 14, 1986, as amended at 55 FR 22790, June 4, 1990; 56 FR 43709, Sept. 4, 1991]

***

§ 410.32 Diagnostic x-ray tests, diagnostic laboratory tests, and other diagnostic tests: Conditions.

(a) Ordering diagnostic tests. All diagnostic x-ray tests, diagnostic laboratory tests, and other diagnostic tests must be ordered by the physician who is treating the beneficiary, that is, the physician who furnishes a consultation or treats a beneficiary for a specific medical problem and who uses the results in the management of the beneficiary's specific medical problem. Tests not ordered by the physician who is treating the beneficiary are not reasonable and necessary (see § 411.15(k)(1) of this chapter).

(2) *Mammography exception.* A physician who meets the qualification requirements for an interpreting physician under section 354 of the Public Health Service Act as provided in § 410.34(a)(7) may order a diagnostic mammogram based on the findings of a screening mammogram even though the physician does not treat the beneficiary.

(3) *Application to non-physician practitioners.* Non-physician practitioners (that is, clinical nurse specialists, clinical psychologists, clinical social workers, nurse-midwives, nurse practitioners, and physician assistants) who furnish services that would be physician services if furnished by a physician, and who are operating within the scope of their authority under State law and within the scope of their Medicare statutory benefit, may be treated the same as physicians treating beneficiaries for the purpose of this paragraph.

(b) Diagnostic x-ray and other diagnostic tests—(1) *Basic rule.* Except as indicated in paragraph (b)(2) of this section, all diagnostic x-ray and other diagnostic tests covered under section 1861(s)(3) of the Act and payable under the physician fee schedule must be furnished under the appropriate level of supervision by a physician as defined in section 1861(r) of the Act. Services furnished without the required level of supervision are not reasonable and necessary (see § 411.15(k)(1) of this chapter).

(2) *Exceptions.* The following diagnostic tests payable under the physician fee schedule are excluded from the basic rule set forth in paragraph (b)(1) of this section:

(i) Diagnostic mammography procedures, which are regulated by the Food and Drug Administration.

(ii) Diagnostic tests personally furnished by a qualified audiologist as defined in section 1861(ll)(3) of the Act.

(iii) Diagnostic psychological testing services when—

(A) Personally furnished by a clinical psychologist or an independently practicing psychologist as defined in program instructions; or

(B) Furnished under the general supervision of a physician or a clinical psychologist.

(iv) Diagnostic tests (as established through program instructions) personally performed by a physical therapist who is certified by the American Board of Physical Therapy Specialties as a qualified electrophysiologic clinical specialist and permitted to provide the service under State law.

(v) Diagnostic tests performed by a nurse practitioner or clinical nurse specialist authorized to perform the tests under applicable State laws.

(vi) Pathology and laboratory procedures listed in the 80000 series of the Current Procedural Terminology published by the American Medical Association.

(3) *Levels of supervision.* Except where otherwise indicated, all diagnostic x-ray and other diagnostic tests subject to this provision and payable under the physician fee schedule must be furnished under at least a general level of physician supervision as defined in paragraph (b)(3)(i) of this section. In addition, some of these tests also require either direct or personal supervision as defined in paragraphs (b)(3)(ii) or (b)(3)(iii) of this section, respectively. (However, diagnostic tests performed by a physician assistant (PA) that the PA is legally authorized to perform under State law require only a general level of physician supervision.) When direct or personal supervision is required, physician supervision at the specified level is required throughout the performance of the test.

(i) *General supervision* means the procedure is furnished under the physician's overall direction and control, but the physician's presence is not required during the performance of the procedure. Under general supervision, the training of the non-physician personnel who actually perform the diagnostic procedure and the maintenance of the necessary equipment and supplies are the continuing responsibility of the physician.

(ii) *Direct supervision* in the office setting means the physician must be present in the office suite and immediately available to furnish assistance and direction throughout the performance of the procedure. It does not mean that the physician must be present in the room when the procedure is performed.

(iii) *Personal supervision* means a physician must be in attendance in the room during the performance of the procedure.

(c) Portable x-ray services. Portable x-ray services furnished in a place of residence used as the patient's home are covered if the following conditions are met:

(1) These services are furnished under the general supervision of a physician, as defined in paragraph (b)(3)(i) of this section.

(2) The supplier of these services meets the requirements set forth in part 486, subpart C of this chapter, concerning conditions for coverage for portable x-ray services.

(3) The procedures are limited to—

(i) Skeletal films involving the extremities, pelvis, vertebral column, or skull;

(ii) Chest or abdominal films that do not involve the use of contrast media; and

(iii) Diagnostic mammograms if the approved portable x-ray supplier, as defined in subpart C of part 486 of this chapter, meets the certification requirements of section 354 of the Public Health Service Act, as implemented by 21 CFR part 900, subpart B.

(d) Diagnostic laboratory tests—(1) *Who may furnish services.* Medicare Part B pays for covered diagnostic laboratory tests that are furnished by any of the following:

(i) A participating hospital or participating RPCH.

(ii) A nonparticipating hospital that meets the requirements for emergency outpatient services specified in subpart G of part 424 of this chapter and the laboratory requirements specified in part 493 of this chapter.

(iii) The office of the patient's attending or consulting physician if that physician is a doctor of medicine, osteopathy, podiatric medicine, dental surgery, or dental medicine.

(iv) An RHC.

(v) A laboratory, if it meets the applicable requirements for laboratories of part 493 of this chapter, including the laboratory of a nonparticipating hospital that does not meet the requirements for emergency outpatient services in subpart G of part 424 of this chapter.

(vi) An FQHC.

(vii) An SNF to its resident under § 411.15(p) of this chapter, either directly (in accordance with § 483.75(k)(1)(i) of this chapter) or under an arrangement (as defined in Sec. 409.3 of this chapter) with another entity described in this paragraph.

(2) *Documentation and recordkeeping requirements*—(i) *Ordering the service.* The physician or (qualified non-physician practitioner, as defined in paragraph (a)(3) of this section), who orders the service must maintain documentation of medical necessity in the beneficiary's medical record.

(ii) *Submitting the claim.* The entity submitting the claim must maintain the following documentation:

(A) The documentation that it receives from the ordering physician or nonphysician practitioner.

(B) The documentation that the information that it submitted with the claim accurately reflects the information it received from the ordering physician or nonphysician practitioner.

(iii) *Requesting additional information.* The entity submitting the claim may request additional diagnostic and other medical information to document that the services it bills are reasonable and necessary. If the entity requests additional documentation, it must request material relevant to the medical necessity of the specific test(s), taking into consideration current rules and regulations on patient confidentiality.

(3) *Claims review.* (i) *Documentation requirements.* Upon request by CMS, the entity submitting the claim must provide the following information:

(A) Documentation of the order for the service billed (including information sufficient to enable CMS to identify and contact the ordering physician or non-physician practitioner).

(B) Documentation showing accurate processing of the order and submission of the claim.

(C) Diagnostic or other medical information supplied to the laboratory by the ordering physician or non-physician practitioner, including any ICD–9–CM code or narrative description supplied.

(ii) *Services that are not reasonable and necessary.* If the documentation provided under paragraph (d)(3)(i) of this section does not demonstrate that the service is reasonable and necessary, CMS takes the following actions:

(A) Provides the ordering physician or non-physician practitioner information sufficient to identify the claim being reviewed.

(B) Requests from the ordering physician or non-physician practitioner those parts of a beneficiary's medical record that are relevant to the specific claim(s) being reviewed.

(C) If the ordering physician or non-physician practitioner does not supply the documentation requested, informs the entity submitting the claim(s) that the documentation has not been supplied and denies the claim.

(iii) *Medical necessity.* The entity submitting the claim may request additional diagnostic and other medical information from the ordering physician or non-physician practitioner to document that the services it bills are reasonable and necessary. If the entity requests additional documentation, it must request material relevant to the medical necessity of the specific test(s), taking into consideration current rules and regulations on patient confidentiality.

(4) *Automatic denial and manual review.* (i) *General rule.* Except as provided in paragraph (d)(4)(ii) of this section, CMS does not deny a claim for services that exceed utilization parameters without reviewing all relevant documentation that is submitted with the claim (for example, justifications prepared by providers, primary and secondary diagnoses, and copies of medical records).

(ii) *Exceptions.* CMS may automatically deny a claim without manual review if a national coverage decision or LMRP specifies the circumstances under which the service is denied, or the service is specifically excluded from Medicare coverage by law.

(e) Diagnostic laboratory tests furnished in hospitals and CAHs. The provisions of paragraphs (a) and (d)(2) through (d)(4), inclusive, of this section apply to all diagnostic laboratory test furnished by hospitals and CAHs to outpatients.

[62 FR 59098, Oct. 31, 1997, as amended at 63 FR 26308, May 12, 1998; 63 FR 53307, Oct. 5, 1998; 63 FR 58906, Nov. 2, 1998; 64 FR 59440, Nov. 2, 1999; 66

FR 58809, Nov. 23, 2001; 69 FR 66421, Nov. 15, 2004; 72 FR 66398, Nov. 27, 2007; 75 FR 73615, Nov. 29, 2010; 77 FR 69361, Nov. 16, 2012]

***

§ 410.34 Mammography services: Conditions for and limitations on coverage.

(a) Definitions. As used in this section, the following definitions apply:

(1) Diagnostic mammography means a radiologic procedure furnished to a man or woman with signs or symptoms of breast disease, or a personal history of breast cancer, or a personal history of biopsy-proven benign breast disease, and includes a physician's interpretation of the results of the procedure.

(2) Screening mammography means a radiologic procedure furnished to a woman without signs or symptoms of breast disease, for the purpose of early detection of breast cancer, and includes a physician's interpretation of the results of the procedure.

(3) Supplier of diagnostic mammography means a facility that is certified and responsible for ensuring that all diagnostic mammography services furnished to Medicare beneficiaries meet the conditions for coverage of diagnostic mammography services as specified in paragraph (b) of this section.

(4) Supplier of screening mammography means a facility that is certified and responsible for ensuring that all screening mammography services furnished to Medicare beneficiaries meet the conditions and limitations for coverage of screening mammography services as specified in paragraphs (c) and (d) of this section.

(5) Certificate means the certificate described in 21 CFR 900.2(b) that may be issued to, or renewed for, a facility that meets the requirements for conducting an examination or procedure involving mammography.

(6) Provisional certificate means the provisional certificate described in 21 CFR 900.2(m) that may be issued to a facility to enable the facility to qualify to meet the requirements for conducting an examination or procedure involving mammography.

(7) The term meets the certification requirements of section 354 of the Public Health Service (PHS) Act means that in order to qualify for coverage of its services under the Medicare program, a supplier of diagnostic or screening mammography services must meet the following requirements:

(i) Must have a valid provisional certificate, or a valid certificate, that has been issued by FDA indicating that the supplier meets the certification requirements of section 354 of the PHS Act, as implemented by 21 CFR part 900, subpart B.

(ii) Has not been issued a written notification by FDA that states that the supplier must cease conducting mammography examinations because the supplier is not in compliance with certain critical certification requirements of section 354 of the PHS Act, implemented by 21 CFR part 900, subpart B.

(iii) Must not employ for provision of the professional component of mammography services a physician or physicians for whom the facility has received written notification by FDA that the physician (or physicians) is (or are) in violation of the certification requirements set forth in section 354 of the PHS Act, as implemented by 21 CFR 900.12(a)(1)(i).

(b) Conditions for coverage of diagnostic mammography services. Medicare Part B pays for diagnostic mammography services if they meet the following conditions:

(1) They are ordered by a doctor of medicine or osteopathy (as defined in section 1861(r)(1) of the Act).

(2) They are furnished by a supplier of diagnostic mammography services that meets the certification requirements of section 354 of the PHS Act, as implemented by 21 CFR part 900, subpart B.

(c) Conditions for coverage of screening mammography services. Medicare Part B pays for screening mammography services if they are furnished by a supplier of screening mammography services that meets the certification requirements of section 354 of the PHS Act, as implemented by 21 CFR part 900, subpart B.

(d) Limitations on coverage of screening mammography services. The following limitations apply to coverage of screening mammography services as described in paragraphs (c) and (d) of this section:

(1) The service must be, at a minimum a two-view exposure (that is, a craniocaudal and a medial lateral oblique view) of each breast.

(2) Payment may not be made for screening mammography performed on a woman under age 35.

(3) Payment may be made for only 1 screening mammography performed on a woman over age 34, but under age 40.

(4) For an asymptomatic woman over 39 years of age, payment may be made for a screening mammography performed after at least 11 months have passed following the month in which the last screening mammography was performed.

[59 FR 49833, Sept. 30, 1994, as amended at 60 FR 14224, Mar. 16, 1995; 60 FR 63176, Dec. 8, 1995; 62 FR 59100, Oct. 31, 1997; 63 FR 4596, Jan. 30, 1998]

§ 410.35 X-ray therapy and other radiation therapy services: Scope.

Medicare Part B pays for X-ray therapy and other radiation therapy services, including radium therapy and radioactive isotope therapy, and materials and the services of technicians administering the treatment.

[51 FR 41339, Nov. 14, 1986. Re-designated at 55 FR 53522, Dec. 31, 1990]

§ 410.36 Medical supplies, appliances, and devices: Scope.

(a) Medicare Part B pays for the following medical supplies, appliances and devices:

(1) Surgical dressings, and splints, casts, and other devices used for reduction of fractures and dislocations.

(2) Prosthetic devices, other than dental, that replace all or part of an internal body organ, including colostomy bags and supplies directly related to colostomy care, including—

(i) Replacement of prosthetic devices; and

(ii) One pair of conventional eyeglasses or conventional contact lenses furnished after each cataract surgery during which an intraocular lens is inserted.

(3) Leg, arm, back, and neck braces and artificial legs, arms, and eyes, including replacements if required because of a change in the individual's physical condition.

(b) As a requirement for payment, CMS may determine through carrier instructions, or carriers may determine, that an item listed in paragraph (a) of this section requires a written physician order before delivery of the item.

[51 FR 41339, Nov. 14, 1986, as amended at 57 FR 36014, Aug. 12, 1992; 57 FR 57688, Dec. 7, 1992]

§ 410.37 Colorectal cancer screening tests: Conditions for and limitations on coverage.

(a) **Definitions.** As used in this section, the following definitions apply:

(1) *Colorectal cancer screening tests* means any of the following procedures furnished to an individual for the purpose of early detection of colorectal cancer:

(i) Screening fecal-occult blood tests.

(ii) Screening flexible sigmoidoscopies.

(iii) In the case of an individual at high risk for colorectal cancer, screening colonoscopies.

(iv) Screening barium enemas.

(v) Other tests or procedures established by a national coverage determination, and modifications to tests under this paragraph, with such frequency and payment limits as CMS determines appropriate, in consultation with appropriate organizations

(2) *Screening fecal-occult blood test* means—

(i) A guaiac-based test for peroxidase activity, testing two samples from each of three consecutive stools, or,

(ii) Other tests as determined by the Secretary through a national coverage determination.

(3) An *individual at high risk for colorectal cancer* means an individual with—

(i) A close relative (sibling, parent, or child) who has had colorectal cancer or an adenomatous polyp;

(ii) A family history of familial adenomatous polyposis;

(iii) A family history of hereditary nonpolyposis colorectal cancer;

(iv) A personal history of adenomatous polyps; or

(v) A personal history of colorectal cancer; or

(vi) Inflammatory bowel disease, including Crohn's Disease, and ulcerative colitis.

(4) *Screening barium enema* means—

(i) A screening double contrast barium enema of the entire colorectum (including a physician's interpretation of the results of the procedure); or

(ii) In the case of an individual whose attending physician decides that he or she cannot tolerate a screening double contrast barium enema, a screening single contrast barium enema of the entire colorectum (including a physician's interpretation of the results of the procedure).

(5) An *attending physician for purposes of this provision* is a doctor of medicine or osteopathy (as defined in section 1861(r)(1) of the Act) who is fully knowledgeable about the beneficiary's medical condition, and who would be responsible using the results of any examination performed in the overall management of the beneficiary's specific medical problem.

(b) Condition for coverage of screening fecal-occult blood tests. Medicare Part B pays for a screening fecal-occult blood test if it is ordered in writing by the beneficiary's attending physician.

(c) Limitations on coverage of screening fecal-occult blood tests. (1) Payment may not be made for a screening fecal-occult blood test performed for an individual under age 50.

(2) For an individual 50 years of age or over, payment may be made for a screening fecal-occult blood test performed after at least 11 months have passed following the month in which the last screening fecal-occult blood test was performed.

(d) Condition for coverage of flexible sigmoidoscopy screening. Medicare Part B pays for a flexible sigmoidoscopy screening service if it is performed by a doctor of medicine or osteopathy (as defined in section 1861(r)(1) of the

Act), or by a physician assistant, nurse practitioner, or clinical nurse specialist (as defined in section 1861(aa)(5) of the Act and §§ 410.74, 410.75, and 410.76) who is authorized under State law to perform the examination.

(e) Limitations on coverage of screening flexible sigmoidoscopies. (1) Payment may not be made for a screening flexible sigmoidoscopy performed for an individual under age 50.

(2) For an individual 50 years of age or over, except as described in paragraph (e)(3) of this section, payment may be made for screening flexible sigmoidoscopy after at least 47 months have passed following the month in which the last screening flexible sigmoidoscopy or, as provided in paragraphs (h) and (i) of this section, the last screening barium enema was performed.

(3) In the case of an individual who is not at high risk for colorectal cancer as described in paragraph (a)(3) of this section but who has had a screening colonoscopy performed, payment may be made for a screening flexible sigmoidosocopy only after at least 119 months have passed following the month in which the last screening colonoscopy was performed.

(f) Condition for coverage of screening colonoscopies. Medicare Part B pays for a screening colonoscopy if it is performed by a doctor of medicine or osteopathy (as defined in section 1861(r)(1) of the Act).

(g) Limitations on coverage of screening colonoscopies. (1) Effective for services furnished on or after July 1, 2001, except as described in paragraph (g)(3) of this section, payment may be made for a screening colonoscopy performed for an individual who is not at high risk for colorectal cancer as described in paragraph (a)(3) of this section, after at least 119 months have passed following the month in which the last screening colonoscopy was performed.

(2) Payment may be made for a screening colonoscopy performed for an individual who is at high risk for colorectal cancer as described in paragraph (a)(3) of this section, after at least 23 months have passed following the month in which the last screening colonoscopy was performed, or, as provided in paragraphs (h) and (i) of this section, the last screening barium enema was performed.

(3) In the case of an individual who is not at high risk for colorectal cancer as described in paragraph (a)(3) of this section but who has had a screening flexible sigmoidoscopy performed, payment may be made for a screening colonoscopy only after at least 47 months have passed following the month in which the last screening flexible sigmoidoscopy was performed.

(h) Conditions for coverage of screening barium enemas. Medicare Part B pays for a screening barium enema if it is ordered in writing by the beneficiary's attending physician.

(i) Limitations on coverage of screening barium enemas. (1) In the case of an individual age 50 or over who is not at high risk of colorectal cancer, payment may be made for a screening barium enema examination performed after at least 47 months have passed following the month in which the last screening barium enema or screening flexible sigmoidoscopy was performed.

(2) In the case of an individual who is at high risk for colorectal cancer, payment may be made for a screening barium enema examination performed after at least 23 months have passed following the month in which the last screening barium enema or the last screening colonoscopy was performed.

[62 FR 59100, Oct. 31, 1997, as amended at 66 FR 55329, Nov. 1, 2001; 67 FR 80040, Dec. 31, 2002; 77 FR 69362, Nov. 16, 2012]

§ 410.38 Durable medical equipment: Scope and conditions.

(a) Medicare Part B pays for the rental or purchase of durable medical equipment, including iron lungs, oxygen tents, hospital beds, and wheelchairs, if the equipment is used in the patient's home or in an institution that is used as a home.

(b) An institution that is used as a home may not be a hospital or a CAH or a SNF as defined in sections 1861(e)(1), 1861(mm)(1) and 1819(a)(1) of the Act, respectively.

(c) Power mobility devices (PMDs)—(1) *Definitions.* For the purposes of this paragraph, the following definitions apply:

Physician has the same meaning as in section 1861(r)(1) of the Act.

Power mobility device means a covered item of durable medical equipment that is in a class of wheelchairs that includes a power wheelchair (a four-wheeled motorized vehicle whose steering is operated by an electronic device or a joystick to control direction and turning) or a power-operated vehicle (a three or four-wheeled motorized scooter that is operated by a tiller) that a beneficiary uses in the home.

Prescription means a written order completed by the physician or treating practitioner who performed the face-to-face examination and that includes the beneficiary's name, the date of the face-to-face examination, the diagnoses and conditions that the PMD is expected to modify, a description of the item (for example, a narrative description of the specific type of PMD), the length of need, and the physician or treating practitioner's signature and the date the prescription was written.

Treating practitioner means a physician assistant, nurse practitioner, or clinical nurse specialist as those terms are defined in section 1861(aa)(5) of the Act, who has conducted a face-to-face examination of the beneficiary.

Supplier means an entity with a valid Medicare supplier number, including an entity that furnishes items through the mail.

(2) *Conditions of payment.* Medicare Part B pays for a power mobility device if the physician or treating practitioner, as defined in paragraph (c)(1) of this section meets the following conditions:

(i) Conducts a face-to-face examination of the beneficiary for the purpose of evaluating and treating the beneficiary for his or her medical condition and determining the medical necessity for the PMD as part of an appropriate overall treatment plan.

(ii) Writes a prescription, as defined in paragraph (c)(1) of this section that is provided to the beneficiary or supplier, and is received by the supplier within 45 days after the face-to-face examination.

(iii) Provides supporting documentation, including pertinent parts of the beneficiary's medical record (for example, history, physical examination, diagnostic tests, summary of findings, diagnoses, treatment plans and/or other information as may be appropriate) that supports the medical necessity for the power mobility device, which is received by the supplier within 45 days after the face-to-face examination.

(3) *Exceptions.* (i) Beneficiaries discharged from a hospital do not need to receive a separate face-to-face examination as long as the physician or treating practitioner who performed the face-to-face examination of the beneficiary in the hospital issues a PMD prescription and supporting documentation that is received by the supplier within 45 days after the date of discharge.

(ii) Accessories for PMDs may be ordered by the physician or treating practitioner without conducting a face-to-face examination of the beneficiary.

(4) *Dispensing a power mobility device.* Suppliers may not dispense a PMD to a beneficiary until the PMD prescription and the supporting documentation have been received from the physician or treating practitioner who performed the face-to-face examination of the beneficiary. These documents must be received within 45 days after the date of the face-to-face examination.

(5) *Documentation.* (i) A supplier must maintain the prescription and the supporting documentation provided by the physician or treating practitioner and make them available to CMS and its agents upon request.

(ii) Upon request by CMS or its agents, a supplier must submit additional documentation to CMS or its agents to support and/or substantiate the medical necessity for the power mobility device.

(6) *Safety requirements.* The PMD must meet any safety requirements specified by CMS.

(d) Medicare Part B pays for medically necessary equipment that is used for treatment of decubitus ulcers if—

(1) The equipment is ordered in writing by the beneficiary's attending physician, or by a specialty physician on referral from the beneficiary's attending physician, and the written order is furnished to the supplier before the delivery of the equipment; and

(2) The prescribing physician has specified in the prescription that he or she will be supervising the use of the equipment in connection with the course of treatment.

(e) Medicare Part B pays for a medically necessary seat-lift if it—

(1) Is ordered in writing by the beneficiary's attending physician, or by a specialty physician on referral from the beneficiary's attending physician, and the written order is furnished to the supplier before the delivery of the seat-lift;

(2) Is for a beneficiary who has a diagnosis designated by CMS as requiring a seat-lift; and

(3) Meets safety requirements specified by CMS.

(f) Medicare Part B pays for transcutaneous electrical nerve stimulator units that are—

(1) Determined to be medically necessary; and

(2) Ordered in writing by the beneficiary's attending physician, or by a specialty physician on referral from the beneficiary's attending physician, and the written order is furnished to the supplier before the delivery of the unit to the beneficiary.

(g) As a requirement for payment, CMS may determine through carrier instructions, or carriers may determine that an item of durable medical equipment requires a written physician order before delivery of the item.

(1) *Items requiring a written order.* As a condition of payment, Specified Covered Items (as described in paragraph (g)(2) of this section) require a written order that meets the requirements in paragraphs (g)(3) and (4) of this section before delivery of the item.

(2) *Specified covered items.* (i) Specified Covered Items are items of durable medical equipment that CMS has specified in accordance with section 1834(a)(11)(B)(i) of the Act. A list of these items is updated annually in the Federal Register.

(ii) The list of Specified Covered Items includes the following:

(A) Any item described by a *Healthcare Common Procedure Coding System (HCPCS)* code for the following types of durable medical equipment:

(*1*) Transcutaneous electrical nerve stimulation (TENS) unit.

(*2*) Rollabout chair.

(*3*) Oxygen and respiratory equipment.

(*4*) Hospital beds and accessories.

(*5*) Traction-cervical.

(B) Any item of durable medical equipment that appears on the Durable Medical Equipment, Prosthetics, Orthotics, and Supplies Fee Schedule with a price ceiling at or greater than $1,000.

(C) Any other item of durable medical equipment that CMS adds to the list of Specified Covered Items through the notice and comment rulemaking process in order to reduce the risk of fraud, waste, and abuse.

(iii) The list of specific covered items excludes the following:

(A) Any item that is no longer covered by Medicare.

(B) Any HCPCS code that is discontinued.

(3) *Face-to-face encounter requirements.* (i) For orders issued in accordance with paragraphs (g)(1) and (2) of this section, as a condition of payment for the Specified Covered Item, all of the following must occur:

(A) The physician must document and communicate to the DME supplier that the physician or a physician assistant, a nurse practitioner, or a clinical nurse specialist has had a face-to-face encounter with the beneficiary on the date of the written order up to 6 months before the date of the written order.

(B) During the face-to-face encounter the physician, a physician assistant, a nurse practitioner, or a clinical nurse specialist must conduct a needs assessment, evaluate, and/or treat the beneficiary for the medical condition that supports the need for each covered item of DME ordered.

(C) The face-to-face encounter must be documented in the pertinent portion of the medical record (for example, history, physical examination, diagnostic tests, summary of findings, diagnoses, treatment plans or other information as it may be appropriate). Physician must sign or cosign the pertinent portion of the medical record indicating the occurrence of a face-to-face encounter for the beneficiary for the date of the face-to-face encounter when performed by a physician assistant, a nurse practitioner, or a clinical nurse specialist. For purposes of this paragraph (g), a face-to-face encounter does not include DME items and services furnished from an "incident to" service.

(ii) For purposes of this paragraph (g), a face-to-face encounter may occur via telehealth in accordance with all of the following:

(A) Section 1834(m) of the Act.

(B)(*1*) Medicare telehealth regulations in § 410.78 and § 414.65 of this chapter; and

(*2*) Subject to the list of payable Medicare telehealth services established by the applicable PFS.

(4) *Written order issuance requirements.* Written orders issued in accordance with paragraphs (g)(1) and (2) of this section must include all of the following:

(i) Beneficiary's name.

(ii) Item of DME ordered.

(iii) Signature of the prescribing practitioner.

(iv) Prescribing practitioner NPI.

(v) The date of the order.

(5) *Supplier's order and documentation requirements.* (i) A supplier must maintain the written order and the supporting documentation provided by the physician, physician assistant, nurse practitioner, or clinical nurse specialist and make them available to CMS upon request for 7 years from the date of service consistent with § 424.516(f) of this chapter.

(ii) Upon request by CMS or its agents, a supplier must submit additional documentation to CMS or its agents to support and substantiate that a face-to-face encounter has occurred.

[51 FR 41339, Nov. 14, 1986, as amended at 57 FR 57688, Dec. 7, 1992; 58 FR 30668, May 26, 1993; 70 FR 50946, Aug. 26, 2005; 71 FR 17030, Apr. 5, 2006; 77 FR 69362, Nov. 16, 2012]

§ 410.39 Prostate cancer screening tests: Conditions for and limitations on coverage.

(a) Definitions. As used in this section, the following definitions apply:

(1) *Prostate cancer screening tests* means any of the following procedures furnished to an individual for the purpose of early detection of prostate cancer:

(i) A screening digital rectal examination.

(ii) A screening prostate-specific antigen blood test.

(iii) For years beginning after 2002, other procedures CMS finds appropriate for the purpose of early detection of prostate cancer, taking into account changes in technology and standards of medical practice, availability, effectiveness, costs, and other factors CMS considers appropriate.

(2) A *screening digital rectal examination* means a clinical examination of an individual's prostate for nodules or other abnormalities of the prostate.

(3) A *screening prostate-specific antigen blood test* means a test that measures the level of prostate-specific antigen in an individual's blood.

(4) A physician for purposes of this provision means a doctor of medicine or osteopathy (as defined in section 1861(r)(1) of the Act) who is fully knowledgeable about the beneficiary, and who would be responsible for explaining the results of the screening examination or test.

(5) A physician assistant, nurse practitioner, clinical nurse specialist, or certified nurse midwife for purposes of this provision means a physician assistant, nurse practitioner, clinical nurse specialist, or certified nurse midwife (as defined in sections 1861(aa) and 1861(gg) of the Act) who is fully knowledgeable about the beneficiary, and who would be responsible for explaining the results of the screening examination or test.

(b) Condition for coverage of screening digital rectal examinations. Medicare Part B pays for a screening digital rectal examination if it is performed by the beneficiary's physician, or by the beneficiary's physician assistant, nurse practitioner, clinical nurse specialist, or certified nurse midwife as defined in paragraphs (a)(4) or (a)(5) of this section who is authorized to perform this service under State law.

(c) Limitation on coverage of screening digital rectal examinations. (1) Payment may not be made for a screening digital rectal examination performed for a man age 50 or younger.

(2) For an individual over 50 years of age, payment may be made for a screening digital rectal examination only if the man has not had such an examination paid for by Medicare during the preceding 11 months following the month in which his last Medicare-covered screening digital rectal examination was performed.

(d) Condition for coverage of screening prostate-specific antigen blood tests. Medicare Part B pays for a screening prostate-specific antigen blood test if it is ordered by the beneficiary's physician, or by the beneficiary's physician assistant, nurse practitioner, clinical nurse specialist, or certified nurse midwife as defined in paragraphs (a)(4) or (a)(5) of this section who is authorized to order this test under State law.

(e) Limitation on coverage of screening prostate-specific antigen blood test. (1) Payment may not be made for a screening prostate-specific antigen blood test performed for a man age 50 or younger.

(2) For an individual over 50 years of age, payment may be made for a screening prostate-specific antigen blood test only if the man has not had such an examination paid for by Medicare during the preceding 11 months following the month in which his last Medicare-covered screening prostate-specific antigen blood test was performed.

[64 FR 59440, Nov. 2, 1999, as amended at 65 FR 19331, Apr. 11, 2000]

§ 410.40 Coverage of ambulance services.

(a) Basic rules. Medicare Part B covers ambulance services if the following conditions are met:

(1) The supplier meets the applicable vehicle, staff, and billing and reporting requirements of Sec. 410.41 and the service meets the medical necessity and origin and destination requirements of paragraphs (d) and (e) of this section.

(2) Medicare Part A payment is not made directly or indirectly for the services.

(b) Levels of services. Medicare covers the following levels of ambulance service, which are defined in Sec. 414.605 of this chapter:

(1) Basic life support (BLS) (emergency and nonemergency).

(2) Advanced life support, level 1 (ALS1) (emergency and nonemergency).

(3) Advanced life support, level 2 (ALS2).

(4) Paramedic ALS intercept (PI).

(5) Specialty care transport (SCT).

(6) Fixed wing transport (FW).

(7) Rotary wing transport (RW).

(c) Paramedic ALS intercept services. Paramedic ALS intercept services must meet the following requirements:

(1) Be furnished in an area that is designated as a rural area by any law or regulation of the State or that is located in a rural census tract of a metropolitan statistical area (as determined under the most recent Goldsmith Modification). (The Goldsmith Modification is a methodology to identify small towns and rural areas within large metropolitan counties that are isolated from central areas by distance or other features.)

(2) Be furnished under contract with one or more volunteer ambulance services that meet the following conditions:

(i) Are certified to furnish ambulance services as required under Sec. 410.41.

(ii) Furnish services only at the BLS level.

(iii) Be prohibited by State law from billing for any service.

(3) Be furnished by a paramedic ALS intercept supplier that meets the following conditions:

(i) Is certified to furnish ALS services as required in § 410.41(b)(2).

(ii) Bills all the recipients who receive ALS intercept services from the entity, regardless of whether or not those recipients are Medicare beneficiaries.

(d) Medical necessity requirements—(1) *General rule.* Medicare covers ambulance services, including fixed wing and rotary wing ambulance services, only if they are furnished to a beneficiary whose medical condition is such that other means of transportation are contraindicated. The beneficiary's condition must require both the ambulance transportation itself and the level of service provided in order for the billed service to be considered medically necessary. Nonemergency transportation by ambulance is appropriate if either: the beneficiary is bed-confined, and it is documented that the beneficiary's condition is such that other methods of transportation are contraindicated; or, if his or her medical condition, regardless of bed confinement, is such that transportation by ambulance is medically required. Thus, bed confinement is not the sole criterion in determining the medical necessity of ambulance transportation. It is one factor that is considered in medical necessity determinations. For a beneficiary to be considered bed-confined, the following criteria must be met:

(i) The beneficiary is unable to get up from bed without assistance.

(ii) The beneficiary is unable to ambulate.

(iii) The beneficiary is unable to sit in a chair or wheelchair.

(2) *Special rule for nonemergency, scheduled, repetitive ambulance services.* (i) Medicare covers medically necessary nonemergency, scheduled, repetitive ambulance services if the ambulance provider or supplier, before furnishing the service to the beneficiary, obtains a written order from the beneficiary's attending physician certifying that the medical necessity requirements of paragraph (d)(1) of this section are met. The physician's order must be dated no earlier than 60 days before the date the service is furnished.

(ii) In all cases, the provider or supplier must keep appropriate documentation on file and, upon request, present it to the contractor. The presence of the signed physician certification statement does not alone demonstrate that the ambulance transport was medically necessary. All other program criteria must be met in order for payment to be made.

(3) *Special rule for nonemergency ambulance services that are either unscheduled or that are scheduled on a non-repetitive basis.* Medicare covers medically necessary nonemergency ambulance services that are either unscheduled or that are scheduled on a non-repetitive basis under one of the following circumstances:

(i) For a resident of a facility who is under the care of a physician if the ambulance provider or supplier obtains a written order from the beneficiary's attending physician, within 48 hours after the transport, certifying that the medical necessity requirements of paragraph (d)(1) of this section are met.

(ii) For a beneficiary residing at home or in a facility who is not under the direct care of a physician. A physician certification is not required.

(iii) If the ambulance provider or supplier is unable to obtain a signed physician certification statement from the beneficiary's attending physician, a signed certification statement must be obtained from either the physician assistant (PA), nurse practitioner (NP), clinical nurse specialist (CNS), registered nurse (RN), or discharge planner, who has personal knowledge of the beneficiary's condition at the time the ambulance transport is ordered or the service is furnished. This individual must be employed by the beneficiary's attending physician or by the hospital or facility where the beneficiary is being treated and from which the beneficiary is transported. Medicare regulations for PAs, NPs, and CNSs apply and all applicable State licensure laws apply; or,

(iv) If the ambulance provider or supplier is unable to obtain the required certification within 21 calendar days following the date of the service, the ambulance supplier must document its attempts to obtain the requested certification and may then submit the claim. Acceptable documentation includes a signed return receipt from the U.S. Postal Service or other similar service that evidences that the ambulance supplier attempted to obtain the required signature from the beneficiary's attending physician or other individual named in paragraph (d)(3)(iii) of this section.

(v) In all cases, the provider or supplier must keep appropriate documentation on file and, upon request, present it to the contractor. The presence of the signed certification statement or signed return receipt does not alone demonstrate that the ambulance transport was medically necessary. All other program criteria must be met in order for payment to be made.

(e) Origin and destination requirements. Medicare covers the following ambulance transportation:

(1) From any point of origin to the nearest hospital, CAH, or SNF that is capable of furnishing the required level and type of care for the beneficiary's illness or injury. The hospital or CAH must have available the type of physician or physician specialist needed to treat the beneficiary's condition.

(2) From a hospital, CAH, or SNF to the beneficiary's home.

(3) From a SNF to the nearest supplier of medically necessary services not available at the SNF where the beneficiary is a resident, including the return trip.

(4) For a beneficiary who is receiving renal dialysis for treatment of ESRD, from the beneficiary's home to the nearest facility that furnishes renal dialysis, including the return trip.

(f) Specific limits on coverage of ambulance services outside the United States. If services are furnished outside the United States, Medicare Part B covers ambulance transportation to a foreign hospital only in conjunction with the beneficiary's admission for medically necessary inpatient services as specified in subpart H of part 424 of this chapter.

[64 FR 3648, Jan. 25, 1999, as amended at 65 FR 13914, Mar. 15, 2000; 67 FR 9132, Feb. 27, 2002; 77 FR 69362, Nov. 16, 2012]
***

§ 410.42 Limitations on coverage of certain services furnished to hospital outpatients.

(a) General rule. Except as provided in paragraph (b) of this section, Medicare Part B does not pay for any item or service that is furnished to a hospital outpatient (as defined in § 410.2) during an encounter (as defined in § 410.2) by an entity other than the hospital unless the hospital has an arrangement (as defined in § 409.3 of this chapter) with that entity to furnish that particular service to its patients. As used in this paragraph, the term "hospital" includes a CAH.

(b) Exception. The limitations stated in paragraph (a) of this section do not apply to the following services:

(1) Physician services that meet the requirements of § 415.102(a) of this chapter for payment on a fee schedule basis.

(2) Physician assistant services, as defined in section 1861(s)(2)(K)(i) of the Act.

(3) Nurse practitioner and clinical nurse specialist services, as defined in section 1861(s)(2)(K)(ii) of the Act.

(4) Certified nurse mid-wife services, as defined in section 1861(gg) of the Act.

(5) Qualified psychologist services, as defined in section 1861(ii) of the Act.

(6) Services of an anesthetist, as defined in § 410.69.

(7) Services furnished to SNF residents as defined in § 411.15(p) of this chapter.

[65 FR 18536, Apr. 7, 2000]
***

§ 410.45 Rural health clinic services: Scope and conditions.

(a) Medicare Part B pays for the following rural health clinic services, if they are furnished in accordance with the requirements and conditions specified in part 405, subpart X, and part 491 of this chapter:

(1) Physicians' services.

(2) Services and supplies furnished as an incident to physicians' professional services.

(3) Nurse practitioner and physician assistant services.

(4) Services and supplies furnished as an incident to nurse practitioners' or physician assistants' services.

(5) Visiting nurse services.

(b) Medicare pays for rural health clinic services when they are furnished at the clinic, at a hospital or other medical facility, or at the beneficiary's place of residence.

***

§ 410.50 Institutional dialysis services and supplies: Scope and conditions.

Medicare Part B pays for the following institutional dialysis services and supplies if they are furnished in approved ESRD facilities:

(a) All services, items, supplies, and equipment necessary to perform dialysis and drugs medically necessary and the treatment of the patient for ESRD and, as of January 1, 2011, renal dialysis services as defined in § 413.171 of this chapter.

(b) Routine dialysis monitoring tests (i.e., hematocrit and clotting time) used by the facility to monitor the patients' fluids incident to each dialysis treatment, when performed by qualified staff of the facility under the direction of a physician, as provided in § 494.130 of this chapter, even if the facility does not meet the conditions for coverage of services of independent laboratories in part 494 of this chapter.

(c) Routine diagnostic tests.

(d) Epoetin (EPO) and its administration.

[51 FR 41339, Nov. 14, 1986, as amended at 56 FR 43709, Sept. 4, 1991; 59 FR 1285, Jan. 10, 1994; 73 FR 20474, Apr. 15, 2008; 75 FR 49197, Aug. 12, 2010]

***

§ 410.52 Home dialysis services, supplies, and equipment: Scope and conditions.

(a) Medicare Part B pays for the following services, supplies, and equipment furnished to an ESRD patient in his or her home:

(1) Purchase or rental, installation, and maintenance of all dialysis equipment necessary for home dialysis, and reconditioning of this equipment. Dialysis equipment includes, but is not limited to, artificial kidney and automated peritoneal dialysis machines, and support equipment such as blood pumps, bubble detectors, and other alarm systems.

(2) Items and supplies required for dialysis, including (but not limited to) dialyzers, syringes and needles, forceps, scissors, scales, sphygmomanometer with cuff and stethoscope, alcohol wipes, sterile drapes, and rubber gloves.

(3) Home dialysis support services furnished by an approved ESRD facility, including periodic monitoring of the patient's home adaptation, emergency visits

by qualified provider or facility personnel, any of the tests specified in paragraphs (b) through (d) of § .410.50, personnel costs associated with the installation and maintenance of dialysis equipment, testing and appropriate treatment of water, and ordering of supplies on an ongoing basis.

(4) On or after July 1, 1991, erythropoeisis-stimulating agents for use at home by a home dialysis patient and, on or after January 1, 1994, by a dialysis patient, if it has been determined, in accordance with § .494.90(a)(4) of this chapter, that the patient is competent to use the drug safely and effectively.

(b) Home dialysis support services specified in paragraph (a)(3) of this section must be furnished in accordance with a written treatment plan that is prepared and reviewed by a team consisting of the individual's physician and other qualified professionals. (§ 494.90 of this chapter contains details on patient plans of care).

[51 FR 41339, Nov. 14, 1986, as amended at 56 FR 43709, Sept. 4, 1991; 59 FR 26959, May 25, 1994; 73 FR 20474, April 15, 2008]

***

§ 410.55 Services related to kidney donations: Conditions.

Medicare Part B pays for medical and other health services covered under this subpart that are furnished in connection with a kidney donation—

(a) If the kidney is intended for an individual who has end-stage renal disease and is entitled to Medicare benefits; and

(b) Regardless of whether the donor is entitled to Medicare.

***

§ 410.57 Pneumococcal vaccine and flu vaccine.

(a) Medicare Part B pays for pneumococcal vaccine and its administration when reasonable and necessary for the prevention of disease, if the vaccine is ordered by a doctor of medicine or osteopathy.

(b) Medicare Part B pays for the influenza virus vaccine and its administration.

[63 FR 35066, June 26, 1998]

§ 410.58 Additional services to HMO and CMP enrollees.

Services not usually covered under Medicare Part B may be covered as medical and other health services if they are furnished to an enrollee of an HMO or a CMP and the following conditions are met:

(a) The services are—

(1) Furnished by a physician assistant or nurse practitioner as defined in § 491.2 of this chapter, or are incident to services furnished by such a practitioner; or

(2) Furnished by a clinical psychologist as defined in § 417.416 of this chapter to an enrollee of an HMO or CMP that participates in Medicare under a risk-sharing contract, or are incident to those services.

(b) The services are services that would be covered under Medicare Part B if they were furnished by a physician or as incident to a physician's professional services.

***

§ 410.60 Outpatient physical therapy services: Conditions.

(a) Basic rule. Except as specified in paragraph (a)(3)(iii) of this section, Medicare Part B pays for outpatient physical therapy services only if they are furnished by an individual meeting the qualifications in part 484 of this chapter for a physical therapist or an appropriately supervised physical therapist assistant but only under the following conditions:

(1) They are furnished to a beneficiary while he or she is under the care of a physician who is a doctor of medicine, osteopathy, or podiatric medicine.

(2) They are furnished under a written plan of treatment that meets the requirements of § 410.61.

(3) They are furnished—

(i) By a provider as defined in § 489.2 of this chapter, or by others under arrangements with, and under the supervision of, a provider; or

(ii) By, or under the direct supervision of a physical therapist in private practice as described in paragraph (c) of this section; or

(iii) By, or incident to the service of, a physician, physician assistant, clinical nurse specialist, or nurse practitioner when those professionals may perform physical therapy services under State law. When a physical therapy service is provided incident to the service of a physician, physician's assistant, clinical nurse specialist, or nurse practitioner, by anyone other than a physician, physician assistant, clinical nurse specialist, or nurse practitioner, the service and the person who furnishes the service must meet the standards and conditions that apply to physical therapy and physical therapists, except that a license to practice physical therapy in the State is not required.

(4) Claims submitted for furnished services contain prescribed information on patient functional limitations.

(b) Condition for coverage of outpatient physical therapy services furnished to certain inpatients of a hospital or a CAH or SNF. Medicare Part B pays for outpatient physical therapy services furnished to an inpatient of a hospital, CAH, or SNF who requires them but who has exhausted or is otherwise ineligible for benefit days under Medicare Part A.

(c) Special provisions for services furnished by physical therapists in private practice—(1) *Basic qualifications.* In order to qualify under Medicare as a supplier of outpatient physical therapy services, each individual physical therapist in private practice must meet the following requirements:

(i) Be legally authorized (if applicable, licensed, certified, or registered) to engage in the private practice of physical therapy by the State in which he or she practices, and practice only within the scope of his or her license, certification, or registration.

(ii) Engage in the private practice of physical therapy on a regular basis as an individual, in one of the following practice types:

(A) An unincorporated solo practice.

(B) An unincorporated partnership or unincorporated group practice.

(C) An unincorporated solo practice, partnership, or group practice, or a professional corporation or other incorporated physical therapy practice.

(D) An employee of a physician group.

(E) An employee of a group that is not a professional corporation.

(iii) Bill Medicare only for services furnished in his or her private practice office space, or in the patient's home. A therapist's private practice office space refers to the location(s) where the practice is operated, in the State(s) where the therapist (and practice, if applicable) is legally authorized to furnish services, during the hours that the therapist engages in practice at that location. When services are furnished in private practice office space, that space must be owned, leased, or rented by the practice and used for the exclusive purpose of operating the practice. A patient's home does not include any institution that is a hospital, a CAH, or a SNF.

(iv) Treat individuals who are patients of the practice and for whom the practice collects fees for the services furnished.

(2) *Supervision of physical therapy services.* Physical therapy services are performed by, or under the direct supervision of, a physical therapist in private practice. All services not performed personally by the therapist must be performed by employees of the practice, directly supervised by the therapist, and included in the fee for the therapist's services.

(d) Excluded services. No service is included as an outpatient physical therapy service if it would not be included as an inpatient hospital service if furnished to a hospital or CAH inpatient.

(e) Annual limitation on incurred expenses. (1) Amount of limitation. (i) In 1999, 2000, and 2001, no more than $1,500 of allowable charges incurred in a calendar year for outpatient physical therapy services are recognized incurred expenses.

(ii) In 2002 and thereafter, the limitation shall be determined by increasing the limitation in effect in the previous calendar year by the increase in the Medicare Economic Index for the current year.

(iii) The limitation is not applied for services furnished from December 8, 2003 through December 31, 2005.

(2) For purposes of applying the limitation, outpatient physical therapy includes:

(i) Except as provided in paragraph (e)(3) of this section, outpatient physical therapy services furnished under this section;

(ii) Except as provided in paragraph (e)(3) of this section outpatient speech-language pathology services furnished under § 410.62;

(iii) Outpatient physical therapy and speech-language pathology services furnished by a comprehensive outpatient rehabilitation facility;

(iv) Outpatient physical therapy and speech-language pathology services furnished by a physician or incident to a physician's service;

(v) Outpatient physical therapy and speech-language pathology services furnished by a nurse practitioner, clinical nurse specialist, or physician assistant or incident to their services.

(3) For purposes of applying the limitation, outpatient physical therapy excludes services furnished by a hospital or CAH directly or under arrangements.

[63 FR 58906, Nov. 2, 1998, as amended at 67 FR 80041, Dec. 31, 2002; 69 FR 66422, Nov. 15, 2004; 72 FR 66399, Nov. 27, 2007; 77 FR 69363, Nov. 16, 2012]

***

§ 410.62 Outpatient speech-language pathology services: Conditions and exclusions.

(a) Basic rule. Except as specified in paragraph (a)(3)(ii) of this section, Medicare Part B pays for outpatient speech-language pathology services only if they are furnished by an individual who meets the qualifications for a speech-language pathologist in § 484.4 of this chapter and only under the following conditions:

(1) They are furnished to a beneficiary while he or she is under the care of a physician who is a doctor of medicine or osteopathy.

(2) They are furnished under a written plan of treatment that meets the requirements of § 410.61.

(3) They are furnished by one of the following:

(i) A provider as defined in § 489.2 of this chapter, or by others under arrangements with, and under the supervision of, a provider.

(ii) A speech-language pathologist in private practice as described in paragraph (c) of this section.

(iii) Incident to the service of, a physician, physician assistant, clinical nurse specialist, or nurse practitioner when those professionals may perform speech-language pathology services under State law. When a speech-language pathology service is provided incident to the services of a physician, physician assistant, clinical nurse specialist, or nurse practitioner, by anyone other than a physician,

physician assistant, clinical nurse specialist, or nurse practitioner, the service and the person who furnishes the service must meet the standards and conditions that apply to speech-language pathology and speech-language pathologists, except that a license to practice speech-language pathology services in the State is not required.

(4) Claims submitted for furnished services contain prescribed information on patient functional limitations.

(b) Condition for coverage of outpatient speech-language pathology services furnished to certain inpatients of a hospital, CAH, or SNF. Medicare Part B pays for outpatient speech-language pathology services furnished to an inpatient of a hospital, CAH, or SNF who requires the services but has exhausted or is otherwise ineligible for benefit days under Medicare Part A.

(c) Special provisions for services furnished by speech-language pathologists in private practice.

(1) Basic qualifications. In order to qualify under Medicare as a supplier of outpatient speech-language pathology services, each individual speech-language pathologist in private practice must meet the following requirements:

(i) Be legally authorized (if applicable, licensed, certified, or registered) to engage in the private practice of speech-language pathology by the State in which he or she practices, and practice only within the scope of his or her license and/or certification.

(ii) Engage in the private practice of speech-language pathology as an individual, in one of the following practice types:

(A) An unincorporated solo practice.

(B) An unincorporated partnership or unincorporated group practice.

(C) An unincorporated solo practice, partnership, or group practice, or a professional corporation or other incorporated speech-language pathology practice.

(D) An employee of a physician group.

(E) An employee of a group that is not a professional corporation.

(iii) Bill Medicare only for services furnished in one of the following:

(A) A speech-language pathologist's private practice office space that meets all of the following:

(1) The location(s) where the practice is operated, in the State(s) where the therapist (and practice, if applicable) is legally authorized to furnish services and during the hours that the therapist engages in practice at that location.

(2) The space must be owned, leased, or rented by the practice, and used for the exclusive purpose of operating the practice.

(B) A patient's home not including any institution that is a hospital, a CAH, or a SNF.

(iv) Treat individuals who are patients of the practice and for whom the practice collects fees for the services furnished.

(d) Excluded services. No service is included as an outpatient speech-language pathology service if it is not included as an inpatient hospital service if furnished to a hospital or CAH inpatient.

[63 FR 58906, Nov. 2, 1998, as amended at 67 FR 80041, Dec. 31, 2002; 69 FR 66422, Nov. 15, 2004; 72 FR 66399, Nov. 27, 2007; 77 FR 69363, Nov. 16, 2012]

APPENDIX 6-6 TITLE 42—PUBLIC HEALTH (CODE OF FEDERAL REGULATIONS):

PART 411—EXCLUSIONS FROM MEDICARE AND LIMITATIONS ON MEDICARE PAYMENT

(Subpart K—Payment for Certain Excluded Services)*

§ 411.400 Payment for custodial care and services not reasonable and necessary.

(a) Conditions for payment. Notwithstanding the exclusions set forth in § 411.15(g) and (k), Medicare pays for "custodial care" and "services not reasonable and necessary" if the following conditions are met:

(1) The services were furnished by a provider or by a practitioner or supplier that had accepted assignment of benefits for those services.

(2) Neither the beneficiary nor the provider, practitioner, or supplier knew, or could reasonably have been expected to know, that the services were excluded from coverage under § 411.15(g) or (k).

(b) Time limits on payment. (1) *Basic rule.* Except as provided in paragraph (b)(2) of this section, payment may not be made for inpatient hospital care, post hospital SNF care, or home health services furnished after the earlier of the following:

(i) The day on which the beneficiary has been determined, under § 411.404, to have knowledge, actual or imputed, that the services were excluded from coverage by reason of § 411.15(g) or § 411.15(k).

(ii) The day on which the provider has been determined, under § 411.406, to have knowledge, actual or imputed, that the services are excluded from coverage by reason of § 411.15(g) or § 411.15(k).

(2) *Exception.* Payment may be made for services furnished during the first day after the limit established in paragraph (b)(1) of this section, if the QIO or the intermediary determines that the additional period of one day is necessary for planning post-discharge care. If the QIO or the intermediary determines that yet another day is necessary for planning post-discharge care, payment may be made for services furnished during the second day after the limit established in paragraph (b)(1) of this section.

***

---

* *See* www.ecfr.gov/cgi-bin/text-idx?tpl=/ecfrbrowse/title42/42cfr411_main_02.tpl (site visited Oct. 18, 2015).

§ 411.404 Criteria for determining that a beneficiary knew that services were excluded from coverage as custodial care or as not reasonable and necessary.

(a) Basic rule. A beneficiary who receives services that constitute custodial care under § 411.15(g) or that are not reasonable and necessary under § 411.15(k), is considered to have known that the services were not covered if the criteria of paragraphs (b) and (c) of this section are met.

(b) Written notice. (1) Written notice is given to the beneficiary, or to someone acting on his or her behalf, that the services were not covered because they did not meet Medicare coverage guidelines.

(2) A notice concerning similar or reasonably comparable services furnished on a previous occasion also meets this criterion.

(3) After a beneficiary is notified that there is no Medicare payment for a service that is not covered by Medicare, he or she is presumed to know that there is no Medicare payment for any form of subsequent treatment for the non-covered condition.

(c) Source of notice. The notice was given by one of the following:

(1) The QIO, intermediary, or carrier.

(2) The group or committee responsible for utilization review for the provider that furnished the services.

(3) The provider, practitioner, or supplier that furnished the service.

[54 FR 41734, Oct. 11, 1989, as amended at 69 FR 66423, Nov. 15, 2004]

***

§ 411.406 Criteria for determining that a provider, practitioner, or supplier knew that services were excluded from coverage as custodial care or as not reasonable and necessary.

(a) Basic rule. A provider, practitioner, or supplier that furnished services which constitute custodial care under Sec. 411.15(g) or that are not reasonable and necessary under § 411.15(k) is considered to have known that the services were not covered if any one of the conditions specified in paragraphs (b) through (e) of this section is met.

(b) Notice from the QIO, intermediary or carrier. The QIO, intermediary, or carrier had informed the provider, practitioner, or supplier that the services furnished were not covered, or that similar or reasonably comparable services were not covered.

(c) Notice from the utilization review committee or the beneficiary's attending physician. The utilization review group or committee for the provider or the beneficiary's attending physician had informed the provider that these services were not covered.

(d) Notice from the provider, practitioner, or supplier to the beneficiary. Before the services were furnished, the provider, practitioner or supplier informed the beneficiary that—

(1) The services were not covered; or

(2) The beneficiary no longer needed covered services.

(e) Knowledge based on experience, actual notice, or constructive notice. It is clear that the provider, practitioner, or supplier could have been expected to have known that the services were excluded from coverage on the basis of the following:

(1) Its receipt of CMS notices, including manual issuances, bulletins, or other written guides or directives from intermediaries, carriers, or QIOs, including notification of QIO screening criteria specific to the condition of the beneficiary for whom the furnished services are at issue and of medical procedures subject to preadmission review by a QIO.

(2) Federal Register publications containing notice of national coverage decisions or of other specifications regarding noncoverage of an item or service.

(3) Its knowledge of what are considered acceptable standards of practice by the local medical community.

[54 FR 41734, Oct. 11, 1989, as amended at 60 FR 48425, Sept. 19, 1995]

APPENDIX 6-7 TITLE 20—EMPLOYEES' BENEFITS (CODE OF FEDERAL REGULATIONS):

PART 418—MEDICARE SUBSIDIES

(Subpart B—Medicare Part B Income-Related Monthly Adjustment Amount)*

§ 418.1001 What is this subpart about?

This subpart relates to section 1839(i) of the Social Security Act (the Act), as added by section 811 of the Medicare Prescription Drug, Improvement, and Modernization Act of 2003 (Pub. L. 108–173). Section 1839(i) establishes an income-related monthly adjustment to the Medicare Part B premium. Beneficiaries enrolled in Medicare Part B who have modified adjusted gross income over a threshold amount established in the statute will pay an income-related monthly adjustment amount in addition to the Medicare Part B standard monthly premium and any applicable premium increases as described in 42 CFR 408.20. The regulations in this subpart explain how we decide whether you are required to pay an income-related monthly adjustment amount, and if you are, the amount of your adjustment. The rules are divided into the following groups of sections:

(a) Sections 418.1001 through 418.1010 contain the introduction, a statement of the general purpose of the income-related monthly adjustment amount, general provisions that apply to the income-related monthly adjustment amount, and definitions of terms that we use in this subpart.

(b) Sections 418.1101 through 418.1150 describe what information about your modified adjusted gross income we will use to determine if you are required to pay an income-related monthly adjustment amount. In these sections, we also describe how the income-related monthly adjustment amount will affect your total Medicare Part B premium. These sections also explain how the income-related monthly adjustment amount will be phased in from calendar year 2007 through calendar year 2009.

(c) Sections 418.1201 through 418.1270 contain an explanation of the standards that you must meet for us to grant your request to use modified adjusted gross income information that you provide for a more recent tax year rather than the information described in paragraph (b) of this section. These sections explain when we may consider such a request, and the evidence that you will be required to provide. These sections also explain when income-related monthly adjustment amount determinations based on information you provide will be effective, and how long they will remain in effect. Additionally, these sections describe how retroactive adjustments of the income-related monthly adjustment amount will be

---

* *See* www.ecfr.gov/cgi-bin/text-idx?tpl=/ecfrbrowse/title23/20cfr418_main_02.tpl (site visited Oct. 18, 2015).

made based on information you provide, updated information you provide, and information we later receive from the Internal Revenue Service (IRS).

(d) Sections 418.1301 through 418.1355 contain the rules that we will apply when you disagree with our determination regarding your income-related monthly adjustment amount. These sections explain your appeal rights and the circumstances under which you may request that we make a new initial determination of your income-related monthly adjustment amount.

APPENDIX 6-8 COMPARISON OF REDESIGNED MEDICARE SUMMARY NOTICE WITH ITS PREDECESSOR

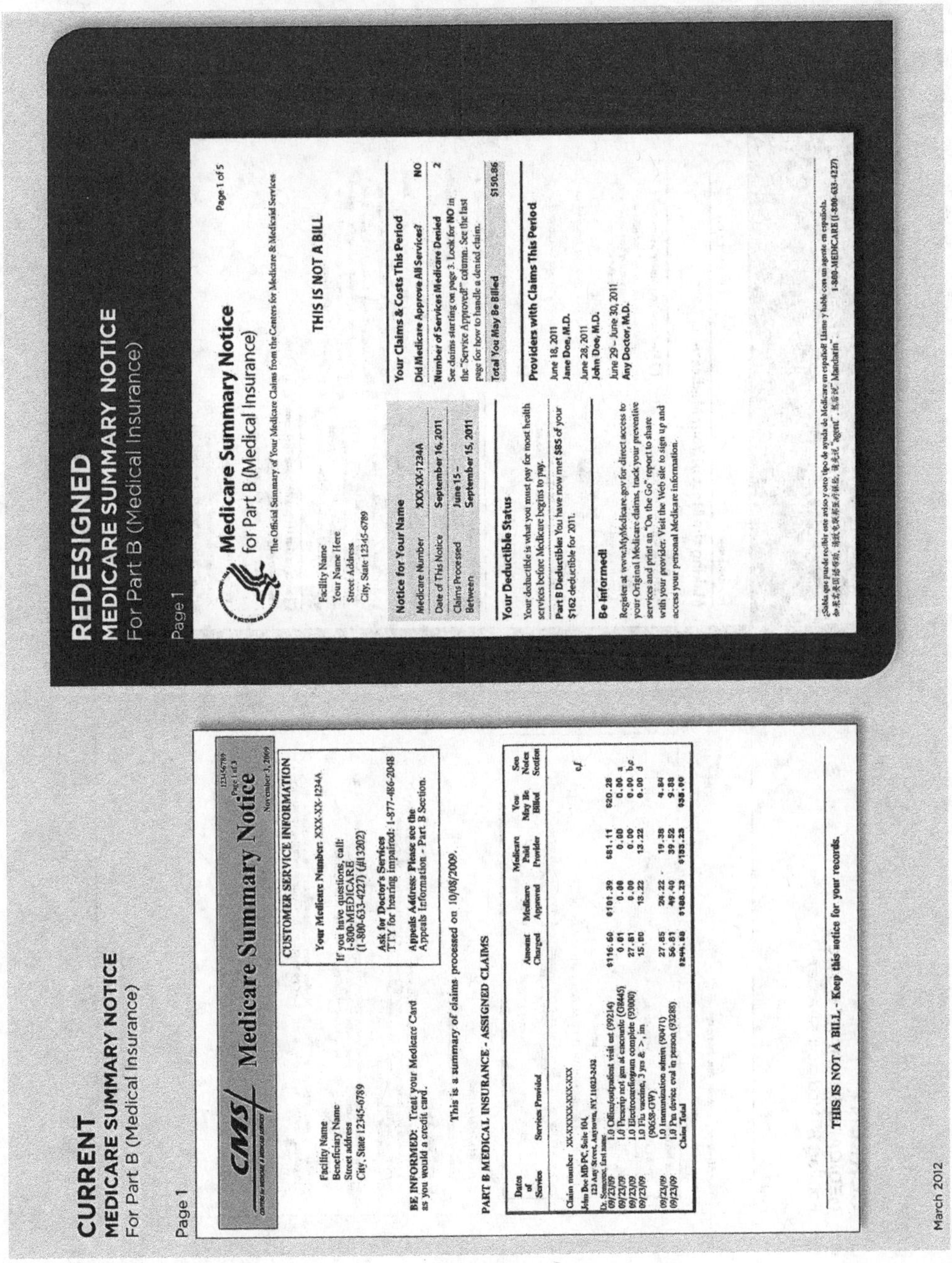

CURRENT
MEDICARE SUMMARY NOTICE
For Part B (Medical Insurance)

Page 1

CMS — Medicare Summary Notice
123456789
Page 1 of 3
November 3, 2009

Facility Name
Beneficiary Name
Street address
City, State 12345-6789

CUSTOMER SERVICE INFORMATION

Your Medicare Number: XXX-XX-1234A

If you have questions, call:
1-800-MEDICARE
(1-800-633-4227) (#13202)

Ask for Doctor's Services
TTY for hearing impaired: 1-877-486-2048

Appeals Address: Please see the Appeals Information - Part B Section.

BE INFORMED: Treat your Medicare Card as you would a credit card.

This is a summary of claims processed on 10/08/2009.

PART B MEDICAL INSURANCE - ASSIGNED CLAIMS

Dates of Service	Services Provided	Amount Charged	Medicare Approved	Medicare Paid Provider	You May Be Billed	See Notes Section
Claim number XX-XXXXX-XXX-XXX						
John Doe MD PC, Suite 104, 123 Any Street, Anytown, NY 11023-2432						c,f
Dr. Someone, first name						
09/23/09	1.0 Office/outpatient visit est (99214)	$116.60	$101.39	$81.11	$20.28	
09/23/09	1.0 Prescrip not gen at encounte (G8445)	0.01	0.00	0.00	0.00	a
09/23/09	1.0 Electrocardiogram complete (93000)	27.81	0.00	0.00	0.00	b,c
09/23/09	1.0 Flu vaccine, 3 yrs & >, im (90658-GW)	15.00	13.22	13.22	0.00	d
09/23/09	1.0 Immunization admin (90471)	27.85	24.22	19.38	4.84	
09/23/09	1.0 Pm device eval in person (93288)	56.81	49.40	39.52	9.88	
	Claim Total	$244.08	$188.23	$153.23	$35.00	

THIS IS NOT A BILL - Keep this notice for your records.

REDESIGNED
MEDICARE SUMMARY NOTICE
For Part B (Medical Insurance)

Page 1

Medicare Summary Notice
for Part B (Medical Insurance)
The Official Summary of Your Medicare Claims from the Centers for Medicare & Medicaid Services

Page 1 of 5

Facility Name
Your Name Here
Street Address
City, State 12345-6789

THIS IS NOT A BILL

Notice for Your Name

Medicare Number	XXX-XX-1234A
Date of This Notice	September 16, 2011
Claims Processed Between	June 15 – September 15, 2011

Your Claims & Costs This Period

Did Medicare Approve All Services?	NO
Number of Services Medicare Denied	2

See claims starting on page 3. Look for NO in the "Service Approved?" column. See the last page for how to handle a denied claim.

Total You May Be Billed	$150.86

Your Deductible Status

Your deductible is what you must pay for most health services before Medicare begins to pay.

Part B Deductible: You have now met $85 of your $162 deductible for 2011.

Be Informed!

Register at www.MyMedicare.gov for direct access to your Original Medicare claims, track your preventive services and print an "On the Go" report to share with your provider. Visit the Web site to sign up and access your personal Medicare information.

Providers with Claims This Period

June 18, 2011
Jane Doe, M.D.

June 28, 2011
John Doe, M.D.

June 29 – June 30, 2011
Any Doctor, M.D.

¿Sabía que puede recibir este aviso y otro tipo de ayuda de Medicare en español? Llame y hable con un agente en español. 1-800-MEDICARE (1-800-633-4227)

March 2012

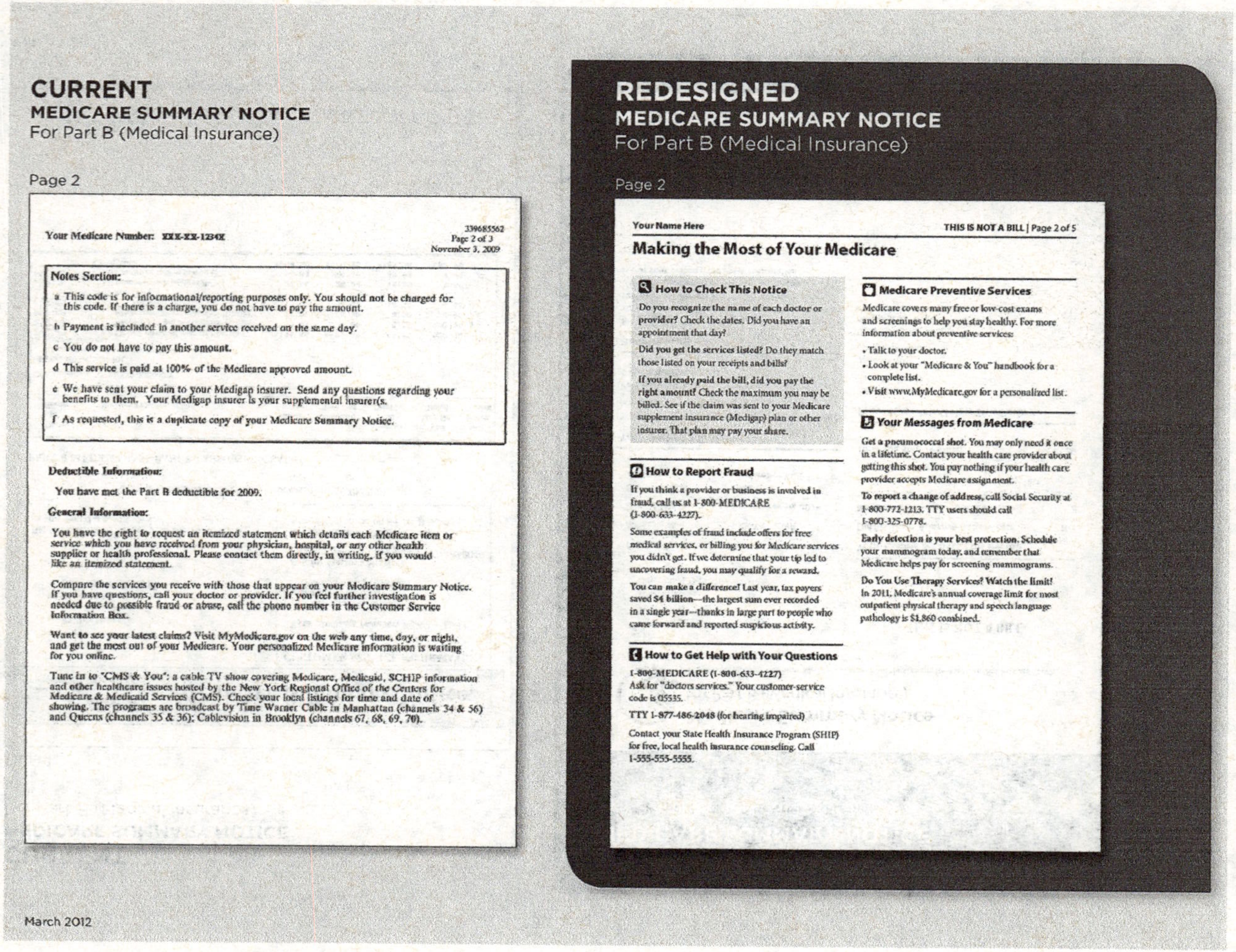

CURRENT
MEDICARE SUMMARY NOTICE
For Part B (Medical Insurance)

Page 2

Your Medicare Number: XXX-XX-1234X

339685562
Page 2 of 3
November 3, 2009

Notes Section:

a This code is for informational/reporting purposes only. You should not be charged for this code. If there is a charge, you do not have to pay the amount.

b Payment is included in another service received on the same day.

c You do not have to pay this amount.

d This service is paid at 100% of the Medicare approved amount.

e We have sent your claim to your Medigap insurer. Send any questions regarding your benefits to them. Your Medigap insurer is your supplemental insurer(s.

f As requested, this is a duplicate copy of your Medicare Summary Notice.

Deductible Information:

You have met the Part B deductible for 2009.

General Information:

You have the right to request an itemized statement which details each Medicare item or service which you have received from your physician, hospital, or any other health supplier or health professional. Please contact them directly, in writing, if you would like an itemized statement.

Compare the services you receive with those that appear on your Medicare Summary Notice. If you have questions, call your doctor or provider. If you feel further investigation is needed due to possible fraud or abuse, call the phone number in the Customer Service Information Box.

Want to see your latest claims? Visit MyMedicare.gov on the web any time, day, or night, and get the most out of your Medicare. Your personalized Medicare information is waiting for you online.

Tune in to "CMS & You": a cable TV show covering Medicare, Medicaid, SCHIP information and other healthcare issues hosted by the New York Regional Office of the Centers for Medicare & Medicaid Services (CMS). Check your local listings for time and date of showing. The programs are broadcast by Time Warner Cable in Manhattan (channels 34 & 56) and Queens (channels 35 & 36); Cablevision in Brooklyn (channels 67, 68, 69, 70).

March 2012

REDESIGNED
MEDICARE SUMMARY NOTICE
For Part B (Medical Insurance)

Page 2

Your Name Here — THIS IS NOT A BILL | Page 2 of 5

Making the Most of Your Medicare

How to Check This Notice

Do you recognize the name of each doctor or provider? Check the dates. Did you have an appointment that day?

Did you get the services listed? Do they match those listed on your receipts and bills?

If you already paid the bill, did you pay the right amount? Check the maximum you may be billed. See if the claim was sent to your Medicare supplement insurance (Medigap) plan or other insurer. That plan may pay your share.

How to Report Fraud

If you think a provider or business is involved in fraud, call us at 1-800-MEDICARE (1-800-633-4227).

Some examples of fraud include offers for free medical services, or billing you for Medicare services you didn't get. If we determine that your tip led to uncovering fraud, you may qualify for a reward.

You can make a difference! Last year, tax payers saved $4 billion—the largest sum ever recorded in a single year—thanks in large part to people who came forward and reported suspicious activity.

How to Get Help with Your Questions

1-800-MEDICARE (1-800-633-4227)
Ask for "doctors services." Your customer-service code is 05535.

TTY 1-877-486-2048 (for hearing impaired)

Contact your State Health Insurance Program (SHIP) for free, local health insurance counseling. Call 1-555-555-5555.

Medicare Preventive Services

Medicare covers many free or low-cost exams and screenings to help you stay healthy. For more information about preventive services:

- Talk to your doctor.
- Look at your "Medicare & You" handbook for a complete list.
- Visit www.MyMedicare.gov for a personalized list.

Your Messages from Medicare

Get a pneumococcal shot. You may only need it once in a lifetime. Contact your health care provider about getting this shot. You pay nothing if your health care provider accepts Medicare assignment.

To report a change of address, call Social Security at 1-800-772-1213. TTY users should call 1-800-325-0778.

Early detection is your best protection. Schedule your mammogram today, and remember that Medicare helps pay for screening mammograms.

Do You Use Therapy Services? Watch the limit! In 2011, Medicare's annual coverage limit for most outpatient physical therapy and speech language pathology is $1,860 combined.

CURRENT
MEDICARE SUMMARY NOTICE
For Part B (Medical Insurance)

Page 3

Your Medicare Number: XXX-XX-1234A — 339685562, Page 3 of 3, November 3, 2009

General Information (continued):

If you aren't due a payment check from Medicare, your Medicare Summary Notices (MSN) will now be mailed to you on a quarterly basis. You will no longer get a monthly statement in the mail for these types of MSNs. You will now get a statement every 90 days summarizing all of your Medicare Claims. Your provider may send you a bill that you may need to pay before you get your MSN. When you get your MSN, look to see if you paid more than the MSN says is due. If you paid more, call your provider about a refund. If you have any questions about the bill from your provider, you should call your provider.

If you change your address, contact the Social Security Administration by calling 1-800-772-1213.

The Medicare Summary Notice is now available in Spanish. If you or someone you know would like to receive the Medicare Summary Notice in Spanish, please contact us at: 1-800-MEDICARE (1-800-633-4227).

Si usted o alguien que usted conoce dese recibir el Resumen de Medicare en Espa ol, favor de llamarnos al: 1-800-MEDICARE (1-800-633-4227).

Please have your complete Medicare number with you when you call 1-800-MEDICARE so your record can be located. For your protection this MSN does not include your entire number.

Colorectal cancer is the second leading cancer killer in the United States. Medicare helps pay for colorectal cancer screening tests. Talk to your doctor about screening options that are right for you.

Appeals Information - Part B

If you disagree with any claims decision on this notice, your appeal must be received by **March 8, 2010.** Follow the instructions below:

1) Circle the item(s) you disagree with and explain why you disagree.
2) Send this notice, or a copy, to National Government Services, Inc., P.O. Box 7111, Indianapolis, IN 46207-7111. (You may also send any additional information you may have about your appeal.)
3) Sign here_______________ Phone number (___)________
4) Medicare Number_______________

REDESIGNED
MEDICARE SUMMARY NOTICE
For Part B (Medical Insurance)

Page 3

Your Name Here — **THIS IS NOT A BILL** | Page 3 of 5

Your Claims for Part B (Medical Insurance)

Part B Medical Insurance helps pay for doctors' services, diagnostic tests, ambulance services, and other health care services.

Definitions of Columns

Service Approved?: This column tells you if Medicare covered this service.

Amount Provider Charged: This is your provider's fee for this service.

Medicare-Approved Amount: This is the amount a provider can be paid for a Medicare service. It may be less than the actual amount the provider charged. Your provider has agreed to accept this amount as full payment for covered services. Medicare usually pays 80% of the Medicare-approved amount.

Amount Medicare Paid: This is the amount Medicare paid your provider. This is usually 80% of the Medicare-approved amount.

Maximum You May Be Billed: This is the total amount the provider is allowed to bill you, and can include a deductible, coinsurance, and other charges not covered. If you have Medicare Supplement Insurance (Medigap policy) or other insurance, it may pay all or part of this amount.

June 18, 2011
Jane Doe, M.D., (XXX)XXX-XXXX
Physical Therapy, Main Street, Any Town, Any State XXXXX

Service Provided & Billing Code	Service Approved?	Amount Provider Charged	Medicare-Approved Amount	Amount Medicare Paid	Maximum You May Be Billed	See Notes Below
Therapeutic exercise to develop strength, endurance, range of motion, and flexibility, each 15 minutes (97110)	Yes	$45.00	$28.54	$22.83	$5.71	
Total for Claim #99-99999-999-999		$45.00	$28.54	$22.83	**$5.71**	A

Continued →

Notes for Claims Above

A **Your claim was sent to your Medicare Supplement Insurance (Medigap policy), Wellmark BlueCross BlueShield of N. Carolina.** Send any questions regarding your benefits to them.

March 2012

CURRENT
MEDICARE SUMMARY NOTICE
For Part B (Medical Insurance)

Supplement Page

IMPORTANT INFORMATION YOU SHOULD KNOW ABOUT YOUR MEDICARE PART B BENEFITS

For more information about services covered by Medicare, please see your Medicare Handbook.

MEDICARE PART B MEDICAL INSURANCE: Medicare Part B helps pay for doctors' services, diagnostic tests, ambulance services, durable medical equipment, and other health care services. Medicare Part A Hospital Insurance helps pay for inpatient hospital care, inpatient care in a skilled nursing facility following a hospital stay, home health care and hospice care. You will be sent a separate notice if you received Part A services or any outpatient facility services.

MEDICARE ASSIGNMENT: Medicare Part B claims may be **assigned or unassigned.** Providers who accept assignment agree to accept the Medicare approved amount as total payment for covered services. Medicare pays its share of the approved amount directly to the provider. You may be billed for unmet portions of the annual deductible and the coinsurance. You may contact us at the address or telephone number in the Customer Service Information box on the front of this notice for a list of **participating providers** who always accept assignment. You may save money by choosing a participating provider.

Doctors who submit **unassigned claims** have not agreed to accept Medicare's approved amount as payment in full. Generally, Medicare pays you 80% of the approved amount after subtracting any part of the annual deductible you have not met. A doctor who does not accept assignment may charge you up to 115% of the Medicare approved amount. This is known as the Limiting Charge. Some states have additional payment limits. The NOTES section on the front of this notice will tell you if a doctor has exceeded the Limiting Charge and the correct amount to pay your doctor under the law.

YOUR RESPONSIBILITY: The amount in the You May Be Billed column is your share of cost for the services shown on this notice. You are responsible for:

- **annual deductible:** taken from the first Medicare Part B approved charges each calendar year,
- **coinsurance:** 20% of the Medicare approved amount, after the deductible has been met for the year,
- the amount billed, up to the **limiting charge**, for unassigned claims, and
- charges for services/supplies that are **not covered** by Medicare. You may not have to pay for certain denied services. If so, a NOTE on the front will tell you.

If you have supplemental insurance, it may help you pay these amounts. If you use this notice to claim supplemental benefits from another insurance company, make a copy for your records.

WHEN OTHER INSURANCE PAYS FIRST: All Medicare payments are made on the condition that you will pay Medicare back if benefits could be paid by insurance that is primary to Medicare. Types of insurance that should pay before Medicare include employer group health plans, no-fault insurance, automobile medical insurance, liability insurance and workers compensation. Notify us right away if you have filed or could file a claim with insurance that is primary to Medicare.

YOUR RIGHT TO APPEAL: If you disagree with what Medicare approved for these services, you may appeal the decision. You must file your appeal within 120 days of the date you receive this notice. Unless you show us otherwise, we assume you received this notice 5 days after the date of this notice. Follow the appeal instructions on the front of the last page of the notice. If you want help with your appeal, a friend or someone else can help you. Also, groups such as legal aid services may provide free assistance. To contact us for the names and telephone numbers of groups in your area, please see our Customer Service Information box on the front of this notice.

HELP STOP MEDICARE FRAUD: Fraud is a false representation by a person or business to get Medicare payments. Some examples of fraud include:

- offers of goods or money in exchange for your Medicare Number,
- telephone or door to door offers of free medical services or items, and
- claims for Medicare services or items you did not receive.

If you think a person or business is involved in fraud, you should call Medicare at the Customer Service telephone number on the front of this notice.

INSURANCE COUNSELING AND ASSISTANCE: Insurance Counseling and Assistance programs are located in every State. These programs have volunteer counselors who can give you free assistance with Medicare questions, including enrollment, entitlement, Medigap and premium issues. If you would like to know how to get in touch with your local Insurance Counseling and Assistance Program Counselor, please call us at the number shown in the Customer Service Information box on the front of this notice.

CENTERS for MEDICARE & MEDICAID SERVICES

REDESIGNED
MEDICARE SUMMARY NOTICE
For Part B (Medical Insurance)

NEW Page 4

Your Name Here — **THIS IS NOT A BILL** | Page 4 of 5

June 28, 2011
John Doe, M.D., (XXX)XXX-XXXX
Eye Glass Center, Any Town, Any State, XXXXX

Service Provided & Billing Code	Service Approved?	Amount Provider Charged	Medicare-Approved Amount	Amount Medicare Paid	Maximum You May Be Billed	See Notes Below
Eye and medical examination for diagnosis and treatment, established patient, 1 or more visits (92014)	Yes	$143.00	$107.97	$86.38	$21.59	
Computerized mapping of corneal curvature (92025)	Yes	0.00	0.00	0.00	0.00	B
Total for Claim #99-99999-999-999		$143.00	$107.97	$86.38	$21.59	C

June 29 – June 30, 2011
Any Doctor, M.D., (XXX)XXX-XXXX
Cardiology, Any Town, Any State, XXXXX
Referred by Jane Doe

Service Provided & Billing Code	Service Approved?	Amount Provider Charged	Medicare-Approved Amount	Amount Medicare Paid	Maximum You May Be Billed	See Notes Below
June 29, 2011						
Routine electrocardiogram (EKG) using at least 12 leads with interpretation and report (93010)	NO	$55.00	$0.00	$0.00	$55.00	D,E
June 30, 2011						
Destruction of skin growth (17000)	NO	68.56	0.00	0.00	68.56	D
Total for Claim #99-99999-999-999		$123.56	$0.00	$0.00	$123.56	C

Notes for Claims Above

B This line is for reporting purposes only. You should not be charged. If there is a fee listed, you do not have to pay.

C **Your claim was sent to your Medicare Supplement Insurance (Medigap policy), Wellmark BlueCross BlueShield of N. Carolina.** Send any questions regarding your benefits to them.

D **This service was denied.** The information provided does not support the need for this service or item.

E A National Coverage Determination (NCD) or Local Coverage Determination (LCD), was used when we made this decision. These policies provide a guide to help in determining whether a particular item or service is covered by Medicare. A copy of this policy is available by calling 1-800-MEDICARE (1-800-633-4227). Policy #L27490.

March 2012

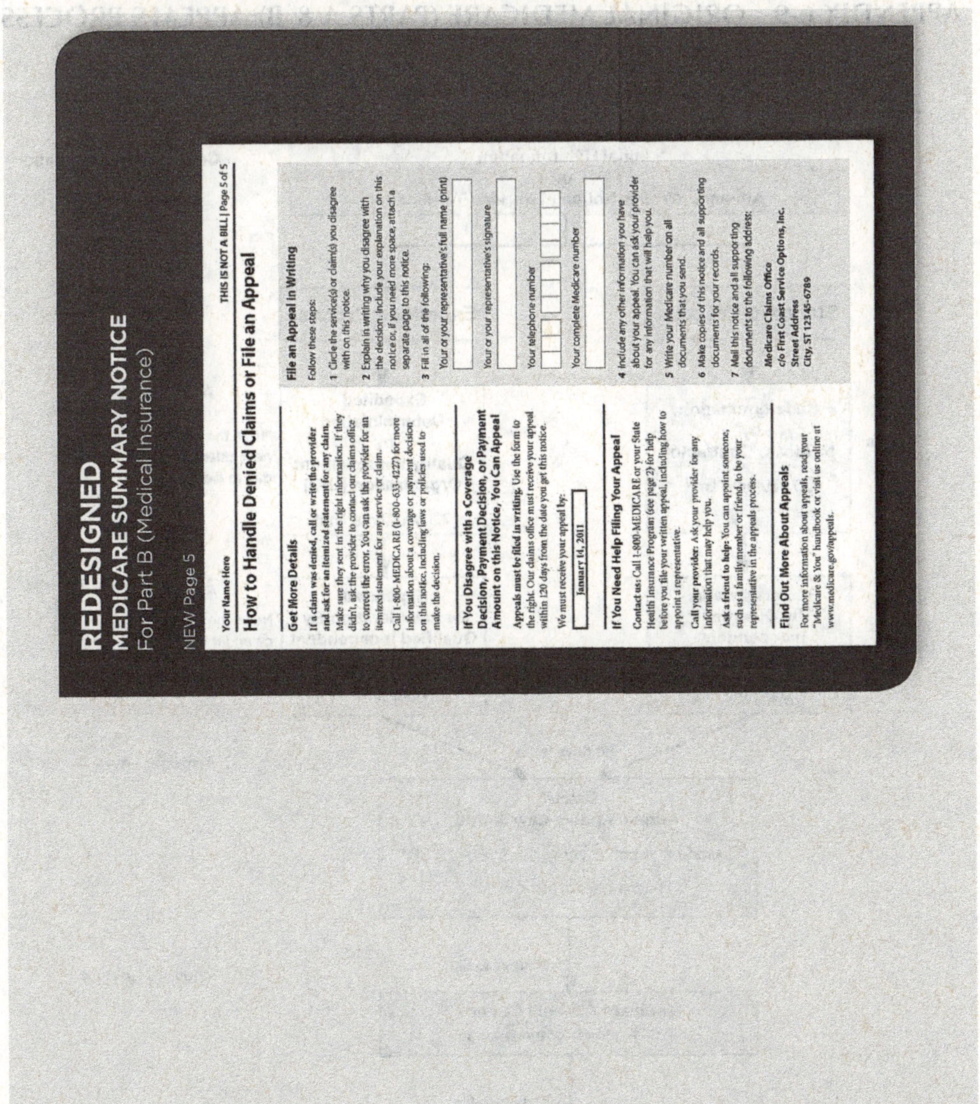

REDESIGNED
MEDICARE SUMMARY NOTICE
For Part B (Medical Insurance)

NEW Page 5

Your Name Here — THIS IS NOT A BILL | Page 5 of 5

How to Handle Denied Claims or File an Appeal

Get More Details

If a claim was denied, call or write the provider and ask for an itemized statement for any claim. Make sure they sent in the right information. If they didn't, ask the provider to contact our claims office to correct the error. You can ask the provider for an itemized statement for any service or claim.

Call 1-800-MEDICARE (1-800-633-4227) for more information about a coverage or payment decision on this notice, including laws or policies used to make the decision.

If You Disagree with a Coverage Decision, Payment Decision, or Payment Amount on this Notice, You Can Appeal

Appeals must be filed in writing. Use the form to the right. Our claims office must receive your appeal within 120 days from the date you get this notice.

We must receive your appeal by:

January 14, 2011

If You Need Help Filing Your Appeal

Contact us: Call 1-800-MEDICARE or your State Health Insurance Program (see page 2) for help before you file your written appeal, including how to appoint a representative.

Call your provider: Ask your provider for any information that may help you.

Ask a friend to help: You can appoint someone, such as a family member or friend, to be your representative in the appeals process.

Find Out More About Appeals

For more information about appeals, read your "Medicare & You" handbook or visit us online at www.medicare.gov/appeals.

File an Appeal in Writing

Follow these steps:

1 Circle the service(s) or claim(s) you disagree with on this notice.

2 Explain in writing why you disagree with the decision. Include your explanation on this notice or, if you need more space, attach a separate page to this notice.

3 Fill in all of the following:

Your or your representative's full name (print)

Your or your representative's signature

Your telephone number

Your complete Medicare number

4 Include any other information you have about your appeal. You can ask your provider for any information that will help you.

5 Write your Medicare number on all documents that you send.

6 Make copies of this notice and all supporting documents for your records.

7 Mail this notice and all supporting documents to the following address:

Medicare Claims Office
c/o First Coast Service Options, Inc.
Street Address
City, ST 12345-6789

March 2012

For a discussion of the MSN, see Center for Medicare Advocacy, "New Medicare Summary Notice," *available at* http://www.medicareadvocacy.org/new-medicare-summary-notice/ (site visited Sept. 23, 2016).

APPENDIX 6-9 ORIGINAL MEDICARE (PARTS A & B) APPEALS PROCESS

The following chart provides an overview of the appeals process for Original Medicare (Parts A&B). For more information on each level, click on the level name on the left hand side of this document or visit http://www.hhs.gov/omha/

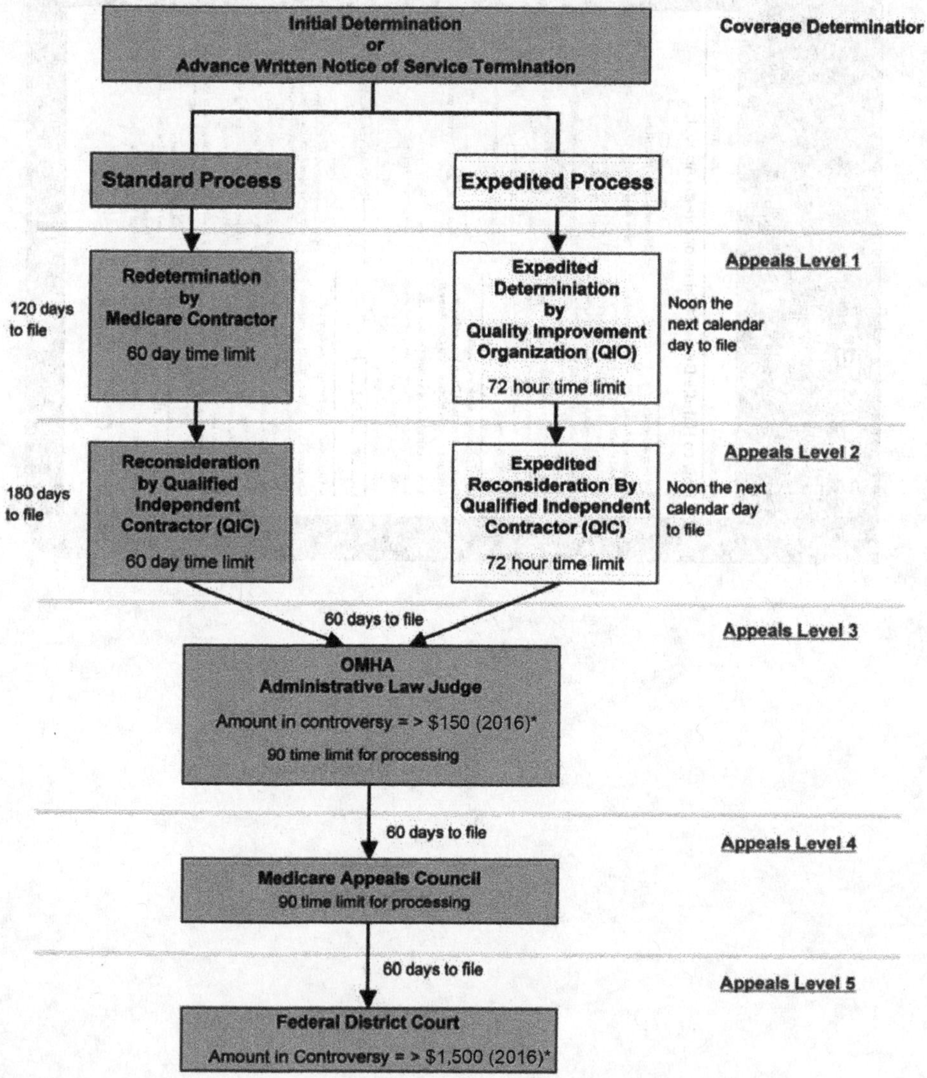

*The AIC requirements for an ALJ hearing and Federal District Court are annually in accordance with the medical care component of the Consumer Price Index.

CHAPTER 7

MEDICARE ADVANTAGE: COORDINATED CARE PLANS, PRIVATE FEE-FOR-SERVICE, AND OTHER DELIVERY OF SERVICES OPTIONS

Some helpful resources often referred to when discussing Medicare are:

- **The Medicare Statute**, Title XVIII of the Social Security Act (with parallel citations to the United States Code), can be found at http://ssa.gov/OP_Home/ssact/title18/1800.htm.
- **Code of Federal Regulations, Title 42** (most Medicare regulations are in Parts 405–426), can be found at http://www.ecfr.gov/cgi-bin/text-idx?c=ecfr&tpl=/ecfrbrowse/Title42/42tab_02.tpl. The Medicare Advantage regulations (in Part 422) can be found at http://www.ecfr.gov/cgi-bin/text-idx?SID=8d866696bbaf69e90e0557482ce3c33&mc=true&node=pt42.3.422&rgn=div5.
- **Medicare Manuals** can be found at https://www.cms.gov/Regulations-and-Guidance/Guidance/Manuals/Internet-Only-Manuals-IOMS.html.
  - The Medicare Managed Care Manual (CMS Pub. No. 100-16) is at https://www.cms.gov/Regulations-and-Guidance/Guidance/Manuals/Internet-Only-Manuals-IOMs-Items/CMS019326.html, and
  - Chapter 2 (enrollment and disenrollment guidance, 2017 updates) of the Medicare Managed Care Manual is at https://www.cms.gov/Medicare/Eligibility-and-Enrollment/MedicareMangCareEligEnrol/Downloads/CY_2017_MA_Enrollment_and_Disenrollment_Guidance_06-03-2016.pdf.

§ 7.01 INTRODUCTION

[A] What Is Medicare Advantage?

Medicare provides for a variety of delivery of care options for the receipt of Medicare-covered services, including managed care.[1] These services are found in Part C of the Medicare Statute, formerly known as the Medicare+Choice (M+C) Program[2] and now known as Medicare Advantage (MA). Medicare Advantage plans are a type of Medicare health plan that are administered and run by private

[1] 42 U.S.C. § 1395w-21; The Balanced Budget Act of 1997 (BBA '97), Pub. L. No. 105-33 (Aug. 5, 1997), § 4001; *see also* The Medicare Prescription Drug, Improvement, and Modernization Act of 2003 (MMA), Pub. L. No. 108-173 (Dec. 8, 2003), § 201(c). Managed care is used generally in this chapter to refer to all Medicare Part C plans. Manual provisions concerning Medicare managed care are found in the Centers for Medicare & Medicaid Services (CMS) online manuals which are available on the CMS website: http://cms.hhs.gov/Regulations-and-Guidance/Guidance/Manuals/Internet-Only-Manuals-IOMs.html (site visited May 25, 2016). *See* Medicare Managed Care (MMC) Manual, CMS Pub. 100-16, *available at* https://www.cms.gov/Regulations-and-Guidance/Guidance/Manuals/Internet-Only-Manuals-IOMs-Items/CMS019326.html?DLPage=2&DLEntries=10&DLSort=0&DLSortDir=ascending (site visited May 25, 2016).

[2] 42 U.S.C. § 1395w-21.

insurers that contract with Medicare to provide an individual with all of their Part A and Part B benefits. The private MA health plans are approved by Medicare and regulated by the federal government. Someone who joins an MA plan is still in the Medicare program and still has Medicare rights and protections. An MA enrollee will get his or her Medicare Part A, Part B, and sometimes Part D benefits covered through the private MA plan and not traditional Medicare.

The Secretary of the Department of Health and Human Services (HHS) is required to establish standards, regulations, and rules for Medicare Part C that are consistent with existing standards and regulations governing health maintenance organizations (HMOs) and competitive medical plans (CMPs).[3]

Each MA organization must provide the benefits currently available under Medicare Parts A and B, except hospice.[4] The MA organization, through its MA plan[5] or plans, however, may impose copayments and deductibles different from those under Parts A and B of traditional Medicare, as long as the monthly premium and cost-sharing are actuarially equivalent to cost-sharing under traditional Medicare.[6] Since 2011, local MA plans (and, since 2012 regional preferred provider plans, or PPOs) must establish a yearly maximum out-of-pocket (MOOP) liability amount for enrollees for all Part A and B services that does not exceed the maximum set yearly by CMS.[7] MA plans must also pass on to beneficiaries a percentage of any cost savings in the form of additional health benefits or reduced premiums.[8] Plans may offer supplemental benefits for which a separate premium may be charged, but the separate premium may not vary among individuals within the plan and must not exceed certain actuarial and community rating requirements.[9]

With respect to Medicare Part D drug coverage, MA sponsors must offer drug coverage unless the sponsor offers plans with and without drug coverage. Private fee-for-service (PFFS) plans do not have to offer drug coverage.[10] The

---

[3] 42 U.S.C. § 1395w-26(b)(1)–(2); *see also* 42 U.S.C. § 1395mm (payments to health plan organizations and competitive medical plans); 42 C.F.R. § 422.312.

[4] *See* **§ 7.04[C][1]** for a discussion of hospice coverage. 42 U.S.C. § 1395w-22(a);42 C.F.R. § 422.100(c)(1); 42 C.F.R. § 422.101. Note that 42 C.F.R. § 422.2 (MA definitions) and 42 C.F.R. § 423.4 (Voluntary Prescription Drug Benefit, Medicare Part D, definitions) contain an important explanatory list of terms of importance in discussing and understanding the MA program.

[5] An MA plan means health benefits coverage offered through a policy or contract with an MA organization that includes a specific set of health benefits offered at a uniform premium and uniform level of cost-sharing to all Medicare beneficiaries residing in the service area of the MA plan (or individual segments of a service area). 42 C.F.R. § 422.2 (definitions). Though different in meaning, "MA organization" and "MA plan" are often used interchangeably. In general, an MA organization is the overarching structure that may comprise one or more MA plans.

[6] 42 U.S.C. § 1395w-24(e).

[7] 42 C.F.R. §§ 422.100 and 422.101. In 2017, the mandatory MOOP is $ 6,700. Plans that use a lower, voluntary MOOP of $3,400 have greater flexibility in establishing cost-sharing amounts.

[8] 42 C.F.R. § 422.266.

[9] 42 U.S.C. § 1395w-22; 42 C.F.R. § 422.102.

[10] 42 C.F.R. § 422.4(c)(3).

type of MA plan an individual is enrolled in determines whether the individual can also enroll in a stand-alone Part D plan if his or her MA plan does not offer Part D coverage.[11]

Although there are some benefits to enrolling in an MA plan, those who do enroll in a plan have additional issues to consider than those who remain in the traditional Medicare program. MA enrollees must understand the various rules and guidelines associated with enrollment in an MA plan that might involve network restrictions and other rules for getting coverage for certain services like referrals to see specialists. Enrollees must also review MA plan material with a vigilant eye toward changes to plan premiums, benefits, and copayments that can change each year. MA enrollees should also be aware of the various enrollment periods that occur during the year and when they can make changes to their coverage.

[B] Background and History of Medicare Advantage Program

Although some form of managed care has existed in Medicare since the program's inception, the Balanced Budget Act of 1997 (BBA '97) formalized private plan contracting in Medicare by adding "Part C" to the Medicare statute and creating the Medicare+Choice (M+C) program.[12] Between 1999 and 2003, the early years of the introduction of a broader array of private plan offerings, almost half of all M+C plans stopped offering services completely or cut back on the counties served, affecting about 2.4 million beneficiaries.[13] To address this instability, the Medicare Prescription Drug, Improvement, and Modernization Act of 2003 (MMA) made significant changes to the M+C program, including substantial increases to plan payment rates and a change in the program's name from M+C to Medicare Advantage (MA).[14] The number of MA plan offerings grew tremendously in the years following passage of the MMA, and while the average number of plans available to enrollees nationwide has declined since 2009, overall

[11] *See* 42 C.F.R. § 423.30(b). Individuals enrolled in an MA coordinated care plan (HMO, PPO, Provider Service Organization (PSO)) cannot also be enrolled in a stand-alone Part D plan, even if the MA plan does not provide Part D coverage. If a private fee-for-service (PFFS) plan does not offer Part D coverage, enrollees can enroll in a separate Part D plan. Medical Savings Accounts (MSAs) cannot offer Part D coverage, so enrollees can also enroll in a Part D plan.

[12] Balanced Budget Act (BBA '97) of 1997, Pub. L. No. 105-33. For a history of private managed care plans in the Medicare program, see, e.g., Zarabozo, Carlos, "Milestones in Medicare Managed Care" Health Care Financing Review, Fall 2000, Vol. 22, Number 1, *available at* https://www.cms.gov/Research-Statistics-Data-and-Systems/Research/HealthCareFinancingReview/downloads/00fallpg61.pdf (site visited May 25, 2016).

[13] Public Citizen, "Private Insurance Plans & Medicare: The Disappointing History" (June 2003), *available at* www.citizen.org/documents/privatemedicare.pdf (site visited May 25, 2016).

[14] 42 U.S.C. § 1395w-23(k)(2)(B)(iv)(III); *see also* § 211 of the MMA, amending 42 U.S.C. § 1395w-23 (Payment to Medicare+Choice Organizations). 42 C.F.R. §§ 422.304–422.311. Rates and related data are posted on the CMS website at http://www.cms.gov/Medicare/Health-Plans/MedicareAdvtgSpecRateStats/index.html?redirect=/MedicareAdvtgSpecRateStats/ (site visited

enrollment in MA plans has increased.[15] As of May 2016, almost one in three (31 percent) people on Medicare were enrolled in an MA plan.[16] Payment rates for MA plans currently remain higher than those for traditional Medicare (sometime referred to as "original Fee-for-Service [FFS] Medicare"), even while, as discussed in the **§ 7.01[C]**, MA payment reform pursuant to the Affordable Care Act of 2010 is phased in.[17] There is, however, widespread concern that MA plans, despite increased rates, may not provide sufficient services even though they have been significantly overpaid.[18] The Affordable Care Act provides steps toward

---

May 26, 2016); *see also* Statement of Peter R. Orszag, Director, Congressional Budget Office (CBO), pp. 14–17 (June 28, 2007), *available at* http://www.cbo.gov/sites/default/files/cbofiles/ftpdocs/82xx/doc8268/06-28-medicare_advantage.pdf (site visited May 26, 2016).

[15] *See, e.g.*, Kaiser Family Foundation, "Medicare Advantage 2016 Spotlight: Enrollment Market Update" (May 11, 2016), *available at* http://kff.org/medicare/issue-brief/medicare-advantage-2016-spotlight-enrollment-market-update/ (site visited May 26, 2016).

[16] Kaiser Family Foundation, "Medicare Advantage 2016 Spotlight: Enrollment Market Update" (May 11, 2016), *available at* http://kff.org/medicare/issue-brief/medicare-advantage-2016-spotlight-enrollment-market-update/ (site visited May 26, 2016).

[17] The Medicare Payment Advisory Commission (MedPAC), an independent federal body established by the BBA '97 to advise Congress, releases annual reports to Congress and other publications. MedPAC projected that 2016 MA payments would be 102 percent of fee-for-service spending. *See* MedPAC, "A Data Book: Health Care Spending and the Medicare Program" (June 2016), *available at* http://medpac.gov/documents/data-book/june-2016-data-book-health-care-spending-and-the-medicare-program.pdf?sfvrsn=0 (site visited Aug. 2, 2016). This is down from, for example, 113 percent in 2009. *See* "Report to the Congress: Medicare Payment Policy" (Mar. 2009), *available at* http://medpac.gov/documents/reports/march-2009-report-to-congress-medicare-payment-policy.pdf?sfvrsn=0 (site visited May 26, 2016).

[18] *See, e.g.*, Austin Frakt, "Sicker Patients Seen at a Disadvantage with Medicare Advantage," *New York Times* (Apr. 4, 2016), *available at* http://www.nytimes.com/2016/04/05/upshot/sicker-patients-signal-a-drawback-of-medicare-advantage.html?emc=eta1; Momotazur Rahman et al., *High-Cost Patients Had Substantial Rates of Leaving Medicare Advantage and Joining Traditional Medicare,* Health Affairs 34(10):1676-82 (2015); Gerald F. Riley, "Impact of Continued Biased Disenrollment from the Medicare Advantage Program to Fee-for-Services," CMS, Medicare & Medicaid Research Review (MMRR) Vol. 2 No. 4 (2012), *available at* http://www.cms.gov/mmrr/Articles/A2012/mmrr-2012-002-04-a08.html (site visited May 26, 2016). *See also* Kaiser Family Foundation, "What Do We Know About Health Care Access and Quality in Medicare Advantage Versus the Traditional Medicare Program?" (Nov. 2014), which notes that "beneficiaries continue to rate traditional Medicare more favorably than Medicare Advantage plans in terms of quality and access. . . . [and] Among beneficiaries who are sick, the differential between traditional Medicare and Medicare Advantage is particularly large (relative to those who are healthy), favoring traditional Medicare;" this report is available at http://kff.org/medicare/report/what-do-we-know-about-health-care-access-and-quality-in-medicare-advantage-versus-the-traditional-medicare-program/ (site visited May 26, 2016).

See also GAO, "Medicare Advantage: Comparison of Plan Bids to Fee-for-Service Spending by Plan and Market Characteristics," GAO-11-247R (Feb. 2011), *available at* http://www.gao.gov/new.items/d11247r.pdf (site visited May 26, 2016). *See also* GAO, "Medicare Advantage: Higher Spending Relative to Medicare Fee-for-Service May Not Ensure Lower Out-of-Pocket Costs for Beneficiaries," GAO-08-522T (Feb. 2008), *available at* http://www.gao.gov/products/GAO-08-522T (site visited May 26, 2016). *See also* GAO, "Medicare Advantage: Increased Spending

addressing overpayment issues.[19] While controversial, their impact over time is expected to bring about more payment equity.

Advocates should watch closely the growth of enrollment in and use of MA options, paying particular attention to plan structure and benefits, scope of coverage, and beneficiary appeal rights, particularly in an environment of increased copayments for services and the push toward premium support ("vouchers") and other defined contribution approaches.[20]

[C] Medicare Advantage Plans and Health Care Reform

In March 2010, President Obama signed into law the Patient Protection and Affordable Care Act (PPACA) and the Health Care and Education Reconciliation Act of 2010 (HCERA) (together, the Affordable Care Act, or ACA).[21] A great deal

Relative to Medicare Fee-for-Service May Not Always Reduce Beneficiary Out-of-Pocket Costs," GAO-08-359 (Feb. 2008), *available at* http://www.gao.gov/products/GAO-08-359 (site visited May 26, 2016); Kathleen M. King & Mark Schlesinger (eds.), Final Report of the Study Panel on Medicare and Markets—The Role of Private Health Plans in Medicare: Lessons from the Past, Looking to the Future (Washington, D.C: National Academy of Social Insurance, Sept. 2003). *See also* COMMONWEALTH FUND ISSUE BRIEF: "The Continuing Cost of Privatization: Extra Payments to Medicare Advantage," (No. 43, Sept. 2008), *available at* http://www.commonwealthfund.org/Publications/Issue-Briefs/2008/Sep/The-Continuing-Cost-of-Privatization--Extra-Payments-to-Medicare-Advantage.aspx (site visited May 26, 2016).

[19] Patient Protection and Affordable Care Act of 2010 (PPACA or ACA), Pub. L. No. 111-148, Mar. 23, 2010, § 3201 *et seq.* and Health Care and Education Reconciliation Act of 2010 (HCERA), Pub. L. No. 111-152, Mar. 30, 2010, § 1102 *et seq.*

[20] *See* Marilyn Moon & Judy Feder, "Proceed with Caution: Renewed Calls to End Medicare as We Know It Because We Can't Afford It Misunderstand the Facts" (May 2011), Center for American Progress, *available at* http://www.americanprogress.org/issues/healthcare/report/2011/05/13/9679/proceed-with-caution/ (site visited May 26, 2016); Marilyn Moon, "Restructuring Medicare: Impacts on Beneficiaries" (Urban Inst., Jan. 1999); *see also* Marilyn Moon, Stephanie Maxwell, & Matthew Storeygard, "Reforming Medicare's Benefit Package: Impact on Beneficiary Expenditures" (Urban Inst., May 1, 2001), *available at* http://www.urban.org/publications/1000313.html (site visited May 26, 2016); and Marilyn Moon et al., "Medicare Extra: A Comprehensive Benefit Option for Medicare Beneficiaries" (Health Affairs, Oct. 4, 2005), *available at* http://www.commonwealthfund.org/Publications/In-the-Literature/2005/Oct/Medicare-Extra--A-Comprehensive-Benefit-Option-for-Medicare-Beneficiaries.aspx (site visited May 26, 2016). Benefit package issues remain key factors in plan utilization and plan satisfaction. Plan flexibility in benefit design, plus favorable reimbursement rates, will continue to be a driver with respect to beneficiary utilization. An important caution is to look carefully at one's overall health status, drug needs, and other factors before making a decision to elect an MA plan. With respect to benefit plan design, costs, and health status, see "MEDICARE ADVANTAGE: Relationship between Benefit Package Designs and Plans' Average Beneficiary Health Status" (Apr. 2010), GAO Study, GAO-10-403, *available at* http://www.gao.gov/new.items/d10403.pdf (site visited May 26, 20016). As has been seen in other studies, this April 2010 study shows that plans with lower premiums tend to have higher cost-sharing requirements and tend to attract healthier beneficiaries.

[21] ACA, Pub. L. No.111-148 (Mar. 23, 2010); Health Care and Education Reconciliation Act of 2010 (HCERA), Pub. L. No. 111-152 (Mar. 30, 2010).

of the discussion surrounding the implications of health care reform for older people and people with disabilities centered on changes in funding for MA plans. Some of the changes have been under consideration for many years.

In order to address payment to MA plans that has been disproportionately higher relative to what traditional Medicare spends on a given beneficiary (or, put more simply, MA overpayments), Section 1102 of HCERA phases in changes to the MA plan payment structure, starting with a freeze in payments to MA plans for 2011. When fully phased in by 2017, payments will be based on national county benchmarks, with plans being paid a fixed percentage of traditional Medicare costs. As a result of the payment scheme, plans in some lower-paid counties, generally rural and suburban areas, will continue to receive payments that exceed the traditional Medicare amount, while plans in higher-paid counties, many of them large cities, may see substantial reductions. The new payment structure also provides for an increase in payments by up to 5 percent for plans that receive four or more stars on the CMS star rating system.[22] Rebates (an amount plans receive if they bid less than the county benchmark) will also be reduced. In an effort to counter some of these payment reductions, there is evidence indicating that some MA plans have sought to improperly inflate payments to plans through overstatements of enrollees' health risks, a practice sometimes referred to as "upcoding."[23]

In addition to attempting to achieve more payment parity between traditional Medicare and MA plans, the ACA also sets limits on how much MA plans can spend on administrative costs. As of 2014, if the Secretary of HHS determines that an MA plan does not maintain a medical loss ratio (MLR) of 85 percent (meaning that 85 percent of its revenues does not go toward benefits), the plan must remit a specified sum to the Secretary.[24]

Note that the provisions of the ACA that apply to stand-alone Part D plans, discussed in **Chapter 11**, also apply to MA plans that offer Part D prescription

---

[22] Each year CMS issues performance quality ratings, using a five-star system where five stars indicate the highest quality, of Part C and D plan sponsors. CMS adopts the authority to terminate the contracts of Part C and D sponsors that fail for three consecutive years to achieve at least a three-star rating. 42 C.F.R. §§ 422.504, 422.510, 423.505, and 423.509. CMS also adopts the authority to deny applications submitted by MA organizations and Part D sponsors that have performed so poorly that CMS terminated or did not renew a contract with the organization in the past. 42 C.F.R. §§ 422.502 and 423.503.

[23] *See, e.g.*, GAO report entitled "Medicare Advantage: Fundamental Improvements Needed in CMS's Effort to Recover Substantial Amounts of Improper Payments" (Apr. 2016), *available at* http://www.gao.gov/assets/680/676441.pdf (site visited Sept. 22, 2016); *see also* Center for Public Integrity's investigative series entitled "Medicare Advantage Money Grab" *available at* https://www.publicintegrity.org/health/medicare/medicare-advantage-money-grab (site visited Sept. 22, 2016).

[24] HCERA § 1103. CMS published a final rule on Medicare Advantage and Part D medical loss ratio (MLR) requirements on May 23, 2013. *See* 78 Fed. Reg. 31,284. Note that if a plan fails to have an MLR of 85 percent for three consecutive years, the Secretary must preclude new enrollment in that plan. The plan's contract must be terminated if the plan fails to have an MLR of 85 percent for five consecutive years.

drug coverage, which are referred to as Medicare Advantage-Prescription Drug (MA-PD) plans. Other changes to the MA program pursuant to the ACA are incorporated into this chapter.[25]

[D] Policy and Technical Changes for 2016

Medicare implements MA plans through a series of regulations[26] and other issuances, particularly its call letters.[27]

[1] Final Regulations

On February 12, 2015, CMS issued final regulations to provide policy and technical changes to the Medicare Part C (Medicare Advantage) and Part D programs for contract year 2016.[28] Similar to the 2014 final rule, this final rule neglected to implement many significant proposed changes to the Parts C and D programs that were suggested in the proposed rule issued in January 2014.[29] The 2016 rule includes, among other things, provisions that:

- require MA-PDs to establish and maintain a process to ensure that appropriate payment is assigned at the point of sale when claims for drugs are made that may be covered under Part A or B, rather than Part D;
- revise the applicable regulations to clarify that plan-initiated extensions of time to issue organization determinations and reconsideration should be permitted in only limited circumstances; and

---

[25] For a summary of changes the ACA made to the Medicare program, see, e.g., Kaiser Family Foundation, "Summary of Key Changes to Medicare in 2010 Health Reform Law" (Apr. 2010), *available at* http://kff.org/health-reform/issue-brief/summary-of-key-changes-to-medicare-in/ (site visited May 26, 2016).

[26] *See generally* 42 C.F.R. Pt. 422, which contains the rules pertaining to Part C (Medicare Advantage).

[27] *See* Medicare's system of call letters used by CMS in setting out its goals and objectives and the operating parameters that plans must use in preparing to offer a plan under programs operated by Medicare. *See generally* 42 C.F.R. Pt. 422 subpt. F and Pt. 423 subpt. F, for the bid submission and plan approval processes. 42 C.F.R. Part 422 contains the rules pertaining to Part C, and 42 C.F.R. Pt. 423 contains the rules pertaining to Part D. It contains information for MA plans and MA-PD plans as well as Part D prescription drug plans. The 2017 "Call Letter," formally known as the Announcement of Calendar Year (CY) 2017 Medicare Advantage Capitation Rates and Medicare Advantage and Part D Payment Policies and Final Call Letter, is *available at* https://www.cms.gov/Medicare/Health-Plans/MedicareAdvtgSpecRateStats/Downloads/Announcement2017.pdf (site visited May 26, 2016).

[28] 80 Fed. Reg. 7912 (Feb. 12, 2015), amending 42 C.F.R. Pts. 422 and 423.

[29] 79 Fed. Reg. 1917 (Jan. 10, 2014). Although there were several proposed changes that would have affected MA plans, most of the proposed changes would have affected Part D and were strongly opposed by industry stakeholders and many members of Congress.

- improve MA enrollees' access to out-of-network facilities in non-extraordinary circumstances.

In addition, CMS clarifies that any individual "not lawfully present" in the United States is no longer eligible to remain enrolled in an MA, Part D, or cost plan.[30] Contrary to customary practice, CMS has not issued a final Part C rule for 2017.

[2] Annual Notice of Payment Rates and Capitation Policies

On April 6, 2016, CMS released its annual Call Letter: "Announcement of Calendar Year (CY) 2017 Medicare Advantage Capitation Rates and Medicare Advantage and Part D Payment Policies and Final Call Letter."[31] This document includes various policy and technical updates, including Part C and Part D payment rates, Part D benefit parameters, and fees and liabilities for vaccine administration, drug dispensing, and negotiated drug pricing. New policies announced in the Call Letter include changes to payments made to Employer Group Waiver Plans (EGWPs) to achieve more parity with payment to other MA plans, and the incorporation of socio-economic and disability status into plans' quality star ratings (which, some advocates fear, could mask health disparities). In addition, CMS reiterated the prohibition on billing individuals dually eligible for Medicare and Medicaid for MA plan cost-sharing.[32]

[3] MA, MA-PD, and PDP Calendar for 2017

CMS's calendar contains dates of importance to beneficiaries and their advocates:

- The annual election period (AEP) begins on October 15 and ends on December 7.[33]
- The former MA open enrollment period (OEP)—now the Medicare Advantage disenrollment period (MADP)—has been changed to a 45-day period at the beginning of the year (January 1 through February 14). During the MADP, beneficiaries enrolled in an MA plan may

[30] For more information about the final 2016 Part C and D rule, *see, e.g.*, Center's Weekly Alert, "2016 Medicare Advantage (Part C) and Part D Final Rule Issued" (Feb. 19, 2015), *available at* http://www.medicareadvocacy.org/2016-medicare-advantage-part-c-and-part-d-final-rule-issued/ (site visited May 26, 2016).

[31] Available on the CMS website at https://www.cms.gov/Medicare/Health-Plans/MedicareAdvtgSpecRateStats/Downloads/Announcement2017.pdf (site visited May 26, 2016).

[32] For more information about the 2017 Call Letter, *see, e.g.*, Center's Weekly Alert, "Center for Medicare Advocacy Submits Comments Regarding Medicare Advantage and Medicare Part D" (Mar.9, 2016), *available at* http://www.medicareadvocacy.org/center-for-medicare-advocacy-submits-comments-regarding-medicare-advantage-and-medicare-part-d/ (site visited Aug. 2, 2016).

[33] ACA § 3204.

disenroll and return to traditional Medicare, with an option to enroll in a Medicare Part D plan.[34]

§ 7.02 ADVANTAGES AND DISADVANTAGES OF MEDICARE ADVANTAGE OPTIONS

As a general matter, MA options by design focus on at least some level of utilization management and cost containment, the savings from which are often passed on to beneficiaries in the form of reduced costs or additional services.

[A] Advantages

There are several advantages in choosing an MA option:

- *No claims.* Generally, a beneficiary need not submit claims unless emergency or urgent care is received while outside the service area.
- *Emphasis on preventive care.* Preventive health care, including annual physical exams, as well as health care screening services not covered under traditional Medicare, even as preventive services benefits under the traditional Medicare program are expanding.
- *Comprehensive services.* These services, which are not covered under traditional Medicare, often include some level of vision care, prescription drugs (but see **Chapter 11**, Medicare Prescription Drug Benefit, Medicare Part D), dental care, and hearing exams.
- *No need for Medigap insurance.* Managed care plans should provide beneficiaries with all or most of the benefits offered by a Medigap policy.
- *Easier to budget health care expenses.* Beneficiaries should know the amount of any premiums and copayments for doctor services in advance. In addition, unlike traditional Medicare, MA plans have beneficiary out-of-pocket spending caps.
- *Avoid unnecessary surgeries.* Plans are interested in avoiding unnecessary risks and have no financial incentive to perform unnecessary procedures. Consequently, if a plan recommends surgery, a beneficiary can be relatively certain that it is necessary.

[B] Disadvantages

Disadvantages include:

- *Plan terminations.* Plans may decide to terminate services and make elections whether to participate in a given market annually.

[34] 42 C.F.R. §§ 422.62, 422.68, 423.38, and 423.40.

- *Limitations on receiving specialized care.* Many plans require a beneficiary to have the prior approval of his or her primary care physician in order to see a specialist. Because of financial incentives and pressures from plan administrators, some primary care physicians resist making referrals.

- *Financial incentives to limit service.* Plans receive a capitated rate per beneficiary member. Some physicians may treat managed care patients differently from traditional Medicare patients. Waiting time may be longer, fewer tests may be performed, or services may be limited. Limiting services based on financial considerations may result in questionable quality of care.

- *Requirement to use plan providers.* In most plans, a beneficiary is not free to go to any physician or hospital he or she may choose. Beneficiaries are often "locked in" and must use the plan's providers and facilities or must pay higher premiums for the privilege of going outside the network. In other plans, a beneficiary must pay more to see "non-network" providers. In addition, plans can terminate providers from their networks mid-year, while a beneficiary's corresponding rights to change plans mid-year are limited.

- *Out-of-area care limitations.* If a beneficiary lives outside the plan service area for more than a specified period of time, the plan may not sell a beneficiary a plan or may disenroll a beneficiary. Plans cover emergency and urgent care if a beneficiary is out of the service area for a brief time, but a beneficiary must return to the area for routine care. The plan may offer a separate option that covers out-of-area care, but the beneficiary will have to pay an additional premium.

- *Service locations.* In most plans, there are limited locations where a beneficiary can receive care.

- *Higher copayments and deductibles.* Provided that services and costs are actuarially equivalent, some plans charge higher copayments and deductibles than traditional Medicare, including larger copayments for hospital, skilled nursing facility (SNF),[35] and home health services, and for durable medical equipment (DME), including oxygen. This has been criticized as a way of cherry picking (e.g., forcing heavy care patients out of the managed care plan).

- *Disenrollment.* Most enrollees are locked in to their plan for most of the year. When an individual has a right to leave the plan, it can take up to 30 days to disenroll or other rules may apply, and a beneficiary must continue to use the health plan during this time. Even after the disenrollment

[35] See the discussion of cost-sharing in **§ 7.04[C][2]** of this Handbook.

becomes effective, Medicare's computers may not be updated, and some traditional Medicare claims will be erroneously rejected.

§ 7.03 GUIDELINES FOR CONSIDERING MEDICARE ADVANTAGE OPTIONS

Beneficiaries should make informed decisions before enrolling in an MA plan. Following some general guidelines before enrolling in a plan, beneficiaries can avoid problems and disappointment later. These guidelines will help ensure that beneficiaries make wise decisions about MA options. After careful evaluation, some Medicare beneficiaries will choose managed care, while others may determine that the traditional Medicare program better suits their needs. Beneficiaries should consider the following:

1. Review coverage provided by the traditional Medicare program and by Medigap insurance policies. Beneficiaries should understand the coverage and costs available through the traditional Medicare system combined with an appropriate Medigap policy. Assess whether or not someone is entitled to other insurance coverage that might supplement Medicare, such as retiree coverage, and how such coverage might coordinate (or not) with an MA plan. **Chapter 8** provides more information on Medigap plans.

2. Read each plan's literature to understand the type of plan being considered, what it provides, and what copayments are required for different kinds of services.

3. Determine what plan services are provided at additional cost and how much they cost. In addition, determine the preventive services available under the plan, as well as any limitations associated with visits or services. The beneficiary should fully understand where to go for emergency, urgently needed, and routine care.

4. Review carefully the nature and extent of any offered prescription drug coverage. Identify whether the plan is a stand-alone MA plan or a combined Medicare Advantage-Prescription Drug (MA-PD) plan. If the plan is a stand-alone MA plan, beneficiaries should be aware that they may want a stand-alone prescription drug plan (PDP). For combined MA-PD plans, beneficiaries should scrutinize the prescription drug coverage as if it were a stand-alone PDP. Consideration should be given to whether the plan covers brand names or only generics, imposes different copayments based on the type of drug, or provides coverage on a monthly, quarterly, or yearly basis. In addition, beneficiaries should compare drug coverage with other available PDPs. **Chapter 11** provides more information on PDPs; see in particular **§ 11.03[B]** for rules concerning when an individual can have both an MA plan and a PDP.

5. If plan materials do not provide answers to all questions, contact the plan for additional information. Beneficiaries should make a note of how the plan's staff responds to such inquiries and use that information in evaluating the plan.
6. Ask about plan physicians, determine whether the physicians you use or wish to use are in the plan, and find out how to change physicians if a satisfactory relationship with a plan physician cannot be established. In addition, beneficiaries should inquire as to which hospitals, SNFs, and home care agencies have contracts with the plans under consideration and whether those facilities represent satisfactory choices. Note, though, that current rules allow MA plans to terminate network providers and facilities mid-year without cause.
7. Know how to use the plan's complaint system and how appeals and grievances are handled.
8. Inquire among friends and relatives to determine whether any are currently enrolled in managed care plans or have been enrolled in the past and ascertain whether and to what degree they were satisfied with the services received through those plans. Ask plan representatives whether member satisfaction surveys are conducted and whether the results are available for review.

Contact the Centers for Medicare & Medicaid Services (CMS) Regional Office of Beneficiary Services to determine whether a plan has failed to comply with CMS regulations.[36]

§ 7.04 MEDICARE ADVANTAGE BASICS

[A] Medicare Advantage Eligibility

[1] Eligible Persons

To be eligible for an MA plan, an individual must be entitled to benefits under Part A and enrolled in Medicare Part B.[37] To enroll in an MA plan, an individual must complete and sign an election form or complete a CMS-approved election method offered by the MA organization.[38]

---

[36] For online information about enforcement and compliance actions CMS has taken against individual Part C and D plans, see CMS, "Part C and D Enforcement Actions," *available at* http://www.cms.gov/Medicare/Compliance-and-Audits/Part-C-and-Part-D-Compliance-and-Audits/PartCandPartDEnforcementActions-.html (site visited May 26, 2016).

[37] 42 U.S.C. § 1395w-21; 42 C.F.R. § 422.50(a)(1).

[38] 42 C.F.R. § 422.50(a)(5). *But see* discussion of seamless conversion enrollment at **§ 7.04[D][8]**.

An individual cannot be denied enrollment in an MA plan due to a preexisting condition, unless that individual has end-stage renal disease (ESRD).[39] Individuals with ESRD are excluded, except that an individual who develops ESRD while enrolled in an MA plan may continue to be enrolled in that plan.[40] Such an individual may also enroll in another MA plan if the ESRD beneficiary loses MA plan coverage when his or her plan terminates its contract with CMS or reduces its service area. Note, however, that an individual with ESRD may elect an MA special needs plan as long as that plan has opted to enroll ESRD individuals.[41]

An individual is eligible to enroll in a particular MA plan if the plan serves the geographic area in which the individual resides.[42] If, after enrolling in a plan, the individual leaves the geographic area, the plan can offer the individual the option of staying in the plan if the plan provides the individual with reasonable geographic access to all basic plan benefits.

[2] Persons Ineligible to Enroll

An individual who is a Qualified Medicare Beneficiary (QMB), a Specified Low-Income Medicare Beneficiary (SLMB), a Qualified Disabled and Working Individual (QDWI), or otherwise eligible for Medicaid and entitled to Medicare cost-sharing under a state Medicaid program may not enroll in an MA Medical Savings Accounts (MSA) plan.[43]

Federal Employee Health Benefit Plan (FEHBP) members must make sure that plan choices under consideration are those that have been certified by the Director of the Office of Management and Budget (OMB) to the Secretary that the Office of Personnel Management (OPM) has adopted policies that ensure that the enrollment of FEHBP individuals in such plans will not result in increased expenditures for health benefits under FEHBP.[44] Similar rules may be applied to individuals eligible for health care from either the Veterans Administration (VA) or the Department of Defense (DOD).[45]

---

[39] 42 U.S.C. § 1395w-21(g); 42 C.F.R. § 422.60(a)(1)and(2). For further discussion regarding anti-discrimination and review for discrimination and steering, see Medicare Managed Care (MMC) Manual, CMS Pub. No. 100-16, Ch. 4, §§ 10.5.2 and 10.5.3, *available at* http://www.cms.gov/Regulations-and-Guidance/Guidance/Manuals/downloads/mc86c04.pdf (site visited May 26, 2016).

[40] 42 C.F.R. § 422.50(a)(2). For additional exceptions to the general exclusion of individuals with ESRD, see, e.g., MMC Manual, CMS Pub. No. 100-16, Ch. 2, §§ 20.2.2 and 20.2.3, *available at* http://cms.gov/Medicare/Eligibility-and-Enrollment/MedicareMangCareEligEnrol/Downloads/CY-2014-MA-Enrollment-and-Disenrollment-Guidance-r.pdf (site visited May 26, 2016).

[41] *See* 42 C.F.R. § 422.50(a)(2)(iii). A Medicare Advantage Special Needs Plan (MS-SNP) is defined in 42 C.F.R. § 422.2.

[42] 42 C.F.R. § 422.50(a)(3).

[43] 42 U.S.C. § 1395w-21(b)(3).

[44] 42 U.S.C. § 1395w-21(b)(2)(A).

[45] 42 U.S.C. § 1395w-21(b)(2)(B).

[B] Medicare Advantage Options[46]

There are many different options available under Medicare Advantage. Each MA organization could offer multiple types of plans. Even among similar types of plans benefits and cost-sharing can differ so it is important to read the literature for each plan closely.[47]

[1] Coordinated Care Plans

In order to offer an MA coordinated care plan in an area,[48] the MA organization offering the plan must offer qualified Part D coverage that includes the requirements related to qualified prescription drug coverage.[49] These plans include the following:[50]

---

[46] The types of plans described in this section are available to Medicare beneficiaries through the MA program. Note that the MMA also created Health Savings Accounts (HSAs) outside the Medicare program and under the Internal Revenue Code. MMA § 1201, amending the Internal Revenue Code (Title 26) at § 223. *See also* http://www.irs.gov/publications/p969/ar02.html (site visited May 26, 2016). Under this provision, an individual opens an HSA in connection with the purchase of high-deductible private health insurance. The individual can carry over unspent balances from year to year. Funds deposited in the HSA trust account are to be used for the sole purpose of paying qualified medical expenses of beneficiaries. An individual will be able to withdraw sums from his or her HSA trust account to cover deductibles and other health care expenses in connection with a related high-deductible health insurance policy. Deposits into the trust account each year will be excluded from taxable income; earnings on the accounts are not taxed, nor are amounts withdrawn from the trust account to pay health expenses. MMA § 1201, amending the Internal Revenue Code at § 223. Note that according to an IRS publication, only an "eligible individual" can establish an HSA. An "eligible individual" means, with respect to any month, any individual who (1) is covered under a high-deductible health plan (HDHP) on the first day of such month; (2) is not also covered by any other health plan that is not an HDHP (with certain exceptions for plans providing certain limited types of coverage); (3) is not enrolled in Medicare (generally, has not yet reached age 65); and (4) may not be claimed as a dependent on another person's tax return [emphasis added]. See IRS Publication, Part III-Administrative, Procedural, and Miscellaneous, Section 1, Q2, *available at* http://www.irs.gov/pub/irs-drop/n-04-2.pdf (site visited May 26, 2016).

[47] In order to provide context for the following descriptions of MA plan types, here is a breakdown of plan type by enrollment as of March 2016. Approximately two-thirds (64%) of MA enrollees are in HMOs; almost one-third are in PPOs (23% in local PPOs, 7% in regional PPOs); and the balance are in Private Fee-For Service (PFFS) plans (1%) and other types of MA plans (4%), including cost plans and Medicare Medical Savings Accounts (MSAs). Kaiser Family Foundation, "Medicare Advantage 2016 Spotlight: Enrollment Market Update" (May 11, 2016), *available at* http://kff.org/medicare/issue-brief/medicare-advantage-2016-spotlight-enrollment-market-update/ (site visited Aug. 5, 2016).

[48] 42 U.S.C. § 1395w-21; 42 C.F.R. § 422.4.

[49] 42 C.F.R. § 422.4(c)(1); 42 C.F.R. § 422.104. *See* **Chapter 11** of this Handbook. Note that if an MA organization offers multiple coordinated care plans in a given area, some might not offer Part D prescription drug coverage (e.g., some HMOs might not offer Part D benefits).

[50] 42 C.F.R. § 422.4(a)(1).

- *Health Maintenance Organizations.* A type of managed care plan that can take a variety of forms such as a staff-based facility of service providers and/or a group of independent practice associations that acts as both insurer and provider of services to its members; services and benefits usually financed through a capitated payment; copayments may apply;
- *Provider Sponsored Organizations.* An organization created by health care providers to act as insurer for a defined group of enrollees, including physician-based models, hospital-based models, or a combination of service delivery models; and
- *Preferred Provider Organizations.* Managed care entities that contract with networks or panels of providers for serving the PPOs' enrolled population(s) and are paid on the basis of a contractually specified reimbursement for covered benefits with the organization offering the plan and provide reimbursement for all covered benefits regardless of whether the benefits are provided within the network of providers. A PPO organization does not permit prior notification for out-of-network services (out-of-network services can be obtained without prior notification and without a reduction in the plan's standard cost-sharing levels).[51]

[2] Medicare Medical Savings Accounts

MA organizations offering MSAs are not permitted to offer prescription drug coverage, other than that required under Parts A and B of the Medicare statute.[52] The MMA makes the MA MSA demonstration a permanent Medicare option, starting with contract years beginning January 1, 2006; removes the capacity limits and the deadline for enrollment; and eliminates the requirement for a quality assurance program because MSAs are bank accounts and not plans.[53]

As with the old MSA demonstration, the new option combines the use of a health care savings account with a high deductible catastrophic health plan. To participate in an MA MSA, the beneficiary has to enroll in an MA MSA health plan.[54]

---

[51] 42 C.F.R. § 422.4(a)(1)(v)(A)–(D) (applies to PPOs, MSA plans, and PFFS plans) (Apr. 15, 2010).

[52] 42 C.F.R. § 422.4(c)(2).

[53] MMA § 233, amending §§ 1851(b)(4), 1851(e)(5)(A), 1852, 1852(e)(1), and 1852(k) of the Social Security Act, 42 U.S.C. §§ 1395w-21(b)(4), 1395w-21(e)(5)(A), 1395w-22, 1395w-22(e)(1), and 1395w-22(k); *see also* CMS's guidance document for MA MSAs, *available at* http://www.cms.gov/Medicare/Medicare-Advantage/MedicareAdvantageApps/downloads/2007_MSA_Useful_Information.pdf (site visited May 26, 2016).

[54] 42 C.F.R. § 422.4(a)(2) (types of plans).

Under rules established by the Secretary, an individual is not eligible to enroll (or continue enrollment) in an MA MSA plan for a year unless the individual provides assurances satisfactory to the Secretary that the individual will reside in the United States for at least 183 days during the year.[55] Individuals must enroll during an initial enrollment period or an annual coordinated election period.[56]

[3] Private Fee-for-Service Plans

MA organizations offering PFFS plans may choose to offer qualified Part D coverage that meets the requirement for that coverage.[57] A PFFS plan is an MA plan that:

- Reimburses hospitals, physicians, and other providers at a rate determined by the plan on an FFS basis without placing the provider at financial risk;
- Does not vary such rates for such a provider based on utilization relating to such provider; and
- Does not restrict the selection of providers among those who are lawfully authorized to provide the covered services and who agree to accept the terms and conditions of payment established by the plan. However, effective 2011, PFFS plans in certain areas have an obligation to establish provider networks.[58]

---

[55] 42 C.F.R. § 422.4(a)(2) (types of plans).

[56] 42 C.F.R. § 422.4(a)(2) (types of plans). Note that there are very few Medicare MSA plans offered across the country.

[57] 42 C.F.R. § 422.4(c)(3). See the discussion of Part D drug plan requirements in **Chapter 11** of this Handbook. *See also* CMS, "Private Fee-for-Service: Beneficiary Questions and Answers" (Feb. 10, 2006), *available at* http://www.cms.gov/Medicare/Health-Plans/PrivateFeeforServicePlans/downloads/benqa.pdf (site visited May 26, 2016); CMS, "Your Guide to Medicare Private Fee-for-Service Plans" (CMS Pub. No. 10144, Sept. 2007), *available at* https://www.medicare.gov/pubs/pdf/10144.pdf (site visited May 26, 2016).

[58] 42 U.S.C. § 1395w-28(b)(2); 42 C.F.R. § 422.4(a)(3). PFFS market penetration in both rural and urban areas from 2006 through 2009 was robust, but since the implementation of this MIPPA provision, enrollment in such plans has dramatically decreased and some plans have pulled out of certain markets. Advocates and beneficiaries continue to raise cautions about the scope of services actually available under PFFS when compared to traditional Medicare. Some advocates have reported marketing abuses, particularly with respect to not being clear about the nature of PFFS and its limitations. Reimbursement rates to physicians have been an issue, leading some physicians to decline participation in PFFS plans and thus frustrating patient access to service. These rules also apply to employer-based plans.

The Medicare program will make a capitated payment to the PFFS plan just as it would to an HMO or a PSO.[59] A physician, provider of service, or other entity that has a contract for Medicare services furnished to Medicare enrollees must accept as payment in full for covered services an amount not to exceed (including any permitted deductibles, coinsurance, copayments, or balance billing) 115 percent of its contracted rate.[60] The plan must establish procedures to enforce its billing limits. If the plan fails to adhere to its billing limits, the plan may be subject to sanctions. Beneficiaries must be provided with an appropriate explanation of benefits, consistent with current beneficiary information requirements for Medicare Parts A and B, and for applicable Medicare Supplemental policies.[61] The explanation must include a clear statement of the amount of the enrollee's liability, including any allowable balance billing.

The PFFS plan must provide the Medicare beneficiary with advance balance billing information before incurring inpatient hospital services (and certain other services to be identified by the Secretary) for which balance billing amounts could be substantial.[62]

[4] Religious Fraternal Benefit Society Plans

MA allows a religious fraternal benefit (RFB) society to establish a plan that limits enrollment to members of the church, convention, or group with which it is affiliated.[63] Such plans must be exempt from taxation as provided under the Internal Revenue Code of 1986[64] and be affiliated with, carry out the tenets of, and share a religious bond with a church or convention or association of churches or an affiliated group of churches.[65] In addition, the society must meet certain requirements, and the Secretary can adjust the payment amounts.[66]

---

[59] 42 U.S.C. § 1395w-23.

[60] 42 U.S.C. §§ 1395w-22(k), 1395w-24.

[61] 42 U.S.C. § 1395w-22(k); 42 C.F.R. § 422.111 (disclosure requirements), § 422.112 (access to services), § 422.113 (special rules for ambulance services, emergency and urgently needed services, and maintenance and post-stabilization care services), § 422.114 (access to services under an MA private fee-for-service plan), § 422.133 (return to home skill nursing facility).

[62] Check the websites of specific plans and Medicare.gov or MyMedicare.gov for plan details and locations.

[63] 42 U.S.C. § 1395w-28(c); 42 C.F.R. § 422.57.

[64] 42 C.F.R. § 422.2.

[65] 42 U.S.C. § 1395w-28(e).

[66] 42 U.S.C. § 1395w-28(e).

[5] Local and Regional Medicare Advantage Plans

An MA local plan is defined as an MA plan that is not an MA regional plan.[67] Regional MA plans are structured as PPOs.[68] An MA Regional PPO is an MA plan that has a network of providers that has a contractual agreement with CMS for a specified reimbursement to provide covered benefits regardless of whether such benefits are provided within the network of providers, and the regional PPO service area covers one or more entire MA regions.[69]

There are special cost-sharing rules for MA regional plans. To the extent such plans apply a deductible, they are only permitted to have a single deductible related to Medicare Part A and Part B services.[70] The applicability of the single deductible may be different for specific in-network services and may also be waived for preventative services or other items and services.[71]

MA regional plans are required to provide for a catastrophic limit on beneficiary out-of-pocket expenditures for in-network and out-of-network benefits under the traditional Medicare program.[72] The total out-of-pocket catastrophic limit may be higher than the in-network catastrophic limit but may not increase the total catastrophic limit.[73] MA regional plans are required to track the deductibles and catastrophic limits and are to notify members and health care providers when the limits have been reached.[74] Starting with the January 2012 plan year, regional PPO plans are subject to the mandatory MOOP and catastrophic limit requirements that apply to local MA plans.[75]

MA regional plans are required to provide reimbursement for all covered benefits, regardless of whether those benefits are provided within or outside of the network of contracted providers.[76] In applying the actuarially equivalent level of cost-sharing on MA bids related to benefits under the traditional Medicare program option, only the catastrophic limit on out-of-pocket expenses for in-network benefits will be taken into account.[77]

---

[67] 42 U.S.C. § 1395w-28(b)(5).

[68] *See* CMS, "Medicare Managed Care" (Transmittal 81, CMS Pub. No. 100-16, Apr. 25, 2007), *available at* http://www.cms.gov/Regulations-and-Guidance/Guidance/Transmittals/downloads/R81MCM.pdf (site visited May 26, 2016), for CMS's information on the Regional PPO program; *see also* http://www.cms.gov/Medicare/Prescription-Drug-Coverage/PrescriptionDrugCovGenIn/downloads/MAPDRegions.pdf (site visited May 26, 2016) for a chart of the 26 Medicare Advantage Regional PPO regions. 42 U.S.C. § 1395w-28(b)(5).

[69] 42 C.F.R. § 422.4(a)(1)(v).

[70] 42 C.F.R. § 422.101(d)(1).

[71] 42 C.F.R. § 422.101(d)(1).

[72] 42 C.F.R. § 422.101(d)(2).

[73] 42 C.F.R. § 422.101(d)(3).

[74] 42 C.F.R. § 422.101(d)(4).

[75] 42 C.F.R. §§ 422.100 and 422.101.

[76] 42 C.F.R. § 422.101(c)(1).

[77] 42 C.F.R. § 422.101(e)(2); *see also* § 422.256(b)(3).

[6] Specialized Medicare Advantage Plans for Special Needs Individuals

The MMA adds specialized MA plans for special needs individuals. A SNP is defined as an MA plan that exclusively serves people who are institutionalized; are entitled to medical assistance under a state plan under Title 19 (Medicaid) of the Social Security Act (i.e., those dually eligible for Medicare and Medicaid); or meet such requirements as the Secretary may determine would benefit from enrollment in a specialized MA plan for individuals with severe or disabling chronic conditions.[78] Special rules for SNP enrollment and eligibility have been established by the Secretary.[79]

As set out in MIPPA, there are several types of SNPs.[80] Authority for the existence of SNPs is extended through the end of 2018.[81] In addition, Section 165 of MIPPA prohibits Dual Eligible SNPs from imposing cost-sharing requirements on persons dually eligible for Medicare and Medicaid or Qualified Medicare Beneficiaries (QMB) that would exceed the amounts permitted under the state Medicaid plan if the individual were not enrolled in the Dual Eligible SNP. The provision was effective January 1, 2010. Each type of SNP—Institutional, Dual Eligible, and Disabling Chronic Condition—must enroll only individuals who meet the statutory definition of special needs individual for its SNP type.[82]

- *Institutional SNPs* (I-SNPs) seeking to enroll individuals living in the community but requiring an institutional level of care must use a state assessment tool to determine the need for institutional level of care and must have the assessment performed by an entity other than the organization offering the plan.

---

[78] 42 U.S.C. § 1395w-28(b)(6). MIPPA, Pub. L. No. 110-275, provides that each type of SNP—Institutional (I-SNP), Dual Eligible (D-SNP), and Disabling Chronic Condition (C-SNP)—must, effective January 1, 2010, enroll only individuals who meet the statutory definition of special needs individual for its SNP type. Nothing in the provisions affects benefits to which dual eligible individuals are entitled through their state Medicaid programs. Note that these provisions, taken together, suggest that Congress is inclined to have dual eligible beneficiaries receive all their Medicare and Medicaid services through MA-SNPs. While plans that fully integrate Medicare and Medicaid services have worked well in some situations, these situations have generally evolved with impetus from and a great deal of planning by the states, rather than from private plans.

[79] 42 C.F.R. § 422.52(e). Note that the Secretary may designate certain MA plans that disproportionately serve special needs individuals as SNPs. *See* 42 C.F.R. § 422.52(f). *See also* Halperin, Nemore, & Gottlich, *What's So Special About Special Needs Plans? Assessing Medicare Special Needs Plans for "Dual Eligibles,"* Marquette Elder's Advisor, Vol. 8, No. 2 (Spring 2007). This article discusses the limits of SNPs as a health care delivery vehicle in meeting the needs of low-income people and those with multiple chronic conditions.

[80] MIPPA § 164, Pub. L. No. 110-275.

[81] Medicare Access and CHIP Reauthorization Act of 2015 (MACRA), Pub. L. No. 114-10, § 209 (Apr. 16, 2015).

[82] MIPPA § 164 (effective Jan. 1, 2010).

- *Dual-Eligible SNPs* (D-SNPs) must provide each prospective enrollee, prior to enrollment, with a comprehensive written statement of benefits and cost-sharing protections under the relevant state Medicaid plan and an explanation of which such benefits and cost-sharing protections are available under the plan.[83] D-SNPs must also have a contract with the state Medicaid agency to provide, or arrange for the provision of, benefits to which the individual is entitled under Medicaid. Such benefits may, but apparently are not required to, include long-term care services. Those D-SNPs that do not have such a contract, which had to be in effect by January 1, 2010, may continue to operate but cannot expand their service areas. Also note that beginning in CY 2013, all MA organizations that offer D-SNPs (existing, new, and expanding) are required to have contracts with the state Medicaid agencies in the states in which they operate. D-SNPs that fail to secure a State Medicaid agency contract will not be permitted to operate.
- *Severe or Disabling Chronic Condition SNPs* (C-SNPs). The definition for persons eligible for the services of C-SNPs is amended to include having "one or more [co-morbid] and medically complex chronic conditions that are substantially disabling or life threatening, have a high risk of hospitalization or other significant adverse health outcomes, and require specialized delivery systems across domains of care." The Secretary is directed to convene a panel including the Director of the Agency for Healthcare Research and Quality to determine conditions that meet this new definition.

All SNPs, regardless of type, must meet new requirements for care management. They must have in place an evidence-based model of care with appropriate networks of providers and specialists; conduct an initial assessment and annual reassessment of each individual's physical, psychosocial, and functional needs; develop a care plan, in consultation with the individual, as feasible, that identifies goals and objectives and specific services and benefits to be provided; and use an interdisciplinary team in the management of care. The Secretary is directed to review each plan's care management compliance as part of a periodic audit.

All SNPs, regardless of type, must meet data collection and reporting requirements relating to their compliance with the plan requirements introduced by MIPPA. Such data "may be based on claims data" and must be reported at the

[83] Note that this provision presumably would allow a prospective dual enrollee to determine whether he or she will receive any value from a dual SNP that is not already available under his or her state Medicaid program. One challenge for those helping individuals make choices is to determine whether the plan has accurately presented state Medicaid coverage, which is not an easy undertaking. Note, too, that the Secretary of the Department of Health and Human Services (HHS) is directed to designate staff and resources to assist states that are inquiring about coordination with SNPs. However, states are not required to enter into contracts with SNPs.

plan, rather than sponsor, level. Nothing in the provisions affects benefits to which dual eligible individuals are entitled through their state Medicaid programs.

For more information about managed care issues for dual eligible individuals, see **§ 10.7** in this Handbook.

[7] Cost Plans

Cost plus plans should not be confused with MA plans. Note that "Section 1876 cost plans" are a health plan option for some Medicare beneficiaries that are sometimes confused with MA plans. Cost plans, though, are not MA plans and are authorized under a different section of the Social Security Act than are MA plans. As noted in the MMC Manual:

> Section 1876 cost plans are plans operated by an HMO or Competitive Medical Plan (CMP) in accordance with a cost reimbursement contract under section 1876 of the Act and Title 42, Part 417 of the Code of Federal Regulations. Medicare cost plan enrollees are not restricted to the HMO or CMP network for receipt of covered Medicare services (i.e., Original Medicare services may be received through non-HMO/CMP sources and are reimbursed separately by Medicare intermediaries and carriers). Medicare payment to the HMO/CMP is based on the reasonable costs of providing services to the Medicare beneficiaries.[84]

Note that cost contracts are currently authorized through 2018. Section 209 of the Medicare Access and CHIP Reauthorization Act of 2015, Pub. L. No. 114-10, signed into law by President Obama on April 16, 2015, requires that cost contract plans transition to MA plans by 2019. Also note that the 2015 Final Rule closes certain cost plans to new enrollment.[85]

[C] Medicare Advantage Coverage, Costs, and Access to Care

An MA plan is required to clearly communicate to enrollees through the Evidence of Coverage (EOC) and Summary of Benefits (SB) the MA plan's service area, benefits offered under the plan including premiums and cost-sharing, and information related to access to services.[86] This must be done at the time of enrollment and at least annually thereafter, 15 days before the annual coordinated election period.[87] An MA enrollee will receive an Annual Notice of Change

[84] MMC Manual, Ch. 1, § 40, *available at* http://www.cms.gov/Regulations-and-Guidance/Guidance/Manuals/Downloads/mc86c01.pdf (site visited May 26, 2016).

[85] 79 Fed. Reg. 29,844, 28,850 (May 23, 2014).

[86] 42 C.F.R. § 422.111(a) and (b).

[87] 42 C.F.R. § 422.111(a)(3).

(ANOC) each fall that will include any changes to the MA's rules.[88] The MA plan typically sends out the ANOC sometime in September. Upon receipt, an enrollee should review the changes for the following year and decide whether the plan's terms continue to meet their needs.

[1] Coverage of Benefits

MA plans offer a specific set of health benefits at a uniform premium and uniform level of cost-sharing to all Medicare beneficiaries residing in the service area of the MA plan.[89] Each MA organization must provide the benefits currently available under Medicare Parts A and B, except for hospice, as discussed below.[90] As a practical matter, most of the rules that apply to coverage under Parts A and B as discussed in other chapters of this Handbook also apply to MA plans. MA plans generally impose the same coverage limits set in traditional Medicare (e.g., limit on number of consecutive covered days in hospitals and skilled nursing facilities, outpatient therapy caps), but plans have some discretion to ease such restrictions (e.g., most MA plans waive the three-day prior hospitalization requirement for subsequent coverage of a SNF stay, as is required under Part A). MA plans are required to provide in-network Medicare-covered preventive benefits at zero cost-sharing.[91]

MA plans may not deny, limit, or condition the coverage or provision of benefits based on any health status-related factor; similarly, MA plans cannot design plan benefits in such a way that is likely to substantially discourage enrollment by certain individuals.[92]

With respect to Medicare Part D prescription drug coverage, MA sponsors may not offer an MA plan in an area unless either that plan (or another MA plan offered by the organization in that same service area) includes required prescription drug coverage.[93] MA plans offering Part D prescription drug coverage are known as MA-PD plans and must follow Part D rules concerning drug coverage, as outlined in **Chapter 11**.[94] If an MA plan does not offer Part D coverage, then

[88] 42 C.F.R. § 422.111(d).

[89] 42 C.F.R. § 422.2.

[90] 42 U.S.C. § 1395w-22(a); 42 C.F.R. § 422.101. Note that 42 C.F.R. § 422.2 (MA definitions) and 42 C.F.R. § 423.4 (Voluntary Prescription Drug Benefit, Medicare Part D, definitions) contain an important explanatory list of terms important in discussing and understanding the MA program.

[91] 42 C.F.R. §§ 417.454 and 422.100. *See also* ACA § 4103 (annual wellness visit and personalized prevention plan).

[92] 42 U.S.C. § 1395w-22(b).

[93] 42 U.S.C.§ 1395w-131(a).

[94] Note that in 2016 the vast majority of MA enrollees (89 percent) are in MA-PDs. Kaiser Family Foundation, "Medicare Advantage 2016 Spotlight: Enrollment Market Update" (May 2016), *available at* http://kff.org/medicare/issue-brief/medicare-advantage-2016-spotlight-enrollment-market-update/ (site visited May 26, 2016).

the type of MA plan an individual is enrolled in determines whether the individual can also enroll in a stand-alone Part D plan.[95] Individuals enrolled in an MA coordinated care plan (HMO, PPO, PSO) cannot also be enrolled in a stand-alone Part D plan, even if the MA plan does not provide Part D coverage. Private fee-for-service (PFFS) plans are not required to offer Part D coverage. If PFFS plan does not offer Part D coverage, enrollees can enroll in a separate Part D plan. MSAs cannot offer Part D coverage, so enrollees can also enroll in a Part D plan.

On an annual basis, insurance companies that wish to offer MA coverage in the following calendar year submit bids to CMS, which are compared to a CMS-established local benchmark rate. Whether a plan's bid is below or above the benchmark determines, in part, a plan's premiums and supplemental benefits it may offer.[96] If a plan's bid is below the CMS-established benchmark, the plan receives a rebate payment from Medicare, a percentage of which must be passed along to plan enrollees in the form of either lower premiums or supplemental benefits.[97] Plans may offer supplemental benefits for which a separate premium may be charged, but the separate premium may not vary among individuals within the plan and must not exceed certain actuarial and community rating requirements.[98] It is largely due to these rebates that many MA plans offer supplemental benefits—things not covered under Part A or B—such as limited vision, hearing, and dental services.

MA plans are not required to cover hospice services, which is a benefit available under Part A of Medicare.[99] MA plans must tell an enrollee about hospice care, if a hospice program is located within the MA organization's service area, or, if not located within the service area, if it is common to refer patients to hospice programs outside the service area.[100] Medicare fee-for-service contractors are required by federal regulations to maintain payment responsibility for MA enrollees who elect hospice.[101] If the patient elects hospice care, CMS makes payments directly to the hospice program and makes monthly payments to the MA organization for additional benefits not provided by hospice care.[102]

---

[95] *See* 42 C.F.R. § 423.30(b).

[96] *See, e.g.*, Medicare Payment Advisory Commission (MedPAC), "Medicare Advantage Program Payment Basics" (Oct. 2014), *available at* http://medpac.gov/documents/payment-basics/medicare-advantage-program-payment-system-14.pdf?sfvrsn=0 (site visited May 26, 2016).

[97] 42 C.F.R. § 422.266.

[98] 42 U.S.C. § 1395w-22; 42 C.F.R. § 422.102.

[99] 42 C.F.R. § 422.100(c)(1). See **Chapter 5** of this Handbook regarding Medicare coverage of hospice services.

[100] 42 U.S.C. § 1395w-23(h); 42 C.F.R. § 422.320; *see also* **Chapter 5** of this Handbook for discussion of the Medicare hospice program.

[101] 42 C.F.R. §§ 417.585 and 417.531.

[102] 42 U.S.C. § 1395w-23(h); 42 C.F.R. § 422.320(c). Note that when an MA enrollee elects hospice care and requires nonterminal care or treatment, the individual might have to pay cost-sharing rates under traditional Medicare, which might be greater than cost-sharing through the MA plan; additionally, if an individual opts out of hospice care and wishes to return to the MA plan, MA

[2] Premiums and Cost-Sharing

Out-of-pocket costs in an MA plan depend on whether the plan charges a monthly premium, whether the plan has a yearly deductible, how much an individual pays for each visit or service (copayments or coinsurance), the type of health care services needed and how often and whether network providers are used. MA plans can differ with respect to expected costs so it is imperative to read each plan's literature to see what kind of plan it is and what it pays for.

As noted in the previous section, MA premiums are based on the difference between Medicare payments to the plan and the plan's bid submitted to Medicare. These amounts vary by county.[103] MA plan enrollees must continue to pay their Part B premium regardless of any additional premium amount charged by the MA plan, however MA plans are allowed to offer reduced Medicare Part B premiums as an additional benefit to their enrollees. Information about Part B premium reductions would be included with the information beneficiaries receive about plans during the annual open enrollment period.[104]

The MA organization, through its MA plan or plans, may impose copayments and deductibles different from those under Parts A and B, as long as the monthly premium and cost-sharing are actuarially equivalent to cost-sharing under traditional Medicare.[105] However, cost-sharing under MA plans cannot exceed the cost-sharing imposed under traditional Medicare for three specific services—chemotherapy administration, renal dialysis services, and skilled nursing care.[106] Cost-sharing can vary depending on what type of plan an

coverage might not begin until the following month. *See* MMC Manual, Ch. 4, § 10.4, *available at* http://www.cms.gov/Regulations-and-Guidance/Guidance/Manuals/Downloads/mc86c04.pdf, and Medicare Claims Processing (MCP) Manual, Ch. 11, § 30. 4, *available at* http://www.cms.gov/Regulations-and-Guidance/Guidance/Manuals/Downloads/clm104c11.pdf (site visited May 26, 2016).

[103] In 2016, the average MA-PD enrollee pays a monthly premium of about $37; however, 49 percent of MA-PD enrollees are in zero-premium plans. Kaiser Family Foundation, "Medicare Advantage 2016 Spotlight: Enrollment Market Update" (May 2016), *available at* http://kff.org/medicare/issue-brief/medicare-advantage-2016-spotlight-enrollment-market-update/ (site visited May 26, 2016).

[104] Medicare, Medicaid, and SCHIP Benefits Improvement and Protection Act of 2000 (BIPA), Pub. L. No. 106-554, § 606 (Dec. 21, 2000).

[105] 42 U.S.C. § 1395w-24(e).

[106] ACA § 3203; 42 C.F.R. §§ 417.454, and 422.100 (effective Jan. 2011). Note that the Secretary of HHS has discretion to require that cost-sharing for other services also not exceed traditional Medicare cost-sharing but, to date, has not exercised this discretion. In the preamble to the final rules, CMS clarified that this limitation to MA cost-sharing applies only to in-network services. Under traditional Medicare, beneficiaries are not charged any cost-sharing for a covered SNF stay for the first 20 days. Current CMS policy, however, allows MA plans to charge cost-sharing during this 20-day period.

individual is enrolled in and whether in-network or out-of-network providers are used.[107]

Since 2011, local MA plans (and since 2012 regional PPOs) must establish a MOOP liability amount for enrollees for all Part A and B services to be set yearly by CMS.[108] In 2017, the mandatory MOOP is $6,700. Plans that use a lower, voluntary MOOP of $3,400 have greater flexibility in establishing cost-sharing amounts.[109]

Note that low-income MA enrollees, similar to other low-income Medicare beneficiaries, may be entitled to assistance with certain premiums and cost-sharing. See **§ 10.04[B]** of this Handbook for information concerning MA plans and the QMB benefit; also see **§ 11.06** of this Handbook concerning the Part D low-income subsidy.

[3] Access to Care

By virtue of their design, most MA plans impose restrictions on enrollees' access to Medicare-covered services. Coordinated care plans (e.g., HMOs) can use mechanisms to control use of services, such as referrals from a gatekeeper for an enrollee to receive services within the plan.[110] While such plans may specify the networks of providers from whom enrollees may obtain services, such networks must be sufficient to provide adequate access to covered services to meet the needs of the population served.[111]

---

[107] Note that in the final 2016 Parts C and D rule issued on February 12, 2015, CMS revises 42 C.F.R. § 422.100 to codify and further clarify an MA plan's obligations when plan services are affected by public health emergencies or disasters. The clarification includes a requirement that MA plans "ensure access, at in-network cost-sharing, to covered services even when furnished by non-contracted providers when disruption in the service area impedes enrollees' ability to access contracted providers and/or contracted providers' ability to provide needed services." 80 Fed. Reg. 7912-58, 7953 (Feb. 12, 2015).

[108] 42 C.F.R. §§ 422.100 and 422.101.

[109] *See* CMS, "Announcement of Calendar Year (CY) 2017 Medicare Advantage Capitation Rates and Medicare Advantage and Part D Payment Policies and Final Call Letter," pp. 167 (Apr. 4, 2016), *available at* https://www.cms.gov/Medicare/Health-Plans/MedicareAdvtgSpecRateStats/Downloads/Announcement2017.pdf (site visited May 26, 2016).

[110] 42 C.F.R. § 422.4(a)(1)(ii).

[111] 42 C.F.R. § 422.112(a). Ongoing concerns have been raised regarding both the scope of MA network adequacy rules and regulatory oversight. *See, e.g.,* General Accounting Office (GAO), "Medicare Advantage: Actions Needed to Enhance CMS Oversight of Provider Network Adequacy," GAO-15-710 (Aug. 31, 2015), *available at* http://www.gao.gov/products/GAO-15-710 (accessed May 2016). For an analysis of network adequacy relating to hospitals, see Kaiser Family Foundation, "Medicare Advantage Hospital Networks: How Much Do They Vary?" (June 2016), *available at* http://kff.org/medicare/report/medicare-advantage-hospital-networks-how-much-do-they-vary/ (Aug. 5, 2016).

Specialist referral policies are set by plans, however plans must provide or arrange for necessary specialist care, and in particular give female enrollees the option of direct access to a women's health specialist within the network for women's routine and preventive health care services. In addition, the plan must arrange for specialty care outside of the plan provider network when network providers are unavailable or inadequate to meet a member's medical needs.[112]

The distinction between "in-network" vs. "out-of-network" providers is relevant to the type of MA plan, coverage of services and enrollees' out-of-pocket liabilities. PPOs have networks of contracting providers but, unlike HMOs, also provide for reimbursement for all covered benefits regardless of whether the benefits are provided within the network of providers (i.e., out-of-network care).[113] PFFS plans in non-network areas and MSAs do not need to establish networks.

MA plans generally have a prior-authorization process: if an enrollee wishes to receive a service from an in-network provider, the provider must seek prior authorization from the plan and inform the enrollee if the plan makes an adverse determination, triggering appeal rights; if, however, the provider furnishes the service and without seeking prior authorization from the plan and the service is not covered, the provider cannot bill the enrollee for more than standard in-plan cost-sharing.[114] Similarly, plan enrollees are protected against balance billing (meaning they generally pay only plan-allowed cost-sharing) when they obtain services that are covered by the plan (either by a plan decision or through an appeal), including from noncontracted providers.[115]

MA plans can change their provider networks any time during the year, as long as they continue to meet network adequacy standards, provide timely notice (at least 30 days advance notice to affected enrollees), and ensure continuity of care for enrollees.[116] In response to significant mid-year network provider terminations by certain MA plan sponsors starting in the fall of 2013, CMS created a new, but limited, special enrollment period (SEP) right to change MA plans available to certain plan enrollees affected by mid-year provider terminations, effective in 2015.[117]

---

[112] 42 C.F.R. § 422.112(a)(3); *see also* MMC Manual, Ch. 4, § 110.1, *available at* http://www.cms.gov/Regulations-and-Guidance/Guidance/Manuals/Downloads/mc86c04.pdf (site visited May 26, 2016).

[113] 42 C.F.R. § 422.4(a)(1)(v).

[114] 42 C.F.R. § 422.105(a); *see also* MMC Manual, Ch. 4, §§ 170-180.2, *available at* http://www.cms.gov/Regulations-and-Guidance/Guidance/Manuals/Downloads/mc86c04.pdf (site visited May 26, 2016).

[115] MMC Manual, Ch. 4, § 170, *available at* http://www.cms.gov/Regulations-and-Guidance/Guidance/Manuals/Downloads/mc86c04.pdf (site visited May 26, 2016).

[116] *See, generally,* MMC Manual, Ch. 4 (Part II), *available at* http://www.cms.gov/Regulations-and-Guidance/Guidance/Manuals/Downloads/mc86c04.pdf (site visited May 26, 2016).

[117] *See* MMC Manual, Ch. 2, § 30.4.6, *available at* http://www.cms.gov/Medicare/Eligibility-and-Enrollment/MedicareMangCareEligEnrol/Downloads/CY_2016_MA_Enrollment_and_Disenrollment_Guidance.pdf (site visited May 26, 2016).

Emergency services obtained out-of-network are covered by plans with a limit on charges to enrollees (to an amount determined by CMS annually ($75 for 2017), or what the plan would charge the enrollee if he or she obtained the services through the MA organization, whichever is less).[118] Urgently needed services that are medically necessary and immediately required can also be covered if provided when an enrollee is temporarily absent from the MA plan's service area, or provided when the enrollee is in the service area but the organization's provider network is temporarily unavailable or inaccessible.[119]

With respect to drug coverage, MA-PD plans are required to establish and maintain a process to ensure that appropriate payment is assigned at the point of sale (POS) so that claims for drugs that may be covered under Part A or B, rather than Part D, are properly adjudicated. If a denial under Part D is based on the existence of coverage under Parts A or B, the MA-PD plan should authorize or provide the drug under that other benefit without requiring the enrollee to make a subsequent request for coverage under that other benefit.[120]

[D] Process for Exercising Choice

The Secretary of HHS must establish a process through which Medicare beneficiaries can elect how they wish to obtain their Medicare covered services. Elections are made or changed only during coverage election periods.[121]

At the time of enrollment and every year thereafter, MA plans must disclose to enrollees their service area emergency service options and procedures for obtaining emergency services; out-of-state service coverage; optional supplemental coverage and costs; prior authorization rules; grievance and appeals procedures; quality

[118] 42 C.F.R. § 422.113(b). For both MA plan and enrollee responsibilities concerning post-stabilization care related to an emergency medical condition, see 42 C.F.R. § 422.113(c).

[119] 42 C.F.R. § 422.113(b). Note that in the final 2016 Parts C and D rule issued on February 12, 2015, CMS finalized a proposal to improve MA enrollees' access to out-of-network facilities in non-extraordinary circumstances by revising 42 C.F.R. § 422.113 to remove the phrase "under extraordinary and unusual circumstances." As noted in the preamble, this revision is meant to encourage plans to cover care provided in clinics that operate on weekends and outside of normal business hours when the plan network is not available. 80 Fed. Reg. 7912-58, 7949 (Feb. 12, 2015).

[120] 42 C.F.R. § 422.112(b)(7). According to the preamble of the final 2016 rule for Medicare Part C, CMS amended 42 C.F.R. § 422.112(b)(7) to "require MA-PDs to coordinate with their network pharmacies and prescribers to improve existing processes and develop new ones in order to ensure that enrollees receive their Medicare-covered prescription medications, without delay, when they present at the network pharmacy." 80 Fed. Reg. 7912-58, 7941 (Feb. 12, 2015).

[121] 42 U.S.C. § 1395w-21(c); 42 C.F.R. §§ 422.60 (election process), 422.62 (election of coverage under an MA plan), 422.66 (coordination of enrollment and disenrollment through MA organizations), 422.74 (disenrollment by the MA organization). *But see* **§ 7.04[D][5]** of this Handbook for a discussion of special enrollment periods (SEPs).

assurance mechanisms; the number of grievances and appeals and their disposition; and a summary of the method of compensating doctors.[122]

[1] Medicare Advantage Disenrollment Period

Before 2011, individuals enrolled in an MA plan, including an MA-PD, could change plans once during the open enrollment period, which ran for the first three months of each year, as long as they did not add or drop prescription drug coverage.[123] Beginning in 2011, beneficiaries who are in an MA plan have a 45-day Medicare Advantage disenrollment period (MADP).[124] During this period, they may only drop the MA plan and return to traditional Medicare and enroll in a PDP; they are not able to enroll in a different MA plan. Beneficiaries who are in traditional Medicare with a PDP are not able to change to an MA-PD during this time period.[125] As in previous years, a beneficiary in traditional Medicare with a PDP cannot change to a different PDP. Those in traditional Medicare without drug coverage cannot use this time period to enroll in a PDP.

[2] Initial Coverage Election Period

If there are one or more MA plans offered in an individual's service area at the time the individual first becomes entitled to benefits under Part A and enrolled under Part B, the individual must make the election during a defined election period beginning three months before the individual is entitled to both Parts A and B and ending the last month preceding the month of entitlement.[126] An election is considered to have been made on the date the election form is received by the MA plan.[127] An election made during an initial coverage election period (ICEP) is effective as of the first day of the month of entitlement to both Part A and Part B.[128]

Beneficiaries who do not make an election will remain in the traditional Medicare program. If an individual is in a non-Medicare health plan the month before enrolling in Part B, that individual will be entitled to remain in the health plan if the plan sponsor also offers an MA plan.[129]

---

[122] 42 U.S.C. § 1395w-22(c); 42 C.F.R. § 422.111.

[123] 42 C.F.R. § 422.62(a)(3)–(5) (Apr. 2010 amendments).

[124] 42 C.F.R. § 422.62(a)(7).

[125] ACA § 3204.

[126] 42 U.S.C. § 1395w-22(c); 42 C.F.R. §§ 422.60 (election process), 422.62(a) (election of coverage under an MA plan).

[127] 42 C.F.R. § 422.60 (election process).

[128] 42 C.F.R. § 422.68(a).

[129] 42 U.S.C. § 1395w-21(c)(3) (default); 42 C.F.R. § 422.66(d). However, persons who fail to make an election during the initial coverage election period (have not joined an MA plan) are deemed to have elected traditional Medicare. 42 C.F.R. § 422.66(c). *See also* **§ 7.04[D][8]** of this Handbook.

[3] Annual Coordinated Election Period

Starting in fall of 2011, the annual coordinated election period (ACEP) has been changed from November 15 through December 31 every year so that it begins on October 15 and ends on December 7.[130] Each October, the Secretary of HHS must conduct an ACEP during which time a beneficiary may choose to enroll in an MA plan, change to a different MA plan, or return to traditional Medicare.[131] An election made during this time period becomes effective on January 1 of the following year.[132] A beneficiary who makes no election will remain in traditional Medicare or in the MA plan in which she or he is enrolled. The Secretary of HHS must mail written comparative information about plan choices to all beneficiaries who live in an area in which at least one MA plan is offered at least 15 days before the annual coordinated enrollment period.[133]

During the annual coordinated election period, an individual eligible to enroll in an MA plan may change his or her election from an MA plan to traditional Medicare or to a different MA plan, or from traditional Medicare to an MA plan; and if an individual changes his or her election from an MA plan that offers prescription drug coverage to traditional Medicare, he or she may also elect a PDP.[134]

[4] Open Enrollment Period for Institutionalized Individuals

An individual who is eligible to elect an MA plan and who is institutionalized is not limited, except as provided for in special rules for MA MSA plans, in the number of elections or changes he or she may make.[135] Subject to the MA plan being open to enrollees, an MA eligible institutionalized individual may at any time elect an MA plan or change his or her election from an MA plan, or from traditional Medicare to an MA plan.[136] A beneficiary is considered institutionalized if they continuously reside or are expected to continuously reside for 90 days or longer in a long-term care facility, which is a skilled nursing facility or nursing facility; an intermediate care facility for individuals with intellectual disabilities; or an inpatient psychiatric facility.[137]

---

[130] 42 C.F.R. § 422.62(a)(2).

[131] 42 U.S.C. § 1395w-21(c)(1)–(3).

[132] 42 C.F.R. § 422.68(b).

[133] 42 U.S.C. § 1395w-21(d)(1)–(7).

[134] *See* 42 C.F.R. § 422.62(a)(2).

[135] 42 C.F.R. § 422.62(a)(6).

[136] *See* 42 C.F.R. § 422.62(a)(6). *See also* MMC Manual, Ch. 2, § 30.3, *available at* http://cms.gov/Medicare/Eligibility-and-Enrollment/MedicareMangCareEligEnrol/Downloads/CY-2014-MA-Enrollment-and-Disenrollment-Guidance-r.pdf (site visited May 27, 2016).

[137] 42 C.F.R. § 422.2.

[5] Special Election Periods

An individual may also change his or her election in the form and manner specified by CMS, from an MA plan to traditional Medicare or to a different MA plan under several special circumstances during a special election period (SEP), including the following:[138]

(1) CMS or the organization has terminated the organization's contract for the plan, discontinued the plan, discontinued the plan in the area in which the individual resides, or the organization has notified the individual of the impending termination of the plan, or the impending discontinuation of the plan in the area in which the individual resides;

(2) The individual is not eligible to remain enrolled in the plan because of a change in his or her place of residence to a location out of the service area or continuation area or other change in circumstances as determined by CMS but not including terminations resulting from a failure to make timely payment of an MA plan monthly or supplemental beneficiary premium, or from disruptive behavior;

(3) The individual demonstrates to CMS, that—

(i) the organization offering the plan substantially violated a material provision of its contract in relation to the individual, such as (a) failing to provide the beneficiary on a timely basis medically necessary services for which benefits are available under the plan;

---

[138] 42 C.F.R. § 422.62(b). Note that CMS has exercised its discretion to SEPs in a number of additional situations; for a complete list of SEPs, see CMS MMC Manual, CMS Pub. 100-16, Ch. 2, §§ 30.4, *et seq.*, *available at* https://www.cms.gov/Medicare/Eligibility-and-Enrollment/MedicareMangCareEligEnrol/Downloads/CY_2017_MA_Enrollment_and_Disenrollment_Guidance_06-03-2016.pdf (site visited Aug. 5, 2016).

As of 2015 there is a new SEP, which occurs when an MA plan terminates providers from its network. In its 2015 Call Letter, CMS describes the SEP:

> CMS will [. . .] find that an enrollee meets exceptional conditions sufficient to justify a special enrollment period (SEP) when the enrollee is affected by substantial mid-year provider network terminations initiated by an [MA plan] without cause. CMS will determine whether the terminations are substantial and require the granting of an SEP. CMS will use a variety of criteria for determining whether or not the network terminations are substantial, such as: (1) the number of enrollees affected; (2) the size of the service area affected; (3) the timing of the termination; (4) whether adequate and timely notice is provided to enrollees, (5) and any other information that may be relevant to the particular circumstance(s). In addition, the enrollee must demonstrate that the enrollee has been affected by this change. SEPs will not be granted when [MA plans] make changes to their network that are effective on January 1 of the following contract year, as long as affected enrollees are notified of the changes prior to the start of the AEP.

2015 Call Letter, p. 104, *available at* http://www.cms.gov/Medicare/Health-Plans/MedicareAdvtgSpecRateStats/Downloads/Announcement2015.pdf (site visited May 27, 2016). This SEP is incorporated in the MMC Manual, Ch. 2, at § 30.4.6, *available at* https://www.cms.gov/Medicare/Eligibility-and-Enrollment/MedicareMangCareEligEnrol/Downloads/CY_2017_MA_Enrollment_and_Disenrollment_Guidance_06-03-2016.pdf (site visited Aug. 5, 2016).

(b) failing to provide medical services in accordance with applicable quality standards; or the organization (or its agent, representative, or plan provider) materially misrepresented the plan's provisions in marketing the plan to the individual,

(ii) the organization (or its agent, representative, or plan provider) materially misrepresents the plan's provisions in marketing the plan to an individual.

(4) The individual meets such other exceptional conditions as CMS may provide.

[6] Retroactive Disenrollments

CMS may grant a request for disenrollment when an enrollment was never legally valid or if a valid request for disenrollment was properly made, but not processed or acted upon which includes both system error and plan error.[139] A retroactive disenrollment may also be allowed if the reason for disenrollment is related to a permanent move out of the plan service area, a contract violation or other limited exceptional conditions established by CMS which may include fraudulent enrollment or misleading marketing practices.[140] The beneficiary or an MA organization can submit a retroactive disenrollment request to CMS.[141] If a request for retroactive disenrollment is approved by CMS the MA organization must return any premium paid by the enrollee for any month for which CMS processed a retroactive disenrollment.[142]

[7] Coordination of Enrollment and Disenrollment Through Medicare Advantage Organizations

The enrollment and disenrollment of an individual in an MA plan of an MA organization is governed by the election of coverage under MA plans.[143] An individual may elect a different MA plan by filing the appropriate election with the MA organization;[144] or submit a request for disenrollment to the MA in the form and manner prescribed by CMS, or file the appropriate disenrollment form through other mechanisms as determined by CMS.[145] A disenrollment request is considered to have been made on the date the disenrollment request is received by the MA organization.[146]

---

[139] 42 C.F.R. § 422.66(b)(5) and Medicare Managed Care Manual, Ch. 2, § 60.5.

[140] 42 C.F.R. § 422.66(b)(5) and Medicare Managed Care Manual, Ch. 2, § 60.5.

[141] 42 C.F.R. § 422.66(b)(5) and Medicare Managed Care Manual, Ch. 2, § 60.5.

[142] 42 C.F.R. § 422.66(b)(5) and Medicare Managed Care Manual, Ch. 2, § 60.5.

[143] 42 C.F.R. § 422.66(a)–(b).

[144] 42 C.F.R. § 422.66(b)(i).

[145] 42 C.F.R. § 422.66(b)(ii).

[146] 42 C.F.R. § 422.66(b)(2).

The MA organization or plan must submit a disenrollment notice to CMS within time frames specified by CMS;[147] provide the enrollee with notice of disenrollment; include in the notice a statement explaining that the enrollee remains enrolled until the effective date of disenrollment and that until that date, neither the MA organization nor CMS pays for services not provided or arranged for by the MA plan in which the enrollee is enrolled; and file and retain disenrollment request for the period specified in CMS instructions.[148]

[a] *Failure to Submit Disenrollment Notice to CMS Promptly*

If the MA organization fails to submit the correct and complete required notice, the MA organization must reimburse CMS for any capitation payments received after the month in which payment would have ceased if the requirement had been met timely.[149] Note that an individual who fails to make an election during the initial coverage election period is deemed to have elected traditional Medicare.[150]

[8] Conversion of Enrollment (Seamless Continuation of Coverage)

The Medicare statute allows the Secretary of HHS to establish procedures under which an individual who is enrolled in a health plan (offered by an organization that also offers MA plans) at the time of the initial election period and who fails to elect to receive coverage other than through the organization to be deemed to have elected the MA plan offered by the organization.[151] In other words, subject to CMS approval, an insurance company can enroll an individual who is covered by the company's product into the same company's MA product upon becoming eligible for Medicare unless the individual "opts out." Given the minimal notice requirements related to such enrollments, it is possible for individuals to be enrolled in an MA plan without express consent.[152]

---

[147] 42 C.F.R. § 422.66(b)(3)(i).

[148] 42 C.F.R. § 422.66(b)(3)(i)–(iv).

[149] 42 C.F.R. § 422.66(b)(4).

[150] 42 C.F.R. § 422.66(c). The MMC Manual defines "passive" election as when the beneficiary has been informed by the MA plan that he or she may make an election of a different plan but takes no action. *See* MMC Manual, Ch. 2, § 20.4.2.

[151] 42 U.S.C. § 1395w-21(c)(3)(A)(ii); *see also* 42 C.F.R. § 422.66(d) and MMC Manual, Ch. 2, § 40.1.4, *available at* https://www.cms.gov/Medicare/Eligibility-and-Enrollment/MedicareMangCareEligEnrol/Downloads/CY_2017_MA_Enrollment_and_Disenrollment_Guidance_06-03-2016.pdf (site visited Aug. 5, 2016).

[152] *See, e.g.*, the Center Medicare Advocacy's Weekly Alert "Case Study: Enrolled in a Medicare Advantage Plan Without Her Knowledge Through 'Seamless Conversion Enrollment'" (June 1, 2016) *available at* http://www.medicareadvocacy.org/case-study-enrolled-in-a-medicare-advantage-plan-without-her-knowledge-through-seamless-conversion-enrollment/ (site visited Aug. 5, 2016).

An MA plan offered by an MA organization must accept any individual (regardless of whether the individual has end-stage renal disease) who is enrolled in a health plan offered by the MA organization during the month immediately preceding the month in which he or she is entitled to both Part A and Part B and who meets the MA plan eligibility requirements.[153]

Subject to CMS's approval, an MA organization may set aside a reasonable number of vacancies in order to accommodate enrollment of conversions. Any set aside vacancies that are not filled within a reasonable time must be made available to other MA eligible individuals.[154]

If an individual chooses to remain enrolled with the MA organization as an MA enrollee, the individual's conversion to an MA enrollee is effective the month in which he or she is entitled to both Part A and Part B.[155] With respect to conversions, the MA organization may only disenroll an individual in accordance with applicable disenrollment provisions.[156] Moreover, the individual who is converting must complete an election as prescribed in the MA election process.[157] The MA organization must transmit the information necessary for CMS to add the individual to its records as specified in the election requirements.[158]

[9] Maintenance of Enrollment

An individual who has made an election is considered to have continued that election until either (1) the individual changes the election; (2) the elected MA plan is discontinued or no longer serves the area in which the individual resides; or (3) the organization does not offer or the individual does not elect the option of continuing enrollment.[159] An individual enrolled in an MA-PD plan as of December 31 of a year is deemed to have elected to remain enrolled in that plan on January 1 of the following year.[160]

[10] Exception for Employer Group Health Plans

In cases when an MA organization has both a Medicare contract and a contract with an employer group health plan, and in which the MA organization arranges for the employer to process election forms for Medicare-entitled group members who wish to disenroll from the Medicare contract, the effective date of

---

[153] 42 C.F.R. § 422.66(d)(1). Note that eligibility requirements to elect an MA plan are at 42 C.F.R. § 422.50.

[154] 42 C.F.R. § 422.66(d)(2).

[155] 42 C.F.R. § 422.66(d)(3).

[156] 42 C.F.R. § 422.66(d)(4); *see* 42 C.F.R. § 422.74 (disenrollment by the MA organization).

[157] 42 C.F.R. § 422.66(d)(5); *see* 42 C.F.R. § 422.60 (election process requirements).

[158] 42 C.F.R. § 422.66(d)(6).

[159] 42 C.F.R. § 422.66(e)(1)(i)–(ii).

[160] 42 C.F.R. § 422.66(e)(5).

the election may be retroactive; a retroactive effective date may be made for up to a 90-day period.[161] Upon receipt of the election from the employer, the MA organization must submit a disenrollment notice to CMS.[162]

[11] Disenrollment by the MA Organization

[a] Basis for Disenrollment

An MA organization may not disenroll an individual from any MA plan it offers nor, by any action or inaction, request or encourage an individual to disenroll,[163] except as follows:

[i] Optional Disenrollment. An MA organization may disenroll an individual from an MA plan it offers in any of the following circumstances: (1) any monthly basic and supplementary beneficiary premiums are not paid on a timely basis, subject to the grace period for late payment; (2) the individual has engaged in disruptive behavior; and (3) the individual provides fraudulent information on his or her election form or permits abuse of his or her enrollment card.[164]

[ii] Required Disenrollment. An MA organization must disenroll an individual from any MA plan it offers in any of the following circumstances: (1) the individual no longer resides in the MA plan's service area as specified in the plan, is no longer eligible under the plan, and optional continued enrollment has not been offered or elected; (2) the individual loses entitlement under Part A or Part B benefits; (3) death of the individual; and (4) the individual enrolled in a specialized MA plan for special needs individuals that exclusively serves and enrolls special needs individuals no longer meets the special needs status of that plan (or deemed continued eligibility, if applicable).[165]

[b] Plan Termination or Reduction of Area Where Plan Is Available

General rule. An MA organization that has its MA plan terminated, or terminates an MA plan, or that discontinues offering the plan in any portion of the area where the plan had previously been available, must disenroll affected enrollees.[166]

---

[161] 42 C.F.R. § 422.66(f)(1).

[162] 42 C.F.R. § 422.66(f)(2).

[163] 42 C.F.R. § 422.74(a)(1)–(2).

[164] 42 C.F.R. § 422.74(b)(i)–(iii). Note that 42 C. F. R. § 422.74((d)(2) defines "disruptive behavior."

[165] 42 C.F.R. § 422.74(b)(2).

[166] 42 C.F.R. § 422.74(b)(3).

Exception. When an MA organization discontinues offering an MA plan in a portion of its service area, the MA organization may elect to offer enrollees residing in all or portions of the affected area the option to continue enrollment in plan offered by the organization, provided that there is no other MA plan offered in the affected area at the time of the discontinuation.[167] The organization may require an enrollee who chooses to continue enrollment to agree to receive the full range of basic benefits (excluding emergency and urgently needed care) exclusively through facilities designated by the organization within the plan service area.[168]

Note, however, that if the MA plan (organization) offers a *visitor/traveler benefit*, the 2010 regulations require that when the individual is out of the service area but within the United States (as defined in 42 C.F.R. § 400.200) for a period of consecutive days longer than 6 months but less than 12 months, the plan may elect to offer to the individual the option of remaining enrolled in the MA plan if:[169]

> (A) The individual is disenrolled on the first day of the 13th month after the individual left the service area (or residence, if paragraph (d)(4)(i)(B) of this section applies);
>
> (B) The individual understands and accepts any restrictions imposed by the MA plan on obtaining these services while absent from the MA plan's service area for the extended period, consistent with paragraph (d)(4)(i)(C) of the section;
>
> (C) The MA organization makes this visitor/traveler option available to all Medicare enrollees who are absent for an extended period from the MA plan's service area. MA organizations may limit this visitor/traveler option to enrollees who travel to certain areas, as defined by the MA organization, and who receive services from qualified providers who directly provide, arrange for, or pay for health care; and
>
> (D) The MA organization furnishes all Medicare Parts A and B services and all mandatory and optional supplemental benefits at the same cost sharing levels as apply within the plan's service area; and
>
> (E) The MA organization furnishes the services in paragraph (d)(4)(iii)(D) of this section consistent with Medicare access and availability requirements at § 422.112 of this part.[170]

---

[167] 42 C.F.R. § 422.74(b)(3). Note that an individual who is disenrolled from a plan due to the plan's termination or area reduction has a SEP right to enroll in another plan. *See* 42 C.F.R. § 422.74(e)(2).

[168] 42 C.F.R. § 422.74(b)(3).

[169] 42 C.F.R. § 422.74(d)(4)(iii)(A)–(E) (Apr. 2010 amendments).

[170] 42 C.F.R. § 422.74(d)(4)(iii)(A)–(E) (Apr. 2010 amendments).

[c] Notice Requirement

If the disenrollment is for reasons such as failure to pay premiums, disruptive behavior, or provision of fraudulent information with respect to plan election (other than death or loss of entitlement to Part A or Part B), the MA organization must give the individual a written notice of the disenrollment, with an explanation of the reasons for disenrollment provided to the individual before submission of the disenrollment to CMS. Moreover, the notice must include an explanation of the individual's right to a hearing under MA organization's grievance procedures.[171]

[d] Process for Disenrollment

[i] Monthly Basic and Supplementary Premiums Are Not Paid Timely. An MA organization may disenroll an individual from the MA plan for failure to pay basic and supplemental premiums if:

1. The MA organization can demonstrate to CMS that it made reasonable efforts to collect the unpaid premium amount. Such efforts include alerting the individual that the premiums are due and providing the individual with a grace period, that is, an opportunity to pay past due premiums in full; (2) the length of the grace period will be at least two months and will begin on the first day of the month for which the premium is unpaid or the first day of the month following the date on which premium payment is requested, whichever is later.[172]
2. Beneficiaries who establish good cause for failure to pay a premium that leads to disenrollment from an MA plan or a PDP and who pay the arrearage in full within three months of the disenrollment may be reinstated into the plan. The failure to pay the premiums must have been due to circumstances beyond the beneficiary's control. CMS will provide further guidance on what constitutes good cause.[173] With respect to a PDP, if a beneficiary is disenrolled from the PDP for failure to pay his or her monthly premiums, the PDP has the option to decline future enrollment until the past due premiums are paid.[174] Until now, the process of accepting, reviewing, and processing beneficiary requests for reinstatement for good cause has been carried out exclusively by CMS. Despite concerns about impartiality and the "quality of work currently performed by plans and CMS contractors" raised by beneficiary

---

[171] 42 C.F.R. § 422.74(c).

[172] 42 C.F.R. § 422.74(d)(1)(i)(B) (Apr. 2010 amendments).

[173] 42 C.F.R. §§ 422.74(d)(v) and 423.44. *See also* MMC Manual, Ch. 2, § 60.3.4.

[174] 42 C.F.R. § 423.44(d)(iv).

advocates, CMS will assign the responsibility to effectuate reinstatements when good cause criteria are met to a third party, which can include an MA or Part D plan sponsor.[175]

Further, the MA organization must demonstrate to CMS that it has provided the enrollee with notice of disenrollment.[176] If the enrollee fails to pay the premiums for optional services, but pays the premium for basic and mandatory supplemental services, the MA organization has the option to discontinue the optional supplemental benefits and retain the individual as an MA enrollee.[177]

[ii] Disruptive Behavior. An MA plan enrollee is disruptive if his or her behavior substantially impairs the plan's ability to arrange for or provide services to the individual or other plan members.[178] An individual cannot be considered disruptive if such behavior is related to the use of medical service or compliance (or noncompliance) with medical advice or treatment. Plans must make efforts to resolve the problems and document the enrollee's behavior and its efforts to resolve the problem. In addition, CMS will review the information on the matter as submitted by the plan and the enrollee and make a decision whether to approve or deny the disenrollment. If CMS permits the disenrollment of a disruptive individual, disenrollment is the first day of the calendar month after the month in which the MA organization gives the individual notice of its plan to disenroll the individual for disruptive behavior.[179]

[E] Appeal and Grievance in Medicare Advantage Plans

MA appeal procedures include an internal grievance process and a formal appeal process with external review. The grievance and appeal processes are intended for different kinds of complaints. MA organizations must ensure that all enrollees receive written information about the grievance and appeal procedures that are available to them.[180]

CMS has modified its regulations to clarify that a *representative* is an individual appointed by an enrollee or other party, or authorized under state or other applicable law, to act on behalf of an enrollee or other party involved in the grievance or appeal. Generally, unless otherwise stated, the representative will have all the rights and responsibilities of an enrollee or party in filing a grievance, and in

[175] See discussion at 80 Fed. Reg. 7912-58, 7942-43 (Feb. 12, 2015).

[176] 42 C.F.R. § 422.74(c).

[177] 42 C.F.R. § 422.74(d)(1)(C)(iii).

[178] 42 C.F.R. § 422.74(d)(2)(i)–(vi).

[179] 42 C.F.R. § 422.564(a)(1).

[180] 42 C.F.R. § 422.562(a)(2). *See* Transmittal 88, effective Sept. 21, 2007, through which CMS clarifies various notice and other procedures applicable to the review and appeal of a managed care (MA) claim.

obtaining an organization determination or in dealing with any of the levels of the appeals process, as provided under the regulations.[181]

[1] Grievances

[a] Generally

Each MA organization must provide meaningful procedures for timely hearing and resolving grievances between enrollees and the organization or any other entity or individual through which the organization provides health care services under any MA plan it offers.[182] Grievance procedures are separate and distinct from appeals.[183] Appeals address concerns and disagreements with organizational determinations (whether an item, service, or procedure is covered). Grievances go to issues about the quality of services received, time and location of services, and related matters.[184] In addition, the MA plan's grievance process is separate from the quality of care complaint filed with a Quality Improvement Organization (QIO), which address beneficiaries' written complaints about the quality of services received under the Medicare program. For quality of care issues, the beneficiary may file a written complaint with the MA organization or the QIO, or both.[185]

Further, the MA organization must have an established recordkeeping process for tracking records on all grievances received, both orally and in writing. The record is to contain, at a minimum, the date of receipt of the grievance, and the final disposition of the grievance, and the date that the MA organization notified the enrollee of the disposition.[186]

[b] Expedited Grievances

Expedited grievances must be responded to within 24 hours. This process is available if the complaint involves an MA organization's decision to invoke an extension relating to an organization determination or reconsideration, or the MA organization's refusal to grant an enrollee's request for an expedited organization determination.[187]

---

[181] 42 C.F.R. § 422.561 (Apr. 15, 2010).

[182] 42 C.F.R. § 422.564(a).

[183] 42 C.F.R. § 422.564(b); *see also* 42 C.F.R. § 422.566(a)–(b) (definition of an organization determination).

[184] 42 C.F.R. § 422.564(b).

[185] 42 C.F.R. § 422.564(c); for the functions of the Quality Improvement Organization (QIO), see 42 U.S.C. 1320c-3(a)(14).

[186] 42 C.F.R. § 422.564(g).

[187] 42 C.F.R. § 422.564(f).

[c] Grievance Process

CMS defines a grievance as an issue that does not involve organization determinations, and that is:

> any complaint or dispute, other than one that constitutes an organization determination, expressing dissatisfaction with any aspect of an MA Organization's or provider's operations, activities, or behavior, regardless of whether remedial action is requested.[188]

The grievance process is designed to provide a remedy for MA beneficiaries who have concerns about things other than coverage of benefits. For example, a grievance might be brought concerning rudeness of staff members, inconvenience of facilities, location and hours of service, or receipt of membership materials. Every MA organization is required to provide "meaningful procedures for timely hearing and resolving grievances between enrollees and the organization."[189] Grievances also include disputes with "any other entity or individual through which the organization provides health care services."[190]

An enrollee may file a grievance with an MA plan either orally or in writing. The grievance must be filed no later than 60 days after the event or incident that precipitates the grievance.[191] The MA plan must notify the enrollee of its decision as expeditiously as possible, based on health status, but no later than 30 days of receipt of grievance.[192] The MA organization may extend the 30-day time frame by up to 14 days if the enrollee requests the extension, or if the MA organization justifies a need for additional information and documents how the delay is in the interest of the enrollee. If the MA organization extends the deadline, it must notify the enrollee in writing of the reasons for the delay.[193]

Grievances submitted in writing must be responded to in writing; grievances submitted orally may be responded to either orally or in writing, unless the enrollee requests a written response.[194] Grievances related to quality of care, regardless of how filed, must be responded to in writing and must include a description of the enrollee's right to file a written complaint with the QIO. In addition, the MA organization must cooperate with the QIO in resolving the complaint.[195]

---

[188] 42 C.F.R. § 422.561.
[189] 42 C.F.R. § 422.564(a).
[190] 42 C.F.R. § 422.564(a).
[191] 42 C.F.R. § 422.564(d).
[192] 42 C.F.R. § 422.564(e)(1).
[193] 42 C.F.R. § 422.564(e)(2).
[194] 42 C.F.R. § 422.564(e)(3)(i)–(ii).
[195] 42 C.F.R. § 422.564(e)(3)(iii).

Upon receiving a complaint, an MA organization must promptly determine and inform the enrollee whether the complaint is subject to its grievance procedures or its appeal procedures.[196]

[2] Organization Determinations

[a] Generally

Each MA organization must have a procedure for making timely organization determinations regarding the benefits to which the enrollee is entitled under the MA plan, including such things as basic benefits, mandatory and optional supplemental benefits, and the amount, if any, the beneficiary is to pay.[197]

An organization determination is any determination made by an MA organization with respect to (1) payment for temporary out of the area renal dialysis services, emergency services, post-stabilization care or urgent care; (2) payment for any other health services furnished by a provider other than the MA organization that the enrollee believes are covered under Medicare or if not covered under Medicare, should be furnished, arranged for, or reimbursed by the MA organization; (3) the MA organization's refusal to provide or pay for services, in whole or in part, including the type or level of services, that the enrollee believes should be furnished or arranged for by the MA organization; (4) reduction, or premature discontinuation, of a previously authorized ongoing course of treatment;[198] or (5) the failure of the MA organization to approve, furnish, arrange for, or provide payment for health care services in a timely manner, or to provide the enrollee with timely notice of an adverse determination, such that a delay would adversely affect the health of the enrollee.[199]

[b] Who Can Request an Organization Determination?

Individuals or entities who can request an organization determination are the enrollee (including his or her authorized representative); any provider that

---

[196] 42 C.F.R. § 422.564(b).

[197] 42 C.F.R. § 422.566(a).

[198] 42 C.F.R. § 422.566(b) (Apr. 2010 amendments). The settlement in *Jimmo v. Sebelius*, Civil Action No. 5:11-cv-17-CR (D. Vt. Jan. 24, 2013), applies to MA plans. With appropriate documentation, Medicare-covered skilled nursing and skilled therapy services are available to improve, maintain, or slow deterioration of a patient's condition. *See* Center for Medicare Advocacy, "*Jimmo v. Sebelius*, the Improvement Standard Case FAQs," *available at* http://www.medicareadvocacy.org/jimmo-v-sebelius-the-improvement-standard-case-faqs/ (site visited May 27, 2016). *See also* **Appendix 1-9** of this Handbook.

[199] 42 C.F.R. § 422.566(b).

furnishes, or intends to furnish, services to the enrollee; or the legal representative of a deceased enrollee's estate).[200]

An expedited organization determination, as explained below, can be requested by an enrollee (including his or her authorized representative) or a physician (regardless of whether the physician is affiliated with the MA organization).[201]

[c] Standard Time Frames and Notice—Organization Determinations

An enrollee must ask for a standard organization determination by making a request with the MA organization or, if applicable, to the entity responsible for making the determination (as directed by the MA organization), in accordance with the following: (1) the request may be made orally or in writing, and (2) requests for payment must be made in writing (unless the MA organization or entity responsible for making the determination has implemented a voluntary policy of accepting verbal payment requests).[202]

The MA organization must give the enrollee a written notice if (1) an MA organization decides to deny service or payment in whole or in part, or reduce or prematurely discontinue the level of care for a previously authorized ongoing course of treatment or (2) an enrollee requests an MA organization to provide an explanation of a practitioner's denial of an item or service, in whole or in part.[203] Parties to the organization determination include the enrollee (including his or her representative); an assignee of the enrollee (a physician or other provider who has furnished a service to the enrollee and formally agrees to waive any right to payment from the enrollee for that service), the legal representative of a deceased enrollee's estate; or any other provider or entity (other than the MA organization) determined to have an appealable interest in the proceeding.[204]

[i] Time Frame for Requests for Service. When a party has made a request for a service, the MA organization must notify the enrollee of its determination as expeditiously as the enrollee's health condition requires, but no later than 14 calendar days after the day the organization receives a request for a

---

[200] 42 C.F.R. § 422.566(c)(1)(i)–(iii). *See also* § **7.04[C][3]**. 42 C.F.R. § 422.112(b)(7) requires MA-PD plans to coordinate all benefits administered by the plan including drugs available under Part A or Part B, or under Part D. MA-PDs must establish a process to ensure timely and accurate point-of-sale transactions and issue a determination and authorize or provide the benefit under Part A, B, or D as expeditiously as the enrollee's health condition requires, in accordance with the requirements of 42 C.F.R. Pt. 423, subpt. M when a party requests a coverage determination.

[201] 42 C.F.R. § 422.566(c)(2)(i)–(ii).

[202] 42 C.F.R. § 422.568(a)(1)–(2).

[203] 42 C.F.R. § 422.568(d)(1)–(2).

[204] 42 C.F.R. § 422.574.

standard review.[205] The MA organization may extend the time frame by up to 14 calendar days upon request of the enrollee, if the extension is both justified and in the enrollee's interest because it is necessary to obtain additional medical evidence from a noncontract provider that might change the decision from the MA organization to deny an item or service, or if the extension is both justified due to extraordinary, exigent, or other nonroutine circumstances and is also in the enrollee's interest.[206] The enrollees must be informed in writing of the MA organization's decision to extend the time frame, and its reasons, and the MA organization must inform the beneficiary of his or her right to file an expedited grievance if he or she disagrees with the MA organization's decision.[207]

[ii] Time Frame for Request for Payment. The MA organization must process requests for payment according to the Secretary's "prompt payment" provisions which call for paying 95 percent of clean claims (no obvious errors on the face of the claim) within 30 days, with all other claims to be paid, or denied, within 60 days from the date of the request.[208]

---

[205] 42 C.F.R. § 422.568(b).

[206] 42 C.F.R. § 422.568(b)(1)(i)–(iii), In the preamble to the final 2016 rules for Medicare Part C, CMS explains that some MA plans are inappropriately extending their own deadlines:

> [W]e believe the current language that permits extension of the adjudication timeframes set forth in § 422.568(b), § 422.572(b), § 422.590(a)(1), and § 422.590(d)(2) is being interpreted more broadly than we intended and that MA organizations are regularly invoking extensions of the adjudication timeframes for organization determinations and reconsiderations. Based on information ascertained during recent MA program audits, we have seen circumstances in which MA organizations are routinely and inappropriately invoking the 14-day extension in cases where the plan: (1) Lacks adequate internal controls to ensure coverage requests are reviewed and adjudicated within the required regulatory timeframe; and (2) is awaiting receipt of supporting clinical documentation from one of its contract providers. [CMS goes on to state:] Routinely invoking an extension of the applicable adjudication timeframe is counter to the intent of the statutory and regulatory requirements for timely determinations that emphasize the health needs of the beneficiary in determining the appropriate adjudication timeframe. Extensions that are not affirmatively requested by the enrollee should be permitted only in limited circumstances, and only if the extension is in the enrollee's interest.

80 Fed. Reg. 7912-58, 7943 (Feb. 12, 2015).

Accordingly, CMS revised the applicable regulations to clarify that extensions should be permitted in only limited circumstances. CMS revisions included clarifying in § 422.568(b)(1)(ii), § 422.572(b)(1)(ii), and § 422.590(e)(1)(ii) that an extension may be justified and in the enrollee's interest due to the need to obtain additional medical information, which may result in changing the denial of coverage only from a non-contract provider. New sections were added at § 422.568(b)(1)(iii), § 422.572(b)(1)(iii), and § 422.590(e)(1)(iii) to clarify that the adjudication time frame extension may be permitted when the extension is both justified due to extraordinary, exigent, or other non-routine circumstances and that the extension is in the enrollee's interest. 80 Fed. Reg. 7912-58, 7943 (Feb. 12, 2015).

[207] 42 C.F.R. § 422.566(b)(2).

[208] 42 C.F.R. § 422.568(c)).

[iii] Written Notification of Organization Denials. If the MA organization decides to deny service or payment in whole or in part, or if an enrollee disagrees with an MA organization's decision to discontinue or reduce the level of care for an ongoing course of treatment, the organization must give the enrollee written notice of the determination.[209]

[iv] Parties to the Organization Determination. Parties to an organization determination include the enrollee (including his or her representative) or an assignee of the enrollee (a physician or other service provider who waives any right to payment from the enrollee for that service) and the legal representative of a deceased enrollee's estate, as well as any provider or entity (other than the MA organization) determined to have an appealable interest.[210] The effect of an organization determination is binding on all parties unless it is reconsidered or reopened.[211]

[v] Expediting Certain Organization Determinations. An enrollee or a physician must submit an oral or written request directly to the MA organization or, if applicable, to the entity responsible for making the determination as directed by the MA organization. A physician may provide oral or written support for a request for an expedited determination.[212]

To ask for an expedited determination, an enrollee or a physician must submit an oral or written request directly to the MA organization; if applicable, to the entity responsible for making the determination, as directed by the MA organization.[213] A physician may provide oral or written support for a request for an expedited determination.[214]

An MA plan that processes expedited requests must establish an efficient and convenient means for individuals to submit oral or written requests, and document in case files requests made by enrollees. In addition, the MA organization must determine that using the standard time frame could seriously jeopardize the life or health of the enrollee or the enrollee's ability to regain maximum function.[215]

The MA organization must provide an expedited determination if the physician indicates that applying the standard time frame for making a determination could seriously jeopardize the life or health of the enrollee or the enrollee's ability to regain maximum function.[216]

---

[209] 42 C.F.R. § 422.568(d)(1).

[210] 42 C.F.R. § 422.574.

[211] 42 C.F.R. § 422.576. *See* 42 C.F.R. §§ 422.578–422.596 (reconsideration), 42 C.F.R. § 422.616 (reopening).

[212] 42 C.F.R. § 422.570(a).

[213] 42 C.F.R. § 422.570(b)(1).

[214] 42 C.F.R. § 422.570(b)(2).

[215] 42 C.F.R. § 422.570(c).

[216] 42 C.F.R. § 422.570(c)(2)(ii).

[vi] Actions Following a Denial. The MA plan is to transfer automatically a request to the standard time frame and make the determination within 14 days (from the date the MA organization received the request), give the enrollee prompt oral notice of the denial, and within 3 days, a written letter explaining that the request will be processed using the 14-day standard time frame, as well as explain that the enrollee has the right to submit an expedited grievance and a right to re-submit the request with physician support.[217]

[vii] Timeline for Expedited Organization Determinations. MA plans must make adverse or favorable determination as expeditiously as the enrollee's health condition requires, but not later than 72 hours.[218] The MA organization may extend the time frame by up to 14 calendar days upon request of the enrollee, if the extension is both justified and in the enrollee's interest because it is necessary to obtain additional medical evidence from a noncontract provider that might change the decision from the MA organization to deny an item or service, or if the extension is both justified due to extraordinary, exigent, or other nonroutine circumstances and is also in the enrollee's interest.[219] The enrollee must be informed in writing of reasons for the delay and that he or she can file an expedited grievance.[220] Moreover, if notice is oral, the MA must confirm it in writing within three days of oral notice.[221]

[d] Right to Reconsideration

Any party to an organization determination may request that the determination be reconsidered under the procedures described in 42 C.F.R. § 422.582 (requests for a standard reconsideration).[222] An enrollee or a physician (acting on behalf of an enrollee) can request an expedited reconsideration.[223]

[i] Reconsideration Defined. A reconsideration is defined as consisting of a review of an adverse organization determination, the evidence and findings upon which it was based, and any other evidence the parties submit or the MA organization or CMS obtains.[224] A party to an organization determination must ask for a reconsideration of the determination by making a written request to the

[217] 42 C.F.R. § 422.570(d).
[218] 42 C.F.R. § 422.572(a).
[219] 42 C.F.R. § 422.572(b)(1)(i)–(iii).
[220] 42 C.F.R. § 422.572(b)(2).
[221] 42 C.F.R. § 422.572(c).
[222] 42 C.F.R. § 422.578.
[223] 42 C.F.R. § 422.584.
[224] 42 C.F.R. § 422.580.

MA organization that made the organization determination. The MA organization may adopt a policy for accepting oral requests.[225]

[ii] Filing a Request for Reconsideration. A party must file a request for reconsideration within 60 calendar days from the date of the notice of the organization determination.[226] If a party shows good cause, the MA organization may extend the time frame for filing a request for reconsideration.[227]

If the 60-day period in which to file a request for reconsideration has expired, a party to the organization determination may file a request for a reconsideration with the MA organization. The request for reconsideration and to extend time must be in writing and must state why the request for reconsideration was not filed timely.[228]

[iii] Parties to Reconsideration. The parties to the reconsideration are the parties to the organization determination, and any other provider or entity (other than the MA organization) whose rights with respect to the organization determination may be affected by the reconsideration, as determined by the entity that conducts the reconsideration.[229] The party who files a request for reconsideration may withdraw it by filing a written request for withdrawal to the MA organization.[230]

[iv] Time Frames and Responsibilities for Reconsiderations. *Standard reconsideration: Requests for services*—determinations completely favorable to the enrollee must be issued as expeditiously as the beneficiary's health condition requires, but not later than 30 calendar days from the date the MA organization received the request for a standard review.[231]

If the MA organization affirms, in whole or in part, its adverse organization determination, it must prepare a written explanation and send the case file to the independent entity contracted by CMS as expeditiously as the enrollee's health condition requires, but no later than 30 calendar days from the date it receives the request for a standard reconsideration.[232] The organization must make reasonable and diligent efforts to assist in gathering and forwarding information to the independent entity.[233]

---

[225] 42 C.F.R. § 422.582(a).

[226] 42 C.F.R. § 422.582(b).

[227] 42 C.F.R. § 422.582(c).

[228] 42 C.F.R. § 422.582(c)(2).

[229] 42 C.F.R. § 422.582(d).

[230] 42 C.F.R. § 422.582(e).

[231] 42 C.F.R. § 422.590(a)(1).

[232] 42 C.F.R. § 422.590(a)(2).

[233] 42 C.F.R. § 422.590(a)(2).

Standard reconsideration: Requests for payment—determinations completely favorable to the enrollee must be issued (and effectuated) no later than 60 calendar days from the date it receives the request for a standard reconsideration.[234]

If the MA organization affirms, in whole or in part, its adverse organization determination, it must prepare a written explanation and send the case file to the independent entity contracted by CMS no later than 60 calendar days from the date it receives the request for a standard reconsideration.[235] The organization must make reasonable and diligent efforts to assist in gathering and forwarding information to the independent entity.[236]

If the MA organization fails to provide a reconsideration determination within the specified time frames, the failure constitutes an affirmation of its adverse organization determination, and the organization must submit the file to the Independent Review Entity (IRE).[237]

Expedited reconsideration: The MA organization that approves a request for expedited reconsideration must complete its reconsideration and give the enrollee (and physician if involved) notice of its decision as expeditiously as the enrollee's health condition requires but no later than 72 hours after receiving the request.[238]

If the MA organization first notifies an enrollee of a completely favorable expedited reconsideration, it must mail written confirmation to the enrollee within three calendar days.[239]

If the MA organization must receive medical information from noncontract providers, the MA organization must request the necessary information from the noncontract provider within 24 hours of the initial request for an expedited reconsideration.[240] Noncontract providers must make reasonable and diligent efforts to expeditiously gather and forward all necessary information to assist the MA organization in meeting the required time frame.[241]

If, as a result of its reconsideration, the MA organization affirms, in whole or in part, its adverse expedited organization determination, the MA organization must submit a written explanation and the case file to the independent entity contracted by CMS as expeditiously as the enrollee's health condition requires, but not later than within 24 hours of its affirmation.[242] The organization must make

---

[234] 42 C.F.R. § 422.590(b)(1).
[235] 42 C.F.R. § 422.590(b)(2).
[236] 42 C.F.R. § 422.590(b)(2).
[237] 42 C.F.R. § 422.590(c).
[238] 42 C.F.R. § 422.590(d)(1).
[239] 42 C.F.R. § 422.590(d)(2).
[240] 42 C.F.R. § 422.590(d)(3).
[241] 42 C.F.R. § 422.590(d)(3).
[242] 42 C.F.R. § 422.590(d)(4).

reasonable and diligent efforts to assist in gathering and forwarding information to the independent entity.[243]

The MA organization may extend the standard or expedited reconsideration deadline time frame by up to 14 calendar days upon request of the enrollee, if the extension is both justified and in the enrollee's interest because it is necessary to obtain additional medical evidence from a noncontract provider that might change the decision from the MA organization to deny an item or service, or if the extension is both justified due to extraordinary, exigent, or other nonroutine circumstances and is also in the enrollee's interest.[244] The enrollee must be informed in writing of reasons for the delay and that he or she can file an expedited grievance.[245]

[v] Expediting Certain Reconsiderations. Excluding requests for payment for services already furnished, an enrollee or a physician (regardless of whether he or she is affiliated with the MA organization) may request an expedited reconsideration.[246] An enrollee, or a physician acting on behalf of an enrollee, must submit an oral or written request directly to the MA organization

---

[243] 42 C.F.R. § 422.590(d)(4).

[244] 42 C.F.R. § 422.590(e)(1)(i)–(iii). In the preamble to the final 2016 rules for Medicare Part C, CMS explains that some MA plans are inappropriately extending their own deadlines:

> [W]e believe the current language that permits extension of the adjudication timeframes set forth in § 422.568(b), § 422.572(b), § 422.590(a)(1), and § 422.590(d)(2) is being interpreted more broadly than we intended and that MA organizations are regularly invoking extensions of the adjudication timeframes for organization determinations and reconsiderations. Based on information ascertained during recent MA program audits, we have seen circumstances in which MA organizations are routinely and inappropriately invoking the 14-day extension in cases where the plan: (1) Lacks adequate internal controls to ensure coverage requests are reviewed and adjudicated within the required regulatory timeframe; and (2) is awaiting receipt of supporting clinical documentation from one of its contract providers. [CMS goes on to state:] Routinely invoking an extension of the applicable adjudication timeframe is counter to the intent of the statutory and regulatory requirements for timely determinations that emphasize the health needs of the beneficiary in determining the appropriate adjudication timeframe. Extensions that are not affirmatively requested by the enrollee should be permitted only in limited circumstances, and only if the extension is in the enrollee's interest.

80 Fed. Reg. 7912-58, 7943 (Feb. 12, 2015).

Accordingly, CMS revised the applicable regulations to clarify that extensions should be permitted in only limited circumstances. CMS revisions included clarifying in § 422.568(b)(1)(ii), § 422.572(b)(1)(ii), and § 422.590(e)(1)(ii) that an extension may be justified and in the enrollee's interest due to the need to obtain additional medical information, which may result in changing the denial of coverage only from a noncontract provider. New sections were added at § 422.568(b)(1)(iii), § 422.572(b)(1)(iii), and § 422.590(e)(1)(iii) to clarify that the adjudication time frame extension may be permitted when the extension is both justified due to extraordinary, exigent, or other nonroutine circumstances and that the extension is in the enrollee's interest. 80 Fed. Reg. 7912-58, 7943 (Feb. 12, 2015).

[245] 42 C.F.R. § 422.590(e)(2).

[246] 42 C.F.R. § 422.584(a).

or, if applicable, to the entity responsible for making the reconsideration, as directed by the MA organization.[247] A physician may provide oral or written support for the request.[248]

The MA organization must establish and maintain efficient and convenient means to submit oral and written requests and documents and maintain the documentation in the case file, and make prompt decisions whether to expedite the reconsideration or follow the standard time frame.[249] When requested by an enrollee, the MA organization must decide whether to expedite its decision or, where the request is made or supported by a physician, make its reconsideration on an expedited basis.[250]

If the request for expedited reconsideration is denied, the MA organization must transfer a request to a standard time frame and make determination within the 30 days that begins the day the MA organization received the request for expedited reconsideration and must give the enrollee prompt oral notice, followed within 3 calendar days by written letter, explaining that the request will be processed using the 30-day standard time frame for reconsiderations.[251]

If an MA organization grants a request for expedited reconsideration, it must conduct the reconsideration and give notice as required by the regulations.[252] Moreover, if the MA organization must receive medical information from noncontract providers, the organization must request the necessary information within 24 hours of the initial request for an expedited reconsideration.[253] Noncontractors are to make a diligent effort to supply the information, and the MA organization is still responsible for meeting the time frame and notice requirements.[254]

If the MA organization affirms in whole or in part, it must submit a written explanation and the case file to the independent review entity (IRE) contracted by CMS as expeditiously as the enrollee's health condition requires, but not later than within 24 hours of its affirmation. In addition, the organization must make a reasonable and diligent effort to gather and forward the information to the IRE.[255] If the MA organization refers the matter to the IRE, it must concurrently notify the enrollee of that action.[256]

If the MA organization fails to provide the enrollee with timely results of its reconsideration within the time frame set out above, the failure constitutes an adverse reconsideration predetermination, and the MA organization must submit

[247] 42 C.F.R. § 422.584(b).
[248] 42 C.F.R. § 422.584(b)(2).
[249] 42 C.F.R. § 422.584(c).
[250] 42 C.F.R. § 422.584(c).
[251] 42 C.F.R. § 422.584(d).
[252] 42 C.F.R. § 422.584(d); *see also* 42 C.F.R. § 422.590.
[253] 42 C.F.R. § 422.584(d); *see also* 42 C.F.R. § 422.590.
[254] 42 C.F.R. § 422.584(d); *see also* 42 C.F.R. § 422.590.
[255] 42 C.F.R. § 422.590(d)(4).
[256] 42 C.F.R. § 422.590(f).

the file to the IRE within 24 hours of expiration of the above-described time frame.[257]

[vi] Who Can Hear an Adverse Medicare Advantage Organization Determination. Persons not involved in the organization determination may hear an adverse MA organization determination; medical necessity determinations must be made by a physician with expertise in the field of medicine that is appropriate for the service at issue,[258] although the physician need not in all cases be of the same specialty or subspecialty as the treating physician.[259]

[e] Reconsideration by an Independent Entity

When the MA organization affirms, in whole or part, its adverse organization determinations, the issues that remain in dispute must be reviewed and resolved by an independent, outside entity that contracts with CMS; the entity must meet contract deadlines for its decisions; the parties to a reconsideration are the same as those before the MA organization's reconsideration, with the addition of the MA organization.[260] The independent entity is responsible for mailing a notice of its reconsideration determination to the parties and for sending a copy to CMS. The notice must state the specific reasons for the entity's decision in understandable language; and if the decision is adverse, it must inform the parties of their right to review by an Administrative Law Judge (ALJ) if the amount in controversy is $160 (in 2017) or more and describe the procedures for obtaining ALJ review.[261]

A reconsidered determination is final and binding on all parties unless a party other than the MA organization files a request for a hearing under the provisions for request for an ALJ review, or unless the reconsidered determination is revised.[262] If the amount remaining in controversy after reconsideration meets the threshold requirement established annually by the Secretary, any party to the reconsideration (except the MA organization) who is dissatisfied with the reconsideration determination has a right to a hearing before an ALJ.[263]

---

[257] 42 C.F.R. § 422.590(g).

[258] 42 C.F.R. § 422.590(h)(2).

[259] 42 C.F.R. § 422.590(h)(2).

[260] 42 C.F.R. § 422.592.

[261] The amount in controversy (AIC) for administrative law judge (ALJ) hearings is $160 in 2017. The AIC for federal court review increases to $1,560 in 2017. *See* 81 Fed. Reg. 185, P. 65,653 (Sept. 23, 2016), *available at* https://www.gpo.gov/fdsys/pkg/FR-2016-09-23/pdf/2016-23002.pdf (site visited Sept. 27, 2016).

[262] 42 C.F.R. § 422.596; *see* 42 C.F.R. § 422.616 (reopening and revising determinations and decisions).

[263] 42 C.F.R. § 422.600(a).

[f] *Right to Administrative Law Judge Hearing and Amount in Controversy*

When an MA appeal reaches the ALJ level of review, the appeal system merges with claims originating from traditional Medicare. At this stage, absent a regulation specific to MA appeals, the regulations governing administrative review of Part A and B claims apply.[264] Since there are almost no regulations specific to MA claims for the ALJ level of review, the rules for traditional Medicare claims are incorporated to fill the vacuum. This includes the requirement that an ALJ decision be issued within 90 days of the receipt of a request for a hearing unless the parties waive their rights to such a timely decision.[265]

Any party to the reconsideration (except the MA organization) who is dissatisfied with the reconsidered determination has a right to a hearing before an ALJ, so long as the amount remaining in controversy meets the threshold requirement established annually by the Secretary.[266] The amount remaining in controversy, which can include any combination of Part A and Part B services, is computed by the Secretary.[267]

A party must file a written request for a hearing with the entity specified in the IRE's reconsideration notice, and except when an ALJ extends the time frame, a party must file a request within 60 days of the notice of a reconsideration determination.[268] The parties to a hearing are the parties to the reconsideration, the MA organization, and any other party or entity whose rights with respect to the reconsideration may be affected by the hearing, as determined by the ALJ.[269]

---

[264] 42 C.F.R. § 422.562(d).

[265] 42 C.F.R. § 405.1016(a). In Exley v. Burwell, No. 3:14-cv-1230, 2015 WL 3649632 (D. Conn. June 10, 2015), the Secretary of HHS argued that the 90-day deadline for ALJ decisions was not applicable to MA appeals. In an order granting class certification, however, the court concluded that 42 C.F.R. § 422.562(d) made the 90-day deadline applicable to "all Medicare beneficiaries," including those in MA plans, at least for the purposes of the class motion. *Exley*, 2015 WL 3649632, at *4. *See also* Medicare.gov, "Appeals—Level 3: Hearing Before an Administrative Law Judge (ALJ)," *available at* http://medicare.gov/claims-and-appeals/file-an-appeal/appeals-level-3.html (site visited May 27, 2016) (making no distinction between beneficiaries of the different parts of Medicare for purposes of the 90-day deadline for ALJ decisions). Note that on August 1, 2016, the court granted final approval of the *Exley* settlement agreement which will ensure timely ALJ decisions for Medicare beneficiaries. *See, e.g.,* the Center for Medicare Advocacy's Weekly Alert, which includes a link to the settlement agreement, "*Exley v. Burwell*: Settlement In Medicare Appeals Delay Case Granted Final Approval" (Aug. 4, 2016) *available at* http://www.medicareadvocacy.org/exley-v-burwell-settlement-in-medicare-appeals-delay-case-granted-final-approval/ (site visited Aug. 5, 2016).

[266] 42 C.F.R. § 422.600(a).

[267] 42 C.F.R. § 422.600(b).

[268] 42 C.F.R. §§ 422.602(a)–(b).

[269] 42 C.F.R. § 422.602(c).

If a request for a hearing clearly shows that the amount in controversy is less than the required jurisdictional amount, the ALJ dismisses the request; if the hearing is initiated, and the ALJ finds the amount in controversy is less than the required jurisdictional amount, the ALJ discontinues the hearing and does not rule on the substantive issues raised in the appeal.[270]

[g] Medicare Appeals Council Review

Any party to the hearing, including the MA organization, who is dissatisfied with the ALJ hearing decision may request that the Medicare Appeals Council (MAC) review the ALJ's decision or dismissal. The regulations under Part 405 apply to matters addressed by this subpart to the extent they are appropriate.[271]

[h] Judicial Review

Any party, including the MA organization, may request judicial review (upon notifying the other parties) of an ALJ's decision if the MAC denied the party's request for review and the amount in controversy meets the threshold requirement established annually by the Secretary.[272]

With respect to a review of a MAC decision, any party, including the MA organization, may request judicial review (upon notifying the other parties) of the MAC decision if it is the final decision of CMS and the amount in controversy meets the threshold established by the Secretary ($1,560 in 2017).[273]

In order to request judicial review, a party must file a civil action in a district court of the United States in accordance with Section 205(g) of the Social Security Act.[274]

[i] Reopening and Revising Determinations and Decisions

An organization or reconsidered determination made by an MA organization, a reconsidered determination made by the IRE, or the decision of an ALJ or

---

[270] 42 C.F.R. § 422.602(d). This provision implements § 1869(b)(1)(E)(iii) (Amount in Controversy) (MMA) of the Social Security Act, 42 U.S.C. § 1395w-22(g)(5). The amount in controversy (AIC) requirement for ALJ hearing requests and judicial review is amended so that it will be adjusted annually by the Secretary, beginning January 1, 2005, by the percentage increase in the medical care component of the consumer price index (CPI) for all urban consumers and rounded to the nearest multiple of $10. *See* 42 C.F.R. §§ 405.950(a), 405.970(a), and 405.1006. The 2017 AIC threshold amounts are $160 for ALJ hearings and $1,560 for judicial review.

[271] 42 C.F.R. § 422.608.

[272] 42 C.F.R. § 422.612(a).

[273] 42 C.F.R. § 422.612(b).

[274] 42 C.F.R. § 422.612(c). (*See* 42 C.F.R. Pt. 405 for a description of the procedures to follow in requesting judicial review.)

of the MAC may be reopened and revised by the entity that made the determination or decision.[275]

[j] Effectuating Standard Reconsidered Determinations and Decisions

For a request for service, if on reconsideration, the MA organization completely reverses its organization determination, the MA organization must authorize or provide the service under dispute as expeditiously as the enrollee's condition requires, but no later than 30 calendar days after the date the MA organization receives the request for reconsideration (or no later than the end of an extension).[276]

For a request for payment, if on reconsideration, the MA organization completely reverses its organization determination, the organization must pay for the service no later than 60 days after the date the MA organization receives the request for reconsideration.[277]

[k] Effectuating Reversals by the Independent, Outside Review Entity

For a request for service, the IRE must authorize the service within 72 hours from the date it receives notice reversing the determination; with respect to request for payment, the IRE must authorize payment within 30 calendar days from the date it receives notice reversing the organization determination.[278]

[i] Effectuating Standard Reconsiderations. For reversals other than by the MA organization or the IRE, decisions by an ALJ or higher level of appeal must be effectuated as expeditiously as the enrollee's health requires, but no later than 60 calendar days from the date it receives notice reversing the decision.[279] When, however, the MA organization files an appeal with the MAC, the MA organization may await the outcome of the review before it pays for, authorizes, or provides the service under dispute. The MA organization must concurrently send a copy of its appeal request and any accompanying documents to the enrollee and must notify the outside entity that it has requested an appeal.[280]

---

[275] 42 C.F.R. § 422.616.
[276] 42 C.F.R. § 422.618(a)(1).
[277] 42 C.F.R. § 422.618(a)(2).
[278] 42 C.F.R. § 422.618(b)(1)–(2).
[279] 42 C.F.R. § 422.618(c)(1).
[280] 42 C.F.R. § 422.618(c)(2).

[ii] Effectuating Expedited Reconsidered Determinations. If the MA organization completely reverses its determination, the service must be authorized as expeditiously as the enrollee's health condition requires, but no later than 72 hours after receipt of the request for reconsideration (or no later than upon expiration of any extension).[281]

[iii] Effectuating Reversals by the Independent Review Entity, Expedited Reconsideration. If the MA organization's decision is reversed in whole or in part, the decision must be effectuated as expeditiously as the enrollee's condition requires, but no later than 72 hours from the date it receives the notice reversing the determination.[282]

[iv] Effectuating Expedited Reversals by Other Than the MA Organization or the Independent Review Entity. If reversed in whole or in part by the ALJ or higher level of appeal, the MA organization must authorize payment as expeditiously as the enrollee's condition requires, but no later than 60 days from the date it receives the notice reversing the determination.[283] The MA organization may await the outcome of the review before it authorizes or provides the service under dispute, and if the MA organization files an appeal with the MAC, it must concurrently notify the enrollee and notify the IRE.[284]

[I] Medicare Advantage Organization Enrollee Notice of Non-Covered Inpatient Hospital Care

[i] Notice Requirement. Beginning July 1, 2007, hospitals must deliver a revised version of the Important Message from Medicare (IM) (CMS-R-193) (approved July 2010) and the Detailed Notice of Discharge (CMS 10066) (approved July 2010).[285] Under 42 C.F.R. § 405.1205 (Traditional Medicare) and 42 C.F.R. § 422.620 (Medicare Advantage), Medicare participating hospitals must deliver valid, written notice (the "Important Message from Medicare" (IM)) of a patient's rights as a hospital patient, including discharge appeal rights, within 2 calendar days of admission. A follow-up copy of the signed IM is given again as far as possible in advance of discharge, but no more than 2 calendar days before discharge.[286] Follow-up notice is not required if the provision of the admission IM falls within 2 calendar days of discharge.[287]

---

[281] 42 C.F.R. § 422.619(a).

[282] 42 C.F.R. § 422.619(b).

[283] 42 C.F.R. § 422.619(c)(1).

[284] 42 C.F.R. § 422.619(c)(2).

[285] 72 Fed. Reg. 17,169 (Apr. 6, 2007); *see also* MCP Manual, CMS Pub. No. 100–4, Ch. 30 §§ 200.6.2 and 200.6.3, *available at* http://www.cms.gov/Regulations-and-Guidance/Guidance/Manuals/downloads/Clm104c30.pdf (site visited May 31, 2016).

[286] 42 C.F.R. § 422.620(c)(1).

[287] 42 C.F.R. § 422.620(c)(2).

For a hospital stay, a beneficiary must request immediate (expedited) review, orally or in writing, no later than the day of discharge.[288] The beneficiary (or his or her authorized representative), upon request by the QIO, must be prepared to discuss the case with the QIO.[289] On the date that the QIO receives the beneficiary's request, the QIO must notify the hospital that the beneficiary has filed a request for immediate review.[290] The hospital must supply any information, including medical records, that the QIO requires to conduct its review and must make the information available, by phone or in writing, by the close of business of the first full working day after the day the beneficiary receives notice of the planned discharge.[291] When the beneficiary requests an expedited determination in accordance with 42 C.F.R. § 422.622(b)(1), the QIO must make a determination and notify the beneficiary, the hospital, and the physician of its determination by close of business of the first working day after it receives all requested pertinent information.[292]

[ii] Coverage During QIO Immediate (Expedited) Review. If the beneficiary remains in the hospital after receiving the hospital-issued notice of non-coverage and the hospital and the physician who concurred in the hospital's determination of non-coverage and subsequent advanced notice of non-coverage, or the QIO subsequently finds that the beneficiary requires an acute level of inpatient hospital care, the beneficiary is not financially responsible for continued care until the hospital once again determines that the beneficiary no longer requires inpatient care, secures concurrence from the physician responsible for the beneficiary's care or the QIO, and notifies the beneficiary.[293]

If a beneficiary files a request for an expedited determination by the QIO in accordance with 42 C.F.R. § 422.622(b)(1) and meets the "waiver of liability" provisions of Section 1879(a)(2) of the Social Security Act[294] (did not know or could not reasonably have been expected to know, that payment would not be made for such items or service under Part A or Part B), the beneficiary is not financially responsible for inpatient hospital services furnished until noon of the day after the QIO provides the beneficiary with notice (either orally or in writing) of the immediate determination of the QIO.[295] If the QIO determines that a beneficiary still requires inpatient hospital care, the hospital must provide the enrollee with a notice consistent with 42 C.F.R. § 422.620(c).[296]

---

[288] 42 C.F.R. § 422.662(b)(1).

[289] 42 C.F.R. § 422.662(b)(2).

[290] 42 C.F.R. § 422.662(d)(1).

[291] 42 C.F.R. § 422.662(e)(2).

[292] 42 C.F.R. § 422.622(d)(8). Notice is by telephone, with a written follow-up notice.

[293] 42 C.F.R. § 422.622(f)(3).

[294] *See* 42 U.S.C. § 1395pp(a)(2).

[295] 42 C.F.R. § 422.622(f)(1).

[296] 42 C.F.R. § 422.622(f)(3) (Apr. 2010 amendments).

When a beneficiary does not request an immediate QIO review in accordance with 42 C.F.R. § 422.622(b)(1), he or she may request expedited reconsideration by the MA organization (42 C.F.R. § 422.584), but the financial liability rules of 42 C.F.R. § 422.622(f) do not apply.[297]

A beneficiary who fails to request an expedited determination in accordance with 42 C.F.R. § 422.622(b)(1) above and who is no longer an inpatient in the hospital and is dissatisfied with the determination of the QIO may appeal to an ALJ, the MAC, or a federal court, as provided under Subpart M.[298]

[m] Notifying Enrollees of MA Organization Provider Termination of Services

[i] Timing of Notice. Before terminating covered services authorized by an MA organization, an advance written notice must be provided to an enrollee by providers of service, including Home Health Agencies (HHAs), SNFs, and Comprehensive Outpatient Rehabilitation Facilities (CORFs).[299] This includes the cessation of coverage at the end of a course of treatment, regardless of whether the enrollee agrees with the termination.[300] Prior to any termination of service, the provider must deliver advance written notice to the enrollee of the MA's decision to terminate services; provider must use a standardized notice, required by the Secretary.[301] The notice is to be provided no later than two days before the proposed end of services.[302] If services are expected to be fewer than two days in duration, notify the enrollee at the time of admission to the provider; for non-institutional settings if the span of time between services exceeds two days, the notice should be given no later than the next to last time services are furnished.[303]

[ii] Content of Notice. Standardized notice should include date that coverage ends; date of enrollee's liability; a description of the enrollee's right to a fast-track appeal, described below, to the IRE; an enrollee's right to submit evidence that services should continue; availability of other MA appeal procedures; the right to receive detailed information about the IRE process; and other information required by the Secretary.[304]

[iii] When Delivery of Notice Is Valid. Delivery is not valid unless (1) the enrollee (or authorized rep) has signed and dated the notice to indicate

[297] 42 C.F.R. § 422.622(b)(5).
[298] 42 C.F.R. § 422.622(g)(2).
[299] 42 C.F.R. § 422.624(a).
[300] 42 C.F.R. § 422.624(a)(2).
[301] 42 C.F.R. § 422.624(b).
[302] 42 C.F.R. § 422.624(b)(1).
[303] 42 C.F.R. § 422.624(b)(1).
[304] 42 C.F.R. § 422.624(b)(2).

receipt and comprehension of content, and (2) the notice is delivered as described above and has the notice content described above in §§ **7.04[E][2][m][i]** and **7.04[E][2][m][ii]**.[305] Moreover, with respect to notifying enrollees of termination of provider services, the MA plan is to ensure that the enrollee (or the enrollee's representative) has signed and dated the notice to indicate that he or she has received the notice and can comprehend its contents.[306]

[iv] Financial Liability for Failure to Deliver Valid Notice. An MA organization is financially liable for continued services until two days after the enrollee receives valid notice; an enrollee may waive continuation of service if he or she agrees with being discharged sooner than two days after receiving the notice.[307]

[n] Fast-Track Appeals to Independent Review Entities

[i] Right to Fast-Track Appeal. An enrollee of an MA organization has a right to a fast-track appeal of an MA organization decision to terminate provider services, which can be requested of the IRE in writing or by telephone by noon of the first day after the day of delivery of the termination notice (or by noon of the next day that the IRE is open for business).[308] If the enrollee fails to make a timely request to the IRE, he or she may request an expedited reconsideration by the MA organization.[309] If, after delivery of the termination notice, the enrollee chooses to leave a provider or discontinue receipt of services on or before the proposed termination, the enrollee cannot later assert a right to IRE appeal for the services at issue.[310]

[ii] Continuation of Coverage. Coverage of provider services continues until the date and time designated on the termination notice, unless the enrollee appeals and the IRE reverses the MA organization decision.[311] If the decision is delayed because the provider did not submit requested information timely, the MA organization is liable for any additional coverage required by the delayed IRE decision; if the IRE finds that enrollee did not receive valid notice, coverage continues until at least two days after valid notice is received, unless the continued coverage poses a threat to the enrollee's health and safety.[312]

---

305 42 C.F.R. § 422.624(c).

306 42 C.F.R. § 422.624(c)(1).

307 42 C.F.R. § 422.624(d).

308 42 C.F.R. § 422.626(a); CMS Manual Provisions on Fast Track can be found in the MMC Manual, Ch. 13, § 90.8.

309 42 C.F.R. § 422.626(a)(2)–(3).

310 42 C.F.R. § 422.626(a)(2)–(3).

311 42 C.F.R. § 422.626(b).

312 42 C.F.R. § 422.626(b).

[iii] Burden of Proof. The burden of proof rests with the MA organization to demonstrate that termination of coverage is the correct decision, either based on medical necessity or on other Medicare coverage policies.[313]

[iv] Procedures Independent Review Entity Must Follow. On the date of receipt of enrollee's request for an appeal, the IRE must immediately notify the MA organization and the provider of the appeal request and of its responsibility to submit documentation as requested by the IRE.[314] The IRE must make a decision and notify the enrollee, the MA organization, and the provider, by close of business of the day after it receives the necessary information for decision.[315] It can defer the decision until it receives necessary information from the MA, and until it does, coverage continues until the IRE makes its decision.[316] If an IRE reverses an MA organization's termination decision, the provider must provide the enrollee with a new notice as provided in 42 C.F.R. § 422.624(b).[317]

[v] Responsibilities of the Medicare Advantage Organization. The MA organization is to provide detailed notice to the enrollee about why services are either no longer reasonable and necessary or no longer covered and is to include in the notice a description of any applicable Medicare coverage rule, instruction, policy, including citation, or any applicable MA rationale or contract provision, or facts specific to the enrollee, and other information required by CMS, including cost for copying documents, as well as any information required by the IRE.[318]

[vi] Reconsiderations of Independent Review Entity Decisions. An enrollee may request reconsideration no later than 60 days after notification that the IRE has upheld the decision.[319] The reconsideration must be rendered expeditiously, but no later than within 14 days of receipt of the enrollee's request.[320] If affirmed in whole or part, the enrollee may appeal to the ALJ, the MAC, or a federal court as provided in these rules.[321]

---

[313] 42 C.F.R. § 422.626(c).
[314] 42 C.F.R. § 422.626(d).
[315] 42 C.F.R. § 422.626(d).
[316] 42 C.F.R. § 422.626(d).
[317] 42 C.F.R. § 422.626(f) (Apr. 2010 amendments).
[318] 42 C.F.R. § 422.626(e).
[319] 42 C.F.R. § 422.626(g).
[320] 42 C.F.R. § 422.626(g)(2).
[321] 42 C.F.R. § 422.626(g)(3).

APPENDIX 7-1 MEDICARE ADVANTAGE (PART C) DETERMINATION/APPEALS PROCESS

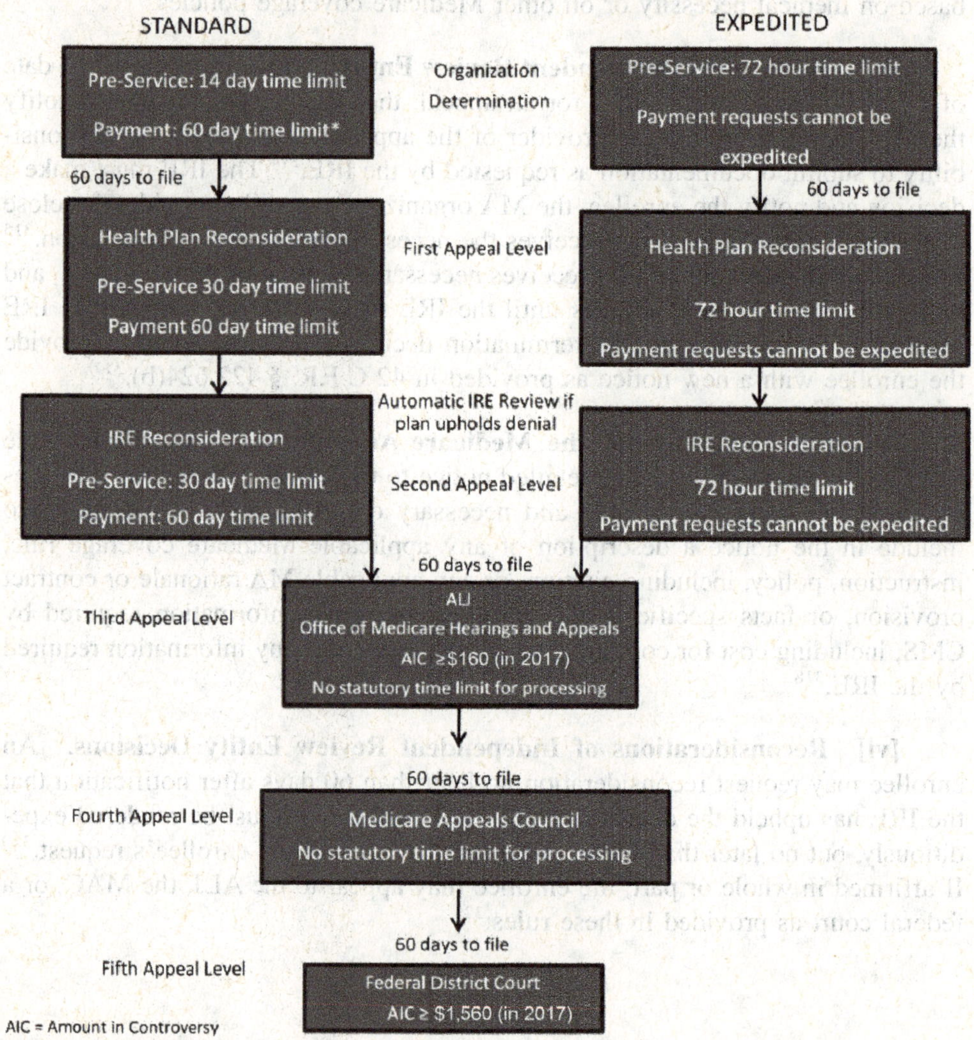

AIC = Amount in Controversy

ALJ=Administrative Law Judge

IRE=Independent Review Entity

*Plans must process 95% of all clean claims from out-of-network providers within 30 days. All other claims must be processed within 60 days.

APPENDIX 7-2

FORMS

FORM 7A INTEGRATED DENIAL NOTICE (IDN)

Important: This notice explains your right to appeal our decision. Read this notice carefully. If you need help, you can call one of the numbers listed on the last page under "Get help & more information."

Notice of Denial of Medical Coverage

{Replace *Denial of Medical Coverage* with *Denial of Payment*, if applicable}

Date: **Member number:**

Name:

[Insert other identifying information, as necessary (e.g., provider name, enrollee's Medicaid number, service subject to notice, date of service)]

Your request was denied

We've {Insert appropriate term: *denied, stopped, reduced, suspended*} the {*payment of*} medical services/items listed below requested by you or your doctor [*provider*]:

Why did we deny your request?

We {Insert appropriate term: *denied, stopped, reduced, suspended*} the {*payment of*} medical services/items listed above because {Provide specific rationale for decision and include State or Federal law and/or Evidence of Coverage provisions to support decision}:

You have the right to appeal our decision

You have the right to ask {health plan name} to review our decision by asking us for an appeal [Insert Medicaid information, if applicable: *and/or you can request a State Fair Hearing. You can ask for both types of review at the same time, as long as you meet the deadlines. If you ask us for an appeal first, you may miss the deadline for requesting a State Fair Hearing.*]:

Appeal: Ask {health plan name} for an appeal within **60 days** [Insert State Medicaid timeframe, if different] of the date of this notice. We can give you more time if you have a good reason for missing the deadline.

State Fair Hearing: *Ask for a State Fair Hearing within ( ) days of the date of this notice. You have up to ( ) days if you have a good reason for being late.*

If we're stopping or reducing a service, you can keep getting the service while your case is being reviewed. ***If you want the service to continue, you must ask for an appeal*** (Insert, if applicable: ***or a State Fair Hearing***) ***within 10 days*** *of the date of this notice or before the service is stopped or reduced, whichever is later. Your provider must agree that you should continue getting the service. If you lose your State Fair Hearing appeal, you may have to pay for these services.*

Form CMS 10003-NDMCP (Iss. 06/2013) OMB Approval 0938-0829

If you want someone else to act for you

You can name a relative, friend, attorney, doctor, or someone else to act as your representative. If you want someone else to act for you, call us at: {number(s)} to learn how to name your representative. TTY users call {number}. Both you and the person you want to act for you must sign and date a statement confirming this is what you want. You'll need to mail or fax this statement to us.

Important Information About Your Appeal Rights

There are 2 kinds of appeals

Standard Appeal – We'll give you a written decision on a standard appeal within **30 days** [Insert timeframe for standard Medicaid appeals, if different] after we get your appeal. Our decision might take longer if you ask for an extension, or if we need more information about your case. We'll tell you if we're taking extra time and will explain why more time is needed. If your appeal is for payment of a service you've already received, we'll give you a written decision within **60 days.**

Fast Appeal – We'll give you a decision on a fast appeal within **72 hours** after we get your appeal. You can ask for a fast appeal if you or your doctor believe your health could be seriously harmed by waiting up to 30 days for a decision.

We'll automatically give you a fast appeal if a doctor asks for one for you or supports your request. If you ask for a fast appeal without support from a doctor, we'll decide if your request requires a fast appeal. If we don't give you a fast appeal, we'll give you a decision within 30 days.

How to ask for an appeal with {health plan name}

Step 1: You, your representative, or your doctor [*provider*] must ask us for an appeal [*or State Fair Hearing*]. Your {*written*} request must include:

- Your name
- Address
- Member number
- Reasons for appealing
- Any evidence you want us to review, such as medical records, doctors' letters, or other information that explains why you need the item or service. Call your doctor if you need this information.

[Insert, if applicable: *You can ask to see the medical records and other documents we used to make our decision before or during the appeal. At no cost to you, you can also ask for a copy of the guidelines we used to make our decision.*]

Step 2: Mail, fax, or deliver your appeal {*or call us*}.

For a Standard Appeal: Address:
{Phone:} Fax:

{Insert, if applicable: *If you ask for a standard appeal by phone, we will send you a letter confirming what you told us.*}

For a Fast Appeal: Phone: Fax:

Form CMS 10003-NDMCP (Iss. 06/2013) OMB Approval 0938-0829

What happens next?

If you ask for an appeal and we continue to deny your request for {*payment of*} a service, we'll send you a written decision and automatically send your case to an independent reviewer. **If the independent reviewer denies your request, the written decision will explain if you have additional appeal rights.**

[Insert additional State-specific Medicaid rules, as applicable.]

How to ask for a Medicaid State Fair Hearing

[You have the right to ask for a State Fair Hearing without asking us (health plan) to review our decision first.]

Step 1: *You or your representative must ask for a State Fair Hearing (in writing) within (   ) days of the date of this notice. You have up to (   ) days if you have a good reason for your request being late.*

Your {written} request must include:

- Your name
- Address
- Member number
- Reasons for appealing
- Any evidence you want us to review, such as medical records, doctors' letters, or other information that explains why you need the item or service. Call your doctor if you need this information.

Step 2: *Send your request to:* Address:
Phone: Fax:

What happens next?

The State will hold a hearing. You may attend the hearing in person or by phone. You'll be asked to tell the State why you disagree with our decision. You can ask a friend, relative, advocate, provider, or lawyer to help you. You'll get a written decision within (   ) days. The written decision will explain if you have additional appeal rights.

[A copy of this notice has been sent to:]

Get help & more information

- {Health Plan Name} Toll Free: TTY users call:
  {Insert plan hours of operation}
- 1-800-MEDICARE (1-800-633-4227), 24 hours, 7 days a week. TTY users call: 1-877-486-2048
- Medicare Rights Center: 1-888-HMO-9050
- Elder Care Locator: 1-800-677-1116
- [Medicaid/State contact information]

Form CMS 10003-NDMCP (Iss. 06/2013) OMB Approval 0938-0829

MA plans are required (effective November 1, 2013) to issue the Integrated Denial Notice (IDN) upon denial, in whole or in part, of an enrollee's request for coverage and upon discontinuation or reduction of a previously authorized course of treatment.

FORM 7B NOTICE OF DISCHARGE

Patient Name: OMB Approval No. 0938-1019
Patient ID Number: Date Issued:
Physician:

{Insert Hospital or Plan Logo here}

Detailed Notice Of Discharge

You have asked for a review by the Quality Improvement Organization (QIO), an independent reviewer hired by Medicare to review your case. This notice gives you a detailed explanation about why your hospital and your managed care plan (if you belong to one), in agreement with your doctor, believe that your inpatient hospital services should end on ______________________. This is based on Medicare coverage policies listed below and your medical condition.

This is not an official Medicare decision. The decision on your appeal will come from your Quality Improvement Organization (QIO).

- Medicare Coverage Policies:

  _____ Medicare does not cover inpatient hospital services that are not medically necessary or could be safely furnished in another setting. (Refer to 42 Code of Federal Regulations, 411.15 (g) and (k)).

  _____ Medicare Managed Care policies, if applicable: ______________________
  ______________________ {insert specific managed care policies}

  _____ Other ______________________ {insert other applicable policies}

- Specific information about your current medical condition:

- If you would like a copy of the documents sent to the QIO, or copies of the specific policies or criteria used to make this decision, please call ______________________{insert hospital and/or plan telephone number}.

According to the Paperwork Reduction Act of 1995, no persons are required to respond to a collection of information unless it displays a valid OMB control number. The valid OMB control number for this information collection is 0938-1019. The time required to complete this information collection is estimated to average 60 minutes per response, including the time to review instructions, search existing data resources, gather the data needed, and complete and review the information collection. If you have comments concerning the accuracy of the time estimate(s) or suggestions for improving this form, please write to: CMS, 7500 Security Boulevard, Attn: PRA Reports Clearance Officer, Mail Stop C4-26-05, Baltimore, Maryland 21244-1850.

CMS 10066 (approved 07/10)

Instructions for Completing the Detailed Notice of Discharge

CMS 10066

This is a standardized notice. Hospitals may not deviate from the content of the form except where indicated. Please note that the OMB control number must be displayed on the notice. Insertions must be typed or legibly hand-written in 12-point font or the equivalent.

Hospitals or plans may modify the following sections to incorporate use of a sticker or label that includes this information:

Patient Name: Fill in the patient's full name.

Patient ID number: Fill in the patient's ID number. This should not be, nor should it contain, the patient's social security or HICN number.

Physician: Fill in the name of the patient's physician.

Date Issued: Fill in the date the notice is delivered to the patient by the hospital/plan.

Insert logo here: Hospitals/plans may elect to place their logo in this space. However, the name, address, and telephone number of the hospital/plan must be immediately under the logo, if not incorporated into the logo. If no logo is used, the name and address and telephone number (including TTY) of the hospital/plan must appear above the title of the form.

BLANK 1: **"This notice gives you a detailed explanation of why your hospital and your managed care plan (if you belong to one), in agreement with your doctor, believe that your inpatient hospital services should end on ______________________________.** In the space provided, fill in planned date of discharge.

First Bullet: **"Medicare Coverage Policies:"** Place a check next to the applicable Medicare and/or managed care policies. If necessary, hospitals may also use the selection "Other" to list other applicable policies, guidelines or instructions. Hospitals or plans may also preprint frequently used coverage policies or add more space below this line, if necessary. Policies should be written in full sentences and in plain language. In addition, the hospital or plan may attach additional pages or specific policies or discharge criteria to the notice. Any attachments must be included with the copy sent to the QIO as well.

Second Bullet: **"Specific information about your current medical condition"** Fill in detailed and specific information about the patient's current medical condition and the reasons why services are no longer reasonable or necessary for this patient or are no longer covered according to Medicare or Medicare managed care coverage guidelines. Use full sentences and plain language.

Third Bullet: **"If you would like a copy of the documents sent to the QIO, or copies of the specific policies or criteria used to make this decision, please call ______________________________."** The hospital/plan should also supply a telephone number for patients to call to get a copy of the relevant documents sent to the QIO. If the hospital/plan has not attached the Medicare policies and/or the Medicare managed care plan policies used to decide the discharge date, the hospital should supply a telephone number for patients to call to obtain copies of this information.

Hospitals or plans may add space below this section to insert a signature line and date, if they so choose.

FORM 7C WAIVER OF LIABILITY STATEMENT

(Rev. 105, Issued: 04-20-12, Effective Date: 04-20-12; Implementation Date: 04-20-12)

WAIVER OF LIABILITY STATEMENT

Medicare/HIC Number

Enrollee's Name

Provider *Dates of Service*

Health Plan

I hereby waive any right to collect payment from the above-mentioned enrollee for the aforementioned services for which payment has been denied by the above-referenced health plan. I understand that the signing of this waiver does not negate my right to request further appeal under 42 CFR 422.600.

Signature *Date*

FORM 7D NOTICE OF MEDICARE NON-COVERAGE

{Insert provider contact information here}
Notice of Medicare Non-Coverage

Patient name: **Patient number:**

The Effective Date Coverage of Your Current **{insert type}** Services Will End: **{insert effective date}**

- Your Medicare provider and/or health plan have determined that Medicare probably will not pay for your current {insert type} services after the effective date indicated above.
- You may have to pay for any services you receive after the above date.

Your Right to Appeal This Decision

- You have the right to an immediate, independent medical review (appeal) of the decision to end Medicare coverage of these services. Your services will continue during the appeal.
- If you choose to appeal, the independent reviewer will ask for your opinion. The reviewer also will look at your medical records and/or other relevant information. You do not have to prepare anything in writing, but you have the right to do so if you wish.
- If you choose to appeal, you and the independent reviewer will each receive a copy of the detailed explanation about why your coverage for services should not continue. You will receive this detailed notice only after you request an appeal.
- If you choose to appeal, and the independent reviewer agrees services should no longer be covered after the effective date indicated above;
  - Neither Medicare nor your plan will pay for these services after that date.
- If you stop services no later than the effective date indicated above, you will avoid financial liability.

How to Ask For an Immediate Appeal

- You must make your request to your Quality Improvement Organization (also known as a QIO). A QIO is the independent reviewer authorized by Medicare to review the decision to end these services.
- Your request for an immediate appeal should be made as soon as possible, but no later than noon of the day before the effective date indicated above.
- The QIO will notify you of its decision as soon as possible, generally no later than two days after the effective date of this notice if you are in Original Medicare. If you are in a Medicare health plan, the QIO generally will notify you of its decision by the effective date of this notice.
- Call your QIO at: {insert QIO name and toll-free number of QIO} to appeal, or if you have questions.

See page 2 of this notice for more information.

Form CMS 10123-NOMNC (Approved 12/31/2011) OMB approval 0938-0953

If You Miss The Deadline to Request An Immediate Appeal, You May Have Other Appeal Rights:

- If you have Original Medicare: Call the QIO listed on page 1.
- If you belong to a Medicare health plan: Call your plan at the number given below.

Plan contact information ____

____

Additional Information (Optional):

Please sign below to indicate you received and understood this notice.

I have been notified that coverage of my services will end on the effective date indicated on this notice and that I may appeal this decision by contacting my QIO.

_______________________________________ _______________

Signature of Patient or Representative Date

Form CMS 10123-NOMNC (Approved 12/31/2011) OMB approval 0938-0953

FORM 7E DETAILED EXPLANATION OF NON-COVERAGE

Insert contact information here

Detailed Explanation of Non-coverage

Date:

Patient name: Patient number:

This notice gives a detailed explanation of why your Medicare provider and/or health plan has determined Medicare coverage for your current services should end. ***This notice is not the decision on your appeal.*** The decision on your appeal will come from your Quality Improvement Organization (QIO).

We have reviewed your case and decided that Medicare coverage of your current {insert type} services should end.

- **The facts used to make this decision:**

- **Detailed explanation of why your current services are no longer covered, and the specific Medicare coverage rules and policy used to make this decision:**

- **Plan policy, provision, or rationale used in making the decision (health plans only):**

If you would like a copy of the policy or coverage guidelines used to make this decision, or a copy of the documents sent to the QIO, please call us at: {insert provider/plan toll-free telephone number}

Form CMS-10124-DENC (Approved 12/31/2011) OMB Approval No. 0938–0953

CHAPTER 8

MEDIGAP SERVICES

§ 8.01 INTRODUCTION

Despite the protections offered by Medicare, there are gaps in the traditional (or original) Medicare benefit package in the form of deductibles, copayments, and other limitations. Medigap insurance is provided by private insurance companies to supplement Medicare coverage and, sometimes, to cover services not included in Medicare's benefit package.[1] Since Medicare generally pays only a portion of a beneficiary's medical expenses, Medigap insurance is intended to "bridge the gap" between what Medicare pays and the balance of a beneficiary's medical bills.[2]

Medigap insurance is meant to work in tandem with the fee-for-service Medicare program and generally covers only services that Medicare has already approved for payment. Generally, if Medicare denies coverage for an item or a service, the Medigap policy will also refuse to pay its portion of the bill, unless coverage is specified in the policy.[3]

Medigap coverage is a key component of health insurance protection for individuals who rely on the original Medicare program to finance their health care. Consumers must be clear about the benefits they need and what the various plans cover to ensure that they pay for only what they need and get the coverage to which they are entitled.[4]

§ 8.02 MEDICARE CERTIFICATION OF POLICIES

Beginning in 1990, the Health Care Financing Administration (HCFA), now the Centers for Medicare & Medicaid Services (CMS), began a program of mandatory certification of Medigap policies and created ten standard plans.[5] Under

---

[1] *See* Medicare.gov, "What's Medicare Supplement Insurance (Medigap)?," *available at* http://www.medicare.gov/supplement-other-insurance/medigap/whats-medigap.html (site visited June 8, 2016); *see also* http://www.cms.gov/Medicare/Health-Plans/Medigap/index.html (site visited July 8, 2016).

[2] *See* CMS.gov, "Medigap (Medicare Supplement Insurance)," *available at* http://www.cms.gov/Medicare/Health-Plans/Medigap/index.html?redirect=/Medigap/ (site visited June 8, 2016).

[3] *See* Medicare.gov, "What's Medicare Supplement Insurance (Medigap)?," *available at* http://www.medicare.gov/supplement-other-insurance/medigap/whats-medigap.html (site visited June 8, 2016).

[4] A helpful resource is "2016 Choosing a Medigap Policy: A Guide to Health Insurance for People with Medicare," *available at* https://www.medicare.gov/Pubs/pdf/02110-Medicare-Medigap.guide.pdf (site visited June 8, 2016).

[5] See § 4353(a) of the Omnibus Budget Reconciliation Act of 1990 (OBRA '90), Pub. L. No. 101-508 (Nov. 5, 1990) (codified at 42 U.S.C. § 1395ss(a)), applicable to policies sold after July 1992; such policies must conform to one of the 10 standardized model policies developed by the National Association of Insurance Commissioners (NAIC). Previously, certification was voluntary as provided in § 507(a) of the Social Security Disability Amendments of 1980, Pub. L. No. 96-265 (June 9, 1980). (*See* 42 U.S.C. § 1395ss(b)–(f) for a full discussion of the state and federal certification processes and § 1395ss(i)–(n) for a full discussion and history of the effective dates for

this authority, the Secretary is required to establish a procedure whereby Medigap policies are certified as meeting minimum standards and requirements.[6] The Medicare statute deems the certification of Medigap policies by the Secretary of Health and Human Services (the Secretary) as meeting regulatory requirements established under state law if the state regulatory programs provide for the application and enforcement of standards that are equal to or more stringent than the model standards of the National Association of Insurance Commissioners (NAIC).[7] The Secretary is to review periodically the compliance of states with these requirements[8] and is also to submit a report to Congress at least once every two years that evaluates the effectiveness of the certification process.[9]

The Medicare Prescription Drug, Improvement, and Modernization Act of 2003 (MMA) added two new standardized plans and changed the benefits under three existing plans, starting in 2006.[10] In addition, the MMA authorized the NAIC to review and revise the model standards to incorporate the new plans and reflect the changes in the existing plans.[11]

The Genetic Information Nondiscrimination Act of 2008 (GINA),[12] applicable in states as of July 1, 2009, prohibits the denial, conditioning, or discrimination in pricing of a Medigap plan on the basis of genetic information. GINA also limits the ability of Medigap issuers to request or require genetic testing and prohibits the collection of genetic information for underwriting or other purposes prior to enrollment.

---

adopting and meeting the NAIC Model Regulation or federal model standards.) *See also* http://www.cms.gov/Medicare/Health-Plans/Medigap/Downloads/ModelMedigapRegulation2008.pdf (site visited June 8, 2016). Please visit the NAIC website for updated information, particularly on the work of its several committees. *See* NAIC, "2015 Charges," *available at* http://www.naic.org/committees_b_senior_issues.htm (site visited June 8, 2016).

[6] 42 U.S.C. § 1395ss(a)(1). The Secretary's authority to promulgate rules for the administration of its certification program for Medigap policies is found at 42 U.S.C. § 1395ss(h). The requirements for certification by the Secretary are found at 42 U.S.C. § 1395ss(c). Procedures for certification are found in the regulations at 42 C.F.R. § 403.232.

[7] *See* 42 U.S.C. § 1395ss(g)(2)(A). NAIC Model Standards for 2015 are found at 42 C.F.R. § 403.210. *See* http://www.naic.org/documents/committees_models_table_of_contents.pdf (site visited June 8, 2016).

[8] 42 U.S.C. § 1395ss(b).

[9] 42 U.S.C. § 1395ss(f)(2).

[10] Medicare Prescription Drug, Improvement, and Modernization Act of 2003 (MMA), Pub. L. No. 108-173 (Dec. 8, 2003), amending 42 U.S.C. § 1395ss.

[11] Legislation required implementation of the modifications made by NAIC to the standard Medigap plans, which include restructuring of the current benefit packages. NAIC had until October 31, 2008, to complete its modifications; the states then had one year from the time NAIC adopted the revised model law to conform. The Medicare Improvements for Patients and Providers Act of 2008 (MIPPA), Pub. L. No. 100-275 (July 15, 2008).

[12] The Genetic Information Nondiscrimination Act of 2008 (GINA), Pub. L. No. 110-233 (May 21, 2008).

The Medicare Improvements for Patients and Providers Act of 2008 (MIPPA)[13] approved recommendations made by the NAIC and authorized a number of changes to standardized Medigap plans. States were required to adopt all NAIC Medigap model changes as authorized by MIPPA by July 1, 2009. Effective June 1, 2010, modernized Medigap plans were available for sale. The Medicare Access and CHIP Reauthorization Act of 2015 (MACRA) made changes to what plans will be available for purchase for those who are newly eligible for Medicare on or after January 1, 2020.[14]

§ 8.03 STANDARDIZED PLANS OFFERED BEFORE JUNE 1, 2010

In all states except Minnesota, Massachusetts, and Wisconsin,[15] federal law requires insurers to sell Medigap policies that are one of the 12 standard supplemental plans.[16] These 12 plans are labeled with the letters A through L to make it easier for consumers to compare plans.[17] Medigap policies pay most, if not all, of traditional Medicare's coinsurance amounts and may provide coverage for deductibles as well. Some of the 12 standardized plans pay for services not covered by Medicare, such as some preventive screening services, extended hospital coverage, and emergency medical care while traveling outside the United States.[18] When describing the benefits of each of the Medigap policies, insurance companies must use the same format, language, and definitions to make it easier for consumers to compare policies.[19]

Plan A contains the basic or "core" benefits. The other 11 policies contain the core benefits plus one or more additional benefits. The following is a list of

---

[13] The Medicare Improvements for Patients and Providers Act of 2008 (MIPPA), Pub. L. No. 110-275 (July 15, 2008).

[14] The Medicare Access and CHIP Reauthorization Act of 2015 (MACRA), Pub. L. No. 114-10 (Apr. 16, 2015).

[15] Information on these three states' Medigap plans for 2017 as well as the 12 standardized plans can be found on the Medicare website "2016: Choosing a Medigap Policy," *available at* https://www.medicare.gov/Pubs/pdf/02110-Medicare-Medigap.guide.pdf (site visited June 9, 2016).

Visit the NAIC website (http://www.naic.org/ (site visited June 8, 2016)) for 2017 updates.

[16] 42 U.S.C. § 1395ss(a).

[17] Policies sold before July 31, 1992, were not standardized, and although these policies are no longer offered for sale, many beneficiaries continue to renew their existing pre-standardization policies.

[18] Some Medigap polices offered coverage for outpatient prescription drugs. Effective January 1, 2006, no new standardized Medigap policies that provide outpatient prescription drug benefits will be sold. Consumers who were enrolled in those plans as of December 1, 2005, may retain and renew those policies. 42 U.S.C. § 1395ss(v), as added by the MMA.

[19] 42 U.S.C. § 1395ss(e).

the benefits that are contained in the core policy and that must be contained in all new Medigap policies sold since July 31, 1992:[20]

1. Part A hospital coinsurance for days 61 to 90 ($329 per day in the year 2017);
2. Part A lifetime reserve coinsurance for days 91 to 150 ($658 in 2017);
3. 365 lifetime hospital days beyond Medicare coverage;
4. Parts A and B Three Pint Blood Deductible;
5. Part B 20 percent coinsurance.

Additional benefits are offered in Policies B through L. Each plan offers a different combination of these benefits in addition to the core benefits. A chart on the Medicare website compares the Medigap plans and shows which plans contain which benefits.[21] Additional benefits are:

1. Part A Skilled Nursing Facility (SNF) coinsurance for days 21 to 100 ($161.00 per day in 2016);
2. Part A hospital deductible ($1,316 in 2017);
3. Part B deductible ($183 in 2017);
4. Part B charges above the Medicare approved amount (if the provider does not accept assignment);
5. Foreign travel emergency coverage;
6. At-home recovery (home health aide services);
7. Prescription drug coverage (basic or extended);[22]
8. Preventive medical care.

---

[20] 42 U.S.C. § 1395ss(o). Please check for updated numbers, https://www.medicare.gov/supplement-other-insurance/medigap/whats-medigap.html (site visited June 8, 2016).

[21] *See* https://www.medicare.gov/supplement-other-insurance/compare-medigap/compare-medigap.html. The plans for Massachusetts, Minnesota, and Wisconsin are different. *See* http://www.medicare.gov/supplement-other-insurance/compare-medigap/massachusetts/medigap-massachusetts.html, http://www.medicare.gov/supplement-other-insurance/compare-medigap/minnesota/medigap-minnesota.html; *and* http://www.medicare.gov/supplement-other-insurance/compare-medigap/wisconsin/medigap-wisconsin.html (sites visited June 8, 2016).

[22] No new policies offering prescription drug coverage may be sold on or after January 1, 2006. 42 U.S.C. § 1395ss(v).

§ 8.04 HIGH DEDUCTIBLE PLANS

Medigap policies F and J also have a high deductible option. After June 1, 2010, however, Plan J is no longer offered for sale. These high deductible options offer the same basic benefits as Plan F, but the beneficiary enrolled in the high deductible option must pay a deductible ($2,200.00 in 2017)[23] each year before the policy pays anything. Additional deductibles must be met, including a separate foreign travel emergency deductible per year for Plans F and J.[24] Because of these additional deductibles, the premiums for these plans may be significantly lower than for plans without the high deductible.

§ 8.05 MEDICARE SELECT

Sections 4358(a) and (b) of the Omnibus Budget Reconciliation Act of 1990 (OBRA '90)[25] authorize approval of certain Medigap policies as Medicare SELECT[26] policies if the policies meet the NAIC model standards and otherwise comply with the statute. Medicare SELECT is the same as standard Medigap insurance in nearly all ways. Medicare SELECT policies limit full benefits to only those items and services furnished by a network of providers (hospitals and other entities), except in emergency situations. Reduced benefits may be provided for items and services furnished by non-network providers. Medicare SELECT policies generally have lower premiums because of this limitation.[27]

---

[23] *See* CMS, "Deductible Amount for Medigap High Deductible Options F & J for Calendar Year 2017 www.cms.gov/Medicare/Health-plans/Medigap/FandJ.html." The deductible is increased by the percentage increase in the Consumer Price Index for all urban consumers for the 12-month period ending with August of the preceding year. *See* 42 U.S.C. § 1395ss(p)(11)(C)(ii).

[24] 42 U.S.C. § 1395ss(p)(11). For updated information, check http://www.medicare.gov (site visited June 8, 2016).

[25] *See* § 4353(a) of the Omnibus Budget Reconciliation Act of 1990 (OBRA '90), Pub. L. No. 101-508 (Nov. 5, 1990) (codified at 42 U.S.C. § 1395ss(a)), applicable to policies sold after July 1992; such policies must conform to one of the ten standardized model policies developed by the National Association of Insurance Commissioners (NAIC). Previously, certification was voluntary as provided in § 507(a) of the Social Security Disability Amendments of 1980, Pub. L. No. 96-265 (June 9, 1980). (*See* 42 U.S.C. § 1395ss(b)–(f) for a full discussion of the state and federal certification processes and § 1395ss(i)–(n) for a discussion and history of the effective dates for adopting and meeting the NAIC Model Regulation or federal model standards.)

[26] *See* Medicare.gov, "How to Compare Medigap Policies," *available at* http://www.medicare.gov/supplement-other-insurance/compare-medigap/compare-medigap.html (site visited June 8, 2016). *See also* CMS, "2016 Choosing a Medigap Policy," *available at* https://www.medicare.gov/Pubs/pdf/02110-Medicare-Medigap.guide.pdf (site visited June 8, 2016).

[27] 42 U.S.C. § 1395ss(t)(1).

Medicare SELECT policies meet the NAIC or federal regulations if:

- Full benefits are provided for items and services furnished through a network of entities that have entered into contracts or agreements with the issuer of the policy;
- Full benefits are provided for medically necessary and immediately required services because of an unforeseen illness, injury, or condition, and it is not reasonable given the circumstances to obtain the services through the network;
- The network offers sufficient access;
- The issuer of the policy has arrangements for an ongoing quality assurance program for items and services furnished through the network;
- The insurer provides each enrollee at the time of enrollment (and the enrollee acknowledges receipt of) an explanation of the restrictions on obtaining services through the network, out-of-network services, coverage of emergency services, and urgently needed care; and
- The insurer provides each enrollee an explanation regarding the availability and cost of other Medigap policies offered by the insurer that do not include the network restrictions.[28]

The Secretary is authorized to impose civil money penalties against the issuer of a policy up to $25,000 for each of the following violations:[29]

- Substantial failure to provide medically necessary items and services to enrollees through the network, if the failure has adversely affected or has a substantial likelihood of adversely affecting the enrollee;
- Imposition of premiums on enrollees in excess of premiums approved by the state;
- Actions to expel an enrollee for reasons other than nonpayment of premiums;
- Failure to provide the enrollee with a written explanation of the policy's restrictions on payment outside the network, out-of-area coverage, coverage of emergency and urgently needed care, and availability and cost of a policy without a network restriction; and
- Failure to obtain an acknowledgment from the enrollee that he or she received the above-described explanation at the time of enrollment.

---

[28] 42 U.S.C. § 1395ss(t)(1)(A)–(F).

[29] 42 U.S.C. § 1395ss(t)(2).

§ 8.06 LEGISLATED POLICY CHANGES: A BRIEF HISTORY

[A] Changes to Policies Effective in 2006

Congress, in the MMA, made changes to existing standard plans H, I, and J and created two new Medigap plans. The changes to the existing plans and the sale of the new plans became effective on January 1, 2006, the day that the new Medicare drug provisions (Part D) went into effect.

On or after that date, Medigap plans H, I, and J cannot be sold, issued, or renewed to anyone with Medicare who is enrolled in or eligible for Medicare Part D. The Act created an exception for people with a plan H, I, or J policy that was issued before January 1, 2006.[30] Those policies may be renewed for such individuals as long as the individuals are not enrolled in a Medicare Part D prescription drug plan. If someone decides to keep a Medigap prescription drug plan, upon enrollment in a Medicare Part D drug plan, the Medigap plan's coverage will be modified to eliminate prescription drug coverage for expenses of prescription drugs incurred after the effective date of coverage under Part D. Premiums will also be adjusted to reflect the elimination of this coverage. Note that individuals who retained a Medigap policy with drug coverage and who later enroll in a Part D drug plan will have to pay a late enrollment penalty.[31] Two additional Medigap policies were introduced. The first benefit package, Plan K, covers 50 percent of cost-sharing applicable under Medicare Parts A and B, except for the Part B deductible. It covers 100 percent of cost-sharing for preventive benefits, all inpatient hospital coinsurance, and 365 extra lifetime days of coverage of inpatient hospital services. There is also a limitation on annual out-of-pocket expenses under Parts A and B.[32] The second benefit package, Plan L, is the same as the first except that it covers 75 percent of cost-sharing applicable under Parts A and B.[33]

The MMA authorized the NAIC to review and revise the standard benefit packages, taking into account the changes to Plans H, I, and J, and the addition of the two new benefit packages. The revisions were to be consistent with existing NAIC model regulations. The Act required that the revised standards be implemented as of January 1, 2006.[34]

Note that the MMA did not modify the standard plans to require that any or all of them pay the cost-sharing under the new Medicare Part D prescription drug benefit. Thus, neither existing nor newer Medigap policies will cover any of the

[30] 42 U.S.C. § 1395ss(v).

[31] *See* https://www.medicare.gov/part-d/costs/penalty/part-d-late-enrollment-penalty.html (site visited June 15, 2016),

[32] *See* Medicare.gov, "How to Compare Medigap Policies," *available at* http://www.medicare.gov/supplement-other-insurance/compare-medigap/compare-medigap.html (site visited June 8, 2016).

[33] 42 U.S.C. § 1395ss(w)(2). Please check http://www.cms.gov or https://www.medicare.gov for updated information (site visited June 8, 2016).

[34] 42 U.S.C. § 1395ss(w)(1).

out-of-pocket costs associated with prescription drug benefits provided under Part D.

[B] Changes to Policies Effective in June 2010

The Medicare Improvement for Patients and Providers Act of 2008 (MIPPA)[35] made changes to the standardized Medigap policies that may be sold on or after June 1, 2010. MIPPA authorizes a reduction in the number of standardized plans offered from 12 to ten. Plans E, H, I, and J are eliminated. Plans H, I, and J became duplicative of other plans after the Medicare Prescription Drug, Improvement, and Modernization Act of 2003 (MMA) added a prescription drug benefit to Medicare.[36] Plan E became unnecessary as a result of the other MIPPA changes. MIPPA also eliminates the "at-home recovery" and "preventive care" benefits as additional benefits Medigap plans could offer. A new hospice benefit, which covers all cost-sharing for Part A eligible hospice care and respite care expenses, was added as a core benefit available with every Medigap plan offered for purchase. Before June 1, 2010, Plan G paid 80 percent of the excess charges that a provider who does not accept Medicare assignment is allowed to charge. The excess charge benefit in the new Plan G is increased to 100 percent.

The two new plans, M and N, offer options with higher beneficiary cost-sharing and lower anticipated premiums. Plan M offers the basic core benefits required of every Medigap plan and additionally covers skilled nursing facility copayments, medically necessary emergency care in a foreign country, and 50 percent of the Medicare Part A deductible.[37]

Plan N offers the basic core benefits required of every Medigap plan and additionally covers 100 percent of the Medicare Part A deductible, skilled nursing facility copayments, and medically necessary emergency care in a foreign country. Plan N also includes copayments for covered services as follows: (1) the lesser of $20 or the Medicare Part B coinsurance or copayment for each covered health care provider office visit and (2) the lesser of $50 or the Medicare Part B coinsurance or copayment for each covered emergency room visit. However, this copayment for an emergency room visit is waived if the insured is admitted to any hospital and the emergency visit is subsequently covered as a Part A expense.[38]

In order to help define what constitutes an office visit for purposes of determining whether the beneficiary must pay the Plan N cost-sharing amount, CMS

---

[35] MIPPA, Pub. L. No. 110-275 (July 25, 2008).

[36] MMA, Pub. L. No. 108-173 (Dec. 8, 2003).

[37] *See* Medicare.gov, "How to Compare Medigap Policies," ***available at*** http://www.medicare.gov/supplement-other-insurance/compare-medigap/compare-medigap.html (site visited June 8, 2016).

[38] *See* http://www.medicareadvocacy.org/medicare-info/medigap/(site visited June 15, 2016).

has identified the codes for services that fall within the appropriate category.[39] These are codes for office visits or evaluation and management visits. Codes for laboratory, x-ray, durable medical equipment, or other services are not subject to the cost-sharing. However, if the physician bills for multiple Medicare-covered office visits in one day, the coinsurance or copayment amount is applicable to each Medicare-covered office visit.

[C] Sales of New Policies After June 2010

After June 1, 2010, only the new Medigap policies may be sold. Beneficiaries who have a pre-June 1, 2010 Medigap policy are allowed to keep and renew their older Medigap policies after that date. However, these policies may become more expensive over time as the number of policyholders decreases.

It is up to each individual insurance company to decide whether it will offer beneficiaries who have pre-June 1, 2010 policies the opportunity to purchase one of the new policies without medical underwriting. According to the NAIC, the entity that develops the standardized Medigap policies, this may depend on whether the insurance company chooses not to underwrite existing policyholders into the new standard policies.[40] If the insurance company does not exercise this option, a beneficiary may still apply for a new policy, but the application would be subject to medical underwriting unless other protections apply.[41]

If an insurer provides a period for policyholders to change to a new plan, or sells a new policy to replace a policy of equivalent or lesser coverage, the insurer must waive pre-existing condition time periods, waiting periods, and probationary periods for people whose previous policy was in effect for at least six months. Agents are prohibited from selling duplicate Medicare policies; one of the new Medigap policies cannot be sold to someone who already has a policy unless the new policy will replace the existing policy.[42]

[D] Sales of Policies for Those Newly Eligible as of January 2020

The Medicare Access and CHIP Reauthorization Act of 2015 (MACRA) made changes to those who will be eligible for certain Medigap policies starting in 2020.[43] Beginning in 2020, newly eligible Medicare beneficiaries will not be able to purchase Medigap policies that cover the Part B deductible ($183 in 2017).

[39] *See* http://www.medicareadvocacy.org/medicare-info/medigap/(site visited June 15, 2016).

[40] Implementation Materials for Revision to Medigap Model (NAIC, Oct. 7, 2008), *available at* http://www.naic.org/documents/committees_b_senior_issues_medigap_impl_guide.pdf (site visited June 8, 2016).

[41] *See* http://www.medicareadvocacy.org/medicare-info/medigap/(site visited June 15, 2016).

[42] *See* https://www.medicare.gov/find-a-plan/staticpages/learn/rights-and-protections.aspx (site visited June 15, 2016).

[43] MACRA, § 401, Pub. L. No.114-10 (Apr.16, 2015).

This includes individuals who become eligible for Medicare due to age, disability or end-stage renal disease on or after January 1, 2020. For these newly eligible beneficiaries, plans C and F will be referred to as plans D and G, respectively. All persons eligible for Medicare before January 1, 2020 may continue to be offered and to purchase policies that cover the Part B deductible.

§ 8.07 CONSUMER PROTECTIONS

Pursuant to federal law, all Medicare beneficiaries have an "open enrollment" period during the first six months they are both at least 65 years of age and enrolled in Medicare Part B. During this time period, a Medicare beneficiary can purchase any of the standard Medigap policies. This is a "guaranteed issue period," which means that insurance companies are prohibited from denying a policy to any Medicare beneficiary who meets the open enrollment requirements.[44]

Medicare beneficiaries who are at least 65 years old are also guaranteed issuance of certain Medigap policies if they apply within 63 days of the following events:

- A Medicare beneficiary who enrolled in a Medicare Advantage (MA) (formerly Medicare+Choice) plan upon first becoming eligible for Medicare who subsequently disenrolled within 12 months is guaranteed issuance of any Medigap policy offered for sale in the beneficiary's state. That period is extended for another 12 months if the MA plan terminated its contract with CMS or the beneficiary was otherwise involuntarily disenrolled within the first 12 months of enrollment and enrolled in another MA plan.[45]

- A Medicare beneficiary who dropped a Medigap policy upon enrolling for the first time in an MA plan but who subsequently disenrolled within 12 months is guaranteed issuance of the same Medigap policy from the same insurance company *if that policy* is still being offered for sale. Otherwise, such an individual is entitled to guaranteed issuance of Medigap plans A, B, C, or F. That period is extended for an additional 12 months if the MA plan terminated its contract with CMS or the beneficiary was otherwise involuntarily disenrolled within the first 12 months of enrollment and enrolled in another MA plan.[46]

- A Medicare beneficiary who moved out of the area or whose plan terminated service to the beneficiary's area, became bankrupt, or violated

[44] For a useful chart on guaranteed issue rules, *see* Medicare.gov, "How to Compare Medigap Policies," *available at* https://www.medicare.gov/supplement-other-insurance/compare-medigap/compare-medigap.html (site visited June 8, 2016).

[45] 42 U.S.C. § 1395ss(s).

[46] 42 U.S.C. § 1395ss(s).

or misrepresented a provision of the plan, or engaged in marketing violations is guaranteed issuance of Medigap plans A, B, C, or F. These same rights apply to Medicare beneficiaries whose employer stops providing employee or retiree health insurance coverage, or when COBRA health care continuation insurance ends.[47]

Once a beneficiary purchases a Medigap policy, he or she is also guaranteed renewal of that policy unless he or she does not pay the policy premiums or there has been some material misrepresentation of information leading to obtaining the policy. The health status of the individual is not a valid reason to cancel or to refuse to renew a policy.[48]

Each Medigap policy shall provide that benefits and premiums can be suspended at the request of the policy holder for a period up to 24 months when the policy holder has applied for and is determined to be eligible for medical assistance under the Medicaid program, provided the policy holder notifies the issuer of the policy within 90 days after the entitlement to such assistance. If the beneficiary's Medicaid entitlement is suspended or terminated, the Medigap policy can be automatically reinstated effective the day of the suspension or termination.[49] There are penalties for insurers who fail to abide by these provisions.[50] The Ticket to Work and Work Incentives Improvement Act of 1999[51] provides for suspension of Medigap coverage and premiums for disabled workers entitled to Medicare Part A covered under certain group health plans. It also requires reinstatement of a Medigap policy if group coverage is lost provided that the policyholder gives notice of the loss of such coverage within 90 days.[52]

Note that federal law provides a minimum level of consumer protections concerning when individuals have a right to purchase Medigap policies. States may expand such protections through state law, including requiring that certain Medigap policies be sold to individuals under 65 who are eligible for Medicare, and/or those eligible based upon having end-stage renal disease (ESRD), or when other designated triggering events occur.[53] Individuals should consult their state law relating to any expanded Medigap rights as such rights vary considerably by state.

---

[47] 42 U.S.C. § 1395ss(s).

[48] 42 U.S.C. § 1395ss(q)(1)(A)–(B).

[49] 42 U.S.C. § 1395ss(q)(5)(A).

[50] 42 U.S.C. § 1395ss(q)(5)(C).

[51] The Ticket to Work and Work Incentives Improvement Act of 1999, Pub L. No. 106-170 (Dec. 17, 1999), *available at* http://www.gpo.gov/fdsys/pkg/PLAW-106publ170/html/PLAW-106publ170.htm (site visited June 8, 2016); *see also* Social Security Legislative Bulletin, December 3, Subject: 1999 Congress Passes the Ticket to Work and Work Incentives Improvement Act of 1999, *available at* http://www.ssa.gov/legislation/legis_bulletin_120399.html (site visited June 8, 2016).

[52] 42 U.S.C. § 1395ss(q)(6).

[53] For an overview of additional state law protections, *see, e.g.*, Appendix I in Kaiser Family Foundation's report "Medigap: Spotlight on Enrollment, Premiums and Recent Trends" (Apr. 2013) *available at* http://kff.org/medicare/report/medigap-enrollment-premiums-and-recent-trends/ (site visited Sept. 22, 2016).

§ 8.08 PROHIBITION AGAINST SALE OF DUPLICATE POLICIES

Another important consumer protection found in federal law is the prohibition against the sale of a second Medigap policy to a beneficiary.[54] It is also unlawful for a person to knowingly sell or issue a Medigap policy that duplicates health benefits to which the individual is entitled under Title 19 (Medicaid) or other benefit programs under a state or federal law.[55] An insurance agent is required to disclose this provision of the law to Medicare beneficiaries and must obtain a written acknowledgment of their receipt of this information. A new policy may be sold to replace an existing policy, but this fact must also be acknowledged in writing. However, a beneficiary may keep or purchase another medical insurance policy that is not a Medigap policy. Such policies include hospital indemnification coverage, which provides benefits only for hospitalization and nothing else, and long-term care insurance.[56] When an insurance company or independent insurance agent sells such a policy, the specific coverage must be disclosed, and it must be certified that the policy is not a Medigap policy.[57]

In addition, since January 2006, issuers of Medigap policies are required to eliminate coverage that duplicates prescription drug benefits for individuals who have a Medigap prescription drug policy and who enroll in a Medicare Part D prescription drug plan.[58] Affected individuals could either enroll in a Medicare supplemental policy without prescription drug coverage or remain in their current plan if that plan has been modified to eliminate the drug benefit.[59]

§ 8.09 REQUIRED RATIO OF AGGREGATE BENEFITS TO AGGREGATE PREMIUMS

Medigap policies may not be issued or renewed in any state unless the policy can be expected to provide a return to policyholders in the form of aggregate benefits provided under the policy of at least 75 percent of the aggregate amount of premiums collected in the case of group policies, and at least 65 percent in the case

[54] It is not illegal for a beneficiary to renew existing policies. For that reason, there are a few beneficiaries who do have more than one Medigap policy because the policies were purchased before this provision of the law took effect.

[55] 42 U.S.C. § 1395ss(d)(3).

[56] 42 U.S.C. § 1395ss(d)(3).

[57] State law can and does, in many instances, offer additional consumer protections to beneficiaries purchasing Medigap policies. Medicare beneficiaries should check with their state's insurance commissioner for additional information.

[58] A Medigap prescription drug policy is defined as Plans H, I, and J, including a high deductible Plan J, or a policy to which the standards do not apply but which provides prescription drug benefits. 42 U.S.C. § 1395ss(v)(6)(A).

[59] 42 U.S.C. § 1395ss(v)(2)(A).

of individual policies.[60] Issuers of policies must provide for a proportional refund or credit against future premiums in order to ensure this required ratio of aggregate benefits provided as compared to the aggregate premiums collected, also known as loss ratios.[61] Refunds or credits must include interest from the end of the calendar year involved until the date of the refund or credit at a rate specified by the Secretary.[62]

Since 1993 the Secretary has been required to submit an annual report each October on loss ratios under Medigap policies to the Committees on Energy and Commerce and Ways and Means of the House of Representatives and the Committee on Finance of the Senate.[63] The Comptroller General is required to perform audits to ascertain compliance with the loss ratio requirements at least once every three years and to report the results of the audits to the state involved and to the Secretary.[64] The Secretary also has independent audit authority.[65] An insurer who fails to provide the required premium refunds or credits is subject to fines of up to $25,000 for each policy issued for which such failure occurred.[66]

§ 8.10 COVERAGE OF PREEXISTING CONDITIONS

In general, insurance companies are permitted to sell Medigap policies with exclusions for coverage of preexisting conditions for a period of up to six months.[67] A preexisting condition is a medical condition present prior to obtaining the health insurance coverage. Under the Health Insurance Portability and

---

[60] 42 U.S.C. § 1395ss(r)(1)(A). For purposes of this provision, only policies issued as a result of solicitations of individuals through the mail or by mass media advertising shall be deemed to be individual policies.

[61] 42 U.S.C. § 1395ss(r)(1)(B), *available at* http://www.ssa.gov/OP_Home/ssact/title18/1882.htm (site visited June 8, 2016).

[62] 42 U.S.C. § 1395ss(r)(2)(A)–(D), *available at* http://www.ssa.gov/OP_Home/ssact/title18/1882.htm (site visited June 8, 2016).

[63] 42 U.S.C. § 1395ss(r)(4)–(5), *available at* http://www.ssa.gov/OP_Home/ssact/title18/1882.htm (site visited June 8, 2016). *See also* HHS, ASPE, "Variations and Trends in Medigap Premiums" (Dec. 16, 2011), *available at* http://aspe.hhs.gov/health/reports/2011/medigappremiums/index.pdf (site visited June 8, 2016).

[64] 42 U.S.C. § 1395ss(r)(5)(A).

[65] 42 U.S.C. § 1395ss(r)(5)(B).

[66] 42 U.S.C. § 1395ss(r)(6)(A).

[67] GINA, Pub. L. No. 110-233 (May 21, 2008), prohibits Medigap issuers from denying or conditioning the issuance or effectiveness of a policy on the basis of a beneficiary's genetic information. Issuers are also prohibited from requesting, requiring, or purchasing a beneficiary's genetic information and from using that information in discriminating in the pricing of a policy. However, issuers may raise the premiums for beneficiaries with pre-existing conditions, except as indicated in this chapter. A temporary, high risk pool is created by the Affordable Care Act (ACA) (effective 90 days after enactment of the Act) for individuals who have been uninsured for six months or who have been denied insurance because of a preexisting condition. This funding is capped at $5 billion

Accountability Act (HIPAA)[68] such exclusions *cannot* be imposed on an individual who applies for a Medigap policy during his or her initial open enrollment period, who has at least six months of creditable coverage, and who has not had a break in creditable coverage of more than 63 days prior to applying for the Medigap policy.[69]

A beneficiary's initial open enrollment period occurs during the first six months the beneficiary is both age 65 or older and enrolled in Medicare Part B.[70] Creditable coverage is defined as coverage under:

- A group health plan;
- Health insurance coverage;
- Part A or Part B of Medicare;
- Medicaid;
- A medical program on the Indian Health Service or tribal organization;
- A state health benefits risk pool;
- CHAMPUS (Civilian Health and Medical Program of the Uniformed Services);
- The Federal Employees Health Benefit Plan;
- A public health plan; or
- A health plan under the Peace Corps Act.[71]

For beneficiaries who are switching from one Medigap policy to another, the issuer of the replacement Medigap policy must waive any time periods applicable to preexisting conditions, waiting periods, elimination periods, and probation periods in the new Medigap policy for similar benefits to the extent of time spent under the original policy.[72]

---

and expired on January 1, 2014. *See* ACA § 1101. Note, too, that for plan years starting on or after January 1, 2014, group health plans and health insurers that offer group or individual health insurance coverage are prohibited from imposing any preexisting condition exclusion. *See* ACA § 1201(2)(A). *See also* Medicare.gov, "When Can I Buy Medigap?" *available at* http://www.medicare.gov/supplement-other-insurance/when-can-i-buy-medigap/when-can-i-buy-medigap.html (site visited June 8, 2016).

[68] 42 U.S.C. § 300gg.

[69] 42 U.S.C. § 1395ss(s)(2)(D).

[70] State law can and does, in many instances, offer additional consumer protections to beneficiaries purchasing Medigap policies, including requiring a similar open enrollment period for individuals under 65.

[71] 42 U.S.C. § 300gg(c)(1).

[72] 42 U.S.C. § 1395ss(s)(1).

Since 1997, pursuant to the Balanced Budget Act of 1997 (BBA '97),[73] Medicare beneficiaries who are at least 65 years old are also guaranteed issuance of certain Medigap policies with no wait for coverage of preexisting conditions if they apply within 63 days under certain circumstances.[74] The circumstances under which these rights exist are as follows:

- A Medicare beneficiary whose employer stopped providing employee retirement health benefits or whose COBRA health care continuation insurance coverage ends is guaranteed issuance of Medigap policies A, B, C, or F.
- A Medicare beneficiary who enrolled in an MA plan upon first becoming eligible for Medicare who subsequently disenrolled within 12 months is guaranteed issuance of any Medigap policy sold in his or her state.
- A Medicare beneficiary who dropped a Medigap policy upon enrolling for the first time in an MA plan but who subsequently disenrolled within 12 months is guaranteed issuance of the same Medigap policy from the same insurance company if that policy is still being offered for sale. Otherwise, such an individual is entitled to "guaranteed issuance" of Medigap policies A, B, C, or F from any insurance company selling Medigap policies in his or her state.
- A Medicare beneficiary who moved out of the area served by his or her MA plan or whose MA plan terminated service to his or her area, became bankrupt, or violated or misrepresented a provision of the plan is guaranteed issuance of Medigap policies A, B, C, or F.

§ 8.11 DISSEMINATION OF INFORMATION ABOUT MEDIGAP POLICY BENEFITS

The Secretary is required to provide Medicare beneficiaries with information that will assist them in evaluating whether a Medigap policy will be of value to them and with information that will be helpful in comparing Medigap policies.[75] Pursuant to this requirement, beneficiaries are to be provided information about the actions and practices that are subject to sanctions under Medicare, the manner in which such actions and practices may be reported, and a toll-free telephone number for individuals to report suspected violations.[76] In addition, beneficiaries are to be provided a listing, including addresses and telephone numbers, of state and federal agencies and offices that provide information and assistance

[73] The Balanced Budget Act of 1997 (BBA '97), Pub. L. No. 105-33 (Aug. 5, 1997).

[74] 42 U.S.C. § 1395ss(s)(3).

[75] 42 U.S.C. § 1395ss(e)(1).

[76] 42 U.S.C. § 1395ss(e)(2)(A).

to individuals on selecting Medigap policies.[77] The Secretary is also to provide a toll-free telephone number for information about Medigap policies, including the relationship of state Medicaid programs to Medigap policies.[78] Much of this required information is found on the Medicare website: *www.medicare.gov*.

The MMA required issuers of Medicare prescription drug policies[79] to provide written notice, during the 60 days immediately before the initial Medicare Part D prescription drug enrollment period to everyone who held a Medigap prescription drug policy.[80] The standard notice, approved by the Secretary and by NAIC, advised policy holders of the effects on the new Medicare prescription drug benefit on their policies, and their rights to either retain or change Medigap coverage. The notice also explained that the coverage under the Medigap drug policy may not count as creditable coverage, raising the possibility of limited enrollment periods and a late enrollment penalty should they subsequently decide to enroll in a Part D plan.[81]

§ 8.12 CONCLUSION

In 2011, one in five Medicare beneficiaries had a Medigap policy that provided his or her only coverage supplemental to Medicare.[82] The changes to the benefit structure of the standardized Medigap policies effective for plans sold after June 1, 2010, reflect changes to the Medicare program and service utilization and provide cost-sharing protections in the hospice benefit. Preventive services has expanded, and MIPPA and ACA give the Secretary greater authority to expand Medicare coverage of preventive services. The opportunity to sell Medigap policies brings with it the opportunity for marketing abuses. Advocates should ensure that a client who purchases a Medigap policy has done so because the client believes the policy best suits his or her needs and not because of pressure from sales tactics and other marketing abuses.

---

[77] 42 U.S.C. § 1395ss(e)(3).

[78] 42 U.S.C. § 1395ss(f)(3).

[79] State law can and does, in many instances, offer additional consumer protections to beneficiaries purchasing Medigap policies. Medicare beneficiaries should check with their state's insurance commissioner for additional information.

[80] The initial enrollment period for Part D began November 15, 2005. MMA § 101(a), adding § 1860D-1(b)(2)(A) to the Social Security Act.

[81] 42 U.S.C. § 1395ss(v)(2)(B).

[82] Kaiser Family Foundation (KFF), "Medigap Reform: Setting the Context" (Sept. 2011), *available at* http://kaiserfamilyfoundation.files.wordpress.com/2013/01/8235-2.pdf (site visited June 8, 2016); *see also* KFF, "Medigap Reform: Setting the Context for Understanding Recent Proposals" (Jan. 13, 2014), *available at* http://kff.org/medicare/issue-brief/medigap-reform-setting-the-context/ (site visited June 8, 2016); *and* KFF, "Medigap Enrollment Among New Medicare Beneficiaries: How Many 65-Year Olds Enroll in Plans with First-Dollar Coverage?" (Apr. 13, 2015), *available at* http://kff.org/medicare/issue-brief/medigap-enrollment-among-new-medicare-beneficiaries/ (site visited June 8, 2016).

APPENDIX 8-1 TITLE 42—PUBLIC HEALTH (CODE OF FEDERAL REGULATIONS):

PART 403—SPECIAL PROGRAMS AND PROJECTS

Subpart B—Medicare Supplemental Policies

Sec. 403.215 Loss ratio standards.

(a) The policy must be expected to return to the policyholders, in the form of aggregate benefits provided under the policy—

(1) At least 75 percent of the aggregate amount of premiums in the case of group policies; and

(2) At least 60 percent of the aggregate amount of premiums in the case of individual policies.

(b) For purposes of loss ratio requirements, policies issued as a result of solicitation of individuals through the mail or by mass media advertising are considered individual policies.

***

Sec. 403.232 Requirements and procedures for obtaining certification.

(a) To be certified by CMS, a policy must meet—

(1) The NAIC model standards specified in Sec. 403.210;

(2) The loss ratio standards specified in Sec. 403.215; and

(3) Any State requirements applicable to a policy—

(i) Issued in that State; or

(ii) Marketed in that State.

(b) An insuring organization requesting certification of a policy must submit the following to CMS for review—

(1) A copy of the policy form (including all the documents that would constitute the contract of insurance that is proposed to be marketed as a certified policy).

(2) A copy of the application form including all attachments.

(3) A copy of the uniform certificate issued under a group policy.

(4) A copy of the outline of coverage, in the form prescribed by the NAIC model standards.

(5) A copy of the Medicare supplement buyers' guide to be provided to all applicants if the buyers' guide is not the CMS/NAIC buyers' guide.

(6) A statement of when and how the outline of coverage and the buyers' guide will be delivered and copies of applicable receipt forms.

(7) A copy of the notice of replacement and statement as to when and how that notice will be delivered.

(8) A list of States in which the policy is authorized for sale. If the policy was approved under a deemer provision in any State, the conditions involved must be specified.

(9) A copy of the loss ratio calculations, as specified in Sec. 403.250.

(10) Loss ratio supporting data, as specified in Sec. 403.256.

(11) A statement of actuarial opinion, as specified in Sec. 403.258.

(12) A statement that the insuring organization will notify the policyholders in writing, within the period of time specified in Sec. 403.245(c), if the policy is identified as a certified policy at the time of sale and later loses certification.

(13) A signed statement in which the president of the insuring organization, or a designee, attests that—

(i) The policy meets the requirements specified in paragraph (a) of this section; and

(ii) The information submitted to CMS for review is accurate and complete and does not misrepresent any material fact.

APPENDIX 8-2 TITLE 42—THE PUBLIC HEALTH AND WELFARE (UNITED STATES CODE):

CHAPTER 7—SOCIAL SECURITY: SUBCHAPTER XVIII—HEALTH INSURANCE FOR AGED AND DISABLED

(Subpart D—Miscellaneous Provisions)*

Sec. 1395ss Certification of Medicare supplemental health insurance policies.

(a) Submission of policy by insurer.

(1) The Secretary shall establish a procedure whereby Medicare supplemental policies (as defined in subsection (g)(1) of this section) may be certified by the Secretary as meeting minimum standards and requirements set forth in subsection (c) of this section. Such procedure shall provide an opportunity for any insurer to submit any such policy, and such additional data as the Secretary finds necessary, to the Secretary for his examination and for his certification thereof as meeting the standards and requirements set forth in subsection (c) of this section. Subject to subsections (k)(3), (m), and (n) of this section, such certification shall remain in effect if the insurer files a notarized statement with the Secretary no later than June 30 of each year stating that the policy continues to meet such standards and requirements and if the insurer submits such additional data as the Secretary finds necessary to independently verify the accuracy of such notarized statement. Where the Secretary determines such a policy meets (or continues to meet) such standards and requirements, he shall authorize the insurer to have printed on such policy (but only in accordance with such requirements and conditions as the Secretary may prescribe) an emblem which the Secretary shall cause to be designed for use as an indication that a policy has received the Secretary's certification. The Secretary shall provide each State commissioner or superintendent of insurance with a list of all the policies which have received his certification.

(2) No Medicare supplemental policy may be issued in a State on or after the date specified in subsection (p)(1)(C) of this section unless—

(A) the State's regulatory program under subsection (b)(1) of this section provides for the application and enforcement of the standards and requirements set forth in such subsection (including the 1991 NAIC Model Regulation or 1991 Federal Regulation (as the case may be)) by the date specified in subsection (p)(1)(C) of this section; or

---

* *See* http://www.gpo.gov/fdsys/pkg/USCODE-2011-title42/pdf/USCODE-2011-title42-chap7-subchapXVIII-partE-sec1395ss.pdf (site visited June 8, 2016)

(B) if the State's program does not provide for the application and enforcement of such standards and requirements, the policy has been certified by the Secretary under paragraph (1) as meeting the standards and requirements set forth in subsection (c) of this section (including such applicable standards) by such date. Any person who issues Medicare supplemental policy, on and after the effective date specified in subsection (p)(1)(C) of this section, in violation of this paragraph is subject to a civil money penalty of not to exceed $25,000 for each such violation. The provisions of section 1320a–7a of this title (other than the first sentence of subsection (a) and other than subsection (b)) shall apply to a civil money penalty under the previous sentence in the same manner as such provisions apply to a penalty or proceeding under section 1320a–7a(a) of this title.

CHAPTER 9

MEDICARE'S RELATIONSHIP WITH PRIVATE INSURANCE

§ 9.01 INTRODUCTION

In 1980, Congress prohibited Medicare from paying for health services that are also covered by other insurers through its creation of the Medicare Secondary Payer (MSP; not to be confused with the acronym for "Medicare Savings Program," discussed in **Chapter 10**) program.[1] The MSP program has been modified and expanded by subsequent legislation in order to shift more health care costs from the federal government to private insurers.

The MSP law makes Medicare payment secondary to payment by two kinds of private insurers: first, insurers providing group health insurance for currently working employees;[2] and second, insurers providing coverage under automobile, liability, and workers' compensation policies.[3] Moreover, an employer or other entity is prohibited from offering Medicare beneficiaries financial or other benefits as incentives not to enroll in or to terminate enrollment in a group health plan (GHP) or large group health plan (LGHP) that is or would be primary to Medicare.[4] Such financial or other incentives are a violation of the Medicare law every time a prohibited offer is made regardless of whether it is oral or in writing and is subject to a civil money penalty of up to $5,000 for each violation.[5]

§ 9.02 EMPLOYER GROUP HEALTH PLANS

[A] Medicare Secondary to Employer Group Health Plans

The Medicare statute makes Medicare secondary to employer group health insurance in a number of situations. Employer group health plans (EGHPs) of specified sizes are prohibited from discriminating in health insurance benefits available to workers and their spouses who are eligible for Medicare because they are disabled or age 65 or older.[6]

Medicare is secondary to LGHPs for individuals under age 65 entitled to Medicare on the basis of disability and whose LGHP coverage is based on the individual's *current* employment status or the *current* employment status of a

---

[1] Omnibus Budget Reconciliation Act (OBRA) of 1980, Pub. L. No. 96-499 (Dec. 5, 1980), § 953.

[2] 42 U.S.C. § 1395y(b)(2)(A)(i).

[3] 42 U.S.C. § 1395y(b)(2)(A)(ii).

[4] *See* Medicare Secondary Payer (MSP) Manual, Ch. 1, § 70, *available at* http://www.cms.gov/Regulations-and-Guidance/Guidance/Manuals/downloads//msp105c01.pdf (site visited May 31, 2016).

[5] MSP Manual, Ch. 1, § 70.1.

[6] 42 U.S.C. § 1395y(b)(1)(A)(i). *See also* **§ 9.02[C]** of this Handbook for defining EGHPs that are affected by Medicare secondary payer (MSP) rules.

family member. An LGHP may not "take into account" that such an individual is eligible for, or receives, Medicare benefits based on disability.[7]

An LGHP is a GHP that covers at least 100 full-time or part-time employees on 50 percent or more of its regular business days during the previous calendar year and includes individual policies (including Medigap policies) purchased by or through an employer or former employer of the individual or family member.[8]

Medicare is secondary payer to GHPs for individuals eligible for, or entitled to, Medicare benefits based on end-stage renal disease (ESRD) during the 30-month coordination period during which Medicare may be secondary payer.[9] A GHP is an arrangement of one or more employers or employee organizations to provide health benefits to the employee or medical care directly or indirectly to current or former employees, the employer, others associated or formerly associated with the employer in a business relationship, or their families.[10]

If Medicare was not the proper primary payer for an individual on the basis of age or disability at the time the individual became eligible for or entitled to Medicare on the basis of ESRD, Medicare is the secondary payer to GHPs for items and services furnished during a period of up to 30 consecutive months that begins with the earlier of: the month in which a regular course of renal dialysis is initiated or, if the patient undergoes a course of self-dialysis training, the first day of the month in which the training occurred or, if the individual received a kidney transplant, the first month in which the individual became entitled.[11] Eligibility refers to the first month that the individual would have become entitled to Medicare Part A on the basis of ESRD if he or she had filed an application for such benefits.[12] Medicare entitlement usually begins with the third month after the month in which the individual starts a regular course of dialysis.[13] This provision applies regardless of the number of employees employed by the employer and

---

[7] *See* MSP Manual, Ch. 1, § 10.3, *available at* http://www.cms.gov/Regulations-and-Guidance/Guidance/Manuals/downloads//msp105c01.pdf (site visited May 31, 2016).

[8] *See* MSP Manual, Ch. 1, § 20 (definitions), *available at* http://www.cms.gov/Regulations-and-Guidance/Guidance/Manuals/downloads//msp105c01.pdf (site visited May 31, 2016).

[9] *See* MSP Manual, Ch. 2, § 20, *available at* http://www.cms.gov/Regulations-and-Guidance/Guidance/Manuals/downloads//msp105c02.pdf (site visited May 31, 2016).

[10] *See* MSP Manual, Ch. 1, § 20 (definitions), *available at* http://www.cms.gov/Regulations-and-Guidance/Guidance/Manuals/downloads//msp105c01.pdf (site visited May 31, 2016).

[11] *See* MSP Manual, Ch. 2, § 20.1, *available at* http://www.cms.gov/Regulations-and-Guidance/Guidance/Manuals/downloads//msp105c02.pdf (site visited May 31, 2016).

[12] See MSP Manual, Ch. 2, § 20, *available at* www.cms.gov/Regulations-and-Guidance/Guidance/Manuals/downloads//msp105c02.pdf (site visited May 31, 2016).

[13] *See* MSP Manual, Ch. 2, § 20.1, *available at* http://www.cms.gov/Regulations-and-Guidance/Guidance/Manuals/downloads//msp105c02.pdf (site visited May 31, 2016).

regardless of whether the individual or the family member has current employment status. The provision applies to former as well as current employees.[14]

Medicare provides only limited, secondary coverage for EGHP-eligible beneficiaries.[15] It will take steps to recover payments previously made when it discovers that an EGHP should have paid as primary insurer.[16]

[B] Which Medicare Beneficiaries Are Covered Under an EGHP?

A Medicare beneficiary may be able to obtain coverage under an EGHP offered to currently working employees, their spouses, and their dependents; under a retiree health plan offered to retirees, their spouses, and their dependents; or under the health care continuation coverage of the Consolidated Omnibus Budget Reconciliation Act (COBRA).[17] In all three situations, if the plan is offered by a private employer or union, the plan must meet the requirements of another federal law known as the Employee Retirement Income Security Act (ERISA),[18] which sets certain standards for employment-related health insurance.

ERISA and other federal laws currently do not require employers to offer group health insurance to their employees.[19] Employers that offer health insurance do so voluntarily.[20] If a health insurance plan is offered, ERISA generally allows the plan sponsor, that is, the employer or union, to set the eligibility criteria for participation in the health plan offered to active employees. Someone who does not meet the criteria established by the plan sponsor is not eligible to join in the health plan, and Medicare is the primary insurer.

Similarly, employers who offer group health insurance to currently working employees are not required to offer retiree health insurance to retired workers.[21]

---

[14] *See* MSP Manual, Ch. 2, § 20.1, *available at* http://www.cms.gov/Regulations-and-Guidance/Guidance/Manuals/downloads//msp105c02.pdf (site visited May 31, 2016).

[15] Individuals with end-stage renal disease (ESRD) may be entitled to primary coverage through an EGHP for a limited time. *See* **§ 9.02[C][1]** of this Handbook.

[16] 42 U.S.C. § 1395y(b)(2)(B)(iii).

[17] 29 U.S.C. § 1161; 42 U.S.C. §§ 300bb-1 *et seq. See* discussion at **§ 9.05** of this Handbook.

[18] 29 U.S.C. § 1001.

[19] The Patient Protection and Affordable Care Act (PPACA, also known as the Affordable Care Act, or ACA), Pub. L. No. 111-148, §§ 1511 *et seq.* (Mar. 23, 2010), *available at* http://www.gpo.gov/fdsys/pkg/PLAW-111publ148/pdf/PLAW-111publ148.pdf (site visited May 31, 2016), amended the Fair Labor Standards Act of 1938 (29 U.S.C. § 218) to require that employers with 200 or more employees automatically enroll all new employees in health care coverage. The ACA also requires employers with more than 50 employees to offer qualified coverage, and it sets minimum standards for coverage.

[20] Hawaii is the only state permitted to require employers to offer health insurance. General Accounting Office (GAO), "Employment-Based Health Insurance: Medium and Large Employers Can Purchase Coverage, but Some Workers Are Not Eligible," GAO/HEHS-98-184 (July 1998), *available at* http://gao.gov/assets/230/226058.pdf (site visited May 31, 2016).

[21] ACA § 1102(a)(1) establishes the Early Retiree Reinsurance Program to provide reimbursement to health plan sponsors for a portion of the cost of providing health coverage to early retirees

An employer may choose to offer retiree health insurance to some classes of retirees and not others. The Equal Employment Opportunity Commission (EEOC) issued final regulations indicating that employers may reduce health benefits for retirees aged 65 and older without violating the Age Discrimination in Employment Act.[22]

Unlike Medicare, which specifies that some benefits and services are covered, an EGHP generally is not required to provide a specific level of services or coverage. Congress originally intended ERISA to protect pension benefits.[23] Only the fiduciary duty provisions of ERISA, its disclosure provisions, and its cause-of-action provisions were made applicable to health plans.[24] This has left employers free, with some exceptions, to decide what benefits to offer, to change health insurance, to reduce the level of benefits, and even to eliminate coverage entirely without any protection for employees or retirees.[25] Most pertinent to Medicare beneficiaries, the addition of a Medicare prescription drug benefit has caused some employers and unions to reconsider the prescription drug coverage they provide through their retiree health plans. Because the drug coverage is not separate from the rest of the retiree health benefit package offered by an employer or a union, retirees who enroll in a Medicare Part D drug plan can lose all their retiree health coverage for themselves and for their dependents who are also covered under the retiree health plan. This has created problems for some individuals with retiree health coverage who are dually eligible for Medicare and Medicaid and who were automatically enrolled in a Part D plan.[26]

Some states require that health plans offered in their state cover certain benefits. However, ERISA preempts such state law requirements for self-insured plans, that is, plans that set aside their own funds and assume the risk of meeting the health claims of employees and dependents.[27] As a result, even if state law mandates that certain services such as home health benefits be included in the benefit package, a self-insured health plan subject to ERISA does not have to offer the mandated benefit.

---

and their dependents. *See also* http://www.cms.gov/CCIIO/Resources/Files/Downloads/gate.pdf (site visited May 31, 2016) and http://www.errp.gov/about_errp.shtml (site visited May 31, 2016).

[22] 29 C.F.R. § 1625.32, Appendix to § 1625.32.

[23] 29 U.S.C. § 1001(c).

[24] 29 U.S.C. §§ 1003, 1051, 1081, and 1101.

[25] *See, e.g.*, Coffin v. Bowater, Inc., 501 F.3d 80 (1st Cir. 2007); Stearns v. NCR Corp., 297 F.3d 706 (8th Cir. 2002); Sprague v. General Motors Corp., 133 F.3d 388 (6th Cir. 1998); McGann v. H&H Music, 946 F.2d 401 (5th Cir. 1991). *See also* D & H Therapy Assocs. v. Boston Mut. Life Ins. Co., 640 F.3d 27 (1st Cir. 2011) (administrator abuse of discretion to interpret "income" as money gained outside of W-2 form; distinguished *Coffin*, 501 F.3d 80, which only addressed interpretation by administrator that was "significantly more persuasive," not equally or less persuasive).

[26] *See* discussion on Medicare Part D in **Chapter 11** of this Handbook.

[27] 29 U.S.C. § 1144.

[C] Definitions of MSP EGHPs

[1] Health Plans That Are Affected by MSP Rules

An EGHP, regardless of whether it is subject to ERISA, is included within the scope of the basic MSP program when the sponsoring employer employs 20 or more full- or part-time employees, one of whom is age 65 or older or is married to a spouse who is age 65 or older.[28] In addition, a large group health plan with 100 or more full- or part-time employees is subject to the MSP statute when an employee is disabled or has a family member who is disabled.[29] EGHPs, regardless of size, and including COBRA plans, are primary under MSP rules for Medicare beneficiaries with ESRD only for 30 months.[30]

Beginning on January 1, 2014, small employers (fewer than 50 full-time employees) will be permitted to buy coverage through health insurance marketplaces, known as Small Business Health Options Plan (SHOP) exchanges.[31] Insurance purchased by small employers through SHOP exchanges will be subject to MSP rules the same as other EGHPs.[32]

[2] Health Insurance That Is Not Affected by MSP Rules

Certain kinds of health insurance are not made primary to Medicare under the MSP statute and regulations. These unaffected types of insurance include retiree health insurance benefits and insurance that is purchased voluntarily by a former employee or spouse. Private health insurance purchased under COBRA by a beneficiary eligible for Medicare when initially purchased, other than a beneficiary with ESRD, would not be affected. Private health insurance unrelated to employment, including Medicare supplemental health insurance (Medigap) that is privately purchased is also not affected by the EGHP law.

Persons insured under health insurance that is not subject to MSP requirements are entitled to receive Medicare benefits as their primary source of health insurance, and their private health insurer can be secondary to Medicare. In other words, Medicare pays first for individuals covered by retiree health plans and by COBRA. Beneficiaries who are covered by these plans and who did not enroll in

---

[28] 42 U.S.C. § 1395y(b)(1)(A).

[29] 42 U.S.C. § 1395y(b)(1)(B).

[30] 42 U.S.C. § 1395y(b)(1)(C); 42 C.F.R. §§ 411.161(a)(3) and 411.162(a)(3).

[31] ACA § 1312(f)(2). *See also* "Overview of the SHOP Marketplace," *available at* https://www.healthcare.gov/what-is-the-shop-marketplace/ (site visited June 2, 2016).

[32] At least 70 percent of an employer's full-time employees must choose to participate in order for the employer to be eligible to purchase coverage through the federally facilitated SHOP exchanges. Federal regulations permit federally facilitated SHOP exchanges to exclude Medicare beneficiaries from the participation requirement. Individual state SHOP exchanges have somewhat more flexibility in determining minimum participation requirements and exclusions *See* 45 C.F.R. 155.705(b)(10)(I).

Part B when first eligible may find themselves without insurance coverage for doctor visits and other Part B covered services, since many employer-sponsored health plans will not pay for services for which Medicare is primary. Beneficiaries may be eligible to enroll in Part B during a special enrollment period (SEP) when their employment ends; however, there is no SEP for Part B when COBRA coverage ends.[33]

§ 9.03 CALCULATION OF MEDICARE SECONDARY PAYMENT AMOUNT IN EGHP CASES

The Medicare statute and regulations set out a complex set of formulas for determining how much Medicare will pay when it is secondary to an EGHP.[34] Under these rules, Medicare will pay when the provider's charge for the service is not fully paid by the primary plan. The amount that Medicare will pay is the lowest of the following amounts, calculated without reduction by the usual coinsurance or deductibles:

1. The Medicare payment amount if there were no EGHP;
2. For payments calculated by Medicare on a cost-related basis (mostly Part A), the Medicare payment amount minus the EGHP payment;
3. For payments calculated by Medicare on a basis other than cost (mostly reasonable charge basis payments under Part B), the higher of the EGHP allowed amount or the Medicare allowed amount, minus the payment actually paid by the EGHP.

When the EGHP is a managed care organization (MCO), Medicare will not pay for services for which the MCO denied coverage, unless the beneficiary was unaware that Medicare would not pay.[35] This has caused problems for beneficiaries who have gone out of plan for services or counted on Medicare's less restrictive application of coverage rules to fill gaps in services available from the employer's managed care plan. Note, also, that the restriction applies only to EGHP MCOs that are not Medicare Advantage plans under Part C. If the employer or union sponsoring the group health plan contracts with a Medicare

[33] *See* Centers for Medicare & Medicaid Services (CMS), The Center for Consumer Information & Insurance Oversight, "COBRA Continuation Coverage," *available at* https://www.cms.gov/CCIIO/Programs-and-Initiatives/Other-Insurance-Protections/cobra_fact_sheet.html (site visited June 2, 2016); *see also* Center for Medicare Advocacy, "COBRA and Medicare, Part II," *available at* http://www.medicareadvocacy.org/cobra-and-medicare-part-ii/ (site visited June 2, 2016).

[34] 42 U.S.C. § 1395y(b)(4); 42 C.F.R. § 411.33.

[35] MSP Manual, CMS Pub. 100-05, Ch. 5, §§ 40.1.2 and 40.1.2.1, *available at* https://www.cms.gov/Regulations-and-Guidance/Guidance/Manuals/downloads/msp105c05.pdf (site visited June 2, 2016).

Advantage plan to offer retiree health benefits, then regular Medicare Advantage rules concerning network use apply.[36]

§ 9.04 ENFORCEMENT OF EGHP CLAIMS

[A] EGHP Enforcement and Recovery Powers

When Medicare believes that an EGHP is liable as primary insurer for a Medicare beneficiary, it will refuse to make payment. If the EGHP refuses to pay for health services, Medicare has the statutory authority to seek double damages from the plan.[37]

The Centers for Medicare & Medicaid Services (CMS) also has the authority to seek a recovery of payments for health services it made by mistake ("overpayments") when an EGHP should have been the primary payer. It can recover overpayments from the EGHP or from a beneficiary in situations where the beneficiary is deemed not to be cooperating with CMS in a recovery action.

[B] Individual Enforcement of EGHP Claims

An individual who believes that the EGHP is responsible for a health claim may file an appeal through the EGHP's appeals process. A worker or beneficiary, upon becoming covered by a health plan and periodically thereafter, is given a summary plan description (SPD), or plan brochure.[38] The SPD describes in plain terms the coverage under the plan, how to apply for benefits, and how to file an appeal if a claim is denied.[39] Individuals should consult their SPD to determine the proper procedure for filing an appeal.

An EGHP that is subject to ERISA must comply with the claims procedure established under that statute and implementing regulations issued by the Department of Labor.[40] The worker or beneficiary must complete any internal administrative appeal rights available under the plan before going to court.[41] The worker or beneficiary may not need to exhaust or complete the health plan's appeal process if serious procedural violations are shown or where exhaustion would be futile.[42]

---

[36] MSP Manual, CMS Pub. 100-05, Ch. 5, § 40.1.2, *available at* https://www.cms.gov/Regulations-and-Guidance/Guidance/Manuals/downloads/msp105c05.pdf (site visited June 2, 2016). *See also* **Chapter 7** of this Handbook for a discussion of the rules pertaining to Medicare Advantage plans.

[37] 42 U.S.C. § 1395y(b)(2)(B)(iii).

[38] 29 U.S.C. §§ 1021 and 1024(b).

[39] 29 U.S.C. § 1022.

[40] 29 U.S.C. §§ 1132 and 1133; 29 C.F.R. § 2560.503-1.

[41] 29 U.S.C. § 1132.

[42] *See, e.g.*, Hill v. Blue Cross & Blue Shield of Mich., 409 F.3d 710 (6th Cir. 2005); Curry v. Contract Fabricants Profit Sharing Plan, 891 F.2d 842 (11th Cir. 1990).

When health care has been denied, the individual or his or her advocate should request a review of the adverse decision pursuant to the claims procedures described in the SPD. Department of Labor regulations require that decisions on review be within a "reasonable amount of time," which they define as no more than 90 days.[43] Plans may extend the time period for response to 90 days after receipt of the request for review if there are special circumstances, such as the need to hold a hearing or wait for a meeting of the board of trustees.[44] Expedited consideration is available for claims involving urgent care.[45]

If the plan denies the appeal, the individual may file a court action. Civil actions that may be brought under ERISA include suits to recover benefits due under the plan, to enforce rights under the plan, or to clarify rights to future benefits. Affected individuals may also seek to enjoin violations of ERISA as well as to obtain any other equitable relief to redress violations or to enforce provisions of the statute.[46]

§ 9.05 COORDINATION OF COBRA RIGHTS AND MEDICARE

Medicare beneficiaries who want to exercise their option to purchase health care under the COBRA continuation of care provisions[47] should review how COBRA coordinates with Medicare.[48]

[A] What Is COBRA?

Private employers who offer an EGHP and who normally employed 20 or more workers on a typical business day during the preceding calendar year must offer COBRA to employees and their dependents who lose their health insurance because of certain specified events, discussed below.[49] State and local governments employing 20 or more employees also must offer continuation coverage.[50]

---

[43] 29 C.F.R. § 2560.503-1(f)(1).

[44] 29 C.F.R. § 2560.503-1(f)(1).

[45] 29 C.F.R. § 2560.503-1(f)(2)(i), (m)(1).

[46] 29 U.S.C. § 1132(a)(2), (3).

[47] Consolidated Omnibus Budget Reconciliation Act of 1985 (COBRA), Pub. L. No. 99-272 (Apr. 7, 1986), 100 Stat. 222, codified at 26 U.S.C. § 4980(b), 29 U.S.C. §§ 1161 *et seq.*, 42 U.S.C. §§ 300bb-1 *et seq.*

[48] Advocates should be aware that COBRA coverage is not available to an active employee. For a discussion, see Center for Medicare Advocacy, "People with Medicare Beware: COBRA Is Not Coverage as a 'Current' Employee," *available at* http://www.medicareadvocacy.org/people-with-medicare-beware-cobra-is-not-coverage-as-a-current-employee/ (site visited June 2, 2016).

[49] 29 U.S.C. § 1161(b).

[50] 42 U.S.C. § 300bb-1(a), (b)(1). Federal employees have their own health care continuation coverage. 5 U.S.C. § 8905a.

[B] Eligibility and Coverage

An individual eligible to purchase COBRA is referred to as a "qualified beneficiary."[51] In order to be a qualified beneficiary, the individual must have been covered under a group health plan on the day before a "qualifying event."[52] Qualified beneficiaries include:

- Covered employees;
- Spouses;
- Dependent children; and
- Retirees, their dependents, or their surviving spouses if the retiree's former employer files a petition for bankruptcy.[53]

Covered employees, or workers, are only eligible for COBRA based on termination of their employment or reduction in their hours.[54]

Eligibility to elect COBRA continuation coverage arises upon the occurrence of one of six "qualifying events" that result in the loss of health coverage:

1. The death of the covered employee;
2. The termination, other than for gross misconduct, or reduction in hours of the covered employee's employment;[55]
3. The divorce or legal separation of the covered employee from the employee's spouse;
4. The covered employee's entitlement to Medicare;[56]
5. A dependent child's losing dependent status;
6. The filing for bankruptcy by a retiree's former employer.[57]

[51] 29 U.S.C. § 1161(a). The COBRA premium may not exceed 102 percent of the applicable premium for the continuation period. 29 U.S.C. § 1162(3).

[52] 29 U.S.C. § 1167(3). *See* discussion of qualifying events below.

[53] 29 U.S.C. § 1167(2), (3).

[54] 29 U.S.C. §§ 1163(2) and 1167(2).

[55] For a discussion of COBRA and cautions for employees of small businesses, see Center for Medicare Advocacy, "COBRA III: Cautions for Employees of Small Businesses," *available at* http://www.medicareadvocacy.org/cobra-iii-cautions-for-employees-of-small-businesses/ (site visited June 2, 2016).

[56] For a discussion of Medicare entitlement and COBRA, see Center for Medicare Advocacy, "COBRA and Medicare, Part II," *available at* http://www.medicareadvocacy.org/cobra-and-medicare-part-ii/ (site visited June 2, 2016).

[57] 29 U.S.C. § 1163.

Covered employees and their dependents must be given notice of their COBRA rights when first eligible to participate under the plan.[58] Often the notice is included in the SPD that describes plan benefits and plan rights. The covered employees and their dependents receive a second notice of COBRA rights generally within 45 days after they experience a qualifying event.[59] The qualified beneficiaries then have 60 days in which to elect COBRA coverage.[60]

The coverage offered to qualified beneficiaries must be identical to the coverage provided to employees in the same kind of job who have not experienced a qualifying event.[61] Thus, an employer cannot offer Medicare wrap-around coverage as a COBRA benefit when similarly situated active employees are entitled to full health insurance coverage. If, however, coverage is expanded or reduced for current workers, it must be modified in the same manner for qualified beneficiaries.[62]

A plan may not condition COBRA coverage upon, nor discriminate because of, a lack of evidence of insurability.[63] Thus, a plan may not deny COBRA coverage or limit the scope of coverage available to qualified beneficiaries because of their health status or medical conditions.

COBRA coverage lasts 18 or 36 months, depending on the qualifying event.[64] For events that have an 18-month period, coverage may be extended beyond that period, for a total of 36 months, if the qualified beneficiary experiences another qualifying event during that time frame.[65]

However, an Internal Revenue Service (IRS) ruling clarifies that where the second qualifying event is the covered employee's becoming entitled to Medicare, and where Medicare entitlement would not result in a loss of coverage, the qualified beneficiary is not entitled to an extension of COBRA coverage.[66]

COBRA coverage will end early if:

1. The employer stops offering group health coverage;
2. The qualified beneficiary fails to pay premiums;

---

[58] 29 U.S.C. § 1166(a); 26 C.F.R. §§ 2590.606-1, 2590.606-4, and appendices.

[59] 29 U.S.C. § 1166(a); 26 C.F.R. §§ 2590.606-1, 2590.606-4, and appendices.

[60] 29 U.S.C. § 1166(a)(2), (4)(b).

[61] 29 U.S.C. § 1162(1). Note that while coverage offered must be identical, individuals are responsible for covering up to 102 percent of the premium (the COBRA premium may not exceed 102 percent of the applicable premium for the continuation period, *see* 29 U.S.C. § 1162(3)); this often is a surprise to individuals who previously had most or all of their premiums paid by their employer.

[62] 29 U.S.C. § 1162(1).

[63] 29 U.S.C. § 1162(4).

[64] 29 U.S.C. § 1162(2)(A). Coverage for retirees whose employer filed for bankruptcy extends for the lifetime of the retiree.

[65] 29 U.S.C. § 1162(2)(A)(ii).

[66] IRS Rev. Rul. 2004-22, 2004-10 I.R.B. 553 (Mar. 8, 2004), *available at* http://www.irs.gov/pub/irs-irbs/irb04-10.pdf (site visited June 2, 2016).

3. The qualified beneficiary becomes entitled to Medicare;
4. The qualified beneficiary becomes covered under another group health plan that contains no limitation for preexisting conditions.[67]

[C] Coordination of COBRA and Medicare

As explained earlier, Medicare is the primary payer for a Medicare beneficiary who is also covered under COBRA health care continuation insurance.[68] The more confusing relationship involves the role Medicare entitlement plays in determining whether an individual may elect COBRA and the duration of COBRA coverage.

[1] What Is "Medicare Entitlement"?

Both the statutory sections on COBRA qualifying events and COBRA maximum coverage periods use the term "Medicare entitlement" rather than Medicare eligibility.[69] COBRA regulations clarify that being eligible to enroll in Medicare does not constitute being entitled to Medicare for purposes of electing COBRA.[70] A qualified beneficiary becomes entitled to Medicare on the effective date of enrollment in either Part A or Part B, whichever occurs first.[71] Thus, an individual who continues working at age 65 and does not elect to receive Social Security benefits and Medicare at that time is not entitled to Medicare for purposes of COBRA eligibility.

[2] Coverage Period If the Qualifying Event Is Medicare Entitlement

The maximum coverage period for a qualified beneficiary who loses health insurance as a result of a covered employee's becoming entitled to Medicare is

[67] 29 U.S.C. § 1162(2)(B)–(D). Note that health care reform rules on preexisting conditions went into effect on January 1, 2014. Also, after September 23, 2010, new plans and existing group health plans cannot deny coverage to children based on preexisting condition exclusions. See the timeline for the Affordable Care Act at http://www.hhs.gov/healthcare/facts-and-features/key-features-of-aca-by-year/index.html# (site visited June 2, 2016).

[68] Note that for individuals who qualify for Medicare because of ESRD and are also entitled to health coverage under an employer plan, the group plan will be the primary payer for a 30-month coordination of benefits period. *See* 42 U.S.C. § 1395y(b)(1)(C); 42 C.F.R. § 411.162. This rule applies regardless of whether the individual is a current or former employee and regardless of whether the individual has coverage through COBRA. Also note that if an individual enrolls in Medicare after electing COBRA coverage, the employer can elect to terminate the COBRA coverage.

[69] 29 U.S.C. §§ 1162(2)(A) and 1163.

[70] 26 C.F.R. § 54.4980B-7, Q & A-3.

[71] 26 C.F.R. § 54.4980B-7, Q & A-3.

36 months.[72] The 36-month period begins to run at the time of Medicare entitlement, even if the qualified beneficiary does not lose health coverage until he or she experiences a subsequent qualifying event that occurs less than 18 months after the Medicare entitlement.[73] As a result of this complicated provision, the qualified beneficiary often will not be covered for the full 36-month period.

Consider the following examples involving Medicare entitlement as a qualifying event:

■ **EXAMPLE 1:** An employee becomes entitled to Medicare on May 1, 2017, causing his dependents to lose health insurance as of that date. In this situation the dependents are entitled to 36 months of COBRA, starting on May 1, 2017.

■ **EXAMPLE 2:** Again, the employee becomes entitled to Medicare on May 1, but the dependents do not lose their health coverage until the employee retires on October 1, 2017. They are technically entitled to 36 months of COBRA starting on May 1, 2017, the date of Medicare entitlement. Because of the way the coverage period is calculated, and because they do not lose insurance until October 1, they have COBRA coverage only for the 31-month period starting in October.

■ **EXAMPLE 3:** If the same dependents do not lose health insurance until the employee retires on May 1, 2017, they are not entitled to the coverage period for a qualifying event based on Medicare entitlement. The subsequent qualifying event that caused the loss of health coverage occurred more than 18 months after the employee became entitled to Medicare. The dependents are entitled to the coverage period for a qualifying event of termination of employment, which is 18 months from the date of retirement, May 1, 2017.[74]

[3] Extended COBRA Coverage Until Medicare Entitlement

To avoid a gap in health coverage before Medicare entitlement begins,[75] workers or their dependents determined to be disabled under Title II or Title XVI of the Social Security Act may receive 29 months of extended COBRA coverage if certain conditions are met.[76] The disability onset date, that is, the date the individual is found disabled, must occur sometime during the first 60 days of

---

[72] 29 U.S.C. § 1162(2)(A)(vii).

[73] 29 U.S.C. § 1162(2)(A)(vii).

[74] 29 U.S.C. § 1162(2)(A)(i).

[75] Individuals under age 65 become entitled to Medicare if they have been entitled to Social Security disability benefits for 24 months. Eligibility begins in the 25th month. 42 C.F.R. § 406.12.

[76] 29 U.S.C. § 1162(2)(A). *See also* Marsh v. Omaha Printing Co., 218 F.3d 854 (8th Cir. 2000); Meadows v. Cagle's, 954 F.2d 686 (11th Cir. 1992).

continuation coverage.[77] The individual must also notify the health plan administrator within 60 days of the determination. Individuals who do not meet these requirements because, for example, their disability onset date is later than the first 60 days of COBRA or they fail to notify the plan administrator in a timely manner are not eligible for extended coverage. Health plans may increase the COBRA premium for the 19th through the 29th month of extended coverage,[78] making it difficult for some individuals to continue purchasing coverage.

[4] COBRA Eligibility for Beneficiaries Already on Medicare

Individuals who were already receiving Medicare or who were covered under a second group health plan at the time of their qualifying event are eligible to elect COBRA.[79] If the health plan requires participants to enroll in all other health benefits for which they are eligible, the plan may require them to enroll in Medicare Part B.

[5] COBRA and Special Enrollment Periods

COBRA-qualified beneficiaries who have delayed enrollment in Medicare Part B do not qualify for a SEP to enroll in Part B after their COBRA coverage ends.[80] Only individuals who delayed enrolling in Part B because they were covered under an EGHP by reason of current employment may take advantage of the SEP rules.[81] Individuals on COBRA do not meet the definition of having current employment status.[82] Thus, they have to wait to enroll in Part B until the general enrollment period, and they have to pay the applicable premium for delayed enrollment.

Some COBRA-qualified beneficiaries may have delayed enrollment in a Part D drug plan because the drug coverage they had under COBRA constitutes creditable coverage, that is, was determined to be as good as Medicare drug coverage. Because these individuals will lose their creditable drug coverage when their COBRA coverage ends, they may have a SEP that would allow them to

---

[77] 29 U.S.C. § 1162(2)(A).

[78] 29 U.S.C. § 1162(3)(B); *see also* 26 C.F.R. § 54.4980B-8, Q & A-1.

[79] Geissal v. Moore Med. Corp., 524 U.S. 74 (1998); Miles-Hickman v. David Powers Homes, Inc., 589 F. Supp. 2d 849, 877 (S.D. Tex. 2008); 26 C.F.R. § 54.4980B-7 Q 3(a), *available at* http://www.gpo.gov/fdsys/pkg/CFR-2012-title26-vol17/pdf/CFR-2012-title26-vol17-sec54-4980B-7.pdf (site visited June 2, 2016).

[80] 42 C.F.R. §§ 407.20 and 406.24(a)(3). See also, Center for Medicare Advocacy, "People with Medicare Beware: COBRA Is Not Coverage as a 'Current' Employee," *available at* http://www.medicareadvocacy.org/people-with-medicare-beware-cobra-is-not-coverage-as-a-current-employee/ (site visited June 27, 2016).

[81] 42 C.F.R. § 407.20(b), (c).

[82] 42 C.F.R. § 411.104.

choose and enroll in a Part D plan before the next annual coordinated enrollment period. The SEP begins with the month they are advised of the loss of creditable drug coverage and ends 60 days from the loss of coverage or from the date of the notice, whichever is later.[83]

§ 9.06 MSP RULES APPLICABLE TO MEDICARE ADVANTAGE PLANS

Medicare Advantage (MA) plans are also subject to MSP rules.[84] The statute and regulations require MA plans to identify other payers that should be primary and coordinate benefits to Medicare enrollees with them.[85]

The MA plan is authorized to charge or allow its providers to charge any other insurer that should be primary—liability insurers, workers' compensation insurers, and EGHPs—for Medicare-covered services. The MA plan and its providers are also authorized to collect for services rendered by them from either the primary insurer or from the beneficiary, if he or she has received payment from the primary insurer.[86] Decisions have held, however, that there is no cause of action to allow an MA plan to bring suit in federal court to recover the cost of care it provided to a beneficiary.[87]

Surprisingly, the statute and regulation do not limit the MSP amount that the MA plans and their providers can charge or recover to the rates that they receive under the Medicare program. Beneficiary advocates should keep in mind that they have the opportunity to appeal and/or request waiver of MSP recovery claims. Beneficiaries must be informed of this right at the time repayment is requested; however, MA collection notices may not advise them of this right. They should be prepared to cite the criteria for waiver and the appeal rights set out in the CMS MSP Manual.[88]

---

[83] 42 C.F.R. §§ 423.38(c) and 423.46; *see also* Medicare Prescription Drug Benefit (MPDB) Manual, CMS Pub. 100-18, Ch. 3, §§ 30.3.5 and 30.3.8.1, *available at* https://www.cms.gov/Medicare/Eligibility-and-Enrollment/MedicarePresDrugEligEnrol/Downloads/CY_2017_PDP_Enrollment_and_Disenrollment_Guidance_06-03-2016.pdf (site visited Aug. 11, 2016).

[84] 42 U.S.C. § 1395w-22(a)(4).

[85] 42 C.F.R. § 422.108(b).

[86] 42 C.F.R. §§ 422.108(c) and 411.204 (LGHP).

[87] Care Choices HMO v. Engstrom, 330 F.3d 786 (6th Cir. 2003); Nott v. Aetna U.S. Healthcare, Inc., 303 F. Supp. 2d 565, 571 (E.D. Pa. 2004). *See also In re* Avandia Mktg., Sales Practices & Prods. Liab. Litig., 11-2664, 2012 WL 2433508 (3d Cir. June 28, 2012) (MA insurance company could bring private cause of action for reimbursement under MSP Act. Court noted that Medicare-substitute HMO in Care Choices never addressed whether it could bring suit as a private actor under MSP Act). *See also* the CMS memo from Danielle R. Moon, Director, Medicare Drug & Health Plan Contract Administration Group, "Medicare Secondary Payment Subrogation Rights" (Dec. 5, 2011), *available at* https://www.cms.gov/Medicare/Health-Plans/HealthPlansGenInfo/downloads/21_MedicareSecondaryPayment.pdf (site visited June 2, 2016).

[88] MSP Manual, Ch. 7, §§ 50.5.4.4–50.6.5.4, and 50.8. *See also* Center for Medicare Advocacy, "CMS Revises Its Medicare Secondary Payer Collection Letters Following *Haro v. Sebelius* Decision," *available at* http://www.medicareadvocacy.org/cms-revises-its-medicare-secondary-payer-collection-letters-following-haro-v-sebelius-decision/ (site visited June 2, 2016).

§ 9.07 CONDITIONAL PAYMENT AND THIRD-PARTY RECOVERY

If an injured Medicare beneficiary's medical expenses are covered by liability insurance, including no-fault and med-pay, Medicare will pay for medical services only when the third-party insurance payment will not be "prompt."[89] "Prompt" is defined as within 120 days.[90] Such Medicare payments are described as "conditional," and the program expects to recover them when the private insurance payment "has been or could be made."[91] Medicare is entitled to reimbursement from liability payments to the beneficiary and also to the family of a deceased beneficiary.[92] Reimbursement to Medicare must be made within 60 days of receipt of information about the insurer's responsibility.[93] When there has been a conditional Medicare payment, the hospital must accept payment at the Medicare rate and cannot seek additional payment from the liability insurance recovery.[94]

The Medicare program through CMS is given specific collection powers with respect to its conditional payment recovery claims by statute. CMS has both subrogation rights and the right to bring an independent action to recover its conditional payments.[95] It is authorized to bring such actions against "any or all entities that are or were required or responsible (directly, as an insurer or self-insurer, as a third-party administrator . . . or otherwise) to make payment with respect to the same item or service . . . under a primary plan" and to collect double damages against that primary plan entity.[96] It is further authorized to bring actions against "any entity that has received payment from a primary plan or from the proceeds of a primary plan's payment to any entity."[97] Since April 2010, liability insurers

---

[89] MSP Manual, Ch. 1, § 10.7, *available at* http://www.cms.gov/Regulations-and-Guidance/Guidance/Manuals/Downloads/msp105c01.pdf (site visited June 2, 2016). *See also* MLN Matters, "Clarification of Medicare Conditional Payment Policy and Billing Procedures for Liability, No-Fault and Workers' Compensation (WC) Medicare Secondary Payer (MSP) Claims" (2012), *available at* http://www.cms.gov/Outreach-and-Education/Medicare-Learning-Network-MLN/MLNMattersArticles/Downloads/MM7355.pdf (site visited June 2, 2016).

[90] MSP Manual, Ch. 1, § 20.

[91] 42 U.S.C. § 1395y(b)(2)(A)(ii), (b)(2)(B); 42 C.F.R. § 411.20, .50(c).

[92] Mathis v. Leavitt, No. 07-0062-CV-W-RED, 2007 WL 4205815 (W.D. Mo. 2007).

[93] 42 U.S.C. § 1395y(b)(2)(B)(ii).

[94] Rybicki v. Hartley, 792 F.2d 260 (1st Cir. 1986); Holle v. Moline Pub. Hosp., 598 F. Supp. 1017 (C.D. Ill. 1984). If, however, payment by the primary payer will be made promptly, a provider can choose not to bill Medicare but instead to bill the liability insurer or assert a lien on the beneficiary's insurance settlement. Medicare Program: Third Party Liability Insurance Regulations, 68 Fed. Reg. 43,940 (2003), modifying 42 C.F.R. §§ 411.54 and 489.20; *see also* Wentz v. Kindred Hosps. East, 333 F. Supp. 2d 1298 (S.D. Fla. 2004).

[95] *See* 42 C.F.R. § 411.26.

[96] 42 U.S.C. § 1395y(b)(2)(B)(iii).

[97] 42 U.S.C. § 1395y(b)(2)(B)(iii) and (3)(A); *see also* 42 C.F.R. § 411.24.

and workers' compensation plans have been required to determine, and supply CMS with, information about the Medicare status of their claimants.[98]

Several court decisions restricted MSP recovery by interpreting the statute to prevent Medicare from recovering conditional payments from settlement funds established in class action litigation.[99] Congress responded in 2003 by amending the Medicare statute to expand the definitions of self-insured entities and responsible primary plans from which MSP recovery could be required.[100] The courts have also held that the MSP statute does not authorize *qui tam* suits brought by individuals who have suffered no personal harm.[101]

The Fixed Percentage Option for repayment is available to beneficiaries who have experienced a physical trauma–based injury. If the expected settlement, judgment, award, or other payment is $5,000 or less in these cases, Medicare offers the option to pay a fixed percentage (25%). This eliminates the time and resources associated with the MSP recovery process and allows beneficiaries to settle claims with Medicare quickly, prior to settlement.[102]

[A] Amount of Medicare Recovery

In general, "CMS may recover an amount equal to the Medicare payment or the amount payable by the third party, whichever is less."[103] CMS has contracted with a private entity, the Benefits Coordination & Recovery Center (BCRC), to handle MSP collections from beneficiaries.[104] The amount of the Medicare recovery for medical expenses caused by torts stops accruing at the time of settlement.

---

[98] 42 U.S.C. § 1395y(b)(8). *See* CMS guidance and instructions on reporting at http://cms.gov/Medicare/Coordination-of-Benefits-and-Recovery/Mandatory-Insurer-Reporting-For-Group-Health-Plans/Overview.html ("Mandatory Insurer Reporting for Group Health Plans (GHP)") (site visited June 2, 2016) *and* http://www.cms.gov/Medicare/Coordination-of-Benefits-and-Recovery/Mandatory-Insurer-Reporting-For-Non-Group-Health-Plans/Overview.html ("Mandatory Insurer Reporting for Non-Group Health Plans (NGHP)") (site visited June 2, 2016). *See* 73 Fed. Reg. 45,013 (Aug. 1, 2008).

[99] Thompson v. Goetzmann, 337 F.3d 489 (5th Cir. 2003); Mason v. American Tobacco Co., 346 F.3d 36 (2d Cir. 2003); United States v. Phillip Morris, 116 F. Supp. 2d 131, 145 (D.D.C. 2000).

[100] 42 U.S.C. § 1395y(b)(2)(A) and (B), Medicare Prescription Drug, Improvement, and Modernization Act of 2003 (MMA), Pub. L. No. 108-173 (Dec. 8, 2003), § 301(b)(1) and (2). These changes are retroactive to 1980.

[101] Stalley v. Catholic Health Initiative, 509 F.3d 517 (8th Cir. 2007).

[102] *See* Fixed Percentage Option, *available at* https://www.cms.gov/Medicare/Coordination-of-Benefits-and-Recovery/Beneficiary-Services/Downloads/FixedPercOptionInfo070113d.pdf (site visited June 2, 2016).

[103] 42 C.F.R. § 411.24(c).

[104] *See* https://www.cms.gov/Medicare/Coordination-of-Benefits-and-Recovery/Coordination-of-Benefits-and-Recovery-Overview/Overview.html (site visited Sept. 21, 2016). Note that the entity was previously called the Medicare Secondary Payer Recovery Contractor (MSPRC). *See also* CMS, "Attorney Services," *available at* http://www.cms.gov/Medicare/Coordination-of-Benefits-and-Recovery/Attorney-Services/Attorney-Services.html (site visited June 2, 2016).

There is no MSP recovery for such services covered by Medicare after that time, unless the settlement includes a specific allocation for future medical services.[105] In cases involving liability insurers, "Medicare reduces its recovery to take account of the cost of procuring the judgment or settlement[106] Under this provision, a proportionate share of attorney's fees and costs should be subtracted from the amount recovered by Medicare. If the primary insurer's payment is less than the MSP claim, Medicare will take it all, minus the costs of procurement.

> ■ **EXAMPLE:** Following her auto accident, for which liability was disputed, Vicki Victim received a settlement of $50,000. Her medical expenses were $40,000, of which Medicare paid $25,000; her pain and suffering were valued at $10,000; lost wages were $20,000; and her permanent loss of limb was valued at $30,000.

Despite the fact that Vicki's settlement was only 50 percent of her $100,000 damages, Medicare would demand recovery of its entire $25,000 outlay, reduced only by its proportionate share of the procurement costs. Assuming a 30 percent contingency fee arrangement, Medicare would actually take $17,500, Vicki's personal injury attorney would receive a fee of $15,000, and Vicki would receive only $17,500, leaving $82,500 in uncompensated losses.

This basic formula is limited to Medicare outlays for health services resulting from the accident or other incident that gave rise to liability. Thus, Medicare should not recover for health services to the extent that they were aggravated by, for example, a preexisting heart condition. Advocates should examine the list of conditional payments presented by Medicare and object to the inclusion of any that were not caused entirely by the incident that triggered third-party insurer liability.[107]

In addition, advocates should be aware that on June 15, 2012, CMS issued an advance notice of proposed rulemaking (ANPRM) for the treatment of funds set aside for future medical expenses related to an accident or injury.[108] CMS's

See also CMS, "Medicare Secondary Payer Recovery Portal," *available at* http://www.cms.gov/Medicare/Coordination-of-Benefits-and-Recovery/Coordination-of-Benefits-and-Recovery-Overview/MSPRP/Medicare-Secondary-Payer-Recovery-Portal.html (site visited June 2, 2016).

[105] *See* CMS, Memorandum, "Medicare Secondary Payer—Liability Insurance (Including Self-Insurance) Settlements, Judgments, Awards, or Other Payments and Future Medicals—INFORMATION (Sept. 30, 2011), *available at* http://www.cms.gov/Medicare/Coordination-of-Benefits-and-Recovery/Coordination-of-Benefits-and-Recovery-Overview/Non-Group-Health-Plan-Recovery/Downloads/Future-Medicals.pdf (site visited June 2, 2016).

[106] 42 C.F.R. § 411.37.

[107] One court held that a beneficiary could dispute whether the health services for which MSP recovery is sought actually resulted from the accident producing the award even if the original liability claim alleged that they had. United States v. Weinberg, No. 01-CV-0679, Medicare & Medicaid Guide (CCH) 301,136, 2002 WL 32356399 (E.D. Pa. 2002).

[108] *See* 77 Fed. Reg. 35,917 (CMS-6047-ANPRM), *available at* http://www.gpo.gov/fdsys/pkg/FR-2012-06-15/pdf/2012-14678.pdf (site visited June 2, 2016) 14, 2015). *See also* the Center for

proposed regulation, following its June 15, 2012, ANPRM, was scheduled to be published in the *Federal Register* in September 2013. The proposal was withdrawn on October 8, 2014.[109] The extension of a Medicare set-aside requirement in liability cases remains a subject of interest within CMS[110] and among federal legislators.[111]

[B] MSP Collection Duties of Personal Injury Attorneys

CMS asserts that personal injury attorneys have statutory obligations to affirmatively assist Medicare in its MSP recovery efforts,[112] but beneficiary advocates question the extent of attorneys' obligations. Advocates believe the CMS position is based on a misreading of the Medicare statute that incorrectly gives MSP recovery claims the status of liens and confuses insurers' obligations with those of attorneys. Also note that there is a Congressionally mandated website for the collection and reporting of information about Medicare's conditional payments on behalf of beneficiaries.[113]

Medicare Advocacy, Weekly Alert, "Medicare Secondary Payer (MSP) Program: Proposed Rules for the Treatment of Funds Intended for Future Medical Expenses," *available at* http://www.medicareadvocacy.org/medicare-secondary-payer-msp-program-proposed-rules-for-the-treatment-of-funds-intended-for-future-medical-expenses/ (site visited June 3, 2016).

[109] On October 8, 2014, CMS withdrew its proposal on future medicals. *See* http://www.reginfo.gov/public/do/eoDetails?rrid=123255 (site visited June 3, 2016). The CMS proposal was called "Medicare Secondary Payer and 'Future Medicals'" (CMS-6047-P).

[110] *See* Center for Medicare Advocacy, "Medicare Second Payer (MSP) Program: Proposed Rules for the Treatment of Funds Intended for Future Medical Expenses," *available at* http://www.medicareadvocacy.org/medicare-secondary-payer-msp-program-proposed-rules-for-the-treatment-of-funds-intended-for-future-medical-expenses/(site visited June 3, 2016).

[111] *See* Medicare Secondary Payer and Workers' Compensation Settlement Agreements Act of 2013, H.R. 1982, 113th Cong. (2013). *See also* S. 2731, 113th Cong. (2014) (introduced by Sen. Bill Nelson, D-Fla.).

[112] *Compare* Thomas J. Nyzio, *Medicare Recovery in Liability Cases*, S.C. Law. 20-24 (May/June 1996) *and* Glenn E. Bradford & Melinda M. Ward, *The Medicare "Super Lien" Revisited*, Mo. Bar J. 44-49 (Jan./Feb. 2000).

[113] Medicare IVIG Access and Strengthening Medicare and Repaying Taxpayers Act of 2012 (SMART Act), Pub. L. No. 112-242 (Jan. 3, 2013), *available at* http://beta.congress.gov/112/plaws/publ242/PLAW-112publ242.pdf (site visited June 3, 2016). *See also* Center for Medicare Advocacy, "New CMS Website: Medicare Secondary Payer Conditional Payment Information," *available at* http://www.medicareadvocacy.org/new-cms-website-medicare-secondary-payer-conditional-payment-information/ (site visited June 3, 2016). Regulations implementing Pub. L. No. 112-242 are available in 78 Fed. Reg. 57,800-806 (Sept. 20, 2013). See additional discussion at Center for Medicare Advocacy, "Medicare Secondary Payer: Web Portal to Collect Data on Conditional Payment Amounts and Claims Detail, *available at* http://www.medicareadvocacy.org/medicare-secondary-payer-web-portal-to-collect-data-on-conditional-payment-amounts-and-claims-detail/ (site visited June 3, 2016). With respect to the web portal system being developed, conditional payment information will reflect claims that CMS has already made and will not address future medical expenses.

In *Zinman v. Shalala*, a nationwide class action, a federal district court held that Medicare has no lien rights with respect to its MSP recovery claims and ordered Medicare to stop using the term "lien" in its collection efforts.[114]

The Medicare statute and regulations do require that a beneficiary, provider, supplier, physician, attorney, or private insurer that has received a third-party payment reimburse Medicare within 60 days of receipt.[115] The Medicare statute gives CMS a right of action to recover from an attorney who has liability proceeds in his or her possession. In contrast, it gives CMS a broader right of action to recover from an insurance company (a "primary payer") that has transferred proceeds, for example, to its insured, without paying Medicare.[116] The key to understanding this statutory language is the cross-reference to 42 U.S.C. § 1395y(b)(3)(A), which imposes double damages only on primary plans, together with the broad definition of entities responsible under a "primary plan" in the preceding section.[117] Carefully read, the statute clearly distinguishes between actions against insurers, which can be for double damages, and actions against other entities, such as attorneys who have received a payment from the insurer, which are limited to the payment itself.[118]

The language of the regulations makes the same distinction between Medicare's double collection rights against third-party payers and its rights against others such as attorneys.[119] Like the statute, the regulations define "third-party payer" as "an insurance policy, plan, or program that is primary to Medicare."[120] Thus, they provide no authority for Medicare to recover double damages from attorneys who have received liability insurance proceeds but then passed them on to their clients.

Two courts applying these requirements have held that attorneys who had received insurance proceeds and were apparently still holding them could be required to reimburse Medicare for its MSP claims.[121] A third court went further and held that Medicare could bring suit to recover MSP claims from an attorney

---

[114] 835 F. Supp. 1163, 1171 (N.D. Cal. 1993), *aff'd*, 67 F.3d 841 (9th Cir. 1995).

[115] 42 C.F.R. § 411.24(g), (h).

[116] 42 U.S.C. § 1395y(b)(2)(B)(iii); Manning v. Utilities Mut. Ins. & Niagara Mohawk Dist. Power Co., 254 F.3d 387 (2d Cir. 2001).

[117] 42 U.S.C. § 1395y(b)(2)(A), (b)(2)(B)(iii).

[118] *See also* Health Ins. Ass'n of Am. & Blue Cross & Blue Shield Ass'n of Am. v. Shalala, 23 F.3d 412 (D.C. Cir. 1994). In that case the D.C. Circuit struck down several MSP regulations as going too far in imposing collection liability on insurance companies, including one extending MSP recovery provisions against insurance companies to such companies when they act as administrators for self-insured employer plans, and another authorizing recovery against insurance companies even when policy filing deadlines had passed.

[119] *Compare* closely the provisions of 42 C.F.R. § 411.24(g), which confers collection rights against attorneys, *with* 42 C.F.R. § 411.24(i), which confers broader collection rights against third-party payers.

[120] 42 C.F.R. § 411.21. For MSP enforcement, use the analogous state statute of limitations.

[121] United States v. Sosnowska, 822 F. Supp. 570 (W.D. Wis. 1993); United States v. Weinberg, No. 01-CV-0679, 2002 WL 32356399 (E.D. Pa. July 1, 2002).

who failed to follow the procedures for administratively appealing the MSP claim. The court held this attorney responsible for reimbursement even though he had disbursed the proceeds to his client, a point that the attorney apparently did not contest.[122]

Some commentators have suggested that attorneys for Medicare beneficiaries should make provision for payment of future as well as past medical expenses when liability claim proceeds are received. There is no authority in the Medicare statute, regulations, or manuals for such payment, or discussion of the use of set-aside arrangements for payment of future medical expenses in liability cases.[123] Medicare requirements for liability cases differ in this respect from those in workers' compensation situations, discussed in **§ 9.08** of this Handbook.

§ 9.08 MSP WORKERS' COMPENSATION RECOVERY

The MSP program also makes workers' compensation insurers primary payers of medical expenses for persons receiving workers' compensation benefits.[124] A workers' compensation insurer is responsible for reimbursing Medicare's past payments and paying for future medical care required to treat an accident or illness that is work-related. The obligation does not arise until there has been a workers' compensation system determination that the accident or illness is work-related.[125] Information about workers' compensation recovery can be obtained from the Coordination of Benefits (COB) contractor at (800) 999-1118, P.O. Box 33847, Detroit, MI, 43232-5849.[126]

Sometimes workers' compensation claims are settled by agreement for a lump sum commutation of future benefits rather than continuing payments for the lifetime of the disabled worker. In such cases, unlike its policy with respect to liability insurance settlements, Medicare will recognize an apportionment set out in the settlement agreement of the lump sum between future medical expenses and other damages (lost wages), so long as the amount allocated to future medical expenses appears to be reasonable and not an attempt to shift the burden of payment for work-related medical services to Medicare.[127] If the amount of the lump

---

[122] United States v. Harris, No. 5:08CV102, 2009 WL 891931 (N.D. W. Va. Mar. 26, 2008), *aff'd*, 334 Fed. Appx. 569 (4th Cir. 2009) (not for publication).

[123] *See* Center for Medicare Advocacy, "Medicare Secondary Payer Program," *available at* http://www.medicareadvocacy.org/medicare-info/medicare-secondary-payer-program/ (site visited June 3, 2016).

[124] 42 U.S.C. § 1395y(b)(2)(B); MSP Manual, Ch. 7, § 40.3.

[125] Fisher v. Clarendon Nat'l Ins. Co., No. 07-4092-CV-C-NKL, 2008 WL 191813 (W.D. Mo. Jan. 18, 2008).

[126] *See* CMS, "Reporting a Case" (Mar. 5, 2012), *available at* http://www.cms.gov/Medicare/Coordination-of-Benefits-and-Recovery/Attorney-Services/Reporting-a-Case/Reporting-a-Case.html (site visited June 3, 2016).

[127] MSP Manual, Ch. 7, § 40.3.4–40.3.5.

sum exceeds $250,000 and Medicare enrollment is likely within 30 months, approval of the apportionment must be obtained from the CMS regional office.[128]

Medicare will pay for all the beneficiary's covered health care after the portion of the settlement allocated to medical expenses for work-related conditions has been spent for such services. Beneficiaries should keep records of their expenditures for medical services from this portion of the settlement so they can establish when it has been exhausted and Medicare should become primary payer. This record keeping could be done under a "set-aside arrangement" established to administer the medical expense portion of the settlement in cases where the settlement is a commutation of future benefits rather than a compromise, but there is no requirement for doing so.[129]

§ 9.09 MSP COLLECTION PROCEDURES

The Medicare Secondary Payer Manual is an online program guide for the administration of the MSP law posted on the CMS website.[130] It is used by providers, insurers, and advocates in working through the day-to-day administration of the Medicare program. The Manual includes a form letter for use by entities under contract with CMS in making initial MSP recovery demands to beneficiaries.[131] Usually, Medicare initiates collection procedures when a beneficiary's personal injury attorney notifies it that a settlement is expected.[132] Medicare also may learn about the existence of third-party liability claims through questionnaires to beneficiaries and Medicare Administrative Contractors (MACs),[133]

---

[128] MSP Manual, Ch.7, § 40.3.5.1.

[129] Procedures for obtaining CMS approval of a set-aside arrangement from the Regional Office are described in the MSP Manual, Ch. 7, § 40.3.5–40.3.5.1. For a discussion of CMS's revision of its MSP collection letters, see Center for Medicare Advocacy, "CMS Revises Its Medicare Secondary Payer Collection Letters Following *Haro v. Sebelius* Decision," *available at* http://www.medicareadvocacy.org/cms-revises-its-medicare-secondary-payer-collection-letters-following-haro-v-sebelius-decision/ (site visited June 3, 2016).

[130] *See* http://www.medicareadvocacy.org/cms-revises-its-medicare-secondary-payer-collection-letters-following-haro-v-sebelius-decision/ (site visited June 3, 2016).

[131] MSP Manual, Ch. 7, § 50.5.1.1, Exhibit 2; *see also* http://www.medicareadvocacy.org/cms-revises-its-medicare-secondary-payer-collection-letters-following-haro-v-sebelius-decision/ (site visited June 3, 2016).

[132] *See* CMS, "Medicare Secondary Payer for Providers, Physicians, Other Suppliers, and Billing Staff," ICN 006902 (July 2014), *available at* http://www.cms.gov/Outreach-and-Education/Medicare-Learning-Network-MLN/MLNProducts/downloads/msp_fact_sheet.pdf (site visited June 3, 2016).

[133] Claims are reviewed by Medicare Administrative Contractors (MACs) chosen by CMS through a competitive bidding process. As of September 6, 2011, if a beneficiary received a lump sum settlement of $1,000 or less, and certain conditions are met, Medicare will not seek recovery of the settlement. *See* CMS, "Reporting a Case," *available at* http://www.cms.gov/Medicare/Coordination-of-Benefits-and-Recovery/Attorney-Services/Reporting-a-Case/Reporting-a-Case.html

screening of claims for injury-related services, insurance company reporting, and information-sharing with the IRS.

The CMS collection letter advises beneficiaries of the amount claimed as an overpayment by Medicare, sets out the repayment process, and describes the beneficiary waiver and appeal procedures.[134]

§ 9.10 MANDATORY REPORTING BY INSURERS

Mandatory reporting obligations were imposed on private insurers by the Medicare, Medicaid, and SCHIP Extension Act of 2007.[135] Guidance from CMS for implementation of these reporting obligations is provided on the CMS website rather than in regulations.[136]

Group health plan (GHP) arrangements, including self-insured plans, are required to obtain information "to identify situations where the GHP is primary to

---

(site visited June 3, 2016); *see also* "Revised Alert" (Feb. 28, 2014), *available at* https://www.cms.gov/Medicare/Coordination-of-Benefits-and-Recovery/Coordination-of-Benefits-and-Recovery-Overview/Non-Group-Health-Plan-Recovery/Downloads/Alert-Change-in-Recovery-Threshold-for-Certain-Liability-Insurance.pdf (site visited June 3, 2016).

[134] The data compilation function of the MSP recovery program is performed by a coordination of benefits (COB) contractor. *See also* Medicare's reorganization of its Coordination of Benefits for MSP. Several links to websites for it can be found at Coordination of Benefits & Recovery Overview, http://go.cms.gov/cobro. Links for Attorney Services are *available at* http://go.cms.gov/attorney; links for Beneficiary Services are *available at* http://www.cms.gov/Medicare/Coordination-of-Benefits-and-Recovery/Beneficiary-Services/Overview.html; and links for Insurer Services are *available at* http://go.cms.gov/insurer (sites visited June 3, 2016).

[135] Final rules as of February 2015 can be found at https://www.francosignor.com/wp-content/uploads/2015/02/SMART-Act-Appeal-Final-Rule.pdf (site visited June 3, 2016). *See also* 42 U.S.C. § 1395y(b)(7), (8). *See* 43 Fed. Reg. 45,013–14 (Aug. 1, 2008). *See also* CMS, "MSP Beneficiary Overpayment: Request for 'Waiver of Recovery' Flow Chart," *available at* http://www.cms.gov/Medicare/Coordination-of-Benefits-and-Recovery/Beneficiary-Services/Downloads/MSP-Beneficiary-Overpayment-Request-for-Waiver-of-Recovery-Flow-Chart-.pdf (site visited June 27, 2016).

[136] *See* CMS, "Insurer/Third Party Administrator Services," *available at* http://www.cms.gov/Medicare/Coordination-of-Benefits-and-Recovery/InsurerServices/index.html (site visited June 27, 2016).

In Section 204 of the SMART Act, CMS modified existing requirements to "highly recommend," but not require, NGHP Required Reporting Entities (RREs) to submit beneficiary HICNs and SSNs when they report a settlement, judgment, award, or other payment. Effective January 5, 2015, where an RRE cannot obtain an individual's HICN or full SSN, it may report the following data that will enable CMS to properly identify a Medicare beneficiary: last five digits of SSN; first initial; surname; date of birth; and gender. If the RRE is unable to obtain or does not provide the HICN, full SSN, or any of the above-listed data, it must document its attempts to obtain this information. The CMS Alert on this topic can be found at http://www.cms.gov/Medicare/Coordination-of-Benefits-and-Recovery/Mandatory-Insurer-Reporting-For-Non-Group-Health-Plans/Downloads/Change-in-Reporting-of-Medicare-Health-Insurance-Claim-Numbers-HICNs-and-Social-Security-Numbers-SSNs-for-Non-Group-Health-Plan-NGHPResponsible-Reporting-Entities-RREs-.pdf (site visited June 27, 2016).

Medicare" from plan sponsors and participants. This information must be reported to CMS in the form, manner, and frequency specified by the agency.[137]

Liability and no-fault insurers, as well as workers' compensation plans, are required to determine whether a claimant is entitled to Medicare benefits. These insurers must report the identity and other information about such claimants to CMS so that it can "coordinate Medicare benefits with respect to such insurance."[138]

§ 9.11 BENEFICIARY RIGHTS TO SEEK WAIVER OR APPEAL THE MSP RECOVERY CLAIM

By final rule published February 27, 2015, implementing Section 201 of the SMART Act, CMS has extended to liability insurance (including self-insurance), no-fault insurance, and worker's compensation laws or plans a right of appeal and appeals process when Medicare pursues an MSP recovery claim directly from them.[139] Under the Medicare statute, beneficiaries have the right to appeal the amount of MSP recovery claims if they believe the amount of a claim is not correct.[140] They also have the right to ask Medicare to waive or compromise recovery under several different provisions of the law.[141]

[A] Appeals of MSP Recovery Claims

If it appears that Medicare is demanding more of a beneficiary's award than it is entitled to under these rules, there is an administrative appeals process that

---

[137] *See* CMS, "Mandatory Insurer Reporting for Group Health Plans (GHP)," *available at* http://www.cms.gov/Medicare/Coordination-of-Benefits-and-Recovery/Mandatory-Insurer-Reporting-For-Group-Health-Plans/Overview.html (site visited June 27, 2016).

[138] *See* CMS, "MMSEA Section 111 Medicare Secondary Payer Mandatory Reporting: Liability Insurance (Including Self-Insurance), No-fault Insurance, and Workers' Compensation User Guide, Chapter III: Policy Guidance" (NGHP User Guide) (Aug. 19, 2014), *available at* http://www.cms.gov/Medicare/Coordination-of-Benefits-and-Recovery/Mandatory-Insurer-Reporting-For-Non-Group-Health-Plans/NGHP-User-Guide/NGHP-User-Guide.html (site visited June 27, 2016). At the site, click on the various downloads at the bottom of the page.

[139] 80 Fed. Reg. 10611-18 (Feb. 27, 2015), *available at* https://www.federalregister.gov/articles/2015/02/27/2015-04143/medicare-program-right-of-appeal-for-medicare-secondary-payer-determinations-relating-to-liability (site visited June 3, 2016).

[140] 42 U.S.C. § 1395ff.

[141] 42 U.S.C. § 1395y(b)(2)(B)(v) (waiver provisions in the MSP statute) and 1395gg(c) (general provisions for waiver of Medicare overpayments); 31 U.S.C. § 3711 (Federal Claims Collection Act). A recent court decision has held that CMS should not begin collection procedures while a beneficiary's appeal of CMS's claimed amount is pending. *See* Haro v. Sebelius, 789 F. Supp. 2d 1179 (D. Ariz. 2011). *See also* Center for Medicare Advocacy, "Haro v. Johnson," *available at* http://www.medicareadvocacy.org/haro-v-johnson/ (site visited June 27, 2016).

can be pursued.[142] This is the usual Medicare Part A appeals process, consisting of a paper reconsideration by the MAC, followed by a hearing before an Office of Medicare Hearings and Appeals administrative law judge if the amount in controversy is $160 or more in 2017 and finally judicial review in federal district court if the amount in controversy is $1,560 or more in 2017.[143]

[B] Compromise of MSP Recovery Claims

The second opportunity for a beneficiary to reduce the amount Medicare takes is to request waiver or compromise of the MSP recovery claim.[144] The Medicare statute and regulations set out three grounds for waiver or compromise:[145]

1. When the probability of recovery or the amount involved does not warrant pursuit of the claim;[146]
2. When waiver is in the best interests of the Medicare program;[147]
3. When the beneficiary is without fault (presumed for MSP waivers) and recovery would either defeat the purpose of the Social Security and Medicare programs or would be against equity and good conscience.[148]

[C] Waiver of MSP Recovery Claims

The third ground for waiver is handled by the Medicare contractors, and it is the one commonly used to produce a reduction in MSP recovery claims after a beneficiary has received a personal injury award that is inadequate to compensate him or her fully, or where recovery will otherwise cause the beneficiary to suffer financial hardship.[149]

---

[142] 42 U.S.C. § 1395ff; 42 C.F.R. §§ 404.900 *et seq.*

[143] As is the rule with respect to other Medicare claims, the administrative appeals process must generally be exhausted before a court has jurisdiction. Merrifield v. United States, No. 07-CV-987, 2009 WL 1916328 (D.N.J. Mar. 31, 2008). Amount in controversy information for CY 2017 is available at 81 Fed. Reg. 65651 (september 23, 2016).

[144] 42 U.S.C. § 1395y(b)(2)(B)(iv)-(v).

[145] 42 C.F.R. § 411.28.

[146] Federal Claims Collection Act, 31 U.S.C. § 3711.

[147] *See* MSP section of the Medicare statute, 42 U.S.C. § 1395y (b)(2)(B)(iv).

[148] *See* overpayment recovery provision of the Medicare statute, 42 U.S.C. § 1395gg(c).

[149] *See* CMS, "MSP Beneficiary Overpayment: Request for 'Waiver of Recovery' Flow Chart," *available at* https://www.cms.gov/Medicare/Coordination-of-Benefits-and-Recovery/Beneficiary-Services/Downloads/MSP-Beneficiary-Overpayment-Request-for-Waiver-of-Recovery-Flow-Chart-.pdf (site visited June 27, 2016).

In order to obtain a waiver the beneficiary must supply a list of specific expenses, even when the expenses are for future medical services or other needs. Documentation in the form of sworn statements, actual bills, or canceled checks is required for out-of-pocket medical expenses. Unfortunately, Medicare often denies waiver without comment in cases where it could be justified under the Manual provisions if a particular kind of evidence were supplied. The advocate should ask Medicare MSP collection staff what specific evidence is required to justify granting waiver.

The "defeat the purposes of the Social Security or Medicare laws" criterion under 42 U.S.C. § 1395gg(c) is met when a beneficiary does not have income or resources sufficient to meet his or her ordinary and necessary expenses.[150] Such expenses include food, shelter, utilities, insurance, and medical and other health expenses not covered by other insurance, as well as support payments and other expenses necessary to maintain the beneficiary's standard of living. Examples of financial hardship include a case where the beneficiary has already spent the insurance proceeds and would have inadequate living expenses if the beneficiary repaid Medicare; a case where the beneficiary is living at the poverty level (although preexisting poverty is not in itself enough to justify waiver); and a case where some unforeseen financial circumstance occurs, such as grandchildren becoming the financial responsibility of the beneficiary.[151]

The second 42 U.S.C. § 1395gg(c) waiver ground, "against equity and good conscience," looks to the following factors:

- The degree to which the beneficiary did not contribute to causing the overpayment;
- The degree to which Medicare did contribute to causing the overpayment;
- The degree to which repayment would cause undue hardship to the beneficiary; and
- Whether the beneficiary would be unjustly enriched by waiver, or was harmed by relying on erroneous Medicare information.[152]

---

[150] *See* CMS, "MSP Beneficiary Overpayment: Request for 'Waiver of Recovery' Flow Chart," *available at* http://www.cms.gov/Medicare/Coordination-of-Benefits-and-Recovery/Beneficiary-Services/Downloads/MSP-Beneficiary-Overpayment-Request-for-Waiver-of-Recovery-Flow-Chart.pdf (site visited July 27, 2016). *See also* MSP Manual, Ch. 7, §§ 50.6.5 *et seq.*

[151] MSP Manual, Ch. 7, §§ 50.6.5 *et seq.*

[152] MSP Manual, Ch. 7, §§ 50.6.5 *et seq.*

§ 9.12 MEDICARE AND QUALIFIED HEALTH PLANS OFFERED THROUGH THE AFFORDABLE CARE ACT MARKETPLACE

[A] Definitions and Relationship to the Affordable Care Act

[1] Health Insurance Marketplace (Exchange)

The Affordable Care Act (ACA) requires states to create Health Insurance Marketplaces, also known as exchanges.[153] These Marketplaces offer individuals and small businesses the opportunity to shop for and purchase insurance. The Marketplaces, which were operational by January 1, 2014, are the main way that people gain coverage as mandated by the ACA. It's estimated that in the next few years, Marketplaces could serve as a gateway for an estimated 14.7 million people to find their insurance.[154] A state can choose to establish its own Marketplace, it can partner with the federal government to create one, or it can choose to allow the federal government to entirely facilitate the Marketplace.

[2] Qualified Health Plan

Under the ACA, a qualified health plan (QHP) is an insurance plan that is certified by the Marketplace, provides essential health benefits, follows established limits on cost-sharing (like deductibles, copayments, and out-of-pocket maximum amounts), and meets other requirements.[155] Individuals will be able to purchase QHPs on the Marketplace.

For people between 100 and 400 percent of the federal poverty level (FPL), sliding scale advance premium tax credits will be available to help individuals afford the costs of a QHP.[156] Individuals will also be eligible for cost-sharing reductions (reductions in coinsurance, deductibles, and copayments) based on their income.[157]

[B] Transitioning into Medicare

Individuals enrolled in a QHP must prepare for transitions into Medicare. Delaying Part B enrollment to stay enrolled in a QHP will subject a beneficiary

[153] ACA § 1311.

[154] Larry Levitt, Gary Claxton, Anthony Damico,, and Cynthia Cox. "Assessing ACA Marketplace Enrollment." Kaiser Family Foundation. 04 March 2016. http://kff.org/health-reform/issue-brief/assessing-aca-marketplace-enrollment/ (site visited Aug. 11, 2016). ,

[155] ACA § 1302(a)-(c).

[156] ACA §§ 1401(a)-(e), 10105(a)-(d), 10109(h)(1) and (2).

[157] ACA § 1402(a)-(f).

to a premium penalty if he or she later decides to enroll in Part B.[158] A QHP will not terminate automatically when a beneficiary becomes eligible for Medicare.[159] In order to cancel enrollment in the QHP, an enrollee must give the plan "reasonable notice." Reasonable notice is 14 days or more, and an enrollee should be able to specify a specific termination date if reasonable notice is provided.[160]

Most Medicare eligible individuals are not eligible to receive advance premium tax credits or cost-sharing subsides to help pay for the cost of a QHP.[161] If a beneficiary chooses to keep a QHP upon becoming eligible for Medicare, he or she will be required to pay the full premium and cost-sharing amounts. Unlike enrollment in a QHP, the advance premium tax credit should cancel automatically when the recipient becomes eligible for Medicare.[162] Eligibility criteria for both subsidies in the Marketplace and expansion Medicaid in the states that have chosen to adopt it is less stringent than eligibility criteria for low-income assistance available in Medicare (primarily through the Medicare Savings Programs, or MSPs), leading some individuals transitioning into Medicare to lose cost-sharing and premium assistance.[163]

---

[158] *See* discussion in **§ 6.02[B][2]** of this Handbook. *See also* CMS Frequently Asked Questions re: transitions from Medicare to Marketplace plans (updated Apr. 2016), *available at* http://www.cms.gov/Medicare/Eligibility-and-Enrollment/Medicare-and-the-Marketplace/Overview1.html.

[159] ACA; Establishment of Exchanges and Qualified Health Plans; Exchange Standards for Employers; Final Rule and Interim Final Rule, 77 Fed. Reg. 18,371–74, 18,394, 18,395, 18,463 (to be codified at 45 C.F.R. §§ 155.330 and 155.430); Health Insurance Premium Tax Credit, 76 Fed. Reg. 50,933, 50,934, 50,941 (Aug. 17, 2011).

[160] 77 Fed. Reg. 18,371, 18,394, 18,395, 18,463 (to be codified at 45 C.F.R. § 155.430).

[161] Medicare is considered minimum essential coverage. 26 U.S.C. § 5000A(f)(1)(A)(i). *See also* CMS, "The Center for Consumer Information & Insurance Oversight: Minimum Essential Coverage," *available at* http://www.cms.gov/CCIIO/Programs-and-Initiatives/Health-Insurance-Market-Reforms/minimum-essential-coverage.html (site visited June 3, 2016). An exception to the prohibition on receiving premium tax credits exists for people eligible for Medicare based on end-stage renal disease (ESRD) and those who must pay a premium for Part A. IRS guidance allows these individuals to forego enrollment in Part A in favor of a QHP with a tax credit. Internal Revenue Service, "Eligibility for Minimum Essential Coverage for Purposes of the Premium Tax Credit," Notice 2013-41, *available at* http://www.irs.gov/pub/irs-drop/n-13-41.pdf (site visited June 3, 2016).

[162] ACA § 1401, as modified by the Federal Aviation Administration Extension Act of 2010, Pub. L. No. 111-153 (Mar. 3, 2010), § 1001; Health Insurance Premium Tax Credit. Medicare is considered minimum essential coverage. 26 U.S.C. § 5000A(f)(1)(A)(i). *See also* CMS, "The Center for Consumer Information & Insurance Oversight: Minimum Essential Coverage," *available at* http://www.cms.gov/CCIIO/Programs-and-Initiatives/Health-Insurance-Market-Reforms/minimum-essential-coverage.html (site visited June 3, 2016).

[163] This is sometimes referred to as the "Medicare Cliff." *See, e.g.*, Kaiser Family Foundation, "Comparison of Consumer Protections in Three Health Insurance Markets: Medicare Advantage, Qualified Health Plans and Medicaid Managed Care Organizations" (Mar. 2015), Appendix B, *available at* http://kff.org/medicare/report/comparison-of-consumer-protections-in-three-health-insurance-markets/.

[C] Coordination of Qualified Health Plans and Medicare

Under the ACA, QHPs offered through the health insurance Marketplace may not refuse to sell coverage to any applicant.[164] Federal Medicare anti-duplication provisions, however, require private insurers to either refuse to sell to people with Medicare or to pay out benefits regardless of Medicare enrollment. Under these anti-duplication rules, in general, it is unlawful to sell or issue someone *eligible for* Medicare Part A or *enrolled* in Medicare Part B any individual market health insurance policy that duplicates Medicare benefits, unless the policy is a standardized Medicare Supplement (Medigap) policy.[165] Thus, insurers cannot sell individual policies to Medicare-eligible persons if the policy will pay secondary to Medicare.[166]

Language provided by the Department of Health and Human Services through Healthcare.gov and a CMS fact sheet appears to signal that the anti-duplication rules govern the sale of QHPs to people with Medicare.[167] The language provided indicates that " . . . it's against the law for someone who knows you have Medicare to sell you a Marketplace plan." Further, the ACA did not seemingly intend for QHPs to be sold to people with Medicare. The law states that premium tax credits and other Marketplace cost-sharing subsidies are not available to most Medicare-eligible individuals.[168]

---

[164] Sec. 2702 of the PHS Act (42 U.S.C. § 300gg), 42 C.F.R. § 147.104.

[165] 42 U.S.C. § 1395ss(d)(3)(A)(i). *See* Chapter 8.

[166] Based on the authors' interpretation of the anti-duplication rules, QHPs offered on the health insurance Marketplaces could be purchased by Medicare beneficiaries only if the QHPs comply with 42 U.S.C. § 1395ss(d)(3)(A)(i) and *do not* coordinate benefits with Medicare, meaning that insurers could sell products to people with Medicare only if the products would pay primary regardless of whether the person had Medicare Part A or B. Based on our experience serving individuals with private health plans, we believe it is highly unlikely that QHPs would opt to pay primary regardless of Medicare eligibility or enrollment. However, the law seems to permit this possibility.

[167] Healthcare.gov, Medicare & the Marketplace, *available at* https://www.healthcare.gov/if-i-have-medicare-do-i-need-to-do-anything (site visited June 3, 2016); CMS, "People with Medicare and the Health Insurance Marketplace" (Aug. 2013), *available at* http://www.cms.gov/Center/Special-Topic/Open-Enrollment/Downloads/Medicare-Marketplace-FAQs.pdf (site visited June 3, 2016).

[168] Medicare Part A is considered minimum essential coverage. Those eligible for other minimum essential coverage are not eligible for a premium tax credit. 26 U.S.C. § 5000A(f)(1)(A)(i); 77 Fed. Reg. 30,388 (to be codified at 26 U.S.C. § 1.36B-2(c)). An exception to the prohibition on receiving premium tax credits exists for those eligible for Medicare based on end-stage renal disease (ESRD) and those who must pay a premium for Part A. IRS guidance allows these individuals to forego enrollment in Part A in favor of a QHP with a tax credit. Internal Revenue Service, "Coordination of Benefits Model Regulation," *available at* http://www.naic.org/store/free/MDL-120.pdf (site visited June 3, 2016).

Nevertheless, some Medicare-eligible individuals will become enrolled in a qualified health plan either by accident or through small loop-holes in the law.[169] It remains unclear how coordination between a QHP and Medicare will function in these scenarios.[170]

[169] For example, someone already enrolled in a QHP who becomes eligible for, and enrolls in, Medicare would not necessarily be governed by the anti-duplication statute and could therefore retain a QHP while also enrolling in Medicare. Likewise, someone with Part B who is eligible only for premium Part A may decide to keep Part B and enroll in a QHP with or without a tax credit.

[170] Confusion exists about how QHPs will work with Medicare because the National Association of Insurance Commissioners (NAIC) Coordination of Benefits scheme, adopted by 40 states, seems to be in direct conflict with the federal anti-duplication law. On the one hand, the anti-duplication law prohibits insurers from selling products, with certain exceptions, that coordinate with Medicare to persons who have Medicare or qualify for it. On the other hand, the NAIC model rules allow individual plans to require Medicare B enrollment and to pay as if secondary to Medicare. *See* NAIC, Coordination of Benefits Model Regulation, *available at* http://www.naic.org/store/free/MDL-120.pdf (site visited June 3, 2016).

APPENDIX 9-1 TITLE 29—LABOR (CODE OF FEDERAL REGULATIONS): SUBCHAPTER G—ADMINISTRATION AND ENFORCEMENT UNDER THE EMPLOYEE RETIREMENT INCOME SECURITY ACT OF 1974

PART 2560—RULES AND REGULATIONS FOR ADMINISTRATION AND ENFORCEMENT

Sec. 2560.503-1 Claims procedure.

(a) Scope and purpose. In accordance with the authority of sections 503 and 505 of the Employee Retirement Income Security Act of 1974 (ERISA or the Act), 29 U.S.C. 1133, 1135, this section sets forth minimum requirements for employee benefit plan procedures pertaining to claims for benefits by participants and beneficiaries (hereinafter referred to as claimants). Except as otherwise specifically provided in this section, these requirements apply to every employee benefit plan described in section 4(a) and not exempted under section 4(b) of the Act.

(b) Obligation to establish and maintain reasonable claims procedures. Every employee benefit plan shall establish and maintain reasonable procedures governing the filing of benefit claims, notification of benefit determinations, and appeal of adverse benefit determinations (hereinafter collectively referred to as claims procedures). The claims procedures for a plan will be deemed to be reasonable only if—

(1) The claims procedures comply with the requirements of paragraphs (c), (d), (e), (f), (g), (h), (i), and (j) of this section, as appropriate, except to the extent that the claims procedures are deemed to comply with some or all of such provisions pursuant to paragraph (b)(6) of this section;

(2) A description of all claims procedures (including, in the case of a group health plan within the meaning of paragraph (m)(6) of this section, any procedures for obtaining prior approval as a prerequisite for obtaining a benefit, such as preauthorization procedures or utilization review procedures) and the applicable time frames is included as part of a summary plan description meeting the requirements of 29 C.F.R. 2520.102-3;

(3) The claims procedures do not contain any provision, and are not administered in a way, that unduly inhibits or hampers the initiation or processing of claims for benefits. For example, a provision or practice that requires payment of a fee or costs as a condition to making a claim or to appealing an adverse benefit determination would be considered to unduly inhibit the initiation and processing of claims for benefits. Also, the denial of a claim for failure to obtain a prior approval under circumstances that would make obtaining such prior approval impossible or where application of the prior approval process could seriously jeopardize the life or health of the claimant (e.g., in the case of a group health

plan, the claimant is unconscious and in need of immediate care at the time medical treatment is required) would constitute a practice that unduly inhibits the initiation and processing of a claim;

(4) The claims procedures do not preclude an authorized representative of a claimant from acting on behalf of such claimant in pursuing a benefit claim or appeal of an adverse benefit determination. Nevertheless, a plan may establish reasonable procedures for determining whether an individual has been authorized to act on behalf of a claimant, provided that, in the case of a claim involving urgent care, within the meaning of paragraph (m)(1) of this section, a health care professional, within the meaning of paragraph (m)(7) of this section, with knowledge of a claimant's medical condition shall be permitted to act as the authorized representative of the claimant; and

(5) The claims procedures contain administrative processes and safeguards designed to ensure and to verify that benefit claim determinations are made in accordance with governing plan documents and that, where appropriate, the plan provisions have been applied consistently with respect to similarly situated claimants.

(6) In the case of a plan established and maintained pursuant to a collective bargaining agreement (other than a plan subject to the provisions of section 302(c)(5) of the Labor Management Relations Act, 1947 concerning joint representation on the board of trustees)—

(i) Such plan will be deemed to comply with the provisions of paragraphs (c) through (j) of this section if the collective bargaining agreement pursuant to which the plan is established or maintained sets forth or incorporates by specific reference—

(A) Provisions concerning the filing of benefit claims and the initial disposition of benefit claims, and

(B) A grievance and arbitration procedure to which adverse benefit determinations are subject.

(ii) Such plan will be deemed to comply with the provisions of paragraphs (h), (i), and (j) of this section (but will not be deemed to comply with paragraphs (c) through (g) of this section) if the collective bargaining agreement pursuant to which the plan is established or maintained sets forth or incorporates by specific reference a grievance and arbitration procedure to which adverse benefit determinations are subject (but not provisions concerning the filing and initial disposition of benefit claims).

(c) Group health plans. The claims procedures of a group health plan will be deemed to be reasonable only if, in addition to complying with the requirements of paragraph (b) of this section—

(1)(i) The claims procedures provide that, in the case of a failure by a claimant or an authorized representative of a claimant to follow the plan's procedures for filing a pre-service claim, within the meaning of paragraph (m)(2) of this section, the claimant or representative shall be notified of the failure and the proper procedures to be followed in filing a claim for benefits. This notification shall be provided to the claimant or authorized representative, as appropriate, as soon as possible, but not later than 5 days (24 hours in the case of a failure to file a claim involving urgent care) following the failure. Notification may be oral, unless written notification is requested by the claimant or authorized representative.

(ii) Paragraph (c)(1)(i) of this section shall apply only in the case of a failure that—

(A) Is a communication by a claimant or an authorized representative of a claimant that is received by a person or organizational unit customarily responsible for handling benefit matters; and

(B) Is a communication that names a specific claimant; a specific medical condition or symptom; and a specific treatment, service, or product for which approval is requested.

(2) The claims procedures do not contain any provision, and are not administered in a way, that requires a claimant to file more than two appeals of an adverse benefit determination prior to bringing a civil action under section 502(a) of the Act;

(3) To the extent that a plan offers voluntary levels of appeal (except to the extent that the plan is required to do so by State law), including voluntary arbitration or any other form of dispute resolution, in addition to those permitted by paragraph (c)(2) of this section, the claims procedures provide that:

(i) The plan waives any right to assert that a claimant has failed to exhaust administrative remedies because the claimant did not elect to submit a benefit dispute to any such voluntary level of appeal provided by the plan;

(ii) The plan agrees that any statute of limitations or other defense based on timeliness is tolled during the time that any such voluntary appeal is pending;

(iii) The claims procedures provide that a claimant may elect to submit a benefit dispute to such voluntary level of appeal only after exhaustion of the appeals permitted by paragraph (c)(2) of this section;

(iv) The plan provides to any claimant, upon request, sufficient information relating to the voluntary level of appeal to enable the claimant to make an informed judgment about whether to submit a benefit dispute to the voluntary level of appeal, including a statement that the decision of a claimant as to whether or not to submit a benefit dispute to the voluntary level of appeal will have no effect on the claimant's rights to any other benefits under the plan and information about the applicable rules, the claimant's right to representation, the process for selecting the decision maker, and the circumstances, if any, that may affect the impartiality of the decision maker, such as any financial or personal interests in the result or any past or present relationship with any party to the review process; and

(v) No fees or costs are imposed on the claimant as part of the voluntary level of appeal.

(4) The claims procedures do not contain any provision for the mandatory arbitration of adverse benefit determinations, except to the extent that the plan or procedures provide that:

(i) The arbitration is conducted as one of the two appeals described in paragraph (c)(2) of this section and in accordance with the requirements applicable to such appeals; and

(ii) The claimant is not precluded from challenging the decision under section 502(a) of the Act or other applicable law.

(d) Plans providing disability benefits. The claims procedures of a plan that provides disability benefits will be deemed to be reasonable only if the claims procedures comply, with respect to claims for disability benefits, with the requirements of paragraphs (b), (c)(2), (c)(3), and (c)(4) of this section.

(e) Claim for benefits. For purposes of this section, a claim for benefits is a request for a plan benefit or benefits made by a claimant in accordance with a plan's reasonable procedure for filing benefit claims. In the case of a group health plan, a claim for benefits includes any pre-service claims within the meaning of paragraph (m)(2) of this section and any post-service claims within the meaning of paragraph (m)(3) of this section.

(f) Timing of notification of benefit determination. (1) *In general.* Except as provided in paragraphs (f)(2) and (f)(3) of this section, if a claim is wholly or partially denied, the plan administrator shall notify the claimant, in accordance with paragraph (g) of this section, of the plan's adverse benefit determination within a reasonable period of time, but not later than 90 days after receipt of the claim by the plan, unless the plan administrator determines that special circumstances require an extension of time for processing the claim. If the plan administrator determines that an extension of time for processing is required, written notice of the extension shall be furnished to the claimant prior to the termination of the initial 90-day period. In no event shall such extension exceed a period of 90 days from the end of such initial period. The extension notice shall indicate the special circumstances requiring an extension of time and the date by which the plan expects to render the benefit determination.

(2) *Group health plans.* In the case of a group health plan, the plan administrator shall notify a claimant of the plan's benefit determination in accordance with paragraph (f)(2)(i), (f)(2)(ii), or (f)(2)(iii) of this section, as appropriate.

(i) *Urgent care claims.* In the case of a claim involving urgent care, the plan administrator shall notify the claimant of the plan's benefit determination (whether adverse or not) as soon as possible, taking into account the medical exigencies, but not later than 72 hours after receipt of the claim by the plan, unless the claimant fails to provide sufficient information to determine whether, or to what extent, benefits are covered or payable under the plan. In the case of such a failure, the plan administrator shall notify the claimant as soon as possible, but not later than 24 hours after receipt of the claim by the plan, of the specific information necessary to complete the claim. The claimant shall be afforded a reasonable amount of time, taking into account the circumstances, but not less than 48 hours, to provide the specified information. Notification of any adverse benefit determination pursuant to this paragraph (f)(2)(i) shall be made in accordance with paragraph (g) of this section. The plan administrator shall notify the claimant of the plan's benefit determination as soon as possible, but in no case later than 48 hours after the earlier of—

(A) The plan's receipt of the specified information, or

(B) The end of the period afforded the claimant to provide the specified additional information.

(ii) *Concurrent care decisions.* If a group health plan has approved an ongoing course of treatment to be provided over a period of time or number of treatments—

(A) Any reduction or termination by the plan of such course of treatment (other than by plan amendment or termination) before the end of such period of time or number of treatments shall constitute an adverse benefit determination. The plan administrator shall notify the claimant, in accordance with paragraph (g) of this section, of the adverse benefit determination at a time sufficiently in advance of the reduction or termination to allow the claimant to appeal and obtain a determination on review of that adverse benefit determination before the benefit is reduced or terminated.

(B) Any request by a claimant to extend the course of treatment beyond the period of time or number of treatments that is a claim involving urgent care shall be decided as soon as possible, taking into account the medical exigencies, and the plan administrator shall notify the claimant of the benefit determination, whether adverse or not, within 24 hours after receipt of the claim by the plan, provided that any such claim is made to the plan at least 24 hours prior to the expiration of the prescribed period of time or number of treatments. Notification of any adverse benefit determination concerning a request to extend the course of treatment, whether involving urgent care or not, shall be made in accordance with paragraph (g) of this section, and appeal shall be governed by paragraph (i)(2)(i), (i)(2)(ii), or (i)(2)(iii), as appropriate.

(iii) *Other claims.* In the case of a claim not described in paragraphs (f)(2)(i) or (f)(2)(ii) of this section, the plan administrator shall notify the claimant of the plan's benefit determination in accordance with either paragraph (f)(2)(iii)(A) or (f)(2)(iii)(B) of this section, as appropriate.

(A) *Pre-service claims.* In the case of a pre-service claim, the plan administrator shall notify the claimant of the plan's benefit determination (whether adverse or not) within a reasonable period of time appropriate to the medical circumstances, but not later than 15 days after receipt of the claim by the plan. This period may be extended one time by the plan for up to 15 days, provided that the plan administrator both determines that such an extension is necessary due to matters beyond the control of the plan and notifies the claimant, prior to the expiration of the initial 15-day period, of the circumstances requiring the extension of time and the date by which the plan expects to render a decision. If such an extension is necessary due to a failure of the claimant to submit the information necessary to decide the claim, the notice of extension shall specifically describe the required information, and the claimant shall be afforded at least 45 days from receipt of the notice within which to provide the specified information. Notification of any adverse benefit determination pursuant to this paragraph (f)(2)(iii)(A) shall be made in accordance with paragraph (g) of this section.

(B) *Post-service claims.* In the case of a post-service claim, the plan administrator shall notify the claimant, in accordance with paragraph (g) of this section, of the plan's adverse benefit determination within a reasonable period of time, but not later than 30 days after receipt of the claim. This period may be extended one time by the plan for up to 15 days, provided that the plan administrator both determines that such an extension is necessary due to matters beyond the control of the plan and notifies the claimant, prior to the expiration of the initial 30-day period, of the circumstances requiring the extension of time and the date by which the plan expects to render a decision. If such an extension is necessary due to a failure of the claimant to submit the information necessary to decide the claim, the notice of extension shall specifically describe the required information, and the claimant shall be afforded at least 45 days from receipt of the notice within which to provide the specified information.

(3) *Disability claims.* In the case of a claim for disability benefits, the plan administrator shall notify the claimant, in accordance with paragraph (g) of this section, of the plan's adverse benefit determination within a reasonable period of time, but not later than 45 days after receipt of the claim by the plan. This period may be extended by the plan for up to 30 days, provided that the plan administrator both determines that such an extension is necessary due to matters beyond the control of the plan and notifies the claimant, prior to the expiration of the initial 45-day period, of the circumstances requiring the extension of time and the date by which the plan expects to render a decision. If, prior to the end of the first 30-day extension period, the administrator determines that, due to matters beyond the control of the plan, a decision cannot be rendered within that extension period, the period for making the determination may be extended for up to an additional 30 days, provided that the plan administrator notifies the claimant, prior to the expiration of the first 30-day extension period, of the circumstances requiring the extension and the date as of which the plan expects to render a decision. In the case of any extension under this paragraph (f)(3), the notice of extension shall specifically explain the standards on which entitlement to a benefit is based, the unresolved issues that prevent a decision on the claim, and the additional information needed to resolve those issues, and the claimant shall be afforded at least 45 days within which to provide the specified information.

(4) *Calculating time periods.* For purposes of paragraph (f) of this section, the period of time within which a benefit determination is required to be made shall begin at the time a claim is filed in accordance with the reasonable procedures of a plan, without regard to whether all the information necessary to make a benefit determination accompanies the filing. In the event that a period of time is extended as permitted pursuant to paragraph (f)(2)(iii) or (f)(3) of this section due to a claimant's failure to submit information necessary to decide a claim, the period for making the benefit determination shall be tolled from the date on which

the notification of the extension is sent to the claimant until the date on which the claimant responds to the request for additional information.

(g) Manner and content of notification of benefit determination. (1) Except as provided in paragraph (g)(2) of this section, the plan administrator shall provide a claimant with written or electronic notification of any adverse benefit determination. Any electronic notification shall comply with the standards imposed by 29 C.F.R. 2520.104b-1(c)(1)(i), (iii), and (iv). The notification shall set forth, in a manner calculated to be understood by the claimant—

(i) The specific reason or reasons for the adverse determination;

(ii) Reference to the specific plan provisions on which the determination is based;

(iii) A description of any additional material or information necessary for the claimant to perfect the claim and an explanation of why such material or information is necessary;

(iv) A description of the plan's review procedures and the time limits applicable to such procedures, including a statement of the claimant's right to bring a civil action under section 502(a) of the Act following an adverse benefit determination on review;

(v) In the case of an adverse benefit determination by a group health plan or a plan providing disability benefits,

(A) If an internal rule, guideline, protocol, or other similar criterion was relied upon in making the adverse determination, either the specific rule, guideline, protocol, or other similar criterion; or a statement that such a rule, guideline, protocol, or other similar criterion was relied upon in making the adverse determination and that a copy of such rule, guideline, protocol, or other criterion will be provided free of charge to the claimant upon request; or

(B) If the adverse benefit determination is based on a medical necessity or experimental treatment or similar exclusion or limit, either an explanation of the scientific or clinical judgment for the determination, applying the terms of the plan to the claimant's medical circumstances, or a statement that such explanation will be provided free of charge upon request.

(vi) In the case of an adverse benefit determination by a group health plan concerning a claim involving urgent care, a description of the expedited review process applicable to such claims.

(2) In the case of an adverse benefit determination by a group health plan concerning a claim involving urgent care, the information described in paragraph (g)(1) of this section may be provided to the claimant orally within the time frame prescribed in paragraph (f)(2)(i) of this section, provided that a written or electronic notification in accordance with paragraph (g)(1) of this section is furnished to the claimant not later than 3 days after the oral notification.

(h) Appeal of adverse benefit determinations. (1) *In general.* Every employee benefit plan shall establish and maintain a procedure by which a claimant shall have a reasonable opportunity to appeal an adverse benefit determination to an appropriate named fiduciary of the plan, and under which there will be a full and fair review of the claim and the adverse benefit determination.

(2) *Full and fair review.* Except as provided in paragraphs (h)(3) and (h)(4) of this section, the claims procedures of a plan will not be deemed to provide a claimant with a reasonable opportunity for a full and fair review of a claim and adverse benefit determination unless the claims procedures—

(i) Provide claimants at least 60 days following receipt of a notification of an adverse benefit determination within which to appeal the determination;

(ii) Provide claimants the opportunity to submit written comments, documents, records, and other information relating to the claim for benefits;

(iii) Provide that a claimant shall be provided, upon request and free of charge, reasonable access to, and copies of, all documents, records, and other information relevant to the claimant's claim for benefits. Whether a document, record, or other information is relevant to a claim for benefits shall be determined by reference to paragraph (m)(8) of this section;

(iv) Provide for a review that takes into account all comments, documents, records, and other information submitted by the claimant relating to the claim, without regard to whether such information was submitted or considered in the initial benefit determination.

(3) *Group health plans.* The claims procedures of a group health plan will not be deemed to provide a claimant with a reasonable opportunity for a full and fair review of a claim and adverse benefit determination unless, in addition to complying with the requirements of paragraphs (h)(2)(ii) through (iv) of this section, the claims procedures—

(i) Provide claimants at least 180 days following receipt of a notification of an adverse benefit determination within which to appeal the determination;

(ii) Provide for a review that does not afford deference to the initial adverse benefit determination and that is conducted by an appropriate named fiduciary of the plan who is neither the individual who made the adverse benefit determination that is the subject of the appeal, nor the subordinate of such individual;

(iii) Provide that, in deciding an appeal of any adverse benefit determination that is based in whole or in part on a medical judgment, including determinations with regard to whether a particular treatment, drug, or other item is experimental, investigational, or not medically necessary or appropriate, the appropriate named fiduciary shall consult with a health care professional who has appropriate training and experience in the field of medicine involved in the medical judgment;

(iv) Provide for the identification of medical or vocational experts whose advice was obtained on behalf of the plan in connection with a claimant's adverse benefit determination, without regard to whether the advice was relied upon in making the benefit determination;

(v) Provide that the health care professional engaged for purposes of a consultation under paragraph (h)(3)(iii) of this section shall be an individual who is neither an individual who was consulted in connection with the adverse benefit determination that is the subject of the appeal, nor the subordinate of any such individual; and

(vi) Provide, in the case of a claim involving urgent care, for an expedited review process pursuant to which—

(A) A request for an expedited appeal of an adverse benefit determination may be submitted orally or in writing by the claimant; and

(B) All necessary information, including the plan's benefit determination on review, shall be transmitted between the plan and the claimant by telephone, facsimile, or other available similarly expeditious method.

(4) *Plans providing disability benefits.* The claims procedures of a plan providing disability benefits will not, with respect to claims for such benefits, be deemed to provide a claimant with a reasonable opportunity for a full and fair review of a claim and adverse benefit determination unless the claims procedures comply with the requirements of paragraphs (h)(2)(ii) through (iv) and (h)(3)(i) through (v) of this section.

(i) Timing of notification of benefit determination on review. (1) *In general.* (i) Except as provided in paragraphs (i)(1)(ii), (i)(2), and (i)(3) of this section, the plan administrator shall notify a claimant in accordance with paragraph (j) of this section of the plan's benefit determination on review within a reasonable period of time, but not later than 60 days after receipt of the claimant's request for review by the plan, unless the plan administrator determines that special circumstances (such as the need to hold a hearing, if the plan's procedures provide for a hearing) require an extension of time for processing the claim. If the plan administrator determines that an extension of time for processing is required, written notice of the extension shall be furnished to the claimant prior to the termination of the initial 60-day period. In no event shall such extension exceed a period of 60 days from the end of the initial period. The extension notice shall indicate the special circumstances requiring an extension of time and the date by which the plan expects to render the determination on review.

(ii) In the case of a plan with a committee or board of trustees designated as the appropriate named fiduciary that holds regularly scheduled meetings at least quarterly, paragraph (i)(1)(i) of this section shall not apply, and, except as provided in paragraphs (i)(2) and (i)(3) of this section, the appropriate named fiduciary shall instead make a benefit determination no later than the date of the meeting of the committee or board that immediately follows the plan's receipt of a request for review, unless the request for review is filed within 30 days preceding the date of such meeting. In such case, a benefit determination may be made by no later than the date of the second meeting following the plan's receipt of the request for review. If special circumstances (such as the need to hold a hearing, if the plan's procedures provide for a hearing) require a further extension of time for processing, a benefit determination shall be rendered not later than the third meeting of the committee or board following the plan's receipt of the request for review. If such an extension of time for review is required because of special circumstances, the plan administrator shall provide the claimant with written notice of the extension, describing the special circumstances and the date as of which the benefit determination will be made, prior to the commencement of the extension. The plan administrator shall notify the claimant, in accordance with paragraph (j) of this section, of the benefit determination as soon as possible, but not later than 5 days after the benefit determination is made.

(2) *Group health plans.* In the case of a group health plan, the plan administrator shall notify a claimant of the plan's benefit determination on review in accordance with paragraphs (i)(2)(i) through (iii), as appropriate.

(i) *Urgent care claims.* In the case of a claim involving urgent care, the plan administrator shall notify the claimant, in accordance with paragraph (j) of this section, of the plan's benefit determination on review as soon as possible, taking into account the medical exigencies, but not later than 72 hours after receipt of the claimant's request for review of an adverse benefit determination by the plan.

(ii) *Pre-service claims.* In the case of a pre-service claim, the plan administrator shall notify the claimant, in accordance with paragraph (j) of this section, of the plan's benefit determination on review within a reasonable period of time appropriate to the medical circumstances. In the case of a group health plan that provides for one appeal of an adverse benefit determination, such notification shall be provided not later than 30 days after receipt by the plan of the claimant's request for review of an adverse benefit determination. In the case of a group health plan that provides for two appeals of an adverse determination, such notification shall be provided, with respect to any one of such two appeals, not later than 15 days after receipt by the plan of the claimant's request for review of the adverse determination.

(iii) *Post-service claims.* (A) In the case of a post-service claim, except as provided in paragraph (i)(2)(iii)(B) of this section, the plan administrator shall notify the claimant, in accordance with paragraph (j) of this section, of the plan's benefit determination on review within a reasonable period of time. In the case of a group health plan that provides for one appeal of an adverse benefit determination, such notification shall be provided not later than 60 days after receipt by the plan of the claimant's request for review of an adverse benefit determination. In the case of a group health plan that provides for two appeals of an adverse determination, such notification shall be provided, with respect to any one of such two appeals, not later than 30 days after receipt by the plan of the claimant's request for review of the adverse determination.

(B) In the case of a multiemployer plan with a committee or board of trustees designated as the appropriate named fiduciary that holds regularly scheduled meetings at least quarterly, paragraph (i)(2)(iii)(A) of this section shall not apply, and the appropriate named fiduciary shall instead make a benefit determination no later than the date of the meeting of the committee or board that immediately follows the plan's receipt of a request for review, unless the request for review is filed within 30 days preceding the date of such meeting. In such case, a benefit determination may be made by no later than the date of the second meeting following the plan's receipt of the request for review. If special circumstances (such as the need to hold a hearing, if the plan's procedures provide for a hearing) require a further extension of time for processing, a benefit determination shall be rendered not later than the third meeting of the committee or board following the plan's receipt of the request for review. If such an extension of time for review is required because of special circumstances, the plan administrator shall notify the claimant in writing of the extension, describing the special circumstances and the date as of which the benefit determination will be made, prior to the commencement of the extension. The plan administrator shall notify the claimant, in accordance with paragraph (j) of this section, of the benefit determination as soon as possible, but not later than 5 days after the benefit determination is made.

(3) *Disability claims.* (i) Except as provided in paragraph (i)(3)(ii) of this section, claims involving disability benefits (whether the plan provides for one or two appeals) shall be governed by paragraph (i)(1) of this section, except that a period of 45 days shall apply instead of 60 days for purposes of that paragraph.

(ii) In the case of a multiemployer plan with a committee or board of trustees designated as the appropriate named fiduciary that holds regularly scheduled meetings at least quarterly, paragraph (i)(3)(i) of this section shall not apply, and the appropriate named fiduciary shall instead make a benefit determination no later than the date of the meeting of the committee or board that immediately follows the plan's receipt of a request for review, unless the request for review is filed within 30 days preceding the date of such meeting. In such case, a benefit determination may be made by no later than the date of the second meeting following the plan's receipt of the request for review. If special circumstances (such as the need to hold a hearing, if the plan's procedures provide for a hearing) require a further extension of time for processing, a benefit determination shall be rendered not later than the third meeting of the committee or board following the plan's receipt of the request for review. If such an extension of time for review is required because of special circumstances, the plan administrator shall notify the claimant in writing of the extension, describing the special circumstances and the date as of which the benefit determination will be made, prior to the commencement of the extension. The plan administrator shall notify the claimant, in accordance with paragraph (j) of this section, of the benefit determination as soon as possible, but not later than 5 days after the benefit determination is made.

(4) *Calculating time periods.* For purposes of paragraph (i) of this section, the period of time within which a benefit determination on review is required to be made shall begin at the time an appeal is filed in accordance with the reasonable procedures of a plan, without regard to whether all the information necessary to make a benefit determination on review accompanies the filing. In the event that a period of time is extended as permitted pursuant to paragraph (i)(1), (i)(2)(iii)(B), or (i)(3) of this section due to a claimant's failure to submit

information necessary to decide a claim, the period for making the benefit determination on review shall be tolled from the date on which the notification of the extension is sent to the claimant until the date on which the claimant responds to the request for additional information.

(5) *Furnishing documents.* In the case of an adverse benefit determination on review, the plan administrator shall provide such access to, and copies of, documents, records, and other information described in paragraphs (j)(3), (j)(4), and (j)(5) of this section as is appropriate.

(j) Manner and content of notification of benefit determination on review. The plan administrator shall provide a claimant with written or electronic notification of a plan's benefit determination on review. Any electronic notification shall comply with the standards imposed by 29 C.F.R. 2520.104b-1(c)(1)(i), (iii), and (iv). In the case of an adverse benefit determination, the notification shall set forth, in a manner calculated to be understood by the claimant—

(1) The specific reason or reasons for the adverse determination;

(2) Reference to the specific plan provisions on which the benefit determination is based;

(3) A statement that the claimant is entitled to receive, upon request and free of charge, reasonable access to, and copies of, all documents, records, and other information relevant to the claimant's claim for benefits. Whether a document, record, or other information is relevant to a claim for benefits shall be determined by reference to paragraph (m)(8) of this section;

(4) A statement describing any voluntary appeal procedures offered by the plan and the claimant's right to obtain the information about such procedures described in paragraph (c)(3)(iv) of this section, and a statement of the claimant's right to bring an action under section 502(a) of the Act; and

(5) In the case of a group health plan or a plan providing disability benefits—

(i) If an internal rule, guideline, protocol, or other similar criterion was relied upon in making the adverse determination, either the specific rule, guideline, protocol, or other similar criterion; or a statement that such rule, guideline, protocol, other similar criterion was relied upon in making the adverse determination and that a copy of the rule, guideline, protocol, or other similar criterion will be provided free of charge to the claimant upon request;

(ii) If the adverse benefit determination is based on a medical necessity or experimental treatment or similar exclusion or limit, either an explanation of the scientific or clinical judgment for the determination, applying the terms of the plan to the claimant's medical circumstances, or a statement that such explanation will be provided free of charge upon request; and

(iii) The following statement: "You and your plan may have other voluntary alternative dispute resolution options, such as mediation. One way to find out what may be available is to contact your local U.S. Department of Labor Office and your State insurance regulatory agency."

(k) Preemption of State law. (1) Nothing in this section shall be construed to supersede any provision of State law that regulates insurance, except to the extent that such law prevents the application of a requirement of this section.

(2)(i) For purposes of paragraph (k)(1) of this section, a State law regulating insurance shall not be considered to prevent the application of a requirement of this section merely because such State law establishes a review procedure to evaluate and resolve disputes involving adverse benefit determinations under group health plans so long as the review procedure is conducted by a person or entity other than the insurer, the plan, plan fiduciaries, the employer, or any employee or agent of any of the foregoing.

(ii) The State law procedures described in paragraph (k)(2)(i) of this section are not part of the full and fair review required by section 503 of the Act. Claimants therefore need not exhaust such State law procedures prior to bringing suit under section 502(a) of the Act.

(l) Failure to establish and follow reasonable claims procedures. In the case of the failure of a plan to establish or follow claims procedures consistent with the requirements of this section, a claimant shall be deemed to have exhausted the administrative remedies available under the plan and shall be entitled to pursue any available remedies under section 502(a) of the Act on the basis that the plan has failed to provide a reasonable claims procedure that would yield a decision on the merits of the claim.

(m) Definitions. The following terms shall have the meaning ascribed to such terms in this paragraph (m) whenever such term is used in this section:

(1)(i) A "claim involving urgent care" is any claim for medical care or treatment with respect to which the application of the time periods for making non-urgent care determinations—

(A) Could seriously jeopardize the life or health of the claimant or the ability of the claimant to regain maximum function, or,

(B) In the opinion of a physician with knowledge of the claimant's medical condition, would subject the claimant to severe pain that cannot be adequately managed without the care or treatment that is the subject of the claim.

(ii) Except as provided in paragraph (m)(1)(iii) of this section, whether a claim is a "claim involving urgent care" within the meaning of paragraph (m)(1)(i)(A) of this section is to be determined by an individual acting on behalf of the plan applying the judgment of a prudent layperson who possesses an average knowledge of health and medicine.

(iii) Any claim that a physician with knowledge of the claimant's medical condition determines is a "claim involving urgent care" within the meaning of paragraph (m)(1)(i) of this section shall be treated as a "claim involving urgent care" for purposes of this section.

(2) The term "pre-service claim" means any claim for a benefit under a group health plan with respect to which the terms of the plan condition receipt of

the benefit, in whole or in part, on approval of the benefit in advance of obtaining medical care.

(3) The term "post-service claim" means any claim for a benefit under a group health plan that is not a pre-service claim within the meaning of paragraph (m)(2) of this section.

(4) The term "adverse benefit determination" means any of the following: a denial, reduction, or termination of, or a failure to provide or make payment (in whole or in part) for, a benefit, including any such denial, reduction, termination, or failure to provide or make payment that is based on a determination of a participant's or beneficiary's eligibility to participate in a plan, and including, with respect to group health plans, a denial, reduction, or termination of, or a failure to provide or make payment (in whole or in part) for, a benefit resulting from the application of any utilization review, as well as a failure to cover an item or service for which benefits are otherwise provided because it is determined to be experimental or investigational or not medically necessary or appropriate.

(5) The term "notice" or "notification" means the delivery or furnishing of information to an individual in a manner that satisfies the standards of 29 C.F.R. 2520.104b-1(b) as appropriate with respect to material required to be furnished or made available to an individual.

(6) The term "group health plan" means an employee welfare benefit plan within the meaning of section 3(1) of the Act to the extent that such plan provides "medical care" within the meaning of section 733(a) of the Act.

(7) The term "health care professional" means a physician or other health care professional licensed, accredited, or certified to perform specified health services consistent with State law.

(8) A document, record, or other information shall be considered "relevant" to a claimant's claim if such document, record, or other information

(i) Was relied upon in making the benefit determination;

(ii) Was submitted, considered, or generated in the course of making the benefit determination, without regard to whether such document, record, or other information was relied upon in making the benefit determination;

(iii) Demonstrates compliance with the administrative processes and safeguards required pursuant to paragraph (b)(5) of this section in making the benefit determination; or

(iv) In the case of a group health plan or a plan providing disability benefits, constitutes a statement of policy or guidance with respect to the plan concerning the denied treatment option or benefit for the claimant's diagnosis, without regard to whether such advice or statement was relied upon in making the benefit determination.

(n) Apprenticeship plans. This section does not apply to employee benefit plans that solely provide apprenticeship training benefits.

(o) Applicability dates. (1) Except as provided in paragraph (o)(2) of this section, this section shall apply to claims filed under a plan on or after January 1, 2002.

(2) This section shall apply to claims filed under a group health plan on or after the first day of the first plan year beginning on or after July 1, 2002, but in no event later than January 1, 2003.

CHAPTER 10

DUAL ELIGIBILITY: ISSUES FOR MEDICARE BENEFICIARIES ALSO ELIGIBLE FOR MEDICAID

§ 10.01 INTRODUCTION

About 10 million older people and people with disabilities are enrolled in both Medicare and some form of Medicaid.[1] These beneficiaries are referred to as "dual eligibles" because of their simultaneous enrollment in Medicare and Medicaid. Their demographic and health utilization characteristics distinguish them from other Medicare beneficiaries. Generally speaking, they are poorer and sicker than the rest of the Medicare population. They use the emergency room more often, and are less likely to have a regular primary care doctor. They were 20 percent of the traditional Medicare population in 2011 (i.e., those not in private Medicare plans) and accounted for 35 percent of traditional Medicare spending;[2] they are 14 percent of the Medicaid population and account for 34 percent of Medicaid expenditures.[3] Dual eligible beneficiaries with full Medicaid and Medicare make up 13 percent of the combined population of Medicare enrollees and aged, blind, or disabled Medicaid enrollees, but they account for 34 percent of the two programs' total spending.[4]

For those eligible for Medicare Parts A and B and for full Medicaid benefits, Medicaid provides wrap-around coverage—operating as a Medigap policy—both by paying some, or all, of the Medicare cost-sharing, and by extending coverage to services not covered by Medicare. These services include non-skilled long-term care and, in some states, vision, dental, and hearing aid coverage. Ironically, entitlement to the benefits of both Medicare and Medicaid can result in less, rather than more, health care. This is due at least in part to confusion that arises, in efforts to coordinate benefits, from statutory and regulatory differences between the two programs. Medicare and Medicaid are programs with different medical necessity definitions, coverage definitions, provider participation requirements, and reimbursement structures.[5]

---

[1] Medicare Payment Advisory Committee (MedPAC) June 2016 Report to Congress *available at* http://medpac.gov/documents/reports/june-2016-report-to-the-congress-medicare-and-the-health-care-delivery-system.pdf (site visited July 6, 2016) (hereinafter *MedPAC June 2016 Report*).

[2] MedPAC and Medicaid and CHIP Payment and Access Commission (MACPAC), *Data Book: Beneficiaries Dually Eligible for Medicare and Medicaid* (Jan. 2016) § 4, Exhibit 4, *available at* http://www.medpac.gov/documents/publications/january-2016-medpac-and-macpac-data-book-beneficiaries-dually-eligible-for-medicare-and-medicaid.pdf?sfvrsn=0 (site visited June 26, 2015) (hereinafter *MedPAC 2015 Data Book*).

[3] Katherine Young et al., "Medicaid's Role for Dual Eligible Beneficiaries" (using 2010 data), Kaiser Commission on Medicaid and the Uninsured (Aug. 2013), *available at* http://kaiserfamilyfoundation.files.wordpress.com/2013/08/7846-04-medicaids-role-for-dual-eligible-beneficiaries.pdf (site visited June 8, 2016) (hereinafter *Medicaid's Role for Dual Eligibles*).

[4] The Congressional Budget Office (CBO), "Dual-Eligible Beneficiaries of Medicare and Medicaid: Characteristics, Health Care Spending, and Evolving Policies" (June 2013), *available at* https://www.cbo.gov/sites/default/files/113th-congress-2013-2014/reports/44308_DualEligibles2.pdf (site visited June 8, 2016) (hereinafter *CBO Dual-Eligible Beneficiaries*).

[5] MMCO, created by the Patient Protection and Affordable Care Act of 2010 (PPACA, or the Affordable Care Act (ACA)), Pub. L. No. 111-148, solicited comments on a document it created

For those dually eligible who are entitled to full Medicaid benefits, Medicaid is the payer of last resort. Generally, in traditional Medicare, this means that Medicare determines the allowable amount, pays its portion, and then sends the remainder of the bill to Medicaid to pay the balance. However, when the Medicare allowable amount is either more or less than the Medicaid reimbursement for the same service, when the definition of the covered service differs, or when the Medicare beneficiary is enrolled in a private Medicare plan, administrative and other complications can result in the beneficiary's being denied access to care or delays in care.

Prior to January 1, 2006, when Part D took effect, Medicaid also provided prescription drug coverage for dual eligibles since, prior to that date, Medicare provided only very limited drug coverage. Effective January 1, 2006, dually eligible beneficiaries were no longer eligible for prescription drug coverage under Medicaid.[6] They are entitled to Medicare Part D prescription drug coverage and are automatically enrolled in a Part D plan if they do not choose a plan on their own.[7] This coverage change, including automatic qualification of the federal subsidy to help pay for prescription drug costs, is discussed in detail in **Chapter 11,** Prescription Drug Coverage.

The high utilization of health care by, and high levels of spending for, dual eligibles make them a bright target for policy discussion and policy initiatives. There is widespread, but unsubstantiated, belief among policy makers and pundits that dual eligibles' needs can be met at lower cost to public programs.[8] Concomitantly, many believe, with some justification, that the quality of care for those beneficiaries who are dually eligible can be improved by greater care coordination, reduction in duplication of tests, and improved medication management, all of which may result in reduced use of hospitals, emergency rooms, and nursing facilities. The Affordable Care Act (ACA) created an Office for Dual Eligibles (formally called the Medicare and Medicaid Coordination Office) and the

identifying various aspects of Medicare and Medicaid that are misaligned such that they cause difficulties for dual eligibles seeking health care. *See* Medicare and Medicaid Programs: Opportunities for Alignment in Medicaid and Medicare, 76 Fed. Reg. 94, pp. 28196 *et seq.* (May 16, 2011). *See* http://www.cms.gov/Medicare-Medicaid-Coordination/Medicare-and-Medicaid-Coordination/Medicare-Medicaid-Coordination-Office/AlignmentInitiative.html for more information on the Alignment Initiative, including comments on the MMCO document (site visited June 8, 2016).

[6] 42 U.S.C. § 1396u-5(d)(1).

[7] 42 U.S.C. § 1396u-5(c)(6).

[8] The Kaiser Family Foundation, "Best Bets for Reducing Medicare Costs for Dual Eligible Beneficiaries: Assessing the Evidence" (Sept. 19, 2014), *available at* http://kff.org/health-reform/report/best-bets-for-reducing-medicare-costs-for-duals/ (site visited June 8, 2016); Centers for Medicare & Medicaid Services (CMS), "Cost Drivers for Dually Eligible Beneficiaries: Potentially Avoidable Hospitalizations from Nursing Facility, Skilled Nursing Facility, and Home and Community-Based Services Waiver Programs" (Aug. 2010), *available at* https://www.cms.gov/Research-Statistics-Data-and-Systems/Statistics-Trends-and-Reports/Reports/downloads/costdriverstask2.pdf (site visited June 8, 2016).

Center for Medicare and Medicaid Innovation, both of which have focused considerable attention on this population in the past several years. As a result, in many states great changes are underway in the financing and delivery of care for people with Medicare and Medicaid. These changes are discussed in greater detail in **§ 10.09** of this chapter.

This chapter discusses and analyzes issues that affect dually eligible individuals. These issues will continue to affect at least the population in states that are not moving forward to create new delivery systems; some issues will remain alive even in states with new programs. New issues will also arise as the new programs are implemented. In addition, this chapter includes descriptions of Medicaid eligibility and services as they pertain to Medicare beneficiaries.

§ 10.02 PROFILE OF THE DUALLY ELIGIBLE

[A] Demographic Data

Those dually eligible for Medicare and Medicaid are a heterogeneous population. However, some general comparisons with Medicare-only beneficiaries are illustrative. Compared with other Medicare beneficiaries, those who are dually eligible are younger, poorer, more often minorities, disproportionately women, more likely to never have been married, and much more likely to be in an institution.[9] They are considerably less well educated.[10]

- *Younger.* Forty-three percent are under 65, compared with 13 percent of non-dually eligible beneficiaries.
- *Health status.* Nineteen percent of dually eligible beneficiaries reported being in poor health, compared to 7 percent of non-dually eligible beneficiaries, and dually eligible beneficiaries have greater limitations in activities of daily living.
- *Poorer.* In 2012, 61 percent lived below the federal poverty level, and 94 percent lived below 200 percent of the poverty level.

[9] The Kaiser Family Foundation, "Faces of Dually Eligible Beneficiaries: Profiles of People with Medicare and Medicaid Coverage" (July 3, 2013), *available at* https://kaiserfamilyfoundation.files.wordpress.com/2013/07/8446-faces-of-dually-eligible-beneficiaries1.pdf (site visited June 8, 2016).

[10] MedPAC 2016 Data Book, *available at* http://www.medpac.gov/docs/default-source/data-book/june-2016-data-book-health-care-spending-and-the-medicare-program.pdf?sfvrsn=0 (June 2016) (site visited Sept. 7, 2016). *See also* The Medicare-Medicaid Coordination Office (MMCO), CMS, "Data Analysis Brief Medicare-Medicaid Dual Enrollment from 2006 Through 2013" (Dec. 2014), *available at* https://www.cms.gov/Medicare-Medicaid-Coordination/Medicare-and-Medicaid-Coordination/Medicare-Medicaid-Coordination-Office/Downloads/DualEnrollment20062013.pdf (site visited June 8, 2016) (hereinafter *Dual Enrollment Data Analysis Brief*).

- *Ethnic and racial status and gender.* Dually eligible beneficiaries are more likely to be female and more likely to be African American or Hispanic.
- *Educational status.* Close to half of the dually eligible population lacks a high school diploma.
- *More likely to be in an institution.* They are more likely, 17 percent compared to 2 percent, to be in an institution than non-dually eligible Medicare beneficiaries.[11]
- *Health expenditures.* In 2012, $30,619 was spent per dually eligible beneficiary, and $15,583 was spent per non-dually eligible beneficiary.

[B] Health and Functional Status of the Dually Eligible

Compared with other Medicare beneficiaries, dually eligible beneficiaries are more likely to need help with activities of daily living (ADLs), have significantly worse self-reported health status, are more likely to have chronic or serious medical conditions, and are more likely to have cognitive impairments.[12]

- *ADLs.* Thirty-five percent had difficulty with three to six ADLs, compared to 12 percent of non-dually eligible Medicare beneficiaries.
- *Self-reported health status.* They are almost three times more likely to self-report poor health.
- *Chronic or serious medical conditions.* They are more likely to have a stroke, diabetes, and other chronic conditions, especially those who are elderly dual eligibles. They are twice as likely to be diagnosed with three or more chronic conditions.
- *Cognitive impairments.* They are more than twice as likely to have mental illness, mental retardation, or dementia.

[11] Institutionalization, in fact, is likely to *create* dual eligibility, since it is the most common path to Medicaid eligibility for older people. That is to say, people become eligible for Medicaid because the cost of nursing home care far exceeds their income and thus uses up their resources, so, in the parlance of the Medicaid program, they become "medically needy."

[12] These data are taken from MedPAC 2016 Data Book, *available at* http://www.medpac.gov/docs/default-source/data-book/june-2016-data-book-health-care-spending-and-the-medicare-program.pdf?sfvrsn=0 (June 2016) (site visited Sept. 7, 2016). *See Medicaid's Role for Dual Eligibles* and The Kaiser Family Foundation, "Dual Eligibles: Medicaid's Role for Low-Income Medicare Beneficiaries" (May 2011), *available at* https://kaiserfamilyfoundation.files.wordpress.com/2013/01/4091-08.pdf (site visited June 8, 2016); *See also CBO Dual Eligible Beneficiaries.*

§ 10.03 SUMMARY OF MEDICAID ELIGIBILITY AND MEDICAID BENEFITS

Unlike Medicare, Medicaid is a needs-based program, which means all those who receive benefits do so by virtue of having very low incomes or very high medical bills. The ACA substantially changed the structure of the Medicaid program.[13] To qualify for Medicaid prior to health reform, individuals had to meet financial eligibility criteria *and* belong to one of the following specific groups: children, parents, pregnant women, people with a severe disability, seniors, and people in institutions like nursing homes.[14] Additionally, states were required to provide Medicare cost-sharing coverage for poor Medicare beneficiaries called qualified Medicare beneficiaries (QMBs) and premium payments for near-poor Medicare beneficiaries called specified low-income Medicare beneficiaries (SLMBs),[15] qualified disabled and working individuals (QDWIs),[16] and qualified individuals (QIs) under their Medicaid programs.[17] Collectively, these programs are known as the Medicare Savings Programs (MSPs) (not to be confused with the same acronym for "Medicare Secondary Payer," discussed in **Chapter 9**).

For those under 65, non-disabled adults without dependent children were generally excluded from Medicaid unless the state obtained a waiver to cover them.[18] The ACA expanded Medicaid, in the states that have adopted Medicaid expansion,[19] to nearly all people between 19 and 65 who are not eligible for Medicare and have incomes at or below 133 percent of the federal poverty level

---

[13] Although the law as it was passed by Congress mandated all states expand Medicaid to persons below 133 percent of poverty, the Supreme Court ruled in National Federation of Independent Business v. Sebelius, 576 U.S. 1 (2012), that mandatory Medicaid expansion was unconstitutionally coercive. As a result, states have the option to expand their Medicaid program to all persons under 133 percent of FPL. As of June 8, 2016, 32 states and the District of Columbia had adopted Medicaid expansion.

Nineteen states have chosen *not* to expand Medicaid. *See generally* Kaiser Family Foundation, "Status of State Action on the Medicaid Expansion Decision," *available at* http://kff.org/health-reform/state-indicator/state-activity-around-expanding-medicaid-under-the-affordable-care-act/ (site visited June 8, 2016).

[14] ACA § 2001, amending § 1902(a)(10(A)(i) of the Social Security Act, 42 U.S.C. § 1396a(a)(10)(A)(i).

[15] *See* **§ 10.04[B]** of this Handbook.

[16] *See* **§ 10.04[D][2]** of this Handbook.

[17] *See* **§ 10.04[D][1]** of this Handbook. For this group, coverage need only be provided up to the limit of the state's block grant. Authorization for the qualified individual (QI) program was made permanent in April 2015 through the Medicare Access and CHIP Reauthorization Act of 2015 (MACRA), Pub. L. No. 114-10 (Apr. 16, 2015).

[18] States generally pursued this Medicaid through the § 1115 waiver process; § 1115 of the Social Security Act, 42 U.S.C. § 1315.

[19] Kaiser Family Foundation, "Status of State Action on the Medicaid Expansion Decision," *available at* http://kff.org/health-reform/state-indicator/state-activity-around-expanding-medicaid-under-the-affordable-care-act/ (site visited June 8, 2016). As of June 8, 2016, 32 states and the District of Columbia had adopted Medicaid expansion.

(FPL).[20] For this "newly eligible" population, income eligibility is determined based on modified adjusted gross income (MAGI).[21] Reference to MAGI replaces the system of income exclusion and disregards based on the SSI program.[22] Moreover, no asset test is applied to this "newly eligible" adult population.[23]

Categories of eligibility that predated the ACA remain with the old eligibility rules. For people with Medicare, eligibility for Medicaid and the MSP will still adhere to the old, SSI-based income disregard and categorical eligibility system.[24] Income thresholds will continue to be very low (generally around 100 percent of FPL), and an asset test continues to be imposed. For individuals receiving expanded ACA Medicaid who become eligible for Medicare, transitions to Medicare with Medicaid for the aged, blind, and disabled or to Medicare with an MSP can prove problematic.

The disconnect in eligibility rules for those with Medicaid and Medicare, as opposed to those receiving expanded Medicaid, can have profound effects on individuals as they become eligible for Medicare. These individuals are subject to generally lower poverty levels against which their income is measured, to different ways of measuring the income, and to asset tests that otherwise do not apply in expanded Medicaid.[25]

Most Medicare beneficiaries who qualify for Medicaid will do so under pre-ACA aged, blind, and disabled categories. The broad category of aged, blind, and disabled can be further segmented into the following subgroups:

---

[20] Some sources state that the new minimum Medicaid eligibility threshold is 133 percent FPL; other sources state it is 138 percent. Both are correct. The text of the ACA says 133 percent, but the law also calls for a new methodology of calculating income, which makes the effective minimum threshold 138 percent.

[21] ACA § 2002, amending § 1902(e) of the Social Security Act (42 U.S.C. § 1396a(e)).

[22] ACA § 2002, amending § 1902(e) of the Social Security Act (42 U.S.C. § 1396a(e)).

[23] ACA § 2002, amending § 1902(e) of the Social Security Act (42 U.S.C. § 1396a(e)).

[24] This methodology allows a disregard of $20 per month of income from any source, as well as a disregard of the first $65 per month of earned income, plus one-half the remainder. Other disregards are available for individuals with specific circumstances, such as amounts set aside in a plan for achieving self-support. Certain resources are excluded from consideration, including the homestead, personal possessions, a car, a burial plot, a separate burial fund, and a very limited amount of life insurance. States may use methodologies for determining Medicaid and MSP eligibility that are more generous than SSI's, but not less generous.

[25] *See* discussion at **§ 10.06[A]** of this Handbook. *See also* Ilene Stein & Joe Baker, "A Bridge to Health," The Medicare Rights Center (Jan. 2013), *available at* http://www.medicarerights.org/a-bridge-to-health (site visited June 8, 2016). *See also* "AHIP Proposal: Achieving Medicare/Medicaid Integration for Dually Eligible Beneficiaries" (Oct. 2011), *available at* https://kaiserhealthnews.files.wordpress.com/2011/11/dual-eligibles-proposal.pdf (site visited June 9, 2016), *and* Congressional Budget Office, *Dual-Eligible Beneficiaries of Medicare and Medicaid: Characteristics, Health Care Spending, and Evolving Policies* (June 2013), *available at* http://www.cbo.gov/sites/default/files/cbofiles/attachments/44308_DualEligibles2.pdf (site visited June 8, 2016).

1. Individuals who receive SSI or a mandatory state supplement to SSI;[26]
2. Individuals who formerly received SSI and are qualified severely impaired individuals, as defined by law, who qualify for SSI if their earnings are not counted;[27] and
3. Individuals who formerly received SSI and are in one of several categories of people deemed to receive SSI in order to ensure continued Medicaid coverage.[28]

Generally speaking, each of these three paths to Medicaid eligibility must be included in a state's Medicaid program; individuals in these categories are referred to as mandatory categorically eligible.[29] In addition, states have the option of choosing to cover other groups of aged, blind, or disabled individuals:

---

[26] 42 U.S.C. § 1396a(a)(10)(A)(i)(II); 42 U.S.C. § 1396a note referring to § 13(c) of Pub. L. No. 93-233. Individuals are entitled to a mandatory state supplement if they were receiving supplemental assistance from their state prior to the start of the federal Supplemental Security Income (SSI) program. The provision was intended to ensure that such individuals did not receive less assistance under SSI than they had previously received through their state program.

[27] 42 U.S.C. § 1396d(q).

[28] These are "Pickle people," who have received SSI in the past and who would continue to be eligible for SSI but for cost-of-living increases in Title II in 1977 and thereafter, 42 U.S.C. § 1396a note; "Kennelly Widows," who are widows and widowers between age 60 and age 65 who lose SSI due to eligibility for early widows' benefits under the Social Security survivors program and are considered to be receiving SSI for Medicaid eligibility purposes until they are entitled to Medicare at age 65, 42 U.S.C. § 1383c(d); disabled adult children (DACs) who are individuals age 18 and over who had received SSI based on a disability that began before age 22 and who subsequently became eligible for children's benefits under Title II. They are deemed eligible for SSI for Medicaid purposes. 42 U.S.C. § 1383c(c). A fourth category of "deemed SSI recipients" are children who lost SSI due to a change in eligibility rules in the 1996 welfare law. These children are unlikely to be Medicare beneficiaries and therefore are unlikely to be dually eligible.

[29] The exception to coverage of these otherwise mandatory categories is for states that have chosen the so-called 209(b) option. This option, named for the section of the public law in which it was enacted, is set out at 42 U.S.C. § 1396a(f). It permits states to use more restrictive eligibility rules, if they expressly choose to do so. When Congress enacted the all-federal SSI program, replacing federal-state programs of aid to the aged, blind, and disabled, it provided states with an option to otherwise mandatory Medicaid coverage: they may establish eligibility standards in their Medicaid program that are more restrictive than SSI's, but no more restrictive than the eligibility rules that were in effect in the state in January 1972. Congress provided this option to encourage states that would have had dramatic increases in their Medicaid populations due to the higher SSI standards not to drop out of Medicaid altogether. Ten states currently use this option: Connecticut, Hawaii, Illinois, Minnesota, Missouri, New Hampshire, North Dakota, Ohio, Oklahoma, and Virginia. According to a 2016 Kasier Family Foundation Report, two of these states (Connecticut and Ohio) use Section 209(b) to apply more restrictive income eligibility limits than the federal SSI rules, although Connecticut also uses a more generous income disregard than the federal SSI general income disregard ($337 vs. $20) Kaiser Family Foundation, "Medicaid Financial Eligibility for Seniors and People with Disabilities in 2015," *available at* http://kff.org/report-section/medicaid-financial-eligibility-for-seniors-and-people-with-disabilities-in-2015-report/ "site visited Sept. 26, 2016).

1. Individuals who are eligible for, but not receiving, SSI or an optional state supplement.[30]
2. Individuals who have been in an institution for 30 days and who meet an income standard set by the state equal to or less than 300 percent of the SSI federal benefit rate.[31]
3. Individuals who receive home- and community-based services under a waiver of certain Medicaid requirements[32] or under a State Plan Amendment as authorized by the Deficit Reduction Act of 2005 (DRA).[33]
4. Individuals who would be eligible if they were in an institution, who are terminally ill, and who receive only hospice care.[34]
5. Individuals who receive an optional state supplement to SSI.[35]
6. Individuals who are aged or disabled with income under 100 percent of the FPL.[36]
7. Individuals who are aged, blind, or disabled and are "medically needy" due to high medical bills.[37] Individuals in this group must show incurred or paid medical expenses that, when deducted from their income, reduce their income to an amount called the medically needy income level (MNIL), which is often substantially below the SSI benefit rate.[38] The

[30] 42 U.S.C. § 1396a(a)(10)(A)(ii)(I).

[31] 42 U.S.C. § 1396a(a)(10)(A)(ii)(V). Identifying states that have chosen this option is more difficult than one would think. For reasons unfathomable to the authors, every reliable source of information on this subject lists the states somewhat differently. *See* http://www.elderlawanswers.com/how-does-medicaid-treat-income-12017 (site visited June 8, 2016). The harsh effect of an income cap that precludes eligibility of someone even one dollar above the cap has been mitigated by amendments to federal Medicaid law that allow individuals in states with the income cap category and no medically needy program to create a trust (known as a Miller Trust) for their excess income that allows that income to be excluded in determining Medicaid eligibility. *See* 42 U.S.C. § 1396p(d)(4)(B). Additional information is available through the Kaiser Family Foundation at https://kaiserfamilyfoundation.files.wordpress.com/2013/01/8048.pdf (site visited June 8, 2016). According to the website, states with no medically needy program are Alabama, Alaska, Colorado, Delaware, Idaho, Indiana, Mississippi, Missouri, Nevada, New Mexico, Ohio, Oklahoma, Oregon, South Carolina, South Dakota, Texas, and Wyoming. Arizona has a program that is comparable to the medically needy program.

[32] 42 U.S.C. § 1396a(a)(10)(A)(ii)(VI).

[33] The Deficit Reduction Act of 2005 (DRA), Pub. L. No. 109-171 (Feb. 8, 2006), § 6086 amending 42 U.S.C. § 1396n by adding subsection (i).

[34] 42 U.S.C. § 1396a(a)(10)(A)(ii)(VII).

[35] 42 U.S.C. § 1396a(a)(10)(A)(ii)(XI).

[36] 42 U.S.C. § 1396a(a)(10)(A)(ii)(X), referring to § 1396a(m)(1).

[37] 42 U.S.C. § 1396a(a)(10)(C), referring to 42 U.S.C. § 1396d(a).

[38] The medically needy income level (MNIL) has been limited for years by statutory language that prohibits federal Medicaid payments for people with incomes in excess of 133 1/3 percent of the state's standard for a family receiving Aid to Families with Dependent Children (AFDC). 42

amount of incurred or paid medical expense they must document is referred to as their "spend-down."

Individuals in groups 1 through 6 are referred to as the Optional Categorically Needy; individuals in group 7 are referred to as the Medically Needy.

States are required to provide certain services to the Mandatory and Optional Categorically Needy and have the option of including other services. Required Medicaid services are:

- Inpatient hospital services;
- Outpatient hospital services;
- Laboratory and x-ray services;
- Nursing facility services for people age 21 or over;
- Early and periodic screening, diagnosis, and treatment for people under 21;
- Family planning services and supplies for individuals of child-bearing age;
- Physicians' services and some dental services;
- Midwife services;
- Services furnished by certain certified nurse practitioners; and
- Home health services for people entitled to nursing facility services.[39]

Optional services include:

- Prescription drugs (but not after December 31, 2005, for the dually eligible);
- Physical therapy;
- Occupational therapy;

U.S.C. § 1396b(f). This standard, in most states, was substantially below federal poverty levels and even below the SSI level, which is 75 percent of the poverty level. Although AFDC was repealed in 1996 and replaced with a block grant called Temporary Assistance for Needy Families, the old AFDC standard, indexed for inflation, is still used. A separate statutory provision, at 42 U.S.C. § 1396a(r)(2), permits states to use methodologies for determining eligibility for Medicaid that are less restrictive than the income program they relate to, but not more restrictive. The Health Care Financing Administration (HCFA), then the name of the federal agency that administers Medicare and Medicaid (now CMS), interpreted that provision as being circumscribed by the payment limit provision. An amendment to the regulation at 42 C.F.R. § 435.1007 that became effective August 4, 2001, changes that interpretation to allow states to apply their less restrictive methodologies to income *before* measuring it against the payment limit. 66 Fed. Reg. 33,810 (June 25, 2001).

[39] 42 U.S.C. § 1396a(a)(10)(D), referring to 42 U.S.C. § 1396d(a).

- Dentures;
- Prosthetic devices;
- Eyeglasses;
- Personal care;
- Home and community-based attendant services and supports (effective October 1, 2011);[40]
- Podiatry;
- Optometry;
- Transportation; and
- Long-term care support and services provided under a home and community-based services waiver or, with limitations, as an optional service.

Generally speaking, when a state offers an optional service to one group of Optional Categorically Needy individuals, it must offer the same service to all groups.[41] The state does not have to offer all services to the Medically Needy.

Because Medicare is the primary payer for those who are dually eligible, some Medicaid services are more important to these beneficiaries than others. For example, a significant Medicaid service for this population is non-skilled long-term care, both in an institution and in the community. It is, therefore, extremely useful to low-income Medicare beneficiaries to qualify for full Medicaid benefits in addition to assistance with Medicare cost-sharing.

§ 10.04 UNIVERSE OF DUAL ELIGIBILITY

[A] Categories of Dually Eligible Individuals[42]

The term "dually eligible" is used differently depending on the setting or situation. Dual eligibles comprise three primary subgroups of low-income Medicare beneficiaries:

[40] ACA § 2401, amending § 1915 of the Social Security Act (42 U.S.C. 1396n), as amended by Health Care and Education Reconciliation Act of 2010 (HCERA), Pub. L. No. 111-152 (Mar. 30, 2010), § 1205.

[41] 42 U.S.C. § 1396a(a)(10)(B)(i) (services shall be not less in amount, duration, and scope than those available to other categorically needy groups); 42 C.F.R. § 440.240(b). *But see* DRA § 6044 that allows states to establish specific benefit packages for specific groups of people. Dual eligibles are exempt from coverage under this new option.

[42] CMS describes dual eligible categories at http://www.cms.gov/MLNProducts/downloads/Medicare_Beneficiaries_Dual_Eligibles_At_a_Glance.pdf (site visited June 8, 2016).

1. QMBs or SLMBs with full Medicaid benefits and all or some Medicare cost-sharing (QMB-plus or SLMB-plus) or QMBs or SLMBs with all or some Medicare cost-sharing assistance but without any additional Medicaid coverage (QMB-only or SLMB-only);
2. Individuals with full Medicaid benefits but not Medicare cost-sharing as QMBs or SLMBs;
3. Individuals entitled to Medicaid benefits only to pay for Medicare premiums, with no additional Medicaid coverage for other Medicare out-of-pocket costs, and without full Medicaid benefits. This category comprises two groups, in addition to the SLMB-only named above:
   a. QIs[43]
   b. QDWIs[44]

It is useful to understand that the Medicare Prescription Drug, Improvement, and Modernization Act of 2003 (MMA)[45] uses a different nomenclature for dual eligibles. It refers to "full benefit dual eligibles" and defines those people as Medicare beneficiaries entitled to full Medicaid benefits.[46] This definition excludes those in group 3 above, as well as those in group 1 who receive assistance only with Medicare cost-sharing. In this chapter, we will clearly label the groups or subgroups to which we are referring in the various sections.

[B] QMB or SLMB with Full Medicaid Benefits and Medicare Cost-Sharing (QMB/SLMB-Plus) or with Only Medicare Cost-Sharing Assistance (QMB/SLMB-Only)

For 2016, a QMB is an aged or disabled individual with Medicare Part A, whose countable income is at or below the federal poverty level and whose countable resources do not exceed $7,280 for one person and $10,930 for a married

[43] *See* § **10.04[D][1]** of this Handbook. For this group, coverage need only be provided up to the limit of the state's block grant. MACRA makes the QI program permanent, rather than subject to periodic reauthorization tied to Medicare physician payment, as was the case for many years.

[44] QDWI enrollment was estimated to be fewer than 100 beneficiaries as of 2011. Medicaid and CHIP Payment and Access Commission (MACPAC), Report to the Congress on Medicaid and CHIP, Ch. 4, "Medicaid Coverage of Premiums and Cost Sharing for Low-Income Medicare Beneficiaries" (Mar. 2013), *available at* https://www.macpac.gov/wp-content/uploads/2015/01/2013-03-15_MACPAC_Report.pdf (site visited June 8, 2016) (hereinafter *March 2013 MACPAC Report*).

[45] The Medicare Prescription Drug, Improvement, and Modernization Act of 2003 (MMA), Pub. L. No. 108-173 (Dec. 8, 2003), adding 42 U.S.C. §§ 1395w-101 *et seq.* (2008 supplement).

[46] 42 U.S.C. § 1396u-5(c)(6); 42 C.F.R. § 423.902.

couple.[47] The QMB benefit relieves the beneficiary of the cost-sharing that is otherwise imposed on a Medicare beneficiary: the Medicare Part B premium, the Part A premium for voluntary enrollees (i.e., those who do not receive premium-free Part A), and all deductibles and coinsurance imposed under Medicare Part A and Medicare Part B and copayments or other cost-sharing charged by Medicare Advantage (MA) plans. Numerous CMS transmittals over the past 10 years have affirmed this protection[48] A provider is prohibited from billing a QMB for

---

[47] The income eligibility level for 2016 is $1,010 per month for an individual in the 48 states and slightly higher for those in Alaska and Hawaii. The amount includes a $20-per-month federally mandated income disregard that is available to all applicants. In addition to the $20, states must disregard a portion of earned income and may disregard other income, effectively expanding coverage. Likewise, they may offer more generous resource exclusions than federal law requires. About 40 states have some provision for MSP populations that is more generous than the federal rules. Income Poverty Guidelines are published each year between January and March by the Department of Health and Human Services (HHS). The asset test for QMB, SLMB, and QI was changed, effective 2010, to conform to the asset test for Part D full low-income subsidy, found at 42 U.S.C. § 1395w-114(a)(3)(D). MIPPA § 112. For 2016 numbers, see http://www.medicare.gov/your-medicare-costs/help-paying-costs/medicare-savings-program/medicare-savings-programs.html (site visited June 8, 2016).

To review income and resource limits for 2016 for the QMB, SLMB, and QI Medicare Savings Programs and for the QDWI program, see http://www.medicare.gov/your-medicare-costs/help-paying-costs/medicare-savings-program/medicare-savings-programs.html (site visited June 8, 2016). Please check the Medicare.gov site periodically for 2017 updates.

[48] 42 U.S.C. §§ 1396d(p)(3), 1396a(n)(2); State Medicaid Manual (hereinafter SMM), CMS Pub. 45, Ch. 3, Eligibility § 3490.12, *see* **Appendix 10-1** of this Handbook. *See also* MMCO-CMCS Informational Bulletin, June 7, 2013, Subject: Payment of Medicare Cost Sharing for Qualified Medicare Beneficiaries (QMBs), *available at* http://www.medicaid.gov/Federal-Policy-Guidance/downloads/CIB-06-07-2013.pdf (site visited June 8, 2016); MMCO-CMCS Informational Bulletin, January 6, 2012, Subject: Billing for Services Provided to Qualified Medicare Beneficiaries (QMBs), *available at* http://www.medicaid.gov/federal-policy-guidance/downloads/CIB-01-06-12.pdf (site visited June 8, 2016); CMS MLN Matters, "Prohibition on Balance Billing Qualified Medicare Beneficiaries (QMBs)," *available at* http://www.cms.gov/Outreach-and-Education/Medicare-Learning-Network-MLN/MLNMattersArticles/downloads/SE1128.pdf (site visited June 8, 2016); Memorandum of Feb. 27, 2008 from Gale P. Arden, Director, Disabled and Elderly Health Programs Group (DEHPG) to All Associate Regional Administrators, Division of Medicaid and Children's Health, Subject: Medicare Cost Sharing for Medicaid Beneficiaries (hereinafter *Feb. 2008 Memo*) and two attachments, memo *available at* http://www.medicareadvocacy.org/old-site/InfoByTopic/MedicareSavingsPrograms/MedSavProg_08_04.24.ARACostShare.pdf, Balance Billing attachment *available at* http://www.medicareadvocacy.org/old-site/InfoByTopic/MedicareSavingsPrograms/MedSavProg_08_04.24.ARABalanceBilling.pdf, and Capitation attachment *available at* http://www.medicareadvocacy.org/old-site/InfoByTopic/MedicareSavingsPrograms/MedSavProg_08_04.24.ARACapitation.pdf (sites visited June 8, 2016); Memorandum of Nov. 22, 1991, from Director, Office of Medicaid Management, MB, to Deputy Chief Counsel, Office of General Counsel, Subject: State Requirement to Pay Premiums for Qualified Medicare Beneficiaries (QMB)—ACTION (hereinafter *Nov. 1991 Memo*) (**Appendix 10-2**); Memorandum of June 11, 2007, "Cost Sharing for Medicare Advantage Plans," CMS/CMSO/DEHPG/DEEO and Attachment (hereinafter *June 2007 Memo*) (**Appendix 10-3** of this Handbook); and Memorandum of Jan. 6,

Medicare Part A or B deductibles or coinsurance.[49] States have the option of paying premiums or enrollment fees charged by MA plans.[50] In essence, the QMB benefit operates like a basic Medicare supplemental health insurance policy (often called a "Medigap" policy). QMB coverage can save a recipient hundreds or even thousands of dollars each year.[51] Moreover, since all forms of dual eligibility, including receipt of only an MSP, entitle one to the full Part D low income subsidy (LIS), the value of the benefit is increased by the value of the LIS, estimated by the Social Security Administration (SSA) to be $4,000 in 2016.[52] Unlike virtually all other Medicaid benefits, QMB coverage cannot be granted for months prior to the application.[53] The benefit is available in the first month after the month eligibility is determined.[54] An individual can be eligible for both the QMB benefit and full Medicaid coverage, or for only the QMB benefit. Eighty percent of QMBs qualify for full Medicaid benefits in addition to QMB (QMB-plus).[55]

A SLMB is an individual who would be a QMB but for his or her countable income, which must be between 100 and 120 percent of the federal poverty level.[56] The SLMB benefit is payment by Medicaid of the Medicare Part B premium. Thus, a SLMB does not have the Medicare Part B premium ($109.00 in 2017 for most people) deducted from his or her Social Security or Railroad Retirement check each month. However, unlike the QMB benefit, no additional Medicare cost-sharing is included in the SLMB benefit. A SLMB without full Medicaid coverage should consider the need for a Medicare supplemental (Medigap) policy to cover the costs of other Medicare out-of-pocket expenses, such as copayments and deductibles. SLMB coverage can be granted for up to three

---

2012, from Director, MMCO-CMCS Informational Bulletin Concerning Billing for Services Provided to Qualitied Medicare Beneficiaries (QMBs) (hereinafter January 6, 2012 Memo) (**Appendix 10-4** of this Handbook).

[49] *See* discussion at **§ 10.06[B]** of this Handbook.

[50] 42 U.S.C. §§ 1396d(p)(3) and 1396a(n)(2); SMM, Ch. 3.

[51] Out-of-pocket costs for 2012 averaged $3,564 per Medicare-only beneficiary (without supplemental coverage) who reported fair to poor health. MedPAC June 2016 Data Book ch.3, *available at* http://www.medpac.gov/docs/default-source/data-book/june-2016-data-book-health-care-spending-and-the-medicare-program.pdf?sfvrsn=0 (site visited Sept. 26, 2016). Because dual eligibles are three times more likely than non-dual Medicare beneficiaries to report poor health, this number seems like a reasonable proxy for what can be saved by having access to the QMB benefit.

[52] Social Security Administration (SSA), "Extra Help with Medicare Prescription Drug Plan Costs," *available at* http://www.ssa.gov/prescriptionhelp/ (site visited Nov. 20, 2016). Please check the ssa.gov site periodically for 2017 updates.

[53] 42 U.S.C. § 1396d(a).

[54] 42 U.S.C. § 1396d(a).

[55] *March 2013 MACPAC Report* at 134.

[56] 42 U.S.C. § 1396a(a)(10)(E)(iii). The income eligibility limit for SLMB for 2016 was $1,208 per month for an individual in the 48 states, slightly higher for Alaska and Hawaii. This amount includes the $20 income disregard. For updated information, check http://www.medicare.gov/your-medicare-costs/help-paying-costs/medicare-savings-program/medicare-savings-programs.html #slmb (site visited June 8, 2016).

months prior to the date of application if the individual was eligible during those months.[57] An individual could be eligible for both SLMB benefits and full Medicaid benefits or for only SLMB benefits.

[C] Recipients of Full Medicaid Benefits but Not Full Medicare Cost-Sharing as a QMB

These individuals receive Medicare Part A and/or Medicare Part B, and receive full Medicaid benefits. The group comprises two slightly different populations. First, there are those whose incomes are under 100 percent of the FPL but who do not have Part A premium-free and whose state does not pay their Part A premium for them. The lack of Part A prevents them from being QMBs and thus entitled to full Medicare benefits, which may include better hospitalization, home health, or rehabilitation therapy coverage than they have under their state Medicaid program. The Centers for Medicare & Medicaid Services (CMS) has told states they must purchase Part A for their Medicaid recipients whose income is under 100 percent of the FPL to ensure their enrollment as QMBs.[58] CMS has not, however, enforced this requirement.

The second group comprises those whose income is above 100 percent of the FPL who are precluded from QMB coverage for that reason, even if they have Medicare Part A. Generally, these would be individuals entitled to Medicaid under a special income cap, or as medically needy because they are receiving costly long-term care services. If they are not entitled to payment of their Medicare Part B premium as SLMBs, the state nonetheless has the option of paying their Part B premium.[59] If the state chooses not to pay the Part B premium, it cannot receive its federal share of the Medicaid payment for a Medicaid service that is also covered by Medicare Part B if the individual could have been enrolled in Part B but was not.[60]

[D] Recipients of Medicaid Payments for Medicare Premiums Only

In addition to individuals with SLMB-only eligibility who are entitled to payment only of the Medicare Part B premium, two other groups are entitled to

---

[57] 42 U.S.C. § 1396d(a).

[58] SMM, Ch. 3, § 3490.13. *See* **Appendix 10-1** of this Handbook. *See also* Nov. 1991 Memo (**Appendix 10-2** of this Handbook).

[59] 42 U.S.C. § 1395v authorizes states to enter into "buy-in" agreements with the federal CMS through which states purchase Medicare Part B coverage for Medicaid recipients; 42 U.S.C. § 1395i-2(g) authorizes modifications of such agreements to permit the states also to purchase Part A. *See* 42 C.F.R. § 407.42 for the eligibility groups that states can include in their buy-in agreements and 42 C.F.R. § 431.625 for authorization for states to receive federal matching dollars, known as federal financial participation (FFP) for their buy-in costs.

[60] 42 U.S.C. § 1396b(b)(1), 42 C.F.R. § 431.625(d)(3).

Medicaid payments only for Medicare premiums. To be eligible for either of these benefits, an individual cannot be eligible for full Medicaid benefits.

[1] Qualified Individual

This group comprises individuals with Medicare Part A whose countable income is between 120 percent and 135 percent of poverty and whose countable resources are $7,280 for an individual and $10,930 for a couple in 2015.[61] The benefit for a QI is payment of the Part B premium ($109.00/month in 2017 for most people). Payment is made from a block grant to the state that was authorized to be available from January 1998 through December 2002.[62] After a series of short-term extensions, the benefit was permanently extended in April 2015 through the Medicare Access and CHIP Reauthorization Act of 2015 (MACRA).[63]

Although the QI benefit is the same amount as the SLMB benefit, the difference between the two programs, in addition to the higher income eligibility threshold for QI, is that SLMB is an entitlement for the individual and QI is not. Thus, all individuals who are found eligible for SLMB will receive the benefit; individuals found eligible for QI will receive the benefit only as long as the state still has funds in its block grant. States must pay the benefit on a first-come, first-served basis. While individuals must reapply each year, priority is given to those who received the benefit in the previous year.[64] Recipients are entitled to three months retroactive coverage if they were eligible in the three months prior to their application.[65]

[2] Qualified Disabled and Working Individual

A QDWI is an individual who is disabled and working under a work incentive plan, who has exhausted premium-free Part A coverage (available for a period of

---

[61] 42 U.S.C. § 1396a(a)(10)(E)(iv). The 2016 Federal Poverty Guidelines, 81 Fed. Reg. 4036-37 (Jan. 25, 2016), *available at* http://aspe.hhs.gov/poverty/15poverty.cfm (site visited June 8, 2016). The 2017 Federal Poverty Guidelines were not available at the time of publication.

[62] 42 U.S.C. § 1396u-3.

[63] Pub. L. No. 114-10 (Apr. 16, 2015). HHS issued Notice of Proposed Rulemaking on May 9, 2016, as a first step in implementing certain provisions of MACRA. The proposed rule implements changes through a framework called the Quality Payment Program, which includes two paths: the Merit-based Incentive Payment System (MIPS), and Advanced Alternative Payment Models (APMs). The comment period ended on June 27, 2016. Final regulations were published in the Federal Register on November 4, 2016. Final Rule, 81 FRR 7708, available at https://www.federalregister.gov/documents/2016/11/04/2016-25240/medicare-program-merit-based-incentive-payment-system-mips-and-alternative-payment-model-apm (site visited Nov. 20, 2016).

[64] 42 U.S.C. § 1396u-3(b).

[65] 42 U.S.C. § 1396d.

eight and one-half years, including a trial work period) under such plan, whose countable income is not more than 200 percent of poverty, and whose countable resources are not more than twice those allowed for SSI.[66] Resource limits for the program are $4,000 for one person and $6,000 for a married couple. The benefit for a QDWI is payment for the Medicare Part A premium, not the Part B premium. (A QDWI wanting Part B would have to pay for it him- or herself.) Like the QMB and SLMB benefit, the QDWI benefit is an entitlement, so that anyone found eligible should get the benefit. Like SLMB and QI, QDWI is available up to three months prior to application if the individual was eligible during those months. The QDWI benefit is rarely used. Although it is one of the MSPs, citations to MSPs often refer only to QMB, SLMB, and QI. These three programs are the programs that provide automatic enrollment into the Part D Low-Income Subsidy.

LOW INCOME ASSISTANCE*

Program	Income (FPL)	Assets	Benefit
QMB	Up to 100%	$7,280/$10,930	Part A and B premiums, deductibles; cost-sharing
SLMB	Up to 120%	$7,280/$10,930	Part B premium
QI	Up to 135%	$7,280/$10,930	Part B premium
QDWI	Up to 200%	$4,000/$6,000	Part A premium
LIS/Extra Help	Sliding scale up to 150%	$13,640/$27,250 (updated annually)	Most or all of Part D premium; most drug cost-sharing

* CMS, Medicare Savings Program, *available at* https://www.medicare.gov/your-medicare-costs/help-paying-costs/medicare-savings-program/medicare-savings-programs.html (site visited Jul. 8, 2016).

§ 10.05 ENROLLMENT ISSUES FOR MEDICARE SAVINGS PROGRAMS POPULATION

[A] Overview

MSPs—QMB, SLMB, QI, and QDWI—that pay all or some of the Medicare out-of-pocket costs provide critical links to the health care system for low-income Medicare beneficiaries. Yet, an estimated 67 percent of those eligible for QMB-only benefits and about 87 percent of those eligible for SLMB benefits are

[66] 42 U.S.C. §§ 1396a(a)(10)(E)(ii) and 1396d(s). The 2016 Federal Poverty Guidelines, 81 Fed. Reg. 4036-37 (Jan. 25, 2016), *available at* http://aspe.hhs.gov/poverty/15poverty.cfm (site visited June 8, 2016). The 2017 Federal Poverty Guidelines were not available at the time of publication.

not participating in the programs.[67] A 2002 study estimated that fewer than 19 percent of eligible beneficiaries were enrolled in QI.[68] Barriers to program participation have been exhaustively identified in numerous reports that also include policy and practice recommendations.[69] These barriers to enrollment include:

---

[67] CBO, "A Detailed Description of CBO's Cost Estimate for the Medicare Prescription Drug Benefit" (July 2004), *available at* http://www.cbo.gov/sites/default/files/cbofiles/ftpdocs/56xx/doc5668/07-21-medicare.pdf (site visited June 8, 2016). According to a 2013 GAO report and a 2013 MACPAC report, these 2004 numbers are the most recent available.

[68] Laura Summer & Robert Friedland, "The Role of the Asset Test in Targeting Benefits for Medicare Savings Programs" (Oct. 2002), Center on an Aging Society, Georgetown University, *available at* http://ihcrp.georgetown.edu/agingsociety/pdfs/summer_assettest_579.pdf (site visited June 8, 2016)

[69] Medicare Rights Center, "Streamlining Medicare and QMB Enrollment for New Yorkers: Medicare Part A Buy-in Analysis and Policy Recommendations" (Feb. 2011), *available at* http://www.medicarerights.org/pdf/Part-A-Buy-In-Analysis.pdf (site visited June 8, 2016); National Center for Benefits Outreach and Enrollment, "Express Lane Eligibility: New Strategies for Increasing Enrollment," Issue Brief (June 2009), *available at* http://www.ncoa.org/assets/files/pdf/center-for-benefits/express-lane-eligibility.pdf (site visited June 8, 2016); Robert Wood Johnson Foundation, "State Solutions: An Initiative to Improve Enrollment in Medicare Savings Programs" (Oct. 2009), *available at* http://www.rwjf.org/en/research-publications/find-rwjf-research/2009/10/state-solutions.html (site visited June 8, 2016); MedPAC, "Report to the Congress: Medicare Payment Policy," Ch. 5, (Mar. 2008), *available at* http://www.medpac.gov/documents/reports/mar08_entirereport.pdf (site visited Jul. 8, 2016) (hereinafter *MedPAC Report March 2008*); Jack Ebeler, Paul N. Van de Water, & Cyanne Demchak (eds.), "Improving the Medicare Savings Programs" (2006), National Academy of Social Insurance, *available at* http://www.nasi.org/usr_doc/Improving_the_Medicare_Savings_Programs.pdf (site visited June 8, 2016); P.B. Nemore, J.A. Bender, & W. Kwok, "Toward Making Medicare Work for Low-Income Beneficiaries: A Baseline Comparison of the Part D Low-Income Subsidy and Medicare Savings Programs Eligibility and Enrollment Rules" prepared for the Henry J. Kaiser Family Foundation (Apr. 2006), *available at* http://kff.org/medicare/report/toward-making-medicare-work-for-low-income/ (site visited June 8, 2016); Laura L. Summer & Emily S. Ihara, "Simplifying Enrollment in Medicaid and Medicare Savings Programs for the Elderly and Individuals with Disabilities" (Dec. 2005), Georgetown University Health Policy Institute, *available at* http://assets.aarp.org/rgcenter/health/2005_10_medicaid_msp.pdf (site visited June 8, 2016); Kimberley Fox & Jasmine Sia, "Maximizing Medicare Savings Program Enrollment through Medicare Part D" (May 2005), *available at* www.allhealth.org/briefingmaterials/FacilitatiingEnrollmentinMSP-316.pdf (site visited June 8, 2016) but only an abstract is provided at this time); Alex D. Federman, Bruce C. Vladeck, & Albert L. Siu, *Avoidance of Health Care Services Because of Cost: Impact of the Medicare Savings Program*, Health Affairs 24(1):263-270 (2005), *available at* http://content.healthaffairs.org/cgi/content/abstract/24/1/263 (site visited June 8, 2016); Amy M. Tiedemann & Kimberley Fox, "Promising Strategies for Medicare Savings Program Enrollment: Modifying Eligibility Criteria and Documentation Requirements," prepared for the State Solutions Project (Dec. 2004), *available at* http://www.allhealth.org/briefingmaterials/Promising_Strategies_Brief_2005-312.pdf (site visited June 8, 2016); L. Sue Andersen & William F. Benson, "Medicare Savings Programs Outreach in Housing for Elders," prepared for the State Solutions Project (Sept. 2004); GAO, "Medicare Savings Programs: Results of Social Security Administration's 2002 Outreach to Low-Income Beneficiaries," GAO-04-363 (Mar. 2004), *available at* http://www.gao.gov/new.items/d04363.pdf (site visited June 8, 2016); Center for Medicare Education (CME), "Medicare

- Restrictive asset ceilings used in determining eligibility;
- Lack of effective outreach to program beneficiaries;
- Lack of knowledge of the programs on the part of welfare workers, Social Security employees, and community-based organizations;

Savings Programs: Helping Your Clients Get and Use the Benefits," Vol. 5, No. 3 (2004), *available at* http://www.allhealth.org/briefingmaterials/MSPs-Helpingyourclientsgetandusethebenefits-304.pdf (site visited June 8, 2016); GAO-12-871 (Sept. 2012), *available at* http://www.gao.gov/assets/650/648370.pdf (site visited June 8, 2016); Dalia K. Remler & Sherry A. Glied, *What Other Programs Can Teach Us: Increasing Participation in Health Insurance Programs*, Am. J. Pub. Health (Jan. 2003), *available at* http://www.ajph.org/cgi/reprint/93/1/67.pdf (site visited June 8, 2016); Susan G. Haber et al., "Evaluation of Qualified Medicare Beneficiary (QMB) and Specified Low-Income Medicare Beneficiary (SLMB) Programs" (Oct. 2003), RTI International, *available at* https://www.cms.gov/Research-Statistics-Data-and-Systems/Statistics-Trends-and-Reports/Reports/Downloads/HaberVol1.pdf (site visited June 9, 2016); Kim Glaun, "Medicaid Programs to Assist Low-Income Medicare Beneficiaries: Medicare Savings Programs Case Study Findings," prepared for the KCMU (2002), *available at* https://kaiserfamilyfoundation.files.wordpress.com/2013/01/medicaid-programs-to-assist-low-income-medicare-beneficiaries-medicare-savings-programs-case-study-findings-background-paper.pdf (site visited June 8, 2016); Laura Summer & Robert Friedland, "The Role of the Asset Test in Targeting Benefits for Medicare Savings Programs" (Oct. 2002), Center on an Aging Society, Georgetown University, *available at* http://ihcrp.georgetown.edu/agingsociety/pdfs/summer_assettest_579.pdf (site visited June 8, 2016); Jennifer Weiss, Joe Baker, & Diane Archer, "An Investigative Report on Medicare Savings Programs in New York City: Local Involvement in Federal Programs Impedes Access for People with Low Incomes" (Dec. 2001), Medicare Rights Center, *available at* http://www.medicarerights.org/pdf/Investigative_Report_MSPinNYC.pdf (site visited June 8, 2016); CME, "Increasing Enrollment for the Medicare Savings Programs," Vol. 2, No. 7 (2001), *available at* http://ihcrp.georgetown.edu/agingsociety/pdfs/MedicareSavings.pdf (site visited June 8, 2016); Patricia B. Nemore, "Variations in State Medicaid Buy-in Practices for Low-Income Medicare Beneficiaries: A 1999 Update," (Dec. 1999), Kaiser Family Foundation, available upon request from the Center for Medicare Advocacy (hereinafter *Variations in State Medicaid*); GAO, "Low-Income Medicare Beneficiaries: Further Outreach and Administrative Simplification Could Increase Enrollment," GAO/HEHS-99-61 (Apr. 1999), *available at* http://www.gao.gov/archive/1999/he99061.pdf (site visited June 8, 2016); Margo L. Rosenbach & JoAnn Lamphere, *Bridging the Gaps Between Medicare and Medicaid: The Case of QMBs and SLMBs*, AARP Pub. Pol'y Inst. (Jan. 1999), *available at* http://assets.aarp.org/rgcenter/health/9902_qmbs.pdf (site visited June 9, 2015); Families USA, "Shortchanged: Billions Withheld from Medicare Beneficiaries" (1998), *available at* http://research.policyarchive.org/6354.pdf (site visited June 8, 2016); Patricia B. Nemore, "Variations in State Medicaid Buy-In Practices for Low-Income Medicare Beneficiaries" (Nov. 1997), Kaiser Family Foundation (available for copying from the authors); Peter J. Neumann et al., "Identifying Barriers to Elderly Participation in the Qualified Medicare Beneficiary Program," Final Report submitted to HCFA (1994); GAO, "Medicare and Medicaid—Many Eligible People Not Enrolled in Qualified Medicare Beneficiary Program," GAO/HEHS-94-52 (Jan. 1994), *available at* http://archive.gao.gov/t2pbat4/150626.pdf (site visited June 8, 2016); Families USA, "The Medicare Buy-In: A Promise Unfulfilled" (Mar. 1993); Families USA, "The Medicare Buy-In: Still a Government Secret" (Mar. 1992); Families USA, "The Secret Benefit—The Failure to Provide the Medicare Buy-In to Poor Seniors" (1991) (Families USA reports available for copying from the authors).

- Cumbersome and obstacle-laden enrollment processes that require long waits in welfare offices, face-to-face interviews, and extensive documentation of income and assets; and
- Difficulties with language and transportation.

Some of these problems arise because MSP benefits are disconnected from the Medicare program: instead of applying for Medicare and MSP at the same time and place, an individual must go through the SSA for Medicare, and through the state Medicaid or welfare system for MSP benefits.[70] Other issues arise because MSP benefits are needs-based, requiring people both to disclose information about their income and assets, and to provide documentation to support their disclosures. One barrier was eliminated beginning in 2010: Medicaid estate recovery rules no longer apply to MSP benefits.[71] A second barrier, the application disconnect described above, was addressed in part through a provision in the Medicare Improvements for Patients and Providers Act of 2008 (MIPPA). That provision and several other of the more complex issues are discussed below.

[B] Failure of State Medicaid Systems and Workers to Identify Buy-In Eligibility When Processing Medicaid Applications

State Medicaid agencies are required to operate their programs in a manner consistent with simplicity of administration and in the best interests of recipients.[72] The agency, moreover, must consider the applicant's eligibility for *any* program for which he or she qualifies.[73] Yet, eligibility workers are often unfamiliar with the MSPs, and state Medicaid agencies have failed to institute computer prompts during screening. Because each state's Medicaid program has many paths to eligibility, it is difficult, if not impossible, for an applicant to identify with precision the particular coverage group for which he or she is applying, or should be applying. The applicant is unlikely to ask explicitly to be considered for full Medicaid, for QMB, for SLMB, or for QI, although in some states, the

[70] The Medicare, Medicaid, and SCHIP Benefits Improvement and Protection Act of 2000 (BIPA), Pub. L. No. 106-554 (Dec. 21, 2000), included two provisions attempting to address enrollment difficulties experienced by those eligible for MSPs. One provision requires the Secretary of HHS to create a single simplified application form for MSP benefits that states may adopt if they choose. BIPA § 709. This application form is available at http://www.ssa.gov/prescriptionhelp/MSP-Model-Application-ENG.pdf (site visited June 8, 2016). The second provision requires the Commissioner of the SSA to conduct outreach to identify individuals who might be eligible for MSP benefits, to notify them of their potential eligibility, and to notify each state of the names and addresses of those whom the Commissioner had identified who are residents of that state. BIPA § 911. MIPPA § 113 requires additional action with respect to SSA data sent to the states. The MIPPA provision is discussed in **§ 10.05[D]** of this Handbook.

[71] MIPPA § 115, effective Jan. 1, 2010.

[72] 42 U.S.C. § 1396a(a)(19); 42 C.F.R. § 435.902.

[73] 42 U.S.C. § 1396a(a)(10); 42 C.F.R. § 435.902; SMM, Ch. 3, § 3490.3.

applicant must check off on the application all Medicaid categories for which he or she wishes to be considered. An additional complexity is that an individual can receive both full Medicaid and QMB or SLMB benefits.

Being screened for all possible categories of eligibility is essential for applicants to be considered for each one. However, if eligibility determination systems are not fully coordinated with applicants screened for eligibility for all programs, they may be erroneously denied benefits. Another potential MSP eligibility issue arises every January, when Social Security cost-of-living adjustments (COLAs) become effective. The COLAs typically increase individuals' income by a small amount. Because updated income poverty guidelines, on which MSP eligibility is based, may not become effective until a few months into the year, there can be a period of several months when an individual's income may exceed the poverty level standard for the MSP in which the individual is enrolled. Congress recognized the harm caused by the disconnect in the operation of two different annual adjusters and amended the statute to require Social Security cost-of-living increases to be disregarded in determining eligibility until the second month after the month in which new poverty guidelines are published.[74]

Such systems and screening failures often result in dually eligible applicants being found eligible for categories of Medicaid that may not be as useful to them as MSP benefits would be. For example, an individual living in the community may be found eligible for a medically needy coverage group, with an income spend-down requirement, rather than for QMB benefits. This is significant because medically needy individuals must spend precious income on medical bills before their Medicaid entitlement is effective, while remaining liable for all Medicare cost-sharing or perhaps paying for a Medigap supplemental policy to cover some of the Medicare cost-sharing obligation. If the services they use most regularly are covered by Medicare, an MSP may be a more useful benefit for them. Conversely, it may be in an applicant's interest to forgo MSP benefits and use Medicare cost-sharing, especially the monthly Part B premium payment, to meet a spend-down that would then grant access to full Medicaid benefits. Similarly, institutionalized individuals may be found eligible for a long-term care coverage group with a share of cost obligation, without having their MSP entitlement assessed. When this happens, they may incur two potential sources of liability to the nursing facility where none should be occurring: share of cost under Medicaid and a Medicare copayment charge for the 21st through the 100th day of a Medicare Part A covered stay. This issue is addressed in more detail in **§ 10.06** of this Handbook.

The implementation of the ACA provides another application pathway to Medicaid and the MSPs.[75] The Department of Health and Human Services (HHS) has made a new single streamlined application for Medicaid and other insurance

[74] 42 U.S.C. § 1396d(p)(2)(D).

[75] *See* **§ 10.03** of this Handbook.

subsidy programs available.[76] Many people access this application through the federal health insurance marketplace online portal (*www.healthcare.gov*) and through various state-based marketplaces. This single streamlined application, and the health insurance marketplaces more generally, serve as an entry point to all categories of Medicaid, including the MSP. If, after completing the single streamlined application, the individual is found to be potentially eligible for the MSP, the marketplace should transfer the application to the single state Medicaid agency for processing.[77] The applicant may be required to fill out a supplemental application with more detailed questions and submit documentation of income and assets. The application should be processed in 45 days. Practically, however, when counseling clients advocates should continue to encourage people to apply for MSP at the Medicaid office. While an MSP application should in theory be processed through the marketplace, in practice this adds another layer of complexity and delay to a process already fraught with complexity and delay.

[C] Complexities of Enrolling in Medicare Part A for Eligibility for Qualified Medicare Beneficiary Benefits

To be eligible as a QMB for state Medicaid payment of Medicare cost-sharing obligations, applicants must have Medicare Part A.[78] Most Medicare beneficiaries receive Part A without payment of a premium, due to receipt of Social Security income or related benefits, such as Civil Service or Railroad Retirement. Some people, however, are not entitled to premium-free Medicare Part A. For example, individuals who do not have a long enough work history under the Social Security system may not have sufficient quarters of coverage to obtain Social Security benefits. Such individuals can purchase Part A for a premium of $413 per month in 2017 (a slight increase from 2016).[79] Enrollment in Part A by paying a premium is called "voluntary enrollment."

The cost of the Medicare Part A premium represents a significant financial burden for lower income persons: it is more than 50 percent of monthly income

---

[76] *See* http://www.enrollamerica.org/blog/the-single-streamlined-application-is-here (site visited June 8, 2016).

[77] If the Marketplace is a governmental entity, states will have the option to enable their state-based Marketplace to make MSP eligibility determinations for people with Medicare. The Federally Facilitated Exchange/Marketplace will not be making MSP eligibility determinations for non-MAGI groups; the Federally Facilitated Exchange will either do final determinations or assessments for the MAGI eligibility groups. *See* Medicaid/CHIP Affordable Care Act Implementation: Coordination Across Insurance Affordability Programs (May 22, 2012), *available at* http://www.medicaid.gov/State-Resource-Center/FAQ-Medicaid-and-CHIP-Affordable-Care-Act-Implementation/Downloads/Coordination-FAQs.pdf (site visited June 8, 2016).

[78] 42 U.S.C. § 1396d(p).

[79] Those with at least 30 quarters of Social Security coverage pay a lower premium ($227 in 2017, an increase of $1 from 2016). *See* CMS Announcement of Medicare A & B Premiums and Deductibles, available at https://www.cms.gov/Newsroom/MediaReleaseDatabase/Press-releases/2016-Press-releases-items/2016-11-10-2.html.

for a person in poverty. Although states are required to pay the Part A premium for QMBs who must voluntarily enroll,[80] an individual must have Part A to be eligible as a QMB. To circumvent this apparent "Catch-22," in about 1989 the Health Care Financing Administration (HCFA), now CMS, created a "conditional" enrollment process, through which a potential QMB enrolls in Part A conditioned upon his or her being found eligible for QMB benefits.[81]

The conditional enrollment process is complex.[82] The individual must contact a Social Security Administration office to enroll in Part A. He or she should attach a statement to the enrollment application to the following effect:

> I wish to enroll for hospital insurance on a monthly premium basis, and I understand that the hospital insurance premium will be in addition to the monthly premium for supplementary medical insurance. I want this enrollment to be effective only if I am determined to be eligible as a qualified Medicare beneficiary (QMB) and only beginning with the month in which I am eligible as a QMB. I also understand that, if I lose my QMB status, I will have to pay my premiums in order to keep my Medicare hospital insurance.

The individual then takes proof of his or her enrollment to the state Medicaid office, where he or she applies for QMB benefits, appending a copy of the Part A enrollment application to the Medicaid application. If the individual does not already have Part B, he or she will be required to enroll in Part B at the same time.[83]

Generally, persons who fail to voluntarily enroll in Medicare Parts A and B during their initial eligibility period (the seven months surrounding their 65th birthday or, for a person with disabilities under age 65, the seven months beginning when he or she has received disability payments for 21 months) must wait for a general enrollment period to enroll. They are penalized financially for late enrollment and their Medicare coverage is not effective until July 1 of that year. A general enrollment period occurs only once each year from January through March.

---

[80] *See, e.g.*, Notice of Hearing: Reconsideration of Disapproval of Michigan State Plan Amendment, 57 Fed. Reg. 57,469 (Dec. 4, 1992).

[81] Advocates advising clients about conditional enrollment should first check with both their state Medicaid office and their local Social Security office. Despite the legal requirement for states to pay the Part A premium, where necessary, it is not clear that all states honor conditional enrollment, nor that all Social Security offices even know about it in those states that do honor it. Advocates will want to arm their clients with a copy of Social Security Program Operations Manual System (SSA POMS) § HI 00801.140, *available at* https://secure.ssa.gov/poms.nsf/lnx/0600801140 (site visited June 8, 2016).

[82] *See* SSA POMS § HI 00801.140, *available at* https://secure.ssa.gov/poms.nsf/lnx/0600801140 (site visited June 8, 2016).

[83] 42 U.S.C. § 1395i-2; SSA POMS, § HI 00801.138, *available at* https://secure.ssa.gov/poms.nsf/lnx/0600801138 (site visited June 8, 2016).

States can avoid the enrollment limitations, the penalty, and even the complex conditional enrollment process by having buy-in agreements with the federal government that permit them to enroll individuals in Part A or Part B at any time of the year.[84] Not all states have such buy-in agreements for Part A; states without them effectively deny potential beneficiaries access to the QMB benefit during those nine months of the year when Medicare enrollment is closed and subject their applicants to the multi-step and complicated conditional enrollment process during the brief three-month general enrollment period.[85]

Even in the 37 jurisdictions (36 states and the District of Columbia) that do have Medicare Part A buy-in agreements authorizing enrollment in Medicare Part A at any time, significant barriers are sometimes placed in the way of applicants.[86] In some such states, individuals are still directed to the SSA to enroll conditionally in Medicare Part A. For individuals who have not yet enrolled in Part B, the process can be even more complex. Social Security's electronic system will not accept an enrollment for Part B outside the general enrollment period. For states with a Part A buy-in agreement, Social Security has established an emergency process, described in a Policy Instruction, to override its system.[87] Advocates are advised to arm their clients with a copy of this policy instruction when sending them off to the SSA to apply for Parts A and B.

States have the income and resource information to identify whether someone is a potential QMB (i.e., under 100 percent of poverty); if they do not already have it, states can get Medicare information about such persons from CMS. Yet, many states make little effort to identify these individuals in order to enroll them for Medicare Part A automatically. Therefore, even individuals entitled to full *Medicaid* benefits may be put through the conditional enrollment process to get Medicare Part A if they are not already enrolled in Medicare Part A. Part A benefits can be useful even to a recipient of full Medicaid benefits because they entitle the individual to hospital, skilled nursing facility (SNF), home health, and hospice benefits that are often more extensive than those offered by the state Medicaid program. They also enable the individual to reduce his or her Medicaid estate recovery liability by using fewer Medicaid services.

---

[84] 42 U.S.C. § 1395v for Part B, § 1395i-2(g) for Part A; 42 C.F.R. § 406.26. "Buy-in," used in connection with agreements between state Medicaid programs and the federal government to describe a process for paying Medicare premiums, is a term of art, used in regulations.

[85] The states that do *not* have Part A buy-in agreements are AL, AZ, CA, CO, IL, KS, KY, MO, NE, NJ, NM, SC, UT, and VA.

[86] SSA POMS, § HI 00801.140, *available at* https://secure.ssa.gov/poms.nsf/lnx/0600801140 (site visited July 8, 2016). For an excellent detailed analysis of Part A issues in a state with a Part A buy-in agreement, *see* Medicare Rights Center, "Streamlining Medicare and QMB Enrollment for New Yorkers: Medicare Part A Buy-In Analysis and Policy Recommendations" (Feb. 2011), *available at* http://www.medicarerights.org/pdf/Part-A-Buy-In-Analysis.pdf (site visited June 8, 2016).

[87] *See* Social Security Administration Policy Instruction for Individuals in Part A Buy-In States Who Do Not Have Medicare Part B, EM-08071 REV effective Aug. 11, 2008 through Oct. 6, 2012, included as **Appendix 10-6** of this Handbook.

The myriad problems related to getting individuals actually enrolled in QMB and other MSPs and, where relevant, getting the amount of their Part B premium restored to their Social Security checks are addressed in litigation filed in early 2009 against the State of Pennsylvania, the HHS, and the SSA.[88] Settlement was approved by the court on April 23, 2010.[89] Terms of settlement included Pennsylvania's agreement to:

- Send and receive data to and from CMS on a daily basis, instead of monthly as it had prior to the lawsuit;
- Scan its Medicaid rolls monthly to search for individuals eligible for, but not enrolled in, Medicare;
- Submit enrollments for Part B and Part A simultaneously for those individuals with Medicaid who are eligible for, but not enrolled in, either part of Medicare;
- Increase field staff training to promote better understanding of the program and the prompt resolution of data errors that can hold up enrollments; and
- Evaluate all applications for MSP benefits to determine whether the applicant is entitled to retroactive benefits.

[D] MSPs and the Medicare Part D Low-Income Subsidy

The LIS available to Medicare beneficiaries to help with Part D covered drugs[90] is closely related to the MSPs in both design and administration. Eligibility rules for the two programs are similar, though not identical, and states are required by law to make LIS eligibility determinations through their Medicaid programs. Moreover, the law requires states, when they are assisting beneficiaries with LIS applications, to screen them for eligibility for MSPs and, if eligible, offer them an opportunity to enroll.[91] Finally, individuals enrolled in QMB, SLMB, or QI programs are deemed eligible for the LIS without having to apply or separately qualify by meeting the LIS income and asset eligibility rules.

The screen and enroll requirement has great potential for two reasons. First, because it is piggybacked on an application for assistance with paying for prescription drugs (the LIS), it may promote a higher enrollment rate in the MSPs

---

[88] Garcia v. Johnson, Case 2:09-cv-1747 JS (E.D. Pa. Complaint filed Apr. 24, 2009).

[89] The joint motion for approval of the settlement agreement and the order approving the settlement agreement is *available at* https://www.aclusocal.org/wp-content/uploads/2014/04/Notice-of-Proposed-Settlement.pdf, https://www.aclusocal.org/wp-content/uploads/2015/12/Alfaro-Notice-of-Final-Settlement.pdf (sites visited June 9, 2016).

[90] *See* discussion of LIS in **Chapter 11** of this Handbook.

[91] 42 U.S.C. § 1396u-5(a)(3).

themselves, since drug coverage may be viewed as a more attractive and necessary benefit than premium assistance. MSP eligibility rules vary be state, so they can be more liberal in at least some respect than the nationally uniform LIS rules. Therefore, enrollment in an MSP can provide a back-door route to eligibility for the LIS for some who would not otherwise qualify.[92] Unfortunately, this potential is not much realized: staff members at the SSA reported in 2012 that only one state, Colorado, was sending LIS applications to SSA.[93]

Although the SSA does not have a screen and enroll mandate with respect to MSP benefits for those who apply through the SSA for LIS, it does, effective January 1, 2010, have an obligation to send data from the LIS application to the applicant's state.[94] This is done only with the applicant's consent. The state receiving the data must consider it an application for MSP benefits and process it accordingly. States' compliance with the requirement that they treat the data as initiating an application varies considerably throughout the country: some states automatically enroll into MSP virtually all individuals whose data they receive; others merely send a "formal" application to those individuals whose data they receive, or a formal notice requesting additional information or requiring submission of documentation to the state. In some states, community-based organizations are working with the Medicaid eligibility agency to help applicants successfully complete these applications.[95] Advocates are monitoring implementation of this important provision in the law and working with CMS to improve state performance.[96]

Advocates assisting clients with enrolling in MSPs can enhance their assistance by helping clients understand the complexities of enrollment choices for LIS. It may be more expeditious for a client to make one trip to Medicaid rather than two separate trips, one to Medicaid for MSP and one to Social Security for LIS, but clients will need to be clear about what they are seeking when they go

[92] For a detailed discussion of the interrelationships between MSPs and LIS, see The Kaiser Family Foundation, "Toward Making Medicare Work: A Baseline Comparison of the Part D Low-Income Subsidy and Medicare Savings Programs Eligibility and Enrollment Rules" (Apr. 30, 2006), *available at* http://kff.org/medicare/report/toward-making-medicare-work-for-low-income/ (site visited June 8, 2016).

[93] Telephone message from Kojuan Almond, Office of External Affairs, Social Security Administration, left for Patricia Nemore, July 9, 2012.

[94] MIPPA § 113.

[95] *See* Douglas Goggin-Callahan, "Warning Signs: Preliminary Report Highlights Problems with State Implementation of MIPPA Low-Income Reforms" (Feb. 2010), Medicare Rights Center, *available at* http://www.medicarerights.org/pdf/Warning-Signs-MIPPA.pdf (site visited June 8, 2016).

[96] *See* Government Accountability Office, "The Medicare Savings Program: Implementation of Requirements Aimed at Increasing Enrollment" (Sept. 2012), *available at* http://www.gao.gov/assets/650/648370.pdf (site visited June 8, 2016).

to their Medicaid office. Those clients who have access to the Internet can be advised to make their LIS application online.[97]

§ 10.06 ACCESS ISSUES FOR THE DUALLY ELIGIBLE POPULATION

[A] Transition Issues for Certain Medicaid Enrollees upon Becoming Eligible for Medicare

The ACA's expansion and simplification of Medicaid financial eligibility rules, including the increase in Medicaid income limits to 133 percent of FPL and the elimination of asset tests, do not apply to the Medicare population.[98] For individuals receiving expanded ACA Medicaid who become eligible for Medicare, transitions to Medicare with Medicaid for the aged, blind, and disabled or to Medicare with an MSP can be problematic.[99]

When individuals on Medicaid become eligible for Medicare, the agency is required to do an automatic redetermination and reassess them for medical assistance programs for which they may be eligible.[100] Because expanded Medicaid does not have an asset test and relies on a simplified MAGI standard to determine income, new Medicare beneficiaries undergoing a redetermination will be asked for additional documentation of income and assets.[101] Some people with expanded Medicaid may find that they continue to qualify for their state Medicaid program and will become full dual eligibles.[102] Others may qualify for only an MSP and will become partial dual eligibles.[103] Finally, some individuals will

---

[97] Go to https://secure.ssa.gov/i1020/start (site visited June 8, 2016) and look for the button called "Apply Now."

[98] ACA § 2001.

[99] For an excellent analysis of transition issues beneficiaries moving from expanded ACA coverage to Medicare will face, see Ilene Stein & Joe Baker, "A Bridge to Health" (Jan. 2013), The Medicare Rights Center, *available at* http://www.medicarerights.org/pdf/A-Bridge-to-Health.pdf (site visited June 8, 2016). *See also* Amber Cutler & Anna Rich, "Medicaid Expansion in California: Opportunities and Challenges for Older Adults and People with Disabilities" (Nov. 2013), The National Senior Citizens Law Center, *available at* http://nsclcarchives.org/wp-content/uploads/2013/11/1CA-Eligibility-Brief-4.pdf (site visited June 8, 2016).

[100] 42 C.F.R. § 435.930; 42 C.F.R. § 435.916(c)(1) (requires state agency to re-determine eligibility when it receives information about changes in a recipient's circumstances that may affect his/her eligibility). Individuals receiving SSI should be automatically "deemed" for an MSP without going through an ex parte redetermination requiring supplemental documentation. *See* SSA POMS HI 00815.006.

[101] Medicaid Program; Eligibility Changes under the Affordable Care Act of 2010, 77 Fed. Reg. 17,144–217, 17,181–183, 17,210 (Mar. 23, 2013) (to be codified at 42 C.F.R. § 435.916), *available at* http://www.gpo.gov/fdsys/pkg/FR-2012-03-23/pdf/2012-6560.pdf (site visited June 8, 2016).

[102] *See* discussion at **§ 10.04** of this Handbook.

[103] *See* discussion at **§ 10.04** of this Handbook.

lose eligibility for all medical assistance programs upon becoming Medicare eligible. This is the case for people with income below 133 percent of the FPL but assets above MSP resource limits.

[B] Prescription Drug Coverage and Medicare Part D

Prior to January 1, 2006, dually eligible beneficiaries received their prescription drug coverage exclusively from Medicaid, with the exception of drugs covered under Medicare Parts A and B, delivered in institutions or in physicians' offices.

Since January 1, 2006, any individual eligible to enroll in a Medicare Part D plan who is eligible for full Medicaid cannot receive prescription drug coverage through Medicaid.[104] This is true regardless of whether the individual has actually enrolled in a Part D plan, and regardless of whether the plan covers the specific drug needed. Concomitantly, the state cannot receive federal matching payments for such services.

[1] Definition of Dual Eligibles

For purposes of Part D, dual eligibles are defined as individuals who have coverage under a Part D plan and who are eligible for full Medicaid benefits under any category of a state Medicaid plan. Those with full coverage under a Section 1115 Research and Demonstration waiver fall within the definition. This definition is narrower than the definition of dual eligibles offered in **§ 10.04** of this Handbook.

[2] Assignment of Dual Eligibles to Drug Plans

Congress required the automatic enrollment in a drug plan of any dual eligible who does not voluntarily enroll.[105] Auto enrollment must be into Part D plans with premiums at or below the average ("benchmark") plan premium for the region. The difficulties that developed for dual eligibles during the first transition of about 7 million individuals from Medicaid to Medicare in January 2006 led to beneficiaries filing a nationwide class action lawsuit, *Situ v. Leavitt*, challenging the failure of the HHS to implement Part D to ensure drug coverage for dual eligibles.[106] Enrollment for Medicaid-eligible individuals who become eligible for Medicare after January 1, 2006, is effective on the first day of the month

---

[104] 42 U.S.C. § 1396u-5(d)(1). For a more detailed discussion of the entire Medicare drug benefit, see **Chapter 11** of this Handbook.

[105] 42 U.S.C. § 1396u-5(a)(3).

[106] Situ v. Leavitt, C06-02841 TEH (N.D. Cal. Complaint filed Apr. 26, 2006); Defendants' Motion to Dismiss denied, 2000 WL 3734373 (N.D. Cal. Dec. 18, 2006); Plaintiffs' Motion for

the individual becomes eligible for Part D. Enrollment for Part D eligibles who become newly eligible for Medicaid is effective on the first day of the month in which the individual becomes Medicaid eligible.[107] Although coverage is effective the date the individual becomes dually eligible, significant lag times can occur in making the coverage operational, leaving the dually eligible beneficiary in the position of having to pay potentially high copayments with the hope of being reimbursed in the future.[108] Such payments are often not feasible for dual eligibles, due to their very low incomes.

Beginning January 1, 2010, CMS instituted a program called Limited Income Newly Eligible Transition program (LI NET), operated by Humana, Inc. under contract with CMS.[109] The LI NET serves essentially three purposes: it acts as the process for initial auto-enrollment of full-benefit dual eligibles and individuals with Supplemental Security Income; it acts as the point-of-sale (POS) contractor for individuals whose Part D enrollment is not evident in the system when they arrive at the pharmacy to fill a prescription; and it acts as the Part D plan for purposes of retroactive reimbursements that are due to individuals whose enrollment was actually effective before it was available in the system (due, usually, to eligibility for Medicaid benefits retroactive to a period prior to the date of application). Although the point-of-sale enrollment process is not required to be used by pharmacists, CMS did remove the financial liability of pharmacists if their use of the system was in error. This change may make use of the system more attractive to pharmacists.[110] The LI NET demonstration has been extended through the end of 2019. In its 2014 yearly report to Congress, the Medicare-Medicaid Coordination Office (MMCO)[111] recommended that the demonstration be made permanent.[112]

Class Certification granted, 240 F.R.D. 551 (N.D. Cal. 2007); Settlement approved Situ v. Leavitt, No. 06-2841 TEH (N.D. Cal., Order Approving Final Approval of Settlement Agreement, Oct. 22, 2008).

[107] 42 C.F.R. § 423.34(f)(2), (3), effective June 7, 2010.

[108] *See* GAO, "Medicare Part D: Enrolling New Dual-Eligible Beneficiaries in Prescription Drug Plans," GAO-07-824T (May 2007), *available at* http://www.gao.gov/new.items/d07824t.pdf (site visited June 8, 2016).

[109] *See* "The Limited Income Newly Eligible Transition (LI NET) Program," *available at* http://www.cms.gov/LowIncSubMedicarePresCov/Downloads/LINETgeneral100909.pdf (site visited June 8, 2016).

[110] Limited Income Newly Eligible Transition (NET) Program: Four Steps for Pharmacy Providers" (Dec. 10, 2009), *available at* http://apps.humana.com/marketing/documents.asp?file=1285050 (site visited June 8, 2016). *See also* CMS, "Medicare's Limited Income NET Program for People at the Pharmacy Counter," *available at* http://www.cms.gov/partnerships/downloads/11328-P.pdf (site visited June 8, 2016).

[111] *See* **§ 10.09** of this Handbook.

[112] Medicare-Medicaid Coordination Office Fiscal Year 2014 Report to Congress, *available at* https://www.cms.gov/Medicare-Medicaid-Coordination/Medicare-and-Medicaid-Coordination/Medicare-Medicaid-Coordination-Office/Downloads/MMCO_2014_RTC.pdf (site visited June 8, 2016).

Related to the POS system is CMS's best available evidence (BAE) policy.[113] BAE is used when CMS records are incorrect with respect to an individual's LIS status (in contrast with the POS, which relates to whether they are enrolled in a plan), so that they are being charged incorrect cost-sharing. Under the policy, a plan must honor an individual's stated low-income status (and apply appropriate cost-sharing levels) if the individual provides or is able to procure one of five specific types of documentation of Medicaid eligibility, or some other documentation provided by a state Medicaid agency for the relevant period. Requirements on plans with respect to BAE mandate that a plan help beneficiaries establish their LIS status. Although CMS directs plans to use the BAE, including helping beneficiaries, not all plans do so. Advocates would be well advised to have a copy of the policy in hand when they engage the plan.

Both the POS and BAE were subject to the settlement in the *Situ* case and, as such, were subject to ongoing monitoring by plaintiffs' counsel. Official monitoring ended in late 2010, but the Part D advocacy community continues to pay attention to how well these systems are working.

Unlike other Medicare beneficiaries, dual eligibles have the right to switch Part D plans at any time.[114] Thus, individuals assigned to plans whose formularies do not include the prescriptions they use may switch to a more appropriate plan.

[3] Medicaid Wrap-Around

Medicare Part D's complete elimination of coverage for an otherwise covered Medicaid service represents a substantial departure from the historic Medicare-Medicaid relationship for dual eligibles, under which Medicaid has paid Medicare's cost-sharing and provided "wrap-around coverage" for certain services. These include home health, where Medicare coverage is more limited than Medicaid coverage; prescription drugs before January 1, 2006; and non-skilled long-term care because Medicare coverage was or is nearly non-existent. The significance of this situation cannot be overstated. Because of the design of the Medicare drug benefit, many dual eligibles find themselves with less prescription drug coverage than they had under Medicaid and potentially fewer protections during appeals processes to challenge denials or other barriers to coverage. Further, all but those who are receiving long-term care services have to pay copayments for their prescriptions, with the copayment amounts increasing

[113] *See generally* documents at http://www.cms.gov/Medicare/Prescription-Drug-Coverage/PrescriptionDrugCovContra/Best_Available_Evidence_Policy.html. For other documents relevant to Part D and low income subsidies, *see* http://www.cms.gov/PrescriptionDrugCovContra/17_Best_Available_Evidence_Policy.asp (sites visited June 8, 2016).

[114] 42 C.F.R. § 423.38(c).

yearly. Copayments are not required under federal Medicaid law and, in the past, their use was not enforceable, although this is no longer true.[115]

Using both federal and state funding, Medicaid can continue to cover for dual eligibles those drugs that it is permitted, but not required by law, to cover for any Medicaid beneficiary and that are not, by definition, Part D covered drugs. In 2014, such drugs included weight gain and weight loss drugs (used in connection with HIV treatments), prescription vitamins, cough and cold relief drugs, and non-prescription drugs, among others. Prior to January 1, 2013, Part D did not cover benzodiazepines (used for anxiety, panic attacks, seizure disorders, and muscle spasms) or barbiturates (used in the treatment of epilepsy, cancer, or a chronic mental disorder) but has since begun covering these classes of medication.[116] As of January 1, 2014, Medicaid programs may not exclude smoking cessation drugs, barbiturates, and benzodiazepines from coverage under Medicaid.[117] The January 2006 transition from Medicaid to Medicare coverage for prescription drugs was so chaotic for dual eligibles that between 38 and 44 states initiated some sort of emergency coverage programs, some declaring a health care emergency in the state.[118] Few states provide ongoing wrap-around payments—either of Part D copayments or of non-formulary drugs—for their dually eligible residents.[119]

[4] Nursing Facility Residents and Other Beneficiaries Receiving Long-Term Care Services

In addition to experiencing the problems of all dually eligible individuals, those who reside in nursing homes and other institutions experience problems that arise because of the setting in which they live. For example, there is no assurance that a dually eligible resident who does not choose a Part D prescription drug plan will be automatically assigned to a plan that includes the pharmacy used by his or her nursing facility, although plans are required to include long-term care pharmacies in their networks.

---

[115] *See* 42 C.F.R. § 447.53(e). The non-enforceability of copayments was changed by the DRA § 6041.

[116] MIPPA § 175.

[117] ACA § 2502, amending § 1927(d) of the Social Security Act, 42 U.S.C. § 1397r-8(d).

[118] *See* Vernon Smith, Kathleen Gifford, Sandy Kramer, & Linda Elam, "The Transition of Dual Eligibles to Medicare Part D Prescription Drug Coverage: State Actions during Implementation" (Feb. 2006), Kaiser Family Foundation, *available at* http://www.kff.org/medicaid/upload/7467.pdf (site visited June 8, 2016).

[119] The website of the National Conference of State Legislatures, *available at* http://www.ncsl.org/issues-research/health/state-pharmaceutical-assistance-programs.aspx (site visited July 8, 2016), includes discussions of and charts listing various state efforts with respect to prescription drug coverage. It is difficult to discern from this information exactly which states, if any, still have wrap-around drug coverage for dual eligibles, especially for paying Part D copayments and for non-formulary drugs. For a 2013 chart of State Pharmaceutical Assistance Programs, *see* http://www.medicareinteractive.org/uploadedDocuments/mi_extra/SPAP-Chart.pdf (site visited June 8, 2016).

Dually eligible individuals who reside in a nursing facility pay no copayment for their medications.[120] Prior to 2012, this benefit had not been extended to residents of assisted living facilities and others who are receiving home and community-based services pursuant to a Section 1915 waiver, even though these individuals must meet the medical eligibility requirements for a nursing facility to qualify for community-based services. The Affordable Care Act changed this. Effective January 1, 2012, individuals receiving home and community-based services under waiver or state plan provisions of the Medicaid law were relieved of all Part D copayments.[121]

[5] Transitioning into a Part D Plan

When Medicare beneficiaries transition from another source of payment for their prescriptions to a Part D plan, they may encounter difficulties caused by changes in formularies and other utilization management tools used by Part D plans to contain costs. The transition may be particularly difficult for those dual eligibles who transition from more generous Medicaid programs.

All Part D plans are required to establish a transition process for new enrollees who are already taking Medicare-covered drugs that are not on the plan's formulary.[122] The transition process is to ensure access to non-formulary drugs, including those subject to step therapy or prior authorization requirements, during the first 90 days of coverage under a new plan. The transition process is available for new enrollees following the annual coordinated enrollment period, newly eligible Medicare beneficiaries moving from other coverage, individuals who change plans mid-year, and current enrollees who are affected by formulary changes. Eligible enrollees are generally entitled to a 30-day transition fill unless the prescription is for fewer than 30 days. Residents in long-term care facilities are entitled to up to 98-days of transition fills, depending on the dispensing increment. Plans must send enrollees written notice explaining that the prescription has been filled on a transition basis within three business days of approving the transition fill. Plans must also ensure that reasonable notice is made to inform the prescriber of the temporary fill.[123]

[C] Payment of Medicare Cost-Sharing at Medicaid Rates

A provision in the Balanced Budget Act of 1997 (BBA '97), gave states the option to reimburse Medicare cost-sharing to providers for services provided to

[120] 42 C.F.R. §§ 423.772; 423.782(a)(2)(ii).

[121] ACA § 3309, amending § 1860D-14(a)(1)(D)(i) of the Social Security Act, 42 U.S.C. § 1395w-114(a)(1)(D)(i).

[122] 42 C.F.R. § 423.120(b)(3).

[123] 42 C.F.R. § 423.120(b)(3).

dually eligible beneficiaries at their lower Medicaid rate, rather than the full Medicare rate.[124] Federal law also authorizes states to pay at the Medicare rate even if that rate is higher than what the state would pay for a non-dual eligible on Medicaid.[125] Under the BBA '97 provision, if the Medicare share (80 percent of the Medicare allowable amount for most Part B services) is more than the state's Medicaid rate for the same service, the state need pay nothing. This is sometimes referred to as the "lesser-of" policy.

■ **EXAMPLE:** If the *Medicare* approved rate is $100, the Medicare payment would be $80 and the beneficiary coinsurance (for which Medicaid would be responsible for a QMB) would be $20. However, if the *Medicaid* rate for the service is only $75, the state would make no payment for the beneficiary's share, since Medicare has already paid above the state reimbursement rate. Thus, the provider would get $20 less than it would from a non-QMB beneficiary. The QMB is not liable for the unreimbursed state portion.

Since the enactment of BBA '97, courts have held, even in cases that predated BBA '97, that states *may* reimburse at the lower of the two reimbursement rates.[126] Thus, dually eligible beneficiaries are treated as Medicaid rather than Medicare beneficiaries, with respect to provider reimbursement. A July 2015 CMS report, *Access to Care Issues Among Qualified Medicare Beneficiaries (QMB)*, revealed several access to care problems for low-income Medicare beneficiaries enrolled in the QMB program.[127] The report found that QMB enrollees were less likely to use office visits and hospital outpatient services compared to Medicare-only enrollees in states that employed the "lesser-of" policy for reimbursement, thereby limiting access to essential routine and preventive care for beneficiaries. The report provided troubling information regarding barriers to access to care for low-income beneficiaries, something that advocates have long asserted.[128]

---

[124] The Balanced Budget Act of 1997 (BBA '97), Pub. L. No. 105-33 (Aug. 5, 1997), § 4714, amending 42 U.S.C.A. § 1396a(n) (Supp. 2009) by adding subparagraphs (2) and (3).

[125] 42 U.S.C. § 1396a(n)(1).

[126] Beverly Cmty. Hosp. Ass'n v. Belshe, 132 F.3d 1259 (9th Cir. 1997); Stohler v. Menke, 998 F. Supp. 836 (E.D. Tenn. 1997).

[127] CMS, *Access to Care Issues Among Qualified Medicare Beneficiaries (QMB)* (July 2015), *available at* https://www.cms.gov/Medicare-Medicaid-Coordination/Medicare-and-Medicaid-Coordination/Medicare-Medicaid-Coordination-Office/Downloads/Access_to_Care_Issues_Among_Qualified_Medicare_Beneficiaries.pdf (site visited June 8, 2016) (hereinafter *July 2015 QMB Report*).

[128] Letter of July 28, 2009, from Center for Medicare Advocacy and D.C. Legal Aid Society to Ted Gallagher, CMS Region III, concerning specific client issues and general systemic issues with respect to providers billing QMBs for the cost-sharing portion of Medicare payment, available from the Center at kkertesz@medicareadvocacy.org.

A 2003 study of the effects of lesser-of policies on access to services concluded that payment reductions reduced utilization. It did not, however, evaluate the effect of reduced utilization on health outcomes.[129] In 2013 the Medicaid and CHIP Payment and Access Commission (MACPAC) undertook a study of current state payment policies in the 50 states and the District of Columbia.[130] The study found that Medicaid payment for Medicare cost-sharing varied among both states and provider types within individual states. The provider types surveyed were hospital inpatient, hospital outpatient, skilled nursing facility, and physician services. Of the 51 Medicaid programs for which researchers collected information, about half paid the lesser-of amount for all provider types. Only four states (Arkansas, Iowa, Vermont, and Wyoming) pay Medicare's full deductibles and coinsurance for every provider type researchers investigated. The remaining 18 states mix and match policies in almost every possible combination with no clear patterns emerging. The MACPAC report did not address the effect of lesser-of policies on access or health outcomes as suggested by the 2003 BBA report.

The BBA '97 provision authorizing lower payments to providers also expressly prohibits providers from billing dually eligible patients. Providers must accept the Medicare payment and the Medicaid payment, if any, as payment in full.[131]

Until 2008, CMS had interpreted these requirements to permit providers to choose whether to accept a patient as private pay, QMB-only, or, if applicable, full Medicaid.[132] This interpretation eviscerates the statutory protection, since the provider can avoid its reach by telling the beneficiary it will serve him or her only as private pay. Moreover, it appears to violate Medicare law, to the extent the provider in question "accepts assignment" under Medicare,[133] which prohibits the provider from charging the beneficiary anything more than the coinsurance amount. For a QMB, this would be paid for by the state. CMS, in February 2008, issued a Memorandum to its Regional Administrators stating clearly that a provider of services covered by Parts A and B may not bill a QMB either for the balance of the Medicare rate (the 20%) or for the provider's customary charge in

[129] Tommy G. Thompson, Secretary of HHS, "Report to Congress, State Payment Limitations on Medicare Cost-Sharing: Impacts on Dually Eligible Beneficiaries and Their Providers," transmitted by letter of May 20, 2003 to Speaker of the House of Representatives, J. Dennis Hastert, *available at* http://inq.sagepub.com/content/41/4/391.full.pdf+html (site visited June 9, 2016).

[130] *March 2013 MACPAC Report* at 128; *see also March 2015 MACPAC Report* at 103, citing 2013 study.

[131] BBA '97 § 4714(a)(1)(B).

[132] SMM, Ch. 3, § 3490.14B, *available at* http://www.cms.gov/Regulations-and-Guidance/Guidance/Manuals/Paper-Based-Manuals-Items/CMS021927.html (site visited June 8, 2016).

[133] 42 U.S.C. § 1395u(b)(3)(B)(ii). *See generally* **§ 6.04** of this Handbook on the Medicare Assignment Program. While the federal protections only apply with respect to physicians who agree to take assignment, some states require Medicare participating physicians to take assignment. *See also* **§ 1.05[B][2]**.

excess of the Medicare rate.[134] In January 2012, CMS reissued this guidance.[135] The July 2015 CMS Report also underscores this prohibition.

In addition, in 2010, CMS Region III issued letters to two providers in the District of Columbia informing them that their billing of their QMB patients was illegal and could result in sanctions.[136] Advocates have successfully used these letters to educate providers and persuade them to desist from billing their QMB patients. Despite the clear prohibition on balance billing, the July 2015 CMS report shows an alarming trend that low-income beneficiaries enrolled in the QMB program are frequently being illegally balance-billed and that although beneficiaries are not liable for the charges, many of the bills were sent on to collections if unpaid, and most beneficiaries actually paid.[137]

---

[134] *See* 42 U.S.C. §§ 1396d(p)(3) and 1396a(n)(2); SMM, CMS Pub. 45, Ch. 3, Eligibility § 3490.12, *see* **Appendix 10-1** of this Handbook. *See also* Feb. 2008 Memo and two attachments, memo *available at* http://www.medicareadvocacy.org/old-site/InfoByTopic/MedicareSavingsPrograms/MedSavProg_08_04.24.ARACostShare.pdf, Balance Billing attachment *available at* http://www.medicareadvocacy.org/old-site/InfoByTopic/MedicareSavingsPrograms/MedSavProg_08_04.24.ARABalanceBilling.pdf, and Capitation attachment *available at* http://www.medicareadvocacy.org/old-site/InfoByTopic/MedicareSavingsPrograms/MedSavProg_08_04.24.ARACapitation.pdf (sites visited June 8, 2016); Nov. 1991 Memo (**Appendix 10-2** of this Handbook); June 2007 Memo (**Appendix 10-3** of this Handbook); and Memorandum of June 30, 2000 from Director, DEHPG, Subject: Policy Memorandum on Medicaid Obligations to Pay Medicare Cost-sharing Expenses for Qualified Medicare Beneficiaries in Medicare Health Maintenance Organizations or Competitive Medical Plans or Medicare Plus Choice Organizations—Information (hereinafter June 2000 Memo) (**Appendix 10-4** of this Handbook). *See also* 42 U.S.C. § 1396a (a)(25)(C) and (D) concerning non-discrimination by providers serving Medicaid beneficiaries with third party insurance.

[135] MMCO-CMCS Informational Bulletin June 7, 2013, Subject: Payment of Medicare Cost Sharing for Qualified Medicare Beneficiaries (QMBs), *available at* http://www.medicaid.gov/Federal-Policy-Guidance/downloads/CIB-06-07-2013.pdf (site visited June 8, 2016); MMCO-CMCS Informational Bulletin Jan. 6, 2012, Subject: Billing for Services Provided to Qualified Medicare Beneficiaries (QMBs), *available at* http://www.medicareadvocacy.org/wp-content/uploads/2012/01/cib-01-06-12.pdf (site visited June 8, 2016); CMS MLN Matters, "Prohibition on Balance Billing Qualified Medicare Beneficiaries (QMBs)," *available at* http://www.cms.gov/Outreach-and-Education/Medicare-Learning-Network-MLN/MLNMattersArticles/downloads/SE1128.pdf (site visited June 8, 2016).

[136] Letter of February 4, 2010 from John David Smith, Manager, Medicare Operations Branch, Region III Division of Financial Management and FFS Operations, Centers for Medicare & Medicaid Services, Philadelphia, Pennsylvania (the names of providers and beneficiaries are redacted from these documents), *available at* http://www.medicareadvocacy.org/old-site/InfoByTopic/MedicareSavingsPrograms/10_02.04.LtrFromROtoDCproviderReCostSharing.pdf (site visited June 8, 2016).

[137] *July 2015 QMB Report, available at* https://www.cms.gov/Medicare-Medicaid-Coordination/Medicare-and-Medicaid-Coordination/Medicare-Medicaid-Coordination-Office/Downloads/Access_to_Care_Issues_Among_Qualified_Medicare_Beneficiaries.pdf (site visited June 8, 2016)

[D] Skilled Nursing Facilities/Nursing Facilities: Inappropriate Transfers and Obstruction of Medicaid Services

Medicare pays for *skilled* nursing or rehabilitative care, following a three- (or more) day inpatient hospitalization. The care must be provided in a certified skilled nursing facility (SNF) and coverage is available for up to 100 days. After the 20th day, the beneficiary must pay a copayment ($164.50 in 2017). See a full discussion of Medicare coverage of SNF care in **Chapter 3** of this Handbook. *Medicaid* pays for nursing or rehabilitative care that can be provided only in a nursing facility on an inpatient basis. A "nursing facility" in Medicaid is a place that provides both skilled care and "health related care and services."[138] The care must be provided in a certified nursing facility; there is no limit on the number of days of coverage as long as the services are medically necessary. Medicaid requires the individual to pay a "share of cost" that comprises the individual's whole monthly income less certain required and permitted deductions. Medicaid then pays the facility the difference between the individual's share of cost and the Medicaid rate.

Difficulties can arise for dually eligible beneficiaries because facilities may not be certified for both Medicare and Medicaid or may have separate wings certified for each program.[139] If such a beneficiary enters the facility with Medicaid paying for his or her stay and is subsequently hospitalized for three days, the beneficiary may then be eligible for a period of skilled nursing coverage under Medicare. The beneficiary may be told—either by the facility or by the state Medicaid program—that he or she cannot return to his or her Medicaid bed because the beneficiary must be placed in a bed in a Medicare-only certified portion of the facility. The motivation for this could be that the facility may receive higher reimbursement rates under Medicare. The state might try to force the beneficiary to get Medicare coverage because of its interpretation of its obligation under federal law to seek reimbursement from all liable third parties.

Medicare law requires that if a beneficiary's old bed is available or, if not, another bed is available, the facility must readmit the beneficiary to it, regardless of whether the facility can get higher reimbursement if the beneficiary is in a bed in a Medicare-certified portion of the facility.[140] Moreover, with respect to the

[138] 42 U.S.C. § 1396r(a).

[139] Although national data report that about 87 percent of all nursing facility beds and 91 percent of all nursing facilities in the country are certified for both programs, nursing home advocates report that movement between wings separately certified continues to be an issue for dually eligible beneficiaries. *See* American Health Care Association, LTC Stats: Nursing Facility Operational Characteristics Report, March 2013 Update, Table 3: Nursing Facility Certification and Table 6: Nursing Facility Beds by Certification Type (Mar. 2013).

[140] *See* 42 U.S.C. § 1396r(c)(2)(D) concerning a Medicaid resident's right to notice of state bed hold policies when he or she is being transferred to a hospital. Although states are not required to pay nursing facilities to hold beds while residents are absent, they may do so, and the resident must be informed of the state's policy and his or her right to return to the bed the state paid for, if any,

state's concern about third-party liability, CMS has said that states are required to seek third-party coverage only where such coverage exists; if a resident is in a bed in a portion of a facility not certified for Medicare, there would be no Medicare coverage for that bed, and so there would be no third-party liability.[141]

Conversely, a dually eligible beneficiary might enter the facility for the first time needing skilled care after a three-day hospitalization and be entitled to Medicare coverage immediately. When that coverage ends, the beneficiary may be told by the facility that he or she must move because it needs the bed for another Medicare resident. While the law gives the beneficiary an absolute right to refuse this transfer,[142] he or she will not be able to get Medicaid to pay for continued stay unless the bed is also certified for Medicaid.

As a general matter, when a facility asks a resident to move from one part of the facility to another, an advocate or a family member should try to find out what the certification is for both parts of the facility. If they are certified differently—e.g., one is only Medicare-certified and the other is only Medicaid-certified—the resident is entitled to a notice of the reasons for the transfer and an opportunity for a fair hearing to challenge the transfer.[143] If the move is merely from one room to another within a certified portion of the facility, the resident is entitled only to notification, not to a hearing, but may nonetheless be able to prevent the relocation by invoking federal standards that promote self-determination, participation, and accommodation of the resident's need.[144]

---

or to the first available bed in the facility. In addition to this right of the nursing home resident, Medicaid provides a generic right of free choice of provider to all beneficiaries. 42 U.S.C. § 1396a(a)(23).

[141] Letter of March 31, 1999, from Associate Regional Administrator, Region I, HCFA to Center for Medicare Advocacy, Inc (hereinafter Preston letter). *See* **Appendix 10-5** of this Handbook. Advocates are cautioned that while the principles enunciated in this letter are embodied in the law, actual state policy and practice is likely to be less favorable and the state may refuse to pay for a resident who has declined Medicare coverage. Advocates are encouraged, nonetheless, to make these arguments for clients who wish to return to a non-Medicare-certified bed.

[142] 42 U.S.C. §§ 1395i-3(c)(1)(A)(x) (Medicare) and 1396r(c)(1)(A)(x) (Medicaid).

[143] Federal law limits the permissible reasons for transfers. The reasons, which apply to all nursing home residents, not just to those dually eligible, are: (1) the resident's welfare cannot be met by the facility, (2) the resident no longer needs the facility's services because of improved health, (3) safety of individuals in the facility is endangered, (4) health of individuals in the facility would be endangered, (5) resident has failed to pay, and (6) facility ceases to operate. 42 U.S.C. §§ 1396r(c)(2)(A)(i)–(vi) and 1395i-3(c)(2)(A)(i)–(vi). In addition, a resident can refuse a transfer to or from a Medicare-certified portion of the facility when the purpose is to relocate him or her from or to a non-Medicare certified portion of the facility. 42 U.S.C. §§ 1395i-3(c)(1)(A)(x) (Medicare), 1396r(c)(1)(A)(x) (Medicaid). *See also* Eric Carlson, "20 Common Nursing Home Problems and How to Solve Them" (June, 2010), National Senior Citizens Law Center, *available at* http://www.elderlawanswers.com/20-common-nursing-home-problems--and-how-to-resolve-them-5166 (site visited Sept. 21, 2016).

[144] *See, e.g.*, 42 C.F.R. § 483.15(b), (e).

From the resident's perspective, these problems would be eliminated by the state's requiring that all beds in facilities be certified for both Medicare and Medicaid. Data suggest that no state does this, but that the District of Columbia, Idaho, Montana, North Dakota, and Vermont come very close.[145]

[E] Medicaid Individual Share of Cost Issues During a Skilled Nursing Facility Benefit Period

If a dually eligible individual's nursing home stay is paid for by Medicaid, he or she will pay all of his or her income, less deductions allowed for personal needs, the support of family members, and a few other purposes,[146] to the facility as his or her share of cost. This payment is also called net available monthly income (NAMI), patient pay amount, or applied income. Medicaid then pays the difference between the share of cost and the established Medicaid rate for the facility.

However, when a portion of the stay is paid for by Medicare, different rules apply. If the individual is a QMB, he or she should have no share of cost for any portion of the nursing home stay that is covered by Medicare. This is because Medicare will cover fully the first 20 days of the Medicare-covered stay, and the copayment ($164.50 in 2017) for days 21 to 100 is Medicaid's responsibility.[147] Even if Medicaid does not pay the full Medicare cost-sharing amount, the nursing home can neither charge the individual for the copayment nor receive his or her Medicaid share of cost for that period of time. Sometimes, nursing facilities and Medicaid agencies are not as clear as they could be in informing residents about their rights and obligations with respect to share of cost.[148]

---

[145] *See* American Health Care Association, LTC Stats: Nursing Facility Operational Characteristics Report, Mar. 2013 Update, Table 6: Nursing Facility Beds by Certification Type, Mar. 2013).

[146] 42 U.S.C. §§ 1396a(r)(1) and 1396r-5(d)(1); 42 C.F.R. §§ 435.725, 435.733, and 435.832. The deductions from gross income include incurred medical expenses, a personal needs allowance of at least $30 a month, monies diverted to create a minimum monthly needs allowance for a community spouse, and/or a family allowance for other dependents, if any, and certain reparation payments. Although the above-cited regulations do, indeed, describe certain required and permissible deductions from income before determining share of cost, advocates should not rely on them as they do not reflect changes that have been made in the law since 1987.

[147] *See* http://www.medicare.gov/coverage/skilled-nursing-facility-care.html (site visited June 8, 2016). Data in the *March 2013 MACPAC Report* show that 12 states pay nursing homes the full Medicare copayment rate. The rest pay the lesser-of amount (see discussion at **§ 10.06[C]**).

[148] *See, e.g.*, Conrad v. Perales, 92 F. Supp. 2d 175 (W.D.N.Y. 2000) for discussion of a variation on this theme

[F] Wheelchairs, Supplies, and Other Durable Medical Equipment

Generally, Medicare pays for wheelchairs only if the wheelchair will improve the mobility of the beneficiary and improve his or her ability to undertake activities of daily living (ADLs). ADLs include personal feeding, dressing, and bathing. Other items that might be thought of as durable medical equipment (DME), such as bathroom grab bars, are explicitly excluded from Medicare coverage. DME is covered when needed for use in the home.[149] Medicaid coverage rules may be more expansive and must include a process for a beneficiary to request coverage for a non-covered item.[150]

When a physician believes that a patient requires Medicare-covered DME, the physician refers the patient to a medical equipment supplier who then obtains a Certificate of Medical Necessity from the physician.[151] The supplier provides the equipment to the patient and then submits a claim to the regional DME carrier for a determination as to Medicare coverage. As with most Medicare coverage decisions, determinations as to whether DME will be covered are generally made after the equipment has been provided to the patient. If Medicare coverage is denied, the patient, or a third-party payer such as Medicaid, may be liable.

Advocates have reported misalignment of coverage and payment procedures in Medicare and Medicaid that lead to denials and delays for important DME for this vulnerable population. While having both types of coverage should enhance benefits, the logistical problems created by this misalignment lead to barriers in accessing needed care.

Often these problems arise when beneficiaries transition from Medicaid-only status to dual Medicare-Medicaid status. In these instances, individuals who previously had no difficulty obtaining their DME through Medicaid, may face vendors who refuse to deliver the same DME once they become eligible for Medicare.

Advocates report that Medicaid's practice of only processing payment after issuance of a Medicare coverage decision, coupled with Medicare's lack of a coverage decision until after delivery of the DME, often creates an insurmountable barrier to an essential element of care for those individuals who are most in need. Advocates also report challenges due to the mismatch between Medicaid and Medicare suppliers, and how the competitive bidding process may affect availability of suppliers.[152]

---

[149] 42 C.F.R. §§ 410.38 (regulations for durable medical equipment) and 414.224 (regulations governing customized durable medical equipment).

[150] *See, e.g.*, Lankford v. Sherman, 451 F.3d 496 (8th Cir. 2006); State Medicaid Director Letter, Sept. 4, 1998, *available at* http://downloads.cms.gov/cmsgov/archived-downloads/SMDL/downloads/SMD090498.pdf (site visited June 8, 2016).

[151] See **Chapter 6** of this Handbook for a general discussion of Medicare's coverage of durable medical equipment (DME), including wheelchairs.

[152] On June 30, 2016, CMS published a proposed rule seeking information about the difficulties of dually eligible people obtaining DME. CMS also seeks information about potential solutions. 81 Fed.

In addition to limiting coverage for wheelchairs, Medicare may reimburse for wheelchairs and other mobility devices at a rate lower than that of many state Medicaid programs, whose fee structures for such items are often more generous.[153] Medical supplies may also be treated differently by the two programs: for example, a month's supply of catheters under Medicare is 30; a state Medicaid program may pay for 31 in a 31-day month. These disparities result in claims for dually eligible individuals being denied or reduced by Medicare, with complications ensuing when the individual seeks Medicaid coverage.

In the past, states told providers serving dually eligible individuals that they were required to serve them on an assignment-related basis, even though this is only required for physicians.[154] "Assignment-related basis" means they cannot receive more than the Medicare-approved amount for the supply or service. Because this amount is often less than they would receive from Medicaid for a Medicaid-only client, and because they are prohibited from billing a dually eligible person the way they would a non-dually eligible Medicare beneficiary, providers are often reluctant to serve dually eligible individuals. These state practices can be challenged as violations of comparability requirements in the Medicaid program and possibly as violations of state medical necessity law.[155]

Several states have addressed this issue by creating, in their Medicaid programs, a three-step process that promotes better access to DME coverage for dual eligibles. First, the individual gets prior authorization from the state for the wheelchair he or she needs. Then the individual gets the wheelchair from the supplier, who bills Medicare. If Medicare denies coverage, the supplier can still bill Medicaid because the prior authorization established Medicaid coverage.[156]

Reg. 42801 (June 30, 2016), Request for information (Section IX. Access to Care Issues for DME, page 42864-5.), *available at* https://www.federalregister.gov/articles/2016/06/30/2016-15188/medicare-program-end-stage-renal-disease-prospective-payment-system-coverage-and-payment-for-renal (site visited Sept. 21, 2016).

[153] As a general matter, in most states, Medicaid pays less for similar services than does Medicare. Customized wheelchairs and certain medical supplies are anomalous in this regard.

[154] 42 U.S.C. § 1395w-4(g)(3).

[155] *See, e.g.*, Charpentier v. Belshe, Civ. No. 90-758 EJG/PAN, Medicare & Medicaid Guide (CCH) 43,123 (N.D. Cal. 1994), holding that policies resulting in no access to certain Medicaid services for categorically needy individuals who were also eligible for Medicare, where such access was not so limited for individuals not "dually eligible," violated comparability requirements. *But see* Ralabate v. Wing, 1996 WL 377204, Medicare & Medicaid Guide (CCH) 44,550 (W.D.N.Y. 1996).

[156] *See, e.g.*, Connecticut law at C.G.S.A. § 17b-281a:

> (a) The Commissioner of Social Services shall extend the procedure in effect on October 1, 1998, for the preauthorization of the purchase or rental of new durable medical **equipment** and modification or repair of existing **equipment** to include services provided to **Medicaid** recipients who are also recipients of **Medicare.** The commissioner may enter into any necessary agreements with the Centers for **Medicare** and **Medicaid** Services to ensure the coordination of **authorization** and payment for durable medical **equipment** for such recipients.

The BBA '97 prohibits providers from billing dually eligible beneficiaries who are QMBs more than the provider receives from Medicare and Medicaid together, regardless of what that amount is.[157] It is not as clear whether the prohibition on billing *QMBs* includes within its meaning a prohibition on the provider receiving a payment *from the state* that is higher than the Medicare rate.[158]

[G] Differing Home Care Coverage Standards in Medicare and Medicaid Programs

Medicare covers a defined package of home health services when specified coverage criteria are met.[159] It covers a finite amount (no more than 35 hours per week) of skilled nursing care and home health aide services combined. In addition, the Medicare home health benefit covers skilled physical therapy, occupational therapy, speech language, pathology services, medical social work services, and some medical equipment and supplies.

Several Medicare requirements restrict the availability of the Medicare home health benefit. To qualify for home health services, a Medicare beneficiary must be homebound[160] and must require a skilled service.[161] The requirement that an individual be homebound is included in the statute.[162] Homebound status does

---

(b) Access to such procedure shall not be denied to a recipient on the basis that a **Medicare** coverage determination has not been made prior to the submission of a request for preauthorization to the commissioner. The commissioner shall not make payment for an item to a supplier of durable medical **equipment** on behalf of a **Medicare** recipient until the commissioner has received documentation establishing that a claim has been filed with, and a coverage and reimbursement decision has been rendered, under the **Medicare** program.

[157] BBA '97 § 4714(a)(1)(B), amending 42 U.S.C. § 1396a(n) by adding subparagraphs (2) and (3) (2009 Supp.). Note that this provision applies explicitly to QMBs, not necessarily to other dual eligibles. This particular protection is one reason that advocates should assure that their dually eligible clients with incomes under the state's QMB qualifying level are enrolled in the QMB program even though such enrollment might otherwise seem unnecessary.

[158] An additional wrinkle in this thorny issue is raised in CMS guidance from early 2008 that states that all providers must take assignment for all dual eligibles. *See, e.g.*, Feb. 2008 Memo. While providers are, by virtue of 42 U.S.C. § 1395cc(a)(1)(A)(i), prohibited from charging any QMB more than the Medicare and Medicaid payments (if any from the latter source), other provisions of Medicare law require only that physicians, not other providers, take assignment for dual eligibles. 42 U.S.C. § 1395w-4(g)(3).

[159] 42 U.S.C. §§ 1395f(a)(2)(C), 1395x(m). *See* **Chapter 4** of this Handbook for a thorough discussion of Medicare home health coverage criteria.

[160] 42 U.S.C. §§ 1395f(a)(2)(c) and 1395n(a)(2)(A).

[161] 42 U.S.C. § 1395f(a)(2)(C).

[162] 42 U.S.C. §§ 1395f(a)(8) and 1395n(a)(2)(F). The statutory language is "confined to the home." Under an amendment to this section passed in 2000, beneficiaries receiving therapeutic, psychosocial, or medical treatment in an adult day care program may still be considered "homebound." Moreover, absences from home for the purpose of attending a religious service are deemed to be of infrequent or short duration, in keeping with the statutory standard.

not preclude infrequent absences from the home for non-medical reasons such as hair dresser appointments, religious services, weddings, an occasional dinner, etc. To meet the statutory definition there must remain a normal inability to leave home without a considerable and taxing effort, or the assistance of another.

However, interpretations by both home health providers and Medicare Administrative Contractors (formerly, and sometimes still, called Fiscal Intermediaries) are often narrower than necessary and operate to limit the availability of the Medicare home health benefit.

For example, *any* absence from the home setting may lead to a decision by the home health agency that the patient is not homebound and therefore does not qualify for Medicare coverage. As a result of such a determination, the agency will no longer bill Medicare. If the beneficiary can pay to continue the services, he or she can ask the agency to submit a "demand bill" to Medicare to get an official coverage determination by Medicare. A demand bill is submitted when the agency itself does not believe there is Medicare coverage but the beneficiary seeks an official determination, which is a condition precedent to a Medicare appeal. There is no right under Medicare, as there is in Medicaid,[163] to continued coverage pending the outcome of an appeal. Accordingly, unless another payment source exists, as a practical matter, the home health agency makes final decisions regarding Medicare coverage.

Individuals who are dually eligible may need to look to Medicaid home care benefits to meet some or all of their needs, as well as to sustain their Medicare appeals. Medicaid mandatory home health care coverage rules are similar to Medicare rules, with two significant exceptions: they require neither homebound status nor that a skilled service be needed.[164] In addition to mandatory home health, all states include in their Medicaid programs home- and community-based services provided to limited populations through waiver of certain federal Medicaid requirements or modifications of their Medicaid State Plan.[165] These programs vary widely in their eligibility and services. They usually offer

---

[163] 42 U.S.C. § 1396a(a)(3); 42 C.F.R. § 431.220; Goldberg v. Kelly, 397 U.S. 254 (1970). This concept is often referred to as aid paid pending. It is a hallmark of the Medicaid program that advocates seek to have expanded to all health care recipients.

[164] 42 U.S.C. §§ 1396a(a)(10)(D), 1396d. Although neither the Medicaid statute nor the Medicaid regulations use the "homebound" standard, states have, in the past, incorporated it into their Medicaid home health programs. CMS has informed states that such a requirement is impermissible under Medicaid regulations at 42 C.F.R. §§ 440.230(c) and 440.240(b). State Medicaid Director Letter of July 25, 2000, Olmstead Update No. 3, Attachment 3-g, *available at* http://www.cms.gov/smdl/downloads/smd072500b.pdf (site visited Sept. 21, 2016). To the author's knowledge, the most recent action by CMS with respect to this issue came in a letter sent to the Director of the Missouri Department of Social Services in February 2010 informing the state that it was out of compliance with federal Medicaid law by requiring homebound status for the receipt of Medicaid home health services.

[165] 42 U.S.C. § 1396a(a)(10)(D). These programs are referred to as waiver programs because certain Medicaid statutory requirements are waived by the federal government for limited purposes.

"nonmedical" services, such as companion services, chore services, or adult day care, in addition to the more traditional home health care services offered by Medicare and the Medicaid mandatory home health benefit.

While some dual eligibles may need the services of one or the other program, many could benefit from enhanced coordination of the services offered by Medicare and Medicaid. This is particularly true with respect to coordination between Medicare and the Medicaid waiver home care programs. BBA '97 imposed a statutory limit on the amount of certain key home health services for which Medicare will pay. BBA '97 explicitly defined the "part-time or intermittent" quantitative standard for Medicare home health services to mean less than 35 hours a week of a combination of skilled nursing and home health aide services. That is the maximum amount of those services that Medicare will cover. Although Medicaid home health regulations adopt the "part-time or intermittent" language from Medicare, the Medicaid statute contains no such limitation. The regulations, therefore, may be subject to challenge. Most waiver programs also limit coverage through a cap on the amount of money or hours of care available to a beneficiary. Coordination of Medicare and Medicaid benefits can thus enhance the total quantity of care that may be offered to an individual and, in doing so, can also enhance the quality of care and quality of life for the beneficiary. Indeed, it can make the difference between being able to remain in a home setting and being forced to accept a residential long-term care placement.

§ 10.07 MANAGED CARE ISSUES FOR DUALLY ELIGIBLE INDIVIDUALS

[A] Overview

Dual eligibility presents a particularly wide spectrum of complexity when enrollment in managed care is introduced into the mix of possibilities. While both Medicare and Medicaid offer managed care options, with limited exceptions, neither program requires those who are dually eligible to enroll. Changes in payment for, and structure of, MA plans made in the MMA have resulted in a surge in the number of dually eligible beneficiaries participating in such plans. According to the *MACPAC March 2015 Report*, more than 20 percent of dual eligibles were enrolled for at least part of 2010 in a Medicare Advantage plan. This is up from only 7 percent in 1998.[166] Programmatic differences between Medicare and

The DRA authorizes states to provide such services as part of their regular Medicaid program, without having to seek a waiver. DRA, § 6086, amending 42 U.S.C. § 1396n by adding subsection (i). ACA § 2401, amending § 1915 of the Social Security Act, 42 U.S.C. § 1396n, further expands home and community-based options for care.

[166] MMA §§ 201, 211; 42 U.S.C. § 1395w-23. According to *MACPAC March 2015 Report*, among the 9.6 million dually eligible, 2 million were enrolled for at least part of the year in an MA plan. Of those in an MA plan, 1.5 million were in MSP or full-benefit Medicaid. For June 2015, CMS reports that 1,693,593 individuals are enrolled in Medicare Advantage (MA) Special Needs

Medicaid in requirements for beneficiaries and for participating managed care organizations have made coordination between the two programs difficult. Due to this and other coordination difficulties, few states have promoted enrollment of dually eligible individuals into Medicaid managed care; fewer states require them to enroll.[167]

Policy initiatives developing under provisions of the ACA favor an integrated approach to care for the dually eligible that blends Medicare and Medicaid dollars and covers both acute care (now primarily paid for by Medicare) and non-skilled long-term care (now primarily paid for by Medicaid).[168] Programs of All-Inclusive Care for the Elderly (PACE), which have operated for more than 20 years, are one such model, but PACE programs are limited in their scope,

---

Plans (SNPs) for Dual Eligibles. This number is about 15 to 20 percent of the total population of dual eligibles. CMS, "Special Needs Plans Comprehensive Report" (2014-05), *available at* http://www.cms.gov/Research-Statistics-Data-and-Systems/Statistics-Trends-and-Reports/MCRAdvPartDEnrolData/Special-Needs-Plan-SNP-Data-Items/SNP-Comprehensive-Report-2014-05.html?DLPage=1&DLSort=1&DLSortDir=descending (site visited June 8, 2016). This number does not account for duals who are enrolled in other types of MA plans. For a discussion of this, see, e.g., Kaiser Family Foundation, "Medicare's Role for Dual Eligible Beneficiaries" (Apr. 2012), *available at* http://www.kff.org/medicare/upload/8138-02.pdf (site visited June 8, 2016). *See also* CBO, "Dual Eligible Beneficiaries of Medicare and Medicaid: Characteristics, Health Care Spending and Evolving Policies" (June 2013), *available at* http://www.cbo.gov/publication/44308 (site visited June 8, 2016). In a more general discussion of dual eligibles in managed care (either Medicare, or Medicaid, or both) the March 2010 report from the Center for Health Care Strategies called *Options for Integrating Care for Dual Eligible Beneficiaries* reports that over 80 percent of dual eligibles get their care through fee-for-service delivery systems. The report does not distinguish between Medicare and Medicaid enrollments, though it is possible for a dual eligible to receive Medicare services outside a managed care plan but receive Medicaid through a plan, and vice versa. For historical experience of duals in managed care, see, e.g., Edith Walsh et al., "Case Studies of Managed Care Arrangements for Dually Eligible Beneficiaries," Research Triangle Institute for CMS (Sept. 26, 2003), *available at* http://spectra.rti.org/pubs/ManagedCareStudies.pdf (site visited June 9, 2016) (hereinafter Case Studies). The range of participation among the states historically is remarkable: in 1998, Oregon had 36.5 percent of its dual eligibles in MA plans while Mississippi had 0.1 percent (one-tenth of one percent). To this author's knowledge, similar data do not exist for later years. With respect to Medicare Advantage Dual Eligible SNPs, in 2016, the following states had no dual eligible SNPs at all (Alaska, Kansas, Nebraska, Nevada, New Hampshire, North Dakota, Oklahoma, Rhode Island, South Dakota, Vermont, Wyoming); five states have between 13 and 24 SNPs for dual eligibles (California, Florida, New York, Texas, Wisconsin). *See* CMS 2016 SNP Landscape, *available at* https://www.cms.gov/Medicare/Prescription-Drug-Coverage/PrescriptionDrugCovGenin/ (site visited Sept.28, 2016).

[167] *See, e.g.*, The Kaiser Family Foundation, "Dual Eligible Enrollment in Medicaid Managed Care, by Plan Type" (2011 data), *available at* http://kff.org/medicaid/state-indicator/dual-eligible-enrollment-in-medicaid-managed-care-by-plan-type/ (site visited June 8, 2016).

[168] *See, e.g.*, Medicare and Medicaid Coordination Office website at https://www.cms.gov/Medicare-Medicaid-Coordination/Medicare-and-Medicaid-Coordination/Medicare-Medicaid-Coordination-Office/ (site visited June 8, 2016).

currently serving less than one percent of the dually eligible population.[169] The ACA moved this agenda forward in significant ways by mandating the establishment of two new Centers within the CMS, both of which focus attention on such integrated care.[170] The Medicare-Medicaid Coordination Office (MMCO) and the Center for Medicare and Medicaid Innovation (Innovation Center, or CMMI) will be discussed more fully at the end of this section.

The MMA's authorization of Medicare Advantage SNPs, including such plans for dual eligibles, has changed the landscape with respect to dual eligibles in Medicare managed care.[171] In June 2016, 568 SNPs were available to "special needs" Medicare beneficiaries (down from 769 in 2008, up from 541 in 2015); 350 of those are designed to serve dually eligible beneficiaries (down from 443 in 2008, up from 336 in 2015).[172] Some are Medicaid managed care plans entering the Medicare market. In many respects these plans, with their state contracts and experience serving special needs individuals such as dual eligibles, represent the SNPs with the most promise of actually meeting the special needs of the dually eligible population. Many approved SNPs, however, do not have contracts with state Medicaid agencies and are new to serving special needs individuals. Although it is clear that the SNP option is popular with private MA health plan sponsors, little is known about what SNPs are actually providing that distinguishes them from other MA plans or from traditional Medicare, and it is not known whether fully integrated care that benefits the beneficiary will result.[173]

---

[169] Notably, in its 2013 report to Congress, the Medicare-Medicaid Coordination Office recommended a PACE pilot program for individuals between the ages of 21 and 55. Currently PACE programs are available only to those 55 and older. Recent data from the National PACE organization show 121 PACE programs operating in 31 states. National PACE Association, *available at* http://www.npaonline.org/pace-you/find-pace-program-your-neighborhood (site visited Sept. 28, 2016).

[170] ACA §§ 2602 and 3021.

[171] MMA § 231, amending 42 U.S.C. §§ 1395w-21(a)(2)(A) and 1395w-28.

[172] *See* CMS, SNP Comprehensive Report—June 2016, *available at* https://www.cms.gov/Research-Statistics-Data-and-Systems/Statistics-Trends-and-Reports/MCRAdvPartDEnrolData/Special-Needs-Plan-SNP-Data-Items/SNP-Comprehensive-Report-2016-06.html?DLPage=1&DLEntries=10&DLSort=1&DLSortDir=descending (site visited July 7, 2016) (hereinafter *2016 Special Needs Plans Comprehensive Report*), *and*, for 2015 data, SNP Comprehensive Report—June 2015, *available at* https://www.cms.gov/Research-Statistics-Data-and-Systems/Statistics-Trends-and-Reports/MCRAdvPartDEnrolData/Special-Needs-Plan-SNP-Data-Items/SNP-Comprehensive-Report-2015-01.html (site visited June 8, 2016); for 2008 data, SNP Comprehensive Report—June 2008, *available at* http://www.cms.gov/Research-Statistics-Data-and-Systems/Statistics-Trends-and-Reports/MCRAdvPartDEnrolData/Special-Needs-Plan-SNP-Data-Items/CMS1211836.html (site visited June 8, 2016).

[173] *See, e.g.*, Alissa Halperin, Patricia Nemore & Vicki Gottlich, *What's So Special About Medicare Advantage Special Needs Plans? Assessing Medicare Special Needs Plans for Dual Eligibles*, Marquette Elder's Advisor, Vol. 8, No. 2 (Spring 2007); Christie Provost Peters, "Medicare Advantage SNPs: A New Opportunity for Integrated Care?" National Health Policy Forum, Issue Brief #808 (Nov. 11, 2005), *available at* http://www.nhpf.org/library/details.cfm/2503 (site visited June 8, 2016); Memo from Danielle Moon, Director, Medicare Drug and Health Plan Contract Administration Group to Medicare Advantage Organizations offering Special Needs Plans, "CMS

MIPPA included new requirements for SNPs, effective beginning the 2010 plan year.[174] All SNPs must exclusively enroll individuals who meet the definition of the population for which they are designated. All plans must have in place an evidence-based model of care with appropriate networks of providers and specialists and must provide care management that includes an annual assessment of the enrollee's needs, a plan of care, and the provision of care by an interdisciplinary team. Dual Eligible SNPs (D-SNPs) must provide each enrollee a comprehensive statement about his or her coverage under Medicaid and cost-sharing requirements/protections. Any D-SNP wishing to start up or expand its existing coverage area must have a contract with the state Medicaid agency under which the plan will provide or arrange for the provision of benefits to which the enrollee is entitled under the state Medicaid plan. Contracts with the state may, but are not required to, include coverage for long-term care services.[175] Beyond the state contract issue for D-SNPs, the fate of SNPs, especially D-SNPs, may be partially linked to the success or lack of success of initiatives being proposed by some states to integrate financing and care delivery systems for the dually eligible, discussed in **§ 10.09**. Some states propose to rely on D-SNPs in the design of their delivery systems. To the extent states are permitted to enroll all their dually eligible beneficiaries into their new systems, SNPs may gain or lose enrollees.

The MMA required ongoing Congressional reauthorization of SNPs. Most recently, SNPs were reauthorized through 2018 by MACRA.[176] Without Congressional reauthorization, SNPs lose the authority to restrict enrollment to certain populations and must be open to all Medicare beneficiaries. Congressional reauthorization provides a unique opportunity for advocates to seek legislative improvements, such as those included in MIPPA, to strengthen SNPs.[177] One such improvement—an integrated appeals process—was proposed, but not adopted, in recent reauthorizing legislation.[178]

Expectations of Special Needs Plans for 2010," *available at* http://www.medicareadvocacy.org/old-site/InfoByTopic/MedicareAdvantageAndHMOs/10_01.11.SNPMemo.pdf (site visited June 8, 2016).

[174] MIPPA §§ 164 and 165, amending § 1859 of the Social Security Act, 42 U.S.C. § 139w-28(f).

[175] 42 C.F.R. §§ 422.2, 422.4, 422.52, 422.107, and 422.504 for new requirements on SNPs.

[176] MACRA § 206.

[177] For a discussion of recommendations for 2014 reauthorization, see Center for Medicare Advocacy, "Dual Eligible Special Needs Plans: Considerations for Reauthorization" (Dec. 5, 2013), *available at* http://www.medicareadvocacy.org/dual-eligible-special-needs-plans-considerations-for-reauthorization/ (site visited June 8, 2016).

[178] An integrated Medicare-Medicaid appeals process for dual eligible SNPs was recommended in MMCO's 2012 report to Congress and included in the Senate bill S. 1871: The SGR Repeal and Medicare Beneficiary Access Improvement Act of 2013. This provision did not, however, make it into the final reconciled bill, the aforementioned Protection Access to Medicare Act of 2014 Pub. L. No. 133-93. *See* CMS, "Medicare-Medicaid Coordination Office FY 2012 Report to Congress," *available at* http://www.cms.gov/Medicare-Medicaid-Coordination/Medicare-and-Medicaid-Coordination/Medicare-Medicaid-Coordination-Office/Downloads/MMCO_2012_RTC_v2.pdf (site visited June 8, 2016).

[B] Managed Care/Fee-for-Service Matrix

At least four combinations of health care coverage for dually eligible individuals are possible when managed care is offered in the mix. A dually eligible individual can be in:

1. Medicaid fee-for-service/traditional Medicare
2. Medicaid fee-for-service/Medicare Advantage
3. Medicaid managed care/traditional Medicare
4. Medicaid managed care/Medicare Advantage

In the last case, the individual could be enrolled in two different managed care plans and become very confused as to which plan he or she should look to for coverage. Dually eligible individuals may increasingly find themselves in this situation as more states move their Medicaid, and especially Medicaid Long Term Services and Supports (LTSS) programs into managed care.[179] Managed care issues arise concerning state obligations to pay Medicare managed care cost-sharing for QMBs, as well as concerning MA organizations' efforts to limit their liability for providing care by trying to shift coverage to the Medicaid program. Additional issues arise with respect to a dually eligible individual's right to choose a nursing facility if he or she is in an MA plan that has a network of nursing facilities. These issues are discussed below.

[C] State Medicaid Payment of Cost-Sharing for Medicare Managed Care Enrollees

Dual eligibles who are enrolled in MA plans and who are QMBs are entitled to have their states pay MA plan copayments and are excused from liability for such payments; other dual eligibles are entitled to have at least some copayments paid.[180] Little is known, however, about whether, and how, states actually make

---

[179] *See generally* National Senior Citizens Law Center, "LTSS in Managed Care," *available at* http://nsclcarchives.org/index.php/mltss/#.VipV6H6rTct (site visited June 8, 2016). Traditionally, Medicaid beneficiaries in need of Long Term Services and Supports were exempt from state mandatory Medicaid managed care. Increasingly, this exemption is being lifted as states transition their entire Medicaid populations into managed care.

[180] 42 U.S.C. § 1396d(p)(3); SMM, Chap. 3, § 3490.12; MMCO-CMCS Informational Bulletin June 7, 2013, Subject: Payment of Medicare Cost Sharing for Qualified Medicare Beneficiaries (QMBs), *available at* http://www.medicaid.gov/Federal-Policy-Guidance/downloads/CIB-06-07-2013.pdf (site visited June 8, 2016); MMCO-CMCS Informational Bulletin Jan. 6, 2012, Subject: Billing for Services Provided to Qualified Medicare Beneficiaries (QMBs), *available at* http://www.medicareadvocacy.org/wp-content/uploads/2012/01/cib-01-06-12.pdf (site visited June 8, 2016); CMS MLN Matters, "Prohibition on Balance Billing Qualified Medicare Beneficiaries

such copayments.[181] Information is available from CMS to identify MA plan enrollees.[182] Until a state has a formal system in place, advocates should advise clients to inform their state of their MA plan enrollment and have the MA plan providers bill the state for any copayments for which the individual is responsible.[183] Recent regulations governing Medicare Advantage plans should improve this situation as well because plans must include provisions in contracts with all providers in their networks prohibiting providers from charging dual eligibles cost-sharing that is not due under their state Medicaid program.[184]

(QMBs), *available at* http://www.cms.gov/Outreach-and-Education/Medicare-Learning-Network-MLN/MLNMattersArticles/downloads/SE1128.pdf (site visited June 8, 2016); Feb. 2008 Memo and two attachments, memo *available at* http://www.medicareadvocacy.org/old-site/InfoByTopic/MedicareSavingsPrograms/MedSavProg_08_04.24.ARACostShare.pdf, Balance Billing attachment *available at* http://www.medicareadvocacy.org/old-site/InfoByTopic/MedicareSavingsPrograms/MedSavProg_08_04.24.ARABalanceBilling.pdf, and Capitation attachment *available at* http://www.medicareadvocacy.org/old-site/InfoByTopic/MedicareSavingsPrograms/MedSavProg_08_04.24.ARACapitation.pdf (sites visited June 8, 2016); June 2007 Memo (**Appendix 10-3** of this Handbook); January 2012 Memo (**Appendix 10-4** of this Handbook).

[181] *See Variations in State Medicaid.* Only 19 states responded affirmatively to a 1999 survey question asking whether the state pays copayments in Medicare managed care. Eighteen states reported that they did not; the remaining states either did not answer or do not have Medicare managed care in their state. The author is not aware of more recent data on this subject.

[182] According to one CMS official, "States still do get that information on their MMA response file. If they'd like, they can also query our system on an ad hoc basis (i.e., when they need it, not just when MMA response file is returned)." E-mail of July 3, 2012, from Sharon Donovan, Medicare-Medicaid Coordination Office CMS, to Patricia B. Nemore, Center for Medicare Advocacy, *available from* kkertesz@medicareadvocacy.org. CMS now accepts MMA files from states on a daily basis.

[183] Guidance from CMS issued in February 2008 discusses potential complexities associated with paying cost-sharing for services delivered through MA plans. *See* 42 U.S.C. §§ 1396d(p)(3), 1396a(n)(2); SMM, CMS Pub. 45, Ch. 3, Eligibility § 3490.12, *see* **Appendix 10-1** of this Handbook. *See also* Feb. 2008 Memo and two attachments, memo *available at* http://www.medicareadvocacy.org/old-site/InfoByTopic/MedicareSavingsPrograms/MedSavProg_08_04.24.ARACostShare.pdf, Balance Billing attachment *available at* http://www.medicareadvocacy.org/old-site/InfoByTopic/MedicareSavingsPrograms/MedSavProg_08_04.24.ARABalanceBilling.pdf, and Capitation attachment *available at* http://www.medicareadvocacy.org/old-site/InfoByTopic/MedicareSavingsPrograms/MedSavProg_08_04.24.ARACapitation.pdf (sites visited June 8, 2016); Nov. 1991 Memo (**Appendix 10-2** of this Handbook); June 2007 Memo (**Appendix 10-3** of this Handbook); and Memorandum of June 30, 2000 from Director, DEHPG, Subject: Policy Memorandum on Medicaid Obligations to Pay Medicare Cost-sharing Expenses for Qualified Medicare Beneficiaries in Medicare Health Maintenance Organizations or Competitive Medical Plans or Medicare Plus Choice Organizations—Information (hereinafter Jan. 6, 2000 Memo) (**Appendix 10-4** of this Handbook).

[184] 42 C.F.R. § 422.504(g)(1)(iii).

[D] Managed Long-Term Care

Several problematic scenarios can arise if an individual enrolled in an MA plan needs or is receiving nursing home care.

> ■ **SCENARIO ONE:** A dually eligible beneficiary living at home and enrolled in an MA plan needs skilled nursing home care. The MA plan waives the Medicare three-day prior hospitalization requirement. The beneficiary wants to move to an out-of-network nursing home. The MA plan says it will not cover such care. The state Medicaid agency refuses to pay for Medicaid coverage since the individual could have received Medicare coverage through the MA plan in which she chose to enroll.

A solution to this problem is to disenroll from the MA plan. Disenrollment is effective the month following the individual's notice to disenroll; the beneficiary is then free to choose a nursing facility and have Medicaid pay, since she would not have met the three-day prior hospitalization requirement for Medicare coverage. This solution will not work for most Medicare beneficiaries because they are generally "locked" into MA plans for most of the plan year, but dual eligibles are able to change enrollment monthly.[185]

> ■ **SCENARIO TWO:** The same beneficiary needs a nursing home placement but does not need skilled care. There is no possibility of Medicare coverage for the nursing home stay.

Even though she chooses an out-of-network nursing facility, Medicaid will pay because the MA plan has no liability for non-Medicare-covered nursing facility care.[186] But, note that this outcome assumes the beneficiary is not also enrolled in a Medicaid managed care plan that has its own network of facilities, which may exclude this facility. This is unlikely, however, as few states include nursing facility care in their Medicaid managed care coverage, and few dual eligibles are enrolled in Medicaid managed care. However, this scenario is rapidly changing as states look to managed care to provide long-term care.

---

[185] 42 C.F.R. § 422.62(b)(4) authorizes CMS to establish a special enrollment period for an individual who meets "such other exceptional conditions" as CMS may provide. Through informal guidance, CMS has established a permanent special enrollment period for dual eligibles. *See* Medicare Managed Care Manual Chapter 2—Medicare Advantage Enrollment and Disenrollment § 30.4.4 #5, *available at* https://www.cms.gov/MedicareMangCareEligEnrol/Downloads/FINALMAEnrollmentandDisenrollmentGuidanceUpdateforCY2011.pdf (site visited June 8, 2016).

[186] *See, e.g.*, Preston letter. Advocates are cautioned that while the principles enunciated in this letter are embodied in the law, actual state policy and practice is likely to be less favorable and the state may refuse to pay for a resident who has declined Medicare coverage. Advocates are encouraged, nonetheless, to make these arguments for clients who wish to return to a non-Medicare-certified bed. A copy of the letter can be found in **Appendix 10-5** of this Handbook.

■ **SCENARIO THREE:** A dually eligible individual enrolled in an MA plan resides in a non-Medicare-certified bed in a nursing facility. She becomes eligible for the Medicare SNF benefit after a three-day hospitalization. Would she be required to move to an in-network Medicare certified bed or would she be allowed to waive her right to Medicare coverage and remain in the non-Medicare-certified bed, with Medicaid as the payer?

The Medicaid law requires states to allow beneficiaries to receive services from any certified provider who chooses to serve them.[187] While there is legal support for the view that if the individual chooses to remain in a bed in which she could not receive Medicare services, there is no Medicare liability and Medicaid must pay, it is unlikely that many states interpret their obligations that way, so advocates should be cautious about advising their clients in this regard.[188]

Legislation enacted in December 2000 addressed a fourth variation of the nursing home musical bed game for dually eligible beneficiaries enrolled in an MA plan: the situation where an MA plan enrollee in a non-network SNF is transferred to a hospital and seeks to return to his or her former SNF instead of going to an in-network facility.[189] The legislation permits the enrollee to choose to return to the former (out-of-network) facility if the facility agrees to accept the MA plan payment for services. This provision appears to actually undermine existing rights of dually eligible individuals, although the situation it addresses seems unlikely to arise very often.

Historically, enrollment of dually eligible beneficiaries in Medicare and Medicaid managed care has been considerably more limited than such enrollment of non-dual populations in both programs. Even states that have used managed care for this population may "carve out" long-term care for different treatment. As noted above, this situation appears to be shifting, bolstered by the MMA provision for MA plans for special populations, including plans for institutionalized individuals (I-SNPs), and by state Medicaid programs' increased interest in using managed care for this population in need of long-term services and supports. Current enrollment in I-SNPs is relatively low: 59,364 (down from 138,097 in 2008, up from 50,474 in 2015) individuals were enrolled in 79 (down from 89 in 2008, up from 57 in 2015) plans as of June 2016.[190] This author has no data on how many of these individuals are dually eligible. More importantly, little is known about what I-SNPs offer by way of extra or "special" benefits that would not be

[187] 42 U.S.C. § 1396a(a)(23).

[188] *But see* Preston letter at **Appendix 10-5** of this Handbook. Advocates are cautioned that while the principles enunciated in this letter are embodied in the law, actual state policy and practice is likely to be less favorable and the state may refuse to pay for a resident who has declined Medicare coverage.

[189] BIPA § 621.

[190] *See also 2016 Special Needs Plans Comprehensive Report.*

required either through the Medicaid program of the state in which they operate or by the federal nursing home reform law.[191]

§ 10.08 PROGRAMS OF ALL-INCLUSIVE CARE FOR THE ELDERLY

As noted briefly earlier, PACE programs are operated under both the Medicare and Medicaid programs[192] to replicate the comprehensive services delivery and financing model for acute and long-term care created by On Lok Senior Health Services in San Francisco in the late 1970s. Until the BBA '97, PACE programs were operated under waivers of both Medicare and Medicaid requirements. The BBA '97 amended both Medicare and Medicaid to establish PACE as a non-waiver program, with states having the option to include PACE in their Medicaid program. PACE is the embodiment of the "integrated" approach to serving dually eligible older people, putting Medicare and Medicaid dollars and acute and long-term care services together and thus avoiding many of the confusions and complexities described elsewhere in this chapter. A goal of PACE is to provide a full range of long-term care services to frail older people in a community-based setting.

To be eligible for PACE services, enrollees must need the level of health care required from a nursing facility under Medicaid.[193] But PACE programs are not merely long-term care programs; generally speaking, they must provide the full array of both acute and long-term care services required under Medicare and Medicaid as well as any services determined necessary for the individual enrollee by his or her interdisciplinary team.[194]

Based on a study released in May 2015, HHS can no longer limit PACE programs to nonprofit entities. The CMS study found "no statistically significant difference" between seniors enrolled in PACE through Senior LIFE and those in other PACE programs in regard to frailty, access to care, and quality of care received. Expenditures for both the nonprofit and for-profit programs also were similar.[195]

---

[191] *See, e.g.*, Alissa Eden Halperin, Patricia Nemore, Vicki Gottlich & Toby Edelman, *Medicare Advantage Special Needs Plans for "Institutionalized Individuals": What Advantage to Enrollment?*, 1 St. Louis U.J. Health L. & Pol'y 175 (2007).

[192] The principal statutory provisions governing PACE, 42 U.S.C. § 1395eee (Medicare) and 42 U.S.C. § 1396u-4 (Medicaid), are substantially the same. Final regulations are at 42 C.F.R. Pt. 460, 71 Fed. Reg. 71,334 (Dec. 8, 2006). While most enrollees in PACE programs will be dually eligible, such dual enrollment is not a requirement for the program. However, for those who are enrolled in either Medicare or Medicaid or both, regulations for those programs will govern beneficiaries' rights and entitlements, in addition to the provisions of the PACE regulations.

[193] 42 C.F.R. § 460.150(b)(2).

[194] *See generally* 42 C.F.R. § 460.92.

[195] CMS, "Report to Congress: The Centers for Medicare & Medicaid Services' Evaluation of For-Profit PACE Programs under Section 4804(b) of the Balanced Budget Act of 1997," *available*

As noted above, PACE is a paradigm of integrated care for dual eligibles. However it has been very slow to develop. A document on the website of the National PACE Association lists 121 PACE programs (up from 114 in 2015) in 31 states enrolling about 38,072 participants in January 2015 (an increase from 2014).[196]

§ 10.09 MEDICARE-MEDICAID COORDINATION OFFICE AND CENTER FOR MEDICARE AND MEDICAID INNOVATION

The ACA created two new centers within CMS, both of which have an impact on the care for dual eligibles.[197]

The purpose of the Medicare-Medicaid Coordination Office (MMCO) (originally called the Federal Coordinated Health Care Officer) is to integrate benefits under Medicare and Medicaid and to improve coordination between the federal government and the states on behalf of individuals dually eligible for Medicare and Medicaid. The Office has eight statutory goals:

1. Provide dual eligibles full access to all benefits of both programs;
2. Simplify access to services;
3. Improve quality;
4. Eliminate regulatory conflicts;
5. Improve continuity of care and safe transitions;
6. Increase dual eligibles' understanding of the programs;
7. Eliminate cost-shifting between the two programs and among providers; and
8. Improve performance of providers.

Specific responsibilities are to:

- Provide states, Medicare Advantage SNPs, plan sponsors, and others with the tools to develop programs that align Medicare and Medicaid benefits;
- Support state efforts to align acute and long-term care services for duals with Medicare service;

at http://innovation.cms.gov/Files/reports/RTC_For-Profit_PACE_Report_to_Congress_051915_Clean.pdf (site visited June 8, 2016).

[196] National PACE Association, *available at* http://www.npaonline.org/pace-you/find-pace-program-your-neighborhood (site visited June 9, 2016).

[197] ACA §§ 2602 (Federal Coordinated Health Care Office) and 3021 (Center for Medicare and Medicaid Innovation). The latter section amends the Social Security Act by adding, after § 1115, a new § 1115A.

- Support coordination of contracting and oversight with respect to Medicare and Medicaid to promote the statutory goals;
- Consult and coordinate with the Medicare Payment Advisory Commission (MedPac); and
- Study drug coverage for new full-benefit dual eligibles.

The Secretary is directed to report annually to Congress on recommendations for legislation to improve care for dual eligibles.[198]

The MMCO has no authority, per se, with respect to Medicare or Medicaid. The authority rests with the Secretary of HHS, but on a practical basis, with CMS, which has jurisdiction over Medicare and Medicaid within HHS.

The purpose of the Innovation Center "is to test innovative payment and service delivery models to reduce program expenditures under the applicable titles while preserving or enhancing the quality of care furnished to individuals under such titles."[199] Among the 18 models to be tested by the new Center is one that allows states "to test and evaluate fully integrating care for dual eligible individuals in the state, including the management and oversight of all funds under the applicable titles with respect to such individuals."[200] Through the section of the law that created the Innovation Center, the Secretary of HHS is given broad authority to waive provisions of the Medicare law to advance the specific models identified in the legislation.

In July 2011, the MMCO, in partnership with the Innovation Center, launched a demonstration initiative intended to better serve dual eligibles by increasing coordination and integration between Medicare and Medicaid.[201] The MMCO has also shown willingness to explore alternative demonstration models with states.

It is an ambitious initiative: MMCO aims to have as many as 2 million of the roughly 7 million full dual eligibles enrolled in demonstrations once all are fully operational. The demonstrations are jointly managed by CMS and the participating states. The centerpiece of the capitated model is the Medicare–Medicaid Plan (MMP), a health plan that provides all Medicare-covered and all or most

[198] Medicare-Medicaid Coordination Office Fiscal Year 2012 Report to Congress, *available at* http://www.cms.gov/Medicare-Medicaid-Coordination/Medicare-and-Medicaid-Coordination/Medicare-Medicaid-Coordination-Office/Downloads/MMCO_2012_RTC_v2.pdf (site visited June 8, 2016); Medicare-Medicaid Coordination Office Fiscal Year 2013 Report to Congress, *available at* http://www.cms.gov/Medicare-Medicaid-Coordination/Medicare-and-Medicaid-Coordination/Medicare-Medicaid-Coordination-Office/Downloads/MMCO_2013_RTC.pdf (site visited June 8, 2016).

[199] ACA § 3021(a).

[200] ACA § 3021(b)(2)(B)(x).

[201] For updates on states with innovation models, see http://innovation.cms.gov/ (site visited June 9, 2016).

Medicaid-covered services to dual eligibles. MMPs receive a blended capitation rate that combines Medicare Part A, Part B, and Part D and Medicaid payments. The aim is that the integration of Medicare and Medicaid financing, combined with extensive requirements for care coordination, will lead to better care for this vulnerable population, while maintaining or reducing Medicare and Medicaid spending.[202]

Though the initiative is in its early stages, it has gotten off to a rough start with delays in enrollment, high costs, and withdrawals of states and plans from the program.[203] The demonstrations were initially set to run for three years, but CMS announced in July 2015 that states may extend their demonstrations by two years.[204]

As of June 2016, about 370,000 beneficiaries were enrolled and receiving services from health plans in 9 states with capitaled financial alignment demonstrations.[205] The capitated financial alignment demonstrations are in nine states as of June 2016. These states include California, Illinois, Massachusetts, Michigan, New York, Ohio, South Carolina, Texas, and Virginia.[206]

All states that currently have demonstrations approved by CMS have now started to enroll beneficiaries, and enrollment will continue. In addition, Colorado and Washington are enrolling beneficiaries in managed fee-for-service (FFS) demonstrations, and Minnesota is implementing an administrative alignment demonstration using Medicare Advantage Special Needs Plans for Dual Eligible Beneficiaries.[207]

As of June 2016, California's demonstration had the largest enrollment, with nearly 123,000 beneficiaries, followed by Ohio, Texas, Illinois, Michigan, Virginia, Massachusetts, New York, and South Carolina. These states' demonstrations have been in effect for different lengths of time, with Massachusetts first

---

[202] *MedPAC June 2016 Report* at 264-5.

[203] Virgil Dickson, *Future of Dual-Eligible Demonstrations Questioned Due to Low Enrollment,* Modern Healthcare (Apr. 21, 2015), *available at* http://www.modernhealthcare.com/article/20150421/NEWS/150429978 (site visited June 8, 2016).

[204] CMS letter July 16, *available at* http://www.modernhealthcare.com/assets/pdf/CH10117592.PDF (site visited June 8, 2016).

[205] Kaiser Family Foundation, "Health Plan Enrollment in the Capitated Financial Alignment Demonstrations for Dual Eligible Beneficiaries," *available at* http://kff.org/medicaid/fact-sheet/health-plan-enrollment-in-the-capitated-financial-alignment-demonstrations-for-dual-eligible-beneficiaries/ (site visited Nov. 21, 2016).

[206] Kaiser Family Foundation, "Health Plan Enrollment in the Capitated Financial Alignment Demonstrations for Dual Eligible Beneficiaries," *available at* http://kff.org/medicaid/fact-sheet/health-plan-enrollment-in-the-capitated-financial-alignment-demonstrations-for-dual-eligible-beneficiaries/ (site visited Nov. 21, 2016).

[207] Kaiser Family Foundation, "Health Plan Enrollment in the Capitated Financial Alignment Demonstrations for Dual Eligible Beneficiaries," *available at* http://kff.org/medicaid/fact-sheet/health-plan-enrollment-in-the-capitated-financial-alignment-demonstrations-for-dual-eligible-beneficiaries/ (site visited Nov. 21, 2016).

enrolling beneficiaries in October, 2013 and Michigan beginning voluntary enrollment in April 2015.

In all states, beneficiaries can opt out of the demonstration.[208]

[208] CMS letter July 16, *available at* http://www.modernhealthcare.com/assets/pdf/CH10117592.PDF (site visited June 8, 2016).

APPENDIX 10-1 CMS PUB. 45: STATE MEDICAID MANUAL, CHAPTER 3 ELIGIBILITY

Sec. 3490.12 Medicare Cost-Sharing Expenses and Federal Financial Participation

Sec. 3490.13 Payment of Monthly Premiums for Medicare Part B and for Premium Hospital Insurance Under Medicare Part A

3490.12 Medicare Cost Sharing Expenses and Federal Financial Participation.—FFP is available for medical assistance for Medicare cost sharing expenses. These expenses are defined as:

- Monthly premiums for Medicare Part B and, where applicable, for Premium Hospital Insurance under Medicare Part A;
- Medicare Part A and Part B deductibles and coinsurance, including deductibles and coinsurance that HMOs and CMPs charge their Medicare enrollees in lieu of the Medicare deductibles and coinsurance that the beneficiaries would pay if they were not enrolled in an HMO or CMP; and
- At your option, premiums for enrollment with a Health Maintenance Organization (HMO) or a Competitive Medical Plan (CMP) under § 1876 of the Act.

Note that FFP is available for Medicare cost sharing expenses at the beginning of the month after the month in which you determine an individual is eligible for Medicaid as a QMB.

3490.13 Payment of Monthly Premiums for Medicare Part B and for Premium Hospital Insurance Under Medicare Part A.—You are required to pay the full amount of monthly premiums for Medicare Part B and, where applicable, for Premium Hospital Insurance under Medicare Part A. You may enroll QMBs and pay the Medicare Part B premiums under the State buy-in process under § 1843 of the Act. Effective January 1, 1990, a State may request and obtain a buy-in agreement modification to include payment of Part A premiums on behalf of QMBs. Payment of premiums through buy-in is advantageous because premiums paid through this method are not subject to the increases otherwise applicable in the case of late enrollment or re-enrollment. States without a buy-in agreement for Part B and/or Part A, are billed for the premiums (which may include any penalty applicable to the QMB for late enrollment) when the State seeks to enroll the QMB in Part A or Part B.

APPENDIX 10-2 NOVEMBER 22, 1991, MEMORANDUM FROM DIRECTOR OF OFFICE OF MEDICAID MANAGEMENT, MB, TO DEPUTY CHIEF COUNSEL, OFFICE OF THE GENERAL COUNSEL, RE: STATE REQUIREMENT TO PAY MEDICARE PREMIUMS FOR QUALIFIED MEDICARE BENEFICIARIES (QMB)—ACTION

DEPARTMENT OF HEALTH & HUMAN SERVICES

Health Care Financing Administration

Memorandum

Date NOV 22 1991

Refer to: FMC-33

From Director
Office of Medicaid Management, MB

Subject State Requirement to Pay Medicare Premiums for Qualified Medicare Beneficiaries (QMB)--ACTION

To Deputy Chief Counsel
Office of the General Counsel

ISSUE

It has come to our attention that as many as 3 million Medicare beneficiaries may not be receiving the benefits to which they are entitled under section 1902(a)(10)(E) of the Social Security Act (the QMB provision).

We seek to confirm that the Federal Government has the authority necessary to compel States to: (a) enroll these individuals as QMBs, and (b) provide such individuals with all the benefits to which they are entitled under the QMB provision. Can the Health Care Financing Administration (HCFA) unilaterally accrete likely QMBs in Part A buy-in States and all other States without any State approval up front?

BACKGROUND

The Medicare Catastrophic Coverage Act of 1988 amended the Social Security Act to make coverage of certain Medicare beneficiaries for Medicare cost sharing expenses a mandatory Medicaid coverage group.

The State Medicaid Manual (SMM), Part 3, Eligibility, was revised to instruct the States as to their obligations under this section. A QMB is defined as an individual who:

- is entitled to Medicare hospital insurance benefits under Part A, with or without payment of premiums;
- has income (as determined for Supplemental Security Income (SSI) purposes) that does not exceed 100 percent of the Federal poverty level; and
- has resources (as determined for SSI purposes) that do not exceed twice the maximum amount established for SSI eligibility.

Page 2 - Deputy Chief Counsel, OGC

Potential QMBs Currently Without Part A

Part A Buy-in States

As a result of the Omnibus Budget Reconciliation Act of 1989, States are permitted, at their option, to modify their Part B buy-in agreement (copy attached) to include paying Part A premiums for QMBs. On February 7, 1990, we sent a letter to all State Medicaid Directors informing States of this option.

Thirty-Four States currently participate in Part A buy-in. The buy-in process allows States to accrete individuals as QMBs and to automatically enroll them in Part A. States are required (SMM section 3490.5) to conduct a review of all recipients currently eligible under the State plan and who also are entitled under Part A of Medicare to determine whether they meet the eligibility requirements for QMB status.

At the time the buy-in process became effective, there were 270,000 individuals in the 34 buy-in States for whom the States were purchasing Part B coverage on their behalf but who lacked Part A coverage and should have been accreted as QMBs through the Part A buy-in process. Of these, only 124,458 individuals have been accreted as QMBs. These States have had more than 15 months to perform the required review of their records, and accrete the remaining 145,000 individuals as QMBs, but have failed to do so.

We have sent a letter to the 18 most egregious States asking that they review the records of the remaining individuals in order to make the QMB determination and accrete them as QMBs. We have asked that they let us know what they plan to do in this regard.

It is our intention that after a period of 6 weeks from the date of our letter (October 10) HCFA will accrete the remaining individuals as QMBs and bill the State for the Part A premium. The State will then have an opportunity to delete any individuals they have determined do not meet the QMB eligibility criteria.

Page 3 - Deputy Chief Counsel, OGC

<u>Non-Part A Buy-in States</u>

In the 16 States which did not modify their buy-in agreement, there were 250,000 individuals who could have been QMBs except for their lack of enrollment in Part A. In these States the individual must enroll in Part A. In 1989 we made available an easy method for the States to have these individuals enroll in Part A. An SSA-795 contact form was modified permitting the individual to sign a preprinted statement asking to be enrolled in Part A with the understanding that the State would be billed for the premium. To date, only 34,962 individuals have enrolled using this process. This is due, we believe, to State failure to inform the individual of this process.

It is our intention to mail the form directly to the remaining individuals, explaining the benefit to them, and instructing them to sign and return the form to us. Having thus established their enrollment in Part A, we intend to accrete these individuals as QMBs in a manner similar to that described earlier for the Part A buy-in States.

<u>Potential QMBs Already Entitled to Part A</u>

Finally, approximately 3.2 million Medicaid recipients are currently covered under Part A and have their Part B coverage purchased by States on their behalf. The vast majority of these individuals are SSI recipients. Of these, only 845,000 have been identified as QMBs.

Although States are paying the $358.80 annual Part B premium, the beneficiary is not <u>guaranteed</u> the financial protection afforded under the statute for other costs; e.g., the $100 annual Part B deductible and 20-percent copayment for physician charges in excess of the deductible.

It is our intention to insert the required QMB identifier in the records of these 3.2 million individuals, and to inform the State of the QMB status of these individuals.

We are writing seeking your concurrence with these intended actions. Your prompt reply is appreciated. Should you have any questions please contact Mike Sparacino on extension 6-5918.

/S/
David McNally

Attachment

FMC-33:MSparacino:SGullick:MPSMISC DISK:A:OGCNOTE:11-12-91

APPENDIX 10-3 JUNE 11, 2007, MEMORANDUM FROM GALE P. ARDEN, DIRECTOR, DISABLED AND ELDERLY HEALTH PROGRAMS GROUP, TO ALL ASSOCIATE REGIONAL ADMINISTRATORS, DIVISION OF MEDICAID AND CHILDREN'S HEALTH, RE: MEDICAID OBLIGATIONS FOR COST-SHARING IN MEDICARE PART C PLANS

DEPARTMENT OF HEALTH & HUMAN SERVICES
Centers for Medicare & Medicaid Services
7500 Security Boulevard, Mail Stop S2-14-26
Baltimore, Maryland 21244-1850

CMS
CENTERS for MEDICARE & MEDICAID SERVICES

Center for Medicaid and State Operations
Disabled and Elderly Health Programs Group (DEHPG)

DATE: JUN 1 1 2007

FROM: Gale P. Arden, Director
Disabled and Elderly Health Programs Group

SUBJECT: Medicaid Obligations for Cost–Sharing in Medicare Part C Plans

TO: All Associate Regional Administrators
Division of Medicaid and Children's Health

Many questions have been raised by States, providers and Medicare Part C plans regarding Medicaid's obligation to pay cost-sharing for individuals who are eligible for both Medicare and Medicaid (dual eligibles) and who are enrolled in Medicare Part C, i.e. Medicare Advantage (MA) plans. Over the years CMS has issued guidance on various aspects of this question; however there has been no single document that brings this guidance together. The purpose of this memorandum is to provide a compilation of pertinent information found in statute, regulation and guidance in a concise format.

Dual eligibles are individuals enrolled in Medicare and eligible for Medicaid coverage, whether that Medicaid coverage is limited to certain costs, such as Medicare premiums, or the full benefits covered under the State Plan. Dual eligibles whose benefits are limited include Qualified Medicare Beneficiaries (QMB), Specified Low-income Medicare Beneficiaries (SLMB), Qualifying Individuals (QI), and Qualified Disabled Working Individuals (QDWI). Those eligible for full Medicaid benefits are called Full Benefit Dual Eligibles (FBDE). At times individuals may qualify for both limited coverage of Medicare cost sharing as well as full Medicaid benefits.

MA plans are health plan options approved by Medicare and run by private companies. These plans must provide all Part A and Part B services, and may offer additional services including Part D drug coverage. MA plans include Medicare Preferred Provider Organizations (PPO), Medicare Health Maintenance Organizations (HMO), Medicare Private Fee-for-Service (PFFS) plans, Medicare Medical Savings Account (MSA) plans and Medicare Special Needs Plans (SNP).

Medicare cost-sharing includes Part A and B premiums and Part C premiums for those enrolled in an MA plan. Medicare cost sharing also includes deductibles, co-insurance and, for MA plans, may include co-pays. Deductibles are fixed dollar amounts that an individual must pay out-of-pocket before the costs of services are covered. Co-insurance is a percentage of the cost of services. Co-payments are fixed dollar amounts that an individual must pay each time a service is received.

Page 2- All Associate Regional Administrators

Several factors determine whether or not Medicaid is liable for coverage of cost-sharing in MA plans. These factors include the dual eligible's coverage category, the type of cost-sharing, the options elected by the State, and payment limitations specified in the State Plan. The attached chart is intended to clarify how these factors affect whether or not the State Medicaid program has a liability for cost-sharing for dual eligibles in MA plans.

The information presented in this policy clarification is not intended to address all issues related to Part C cost-sharing for dual eligibles. This clarification is limited to State Medicaid program cost-sharing obligations, and does not address issues related to provider billing practices or beneficiary obligations.

Please share this information with the States in your regions. If you have any questions regarding this memorandum, please contact Christine Gerhardt at 410-786-0693, or christine.gerhardt@cms.hhs.gov.

Attachment

CMS/CMSO/DEHPG/DEEO: 5/9/07

Cost Sharing for Medicare Advantage Plans

Questions have been raised by States, providers and Medicare Advantage plans regarding the obligations of State Medicaid programs, and the availability of Federal Financial Participation (FFP), for dual-eligibles enrolled in Medicare Advantage plans.[1] In the past, guidance has been issued in the State Medicaid Manual, letters to CMS Associate Regional Administrators and other correspondence that addressed various aspects of this issue. To properly determine Medicaid liability for Part C cost sharing for a dual-eligible it is necessary to determine the individual's Medicaid coverage group and the type of Part C cost-sharing. Below is a description of the various coverage groups in which a dual-eligible could be certified. The chart that follows identifies the Medicaid liability by coverage group and type of Part C cost-sharing. The purpose of the chart is to clarify existing Centers for Medicare and Medicaid Services (CMS) policy by combining material from previously issued guidance, statute and regulation into a concise format, addressing all categories of dual-eligibles and all forms of Medicare Part C cost-sharing.

Description of Coverage Groups

Qualified Medicare Beneficiary (QMB Only)

A "QMB" is an individual who is entitled to Medicare Part A, has income that does not exceed 100% of the Federal Poverty Level (FPL), and whose resources do not exceed twice the Supplemental Security Income (SSI) limit. A QMB is eligible for Medicaid payment of Medicare premiums, deductibles, co-insurance and co-pays (except for Part D). QMBs who do not qualify for any additional Medicaid Benefits are called "QMB Only."

QMB Plus

A "QMB Plus" is an individual who meets all of the standards for QMB eligibility as described above, but who also meets the financial criteria for full Medicaid coverage. Such individuals are entitled to all benefits available to a QMB, as well as all benefits available under the State Plan to a fully eligible Medicaid recipient. These individuals often qualify for full Medicaid benefits by meeting the Medically Needy standards, or through spending down excess income to the Medically Needy level.

Specified Low-income Medicare Beneficiary (SLMB Only)

A "SLMB" is an individual who is entitled to Medicare Part A, has income that exceeds 100% FPL but is less than 120% FPL, and whose resources do not exceed twice the SSI limit. The only Medicaid benefit a SLMB is eligible for is payment of Medicare Part B premiums. SLMBs who do not qualify for any additional Medicaid benefits are called "SLMB Only".

[1] Sec. 201 of P. L. 108-173 established the Medicare Advantage program, consisting of the program under part C of Medicare. Any references to part C or "Medicare + Choice" were deemed to be references to "Medicare Advantage" or "MA". Thus, any references in past policy documents to "Medicare + Choice" plans are applicable to Medicare Advantage plans.

SLMB Plus

A "SLMB Plus" is an individual who meets the standards for SLMB eligibility, but who also meets the financial criteria for full Medicaid coverage. Such individuals are entitled to payment of Medicare Part B premiums, as well as all benefits available under the State Plan to a fully eligible Medicaid recipient. These individuals often qualify for Medicaid by meeting the Medically Needy standards, or though spending down excess income to the Medically Needy level.

Qualifying Individual (QI)

A "QI" is an individual who is entitled to Part A, has income that is at least 120% FPL but less than 135% FPL, resources that do not exceed twice the SSI limit, and who is not otherwise eligible for Medicaid. A QI is similar to a SLMB, in that the only benefit available is Medicaid payment of the Medicare Part B premium, however expenditures for QIs are 100% federally funded and the total expenditures are limited by statute.

Other Full Benefit Dual Eligibles (FBDE)

An individual who is eligible for Medicaid either categorically or through optional coverage groups such as medically needy or special income levels for institutionalized or home and community-based waivers, but who does not meet the income or resource criteria for QMB or SLMB.

Qualified Disabled and Working Individual (QDWI)

A QDWI is an individual who lost Medicare Part A benefits due to returning to work, but who is eligible to enroll in and purchase Medicare Part A. The individual's income may not exceed 200% FPL and resources may not exceed twice the SSI limit. The individual may not be otherwise eligible for Medicaid. QDWIs are eligible only for Medicaid payment of Part A premiums.

Description of Medicare Part C Benefits

Mandatory Supplemental Benefits

Mandatory supplemental benefits are non-drug benefits that are not covered by Medicare, but are covered by the plan for every enrollee of the plan. Mandatory supplemental benefits are paid for in full, directly by (or on behalf of) Medicare enrollees, in the form of premiums, cost sharing or through application of rebate dollars.

Optional Supplemental Benefits

Optional supplemental benefits are non-drug benefits that are not covered by Medicare. However, plan enrollees may choose whether to elect and pay for optional supplemental benefits. These services may be grouped or offered individually.

Deductibles, Coinsurance and Co-payments

Deductibles are fixed dollar amounts that an individual must pay out-of-pocket before the cost of services are covered by the MA organization. Coinsurance charges are a percentage of the costs for services. Co-payments are fixed dollar amounts that a beneficiary must pay when he or she uses a particular service. For purposes of this memorandum, co-payments charged by a Part C plan are considered to be coinsurance.

Medicare Part C Cost Sharing Chart

	Part C Premium for Basic Medicare Part A and Part B Benefits and Mandatory Supplemental Benefits	Part C Premium for Optional Supplemental Benefits	Medicare Deductibles, Coinsurance & Co-pays* (except Part D) **
QMB Only	Optional [1]	Not allowed [2]	Required [3]
QMB Plus	Optional [4]	Optional [5]	Required [6]
SLMB Only	Not allowed [7]	Not allowed [8]	Not allowed [9]
SLMB Plus	Not allowed [10]	Optional [11]	Conditional [12]
QI	Not allowed [13]	Not allowed [14]	Not allowed [15]
Other FBDEs	Not allowed [16]	Optional [17]	Conditional [18]
QDWI	Not allowed [19]	Not allowed [20]	Not allowed [21]

*Section 1902(n)(2) of the Social Security Act provides that a State is not required to provide any payment for any expenses incurred relating to payment for deductibles, coinsurance, or co-payment for Medicare cost-sharing to the extent that payment under Medicare for the service would exceed the payment amount that otherwise would be made under the State Medicaid plan. In any case where Medicare deductibles, coinsurance or co-payments are required to be paid or may be paid conditionally, the State may limit Medicaid payment as specified in Supplement 1 to Attachment 4.19-B of the State Plan, including nominal cost sharing amounts as permitted under Section 1916 of the Social Security Act and specified in attachment 4.18 of the State Plan. These payment limitations may result in a Medicaid payment of zero.

** Section 1935(d)(1) of the Social Security Act specifies that FFP is not available for the coverage of Part D drugs for Part D eligible individuals.

Notes to Cost Sharing Chart

1. Section 1905(p)(3) of the Social Security Act (the Act) provides that the State may opt to cover premiums for enrollment of QMBs in organizations under §1876. In a June 30, 2000 Policy Memorandum, from the Director of the Disabled and Elderly Health Programs Group, Thomas E. Hamilton, to Associate Regional Administrators (Hamilton Memo), CMS affirmed that §1905(p)(3) may be read to permit Medicare + Choice (now known as Medicare Advantage) to be included, at State option, under the same terms as §1876 contracts. States may make this election on page 29, 3.2(a)(1) of their Medicaid State Plan.

2. Section 1902(a)(10)(E)(i) specifies that QMB coverage is limited to the cost sharing described in §1905(p)(3) of the Act, and does not include coverage of additional services.

3. Coverage of Medicare deductibles and coinsurance are required for QMBs under §1902(a)(10)(E)(i) and §1905(p)(3) of the Act. Hamilton Memo, page 3, Medicare Cost Sharing, "... coinsurance includes the co-payments that M+C organizations charge when beneficiaries use services."

4. See note #1.

5. Section 1905(a) of the Act permits coverage of health insurance premiums, other than Medicare Part B, for medical or remedial care, except for individuals who could be enrolled in Part B but are not. Hamilton Memo, page 3, Monthly premiums in Medicare +Choice Organizations, "...since QMB Plus is also eligible for full Medicaid benefits, Medicaid may also pay premiums for supplemental benefits not covered by Medicare, but which are covered by Medicaid, if so elected in the State Plan (page 29b, 3.2(a)(2))."

6. See note #3.

7. Section 1902(a)(10)(E)(iii) and §1905(p)(3)(A)(ii) limit SLMB coverage to Part B premiums.

8. See note #7.

9. See note #7.

10. See note #7. For non-QMB dual-eligibles, FFP is not available for Medicaid coverage of Medicare Advantage premiums for basic Medicare services.

11. Section 1905(a) of the Act permits payment of health insurance premiums, other than Medicare Part B, for coverage of medical or remedial services, except for individuals who could be enrolled in Part B but are not. States may elect this option in their State Plan, page 29b, 3.2(a)(2).

12. For non-QMB eligibles, there is no Medicaid liability for cost sharing in a Medicare Advantage plan, however, States are liable for payment for Medicaid covered services rendered by Medicaid providers to Medicaid eligible individuals in excess of any third party (including Medicare Part C) liability. When the following conditions are met, there may be a liability for a specific service received through a Medicare Advantage plan:

- The Medicare service is also a covered service under the State Plan;
- The Medicare provider is also a Medicaid provider; and
- The amount specified in the State plan is greater than the Medicare payment amount.

13. Sections 1902(a)(10)(E)(iv) and §1905(p)(3)(A)(ii) of the Act limit QI coverage to Part B premiums.

14. See note #13.

15. See note #13.

16. For non-QMB dual-eligibles, there is no FFP available for Medicaid coverage of Medicare Advantage premiums for basic Medicare services.

17. See note #11.

18. See note #12.

19. Section 1902(a)(10)(E)(ii) and §1905(p)(3)(A)(i) limit QDWI coverage to Part A premiums.

20. See note #19.

21. See note #19.

APPENDIX 10-4 JANUARY 6, 2012, MEMORANDUM FROM DIRECTOR, MMCO-CMCS INFORMATIONAL BULLETIN CONCERNING BILLING FOR SERVICES PROVIDED TO QUALIFIED MEDICARE BENEFICIARIES (QMBs)

DEPARTMENT OF HEALTH AND HUMAN SERVICES
Centers for Medicare & Medicaid Services
7500 Security Boulevard, Mail Stop S2-26-12
Baltimore, MD 21244-1850

Center for Medicaid and CHIP Services

MMCO - CMCS Informational Bulletin

DATE: January 6, 2012

FROM: Melanie Bella, Director
Medicare-Medicaid Coordination Office

Cindy Mann, Director
Center for Medicaid and CHIP Services (CMCS)

SUBJECT: **Billing for Services Provided to Qualified Medicare Beneficiaries (QMBs)**

This Informational Bulletin provides information for State Medicaid Agencies and other interested parties regarding the prohibition on "balance-billing" Qualified Medicare Beneficiaries (QMB) for Medicare cost-sharing, including deductible, coinsurance, and copayments. This Bulletin is provided as a companion to a communication on this topic to Medicare providers in the form of a recently published Medicare Learning Network Matters article which is available at: http://www.cms.gov/MLNMattersArticles/Downloads/SE1128.pdf

Background on QMBs and Benefits
QMBs are persons who are entitled to Medicare Part A and are eligible for Medicare Part B; have incomes below 100 percent of the Federal Poverty Level; and have been determined to be eligible for QMB status by their State Medicaid Agency. Medicaid pays the Medicare Part A and B premiums, deductibles, co-insurance and co-payments for QMBs. At the State's discretion, Medicaid may also pay Part C Medicare Advantage premiums for those who join a Medicare Advantage plan that covers Medicare Part A and B benefits and Mandatory Supplemental Benefits. Regardless of whether the State Medicaid Agency opts to pay the Part C premium, the QMB is not liable for any co-insurance or deductibles for Part C benefits. States also have the authority to pay cost-sharing for QMBs for either the Medicare cost-sharing amount, the Medicaid State plan rate for the same service, or a rate between those amounts that is established by the State and approved by CMS.

Balance-billing Is Prohibited by Federal Law
Section 1902(n)(3)(B) of the Social Security Act (the Act), as modified by section 4714 of the Balanced Budget Act of 1997, prohibits Medicare providers from balance-billing QMBs for Medicare cost-sharing. All Medicare physicians, providers, and suppliers who offer services and supplies to QMBs are prohibited from billing QMBs for Medicare cost-sharing, including deductible, coinsurance, and copayments. This section of the Act is available at:

CMCS Informational Bulletin
January 6, 2012
Page 2

http://www.ssa.gov/OP_Home/ssact/title19/1902.htm. QMBs have no legal obligation to make further payment to a provider or Medicare managed care plan for Part A or Part B cost sharing. Providers who inappropriately bill QMBs for Medicare cost-sharing are subject to sanctions. Please note that the statute referenced above supersedes Section 3490.14 of the State Medicaid Manual, which is no longer in effect, but may be causing confusion about QMB billing.

How State Medicaid Agencies Process QMB Claims
Providers who serve QMBs are responsible for billing the State Medicaid Agency for any Medicare cost-sharing amounts the State is responsible for covering. When the State receives the claim, the Medicaid processing system determines whether the QMB is eligible and to which services they are entitled. Next, the system determines whether the provider is registered as a Medicaid-participating provider for the service. Particularly for QMB claims, the provider might only be a participating Medicare provider, and not a Medicaid-enrolled provider. The process for a Medicare provider to become enrolled as a Medicaid provider varies by State, and providers must follow each State's specific rules for provider enrollment to receive payment. Once the provider's registration is confirmed, the system uses the State's Medicaid payment policy to determine the State's cost-sharing contribution.

Ways to Improve the Claims Process
Effective communications between State Medicaid Agencies and QMB providers can improve the claims process for beneficiaries, States, and providers.

Below are strategies State Medicaid Agencies can consider to both improve communication with QMB providers and reinforce the provider prohibition on QMB balance-billing:

1. Offer separate enrollment forms for QMB-only providers, or allow providers to identify as "QMB-only" on provider enrollment applications.

2. Include guidance in all communications with QMB providers to emphasize that balance-billing of QMBs is a violation of the provider's Medicare agreement.

3. Provide clear guidelines for QMB providers on Medicaid provider enrollment and billing processes.

Additionally, CMS suggests the following for providers to improve communications with State Medicaid Agencies and better understand the billing process for services provided to QMBs:

1. Recognize that you must complete the State's provider enrollment process to be entered into the State payment system.

2. Contact the State Medicaid Agency directly to determine the process you need to follow to begin submitting claims and receiving payment.

CMCS Informational Bulletin
January 6, 2012
Page 3

Additional Information
More information about QMBs and other people dually eligible for Medicare and Medicaid is available through the Medicare Learning Network:
http://www.cms.gov/mlnproducts/downloads/medicare_beneficiaries_dual_eligibles_at_a_glance.pd

For more information about Medicare cost-sharing, see the "Get Help with Your Medicare Costs" publication:
http://www.medicare.gov/Publications/Pubs/pdf/10126.pdf

We hope this information is helpful. Please address any questions to Nancy Dieter at nancy.dieter@cms.hhs.gov or Edo Banach at edo.banach@cms.hhs.gov.

APPENDIX 10-5 LETTER OF MARCH 31, 1999, FROM THE ASSOCIATE REGIONAL ADMINISTRATOR, REGION 1, HEALTH CARE FINANCING ADMINISTRATION, TO HILARY S. DALIN, STAFF ATTORNEY, CENTER FOR MEDICARE ADVOCACY, INC., CONCERNING DUALLY ELIGIBLE INDIVIDUALS IN NURSING FACILITIES

Region I
J.F.K. Federal Building Government Center
Boston, MA 02203

March 31, 1999

Hilary S. Dalin
Staff Attorney
Center for Medicare Advocacy, Inc.
P.O. Box 350
Willimantic, Connecticut 06226

Dear Ms. Dalin:

This letter is the response to the questions you asked us by letter, dated February 10, 1999. Your questions and our responses follow below.

1. If a dually eligible individual who is enrolled in a Medicare HMO sought nursing home admission due solely to a need for custodial care and the Medicare HMO denied Medicare coverage on the grounds that the nursing facility was out-of-network, would Medicaid reimbursement also be precluded?

Neither Medicaid nor Medicare cover custodial care. However, if the individual met the nursing facility (NF) level of care requirements for Medicaid, then coverage by Medicaid would not be precluded. Medicare only covers skilled nursing facility (SNF) services, so Medicare or the Medicare HMO would not be a liable third party in this situation.

2. If a dually eligible individual who was enrolled in a Medicare HMO and resided in a non-Medicare-certified bed in a NF became eligible for the Medicare SNF benefit, would the resident be compelled to move to an in-network Medicare-certified bed or would such an individual be allowed to waive her right to Medicare coverage and remain in the non-Medicare-certified bed, with Medicaid as the payor?

Our answer is that the individual would not have to move, and thus Medicare would not be an available third party resource. A State may not, as a condition of eligibility, require an individual entitled to Medicare to obtain a "Medicare bed" in order to utilize her Medicare benefits. A liable third party resource exists for Medicaid purposes only to the extent that the services the individual receives from the provider of her choice are covered by the third party entity. According to section 1902(a)(23) of the Social Security Act (the Act), a Medicaid eligible individual may obtain Medicaid covered services from any qualified provider who undertakes to provide her the services.

In general, if the individual is in a "Medicaid bed" that is not also a "Medicare bed," then Medicare is not a liable third party and the Medicaid agency must pay the full amount allowed under the Medicaid payment schedule (42 CFR 433.139(c)). However, if a Medicaid/Medicare bed is available *at no cost* to the individual, *at the time of placement in a facility*, then the State may deny or reduce payment for a Medicaid only bed in an amount corresponding to the value of the available resource (section 1902(a)(17)(B) of the Act). In other words, Medicaid would only be liable for that amount of the Medicaid rate which exceeded the amount the third party would have paid, if any, had the individual been placed in an available Medicare covered bed.

I trust I have answered your questions fully. Should you have further questions, do not hesitate to contact me.

Sincerely

Ronald Preston
Associate Regional Administrator

APPENDIX 10-6 SOCIAL SECURITY ADMINISTRATION POLICY INSTRUCTION FOR INDIVIDUALS IN PART A BUY-IN STATES WHO DO NOT HAVE MEDICARE PART B

Identification Number:	**EM-08071 REV**	**Effective Date: 08/11/2008**
Intended Audience:	**All RCs/ARCs/ADs/FOs/TSCs/PSCs/ OCO//OCO-STs/ODARHQ/CMS**	
Originating Office:	**ORDP OISP**	
Title:	**Processing Instructions—Premium HI for Individuals in Part A Buy-In States Who Do Not Have Medicare Part B—Instructions Will Follow Shortly**	
Type:	**EM—Emergency Messages**	
Program:	**Medicare**	
Link To Reference:	**HI 00801.134, HI 00801.138, HI 00801.139, HI 00801.140, HI 00815.023, SM 00850.355, SM 00850.700, SM 03040.025**	

Retention Date: November 8, 2013

In Part A buy-in states, some low income individuals that appear eligible for Medicare Part A and Part B buy-in as qualified Medicare beneficiaries (QMB) are experiencing difficulty enrolling in Part B at their local Social Security offices. QMB's are individuals who are eligible for Medicaid payment of their Medicare premiums, deductibles, and coinsurance. The confusion seems to occur with individuals who want to file for Premium Part A, do not have Part B, and are outside of an enrollment period.

If an individual contacts the field office (FO) and appears to meet the QMB eligibility requirements, resides in a Part A buy-in State, wishes to file for Premium Part A, and does not have Part B, the individual may file an application for Part B and conditional enrollment in Premium Part A. Since the individual resides in a Part A buy-in State, the application does not have to be filed in an enrollment period; it may be filed at any time.

Currently, MCS will not accept a Part B and conditional Part A enrollment filed outside of an enrollment period for an individual who resides in a Part A Buy-in State. MCS will generate exception message number 20604—Check BIC M Decision Status—SMI Application Not in Enrollment Period. To address this exception, the FO needs to input the claim into MCS and then prepare an A101/ EF101 for the Part B and conditional Part A award when the exception is received.

POMS instructions are being updated. Until national instructions are published, follow these processing instructions:

FO Processing Instructions:

- Take an initial claim for Part B and conditional Part A through MCS (i.e. select claim type 5 = UNINS MED ONLY on APPL screen)
- Develop proofs of age, citizenship or LAPR, and residency.
- Review the earnings record for accuracy. A reduced Hospital Insurance Premium (HI) may apply if the individual or spouse has 30–39 quarters of coverage (see HI 01005.007, Reduced Hospital Insurance (HI) Premium).
- Prepare an A101. If problems occur with the A101 prepare an EF101. Instructions for screen completion for the A101 are in MCS 014.000 and EF101 are in T2PE 009.000.

Include the following entries:

➢ Part A entitlement on the HI Data screen (HIDA or EFHIDA);

- ■ START equal to the current operating month (COM)
- ■ BASIS of 'A'
- ■ TYPE of 'P'
- ■ PERIOD of 'Q'
- ■ FILING date;

➢ HI THIRD PARTY DATA (HITP or EFHITP);

- ■ START equal to PREMIUM HI START
- ■ CODE of Z99
- ■ CATEGORY of 'Q'

➢ HI Premium/Reduction (HIPR or EFHIPR)

- ■ START equal to PREMIUM HI START
- ■ PENALTY PERCENTAGE OF 00
- ■ Complete the following fields if applicable:
  - HAS 30 QTR
  - STOP
  - 30 QTR SSN

➢ Part B entitlement on the SMI Data screen (SMID or EFSMID);

- ■ START equal to COM
- ■ BASIS of 'A'
- ■ PERIOD of 'Q'

- ■ FILING date
- ■ MED-RET-US, if applicable

➢ SMI THIRD PARTY DATA (SMTP or EFSMTP);

- ■ Do not code THIRD PARTY DATA for Part B. See NOTE below.

➢ SMI PREMIUM HISTORY/VARIABLE SMI (SMPR or EFSMPR);

- ■ START equal to SMI START
- ■ PENALTY PERCENTAGE of 000

NOTE:
Refer the individual to the appropriate State office to file for QMB benefits. Emphasize the importance of promptly contacting the State. The individual may be billed for Part B premiums until state buy-in begins.

PSC Processing Instructions:

- Propagate A101/EF101 into MACADE.
- NOTE: Technicians should ensure that all coding referred to above are included on the screens of their MACADE action (see SM 00850.700).

If the enrollee does not contact the State and does not pay the Part B premiums when billed, Part B will terminate for nonpayment of premiums (HI 00820.035). Conditional Premium Part A will not generate a bill.

Direct all program-related and technical questions to your RO support staff or PSC OA staff. RO support staff or PSC OA staff may refer questions or problems to their Central Office contacts.

CHAPTER 11

PRESCRIPTION DRUG COVERAGE

§ 11.01 INTRODUCTION

On January 1, 2006, Medicare began providing limited assistance in paying for prescription drugs through Medicare Part D. The drug benefit, added by the Medicare Prescription Drug, Improvement, and Modernization Act of 2003 (MMA),[1] is not part of the traditional Medicare program but rather is offered through private insurance plans.

The Part D benefit is premised on the notion that individual Medicare beneficiaries should have a choice of private drug plans in order to select a drug benefit that best meets their needs. The statute creates three categories of drug plans: (1) stand-alone plans that offer only prescription drug coverage, (2) Medicare Advantage (MA) plans with a drug benefit, and (3) fallback plans. The categories of drug plans are discussed below.

Most significantly, the MMA established a low-income subsidy (LIS) for beneficiaries with incomes up to 150 percent of the federal poverty level (FPL) and with limited resources. The Act also eliminated, beginning January 1, 2006, all Medicaid drug coverage for the more than 10 million individuals who are dually eligible for Medicare and some form of Medicaid (dual eligibles). Moreover, it required states to pay back to the federal government (also known as the "claw back" provision) much of the savings they would otherwise realize from their reduced Medicaid obligation to dual eligible individuals. The Act also included other provisions that affect state budgets.

In 2017 private companies continue to offer a wide array of Part D plans throughout the country.[2] However, premiums are higher than in 2006. The average Part D premium (weighted by 2016 plan enrollment) is projected to increase by 9 percent from 2016 to 2017, up to $42.17 per month.[3]

§ 11.02 ELIGIBILITY FOR PART D COVERAGE

Prescription drug coverage under Part D is voluntary. A beneficiary may purchase Part D coverage if he or she has Part A or Part B. Beneficiaries do not have to have both Part A and Part B coverage to choose prescription drug

---

[1] Medicare Prescription Drug, Improvement, and Modernization Act of 2003 (MMA), Pub. L. No. 108-73 (Dec. 8, 2003); 42 U.S.C. §§ 1395w-101 *et seq.* (2004 Supp.); 42 C.F.R. § 423.506.

[2] For detailed information about Part D plans available in 2017, see the plan finder at http://www.medicare.gov (site visited June 3, 2016) and CMS's website at https://www.cms.gov/PrescriptionDrugCovGenIn/ (site visited June 3, 2016). Note that rules may change as CMS issues additional program guidance to clarify how the Part D program operates. *See, e.g.*, http://www.cms.gov/Medicare/Prescription-Drug-Coverage/PrescriptionDrugCovContra/index.html?redirect=/prescriptiondrugcovcontra/ (site visited June 3, 2016).

[3] *See* Henry J. Kaiser Family Foundation, J. Hoadley et al., "Medicare Part D: A First Look at Plan Offerings in 2017" (Oct. 2016), *available at* kff.org/medicare/issue-brief/medicare-part-d-a-first-look-at-presending-plans-in-2017 (site visited November 22, 2016).

coverage, unless they choose to enroll in an MA plan, in which case they must be in both Parts A and B.[4] The beneficiary must enroll in a Part D plan that serves the geographic region in which he or she resides.[5] Beneficiaries who are incarcerated are not eligible to participate in Part D, nor are beneficiaries who live outside the United States.[6]

§ 11.03 CHOICE OF DRUG PLANS

[A] Prescription Drug Plans

Medicare beneficiaries who remain in the traditional Medicare program will be able to purchase drug coverage through prescription drug plans (PDPs) that offer only prescription drug coverage. PDPs are offered by sponsoring organizations pursuant to a one-year contract with the Centers for Medicare & Medicaid Services (CMS).[7]

[B] Medicare Advantage Plans

Individuals who are enrolled in an MA plan established under Medicare Part C must receive their prescription drug coverage through their MA plan, known as a Medicare Advantage-Prescription Drug (MA-PD) plan. They may not purchase a separate PDP. However, individuals who are enrolled in a Medicare Medical Savings Account (MSA) or an MA Private Fee-for-Service (PFFS) plan that does not include a prescription drug option may purchase a PDP for their Part D coverage. Individuals who want to join an MA-PD must have both Medicare Part A and Part B.[8]

[C] Fallback Plans

The MMA authorized the creation of a fallback PDP in any prescription drug region[9] in which beneficiaries did not have a choice of enrollment in at least two

---

[4] 42 C.F.R. § 423.30.

[5] 42 U.S.C. § 1395w-101(b)(1)(b)(i).

[6] 42 C.F.R. §§ 423.4 and 423.30(a).

[7] 42 U.S.C. §§ 1395w-101(a)(1)(A), 1395w-112(b)(1), and 1395w-151(a)(14).

[8] 42 U.S.C. § 1395w-101(a)(1)(B). Note that individuals enrolled in a Medicare Part C Medical Savings Account (MSA) may also purchase a prescription drug plan (PDP) to obtain drug coverage, as may individuals who are enrolled in "cost plans" that do not offer drug coverage.

[9] 42 C.F.R. § 423.112. CMS has established 34 PDP regions, several of which include more than one state. Each PDP must offer coverage to all beneficiaries in the region that it serves. A PDP may also offer a plan that serves more than one region or that is national in scope. 42 U.S.C. § 1395 w-111(a).

plans.[10] However, since the beginning of the Part D program, there have been substantially more than two drug plans in each PDP region and CMS has not needed to contract with fallback plans. CMS anticipates that sufficient drug plans will be available for the foreseeable future.

§ 11.04 THE PART D DRUG BENEFIT

[A] Covered Part D Drugs

The MMA defines the drugs that are covered under Part D and therefore the drugs for which payment will be made under Part D in relationship to their coverage under Medicaid and under other parts of Medicare. A Part D drug is a drug that is approved by the Food and Drug Administration, for which a prescription is required, which is medically necessary and for a medically accepted indication, and for which payment is required under Medicaid.[11] Only compounds that contain at least one ingredient that is a Part D covered drug may be covered under Part D.[12] Biological products, including insulin and insulin supplies and smoking cessation drugs, are also covered under Part D.[13]

The MMA excludes from coverage those categories of drugs for which Medicaid payment is optional.[14] Excluded drugs may include drugs for erectile dysfunction (ED), drugs for weight gain or loss,[15] vitamins, and over-the-counter medications. Note that benzodiazepines and barbiturates, classes of drugs previously excluded from Part D coverage, are now considered Part D covered drugs.[16] Also note that some of the excluded drugs may be covered if prescribed for a purpose other than those prohibited by the MMA. For example, Viagra is an excluded drug if it is prescribed for ED, but it may be coverable if it is prescribed

[10] 42 U.S.C. §§ 1395w-103(a) and 1395w-111(g)(4). At least one of the available plans must be a PDP.

[11] 42 U.S.C. §§ 1395w-102(e)(1) and 1396r-8(d), (k).

[12] For low-income subsidy (LIS)-eligible individuals (*see* **§ 11.06** of this Handbook), the copayment amount is based on whether the most expensive Part D covered component of the compound drug is a generic or brand name drug. 42 C.F.R. § 423.120(d).

[13] 42 U.S.C. § 1395w-102(e)(1)(B), (2)(A).

[14] Congress added an exclusion for drugs used to treat sexual or erectile dysfunction unless prescribed for a different use approved by the Food and Drug Administration. QI, TMA, and Abstinence Programs Extension and Hurricane Katrina Unemployment Relief Act of 2005, Pub. L. No. 109-91 (Oct. 20, 2005), § 103; 42 U.S.C. §§ 1395w-102(e)(2)(A) and 1396r-8(d)(2).

[15] Drugs for weight gain will be covered to treat wasting diseases for people with HIV/AIDS, but weight loss drugs are not covered for treatment of obesity. 73 Fed. Reg. 20,486 (Apr. 15, 2008).

[16] Effective January 1, 2013, benzodiazepines and barbiturates (used for treating epilepsy, cancer, or a chronic mental health disorder) are included as Part D covered drugs. Medicare Improvements for Patients and Providers Act of 2008 (MIPPA), Pub. L. No. 110-275 (July 15, 2008), § 175. Effective January 1, 2014, all barbiturates are covered by Medicaid and therefore are covered by Medicare Part D. Patient Protection and Affordable Care Act of 2010 (PPACA; also known as the Affordable Care Act, or ACA), Pub. L. No. 111-148 (Mar. 23, 2010), § 2502.

for pulmonary hypertension. The MMA also excludes from Part D coverage those drugs for which payment could be made under Medicare Part A or Part B. CMS has determined that such drugs are excluded from Part D coverage even if the beneficiary does not have coverage under the part of Medicare (either Part A or Part B) that would generally pay for the drug.[17]

When certain conditions are met, Part D plans can cover drugs that are FDA-approved but prescribed in a manner not specifically approved by the FDA (in other words, for a diagnosis or condition that is not approved for that specific drug), sometimes called "off-label" use. Peer-reviewed medical journals that are identified by Medicare may be used to establish a medically accepted indication for off-label drugs, but only for those used in an anticancer chemotherapeutic regimen covered under Medicare Part D. For other uses, Part D covers drugs prescribed for off-label use only if the drugs are identified as safe and effective for that use in an officially recognized drug compendia.[18] "Compendia" are encyclopedias of drug chemicals, with information on dosage and usage. Part D rules concerning peer-reviewed medical journals differ from Part B rules, which allow reliance on such peer-reviewed medical journals for all categories and classes of drugs.[19]

Since 2011, all drug manufacturers must enter into an agreement with CMS to offer a 50 percent discount on brand name drugs filled in the coverage gap known as the "donut hole."[20] Drugs for which no manufacturer's agreement is in effect will no longer be considered covered drugs, even if they otherwise meet the definition of a Part D covered drug. CMS has authority to allow coverage of drugs not subject to a manufacturer discount agreement if CMS determines that the availability of the drug is essential to the health of Part D enrollees, or if there are extenuating circumstances.[21] Virtually all manufacturers signed agreements for 2017

---

[17] 42 C.F.R. § 423.100. *See also* Medicare Prescription Drug Benefit (PDB) Manual, Ch. 6 § 20.2, *available at* https://www.cms.gov/Medicare/Prescription-Drug-Coverage/PrescriptionDrugCovContra/downloads/chapter6.pdf.

[18] 42 U.S.C. § 1395w-102(e)(4); 42 C.F.R. § 423.100 (see definition of "Part D drug"); Medicare Prescription Drug Benefit (PDB) Manual, Ch. 6 § 10.6, *available at* https://www.cms.gov/Medicare/Prescription-Drug-Coverage/PrescriptionDrugCovContra/downloads/chapter6.pdf. *See also* the following materials from the Center for Medicare Advocacy: "CMA Report: Medicare Coverage for Off-Label Drug Use" (Sept. 2010), *available at* http://www.medicareadvocacy.org/cma-report-medicare-coverage-for-off-label-drug-use/; Weekly Alert "Federal Court Issues Favorable Off-label Part D Drug Coverage Decision" (May 18, 2016) *available at* http://www.medicareadvocacy.org/federal-court-issues-favorable-off-label-part-d-drug-coverage-decision/; and Weekly Alert "Medicare Part D and Off-Label Rx Denials" (June 29, 2016) *available at* http://www.medicareadvocacy.org/medicare-part-d-and-off-label-rx-denials/.

[19] 42 U.S.C. § 1395(t)(2)(B).

[20] Health Care and Education Reconciliation Act of 2010 (HCERA), Pub. L. No. 111-152 (Mar. 30, 2010), § 1101. *See* **§ 11.04[B][2]** of this Handbook.

[21] CMS, "The Medicare Coverage Gap Discount Program: Part D Sponsor Guidance" (May 21, 2010), § 50.2, *available at* https://www.cms.gov/PrescriptionDrugCovContra/downloads/MedicareCoverageGapDiscountProgramGuidance.zip (site visited June 6, 2016).

Part D plans are not required to pay for all covered Part D drugs. They may establish their own formularies, or list of covered drugs for which they will make payment, as long as their formularies and benefit structures are not found by CMS to discourage enrollment by certain Medicare beneficiaries.[22] Part D plans that follow the formulary classes and categories established by the United States Pharmacopoeia will pass the first discrimination test. However, CMS indicates it will still review formularies to determine whether the placement of specific drugs in each category or class, as well as other benefit design issues, discriminates against particular individuals. Plans also have the flexibility to change the drugs on their formulary during the course of the year, provided the change is approved by CMS.

Additionally, drug plan sponsors must include in their plans' formularies substantially all covered Part D drugs in a category or class identified by CMS. CMS has discretion to establish exceptions that allow a plan sponsor to exclude or attach utilization management requirements to a drug within a protected category or class.[23] The current six protected classes of drugs remain protected until such time as CMS establishes new criteria. They are:

1. antidepressant,
2. antipsychotic,
3. anticonvulsant,
4. anticancer,
5. immunosuppressant, and
6. anti-retroviral drugs.[24]

In response to the national issue of opioid abuse, Congress passed a bill in 2016 that allows Part D plan sponsors to establish drug management programs for enrollees who are deemed to be at-risk of prescription drug abuse that can limit access to coverage for frequently abused drugs, in part, by limiting the number of prescribers and pharmacies from which such drugs can be obtained.[25]

---

[22] 42 C.F.R. §§ 423.120(b) and 423.272(b).

[23] ACA § 3307.

[24] Medicare Prescription Drug Benefit (PDB) Manual, Ch. 6, § 30.2.5, *available at* https://www.cms.gov/Medicare/Prescription-Drug-Coverage/PrescriptionDrugCovContra/Downloads/Chapter6.pdf (site visited June 6, 2016).

[25] Title VII, § 704, Comprehensive Addiction and Recovery Act of 2016 (CARA), Pub. L. No. 114-198 (signed into law by President Obama on July 22, 2016).

[B] Structure of the Drug Benefit

[1] Introduction

PDPs are given a great deal of flexibility to design their own benefit structure.[26] Thus, the majority of plans have chosen not to offer the statutory "standard" benefit and instead offer an alternative benefit structure.[27] Variations in plan benefit structure, along with the substantial number of plans available, have adversely affected the ability of Medicare beneficiaries to compare plans that may best meets their needs. Beneficiaries are encouraged to use CMS's Plan finder tool (*www.medicare.gov/find-a-plan/questions/home.aspx*) or to avail themselves of the counseling services of their local State Health Insurance Assistance (SHIP) agencies.

[2] The Standard Drug Benefit

The MMA establishes a standard drug benefit that Part D plans may offer. The standard benefit is defined in terms of the financial structure of the cost-sharing and not in terms of the drugs that must be covered. In 2017, this standard benefit requires payment of a $400 deductible (an increase of $40 from 2016). The beneficiary then pays 25 percent of the cost of a covered Part D prescription drug up to the initial coverage limit of $3,700.[28] The initial coverage limit is calculated based on the total cost of the drugs used by the beneficiary.

Once the initial coverage limit is reached, the beneficiary enters a second deductible period known as the "donut hole" or coverage gap during which he or she is required to pay the full cost of his or her medicine.[29] The Health Care and

---

[26] All prescription drug plans, regardless of their benefit design, are supposed to provide beneficiaries with access to negotiated prices for the covered Part D drugs they include in their formulary, even if the beneficiary is required to pay the full cost of the prescription. 42 C.F.R. § 423.104(g)(1). Note that CMS revised the definition of "negotiated price" at 42 C.F.R. § 423.100 to reflect pharmacy price concessions. 79 Fed. Reg. 29844, 29876 (May 23, 2014).

[27] The Henry J. Kaiser Family Foundation (KFF), "The Medicare Part D Prescription Drug Benefit" (Oct. 2015), *available at* http://kff.org/medicare/fact-sheet/the-medicare-prescription-drug-benefit-fact-sheet/ (site visited June 6, 2016).

[28] The beneficiary's share of cost is $825, or 25 percent of the difference between $3,700 and $400. When added to the deductible, the beneficiary's total cost-sharing for formulary drugs up to the initial coverage limit is $1,225.

[29] CMS estimates that the total spending (both plan and beneficiary) needed to reach catastrophic coverage will increase from $7,515.22 (the 2016 figure) to $8,071.16. CMS, "Announcement of Calendar Year (CY) 2017 Medicare Advantage Capitation Rates and Medicare Advantage and Part D Payment Policies and Final Call Letter" (Apr. 4, 2016), *available at* https://www.cms.gov/Medicare/Health-Plans/MedicareAdvtgSpecRateStats/Downloads/Announcement2017.pdf (site visited June 6, 2016).

Education Reconciliation Act of 2010 (HCERA)[30] provides for the gradual phasing down of the donut hole until 2020, when it will be eliminated. Beginning in 2020, beneficiaries in the standard drug plan who have met their deductible will then pay 25 percent coinsurance for prescriptions until they reach the catastrophic level. To further the goal of eliminating the donut hole, drug manufacturers are now required to offer what amounts to a 50 percent discount on brand name drugs used during the donut hole. Beginning in 2013, additional subsidies apply to brand name drugs in the coverage gap, further reducing beneficiaries' costs. In 2017, beneficiaries will pay 40 percent of the cost-sharing for brand name drugs, plus applicable dispensing fees charged by the pharmacy. Note that even though the beneficiary is paying a discounted price, the full cost of brand name drugs counts toward meeting the annual out-of-pocket threshold. Also in 2017, the coinsurance for generic drugs in the donut hole will be reduced from 65 percent to 51 percent.

When the beneficiary's total out-of-pocket expenses for the year, including the deductible and initial coinsurance, reach $4,950, the beneficiary enters the catastrophic coverage period. The beneficiary then pays $3.30 for a generic or preferred drug and $8.25 for other drugs, or 5 percent coinsurance, whichever is greater.[31] Note that the $4,950 amount is calculated on a calendar year basis; a beneficiary who amasses $4,950 in out-of-pocket costs on December 31 will have to start all over again on January 1. The deductible, initial coverage limit, and annual out-of-pocket threshold have usually increased each year by the increase in expenditures for Part D drugs.

The MMA does not mandate a set premium amount. Premiums are determined by a bidding process and vary from plan to plan and from region to region. Private insurance companies that want to continue participating in the Part D drug benefit must submit new bids each year. Thus, the premiums they charge are likely to change on a yearly basis. Premium amounts are especially critical for individuals with low incomes, as they receive full LIS premium assistance only for plans that offer the standard benefit and that charge the lowest premiums.[32]

Beneficiaries with higher incomes who pay the Part B income-related premium are also subject to a Part D income-related premium. The increased premium amount is based on a percentage of the base beneficiary premium for that year as determined by CMS.[33]

---

[30] HCERA § 1101. On April 15, 2011, CMS issued final regulations implementing the Act's provisions that close the Part D coverage gap between 2011 and 2019. 42 C.F.R. §§ 423.104, 423.884.

[31] 42 U.S.C. § 1395w-102(b)(4)(A)(i)(II). *See also* CMS, "Announcement of Calendar Year (CY) 2017 Medicare Advantage Capitation Rates and Medicare Advantage and Part D Payment Policies and Final Call Letter" (Apr. 4, 2016), *available at* https://www.cms.gov/Medicare/Health-Plans/MedicareAdvtgSpecRateStats/Downloads/Announcement2017.pdf (site visited June 6, 2016).

[32] *See* **§ 11.06[B][1]** in this Handbook.

[33] ACA § 3308. *See* **Appendix 1-4** of this Handbook for the 2017 income-related adjustment amounts.

[3] Alternative Coverage and Enhanced Alternative Coverage

Part D drug plans are not required to offer the standard benefit, but they can offer alternative prescription drug coverage. Alternative coverage must be "actuarially equivalent" to the standard benefit. In other words, the value of the benefit package must be equal to the value of the standard benefit package.[34] In an actuarially equivalent plan, the cost-sharing varies through the use of such mechanisms as tiered copayments.[35] For example, a beneficiary's share of cost may be less for a generic or preferred brand name drug than for a non-preferred brand name drug. However, a plan that offers an alternative benefit package cannot impose a higher deductible ($400 in 2017) or require a higher out-of-pocket limit ($4,950 in 2017) than required by the standard benefit.

Plans can also offer enhanced alternative coverage that might include changes to the deductible and the initial coverage limit, although the deductible cannot be higher than the amount set in the statute ($400 in 2017). Enhanced alternative coverage might also include coverage of drugs that are excluded under Part D or coverage of some drugs in the coverage gap or donut hole. If supplemental coverage includes payment or discounted prices for brand name drugs in the donut hole, the supplemental coverage will pay first, before the manufacturer discount, and will include the dispensing fee. The beneficiary would then be responsible for any remainder of the negotiated price after the supplemental coverage, dispensing fee, and discounted price have been calculated.[36]

A PDP that wants to offer a drug plan with enhanced alternative coverage in a region must also offer a PDP with the basic benefit package in that region.[37]

[4] Calculating Beneficiary Expenses

As indicated above, only the costs of Part D covered drugs that are included on a plan's formulary (or that are approved through a formulary exception or

[34] 42 C.F.R. §§ 423.4, 423.100 and 423.104(e).

[35] Tiered cost-sharing above an amount set annually by CMS will be considered to be discriminatory. 42 C.F.R. § 423.104(d)(2)(iii).

[36] The manufacturer would be responsible for a 50 percent discount on the difference between the negotiated drug price and the supplemental benefit. CMS, "The Medicare Coverage Gap Discount Program: Part D Sponsor Guidance" (May 21, 2010), § 70.1, *available at* http://www.cms.gov/PrescriptionDrugCovContra/Downloads/MedicareCoverageGapDiscountProgramGuidance.zip (site visited June 6, 2016). Note that CMS revised the definition of "negotiated price" at 42 C.F.R. § 423.100 to reflect pharmacy price concessions. 79 Fed. Reg. 29,844, 29,876 (May 23, 2014).

[37] 42 C.F.R. § 423.104(f).

appeal) count toward the deductible and out-of-pocket limits.[38] For example, a beneficiary whose only drug expense in January 2017 is $500 for a Part D drug that is not on his or her plan's formulary will not meet the deductible, and the $4,950 in out-of-pocket expenses he or she will incur for the year for the non-formulary drug do not qualify for the reduced cost-sharing for high out-of-pocket costs.

Payments that count toward the yearly out-of-pocket limit are referred to as true out-of-pocket expenses, or TrOOP. Only out-of-pocket costs for formulary drugs that are paid for by the beneficiary; by a family member or other person acting on the beneficiary's behalf; or by a State Pharmaceutical Assistance Program (SPAP), AIDS Drug Assistance Programs (ADAPs), and the Indian Health Service are considered TrOOP and are counted toward the out-of-pocket limit.[39] Payments made by other insurance, including employer-sponsored plans, do not count toward the limit. Such uncounted payments increase the amount the beneficiary must spend before the reduced cost-sharing for high drug expenses begins. In sum, the beneficiary is responsible for paying premiums and the full costs of non-formulary prescriptions and gets no credit for these payments toward the out-of-pocket limit.

Calculating TrOOP gets more complicated as the donut hole is being phased down. The 50 percent manufacturer rebate for brand name drugs in the donut hole counts toward TrOOP. This is because the beneficiary is still responsible for the full cost of the drug. The manufacturer's rebate is treated the same as a payment by an SPAP or ADAP. However, the additional subsidy paid by the plan (5 percent in 2017) does not count toward TrOOP. In addition, the 40 percent reduction in the cost of a generic drug in the donut hole does not count toward TrOOP. This is because the beneficiary is responsible for only 51 percent of the drug's cost, not 100 percent.[40]

[C] Access to Pharmacies

A drug plan may establish a network of retail pharmacies with which it enters into contracts in its service area as long as the pharmacies are conveniently

---

[38] The regulations discuss beneficiary cost-sharing in terms of "covered Part D drugs." 42 C.F.R. § 423.104. CMS uses the term to describe Part D drugs that are on a plan's formulary. 70 Fed. Reg. 4228 (Jan. 28, 2005).

[39] 42 U.S.C. § 1395w-102(b)(4)(C)(ii), as amended by ACA § 3314; 42 C.F.R. §§ 423.100 and 423.464. Note that a final rule issued in 2015 amends § 423.464 to codify the requirement that Part D plans transfer and apply TrOOP-related data when an individual changes Part D plans mid-year. 80 Fed. Reg. 7912, 7934 (Feb. 12, 2015).

[40] *See, e.g.*, CMS, "Announcement of Calendar Year (CY) 2017 Medicare Advantage Capitation Rates and Medicare Advantage and Part D Payment Policies and Final Call Letter" (Apr. 4, 2016), *available at* https://www.cms.gov/Medicare/Health-Plans/MedicareAdvtgSpecRateStats/Downloads/Announcement2017.pdf (site visited June 6, 2016).

located for all enrollees in the drug plan. The network must include access to long-term care (LTC) pharmacies that serve residents of nursing facilities.[41] A plan that does not offer the standard benefit can offer reduced copayments to enrollees who use its preferred pharmacies. A plan may also offer access to formulary drugs through a mail-order pharmacy.[42]

A Part D plan must provide coverage for formulary drugs purchased at an out-of-network pharmacy if a beneficiary cannot reasonably be expected to obtain the drugs through a network pharmacy. A beneficiary may not use an out-of-network pharmacy on a routine basis. A beneficiary may also have to pay a larger copayment or coinsurance for using an out-of-network pharmacy.[43] Plans may establish policies and procedures, including contracting with pharmacies that are outside of their service areas, to accommodate seasonal residents, often known as "snowbirds," and travelers.[44]

In an effort to reduce the amount of unused prescription drugs in LTC facilities, a rule effective in January 2013 requires all Part D plan sponsors to contract with network pharmacies servicing LTC facilities to dispense nonexempt brand name medications in 14-day-or-less increments, rather than in 30-day supplies.[45]

§ 11.05 ENROLLING IN A PART D PLAN

[A] Introduction

Enrollment in Medicare Part D differs dramatically from enrollment in Medicare Part B, which is also voluntary. A beneficiary who becomes entitled to Part A is automatically enrolled in Part B unless he or she takes steps to notify the Social Security Administration (SSA) that he or she does not want Part B coverage. Enrollment in Part D requires the beneficiary to take affirmative steps to enroll and get Part D coverage. The beneficiary must first choose a drug plan from the options available in his or her area. Then, the beneficiary must enroll through the plan he or she chooses. If the beneficiary may be eligible for the LIS, he or she must file a separate application for the subsidy either with his or her state Medicaid agency or with SSA.

---

[41] *See* 73 Fed. Reg. 20,486 (Apr. 15, 2008).

[42] 42 C.F.R. § 423.120(a).

[43] 42 C.F.R. § 423.124.

[44] 70 Fed. Reg. 4193, 4249 (Jan. 28, 2005).

[45] 76 Fed. Reg. 21,573 (Apr. 15, 2011), adding 42 C.F.R. § 423.154. In response to comments from advocates and others, CMS clarified that regardless of the number of incremental dispensing events, the total cost-sharing for a Part D drug to which the 14-day-or-less dispensing requirements apply shall be no greater than the total cost-sharing that would be imposed for such Part D drug if the 14-day-or-less requirements did not apply.

[B] Enrollment Periods

[1] Initial Enrollment Period

The initial enrollment period (IEP) for Part D for individuals who are newly eligible for Medicare corresponds to the initial enrollment period for Part B, that is, the seven-month period running from three months before the month the individual first becomes eligible and ending three months after the first month of eligibility.[46] Individuals who are not eligible to enroll in Part D during their initial enrollment period, generally because they were living out of the country or were incarcerated, have an initial enrollment period that begins three months before they meet the eligibility criteria for Part D, the month of Part D eligibility, and three months afterward.[47]

There are two exceptions to the IEP that apply to people whose Medicare entitlement is based on disability, not age. People who become entitled to Medicare retroactively, generally because of a determination of retroactive entitlement to Social Security disability benefits, have a Part D IEP that begins with the month of receipt of notice of Medicare entitlement and continues for three months afterward. Additionally, people whose entitlement to Medicare is based on disability have a second Part D IEP when they turn age 65.[48]

[2] Annual Coordinated Election Period

The annual coordinated election period (ACEP) corresponds to the ACEP for Part C. Starting in 2011, that period runs from October 15 through December 7.[49]

[3] Special Enrollment Periods

Individuals may be eligible for a special enrollment period (SEP)[50] in certain situations, including, but not limited to:

---

[46] 42 C.F.R. §§ 423.38 and 407.14.

[47] PDB Manual, Ch. 3, § 30.1, *available at* http://cms.gov/Medicare/Eligibility-and-Enrollment/MedicarePresDrugEligEnrol/Downloads/CY-2014-PDP-Enrollment-and-Disenrollment-Guidance-r.pdf (site visited June 6, 2016).

[48] PDB Manual, Ch. 3, § 30.1, *available at* http://cms.gov/Medicare/Eligibility-and-Enrollment/MedicarePresDrugEligEnrol/Downloads/CY-2014-PDP-Enrollment-and-Disenrollment-Guidance-r.pdf (site visited June 6, 2016).

[49] ACA § 3204, amending 42 U.S.C. §§ 1395w-21(e)(2)(C) and 1395w-101(b)(1)(iii).

[50] 42 C.F.R. § 423.38(c). For a complete list of available SEPs, see PDB Manual, Ch. 3, *available at* http://cms.gov/Medicare/Eligibility-and-Enrollment/MedicarePresDrugEligEnrol/Downloads/CY-2014-PDP-Enrollment-and-Disenrollment-Guidance-r.pdf (site visited June 6, 2016). Note that effective December 2011, there is a SEP to join a PDP or MA plan with a 5 star performance rating (*see* PDB Manual, Ch. 3, § 30.3.8.8.H).

- They did not enroll in Part D during their initial enrollment because they had other prescription drug coverage deemed to be "creditable coverage," and they lose the creditable coverage;
- They were given incorrect information concerning the status of their other prescription drug coverage as creditable coverage;
- They were given incorrect information about enrollment by a federal employee;
- They have Medicare and full Medicaid coverage or a Medicare Savings Program (MSP) or are otherwise eligible for the Part D LIS;
- They move out of a plan's service area;
- Their PDP's or Medicare Advantage plan's contract with Medicare is terminated;
- They enrolled in an MA-PD during the first year of eligibility and want to return to traditional Medicare and a PDP;
- Their eligibility for an SPAP changes;
- They move into, reside in, or move out of a nursing home.

[4] Effective Date of Enrollment

Part D coverage becomes effective:[51]

- For an enrollment made prior to the month of eligibility, the first month of Part D eligibility;
- For an enrollment made subsequently, the month after the election of the Part D plan;
- For an enrollment made during the Annual Enrollment Period, January 1 of the following year;
- The effective date of an enrollment made during a SEP, including a SEP for someone who becomes eligible for the LIS, depends on the SEP.[52]

[51] 42 C.F.R. § 423.40.

[52] 75 Fed. Reg. 19,677 (Apr. 15, 2010), amending 42 C.F.R. § 423.34; CMS, PDB Manual, Ch. 3, § 30.3, "PDP Guidance: Eligibility, Enrollment and Disenrollment," *available at* http://cms.gov/Medicare/Eligibility-and-Enrollment/MedicarePresDrugEligEnrol/Downloads/CY-2014-PDP-Enrollment-and-Disenrollment-Guidance-r.pdf (site visited June 6, 2016).

[5] Involuntary Disenrollment

An individual may be involuntarily disenrolled from a drug plan for reasons similar to the grounds for disenrollment from an MA plan.[53] These include no longer living in the plan's service area, loss of eligibility for Part D, death of the individual, termination of the PDP, failure to pay premiums on a timely basis, and engaging in disruptive behavior that substantially impairs the ability of the plan to arrange for or provide services.[54] Note that a PDP may neither disenroll someone for failure to pay a premium if the enrollee is having premiums withheld from a monthly cash benefit check nor bill the enrollee directly for the premium. As of January 2011, there is a two-month grace period before a beneficiary can be involuntarily disenrolled from a Part D plan for failure to pay premiums. The grace period begins only after the beneficiary is notified that payment is due. It runs from the later of the first day of the month for which the premium is unpaid or the first day of the month after the date on which payment is requested.[55] Note that beneficiaries who establish good cause for failure to pay a premium that leads to disenrollment from a PDP and who pay the arrearage in full within three months of the disenrollment may be reinstated into the plan.[56] To the extent that an individual fails to pay only the Part D Income-Related Monthly Adjusted Amount (IRMAA), if applicable (the additional premium amount based on income, discussed at **§ 11.04[B][2]**), there will be an initial three-month grace period to pay this amount before the individual is disenrolled from the Part D plan.[57]

---

[53] 75 Fed. Reg. 19,677 (Apr. 15, 2010), amending 42 C.F.R. § 423.44. *See* discussion on enrollment and disenrollment in **Chapter 7**, Medicare Advantage, of this Handbook.

[54] 42 C.F.R. § 423.44.

[55] 74 Fed. Reg. 1494 (Jan. 12, 2009), amending 42 C.F.R. §§ 423.44 and 423.293.

[56] 76 Fed. Reg. 21,570 (Apr. 15, 2011), amending 42 C.F.R. § 423.44. Note that the failure to pay premiums must have been due to circumstances beyond the beneficiary's control. CMS provides further guidance on what constitutes good cause in the PDB Manual, Ch. 3, § 60.2.4, *available at* http://cms.gov/Medicare/Eligibility-and-Enrollment/MedicarePresDrugEligEnrol/Downloads/CY-2014-PDP-Enrollment-and-Disenrollment-Guidance-r.pdf (site visited June 6, 2015).

[57] 76 Fed. Reg. 21,456 (Apr. 15, 2011), amending 42 C.F.R. § 423.44. Note that this is similar to the three-month grace period for individuals who fail to pay their Part B IRMAA. If payment is not made during the grace period, an individual will have an additional three months to establish "good cause" for failure to pay the Part D IRMAA and make payment to be reinstated into the Part D plan. The failure to pay the premiums must have been due to circumstances beyond the beneficiary's control. CMS provides further guidance in the PDB Manual, Ch. 3, § 60.2.4, *available at* http://cms.gov/Medicare/Eligibility-and-Enrollment/MedicarePresDrugEligEnrol/Downloads/CY-2014-PDP-Enrollment-and-Disenrollment-Guidance-r.pdf (site visited June 6, 2016).

[6] Ability to Change Plan Mid-Year

[a] Changes During the Annual Coordinated Enrollment Period

All beneficiaries may switch plans once during the ACEP, which runs from October 15th through December 7th each year.[58] Enrollment becomes effective on January 1 of the next year.

In each year, most individuals who enroll in a PDP are "locked in" to their plan for the remainder of the calendar year, even though the plan in which they enroll may change the formulary or cost-sharing arrangements during the year. Enrollees in PDPs must wait until the next ACEP to switch plans, with enrollment in the new plan becoming effective on January 1 of the following year.

[b] Medicare Advantage Annual Disenrollment Period

Before 2011, individuals enrolled in an MA plan, including an MA-PD, could change plans once during the open enrollment period, which ran for the first three months of each year, as long as they did not add or drop prescription drug coverage.[59] Beginning in 2011, beneficiaries who are in an MA plan have an annual 45-day Medicare Advantage Disenrollment Period (MADP). They may only drop the MA plan and return to traditional Medicare and a PDP; they are not able to enroll in a different MA plan. Beneficiaries who are in MA plans that do not include drug coverage and who return to traditional Medicare during this time period are also able to enroll in a PDP. Beneficiaries who are in traditional Medicare with a PDP are not able to change to an MA-PD during this time period.[60] As in previous years, a beneficiary in traditional Medicare with a PDP cannot change to a different PDP. Those in traditional Medicare without drug coverage cannot use this time period to enroll in a PDP.

[c] Special Enrollment Periods

Beneficiaries may also be eligible to change plans mid-year if they qualify for a SEP described above.

[7] Enrollment Process for Individuals Who Are Eligible for Medicare and Medicaid

The MMA established an enrollment process that provides for automatic assignment into drug plans for individuals who are dually eligible for Medicare

[58] 42 C.F.R. § 423.32(a).

[59] 42 C.F.R. § 422.62(a)(3)–(5).

[60] ACA § 3204.

and Medicaid (dual eligibles) and who do not choose their own PDP or MA-PD during their IEP. In addition, dual eligibles are automatically eligible for a continuous SEP and therefore are not ever locked in to a PDP.[61] A similar process provides for the enrollment into a drug plan for individuals who have applied and been found eligible for the LIS and who did not choose their own drug coverage.[62] Every year since the start of Medicare Part D, a large number of dual eligible beneficiaries have had to be reassigned to a new PDP because the plan to which they were originally assigned did not qualify in the following year as a plan eligible for the LIS and a plan to which dual eligibles may be automatically enrolled. The Affordable Care Act (ACA) modified the method for determining which plans qualify as LIS plans in order to reduce the number of LIS-eligible individuals who must be reassigned to a new drug plan each year.[63]

[8] Failure to Enroll on a Timely Basis

[a] Late Penalty

A beneficiary who does not enroll in a Part D plan within 63 days of his or her IEP and has no other "creditable" prescription drug coverage must pay a late penalty if he or she subsequently enrolls in a Part D plan. The penalty is assessed at 1 percent of the national average premium for each month of delayed enrollment, for the remainder of the time in which the beneficiary is enrolled in a Part D plan.[64] Thus, a beneficiary who becomes eligible for Part D at age 65 but who delays enrolling until age 70 may be assessed a 60 percent penalty on his or her premium (5 years × 12 months × 1%). Since the penalty is based on a percentage of the average premium each year, the dollar value of the penalty changes as the national average premium changes.

---

[61] 42 U.S.C. § 1395w-101(b)(3)(D); 42 C.F.R. § 423.38(c)(4).

[62] 75 Fed. Reg. 19,677 (Apr. 15, 2010), amending 42 C.F.R. § 423.34. *See also* the PDB Manual, Ch. 3, § 40.1.4, *available at* http://cms.gov/Medicare/Eligibility-and-Enrollment/MedicarePresDrugEligEnrol/Downloads/CY-2014-PDP-Enrollment-and-Disenrollment-Guidance-r.pdf (site visited June 6, 2016).

[63] ACA §§ 3302 and 3303. Note that this provision codifies existing CMS policy whereby the Secretary may permit a plan whose premium exceeds the benchmark amount by a de minimis amount to waive payment of that portion of the Part D premium that is above the benchmark for LIS-eligible individuals. To the extent that plans choose to waive such increases, the individuals affected would not need to be reassigned to benchmark plans. 76 Fed Reg. 21,451 (Apr. 15, 2011), amending 42 C.F.R. § 423.34.

[64] 42 C.F.R. §§ 423.46 and 423.286(d)(3).

A beneficiary who becomes eligible for Medicare based on disability has a new IEP for Part D upon turning age 65. As a result, any late enrollment penalty assessed against such a beneficiary ends with the new initial enrollment period.[65]

The Medicare Improvements for Patients and Providers Act of 2008 (MIPPA) permanently waived the late enrollment penalty for LIS-eligible individuals, effective January 1, 2009.[66]

Beneficiaries who are assessed a late enrollment penalty may file an appeal with their drug plan.[67]

[b] Creditable Coverage

Someone who delays enrollment because he or she has creditable coverage, that is, coverage through another insurance plan deemed comparable to Part D coverage, will not be assessed a penalty for late enrollment if he or she later decides to enroll in Part D. A determination of whether coverage is creditable involves an actuarial assessment of whether the other insurance provides coverage of the costs of prescription drugs that equals or exceeds the actuarial value of the prescription drug benefit.[68]

Coverage offered through an employer or union-sponsored health plan, the federal employee health benefits program (FEHBP), Medicaid, an SPAP, programs for veterans, and TRICARE may constitute creditable coverage. The entity sponsoring the coverage must inform beneficiaries whether the coverage provided meets the definition of creditable coverage by September 30 of each year.[69]

Coverage offered through some pre-standardized Medicare Supplemental (Medigap) policies may qualify as creditable, as may coverage through some policies sold in Michigan, Minnesota, and Wisconsin, which are not required to sell the standard policies. The standard Medigap policies H, I, and J that offered drug coverage to beneficiaries who purchased them before January 1, 2006, do not meet the definition of creditable coverage. Insurers that offer Medigap policies were required to notify their insured persons concerning the status of their policies. Beneficiaries are advised to check with their insurers about the status of their policies.

---

[65] PDB Manual, Ch. 4, § 10.1.3, *available at* https://www.cms.gov/Medicare/Eligibility-and-Enrollment/MedicarePresDrugEligEnrol/Downloads/FINAL_CY2010_MedicarePrescriptionDrugBenefitManualChapter4_Dec2009.pdf (site visited June 6, 2016).

[66] MIPPA § 114. The section codifies a CMS policy that had waived the late enrollment penalty for this population.

[67] PDB Manual, Ch. 4, *available at* https://www.cms.gov/Medicare/Eligibility-and-Enrollment/MedicarePresDrugEligEnrol/Downloads/FINAL_CY2010_MedicarePrescriptionDrugBenefitManualChapter4_Dec2009.pdf (site visited June 6, 2016).

[68] 42 U.S.C. § 1395w-113(b)(5).

[69] 42 U.S.C. § 1395w-113(b)(4), 42 C.F.R. § 423.56.

[C] Choosing a Part D Plan

CMS is supposed to provide information to all Medicare beneficiaries to help them choose a Part D PDP. Information is made available through the Medicare & You handbook, through the Medicare toll-free number, and through the Medicare website (*www.medicare.gov*). In addition, Part D plan sponsors are required to make available to all individuals eligible to enroll in Part D information about all beneficiary cost-sharing, their formulary and cost control mechanisms, their pharmacy network, and their exceptions and appeals process.[70] Beneficiaries who want this information have to check with each drug plan.

Beneficiaries who have retiree health coverage also must contact their former employers or unions to determine the effect of enrollment in a Part D plan on their retiree health benefits. Some employers and unions will terminate all retiree health coverage, not just the drug benefit, for retirees and their dependents if the retiree enrolls in a Part D plan. Dual eligible beneficiaries who have employer coverage for which a Part D retiree drug subsidy is being paid will be presumed to have declined auto enrollment in a Part D plan.[71] CMS will send such beneficiaries a notice informing them of the option to receive Part D and advising them to contact their plan to discuss the impact of Medicare Part D coverage on their retiree plan.[72]

§ 11.06 PREMIUM AND COST-SHARING SUBSIDIES FOR PART D PRESCRIPTION DRUGS FOR LOW-INCOME INDIVIDUALS

[A] Introduction

For the first time in program history, Medicare has a low-income benefit for people with limited incomes and resources. While the Medicaid program has also played a role in paying Medicare's cost-sharing for beneficiaries dually eligible for both programs, Medicare has never provided direct low-income subsidies. In its design of the benefit, Congress adopted aspects of the federal Supplemental Security Income program (SSI) and of Medicaid's MSPs. Similarly, to administer the benefit, Congress looks to SSA and to state Medicaid agencies.

[B] The Subsidies

To help pay the costs of Medicare Part D, some form of the LIS is available to Medicare beneficiaries with incomes up to 150 percent of the FPL for a family

[70] 42 C.F.R. § 423.128.

[71] 42 C.F.R. § 423.34.

[72] A copy of the model notice is available at http://www.cms.gov/Medicare/Prescription-Drug-Coverage/LimitedIncomeandResources/downloads/11334.pdf (site visited June 6, 2016).

of the size involved.[73] Subsidies vary according to income, Medicaid status, and institutional status. So-called full subsidy eligible individuals are those with full Medicaid status (full-benefit dual eligibles), those with SSI but no Medicaid, those enrolled in one of three MSPs, and individuals with incomes below 135 percent of FPL and countable resources in 2016 of not more than $8,780 for an individual and $13,930 for a couple (including $1,500 per person for burial).[74] Partial subsidy individuals can have incomes up to 150 percent of FPL and resources in 2016 of not more than $13,640 per individual and $27,250 per couple (including $1,500 per person for burial).[75] Resource levels will increase each year based on increases in the consumer price index. Income and resource levels are generally announced in January of each year.

Note that CMS systems do not always reflect a beneficiary's correct subsidy status. In response, CMS created a best available evidence (BAE) policy that requires Part D plans to establish appropriate cost-sharing when presented with evidence that information about the beneficiary is not accurate.[76]

[1] Full Subsidy Eligible Individuals

All full subsidy individuals are entitled to a 100 percent subsidy for the "low-income benchmark premium"[77] for a plan offering the standard Part D benefit, elimination of the deductible, continuation of coverage through the donut hole, and elimination of all cost-sharing after they meet the annual out-of-pocket maximum. In addition, their cost-sharing is reduced as follows:

---

[73] 42 U.S.C. § 1395w-114.

[74] 42 C.F.R. § 423.773(b); CMS, "2015 Resource and Cost-Sharing Limits for Low-Income Subsidy (LIS)" (Feb. 24, 2015), *available at* http://www.cms.gov/Outreach-and-Education/Training/CMSNationalTrainingProgram/Downloads/2015-LIS-Income-and-Resources-Job-Aid.pdf (site visited June 6, 2016). New numbers for 2016 were not available at the time of publication. Check http://www.medicare.gov/your-medicare-costs/help-paying-costs/medicare-savings-program/medicare-savings-programs.html#slmb for updated information (site visited June 19, 2015).

[75] 42 C.F.R. § 423.773(a); CMS, "2015 Resource and Cost-Sharing Limits for Low-Income Subsidy (LIS)" (Feb. 24, 2015), *available at* http://www.cms.gov/Outreach-and-Education/Training/CMSNationalTrainingProgram/Downloads/2015-LIS-Income-and-Resources-Job-Aid.pdf (site visited June 6, 2016). The 2016 Federal Poverty Guidelines are available at https://aspe.hhs.gov/poverty-guidelines (site visited June 6, 2016). The 2017 Federal Poverty Guidelines were not available at the time of publication.

[76] For more information about the BAE, see http://www.cms.gov/Medicare/Prescription-Drug-Coverage/PrescriptionDrugCovContra/Best_Available_Evidence_Policy.html (site visited June 6, 2016).

[77] The "low-income benchmark premium" is the weighted average of plan premiums for the basic benefit package in the region in which the individual lives. As of January 2011, CMS is required to calculate the LIS benchmarks using basic Part D premiums before the application of Part C rebates each year. 42 C.F.R. § 423.780. This provision prevents the artificial lowering of the overall average (benchmark) amount of all Part D plans, which in turn should reduce the number of annual Part D plan reassignments of LIS enrollees.

- Full-benefit dual eligibles who are institutionalized, or who participate in a Home and Community-Based Waiver Program, have no cost-sharing at all.[78]
- Full-benefit dual eligibles with incomes up to 100 percent of FPL initially pay no more than $1.20/generic or preferred brand or $3.70/non-preferred brand, in 2017.[79]
- All other full subsidy individuals initially pay copayments of no more than $3.30/generic or preferred brand or $8.25/non-preferred brand, with copayments indexed annually to the cost of Part D drugs in 2017.[80]

[2] Partial Subsidy Eligible Individuals

In 2017, partial subsidy individuals pay a sliding scale premium; a $82 deductible; coinsurance of 15 percent instead of the full 25 percent, including continued coverage through the donut hole; and a copayment of no more than $3.30/generic or preferred brand or $8.25/non-preferred brand for all drugs after the out-of-pocket threshold is met.[81]

[3] Deemed Subsidy Eligible Individuals

Certain individuals are treated as full subsidy eligible individuals regardless of their actual income and resources. These are full-benefit dual eligibles, recipients of SSI benefits, and beneficiaries of the three MSPs: Qualified Medicare Beneficiaries (QMBs), Specified Low-income Medicare Beneficiaries (SLMBs), and Qualified Individuals (QIs).[82]

---

[78] 42 C.F.R. § 423.782(a).

[79] 42 C.F.R. § 423.782(a); CMS, "Announcement of Calendar Year (CY) 2017 Medicare Advantage Capitation Rates and Medicare Advantage and Part D Payment Policies and Final Call Letter" (Apr. 4, 2016), *available at* https://www.cms.gov/Medicare/Health-Plans/MedicareAdvtgSpecRateStats/Downloads/Announcement2017.pdf (site visited June 8, 2016).

[80] 42 C.F.R. § 423.782(a); CMS, "Announcement of Calendar Year (CY) 2017 Medicare Advantage Capitation Rates and Medicare Advantage and Part D Payment Policies and Final Call Letter" (Apr. 4, 2016), *available at* https://www.cms.gov/Medicare/Health-Plans/MedicareAdvtgSpecRateStats/Downloads/Announcement2017.pdf (site visited June 8, 2016).

[81] 42 C.F.R. § 423.782(b); CMS, "Announcement of Calendar Year (CY) 2017 Medicare Advantage Capitation Rates and Medicare Advantage and Part D Payment Policies and Final Call Letter" (Apr. 4, 2016), *available at* https://www.cms.gov/Medicare/Health-Plans/MedicareAdvtgSpecRateStats/Downloads/Announcement2017.pdf (site visited June 8, 2016).

[82] 42 C.F.R. § 423.773(c). *See* **Chapter 10** of this Handbook for a full discussion of the MSPs.

[4] Length of Eligibility Determination

An initial determination that someone qualifies for the LIS remains in effect for a full year. SSA selects a portion of subsidy-eligible individuals for cyclical redeterminations in August of each year. Individuals are chosen for redetermination based on criteria SSA believes indicate that they are more likely to have had a change in subsidy amount.[83]

An individual who is deemed eligible for LIS between January 1 and June 30 of a given year is deemed LIS-eligible for the rest of the year. An individual who is deemed eligible between July 1 and December 31 of a given year is deemed eligible for the remainder of that calendar year and for the next calendar year.[84] An individual who loses deemed LIS-eligibility will be notified in the fall of the year before LIS-eligibility ends and given the opportunity to apply for LIS. Many people who lose deemed status are "re-deemed" later in the year or are found eligible for LIS based on filing an application.

[C] Eligibility Determinations

[1] Where to Apply

Beneficiaries who are not "deemed eligible" have the choice of filing an application for the LIS either at their state Medicaid office or through SSA.[85] Because of strong encouragement by SSA and CMS, the overwhelming majority of beneficiaries apply through SSA. Applying at Medicaid may have offered some advantages, however, as Medicaid offices screen for other benefits as well as LIS.[86] In a state with more generous income and/or resource limits for its Medicare Savings Program (MSP) than applicable for LIS, someone found ineligible for the LIS might still qualify for MSP benefits. By qualifying for MSP benefits, that individual is deemed eligible for the LIS. Additionally, Medicaid may have speedier determination time frames and more user-friendly appeals systems than SSA.[87] Unlike the Medicaid regulations, the Social Security regulations impose no time restrictions by which SSA must act on applications and appeals.[88]

The choice of location may have less relevance due to changes in LIS eligibility calculation and in information exchanges between SSA and the states.

---

[83] 20 C.F.R. §§ 418.3600 *et seq.*; SSA, Program Operations Manual System (POMS), Section HI 03050.011E, *available at* https://secure.ssa.gov/apps10/poms.nsf/lnx/0603050011 (site visited June 8, 2016).

[84] 75 Fed. Reg. 19,677 (Apr. 15, 2010), amending 42 C.F.R. § 423.773(c)(2).

[85] 42 C.F.R. § 423.774(a).

[86] 42 U.S.C. § 1396a(a)(10); 42 C.F.R. § 435.902.

[87] Eligibility regulations proposed by SSA do not include time frames for making eligibility determinations and include a very limited appeals process. 20 C.F.R. §§ 418.3600 *et seq.*

[88] 20 C.F.R. §§ 418.3110, 418.3220, and 418.3230.

SSA is now required to transmit LIS applications of consenting beneficiaries to the states for purposes of determining eligibility for one of the MSPs.[89] As discussed below, MIPPA modified what counts toward income and resources for LIS eligibility but not for MSP eligibility. Thus, in some states MSP eligibility criteria may not be more generous than LIS criteria.

[2] Eligibility Criteria

In determining eligibility for the LIS, income is to be determined according to MSP rules, which in turn refer to SSI rules. One improvement over both SSI and MSP rules is the definition of "family size," which requires using a standard that reflects the actual number of dependents in an applicant's household. "Dependent" is defined as one who relies on the applicant or spouse for at least one-half of his or her support. "Resources" is defined as liquid resources "such as checking and savings accounts, stocks, bonds, and other resources that can be readily converted to cash within 20 days," and real estate that is neither the primary residence of the applicant nor the land on which the residence is located.[90]

MIPPA also added exemptions from income and resources for determinations of LIS eligibility but not for determinations of MSP eligibility. For applications filed on or after January 1, 2010, non-financial support (in-kind support and maintenance) provided to an LIS applicant will no longer be considered as income, and the cash surrender value of a life insurance policy will no longer be considered as a resource.[91]

[3] Appeals Process

The appeals process for someone who is denied the LIS depends on where the application is filed. When the Medicaid agency makes the decision, any appeal must follow the procedures used for Medicaid appeals. SSA will use its redeterminations and appeals procedures for the determinations it makes.[92] SSA regulations provide for a telephone hearing or a case review. The preamble indicates that the hearings will not be conducted by administrative law judges (ALJs) who hear other Social Security appeals.[93] An individual whose application for LIS has been denied is entitled to judicial review of the final decision to the same extent as other decisions made by SSA.[94]

---

[89] MIPPA § 113, amending 42 U.S.C. § 1396u-5(a)(4).
[90] 42 C.F.R. § 423.772.
[91] 42 U.S.C. § 1395w-114(a)(3)(C), (D), (G).
[92] 42 C.F.R. § 423.774(c).
[93] 70 Fed. Reg. 77,664, 77,674 (Dec. 30, 2005).
[94] 42 U.S.C. § 1395w-114(a)(3)(B)(iv).

[D] Effect of Eligibility Determination for Low-Income Subsidy

CMS will enroll into a Part D plan those individuals who are either deemed or found eligible for the LIS and who have not chosen a Part D plan on their own. These individuals are randomly assigned to a Part D plan in their region that meets the criteria to be a low-income subsidy plan, that is, a plan for which an individual eligible for the full LIS pays no premium.[95] Full-benefit dual eligible individuals who are enrolled in certain retiree health plans may decline automatic enrollment by CMS in a PDP; CMS will not automatically assign to a PDP other LIS-eligible individuals who are enrolled in certain retiree health plans.[96]

§ 11.07 DUAL ELIGIBLES

[A] Introduction

Among the most dramatic aspects of the Medicare drug benefit legislation is its complete elimination of Medicaid prescription drug coverage for all individuals who are dually eligible for both Medicare and Medicaid. Beginning January 1, 2006, any individual eligible to enroll in a Part D plan who is receiving full Medicaid services cannot receive prescription drug coverage through Medicaid.[97] This is true regardless of whether the individual has actually enrolled in a Part D plan and regardless of whether the plan covers the specific drug needed. Concomitantly, the state cannot receive federal matching payments for such services.

[B] Definition of Dual Eligibles

Dual eligibles are defined as individuals who have coverage under a Part D plan and who are eligible for full Medicaid benefits under any category of a state Medicaid plan. Those with full coverage under a so-called Section 1115 research and demonstration waiver fall within the definition.[98]

[C] Assignment of Dual Eligibles to Drug Plans

Presumably because of dual eligibles' loss of Medicaid drug coverage, Congress requires the automatic enrollment in a PDP of any dual eligible who has not

[95] 75 Fed. Reg. 1967 (Apr. 15, 2010), amending 42 C.F.R. § 423.34(d). Such plans are sometimes referred to as "benchmark plans."

[96] 75 Fed. Reg. 1967 (Apr. 15, 2010), amending 42 C.F.R. § 423.34(d)(3). The retiree health plans to which this section applies receive a subsidy from CMS to continue offering drug coverage. Enrollment in a Part D plan terminates the retiree drug benefit and, in most cases, the full retiree health benefit.

[97] 42 U.S.C. § 1396u-5(d)(1).

[98] 42 C.F.R. § 423.772.

voluntarily enrolled.[99] Dual eligible beneficiaries are randomly assigned to Part D plans with premiums at or below the average premium for their region (sometimes referred to as a "benchmark plan"). The effective date of auto-enrollment into a Part D plan for individuals with Medicare who become eligible for Medicaid will be the same as the effective date of Medicaid eligibility. The effective date of auto-enrollment for individuals who become eligible for Medicare and Medicaid in the same month will also be the date of Medicaid eligibility. New dual eligible individuals who have Medicaid first will be auto-enrolled retroactively to the date of their Medicare eligibility. In all situations, retroactive enrollment raises the possibility that dual eligibles may be required to pay for their drugs out of their own pockets and then be reimbursed.[100]

The ACA requires the Office of the Inspector General (OIG) of the Department of Health and Human Services (HHS) to conduct an annual study of the extent to which Part D plan formularies include drugs most commonly used by full-benefit dual eligibles.[101] In its 2016 report, OIG found that the "rate of Part D plan formularies' inclusion of the 198 drugs commonly used by dual eligibles is high, with some variation. On average, Part D plan formularies include 96 percent of the 198 commonly used drugs. In addition, 68 percent of the commonly used drugs are included by all Part D plan formularies. These results are largely unchanged from OIG's findings for formularies reported in the 2015 mandated annual report." OIG also notes that "the percentage of drugs subject to utilization management tools remained relatively the same from 2015 to 2016. On average, formularies applied utilization management tools to 28 percent of the unique drugs we reviewed in 2016, compared to 29 percent of those we reviewed in 2015."[102] Unlike other Medicare beneficiaries, however, dual eligible beneficiaries retain the right to switch plans at any time.[103] Thus, individuals assigned to a plan whose formulary does not include the prescriptions they use may switch to a more appropriate plan. Note, however, that an on-going problem has been the inability of CMS computer systems to process changes from one Part D plan to another quickly enough to ensure that coverage under the new plan would become effective on the first day of the month following the change. In addition, some beneficiaries are enrolled in more than one plan, causing some dual eligible beneficiaries to be assessed a premium by the second plan. CMS has instituted an

---

[99] 42 U.S.C. § 1396u-5(c)(6).

[100] 75 Fed. Reg. 1967 (Apr. 15, 2010), amending 42 C.F.R. § 423.34(f). Effective January 1, 2010, CMS has implemented a new process for retroactive and temporary drug coverage for all LIS-eligible individuals entitled the Limited Income Newly Eligible Transition (NET) Program. For more information, see CMS's website at http://www.cms.gov/Medicare/Eligibility-and-Enrollment/LowIncSubMedicarePresCov/MedicareLimitedIncomeNET.html (site visited June 8, 2016).

[101] ACA § 3313.

[102] OIG, "Part D Plans Generally Include Drugs Commonly Used by Dual Eligibles: 2016 Report" OEI-05-16-00090) (June 29, 2016), *available at* https://oig.hhs.gov/oei/reports/oei-05-16-00090.asp (site visited July 12, 2016).

[103] 42 C.F.R. § 423.38(c).

enrollment reconciliation process to address multiple plan enrollments and/or discrepancies in CMS records of enrollment.

[D] Medicaid Wrap-Around

The elimination of coverage for an otherwise covered Medicaid service represents a substantial departure from the historic Medicare-Medicaid relationship for dual eligibles, under which Medicaid has paid Medicare's cost-sharing and provided "wrap-around coverage" for services where, as with home health, Medicare coverage is more limited than Medicaid's or where, as with LTC, Medicare coverage is nearly nonexistent.[104] The significance of this situation cannot be overstated. Because of the design of the Medicare drug benefit, many dual eligibles who were on Medicaid before becoming eligible for Medicare have less prescription drug coverage than they had under Medicaid and potentially less protection during appeals processes to challenge denials or other barriers to coverage. Further, they have to make copayments for their prescriptions, with the copayment amounts increasing yearly.

Medicaid can continue to cover for dual eligibles, using both federal and state funding, those drugs that it is permitted but not required by law to cover for any Medicaid beneficiary and that are not, by definition, Part D covered drugs. Such drugs include prescription vitamins, cough and cold relief drugs, and nonprescription drugs, among others.[105] States also have the option of paying copayments for dual eligibles and/or for drugs that are not on a plan's formulary. However, they will receive no federal matching payments and must use only state funds if they assist dual eligibles with these costs. Many states continue to cover at least some of the excluded Part D drugs.[106] Few, if any, states also cover Part D cost-sharing.

[E] Nursing Facility Residents

In addition to the problems that may be experienced by other dually eligible individuals, those who reside in nursing and other LTC facilities experience

[104] For a full discussion of dual eligibility, see **Chapter 10** of this Handbook.

[105] As noted above, effective January 1, 2013, benzodiazepines and barbiturates (used for treating epilepsy, cancer, or a chronic mental health disorder) are included as Part D covered drugs. MIPPA § 175. Effective January 1, 2014, all barbiturates are covered by Medicaid and therefore by Medicare Part D. ACA § 2502.

[106] A list of Medicaid coverage of Medicare Part D excluded drugs, by state, as of 2009, is available on the Kaiser Family Foundation's website, statehealthfacts.org. *See* http://kff.org/state-category/medicare/ (site visited June 8, 2016). *See also* "Medicaid Drug Programs Data & Resources," *available at* http://www.medicaid.gov/Medicaid-CHIP-Program-Information/By-Topics/Benefits/Prescription-Drugs/Medicaid-Drug-Programs-Data-and-Resources.html (site visited June 8, 2016).

problems that arise because of the setting in which they live. For example, there is no assurance that a dually eligible resident who does not choose a plan for himself or herself will be automatically assigned to a plan that includes the pharmacy used by his or her nursing facility, although all plans are required to include LTC pharmacies in their networks. Drug plans are not required to provide covered medications in the packaging utilized by nursing facilities or formats utilized by residents, though CMS expects that plan sponsors will do so. CMS also expects plans to allow for at least a 31-day fill for residents in accordance with industry best practices.[107] If access to medically necessary drugs and drug formats is not provided, a beneficiary may need to file an appeal in order to get the prescription ordered by the treating physician. Also, as noted in **§ 11.05[B][3]** of this Handbook, individuals who move into, reside in, or move out of an institution have a special enrollment period right to change Part D plans.[108]

Dually eligible individuals who reside in a nursing facility pay no copayment for their medications. As of January 2012, cost-sharing for covered Part D drugs is also eliminated for full-benefit dually eligible individuals who are receiving home and community-based services (HCBS) under certain home and community-based waivers or a state plan amendment, or if enrolled in certain Medicaid managed care organizations.[109]

[F] Transitioning into a Part D Plan

When Medicare beneficiaries move from another source of payment for their prescriptions to a Part D plan or change to a different Part D plan, they may encounter difficulties caused by changes in formularies and other utilization management tools used by Part D plans to contain costs. The transition may be particularly difficult for nursing home residents and other dual eligibles, and for beneficiaries with chronic conditions who are stabilized on their current treatments.

All Part D plans are required to establish a transition process to ensure access to non-formulary drugs, including those subject to step therapy or prior

[107] PDB Manual, Ch. 6, § 30.2.3, *available at* https://www.cms.gov/Medicare/Prescription-Drug-Coverage/PrescriptionDrugCovContra/Downloads/Part-D-Benefits-Manual-Chapter-6.pdf (site visited June 8, 2016).

[108] *See, e.g.*, PDB Manual, Ch. 3, § 30.3.8.5, *available at* http://cms.gov/Medicare/Eligibility-and-Enrollment/MedicarePresDrugEligEnrol/Downloads/CY-2014-PDP-Enrollment-and-Disenrollment-Guidance-r.pdf (site visited June 8, 2016).

[109] This applies to individuals receiving home and community-based services (HCBS) under § 1115 or § 1915(c) or (d) of the Social Security Act, or under a State Plan Amendment under § 1915(i) of the Act, or if such services are provided through enrollment in a Medicaid managed care organization with a contract under § 1903(m) or § 1932 of the Act. Individuals residing in assisted living facilities are included in the definition of an "individual receiving [HCBS]" if they satisfy the inclusion criteria listed in the previous sentence. 76 Fed. Reg. 21,458–59 (Apr. 15, 2011), amending 42 C.F.R. §§ 423.772 and 423.782(a)(2)(ii).

authorization requirements, during the first 90 days of coverage under a new plan. The transition process is available for new enrollees following the annual coordinated enrollment period; newly eligible Medicare beneficiaries from other coverage; individuals who change plans mid-year; and current enrollees who are affected by formulary changes. Eligible enrollees are generally entitled to a 30-day transition fill, unless the prescription is for fewer than 30 days. Residents in LTC facilities are entitled to up to 93 days of transition fills, in 31-day increments. Plans must also send enrollees written notice explaining that the prescription has been filled on a transition basis within three business days of approving the transition fill. They are also to ensure that reasonable notice is made to inform the prescriber of the temporary fill.[110]

Cost-sharing requirements for transition fills has been modified as follows:

- For low-income subsidy (LIS) enrollees, a plan cannot charge higher cost-sharing for transition supplies than the statutory maximum copayment amounts.
- For non-LIS enrollees, a plan must charge the same cost-sharing for non-formulary Part D drugs provided during the transition that would apply for non-formulary drugs approved through a formulary exception in accordance with 42 C.F.R. § 423.578(b), and the same cost-sharing for formulary drugs subject to utilization management edits provided during the transition that would apply once the utilization management criteria are met.[111]

§ 11.08 STATE PHARMACEUTICAL ASSISTANCE PROGRAMS

States may choose to provide cost-sharing and wrap-around drug coverage for dual eligibles and other low-income residents through an SPAP.[112] Any payments made by the SPAP on behalf of a Part D enrollee will count toward the enrollee's true out-of-pocket costs. In other words, SPAP payments for cost-sharing and for a plan's covered drugs while the beneficiary is in the "donut hole" count toward meeting the $4,950 out-of-pocket limit (in 2017) which, in turn, leads to reduced or eliminated enrollee cost-sharing. State Medicaid programs, including Pharmacy Plus waivers under Section 1115 of the Social Security Act, and any other programs where the majority of the funding is from federal sources, cannot be SPAPs.[113]

[110] 75 Fed. Reg. 19,678 (Apr. 15, 2010), amending 42 C.F.R. § 423.120(b)(3).

[111] 79 Fed. Reg. 29,962 (May 23, 2014), amending 42 C.F.R. § 423.120(b)(3).

[112] 42 C.F.R. §§ 423.454 and 423.464(e)(1).

[113] 42 C.F.R. § 423.464(e)(1)(iv).

SPAPs must not discriminate among drug plans with respect to their supplemental coverage;[114] this requirement prevents an SPAP from automatically enrolling subsidy-eligible individuals into one particular drug plan. Plans must coordinate with SPAPs concerning certain basic elements of the drug benefit they offer.

§ 11.09 GRIEVANCE, APPEALS, AND EXCEPTIONS PROCESSES

[A] Grievance Procedures

All drug plans must establish processes for hearing and resolving grievances similar to the process utilized by MA plans under Medicare Part C.[115] Grievances are separate and distinct from appeals and from quality of service complaints filed with a Quality Improvement Organization (QIO). Grievances may be filed with the drug plan orally or in writing within 60 days after the incident; plans generally must resolve grievances within 30 days. However, plans must resolve within 24 hours a grievance arising from the plan's decision not to expedite a coverage determination or redetermination under the appeals process.[116]

Since January 2012, Part D plans must address complaints received by CMS against the plan by addressing and resolving complaints in the CMS complaint tracking system and displaying a link to the electronic complaint form on the *www.medicare.gov* website on the plan's main web page.[117]

[B] Coverage Determinations and Appeals

[1] The Coverage and Appeals Process

As directed by Congress, the coverage determination and appeals process for Part D also mirrors closely the process utilized by MA plans.[118] The process begins when the beneficiary or prescriber requests a coverage determination, either orally or in writing,[119] and the drug plan issues the formal coverage determination. For appeals filed on or after January 1, 2012, PDP sponsors must make available uniform model forms for requesting coverage determinations and

---

[114] 42 C.F.R. §§ 423.464(e)(1)(ii) and 423.464(e)(1)(ii).

[115] 42 U.S.C. § 1395w-104(f). *See* **§ 7.04[E]** of this Handbook.

[116] 42 C.F.R. § 423.564.

[117] 76 Fed. Reg. 21,470 (Apr. 15, 2011), amending 42 C.F.R. § 423.505.

[118] 42 U.S.C. § 1395w-104(g)–(h).

[119] Plans must establish and maintain a method of documenting all oral requests. 75 Fed. Reg. 19,677 (Apr. 15, 2010), amending 42 C.F.R. § 423.568(a)(3). See discussion about notice at **§ 11.09[D]** of this Handbook.

redeterminations, establish a toll-free telephone number and website for accepting requests for coverage determinations and redeterminations, and arrange with their network providers to distribute written notices at the pharmacy instructing enrollees how to contact their plans to obtain a coverage determination or request an exception if they disagree with the information provided by the pharmacist.[120] The plan may provide oral notice to the beneficiary of a completely favorable coverage determination as long as it sends a written follow-up notice within three calendar days of the oral notification. Notices must meet regulatory requirements. Favorable coverage determination notices must describe in readable and understandable form the conditions of the approval. Unfavorable decisions must use approved notice language that is readable and understandable, that states the specific reason for the denial, and that describes the redetermination process.[121] If the plan intends to issue a partially or fully unfavorable decision, a physician or other appropriate health care professional must be involved in the review.[122]

The beneficiary or prescriber[123] may make an oral or written request for a redetermination, performed by the drug plans, of an unfavorable coverage determination.[124] Individuals or their prescribers who remain dissatisfied after the redetermination can request a further review known as reconsideration; the reconsideration will be performed by the Independent Review Entity (IRE). Following an IRE review, the enrollee may appeal to an ALJ, then to the Medicare Appeals

---

[120] 76 Fed. Reg. 21,573 (Apr. 15, 2011), amending 42 C.F.R. § 423.128; 76 Fed. Reg. 21,575 (Apr. 15, 2011), amending 42 C.F.R. § 423.562. In the final rule, CMS noted its intention to develop separate model forms for coverage determinations and redeterminations, and will continue to allow plan sponsors to develop and make available drug-specific coverage determination request forms to supplement the model forms. In addition, instead of requiring an interactive web-based application for coverage determinations and appeals, CMS will simply require plan enrollees to have the ability to send a secure e-mail via the plan's website in order to initiate a request. In early 2012, CMS issued a model pharmacy notice (CMS-10147), *available at* http://www.cms.gov/Medicare/Appeals-and-Grievances/MedPrescriptDrugApplGriev/PlanNoticesAndDocuments.html (site visited June 8, 2016)

[121] 75 Fed. Reg. 19,677 (Apr. 15, 2010), amending 42 C.F.R. §§ 423.568(d)–(g) and 423.572(b)–(c).

[122] This is required even when the plan uses a claims specialist who is not a physician to conduct the initial review of a Part D coverage determination. 42 C.F.R. §§ 423.562, 423.566, and 423.4.

[123] The prescribing physician or other professional may request a redetermination without having an appointment of representative form filed with the drug plan. An appointment of representative form is still necessary, however, if the prescriber wants to appeal beyond the plan level. 42 C.F.R. § 423.582.

[124] A plan may provide oral notification of either a favorable or an unfavorable expedited redetermination, provided that written confirmation is sent within three calendar days. As with coverage determination notices, redetermination notices must meet regulatory requirements. 75 Fed. Reg. 19,677 (Apr. 15, 2010), amending 42 C.F.R. § 423.590. Note that effective January 1, 2013, prescribers can request a reconsideration on an enrollee's behalf without obtaining an appointed representative form. 77 Fed. Reg. 22,171 (Apr. 12, 2012) amending 42 C.F.R. §§ 600 and 602.

Council (MAC), and finally to federal court. An expedited review is available if the standards set out in Medicare Part C are met.[125]

Plans must notify enrollees of initial coverage determinations involving requests for drug benefits as expeditiously as the enrollee's health condition requires, but no later than 72 hours after receipt of the request. They have seven calendar days in which to notify enrollees of a redetermination decision. Plans must act on requests for expedited coverage determination no later than 24 hours after receiving the request or the physician's supporting statement, and on expedited redeterminations within 72 hours.[126] Note that beneficiaries who file a coverage determination request after paying out of pocket for a needed prescription are not eligible for expedited consideration. Plans in payment cases must notify the beneficiary and make payment no later than 14 calendar days after receipt of the request.[127]

Unlike under Medicare Part C, unfavorable redeterminations on Part D claims are not automatically forwarded to the IRE. The beneficiary must file a request for reconsideration with the drug plan within 60 calendar days of the redetermination decision.[128] The plan must forward the beneficiary's request to the IRE within 24 hours if it does not act in a timely manner on a coverage determination or redetermination request.[129] The IRE must issue its reconsideration decision within the same time frames noted above for issuing a redetermination.[130]

A beneficiary may file a written request for an ALJ hearing with the entity specified in the IRE reconsideration notice within 60 calendar days of receiving an unfavorable reconsideration determination, provided the amount remaining in controversy meets the threshold requirement.[131] In determining whether the jurisdictional amount is met in a claim involving the refusal to provide a covered drug, CMS projects the costs of the drug based on the number of refills prescribed for the disputed drug during the calendar year. The ALJ hearing is conducted pursuant to the procedures for hearings of Part A and B appeals, with some

---

[125] 42 C.F.R. §§ 423.560–423.2140.

[126] 42 C.F.R. §§ 423.568, 423.572, 423.582, and 423.590.

[127] 75 Fed. Reg. 19,677 (Apr. 15, 2010), amending 42 C.F.R. § 423.568(c). CMS encourages plan sponsors to issue unfavorable payment determinations in fewer than 14 days.

[128] 42 C.F.R. § 423.600.

[129] 42 C.F.R. §§ 423.568(h) and 423.590(c), (e). CMS has noted that due to many Part D plans' failure to act in a timely manner, "the volume of cases auto-forwarded to the IRE has been significant and sustained over the past several years." *See* page 153, Announcement of Calendar Year (CY) 2017 Medicare Advantage Capitation Rates and Medicare Advantage and Part D Payment Policies and Final Call Letter (Apr. 4, 2016), *available at* https://www.cms.gov/Medicare/Health-Plans/MedicareAdvtgSpecRateStats/Downloads/Announcement2017.pdf (site visited Sept. 21, 2016).

[130] 42 C.F.R. § 423.600.

[131] The amount in controversy, $160 in 2017, may increase yearly based on increases in health costs. 81 Fed. Reg. 185, P. 65653 (Sept. 27, 2016).

modifications.[132] A beneficiary may appeal further to the MAC and then to federal court, following procedures for MA plans.[133]

Rules that went into effect in 2010 require ALJs and the MAC to issue decisions within the 90-day time frame that applies to Part A and Part B claims. The new rules also add a process for expedited review of all Part D coverage determinations except for those that solely involve a request for payment of drugs already furnished. To qualify for expedited review, the prescriber must indicate, or the ALJ or MAC must determine, that applying the standard 90-day time frame may seriously jeopardize the beneficiary's life, health, or ability to regain maximum function. The ALJ or MAC may consider the standard as having been met if a lower-level adjudicator has granted a request for an expedited hearing.

A beneficiary may make an oral request for an expedited ALJ hearing or MAC review, but only after first receiving the written decision from the IRE, in the case of a request for an ALJ hearing, or the written ALJ decision, in the case of MAC review. The ALJ/MAC must inform the beneficiary, within five days of receipt of the request, as to whether the request for expedited review has been granted. If the request is granted, then the decision must be issued within ten days of receipt of the request for the appeal.[134]

[2] What Constitutes a Coverage Determination

Coverage determinations that trigger appeal rights include a drug plan's decision not to pay for or provide a medication because the drug is not on the plan's formulary, is not considered medically necessary, is furnished by an out-of-network pharmacy, or is not a drug for which Medicare will pay under Part D. Starting in 2011, a dispute involving the availability and amount of the manufacturer discount for brand name drugs in the coverage gap constitutes a coverage determination. An individual may also appeal when a coverage determination is not provided in a timely manner and delay would adversely affect the health of the beneficiary; a request for an exception is rejected; and the individual is dissatisfied with a decision regarding the copayment required for a drug. A coverage determination may be requested by the beneficiary, the beneficiary's appointed

---

[132] 74 Fed Reg. 65,340 (Dec. 9, 2009), adding 42 C.F.R. §§ 423.1968–423.2063. CMS and the IRE cannot be parties at the hearing. They may be participants at the hearing, however, if their request to participate is granted by the ALJ or if the ALJ requests their participation. The limitation on the submission of new evidence at the ALJ hearing in Part A and Part B appeals filed by providers and suppliers also does not apply, although the Part D rules contain some limitations on the submission of new evidence by the beneficiary.

[133] 74 Fed. Reg. 65,340 (Dec. 9, 2009), adding 42 C.F.R. §§ 423.2100–423.2140. The amount in controversy for federal court review in 2017 is $1,560. 80 Fed. Reg. 57,827 (Sept. 25, 2015).

[134] 74 Fed. Reg. 65,340 (Dec. 9, 2009), adding 42 C.F.R. § 423.2016.

representative, the prescribing physician, or another health care professional authorized under state law to write prescriptions.[135]

[C] The Exceptions Process

Part D plans that use formularies to manage drug utilization must also have an exceptions process whereby plan enrollees can seek coverage for a non-formulary drug or request that a formulary drug be provided at a lower tier for cost-sharing (thereby reducing the copayment or coinsurance).[136] As noted above, denial of an exception request constitutes an unfavorable coverage determination from which appeal rights flow. The importance of the exceptions process cannot be overstated; the exceptions process should be used to give beneficiaries access to the medically necessary drugs prescribed for them.

In order to get an exception to require the plan to cover a non-formulary drug, the prescribing doctor or other prescribing professional must show that all of the drugs on any tier of the plan's formulary for treatment of the same condition would not be as effective or would have adverse consequences, or both, for the individual requesting the exception. For this purpose formulary includes the application of cost-savings tools, such as dose restrictions, quantity limits, prior authorization, step therapy, and therapeutic substitution requirements, all of which would result in non-coverage for an otherwise coverable Part D drug. If the plan approves the exception request, the drug will be treated as other drugs on the formulary, so that the beneficiary's cost-sharing counts toward the deductible and the annual out-of-pocket limit. A beneficiary will not have to file a new exception request each time the prescription is refilled. If the beneficiary renews her membership in the plan after the plan year, the plan has the option of continuing coverage of the medicine.[137] If the plan does not adopt this option, the beneficiary would have to reapply for an exception the next year.

Plan enrollees may also use the exceptions process to ask that a drug they require be assigned to a lower tier to reduce their cost-sharing for the drug when the preferred drug would not be as effective or would have adverse consequences. The exceptions process must address situations where a formulary's tiered copayment structure changes during the year and an enrollee is using a drug affected by the change. However, a plan does not have to cover non-preferred drugs at the lower, generic drug copay level if the plan maintains a separate tier dedicated to generic drugs. Further, if the plan maintains a specialty tier, that is, a formulary copay tier in which it places very high cost and unique items such as

[135] 42 C.F.R. §§ 423.560 and 423.566.

[136] 42 U.S.C. § 1395w-104(g), (h); 42 C.F.R. § 423.578.

[137] 42 C.F.R. § 423.578(c)(4).

genomic and biotech products, it may exclude these very high costs or unique drugs from its exceptions process.[138]

Because exceptions requests are coverage determinations and are governed by the rules for coverage determinations, the plan must act within the time frames for standard coverage determinations (72 hours) or expedited coverage determinations (24 hours), depending on which standards are met. A beneficiary may appeal the denial of an exception request through the appeals process.

Despite its importance, the exceptions process has proven to be both burdensome and lengthy to use. Drug plans may require a doctor's or other prescriber's certificate explaining why the plan enrollee needs the non-formulary drug. Each plan has its own criteria for what should be included in the certificate; many plans have different forms a doctor must use depending on the drug in question. CMS has approved a standard exceptions request form developed by the American Medical Association, the Center for Medicare Advocacy, and other groups but has not required that plans honor the standard form. Each plan determines how it will evaluate the doctor's determination that the enrollee requires a non-formulary drug, including establishing a process to compare the medical and scientific evidence about the safety and effectiveness of the non-formulary and formulary drugs. Most plans require extensive documentation, sometimes asking for both the beneficiary's own medical records and medical journals. Because the Part D appeals process follows the appeals process for MA plans, it involves the exhaustion of multiple layers in order to get a face-to-face hearing.

[D] Notice and Other Due Process Issues

The PDP has the responsibility for giving its plan enrollees notice of a change in the formulary or notice that coverage for a requested drug has been denied. The plan must provide written notice of a formulary change, including a change in tiered cost-sharing, 60 days in advance of the change to those enrollees who use the prescription, as well as to CMS, prescribing physicians, and pharmacies. The notice must include the change, other available drugs, and a description of the exceptions process. Alternatively, a plan can choose to give an enrollee the 60 days' notice and a 60-day supply of the drug when a refill request is presented to the plan.[139] When the formulary change is a non-maintenance change—that is, it does not involve changes based on the availability of a new generic drug, new clinical guidelines, or FDA approval—plan enrollees who are currently taking the affected drug are exempt from the change for the plan year.[140]

---

[138] 42 C.F.R. § 423.578(a)(6), (7).

[139] 42 C.F.R. § 423.120(b)(5).

[140] PDB Manual, Ch. 6, § 30.3.3.3, *available at* https://www.cms.gov/Medicare/Prescription-Drug-Coverage/PrescriptionDrugCovContra/Downloads/Part-D-Benefits-Manual-Chapter-6.pdf (site visited June 8, 2016).

How enrollees learn of their rights when coverage of or payment for a prescription is denied at the pharmacy has been problematic. The regulations place the burden on the plan to provide notice of appeal rights for coverage determinations. CMS states that the pharmacy is not required to provide notice of the reasons for the denial or of the appeals process.[141] Until 2012, each drug plan had to arrange with its network pharmacies to either post at the pharmacy or distribute a generic notice that tells enrollees to contact the plan if they disagree with the information provided by the pharmacist; most pharmacies satisfied this obligation by merely posting a written notice about appeal rights. As noted above, though, for appeals filed on or after January 1, 2012, PDP sponsors must arrange with their network providers to distribute written notices at the pharmacy instructing enrollees how to contact their plans to obtain a coverage determination or request an exception if they disagree with the information provided by the pharmacist.[142]

Although the requirement that pharmacies distribute a generic notice at the point of sale is an improvement for enrollees, this approach does not consider the extra burden placed on the enrollee, who must still act on the notice, or the practicalities of providing notice when an enrollee uses a non-network pharmacy.

The appeals process also does not provide adequate protection to someone who must appeal to continue receiving coverage of a drug he or she has been using. Unlike under Medicaid, Part D does not provide for continued access to the medication if an appeal is filed on a timely basis. Thus, dually eligible individuals whose prescription drug coverage will be paid for under Medicare instead of Medicaid may lose an important protection. CMS has indicated in sub-regulatory guidance that Part D plans must provide a continued supply of a medicine to nursing home residents through the exceptions process.

In response to some of these appeals challenges faced by Part D enrollees, CMS announced in its 2016 Call Letter that it plans to move forward with efforts to improve the Medicare Advantage and Part D appeals process for Medicare beneficiaries, including improving Part D denial notices, clarifying plan sponsors' obligations, expanding data collection regarding Part D appeals, and exploring a streamlined Part D appeals process that is initiated when a request for coverage of a prescription drug is denied at the pharmacy counter. Among other things, the Final Call Letter announced a pilot program to help identify options for resolving

---

[141] 70 Fed. Reg. 4194, 4349–50 (Jan. 28, 2005).

[142] 76 Fed. Reg. 21,573 (Apr. 15, 2011), amending 42 C.F.R. § 423.128; 76 Fed. Reg. 21,575 (Apr. 15, 2011), amending 42 C.F.R. § 423.562. In early 2012, CMS issued a model pharmacy notice (CMS-10147), *available at* http://www.cms.gov/Medicare/Appeals-and-Grievances/MedPrescriptDrugApplGriev/PlanNoticesAndDocuments.html (site visited June 8, 2016). Note that a final Part D rule issued in 2015 revises 42 C.F.R. § 423.562(a)(3) to remove reference of an enrollee's "disagreement with information provided by the pharmacist" as a condition requiring delivery of the pharmacy notice. 80 Fed. Reg. 7912, 7952 (Feb. 12, 2015).

certain point-of-sale claims rejections without an enrollee having to request a coverage determination from a plan. In addition, CMS is moving forward with improved data collection concerning Part D appeals data, with an implementation target of 2018.[143]

§ 11.10 CONCLUSION

The Medicare Part D prescription drug program continues to evolve. Advocates should monitor plan changes to their premiums, formularies, and/or cost-sharing structures. Each year a substantial number of LIS-eligible individuals must choose a different plan because their plan no longer qualifies for a subsidy to pay the entire premium; those who are in the drug plans to which they were assigned by CMS are automatically reassigned to a new plan by CMS. All enrollees may need to change plans or pursue exceptions if the plan they chose eliminates drugs from its formulary or adds utilization management tools.

[143] CMS, "Announcement of Calendar Year (CY) 2016 Medicare Advantage Capitation Rates and Medicare Advantage and Part D Payment Policies and Final Call Letter" (Apr. 6, 2015), *available at* http://www.cms.gov/Medicare/Health-Plans/MedicareAdvtgSpecRateStats/Downloads/Announcement2016.pdf (site visited July 2, 2015). CMS noted in its 2017 Call Letter that after analyzing the results of the pilot, it is not imposing any operational requirements for the 2017 plan year. *See* Announcement of Calendar Year (CY) 2017 Medicare Advantage Capitation Rates and Medicare Advantage and Part D Payment Policies and Final Call Letter (Apr. 4, 2016), *available at* https://www.cms.gov/Medicare/Health-Plans/MedicareAdvtgSpecRateStats/Downloads/Announcement2017.pdf (site visited Sept. 21, 2016).

APPENDIX 11-1 MEDICARE PRESCRIPTION DRUG PLAN (PART D) APPEALS PROCESS*

The following chart provides an overview of the appeals process for the Medicare Prescription Drug Plan (Plan D). For more information on each level, click on the level name on the left hand side of this document or visit http://www.hhs.gov/omha/

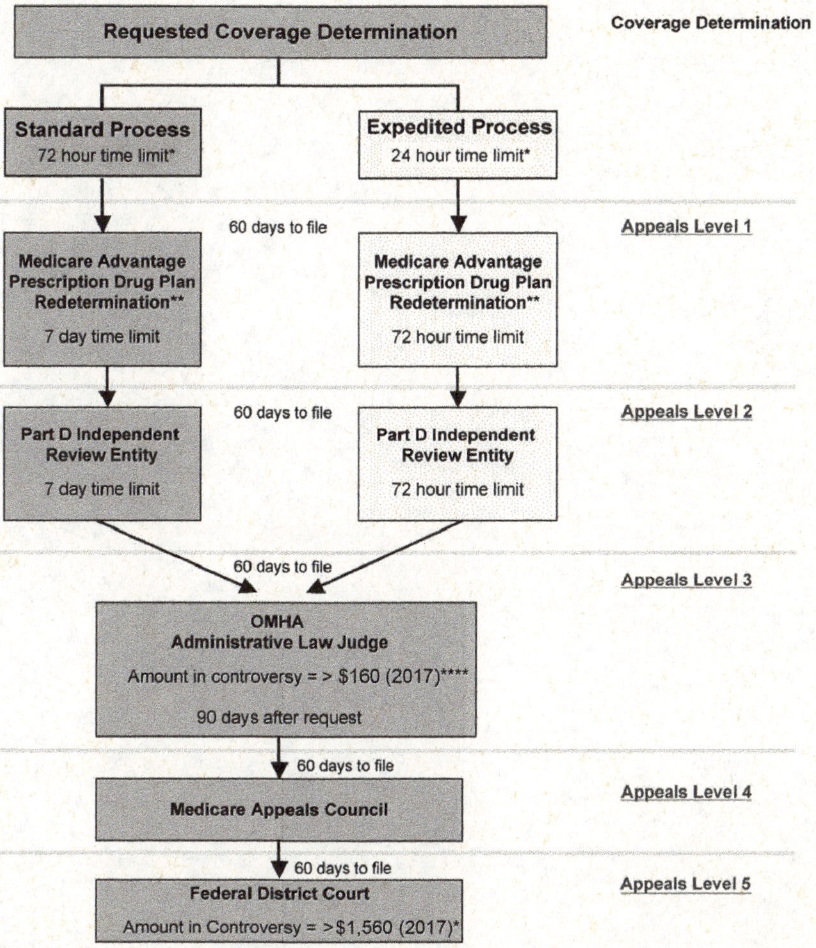

* The adjudication timeframes generally begin when the request is received by the plan sponsor. However, if the request involves an exception request, the adjudication timeframe begins when the plan sponsor receives the physician's supporting statement.

** A request for a coverage determination includes a request for a tiering exception or a formulary exception. A request for a coverage determination may be filed by the enrollee, the enrollee's appointed representative, or the enrollee's physician.

*** Starting in 2005, the AIC requirements for an ALJ hearing and Federal District Court are adjusted in accordance with the medical care component of the consumer price index.

****See 79 Fed. Reg. 57933-935 (Sept. 26, 2014)

* On January 1, 2011, for the standard process in coverage determination level, Part D plan sponsors shall notify an enrollee of a payment decision no later than 14 calendar-days after receiving a reimbursement request instead of within a 72-hour time period. In addition, if the decision is partially or fully favorable, the plan sponsor must also make a payment within the same 14 calendar-day period. 75 Fed. Reg. 19,780 (Apr. 15, 2010), revising 42 C.F.R. § 423.568(b).

TABLE OF CASES

References are to sections.

TABLE OF AUTHORITIES

References are to sections.

UNITED STATES CONSTITUTION

UNITED STATES CODE

BALANCED BUDGET ACT OF 1997 (BBA)

Pub. L. No. 105-33 (1997)

BIPARTISAN BUDGET ACT OF 2015

Pub. L. No. 114-74 (2015)

CONSOLIDATED OMNIBUS BUDGET RECONCILIATION ACT OF 1985

Pub. L. No. 99–272 (1985)

DEFICIT REDUCTION ACT OF 2005 (DRA)

Pub. L. No. 109–171

EXTENSION ACT OF 2010

Pub. L. No. 111–157

GENETIC INFORMATION NONDISCRIMINATION ACT OF 2008

Pub. L. No. 110–233

HEALTH CARE AND EDUCATION RECONCILIATION ACT OF 2010 (HCERA)

Pub. L. No. 111–152

MEDICARE ACCESS AND CHIP REAUTHORIZATION ACT OF 2015

Pub. L. No. 114-10

MEDICARE CATASTROPHIC COVERAGE ACT OF 1988

Pub. L. No. 100–360 (1988)

MEDICARE IMPROVEMENTS FOR PATIENTS AND PROVIDERS ACT OF 2008 (MIPPA)

Pub. L. No. 110–275

MEDICARE, MEDICAID, AND SCHIP BALANCED BUDGET REFINEMENT ACT OF 1999 (BBRA)

Pub. L. No. 106–113

MEDICARE, MEDICAID, AND SCHIP BENEFITS IMPROVEMENT AND PROTECTION ACT OF 2000 (BIPA)

Pub. L. No. 106–554

OMNIBUS BUDGET RECONCILIATION ACT OF 1989

Pub. L. No. 101–239

OMNIBUS BUDGET RECONCILIATION ACT OF 1990

Pub. L. No. 101–508 (1990)

PAPERWORK REDUCTION ACT (PRA)

PATIENT PROTECTION AND AFFORDABLE CARE ACT OF 2010 (PPACA)

Pub. L. No. 111–148 (Mar. 23, 2010)

PROTECTING ACCESS TO MEDICARE ACT OF 2014 (PAMA)

Pub. L. No. 113-93

QI, TMA, AND ABSTINENCE PROGRAMS EXTENSION AND HURRICANE KATRINA UNEMPLOYMENT RELIEF ACT OF 2005

REHABILITATION ACT OF 1973

SOCIAL SECURITY ACT

SOCIAL SECURITY AMENDMENTS OF 1972

SMALL BUSINESS HEALTH OPTIONS PLAN (SHOP) EXCHANGES

STRENGTHENING MEDICARE AND REPAYING TAXPAYERS ACT OF 2012

SOCIAL SECURITY DISABILITY AMENDMENTS OF 1980

TAX RELIEF AND HEALTH CARE ACT OF 2006

TICKET TO WORK AND WORK INCENTIVES IMPROVEMENT ACT OF 1999

IRS RULINGS

INDEX

References are to sections.

A

I